HANDBOOK OF PRICING RESEARCH IN MARKETING

Handbook of Pricing Research in Marketing

Edited by

Vithala R. Rao
Cornell University, USA

Edward Elgar
Cheltenham, UK • Northampton, MA, USA

© Vithala R. Rao 2009

All rights reserved. No part of this publication may be reproduced, stored in a retrieval system or transmitted in any form or by any means, electronic, mechanical or photocopying, recording, or otherwise without the prior permission of the publisher.

Published by
Edward Elgar Publishing Limited
The Lypiatts
15 Lansdown Road
Cheltenham
Glos GL50 2JA
UK

Edward Elgar Publishing, Inc.
William Pratt House
9 Dewey Court
Northampton
Massachusetts 01060
USA

Paperback edition 2010

A catalogue record for this book
is available from the British Library

Library of Congress Control Number: 2008943827

Mixed Sources
Product group from well-managed
forests and other controlled sources
www.fsc.org Cert no. SA-COC-1565
© 1996 Forest Stewardship Council

ISBN 978 1 84720 240 6 (cased)
ISBN 978 1 84980 441 7 (paperback)

Printed and bound by MPG Books Group, UK

Contents

List of contributors	vii
Foreword	xix
Acknowledgments	xxi
Introduction *Vithala R. Rao*	1

PART I INTRODUCTION/FOUNDATIONS

1	Pricing objectives and strategies: a cross-country survey *Vithala R. Rao and Benjamin Kartono*	9
2	Willingness to pay: measurement and managerial implications *Kamel Jedidi and Sharan Jagpal*	37
3	Measurement of own- and cross-price effects *Qing Liu, Thomas Otter and Greg M. Allenby*	61
4	Behavioral pricing *Aradhna Krishna*	76
5	Consumer search and pricing *Brian T. Ratchford*	91
6	Structural models of pricing *Tat Chan, Vrinda Kadiyali and Ping Xiao*	108
7	Heuristics in numerical cognition: implications for pricing *Manoj Thomas and Vicki Morwitz*	132
8	Price cues and customer price knowledge *Eric T. Anderson and Duncan I. Simester*	150

PART II PRICING DECISIONS AND MARKETING MIX

9	Strategic pricing of new products and services *Rabikar Chatterjee*	169
10	Product line pricing *Yuxin Chen*	216
11	The design and pricing of bundles: a review of normative guidelines and practical approaches *R. Venkatesh and Vijay Mahajan*	232

vi *Contents*

12	Pricing of national brands versus store brands: market power components, findings and research opportunities *Koen Pauwels and Shuba Srinivasan*	258
13	Trade promotions *Chakravarthi Narasimhan*	283
14	Competitive targeted pricing: perspectives from theoretical research *Z. John Zhang*	302
15	Pricing in marketing channels *K. Sudhir and Sumon Datta*	319
16	Nonlinear pricing *Raghuram Iyengar and Sunil Gupta*	355
17	Dynamic pricing *P.B. (Seethu) Seetharaman*	384

PART III SPECIAL TOPICS

18	Strategic pricing: an analysis of social influences *Wilfred Amaldoss and Sanjay Jain*	397
19	Online and name-your-own-price auctions: a literature review *Young-Hoon Park and Xin Wang*	419
20	Pricing under network effects *Hongju Liu and Pradeep K. Chintagunta*	435
21	Advance selling theory *Jinhong Xie and Steven M. Shugan*	451
22	Pricing and revenue management *Sheryl E. Kimes*	477
23	Pharmaceutical pricing *Samuel H. Kina and Marta Wosinska*	488
24	Pricing for nonprofit organizations *Yong Liu and Charles B. Weinberg*	512
25	Pricing in services *Stowe Shoemaker and Anna S. Mattila*	535
26	Strategic pricing response and optimization in operations management *Teck H. Ho and Xuanming Su*	557

Index   581

Contributors

Greg M. Allenby is the Helen C. Kurtz Chair in Marketing at Ohio State University. He is a Fellow of the American Statistical Association, and a co-author of *Bayesian Statistics and Marketing* (Wiley, 2005). He is an associate editor of *Marketing Science*, the *Journal of Marketing Research*, *Quantitative Marketing and Economics* and the *Journal of Business and Economic Statistics*. His research has appeared in these and other leading journals.

Wilfred Amaldoss is Associate Professor of Marketing at the Fuqua School of Business of Duke University, Durham, NC. He holds an MBA from the Indian Institute of Management (Ahmedabad), and an MA (Applied Economics) and a PhD from the Wharton School of the University of Pennsylvania. His research interests include behavioral game theory, experimental economics, advertising, pricing, new product development, and social effects in consumption. His recent publications have appeared in *Marketing Science*, *Management Science*, *Journal of Marketing Research*, *Journal of Economic Behavior and Organization* and *Journal of Mathematical Psychology*. His work has received the John D.C. Little award and the Frank Bass award. He serves on the editorial boards of *Journal of Marketing Research* and *Marketing Science*.

Eric T. Anderson is the Hartmarx Research Associate Professor of Marketing at Northwestern University, Kellogg School of Management, Evanston, IL. He holds a PhD in Management Science from MIT Sloan School of Management and previously held appointments at the University of Chicago Graduate School of Business and the W.E. Simon Graduate School of Business at the University of Rochester. Professor Anderson's research interests include pricing strategy, promotion strategy, retailing and channel management. He has conducted field experiments with numerous retailers to investigate customer price perceptions, segmented pricing strategies, long-run effects of promotions and cross-channel effects. He is an area editor for *Operations Research* and on the editorial board of *Marketing Science* and *Quantitative Marketing and Economics*.

Tat Chan is an Associate Professor of Marketing at the Olin Business School, Washington University in St Louis, MO. He received a PhD in Economics at Yale University in 2001. His research interests are in modeling consumer demand and firms' strategies using econometric methodologies. His recent research also includes analyzing the optimal non-linear pricing strategies (e.g. three-part tariff and product bundling) for firms, identifying consumer strategies in making in-store purchase decisions, evaluating the impacts of channel strategies on manufacturers' and retailers' pricing decisions and market share, and using expectations data to infer managerial objectives and choices.

Rabikar Chatterjee is Professor of Business Administration and the Katz Faculty Fellow in Marketing at the University of Pittsburgh, PA. His teaching, research and consulting interests are in the area of customer-focused marketing and product/service strategies, particularly in high-tech and/or engineered products and services. His research has focused on models of market response to new products, with applications in forecasting, product design and pricing, and in methods for measuring and representing customers' perceptions of and preferences for competing products. His articles have appeared in various academic journals, including the *Journal of Marketing Research*, *Management Science* and *Psychometrika*. He has served as an associate editor in the marketing department of *Management Science* and is currently a member of the editorial board of *Marketing Science*.

Yuxin Chen is an Associate Professor of Marketing at New York University. He holds a PhD in Marketing from Washington University in St Louis, MO. His primary research areas include database marketing, Internet marketing, pricing, Bayesian econometric methods and marketing research. His research has appeared in top academic journals such as *Management Science*, *Marketing Science*, the *Journal of Marketing Research* and *Quantitative Marketing and Economics*. His paper, 'Individual marketing with imperfect targetability', won the Frank M. Bass Outstanding Dissertation Award for Contributions to the Discipline of Marketing Science and the John D.C. Little Best Paper Award for Marketing Papers Published in *Marketing Science* and *Management Science*.

Pradeep K. Chintagunta is the Robert Law Professor of Marketing at the University of Chicago Booth School of Business, IL. He is interested in studying strategic interactions among firms in vertical and horizontal relationships. His research also includes measuring the effectiveness of marketing activities in pharmaceutical markets; investigating aspects of technology product markets and analyzing household purchase behavior.

Sumon Datta is a PhD candidate in the Doctoral Program in Marketing at the Yale School of Management, New Haven, CT. Starting in July 2009, he will join Purdue University's Krannert School of Management as an Assistant Professor of Marketing. His research interests include competitive marketing strategy, consumer demand in emerging markets, empirical industrial organization methods, pricing and advertising. His dissertation investigates the market entry and location decisions of retailers. He considers the tradeoff between the benefit of spatial differentiation (lowering competition) and the benefit of agglomeration (increasing the number of consumers who visit a store), as well as the effects of zoning regulations. He is one of the winners of the 2008 Alden G. Clayton Doctoral Dissertation Proposal Competition. He has recently begun to analyze the evolution of consumer demand in emerging markets and its influence on firms' entry decisions.

Sunil Gupta is Edward W. Carter Professor of Business and Head of the Marketing Department at the Harvard Business School, Boston, MA. Before joining Harvard, he taught at Columbia and UCLA. Sunil's research interests include choice models, pricing, customer management, social networking and new media. His articles in these areas have won several awards, including the O'Dell (1993, 2002, 2009) and the Paul Green (1998, 2005) awards for the *Journal of Marketing Research*, and the best paper awards for the *International Journal of Research in Marketing* (1999) and Marketing Science Institute (1999, 2000 and 2003). Sunil is a co-author of two books. His recent book, *Managing Customers as Investments*, won the 2006 annual Berry–AMA book prize for the best book in marketing. In September 1999, Sunil was selected as the best core course teacher at Columbia Business School. He is an area editor for the *Journal of Marketing Research* and serves on the editorial boards of *International Journal of Research in Marketing*, *Journal of Marketing*, *Marketing Letters*, and *Marketing Science*. He is a member of the analytical advisory board of Information Resources, Inc.

Teck H. Ho is the William Halford Jr Family Professor of Marketing at the University of California, Berkeley. He is the chair of the marketing faculty group. Teck's professional leadership includes roles as departmental editor of *Management Science*, area editor of *Journal of Marketing Research* and *Marketing Science* and editorial board member of *Quantitative Marketing and Economics*. Teck has published in *American Economic Review*, *Econometrica*, *Journal of Economic Theory*, *Journal of Marketing Research*, *Marketing Science*, *Management Science*, *Psychological Science* and *Quarterly Journal of Economics*, and has been funded by the National Science Foundation for his innovative research in experimental and behavioral economics since 1995. He won the Best Teacher of the Year Award three years in a row at Haas School of Business, University of California, Berkeley from 2004 to 2006.

Raghuram Iyengar is Assistant Professor of Marketing at the Wharton School of the University of Pennsylvania in Philadelphia, PA. He has an undergraduate degree in engineering from IIT Kanpur, India, and has a PhD in Marketing from Columbia University, New York. His research interests are in pricing, structural models and Bayesian methods.

Sharan Jagpal is Professor of Marketing at Rutgers Business School, Rutgers University, Newark, NJ. He has published widely in top-tier journals in marketing, economics, econometrics and statistics, and is the author of two multidisciplinary books, *Marketing Strategy and Uncertainty* (Oxford University Press, 1998) and *Fusion for Profit: How Marketing and Finance Can Work Together to Create Value* (Oxford University Press, 2008). His theoretical research focuses on developing marketing models for the multiproduct firm under uncertainty, the marketing–finance interface, measuring advertising effectiveness, designing sales force compensation plans, measuring performance in the multiproduct firm, new product models, consumer behavior, forecasting, channels of distribution, strategic alliances, mergers and acquisitions, Internet marketing and pharmaceutical marketing. His methodological research focuses on developing new empirical methods for the multiproduct firm under uncertainty.

Jagpal is president of Strategic Management and Marketing Consultants, a consulting company that focuses on developing customized models for decision-making in the firm. He holds a BSc (Economics Honours) degree from the London School of Economics and MBA, MPhil and PhD degrees from Columbia University.

Sanjay Jain is the Macy's Foundation Professor of Marketing at the Mays Business School, Texas A&M University, College Station, TX. Sanjay's research interests are in the area of product innovation, pricing, competitive strategy, behavioral economics and experimental game theory. His research has been published in *Journal of Marketing Research*, *Marketing Science* and *Management Science*. He has been a finalist for the Paul Green Award in 2001 and won the 2007 ISMS practice prize competition. He serves on the editorial review board of *Decision Sciences*, *Journal of Marketing Research* and *Marketing Science*.

Kamel Jedidi is the John A. Howard Professor of Business and Chair of the Marketing Division at Columbia Business School, Columbia University, New York. He holds a bachelor's degree in Economics from the Faculté des Sciences Economiques de Tunis, Tunisia, and Master's and PhD degrees in Marketing from the Wharton School, University of

Pennsylvania. He has published extensively in leading marketing and statistics journals, the most recent of which have appeared in the *Journal of Marketing Research*, *Marketing Science*, *Management Science*, the *International Journal of Research in Marketing* and *Psychometrika*. His substantive research interests include pricing, product design and positioning, diffusion of innovations, market segmentation, and the long-term impact of advertising and promotions. His methodological interests lie in multidimensional scaling, classification, structural equation modeling, and Bayesian and finite-mixture models. He was awarded the 1998 International Journal of Research in Marketing Best Article Award and the Marketing Science Institute 2000 Best Paper Award.

Vrinda Kadiyali is Professor of Marketing and Economics at Cornell's Johnson School of Management, Ithaca, NY. Her research interests are in empirical models of competition and consumer choices. She has worked with structural and reduced-form econometric models, and laboratory studies. Her interests span various industries, such as residential real estate, movies, Internet bidding, hotels, higher education etc. She has published in journals, including the *Journal of Law and Economics*, *Rand Journal of Economics*, *Journal of Marketing Research*, *Marketing Science* and *Quantitative Marketing and Economics*. She also serves on the editorial boards of the last three.

Benjamin Kartono is an Assistant Professor of Marketing at the Nanyang Technological University in Singapore. He received his BS degrees in Chemical Engineering and Economics from the University of Michigan in 1996 and his PhD from the Johnson Graduate School of Management at Cornell University in 2006. Before entering academia, he worked in the oil and petrochemicals industry. His research focuses on various issues pertaining to branding and pricing.

Sheryl E. Kimes is the Singapore Tourism Board Distinguished Professor of Asian Hospitality Management at the Cornell University School of Hotel Administration, Ithaca, NY. From 2005 to 2006, she served as interim dean of the Hotel School and from 2001 to 2005, as the school's director of graduate studies. She specializes in revenue management with a particular emphasis in the hotel, restaurant, golf and spa industries. She has published in a number of journals including *Interfaces*, *Journal of Operations Management*, *Journal of Service Research*, *Decision Sciences* and the *Cornell Hotel and Restaurant Administration Quarterly*. Kimes earned her doctorate in Operations Management in 1987 from the University of Texas at Austin.

Samuel H. Kina is a doctoral candidate in Health Policy at Harvard University, Boston, MA. He previously held a position at the Congressional Budget Office where he served as an analyst focusing on legislation influencing the pharmaceuticals industry. Mr Kina's research interest is in health economics and includes pricing and strategy in the pharmaceutical industry and physician organization and decision-making.

Aradhna Krishna does research on pricing and promotion policies, sensory marketing and socially relevant marketing. Her work within the area of pricing and promotion focuses on both consumer promotions and trade promotions, e.g. bundling issues, loyalty programs, coupons, price cuts and trade deals. She examines consumer response to promotions, consumers' perceptions of promotions, behavioral pricing issues (e.g. reference price formation, promotion presentation effects), and also builds analytical models for managerial (retailer and manufacturer) promotion policies. Within the area of sensory marketing, she has done a great deal of work on visual stimuli (package design, mall layout, store layout, shelf allocation), haptics (e.g. how the feel of product can affect perceived taste), smell (e.g. whether smell enhances long-term memory for a brand) and taste (e.g. if an advertisement can affect perceived taste). Her research on socially relevant marketing mostly concerns cause marketing. Her research methodology combines experimental techniques with quantitative modeling approaches. She has written numerous articles and her work is cited in NPR, *New York Times*, *Wall Street Journal* and other publications. She is on the editorial boards of the *Journal of Marketing Research*, *International Journal of Research in Marketing*, *Management Science*, *Marketing Science* and *Marketing Letters*.

Hongju Liu is Assistant Professor in Marketing at the University of Connecticut, Storrs, CT. His research interests include empirical industrial organization, dynamic pricing, technology markets and network effects. He received a PhD from the University of Chicago.

Qing Liu is Assistant Professor of Marketing at the University of Wisconsin–Madison. Her research focuses on the application and development of statistical theories and methodology to help solve problems in marketing and marketing research. Areas of interest include conjoint analysis, consumer choice, experimental design and Bayesian methods.

Yong Liu is Assistant Professor of Marketing at the Eller College of Management, University of Arizona, Tucson, AZ. He received a PhD degree in Marketing from the University of British Columbia, Vancouver, Canada. Yong was on the faculty at the Whitman School of Management, Syracuse University, before moving to Tucson, Arizona. His current research interests include social interactions and network effects in the media/entertainment markets, positioning strategies for business and nonprofit organizations, and managing product-harm crisis. His research has been published in journals such as *Marketing Science*, *Journal of Marketing*, *Journal of Public Policy and Marketing*, *Marketing Letters* and *Journal of Cultural Economics*. Yong has served on the editorial boards of *Marketing Science* (2002–05 and 2005–07) and *Canadian Journal of Administrative Sciences* (since 2009), and was selected as a Marketing Science Institute (MSI) Young Scholar in 2007. He was a Fellow at the Center for the Study of Popular Television at the S.I. Newhouse School of Public Communication, Syracuse University.

Vijay Mahajan, former Dean of the Indian School of Business, holds the John P. Harbin Centennial Chair in Business at the McCombs School of Business, University of Texas at Austin. He is a recipient of the American Marketing Association's (AMA) Charles Coolidge Parlin Award for visionary leadership in scientific marketing. The AMA also instituted the Vijay Mahajan Award in 2000 for career contributions to marketing strategy. Mahajan is author or editor of nine books including his recent book on developing countries, *The 86% Solution* (Wharton School Publishing, 2006), which received the 2007 Book-of-the-Year Award from the AMA. He is currently working on a book on Africa, to be released by Wharton School Publishing in 2008. He is a former editor of the *Journal of Marketing Research*. Mahajan received a BTech in Chemical Engineering from the Indian Institute of Technology at Kanpur, and his MS in Chemical Engineering and PhD in Management from the University of Texas at Austin.

xii *Contributors*

Anna S. Mattila is a professor at the School of Hospitality Management at Pennsylvania State University, Philadelphia. She holds a PhD in services marketing from Cornell University. Her research interests focus on service encounters, with a particular interest in service failures and service recovery and cross-cultural research. Her work has appeared in the *Journal of the Academy of Marketing Science, Journal of Retailing, Journal of Service Research, Journal of Consumer Psychology, Psychology & Marketing, Journal of Services Marketing, International Journal of Service Industry Management, Cornell Hotel & Restaurant Administration Quarterly, Journal of Travel Research, International Journal of Hospitality Management, Tourism Management* and in the *Journal of Hospitality & Tourism Research*. Anna has written several book chapters and currently serves on 13 editorial boards in journals specializing in services management. She is also the Chief Editor of *Journal of Hospitality & Tourism Research*. Anna is a recipient of the John Wiley & Sons Lifetime Research Award and The University of Delaware Michael D. Olsen Lifetime Research Achievement Award.

Vicki Morwitz is Research Professor of Marketing at the Stern School of Business, New York University. She received a BS in Computer Science and Applied Mathematics from Rutgers University, an MS in Operations Research from Polytechnic University, and an MA in Statistics and a PhD in Marketing from the Wharton School at the University of Pennsylvania. Her research interests include behavioral aspects of pricing, the relationship between purchase intentions and purchase behavior, and the effects of responding to and exposure to market research surveys on attitudes, intentions and behavior. She teaches the marketing core, marketing research, and doctoral classes in judgment and decision-making. Her work has appeared in *Harvard Business Review, International Journal of Forecasting, Journal of Consumer Psychology, Journal of Consumer Research, Journal of Marketing Research, Management Science* and *Marketing Letters*. She has worked at IBM, Prodigy Services and RCA.

Chakravarthi Narasimhan is the Philip L. Siteman Professor of Marketing and Director of the PhD Program in the Olin Business School at Washington University, in St Louis, MO. His current research interests are in modeling demand in pharmaceutical and telecommunication markets, examining interaction of multiple marketing strategies and supply chain contracts, especially supply chain strategies under uncertainty. He has published in *Marketing Science, Management Science, Journal of Marketing Research, Journal of Marketing, Journal of Business, Journal of Econometrics* and *Harvard Business Review*, among others. He is an area editor of *Marketing Science* and an associate editor of *Management Science* and *Quantitative Marketing and Economics*.

Thomas Otter is Professor of Marketing at Johann Wolfgang Goethe University Frankfurt, Germany. His research focuses on Bayesian modeling with application to marketing. He uses Bayesian statistics and MCMC techniques to develop and refine quantitative marketing models by incorporating psychological and economic theory. His research has been published in *Journal of Marketing Research, Marketing Science, Quantitative Marketing and Economics, Journal of Business & Economic Statistics, International Journal of Research in Marketing, Psychometrika* and *Marketing Letters*.

Young-Hoon Park is Associate Professor of Marketing at the Johnson Graduate School of Management, Cornell University, Ithaca, NY. He holds a PhD in Marketing at the Wharton School of the University of Pennsylvania. His research interests include Bayesian and statistical modeling with application to business problems. His research has been published in *Marketing Science, Management Science*, and *Journal of Marketing Research*, among others. He has been a finalist for the John D.C. Little Award from the INFORMS in 2008. He serves on the editorial board of *Marketing Science*.

Koen Pauwels is Professor of Marketing at Özyeğin University in Istanbul, Turkey, and Associate Professor at the Tuck School of Business at Dartmouth in Hanover, NH, where he teaches and researches return on marketing investment. He won the 2007 O'Dell award for the most influential paper in the *Journal of Marketing Research*, and built his research insights in industries ranging from automobiles and pharmaceuticals to business content sites and fast-moving consumer goods. Current research projects include the predictive power of market dashboard metrics, the impact of brand equity on marketing effectiveness, retailer product assortment, price wars, the dynamics of differentiation and performance turnaround strategies. Professor Pauwels received his PhD in Management from UCLA, won the EMAC 2001 Best Paper Award and publishes in *Harvard Business Review, Journal of Marketing, Journal of Marketing Research, Journal of Retailing, Management Science* and *Marketing Science*. He serves on the editorial boards of the *International Journal of Research in Marketing, Journal of Marketing, Journal of Marketing Research* and *Marketing Science*. Koen is a reviewer for the above journals, and for *Management Science, Marketing Letters, Journal of Retailing, Journal of the Academy of Marketing Science, Journal of Advertising, Statistica Neerlandica* and *International Journal of Forecasting*.

Vithala R. Rao is the Deane W. Malott Professor of Management and Professor of Marketing and Quantitative Methods, Johnson Graduate School of Management, Cornell University, Ithaca, NY. He received his Master's degree in Mathematical Statistics from the University of Bombay and in Sociology from the University of Michigan, and a PhD in Applied Economics/Marketing from the Wharton School of the University of Pennsylvania. He has published over 110 papers on several topics, including conjoint analysis and multidimensional scaling for the analysis of consumer preferences and perceptions, promotions, pricing, market structure, corporate acquisition and brand equity. His current work includes bundle design and pricing, product design, diffusion and demand estimation of pre-announced products, competitive issues of pre-announcement strategies, Internet recommendation systems, linking branding strategies of firms to their financial performance. His research papers have appeared in the *Journal of Marketing Research, Marketing Science, Journal of Consumer Research, Decision Science, Management Science, Journal of Marketing, Multivariate Behavioral Research, Journal of Classification, Marketing Letters, Applied Economics* and *International Journal of Research in Marketing*.

Rao is the co-author of four books, *Applied Multidimensional Scaling* (Holt, Rinehart and Winston, 1972), *Decision Criteria for New Product Acceptance and Success* (Quorum Books, 1991), *New Science of Marketing* (Irwin Professional Pub., 1995) and *Analysis for Strategic Marketing* (Addison-Wesley, 1998).

He currently serves on the editorial boards of *Marketing Science, Journal of Marketing Research, Journal of Marketing* and *Journal of Business to Business Marketng*. He received the 2000–01 Faculty Research Award of the Johnson Graduate School of Management at Cornell University and other awards for his papers. He received the 2008 Charles Coolidge Parlin Marketing Research Award presented by the American Marketing

Association and the American Marketing Association Foundation recognizing his 'outstanding leadership and sustained impact on advancing the evolving profession of marketing research over an extended period of time'.

Brian T. Ratchford. Since 2006 Brian T. Ratchford has been Charles and Nancy Davidson Professor of Marketing, University of Texas at Dallas. From 1999 to 2006 he was Pepsico Chair in Consumer Research, University of Maryland. From 1971 to 1999 he held various academic positions at State University of New York at Buffalo. He has MBA and PhD degrees from the University of Rochester. His research interests are in economics applied to the study of consumer behavior, information economics, marketing productivity, marketing research and electronic commerce. He has published over 70 articles in marketing and related fields, including articles in *Marketing Science, Management Science, Journal of Consumer Research* and *Journal of Marketing Research*. He was editor of *Marketing Science* from 1998 to 2002, is currently an associate editor of *Journal of Consumer Research*, and is currently on the editorial review boards of *Journal of Marketing Research, Journal of Marketing, Journal of Retailing, Journal of Interactive Marketing* and *Journal of Service Research*.

P.B. (Seethu) Seetharaman is Professor of Marketing at the Jesse H. Jones Graduate School of Management, Rice University, Houston, TX. As a marketing researcher, Seethu's interests lie primarily in the area of demand estimation, which aids marketing decision-making. In the area of pricing in particular, Seethu's research deals with understanding both consumers' responses and competitors' reactions to firms' pricing tactics, with particular attention paid to dynamic interdependencies that arise (on account of inertia, variety seeking, reference prices etc.) in consumers' demands for brands over time. Seethu currently serves as the Director of Asian Business Research and Education, and is also the marketing area advisor for the doctoral program in Management at Rice University. He received his PhD at Cornell University and has previously taught at Washington University in St Louis.

Stowe Shoemaker is the Donald Hubbs Distinguished Professor at the University of Houston's Conrad Hilton College of Hotel and Restaurant Management, Houston, TX. He is also on the executive education faculty at the Cornell University School of Hotel Administration. He holds a PhD from Cornell University. He has written numerous academic and popular articles, and is the co-author of a Harvard Business School Case Study on Hilton HHonors. He is the senior author of *Marketing Leadership in Hospitality and Tourism: Strategies and Tactics for a Competitive Advantage* (2007) and senior author of *Marketing Essentials in Hospitality and Tourism* (2008), both published by Prentice-Hall.

Steven M. Shugan, the Russell Berrie Foundation Eminent Scholar and Professor at the University of Florida, Gainesville, FL, teaches multivariate statistics, marketing models and advanced marketing management. His PhD in Managerial Economics is from Northwestern University. Formerly a full professor at University of Chicago (13 years), an assistant professor at the University of Rochester (two years) and an instructor at SDA Bocconi, Milan, he has taught marketing, econometrics (Chicago), statistics (Florida) and computer science (Northwestern). He was editor-in-chief of *Marketing Science* (six years), editor of *Journal of Business* and associate editor of *Management Science*, and served on many editorial boards (including *Journal of Consumer Research, Journal of Marketing* and *Journal of Marketing Research*). He has numerous publications and presentations in over 22 countries, and won several best paper awards, including *Marketing Science* (twice), *Journal of Marketing, Journal of Retailing, Journal of Service Research* (finalist), *Journal of Marketing Research* (finalist), and best teaching awards. He has consulted for over thirty different firms. Website: http://bear.cba.ufl.edu/shugan/.

Duncan I. Simester is a professor at MIT's Sloan School of Management, Cambridge, MA, where he holds the NTU Chair in Management Science. The chapter presented in this volume is one of a series of studies that uses field data from retail settings. These include several studies that focus on evaluating the long-run effect of marketing decisions, together with a stream of work investigating the role of price cues. Duncan edits the marketing science section of *Operations Research*, is on the editorial board of *Journal of Marketing Research*, and serves as an area editor for *Marketing Science* and *Management Science*.

Shuba Srinivasan is Associate Professor of Marketing at Boston University's School of Management. She obtained her MS in Physics from the Indian Institute of Technology and an MBA in Marketing at the Indian Institute of Management. She obtained her PhD in Marketing from the University of Texas at Dallas, where she worked with Dr Frank M. Bass. She was awarded the M/A/R/C Award for Outstanding Doctoral Student from the University of Texas at Dallas in 1998. She has also been a visiting research scholar at UCLA and HEC, Paris. Professor Srinivasan's research focuses on strategic marketing problems, in particular long-term marketing productivity, to which she applies her expertise in econometrics and time-series analysis. She has built her research insights in industries ranging from automobiles to pharmaceuticals and fast-moving consumer goods. Her current research focuses on marketing's impact on financial performance and firm valuation, marketing metrics, and decomposing demand effects of radical innovations, and managing brand equity. Her research won the 2001 EMAC best paper award and her papers have been published in the *Journal of Marketing Research, Marketing Science, Management Science, Journal of Marketing, Harvard Business Review*, the *International Journal of Research in Marketing, Journal of Advertising Research*, and *Journal of Economics and Management Strategy*, among others. Prior to joining Boston University, she served as Associate Professor at the University of California, Riverside. In 2005, the University of California named her a University Scholar for a three-year period. Professor Srinivasan serves on the editorial boards of *Marketing Science, Journal of Marketing Research*, and *International Journal of Research in Marketing*, and also actively reviews for journals such as *Management Science* and the *Journal of Marketing*. She has consulting experience in market-response modeling on customer and marketing databases with a wide spectrum of companies.

Xuanming Su is Assistant Professor at the Haas School of Business at University of California, Berkeley. His areas of research include operations management, revenue management and behavioral decision-making. His recent work studies the impact of consumer behavior on dynamic pricing strategies and supply chain management.

K. Sudhir is Professor of Marketing at the Yale School of Management and Director of the China–India Consumer Insights Program at the Yale Center for Customer Insights, New Haven, CT. After receiving his PhD from Cornell, he was an assistant professor at NYU's Stern School from 1998 to 2001. His research covers a number of substantive and methodological areas, and he is best known for his contributions to empirical industrial organization. He has recently begun a research agenda focused on emerging markets such as China and India. He serves as an area editor at *Marketing Science* and *Management Science*, an associate editor at *Quantitative Marketing and Economics* and is on the editorial board of the *Journal of Marketing Research*. He has received several research awards including the Bass Award at *Marketing Science* (2003), the Lehmann award at the *Journal of Marketing Research* (2007) for best dissertation-based paper, and honorable mentions for the Wittink best paper ward at *Quantitative Marketing and Economics* (2006), and the best paper award in the *International Journal of Research in Marketing* (2001). He was also a finalist for the 2001 Little award at *Marketing Science* (2001) and the Green award at the *Journal of Marketing Research* (2006).

Manoj Thomas is Assistant Professor of Marketing at the S.C. Johnson Graduate School of Management, Cornell University, Ithaca, NY. He received an MBA from the Indian Institute of Management Calcutta and a PhD in Marketing from Stern School of Business, New York University. His current research interests include the role of fluency and nonconscious processes in consumer judgments, mental representation and processing of numerical stimuli, behavioral pricing, and the effects of construal level on judgments. His work has been published in *Journal of Consumer Research* and *Journal of Marketing Research*. He teaches strategic brand management and product management at the S.C. Johnson Graduate School of Management, Cornell University.

R. Venkatesh is Associate Professor of Marketing at the University of Pittsburgh's Katz School of Business, PA. His research interests include pricing, product bundling, co-branding, eCommerce and sales force management. His articles on these topics have appeared or are forthcoming in the *Journal of Business*, *Journal of Marketing*, *Journal of Marketing Research*, *Management Science* and *Marketing Science*. He serves on the editorial review board of the *Journal of Marketing*. Venkatesh has a PhD in Marketing from the University of Texas at Austin, an MBA from the Indian Institute of Management, Ahmedabad, and a BEngg (Honors) degree in Mechanical Engineering from the University of Madras, India.

Xin Wang is Assistant Professor of Marketing at International Business School, Brandeis University, Waltham, MA. Her research interests include online pricing, service quality and consumer learning. Her research investigates consumer behavior under various pricing formats, and helps managers make pricing decisions based on empirical and theoretical analysis. She has published in *Quantitative Marketing and Economics*, *Marketing Letters*, the *Economic Journal*, *Medical Care* and also book chapters on these topics. Before joining the faculty at Brandeis, she was on the faculty at the Krannert School of Management, Purdue University. Her prior professional work experience also includes working as a research fellow and instructor at the Tepper School of Business, Carnegie Mellon University, as well as a research associate at the Wharton School, University of Pennsylvania. She received her PhD in Marketing from Carnegie Mellon University.

Charles B. Weinberg is the Presidents of SME Vancouver and Professor of Marketing at the Sauder School of Business, University of British Columbia, Vancouver, Canada. In 2008, he was selected as one of the first ten fellows of the INFORMS Society for Marketing Science. His research focuses on analytical marketing, services, and public and nonprofit marketing and management. His work in the nonprofit sector includes pricing, the marketing of safer sex practices, portfolio management and competition among nonprofit organizations. For more than 30 years, he has studied the arts and entertainment industries. His early work focused on live entertainment and included the ARTS PLAN model for marketing and scheduling performing arts events for a nonprofit organization. More recently, he has focused on the movie industry in which he has studied such issues as competitive dynamics, scheduling of movies into theaters, sequential release of movies and DVDs, and contract terms. He is a former editor of *Marketing Letters* and area editor of *Marketing Science*. He grew up in New Jersey, but has lived in Vancouver for 30 years. He hopes that all who attended the 2008 Marketing Science conference in Vancouver, which he chaired, will see why he has chosen to make 'Beautiful British Columbia' his home.

Marta Wosinska is the Acting Director for Analysis Staff in the Office of Planning and Informatics at the Food and Drug Administration's Center for Drug Evaluation and Research. Prior to joining FDA, she taught marketing strategy and healthcare marketing at Harvard Business School and Columbia Business School. Her academic research focuses on the impact of various marketing interventions, such as direct-to-consumer advertising and pricing, on patient and physician behavior. Her work has been published in leading marketing and health policy journals.

Ping Xiao is Assistant Professor of Marketing at the Business School at the National University of Singapore. She received a PhD in Marketing at Washington University in St Louis in 2008. Her research focuses on examining the strategic use of nonlinear pricing (e.g. three-part tariffs) and product bundling, both empirically and theoretically.

Jinhong Xie is J.C. Penny Professor of Marketing at the Warrington College of Business Administration, University of Florida, Gainesville, FL. She has taught at a number of universities within and outside of the United States, including the University of Rochester, Carnegie Mellon University, the International University of Japan, Tsinghua University, and Cheung Kong Graduate School of Business. She served as associate editor of *Management Science* and area editor of *Marketing Science*. She is a recipient of INFORMS' John D.C. Little Best Paper Award, the Marketing Science Institute's Research Competition Award, the Product Development and Management Association's Research Competition Award, and the University of Florida's Best Teaching Award. Her research interests include pricing, technology innovation, network effects and standards competition, and consumer social interactions. She has published in *Marketing Science*, *Management Science*, *Journal of Marketing Research*, *Journal of Marketing*, *Journal of Product Innovation Management* and *Journal of Service Research*. She holds a PhD in Engineering and Public Policy from Carnegie Mellon University, an MS in Optimal Control from the Second Academy of the Ministry of Astronautics (China), and a BS in Electrical Engineering from Tsinghua University.

Z. John Zhang is Professor of Marketing and Murrel J. Ades Professor at the Wharton School of the University of Pennsylvania, Philadelphia. He earned a Bachelor's degree in Engineering Automation and Philosophy of Science from Huazhong University of Science and Technology (China), a PhD in History and Sociology of Science from the University of Pennsylvania, and also a PhD in Economics from the University of Michigan.

Before joining Wharton in 2002, John taught pricing and marketing management at the Olin School of Business of Washington University in St Louis for three years and at Columbia Business School for five years. John's research focuses primarily on competitive pricing strategies, the design of pricing structures and channel management. He has published numerous articles in top marketing and management journals on various pricing issues such as measuring consumer reservation prices, price-matching guarantees, targeted pricing, access service pricing, choice of price promotion vehicles, channel pricing, price wars and the pricing implications of advertising. He has also developed an interest in the movie and telecom industries in recent years.

He currently serves as associate editor for *Quantitative Economics and Marketing*. He is also an area editor for *Marketing Science* and *Management Science*. He won the 2001 John D.C. Little Best Paper Award and 2001 Frank Bass Best Dissertation Award, along with his co-authors, for his contribution to the understanding of targeted pricing with imperfect targetability.

Foreword

Editing a handbook is an opportunity to organize a field. My marketing colleague, Vithala Rao, seems to have been preparing for this for 24 years, judging from his paper, 'Review of Pricing Research in Marketing: The State of the Art', written in 1984.

At its finest grain, Vithala's organization of pricing research starts with 26 chapters written by top researchers in areas of their personal expertise. Coverage is remarkably comprehensive. The *Handbook* divides roughly into thirds: Part I – Introduction/Foundations, Part II – Pricing Decisions and Marketing Mix, and Part III – Special Topics, the latter emphasizing recent developments. I am also completely impressed with Vithala's people organizational skills in making 26 chapters with 26 sets of authors and reviewers actually happen.

The *Handbook* takes an active view of pricing, which I applaud. The 'Introduction' contrasts pricing research in marketing with that in microeconomics, pointing out that marketers are oriented toward achieving the objectives of the firm. I relate to this, since I come from the OR/MS tradition, which focuses on decision-making and decision support.

The ubiquity of price as a control variable has pursued me all of my marketing life. In 1969, as a neophyte consultant, I co-built a marketing-mix model at Nabisco for Oreos, 'America's Favorite Cookie'. Our goal was to support marketing management in its annual plan. We had monthly historical data with which to calibrate the model. It was then I first learned that what many academics were interpreting as a price variable was really promotion. Price had not gone away; the marketing mix needs both. I was being introduced to pricing research.

To give the reader a taste of Vithala's *Handbook*, I sample three chapters:

Chapter 20: 'Pricing under network effects' (Liu and Chintagunta)
The hallmark of networks is that they become more valuable to everybody as more people join them. Although network effects are as ancient as a middle-east bazaar, the Internet has newly thrust them in our faces with innovations such as multi-person online games.

Liu and Chintagunta describe pricing issues under network effects as reported in the theoretical literature, including static pricing, dynamic pricing, and nonlinear pricing. The authors, however, lament the state of empirical research in the field. To quote them, 'we are still not well equipped to provide normative guidance on firm's pricing strategies in real industry settings'. Thus one researcher's problem will be a future researcher's challenge.

Chapter 18: 'Strategic pricing: an analysis of social influences' (Amaldoss and Jain)
The authors build models of social phenomena that may variously be called conspicuous consumption, prestige, or snobbishness. The models focus on two basic social needs: a desire for uniqueness on one hand and the countervailing need to conform on the other. People buy conspicuous goods not just to satisfy material needs but also because of social desires. Firms that produce such goods tend to advertise the exclusivity of their products and must find an appropriate pricing strategy for them.

A summer 2008 example was AT&T Wireless, which became an exclusive channel for the Apple's new iPhone 3G. Big introductory promotions (with high prices for the iPhone) produced queues of hundreds of people at Apple stores in shopping malls on July 11. I myself was a purchaser (but through AT&T because I was unwilling to wait in queue). My self-analysis is that I was briefly unique and then sank into conformity.

Chapter 19: 'Online and name-your-own-price auctions: a literature review' (Park and Wang)
The authors review pricing mechanisms that have long been known for selling art objects but have suddenly blossomed into multi-billion dollar Internet businesses. The literature review is a service to all of us interested in this economically significant area, either for research or profit. The chapter covers recent theoretical, empirical, and experimental research on the effect of auction design parameters on outcomes, as well as bidding strategies themselves. The field is rich in results, in part because the theoretical work is well balanced by access to field and experimental data.

Perhaps it is the skill of the authors, but I am heartened to see so many concepts and phenomena from the foundations of pricing (as covered in earlier chapters), from marketing generally, and from consumer behavior in particular, show up in this excellent review.

Challenges ahead
A sub-theme throughout the *Handbook* is future research opportunities. In looking around today, I see many examples of practical pricing problems that seem to beg for investigation. Consider the exploding field of advertising on search engines. In the early days of the Internet, when people were proclaiming a 'new economy', many start-ups planned to pay their bills by selling advertising. This dream disappeared in the collapse of the Internet bubble. Then Google found a way to make advertising generate significant revenue. Its pricing mechanism was auctions. Google's revenue growth brought it a high stock price and a huge market valuation. Now Google competitors are trying to make advertising work too. This sounds like a pricing research challenge. The fundamentals presented in Vithala's *Handbook* will be important building blocks. The world is waiting for the right research team.

John D.C. Little
Institute Professor, MIT Sloan School,
Cambridge, MA, USA

Acknowledgments

I want to thank all the contributors to this *Handbook* for agreeing to contribute and for their care in revising the chapters. I also want to thank all the reviewers, who provided thoughtful comments for revision and thus helped improve the quality of the chapters included here. I sincerely appreciate their support in this venture. Special thanks go to Wilfred Amaldoss, whose encouragement was highly instrumental in my undertaking this project. I am grateful to Professor John D.C. Little for sparing time to compose the foreword to this *Handbook*. I also want to thank my faculty support aides at the Johnson School, Judy Wiiki and Sara Ashman for their administrative guidance in various tasks with lots of cheer. I thank Alan Sturmer of Edward Elgar, who provided invaluable support and guidance in bringing this effort to conclusion, and Caroline Cornish of Edward Elgar for efficiently managing the production of this volume.

Finally, I would also like to thank the reviewers who contributed to this *Handbook*: Asim Ansari (Columbia University), Pradeep Bharadwaj (Kenan-Flagler Business School, University of North Carolina at Chapel Hill), Eric Bradlow (Wharton School of the University of Pennsylvania), Preyas Desai (Fuqua School of Business, Duke University), J.-P. Dubé (The University of Chicago Booth School of Business), Josh Eliashberg (Wharton School of the University of Pennsylvania), Skander Esseghaier (Koç University), Vishal Gaur (The Johnson School at Cornell University), Srinagesh Gavirneni (The Johnson School at Cornell University), Miguel Gomez (Cornell University), Sachin Gupta (The Johnson School at Cornell University), Jim Hess (University of Houston), Teck Ho (Haas School of Business, University of California, Berkeley), Praveen Kopalle (Tuck School of Business at Dartmouth), Angela Y. Lee (Kellogg School of Management, Northwestern University), Tridib Mazumdar (Syracuse University), Carl Mela (Fuqua School of Business, Duke University), Sanjog Misra (University of Rochester), S.P. Raj (Syracuse University), Serdar Sayman (Koç University), Subrata Sen (Yale University), Milind Sohoni (Indian School of Business (ISB)), Manoj Thomas (The Johnson School at Cornell University), Naufel Vilcassim (London Business School), Russ Winer (Leonard N. Stern School of Business, New York University) and Robert Zeithammer (Anderson School of Management, UCLA).

For my wife, Saroj,
and our grandchildren,
Rheya, Vikram, Divya, and Alisha

Introduction
Vithala R. Rao

Introduction
There can be little doubt that pricing decisions are predominant among all the marketing mix decisions for a product (service or business). Pricing decisions interact with other marketing mix decisions and also with the decisions of distribution intermediaries of the firm.

Pricing research occurs in at least two disciplines of microeconomics and marketing. While the pricing research in microeconomics[1] is largely theoretical, research in marketing is primarily oriented toward managerial decisions. Further, pricing research in marketing is interdisciplinary, utilizing economic as well as behavioral (psychological) concepts. Research in marketing emphasizes measurement and estimation issues as well. The environment in which pricing decisions and transactions are implemented has also changed dramatically, mainly due to the advent of the Internet and the practices of advance selling and yield management. Over the years, marketing scholars have incorporated developments in game theory and microeconomics, behavioral decision theory, psychological and social dimensions, and newer market mechanisms of auctions in their contributions to pricing research. Examples include applications of prospect theory, newer conjoint analysis methods for measurement of price effects, newer market mechanisms of auctions, use of game theory in dealing with pricing along the distribution channel, and models that describe practices of advanced selling and yield management.

This *Handbook* consists of 26 chapters and is an attempt to bring together state-of-the-art research by established marketing scholars on various topics in pricing. The chapters are specifically written for this *Handbook*. The chapters cover various developments and concepts as applied to tackling pricing problems. Based on a thorough academic review, the authors have revised their initial drafts of chapters.

Overview of chapters in the *Handbook*
The chapters are organized into three major parts, labeled Parts I (8 chapters), II (9 chapters) and III (9 chapters). Part I covers topics that are in some sense fundamental to pricing research. Part II covers topics that deal with selected pricing decisions and marketing mix, while Part III covers some special topics that are emerging in pricing research.

---

[1] The two volumes of published articles on pricing tactics, strategies and outcomes edited by Waldman and Johnson (2007) epitomize the significant amount of research in microeconomics. A variety of topics is covered in the articles included in these volumes; examples are: pricing product line, pricing and consumer learning, collusive behavior, empirical studies of pricing strategies leasing and couponing.

Part I (eight chapters): fundamental topics

The chapter by Rao and Kartono describes the results and analyses of reported use of some 19 possible pricing strategies based on a survey among pricing decision-makers conducted in three countries. Three most frequently used strategies are the cost-plus, price signaling, and perceived value pricing, with considerable differences among the three countries. Their chapter also shows the relationships between the reported usage of strategies, and several determinants and pricing objectives. These descriptive results may form the basis for developing richer mathematical (possibly game-theoretic) models for optimal choice of pricing strategies.

Chapter 2, by Jedidi and Jagpal, focuses on the methods for measuring willingness to pay (WTP) or reservation price for a product or service, and using those measures in various pricing decisions such as bundling, quantity discounts and product line pricing. This concept is fundamental to both the theory and practice of pricing. In addition to self-stated WTP, the authors discuss methods for estimating WTP from actual purchase data, contingent evaluation data, conjoint methods and experimental auctions. They call for additional research on comparing the methods as well as developing newer methods. One example of a newer method is to measure reservation price as a range (Wang et al., 2007).

Chapter 3 by Liu, Otter and Allenby describes approaches to measure own- and cross-price effects particularly when there is a large number of offerings in a product category. This problem arises particularly in the retail context. They describe methods to reduce the dimensionality of the problem by employing economic theory of choice and demand, and Bayesian methods to augment the information contained in the data. Extension to estimating dynamic price effects is a challenging research issue, as identified by the authors.

Chapter 4 by Krishna focuses on the effects of price that cannot be accounted for by the intrinsic price itself. These effects, called 'behavioral effects', arise due to the way individual consumers are influenced by price presentation in comparison to an externally provided reference price or presentation of a promotional offer as absolute reduction in dollars or as a percentage reduction relative to normal price. The author discusses a variety of these effects using both laboratory experimental data and data of actual purchases. Clearly more work is possible in this fascinating area.

Chapter 5 by Ratchford deals with consumer search behavior and prices. The author reviews empirical studies that support the basic conjecture of Stigler made some 40 years earlier, namely that consumer search is costly and that it will create price dispersion. The review summarizes theoretical models of optimal search, and describes how costly search may affect the behavior of markets. Two of the key results in this literature are that price dispersion should exist in equilibrium, and that differences in search costs provide a motive for price discrimination. Also, there is heterogeneity of search behavior among consumers. The author also reviews the impact of the Internet on price dispersion. As he points out, there is need to develop models of pricing and price dispersion that are more closely related to actual seller behavior.

Chapter 6 by Chan, Kadiyali and Xiao emphasizes the need to specify appropriate assumptions for the behavior of consumers and firms to understand market outcomes. The resulting structural models suitably estimated will be useful for conducting simulations in determining optimal price policies for a varying set of market conditions. While this line of research is distinct from the reduced-form approach often employed in marketing research, it will undoubtedly enrich our understanding of the drivers of market prices. The structural approach offers possibilities to incorporate alternative behavioral assumptions and alternative ways of interactions among agents. It constitutes a step in the right direction for incorporating the impact of competition into pricing research.

Chapter 7 by Thomas and Morwitz describes implications of the anchoring, representativeness and availability heuristics on the judgments consumers make on the magnitude of prices of products or services and the order of numerical digits in the prices. For example, consumers may judge the differences to be large for pairs with easier computations than for pairs with difficult comparisons. These authors comment that pricing managers should decide not only the magnitude of the optimal price but should also pay attention to how the digits are arranged. This general area offers opportunities for exciting experimental research.

In Chapter 8, Anderson and Simester discuss the literature on the effectiveness of price cues that documents examples of firms exploiting their use. A price cue is any marketing tactic used to persuade customers that prices (posted) offer a good value. The authors review extant literature, document the effectiveness of price cues and present evidence for the economic explanation that customers respond to price cues if they lack sufficient knowledge of prices and if they cannot evaluate whether prices offer good value.

Part II (nine chapters): pricing decisions and marketing mix
Chapter 9 by Chatterjee provides a comprehensive review of the normative models developed in the literature on strategic pricing for new products and services that incorporate various factors such as consumer learning, diffusion, cost reduction and competition. This chapter also contains a review of relevant empirical research on the use of penetration pricing or skimming pricing strategies. There are interesting opportunities for building normative models to deal with nontraditional pricing schemes, such as pricing to maximize customer lifetime value and auctions on the Internet.

Chapter 10 by Chen reviews developments in pricing a product line, defined as the set of products or services sold by a firm that provide similar functionalities and serve similar needs and wants of consumers. The products in the line can be vertically or horizontally differentiated, or both. Factors such as customer self-selection and competition are included in the models and results reviewed are intuitively appealing. Various directions for future research are also suggested.

Chapter 11 by Venkatesh and Mahajan provides a comprehensive review of the design and pricing of product bundles, a practice that is growing in the wake of high technology and e-Commerce. The authors have drawn a set of guidelines for bundle pricing based on a large body of traditional models in the literature as well as newer methodologies. Opportunities exist in this area for both behavioral research and analytical modeling.

Chapter 12 by Pauwels and Srinivasan describes the issues involved in pricing of national brands relative to store brands (or private label brands) in light of the increasing quality equivalence between them. The authors suggest that in most cases national brands possess some degree of pricing and market power over store brands. They discuss the sources of such power in terms of price premium, volume premium and margin premium, and suggest directions for future work.

Chapter 13 by Narasimhan describes the tradeoffs involved in using trade promotions versus lowering price or advertising in the B2C markets. The chapter reviews different types of trade promotions, the rationale behind using them, the potential impact on the channel partners, and managerial implications. The chapter concludes with several suggestions for future research such as the need to examine the role of trade promotions in a firm's overall pricing strategy.

Chapter 14 by Zhang discusses how prices can be customized for specific targets. This problem has become quite significant due to the unprecedented capability of firms to store and process past buying information on customers and the ability of firms to tailor prices to individual customers. The chapter answers such questions as 'Is target pricing beneficial to firms?', 'What is the best way of designing incentives if targeted pricing is followed?', and 'Is target pricing beneficial to society as a whole?' Some surprising results are discussed, as well as future directions for research in this emerging area.

Chapter 15 by Sudhir and Datta provides a critical review of research in pricing within a distribution channel. Specifically, the authors review the literature on three decisions, which vary in terms of planning horizon, on retail pass-through, pricing contracts and channel design. They also review the empirical literature on structural econometric models of channels and suggest directions for future research. For example, opportunities exist to study channel behavior in the presence of nonlinear pricing contracts (the topic of Chapter 16) and developing methodologies that endogenize retailers' decision to carry the product.

Chapter 16 by Iyengar and Gupta covers nonlinear pricing and related multi-part pricing paradigms, and reviews the extant literature. The authors point out that while two-part tariffs may be nearly optimal in many settings, there is a need to examine more complex pricing schemes. They also discuss the challenges involved in analyzing pricing schemes due to the two-way relationship between price and consumption (as in telephone pricing) and show some approaches to tackling such problems. They present some empirical generalizations and identify areas for future research.

Chapter 17 by Seetharaman focuses on how state dependence and reference prices affect consumer choices over time and their pricing implications for firms competing in oligopolistic markets. Based on a review of various econometric models of dynamic pricing, he identifies research opportunities for incorporating reference price effects in descriptive models of what firms actually do in practice.

Part III (nine chapters): special topics
Chapter 18 by Amaldoss and Jain focuses on how social needs such as prestige influence purchase decisions. The authors show that snobs can have an upward-sloping demand curve only in the presence of consumers who are conformists. They also investigate how social needs may influence the prices and qualities of the products that consumers choose to buy. There are opportunities to extend their one-period game to deal with multi-period decisions and also to incorporate reference group effects and brand equity.

Chapter 19 by Park and Wang provides a review of recent research on the emerging market mechanism of online auctions. Their survey covers theoretical, empirical and experimental research on the effects of auction design parameters of minimum price, buy price, and duration, bidding strategies and competition. They also discuss the name-your-own-price mechanism. They call for additional empirical research on the effects of auction design parameters, experiments to study the effects of bidder behavior, and studies on bidder learning. Research in this area will undoubtedly proliferate in the future.

Chapter 20 by Liu and Chintagunta deals with the subject matter of pricing under network effects. They review the early literature on static pricing under network effects that focused on the effects of price expectations and the multiple equilibria problem. They state that penetration pricing has been found optimal under various scenarios. Their review of analytical literature of pricing under network effects connects with other literatures. Noting that empirical research is scarce in this area, they identify issues that limit such research.

Chapter 21 by Xie and Shugan covers how prices should be set under the new paradigm of advance selling that has been facilitated by developments in technology. They discuss how the profit advantage of advance selling is quite general and is not severely restricted by industry structures. They also show that simply offering advance selling can improve profits because it separates purchase and consumption, which creates buyer uncertainty about their future product/service evaluation and removes seller information disadvantage. They identify several research opportunities in such areas as the evaluation of consequences and profitability of advance selling in many new situations, and sellers offering multiple advance periods.

Chapter 22 by Kimes discusses the strategic role of price in revenue management. Revenue management has been practiced in the airline, hotel and car rental industries for some time and is receiving attention in other industries such as broadcasting and golf. The chapter reviews the literature on models of revenue management allocation and pricing, and the practices in industry. There are opportunities to incorporate competitive reactions in such models.

Chapter 23 by Kina and Wosinska discusses the various institutional characteristics that affect pricing of prescription drugs. The chapter provides insights on the role of various players in this complex price-setting problem. The authors identify three distinct areas for future research – clarifying the market, ways to optimize the current system, and the influence of changes in the regulatory and institutional environment on pricing pharmaceutical products. Research opportunities in this topic are considerable.

Chapter 24 by Liu and Weinberg describes how pricing decisions particularly challenge not-for-profit organizations, which have a social rather than a profit objective function. The authors show how the pricing models in the nonprofit sector are different from those of for-profit businesses. The chapter surveys findings in the theoretical and empirical research on nonprofit organizations. The authors identify special issues in relating constructs of consumer taste and willingness to pay commonly employed in pricing models for the nonprofit sector. They describe interesting research opportunities in examining the effects of price–quality and product differentiation in the nonprofit sector.

Chapter 25 by Shoemaker and Mattila focuses on the pricing issues in the services sector in general. The authors review how the special characteristics of services such as intangibility and simultaneous production and consumption offer unique challenges to the firm in setting prices. Their framework is an attempt to show how various factors affect consumers' reservation price for a service and how this interacts with the way a firm can formulate service offers to gain maximum revenues. They provide illustrations of practice and suggest research possibilities in this important sector of the economy.

The final chapter, Chapter 26 by Ho and Su, provides a selective review of pricing models that are of interest to operations management researchers. The authors review developments in four specific pricing models, two of which are based on inventory (EOQ and Newsvendor), dynamic pricing models, and queuing models. They show how firms' pricing decisions serve as an important lever to shape consumer behavior and optimize profits. One common theme of this chapter is that consumers respond strategically and actively engage in operational decision-making. The authors suggest opportunities to extend this line of work to conditions that relax the rationality assumptions.

Research directions

Interestingly, several of the research directions identified in my previous reviews of pricing literature (Rao, 1984 and 1993) have been pursued. In a similar manner, I hope that the research topics mentioned in the chapters of this *Handbook* will inspire future researchers. It is possible that future research on pricing will be tilted toward the newer pricing mechanisms that are aided by technology.

References

Rao, Vithala R. (1984), 'Pricing research in marketing: the state of the art', *Journal of Business*, **57** (1, Pt 2), S39–S60.
Rao, Vithala R. (1993), 'Pricing models in marketing', in J. Eliashberg and G.L. Lilien (eds), *Handbooks in Operations Research and Management Science, Volume 5: Marketing*, Amsterdam: North-Holland, pp. 517–52.
Waldman, Michael and Justin P. Johnson (2007) (eds), *Pricing Tactics, Strategies, and Outcomes*, Volumes I and II, Cheltenham, UK and Northampton, MA, USA: Edward Elgar Publishing.
Wang, Tan, R. Venkatesh and Rabikar Chatterjee (2007), 'Reservation price as a range: an incentive-compatible measurement approach', *Journal of Marketing Research*, **44** (May), 200–213.

PART I

INTRODUCTION/ FOUNDATIONS

1 Pricing objectives and strategies: a cross-country survey

*Vithala R. Rao and Benjamin Kartono**

Abstract
This chapter reports the results of a descriptive study on pricing objectives and strategies based on a survey among managers in three countries (USA, India and Singapore). The survey instrument was developed using a conceptual framework developed after an analysis of the extant literature on pricing objectives, strategies and factors that influence the choice of pricing strategies. Data were collected on firms' utilization of 19 possible pricing strategies, pricing objectives and various pricing determinants. The responses were used to estimate logit models of choice of pricing strategies. The results reveal interesting differences among the three countries as well as the use of different strategies. The implications of this descriptive study for guidance of pricing are discussed.

1. Introduction

Pricing is the only element of the marketing mix that brings revenues to a firm. While there are extensive theories/models of how a firm should price its goods and services, descriptive research on how firms make their pricing decisions is sparse in the literature. One may argue that descriptive research can help model builders in developing more realistic models for pricing. Various researchers in the past have been concerned about the practice of pricing and the degree to which it departs from theory. Yet our understanding of the pricing processes is still in its infancy.

The present chapter attempts to contribute to the descriptive pricing literature by not only examining the problem across various industries and countries, but also accounting for the effect of another important element of the pricing decision: the company/product conditions, market conditions, and competitive conditions that influence the pricing strategy adopted by the firm (collectively labeled as 'pricing strategy determinants' by Noble and Gruca, 1999). To complete the analysis, we also consider another element that can play a part in influencing pricing decisions, namely demographic characteristics of the firms in question as well as those of the individuals within the firms. In the sections that follow, we review extant descriptive research on pricing, present a conceptual framework that illustrates how firms determine their choice of pricing strategy, and describe the results of an empirical study that we conducted in three countries to assess the applicability of the framework.

---

* We thank Subrata Sen for providing valuable comments on an earlier draft of this chapter, and Shyam Shankar for his assistance in analysis of the survey data.

10   *Handbook of pricing research in marketing*

2. Selected review of past research

Descriptive research on how firms decide on the specific strategies[1] of pricing is quite limited in the literature. Table 1.1 summarizes the main findings of seven studies beginning with the one by Hall and Hitch (1939) and ending with Avlonitis and Indounas (2005). All of these studies utilized either mail questionnaires and/or personal interviews to obtain data from samples of managers with a view to determining their pricing and profit objectives while pricing their products and services.

Table 1.1   A summary of past studies on pricing objectives and strategies of firms

Author(s)	Date	Objectives of the study	Methodology employed	Some findings
Hall and Hitch	1939	To determine the way business executives decide what price to charge for their products	Use of a questionnaire and lengthy interviews among 38 business executives	Ten of the firms used conventional or full cost policy in setting prices, and methods for computing full cost varied among the firms. A large fraction of firms do not adopt the principle of marginal revenue equals marginal cost in setting prices. Firms take competitor reaction into account while pricing their products.
Lanzillotti	1958	To determine the pricing objectives of a sample of large US industrial firms	Postprandial research – lengthy interviews conducted at two points in time among officials of firms	Several pricing objectives such as achieving a target rate of return, stabilization of price and margin, realizing a target market share, and meeting or preventing competition were uncovered in this study.
Shipley	1981	To determine pricing and profit objectives of British manufacturing firms	Use of a mail questionnaire sent to a stratified sample of sales and marketing directors listed in KOMPASS; responses obtained from 728 firms	General finding that there is a considerable heterogeneity of pricing and profit objectives that vary with size and number of competitors. Firms pursue a multiplicity of objectives while pricing their products. One-third of the firms do not list profit objective.
Samiee	1987	To examine the role of pricing in marketing plans of US- and	Mail survey among 104 US- and 88 foreign-based companies	While there are differences in the role of pricing among the two groups of firms, pricing decisions are found to be more centrally made

[1]   In the literature, the term 'pricing method' is sometimes used in place of the term 'pricing strategy'. For example, Oxenfeldt (1973), Diamantopoulos and Mathews (1995) and Avlonitis and Indounas (2005) use the former while articles such as Tellis (1986) and Noble and Gruca (1999) adopt the latter. In this chapter, we use both terms interchangeably.

Table 1.1 (continued)

Author(s)	Date	Objectives of the study	Methodology employed	Some findings
		foreign-based companies operating in the USA as well as how pricing decisions are made and the objectives for pricing	and personal interviews among executives from 12 such companies	in the US-based companies. Pricing objectives are found to be similar; the major objectives are: satisfactory ROI, maintenance of market share, reaching a specified profit goal, seeking largest market share, and profit maximization.
Jobber and Hooley	1987	To examine pricing objectives for both manufacturing and service companies, differences by stage of market evolution, size of the firm, and the relationship between pricing objectives and performance	Mail survey among 1775 members of the UK Institute of Marketing; questionnaire developed using interviews among 150 executives	Pricing objectives are found to vary by stage of market evolution and size of the firm. For example, maximization of current sales revenues is found to be more important for emerging/new markets as compared to growth markets. Profit maximization and market share attainment/maximization were similar by stage of the market evolution. Small and medium-sized firms used profit maximization as pricing objective more than large firms. Both positive and negative relationships between pricing objectives and performance were found.
Noble and Gruca	1999	To organize the existing theories of pricing and to determine which factors account for the use of specific strategies	Based on extensive literature search, a questionnaire was constructed and administered to 270 managers in industrial firms in the USA. The researchers developed logistic regression models that relate the strategy choices to a variety of factors deemed relevant to pricing strategy.	In general, the authors found that managers' pricing strategy choices are consistent with normative pricing research. This conclusion applies to four specific stets of pricing strategies: new product pricing, competitive pricing, product line pricing and cost-based pricing.

Table 1.1 (continued)

Author(s)	Date	Objectives of the study	Methodology employed	Some findings
Avlonitis and Indounas	2005	To explore the association between pricing objectives and strategies in the services sector	Personal interviews involving 170 companies from six different service sectors in Greece. Logistic regression was used to assess the impact of pricing objectives on the adopted strategies.	The key pricing objectives adopted are fundamentally qualitative in nature and determined with customers' needs and satisfaction in mind, but the pricing strategies used tend to be firm-centric, with the cost-plus method and pricing according to average market prices adopted by most of the firms.

To illustrate, the study by Lanzillotti (1958) utilized personal interviews among officials of a purposive sample of 20 large US corporations and attempted to understand various goals pursued by their pricing policies. He found that these firms had a varied set of goals such as increasing market share, maintenance of market share, achieving a 'fair' return on investment, achieving a minimum rate of return, stabilization of prices, and matching competitor prices. Noble and Gruca (1999) adopted the same basic approach and developed a comprehensive list of factors that affect the choice of pricing strategies of firms. Further, they developed statistical relationships (*à la* the logit model) between the choice of a pricing strategy and a number of determinants of that choice. They identified the factors using normative pricing research and other conjectures about the determinants. More recently, Avlonitis and Indounas (2005) explored the relationship between firms' pricing objectives and their corresponding pricing strategies in the services sector using a sample of 170 Greek companies and found clear associations between specific strategies and objectives.

Several researchers have studied the issue of price stickiness, which is broadly related to that of pricing strategies. The question here is how often firms change prices of products and services they offer. A significant example of this research theme is the extensive study by Blinder et al. (1998), who use interviews among executives to understand why prices are sticky in the US economy; their conclusions are that price stickiness is the rule and not an exception, and that business executives do not adjust prices based on macroeconomic considerations. There is some ongoing work by Bewley (2007), who is conducting interviews among business executives to look at the issue of price stickiness; he reaches a somewhat opposite conclusion that price rigidity is far from being the rule and that prices for a large volume of trade are flexible. In contrast to the studies based on interviews, Lien (2007) analyzes micro-data at the firm level reported in quarterly surveys in Switzerland and concludes that inclusion of macroeconomic variables adds only marginally to the explanatory power of a price adjustment probability model that includes firm-specific variables. A similar study is reported by Cornille and Dossche (2006), who use Belgian data on firm-level prices reported for the computation of the Producers' Price Index and find that one out of four Belgian prices changes in a typical month.

While these studies have offered a number of insights into how firms set prices, more empirical research needs to be done to better understand the price-setting process and, in particular, the relationship between firms' pricing objectives, pricing strategies and other elements of the pricing decision. Indeed, Avlonitis and Indounas (2005) state that their extensive review of the literature revealed a lack of any prior work investigating the potential association between a firm's pricing objectives and pricing methods, and that their work is a first attempt at studying this issue empirically within the context of the service industry. The present chapter attempts to further close this gap in the pricing literature by studying how firms' pricing strategies may be affected by their pricing objectives and various firm, market, and competitive conditions. The study was done on firms operating in three countries (USA, India, and Singapore) across a variety of industries and also examines the relationship between the firms' pricing strategies and selected demographic characteristics of the firm.

3. Conceptual framework for pricing decisions

In general, the factors that affect a firm's choice of a pricing strategy can be classified under two broad categories: the pricing objectives of the firm, and pricing strategy determinants. The latter refers to the various company/product conditions, market and customer (consumer) conditions, and competitive conditions that may influence the pricing strategies adopted. In addition, because the data on pricing choices of firms are usually collected by the survey method from managers, certain demographic characteristics of the individual respondents will also matter. Figure 1.1 shows the conceptual framework we adopt in this chapter. It follows the approach of Noble and Gruca (1999), and develops statistical relationships between the choice of a pricing strategy and various relevant factors. Unlike Noble and Gruca (1999), however, in addition to examining the relationship between pricing strategy determinants and the choice of strategy, our framework also looks into the effect of pricing objectives as well as respondent and firm characteristics (such as the respondent's degree of influence in pricing decisions and the size of the firm) on the pricing strategy adopted.

We established our list of possible pricing objectives for the firm based on Diamantopoulos and Mathews (1995, ch. 5). Based on extensive empirical evidence obtained over a two-year period from an in-depth study of a large, oligopolistic manufacturing firm in the medical supplies industry, the authors developed a comprehensive list of possible objectives that managers may seek to accomplish through their pricing decisions. Next, we developed our list of pricing strategy determinants based on the comprehensive outline given in Noble and Gruca (1999). In addition to the determinants studied by the authors, we extended the list to include a number of other determinants relevant to the pricing decision. The complete list of pricing objectives and pricing strategy determinants is given in our empirical study in the next section. Finally, we developed our list of 19 possible pricing strategies which the firm can adopt (for both consumer and industrial markets) through a detailed review of the pricing strategy literature, in particular Tellis (1986) and Noble and Gruca (1999). These strategies[2] cover a variety of possible pricing situations such as competitive

---

[2] Some of these pricing strategies raise legal issues, but such a discussion is beyond the scope of this chapter; see Nagle and Holden (2006) for discussion.

14 *Handbook of pricing research in marketing*

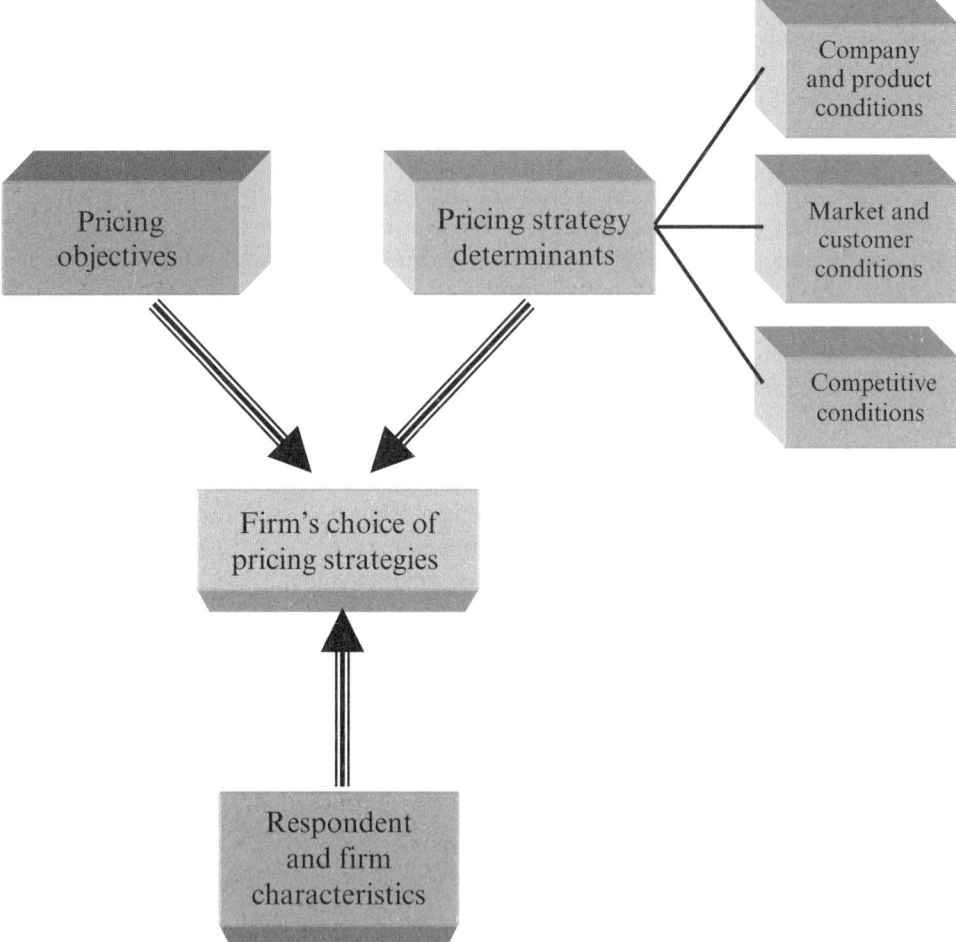

Figure 1.1   The pricing decision: a framework for analyzing a firm's choice of pricing strategies

pricing, cost-based pricing, new product pricing, product line pricing, geographic-based pricing and customer-based pricing. Descriptions of these strategies are given in Table 1.2. One 'new' strategy that we have included, which has not been extensively looked at in the pricing strategy literature, is Internet pricing. We define Internet pricing as the strategy of pricing a product differently on the firm's website compared to the firm's other sales outlets (for example, firms may price their products lower if consumers purchase them online and directly from the firm because of the reduction in costs obtained from not having to pay wholesale and retail margins), and can be thought of as a strategy of pricing differently across channels of distribution (with a focus on direct selling through the Internet). Our reason for including this pricing strategy stems from the increase in Internet commerce that has occurred over the last decade, and we expect this strategy to grow in importance as Internet usage and Internet commerce continue to increase across countries and markets.

Table 1.2 Pricing strategies and their descriptions

Pricing strategy	Description of strategy
1. Price skimming	We set the initial price high and then systematically reduce it over time. Customers expect prices to eventually fall.
2. Penetration pricing	We set the initial price low to accelerate product adoption.
3. Experience curve pricing	We set the price low to build volume and reduce costs through accumulated experience.
4. Leader pricing	We initiate a price change and expect other firms to follow.
5. Parity pricing	We match the price set by the overall market or price leader.
6. Low-price supplier	We always strive to have the lowest price on the market.
7. Complementary product pricing	We price the core product low when complementary items such as accessories, supplies and services can be priced higher.
8. Price bundling	We offer this product as part of a bundle of several products, usually at a total price that is lower than the sum of individual prices.
9. Customer value pricing	We price one version of our product at very competitive levels, offering fewer features than are available on other versions.
10. Cost-plus pricing	We establish the price of the product at a point that gives us a specified percentage profit margin over our costs.
11. Break-even pricing	We establish the price of the product at a point that will allow us to recover the costs of developing the product.
12. Price signaling	We use price to signal the quality of our product to customers.
13. Image pricing	We offer an identical version of the product at a higher price.
14. Premium pricing	We price one version of our product at a premium, offering more features than are available on other versions.
15. Second market discounting	We price this product at very competitive levels for the purpose of exporting or selling in secondary markets.
16. Periodic or random discounts	We periodically or randomly lower the price of this product.
17. Geographic pricing	We price this product differently for different geographic markets.
18. Perceived value pricing	We price this product based on our customers' perceptions of the product's value.
19. Internet pricing	We price this product differently on our Internet website compared to the price we charge through our other sales outlets.

Our review of the extant literature on descriptive, empirical pricing research suggests that ours is the first study that brings together all three key elements of the pricing decision: the pricing objectives, the pricing strategy determinants and, finally, the pricing strategies adopted. In a nutshell, pricing strategies are the means by which the firm's pricing objectives are to be achieved, while the determinants are the internal and external conditions faced by the firm that influence managers' choice of pricing strategies. Our aim is to obtain a more holistic view of the pricing decision, and provide a better understanding of the relationship between each key element of the decision. In addition, the fact that our study was conducted across a number of countries enables us to study any potential differences or similarities in pricing decisions made by firms in different countries. In the next section, we describe our empirical study in detail.

16   *Handbook of pricing research in marketing*

4. Empirical study

The study was conducted via a survey of firms operating in the USA, Singapore and India over a period of about a year beginning in November 2003. The cross-country survey was done primarily by mail and survey questionnaires were sent out to more than 600 firms in each country across a variety of industries. A total of 199 usable responses were obtained, of which 73 were from firms operating in the USA, 54 were from firms operating in Singapore, and 72 were from firms operating in India. The goals of the study were, first, to examine the applicability of our framework in describing the relationship between firms' pricing objectives, pricing strategy determinants and pricing strategies, and, second, to compare the firms' pricing decisions across different countries.

The survey covered products at different stages of the product life cycle (PLC) and spanned a number of different industries and product types. Given the nature of the method used, we cannot claim a representative sample of the population. But the results provide a snapshot of how firms make pricing decisions, as illustrated by the pricing strategies they adopted, their determinants, and the associated pricing objectives. In this section, we first provide a detailed summary of our survey and descriptive statistics of the survey results, and then describe our modeling approach for estimating the statistical relationships between pricing strategy choice and its determinants for several types of pricing strategies. We then present and discuss the results of our estimation and conclude by discussing some directions for future research.

4.1   *Survey and descriptive statistics*

In the survey, the respondents were first asked to name one primary product sold by their firm in the domestic market, provide some background information about the product, and answer all remaining questions in the survey with reference to only the named product. Information on the pricing strategies adopted for this product was then collected by asking the respondents to select up to five strategies from a given list of pricing strategies and to indicate the relative percentage importance of each selected strategy such that the total importance across all selected strategies summed to 100 percent. Next, the respondents were presented with a list of possible pricing objectives that their firm may seek to accomplish by adopting the selected pricing strategies and asked to rate the importance of each objective on a five-point scale. Following that, the respondents were presented with the list of pricing strategy determinants that may play a part in determining the kinds of pricing strategies adopted by the firm and asked to rate the degree to which each condition affects the pricing strategies adopted. Finally, the respondents were asked to provide some information on the profile of the firm and their professional experience.

Product profile   The product information collected in the survey included the name of the product, the price of a unit of the product, the type of product (service or physical product), its stage in the PLC, the price of the product relative to the market, and whether the product was sold to businesses, end-consumers, or both. About 72 percent of the responses obtained were based on physical products, while the rest were based on service products such as financial services or business consultancy services. The products were mostly in the growth (37 percent) or maturity (54 percent) stages of the PLC, although these figures differed somewhat across countries. In terms of the price of the product

Table 1.3 Product profile (all figures in percentages)

	USA	Singapore	India	Full sample
Product type (% physical product)	60.3	68.5	87.5	72.4
Stage of the product life cycle				
Introduction	9.6	9.3	4.2	7.5
Growth	34.2	22.2	50.0	36.7
Maturity	54.8	66.7	43.1	53.8
Decline	1.4	1.9	2.8	2.0
Mean price of product relative to the market*	3.60	3.80	3.66	3.67
Product user				
Individual consumers or households	32.9	27.8	31.9	31.2
Businesses or organizations	42.5	44.4	26.4	37.2
Both	24.7	27.8	41.7	31.7

Note: * Price relative to market: 1 = 5% or more below the market; 2 = 1 to 4% below the market; 3 = same as the market; 4 = 1 to 4% above the market; and 5 = 5% or more above the market.

relative to the market, on a five-point scale where 1 = 5 percent or more below the market, 3 = same as the market, and 5 = 5 percent or more above the market, the sample mean was 3.67, suggesting that most of the products were priced at the same level as or slightly higher than the market. This phenomenon was consistent across all three countries, and the products concerned were distributed fairly evenly among consumer and business markets. Table 1.3 presents a summary of the product profiles.

Pricing strategies Each respondent was presented with the list of 19 pricing strategies encompassing a variety of pricing situations. The respondent was asked to select up to five pricing strategies from the list and to indicate the relative importance of each selected strategy such that they summed to 100 percent. For the sample as a whole, the most frequently used pricing strategy was cost-plus pricing (47.2 percent of firms), with a mean percentage importance of 37.8 percent. This was followed by price signaling (37.7 percent of firms, mean importance of 22.6 percent), perceived value pricing (34.2 percent of firms, mean importance of 33.1 percent), and parity pricing (31.7 percent of firms, mean importance of 36.9 percent). The least frequently used pricing strategies were Internet pricing (3 percent of firms, mean importance of 12.5 percent) and both break-even pricing (7.5 percent of firms, mean importance of 24.7 percent) and second market discounting (7.5 percent of firms, mean importance of 20 percent). In some cases, the frequency of usage and mean importance of certain pricing strategies varied considerably across countries. For example, only 9.7 percent of firms in India used perceived value pricing, while the figure was 52.1 percent in the USA and 42.6 percent in Singapore (the mean importance of perceived value pricing among firms that use this strategy, however, was fairly similar across countries and ranged from about 28 percent to 34 percent). Similarly, almost 42 percent of firms in India used parity pricing (mean importance of 43.2 percent), while

Table 1.4a *Usage frequency (percentage of firms) and mean percentage importance of pricing strategies*

Pricing strategy	Usage frequency (%)				Mean importance (%)			
	USA	S'pore	India	Full sample	USA	S'pore	India	Full sample
1. Price skimming	13.7	16.7	13.9	14.6	22.5	32.8	21.5	25.3
2. Penetration pricing	8.2	18.5	12.5	12.6	25.8	23.0	33.3	27.4
3. Experience curve pricing	12.3	9.3	11.1	11.1	21.1	32.0	30.6	27.0
4. Leader pricing	12.3	13.0	36.1	21.1	35.0	17.1	32.5	30.5
5. Parity pricing	23.3	29.6	41.7	31.7	35.5	26.6	43.2	36.9
6. Low-price supplier	5.5	9.3	6.9	7.0	27.5	28.0	32.0	29.3
7. Complementary product pricing	11.0	7.4	5.6	8.0	27.5	17.5	15.0	21.9
8. Price bundling	16.4	20.4	8.3	14.6	26.3	27.2	20.5	25.4
9. Customer value pricing	12.3	18.5	15.3	15.1	15.0	25.0	22.7	21.2
10. Cost-plus pricing	46.6	42.6	51.4	47.2	41.5	35.1	35.9	37.8
11. Break-even pricing	6.8	7.4	8.3	7.5	23.0	22.5	27.5	24.7
12. Price signaling	31.5	48.1	36.1	37.7	21.1	26.5	20.0	22.6
13. Image pricing	2.7	9.3	5.6	5.5	10.0	14.0	22.5	16.4
14. Premium pricing	31.5	24.1	29.2	28.6	24.9	21.5	22.6	23.3
15. Second market discounting	4.1	5.6	12.5	7.5	18.3	20.0	20.6	20.0
16. Periodic or random discounts	16.4	22.2	13.9	17.1	23.3	20.8	16.0	20.3
17. Geographic pricing	13.7	16.7	26.4	19.1	17.8	21.1	18.4	18.9
18. Perceived value pricing	52.1	42.6	9.7	34.2	34.3	32.8	27.9	33.1
19. Internet pricing	2.7	7.4	0.0	3.0	7.5	15.0	0.0	12.5
20. Other pricing strategies	15.1	5.6	6.9	9.5	54.3	53.3	47.0	52.2

Notes: The above table may be read as follows. As an example, consider price skimming. The column under 'USA usage frequency' shows that 13.7% of the US firms in the sample employ price skimming. Similarly, 16.7% of the Singaporean firms, 13.9% of the Indian firms and 14.6% of all the firms in the sample use price skimming. The column under 'USA mean importance' shows that on average, an importance rating of 22.5% is allocated to price skimming among US firms adopting this strategy (relative to any other pricing strategies that these firms also adopt). Likewise, the mean importance rating for price skimming is 32.8% for Singaporean firms, 21.5% for Indian firms and 25.3% for all firms in the sample employing this strategy. The percentages in each column do not add up to 100% because each firm can select between one to five different pricing strategies.

only about 30 percent of Singapore firms and 23 percent of US firms adopted this pricing strategy (with mean importance of 26.6 percent and 35.5 percent respectively). Detailed information on the usage frequency and mean importance of each pricing strategy are provided in Table 1.4a.

Table 1.4b shows the number (and percentage) of pricing strategies adopted (ranging

Table 1.4b Frequency and percentage of firms using multiple strategies

	USA	S'pore	India	Full sample
No. of firms employing 1 pricing strategy	5 (6.8%)	1 (1.9%)	3 (4.2%)	9 (4.5%)
No. of firms employing 2 pricing strategies	11 (15.1%)	9 (16.7%)	18 (25.0%)	38 (19.1%)
No. of firms employing 3 pricing strategies	20 (27.4%)	14 (25.9%)	13 (18.1%)	47 (23.6%)
No. of firms employing 4 pricing strategies	22 (30.1%)	13 (24.1%)	22 (30.6%)	57 (28.6%)
No. of firms employing 5 (or more) pricing strategies	15 (20.5%)	17 (31.5%)	16 (22.2%)	48 (24.1%)
Total	73 (100%)	54 (100%)	72 (100%)	199 (100%)

Note: * Figures in parentheses show the percentage of firms employing the stated number of pricing strategies as a percentage of the total for that column.

from one strategy up to five or more) by the firms in each country and across the entire sample. Less than 5 percent of firms in the sample employ only one pricing strategy, and indeed, more than half the firms in the sample employ at least four different pricing strategies for the (same) product which they were asked to consider in the survey.

Besides choosing from the given list of pricing strategies, the respondents were also given an option to describe any additional strategies used by their firm that were not part of the given list (about 10 percent of respondents provided such information, with these strategies having a mean importance of 52.2 percent). These strategies included strategies such as contract pricing (where a fixed price for a certain quantity of purchase is agreed upon between the firm and the customer), customer segment pricing (where prices charged depend on the profile or characteristics of the customer), channel member pricing (where prices depend on recommendations or requirements put forth by the firm's distributors in the supply chain), and regulatory pricing (where prices are controlled by the government).

In addition, the respondents were asked if the increase in Internet usage among both consumers and businesses over the last several years has affected their firms' pricing decisions and if their firms have developed any new pricing strategies as a result of this increase. On the whole, the pricing decisions of 16.2 percent of the firms have been affected by the increase in Internet usage. Most of these firms came from Singapore (29.6 percent of firms) compared to 16.7 percent of firms in the USA and 5.6 percent of firms in India. Overall, about 9 percent of firms have developed new pricing strategies due to the increase in Internet usage. Most of these firms came from the USA and Singapore, where about 13 percent of firms reported having developed new pricing strategies, compared to about 3 percent in India.

Pricing objectives To better understand the role of pricing objectives in the firm's choice of pricing strategy, the respondents were presented with a list of 17 possible objectives and asked to rate the importance of achieving each objective with regard to the most

Table 1.5 *Mean ratings of importance of pricing objectives (1 = not at all important, 5 = extremely important)*

Pricing objectives	US mean importance	Singapore mean importance	India mean importance	Full sample mean importance
1. Increase or maintain market share	4.21	4.02	4.15	4.14
2. Increase or maintain sales volume	4.16	4.17	4.14	4.16
3. Project a desired product image	3.57	3.96	3.21	3.55
4. Match competitor pricing	2.85	3.19	3.07	3.02
5. Increase or maintain money gross profit	3.72	4.02	3.86	3.85
6. Maintain level of competition	3.42	3.54	3.18	3.36
7. Avoid price wars	2.50	3.09	2.65	2.72
8. Increase or maintain sales revenue	4.12	4.00	3.72	3.94
9. Maintain distributor support	2.69	2.94	2.60	2.72
10. Increase or maintain gross profit margin	3.88	4.15	3.88	3.95
11. Achieve rational price structure	3.06	3.33	2.93	3.09
12. Erect or maintain barriers to entry	2.28	2.54	2.28	2.35
13. Increase or maintain liquidity	2.21	2.48	2.46	2.37
14. Undercut competitor pricing	1.97	1.98	1.94	1.96
15. Avoid government attention or intervention	1.47	1.94	1.74	1.70
16. Avoid customer complaints about unfair prices	2.11	2.61	2.43	2.36
17. Cover costs	3.57	3.69	3.44	3.56

important pricing strategy they have selected on a five-point scale where 1 represents 'not at all important' and 5 represents 'extremely important'. For the sample as a whole, the most important objectives were those of increasing or maintaining market share (mean importance rating of 4.14) and increasing or maintaining sales volume (mean importance rating of 4.16). These were followed by the objectives of increasing or maintaining gross profit margin (mean importance rating of 3.95) and that of increasing or maintaining sales revenue (mean importance rating of 3.94). The least important objectives were those of avoiding government attention or intervention and undercutting competitor pricing (mean importance rating of 1.70 and 1.96 respectively). The complete list of objectives and the importance ratings of each pricing objective for each country and for the sample as a whole are given in Table 1.5.

Pricing strategy determinants To examine the role of various pricing strategy determinants (expressed in the form of company and product conditions, market and customer conditions, and competitive conditions) in influencing choice of pricing strategy, the respondents were asked to rate the level or intensity of these conditions with regard to

Pricing objectives and strategies 21

the named product. Company and product determinants included the age of the product, issues relating to product design, production costs and capacity utilization, the firm's market share and coverage, the profitability of accompanying and supplementary sales, and the number of intermediaries in the supply chain. Market and customer determinants of pricing strategies included the sensitivity of the firm's customers to price differences between brands, sensitivity of market demand to changes in average price, ease of determining market demand, market growth rate, customer costs and legal constraints. Competitive determinants included the degree of product differentiation between brands, the ease of detecting competitive price changes, and market share concentration of the leading firms in the industry. Table 1.6 presents a summary of the respondents' mean ratings of these pricing strategy determinants, together with the appropriate rating scales.

Table 1.6 Mean ratings of pricing strategy determinants

Pricing strategy determinants	Rating scale	USA	S'pore	India	Full sample
Market conditions					
1. Sensitivity of customers to price differences between brands	1 = Insensitive, 7 = Sensitive	4.92	4.85	4.66	4.81
2. Sensitivity of market demand to changes in average price	1 = Insensitive, 7 = Sensitive	3.85	4.54	4.00	4.09
3. Ease of determining market demand	1 = Difficult, 7 = Easy	3.86	4.04	4.34	4.08
4. Market growth rate	1 = Low, 7 = High	3.92	4.00	4.54	4.16
5. Customer switching costs	1 = Low, 7 = High	3.21	3.94	3.65	3.56
6. Customer search costs	1 = Low, 7 = High	3.21	3.68	3.06	3.28
7. Customer transaction costs	1 = Low, 7 = High	2.96	3.47	3.21	3.18
8. Impact of the Internet on market demand	1 = Low, 7 = High	2.15	2.48	1.38	1.98
9. Legal constraints	1 = Low, 7 = High	2.48	2.28	2.06	2.27
Competitive conditions					
10. Ease of detecting competitive price changes	1 = Difficult, 7 = Easy	4.82	4.50	5.12	4.84
11. Market share concentration of the top three firms in the industry	1 = Less than 5%, 7 = Greater than 80%	5.04	5.09	5.40	5.19
12. Product differentiation between brands	1 = Low, 7 = High	4.08	4.09	3.62	3.92
13. Impact of the Internet on competitive conditions	1 = Low, 7 = High	2.37	2.68	1.42	2.13
Product/company conditions					
14. Estimated age of product in years		7.28	7.61	8.45	7.79
15. Cost disadvantage due to experience curve	Percentage of firms	34.2%	27.8%	43.1%	35.6%

Table 1.6 (continued)

Pricing strategy determinants	Rating scale	USA	S'pore	India	Full sample
16. Cost disadvantage due to economies of scale	Percentage of firms	35.9%	33.3%	47.2%	39.4%
17. Capacity utilization (relative to other products)	1 = Low, 7 = High	4.75	4.71	5.37	4.96
18. Costs (relative to competitors)	1 = Disadvantage 7 = Advantage	4.15	4.28	4.21	4.21
19. Major product change (significance of most current design change)	Percentage of firms	21.4%	20.4%	13.9%	18.2%
20. Market coverage	Percentage of firms serving only one customer segment	8.2%	9.3%	2.8%	6.5%
21. Market share	1 = Low, 7 = High	5.19	5.04	5.59	5.29
22. Per sale/contract pricing	1 = Low, 7 = High	0.53	0.57	0.38	0.49
23. Profitability of accompanying sales	1 = Low, 7 = High	4.34	4.15	3.26	3.89
24. Profitability of supplementary sales	1 = Low, 7 = High	3.15	3.53	2.64	3.06
25. Number of intermediaries in supply chain	1 = Low, 7 = High	2.92	2.69	2.81	2.81
26. Costs of developing the product	1 = Low, 7 = High	4.25	4.22	4.48	4.28
27. Impact of the Internet on product/company conditions	1 = Low, 7 = High	2.73	2.98	1.47	2.34

In terms of market and customer determinants of pricing strategy, the results suggest that customers are fairly sensitive to price differences between brands as well as to changes in the average price. The former is particularly true in the USA and Singapore, possibly due to the higher number of alternative brands available to customers in these highly developed markets, while the latter is especially so for Singapore, due to the small and concentrated nature of its market. All three markets appear to have a moderate growth rate. Customer costs (switching, search and transaction costs) are moderately low across all three markets. Finally, both the impact of the increase in Internet usage on market demand as well as legal constraints on pricing strategies appear to be rather low as well, suggesting, for the former, that most customers still employ traditional methods of shopping and purchase, and, for the latter, that government regulations on pricing are not too restrictive.

The ratings for the competitive determinants of pricing strategy suggest that it is fairly easy for the firms surveyed to detect competitive price changes in the market. Additionally, oligopolistic competition seems to prevail across all three countries, with the top three firms in various industries commanding (in total) more than half the market share in the industry. Product differentiation between brands appears to be moderate and, as before, the impact of the Internet on the competitive conditions faced by the firms appears to be low.

Finally, in terms of the company and product determinants of pricing strategy, the ratings across firms in all three markets appear to be moderate and quite similar across countries, with a couple of exceptions. The first pertains to the frequency of a major product change – more than 20 percent of firms in the USA and Singapore report having made a significant change in their current product design while the figure is about 14 percent for India. The second pertains to market coverage: the products marketed by the Indian firms tend to serve multiple customer segments, with only 2.8 percent of Indian firms reporting that they serve only one segment, vis-à-vis 8.2 percent and 9.3 percent for firms in the USA and Singapore respectively.

Profile of firms and respondents The firms from which the survey responses were obtained cover a diverse range of industries and product categories. They also ranged from small-scale businesses with fewer than ten employees and annual revenues of less than $10 million to large, multinational corporations with several hundred thousand employees and billions of dollars in revenue. Most of the respondents surveyed were middle or senior managers who have had a significant number of years of managerial experience (average of 11.1 years) and have been employed in their present position for a considerable period of time (average of 4.5 years). In addition, most respondents have a fairly high degree of involvement in their firm's pricing decisions, with an average involvement rating of 5.45 on a seven-point scale where 1 represents 'not involved at all' and 7 represents 'strongly involved'. Detailed descriptive statistics on the profile of the firms and respondents are available from the authors.

4.2 Data analysis and discussion

We examined the relationship between the firms' choice of pricing strategies, pricing objectives and pricing strategy determinants by carrying out binary logistic regressions with the choice of the pricing strategy as the dependent variable and relevant variables representing the objectives, determinants, as well as firm and respondent characteristics as the explanatory variables. This section describes our data analysis procedure and its results.

Modeling approach and estimation Given that we collected a large number of variables in the study, we used factor analysis to see if the cumulative set of variables could be reduced to a smaller set of orthogonal factors, which would then be used to estimate the binary choice models for the different pricing strategies. The factor analysis was conducted separately on the groups of variables representing the pricing objectives, the pricing strategy, determinants, as well as the characteristics of the firm and the respondent.

The factor analysis for the 17 variables representing pricing objectives was relatively straightforward. The results shown in Table 1.7 indicate that the 17 objectives can be grouped into nine composite objectives, which explains 78.8 percent of the variance in the data.

The survey had outlined 27 possible determinants of pricing strategy that may influence a firm's choice of pricing strategies, broadly classified under three categories of business conditions: company and product conditions, market and customer conditions, and

24 *Handbook of pricing research in marketing*

Table 1.7 *Factor analysis of the pricing objectives*

Pricing objective	Factor loading	Name for the factor
1. Increase or maintain market share	0.79	Increase or maintain market share
2. Increase or maintain sales volume	0.85	
3. Increase or maintain sales revenue	0.73	
4. Increase or maintain gross profit dollars	0.83	Increase or maintain profit
5. Increase or maintain gross profit margin	0.86	
6. Cover costs	0.52	
7. Match competitor pricing	0.70	Competitor-based pricing
8. Undercut competitor pricing	0.84	
9. Achieve rational price structure	0.82	Rational pricing
10. Increase or maintain liquidity	0.58	
11. Maintain level of competition	0.50	Maintain competitive level
12. Avoid price wars	0.85	
13. Avoid government attention or intervention	0.62	Avoid government attention
14. Avoid customer complaints about unfair prices	0.88	
15. Erect or maintain barriers to entry	0.82	Erect or maintain barriers to entry
16. Maintain distributor support	0.87	Maintain distributor support
17. Project a desired product image	0.96	Project desired product image

competitive conditions. The results of the factor analysis on the 27 variables are shown in Table 1.8, and enabled us to simplify the set of 27 measured variables into 12 factors, which explains 77.4 percent of the variance in the original variables. All but two of the factor loadings are in the expected direction.

In addition to pricing objectives and determinants relating to the business conditions under which the firms are operating, specific demographic characteristics of the survey respondent and the firm may also play a part in affecting the choice of pricing strategy. To account for the effect of such respondent characteristics, we used the size of the firm and the degree of involvement of the respondent with the firm's pricing decisions as two other explanatory variables in the choice model. As with the pricing objectives and determinants, these two variables were based on a factor analysis of the demographic measures we collected in the survey.

The net result of the variable reduction exercise yielded 23 variables[3] (that affect choice of pricing strategy) for the choice model, and is summarized in Table 1.9. In addition, we included two dummy variables to take account of the country differences among the three countries; one dummy variable to represent US respondents and one to represent Singapore respondents.

---

[3] We use variables directly rather than factor scores to retain the specific meaning of the determinants of pricing strategies and ease of interpretation.

Pricing objectives and strategies 25

Table 1.8 *Factor analysis of the measured pricing strategy determinants*

Pricing determinants	Factor loading	Name for the factor
1. Impact of Internet on competitive conditions faced by firm	0.93	Impact of the Internet
2. Impact of Internet on market demand	0.90	
3. Impact of Internet on product/company conditions faced by your firm	0.80	
4. Customer switching costs	0.80	Customer costs
5. Customer search costs	0.76	
6. Customer transaction costs	0.76	
7. Cost disadvantage due to experience curve	0.92	Cost disadvantages
8. Cost disadvantage due to economies of scale	0.91	
9. Profitability of accompanying sales	0.84	Other sources of profit
10. Profitability of supplementary sales	0.74	
11. Sensitivity of customers to price differences between brands	0.79	Customer price sensitivity
12. Sensitivity of market demand to changes in average price	0.78	
13. Legal constraints	0.36	
14. Per sale/contract pricing	0.38	
15. Capacity utilization (relative to other products)	0.74	Capacity utilization
16. Age of product in years	0.64	
17. Costs relative to competitors	0.58	
18. Market share	0.69	Market share
19. Market share concentration of top three firms in the industry	0.68	
20. Ease of detecting competitive price changes	0.52	
21. Number of intermediaries in the supply chain	0.39	Intermediaries in the supply chain
22. Product differentiation between brands	−0.44	Product differentiation
23. Major product change	0.79	
24. Costs of developing the product	0.39	Market development costs
25. Market coverage	0.89	
26. Market growth rate	0.89	Market growth rate
27. Ease of determining market demand	0.60	Market demand determination

Our study examined a list of 19 possible pricing strategies, and we focused our analysis on six of the most important strategies as chosen by the respondents. We first selected the specific pricing strategy deemed by each respondent as the one with largest importance (out of possible five strategies that could be indicated by the respondent) for the product in question. We then identified the following six strategies that are most frequent with this criterion; the frequencies of these six strategies are: 53 for cost-plus pricing, 35 for

Table 1.9 Summary of the various factors affecting the choice of pricing strategy

Category	Factors
Pricing objectives	Increase or maintain market share
	Increase or maintain profit
	Competitor-based pricing
	Rational pricing
	Maintain competitive level
	Avoid government attention
	Erect or maintain barriers to entry
	Maintain distributor support
	Project desired product image
Pricing strategy determinants	*Company and product factors*
	Cost disadvantages
	Other sources of profit
	Capacity utilization
	Intermediaries in the supply chain
	Market and customer factors
	Impact of the Internet
	Customer costs
	Customer price sensitivity
	Market development costs
	Market growth
	Market demand determination
	Competitive factors
	Market share
	Product differentiation
Respondent characteristics	Firm size (number of employees)
	Degree of involvement in pricing

perceived value pricing, 34 for parity pricing, 16 for price signaling, and 14 each for premium pricing and leader pricing. We estimated the choice model in the form of binary logistic regressions for each of the six pricing strategies. Based on the factor analyses done above, there were 25 independent variables: 9 variables were for the objectives of pricing strategies, 12 for the determinants of strategy, 2 country variables and 1 variable each for the size of the firm and the degree of involvement of the respondent. The logistic regression model was run with all the 25 variables. Consequently, even variables that are not significant were a part of the model.

Results and discussion The estimated coefficients for the six pricing strategies are given in Table 1.10. This section discusses the estimation results and the observed relationship between the key elements of the pricing decision.

COST-PLUS PRICING Cost-plus pricing refers to the pricing of a product at a predetermined margin over the product's estimated production costs. Although it is historically a commonly used pricing method, critics have warned against the viability of cost-plus pricing as a profitable pricing strategy because not only does it ignore the customer's valuation of

Table 1.10 *Estimated logistic regression coefficients for six pricing strategies*

Variable name	Cost-plus pricing	Perceived value pricing	Parity pricing	Price signaling	Premium pricing	Leader pricing
Country – USA	0.211	1.882*	−25.397*	−0.199	2.497	0.165
Country – Singapore	0.398	2.417*	−2.178*	1.390	3.072	−23.794
Pricing objectives						
Increase or maintain market share	0.049	0.122	0.152	−0.011	−0.506*	−0.454
Increase or maintain profit	0.473*	−0.100	−0.180*	0.017	0.083	−0.541*
Competitor-based pricing	0.089	−0.307*	0.290*	−0.410	−0.657*	−0.212
Rational pricing	0.213*	−0.116	0.109	−0.194	−0.615*	0.072
Maintain competitive level	−0.161	−0.075	0.337*	0.680*	0.443	−0.557
Avoid government attention	0.097	0.044	−0.135	−0.104	0.395	1.008*
Erect or maintain barriers to entry	−0.384*	0.409*	0.016*	0.092	−0.181	−0.232
Maintain distributor support	0.038	0.042	0.027*	−0.702*	0.858	−0.443
Project desired product image	−0.356*	0.294	−0.194	0.484	0.957*	2.716*
Pricing strategy determinants						
Impact of the Internet	−0.030	−0.038	0.308*	0.112	−0.380*	−0.571
Customer costs	0.041	−0.060	0.597*	−0.074	−0.347*	−0.473*
Cost disadvantages	−0.274	0.053	1.193	−0.733*	−0.200	1.606*
Other sources of profit	−0.028	−0.032	−0.166	0.001	0.211	0.158
Customer price sensitivity	0.016	−0.032	1.181*	0.043	0.131	−0.190
Capacity utilization	−0.040	−0.033	−0.129	0.248	−0.271	0.100
Market share	0.034	−0.046	−0.028	0.199	−0.088	1.476*
Intermediaries in the supply chain	−0.231*	−0.035	−0.252	0.157	−0.058	1.397*
Product differentiation	0.244*	0.097	−0.483	0.531*	−0.091	−1.377*
Market development costs	−0.047	0.055	0.262	0.033	0.157	0.018
Market growth rate	0.011	−0.178	0.249	−0.204	1.378*	0.801
Market demand determination	0.048	0.228	0.490	0.262	−0.379	0.137
Respondent and firm characteristics						
Firm size (number of employees)	0.189*	0.074	0.000	−0.192	0.634*	−0.924*
Degree of involvement in pricing	−0.212*	0.107	−0.009	0.045	0.280	0.053
Constant	−4.828*	−4.433*	−3.696*	−9.881*	−9.200*	−16.727*

Table 1.10 (continued)

Variable name	Cost-plus pricing	Perceived value pricing	Parity pricing	Price signaling	Premium pricing	Leader pricing
Number of observations	199	199	199	199	199	199
2lnL (negative)	168.222	139.532	123.172	68.128	48.268	37.936
Cox & Snell R-square	0.269	0.205	0.256	0.195	0.234	0.273
Hosmer–Lemeshow Chi Square (8 df)	8.867	NA	15.491	26.191	4.619	3.788
Percent correct predictions	79.9	82.9	82.8	93.5	95.5	93.0
Number selecting this strategy	53	35	34	16	14	14

Notes: Values in bold are significant at 0.20 or below.
Values in bold with an asterisk (*) are significant at 0.10 or below.

the product, it may in fact harm profitability by overpricing the product in weak markets and underpricing it when demand is strong. In fact, some researchers argue that using a product's cost to determine its price does not make sense because it is impossible to determine a product's unit cost accurately without first knowing its sales volume (which depends on price), and thus cost-plus pricers are 'forced to make the absurd assumption that they can set price without affecting volume' (Nagle and Hogan, 2006, p. 3). Nevertheless, the results of the present study suggest that it is in fact the most popular pricing strategy used by firms across different industries and countries.

In adopting cost-plus pricing, the estimation results show that the most significant pricing objectives are to increase or maintain profit and to maintain a rational pricing structure. Indeed, one of the key reasons behind the popularity of cost-plus pricing is that it brings with it an air of financial prudence. It is a conservative approach that balances risks and returns by seeking to achieve an acceptable level of financial viability rather than maximum profitability. However, cost-plus pricing tends to go against a firm's objective of erecting or maintaining barriers to entry and maintaining a desired product image. It is difficult for an incumbent to price low enough to deter new entrants if it needs to achieve a predetermined margin over its estimated production costs, and since it is a pricing strategy that accounts for only the firm's supply constraints and fails to consider the customer's perception of the product, it will be difficult to use it to influence the product's image in the customer mindset.

In terms of the pricing strategy determinants, the firm's cost disadvantages have a significant and negative impact on the choice of a cost-plus pricing strategy. This result appears counter-intuitive at first, since the higher a firm's estimated costs of production, the more necessary it will be to cover these costs adequately and, hence, the more one would expect the firm to adopt the cost-plus method. However, as shown in Table 1.4b, most firms use multiple pricing strategies even for the same product. It is likely that the firms are trying to find an optimal balance between cost-plus pricing and other methods that take into account other issues besides costs, particularly when cost-plus pricing on its own leads to unreasonably high and uncompetitive prices. Next, the greater the number of intermediaries in the firm's supply chain, the less likely the firm is to adopt cost-plus pricing. This is because more intermediaries not only leads to more cost disadvantages, but also results in reduced pricing control for the firm with regard to the final price charged to consumers, making it more difficult for the firm to specify a target profit margin for its product. On the other hand, a high level of product differentiation increases the likelihood of a firm adopting cost-plus pricing. This is because competitive pricing pressures are reduced for a unique product, enabling the firm to set a price that is commensurate with the product's costs.

Finally, in terms of respondent and firm characteristics, larger firms are more likely to adopt cost-plus pricing, while the lower the survey respondent's degree of involvement with the pricing decision, the more likely the firm is to adopt this strategy. This may be because larger firms are more likely to have established pricing policies and cost-plus calculation methods in place, developed by their accounting and finance departments, which specify minimum pricing requirements above estimated production costs in order to achieve a certain projected return. In view of these policies, marketing managers are likely to have less flexibility over pricing decisions. As for the country-specific effects, the coefficients on the country dummies suggest no significant difference in a firm's likelihood of adopting cost-plus pricing across the three countries considered, which makes sense given its popularity as a pricing method.

PERCEIVED VALUE PRICING   Perceived value pricing, the next most frequently used pricing strategy, refers to the practice of pricing the product in accordance with what customers perceive the product to be worth. It is a customer-centric approach to pricing that prioritizes the customer's product valuation above cost, competition and other considerations.

Looking at the coefficients for pricing objectives, we observe that competitor-based pricing has a negative relationship with the likelihood of adopting perceived value pricing. This is because the more a firm looks toward the customer in its pricing decisions, the less concerned it is about competitive pricing pressures. Next, the more a firm wants to stop new players from entering the market, the more likely it is to adopt perceived value pricing. Customers who believe that they are getting value for money are more likely to remain loyal to incumbent firms and will hence make the market less attractive for new entrants. Finally, it is interesting to note that maintaining a desired product image does not significantly affect the likelihood of adopting perceived value pricing. An explanation for this could be that product image does not necessarily have to do with a product's value or quality. For instance, in the automobile market, Volvo consistently projects an image of safety, while in the digital music player market, the Apple iPod projects a hip, cool and user-friendly image. In both cases, however, the desired image was established less through the respective firms' pricing strategies and more through consistent and effective advertising messages, word of mouth, and other non-price methods. In other words, a good product image does not necessarily imply an expensive or exclusive product.

In terms of the pricing strategy determinants, the easier it is to determine the market demand, the more likely it is for a firm to use perceived value pricing. No other determinants are observed to significantly affect the likelihood of adopting perceived value pricing. When firms know where their customers come from and are more confident

30   *Handbook of pricing research in marketing*

about their projected sales figures, they can more easily set a price that is more acceptable to customers and at the same time minimizes risks to profitability. Accordingly, in terms of respondent characteristics, the higher the degree of involvement of the respondent with the pricing decision, the more likely it is for the firm to practice perceived value pricing, since this method requires a more flexible approach to pricing. Finally, the results show the presence of significant country-specific effects for perceived value pricing. Firms operating in the USA appear most likely to adopt this method, followed by Singapore and then India.

PARITY PRICING   Parity pricing refers to the practice of setting a price for the product that is comparable to that of the market leader or price leader. In the former case, it means pricing the product close to the prices set by the biggest player(s) in the industry (which may or may not be the lowest or highest price on the market). In the latter case, it means pricing the product close to the prices set by the lowest-price players on the market. It is a strategy that takes into account competitive pricing pressures more than other factors.

Looking at the coefficients on the pricing objective variables, we see that all three objectives that involve meeting competitive pricing pressures (competitor-based pricing, maintaining competitive level, and erecting or maintaining barriers to entry) have a positive relationship with a firm's likelihood of employing parity pricing, which is in line with expectations. Next, the desire to maintain distributor support also increases a firm's likelihood of using parity pricing. This is because in competitive markets, distributors are just as likely as customers to switch to a different supplier if the latter presents them with an opportunity to earn higher margins. Hence it is important for a firm to ensure that its distributors earn competitive margins, and one way of doing this (and demonstrating it to distributors) is by making sure that the (end-user) price of its product is comparable with those of other competing suppliers. Finally, the more a firm wants to increase or maintain its profit, the less likely it is to adopt parity pricing. This is also intuitively reasonable because, in this case, the firm is more concerned with setting prices that are comparable with the competition instead of maintaining or maximizing the product's profitability.

A number of pricing strategy determinants have a positive relationship with a firm's likelihood of using parity pricing. First, the higher the impact of the Internet on the firm's operating and business conditions, the more likely it is to adopt parity pricing. The exponential growth in global Internet usage over the last decade has greatly facilitated the flow of market information and reduced search and transaction costs for customers and distributors, making it easier for the latter to compare prices across potential suppliers. As a result, it has become more necessary for firms to price their products more competitively. Next, the higher the customer costs (in the form of search, transaction and switching costs) and the higher the customer price sensitivity, the more likely it is for a firm to practice parity pricing. The latter is self-explanatory, while the former can be explained by the notion that the more difficult it is for customers to compare or switch between suppliers, the more likely it is for firms to ignore pricing pressures from customers and focus on competitive pressures instead. In addition, high cost disadvantages and market development costs also lead to the increased likelihood of using parity pricing. This could be because firms are trying aggressively to recoup these costs and to make sure that they price in a manner that achieves a balance between per unit profitability (by pricing close to the market leader) and market share (by pricing close to the price leader), which can be more profitable in the long run than pricing at either extreme.

The estimation results also show that, in general, firms in India are most likely to adopt parity pricing, followed by firms in Singapore and then the USA. However, specific respondent and firm characteristics do not appear to have a significant impact on the likelihood of this strategy being adopted.

PRICE SIGNALING   Price signaling is the strategy of using price as an indicator to customers of the product's quality. Although other product attributes (such as brand name) may also influence customers' perceptions of a product's quality, price appears to be particularly influential, and most customers assume that price and quality are positively correlated. Accordingly, price signaling is one of the most popular pricing strategies that firms employ, as not only does it improve customers' quality perceptions of its product, the higher price also translates into larger margins. Like perceived value pricing, it is a customer-centric pricing strategy that focuses more on customers' product perceptions than on other factors.

The only significant pricing objective that increases a firm's likelihood of adopting price signaling appears to be maintaining the level of competition. Since the goal of price signaling is to communicate the quality of your product *vis-à-vis* the competition, it often involves setting a price that is comparable with (if not higher than) than the prices of competing products, thereby maintaining (or reducing) the level of competition and reducing the likelihood of a price war. In the same vein, having competitor-based pricing as a pricing objective significantly reduces the likelihood of price signaling being adopted, as does maintaining distributor support. The reason for the latter can again be attributed to the firm's focus on customers in adopting a price signaling strategy, even at the prospect of having distributors complain that a high retail price affects retail and intermediary sales. As in perceived value pricing, we note that projecting a desired image does not significantly influence the likelihood of price signaling being adopted as a strategy, and a similar reason as discussed previously may also be in effect here.

Looking at the coefficients on the pricing strategy determinants, the following variables increase the likelihood of price signaling being adopted by a firm: impact of the Internet, capacity utilization and product differentiation. As discussed under the section on parity pricing, the Internet has greatly facilitated the availability and flow of information to both firms and their customers. Many customers use the Internet to search for product information prior to purchase, and it serves as an efficient and cost-effective medium for firms to practice price signaling.[4] As for product differentiation, it is reasonable to postulate that firms that use price as an indicator of their product's quality typically have products that are quite differentiated from their competitors (or at least perceived to be so by the firm's customers), thereby justifying the higher relative price. Next, the capacity

---

[4]   Many customers also use the Internet to seek low prices, and this may seem to run contrary to firms' use of price signaling via the Internet to indicate the quality of their product. One explanation could be that firms that use price signaling on the Internet are those whose products are differentiated enough in terms of perceived quality to warrant a price signaling strategy, or those who have a product line, with some lower-quality products priced competitively and others (targeted at the less price-conscious customers) priced relatively higher.

utilization variable encompasses not only how much the product in question makes use of the firm's available production capacity relative to its other products, but also the age of the product and the costs of the product relative to the firm's competitors. The positive coefficient on the variable can thus be explained by the notion that the more the firm has invested in a product, in terms of both time and production costs, the more likely the product is in fact of considerably higher quality than alternative products and, hence, the more likely the firm is to use price signaling to communicate this quality to customers. In further support of this observation, the coefficient on the cost disadvantages variable is negative, indicating that the fewer cost disadvantages the firm has, the more likely it is to produce a better product, which in turn makes it more likely to adopt price signaling.

Finally, the estimation results suggest that firms in all the three countries where the survey was performed are equally likely to use price signaling. Similarly, specific firm and respondent characteristics do not appear to significantly influence the probability that a firm will adopt this strategy.

PREMIUM PRICING Premium pricing is the strategy of pricing one version of a firm's product at a premium, offering more features than are available on the firm's other products. It is a strategy employed by firms that have multiple versions of the same product along a product line, with each version targeted at different customer segments.

We note first that both country-specific effects and respondent and firm characteristics are significant in influencing the likelihood of adopting this strategy. Firms in Singapore are more likely to adopt premium pricing, followed by the USA and India. Larger firms also have a higher likelihood of using this strategy, which makes intuitive sense because larger firms are more likely to have different versions of their product(s) for sale. Likewise, the respondent's degree of involvement in the pricing decision also has a significant and positive impact on the firm's likelihood of using premium pricing.

The following pricing objectives have a negative impact on the likelihood of a firm employing premium pricing: increasing or maintaining market share, competitor-based pricing and rational pricing. Since premium pricing is targeted at customers who value feature-laden products and are generally quite willing to pay a premium for them, firms that use this strategy are less likely to focus on market share or competitive pricing issues, at least not for the product in question. Conversely, maintaining distributor support and projecting a desired product image increase a firm's likelihood of adopting premium pricing. By pricing different versions of its products accordingly, instead of having a 'one-size-fits-all' average price that may overprice some products and underprice others, overall sales should improve as customers are given the flexibility to choose and pay for the value received. In addition, distributors also have the flexibility of carrying some or all of the firm's products. Hence it is likely that improved distributor support can be achieved with this pricing strategy. As for maintaining a desired product image, premium pricing can certainly help to differentiate the premium product from not only other products in the firm's product line but competing firms' products, as well, thereby contributing toward the image desired for the product.

As for the pricing strategy determinants, the following variables are observed to have a negative influence on the likelihood of premium pricing being adopted: customer costs, the impact of the Internet and capacity utilization. Interestingly, the latter two are in contrast to price signaling, which is another strategy that involves the setting of high prices.

The explanation may be as follows. In terms of the impact of the Internet, the ease of obtaining product information provided by the Internet may induce the firm's customers (even the more feature-conscious and less price-conscious ones) to explore other product options, both within the firm's product line and from competing firms, and increase the likelihood that these customers will buy an alternative product. Hence it has a negative impact on the probability of adopting premium pricing. As for capacity utilization, the observed result can be explained by the notion that the less the firm has invested in the product in terms of time and production costs, the less likely it is for the product to be feature-laden and, hence, be priced using premium pricing. Finally, the estimation results show that market growth rate has a positive impact on the likelihood of adopting premium pricing. This is because the faster the market and the firm's customer base grow, the more diverse customer tastes are likely to be. Hence it becomes more likely for firms to introduce, to suit different customers different versions of the product, at least one of which is likely to be premium-priced.

LEADER PRICING   The sixth most frequently used pricing strategy is leader pricing, which refers to the practice of initiating a price change or establishing a benchmark price for a product in a category, and expecting other firms to follow. It is a pricing strategy that market leaders typically adopt, which makes its apparent popularity as a pricing strategy and the observed negative relationship between firm size and the likelihood of adopting leader pricing quite counter-intuitive. One reason for this could be that the firms in our sample are relatively small (Tables 1.7 and 1.9 show that about half the firms have annual revenues of less than $100 million and employ fewer than 500 people), suggesting that many of these firms compete in regional, local or niche markets of limited size where few or no major players dominate (as is the case in larger or global markets) and most players are of comparable footing with one another. In such markets, any price change initiated by a player is likely to be noticed by the other players. As with cost-plus pricing and price signaling, country-specific effects are not significant for leader pricing, suggesting that firms in all three countries are equally likely to adopt this pricing method.

The pricing objectives of increasing or maintaining market share, and increasing or maintaining profit, are observed to have negative relationships with the likelihood of adopting leader pricing. This is because the more competitors follow the benchmark set by the price leader, the more intense the competition and the more fragmented the market. This suggests that firms employ this strategy not as a primary strategy to enhance share or profitability, but more as a secondary strategy to be used when its primary strategies are inappropriate, such as when competition is intense and market demand is at its peak, with little room for further expansion. On the other hand, the more a firm wants to avoid government attention in its pricing decision, the more likely it is to adopt leader pricing. Similarly, leader pricing is more likely to be used when the firm wants to project a certain product image.

Lastly, in terms of the pricing strategy determinants, the observed results show that the higher the firm's market share, the more likely it is to adopt leader pricing since competitors are more likely to follow. Next, the higher the costs are to customers of buying and switching from the product (and presumably competing products), and the higher the degree of product differentiation, the less likely it is that the firm will adopt leader pricing. This may be because, under such situations, firms are less worried about competitors and can price their products more independently of them. However, as with parity pricing, the results suggest that high cost disadvantages lead to an increased probability of adopting leader pricing. This could be because, with high costs of production, firms are more likely to set prices at a level that can cover these costs adequately and hope that its competitors will follow suit. For the same reason, the more intermediaries there are in the supply chain (which translates to a cost disadvantage), the more likely it is that a firm will use leader pricing.

5. Conclusion and future research

The foregoing empirical study has provided a current overview of the kinds of pricing strategies that firms adopt and a discussion of the various factors affecting the adoption of these strategies, across three different countries. It has also made a first attempt at studying the relationship between the three key elements of the pricing decision under an integrated framework: the pricing strategies adopted by a firm, the pricing objectives that these strategies are meant to achieve, and the strategy determinants (in the form of internal and external business conditions) that can influence the firm's choice of pricing strategies. Firms adopt different pricing strategies to achieve a variety of objectives and, contrary to popular belief, pricing to cover costs (or cost-plus pricing) is not always the dominant objective. Many pricing strategies aimed at maximizing earnings, improving customers' product perceptions and addressing competitive pressures (sometimes at the expense of share or profit) are frequently adopted to achieve other objectives. In addition to managerial objectives, the business conditions that the firm is operating under can also greatly influence the type of pricing strategy adopted. These conditions encompass both the firm's internal constraints and competencies as well as the external pressures it faces from competitors, consumers and supply chain partners. While these pricing strategy determinants often go hand in hand with the firm's pricing objectives, at times they are observed to be at odds with one another. This is because firms typically have multiple pricing objectives at any one time, and often some of these objectives are in conflict with one another (e.g. using cost-plus pricing to maintain or increase profit while using parity pricing to meet competitive pricing pressures and deter new entrants). In such a situation, firms have to find the optimal tradeoff between the various objectives and pricing strategies adopted, while taking into account the relevant pricing strategy determinants, in a way that provides the maximum overall 'benefit' to the firm. This benefit may comprise one or more of the following performance indicators: profit, market share, customer support/loyalty and distributor support, among others.

While the study has provided some new insights into the firm's pricing decisions, much further work still needs to be done, particularly to address the limitations of the present study. First, as is the case for much of managerial survey-based research, the small size of the sample used in the study, especially in each country, is an issue. Because of this limitation, the survey data had to be pooled across countries when performing the logistic regression for each pricing strategy, leaving the two country dummies as the only variables to account for country-specific effects. If more responses had been obtained and separate regressions had been performed for each country, deeper insights would have been obtained into the difference in pricing decisions across the three countries.

Next, the logistic regression models estimated in the study also pooled many industries and product types together. While the advantage of such an approach is that it provides a general picture of how a firm (any firm in any industry) makes its pricing decision, the disadvantage is that it overlooks many interesting and critical differences in pricing decision-making that may exist across different industries. Future research can consider estimating separate models for different industries or product types. Along the same lines, various subsets of the array of pricing strategies, objectives and determinants considered may be more applicable to specific industries and products, and this would perhaps explain why many of the estimated coefficients in the regression models are non-significant. To address this limitation, more research needs to be done that first explores the applicability of various pricing strategies, objectives and determinants to various industries and products, after which a similar analysis of the relationships between these elements of the pricing decision can be done for each subset of industries and products.

Finally, while the descriptive study has provided a big picture of the relationship between the key elements of a pricing decision, more complex mathematical models can be developed to study this relationship in greater depth and under more rigorous modeling assumptions. For instance, rather than performing a binary logistic regression for each individual pricing strategy, which implicitly and somewhat unrealistically assumes that the pricing strategy choices within a firm were made independently, multinomial or multivariate pricing strategy choice models can be developed for the firms that would model the firm's strategy choice process more realistically. Other studies could incorporate game-theoretic frameworks that model the firm's optimal choice of pricing strategies, given its strategic considerations of its competitors' choices. The firm's objective function to be used in these game-theoretic models can vary from the popular profit function that is often used in game theory papers to other functions representing the many other objectives that the firm can have. The topic of price rigidity (or stickiness) warrants comprehensive econometric analyses for the US context using data collected for computing consumer price indexes and for other purposes.

References

Avlonitis, George J. and Kostis A. Indounas (2005), 'Pricing objectives and pricing methods in the services sector', *Journal of Services Marketing*, **19** (1), 47–57.
Bewley, Truman (2007), 'Report on an ongoing field study of pricing as it relates to menu costs', a handout prepared for a talk at the Cowles Foundation Conference, 'The Macroeconomics of Lumpy Adjustment', 11–12 June 2007.
Blinder, Alan S., Elie R.D. Canetti, David E. Lebow and Jeremy B. Rudd (1998), *Asking About Prices: A New Approach to Understanding Price Stickiness*, New York: Russell Foundation.
Cornille, David and Maarten Dossche (2006), 'The patterns and determinants of price setting in the Belgian industry', Working Paper No. 618, European Central Bank Working Paper Series.
Diamantopoulos, Adamantios and Brian Mathews (1995), *Making Pricing Decisions: A Study of Managerial Practice*, London: Chapman and Hall.
Hall, R. and C. Hitch (1939), 'Price theory and business behavior', *Oxford Economic Papers*, **2** (1), 12–45.
Jobber, David and Graham Hooley (1987), 'Pricing behavior in UK manufacturing and service industries', *Managerial and Decision Economics*, **8**, 167–71.
Lanzillotti, R.F. (1958), 'Pricing objectives in large companies', *American Economic Review*, **48** (December), 921–40.
Lien (Rupprecht), Sarah M. (2007), 'When do firms adjust prices? Evidence from micro panel data', KOF Working Paper No. 160.
Nagle, Thomas T. and John E. Hogan (2006), *The Strategy and Tactics of Pricing: A Guide to Growing More Profitably*, Princeton, NJ: Pearson Education.
Noble, Peter M. and Thomas S. Gruca (1999), 'Industrial pricing: theory and managerial practice', *Marketing Science*, **18** (3), 435–54.

Oxenfeldt, Alfred R. (1973), 'A decision making structure for price decisions', *Journal of Marketing*, **37** (January), 48–53.
Samiee, Saeed (1987), 'Pricing in marketing strategies of U.S. and foreign-based companies', *Journal of Business Research*, **15** (1), 17–30.
Shipley, David D. (1981), 'Pricing objectives in British manufacturing industry', *Journal of Industrial Economics*, **29** (4), 429–43.
Tellis, Gerard J. (1986), 'Beyond the many faces of price: an integration of pricing strategies', *Journal of Marketing*, **50** (October), 146–60.

2 Willingness to pay: measurement and managerial implications
*Kamel Jedidi and Sharan Jagpal**

Abstract
Accurately measuring consumers' willingness to pay (WTP) is central to any pricing decision. This chapter attempts to synthesize the theoretical and empirical literatures on WTP. We first present the various conceptual definitions of WTP. Then, we evaluate the advantages and disadvantages of alternative methods that have been proposed for measuring it. In this analysis, we distinguish between methods based on purchase data and those based on survey/experimental data (e.g. self-stated WTP, contingent valuation, conjoint analysis and experimental auctions). Finally, using numerical examples, we illustrate how managers can use WTP measures to make key strategic decisions involving bundling, nonlinear pricing and product line pricing.

1. Introduction

Knowledge of consumers' reservation prices or willingness to pay (WTP) is central to any pricing decision.[1] A survey conducted by Anderson et al. (1993) showed that managers regard consumer WTP as 'the cornerstone of marketing strategy', particularly in the areas of product development, value audits and competitive strategy. Consider the following managerial questions you would face as a new product manager:

- How does pricing affect the demand for my new product?
- What price should I charge for my new product?
- What is the likely demand for my new product if I charge this price?
- What are the sources of demand for the new product? What fractions of this demand come from cannibalization, switching from competitors, and market expansion? And which competitors will the new product affect most?
- Which products in my product line should be bundled? And how much should I charge for the bundle and for each of its components?
- How should I determine my product mix and my product-line pricing policy?
- If I can use a one-to-one marketing strategy, how should I customize prices across consumers or consumer segments?
- How should I determine the optimal quantity discount schedule for my product?

From the perspective of the standard economic theory of consumer choice, the key to answering all these questions is knowledge of consumers' WTP for current and new product offerings in a category. Consider, for instance, a phone company that is planning to bundle its landline and wireless services. If the market researcher has information on

---

* The authors thank Vithala Rao, Eric Bradlow and Olivier Toubia for their comments.
[1] Consistent with the literature, we shall use the term 'willingness to pay' interchangeably with 'reservation price'. Alternative definitions will be discussed later in the chapter.

how much each of the target consumers is willing to pay for each of these services and the bundle, then it is straightforward to determine the optimal prices for the bundle and its components. As another example, suppose TiVo is planning to expand its digital video recorder (DVR) product line by offering a high-definition Series 3 DVR model. Suppose the market researcher knows how much each of the target consumers is willing to pay for this new product and each of the existing DVRs in TiVo's product line. Suppose that s/he also knows consumers' WTP for generic boxes from cable companies. Then s/he can determine which consumers will switch away from the cable companies to purchase the new DVR (the customer switching effect), the extent to which TiVo's new product will compete with the other DVRs in its own product line (the cannibalization effect), and how category sales are likely to expand (the market expansion effect) as a result of TiVo's new offering. (See Jedidi and Zhang, 2002 for other examples.)

The practical importance of knowing consumers' WTP is not limited to answering these managerial questions. Knowledge of WTP is also necessary for market researchers in implementing many other nonlinear and customized pricing policies such as bundling, quantity discounts, target promotions and one-to-one pricing (Shaffer and Zhang, 1995). Furthermore, such knowledge bridges the gap between economic theory and marketing practice. Specifically, it enables researchers to study a number of other issues related to competitive interactions, policy evaluations, welfare economics and brand value.

There is a vast literature in marketing and economics on the measurement of WTP and its use for demand estimation, pricing decisions and policy evaluations (see Lusk and Hudson, 2004 for a review). In marketing, we are witnessing a renewed interest in the measurement of WTP (Chung and Rao, 2003; Jedidi et al., 2003; Jedidi and Zhang, 2002; Wertenbroch and Skiera, 2002; Wang et al., 2007). This growing interest stems from three factors. First, pricing and transaction data (e.g. scanner panel data) are readily available to estimate consumer WTP. Second, the advent of e-commerce has made mass customization possible, thus motivating the need for more accurate measurement of WTP (Wang et al., 2007). Third, methodological advances in Bayesian statistics, finite mixture models and experimental economics allow one to obtain more accurate estimates of WTP at the individual or segment levels.

The goal of this chapter is to synthesize the WTP literature, focusing on the measurement of WTP and showing how this information can be used to improve decision-making. The chapter is organized as follows. Section 2 presents the various conceptual definitions of WTP. Section 3 reviews the advantages and disadvantages of alternative methods that have been proposed to measure WTP. Section 4 illustrates how WTP measures can be used for various pricing decisions. Section 5 summarizes the main points and discusses future research directions.

2. Conceptual definitions of WTP

Jedidi and Zhang (2002, p. 1352) define a consumer's reservation price as 'the price at which a consumer is *indifferent* between buying and not buying the product'. Formally, consider a consumer with income y, who is considering whether to buy one unit of product g priced at p or to keep her money. Let $U(g, y - p)$ be her utility from buying the product and $U(0, y)$ the utility from not buying it. Then, by definition, the consumer's reservation price $R(g)$ for product g is implicitly given by

$$U(g, y - R(g)) - U(0, y) \equiv 0 \tag{2.1}$$

This is the standard definition of consumer reservation price in economics, and captures a consumer's maximum WTP for product g, given consumption opportunities elsewhere and the budget constraint she faces. Jedidi and Zhang (2002) show that, under fairly general assumptions about the consumer's utility function, the reservation price $R(g)$ always exists, such that for any $p \leq R(g)$ the consumer is better off purchasing the product. They also show that if the utility function is quasi-linear,[2] then faced with a choice among G products ($g = 1, \ldots, G$), to make the optimal choice decision a utility-maximizing consumer will need to know only her reservation prices for the product offerings and the corresponding prices for these products.

These theoretical properties imply that knowing a consumer's reservation prices for the products in the category is sufficient to predict whether or not she will buy from the product category in question and which of these products she will choose. Specifically, the consumer will choose the product option that provides the maximum surplus ($R(g) - p$) subject to the constraint that $p \leq R(g)$. She will not buy from the category if the maximum surplus across products is negative (i.e. for each product in the category, the consumer's reservation price is always less than the price of that product). Thus knowledge of consumers' reservation prices allows us to distinguish and capture three demand effects that a change in price or the introduction of a new product will generate in a market: the customer switching effect, the cannibalization effect and the market expansion effect. Cannibalization (switching) results when consumers derive more surplus ($R(g) - p$) from a new product offering than from the company's (competitors') existing products. Market expansion results when non-category buyers now derive positive surplus from the new offering.

Other related definitions of WTP have been used in the literature. Kohli and Mahajan (1991) define reservation price as the price at which the consumer's utility (say for a new product) begins to exceed the utility of the most preferred item in the consumer's evoked set (i.e. the set of brands which the consumer considers for purchase). That is, the reservation price for a new product is the price at which the consumer is indifferent between buying the new product and retaining the old one. Hauser and Urban (1986) define reservation price as the minimum price at which a consumer will no longer purchase the product. Varian (1992) defines reservation price as the price at or below which a consumer will purchase one unit of the good. Ariely et al. (2003) argue for a more flexible definition of reservation price. Specifically, they suggest that there is a threshold price up to which a consumer definitely buys the product, another threshold above which the consumer simply walks away, and a range of intermediate prices between these two thresholds in which consumer response is ambiguous.

Implicit in all these definitions of reservation price is a link to the probability of purchase (0 percent in Urban and Hauser's definition, 50 percent in Jedidi and Zhang, and 100 percent in Varian's). In order to reconcile these alternative definitions, Wang et al. (2007) suggest that one should distinguish three reservation prices:

---

[2] That is $U(g, y - p) = u(g) + \alpha(y - p)$ where $u(g)$ is the utility of product g and α is a scaling constant.

(a) *floor reservation price*, the maximum price at or below which a consumer will definitely buy one unit of the product (i.e. 100 percent purchase probability);
(b) *indifference reservation price*, the maximum price at which a consumer is indifferent between buying and not buying (i.e. 50 percent purchase probability); and
(c) *ceiling reservation price*, the minimum price at or above which a consumer will definitely not buy the product (i.e. 0 percent purchase probability).

3. Methods to measure WTP

Reservation prices can be estimated from either purchase data or survey/experimental data. The following methods based on survey/experimental data are commonly used: self-stated WTP, contingent valuation, conjoint analysis and experimental auctions. We consider several factors in evaluating the different measurement methods. The first factor concerns incentive compatibility. That is, how accurate is the method in providing an incentive to consumers to reveal their true WTP? The second factor concerns hypothetical bias. That is, how accurately can the method simulate the actual point-of-purchase context? Note that the issues of incentive compatibility and hypothetical bias are closely related to the conventional criteria of measurement reliability and internal and external validity in psychometric studies. The third factor pertains to the ability of the method to estimate reservation prices for new products with attributes that have not yet been made available in the market or have not varied sufficiently across products in the market to allow reliable estimation. A fourth factor relates to the ability of the method to measure WTP for multiple brands in a given category (e.g. different brands of toothpaste) or for multiple products across product categories (e.g. product bundles). This information is essential for estimating cross-price effects among new and competing products where the competing products could be products within a firm's product line, product items in a bundle, or competitive products.

3.1 Methods based on actual purchase data

These methods analyze scanner/household panel data, test-market data, or simulated test-market data. They provide two important advantages. Because the input data come from actual purchases, these methods are incentive compatible and do not suffer from hypothetical bias. Household panel data, for example, provide useful information about consumers' responses to the price changes of an existing brand and those of its competitors. Such information is useful for predicting the impact of a price change on category incidence, brand choice and quantity decisions (Jedidi et al., 1999). For new products, simulated test market methods such as ASSESSOR (Silk and Urban, 1978) and AC Nielsen BASES provide consumers with the opportunity to buy (real) new products at experimentally manipulated price points. In ASSESSOR, for example, participants are first shown advertisements for the new and existing products. Then they are given seed money that they can keep or use to buy any of the available products displayed in a simulated store. This experimental design provides data on how the demand for the new product varies across the posted prices.

Despite these advantages, however, methods based on actual purchase data have several weaknesses. The main shortcoming is that, because of cost, the firm must choose a limited number of price points for its own product. In addition, the firm can examine only a limited number of price combinations for market prices across competitors. For example, suppose Procter & Gamble (P&G) is competing against three brands in a particular segment of the toothpaste market; in addition, P&G already has one brand of its own (say Crest) in that segment. Let's say that P&G wishes to test the impact of two price points for a new brand that it plans to introduce in this market segment. For simplicity, assume that each of the four incumbent brands (including P&G's own brand) can choose one of two price policies following the new product introduction. The first is to continue with the current price and the second is to reduce price. Then, it will be necessary for P&G to run 32 ($=2^5$) separate experiments to examine all the feasible competitive scenarios before choosing a pricing plan for the new product.

In addition, as Wertenbroch and Skiera (2002) note, data from purchase experiments provide only limited information about WTP. To illustrate, suppose P&G conducts an ASSESSOR study for a new product. Let's say that, for the posted set of prices for the new product and its competitors, 30 percent of the respondents purchase the new product. Then the only inferences that P&G can make are the following. Given the posted set of market prices, 30 percent of the respondents obtain maximum (positive) surplus by purchasing the new product. The remaining 70 percent of the respondents obtain maximum surpluses by buying another brand or not purchasing a brand in the product category. Note that this information is extremely limited. Specifically, since the experiment does not provide estimates of WTP *per se*, P&G cannot estimate new product demand for any other price for the new product or its competitors. Hence P&G cannot use the purchase data to determine the optimal price for the new product or the optimal product line policy.

3.2 Self-stated WTP

This method directly asks a consumer how much she is willing to pay for the product. Consequently, this is perhaps the easiest method to implement. However, for a number of reasons, this method is likely to lead to inaccurate results. Perhaps the most serious problem is that the consumer is not required to purchase the product. Hence the methodology is not incentive compatible. A related problem is that consumers are likely to overstate their WTP for well-known or prestigious brands or for products they are keenly interested in. They are also likely to understate their WTP for less well-known brands or if they anticipate being charged a higher price for the product in the future. Finally, even if consumers are able to correctly state their WTP on average, this method will overstate the degree of heterogeneity in WTP in the population.[3] Hence the firm will make suboptimal pricing decisions using self-stated WTP data.

An interesting managerial question is whether self-stated WTP are similar to the estimates obtained by using other methods. Jedidi and Zhang (2002) examined the correlation between self-stated WTP for different brands of notebook computers and WTP that were estimated using a conjoint experiment. (We shall discuss the conjoint methodology in subsection 3.4.) The results for two brands showed that the correlations were low (0.43 and 0.28 respectively). The correlation coefficient for the third brand was not statistically significant. Furthermore, the self-stated WTP led to excessively high estimates of demand

---

[3] The variance of the observed WTP is always greater than or equal to the variance of the true WTP.

42   *Handbook of pricing research in marketing*

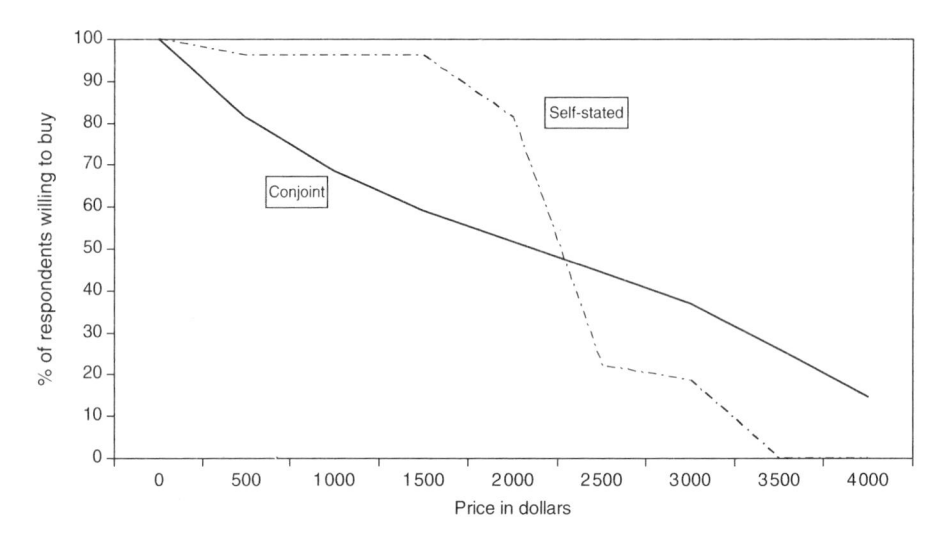

Figure 2.1   Conjoint versus self-stated demand estimates

at low prices and significantly understated the demand at high prices. Figure 2.1 shows the demand functions obtained from both methods for a Dell notebook computer with 266 mHz in speed, 64 MB in memory, and 4 GB in hard drive.[4] These results strongly support the observation in the previous paragraph that the firm should not use self-stated WTP to make pricing decisions.

3.3   Contingent valuation methods

Contingent valuation (CV) is a popular WTP measurement method in agricultural economics and in determining the economic impact of changes in social policy. This method uses dichotomous choice questions to arrive at an estimate of WTP for each respondent in the experiment. In a marketing CV study, the researcher presents consumers with a new product, including its price, and asks them whether they would buy the new product at the listed price (Cameron and James, 1987). Thus a yes response indicates that the consumer is willing to pay *at least* the listed price for the new product. When these yes responses are aggregated across consumers, one obtains a demand curve that shows how the proportion of yes responses varies across the experimentally manipulated price levels.

Estimating WTP from CV data is straightforward using a binary choice model such as logit or probit (Cameron and James, 1987). In such a choice model, the decision of whether to buy or not is modeled through a latent utility function that depends on product characteristics and consumer background variables. Let p_i be the price of the new product given to consumer i. Let I_i be a variable that indicates whether consumer i decided to buy ($I_i = 1$) or not ($I_i = 0$). Let $U_i = x_i'\hat{a} + \varepsilon_i$ be the latent utility of the

---

[4]   The percentage willing to buy is the percentage of respondents whose WTP is higher than the observed price.

product concept, where x_i is a vector of explanatory variables that includes product characteristics (excluding price) and individual-specific consumer background variables, â is a vector of associated parameters, and ϵ_i is an error term. Then the binary choice model is given by

$$I_i = \begin{cases} 1 & \text{if } U_i - p_i > 0 \\ 0 & \text{otherwise} \end{cases} \quad (2.2)$$

Since the price coefficient is set to -1 in equation (2.2), $U_i - p_i$ is a measure of consumer surplus and U_i is therefore a direct measure of WTP. In this model, the â parameters capture the marginal WTP for each of the explanatory variables included in the model.

The main advantage of the CV method is that it is easy to implement. However, the method has several weaknesses. The CV method allows the researcher to observe only whether an individual's WTP is higher or lower than the listed price. Hence it may be necessary to use large samples or multiple replications per respondent to obtain accurate results.

One modification of the basic CV method is to use a sequential approach to obtain more precise information about WTP. In the first step, the researcher asks a consumer to respond to a dichotomous (yes–no) question. Depending on the response, the researcher asks the consumer an additional dichotomous follow-up question. Specifically, if the initial response is no (yes), then the consumer is asked whether she would buy the new product at a lower (higher) price. This data collection procedure is called a double-bounded dichotomous choice question (Lusk and Hudson, 2004). Although this sequential method can provide more information on the true WTP, it is subject to starting-point biases (i.e. the consumer's response to the follow-up question depends on the initial price offered; see Shogren and Herriges, 1996; Hanemann et al., 1991).

Research evaluating the CV method suggests that it is not incentive-compatible and is also subject to hypothetical bias. For example, Bishop and Heberlein (1986) found that WTP in the hypothetical condition were significantly overstated compared to those in the actual cash condition. Finally, in a meta-analysis of 14 valuation studies using the CV method, List and Gallet (2001) found that, on average, subjects overstated their WTP by a factor of 2.65 in hypothetical settings.[5] However, the overstatement factor was much lower for private goods ($=1.65$) compared to public goods ($=5$). This finding is intuitive since most subjects are more confident in valuing products they commonly purchase than in valuing products that they may be unfamiliar with (e.g. public goods).

Most applications of the CV method vary list prices across consumers while holding the product concept description constant. In principle, the basic CV method can be modified so that data on WTP for different combinations of price and product concepts (which are typically multidimensional) are obtained. However, as discussed earlier, the experimental design becomes very expensive and unwieldy. Thus the CV method is not feasible for predicting WTP when the firm is considering several alternative product designs – as is generally the case. Finally, and most importantly from a strategic viewpoint, the CV

---

[5] The overstatement factor is calculated as the ratio of the mean hypothetical WTP to the mean actual WTP. The actual WTP are obtained from experiments with real economic commitments.

method considers only one product. Thus the firm cannot determine the separate effects of the new product (including product design and price) on brand switching, cannibalization and market expansion. Without this disaggregate information across different products and segments in the market, the firm cannot choose its optimal product-line policy. In particular, the firm cannot determine the net effect of its new product policy on product-line sales and profits after allowing for competitive reaction.

3.4 Conjoint analysis
Conjoint analysis is a popular WTP measurement method in marketing, transportation and environmental economics. Two common types of conjoint studies are the rating-based and the choice-based conjoint (CBC) methods. In a rating-based conjoint study, researchers present consumers with a number of hypothetical product profiles (concepts) and ask them to rate *each* of these profiles on a preference scale.[6] Sometimes researchers ask consumers to proceed sequentially (Jedidi et al., 1996). In the first step, consumers decide whether or not they will consider a particular product profile for purchase. In the second step, consumers rate only those profiles that they are willing to consider (i.e. profiles in the consideration set). In contrast, in a CBC study, researchers present consumers with *several sets* of hypothetical product profiles and ask them to choose at most one from each set.

To illustrate the conjoint methodology, consider the following example. Suppose a yogurt manufacturer is planning to introduce a new type of yogurt into the marketplace. The first, and perhaps most important, step is to determine the salient attributes. (See Lee and Bradlow, 2007 for an interesting approach for deriving attributes and levels using online customer reviews.) Let's say that the firm has determined that the relevant attributes are the quantity of yogurt in a container, whether or not the yogurt is fat-free, the flavor of the yogurt, the brand name (e.g. Dannon, Breyers, Yoplait) and the price. Then a product profile (or equivalently product concept) consists of a particular combination of attributes including price. For example, one product profile is the following: a 6-ounce, fat-free, vanilla-flavored yogurt that is made by Yoplait and priced at $1. In a rating-based conjoint experiment, the researcher first determines the set of profiles to be evaluated. Then consumers provide preference rating scores for all profiles that they are asked to evaluate. If a sequential approach is used, consumers first sort profiles and then provide ratings scores for those profiles that they consider acceptable.

In a CBC experiment, the researcher first determines the sets of profiles that consumers will be asked to evaluate. For example, one set of profiles might contain the following options: a 6-ounce, fat-free, vanilla-flavored yogurt made by Yoplait and sold at a price of $1 (Alternative 1); a 10-ounce, full-fat, chocolate-flavored yogurt made by Dannon and sold at a price of $1.50 (Alternative 2); and the no-purchase option (Alternative 3). Then the consumer's task is to choose one of these three alternatives. Similarly, the consumer is offered different sets of profiles and asked to pick the best alternative for each profile in that set. A critical feature of the experimental design is that the no-purchase option must be included in each set of profiles that the consumer is asked to evaluate.

---

[6] Our discussion of conjoint analysis is based on the full-profile method. That is, the consumer is given information about all product attributes simultaneously.

This no-purchase alternative must be included so that we obtain unambiguous monetary values for the WTP. (See appendix in Jedidi et al., 2003.)

Whether the CBC or rating-based conjoint method is used, the product profiles or choice sets included in a study must be carefully chosen using an efficient experimental design (Louviere and Woodworth, 1983). Regardless of the method used for data collection, the end result of a conjoint study is an estimated, individual-level utility function that describes how the consumer trades off different attributes.

The key question is the following: how can one use the conjoint results to infer consumers' WTP for different product designs? Using basic principles from the economic theory of choice, Jedidi and Zhang (2002) show how to derive consumers' reservation prices for a product from the individual-level estimates of conjoint coefficients. Let $\mathbf{x}_j$ be a vector that describes the attribute levels of product profile j and $\hat{\mathbf{a}}_i$ be the vector of the associated parameters (part-worth coefficients) for consumer i.[7] Let p_j be the price of profile j and y_i be consumer i's income.[8] Then the (quasi-linear) utility consumer i derives from purchasing one unit of product j is $U_{ij} = \mathbf{x}_j'\hat{\mathbf{a}}_i + \alpha_i(y_i - p_j)$, where α_i denotes the effect of an increase in income (the income effect) or of a decrease in price (the price effect). For any set of profiles in a choice set, if the consumer chooses the no-purchase option (i.e. she decides to keep the money), then her utility is simply $U_{ij} = \alpha_i y_i$. Using the definition in equation (2.1), Jedidi and Zhang (2002) show that for this utility specification, a consumer's reservation price for product profile j is defined by

$$R(j) = \frac{\mathbf{x}_j'\hat{\mathbf{a}}_i}{\alpha_i} \qquad (2.3)$$

To illustrate the relationships among the conjoint part-worth coefficients and reservation prices, suppose we conduct a CBC study and obtain the following individual-level utility function for consumer i for product j:

$$U_{ij} = 0.2 + 0.15 \text{ Dannon} + 0.05 \text{ Yoplait} + 0.15 \text{ Banana} - 0.10 \text{ Strawberry} - 0.5 \text{ Price}$$

where Breyers and Vanilla, respectively, are the base-level brand and flavor and price is measured in dollars.[9] Thus, for this consumer, the reservation price for the Yoplait brand that has a Banana flavor is $0.80 = (0.2 + 0.05 + 0.15)/0.5$. In addition, a $1 change in price reflects a utility difference of 0.5. Therefore every change of one unit in utility is equal to $2.00 in value (=1/0.5). This ratio is what Jedidi and Zhang (2002) define as the 'exchange rate' between utility and money for the consumer. In the example, the exchange rate implies that, for any product flavor, consumer i is willing to pay up to an additional $0.10 to acquire a Yoplait relative to a Breyers yogurt (=0.05 × $2.00).

Conjoint analysis, in its CBC form, can be viewed as an extension of the conventional

---

[7] For simplicity, we assume that there are no interactions among the product attributes. The analysis can easily be extended to allow for such interactions in conjoint models.
[8] The consumer's income need not be observable, but one has to postulate its existence to develop an economic model.
[9] In any conjoint experiment, it is necessary to choose a base level for each product attribute (e.g. brand and flavor in the yogurt example). The choice of base levels does not affect the results.

contingent valuation (CV) method in two ways. First, in CV, the product to be evaluated is typically fixed across respondents. In contrast, the product profiles in conjoint experiments are experimentally manipulated, hence resulting in a within-subject design. Second, conjoint analysis provides additional information about reservation prices. Thus CV provides information only about whether or not the new product is chosen. In contrast, CBC provides detailed information about the case where the new product is not chosen. Specifically, one can distinguish whether the consumer who does not purchase the new product chooses another product (brand) alternative or the non-purchase option.

Because of this additional information, CBC provides several important advantages over CV. The choice task in CBC is more realistic than in CV and closely mimics the consumer's shopping experience. Hence CBC minimizes hypothetical bias. Interestingly, previous research findings show that the responses to CBC questions are generally similar to those from experiments based on revealed preference (e.g. Carlsson and Martinsson, 2001). In the few cases where the differences in the results from the two methodologies are statistically significant, the differences are small (Lusk and Schroeder, 2004). An additional advantage of CBC is that, when the experiment manipulates several attributes simultaneously, consumers are more likely to consider other attributes than price in making the choice decision. Consequently, the task becomes more incentive-compatible. From a managerial viewpoint, perhaps the most important advantage of CBC is the following. In contrast to CV, CBC provides disaggregate information that allows the firm to distinguish how much of the demand for the new product comes from brand switching, cannibalization and market expansion. Consequently, the firm can choose the optimal product-line policy after allowing for the likely effects of competitive reaction following the new product introduction.

The estimation of conjoint models is straightforward regardless of whether we have choice or preference rating data.[10] With rating-based data, one can use regression to estimate the conjoint model. In the special case where consumers provide rating scores only for profiles that are in their consideration sets, one can use a censored-regression model such as tobit to estimate the conjoint model (see Jedidi et al., 1996). With CBC data, the individual-level conjoint model is typically estimated using a hierarchical Bayesian, multinomial logit (MNL) or probit model (Jedidi et al., 2003; Allenby and Rossi, 1999). The primary advantage of the MNL model is computational simplicity. However, the MNL method makes the restrictive assumption of independence of irrelevant alternatives (i.e. the ratio of the choice probabilities of two alternatives is constant regardless of what other alternatives are in a choice set). If researchers are interested in obtaining segment-level estimates of WTP, they can use finite-mixture versions of these models.

Although the methods described above will work in many cases, there are a number of potential pitfalls that one can encounter when estimating WTP. The quasi-linear utility model that we have discussed above is strictly linear in price. While this specification is consistent with utility theory, a consumer's reaction to price changes need not be linear,

---

[10] Software for estimating conjoint models is readily available (e.g. SAS, SPSS and Sawtooth Software). Note that one does not need to observe consumer's income to infer WTP. Because $\alpha_i y_i$ is specific to consumer i, it cancels out in a choice model and gets absorbed in the intercept in a regression model.

especially when the price differences across alternatives are large. In such cases, Jedidi and Zhang (2002, p. 1354) suggest using the exchange rate that corresponds to the price range that the firm is considering for the new product. Another issue arises if the price coefficient α_i is unconstrained and the estimated coefficient has the wrong sign for some consumers. Thus, suppose some consumers use price as a signal for quality. In such a case, price has two opposing effects. On the one hand, it acts as a constraint since the higher the price paid, the worse off the consumer is. On the other hand, since price is a signal of quality, the higher the price, the higher the utility. Because of these competing effects, it is possible that the estimated WTP measures for these consumers will be negative; see equation (2.3). Another potential difficulty can arise if the price coefficient for a particular respondent is extremely small (close to zero). This can happen if consumers are insensitive to price changes or the data are noisy. In this case, the exchange rate (and hence WTP) may be large and can even approach infinity. One way to address these difficulties is to constrain the price coefficient so that lower prices always have higher utilities. Another frequently used approach is to constrain the price coefficient to be the same across consumers in the sample (e.g. Goett et al., 2000). A third approach is to constrain the price coefficient to 1 (see equation 2.2). In a choice model, this means that consumers maximize surplus instead of utility. The latter two methods are equivalent if the utility function is quasi-linear (see Jedidi and Zhang, 2002). In most practical applications, all three approaches lead to price coefficients that are non-zero and have the proper signs.

3.5 Experimental auctions

Auction-based methods are beginning to gain popularity in marketing because they measure real and not self-stated choices. We discuss below the following auction mechanisms: the Dutch auction; the first-price, sealed-bid auction; the English auction; the nth-price, sealed-bid auction (Vickrey, 1961); the BDM method (Becker et al., 1964); and the reverse auction (see Spann et al., 2004).

In a Dutch auction, the opening price is high and is progressively lowered until one bidder is willing to purchase the item being auctioned. Thus the only information that is available to the firm is that the winner's WTP is at least as high as the price at which the item was sold; in addition, the WTP of all other bidders are lower than this price. Given this auction mechanism, a bidder's bidding strategy will depend on her beliefs about others' bidding strategies; in addition, her strategy will depend on her risk attitude. Consequently, all bidders have an incentive to underbid. In particular, the person with the highest reservation price may not always submit the highest bid. Note that, from a managerial viewpoint, the information from a Dutch auction is extremely limited. All that the firm knows is the (potentially understated) maximum price at which it can sell one unit of its product. Thus, suppose there are three bidders (A, B and C) and A wins the auction at a bid price of $200. Then the only quantitative demand information available to the firm is the following. If it sells one unit, it can obtain a minimum price of $200. However, since bidders have an incentive to underbid, this price may be too low. Furthermore, the results provide no information about market demand if the firm plans to sell more than one unit in the marketplace.

In the first-price, sealed-bid auction, each bidder submits one bid. This information is submitted to the auctioneer and is not provided to the other bidders. The highest bidder wins the auction and pays her bid price. Note that, as in the Dutch auction, each bidder has an incentive to bid less than her reservation price. However, in contrast to the Dutch auction, the firm obtains more detailed information about the demand structure for its product. Thus, suppose there are three bidders (A, B and C) as before. Let's say that the sealed bids are as follows: A bids $100, B bids $160, and C bids $250. Then the firm knows the following information about demand. If it wants to sell one unit, the minimum price that it can charge is $250 per unit. If it wants to sell two units, the minimum price that it can charge is $160 per unit. If it wants to sell three units, the minimum price that it can charge is $100. Note that, in contrast to the Dutch auction, the firm obtains market demand information for different volumes. However, since all bidders have an incentive to underbid, the firm is likely to choose a suboptimal price.

In an English auction, participants offer ascending bids for a product until only one participant is left in the auction. This bidder wins the auction and must purchase the auctioned product at the last offered bid price. Note that, in contrast to the first-price, sealed-bid auction, the English auction is an 'open' auction. Specifically, all bidders know each other's bids. This experimental design is useful in situations where it is important to incorporate market information into participants' valuations (e.g. potential buyers are likely to communicate with each other). However, this method can be a limitation if consumers make independent valuations in real life (Lusk, 2003). In addition, because the bids are 'open', the last bid tends to be only marginally higher than the second-highest bidder's last bid.

Note that, in contrast to the Dutch auction and the first-price, sealed-bid auction, bidders in an English auction have an incentive to reveal their true reservation prices.[11] That is, a bidder will drop out of the auction only when the last bid exceeds her reservation price. From a managerial viewpoint, the firm obtains much more detailed information about the market demand for its product. For simplicity, assume that there are three bidders (A, B and C). Suppose A drops out when the price is $10, B drops out when the price is increased to $15, and C purchases the product at a price of $16. These results imply the following market demand structure. If the firm wants to sell three units, the maximum price it can charge is $10 per unit. If the firm wants to sell two units, the maximum price it can charge is $15 per unit. Note that these results do not imply that the maximum price that the firm can charge for one unit is $16. Specifically, bidder C needs only to bid marginally more ($16) than bidder B, who drops out when the price is raised to $15. The only inference is that bidder C's minimum reservation price is $16. From a practical viewpoint, it is likely that, in most cases, the firm will sell more than one unit. Hence the firm can use the results of an English auction to determine what price to charge for its product.[12]

In an nth-price, sealed-bid auction (Vickrey, 1961), each bidder submits one sealed bid to the seller. None of the other bidders is given this information. Once bids have been made, the $(n - 1)$ highest bidders purchase one unit each of the product and pay an amount equal to the nth-highest bid. Perhaps the most commonly used nth-price auction

---

[11] This conclusion of incentive compatibility holds if the auction is not conducted repeatedly with the same group of bidders and bidders cannot purchase more than one unit. If either of these assumptions does not hold, bidders may behave strategically and systematically choose bid prices that are lower than their WTP.

[12] This analysis assumes that consumers will not purchase multiple items of the product.

is the second-price ($n = 2$) auction in which the highest bidder purchases the product at the second-highest bid amount. Similarly, suppose the firm uses the fourth-price auction (n = 4). Then the three highest bidders will purchase one unit each at the price bid by the fourth-highest bidder. Because of the sealed-bid mechanism, the participants in this auction learn only the market price and whether or not they are buyers in the auction.

As Vickrey (1961) shows, the second-price, sealed-bid auction is isomorphic to the English auction. This is because the final price paid in both auctions is determined by the bid of the second-highest bidder. Furthermore, both the English and nth-price auction mechanisms are incentive compatible. Hence, in principle, the firm can use either the English auction or the nth-price, sealed-bid Vickrey auction to determine the optimal price when it sells more than one unit.[13]

Despite the theoretical advantages of the Vickrey auction methodology, the method has several drawbacks as a marketing research tool for measuring WTP (Wertenbroch and Skiera, 2002). The first limitation concerns the operational difficulties in implementing the method in market research. The second stems from the fact that the bidding process in the auction does not mimic the consumer purchase process (Hoffman et al., 1993). The third limitation stems from the limited stock of products being auctioned. This is not only unrealistic for many products in retail settings; it also encourages participants to bid more than the true worth of the product to ensure that they are placing the winning bid (e.g. Kagel, 1995). Finally, empirical findings suggest that low-valuation participants become quickly disengaged in these auctions when they are conducted in multiple rounds (Lusk, 2003). Thus subjects quickly learn that they will not win the auction and drop out of the auction by bidding zero.

To address some of these limitations, Wertenbroch and Skiera (2002) propose the use of the incentive-compatible, BDM (Becker et al., 1964) method for eliciting WTP. The BDM method is as follows. Each participant submits a sealed bid for one unit of the product. The auctioneer then randomly draws a 'market' price. If the participant's bid exceeds this value, the participant is required to purchase one unit of the product at the market price. If the bid is lower than the market price, the bidder does not purchase the product. Note that, although the BDM method is structurally similar to the standard auction method, there is a fundamental difference. The BDM procedure is not an auction because participants do not bid against one another (Lusk, 2003).

One important practical advantage of the BDM procedure over standard auctions is that it does not require the presence of a group of consumers in a lab for bidding. This feature makes it possible to more accurately mimic the purchase decision process by eliciting WTP at the point-of-purchase (Wertenbroch and Skiera, 2002; Lusk et al., 2001). In addition, because the supply of the product is not limited, every consumer can buy the product as long as his or her WTP is greater than the randomly drawn price. This aspect makes low-valuation participants more likely to be engaged in the experiment. One drawback of the BDM method is the absence of an active market such that participants can incorporate market feedback. Empirical findings, however, suggest that the BDM method and the English auction generate similar results (Lusk et al., 2002; Rutström, 1998).

---

[13] This result holds provided the auction is not repeated with the same group of bidders. For this scenario, bidders may behave strategically and not reveal their true reservation prices.

Another type of auction mechanism is the reverse auction – a method used by such Internet firms as Priceline.com. The reverse auction method works as follows. The seller specifies a time period (e.g. the next seven days from now) during which it will accept bids to purchase a product. During this period, each bidder is allowed to submit one bid for the product.[14] Only the seller has access to bids. The outcome of the auction is as follows. The seller has a secret threshold price below which she will not sell the product. If a consumer bids more than the threshold price, the consumer must purchase one unit of the product at his or her bid price. If the consumer bids less than the seller's threshold price, the seller will not sell the product to the consumer. Note that the reverse auction is similar to the BDM method in that bidders do not compete with each other. However, there is an important difference. In a BDM auction, the buyer pays the randomly drawn market price. In a reverse auction, each buyer pays her bid price if offered the option to purchase.

To illustrate how the reverse auction works, suppose a hotel wishes to sell excess capacity (e.g. three room nights on a given Saturday one month after the auction is conducted). Since the marginal cost of a room night is low, let's say that the hotel's secret threshold price per room night is $20. Suppose the firm conducts the reverse auction over a seven-day period and the room-night bids in descending order are as follows: $60 (Consumer A); $50 (Consumer B); $40 (Consumer C); $30 (Consumer D); and a number of bids less than $30. Then the hotel will choose the following room-night pricing plan. It will charge A a price of $60, B a price of $50, and C a price of $40 for the Saturday night stay. Note that, in contrast to standard auctions, consumers pay different prices for the same product. In our example, the reverse auction method allows the hotel to ration out the limited supply of room nights by using a price discrimination (price-skimming) strategy.

From a managerial viewpoint, reverse auctions are a mixed blessing. On one hand, they allow the firm to extract consumer surplus from the market by charging differential prices. Furthermore, they are a convenient, low-cost method for the firm to sell excess capacity without disrupting the price structure in traditional distribution channels. On the other hand, reverse auctions are not incentive compatible. Specifically, customers will bid less than their true WTP in order to obtain a surplus from the transaction. This lack of incentive compatibility reduces the ability of the firm to extract consumer surplus from the market. To address this problem, some researchers have suggested the following modification: allow bidders to submit multiple bids but require each bidder to pay a bidding fee for each bid submitted (Spann et al., 2004).

3.6 Comparison of WTP methods

Experimental auctions (EAs) can provide several advantages over stated preference methods. Many auction methods are incentive compatible. That is, bidders have an incentive to reveal their true WTP. In contrast to stated preference methods, EAs are conducted in a real context that involves real products and real money. In addition, by putting subjects in an active marketing environment, some EAs allow one to estimate WTP after allowing for a market environment with feedback among buyers. Depending on the purchase context, this feature may be important. WTP from EAs are empirically

---

[14] Some reverse auctions allow bidders to make multiple bids. See, e.g., Spann et al. (2004).

observed. Hence one can obtain individual-level estimates of WTP without making parametric assumptions (e.g. normality) about the distribution of WTP in the population.

However, in spite of these advantages, the EA methodology is not a panacea for measuring WTP. The elicitation process does not mimic the actual purchase process that a consumer goes through, including search for information. The EA method focuses on one product/product design only. Hence one cannot measure the cannibalization, substitution and market-expansion effects of a new product entry. Nor can one determine how consumers trade off attributes. Consequently, the EA method can be used only at a late stage of the product development process when the firm has finalized the product design and the remaining issue is to choose the price conditional on this product design. Since participants in an EA study are expected to pay for the products they purchase, the EA method cannot be used to determine the reservation prices for durables (Wertenbroch and Skiera, 2002). The EA method assumes that reservation prices are deterministic. This may not be the case, especially for new products or products with which the consumer is unfamiliar. It may be difficult to generalize the WTP estimates from an EA study to a national level because it is infeasible to recruit a sufficiently large and representative sample. Subjects must be recruited and paid participatory fees to attend laboratory sessions. This potentially introduces bias into the resulting bids (Rutström, 1998). Depending on the EA method used, bidder values may become affiliated (i.e. a relatively high bid by one auctioneer induces high bids from others). This degrades the incentive compatibility of an auction (Lusk, 2003). In addition, it is not uncommon to observe a large frequency of zero-bidding, potentially because of lack of participant interest (Lusk, 2003). Hence the firm obtains incomplete information about the demand structure in the market.

Empirical studies comparing WTP measures across methods are limited. In three studies, Wertenbroch and Skiera (2002) find that WTP estimates from BDM are lower than those obtained from open-ended and double-bounded contingent valuation methods. Similarly, Balistreri et al. (2001) find that bids from an English auction are significantly lower than those obtained from open-ended and dichotomous CV methods. Lusk and Schroeder (2006) find that the WTP estimates from various auction mechanisms are lower than those from CBC. These findings may be due to the incentive compatibility of the auction methods and to the hypothetical bias inherent in the CV and conjoint analysis methods. In contrast, Fryklom and Shogren (2000) found that they could not reject the null hypothesis that WTP estimates obtained from a non-hypothetical (dichotomous) CV method are equal to those obtained from a second-price auction.

3.7 Emerging approaches

A new stream of research is emerging in marketing that combines the advantages of the stated preference methods with the incentive compatibility of the BDM method. Ding et al. (2005) extended the self-stated WTP and CBC methods using incentive structures that require participants to 'live with' the consequences of their decisions. Using Chinese dinner specials as the context, the authors conducted a field experiment in a Chinese restaurant during dinner time. For the self-stated condition, consumers were presented with a menu of 12 Chinese dinner specials (with no price information) and were asked to state their WTP for each meal in the menu. Consumers were told upfront that a random procedure would be used to select a meal from the menu and that they would receive this meal if their WTP exceeded a randomly drawn price. For the CBC condition, the authors presented consumers with 12 choice sets of three Chinese meals each (with price information) and asked them to choose at most one meal from each choice set. Consumers in this condition were told upfront that a random lottery would be used to draw one choice set and that they would receive the meal that they selected from that choice set. (The consumer would receive no meal if she selected none of the meals in the choice set.) For both experimental conditions, the price of the meal (random price for the self-stated method and menu price for CBC) would be deducted from their compensation for participating in the study. The out-of-sample predictions show that the incentive-aligned conjoint method outperformed both the standard CBC and incentive-aligned, self-stated WTP methods.

More recently, Park et al. (2007) proposed a sequential, incentive-compatible, conjoint procedure for eliciting consumer WTP for attribute upgrades. This method first endows a consumer with a basic product profile and a budget for upgrades. In the next step, the consumer is given the option of upgrading, one attribute at a time, to a preferred product configuration. During this process, the consumer is required to state her WTP for each potential upgrade she is interested in. In addition, the BDM procedure is used to ensure that the incentive-compatibility condition is met. That is, the consumer receives the upgrade only if her self-stated WTP for the upgrade exceeds a randomly drawn price for that upgrade. When no further upgrade is desired by the consumer or the consumer's upgrade budget is exhausted, the consumer receives the final upgraded product. The authors tested their model using data collected from an experiment on the Web to measure consumers' WTP for upgrades to digital cameras. The out-of-sample validation analysis shows that the new method predicted choice better than the benchmark (self-explicated) conjoint approach.

4. Using WTP for pricing decisions

So far, we have focused on empirical methods for measuring WTP. In this section we discuss how managers can use WTP measures to choose pricing policies. We discuss three application areas: bundling, quantity discounts and product line pricing decisions.

4.1 Bundling

Consider a cable company, say Comcast, which sells two services: a basic digital cable service and high-speed online service. Suppose Comcast has conducted market research and obtained the WTP measures shown in Table 2.1 for its bundled and unbundled services for four segments in the market. (We shall discuss empirical methods to estimate the WTP for bundles later in this section.)

Table 2.1 *WTP for individual services and bundle in dollars*

Segment	Average WTP for		
	Cable service	High speed online service	Bundle
1	50	10	55
2	50	43	90
3	45	45	90
4	15	48	55

Suppose all segments are of equal size (1 million customers each) and the marginal cost of providing each service is zero. Then a consumer will only consider buying a particular service or bundle if the price charged is less than her WTP for that service or bundle. In addition, she will choose the alternative that maximizes her surplus (= WTP for any service or bundle – price of that service or bundle). If the maximum surplus is negative, the consumer will not purchase any of the services or the bundle.

Given this information about WTP and costs, Comcast can choose from among three pricing strategies: a uniform pricing strategy, a pure bundling strategy, or a mixed bundling pricing strategy. If Comcast uses uniform pricing, it will sell each service separately at a fixed price per unit. If Comcast uses pure bundling, it will only sell the two services as a package for a fixed price per package. If Comcast uses mixed bundling, it will sell the services separately and as a package.

Suppose Comcast uses a uniform pricing strategy. Then, using the WTP information in Table 2.1, we see that the optimal price for the cable service is $45. If this price is chosen, Comcast's profit from the cable service will be $135 million. Similarly, the optimal price for high-speed online service is $43 and the profit from this service is $129 million. Hence Comcast's product line profit if it uses a uniform pricing strategy is $264 million (= profit from cable service + profit from high-speed online service).

Suppose Comcast uses a pure bundling policy. Then the optimal price for the bundle is $55 and the product line profit is $220 million. Finally, if Comcast uses a mixed bundling strategy, the optimal policy is to charge $90 for the bundle, $50 for the cable service alone, and $48 for the high-speed online service. Hence Comcast's product line profit will be $278 million (= 180 + 50 + 48). Consequently, the optimal product line policy is to use a mixed bundling strategy.

The previous discussion assumed that the manager knows the WTP for the individual products and the bundles. So far, we have discussed only how to estimate WTP for individual products. How can one estimate the WTP for product bundles? One way is to use self-stated WTP. However, as discussed, these are likely to be inaccurate, especially for new products or for products with which the consumer is unfamiliar. Another approach is to use the individual-level, choice-based method developed by Jedidi et al. (2003) or a modified version that allows segment-level estimation. This method is philosophically similar to the choice-based methods discussed earlier. That is, consumers seek to maximize their surpluses. As shown by Jedidi et al., their choice-based method provides more accurate estimates of reservation prices than the self-stated methodology. In practical applications, the data will be more complex than in the example above. For example, there will be many more segments, products and bundles. In such cases, the choice of the optimal bundling policy is complicated. One approach is to use an optimization algorithm (e.g. Hanson and Martin, 1990) to analyze the WTP results and cost data for the products and bundles in question.

4.2 Quantity discounts/nonlinear pricing

Suppose the Marriott Hotel seeks to determine how to price different packages for its standard rooms. Suppose the average WTP measures for stays of different durations in the hotel for three leisure segments are as shown in Table 2.2. Furthermore, assume that Marriott has sufficient room capacity to meet all demand.

Note that for any given consumer segment, the WTP is the highest for the first night

Table 2.2 WTP in dollars for a hotel night for different stay durations

Night	Segment 1	Segment 2	Segment 3
First	90	100	120
Second	60	75	100
Third	35	55	80
Fourth	20	40	60
Fifth	11	15	35

Table 2.3 Pricing of hotel night stays

Night	Optimal price for *n*th night ($)	Number of night stays	Sales revenues ($)
First	90	3000	270,000
Second	60	3000	180,000
Third	55	2000	110,000
Fourth	40	2000	80,000
Fifth	35	1000	35,000
Total		11,000	$675,000

and decreases for every successive night. Suppose the three segments are of equal size (1000 customers) and that the hotel's marginal cost per room is approximately zero. (This is a reasonable assumption since most costs for maintaining hotel rooms are fixed.) Hence any pricing policy that maximizes sales revenue also maximizes profits.

One option for Marriott is to set a uniform price per night, regardless of the duration of stay. Following the same procedure as in the bundling case, we find that the sales-revenue maximizing price is $55 per night. If Marriott uses this uniform pricing plan, it will sell 9000 hotel night stays and obtain a revenue (gross profit) of $495,000. An alternative pricing strategy is to use a quantity discount pricing plan based on the 'price-point' method (see Dolan and Simon, 1996, p. 173). Using this approach, Marriott will proceed sequentially and set the revenue-maximizing price for each successive night stay. Table 2.3 presents the optimal pricing results using the price-point method.

Thus, for the first night the optimal price is $90. This pricing policy leads to 3000 night stays and a revenue of $270,000. Conditional on this pricing policy, the optimal price for the second night is $60, yielding 3000 night stays and a revenue of $180,000. Conditional on the prices for the first two nights, the optimal price for the third night is $55. Note that Segment 1 will not stay for a third night because its WTP for the third night ($35) is lower than the price for the third night ($55). Hence the hotel will sell 2000 night stays and obtain a revenue of $110,000. Similarly, we can determine the number of night stays and the corresponding revenues for the fourth and fifth nights (see Table 2.3). Given this price-point strategy, Marriott will sell 11,000 night stays and make a gross profit of $675,000. Note that, when Marriott uses a quantity discount pricing plan, it sells more hotel room nights and obtains a higher profit than if it uses uniform pricing. Specifically, the number of hotel night stays increases from 9000 to 11,000 (a 22 percent increase)

Table 2.4 WTP for different models of notebook computers by Dell and Hewlett-Packard ($)

Segment	WTP for			
	DELL	HP_C	HP_L	HP_H
1	1700	1200	500	1300
2	1600	1100	600	1650
3	1200	1500	700	1700
4	1000	1400	800	1500
5	900	900	900	900

Note: DELL = The notebook model made by Dell; HP_C = The initial notebook made by HP; HP_L = Lower-quality notebook to be made by HP; HP_H = Higher-quality notebook to be made by HP.

and gross profits increase even more sharply from $495,000 to $675,000 (a 36 percent increase).

As discussed, WTP information of the type presented in Table 2.2 can be collected in a number of different ways. For example, one can use conjoint or choice-based experiments where the quantity of product (e.g. different package sizes for a frequently purchased product or the number of hotel nights in the current example) is a treatment variable. See Iyengar et al. (2007) for an example of nonlinear pricing involving the sale of cellphone service. Alternatively, one can use different auction methodologies including the reverse auction method to estimate WTP.[15]

4.3 Product line pricing

In this section, we show how the firm can use information about WTP to determine its optimal product mix and product line pricing strategy after allowing for competition. Consider the following hypothetical example from the PC industry. For simplicity, suppose there are two players in the PC notebook market: Dell and Hewlett-Packard (HP). Let's say that in the first period Dell sells one model of notebook (DELL) and Hewlett-Packard also sells one model (HP_C). Furthermore, there are five segments, each of equal size (1 million), whose WTP for the DELL and HP_C notebooks are as shown in Table 2.4, columns 2 and 3, respectively.

Suppose the marginal costs for the DELL and HP_C notebooks are equal ($800 per unit). In addition, Dell and HP set the prices of their models simultaneously in the first period. Consider the following pricing scenario. Let's say that Dell charges a price of $1200 for the DELL notebook and HP charges a price of $1400 for the HP_C model. Then each consumer will choose the notebook model that maximizes her surplus. If the maximum surplus is negative, the consumer will not purchase either model. Given this set of prices, Segments 1 and 2 will purchase the DELL, Segments 3 and 4 will

---

[15] Internet retailers (e.g. Priceline.com) often sell hotel room nights using the reverse auction methodology. Consequently, bidding information by consumers can be used to infer their WTP for purchasing different quantities of a product.

56 *Handbook of pricing research in marketing*

Table 2.5 *Industry equilibrium in the first period*

DELL price ($)	HP$_C$ price				
	$900	$1100	$1200	$1400	$1500
900	(250, 250)	(300, 600**)	(350, 600**)	(500, 0)	(500, 0)
1000	(400, 300)	(400, 600)	(400, 800**)	(700, 300)	(800, 0)
1200	(800*, 300)	(800*, 600)	(800, 800)	(800, 1200**)	(800, 1200)
1600	(0, 500)	(800*, 900)	(1600*, 800)	(1600*, 1200**)	(1600, 700)
1700	(0, 500)	(0, 1200)	(450, 1000)	(900, 1200**)	(900, 700)

Notes: All entries in parentheses are in millions of dollars. The first entry denotes DELL's gross profits and the second denotes the gross profits for HP$_C$.
* optimal policy for Dell model conditional on price chosen by HP.
** optimal policy for HP conditional on price chosen by Dell.

purchase the HP$_C$ model, and Segment 5 will not purchase a notebook. Hence Dell will make a profit of $800 million (= unit margin × number of customers in Segments 1 and 2 combined) and HP will make a profit of $1200 million (= unit margin × number of customers in Segments 3 and 4 combined; see Table 2.5). Similarly, one can obtain the profits for Dell and HP for different sets of market prices. In the example, we assume that, if the consumer surpluses for any segment are zero for both products, half the segment will purchase the HP product and the other half will purchase the DELL model.

Assume that Dell and HP do not cooperate with each other. In Table 2.5, the * notation denotes the optimal price for DELL conditional on any price for HP$_C$ and the ** notation denotes the optimal price for the HP$_C$ notebook conditional on any price for the Dell notebook. Since the firms do not cooperate with each other, in the first period Dell will charge a price of $1600 per notebook and HP will charge a price of $1400 per notebook. (This is the Nash equilibrium.) Given these prices, Dell will make a gross profit of $1.6 billion and HP will make a gross profit of $1.2 billion. See Table 2.5.

Now, consider the second period. For simplicity, assume that Segment 5 (nonpurchasers in the first period) leaves the market in the second period. In addition, a new cohort of consumers enters the market in the second period. These consumers are clones of those in the first period. That is, there are five segments of equal size (1 million each) in the second period with the same set of reservation prices for notebook computers as the corresponding segments in the first period.

Suppose HP has developed a new technology in the second period which allows it to add a new set of product features to its notebook computers. For simplicity, assume that the marginal costs of adding these new features are approximately zero.[16] Suppose Dell does not have the technology to add these new features; in addition, Dell will continue to charge the same price for its DELL model in the second period ($1600 per unit).[17]

---

[16] This assumption is not an unreasonable approximation since most costs are likely to be developmental.
[17] This assumption can be easily relaxed.

Given HP's new technology, which notebook models should HP sell in the second period and what product line pricing policy should HP use? For simplicity, we assume that HP is considering adding a low-end model and/or a high-end model to its notebook product line. We consider three strategies. One alternative for HP is to continue to sell the old model (HP_C) and to introduce the HP_L model, a low-end notebook (Strategy A). A second alternative is to sell the old model (HP_C) and introduce a high-end notebook, HP_H, aimed at the premium market (Strategy B). A third strategy is to use a 'flanking' strategy (Strategy C). That is, sell a low-end notebook (HP_L) that is of lower quality than the DELL, sell a high-end notebook (HP_H) that is of higher quality than the DELL, and continue selling the old HP model (HP_C).[18]

We begin with Strategy A, where HP augments its product line in the second period by introducing only the low-end notebook. Consumers in the second period now have three choices: they can purchase the old HP model (HP_C), the new low-end HP model (HP_L), or the DELL. As before, consumers will make their purchase decisions to maximize their surpluses: if the maximum surplus from purchase is negative, consumers will not purchase the notebook. Then, following the previous approach, we can show that HP will leave the price of the old model (HP_C) unchanged at $1400 per unit and charge a price of $900 per unit for the low-end model. Given these prices in the second period, consumers in Segments 1 and 2 will purchase the DELL and consumers in Segments 3 and 4 will purchase the old HP model (HP_C). However, consumers in Segment 5 will now purchase the low-end HP notebook (HP_L). Note that the new low-end HP model does not cannibalize HP's old product or steal sales from Dell. In particular, the incremental profit to HP (= $100 million) comes entirely from market expansion since Segment 5 now buys a notebook. Hence, given this product line policy, HP's profits will increase from $1.2 billion in the first period to $1.3 billion.

Suppose HP chooses to augment its product line in the second period by introducing only the new high-end PC notebook, HP_H (Strategy B). Then, following the previous method, we can show that the optimal policy for HP is to discontinue the old model and charge $1500 for the high-end model. Given this product line strategy, Segment 1 will continue to buy the DELL. However, Segments 2, 3 and 4 will buy the high-end HP model. Note that HP gains because of switching from a competitor (Segment 2) and 'good' cannibalization (Segments 3 and 4). Specifically, there are three sources of gain: Segment 2 switches from the DELL to the high-end HP model (additional profit to HP = $700 million), Segment 3 upgrades to the new high-end HP model (additional profit to HP = $100 million), and Segment 4 also upgrades to the new high-end HP model (additional profit to HP = $100 million). Hence HP increases its product line gross profit by $900 million (= 700 + 100 + 100) from $1.2 billion to $2.1 billion.

Finally, suppose HP uses a flanking strategy by simultaneously introducing the low-end and high-end PC notebooks (Strategy C). Now, the optimal policy is to discontinue the old model as in Strategy B. Given this product line strategy, Segments 2, 3 and 4 will purchase the high-end HP notebook and Segment 5 will purchase the low-end HP notebook. Note that, in contrast to the other strategies, there are three sources of

---

[18] We can show that, in our example, a sequential product introduction strategy is dominated by a simultaneous new product introduction strategy.

gain: switching from DELL (Segment 2), 'good' cannibalization (Segments 3 and 4), and market expansion (Segment 5). Specifically, Segment 2 switches from the DELL to the high-end HP notebook (incremental profit = $700 million), Segments 3 and 4 upgrade from the old model to the high-end HP notebook (incremental profit = $200 million), and Segment 5 purchases the low-end HP notebook (incremental profit = $100 million). Hence HP's product-line profit increases by $1 billion (= 700 + 200 + 100) from $1.2 billion in the first period to $2.2 billion in the second.

These results show that Strategy C is optimal for HP. That is, the optimal product mix for HP in the second period is to discontinue its old notebook and to 'flank' DELL by simultaneously introducing two new notebooks: a low-end model (HP_L) that is of lower quality than DELL and a high-end model (HP_H) that is of higher quality than DELL.

In summary, as this example demonstrates, the firm cannot choose its product mix and product line pricing without knowing the distribution of reservation prices for its products *and* those of its competitors. For additional examples and technical details of how to use reservation price data for product-line pricing, see Jedidi and Zhang (2002).

5. Concluding remarks and directions for future research

What can we conclude about the state of the art in WTP research and what are some useful directions for future research in this area? Managerially, the firm needs to know the joint distribution of consumers' reservation prices (WTP) for its products and those of its competitors. As discussed, this information is necessary for the firm to determine how its new product policy affects cannibalization, market growth and the market shares of competing brands. In addition, the firm can use this information to implement nonlinear pricing plans (e.g. quantity discount policies) and to determine its optimal bundling policy (e.g. choose which products to bundle and determine the optimal prices for the individual products and the bundle).

Methodologically, self-stated WTP are likely to be measured with error, regardless of the type of product (e.g. durable or nondurable). When estimating WTP for a public good that is not sold in the market (e.g. the benefits of an environmental policy to reduce pollution), the researcher may have no alternative but to use a contingent valuation method. If, however, the researcher is interested in measuring the WTP for a private good that is sold in the market (as is the case in most market research studies), a better approach is to use an appropriately designed conjoint study, a choice-based experiment, one of the auction methodologies (e.g. the Vickrey auction or the BDM auction method), or the incentive-aligned conjoint methods (e.g. Ding et al., 2005; Park et al., 2007). Given the current state of knowledge, it is not clear which of these methods is superior in general and, if so, in what context (e.g. measuring the WTP for established products or products that are radically new in the marketplace). Hence a better approach for the market researcher may be to use more than one of the methods mentioned above to measure WTP, then use an objective statistical approach to combine results across methods by choosing appropriate weights for each method (e.g. Jedidi et al., 2003).

Future research should focus on several areas. From an applications viewpoint, research should compare different methods for measuring WTP and evaluate the incremental gains from combining different methods in different contexts. This research is necessary so that managers can choose the optimal research design in a particular context, after evaluating the costs and benefits of different methods for measuring WTP.

Additional research is necessary to develop better measures of how consumers' WTP vary with the quantity of product consumed. These measures are necessary for firms to implement nonlinear pricing strategies (e.g. quantity discount policy). Finally, future methodological research should address the issue of optimal bundling strategies when the firm can use nonlinear pricing plans for the individual products and bundles.

References

Allenby, Greg M. and Peter E. Rossi (1999), 'Marketing models of consumer heterogeneity', *Journal of Econometrics*, **89** (March/April), 57–78.
Anderson, J.C., Dipak Jain and Pradeep K. Chintagunta (1993), 'Understanding customer value in business markets: methods of customer value assessment', *Journal of Business-to-Business Marketing*, **1** (1), 3–30.
Ariely, Dan, George Loewenstein and Drazen Prelec (2003), '"Coherent arbitrariness": stable demand curves without stable preferences', *The Quarterly Journal of Economics*, **118** (1), 73–105.
Balistreri, E.C., G. McClelland, G. Poe and W. Schultze (2001), 'Can hypothetical questions reveal true values? A laboratory comparison of dichotomous choice and open-ended contingent values with auction values', *Environmental and Resource Economics*, **18**, 275–92.
Becker, G.M., M.H. DeGroot and J. Marschak (1964), 'Measuring utility by a single-response sequential method', *Behavioral Science*, **9**, 226–32.
Bishop, R. and T.A. Heberlein (1986), 'Does contingent valuation work?', in R. Cummings, D. Brookshire and W. Schulze (eds), *Valuing Environmental Goods: An Assessment of the Contingent Valuation Method*, Totowa, NJ: Rowman & Allanheld, pp. 123–47.
Cameron, Trudy A. and Michelle D. James (1987), 'Estimating willingness to pay from survey data: an alternative pre-test-market evaluation procedure', *Journal of Marketing Research*, **24** (4), 389–95.
Carlsson, F. and P. Martinsson (2001), 'Do hypothetical and actual marginal willingness to pay differ in choice experiments?', *Journal of Environmental Economics and Management*, **41**, 179–92.
Chung, Jaihak and Vithala R. Rao (2003), 'A general choice model for bundles and multiple-category products: application to market segmentation and optimal pricing for bundles', *Journal of Marketing Research*, **40**, 115–30.
Ding, Min, Rajdeep Grewal and John Liechty (2005), 'Incentive aligned conjoint analysis', *Journal of Marketing Research*, **42** (1), 67–82.
Dolan, Robert J. and Hermann Simon (1996), *Power Pricing*, New York: The Free Press.
Frykblom, P. and J.F. Shogren (2000), 'An experimental testing of anchoring effects in discrete choice questions', *Environmental and Resource Economics*, **16** (3), 329–41.
Goett, Andrew A., Kathleen Hudson and Kenneth E. Train (2000), 'Customers' choice among retail energy suppliers: the willingness-to-pay for service attributes', *The Energy Journal*, **21** (4), 1–28.
Hanemann, W. Michael, J. Loomis and B. Kanninen (1991), 'Statistical efficiency of double-bounded dichotomous choice contingent valuation', *American Journal of Agricultural Economics*, **73**, November, 1255–63.
Hanson, Ward A. and R. Kipp Martin (1990), 'Optimal bundle pricing', *Management Science*, **36**, 155–74.
Hauser, John R. and Glen L. Urban (1986), 'The value priority hypotheses for consumer budget plans', *Journal of Consumer Research*, **12** (4), 446–62.
Hoffman, E., D. Menkhaus, D. Chakravarti, R. Field and G. Whipple (1993), 'Using laboratory experimental auctions in marketing research: a case study of new packaging for fresh beef', *Marketing Science*, **12**, Summer, 318–38.
Iyengar, Raghuram, Kamel Jedidi and Rajeev Kohli (2007), 'A conjoint approach to multi-part pricing', Working Paper, Columbia Business School, Columbia University.
Jedidi, Kamel and Z. John Zhang (2002), 'Augmenting conjoint analysis to estimate consumer reservation price', *Management Science*, **48**, 1350–68.
Jedidi, Kamel, Rajeev Kohli and Wayne DeSarbo (1996), 'Consideration sets in conjoint analysis', *Journal of Marketing Research*, **33**, 364–72.
Jedidi, Kamel, Carl F. Mela and Sunil Gupta (1999), 'Managing advertising and promotion for long-run profitability', *Marketing Science*, **18** (1), 1–22.
Jedidi, Kamel, Sharan Jagpal and Puneet Manchanda (2003), 'Measuring heterogeneous reservation prices for bundles', *Marketing Science*, **22**, 107–30.
Kagel, J.H. (1995), 'Auctions: a survey of experimental research', in John H. Kagel and Alvin E. Roth (eds), *The Handbook of Experimental Economics*, Princeton, NJ: Princeton University Press, pp. 501–85.
Kohli, Rajeev and Vijay Mahajan (1991), 'A reservation-price model for optimal pricing of multiattribute products in conjoint analysis', *Journal of Marketing Research*, **28** (3), 347–54.
Lee, Thomas and Eric T. Bradlow (2007), 'Automatic construction of conjoint attributes and levels from online customer reviews', Working Paper, The Wharton School, University of Pennsylvania.

List, John A. and Craig A. Gallet (2001), 'What experimental protocol influence disparities between actual and hypothetical stated values?', *Environmental and Resource Economics*, **20**, 241–54.

Louviere, Jordan J. and George Woodworth (1983), 'Design and analysis of simulated consumer choice or allocation experiments: an approach based on aggregate data', *Journal of Marketing Research*, **20**, 350–67.

Lusk, Jayson L. (2003), 'Using experimental auctions for marketing applications: a discussion', *Journal of Agricultural and Applied Economics*, **35** (2), 349–60.

Lusk, Jayson L. and Darren Hudson (2004), 'Willingness-to-pay estimates and their relevance to agribusiness decision making', *Review of Agricultural Economics*, **26** (2), 152–69.

Lusk, Jayson L. and Ted C. Schroeder (2004), 'Are choice experiments incentive compatible? A test with quality differentiated beef steaks', *American Journal of Agricultural Economics*, **86** (2), 467–82.

Lusk, Jayson L. and Ted C. Schroeder (2006), 'Auction bids and shopping choices', *Advances in Economic Analysis & Policy*, **6** (1), 1539–76.

Lusk, J.L., M.S. Daniel, D.R. Mark and C.L. Lusk (2001), 'Alternative calibration and auction institutions for predicting consumer willingness to pay for non-genetically modified corn chips', *Journal of Agricultural and Resource Economics*, **26** (1), 40–57.

Lusk, Jayson L., T. Feldkamp and T.C. Schroeder (2002), 'Experimental auction procedure: impact of valuation of quality differentiated goods', Working Paper, Department of Agricultural Economics, Purdue University.

Park, Young-Hoon, Min Ding and Vithala R. Rao (2007), 'Eliciting preference for complex products: a web-based upgrading method', Working Paper, Johnson Graduate School of Management, Cornell University.

Rutström, E.E. (1998), 'Home-grown values and incentive compatible auction design', *International Journal of Game Theory*, **27** (3), 427–41.

Shaffer, G. and Z. John Zhang (1995), 'Competitive coupon targeting', *Marketing Science*, **14**, 395–416.

Shogren, J.F. and J.A. Herriges (1996), 'Starting point bias in dichotomous choice valuation with follow-up questioning', *Journal of Environmental Economics and Management*, **30**, 112–31.

Silk, A.J. and G.L. Urban (1978), 'Pre-test-market evaluation of new packaged goods: a model and measurement methodology', *Journal of Marketing Research*, **15**, 171–91.

Spann, M., B. Skiera and B. Schafers (2004), 'Measuring individual frictional costs and willingness-to-pay via name-your-own-price auctions', *Journal of Interactive Marketing*, **18**, 22–36.

Varian, Hal R. (1992), *Microeconomic Analysis*, 3rd edn. New York: Norton.

Vickrey, William (1961), 'Counterspeculation, auctions, and competitive sealed tenders', *Journal of Finance*, **16**, 8–37.

Wang, Tuo, R. Venkatesh and Rabikar Chatterjee (2007), 'reservation price as a range: an incentive-compatible measurement approach', *Journal of Marketing Research*, **44**, 200–213.

Wertenbroch, Klaus and Bernd Skiera (2002), 'Measuring consumers' willingness to pay at the point of purchase', *Journal of Marketing Research*, **39**, 228–41.

3 Measurement of own- and cross-price effects
Qing Liu, Thomas Otter and Greg M. Allenby

Abstract
The accurate measurement of own- and cross-price effects is difficult when there exists a moderate to large number of offerings (e.g., greater than five) in a product category because the number of cross-effects increases geometrically. We discuss approaches that reduce the number of uniquely estimated effects through the use of economic theory, and approaches that increase the information contained in the data through data pooling and the use of informative prior distributions in a Bayesian analysis. We also discuss new developments in the use of supply-side models to aid in the accurate measurement of pricing effects.

Introduction

The measurement of price effects is difficult in marketing because of the many competitive offerings present in most product categories. For J brands, there are J^2 possible effects that characterize the relationship between prices and sales. The number of competitive brands in many product categories is large, taxing the ability of the data to provide reliable estimates of own- and cross-price effects. A recent study by Fennell et al. (2003), for example, reports the median number of brands in 50 grocery store product categories to be 15. This translates into 225 own- and cross-effects that require measurement in the demand system.

Structure-imposing assumptions are therefore required to successfully estimate price effects. At one end of the spectrum, a pricing analyst could simply identify subsets of brands that are thought to compete with each other, and 'zero-out' the cross-effects for brands that are assumed not to compete. While this provides a simple solution to the task of reducing the dimensionality of the measurement problem, it requires strong beliefs about the structure of demand in the marketplace. Moreover, this approach does not allow the data to express contrary evidence.

Alternatively, one might attempt to measure directly all J^2 own- and cross-price effects. However, it is quickly apparent that using a general rule of thumb that one should have n data points for each effect-size measured rules out the use of most commercially available data. Using weekly sales scanning data and the rule that $n = 5$ results in the need for 20 years of data in food product categories such as orange juice or brownies. One could also engage in the generation of data through experimental means, using surveys or field experiments. The data requirements, however, remain formidable.

We discuss approaches to measuring price effects that rely on modeling assumptions to (i) reduce the number of the effects being measured; and/or (ii) increase the information available for measurement. We begin with a brief review of economic theory relevant to price effects, and then discuss the use of economic models to measure them. We then turn our attention to approaches that increase the available information. These approaches are Bayesian in nature, with information being available either through prior information or from data pooled from other sources. We provide a brief review of modern Bayesian methods for pooling data, including the use of hierarchical models, and models that incorporate the price-setting behavior of firms (i.e. supply-side models). We conclude with a discussion of measuring price effects in the presence of dynamic effects and other forms of interactions.

1. Economic models for pricing

According to economic theory, own-price effects should be negative and cross-price effects should be positive for competitive goods. As the price of a brand increases, its own sales should decline. As the price of a competitive brand increases, sales should increase. A commonly encountered problem in the use of regression models for measuring price effects is that cross-effects are often estimated to have the wrong algebraic sign – i.e. they are estimated to be negative when they should be positive. Similarly, but less often, own-price effects are estimated to be positive when they should be negative.

When price effects estimates have erroneous signs and large standard errors, a pricing analyst may be tempted to zero them out and re-estimate the remaining effects as described above. However, doing so imposes strong assumptions about the competitive nature of demand – it means that price of one brand has no effect on another brand, for any price, including zero. While approaches such as Bayesian variable selection (George and McCulloch, 1993) help quantify uncertainty in specification searches (Leamer, 1978) such as this, they require the strong assumptions that some of the effect-sizes have a prior probability of being zero. The assumption of a zero effect is often untenable, especially when deriving estimates from aggregate sales data where at least some customers will react to the price change. So, while the practice of setting coefficients to zero solves the problem of incorrectly signed estimates, it does so by imposing somewhat unbelievable assumptions about the structure of demand.

An alternative approach is to employ economic theory to avoid the direct estimation of the J^2 price effects. As with any theory, the use of an economic model reduces the dimensionality of the effects through model parameters. Economic models of behavior are based on the idea of constrained utility maximization:

$$\text{Max}_x U(x_1,\ldots,x_J) = \sum_{j=1}^{J} \psi_j x_j$$

$$\text{subject to } \sum_{j=1}^{J} p_j x_j \leq E \quad (3.1)$$

where $U(x_1,\ldots,x_J)$ denotes the utility of x_1 units of brand 1, x_2 units of brand 2, ... and x_J units of brand J. In the specification above, utility takes on an additive form that implies that the brands are perfect substitutes. Moreover, this model assumes that utility increases by a constant amount ψ_j as quantity (x_j) increases (i.e. marginal utility is constant). A consumer maximizes utility subject to the budget constraint where p_j is the unit price of brand j, and E is the budgetary allotment – the amount the consumer is willing to spend.

The solution to equation (3.1) can be shown to lead to a discrete choice model, where all expenditure E is allocated to the brand with the biggest bang-for-the-buck, ψ_j/p_j. Assuming that marginal utility has a stochastic component unobservable to the analyst, i.e. $\psi_j = \bar{\psi}_j \exp(\varepsilon_j)$, leads to the demand model:

$$\Pr(x_k > 0) = \Pr\left(\frac{\psi_k}{p_k} > \frac{\psi_j}{p_j} \text{ for all } j\right)$$
$$= \Pr(\ln \psi_k - \ln p_k > \ln \psi_j - \ln p_j \text{ for all } j) \quad (3.2)$$
$$= \Pr(\ln \bar{\psi}_k - \ln p_k + \varepsilon_k > \ln \bar{\psi}_j - \ln p_j + \varepsilon_j \text{ for all } j)$$

The assumption that the error term, ε, is normally distributed leads to a probit model, and the assumption of extreme value errors leads to the logit model. More specifically, if ε is distributed extreme value with location zero and scale σ, then equation (3.2) can be expressed as (McFadden, 1981):

$$\Pr(x_k > 0) = \frac{\exp\left[\frac{\ln \bar{\psi}_k - \ln p_k}{\sigma}\right]}{\sum_{j=1}^{J} \exp\left[\frac{\ln \bar{\psi}_j - \ln p_j}{\sigma}\right]} \quad (3.3)$$
$$= \frac{\exp[V_k]}{\sum_{j=1}^{J} \exp[V_j]}$$

where V_k can be written as $\beta_{0k} - \beta_p \ln p_k$ with $\beta_p = 1/\sigma$ and the intercept β_{0k} equal to $\ln \bar{\psi}_k / \sigma$. Since the sum of all probabilities specified by (3.3) adds up to 1, one of the model intercepts is not identified, and it is customary to set one intercept to zero, leaving $J - 1$ free intercepts and one price coefficient.

Thus the use of an economic model (equations 3.1–3.3) requires J parameters to measure the J^2 own- and cross-price effects. This represents a large reduction in parameters (e.g. from 225 to 15 when $J = 15$) that greatly improves the accuracy of estimates. Given the estimated parameters in equation (3.3), own- and cross-price effects can be computed under the assumption that demand (x) takes on values of only zero or one. With this assumption, we can equate choice probability with expected demand, and we can compute own- and cross-effects as

$$\frac{\partial \ln \Pr_j}{\partial \ln p_j} = -\beta_p(1 - \Pr_j) \quad \text{and} \quad \frac{\partial \ln \Pr_j}{\partial \ln p_k} = \beta_p \Pr_k \quad (3.4)$$

where the former is what economists call own elasticity, and the later is the cross-elasticity. It measures the percentage change in expected demand for a percentage change in price.

Economic models can be used to improve the measurement of own- and cross-price effects in either of two ways. The first is to use the model to suggest constraints for an otherwise purely descriptive model. The second is to directly estimate parameters of the micro economic model, and then use these to measure the price effects.

Using economic theory to constrain descriptive models
Most descriptive models of demand are of log-log or semi-log form. Researchers have extended descriptive models in various ways to achieve more flexible functional forms and to account for uncertainty in the functional form (Kalyanam, 1996; Kalyanam and Shively, 1998). For typical marketing data, where the effective unit of analysis usually

only supplies a limited amount of data, highly flexible descriptive models are especially likely to benefit from constraints derived from economic theory. As we will show, the use of economic theory to derive prior distributions for descriptive models is especially useful in this context. A strong signal in the data can override the implications of economic theory but economic theory will dominate data that are not informative to begin with.

Equation (3.4) suggests a number of constraints on price coefficients that can aid direct estimation of the J^2 own- and cross-price effects using descriptive models. Since β_p is simply the inverse of the scale of the error term, we have $\beta_p > 0$ as $\sigma^2 > 0$, implying that

$$\frac{\partial \ln \Pr_j}{\partial \ln p_j} < 0 \text{ and } \frac{\partial \ln \Pr_j}{\partial \ln p_k} > 0 \qquad (3.5)$$

Constraints of this type, which we call 'ordinal restrictions', occur frequently in the analysis of marketing data. In addition to demand system estimation, the analysis of survey data and use of conjoint analysis are settings in which it is desirable to constrain coefficients so that they are sensible. In addition to expecting that people would rather pay less than more for an offering, researchers also may want to estimate models where preference for a known brand is preferred to an unknown brand, or that respondents prefer better performance assuming all else is held constant.

Natter et al. (2007) describe a decision support system used by bauMax, an Austrian firm in the do-it-yourself home repair industry, which employs ordinal restrictions to derive own effects with correct (negative) algebraic signs. These effects are used by bauMax to derive optimal mark-down policies for the 60,000 stockkeeping units in its stores. Store profits are reported to have increased by 8.1 percent using the decision support system.

Bayesian statistical analysis (see Rossi et al., 2005) offers a convenient solution to incorporating ordinal constraints in models of demand. In a Bayesian analysis, the analyst specifies a prior distribution for the model parameters that reflects his or her beliefs before observing the data. The prior is combined with the data through the likelihood function to arrive at the posterior distribution:

$$\pi(\theta|Data) \propto \pi(Data|\theta)\pi(\theta) \qquad (3.6)$$

where $\pi(\theta)$ denotes the prior distribution, $\pi(Data|\theta)$ denotes the likelihood function; and $\pi(\theta|Data)$ is the posterior distribution. In a regression model, for example, we have

$$y_i = x_i'\beta + \varepsilon_i; \quad \varepsilon_i \sim Normal(0, \sigma^2) \qquad (3.7)$$

and assuming the error terms are normally distributed, the likelihood of the observed data is

$$\pi(Data|\theta = (\beta, \sigma^2)) = \prod_{i=1}^{n} \pi(y_i|x_i, \beta, \sigma^2) = \prod_{i=1}^{n} \frac{1}{\sqrt{2\pi\sigma^2}} \exp\left[\frac{-(y_i - x_i'\beta)^2}{2\sigma^2}\right] \qquad (3.8)$$

where x_i is treated as an independent variable and used as a conditioning argument in the likelihood, and the observations are assumed to be independent given the independent variables x and model parameters, $\theta = (\beta, \sigma^2)$. A prior distribution for the regression coefficients β typically also takes on the form of a normal distribution:

$$\pi(\beta|b, s^2) = \frac{1}{\sqrt{2\pi s^2}} \exp\left[\frac{-(\beta-b)^2}{2s^2}\right] \quad (3.9)$$

where the prior mean, b, and prior variance, s^2, are specified by the analyst. The prior for σ^2 is typically taken to be inverted chi-squared.

Allenby et al. (1995) demonstrate that ordinal constraints can be incorporated into the analysis by specifying a truncated normal prior distribution in (3.9) instead of a normal distribution:

$$\pi(\beta|b, s^2, \text{ordinal restrictions}) = k \exp\left[\sum_{i=1}^{n} \frac{-(\beta-b)^2}{2s^2}\right] I_{\text{ordinal restrictions}} \quad (3.10)$$

where k is an integrating constant that replaces the factor $1/\sqrt{2\pi s^2}$ in equation (3.9), I is an indicator function equal to one when the ordinal constraints are satisfied, and the parameters b and s^2 are specified by the analyst. Examples of ordinal constraints are that an own-price coefficient should be negative, or that a cross-price coefficient should be positive.

From (3.6), the posterior distribution obtained from the likelihood (equation 3.8) and truncated prior (equation 3.10) is:

$$\pi(\theta|Data) \propto \pi(Data|\theta)\pi(\theta) I_{\text{ordinal restrictions}} \quad (3.11)$$

which is the truncated version of the unconstrained posterior. Thus the incorporation of ordinal constraints in an analysis is conceptually simple. The difficulty, until recently, has been in making equation (3.11) operational to the analyst. Analytical expressions for the posterior mean and associated confidence, or credible intervals for the posterior distribution, are generally not available.

Markov chain Monte Carlo (MCMC) estimation offers a tractable approach to working with the truncated posterior distribution in (3.11). The idea is to replace difficult analytic expressions with a series of simple, iterative calculations that result in Monte Carlo draws from the posterior. A Markov chain is constructed with stationary distribution equal to the posterior distribution, allowing the analyst to simulate draws from the posterior. These draws are then used to characterize the posterior distribution. For example, the posterior mean is estimated by taking the mean of the simulated draws from the posterior. Confidence intervals and standard deviations are evaluated similarly.

An important insight about simulation-based methods of estimation (e.g. MCMC) is that once a simulator is developed for sampling from the unconstrained parameter distribution (equation 3.6), it is straightforward to sample from the constrained distribution (equation 3.11) by simply ignoring the simulated draws that do not conform to the restrictions. This is a form of rejection sampling, one of many tools available for generating draws from non-standard distributions.

Economic theory can also be used to impose exact restrictions on own- and cross-price effects. Consider, for example, the constraints implied by equation (3.4). A total of $J^2 - J$ constraints is implied by equation (3.4) because there are J^2 own- and cross-price effects and just J parameters in the logit model in (3.3). One set of constraints is related to the well-known independence of irrelevant alternative (IIA) constraints of logit models. The IIA constraint is typically derived from the logit form in (3.3), where the ratio of choice probabilities of any two brands (e.g. i and j) is unaffected by other brands (e.g. k). Thus changes in the price of brand k must draw proportionally equal choice probability share from brands i and j.

The IIA property is also expressed in equation (3.4) by realizing that the elasticity of demand for brand j with respect to the price of brand k (i.e. η_{jk}) takes the form:

$$\eta_{jk} = \frac{\partial \ln \Pr_j}{\partial \ln p_k} = \beta_p \Pr_k \text{ implying } \eta_{jk} = \eta_{ik} = \ldots = \eta_{Jk} | j \neq k \quad (3.12)$$

Thus the change in the price of brand k has a proportionately equal effect on all other choice probabilities. Equation (3.12) implies a 'proportional draw' property for cross-price effects. In a similar manner it can be shown (see Allenby, 1989) that

$$\frac{\eta_{jk}}{\eta_{ji}} = \frac{\Pr_k}{\Pr_i} \quad (3.13)$$

indicating that the magnitude of price elasticity is proportional to the choice probability. Equation (3.13) implies a 'proportional influence' property where an individual's choice probability is influenced more by price changes of the brands they prefer. At an aggregate level, this implies that brands with greater market share have greater influence.

The constraints implied by equations (3.12) and (3.13) can be incorporated into descriptive regression models either by direct substitution or through the use of a prior distribution. Direct substitution imposes the constraints exactly, and a prior distribution provides a mechanism for stochastically imposing the constraints. For example, in analysis of aggregate data, one could substitute a brand's average market share (m) for the choice probability, and reduce the number of parameters in a regression model by using equation (3.13):

$$\ln m_{jt} = \beta_{0j} + \eta_{jj} \ln p_{jt} + \eta_{jk} \ln p_{kt} + \eta_{ji} \ln p_{it} + \cdots$$

$$= \beta_{0j} + \eta_{jj} \ln p_{jt} + \eta_{jk} \left(\ln p_{kt} + \frac{m_i}{m_k} \ln p_{it} + \cdots \right) \quad (3.14)$$

where t is an index for time. A more formal and flexible approach is to employ a prior distribution that stochastically constrains model parameters to lie close to the subspace implied by the restrictions. Restrictions on the own- and cross-price effects can be expressed as functions of parameters, and priors can be placed on their functional values. To express the equality in equation (3.12), which is equivalent to $\eta_{1k} - \eta_{2k} = \ldots = \eta_{1k} - \eta_{Jk}$, a contrast matrix, R, is used:

$$R = \begin{bmatrix} 1 & -1 & 0 & \cdots \\ 1 & 0 & -1 & \cdots \\ \vdots & \vdots & \cdots & \vdots \\ 1 & 0 & \cdots & -1 \end{bmatrix} \quad (3.15)$$

If equation (3.12) holds exactly, the product $R\eta$ with $\eta = (\eta_{1k}, \ldots \eta_{Jk})$ is a vector of zeros and a prior centered on this belief can be expressed using a normal distribution with mean zero:

$$\pi(R\eta) = (2\pi)^{-(J-1)/2} |S|^{-1/2} \exp\left[-\frac{1}{2}(R\eta) S^{-1}(R\eta)' \right] \quad (3.16)$$

An advantage of this approach is that the prior distribution can be used to control the precision of the restriction through the variance–covariance matrix S.

Montgomery and Rossi (1999) use such an approach to impose restrictions on price elasticities in a descriptive model of demand. This approach assumes that the prior distribution can be constructed with measures that are (nearly) exogenous to the system of study. This assumption is also present in equation (3.14) when employing average market shares, m_i, to impose restrictions. It is reasonable when there are many brands in a category, such that any one brand has little effect on the aggregate expenditure elasticity for the category, when there are sufficient time periods so that the average market share for a brand is reliably measured and when there are no systematic movements in the shares across time.

Formal approaches to demand estimation
The use of linear models to estimate own- and cross-price effects has a long history in economics. Linearity, however, has been limiting research to a restricted number of utility functions. Demand functions, in general, are derived by solving for the demand that maximizes utility subject to the budget (i.e. income) constraint. For the Cobb–Douglas utility function, the demand function can be shown to be of log-log form where the logarithm of quantity is a linear function of logarithm of income and logarithm of price (Simon and Blume, 1994, Example 22.1). Other utility functions do not result in demand functions that are easily estimable with OLS (ordinary least squares).

Some analysts elect to start with the indirect utility function rather than the utility function. The indirect utility function is defined as the maximum utility attainable for a given set of prices and expenditure. It can be shown that differentiating the indirect utility function using Roy's identify (see Simon and Blume, 1994, Theorem 22.5) leads to the demand equation in which demand is expressed as a function of price and income. Varian (1984, ch. 4) demonstrates that this approach usually leads to demand functions that are nonlinear. Some indirect utility functions, such as the translog function of Christensen et al. (1975), lead to linear systems for estimation if a representative economic agent is assumed and consumer heterogeneity is thus ignored. Integrating over a distribution of heterogeneity results in a nonlinear specification that requires the use of alternative methods of estimation (see Allenby and Rossi, 1991 for an exception).

A direct approach to demand estimation is to derive the likelihood of the data corresponding to constrained utility maximization. Distributional assumptions are made about stochastic errors that enter the utility function, understood as information known to the consumer but not observed by the analyst, and from these primitive assumptions the likelihood is derived. Kim et al. (2002) provide an example of such an approach, where utility is specified with diminishing marginal returns:

$$\max_x U(x_1, \ldots, x_J) = \sum_{j=1}^{J} \psi_j (x_j + \gamma_j)^{\alpha_j}$$

$$\text{subject to } \sum_{j=1}^{J} p_j x_j \leq E \tag{3.17}$$

Here, γ_j translates the utility function to allow for corner and interior solutions. Diminishing marginal returns occur if α_j is positive and less than one. The likelihood is obtained by differentiating the Lagrangian $U(x) - \lambda(p'x - E)$ to obtain the Kuhn–Tucker (KT) conditions as follows:

$$\frac{\partial U}{\partial x_1} - \lambda p_1 = \ldots = \frac{\partial U}{\partial x_J} - \lambda p_J = 0, \text{ that is, } \frac{\partial U}{\partial x_1}\frac{1}{p_1} = \ldots = \frac{\partial U}{\partial x_J}\frac{1}{p_J} = \lambda$$

where $\partial U/\partial x_j = \psi_j \alpha_j (x_j + \gamma_j)^{\alpha_j - 1}, j = 1,\ldots, J$. Assuming that log marginal utility can only be measured up to additive error, i.e. $\ln \psi_j = \ln \bar{\psi}_j + \varepsilon_j$, and that the observed data conform to the KT conditions, we have for both x_i and x_j positive:

$$\ln(\bar{\psi}_i \alpha_i (x_i + \gamma_i)^{\alpha_i - 1}) - \ln p_i + \varepsilon_i = \ln(\bar{\psi}_j \alpha_j (x_j + \gamma_j)^{\alpha_j - 1}) - \ln p_j + \varepsilon_j \quad (3.18)$$

or

$$(\ln(\bar{\psi}_i \alpha_i (x_i + \gamma_i)^{\alpha_i - 1}) - \ln p_i) - (\ln(\bar{\psi}_j \alpha_j (x_j + \gamma_j)^{\alpha_j - 1}) - \ln p_j) = \varepsilon_j - \varepsilon_i \quad (3.19)$$

Equation (3.19) provides a basis for deriving the likelihood of the data, $\pi(Data|\theta = (\bar{\psi}, \alpha, \gamma))$ through the distribution of $(\varepsilon_j - \varepsilon_i)$. The distribution of the observed data $\{x_i, x_j\}$ is obtained as the distribution of the calculated errors $\{\varepsilon_i, \varepsilon_j\}$ multiplied by the Jacobian of the transformation from ε to x. Modern Bayesian (MCMC) methods are well suited to estimate such models because they require the evaluation of the likelihood only at specific values of the parameters, and do not require the evaluation of gradients or Hessians of the likelihood. Once the parameters of the utility function are available, estimates of own- and cross-effects can be obtained by solving equation (3.17) numerically for various price vectors and computing numeric derivatives.

Standard discrete choice models such as multinomial logit and probit models are the simplest examples of the direct approach. Utility is assumed to take a linear form with constant marginal utility (equation 3.1), and random error is introduced as shown in equation (3.2). Constant marginal utility implies that as income increases consumers simply consume more of the same brand rather than switching to a higher-quality brand. Allenby and Rossi (1991) use a non-constant marginal utility (non-homothetic), which motivates switching from inferior goods to superior goods as income increases. As a consequence, price responses are asymmetric. Price changes of high-quality brands have a higher impact on low-quality brands than vice versa (see Blattberg and Wisniewski, 1989 for a motivation of asymmetric price response based on heterogeneity).

Chiang (1991) and Chintagunta (1993) remove the 'given purchase' condition inherent to discrete choice models and model purchase incidence, brand choice and purchase quantity simultaneously through a bivariate utility function. A generalized extreme value distribution implies both a probability to purchase and a brand choice probability. A flexible translog indirect utility function is maximized with respect to quantity given a brand is purchased. Variants of this approach have been used by Arora et al. (1998), Bell et al. (1999), and Nair et al. (2005).

The translog approach results in price effects that can be decomposed into three parts: changes in purchase probability, changes in brand choice given purchase occurrence; changes in purchase quantity given purchase occurrence and brand selection. Bell et al. (1999) show that these three components are influenced in different ways by exogeneous consumer-, brand- and category-specific variables.

The linear additive utility specification popular in marketing implies that all brands are perfect substitutes, so that only one brand is chosen as the utility-maximizing solution. Nonlinear utility functions such as (3.17) allow for both corner and interior solutions. That is, a consumer chooses one alternative or a combination of different alternatives as the result of utility maximization. Thus the model quantifies the tradeoff between price and the variety of the product assortment (see Kim et al., 2002, 2007 for details). A different form of nonlinear utility function is used by Dubé (2004), who motivates the choice of more than one brand by multiple consumption occasions that are considered during a customer's shopping trip.

2. Improving measurement with additional information

An alternative to constraining and/or reducing the parameter space through the use of economic models is to use approaches that attempt to increase the available information for estimation. We investigate two approaches to data pooling. The first is with the use of random-effects models that effectively borrow information from other similar units through the random-effects distribution. The second approach pools information from the supply side. This approach views the prices themselves as endogenous to the system of study, and models are specified as a system of demand and supply equations. Both approaches have become practical in applications with the advent of modern Bayesian methods.

Pooling across units

Random-effects models add another layer to the Bayesian prior distribution. Equation (3.9) is the prior associated with one unit of analysis, where the unit might be sales at a specific retailer or in a specific geographic region. When multiple units of analysis are available, it is possible to pool the data by specifying a relationship among the model parameters:

$$\pi(Data_i|\theta_i) \quad \text{for } i = 1, \ldots, N$$

$$\pi(\theta_i|\zeta)$$

$$\pi(\zeta) \tag{3.21}$$

where ζ are known as hyper-parameters – i.e. parameters that describe the distribution of other parameters. For example, $\pi(Data_i|\theta_i)$ could represent a time-series regression model for sales of a specific brand in region i, with own- and cross-effects coefficients θ_i. The second layer of the model, $\pi(\theta_i|\zeta)$, is the random-effects model. A commonly assumed distribution is multivariate normal. Finally, the third layer, $\pi(\zeta)$, is the prior distribution for the hyper-parameters.

Pooling occurs in equation (3.21) because θ_i is present in both the first and second equations of the model, not just the first. The data from all units are used to inform the hyper-parameters, and as the accuracy of the hyper-parameter estimates increases, so does that of the estimates of the individual-level parameters, θ_i. The posterior distribution of the hierarchical model in (3.21) is

$$\pi(\{\theta_i\}, \zeta | \{Data_i\}) \propto \prod_{i=1}^{N} \left(\prod_{t=1}^{T_i} \pi(Data_{it}|\theta_i) \right) \pi(\theta_i|\zeta) \pi(\zeta) \tag{3.22}$$

which highlights a key difference between the Bayeisan and non-Bayesian treatment of random-effects models. In a Bayesian treatment, the posterior comprises the hyperparameters and all individual-level parameters. In a non-Bayesian treatment, parameters are viewed as fixed but unknown constants, the analysis proceeds by forming the marginalized likelihood of the data:

$$\pi(\{Data_i\}|\zeta) = \prod_{i=1}^{N} \int \left(\prod_{t=1}^{T_i} \pi(Data_{it}|\theta_i) \right) \pi(\theta_i|\zeta) d\theta_i \quad (3.23)$$

The Bayesian treatment does not remove the individual-level parameters from analysis, and inferences about unit-specific parameters are made by marginalizing the posterior distribution in equation (3.22):

$$\pi(\theta_i|\{Data_i\}) = \int \pi(\{\theta_i\},\zeta|\{Data_i\}) d\{\theta_{-i},\zeta\} \quad (3.24)$$

Modern Bayesian methods deliver the marginal posterior distribution of model parameters at no additional computational cost. The MCMC algorithm simulates draws from the full posterior distribution of model parameters in (3.22). Analysis for a particular unit, θ_i, proceeds by simply ignoring the simulated draws of the other model parameters, θ_{-i} and ζ. Thus the hierarchical model, coupled with modern Bayesian statistical methods, offers a powerful and practical approach to data pooling to improve parameter estimates.

Allenby and Ginter (1995), and Lenk et al. (1996) demonstrate the efficiency of the estimates obtained from the hierarchical Bayes approach in comparison with the traditional estimation methods. The number of erratic signs on price-elasticity estimates is significantly reduced as more information becomes available via pooling. Montgomery (1997) uses this methodology to estimate store-level parameters from a panel of retailers. Ainslie and Rossi (1998) employ a hierarchical model to measure similarities in demand across categories. Arora et al. (1998) jointly model individual-level brand choice and purchase quantity, and Bradlow and Rao (2000) model assortment choice using hierarchical models.

Bayesian pooling techniques have found their way into practice through firms such as DemandTec (demandtec.com), who specialize in retail price optimization. Current customers of DemandTec include Target, WalMart and leading grocers such as Safeway and Giant Eagle. A major challenge in setting optimal prices at the stockkeeping unit level is the development of demand models that accurately predict the effects of price changes on own sales and competitive sales. Retailers want to set prices to optimize profits in a product category, and a critical element involves estimating coefficients with correct algebraic signs (i.e. own-effects are negative, cross-effects are positive) so that an optimal solution exists. For example, if an own-effect is estimated to be positive, it implies that an increase in price is associated with an increase in demand, and the optimal price is therefore equal to positive infinity. This solution is neither reasonable nor believable. DemandTec uses hierarchical Bayesian models such as equation (3.21) to pool data across similar stockkeeping units to help obtain more accurate price effects with reasonable algebraic signs.

Another industry example of the use of hierarchical Bayesian analysis is Sawtooth Software (sawtoothsoftware.com), the leading supplier of conjoint software. Conjoint analysis is a popular quantitative technique used to evaluate consumer utility for attribute levels, and express them in terms of a common metric. For example, consumer preference for different credit cards can be viewed in terms of utility for different interest rates, grace periods, annual fees, etc. Conjoint analysis estimates the part-worths of the levels of these attributes. In most studies, price is specified as an attribute, and consumer price-sensitivity (β_p) is measured at the individual-respondent level using a hierarchical model. The individual-level estimates are then used to predict changes in demand for all products in a category in response to changes in product attributes, including price. Data pooling via a hierarchical model structure is critical for obtaining individual-level part-worths because of the limited number of conjoint questions that can be asked of a respondent in an interview. Sales for the hierarchical Bayes version of Sawtooth's conjoint software now dominates their non-Bayesian version.

Incorporating supply-side data
Up to this point we have considered models where prices are viewed as explanatory of sales, and also independently determined. This assumption is acceptable when analyzing survey and experimental data because prices are set by the analyst. However, when data are from the marketplace, prices are set in anticipation of demand and profits. Observed prices are influenced by the preferences and sensitivities of consumers, the same factors (e.g. utility function parameters) that influence the magnitude of the own- and cross-price effects.

When explanatory variables are endogenously determined, the likelihood will comprise multiple equations that form a system of equations. Exceptions to this general rule are discussed by Liu et al. (2007). As discussed in the use of formal economic models above, the key in conducting analysis of simultaneous equation systems is to relate primitive assumptions about how errors enter the model to the likelihood for the observed data.

Consider, for example, a monopolist pricing problem using a constant elasticity model, where it is assumed that the variation in prices over time is due to stochastic departures from optimal price-setting behavior. The likelihood for the data is a combination of a traditional demand model:

$$\ln y_t = \beta_0 + \beta_1 \ln p_t + \varepsilon_t; \quad \varepsilon_t \sim Normal(0, \sigma_\varepsilon^2) \qquad (3.25)$$

and a factor for the endogenous price variable. Optimal pricing for the monopolist can be shown to be (see for example, Pashigian, 1998, p. 333):

$$p_t = mc\left(\frac{\beta_1}{1+\beta_1}\right)e^{v_t}; \quad v_t \sim Normal(0, \sigma_v^2) \qquad (3.26)$$

where mc denotes the marginal cost of the brand, and a supply-side error term has been added to account for temporal variation of observed prices from the optimal price. Taking logs of equation (3.26) yields

$$\ln p_t = \ln mc + \ln\left(\frac{\beta_1}{1+\beta_1}\right) + v_t; \quad v_t \sim Normal(0, \sigma_v^2) \qquad (3.27)$$

Equations (3.25) and (3.27) form a system of equations that effectively pools supply-side information and improves the estimation of the own-price effect, β_1, if the marginal cost of the brand is known. That is, the average level of price is informative about β_1 given marginal cost. The likelihood for equations (3.25) and (3.27) is obtained by solving for error terms:

$$\varepsilon_t = \ln y_t - \beta_0 - \beta_1 \ln p_t \sim Normal(0, \sigma_\varepsilon^2)$$

$$v_t = \ln p_t - \ln mc - \ln\left(\frac{\beta_1}{1+\beta_1}\right) \sim Normal(0, \sigma_v^2) \qquad (3.28)$$

and computing:

$$\begin{aligned}
\pi(Data|\theta) &= \prod_{t=1}^{T} \pi(y_t, p_t | \beta_0, \beta_1, \sigma_\varepsilon^2, \sigma_v^2) \\
&= \prod_{t=1}^{T} \pi(\varepsilon_t, v_t | \beta_0, \beta_1, \sigma_\varepsilon^2, \sigma_v^2) \times J_{(\varepsilon_t, v_t) \to (y_t, p_t)} \qquad (3.29) \\
&= \prod_{t=1}^{T} \pi(\varepsilon_t, v_t | \beta_0, \beta_1, \sigma_\varepsilon^2, \sigma_v^2) \times \frac{1}{y_t p_t}
\end{aligned}$$

In this example, the supply-side equation offers additional information that is useful for estimating the own-price effect in two ways. The first way, as mentioned above, is to help locate the value of β_1 if marginal cost is known. The second way is through an ordinal constraint imposed by the supply-side model – i.e. $\beta_1 < -1$ for the supply equation to be valid. If $-1 \le \beta_1 < 0$, $\beta_1/(1+\beta_1)$ is negative, equation (3.26) no longer yields the price that maximizes profits and thus the logarithm in equation (3.27) is not defined. Optimal pricing behavior with positive, finite prices exists only when own-price effects are elastic. Thus the supply-side equation constrains the estimates of price effects by merely ascertaining that optimal pricing with positive, finite prices is possible. This aspect of supply-side analysis is investigated in more detail by Otter et al. (2007).

When the error terms, ε_t and v_t, are correlated, analysis without the supply side leads to inconsistent estimates (Besanko et al. 1998; Villas-Boas and Winer, 1999). The typical rational for correlated demand- and supply-side shocks is the presence of a common omitted variable that raises prices and demand at the same time – e.g. a retailer correctly anticipates a demand shock and simultaneously raises prices. Thus the presence of endogenous price variation requires joint estimation of demand- and supply-side equations to obtain consistent estimates of own- and cross-price effects.

Supply-side equations may be reduced-form linear models (Villas-Boas and Winer, 1999), or structural models where the supply-side equations are obtained through maximizing objective functions of firms and/or retailers. For example, Sudhir (2001a) obtains the supply-side pricing equations by assuming that the firm maximizes the sum of own profits and weighted competitor profits, where the weight on competitor profits characterizes cooperative (positive weight) or aggressive (negative weight) competitive behavior. Chintagunta (2002) obtains the supply-side pricing equations by assuming that retailers set prices to maximize a weighted sum of category profits and store brand share while accounting for manufacturers' actions, store traffic effects and retail competition. Chintagunta and Desiraju (2005) obtain supply-side equations by maximizing a profit function that accounts for firm interactions within a geographic market as well as interactions across all geographic markets. Other examples of structural supply-side models include Besanko et al. (1998), Sudhir (2001b), Draganska and Jain (2004) and Villas-Boas and Zhao (2005).

Techniques to obtain parameter estimates in demand- and supply-side equations include generalized method of moments (GMM) estimation using instrumental variables (see Berry, 1994; Berry et al., 1995; and Nevo, 2001), maximum likelihood estimation (see Villas-Boas and Winer, 1999; Villas-Boas and Zhao, 2005; and Draganska and Jain, 2004), and the Bayesian approach (see Yang et al., 2003).

3. Concluding comments

The measurement of own- and cross-price effects in marketing is complicated by many factors, including a potentially large number of effects requiring measurement, heterogeneity in consumer response to prices, the presence of nonlinear models of behavior, and the fact that prices are set strategically in anticipation of profits by manufacturers and retailers. Over the course of the past 20 years, improvements in statistical computing have allowed researchers to develop new models that improve the measurement of price effects.

The measurement of price effects is inextricably linked to choice and demand models, and more generally consumer decision-making. These are very active research areas, and the implications of many of the more recently published choice models for the measurement of price effects and price setting have yet to be explored. In this chapter we focused on static models that imply (only) an immediate and continuous price response. There is active research on dynamic price effects. Dynamic price effects refer to the effects of price change on future sales as mediated by stockpiling and/or increased consumption. Effects to be measured include immediate, future and cumulative (immediate + future) effects of promotional and/or regular price changes, which may differ in sign and magnitude. For example, as shown by Kopalle et al. (1999), promotions have positive immediate effects but negative future effects on baseline sales. Autoregressive descriptive demand models (see, e.g., Kopalle et al., 1999; Fok et al., 2006) and utility-based demand models (Erdem et al., 2003) have recently been used to account for carry-over effects from past discounts, forward-looking consumer behavior and competitive price reactions. The same approaches are taken to dealing with measurement difficulties – using theory to impose restrictions on parameters, Bayesian pooling, and adding supply-side information.

Finally, there is a large behavioral literature documenting the influence of consumer cognitive capacity, memory, perceptions and attitudes in reaction to price (see Monroe, 2002 for a review). An active area of current research develops demand models that incorporate such behavioral decision theory for an improved measurement of price effects (Gilbride and Allenby, 2004, 2006).

References

Ainslie, A. and P.E. Rossi (1998), 'Similarities in choice behavior across product categories', *Marketing Science*, **17** (2), 91–106.

Allenby, G.M. (1989), 'A unified approach to identifying, estimating and testing demand structures with aggregate scanner data', *Marketing Science*, **8** (3), 265–80.

Allenby, G.M. and J.L. Ginter (1995), 'Using extremes to design products and segment markets', *Journal of Marketing Research*, **32** (4), 392–403.

Allenby, G.M. and P.E. Rossi (1991), 'Quality perceptions and asymmetric switching behavior between brands', *Marketing Science*, **10** (3), 185–204.

Allenby, G.M., N. Arora and J.L. Ginter (1995), 'Incorporating prior knowledge into the analysis of conjoint studies', *Journal of Marketing Research*, **32** (2), 152–62.

Arora, N., G.M. Allenby and J.L. Ginter (1998), 'A hierarchical Bayes model of primary and secondary demands', *Marketing Science*, **17** (1), 29–44.
Bell, D.R., J. Chiang and V. Padmanabhan (1999), 'The decomposition of promotional response: an empirical generalization', *Marketing Science*, **18** (4), 504–26.
Berry, S.T. (1994), 'Estimating discrete-choice models of product differentiation', *Rand Journal of Economics*, **25** (2), 242–53.
Berry, S., J. Levinsohn and A. Pakes (1995), 'Automobile prices in market equilibrium', *Econometrica*, **63** (4), 841–90.
Besanko, D., S. Gupta and D. Jain (1998), 'Logit demand estimation under competitive pricing behavior: an equilibrium framework', *Management Science*, **44** (11), 1533–47.
Blattberg, R.C. and K.J. Wisniewski (1989), 'Price-induced pattern of competition', *Marketing Science*, **8** (4), 291–309.
Bradlow, E.T. and V.R. Rao (2000), 'A hierarchical Bayes model for assortment choice', *Journal of Marketing Research*, **37** (2), 259–68.
Chiang, J. (1991), 'A simultaneous approach to the whether, what and how much to buy questions', *Marketing Science*, **10** (4), 297–315.
Chintagunta, P.K. (1993), 'Investigating purchase incidence, brand choice and purchase quantity decisions of households', *Marketing Science*, **12** (2), 184–208.
Chintagunta, P.K. (2002), 'Investigating category pricing behavior at a retail chain', *Journal of Marketing Research*, **39** (2), 141–54.
Chintagunta, P.K. and R. Desiraju (2005), 'Strategic pricing and detailing behavior in international markets', *Marketing Science*, **24** (1), 67–80.
Christensen, L., D. Jorgenson and L. Lau (1975), 'Transcendental logarithmic utility functions', *American Economic Review*, **3**, 367–83.
Draganska, M. and D. Jain (2004), 'A likelihood approach to estimating market equilibrium models', *Management Science*, **50** (5), 605–16.
Dubé, J.-P. (2004), 'Multiple discreteness and product differentiation: demand for carbonated soft drinks', *Marketing Science*, **23** (1), 66–81.
Erdem, T., S. Imai and M. Keane (2003), 'Brand and quantity choice dynamics under price uncertainty', *Quantitative Marketing and Economics*, **1** (1), 5–64.
Fennell, G., G.M. Allenby, S. Yang and Y. Edwards (2003), 'The effectiveness of demographic and psychographic variables for explaining brand and product use', *Quantitative Marketing and Economics*, **1**, 223–44.
Fok, D., C. Horvath, R. Paap and P.H. Franses (2006), 'A hierarchical Bayes error correction model to explain dynamic effects of price changes', *Journal of Marketing Research*, **43** (3), 443–61.
George, E. and R. McCullloch (1993), 'Variable selection via Gibbs sampling', *Journal of American Statistical Association*, **88**, 881–9.
Gilbride, T.J. and G.M. Allenby (2004), 'A choice model with conjunctive, disjunctive, and compensatory screening rules', *Marketing Science*, **23** (3), 391–406.
Gilbride, T.J. and G.M. Allenby (2006), 'Estimating heterogeneous EBA and economic screening rule choice models', *Marketing Science*, **25** (5), 494–509.
Kalyanam, K. (1996), 'Pricing decisions under demand uncertainty: a Bayesian mixture model approach', *Marketing Science*, **15** (3), 207–21.
Kalyanam, K. and T.S. Shively (1998), 'Estimating irregular price effects: a stochastic spline regression approach', *Journal of Marketing Research*, **35** (1), 16–29.
Kim, J., G.M. Allenby and P.E. Rossi (2002), 'Modeling consumer demand for variety', *Marketing Science*, **21** (3), 229–50.
Kim, J., G.M. Allenby and P.E. Rossi (2007), 'Product attributes and models of multiple discreteness', *Journal of Econometrics*, **138** (1), 208–30.
Kopalle, P.K., C.F. Mela and L. Marsh (1999), 'The dynamic effect of discounting on sales: empirical analysis and normative pricing implications', *Marketing Science*, **18** (3), 317–32.
Leamer, E. (1978), *Specification Searches: Ad-hoc Inference with Non-Experimental Data*, New York: John Wiley & Sons.
Lenk, P.J., W.S. DeSarbo, P.E. Green and M.R. Young (1996), 'Hierarchical Bayes conjoint analysis: recovery of partworth heterogeneity from reduced experimental design', *Marketing Science*, **15** (2), 173–91.
Liu, Q., T. Otter and G.M. Allenby (2007), 'Investigating endogeneity bias in marketing', *Marketing Science*, **26** (5), 642–50.
McFadden, D. (1981), 'Econometric models of probabilistic choice', in C. Manski and D. McFadden (eds), *Structural Analysis of Discrete Data with Econometric Applications*, Cambridge, MA: MIT Press, pp. 198–272.
Monroe K.B. (2002), *Pricing: Making Profitable Decisions*, 3rd edn, Boston, MA: McGraw-Hill/Irwin.

Montgomery, A. (1997), 'Creating micro-marketing pricing strategies using supermarket scanner data', *Marketing Science*, **16** (4), 315–37.
Montgomery, A.L. and P.E. Rossi (1999), 'Estimating price elasticities with theory-based priors', *Journal of Marketing Research*, **36** (4), 413–23.
Nair, H., J.-P. Dubé and P.K. Chintagunta (2005), 'Accounting for primary and secondary demand effects with aggregate data', *Marketing Science*, **24** (3), 444–60.
Natter, M., T. Reutterer, A. Mild and A. Taudes (2007), 'An assortment-wide decision-support system for dynamic pricing and promotion planning in DIY retailing', Working Paper, Univeristy of Frankfurt.
Nevo, A. (2001), 'Measuring market power in the ready-to-eat cereal industry', *Econometrica*, **69** (2), 307–42.
Otter, T., L.-J. Kao, C.-C. Chiu, T. Gilbride and G.M. Allenby (2007), 'Evaluating the effectiveness of marketing expenditures', Working Paper, University of Frankfurt.
Pashigian, P.B. (1998), *Price Theory and Applications*, 2nd edn, New York: McGraw-Hill.
Rossi, P.E., G.M. Allenby and R. McCulloch (2005), *Bayesian Statistics and Marketing*, Hoboken, NJ: John Wiley & Sons.
Simon, C.P. and L. Blume (1994), *Mathematics for Economists*, New York: Norton.
Sudhir, K. (2001a), 'Competitive pricing behavior in the auto market: a structural analysis', *Marketing Science*, **20** (1), 42–60.
Sudhir, K. (2001b), 'Structural analysis of manufacturer pricing in the presence of a strategic retailer', *Marketing Science*, **20** (3), 244–64.
Varian H.R. (1984), *Microeconomic Analysis*, 2nd edn, New York: Norton.
Villas-Boas, J.M. and R.S. Winer (1999), 'Endogeneity in brand choice models', *Management Science*, **45** (10), 1324–38.
Villas-Boas, J.M. and Y. Zhao (2005), 'Retailer, manufacturers, and individual consumers: modeling the supply side in the ketchup marketplace', *Journal of Marketing Research*, **42** (1), 83–95.
Yang, S., Y. Chen and G.M. Allenby (2003), 'Bayesian analysis of simultaneous demand and supply', *Quantitative Marketing and Economics*, **1**, 251–75.

4 Behavioral pricing
Aradhna Krishna

Abstract
The focus is on 'behavioral aspects of pricing', or price effects that cannot be accounted for by the intrinsic price itself. After presenting a broad conceptual framework, I concentrate on two distinct streams of research. The first is composed of laboratory experiments examining the impact of price presentation (e.g. externally provided reference price, whether a deal is presented in absolute dollars off or in percentage off the original price) on perceived price savings. The second stream uses secondary data on consumer purchases (scanner data) and focuses on the effects of internal reference prices, reference prices that are created by consumers themselves, on consumer purchase behavior.

Introduction
Victoria's Secret frequently advertises 'Buy two, get one free'. Storewide sales in Talbots, The Gap, Benetton and others are often announced by signs proclaiming '20–50% off' or 'Up to 70% off'. Are price cuts presented in different ways perceived differently by consumers? If the consumer rationally computes his (her) savings, mental effort could be reduced by simply stating the dollar savings to the consumer. Yet, apparently, the presentation of the promotion has an impact on consumer deal evaluation and hence retail sales. In fact, much research in marketing attests to the effect of price presentation on deal perception (Das, 1992; Lichtenstein and Bearden, 1989; Urbany et al., 1988; Yadav and Monroe, 1993). Non-rational (in the traditional sense) processing of price information is further attested to by Inman et al.'s (1990) finding that the mere presence of a sale announcement, without a reduced price, increased retail sales. Hence, an understanding of price presentation effects is insightful for retailers as well as for brand managers.

In similar vein, if a consumer is fortunate in frequenting a store multiple times when a particular brand is on sale, and then visits the store when it is not on sale, will she be less likely to purchase it – i.e. will the fact that she has purchased the product at a lower price in the past reduce her probability of buying it at regular price in the future? What if she has bought it at regular price for many shopping trips, and now finds it on sale? Will her probability of purchasing the brand increase by the same extent as it would decrease in the previous scenario? Comprehension of internal reference price effects – reference prices that are created by consumers themselves – is important when deciding on price changes over time.

In this chapter, we focus on 'behavioral aspects of pricing' or price effects that cannot be accounted for by the intrinsic price itself. After presenting a broad conceptual framework, we concentrate on two distinct streams of research, price presentation effects and internal reference price effects, that have just been illustrated. The first typically uses laboratory experiments, whereas the second uses secondary data on consumer purchases (scanner data). For price presentation effects, we report results from a meta-analysis (Krishna et al., 2002) where results from past literature are examined to determine the relative importance of different presentation effects (Section 2). For internal reference price effects, we provide a summary of the papers that have been contributed in that area (Section 3). We begin with the framework.

1. Conceptual framework

While much research in marketing and economics has focused on the effect of intrinsic price, only in the last three decades has research focused on behavioral aspects of pricing. However, the latter can be just as significant for consumer choice. We identify a few of the behavioral aspects of special relevance to marketing researchers. By no means is this meant to be an exhaustive review of the literature. Figure 4.1 illustrates our conceptual framework.

The final dependent variables in our conceptual framework are consumer choice among brands, purchase quantity and purchase timing. Two other intermediary dependent variables are identified – subjective price and price fairness. Subjective price is assumed to be affected by many factors, as can be seen in Figure 4.1. Price fairness has also been attributed with many antecedents. We talk about each in turn.

Subjective price

We elaborate in detail on price presentation effects (through a published meta-analysis) and on internal reference price effects in Sections 2 and 3. However, two other price presentation effects not included in the meta-analysis are worthy of mention – these are the effects of (i) '99 cent endings and (ii) temporal pricing and partitioned prices.

99 cent endings Schindler and Kirby (1997) made an analysis of the rightmost digits of selling prices in retail advertisements and found an overrepresentation of 0, 5 and 9. Using the same historical data, they show that this practice cannot be explained by consumers perceiving 9-endings as a round-number price with a small amount given back; instead, it is better explained by underestimation of 9-ending prices with left-to-right processing. Stiving and Winer (1997) provide further proof for the additional utility of 9-endings. Using scanner panel data, they show that 9-ending prices do indeed have additional utility for consumers and that predictive models need to account for this effect for more accuracy.

Temporal pricing and partitioned prices Another area of behavioral pricing research where many puzzles remain unresolved is that of partitioned pricing and temporal pricing. Gourville (1998) shows in his paper that pennies-a-day pricing is a better appeal to consumers for charitable donations than a larger amount paid per month. Similarly, Morwitz et al. (1998) show that separating the total price of a product into the base price and shipping charge is better than presenting it as one combined price. In both the temporal-price-framing case (Gourville, 1998) and the partitioned pricing case, consumers are being asked to pay a larger number of smaller dollar amounts, and this is found to be better valued by consumers. These cases go against Thaler's (1985) segregate losses rule. One explanation may be that very tiny amounts are ignored by consumers – in the pennies-a-day case, all payments are deemed trivial, and in the partitioned pricing case, the shipping charge is small in comparison with the base price and is ignored. Thus, Thaler's arguments do not extend to these cases. Such a hypothesis nevertheless needs further research.

Internal reference prices

- Past prices
- Competitive prices

Price presentation

- 99 cent endings
- Partitioned prices
- Temporal pricing
- Reference price
- Deal plausibility
- Other effects covered in Figure 4.2

Antecedents of perceived price fairness

- Firm reputation
- Inferred relative profit
- Inferred motive of firm
- Direction of price change
- Human or inhuman communication of price change
- Price to self versus price to others

Subjective price

- Perceived savings

Perceived price fairness

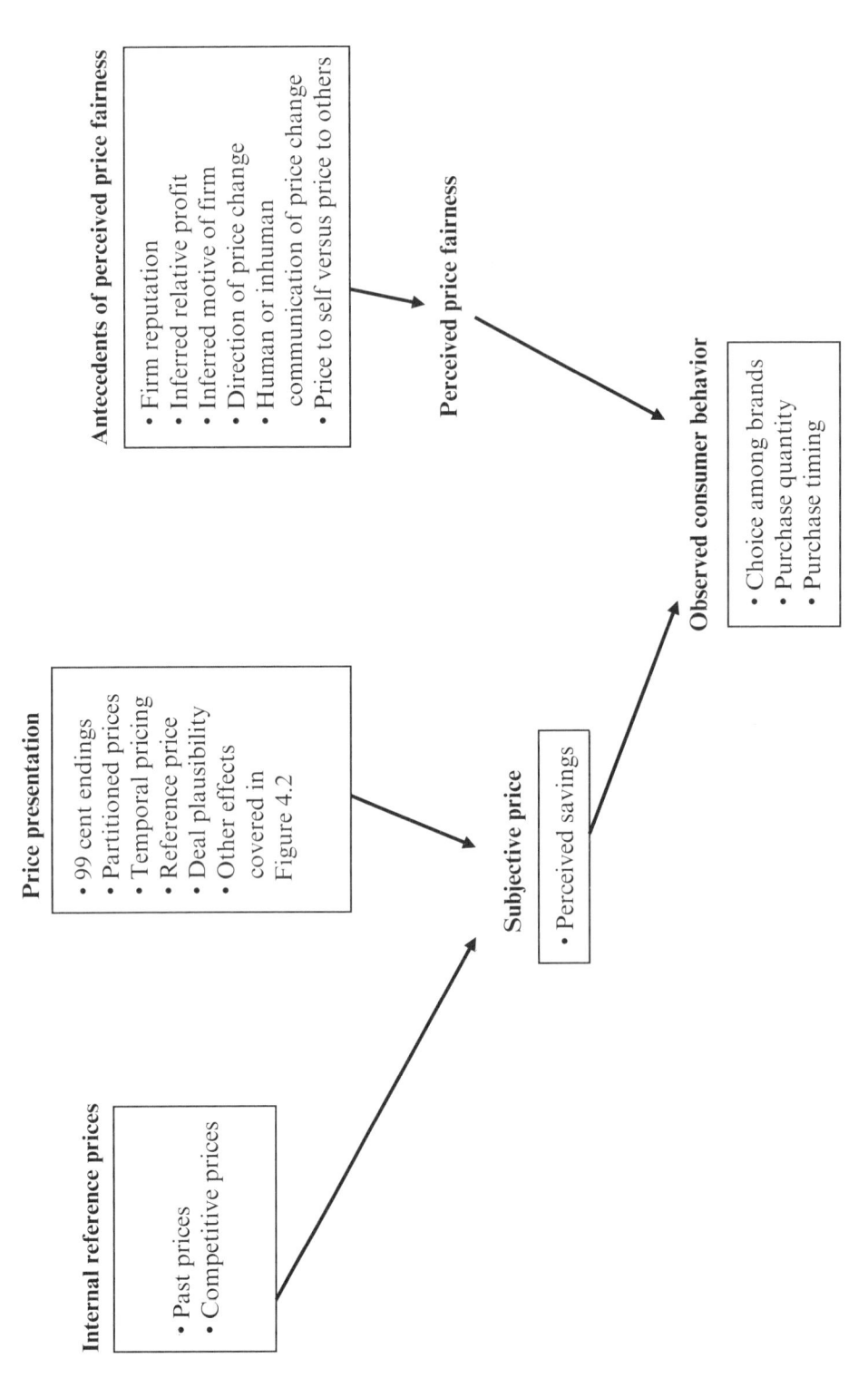

Observed consumer behavior

- Choice among brands
- Purchase quantity
- Purchase timing

Figure 4.1 Conceptual framework

Price fairness
Campbell (1999) provides a rigorous structure for the antecedents and consequences of perceived price fairness. She sets up a scenario where a firm intends to sell a doll by auction just before Christmas because of its rarity. The auction implies a sudden price change (i.e. price increase) compared to the doll's normal market price. Campbell shows in this context that the auction is perceived as more unfair when the firm actually makes more profit than it normally does. Furthermore, when consumers impute a negative motive to the firm (e.g. the firm is making extra profit), the auction is perceived as significantly less fair than the same auction when the firm's motive is seen as positive (e.g. the money is going to a charity). Furthermore, firms with good reputations are more likely to be given the benefit of the doubt by consumers about their motive. More recently, Campbell (2007) further studies the antecedents of price (un)fairness by incorporating the effects of the source of price information and affect on consumers' perceived price (un)fairness. The research shows that whether the price change (increase or decrease) is communicated by human or nonhuman means (e.g. price tag) moderates consumers' fairness perception. This is because the imputed motive of the marketer and affect elicited by such price information both mediate the effect of the price change.

Other authors have studied the effects of perceived price unfairness arising from targeted pricing whereby firms offer different prices to different consumers. Krishna and Wang (2007) demonstrate experimentally that consumers will leave money rather than interact with firms that are perceived to engage in targeted pricing that is believed to be unfair. Feinberg et al. (2002) show that, in this context, the competitive equilibrium will not necessarily be one where firms offer lower prices to new customers to attract them, but can be one where firms offer lower prices to old customers to retain them. Krishna et al. (2007) find a similar result in the context of increasing prices where a constant price is perceived as a deal. Most competitive models in marketing are based on the assumption that consumers are rational utility-maximizers who are motivated only by 'self-regarding preferences'. That is, they care only about their own payoffs. In the papers incorporating fairness, it is shown that consumer behavior may also be affected by 'social preferences'.

We now discuss the meta-analysis of price presentation effects.

2. Meta-analysis of price presentation effects[1]

Krishna et al. (2002) offer a fairly broad meta-analysis of price presentation effects. Their coverage of effects is shown in Figure 4.2. It can be seen that they examined the impact of four broad categories of price presentation factors on consumers' perceived price savings from purchasing on price promotions (see Zeithaml, 1982; Dickson and Sawyer, 1990).

The first set of factors is situational. These factors encompass the overall situation for the price promotion, e.g., is the evaluation for a national brand or a private label brand, is it within a discount store or a specialty store, are consumers comparing prices within or between stores, and/or is this kind of promotion distinct (versus competition) and/or consistent (over time) or not? The second set of factors, presentation effects, addresses whether it matters how the promotions are communicated, and are some ways of doing

---

[1] This part of the chapter is based upon Krishna et al. (2002).

Study effect
- Number of independent variables
- Number of subjects
- Study idiosyncrasies

Price presentation
- Reference price
- Deal frame
- Tensile frame
- Plausibility
- Consistency
- Distinctiveness
- Store frame
- Loss
- Combined prices
- Announce sale

Situation
- Brand type
- Store type
- Good type
- Category experience
- Ad frame

Deal characteristics
- Deal percentage
- Deal amount
- Base price
- Free gift value
- Variance of deals
- Additional savings on bundle
- Size of bundle
- Number of items on deal

Interactions

Subjective price
- Perceived savings

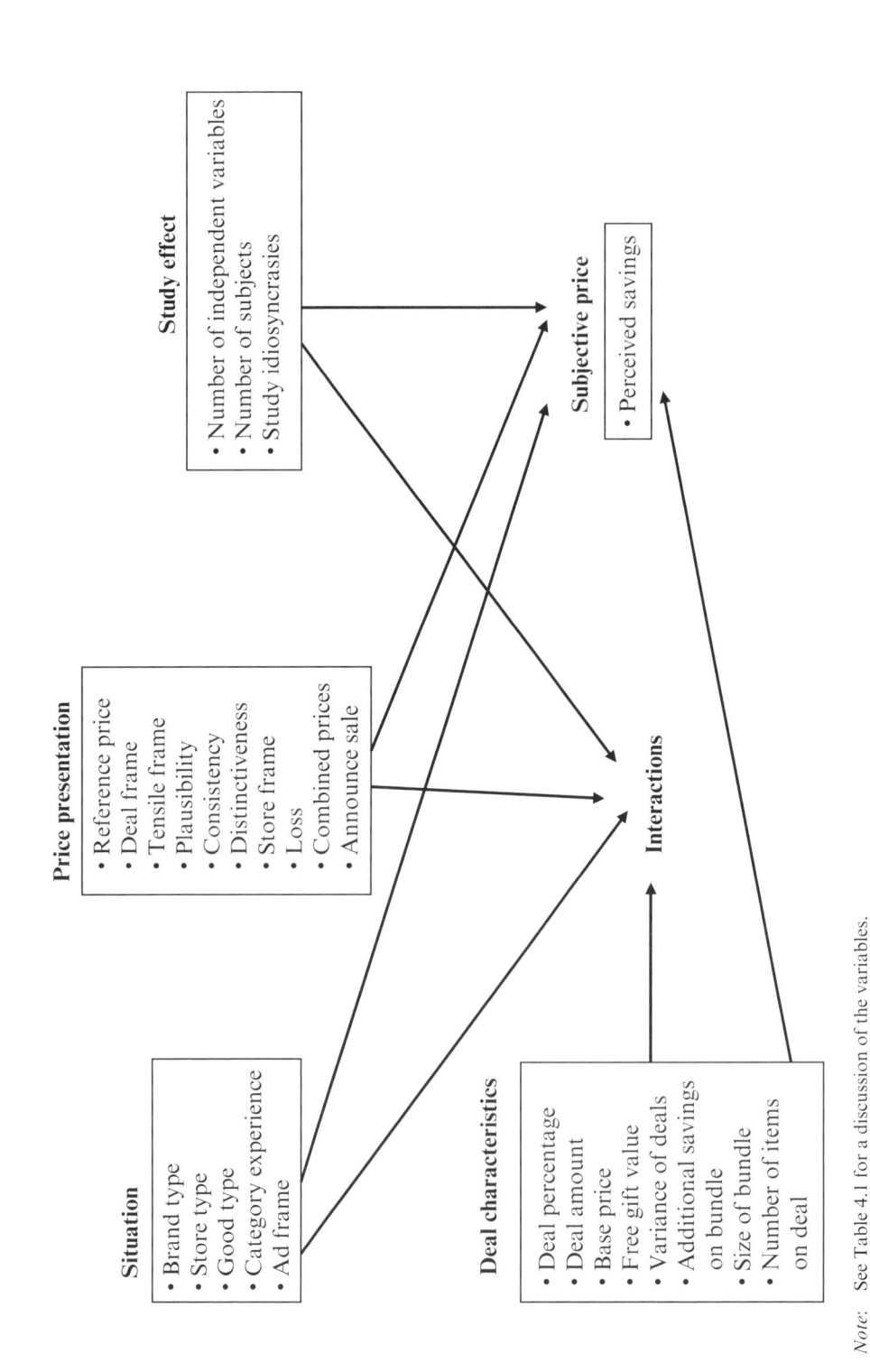

Note: See Table 4.1 for a discussion of the variables.

Figure 4.2   Variables in meta-analysis done by Krishna et al. (2002)

so better than others? For instance, is a tensile claim of 'save up to 70%' better than a claim of 'save 40%'? The third set of factors is the deal characteristics, e.g. how much of a discount is offered to the consumers. The final set of factors relates to the specific studies used in this research and attempts to control for any idiosyncratic effects from a study.

The conceptual model in Figure 4.2 posits that the above four factors may also interact in their effect on the perceived savings. For instance, the type of brand (national or local) may interact with the size of the deal to influence consumers' perceptions of the savings. According to Zeithaml's (1982) conceptual schema, the consumer acquires and encodes the 'objective price' (stimulus) to form the 'subjective price'. In Figure 4.1, the objective price is represented by the 'deal characteristics' and the 'subjective price' by 'perceived savings'. For the meta-analysis, 'perceived savings' was the dependent variable, and 'deal characteristics, situation, price presentation' and 'study effect' were the independent variables.

Data, models and results

Krishna et al. (2002) use published literature where 'perceived savings' was the dependent variable. Further, they required that deal evaluation be actually measured as opposed to inferred. Hence the focus is on experimental and not on scanner-based research (these are considered in Section 3). The ABI Inform and Psychlit indices from 1980 until 1999 were used to search for articles. In addition, they searched through *Journal of Marketing*, *Journal of Marketing Research* and *Journal of Consumer Research*, *American Marketing Association* proceedings and *Association of Consumer Research* proceedings that had been published before December 1999. Twenty articles passed their screening criteria (see Table 4.2). If an author conducted a 2 X 2 experiment, they treat this as four observations. Across all 20 articles, they have 345 observations, i.e. data points.

Across the articles, authors used different measures of 'perceived savings'. To make the different scales comparable, Krishna et al. transformed them to a percentage. Definitions of independent variables and the values of categorical independent variables appear in Table 4.1. The categorical independent variables are coded using dummy variables.

We elaborate on one typical study included in the meta-analysis. Berkowitz and Walton (1980), for instance, asked subjects to evaluate three newspaper advertisements taken from local papers. Subjects were assigned to one of four semantic (price presentation) cues – 'compare at $1.25, now $1.00', 'regular $1.25, sale $1.00', 'total value $1.25, sale $1.00', '20% off, now only $1.00'. Subjects then rated the item in the advertisement on various seven-point scales, e.g. perceived savings, willingness to buy.

Krishna et al. (2002) estimated various models on the data, e.g. a main effects model with all (45) main effects of the design variables plus the study average of 'perceived savings' (to account for idiosyncrasies of each study), and a model with all main effects plus significant interactions. At the aggregate level, all models explained more than 70 percent of the variance. Here we present the major findings from their analysis (detailed results can be obtained from their paper). Table 4.2 summarizes these findings.

- The most important factors influencing consumers' perception of the deal are the deal characteristics and price presentation effects – factors that the manager has the most control over.

Table 4.1 Independent variables

Independent variables and variable levels[a]	Definition	Articles with variance across independent variables[b]
DEAL CHARACTERISTICS		
% of deal[c]		Most studies
Amount of deal		Most studies
Additional savings on bundle		Low and Lichtenstein (1993); Yadav and Monroe (1993); Das (1992)
Base price of item		Between-article variation[d]
No. of items on deal/ no. of deals observed	Number of observations provided to subjects	Between-article variation
Size of the bundle	Number of items in the bundle presented to the subjects	Low and Lichtenstein (1993); Buyukkurt (1986)
Variance of deals	How deal amount varies over time/ uncertainty in deal price	Buyukkurt (1986)
High		
None/low		
Free gift value		
Low	• Value of free gift is small relative to base price of product	Low and Lichtenstein (1993)
High or none	• High if there is a free gift and none if there is no free gift	
SITUATION VARIABLES		
Brand type		
Fictitious		Blair and Landon (1981)
Generic		Dodds et al. (1991)
National		Berkowitz and Walton (1980)
Private		Bearden et al. (1984)
None specified		
Store type		
Department		Dodds et al. (1991)
Discount		Berkowitz and Walton (1980)
Specialty		Buyukkurt (1986)
Supermarket		
None specified		
Type of good		
Packaged		Berkowitz and Walton (1980)
Other	• Durable or soft good	Das (1992)
Category experience		
High	High versus low consumer knowledge/experience with the category	Some between-article variation
Low		
Not specified		

Table 4.1 (continued)

Independent variables and variable levels[a]	Definition	Articles with variance across independent variables[b]
Ad frame		
Advertisement	Catalogue format versus advertisement format versus shopping simulation	Blair and Landon (1981) Grewal et al. (1996) (lots of between-study variance)
Catalogue		
Shopping		
PRICE PRESENTATION VARIABLES		
External reference price		
Manufacture suggested price (MSP)		Blair and Landon (1981); Urbany et al. 1988)
Regular price		Burton et al. (1993); Das (1992)
None		Bearden et al. (1984); Berkowitz and Walton (1980) Della Bitta et al. (1981)
Objective (non-tensile) deal frame		
Coupon	• Deal given as a coupon	Berkowitz and Walton (1980); Della Bitta et al. (1981)
Dollar	• e.g. $__ off	Biswas and Burton (1993, 1994); Burton et al. (1993)
Free gift	• e.g. a free premium	Low and Lichtenstein (1993); Das (1992)
%	• e.g. __% off	Bearden et al. (1984); Chen et al. (1998)
X-For	• e.g. 2 for the price of 1	
None (final price given)		
Tensile deal frame		
Maximum	• Save up to __	Biswas and Burton (1993, 1994)
Minimum	• Save __ and more	Mobley et al. (1988)
Range	• Save __ to __	
Non-tensile (objective) deal frame	• No tensile deal frame	
Plausibility		
Implausible		Lichtenstein and Bearden (1989); Urbany et al. (1988)
Plausible – small		Grewal et al. (1996); Suter and Burton (1996)
Plausible – large		Dodds et al. (1991); Berkowitz and Walton (1980)
Plausible		Low and Lichtenstein (1993); Lichtenstein et al. (1991)

Table 4.1 (continued)

Independent variables and variable levels[a]	Definition	Articles with variance across independent variables[b]
Store frame		
Between stores	• e.g. our price, compare with _ at _	Urbany et al. (1988); Grewal et al. (1996)
Within store	• e.g. regular price _, sale price _	Berkowitz and Walton (1980); Burton et al. (1993)
Both		Lichtenstein et al. (1991)
Consistency		
High	• Of deals over time	Lichtenstein and Bearden (1989)
Low	Three articles specifically discuss manipulating 'consistency'. Lichtenstein and Bearden (1989) manipulate high and low consistency through high and low deal frequency. Burton et al. (1993) and Lichtenstein et al. (1991) depict high consistency by using a within-store frame (was $_, now only $_)	Burton et al. (1993) Lichtenstein et al. (1991)
Neither (not applicable)		
Distinctiveness		
High	• Of deal versus other brands	Lichtenstein and Bearden (1989)
Low	Three articles specifically discuss manipulating 'distinctiveness'. Of these three, Burton et al. (1993) and Lichtenstein et al. (1991) manipulate high distinctiveness through a between-store frame (seen elsewhere for $_, our price $_)	Burton et al. (1993) Lichtenstein et al. (1991)
Neither (not applicable)		
Sale announced?		
Yes	• Offered price is termed a sale	Yadav and Monroe (1993)
No	• Offered price does not state that it is a sale	Burton et al. (1993)
Free gift value		
Low	• Value of free gift is small relative to base price of product	Low and Lichtenstein (1993)
High or none	• High if there is a free gift and none if there is no free gift	
Bundle frame		
Loss		Kaicker et al. (1995)

Table 4.1 (continued)

Independent variables and variable levels[a]	Definition	Articles with variance across independent variables[b]
Mixed (gain and loss) *Gain*		
Combined prices?		
Yes	Single price for bundle	Kaicker et al. (1995);
No	Each item has its own price	Some between-study variation
STUDY EFFECT		
Number of variables manipulated		Between-article variation only
Number of subjects in cell		Within- and between-article variation
Study average		Between-article variation only
Multiple scales for DV		
Yes	• DV is measured as a sum of multiple-scale items	Between-article variation only
No	• DV is measured as a single-scale item	

Notes:
[a] Default level is given in italics.
[b] Some independent variables had variation across articles and some had variation both across and within articles.
[c] Variable is continuous.
[d] Variation in the independent variable occurred across articles, not within the same article.
[e] Variance of deals is coded with dummy variables with none/low as the base case.

- Within deal characteristics, the most important factors are the additional savings on a bundle and the deal percentage. However, as the size of the bundle increases, consumers perceive the deal less favorably. Thus small bundles with high percentage discounts are most significant for consumers.
- Within price presentation effects, Krishna et al. (2002) found several interesting interactions. First, the plausibility of the deal (or size of the deal) interacts with whether or not regular price is given. 'Implausibility' of a deal makes it less attractive. However, a large deal amount more than compensates for its lower plausibility, so that larger deals are evaluated more favorably than smaller deals. A second interesting interaction is that within-store frames (e.g. regular price $1.99, sale price $1.59) are more effective when the consumer is shopping, but between-store frames (e.g. our price $1.59, compare with $1.59 at Krogers) are more effective when communicating with consumers at home.
- Within situational effects, the most important factors are brand (both store and item). Deals on national brands are evaluated more favorably than those on private brands and generics; and consumers value deals less in stores that have higher deal frequency (discount stores) compared to stores perceived to have lower deal frequency (e.g. specialty stores).

Table 4.2 *Important findings from the meta-analysis*

Variables studied	Effect on dependent variables
Deal characteristics	
Amount of deal, % of deal	Both positively influence perceived saving
Variance of deals	High deal variances lead to lower perceived savings
Situational effects	
Brand type: national brands versus private brands and generics	Deals on national brands yield higher perceived savings
Type of good: packaged goods versus other (durable, soft) goods	Deals on packaged goods yield higher perceived savings
Store type: discount store versus department and specialty stores	Deals in discount stores lead to lower perceived savings
Price presentation effects	
External reference price: regular price	Presence of regular price increases perceived savings
Minimum tensile claim versus non-tensile claim	Minimum tensile claims yield lower perceived savings
Plausibility: small and plausible deals versus large but plausible deals and implausible deals	Small and plausible deals yield higher perceived savings
Consistency	Less consistent deals yield higher perceived savings
Distinctiveness	More distinctive deals yield higher perceived savings
Interactions[a]	
Regular price and deal percentage	Presenting a regular price as an external reference price reduces perceived saving when the deal percentage is extremely large
Regular price and plausibility	The presence of a regular price enhances the perceived savings of large but plausible deals and implausible deals but not small plausible deals
MSP and brand type	Presenting MSP increases perceived savings more for national brands than for other brands
Brand type and plausibility	Large but plausible deal on a national brand results in higher perceived savings as opposed to a large plausible deal on other brands
Deal percentage and store type	Large deals in department store yield higher perceived savings than those in discount, specialty stores, or supermarkets

Note: [a] The effects of interactions are explained considering the interaction effect and both the main effects.

The meta-analysis shows that many price features, other than the intrinsic price, significantly influence perceived savings and hence should be taken into account by managers in structuring deals. Another synthesis of reference pricing research has been done by Biswas et al. (1993). In addition to a narrative review, their article presents a meta-analysis based on 113 observations from 12 studies. A major difference between this earlier study and Krishna et al.'s (2002) is that the former study concentrates on statistical significance and variance explained, whereas the latter focuses on the magnitude of the effects. Second, the former study analyzes one variable at a time, whereas the latter analyzes data in a multivariate fashion. A second important reference is an integrative review of comparative advertising studies done by Compeau and Grewal (1998). This review builds upon the meta-analysis done by Biswas et al. (1993) and has 38 studies. This analysis also focuses on statistical significance and variance explained, and does so one variable at a time.

We now turn to a discussion of 'scanner data'-based research that incorporates consumers' internal reference prices.

3. Prediction models incorporating consumer reference prices

As will be clear from this *Handbook*, much research in marketing has focused on predicting consumer choice. These models typically do not use experimental data (and, as such, do not fall within the purview of our meta-analysis), but use scanner data, secondary data on consumer purchases over time. Starting with Winer's (1986) work, some choice models have tried to incorporate the notion of an 'internal reference price' – we call this body of research 'reference price effects in choice models'. Internal reference prices are constructed by consumers themselves and are 'an internal standard against which observed prices are compared' (Kalyanaram and Winer, 1995). They are used to gauge how 'good or fair' the observed price is. Conceptually, they can be construed as a 'fair price' or an 'expected price'. Note that the internal reference price is different from an 'external reference price' provided by the retailer; an external reference price is provided along with a (lower) price the retailer is offering and is used as a means to encourage consumers to purchase the product (or service). The external reference price can be, for example, a manufacturer-suggested retailer price, what the price was, what other retailers are charging, etc.

Operationally, internal reference prices have taken many forms, so that they can be based on current prices (e.g. current price of the last brand purchased), past prices (e.g. the brand's price on the last purchase occasion), or on past prices and other variables (such as market share of the brand). Briesch et al. (1997) offer a comparative analysis of reference price models that use different operationalizations of reference price – they find that models based on past prices do best in terms of fit and prediction.

Reference-price choice models are constructed so that, if the observed price is lower than the reference price, then choice probability increases; if the observed price is higher, then the choice probability decreases. While Winer (1986) incorporated a reference price effect, Lattin and Bucklin (1989) introduced a reference promotion effect so that there is a reference level of promotion frequency which dictates how the consumer responds to a promotion. Kalyanaram and Little (1994) estimate a latitude of acceptance around the reference price, and show that it is wider for consumers with higher average reference price, lower purchase frequency, and higher average brand loyalty.

Some researchers have taken the notion of reference prices one step further and have built the concepts of prospect theory on top of reference price effects, since they lend themselves quite easily to such interpretation. A lower observed price versus the 'reference price' is seen as a 'gain' whereas a higher observed price is seen as a 'loss'. Further, 'gains' and 'losses' are predicted to have different effects on choice. According to prospect theory, 'losses loom larger than gains', i.e. losses have stronger effects compared to equivalent gains. This is tested within the context of brand-choice models by Kalwani et al. (1990) and Hardie et al. (1993), and both brand-choice and purchase and quantity models by Krishnamurthi et al. (1992). Different parameters are estimated for the effect of 'gains' versus 'losses' on choice. Most researchers find significant and predicted effects for gains and losses (losses have larger negative than gains have positive effects). Krishnamurthi et al. (1992) also show that sensitivity to gains and losses is a function of loyalty toward the brand for both choice and quantity models, and is also a function of household stock-outs for quantity models. Hardie et al. (1993) also introduce the notion of a reference brand, so that the current price of any brand is compared to the current price of the referent brand. While the aforementioned articles focus on empirical estimation, Putler (1992) incorporates the effects of reference price into the traditional theory of consumer choice and then tests it on egg sales data. Like other researchers, he too finds asymmetry for egg price increases versus decreases.

For more detailed and excellent summaries of research on reference price effects, the reader should consult Kalyanaram and Winer (1995) and Mazumdar et al. (2005).

4. Future research

This chapter shows that the price of a product can affect observed consumer behavior in various ways other than through the actual price. Both subjective price and price fairness affect consumer choice of product, purchase quantity and purchase timing. Subjective price is affected by price presentation and internal reference price, which are each composed of a host of factors, and also by '99 cent' endings, partitioned prices and temporal pricing. Similarly, perceived price unfairness has several antecedents.

We focus on price presentation effects and summarize a meta-analysis of 20 published articles in marketing that focus on price presentation. We also provide a summary of the effect of internal reference price (formed as a function of observing different prices over time) on consumer behavior.

In terms of predictive models, besides price presentation effects, there is much scope for incorporating other behavioral effects – internal reference price is just one single behavioral pricing aspect. Thus an important direction for future research is to see how price presentations affect 'consumer behavior' as opposed to 'consumer perceptions'. The studies in the meta-analysis were based upon laboratory experiments. Few studies have assessed the effect of different price presentations on consumer behavior (for an exception, see Dhar and Dutta, 1997). Of course, a major reason for this is lack of data. While scanner data record a host of information, price presentation is still not included in the data. Future research should try to obtain these additional data within the context of scanner data, and replicate the laboratory-experiment results in the field. Additionally, future research should incorporate other behavioral aspects, besides internal reference prices and price presentation effects, within predictive models.

While normative models have begun to incorporate the effects of perceived price fairness (e.g. Feinberg et al., 2002), predictive models have still not followed suit and this is another area for future research. Yet another area fruitful for research is the behavioral aspects of online shopping, e.g. how shopping bots may have altered price response behaviors online as well as influenced responses in physical stores. Researchers could also further examine the lower relevance of price when the product is linked to a 'cause' (e.g. part of proceeds from the sales of the product go towards AIDS research). Arora and Henderson (2007) show that these 'embedded premiums' are in a sense a price deal not to the consumer but to the cause. This needs additional work. Besides brand choice, purchase quantity and timing, another construct to focus on is consumption and how perceived price affects it. Clearly, there is much left to study in the area of behavioral pricing.

References

Arora, Neeraj and Ty Henderson (2007), 'Embedded premium promotion: why it works and how to make it more effective', *Marketing Science*, **26** (4), 514–31.

Bearden, William O., Donald R. Lichtenstein and Jesse E. Teel (1984), 'Comparison price, coupon, and brand effects on consumer reactions to retail newspaper advertisements', *Journal of Retailing*, **60** (Summer), 11–34.

Berkowitz, Eric N. and John R. Walton (1980), 'Contextual influences on consumer price responses: an experimental analysis', *Journal of Marketing Research*, **17** (August), 349–58.

Biswas, Abhijit and Scot Burton (1993), 'Consumer perceptions of tensile price claims in advertisements: an assessment of claim types across different discount levels', *Journal of the Academy of Marketing Science*, **21** (3), 217–29.

Biswas, Abhijit and Scot Burton (1994), 'An experimental assessment of effects associated with alternative tensile price claims', *Journal of Business Research*, **29**, 65–73.

Biswas, Abhijit, Elizabeth J. Wilson and Jane W. Licata (1993), 'Reference pricing studies in marketing: a synthesis of research results', *Journal of Business Research*, **27** (3), 239–56.

Blair, Edward and E. Laird Landon, Jr (1981), 'The effects of reference prices in retail advertisements', *Journal of Marketing*, **45** (Spring), 61–9.

Briesch, Richard, Lakshman Krishnamurthi, Tridib Mazumdar and S.P. Raj (1997), 'A comparative analysis of consumer internal reference price formulation', *Journal of Consumer Research*, **24** (2), 202–14.

Burton, Scot, Donald R. Lichtenstein and Paul M. Herr (1993), 'An examination of the effects of information consistency and distinctiveness in a reference-price advertisement context', *Journal of Applied Social Psychology*, **23** (24), 2074–92.

Buyukkurt, B. Kemal (1986), 'Integration of serially sampled price information: modeling and some findings', *Journal of Consumer Research*, **13** (December), 357–73.

Campbell, Margaret C. (1999), 'Perceptions of price unfairness: antecedents and consequences', *Journal of Marketing Research*, **36** (May), 187–99.

Campbell, Margaret C. (2007), '"Says who?!" How the source of price information and affect influence perceived price (un)fairness', *Journal of Marketing Research*, **44** (May), 261–271.

Chen, Shih-Fen S., Kent B. Monroe and Yung-Chein Lou (1998), 'The effects of framing price promotion messages on consumers' perceptions and purchase intentions', *Journal of Retailing*, **74**(3), 353–72.

Compeau, Larry D. and Dhruv Grewal (1998), 'Comparative price advertising: an integrative review', *Journal of Public Policy and Marketing*, **17** (2), 257–73.

Das, Priya Raghbour (1992), 'Semantic cues and buyer evaluation of promotional communication', *American Marketing Association Educator's Proceedings: Enhancing Knowledge Development in Marketing*, eds Robert P. Leone and V. Kumar, pp. 12–17.

Della Bitta, Albert J., Kent B. Monroe and John M. McGinnis (1981), 'Consumer perceptions of comparative price advertisements', *Journal of Marketing Research*, **18** (November), 416–27.

Dhar, Sanjay K. and Shantanu Dutta (1997), 'The effects of newspaper price advertisements on department store sales', Working Paper, University of Chicago.

Dickson, Peter R. and Alan G. Sawyer (1990), 'The price knowledge and search of supermarket shoppers', *Journal of Marketing*, **54** (July), 42–53.

Dodds, William B., Kent B. Monroe and Dhruv Grewal (1991), 'Effect of price, brand, and store information on buyers' product evaluations', *Journal of Marketing Research*, **28** (August), 307–19.

Feinberg, Fred, Aradhna Krishna and John Z. Zhang (2002), 'Do we care what others get?: A behaviorist approach to targeted promotions', *Journal of Marketing Research*, **39** (3), 277–91.

Gourville, John (1998), 'Pennies-a-day: the effect of temporal reframing on transaction evaluation', *Journal of Consumer Research*, **24** (March), 395–408.
Grewal, Dhruv, Howard Marmorstein and Arun Sharma (1996), 'Communicating price information through semantic cues: the moderating effects of situation and discount size', *Journal of Consumer Research*, **23** (2), 148–55.
Hardie, Bruce G.S., Eric J. Johnson and Pete S. Fader (1993), 'Modeling loss aversion and reference dependence effects on brand choice', *Marketing Science*, **12** (4), 378–94.
Inman, J. Jeffrey, Leigh McAlister and Wayne D. Hoyer (1990), 'Promotion signal: proxy for a price cut?', *Journal of Consumer Research*, **17** (June), 74–81.
Kaicker, Ajit, William O. Bearden and Kenneth C. Manning (1995), 'Component versus bundle pricing: the role of selling price deviations from price expectations', *Journal of Business Research*, **33**, 231–9.
Kalyanaram, Gurumurthy and John D.C. Little (1994), 'An empirical analysis of latitude of price acceptance in consumer packaged goods', *Journal of Consumer Research*, **21** (December), 408–18.
Kalyanaram, Gurumurthy and Russell S. Winer (1995), 'Empirical generalizations from reference price research', *Marketing Science*, **14** (3), G161–G169.
Kalwani, Manohar U., Chi Kin Yim, Heikke J. Rinne and Yoshi Sugita (1990), 'A price expectations model of customer brand choice', *Journal of Marketing Research*, **27** (August), 251–62.
Krishna, Aradhna and Yu Wang (2007), 'Costly punishment: an experimental test of consumer resistance to discriminating firms', Working Paper, University of Michigan.
Krishna, Aradhna, Fred Feinberg and John Z. Zhang (2007), 'Pricing power and selective versus across-the-board price increases', *Management Science*, **53** (9), September, 1407–23.
Krishna, Aradhna, Richard Briesch, Donald Lehmann and Hong Yuan (2002), 'A meta-analysis of the effect of price presentation on deal evaluation', *Journal of Retailing*, **78**, 101–18.
Krishnamurthi, Lakshman, Tridib Mazumdar and S.P. Raj (1992), 'Asymmetric response to price in consumer brand choice and purchase quantity decisions', *Journal of Consumer Research*, **19** (3), 387–400.
Lattin, James M. and Randolph E. Bucklin (1989), 'Reference price effects of price and promotion on brand choice behavior', *Journal of Marketing Research*, **26** (August), 299–310.
Lichtenstein, Donald R. and William O. Bearden (1989), 'Contextual influences on perceptions of merchant-supplied reference prices', *Journal of Consumer Research*, **16** (June), 55–66.
Lichtenstein, Donald, Scot Burton and Eric J. Karson (1991), 'The effect of semantic cues on consumer perceptions of reference price ads', *Journal of Consumer Research*, **18** (December), 380–91.
Low, George S. and Donald R. Lichtenstein (1993), 'The effect of double deals on consumer attitudes', *Journal of Retailing*, **69** (4), 453–66.
Mazumdar, Tridib, S.P. Raj and Indrajit Sinha (2005), 'Reference price research: review and propositions', *Journal of Marketing*, **69** (October), 84–102.
Mobley, Mary F., William O. Bearden and Jesse E. Teel (1988), 'An investigation of individual responses to tensile price claims', *Journal of Consumer Research*, **15** (September), 273–9.
Morwitz, Vicki G., Eric A Greenleaf and Eric J. Johnson (1998), 'Divide and prosper: consumers' reactions to partitioned prices', *Journal of Marketing Research*, **35** (November), 453–63.
Putler, Daniel S. (1992), 'Incorporating reference price effects into a theory of consumer choice', *Marketing Science*, **11** (Summer), 287–309.
Schindler, Robert M. and Patrick N. Kirby (1997), 'Patterns of rightmost digits used in advertised prices: implications for nine-ending effects', *Journal of Consumer Research*, **24** (September), 192–201.
Stiving, Mark and Russell S. Winer (1997), 'An empirical analysis of price endings with scanner data', *Journal of Consumer Research*, **24** (June), 57–67.
Suter, Tracy and Scot Burton (1996), 'Believability and consumer perceptions of implausible reference prices in retail advertisements', *Psychology and Marketing*, **13** (1), 37–54.
Thaler, Richard H. (1985), 'Mental accounting and consumer choice', *Marketing Science*, **4** (Summer), 199–214.
Urbany, Joel E., William O. Bearden and Dan C. Weilbaker (1988), 'The effect of plausible and exaggerated reference prices on consumer perceptions and price search', *Journal of Consumer Research*, **15** (June), 95–110.
Winer, Russell S. (1986), 'A reference price model of brand choice for frequently purchased products', *Journal of Consumer Research*, **13** (September), 250–56.
Yadav, Manjit S. and Kent B. Monroe (1993), 'How buyers perceive savings in a bundle price: an examination of a bundle's transaction value', *Journal of Marketing Research*, **30** (August), 350–58.
Zeithaml, Valerie A. (1982), 'Consumer response to in-store price information environments', *Journal of Consumer Research*, **8** (March), 357–69.

5 Consumer search and pricing
Brian T. Ratchford*

Abstract
In most cases, consumers must search for information about prices and product attributes, and find it too costly to become perfectly informed. The consequent departure from perfect information affects the pricing behavior of sellers in a variety of ways. The purpose of this chapter is to review the literature on consumer search, and on the consequences of consumer search behavior for the behavior of markets. The review first focuses on summarizing theoretical models optimal search, and on how costly search may affect the behavior of markets. Two of the key results in this literature are that price dispersion should exist in equilibrium, and that differences in search costs provide a motive for price discrimination. After summarizing the theoretical models, the review presents empirical results on consumer search, and on pricing by sellers given differences in consumer search costs. Specific results for different information sources, including word of mouth, advertising, retailing and the Internet are discussed.

Introduction
In his seminal paper Stigler (1961) pointed out that there appears to be substantial and persistent price dispersion in markets for commodities such as coal. This is a direct contradiction of the standard model of perfect competition, in which the law of one price should prevail. Setting out to explain this anomaly, Stigler pointed out that the standard assumption that consumers are informed about all alternatives should be violated if search is costly. Since it only pays to search up to the point where the marginal benefits of search equal its marginal costs, a rational consumer will accept a price above the minimum when the expected gain from searching further is less than the cost. Therefore rational consumers can pay a price higher than the minimum, and price dispersion can result.

Thus began the study of the relationship between consumer search and market prices, which has burgeoned into a large and diverse literature over the past 40+ years. The objective of this review is to summarize this literature. Since the initial literature, including Stigler's article, was focused on the consumer side of the market, I shall consider models of optimal consumer search first. Then I shall discuss equilibrium models of search and price dispersion, and the empirical literatures on pricing and search that are related to these models. Finally I shall consider research that explores the relationship between search, pricing and different institutions that provide information and facilitate sales. My intent is to provide a broad overview of these very diverse areas that shows how they fit together rather than to provide a detailed review of each that cites all of the available references.

---

* The author is grateful for the helpful comments of the editor and an anonymous reviewer.

Models of consumer search

Stigler (1961) considered a decision rule in which the searcher sets the number of items to be searched as the number at which the expected gains from an additional search are equal to the expected cost of that search. In this model all alternatives are assumed to be equally promising *a priori*, and search for an item is assumed to yield a complete understanding of that item. While this is sufficient to prove the point that expected-utility-maximizing consumers with positive search costs should not be fully informed, Stigler's formulation is a very simplified model of search that does not capture the more general case in which priors on alternatives may be different, and search may be sequential. Nevertheless Stigler's model may be a reasonable approximation to search in some situations; for example when soliciting bids for repair work when the bidder has time to prepare a proposal, and the purchase is not made until proposals are received. In this case, if one knew the variance of payoffs prior to searching, and the costs of soliciting and evaluating each contractor's proposal, tables in Stigler's article or in David (1970) and Ratchford (1980) could be used to determine the number of contractors to solicit bids from.

While still restrictive in many respects, the model of Weitzman (1979) considers the more general case in which the consumer may have different priors across alternatives, and in which the consumer can search sequentially. Weitzman assumes expected utility maximization, that search for an item uncovers all information about it, that there is recall, that there is no parallel search, and that there are no joint costs of search in which several alternatives can be inspected for the price of one. Given these assumptions, Weitzman proves the optimality of a stopping rule in which alternatives are searched in order of their reservation utility, and the consumer stops searching if the payoff exceeds the reservation utility of the next best alternative. Otherwise the consumer searches the alternative that is next in the ranking, and repeats the process until an alternative that meets the stopping criterion is found.

The reservation utility for alternative i, V_i^R, is the payoff value at which the consumer would be indifferent between searching the item at a cost of C_i or accepting the payoff V_i^R. The value of V_i^R is the one that equates the cost of searching i with the expected gain from looking for a payoff that exceeds V_i^R:

$$C_i = \int_{V_i^R}^{\infty} (V_i - V_i^R) f(V_i) dV_i$$

If the consumer already has an item with a payoff greater than V_i^R, he/she should stop since the expected gain from search is less that the cost. If the consumer does not have a payoff as high as V_i^R, he/she should continue to search because the expected gain will exceed the expected cost.

As an example, consider the case where V_i is normally distributed, with a mean $\overline{V}_i$, standard deviation σ_{V_i}. Then the integral on the right becomes σ_{V_i} times the value of the unit loss integral L_i^R that equates the right side with C_i:

$$C_i = \int_{V_i^R}^{\infty} (V_i - V_i^R) f(V_i) dV_i = \sigma_{V_i} L_i^R$$

The reservation value of i can then be calculated as

$$V_i^R = \overline{V}_i + \sigma_{V_i} z_i^R$$

Table 5.1 Example of application of the Weitzman model

Rank	c	σ_{vi}	$L^R = c/\sigma_{vi}$	z^R	$\overline{V}_i$	$V_i^R = \overline{V}_i + \sigma_{vi} z_i^R$	$\Pr(V_i > V_{i+1}^R)$
1	3	15	0.20	0.49	50	57.35	0.3156
2	3	10	0.30	0.22	55	57.20	0.6179
3	6	20	0.30	0.22	50	52.02	

Consider the example in Table 5.1. The reservation utilities V_i^R are seen to depend on the costs of search, standard deviation of utilities and expected utility. Although the second alternative has the highest expected utility, the first has a larger standard deviation, which leads it to have the highest reservation utility. Basically the first alternative offers a better chance of 'striking it rich'. The third alternative gets set back in the order of reservation utilities because it has a high search cost (6). Weitzman's rule dictates that consumers should search the ranked first alternative first, with a probability of being able to stop after one search of 0.3156. If the payoff from the first search is less than 57.2, the reservation utility of the second alternative, the consumer should continue searching. Similarly, if the payoffs from both the first and second searches are less than 52.02 the consumer should go on to the third alternative. At this point the consumer should choose the best of the three items. The expected number of searches = 1*(0.3156) + 2*(1 − 0.3156)*(0.6179) + 3*(1 − 0.3156)*(1 − 0.6179) = 1.95

Moorthy et al. (1997) applied the Weitzman model to develop an explanation of the relationship between prior brand perceptions and search. In their model, prior brand perceptions govern search, and these are expected to vary with experience. In particular, they show that prior brand perceptions can create the U-shaped relationship between knowledge and search that is often uncovered in laboratory experiments (Johnson and Russo, 1984). They tested their hypotheses on a panel of automobile shoppers in which data were obtained as the search progressed. They found that priors and search effort, and brands and attributes searched, vary with experience as hypothesized.

Around the time of Weitzman's article, labor economists began using hazard models to model search for a job and the duration of unemployment; good examples of these models are Lancaster (1985), Wolpin (1987), Jones (1988) and Eckstein and Wolpin (1990, 1995). Since there is a direct analogy between searching for the highest wage for a job and for the lowest price for a product, and since the structure of the search problem is similar in both cases, these job search models can also be applied to consumer price search with only minor modifications.

An application drawn from the labor economics literature to modeling the duration of search for automobiles was presented by Ratchford and Srinivasan (1993). In their model, price offers arrive at a constant rate, with the distribution of price offers following a Pareto distribution. The hazard of terminating the search and buying a car is then the product of the arrival rate of offers and the probability that an offer exceeds the reservation price. The observed outcomes of prices paid and time devoted to search result from two equations: an equation that determines the level and rate of arrival of offers, which depends on seller characteristics and the consumer's efficiency at search; and an equation that determines the reservation price, which depends on the same factors plus the cost of search per unit of time. Ratchford and Srinivasan (1993) employ these equations in estimating the determinants of observed prices and search time, and in calculating monetary returns to additional search time.

The job search models of Wolpin (1987) and Eckstein and Wolpin (1990) are early examples of dynamic structural models. Their structural modeling approach has carried over into the literature on packaged goods choice in the form of models that postulate Bayesian learning of brand attributes through consumption (Erdem and Keane, 1996; Erdem et al., 2003; Mehta et al., 2003).

This structural approach has recently been applied to consumer search prior to purchase by Erdem et al. (2005). Using a very rich panel dataset that tracks a sample of potential computer buyers from early in their search to purchase, the authors simultaneously model gathering information from retailers, and the final choice of a computer. The panel has six waves in which respondents report the sources that they consulted, their quality perceptions of the competing brands, their price expectations, and, if applicable, their choice. Respondents are assumed to follow a Bayesian updating process for incorporating quality information from five information sources. Specifically, if L_{ikt} is a dummy variable indicating whether consumer i visits information source k at time t, if x_{ijkt} is a similarly defined noisy but unbiased signal from a given source, z_{ijt} is consumer i's quality perception error at t, and σ^2_{ijt} is the variance of perceptions at time t, the Bayesian updating formula for quality perceptions is given by (Erdem et al., 2005, p. 219):

$$\sigma^2_{ijt} = \left[\frac{1}{\sigma^2_{j0}} + \sum_{s=1}^{t} \sum_{k=1}^{5} \frac{L_{iks}}{\sigma^2_k} \right]^{-1}$$

$$z_{ijt} = z_{ijt-1} + \sum_{k+1}^{5} L_{iks} \frac{\sigma^2_{ijt-1}}{\sigma^2_{ijt-1} + \sigma^2_k} (x_{ijt} - z_{ijt-1})$$

where σ^2_{j0} is the variance of prior information, σ^2_k is a measure of the reliability of source k, and information signals are assumed to be independent across sources. Smaller values of σ^2_k lead to smaller σ^2_{ijt} and more complete updating.

Given the above Bayesian updating mechanism for information sources, and an adaptive model of price expectations, Erdem et al. estimate a structural model in which each consumer optimizes the choice of the five information sources over the six periods of the panel, optimizes the timing of the choice given price expectations, and optimizes the make and quality level of computer chosen. While this model assumes that consumers can make very complex calculations, it also represents a direct empirical application of an optimizing model of search. Since this paper represents the state of the art in combining theoretical and empirical analysis of consumer search, it deserves careful study.

Models of search and pricing
If many consumers do not search much, there is a potential opportunity to exploit their ignorance by charging higher prices, so that price levels should be inversely related to search. Conversely, while some consumers may not search, those who can afford to search extensively will attempt to locate lower prices. This leads to the possibility that price dispersion, which is commonly observed in actual markets, will exist in equilibrium.

For our purposes, price dispersion may be defined as offering physically identical items for sale at different prices. Price dispersion may be either spatial (across sellers at one point in time), or temporal (prices vary within a seller over time). There are at least four explanations for equilibrium price dispersion in the literature:

- Price dispersion due to differences in search costs and seller costs (Carlson and McAfee, 1983).
- Periodic sales due to adoption of mixed strategies by competing sellers to capture sales from high and low search cost segments (Varian, 1980).
- Markdowns due to demand uncertainty (Lazear, 1986; Pashigian, 1988; Smith and Achabal, 1998).
- Differences in services provided by sellers (Ehrlich and Fisher, 1982; Ratchford and Stoops, 1988, 1992).

Each of these explanations is discussed below.

While earlier equilibrium models of price dispersion had been developed (e.g. Salop and Stiglitz, 1977), Carlson and McAfee (1983) presented a model that was amenable to empirical testing, and was later tested by Dahlby and West (1986). The model of Carlson and McAfee addresses a homogeneous commodity sold by different sellers. Each buyer in the market will buy one unit. *A priori*, consumers know the distribution of prices, but not the specific price of any item. They search sequentially for the lowest price using a stopping rule in which search is terminated when the expected gain from additional search is less than the constant cost of the additional search. This cost per item searched is assumed to vary across consumers with a uniform distribution bounded at 0 on the low end. In this framework, a consumer with the highest search cost still has a $1/n$ (n = number of items) chance of getting any price, including the lowest one. A consumer with a search cost low enough to justify searching further if the highest price is encountered has a $1/(n-1)$ chance of getting any of the other prices, and so on. Given the uniform distribution of search costs, Carlson and McAfee derive a demand function of the following form:

$$(q_j/\bar{q}) = 1 - (1/T)(p_j - \bar{p})$$

where j refers to firm, 'bar' denotes mean, q is quantity, p is price, and T is the upper bound of the uniform distribution of search costs. Increases in T (upward shifts in the distribution of search costs) make demand less sensitive to price changes.

On the supply side, Carlson and McAfee assume that unit costs differ across firms by a parameter α_j. Given the demand curve outlined above, their assumed cost function, and n competing sellers, they derive Nash equilibrium prices for each seller. Given that firms earn nonnegative profits, they show that the variance of prices in this model is proportional to the variance in the unit cost parameters α_j. If this variance is 0 and all firms have the same cost function, there will be no price dispersion: price dispersion is driven entirely by differences in unit costs in this model. However, if costs are the same for all firms, each firm will charge an equilibrium markup that is proportional to T, the highest search cost. Thus search costs affect price levels, and the variation in costs drives price dispersion.

While the Carlson and McAfee model leads to demand and cost functions that can be estimated empirically, it does not readily extend to differentiated products. Given the potential for empirical application, efforts to make this model applicable to products with different attributes may be worthwhile.

Salop and Stiglitz (1977) considered a monopolistically competitive market in which there were two segments of consumers – completely informed and completely uninformed, and showed that two prices could emerge in the market even though the competing sellers have identical U-shaped cost curves. As noted by Varian (1980), this a model of spatial competition.

A weakness of this model is that consumers never learn about the existence of the lower prices. To address this problem, Varian (1980) formulated a model of temporal price discrimination in the face of segments of informed and uninformed consumers, and a market with identical firm cost functions and free entry. Since firms are torn between the desire to extract surplus from the uninformed consumers and the desire to capture all of the business of the informed consumers by charging the lowest price, there is no pure strategy equilibrium in this model. The Nash equilibrium solution that maximizes expected profit for each firm is to select prices at random from an equilibrium distribution function. This allows each firm to capture a surplus from the uninformed consumers, while occasionally having the lowest price and therefore getting the business of the informed consumers. One way to interpret the practice of randomly offering relatively low prices in an effort to capture the informed consumers is that these low offers represent sales or promotions. Thus Varian's analysis provides a rationale for sales and promotions as the outcome of mixed strategies in a competitive market when there are differences in the degree to which consumers are informed. In the Varian model, price dispersion exists over time even though firms have identical costs. A testable outcome of the model is that the rank order of prices charged by firms in a market should fluctuate randomly over time.

The mixed strategy model has become a staple of models that explain price dispersion, promotions, advertising and other phenomena. For example, although he uses the terminology 'loyals' and 'switchers' instead of 'uninformed' and 'informed', Narasimhan (1988) employs a mixed strategy model similar in structure to Varian's to study the frequency and depth of promotions. Another example is Iyer and Pazgal (2003), who present a mixed strategy model that explains the dispersion of posted prices at Internet shopping agents. Recently, Baye and Morgan (2004) have shown that a mixed strategy model, and dispersion of offer prices, can be generated if firms depart from maximizing behavior, even if all consumers have zero search costs.

While the mixed strategy model based on segments with different amounts of information or brand loyalty provides one explanation for the existence of periodic promotions and sales, an alternative explanation is based on seller efforts to determine what consumers will pay for an item. The basic idea is that sellers who are uncertain about demand may initially charge a high price to see if any customers will pay it. Failure to sell the item at that price conveys to the seller that the distribution of consumer willingness to pay must lie below it. It becomes optimal to reduce the price. Failure to sell at the lower price conveys information that the distribution of willingness to pay lies below the reduced price, triggering a further price cut, and so on. This approach is feasible for goods like fashion merchandise because the consumer knows that inventories of the item will not be replenished once it sells, which makes it risky to wait for prices to be reduced further. A complete model of clearance sales is provided by Lazear (1986), and empirical studies based on this model are provided in Pashigian (1988), Pashigian and Bowen (1991) and Pashigian et al. (1995). A decision support system for optimal clearance pricing was developed by Smith and Achabal (1998).

A final potential determinant of price dispersion that is unrelated to differences in physical product characteristics is differences in advertising or other services provided by sellers. The basic idea, first developed by Ehrlich and Fisher (1982), is that advertising and other services are valued by consumers because they cut down on search costs, and that consumers will therefore willingly pay a higher price for goods that are bundled with the services. If the marginal costs of providing the services are non-decreasing in both amount per customer and number of customers, optimal trade between customer i and firm j can be expressed (Ehrlich and Fisher, 1982) as

$$- dL_i/dS_j = dp_j/dS_j = dC_j/dS_j$$

This implies that the marginal reduction in search costs (L) of consumer i due to advertising or other services provided by firm j ($- dL_i/dS_j$) is equal to the marginal increase in price that firm j can command on the market resulting from a marginal increase in services (dp_j/dS_j), which in turn is equal to the marginal cost to firm j of supplying the services (dC_j/dS_j). If the above assumptions about the marginal costs of services are satisfied, and there is free entry, an equilibrium with consumers choosing service levels that satisfy the above conditions, and prices equal to average cost including the cost of providing the services ($p_j = AC_j$) will result. Thus differences in observed prices across sellers result from differences in advertising or other services provided by firms. In turn these differences result from differences in consumer demand for the services.

Thus we have four potential explanations for price dispersion in markets. Spatial price dispersion may be related to differences in search costs between buyers coupled with cost differences between sellers, and to differences in use of advertising and other services provided by sellers. Both spatial and temporal price dispersion may be related to differences in search costs and mixed strategies over time, and temporal price dispersion may be related to reducing prices over time in response to information about willingness to pay. Aside from these explanations of price dispersion, there is a consistent finding that increases in the mass of consumers with high search costs will lead to higher prices and possibly to a higher supply of services that reduce search costs.

Empirical evidence on price dispersion and search
We shall first discuss the extensive empirical literature that tests various hypotheses about price dispersion suggested by the models of price dispersion outlined in the preceding section. Since the results of these models depend on consumer behavior, we shall also examine evidence in the literature on consumer search that is related to the empirical results about price dispersion and its antecedents.

Price dispersion
The dispersion of offer prices of physically identical items in retail markets has been consistently found to be quite large, even for relatively expensive items. For example, Sorenson (2000) found an average coefficient of variation of prices of prescription drugs across retailers in a particular market to be 22 percent. Dahlby and West (1986) found a coefficient of variation of auto insurance prices across insurers in a particular market of between 7 and 18 percent. In their study of 39 products in the Boston market, Pratt et al. (1979) found coefficients of variation ranging across products from 4.38 percent to 71.35

percent, with a mean of 21.6 percent across the 29 items. In their study of prices posted at Biz Rate, Pan et al. (2002) found average coefficients of variation across eight broad categories of between 8.3 and 15.4 percent. Although these measures of dispersion do decline somewhat with price levels (Pan et al., 2006), they are still substantial for high-ticket items.

The existing evidence indicates that most of the variation in prices across retailers cannot be explained by differences in retail services, at least with existing measures of services. Pan et al. (2002) found that between 5 and 43 percent of the variation in prices of homogeneous items across the eight categories studied could be explained by differences in services across sellers, and that this percentage of explained variation was under 25 percent for seven of the eight categories. Across different products in a category, evidence in the extensive literature on price–quality relations also indicates that differences in prices across items are not closely related to differences in their quality. This literature consistently indicates that the correlation between price and overall quality is low (e.g. Tellis and Wernerfelt, 1987), or that many brands have a price that is well above a frontier that defines the minimum price for a given quality or set of attributes (Maynes, 1976; Kamakura et al., 1988).

Although uncontrolled differences in service or product attributes may be part of the explanation for observed price dispersion and low price–quality correlations, the existing evidence seems more consistent with costly search. For example, Sorenson (2000) found that prices for repeatedly purchased prescription drugs had lower margins and less dispersion than less frequently purchased ones. Because the annual expenditure is higher, incentives to search for drugs are greater, and Sorenson's evidence is therefore consistent with consumer incentives to search for lower prices. Sorenson also concluded that at most one-third of the observed price dispersion can be attributed to pharmacy fixed effects, which may be due to some combination of cost and service level differences across pharmacies.

Dahlby and West (1986) employed the model of Carlson and McAfee (1983) in their study of price dispersion in an automobile insurance market, and concluded that price dispersion in this market can be explained by costly consumer search. Employing a unique dataset on market shares and prices, Dahlby and West (1986) estimated distributions of search costs for buyers of auto insurance that explained the observed variation in prices and market shares.

However, data on sales and market shares of items are generally difficult to obtain for specific sellers. To remedy this problem, Hong and Shum (2006) showed that, if one assumes optimal search by consumers and pricing according to an optimal mixed strategy by each seller, the distribution of search costs can be recovered from the observed distribution of prices. The basic idea is that a given distribution of search costs implies a particular frequency distribution of prices that arise from the optimal mixed strategies. If the observed frequency distribution corresponds to the optimal one, the distribution of search costs can be recovered. Using this approach, the authors developed a non-parametric estimator of the distribution of search costs for a fixed sample size model of search, and a maximum likelihood estimator for a sequential search model, under the maintained assumption that the distribution of search costs follows a gamma distribution. The authors presented some limited empirical evidence on search costs derived from observed price distributions of four books.

Search
Articles that are representative of the literature that examines the overall extent of pre-purchase search for consumer durables are: Punj and Staelin (1983); Wilkie and Dickson (1985); Beatty and Smith (1987); Srinivasan and Ratchford (1991); Ratchford and Srinivasan (1993); Moorthy et al. (1997); Lapersonne et al. (1995). A consistent finding of this literature is that the overall extent of search is limited for many buyers, and that the number of alternatives seriously considered for purchase is typically a small fraction of the number available. Despite the limited search, Ratchford and Srinivasan (1993) estimated that consumers tend to search until they are reasonably close to the point where the marginal saving in price equals the marginal costs of search. The U-shaped relationship between knowledge and search (Moorthy et al., 1997) discussed earlier suggests that price dispersion may result partly from price discrimination against consumers with low knowledge.

A number of studies have addressed price search by grocery shoppers. Carlson and Gieseke (1983) found that the percentage saved increases with stores shopped. Urbany et al. (1996), and Putrevu and Ratchford (1997), studied the relation between self-reported grocery search activities and attitudinal and demographic variables. They found that perceived price dispersion, knowledge of prices, ability to search and access to price information are positively related to search, while measures of time costs are negatively related. Fox and Hoch (2005) studied the impact of shopping more than one store on the same day, which they defined as cherry picking, and found that the savings resulting from the additional trip averaged $14.66, which is high enough to justify the extra trip for the average consumer (the trip is justified as long as its opportunity cost is less than $14.66).

While other authors employed either panel data on actual prices, or survey data, Gauri et al. (2007) collected both types of data. They studied both spatial (more than one store in a time period) and temporal (stocking up at one store when promotions are offered) dimensions of search and found that each search strategy can generate about the same level of savings, while a combination of the two strategies can generate the highest savings. They also found that patterns of search were largely driven by consumer geographical locations relative to stores.

There is a more micro body of research that infers how consumers search for repeatedly purchased items that are sold in a supermarket. As with consumer durables, survey research indicates that consumers do not search extensively for specific grocery items. For example, Dickson and Sawyer (1990) found that only about 60 percent of consumers checked the price of the item they bought before purchase, and that less than 25 percent checked the price of any competing brand. A majority of consumers could not accurately recall prices that they paid.

Consistent with these findings, models of costly and incomplete search have been estimated on scanner panel data. Murthi and Srinivasan (1999) built a model in which consumers evaluate alternatives only part of the time, and show that this provides better predictive performance than models that do not incorporate this partial evaluation behavior. Bayesian learning models were employed by Erdem and Keane (1996), Erdem et al. (2003), and Horsky et al. (2006) to represent the evolution of consumer preferences as they gain more experience with different brands. Mehta et al. (2003) combined the extensive body of literature on consideration sets (see the references in their paper),

Bayesian updating of quality and price perceptions, and a search model that balances benefits and costs of search, to determine which brands are considered on a particular occasion.

Summary of empirical results
The extensive theoretical literature on how consumers should search indicates that they should terminate their search at the point where the expected gain from additional search is less than the expected cost. If this search is costly, consumers should not gather complete information on all alternatives, and if it is costly enough, they should not search at all. Differences in gains and costs of search across consumers should determine differences in the amount of search that they undertake.

While individual consumers may not behave optimally according to a normative decision rule, the empirical literature on search generally indicates that differences in search across consumers are consistent with the predictions of the normative models. In both durables and grocery markets, it appears that consumers who perceive more gains from search actually do search more, and that more search is associated with savings. In durables markets, there is a group of consumers, generally knowledgeable and experienced, who do not search extensively. Nevertheless, while this limited search appears to be partly due to prior information that makes further search unnecessary, and may also be due to high search costs, one wonders if there is more to the story.

Search, sources of information and pricing
While the market models of search and pricing outlined above usually abstract from specific sources of information, it is clear that consumers use a variety of sources in the course of their search. Following Klein and Ford (2003), these information sources can be broadly classified as personal (word-of-mouth, talking to salesperson, inspection at the retail outlet), and impersonal (advertising, *Consumer Reports*). They can be further classified as seller-sponsored attempts to influence sales (advertising, salesperson), and neutral or objective (friend/relative, *Consumer Reports*). Finally, the impersonal sources can be classified by medium (Internet, print). Because they involve considerations related to search and pricing that have not yet been incorporated into this review, we shall concentrate our discussion on word-of-mouth, advertising, retail and the Internet.

Word of mouth
There has been extensive study of word of mouth as a source of information in automobile purchases, with the results generally indicating that heavy users of this source tend to be young, female, inexperienced at buying cars, and low in confidence about their ability to judge them (Furse et al., 1984; Ratchford et al., 2007). They are likely to employ a purchase pal who is viewed as having more knowledge of car buying in their search (Furse et al., 1984).

The latter indicates an important consideration in studying word of mouth as an information source: someone must supply the information. This role of information supplier often appears to be filled by persons described as market mavens (Feick and Price, 1987). Market mavens are individuals who tend to collect a broad array of marketplace information with the intent of sharing it with others (Urbany et al., 1996). They appear to collect more information about food, drug, and other items sold at grocery stores (Feick and Price, 1987; Urbany et al., 1996). The implication is that market mavens, who appear to enjoy gathering and sharing marketplace information, may play a significant role in enhancing the efficiency of consumer markets.

Advertising
Since the advertiser is normally engaging in this activity in order to make money, and consumers are likely to be aware of this, the possibility that advertising may be a signal rather than a direct source of information needs to be discussed. The possible role of advertising in cutting down on search costs has been discussed above. But there are cases in which the veracity of advertising cannot be verified through pre-purchase search (Nelson, 1974). There have been many attempts to develop formal arguments about the role of advertising and price as signals of quality in cases where consumers do not find it cost-effective to learn about quality prior to purchase (this work is reviewed by Kirmani and Rao, 2000). One of the major arguments in this literature is that advertising serves as a performance bond to motivate the firm to maintain its quality: firms advertise up front to convince consumers that they will maintain their quality; in return they get a price premium that is forfeited if their quality deteriorates. Since the firm cannot earn an adequate return on the advertising investment if it allows quality to decline, the advertising signal is credible (Klein and Leffler, 1981; Shapiro, 1983). While the rationale for the result is different from the case of informative advertising, the outcome is similar: in Ehrlich and Fisher (1982) consumers pay a higher price to avoid search costs; in signaling models they pay a higher price to get insurance of high quality.

In contrast to the signaling models discussed above, which have the most direct application to manufactured goods, Bagwell and Ramey (1994) modeled the use of advertising as a signal in retail markets. Their clear prediction is that advertising will be associated with lower prices and better buys. In their model, investments in selling technology lower costs, expansion of product line increases sales from any given set of customers, and marginal selling costs are constant or declining. All of these factors are complementary and allow the larger retailer to offer lower prices. Consumers who are aware of the heaviest advertiser employ advertising as a signal to patronize that retailer. They are rewarded with the lowest prices, while that retailer achieves the best information technology, broadest product line and lowest marginal costs. Other research related to search in retail markets is discussed in the next section.

Retailing
Since retailers not only function as an information source, but also set or negotiate prices, provide locational convenience, assemble assortments, hold inventory and finalize transactions (Betancourt, 2004), their role in the search process is unique. All of these activities have an impact on the full price of the product (price plus search and transaction costs). In general, since information, convenience, assortments, inventories and other services reduce search costs, retailers who provide them can cover their cost through higher prices. We shall review a number of studies that have addressed these tradeoffs between services that reduce search costs and price.

Messinger and Narasimhan (1997) studied the impact of large assortments that create economies of one-stop shopping. In their model, which is similar in structure to the model of Ehrlich and Fisher (1982) discussed above, the equilibrium assortment of a supermarket is the assortment that equates the marginal saving in consumer shopping costs with the marginal cost to the store of providing a larger assortment. The cost saving to consumers comes from spreading a fixed travel cost over a higher number of items bought. The authors estimate that consumers trade a 1–2 percent increase in store margin for a 3–4 percent decrease in shopping costs that results from the large supermarket assortments.

The desire of buyers to shop in one location to minimize search costs often leads retailers of a given type to locate proximate to one another even though this creates more competition between them. For example, automobile retailers often cluster together, and major specialty stores for clothing and sporting goods tend to locate in the same mall. This clustering benefits buyers by lowering the cost of shopping for multiple items, or the cost of comparison shopping. In the latter case, it also makes the clustered retailers more competitive, which they endure because the clustered site is attractive to consumers (Wernerfelt, 1994b). A study by Arentze et al. (2005) provides a framework for the estimation of these retail agglomeration effects, and a case analysis that indicates that the effects on demand are substantial.

Once a potential buyer incurs the cost of a trip to a retailer, the retailer gains a measure of monopoly power over the buyer: if the buyer does not purchase, the cost of going to the next store must be incurred. Knowing this, the buyer will be more likely to patronize the retailer if the retailer can commit to not exploiting the buyer's sunk costs of traveling to the retailer. Wernerfelt (1994b) explains that such a commitment can be achieved by the co-location described above (the cost of going to the next seller becomes low), and also by price advertising that provides a legal commitment to provide the advertised price. Conversely, Wernerfelt (1994b) shows that retailers can employ negotiated prices to soften price competition. Manufacturers can also soften price competition between retailers by making the models available at competing retailers slightly different, thereby making it difficult for consumers to make price comparisons (Bergen et al., 1996).

One case in which the buyer's sunk travel costs may be exploited is when a stock-out is encountered. In this case, because the cost of the extra trip may not be worth it, the consumer may still buy other items from the retailer and may substitute for the item that is subject to the stock-out (see Anupindi et al., 1998 for a method for estimating substitution effects when stock-outs occur). Hess and Gerstner (1987) show that retailers may be able to induce an extra trip by using a rain check policy when there is a stock-out.

Since retail salespeople appear to be a key source of consumer information for appliances and durables (Wilkie and Dickson, 1985), it is important to examine the circumstances under which salespeople will be used as an information source. Wernerfelt (1994a) presents a model in which salespeople will be the preferred source of information for complex products in which a dialog between salesperson and consumer is needed to establish a match, and in which the salesperson is motivated to give honest answers by the prospect of repeat business.

Search and the Internet
Since the advent of the Internet provided an altogether new information source and form of retailing that quickly received widespread use by buyers and sellers, it is not surprising that this medium has been the subject of a great deal of theoretical and empirical research. The early expectation was that the Internet would reduce search costs and lead

to something approaching Bertrand competition. For example, Bakos (1997) predicted that the Internet would increase the participation of consumers in markets, and create improved matches between buyers and sellers. However, it did not take long for more sober views to emerge. The paper by Lal and Sarvary (1999) provides one important exception to the belief that the Internet will always increase competition. The authors show that, by making it easy to order over the Internet, the cost of acquiring a brand that has been bought in the past relative to an unknown brand that requires inspection before purchase is altered. One can acquire the known brand over the Internet at a low cost but must incur the cost of traveling to a retailer to get the needed information about the unknown brand. This gives the seller of the known brand a cost advantage that he/she can exploit in setting prices. Thus the Internet can promote brand loyalty and lessen competition.

Internet shopping agents (ISAs) that present comparative price data for competing sellers have become a common feature of Internet commerce. Despite the fact that users of an ISA should have no trouble determining which seller charges the lowest price, a large number of studies have shown that prices listed on ISAs typically exhibit a large degree of dispersion, similar in magnitude to 'brick and mortar' retail prices (see the review in Pan et al., 2006). Baye and Morgan (2001) and Iyer and Pazgal (2003) have explained this apparent anomaly as the adoption of mixed strategies. Firms want to trade off between extracting surplus from non-searching (loyal) customers and obtaining the business of those who consult the ISA. Similar to Varian (1980), this leads sellers who belong to the ISA to choose mixed strategies, which leads to the observed dispersion in posted prices. Because the chance of having the lowest price declines as the number of sellers increases, Iyer and Pazgal (2003) show that, as long as the reach of the ISA does not increase substantially with the number of members, ISA members will give more weight to loyal customers and charge higher prices as the number of members of the ISA increases. Since the chance of getting the business of ISA shoppers declines as the number of sellers increases, at some point it will be more profitable to cater exclusively to the non-ISA customers. Thus not all sellers will join an ISA. For the three categories they studied (books, music CDs and movie videos), Iyer and Pazgal (2003) did find evidence of variation in the identity of the seller offering the minimum price that is consistent with mixed strategies, and a tendency of prices to increase with the number of sellers.

Aside from the evidence of considerable dispersion of posted prices among Internet retailers, there is a body of evidence that indicates that the Internet does lead to lower prices and more efficient search on the part of consumers. For example, for data collected from early 1998 through early 1999, Brynjolfsson and Smith (2000) found that online book and CD prices were 9–16 percent below the offline prices of the same items. Garbarino (2006) shows that the lower online book and CD prices have persisted though 2006, although the gap has narrowed in recent years. Additional evidence that the Internet leads to lower prices is provided by Brown and Goolsbee (2002) and Zettelmeyer et al. (2006). Using micro-level data on transaction prices for term insurance that allows estimation of relationships between prices paid and differences in Internet use, Brown and Goolsbee (2002) determined that the Internet lowered term insurance prices by 8–15 percent from 1995 to 1997. Using a matched set of data on transaction prices and survey data on search behavior, Zettelmeyer et al. (2006) estimated that access to price data and referrals through the Internet leads to a decline in transaction prices of about 1.5 percent, and that the benefits of the Internet accrue mainly to those who dislike bargaining.

As pointed out by Bakos (1997), the Internet need not lower prices if it makes it easier to locate sellers that provide a better match to consumer preferences. The better match can allow the seller to command a higher price. Lynch and Ariely (2000) found evidence of this in their experimental study of wine purchasing. More accessible quality information did lead to decreased price sensitivity in their experiments.

In addition to influencing prices, the Internet can affect other aspects of search. In particular, it may affect the total amount of effort that consumers put into their search in either direction: by allowing consumers to search more efficiently, the Internet should lead to a reduction in the effort required to obtain a given amount of information; however, the increased efficiency may make it cost-effective to attempt to locate more information than would otherwise be the case. Evidence from data on search for automobiles before and after the Internet appeared suggests that the latter effect predominates and that the Internet tends to lead to increased total search (Ratchford et al., 2003; Ratchford et al., 2007).

In addition to affecting the total amount of search, the Internet should also alter the allocation of effort between sources. Evidence for automobile search in Ratchford et al., (2003) and Ratchford et al. (2007) indicates that the Internet has had a major impact on time spent with the dealer, considerably reducing this time, and specifically reducing time spent in negotiating price with the dealer. This is consistent with the finding cited above that the Internet leads to lower prices for automobiles. Consumers do appear to come to the dealer with price information obtained from the Internet, making the price negotiation more efficient in terms of time spent, while at the same time neutralizing the salesperson's advantage in negotiating price. This should ultimately have an impact on margins that can be obtained by dealers, and on the number and skill of salespeople that they retain.

Conclusions and future research
Forty-plus years after his original article, Stigler's basic insight that search is costly, and that this will create price dispersion, still holds. Since the dispersion of offer prices for physically identical items is a pervasive phenomenon, even in cases where prices are easy to compare, models that fail to account for this may be assuming away something important and should be treated with caution.

The existing evidence about consumer search for both durables and groceries indicates that buyers stop well short of obtaining complete information, and in many cases obtain almost no new information. However, given that search is costly, it is not clear that consumers systematically search less than some normative model might tell them to. In fact, evidence presented in Ratchford and Srinivasan (1993), Fox and Hoch (2005) and Gauri et al. (2007) indicates that marginal gains to search are not far out of line with marginal costs. Moreover, empirical studies of search behavior generally indicate that search varies across consumers in ways that are consistent with fundamental search models.

One reason why it is hard to determine whether consumers search too little or too much compared to a normative model is that costs of search are difficult to measure. Time costs appear to differ considerably from wage rates, and shopping time may be a consumption good in itself (Marmorstein et al., 1992). Moreover, while there are obvious constraints on consumers' ability to process information, this information-processing capacity generally is not incorporated into estimates of search costs. Learning more about the nature and magnitude of search costs would seem to be a potentially fruitful area for further research.

Existing models indicate that average and minimum prices, and price dispersion, increase with the variation in search costs across consumers (an assumption that the lowest search cost is 0 – some consumers are fully informed – is generally required to solve for equilibrium). Price dispersion may arise from heterogeneity of consumer search costs, accompanied either with cost differences among sellers or mixed strategies aimed at targeting consumers with different levels of search costs. It may also arise from heterogeneity in demand for services that reduce search costs, with consumers that demand more services paying higher prices. Finally, temporal price dispersion may arise from seller efforts to learn the maximum price at which an item will sell.

While the mixed strategy explanation for price dispersion is commonly used, and there is some evidence that the identity of the minimum-priced seller does fluctuate through time, one must worry about the realism of this explanation. It seems questionable that sellers really do randomize their prices through time, although possibly this is a good approximation. Development of a model of pricing and price dispersion that is more closely related to actual seller behavior, and that incorporates services provided by the seller that may reduce search costs, would seem a good area for further research. Possibly, extension of the model of Carlson and McAfee (1983) to the case where sellers are differentiated on the services they offer would be a good way to proceed.

References

Anupindi, R., M. Dada and S. Gupta (1998), 'Estimation of consumer demand with stock-out based substitution: an application to vending machine products', *Marketing Science*, **17** (4), 406–23.
Arentze, T., H. Oppewal and H. Timmermans (2005), 'A multipurpose shopping trip model to assess retail agglomeration effects', *Journal of Marketing Research*, **42** (February), 109–15.
Bagwell, K. and G. Ramey (1994), 'Coordination economies, advertising and search behavior in retail markets', *American Economic Review*, **84** (June), 498–517.
Bakos, Y. (1997), 'Reducing buyer search costs: implications for electronic marketplaces', *Management Science*, **43** (December), 1676–92.
Baye, M. and J. Morgan (2001), 'Information gatekeepers on the Internet and the competitiveness of homogeneous product markets', *American Economic Review*, **91**, 454–74.
Baye, M. and J. Morgan (2004), 'Price dispersion in the lab and on the Internet: theory and evidence', *Rand Journal of Economics*, **35** (3), 4449–66.
Beatty, S. and S. Smith (1987), 'External search effort: an investigation across several product categories', *Journal of Consumer Research*, **14** (1), 83–95.
Bergen, M., S. Dutta and S. Shugan (1996), 'Branded variants: a retail perspective', *Journal of Marketing Research*, **33** (February), 9–19.
Betancourt, R. (2004), *The Economics of Retailing and Distribution*, Cheltenham, UK and Northampton, MA, USA: Edward Elgar Publishing.
Brown, J. and A. Goolsbee (2002), 'Does the Internet make markets more competitive? Evidence from the life insurance industry', *Journal of Political Economy*, **110**, 481–507.
Brynjolfsson, E. and M. Smith (2000), '"Frictionless commerce": a comparison of Internet and conventional retailers', *Management Science*, **46** (4), 563–85.
Carlson, J. and R. Gieseke (1983), 'Price search in a product market', *Journal of Consumer Research*, **9** (March), 357–65.
Carlson, J. and R. McAfee (1983), 'Discrete equilibrium price dispersion', *Journal of Political Economy*, **91** (June), 480–93.
Dahlby, B. and D. West (1986), 'Price dispersion in an automobile insurance market', *Journal of Political Economy*, **94** (2), 418–38.
David, H.A. (1970), *Order Statistics*, New York: John Wiley & Sons.

Dickson, P. and A. Sawyer (1990), 'The price knowledge and search of supermarket shoppers', *Journal of Marketing*, **54** (3), 42–53.

Eckstein, Z. and K. Wolpin (1990), 'Estimating a market equilibrium search model from panel data on individuals', *Econometrica*, **58** (4), 783–808.

Eckstein, Z. and K. Wolpin (1995), 'Duration to first job and the turn to schooling: estimates from a search-matching model', *The Review of Economic Studies*, **62** (2), 263–86.

Ehrlich, I. and L. Fisher (1982), 'The derived demand for advertising: a theoretical and empirical investigation', *American Economic Review*, **72** (June), 366–88.

Erdem, T. and M. Keane (1996), 'Decision making under uncertainty: capturing dynamic brand choice processes in turbulent consumer goods markets', *Marketing Science*, **15** (1), 1–20.

Erdem, T., S. Imai and M. Keane (2003), 'Brand and quantity choice dynamics under price uncertainty', *Quantitative Marketing and Economics*, **1** (1), 5–64.

Erdem, T., M. Keane, T. Öncü and J. Strebel (2005), 'Learning about computers: an analysis of information search and technology choice', *Quantitative Marketing and Economics*, **3** (September), 207–47.

Feick, L. and L. Price (1987), 'The market maven: a diffuser of marketplace information', *Journal of Marketing*, **51** (January), 83–97.

Fox, E. and S. Hoch (2005), 'Cherry picking', *Journal of Marketing*, **69** (1), 46–62.

Furse, D., G. Punj and D. Stewart (1984), 'A typology of individual search strategies among purchasers of new automobiles', *Journal of Consumer Research*, **10** (March), 417–31.

Garbarino, E. (2006), 'Then and now: reality and perceptions in the evolution of online and offline pricing', Working Paper, Weatherhead School of Management, Case Western Reserve University.

Gauri, D., K. Sudhir and D. Talukdar (2007), 'The temporal and spatial dimensions of price search: insights from matching household survey and purchase data', *Journal of Marketing Research*, **45** (April), 226–40.

Hess, J. and E. Gerstner (1987), 'Loss leader pricing and rain check policy', *Marketing Science*, **6** (Autumn), 358–74.

Hong, H. and M. Shum (2006), 'Using price distributions to estimate search costs', *Rand Journal of Economics*, **37** (2), 257–75.

Horsky, D., S. Misra and P. Nelson (2006), 'Observed and unobserved preference heterogeneity in brand-choice models', *Marketing Science*, **25** (July–August), 322–35.

Iyer, G. and A. Pazgal (2003), 'Internet shopping agents: virtual co-location and competition' *Marketing Science*, **22** (Winter), 85–106.

Johnson, E. and J. Russo (1984), 'Product familiarity and learning new information', *Journal of Consumer Research*, **11** (1), 542–50.

Jones, S. (1988), 'The relationship between unemployment spells and reservation wages as a test of search theory', *Quarterly Journal of Economics*, **103** (November), 741–65.

Kamakura, W., B. Ratchford and J. Agrawal (1988), 'Measuring market efficiency and welfare loss', *Journal of Consumer Research*, **15** (December), 289–302.

Kirmani, A. and A. Rao (2000) 'No pain, no gain: a critical review of the literature on signaling unobservable product quality', *Journal of Marketing*, **64** (2), 66–79.

Klein, B. and K. Leffler (1981), 'The role of market forces in assuring contractual performance', *Journal of Political Economy*, **89** (August), 615–41.

Klein, L. and G. Ford (2003), 'Consumer search for information in the digital age: an empirical study of pre-purchase for automobiles', *Journal of Interactive Marketing*, **17** (3), 29–49.

Lal, R. and M. Sarvary (1999), 'When and how is the Internet likely to decrease price competition?', *Marketing Science*, **18** (Fall), 485–503.

Lancaster, T. (1985), 'Simultaneous equation models in applied search theory', *Journal of Econometrics*, **28**, 113–26.

Lapersonne, E., G. Laurent and J. Le Goff (1995), 'Consideration sets of size one: an empirical investigation of automobile purchases', *International Journal of Research in Marketing*, **12** (1), 55–66.

Lazear, E. (1986), 'Retail pricing and clearance sales', *American Economic Review*, **76** (March), 14–32.

Lynch, J. and D. Ariely (2000), 'Wine online: search costs affect competition on price, quality, and distribution', *Marketing Science*, **19** (1), 83–103.

Maynes, E. (1976), *Decision Making for Consumers*, New York: Macmillan.

Marmorstein, H., D. Grewal and R. Fishe (1992), 'The value of time spent in price comparison shopping: survey and experimental evidence', *Journal of Consumer Research*, **19** (June), 52–61.

Mehta, R., S. Rajiv and K. Srinivasan (2003), 'Price uncertainty and consumer search: a structural model of consideration set formation', *Marketing Science*, **22** (Winter), 58–84.

Messinger, P. and C. Narasimhan (1997), 'A model of retail formats based on consumers' economizing on shopping time', *Marketing Science*, **16** (Winter), 1–23.

Moorthy, S., B. Ratchford and D. Talukdar (1997), 'Consumer information search revisited: theory and empirical analysis', *Journal of Consumer Research*, **23** (March), 263–77.

Murthi, B. and K. Srinivasan (1999), 'Consumers' extent of evaluation in brand choice', *The Journal of Business*, **72** (April), 229–56.
Narasimhan, C. (1988), 'Competitive promotional strategies', *Journal of Business*, **61** (4), 427–49.
Nelson, P. (1974), 'Advertising as information', *Journal of Political Economy*, **82** (July–August), 729–54.
Pan, X., B. Ratchford and V. Shankar (2002), 'Can price dispersion in online markets be explained by differences in e-tailer service quality?', *Journal of the Academy of Marketing Science*, **30** (Fall), 433–45.
Pan, X., B. Ratchford and V. Shankar (2006), 'Drivers of price dispersion among e-tailers', Working Paper, Texas A&M University.
Pashigian, B. (1988), 'Demand uncertainty and sales: a study of fashion and markdown pricing', *American Economic Review*, **78** (5), 936–53.
Pashigian, B. and B. Bowen (1991), 'Why are products sold on sale?: Explanations of pricing regularities', *Quarterly Journal of Economics*, **106** (4), 1015–38.
Pashigian, B., B. Bowen and E. Gould (1995), 'Fashion, styling, and the within-season decline in automobile prices', *Journal of Law and Economics*, **38** (2), 281–309.
Pratt, J., D. Wise and R. Zeckhauser (1979), 'Price differences in almost competitive markets', *Quarterly Journal of Economics*, **93** (2), 189–211.
Punj, G. and R. Staelin (1983), 'A model of consumer information search behavior for new automobiles', *Journal of Consumer Research*, **9** (4), 366–80.
Putrevu, S. and B. Ratchford (1997), 'A model of search behavior with an application to grocery shopping', *Journal of Retailing*, **73** (Winter), 463–86.
Ratchford, B. (1980), 'The value of information for selected appliances', *Journal of Marketing Research*, **17** (1), 14–25.
Ratchford, B. and N. Srinivasan (1993), 'An empirical investigation of returns to search', *Marketing Science*, **12** (Winter), 73–87.
Ratchford, B. and G. Stoops (1988), 'A model and measurement approach for studying retail productivity', *Journal of Retailing*, **64** (Fall), 241–63.
Ratchford, B. and G. Stoops (1992), 'An econometric model of a retail firm', *Managerial and Decision Economics*, **13**, 223–31.
Ratchford, B., M. Lee and D. Talukdar (2003), 'The impact of the Internet on information search for automobiles', *Journal of Marketing Research*, **40** (May), 193–209.
Ratchford, B., D. Talukdar and M. Lee (2007), 'The impact of the Internet on consumers' use of information sources for automobiles', *Journal of Consumer Research*, **34** (June), 111–19.
Salop, S. and J. Stiglitz (1977), 'Bargains and ripoffs: a model of monopolistically competitive price dispersion', *Review of Economic Studies*, **44** (October), 493–510.
Shapiro, C. (1983), 'Premiums for high quality products as returns to reputations', *Quarterly Journal of Economics*, **98** (November), 659–79.
Smith, S. and D. Achabal (1998), 'Clearance pricing and inventory policies for retail chains', *Management Science*, **44** (March), 285–300.
Sorenson, A. (2000), 'Equilibrium price dispersion in retail markets for prescription drugs', *Journal of Political Economy*, **108** (4), 833–50.
Srinivasan, N. and B. Ratchford (1991), 'An empirical test of a model of external search for automobiles', *Journal of Consumer Research*, **18** (September), 233–42.
Stigler, G. (1961), 'The economics of information', *Journal of Political Economy*, **69** (June), 213–25.
Tellis, G. and B. Wernerfelt (1987), 'Competitive price and quality under asymmetric information', *Marketing Science*, **6** (Summer), 240–53.
Urbany, J., P. Dickson and R. Kalapurakal (1996), 'Price search in the retail grocery market', *Journal of Marketing*, **60** (April), 91–104.
Varian, H. (1980), 'A model of sales', *American Economic Review*, **70** (September), 651–9.
Weitzman, M. (1979), 'Optimal search for the best alternative', *Econometrica*, **47** (May), 641–54.
Wernerfelt, B. (1994a), 'On the function of sales assistance', *Marketing Science*, **13** (Winter), 68–82.
Wernerfelt, B. (1994b), 'Selling formats for search goods', *Marketing Science*, **13** (Summer), 298–309.
Wilkie, W. and P. Dickson (1985), 'Shopping for appliances: consumers strategies and patterns of information search', Working Paper 85–108, Marketing Science Institute.
Wolpin, K. (1987), 'Estimating a structural search model: the transition from school to work', *Econometrica*, **55** (4), 810–17.
Zettelmeyer, F., F. Scott Morton, and J. Silva-Risso (2006), 'How the Internet lowers prices: evidence from matched survey and automobile transaction data', *Journal of Marketing Research*, **43** (May), 168–81.

6 Structural models of pricing
Tat Chan, Vrinda Kadiyali and Ping Xiao*

Abstract
In this chapter, we first describe how structural pricing models are different from reduced-form models and what the advantages of using structural pricing models might be. Specifically, we discuss how structural models are based on behavioral assumptions of consumer and firm behavior, and how these behavioral assumptions translate to market outcomes. Specifying the model from these first principles of behavior makes these models useful for understanding the conditions under which observed market outcomes are generated. Based on the results, managers can conduct simulations to determine the optimal pricing policy should the underlying market conditions (customer tastes, competitive behavior, production costs etc.) change.

1. Introduction

Pricing is a critical marketing decision of a firm – witness this entire *Handbook* devoted to the topic. And increasingly, structural models of pricing are being used for understanding this important marketing decision, making them a critical element in the toolkit of researchers and managers. Starting in the early 1990s (for example see Horsky and Nelson, 1992), there has been a steady increase in structural modeling of pricing decisions in the marketing literature. These models have accounted for firm and consumer decision-making processes, with topics ranging from product-line pricing, channel pricing, non-linear pricing, price discrimination and so on (see Table 6.1 for a sample of these papers).

So what precisely are structural models of pricing? And how do they help the pricing decisions of a firm? In these models, researchers explicitly state the behaviors of agents based on economic or behavioral theory. In marketing, these agents are typically consumers and/or firms who interact in the market. Market data of quantity purchased and/or prices and other types of promotions are treated as outcomes of these interactions. In contrast to structural models, reduced-form models do not need to articulate precisely what behaviors of consumers and/or managers lead to the observed quantity purchased and/or market prices. There is a rich tradition of such reduced-form studies in marketing, with the profit impact of marketing strategies or PIMS studies as a leading example. In these studies, researchers examined how profits were affected by factors such as advertising and market concentration. Such reduced-form studies are very useful in establishing stylized facts (e.g. high firm concentration is associated with higher prices). Also, if the researcher's primary interest is in determining comparative statics (e.g. whether prices go up when excess capacity is more concentrated), reduced-form studies are perfectly adequate.

That said, there are several issues with these reduced-form models – the use of accounting data (which do not always capture economically relevant constructs, e.g. economic

---

* The chapter has benefited from excellent comments from a referee and the editor.

Table 6.1 A survey of structural pricing papers

Author	Pricing issue examined	Model	Managerially relevant findings
Besanko et al. (2003)	Third-degree price discrimination under competition by manufacturers and a retailer in the ketchup market	Demand side: aggregate logit model with latent-class heterogeneity structure Supply side: the retailer as a monopolist decides prices to maximizes the category profit while manufacturers maximize their profit by acting as a Stackelberg leader in the channel	The retailer can increase the profit by discriminating a finite number of customer segments; manufacturers are better off because of the retailer's use of price discrimination Price discrimination under competition does not lead to all-out price competition
Besanko et al. (1998)	Competitive pricing behavior of manufacturers in the yogurt and ketchup markets	Demand side: aggregate logit model Supply side: Bertrand–Nash pricing behavior by manufacturers and the common retailer	Firm can use alternative value creation strategies to accomplish competitive advantage
Che et al. (2007)	Competitive pricing behaviors of manufacturers and retailers when the demand is state-dependent in the breakfast cereal market	Demand side: logit model with a latent-class heterogeneity structure Supply side: menu of different pricing behaviors by manufacturers – Bertrand and collusive; menu of different interactions between manufacturers and the retailer – manufacturer Stackelberg and vertical Nash	Ignoring demand dependence will lead to wrong firm behavior inferences The observed retail pricing in this market is consistent with the assumption that manufacturers and retailers are one-period-forward-looking in price-setting
Chintagunta (2002)	Drivers of retailer pricing behavior in OTC analgesics category	Demand side: aggregate mixed logit model Supply side: retailers maximize the profit function by accounting for store retail competition, side payment and share of the store brand	The effects of different drivers differ across brands within the category
Chintagunta et al. (2003)	Price discrimination in a retail chain	Demand side: aggregate mixed logit model	Store-level pricing may increase firm's profit but not reduce consumers' surplus relative to chain-level pricing

Table 6.1 (continued)

Author	Pricing issue examined	Model	Managerially relevant findings
Chu et al. (2006)	Effects of various product bundle pricing strategies, including bundle-size pricing[a] (BSP), discounted component pricing[b] (DCP), mixed bundling and simple component pricing	Demand side: the market share for each option is derived from consumer utility maximization while consumers' preferences are assumed to follow bimodal normal distribution	Bundling strategies like BSP and DCP dominate simple component pricing. Although fewer bundles are offered, DCP can generate almost the same profit as mixed bundling. BSP is also a profitable pricing strategy
Draganska and Jain (2005)	Optimal pricing strategies across product lines and within product lines in the yogurt industry	Demand side: aggregate nested logit model with latent-class heterogeneity structure Supply side: Bertrand–Nash pricing behavior by manufacturers and the common retailer	Pricing differently across product lines but uniformly within product lines is an optimal strategy, which is consistent with current pricing practice
Iyengar (2006)	Increasing block pricing (three-part tariff pricing) in the wireless service industry in USA	Demand side: mixed logit model	Changes in access price affect consumer churn and long-term profitability more than changes in marginal prices Changes in access prices affect the CLV of the light users more than that of the heavy users
Kadiyali et al. (1996)	Product line pricing in the laundry detergents market	Demand side: linear function of prices and other variables Supply side: menu of different pricing strategy assumptions – Bertrand–Nash, Stackelberg etc.	Stackelberg leader–follower pricing better explains data than Bertrand–Nash pricing. Each firm positions its strong brand as a Stackelberg leader, with the rival's minor brand being the follower
Lambrecht et al. (2007)	The impact of demand uncertainty on how consumers choose Internet service plans	Demand side: mixed logit model	Demand uncertainty drives the consumer plan choice, which favors three-part tariffs Three-part tariff will increase firm's profit but reduce consumer surplus

Table 6.1 (continued)

Author	Pricing issue examined	Model	Managerially relevant findings
Leslie (2004)	Monopoly second- and third-degree price discrimination of Broadway theaters	Demand side: aggregate mixed logit model	Observed practices of price discrimination increase firms' profit by 5% relative to uniform pricing. The theater can further improve firms' profit if they offer 30% discount instead of the current 50% Consumer welfare gain from price discrimination is relatively small
McManus (2004)	Second-degree price discrimination under competition in specialty coffee market	Demand side: aggregate mixed logit model	Quality distortion is the lowest for the top qualities, which is consistent with economic theory
Narayanan et al. (2007)	Two-part tariff pricing in the telecommunication industry	Demand side: random coefficient probit model, accounts for consumer learning	Consumers learn much faster when they are on the measured plan than when they are on the fixed plan
Pancras and Sudhir (2007)	Evaluate the optimal customer, product and pricing strategy for the coupon service provided by Catalina in the ketchup market	Demand side: logit model with a latent-class heterogeneity structure Supply side: the retailer sets prices to maximize category profits given the manufacturer's decision to buy one-to-one coupon service. The manufacturer sets wholesale price and the coupons' face value to consumers	Catalina can increase its profit by selling nonexclusively Catalina can increase the profit by using longer purchase history data to target Retailer will benefit from undercutting the prices of Catalina for the one-to-one service
Richards (2007)	Strategic pricing promotion in perishable product market	Demand side: nested logit model Supply side: multiproduct retailers maximize profits by making strategic decisions including shelf price, promotion price and frequency of promotion	Retailers set prices and promotion strategies moderately cooperatively, which is less competitive than Bertrand Price promotions affect store revenue most when stores are highly substitutable but products are not

Table 6.1 (continued)

Author	Pricing issue examined	Model	Managerially relevant findings
Roy et al. (1994)	Competitive pricing in the US automobile market	Demand side: a function of lagged quantities and current prices Supply side: firms choose prices to minimize the difference between the real sales and the preset target	Stackelberg leader–follower game is more consistent with the pricing behavior in some segments of the US automobile market than Bertrand–Nash pricing
Sudhir (2001)	Competitive pricing behavior in various segments of the automobile market	Demand side: aggregate mixed logit model Supply side: firms maximize the profit by allowing a menu of possible pricing behaviors	The larger car and luxury segments show evidence of more collusive pricing; the small car segment is much more competitive
Sudhir et al. (2005)	How prices change with changes in demand, costs and competition in the US photographic film industry	Demand side: aggregate mixed logit model Supply side: Bertrand pricing behavior by firms	Competitive intensity is higher in periods of high demand and low cost The information of competitor prices can help determine how demand and cost conditions affect the competitive intensity
Verboven (2002)	Quality-based price discrimination in the European car market	Demand side: aggregate mixed logit model Supply side: pricing difference is the sum of the marginal cost differences and mark-up differences	Find evidence to support the existence of the second-degree price discrimination between high- and low-mileage drivers
Xiao et al. (2007)	Service bundles (voice and text services) under three-part tariff pricing in the wireless market	Demand side: mixed logit model accounting for switching cost and learning	Consumer preference for voice call is positively correlated with that for text Changes in switching cost or consumers' information of own usage preferences significantly affect the penetration of the two service plans offered by the firm

Notes:
[a] Bundle-size pricing means that firm sets prices that depend only on the number of products purchased.
[b] Discounted component pricing means that firm sets component pricing and offers discounts by the total number of products purchased at the same time.

profits are not the same as accounting profits) and the reverse causality issue. As an example of the latter, estimating a simple market demand function treating firm prices as exogenous ignores the fact that a change of the firm's pricing decisions may be caused by a change in the market environment, such as competition and consumer preference. Another important issue with reduced-form models relates to Lucas's critique – the behavior of players (firms or consumers) is likely to be a function of the behaviors of other players. For example, if firms are in a price war, consumers may come to expect low prices and will change their shopping behaviors accordingly. If firms are able to stop this price war, how might the behaviors of consumers change as their price expectations change? These issues cannot be addressed with reduced-form models unless we have reasonable assumptions about the behaviors of consumers and/or firms in the market and unless we have regime-invariant estimates of consumer behavior.

In contrast, using the structural approach to build pricing models, we assume that the observed market outcomes such as quantity sales and/or prices are generated from some explicit economic or behavioral theory of consumers' and firms' behaviors. There is an explicit linkage between theory and empirics. To build theory models of pricing (e.g. for third-degree price discrimination) that are tractable, researchers usually have to choose simple demand specifications and firm-conduct specifications. To understand comparative statics in such models, researchers sometimes also have to resort to selecting what might seem like arbitrary parameter values and conduct numerical simulations. An advantage of structural empirical models is that they can build realistic consumer and firm behavior models, and estimate them even when the models are intractable. Parameter estimates are obtained from actual data and linked to behavioral interpretations. The estimated parameters can then provide a sound basis for conducting policy simulations, such as understanding the impact of new pricing policies from existing firms, entry and exit, mergers and acquisitions and so on, and, based on that, provide managerial recommendations that might not be possible using the reduced-form approach.

This is especially true if the policy experiments are related to new price regimes, i.e. prices assumed in experiments are out of the range of the current sample data. This is because a reduced-form regression model typically tries to match the model with the observed data; there is no guarantee that the model will still perform well when new prices lie outside the range of the current data. Further, when the data are incomplete researchers can sometimes impose restrictions based on economic theory to recover the parameters they are interested in. A typical example in marketing is to infer marginal costs based on pricing equations. Thomadsen (2007) demonstrated that using a structural model, one can infer the demand and production functions in the fast-food industry solely from observed prices (and not units sold or market shares). One major constraint of structural models is the need to impose potentially restrictive behavioral assumptions. Hence they might be less flexible compared with the reduced-form approach; researchers should examine the reasonableness of these assumptions from the data.

It is important to recognize that the distinction between a structural model of pricing and its reduced-form counterpart is less stark. That is, structural modeling is really a continuum where more details of consumer and firm behaviors are modeled, as data and estimation methodology permit. Most empirical models lie between 'pure' reduced-form and structural models. For example, if pricing is the real interest, researchers may focus on modeling how the behaviors of consumers are affected by the firm pricing strategies, or how firms compete in the market through pricing strategies, and treat the impact of other firm strategies such as advertising and non-price promotions in a reduced-form manner as simple control variables (see Chintagunta et al., 2006b). On the other hand, we should also recognize that some sort of causal relationships are implicitly assumed in most reduced-form models, especially when the results lead to policy recommendations. Suppose a researcher estimates a simple model of price as a function of firm concentration, and uses the result to infer the optimal price for a firm. This researcher assumes that concentration changes prices and not the other way round. Further, the assumption of firm behavior is current period profit or revenue maximization. When the researcher suspects that there may be a correlation between the error term and the price in the regression model, instrumental variables may be used in model estimation. However, the choice of instrumental variables implies certain assumptions about why they are correlated with prices and not the error term in the model. In summary, the major difference between structural and reduced-form models is whether behavioral assumptions are explicitly specified in the model (see detailed discussion in Pakes, 2003).

We now turn to the discussion of various parts of a structural model. The purpose of this chapter is not to provide an exhaustive survey of the marketing literature. We select some marketing and economic works in our discussion for illustration purposes, and refer the reader to Chintagunta et al. (2006b), which provides a more complete survey. Our purpose here is to explain the procedure of building a structural model that relates to pricing issues in marketing, and to discuss some important but understudied issues. For greater detail, especially on econometric issues, we refer the reader to excellent surveys in Reiss and Wolak (2007) and Ackerberg et al. (2007).

We first discuss in the next section the four basic steps in constructing a structural pricing model, which involves (1) specifying model primitives including consumer preferences and/or firm production technologies; (2) specifying the maximands or objective functions for consumers and/or firms; (3) specifying model decision variables, which include consumers' quantity purchased and/or firms' pricing decisions. Sometimes other strategic decisions such as advertising, display promotions etc. will also be modeled. The final step is (4) specifying price-setting interactions, i.e. how firms compete against each other through setting prices. With this structural model we explore further issues in model estimation and application, including (1) the two major types of error terms that researchers typically add in the estimation model and their implications; (2) various techniques used in the econometric estimation and other issues such as endogeneity, the choice of instruments and model identification; (3) model specification analysis, i.e. the test of the behavioral assumptions in the model; and (4) policy analysis based on the estimation results. We also discuss some general marketing applications of the structural model there. Finally we conclude and offer some thoughts on future research directions.

2. Specifying a structural pricing model

We use two papers as illustrations to show various aspects of structural modeling for setting prices. These are the studies by Besanko et al. (2003) on competitive price discrimination and Xiao et al. (2007) on pricing for wireless services in the communication industry. Competitive price discrimination cannot be grasped without an understanding of underlying consumer behaviors and firm strategies. Therefore Besanko et al. build a consumer choice model with the assumption of utility maximization. Further, manufacturers and retailer price decisions are modeled as the outcome of profit maximization, with dependencies between them explicitly modeled. Besanko et al. use model estimates to conduct policy simulations, as we discuss in later sections.

Xiao et al.'s study of wireless pricing includes an analysis of three-part tariff pricing (a fixed fee, a free usage and a marginal price that is charged with usage above the free usage) is typically used in the industry. Firms in the industry also typically offer consumers service plans that bundle several services such as voice and text message. In their data, the focal firm introduced a new service plan in the middle of the sample period. While most consumers finally choose the service plan that minimizes the total cost conditional on their observed usages, switching from one to another service plan took time. It is difficult to use a reduced-form demand model of service plans to estimate the data given the complex pricing structure and the entry of the new plan during the sample period. The authors therefore build a structural model in which consumers choose a service plan that maximizes their utility. The authors are agnostic about the firm pricing strategy; however, based on their estimated consumers' responses to the new service bundle under a three-part tariff they are able to explore interesting managerial issues such as whether or not bundling services in a plan under a three-part tariff will be more profitable than selling services separately under various pricing mechanisms, including linear and two-part tariff pricing. They can further compute the optimal pricing structure based on estimated consumer preference.

In anticipation of the coming discussion, Table 6.2 lists the steps needed to build a structural model and provides a quick summary of how our two illustrative papers perform each of these steps.

2.1 Specifying model primitives

As mentioned in the introduction, the starting point of a structural model is to specify the behaviors of the agents being studied. In Besanko et al. the agents being studied are consumers, retailers and manufacturers, whereas in Xiao et al. the focus is consumer choice behavior for wireless service plans; therefore the agents studied are only consumers.

A structural model usually begins with the following model primitives: consumer preferences and firm production technologies. Consumer preferences are a function of variables exogenous to them, such as attributes of products, and variables that are decision outcomes of firms such as market prices. Firms face factor prices that are exogenous to them. A richer model usually allows for heterogeneity in the consumer preferences and/or firm technologies. It is important to identify which variables in the data are assumed to be exogenous and which are not, and examine how reasonable these assumptions are. In this way we make the implied causality explicit (i.e. changes in exogenous variables cause changes in endogenous variables), and also examine how restrictive the model assumptions are. For example, it might be reasonable for researchers to assume product attributes as exogenous given a sufficiently short time horizon, but allow pricing and other promotion decisions to be endogenous, resulting from consumer preferences and the production technologies and competition behaviors of firms based on these primitives. Another example is that in the short run it is reasonable to treat the number of competitors as exogenous. Pricing decisions do not depend on fixed costs. This is a common

Table 6.2 *Steps in building a structural model: Bensanko et al. and Xiao et al.*

Step in modeling	Besanko et al.	Xiao et al.
Specify model primitives	Heterogeneity of consumers' preferences for ketchup products, cost functions faced by retailers and manufacturers	Heterogeneity of consumer preferences for voice and text offered from wireless phone
Specify agent maximands	Consumers maximize utility; retailers and manufacturers maximize profits	Consumers maximize utility under nonlinear pricing and budget constraint
Specify model decision variable	Consumers choose which brand to purchase; manufacturers choose wholesale price; retailer chooses retail price	Consumers choose service plan at the beginning of the period, then choose usage levels for both voice and text
Model price-setting interactions	Consumers are price-takers; Stackelberg game between manufacturers and retailer, Bertrand–Nash price competition among manufacturers	Consumers are price price-takers; firm behavior is not modeled

assumption used in most of the structural pricing models in marketing. However, in the long run, entry and exit can be expected to happen. Fixed costs can affect the number of competing firms in a market and hence also market prices.

Besanko et al. model the consumer preference for ketchup products. They allow for latent class consumer heterogeneity in brand preferences as well as responsiveness to marketing variables including price. They assume an exogenous number of manufacturers in the ketchup market and a monopoly retailer. Each manufacturer may produce several brands and must sell their products through the retailer. The marginal cost of producing one unit of the product is constant and differs across the manufacturers. The marginal cost of selling one unit of the product is the wholesale price charged by the manufacturers. They assume that other costs for the retailer are fixed costs. Fixed costs of manufacturers and the retailer have no impact on market prices in their data. Further discussion of the details of the model is provided below.

The consumer utility in Xiao et al. is a function of the consumption of two types of services – voice and text message usages (voice and text henceforward). They assume that the preferences for the two services are continuously distributed, and these preferences might be correlated. The assumption of the preference distributions for the two services is important as they determine the firm's optimal bundling and non-linear pricing strategies to target different consumer segments. The firm decision of new service plan introduction is treated as exogenous. Because the charges for the two service plans vary according to the specific levels of access fee, free usages and marginal prices, the consumer cost will be different depending on the usage levels of voice and text and which service plan they sign up to. Again, further discussion of the details of the model is provided below.

2.2 Specifying agent maximands

Next, modelers specify objective functions for agents. Objective functions can be treated as a bridge connecting the changes of exogenous variables to changes of endogenous variables that we are interested in (quantity purchased, prices etc.) Consumers are typically modeled as utility maximization agents within a time horizon. The time horizon can vary from single period to infinite period. Firms are typically assumed to maximize profits, again within a single or infinite period. They are called dynamic models if multiple periods are involved and there exists linkage between current (purchase or pricing) decisions and state variables in future periods that will affect the utility or profit function; otherwise they are called static models. The major examples we discuss in this chapter are static models. We refer readers interested in dynamic models to another review paper by Chintagunta et al. (2006b). We visit the dynamic issues in the conclusion section.

The assumptions of the objective functions of consumers and firms in Besanko et al. are common in most marketing papers on pricing strategy. On the demand side, they assume that myopic consumers maximize their utility from purchasing brand j on each shopping trip. The indirect utility for consumer i from brand j on shopping trip t, u_{ijt} is given by

$$u_{ijt} = \gamma_{ij} + x_{jt}\beta_i - \alpha_i p_{jt} + \xi_{jt} + \varepsilon_{ijt} \tag{6.1}$$

where γ_{ij} is consumer i's brand preference, α_i is consumer i's sensitivity to price p_{jt}. The parameter β_i measures consumer i's responsiveness to other marketing variables x_{jt} such as feature and display. The indirect utility for the outside option is normalized to be mean zero with a random component ε_{i0t}. The myopic consumer assumption may be reasonable for ketchup, given that it is a small-price item in the shopping basket. A latent-class structure is used to capture consumer heterogeneity: there are K latent-class consumer segments, and every segment has its own parameters $(\gamma_{ij}^k, \beta_i^k, \alpha_i^k)$ and a probability weight λ^k, $k = 1, \ldots, K$. On the supply side, the manufacturer is assumed to maximize her current period profit by charging wholesale prices for her products, given other manufacturers' pricing strategies and the expected retailer's reaction to wholesale prices. The monopoly retailer is assumed to maximize her profit conditional on manufacturers' wholesale prices. The monopoly retailer r's objective function is modeled as follows:

$$\Pi_r = \sum_{j=1}^{J} (p_j - w_j) \sum_{k=1}^{K} \lambda^k S_j^k M \tag{6.2}$$

The manufacturer m's objective function is the following:

$$\Pi_m = \sum_{j \in B_m} (w_j - mc_j) \sum_{k=1}^{K} \lambda^k S_j^k M \tag{6.3}$$

where p_j is the retail price for brand j, w_j is the wholesale price, mc_j is the marginal cost, λ^k is the size of segment k, S_j^k is the share for brand j within segment k, and B_m is the number of brands offered by manufacturer m with $\sum_m B_m = J$. Finally, M is the quantity of total potential demand in the local market.

In Xiao et al., consumers are assumed to choose a service plan at the beginning of each period to maximize the expected utility within the period (rather than maximize intertemporal utility). If consumer i chooses a service plan j, $j = 1, \ldots, J$, from the focal firm at time t, she will then choose the number of voice minutes x_{it}^V, the number of text messages

x_{it}^D, and quantity of the outside good x_{it}^0 which is the consumption of products and services other than the wireless services. To consume a bundle $\{x_{it}^V, x_{it}^D\}$ from service plan j, the consumer pays an access fee A_j, enjoys a free usage for voice F_j^V and for text F_j^D, and then pays a marginal price for voice p_j^V if $x_{it}^V > F_j^V$, and for text p_j^D if $x_{it}^D > F_j^D$. The authors assume that the utility function is additively separable in voice and text. The consumer's direct utility from the consumption and choosing the service plan, $U_j^i(x_{it}^0, x_{it}^V, x_{it}^D)$ is as follows:

$$U_j^i(x_{it}^0, x_{it}^V, x_{it}^D) = \delta_j + x_{it}^0 + \left[\theta_{it}^V \beta_i^V x_{it}^V - \beta_i^V \frac{(x_{it}^V)^2}{2}\right] + \left[\theta_{it}^D \beta_i^D x_{it}^D - \beta_i^D \frac{(x_{it}^D)^2}{2}\right] + \varepsilon_{ijt} \quad (6.4)$$

where δ_j is a plan-specific preference intercept. θ_{it}^L is the preference parameter of consuming service L, $L = \{V, D\}$, with the following specification:

$$\theta_{it}^L = \theta_i^L + \xi_{it}^L \quad (6.5)$$

where θ_i^L is the mean preference, and ξ_{it}^L is the time-varying usage shock. The heterogeneity of preferences $\theta_i \equiv (\theta_i^V, \theta_i^D)'$ among consumers is assumed to follow a continuous bivariate normal distribution with mean $(\bar{\theta}^V, \bar{\theta}^D)'$ and covariance matrix

$$\begin{bmatrix} \sigma_V^2 & \sigma_{VD} \\ \sigma_{VD} & \sigma_D^2 \end{bmatrix}.$$

Finally, β_i^L, $L = V, D$ are the price sensitivity parameters for voice and text, respectively. The consumer will maximize the above direct utility function subject to the budget constraint:

$$\max_{\{x_{it}^0, x_{it}^V, x_{it}^D\}} U_j^i(x_{it}^0, x_{it}^V, x_{it}^D | d_{it} = j) \quad (6.6)$$

subject to $x_{it}^0 + [p_j^V \cdot (x_{it}^V - F_j^V)]\{x_{it}^V \geq F_j^V\} + [p_j^D \cdot (x_{it}^D - F_j^D)]\{x_{it}^D \geq F_j^D\} + A_j \leq Y_i$

where Y_i is the income of the consumer, and $\{\cdot\}$ is an indicator function that equals one if the logical expression inside is true, and zero otherwise. The variable d_{it} is the consumer's choice at time t. Solving this constrained utility maximization problem, Xiao et al. obtain the consumer's optimal usage decision x_{it}^{L*} as follows:

$$x_{it}^{L*} = \begin{cases} \theta_{it}^L - \frac{1}{\beta_i^L} p_j^L & \text{if } \left\{\theta_{it}^L > F_j^L + \frac{1}{\beta_i^L} p_j^L\right\} \\ F_j^L & \text{if } \left\{F_j^L < \theta_{it}^L \leq F_j^L + \frac{1}{\beta_i^L} p_j^L\right\}, L = V, D \\ \theta_{it}^L & \text{if } \{0 < \theta_{it}^L \leq F_j^L\} \\ 0 & \text{if } \{\theta_{it}^L \leq 0\} \end{cases} \quad (6.7)$$

The consumer's optimal usage is a non-linear function depending on which interval her θ_{it}^L is in. Plugging equation (6.7) into the direct utility function (6.4), the authors obtain consumer i's indirect utility $V_{j,it}$ from choosing the service plan j.

The above examples assume fully rational consumers and firms. Recently there has been a call in marketing to incorporate psychological and sociological theories into modeling consumers' and firms' behaviors, e.g. including reference dependence, fairness, confirmatory bias (see Narasimhan et al., 2005). Such richer specifications will help to explain the observed data which may not be explained by standard economic theory – for example, market response to price increases versus decreases may be asymmetric. This may relate to reference dependence or other psychological factors.

On the firm behavior modeling front too, researchers have increasingly explored firms going beyond pure profit maximization. Chan et al. (2007) find that the manager of an art-performance theater has a larger preference weight for avant-garde shows, which is consistent with the center's mission statement. Sriram and Kadiyali (2006) study if retailers and manufacturers maximize a weighted combination of shares or sales and profits, and what impact this maximand and behavior have on price setting. They find that across three categories, there is evidence that these firms maximize more than pure profits; as expected, firms that care about sales or shares price lower and firms that have higher prices place a negative weight on sales or shares. Wang et al. (2006) model firm managers' objective function as a linear combination of expected profits and shareholder market value, and their empirical evidence supports this assumption. All three studies point to an issue with static supply-side models, i.e. the difficulty of capturing accurately in a static supply-side model the complexities of competitive pricing in a dynamic game. For example, firms can have long-run objectives that might be a combination of shares, profits, shareholder market value etc. In the short run, the firm might consider building market share and sacrificing profitability to do so, with the goal of market dominance and profitability in the longer run. Also, multiple forms of firm behavior are possible in dynamic games, e.g. entry deterrence, predatory pricing, etc. that are hard to capture in a simple static one-shot game.

Another important assumption in most structural pricing studies that deserves attention is the role of uncertainty or information set of both firms and consumers. The typical assumption has been that consumers know their preferences as well as firm prices, firms know the (distribution of) consumer preferences and their own and rivals' pricing strategies. For example, Besanko et al. (2003) assume that consumers know their own brand preferences and the prices charged by retailers, while firms have good knowledge about the underlying segment structure of consumer preferences (the discrete preference types). It seems a reasonable assumption for stable product markets in their paper. However, this assumption might be unrealistic in many instances. Consumers might be unaware of their own preferences given limited information. For example, Xiao et al. (2007) consider two types of consumer uncertainty: first, consumers do not know the usage shock ξ_{it}^L (see equation (6.5)) when they decide which service plan to choose at the beginning of each period. Second, consumers may not know their mean preference types θ_i; instead, they have to learn their preference over time by observing their usage experience. This behavior assumption is consistent with the fact in the data that consumers only switched to the new data-centric plan several periods after the plan had been introduced (some did not switch even at the end of the sample period) even when their benefits would be large had they switched earlier.

Consumers also may not have perfect information on attributes or quality and prices of all products available in the market. Firms might not know the precise distribution of consumer preferences, and might have incomplete knowledge of their own or rivals' production technologies and pricing strategies. Some structural pricing papers have attempted to incorporate these alternative information set assumptions. Miravete (2002) provides empirical evidence of a significant asymmetry of information between consumers and the monopolist under different tariff pricing schemes in the telecommunication industry. We expect future pricing research to study the impact of limited information on either consumers' or firms' decision-making; the results from these studies are likely to be different from those from models with a perfect information assumption.

2.3 Specifying model decision variables
Given that this chapter is about structural models of pricing, price is of course the firm decision variable that we are focusing on. However, there are at least two layers of complexity in studying pricing – the depth in which pricing is studied, and whether other decision variables are studied simultaneously.

Several studies have examined the case of firms choosing a single price for each product. In Besanko et al. (2003), each manufacturer chooses one wholesale price for each of her own brands. The monopolist retailer decides the retail price for each brand conditional on the wholesale price. While modeling each firm as picking one price is an appropriate place for structural pricing studies to begin their inquiry, researchers must acknowledge that a more complicated pricing structure exists in most industries. Firms may optimize prices of product lines and for various customer segments. Similarly, pricing can be either linear, fixed fee, or a more complicated non-linear scheme. An increasing number of studies examines the issue of price discrimination (e.g. Verboven, 2002; Besanko et al., 2003; Miravete and Roller, 2003; Leslie, 2004; McManus, 2004). Further, pricing for multiple products (product line) leads to the possibility of bundling and charging different prices for different product bundles (e.g. Chu et al., 2006). Under these pricing schemes closed-form optimal solutions usually do not exist, and computational complexity has deterred research efforts in the past. However, with recent development in computation and econometric techniques, researchers are able to estimate complicated models. For instance, Xiao et al. (2007) used simulation-based methods to estimate the demand function for voice and text under service bundling with three-part tariffs. Based on these results they further compute the optimal pricing strategy for the firm under various scenarios.

The other issue in building structural models of price is whether price can be studied independently of other strategic choices of firms. Examples include the study of joint determination of price and advertising (Kadiyali, 1996) and study of the relationship between price and channel choice (Chen et al., 2008; Chu et al., 2007). Often, researchers are constrained by data and the complexity of modeling to examine such joint determination. An additional tricky issue is the possible difference in the periodicity of decision-making regarding price decisions versus other decisions, such as advertising or production capacity. If these decisions are made in different planning cycles, e.g. pricing being made weekly and advertising quarterly, it is difficult to estimate jointly optimal price and advertising rules with a different number of data points. Typically, researchers have assumed the same periodicity of such decisions (e.g. Vilcassim et al., 1999). Another alternative used is to examine the issue sequentially, e.g. studying the choice of price conditional on previous locational choice made by the firm when it entered the market (Venkataraman and Kadiyali, 2005). In this case the first-stage locational choice will take account of its impact on pricing in future periods, leading to a more complicated dynamic model setting.

2.4 Modeling price-setting interactions

Given assumptions about consumers and firms maximizing their objectives, how does the market equilibrium evolve and how do these decision-makers interact with one another? The typical assumption about consumer behavior has been price-taking. For firms, the default has been to assume one form of behavior such as Bertrand–Nash, Stackelberg leader–follower or collusive pricing game. An important point to bear in mind when imposing a particular assumption of how firms interact with each other is to justify why this is an appropriate assumption for the industry, given that the estimation results are very dependent on the assumption made. For example, Besanko et al. (2003) assume a manufacturer Stackelberg (MS) game on the supply side. On this assumption, the retailer chooses retail prices to maximize the objective function (equation 6.2) by taking the wholesale prices as given. The first-order condition for the retailer's objective function is

$$\sum_{j=1}^{J}(p_j - w_j)\left(\sum_{k=1}^{K}\lambda^k \frac{\partial S_j^k}{\partial p_{j'}}M\right) + \sum_{k=1}^{K}\lambda^k S_{j'}^k M = 0 \quad (6.8)$$

Manufacturers decide the wholesale prices to maximize the objective function (equation 6.3) by taking into account the retailer's response to wholesale prices, i.e. $\partial p_l/\partial w_j, j, l = 1, \ldots, J$. The first-order condition for a manufacturer with respect to a brand j' is

$$\sum_{j=1}^{J}(w_j - mc_j)\gamma_{jj'}\left(\sum_{k=1}^{K}\lambda^k \sum_{l=1}^{J}\frac{\partial S_j^k}{\partial p_l}\frac{\partial p_l}{\partial w_{j'}}M\right) + \sum_{k=1}^{K}\lambda^k S_{j'}^k M = 0 \quad (6.9)$$

where $\gamma_{jj'}$ is equal to one if brand j and j' are offered by the same manufacturer; otherwise it is equal to zero, and λ^k is the size of segment k, $k = 1, \ldots, K$.

As we discuss later, Besanko et al. demonstrate that the MS game is a reasonable assumption in their data. The manufacturers are selling in the national market, hence they are likely to be leaders in the vertical channel, while the retailer sells in a local market, so she is likely to be a follower. Further, the retailer sells for all manufacturers, so is assumed to maximize category profits. The monopolist retailer assumption is consistent with the conventional retailer wisdom that most consumers do grocery shopping at the same store.

An alternative to imposing an assumption of how firms interact with each other is to compare various alternative assumptions and let the data suggest which model best represents market outcomes. Gasmi et al. (1992) and Kadiyali (1996) are two of the few studies considering a menu of models (forms) and choosing the one that fits the data best. Gasmi et al. (1992) consider different firm conduct behaviors such as Nash in prices and advertising, Nash in prices and collusion in advertising, Stackelberg leader in price and advertising etc. when they analyze the soft-drink market using data on Coca-Cola and Pepsi-Cola from 1968 to 1986. Using a similar approach, Kadiyali (1996) analyzes pricing and advertising competition in the US photographic film industry.[1]

---

[1] Other studies refer to Roy et al. (1994) and Vilcassim et al. (1999).

3. Estimating and testing a pricing structural model

3.1 Going from deterministic model to market outcomes

Outcomes from the economic models of utility and profit maximization are deterministic. In reality, given any parameter set these outcomes will not perfectly match with the observed prices and quantity purchased in the data. To justify these deviations, and hence to construct an econometric model that can be estimated from the data, researchers have typically added two types of errors: errors that capture agent's uncertainty and errors that capture researcher's uncertainty. The agent's uncertainty is when either consumers or firms (retailers and manufacturers) have incomplete information about marketplace variables that influence their objective functions. Researchers may or may not observe such an error term from their data. For example, before visiting a store consumers might know only the distribution of prices and not the exact prices in the store. The researcher's uncertainty stems from researchers not observing from the data some important variables that affect consumers' or firms' objective functions, but consumers and firms observe these variables and account for them in their optimization behavior. An example of such uncertainty is that shelf-space location of items inside a store may affect consumers' purchase decisions but researchers cannot observe shelf-space locations in the data. Such errors become the stochastic components in the structural models which help researchers to rationalize the deviations of predicted outcomes from their models from observed market data. Economic and managerial implications can be very different under these two error assumptions and, depending on the problem, justifying the distributional assumptions of these errors can be critical, as we discuss below.

In their paper, Besanko et al. (2003) assume researcher's uncertainty only and capture it in two kinds of error terms. One is ε_{ijt} in equation (6.1), which is consumer i's idiosyncratic utility for different product alternatives. This is to capture the factors that affect consumers' purchase decision but are unknown to researchers. Besanko et al. follow the standard assumption that ε_{ijt} is double exponentially distributed. Relying on this distribution assumption, the authors can obtain the probability of type k consumer purchasing brand $j(S_{jt}^k)$ as follows:

$$S_{jt}^k = \frac{\exp(\gamma_{ij} + x_{jt}\beta_i - \alpha_i p_{jt} + \xi_{jt})}{1 + \sum_{j=1}^{J}\exp(x_{jt}\beta^k - \alpha^k p_{jt} + \xi_{jt})} \qquad (6.10)$$

Another error term takes account of the product attributes (e.g. coupon availability, national advertising etc.) observed by the consumers but not by the researchers. It is represented by ξ_{jt} in equation (6.1). There is no agent's uncertainty in their model – consumers know own ε_{ijt} and ξ_{jt}, while firms know ξ_{jt} for all brands and the distribution of ε_{ijt}. The existence of ξ_{jt} causes the endogeneity bias in estimation – since firms may take into account its impact on market demand when they make price decisions, it will lead to the potential correlation between firms' prices and ξ_{jt} in consumers' utility function. Ignoring this price endogenity issue in the estimation will lead to biased estimation results and further biased inferences. See Chintagunta et al. (2006a) for a detailed analysis of this issue. We further discuss how to solve this issue in later sections.

Xiao et al. (2007) include both researcher's uncertainty and agent's uncertainty in their econometric model. One is ε_{ijt} in equation (6.4), which captures the researcher's uncertainty of factors that may affect the consumer's choice of service plan but are unobserved by researchers. Similar to Besanko et al. (2003), ε_{ijt} is assumed to follow the double exponential distribution. Another error term is ξ_{it}^L in equation (6.5), which is consumer i's time-varying preference shock of using service L, $L = V$, D. The exact value is assumed to be unknown to the consumer when she makes the service plan choice, and hence captures the agent's uncertainty. The consumer may also have uncertainty about her mean preference $\theta_i \equiv (\theta_i^V, \theta_i^D)'$. Hence, with uncertainties of θ_i and ξ_{it}^L the consumer has to form an expectation for her indirect utility function $V_{j,it}$ conditional on her information set Ω_{it}, which consists of her past usage experience, i.e. $E[V_{j,it}|\Omega_{it}]$. The consumer will choose the alternative with the highest expected indirect utility. For simplicity let us assume that there is no switching cost. Under the distribution assumption of ε_{ijt} we can write down the probability of consumer i choosing plan j as

$$prob_i(j) = \frac{\exp(E[V_{j,it}|\Omega_{it}])}{1 + \sum_{k=1}^{J}\exp(E[V_{k,it}|\Omega_{it}])} \quad (6.11)$$

Note the difference between (6.10) and (6.11). In Besanko et al.'s (2003) set-up there is no agent's uncertainty, i.e. firms know ξ_{jt} for sure; hence they do not need to form an expectation for $(\gamma_{ij} + x_{jt}\beta_i - \alpha_i p_{jt} + \xi_{jt})$.[2] In Xiao et al. (2007), because of the agent's uncertainty each consumer has to form a conditional expectation for $V_{j,it}$ when she makes the service plan choice. In contrast, when deciding how much voice and text to be used during the period, θ_{it} (see equation (6.5)) is fully revealed to the consumer. Hence there is no agent's uncertainty in the usage decisions (see equation (6.7)). The authors assume that the firm knows only the distribution of θ_i for all consumers and not for each individual consumer, the researchers' information on θ_i is exactly the same as the firm's. Further, any potential unobserved product attributes of the service plans in the data have been accounted for by the plan preference parameter δ_j in the utility function (this effect is assumed as fixed over time; see equation (6.4)). Hence there is no price endogeneity issue in estimating the market share function of service plans. However, if there is an aggregate demand shock (say, a sudden change in the trend of using text message among cellular users) observed by the firm but not by researchers, the pricing structure of the new data-centric plan can be correlated with such a shock, and the endogeneity issue will then arise.

Reiss and Wolak (2007) identify other sources of error terms that could be considered in future research. In general, it is fair to say that the treatment of the nature and source of errors has not received the attention that it merits.

3.2 Econometric estimation

Depending on the type of errors in the model, various econometric techniques have been used in model estimation. Simple OLS or the likelihood approach is widely used when the endogeneity issue does not arise. Structural models typically involve the estimation of simultaneous equation systems. For example, in Besanko et al. (2003) the model involves

---

[2] Here Besanko et al. also implicitly assume that consumers know x_{jt} and p_{jt} for sure.

consumer choice, manufacturers' and the retailer's pricing decisions. In Xiao et al. (2007) the model involves both service plan choice and usage decisions. FIML (full information maximum likelihood) or method of moments has been widely used for estimating simultaneous equations. Advanced simulation-based techniques have been developed recently (e.g. see Gourieroux and Monfort, 1996) in model estimation when there is no closed-form expression of the first-order conditions or likelihood functions. For example, Xiao et al. (2007) find that there is no closed-form expression for the plan choice probability function (see equation (6.11)) when there are agent's uncertainty of own θ_i and preference shocks ξ_{it}. In the model estimation, therefore, they use the simulation approach to integrate out the distribution of θ_i (according to consumers' beliefs) and ξ_{it} to evaluate the probability $prob_i(j)$. In general, allowing for a richer type of errors in the model will complicate the computation of the likelihood of observed market outcomes, and in such situations researchers have to rely on simulation methods. Instead of the classical likelihood approach, marketing researchers have often used the Bayesian approach in model estimation, especially when they want to model a flexible distribution of consumer heterogeneity.

A thorny issue relates to the endogeneity or simultaneity problem when the error terms correlate with prices. In empirical input–output (IO) literature, such as in Berry (1994), Berry et al. (1995) and Nevo (2001), generalized method of moments (GMM) and simulated method of moments estimators are usually used. Various advanced methods including contraction mapping and simulation-based estimation have been developed. The general principle is to use instruments for the endogenous variable price in model estimation. An advantage of using instruments in GMM is that researchers do not need to specify *a priori* the joint distribution of the error terms (e.g. ξ_{jt} in Besanko et al., 2003) and the endogenous variable such as price in their model. Recently, there has been a revival in likelihood-based estimates with the rise of Bayesian estimation in tackling the simultaneity issue (Yang et al., 2003). Another issue relates to the existence of multiple equilibria in the model (this is especially true for many dynamic competition models), where the likelihood function is not well defined. GMM in this case is useful for model estimation since it only uses the optimality condition in any of the equilibria but remains agnostic about which equilibrium is chosen by the markets in data. See related discussion in Ackerberg et al. (2007).

The role of instruments is very important in the econometric estimation of structural pricing models. The requirements for a good instrumental variable are 'relevance', i.e. the variable has to be correlated with the endogenous variable such as price; and 'exogeneity', i.e. the variable has to be uncorrelated with the unobserved error term. If relevance is low, researchers will have weak instruments and the error in the estimation can be large. Without exogeneity the instruments are invalid and researchers will obtain inconsistent estimates. Hence researchers have to examine the quality of the instruments they choose according to these aspects. Because structural models explicitly specify how the data are generated based on behavioral assumptions and hence how error terms and decision variables such as price are potentially correlated in the model, it helps us to understand to what extent the chosen instruments are valid. For example, if firms are involved in Bertrand–Nash pricing competition and their objective is to maximize own profit, cost shifters will be relevant and valid instruments for price in the demand equation (Berry et al., 1995). Bresnahan et al. (1997) specify the 'principles of differentiation' instruments, including counts and means of competing products produced by the same manufacturer and by different manufacturers, for price. They argue that their instruments will be valid under different types of non-cooperative games such as Bertrand and Cournot. Lagged prices are sometimes used as instruments for current prices if the error term is independent over time (e.g. see Villas-Boas and Winer, 1999).

The availability of good instruments is closely related to the identification issue in the model. Usually there are several important behavioral parameters that researchers are interested to estimate, and the others in the model are termed 'nuisance' parameters. Unless there is enough variation in data, the behavioral parameters may not be identifiable. For example, price coefficients in a structural model with both demand and supply functions may not be identified if there is no variation in cost variables (e.g. raw materials cost) across markets or across time periods. Identification is not simply a matter of statistical identification of ensuring exclusion restrictions or overidentification restrictions, but rather more of determining the underlying movement in various market drivers that enables identification. A classic example of such identification is Porter (1983). In a study of rail cartels that ship grain, Porter uses the exogenous shift in demand caused by whether lake steamers were in operation or not – if lakes were frozen, this substitute was not available and therefore rail shipment demand increased predictably. This exogenous shift in demand is easily observed by the cartel members. Therefore, when demand falls with the lake steamers operating, cartel members should not misinterpret the drop in their demand as stemming from another cartel member stealing customers by offering better prices secretly. Therefore this exogenous demand shift is an important instrument in inferring whether pricing is collusive or not. This example illustrates both the importance of finding exogenous demand or cost shifters, and using them in theoretically grounded ways to help identify the pricing strategy of firms rather than a simple statistical identification strategy.

Because of the potential correlation between price and ξ_{jt}, Besanko et al. (2003) would not be able to identify the price coefficient α_i unless they had good instruments for price (see equation (6.1)). They choose product characteristics and factor costs as instruments for prices, and use the GMM to estimate their model. They demonstrate the importance of taking account of the price endogeneity issue by estimating the model without considering it. They find that the price coefficient will be downward-biased in the latter case.

Xiao et al. (2007) face a data problem in identifying the price sensitivity parameters β_i^V and β_i^D in their model (see equation (6.4)) – there is no price variation in either of the service plans during the sample period. To solve this problem, for tractability they first assume that there is no heterogeneity in β_i^V and β_i^D. Then they use the fact that some consumers switch service plans during the sample period. Since the two service plans have different pricing structures, by switching plans these consumers face different marginal prices for voice and text in data. The change of usage levels, once above the free usage levels, of the same consumer will help to infer consumer sensitivity to price changes.

The restriction on agents' objective functions is sometimes necessary for model identification. Suppose one wants to allow for a richer specification with non-profit maximization objectives and other biases in the firm pricing decision, such a model may not be identified solely from the data of market prices and quantity demanded. Similarly a consumer choice model allowing for consumers' imperfect information or bounded rationality may not be identifiable from traditional scanner data. In this case one may need to use other data sources such as self-reported consumers' expectation of future prices or firms' expectation of future profits or revenues (e.g. see Chan et al., 2007a and Horsky et al., 2007).[3] Alternatively, creative field experiments in which price variations are exogenously designed (e.g. see Drèze et al., 1994 and Anderson and Simester, 2004) can help to avoid the endogeneity issue. In these cases researchers are certain that observed prices are not affected by aggregate demand shocks; hence consumers' price sensitivity (short- or long-term) can be estimated without resorting to the structural approach.

3.3 Specification analysis

Related to the above discussion, specifications and hence the estimation results are very dependent on the behavioral assumptions made in the model. While some assumptions have to be made to build structure (e.g. the market demand functional form and the distribution assumption of unobserved errors), when researchers use the reduced-form approach they rely less on the specification of the behavioral assumptions; hence their models may be more flexible to fit with the data. Most studies using the structural approach have not shown too much due diligence in comparing alternative behavioral assumptions or justifying from managerial or other sources why their assumptions are justified. In this regard, some issues to keep in mind are mentioned below.

First, model fit should not be the only criterion in determining whether or not the model assumptions are reasonable. Indeed, if model fit is the only criterion, researchers will often find that reduced-form models dominate structural models whose functional specification relies heavily on restrictive behavioral assumptions. The objective of a structural pricing model should not always be to minimize statistical error but to minimize model assumption error. The former refers to the objective of finding the best fit with the data. The latter refers to identifying a set of economic and behavioral theories that makes sense in explaining the data-generating process. As mentioned in previous sections, some questions related to behavioral assumptions are: are firms competitive or colluding with each other? Are consumers or firms maximizing long-term profit or value functions? Is there asymmetric information between firms and consumers? Does learning better capture firm and consumer behavior than the assumption of perfect information? Are there some 'irrational' behaviors that can be explained by psychological or sociology theory? In deciding which assumption to choose, researchers might have to make a tradeoff in choosing a model that describes the market more reasonably, even if this might mean sacrificing the model fit. For example, Besanko et al. (2003) model the interactions between manufacturers and the retailer in the channel where manufacturers are Stackleberg price leaders. Even if the authors found that a model assuming the retailer as the Stackleberg price leader over national manufacturers fits better with the price data, they might not want to use such a specification, considering the market reality.

So if model fit is not always the best means to judge the performance of a pricing structural model, what is? An important test is whether the model assumptions lead to sensible results when we go from model assumptions to managerial recommendations. For

---

[3] Another stream of literature uses bounded estimators when the structural parameters are not point-estimable.

example, Besanko et al. (2003) compared the equilibrium outcome under their specification with different alternative assumptions. The implied retail margins from their model are face valid and therefore support the feasibility of the manufacturer Stackelberg leader assumption. In another example Xiao et al. (2007) find that with consumer learning and switching cost in their model, they can explain why some consumers switch to the new service plan while the others do not. Another way to see whether results are sensible is to conduct policy simulations and see if those results are sensible. We discuss more on this below.

3.4 Policy analysis

As discussed above, by building the structural model to analyze the underlying consumer preferences and firms' pricing decisions, we can use the structural analyses to answer some questions which cannot be addressed by reduced-form analysis precisely. Specifically, the results of a structural model can be used to conduct managerially useful simulation exercises. These exercises are valuable because the assumed policies can be out of sample (prices set at a level away from the sample observations, change in the mode of interactions between firms and consumers, entry and exit in the market, new government restrictions, and hypothetical consumer preference structure etc.) and will not be subject to the Lucas critique.

Besanko et al. (2003) assume that the retailer sets a uniform price in the model. Based on their demand and supply system estimates, they simulate the effects of two kinds of third-degree price discrimination, which are initiated by either the retailer or manufacturers. Retailer-initiated price discrimination means that the retailer sets segment-specific prices to maximize her profits. Manufacturer-initiated price discrimination means that manufacturers induce the retailer to charge segment-specific prices by offering her scanback discounts. The policy experiments show that firms can increase profit by discriminating a finite number of customer segments under both cases. So in this empirical analysis, price discrimination under competition does not lead to all-out competition (i.e. prices lower than uniform pricing strategy). Allowing for both vertical product differentiation and horizontal differentiation, they find empirical evidence that is against the theoretical finding that price discrimination under competition will lead to the prisoner's dilemma. This provides important managerial insights.

Xiao et al. (2007) illustrate how the firm may use its estimation result of the consumer preferences for voice and text to better segment the market. In particular, they find that preferences for voice and text are weakly positively correlated, indicating that a consumer with high preference for voice is more likely to have high preference for text. Based on their results they calculate the market response to changes in the three-part tariff structure, i.e. access fee, free usages and marginal prices. Finally they compute the optimal pricing structure for the two service plans, and predict the types of consumers, in terms of preferences for voice and text, that each service plan will be able to attract. They further compare the result with the predicted profits when the firm charges a two-part tariff under the bundling case, and when the firm charges two- and three-part tariffs but without bundling the two services. They find that a computed optimal three-part tariff under bundling generates about 38 percent higher revenue than at the current prices, although expected market share is 10 percent lower. Compared with the optimal prices without bundling, the three-part tariff will generate about 8 percent higher revenue. The impact on consumer welfare may vary depending on the consumer segments.

128 *Handbook of pricing research in marketing*

More examples covering different aspects of policy simulations relating to pricing can be found. For example, in addition to Xiao et al. above, Leslie (2004), Lambrecht et al. (2007) and Iyengar (2006) consider non-linear pricing. Draganska and Jain (2005) study the optimal pricing strategies across and within product lines in the yogurt industry. A similar analysis of product-line pricing and assortment decisions is in Draganska et al. (2007). Two papers that cover policy analyses with channel changes are Chen et al. (2008) and Chu et al. (2006). As all these examples indicate, policy analyses form the core of the managerially useful output of structural pricing studies.

4. Summary

Structural models of pricing can be useful in understanding the consumer- and firm-based drivers of market prices. They can also be useful in generating robust and managerially useful implications. That said, given the criticality of behavioral assumptions and instrumental variables in structural price models, researchers need to justify the use of these with great care. More careful analysis of the issues of model comparison and model identification by checking with the data will also be very useful. Yet another area in which structural models can be improved is the modeling of behavioral issues in pricing, relating to both consumers and firms. This is becoming more important following the call to incorporate psychological and sociological theory to better explain the consumer and firm behaviors. Narasimhan et al. (2005) discuss how, despite the demonstration of a variety of behavioral anomalies, very few theoretical models have attempted to incorporate these in their formulation. The same is true of structural pricing work. An exception is Conlin et al. (2007), who show that people are over-influenced by the weather on the day that they make their clothing purchases (rather than accurately forecasting the weather for the days of actual usage of the clothing item).

One way to allow for modeling behavioral issues is to enrich data sources. Additional data may be necessary for researchers to identify a richer set of behavioral assumptions from the data. For example, if we want to model how firms form expectations about their rivals' pricing strategy, we might need to supplement market data with surveys. An example of such a study is Chan et al. (2007a), who use the managerial self-reported expectations of ticket sales and advertising expenditures to understand the bias and uncertainty of managers when they make advertising decisions. Bajari and Hortacsu (2005) use lab experiment data to test if rational economic theories can explain economic outcomes in auction markets. If such data are difficult to obtain, researchers need, at the least, to acknowledge how the behavioral assumptions in their structural models can be tested with additional data.

This summary would be incomplete without consideration of alternatives to structural models of pricing. Reduced-form methods might be useful in providing stylized facts about pricing and other market outcomes. For example, Kadiyali et al. (2007) find that in real-estate deals where the buyer's agent and the seller's agent work for the same company, list prices are strategically set higher (and result in higher sales prices). A full model of buyer and seller dynamics, including the role for buyer and seller agents, accounting for endogenous entries and exits is beyond current methodologies. However, it is still useful to establish these stylized facts because they might reveal market inefficiencies that are important to both buyers and sellers and antitrust authorities. Similarly, natural experiments-based reduced-form models, e.g. Ailawadi et al.'s (2001) research on

P&G's switch to EDLP (everyday low pricing), offer very interesting avenues for understanding markets when full models are hard to build. For other marketing applications also see Drèze et al. (1994) and Anderson and Simester (2004). We expect that, in the future, marketing researchers will spend more effort in data collection though various sources such as survey and lab or natural experiments, and use these additional data to identify a richer set of behavioral assumptions in their models.

Interesting managerial implications may be generated from dynamically modeling the consumer choice and firm pricing behavior. Some of the marketing applications of dynamic models, such as Erdem et al. (2003), Sun (2005), Hendel and Nevo (2006) and Chan et al. (2007b), study how consumers' price expectations change their purchase and inventory-holding behaviors. In the dynamic competition games among firms, the equilibrium concept is typically Markov-perfect Nash equilibrium; that is, agents maximize an objective function, taking into account other agents' behavior and the effect of their current decisions on future state variables (e.g. market share, brand equity and productivity). A wide variety of strategies may be adopted, and some of the equilibrium outcomes are very difficult to model or compute. There has not been much empirical application in the literature due to these issues. However, with the recent development of computation and econometric techniques we start to see growing interest in academic research. For example, Nair (2007) studies the skimming strategies for video games, and Che et al. (2007) study pricing competition when consumer demand is state-dependent (e.g. switching cost, inertia or variety-seeking in consumer behavior) in the breakfast cereal market. These authors have made some interesting findings that would not have emerged from the static models. Studying the interactions of policies with a short-term impact on profitability such as price promotion and others with a long-term impact such as location and R&D investment decisions under the dynamic framework is another important area for future research. Finally, due to the computation complexity researchers might have to make some reduced-form assumptions in their models (e.g. reduced-form price expectation or demand function), and focus on the structural aspect of the strategic behaviors such as strategic inventory-holding among households or entry and exit decisions of firms. As a result the difference between the structural and the reduced-form approach is even less stark, as we discussed in the introduction.

References

Ackerberg, D., C.L. Benkard, S. Berry and A. Pakes (2007), 'Econometric tools for analyzing market outcomes', in J.J. Heckman and E. Leamer (eds), *Handbook of Econometrics*, vol. 6, Amsterdam and Oxford: Elsevier.

Ailawadi, K., D. Lehmann and S. Neslin (2001), 'Market response to a major policy change in the marketing mix: learning from P&G's value pricing strategy', *Journal of Marketing*, **65** (1), 44–61.

Anderson, E. and D. Simester (2004), 'Long-run effects of promotion depth on new versus established customers: three field studies', *Marketing Science*, **23** (1), 4–20.

Bajari, P. and A. Hortacsu (2005), 'Are structural estimates of auction models reasonable? Evidence from experimental data', *Journal of Political Economy*, **4** (113), 703–41.

Berry, S. (1994), 'Estimating discrete-choice models of product differentiation', *Rand Journal of Economics*, **25** (2), 242–62.

Berry, S., J. Levinsohn and A. Pakes (1995), 'Automobile prices in market equilibrium', *Econometrica*, **63**, 841–90.

Besanko, D., S. Gupta and D. Jain (1998), 'Logit demand estimation under competitive pricing behavior: an equilibrium framework', *Management Science*, **44** (11), 1533–47.

Besanko, D., J.-P. Dubé and S. Gupta (2003), 'Competitive price discrimination strategies in a vertical channel using aggregate retail data', *Management Science*, **49**, 1121–38.

Bresnahan, T.F., S. Stern and M. Trajtenberg (1997), 'Market segmentation and the sources of rents from innovation: personal computers in the late 1980s', *Rand Journal of Economics*, **28** (0, Special Issue in Honor of Richard E. Quandt), S17–S44.
Chan, T., B. Hamilton and C. Makler (2007a), 'Managerial expectations and decision makings in a non-profit environment: advertising for the performing arts', Working Paper, Washington University in St Louis.
Chan, T., C. Narasimhan and Q. Zhang (2007b), 'Decomposing promotional effects with a dynamic structural model of flexible consumption', Working Paper, Washington University in St Louis.
Che, H., K. Sudhir and P.B. Seetharaman (2007), 'Bounded rationality in pricing under state dependent demand: do firms look ahead? How far ahead?', *Journal of Market Research*, **44** (3), 434–49.
Chen, X., G. John and O. Narasimhan (2008), 'Assessing the effects of a channel switch', *Marketing Science*, **27** (3), 398–416.
Chintagunta, P.K. (2002), 'Investigating category pricing behavior in a retail chain', *Journal of Marketing Research*, **39** (2), 141–54.
Chintagunta, P. K., J.-P. Dubé and V. Singh (2003), 'Balancing profitability and customer welfare in a supermarket chain', *Quantitative Marketing and Economics*, **1** (1), 111–47.
Chintagunta, P.K., V. Kadiyali and N. Vilcassim (2006a), 'Endogeneity and simultaneity in competitive pricing and advertising: a logit demand analysis', *Journal of Business*, **79** (6), 2761–88.
Chintagunta, P.K., T. Erdem, P. Rossi and M. Wedel (2006b), 'Structural modeling in marketing: review and assessment', *Marketing Science*, **25** (6), 604–16.
Chu, C.H., P. Leslie and A. Sorensen (2006), 'Good enough bundling', Working Paper, Stanford University.
Chu, J., P.K. Chintagunta and N. Vilcassim (2007), 'Assessing the economic value of distribution channels – an application to the PC industry', *Journal of Marketing Research*, **44** (1), 29–41.
Conlin, M., T. O'Donoghue and T. Volgelsang (2007), 'Projection bias in catalog orders', *American Economic Review*, **97** (4), 1217–49.
Draganska, M. and D.C. Jain (2005), 'Consumer preferences and product-line pricing strategies: an empirical analysis', *Marketing Science*, **25** (2), 164–74.
Draganska, M., M. Mazzeo and K. Seim (2007), 'Beyond plain vanilla: modeling joint pricing and product assortment choices', Working Paper, Stanford University.
Drèze, X., S. Hoch and M. Purk (1994), 'EDLP, Hi-Lo, and margin arithmetic', *Journal of Marketing*, **58** (October), 16–29.
Erdem, T., S. Imai and M.P. Keane (2003), 'Consumer price and promotion expectations: capturing consumer brand and quantity choice dynamics under price uncertainty', *Quantitative Marketing and Economics*, **1**, 5–64.
Gasmi, F., J.J. Laffont, and Q. Vuong (1992), 'Econometric analysis of collusive behavior in a soft-drink market', *Journal of Economics and Management Strategy*, **1**, 277–311.
Gourieroux, C. and A. Monfort (1996), *Simulation-based Econometric Methods*, CORE Lectures, New York: Oxford University Press.
Hendel, I. and A. Nevo (2006), 'Measuring the implications of sales and consumer inventory behavior', *Econometrica*, **74**, 1637–73.
Horsky, D. and P. Nelson (1992), 'New brand positioning and pricing in an oligopolistic market', *Marketing Science*, **11** (2), 133–53.
Horsky, D., S. Shin and S. Misra (2007), 'Disentangling preferences and learning in brand choice models', Working Paper, University of Rochester.
Iyengar, R. (2006), 'A structural demand analysis for wireless services under nonlinear pricing schemes', Working Paper, Columbia University.
Kadiyali, V. (1996), 'Entry, its deterrence, and its accommodation: the case of the U.S. photographic film industry', *RAND Journal of Economics*, **78** (3), 452–78.
Kadiyali, V., N. Vilcassim and P.K. Chintagunta (1996), 'Empirical analysis of competitive product line pricing decisions: lead, follow or move together?', *Journal of Business*, **9**, 459–87.
Kadiyali, V., J. Prince and D. Simon (2007), 'The impact of agency on deal price and timing in housing markets', Working Paper, Cornell University.
Lambrecht, A., K. Seim and B. Skiera (2007), 'Does uncertainty matter? Consumer behavior under three-part tariffs', *Marketing Science*, **26** (5), 698–710.
Leslie, P. (2004), 'Price discrimination in Broadway theater', *RAND Journal of Economics*, **35** (3), 520–41.
McManus, B. (2004), 'Nonlinear pricing in an oligopoly market: the case of specialty coffee', Working Paper, Washington University in St Louis.
Miravete, E.J. (2002), 'Estimating demand for local telephone service with asymmetric information and optional calling plans', *Review of Economic Studies*, **69** (241), 943–71.
Miravete, E.J. and L.H. Roller (2003), 'Competitive nonlinear pricing in duopoly equilibrium: the early cellular telephone industry', Working Paper, University of Pennsylvania.

Nair, H. (2007), 'Intertemporal price discrimination with forward-looking consumers: application to the US market for console video-games', *Quantitative Marketing and Economics*, **5** (3), 239–92.
Narasimhan, C., C. He, E. Anderson, L. Brenner, P. Desai, D. Kuksov, P. Messinger, S. Moorthy, J. Nunes, Y. Rottenstreich, R. Staelin, G. Wu and Z. Zhang (2005), 'Incorporating behavioral anomalies in strategic models', *Marketing Letters*, **16**, 361–73.
Narayanan, S., P.K. Chintagunta and E.J. Miravete (2007), 'The role of self selection and usage uncertainty in the demand for local telephone service', *Quantitative Marketing and Economics*, **5** (1), 1–34.
Nevo, A. (2001), 'Measuring market power in the ready-to-eat cereal industry', *Econometrica*, **69**, 307–40.
Pakes, A. (2003), 'Common sense and simplicity in empirical industrial organization', Working Paper, Harvard University.
Pancras, J. and K. Sudhir (2007), 'Optimal marketing strategies for a customer data intermediary', *Journal of Marketing Research*, **44** (4), 560–78.
Porter, R. (1983), 'A study of cartel stability: the JEC 1880–1886', *Bell Journal of Economics*, **14** (2), 301–14.
Reiss, P.C. and F.A. Wolak (2007), 'Structural econometric modeling: rationales and examples from industrial organization', in J.J. Heckman and E. Leamer (eds), *Handbook of Econometrics*, vol. 6, Amsterdam: North-Holland, pp. 4277–416.
Richards, T.J. (2007), 'A nested logit model of strategic promotion', *Quantitative Marketing and Economics*, **5**, 63–91.
Roy, A., D.M. Hanssens and J.S. Raju (1994), 'Competitive pricing by a price leader', *Management Science*, **40** (7), 809–23.
Sriram, S. and V. Kadiyali (2006), 'Manufacturer–retailer competition in grocery retailing channels: an empirical investigation of three categories', Working Paper, Cornell University.
Sudhir, K. (2001), 'Competitive pricing behavior in the auto market: a structural analysis', *Marketing Science*, **20** (1), 42–60.
Sudhir, K, P.K.Chintagunta and V. Kadiyali (2005), 'Time varying competition', *Marketing Science*, **24** (1), 96–109.
Sun, B. (2005), 'Promotion effect on endogenous consumption', *Marketing Science*, **24** (3), 430–43.
Thomadsen, R. (2007), 'Product positioning and competition: the role of location in the fast food industry', *Marketing Science*, **26** (6), 792–804.
Venkataraman, S. and V. Kadiyali (2005), 'Price–location links in consumer and competitive choices: an application of the generalized nested logit', Working Paper, Cornell University.
Verboven, F. (2002), 'Quality-based price discrimination and tax incidence: evidence from gasoline and diesel cars', *Rand Journal of Economics*, **33** (2), 275–97.
Vilcassim, N., V. Kadiyali and P.K. Chintagunta (1999), 'Investigating dynamic multiform market interactions in price and advertising', *Management Science*, **45** (4), 499–518.
Villa-Boas, J.M. and R.S. Winer (1999), 'Endogeneity in brand choice models', *Management Science*, **45**, 1324–38.
Wang, S.S., K.W. Stiegert and T.P. Dhar (2006), 'Strategic pricing behavior under asset value maximization', Working Paper, University of Wisconsin-Madison.
Xiao, P., T. Chan and C. Narasimhan (2007), 'Consumer choice of service plan: switching cost and usage uncertainty', Working Paper, Washington University in St Louis.
Yang, S., G.M. Allenby and Y. Chen (2003), 'A Bayesian analysis of simultaneous demand and supply', *Quantitative Marketing and Economics*, **1**, 251–75.

7 Heuristics in numerical cognition: implications for pricing
Manoj Thomas and Vicki Morwitz

Abstract
In this chapter we review two distinct streams of literature, the numerical cognition literature and the judgment and decision-making literature, to understand the psychological mechanisms that underlie consumers' responses to prices. The judgment and decision-making literature identifies three heuristics that manifest in many everyday judgments and decisions – anchoring, representativeness and availability. We suggest that these heuristics also influence judgments consumers make concerning the magnitude of prices. We discuss three specific instances of these heuristics: the left-digit anchoring effect, the precision effect, and the ease of computation effect respectively. The left-digit anchoring effect refers to the observation that people tend to incorrectly judge the difference between $4.00 and $2.99 to be larger than that between $4.01 and $3.00. The precision effect reflects the influence of the representativeness of digit patterns on magnitude judgments. Larger magnitudes are usually rounded and therefore have many zeros, whereas smaller magnitudes are usually expressed as precise numbers; so relying on the representativeness of digit patterns can make people incorrectly judge a price of $391 534 to be lower than a price of $390 000. The ease of computation effect shows that magnitude judgments are based not only on the output of a mental computation, but also on its experienced ease or difficulty. Usually it is easier to compare two dissimilar magnitudes than two similar magnitudes; overuse of this heuristic can make people incorrectly judge the difference to be larger for pairs with easier computations (e.g. $5.00–$4.00) than for pairs with difficult computations (e.g. $4.97–$3.96). These, and the other reviewed results, reveal that price magnitude judgments entail not only deliberative rule-based processes but also instinctive associative processes

Introduction
The seminal work by Tversky and Kahneman (1974) and Kahneman and Tversky (2000) has identified a set of reasoning heuristics that appear to characterize much of people's everyday judgments and decision-making. Three heuristics, presumably because of their ubiquity, have particularly attracted the attention of researchers – anchoring, availability and representativeness. In this chapter, we review these three heuristics in the context of price cognition. We use the term price cognition as a generic term to refer to the cognitive processes that underlie consumers' judgments concerning the magnitude of a price and their judgments of the magnitude of the difference between two prices. Price magnitude judgment refers to a buyer's subjective assessment of the extent to which an offered price is low or high. Judgments of the magnitude of the difference between two prices are required in many purchase situations; for example, when buyers compare two products, or when they assess the difference between a regular price and sale price of a product on sale.

Price cognition plays a pivotal role in models of consumer behavior postulated in the economics as well as the psychology literature (Monroe, 2003; Winer, 2006). Both streams of literature concur on the following assumption: a buyer's subjective judgment of the magnitude of a price is an important determinant in purchase decisions. However, economists and psychologists differ in the way they characterize the manner in which buyers process the price information. The following two assumptions play a fundamental, though often implicit, role in traditional models of buyer behavior posited by economists: (i) people are aware of the factors that influence their price cognition; and (ii) biases in judgments are caused by volitional inattention or cognitive miserliness and therefore can be prevented at will. In this chapter, we challenge these assumptions about awareness and intentionality (of biases) in price cognition. We begin by reviewing the numerical cognition literature to characterize the price cognition process. We then review evidence to suggest that price magnitude judgments entail not only deliberative rule-based processes, but also instinctive associative processes often referred to as heuristics. Specifically, in this chapter we discuss how anchoring, availability and representativeness heuristics affect the price cognition process.

Our choice of the 'heuristics in numerical cognition' approach to understanding price cognition has been guided by two major considerations. First, we believe an informed characterization of the price cognition process calls for an integration of the numerical cognition literature and the judgment and decision-making literature. Second, the heuristics in the numerical cognition approach could offer a unifying framework to discuss the many seemingly unrelated effects reported in the pricing literature. We explicate each of these considerations in some detail.

First, in order to critically examine the issues of awareness and intentionality in price cognition, we need to examine the two issues in the terms of the underlying representations as well as the processes that operate on these representations.[1] The questions about representations are: what are the different forms in which a multi-digit price is represented in consumers' minds? Are price magnitude judgments based on analog representations or on symbolic representations? The questions about process are: what processes operate on the different types of representations? Are these processes deliberative and rule-based or instinctive and associative? To answer these questions, we review the numerical cognition literature, and then the judgment and decision-making (JDM) literature. The numerical cognition literature elucidates how numbers are represented in people's minds, and some of the basic, lower-level processes that operate on these representations. Research on numerical cognition tends to draw inferences from meticulous analyses of response latency patterns measured down to the milliseconds and error rates in sterile[2] numerical tasks such as binary magnitude judgments and parity judgments. For example, in a typical magnitude judgment task, several numbers are flashed on a computer screen in a random order, and participants have to quickly indicate whether the stimuli are higher or lower than another number, the comparison standard. In a parity judgment task, instead of making magnitude judgments, participants have to indicate whether the stimuli are odd or even. Using such tasks, numerical cognition researchers study how various factors such as magnitude, distance from a comparison standard, and response codes affect participants' response time and error rates. Several robust and reliable effects have emerged from this stream of research: the distance effect (Moyer and Landauer, 1967), the problem size effect (Ashcraft, 1995), the size congruity effect (Henik and Tzelgov,

---

[1] See Markman (1999) for a discussion on the distinction between symbolic and analog representations of knowledge, and the implications of this distinction for the processes that operate on these representations.

[2] We describe them as sterile because it could be argued that many of these tasks are not presented in a practical context and are not representative of everyday judgments.

1982), and the spatial–numerical association effect (also referred to as SNARC; Dehaene et al., 1993), etc. Offering a parsimonious and coherent account for all these effects using the same framework has proved to be a challenge. Competing theoretical models of representations and processing of numerical information continue to strive towards this goal (Dehaene, 1992; McCloskey and Macaruso, 1995).

In contrast, the JDM research tends to be concerned with methods for discerning the nature of everyday judgments and deviations from normative behavior. The JDM literature offers a richer characterization of the cognitive rules that people use in everyday judgments. Research of this nature draws on economics in addition to social and cognitive psychology. Thus the integration of the numerical cognition and the JDM streams of literature, we believe, is not only useful but also necessary for the understanding of the price cognition process.

Second, the heuristics in the numerical cognition approach could serve as a unifying framework for the behavioral pricing literature. To illustrate with an example, research has shown that people's judgments of the magnitude of price differences are anchored on the left-most digits of the prices (Thomas and Morwitz, 2005). People incorrectly judge the difference between 6.00 and 4.95 to be larger than that between 6.05 and 5.00 due to the left-digit anchoring effect. In seemingly unrelated research, it has been shown that incidental prices can affect buyers' valuation of goods and their willingness to pay. Specifically, Nunes and Boatwright (2004) found that the price of a sweatshirt on display at an adjacent seller can influence a shopper's willingness to pay for a music CD. Conceptualizing both these effects as manifestations of a common anchoring heuristic could facilitate the development of some generalizable principles of price cognition.

A caveat is due here. As some readers might have discerned by now, this chapter does not purport to be a comprehensive review of the behavioral pricing literature. Our primary objective is to explore whether focusing on the heuristics used in numerical cognition will bring forth some generalizable principles of price cognition. Further, we hope that this endeavor will contribute to the debate on awareness and intentionality (of biases) in price cognition. In the course of doing this, a review of the numerical cognition literature is necessitated because it provides us with the language (i.e. a typology of processes and representations) to delineate the mechanisms underlying these heuristics. Given this objective, this review will discuss only a few selected research studies in the behavioral pricing area that illustrate the use of anchoring, availability and representativeness in price magnitude judgments and judgments of the magnitude of a price difference. Readers interested in a more comprehensive review of the behavioral pricing literature are referred to Monroe and Lee (1999) for a numerical cognition perspective, Monroe (2003) and Raghubir (2006) for information-processing perspectives, and Winer (2006) for a managerial perspective on behavioral pricing.

Numerical cognition and pricing
An important question that has emerged as a dominant theme in the JDM literature, and of particular relevance to the issue of awareness and intentionality of biases, is whether heuristics are based on quick and associative processes (i.e. system 1) or slow and rule-based processes (i.e. system 2). As discussed by Kahneman and Frederick (2002), the influence of system 1 on judgments is believed to be less deliberate and more automatic than that of system 2. Characterizing the numerical cognition process as an interaction

of slow and rule-based, and fast and associative processes will be helpful in delineating the volitional and unintended elements of the heuristics used in numerical cognition. However, the meaning of 'quick and associative' in the context of numerical cognition is not clear. How can some numerical computations be faster and easier than others? Why are people unable to verbalize some aspects of numerical cognition processes? To understand more about associative processes in numerical cognition, we focus on two important findings in the numerical cognition literature in this review: (i) cognitive arithmetic is not always based on online computations; instead it involves associative knowledge structures stored in memory; and (ii) numbers can also be represented as analog magnitudes and processed non-verbally, in much the same manner as other analog stimuli such as light and sound are represented and processed.

Evidence for associative processes in cognitive arithmetic
The area of cognitive psychology that examines the mental representation and the cognitive processes that underlie responses to a math task is referred to as cognitive arithmetic. Although researchers in this area have traditionally focused on the study of addition and multiplication, we believe that in the context of price cognition, since consumers often consider differences in prices of comparable products, subtraction is perhaps the most ubiquitous arithmetic operation. Some of the findings reviewed below were initially studied in the context of addition and multiplication; however, subsequent research has revealed that they are relevant to subtraction (Zbrodoff and Logan, 2005).

Ashcraft (1995) describes several pieces of evidence to suggest that responses to arithmetic problems are based not only on online computations but also on retrieval from associative knowledge structures. First, it has been shown that some problems can be solved faster than others. Problems that entail smaller numbers (e.g. $2 + 3$) are solved faster than problems that entail larger numbers (e.g. $7 + 9$); problems that include the number 5 are solved faster than problems that do not; and problems with identical operands (e.g. 8×8) are solved faster than other problems (e.g. 8×7). These patterns of response times for mental computations are comparable to the word frequency effects in language; they reflect the frequency with which arithmetic facts are acquired and practiced. Second, as in word recognition, repetition affects arithmetic fact retrieval: it is easier to respond to $7 + 9 = 16$ when it is presented the second time. Third, there is evidence for unintended interference in mental calculations by automatic activation of irrelevant arithmetic facts. For example, in a verification task, participants are less likely to respond 'false' to problems such as $3 + 4 = 12$ and $3 \times 4 = 7$ because the incorrect solutions to these problems are correct solutions to similar problems stored in the memory. This and other evidence reviewed by Ashcraft (1995) lead to an important conclusion about mental arithmetic: solutions to arithmetic problems are not always computed online; instead, mental arithmetic is based on associative knowledge structures in the memory.

The representation of arithmetic facts as associative knowledge structures has implications for price cognition processes. The spontaneous activation of arithmetic facts could influence consumers' judgments. For example, while computing the difference between \$4.00 and \$2.99, the left-digit difference ($4 - 2 = 2$) might spontaneously 'pop up' in the consumer's mind and might serve as an unintended anchor in numerical judgments. Such left-digit anchoring could cause consumers to incorrectly judge the difference between \$4.00 and \$2.99 to be larger than that between \$4.01 and \$3.00. Further, the spontaneous

136 *Handbook of pricing research in marketing*

activation of arithmetic facts makes some mental problems easier than others. For example, consumers will be able to assess the price difference between $500 and $400 much faster than that between $497 and $394. As we discuss later in this chapter, this ease by itself could influence consumers' price magnitude judgments.

Evidence for non-verbal processing of numbers
The arithmetic tasks discussed in the preceding section assume symbolic representations of numbers; the strings of digits in a multi-digit number are assumed to be represented in the working/long-term memory, preserving the syntactic structure of tens and units. However, magnitude judgments might not always entail such symbolic representations; instead they are assumed to entail analog representations. Analog representations refer to non-symbolic magnitude representations of the numbers on a subjective 'small–large'

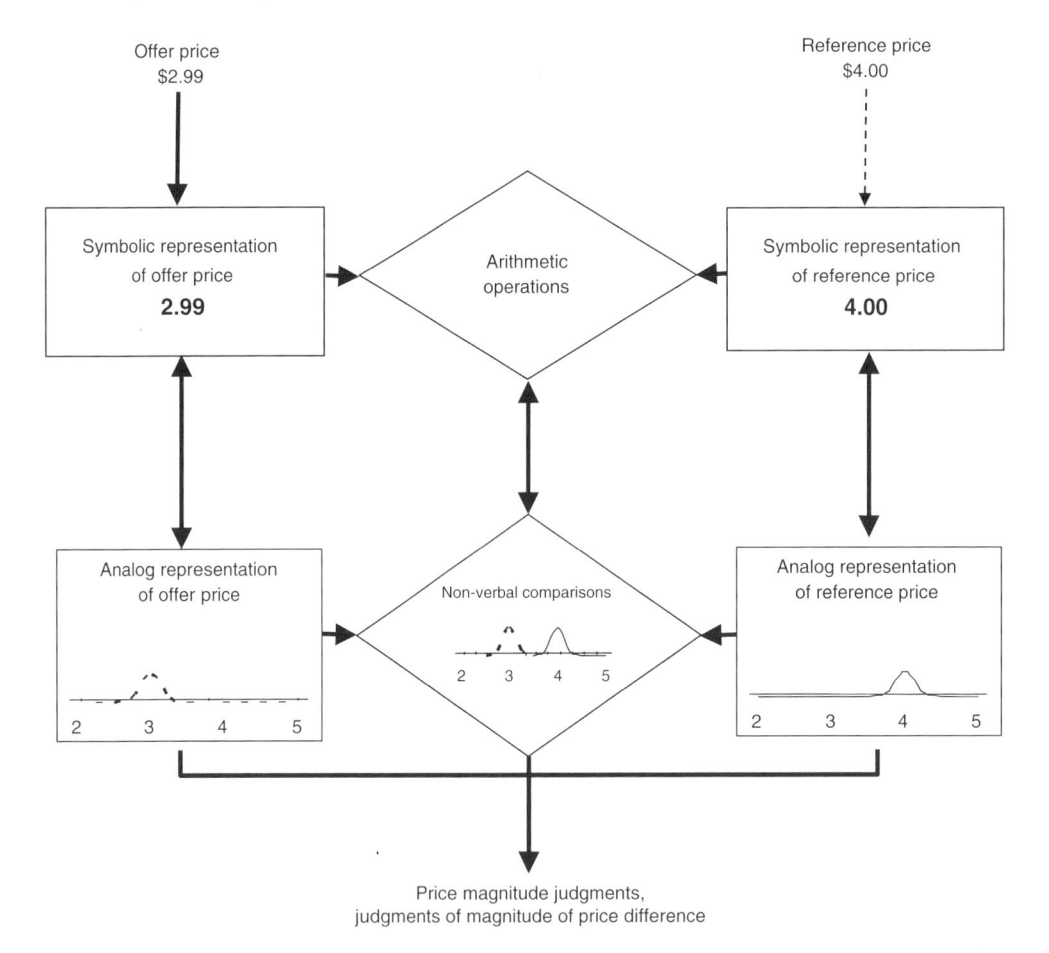

Note: Price cognition is postulated to entail symbolic and analog representations. The arithmetic processes that operate on symbolic representations could be deliberative and rule-based or instinctive and associative. The non-verbal processes that operate on analog representations are likely to be instinctive and associative.

Figure 7.1 Putative processes in price cognition

mental number line (see Figure 7.1). In this section, we discuss the relevance of analog representations for price cognition.

When asked why she did not buy her usual brand of laundry detergent this week, a consumer might respond that her decision was based on the size of the difference between this week's price and the previous week's price. Such a response might mislead an observer to conclude that the numerical cognition process that led to this response might have entailed a symbolic comparison of two weekly prices: this week's price $4.49 minus the previous week's price $3.99 = 50 cents. While such a response could indeed be based on mental subtraction of symbolic representations, it is also possible that the response might have been based on the analog representations, in much the same way as she would judge the difference in hues of a light and a dark color, or the difference in the luminosity of a 30 watt bulb and a 60 watt bulb. Analog representations refer to semantic magnitude representations of the numbers on a subjective mental scale. Such analog representations are assumed to be similar to the representations of psychophysical stimuli such as light, sound, size etc. Dehaene (1992, p. 20) suggests that many of our daily numerical cognition tasks are based on analog judgments: 'tasks such as measurement, comparison of prices, or approximate calculations, solicit an approximate mode in which we access and manipulate a mental model of approximate quantities similar to a mental number line'.

Several pieces of evidence support the notion that numerical cognition entails analog representations. The most frequently cited evidence for the use of analog representations is the distance effect. In a typical distance effect experiment (e.g. Moyer and Landauer, 1967), pairs of digits such as 7 and 9 are flashed on the screen, and participants are asked to identify the higher digit by pressing one of two keys. The main finding from this experiment is that when the two digits stand for very different analog quantities such as 2 and 9, subjects respond quickly and accurately. But their response time slows down by more than 100 milliseconds when the two digits are numerically closer, such as 7 and 9. The distance effect has been interpreted by many cognitive psychologists as evidence for the proposition that magnitude judgments entail an internal analog scale. Dehaene suggests (p. 74):

> the brain does not stop at recognizing digit shapes. It rapidly recognizes that at the level of their quantitative meaning, digit 4 is indeed closer to 5 than 1 is. An analogical representation of the quantitative properties of Arabic numerals, which preserve the proximity relations between them, is hidden somewhere in the cerebral sulci and gyri. Whenever we see a digit, its quantitative representation is immediately retrieved and leads to greater confusion over nearby numbers.

The distance effect manifests even when the comparison standard is not shown on the screen. For example, Dehaene et al. (1990) flashed randomly selected numbers between 31 and 99 on the screen, one at a time, and asked participants to judge whether the shown number was lower or higher than 65. That the distance effect has been shown to occur with all sorts of psychophysical stimuli such as light, sound, size etc. suggests that numbers also can be processed as psychophysical stimuli.

Additional support for the existence of analog representations of numbers comes from the fact that numerical cognition is non-verbal: it does not require linguistic capabilities. Infants and animals can also comprehend magnitude information. Based on the differences in the time that infants take to look at displays with different numbers of dots, Starkey and Cooper (1980) suggest that four- to seven-month-old infants can discriminate between quantities of two and three. Similar results were presented by Lipton and Spelke (2003). Gallistel and Gelman (2005) found that the distance effect manifests in animals. This observation, once again, implies that linguistic ability is not necessary for representing the magnitude information. Based on such findings, Gallistel and Gelman (2005, p. 559) suggest that the human ability to think mathematically might draw on a primitive, non-verbal system: 'the verbal expression of number and of arithmetic thinking is based on a non-verbal system for estimating and reasoning about discrete and continuous quantity, which we share with many non-verbal animals'.

Researchers have also found evidence for the association of spatial orientation and numerical information. Several studies have shown that people's spatial orientation affects their ability to make magnitude judgments, a result known as the SNARC (spatial–numerical association of response codes) effect. Dehaene et al. (1993) showed participants in their experiment numbers between 0 and 9, one at a time, on a computer screen and asked them to judge whether the shown number is odd or even (i.e. parity). The assignment of the 'odd' and 'even' responses to response keys was varied within subjects such that for each number, participants responded using the left key in one half of the experiment and the right key in the other half. Results showed that, regardless of the parity, larger numbers yielded faster responses with the right hand than with the left, and the reverse was true for smaller numbers. The large–right and small–left associations are consistent with the notion that numbers are represented non-verbally. These spatial magnitude associations suggest that numbers activate semantic magnitude representations on a horizontal number line that extends from left to right, with smaller numbers on its left and larger numbers on its right.

The representation of numbers as analog representations raises new challenges as well as opportunities for theories of price cognition. An inevitable question that surfaces from this discussion is: when are prices likely to be represented and processed as analog representations or as symbolic representations? There is some evidence to suggest that price magnitude judgments are influenced by both analog and symbolic representations. Left-digit anchoring could be considered a signature of symbolic processing. If consumers were to ignore the numerical symbols and focus only on the underlying magnitudes, then they should perceive the difference between $4.00 and $2.99 to be the same as that between $4.01 and $3.00. The abundant evidence for left-digit anchoring (Schindler and Kirby, 1997; Stiving and Winer, 1997; Thomas and Morwitz, 2005) suggests that price cognition does entail symbolic processing. However, some studies have also found evidence for the distance effect in price magnitude judgments (Thomas and Morwitz, 2005, experiment 3; but see Viswanathan and Narayan, 1994), which is a signature of analog processing. Further, Thomas and Menon (2007) found that phenomenological experiences can affect consumers' price magnitude judgments even when the articulated price expectation remains unchanged. They interpreted this evidence as suggesting that while price magnitude judgments entail analog representations of reference prices, articulated price expectations draw on symbolic representations of prices in memory. Such a distinction between analog and symbolic representations of prices offers a promising framework to address a long-standing conundrum in the pricing literature: consumers are not very good at recalling the past prices of products (Dickson and Sawyer, 1990; Gabor, 1988; Urbany and Dickson, 1991), yet their brand choices are very sensitive to small changes in prices relative to past prices (Kalyanaram and Winer, 1995; Winer, 1988; also see Monroe and Lee, 1999). Exploring the dissociation between analog and symbolic representations of price knowledge, understanding when one representation is likely to be more influential than the other, and examining how these two distinct types of price knowledge interact with each other could be promising avenues for future research.

A putative model of price cognition
The literature reviewed in the preceding paragraphs suggests that price magnitude judgments might be based on symbolic representations, analog representations, or on a combination of the two (see Figure 7.1). The processes that operate on these representations can be grouped into two distinct families: they can either be deliberative and rule-based or instinctive and associative. The non-verbal processes that operate on analog representations are likely to be instinctive and associative. For example, although we can easily identify the more luminous bulb when presented with two lighted bulbs of differing luminosities, it is difficult to explain how we made the judgment. In a similar vein, when people judge the magnitudes of two numbers using analog representations, they are likely to be aware of the final judgment without knowing how they arrived at it. However, the arithmetic processes that operate on symbolic representations could either be deliberative and rule-based or instinctive and associative. Specifically, they are likely to be deliberative and rule-based when people have to do online computations to respond to an arithmetic problem, but they are likely to be instinctive and associative when the response can be retrieved from associative knowledge structures in the long-term memory. People might have introspective access to the deliberative and rule-based cognitive processes, and therefore might be able to report the cognitive strategies used in such processes.

Figure 7.1 adapts Dehaene's (1992; also discussed in McCloskey and Macaruso, 1995) framework of numerical comparison to represent the putative processes in price magnitude judgments. These processes are best illustrated by an example. Consider a consumer who is evaluating a stimulus price, $2.99. Numerical judgments usually involve comparisons with a reference point (Thomas and Menon, 2007; Winer, 1988). The broken line connecting the reference price to its internal representation indicates that it could either be retrieved from memory (an internal reference price), or it could be the most relevant comparison standard at the point of sale (an external reference price). During the encoding stage, the numerical symbols are transcoded to an analog representation in consumers' working memory. As discussed in the preceding paragraphs, the three digits in the numerical stimulus (2, 9 and 9) could be represented holistically as a discriminal dispersion on the psychological continuum used to represent magnitudes (see Figure 7.1). Also activated on the mental number line is the analog representation of the comparison standard associated with the stimulus product. The final response toward the stimulus price could be based on arithmetic operations on the symbolic representations, non-verbal comparisons of analog representations, or on a combination of these processes.

Heuristics in price cognition
Having characterized the representations and processes that underlie the price cognition process, we now review some of the heuristics used in price magnitude judgments and judgments of the magnitudes of price differences. Specifically, we focus on three heuristics: anchoring, representativeness and availability.

Anchoring in price cognition
The anchoring effect, which was first demonstrated in the context of numeric estimates, refers to the influence of uninformative or irrelevant numbers in numerical cognition. In their classic study, Tversky and Kahneman (1974) asked participants to estimate the percentage of African nations in the UN. Before they indicated their response, participants were first asked to indicate whether their estimate was higher or lower than a random number between 0 percent and 100 percent generated by spinning a wheel of fortune. These arbitrary numbers had a significant effect on participants' estimates. For example, participants who were first asked 'Was it more or less than 45 percent?' guessed lower values than those who had been asked if it was more or less than 65 percent. Since the publication of these results, several studies have documented the effect of anchoring in the context of price cognition (Adaval and Monroe, 2002; Bolton et al., 2003; Morwitz et al., 1998; Chapman and Johnson, 1999; Mussweiler and Englich, 2003; Northcraft and Neale, 1987; Raghubir and Srivastava, 2002; Schkade and Johnson, 1989; Thomas and Morwitz, 2005).

Mussweiler and Englich (2003) found that anchoring effects are more likely when people use an unfamiliar currency than a familiar currency. The introduction of the euro as a new currency in Germany offered them a natural setting to test the moderating role of currency familiarity in anchoring effects. Participants in their experiment were asked to estimate the price of a mid-sized car, immediately before and about half a year after the introduction of the euro. The researchers found that immediately before the introduction of the euro, the anchoring bias was more likely to manifest when German participants made price estimates in euros than in German marks. However, six months after the introduction of the euro, this pattern was completed reversed: euro estimates were less biased than mark estimates. Similar results were reported by Raghubir and Srivastava (2002). In a series of experimental studies, they found that people's valuation of a product in an unfamiliar foreign currency is anchored on its face value, with inadequate adjustment for the exchange rate. As a consequence, an American consumer is likely to underspend in Malaysia (because 1 US dollar = 4 Malaysian ringgits) and overspend in Bahrain (because 1 US dollar = 0.4 Bahraini dinar). As in Mussweiler and Englich's research, familiarity with the foreign currency was found to be a moderator of the face value anchoring effect. Morwitz et al. (1998) demonstrated anchoring effects in the context of partitioned prices. They found that charging the shipping and handling fee as a separate component from the catalog price reduced recall of total cost because of the propensity to anchor on the base price. In another experiment, Morwitz et al. (1998) found that auction bidders agreed to pay more in total cost in an auction when a 15 percent buyer's premium was charged separately than in one in which there was no buyer's premium. The anchoring effect observed in partitioned pricing has subsequently been replicated and extended in several studies (e.g. Bertini and Wathieu, 2008; Chakravarti et al., 2002).

Although these studies demonstrate the pervasiveness of the anchoring heuristic in price cognition, it is not clear whether the observed anchoring effects are the results of volitional cognitive strategies, or a consequence of the associative and non-verbal processes in price cognition. Some studies have explicitly addressed the issue of awareness and intentionality in anchoring.

Unaware anchoring   Northcraft and Neale (1987) examined the effect of the anchoring heuristic in price estimates in an information-rich, real-world setting. They asked students and real-estate agents to tour a house and appraise it. Their results revealed that not only the students' but also the real-estate agents' price estimates were anchored on the list price of the house. It could be argued that the use of an anchoring strategy in this example is not completely unwarranted. Since list prices are usually correlated with the real-estate value, participants in this experiment might have considered list price as relevant information. However, analysis of the decision processes based on participants' verbal protocols revealed that the real-estate agents seemed to be unaware of the anchoring effect of the list price: a majority of them flatly denied that they considered the list price while appraising the property.

Unintentional anchoring The proposition that anchoring might be occurring unintentionally is supported by the finding that completely irrelevant anchors can also affect people's price estimates and magnitude judgments. Nunes and Boatwright (2004) suggest that incidental prices (i.e. prices advertised, offered or paid for unrelated goods that neither sellers nor buyers regard as relevant to the price of an item that they are engaged in buying) can affect buyers' valuation of goods and their willingness to pay. They find that the price of a sweatshirt on display at an adjacent seller can influence a shopper's willingness to pay for a music CD. Adaval and Monroe (2002) show that even subliminally primed numbers can affect consumers' price magnitude judgments. The researchers demonstrate that exposing subjects to high numbers below the consumer's threshold of perception can make the price of a product seen later seem less expensive. This effect manifests even when the subliminal information is completely irrelevant (e.g. weight in grams) to the price judgment task. Their results suggest that numerical information is translated into a magnitude representation regardless of the associated attribute dimension (e.g. grams or dollars).

Another example of unintentional anchoring in price cognition is the left-digit effect in judgments of the magnitude of price differences. Research has revealed that the propensity to read from left to right leads to anchoring in judgments of the magnitude of the numerical difference. Thomas and Morwitz (2005) demonstrated that using a 9-ending price can affect judgments of the magnitude of the difference between two prices when the use of such an ending leads to a change in the left-most digit (e.g. $3.00 versus $2.99), but has no effect on the perceived magnitude when the left-most digit remains unchanged (e.g. $3.50 versus $3.49). More recently, these researchers found that participants in an experiment judged the numerical difference to be larger when the left-digit difference is larger (e.g. 6.00 minus 4.95) than when the left-digit difference is smaller (e.g. 6.05 minus 5.00), even though the holistic differences are identical across the pairs. Evidence for the left-digit effect has also come from analyses of scanner panel data (Stiving and Winer, 1997) and a survey of retailers' pricing practices (Schindler and Kirby, 1997).

Cognitive miserliness or numeric priming? Economists and like-minded marketing researchers have suggested that such left-digit anchoring in judgments is on account of volitional cognitive miserliness. This stream of literature suggests that the left-digit effect occurs because consumers volitionally ignore the right digits. Characterizing a model of rational consumer behavior, Basu (2006, p. 125) suggested that consumers do not ignore the right digits 'reflexively or out of irrationality, but only when they expect the time cost of acquiring full cognizance of the exact price to exceed the expected loss caused by the slightly erroneous amount that is likely to be purchased or the slightly higher price that may be paid by virtue of ignoring the information concerning the last digits of prices'. In a similar vein, Stiving and Winer (1997, p. 65) suggest that consumers ignore the pennies digits in a price because they might be 'trading off the low likelihood of making a mistake against the cost of mentally processing the pennies digits'.

However, the price cognition model described earlier in this review suggests that the left-digit effect can manifest even when consumers diligently compute holistic numerical differences. Mental subtraction of multi-digit numbers proceeds from left to right, and entails several intermediate steps. One such step is the retrieval/computation of the difference between left-most digits as an initial anchor. For example, when a consumer tries to compute the holistic difference between $6.00 and $4.95, the difference between the left-most digits 6 and 4 might 'pop up' in her mind. Thus the left-digit difference is activated in the consumer's working memory as an intermediate step. Even when the consumer corrects this intermediate output for the right digits, the activation of this left-digit difference in working memory can unobtrusively prime the consumer's judgments. Thus the subjective numerical judgment is affected not only by the final corrected output (i.e. 1.05) but is also contaminated by the initial anchor (i.e. 2) generated during the mental subtraction process. This example illustrates the divergence in the predictions from the traditional economic models based on assumptions of deliberative and controlled thinking, and the price cognition model characterized by associative and non-verbal processes.

In conclusion, the evidence reviewed in this section supports the proposition that consumers' responses to prices are often influenced by irrelevant anchors. Further, in many instances, this influence seems to be occurring unintentionally and without consumers' awareness.

Representativeness heuristic in price cognition
According to Gilovich and Savitsky (2002, p. 618), the representativeness heuristic refers to the 'reflexive tendency to assess the fit or similarity of objects and events along salient dimensions and to organize them on the basis of one overarching rule: Like goes with like.' The classic engineer–lawyer study, discussed by Tversky and Kahneman (1974), offers an excellent illustration of the use of representativeness heuristic in everyday judgments. Participants in their experiment were provided with the non-diagnostic descriptions of several individuals, such as:

> Dick is a 30 year old man. He is married with no children. A man of high ability and high motivation, he promises to be quite successful in his field. He is well liked by his colleagues.

Further, the participants were informed that the described individuals were sampled at random from a group of 100 professionals – engineers and lawyers. Half the participants were told that this group consisted of 70 engineers and 30 lawyers, while the other half were told that the group comprised 30 engineers and 70 lawyers. Tversky and Kahneman (1974) found, as they predicted, that the base rate manipulation had little effect on participants' judgment of the probability of Dick being an engineer. The results suggest that participants in the experiment might have judged the probability based on the degree to which the description was representative of the two stereotypes, without considering the base rates for the two categories.

Although in this experiment participants relied only on the representativeness heuristic and ignored rule-based reasoning, as Kahneman and Frederick (2002) suggest, this may not always be the case. In many instances, rule-based reasoning and heuristic thinking can co-occur.[3] In our view, it is almost impossible to ignore rule-based thinking while evaluating numeric information such as price. The effects of representativeness-based thinking are likely to surreptitiously influence judgments as consumers engage in systematic rule-based evaluation of prices, so their final magnitude judgments are likely to be conjointly influenced by rule-based and representativeness-based thinking.

Representativeness of font size Although the use of the representativeness heuristic has not been specifically implicated in price cognition, some published results could be reinterpreted as evidence for the use of representativeness. In our view, the size congruity effect reported by Coulter and Coulter (2005) is a good example of the influence of the representativeness heuristic in price cognition. Coulter and Coulter's (2005) results indicate that price magnitude judgments are not only influenced by the magnitude of the price but also by the physical size of the symbolic representation. The researchers predicted that consumers are likely to perceive an offered price to be lower when the price is represented in smaller than in larger font. To test this hypothesis, they presented participants with an advertisement for a fictitious brand of an in-line skate sold on sale; in addition to the usual product details, the advertisement also displayed the regular ($239.99) and the sale prices ($199.99) for the product. For half the participants, the font used for the sale price was smaller than that used for the regular price ($239.99 versus $199.99). For the other half, the font used for the sale price was larger ($239.99 versus $199.99). The results revealed that participants' evaluations of the sale price magnitude and their purchase intentions were influenced by this font manipulation. Participants judged the sale price magnitude to be lower when the font size for the sale price was smaller. Interestingly, participants' self-reports of their decision-making processes revealed that the effect occurred nonconsciously: they could not recall details of the font size manipulation, and a majority reported that font size did not influence their judgments at all. These results suggest that participants might have nonconsciously inferred smaller font size to be representative of lower price magnitudes.

Representativeness of digit patterns Consumers might also rely on representativeness of digit patterns to make magnitude judgments. Thomas et al. (2007) examine whether precision or roundedness of prices affects consumers' magnitude judgments. They found that consumers incorrectly perceive precise prices ($395 425) to be lower than round prices (e.g. $395 000) of similar magnitude. Previous research on the distribution of numbers has shown that all numbers do not occur with uniform frequency in printed or spoken communication. Dehaene and Mehler (1992) analyzed the frequency of number words in word frequency tables for English, Catalan, Dutch, French, Japanese, Kannada and Spanish languages. They found an overrepresentation of small, precise numbers (e.g. 1, 2, 3, . . ., 8 and 9) and large numbers rounded to the nearest multiple of 10 (e.g. 10, 20, . . ., 100, 110). Stated differently, precise large numbers (e.g. 101, 102, 103, . . .,1011, 1121)

---

[3] See Gilbert (1999) for a discussion on consolidative and competitive models of dual process systems.

are used relatively infrequently in our daily communication. This finding was replicated in studies on the patterns of number usage in the World Wide Web and in newspapers. Given this evidence of greater prevalence of precision in smaller numbers and roundedness in larger numbers, Thomas et al. (2007) hypothesized that the representativeness of digit patterns might influence judgments of magnitude. Specifically, drawing on previous research on the distribution of numbers and on the role of representativeness in everyday judgments, they suggest that people nonconsciously learn to associate precise prices with smaller magnitudes. They tested this hypothesized precision heuristic in a laboratory experiment. Participants in their experiment were asked to evaluate 12 different list prices of a house listed for sale in a neighboring city. Six of these prices were precise and the other six round. Participants were randomly assigned to two groups and each group evaluated six of the 12 prices, one at a time, in a random order on computer screens. Specifically, one of the groups evaluated the prices $390 000, $395 000, $400 000, $501 298, $505 425 and $511 534, while the other group evaluated $391 534, $395 425, $401 298, $500 000, $505 000 and $510 000. Consistent with their prediction, the researchers found that participants, systematically but incorrectly, judged the magnitudes of the precise prices to be significantly smaller than the round prices. This result suggests that magnitude judgments are influenced by the representativeness of digit patterns: precise digit patterns are considered to be representative of smaller magnitudes.

In conclusion, the evidence reviewed in this section suggests that price magnitude judgments can be influenced by representativeness-based thinking. The research we reviewed suggests a reflexive tendency in consumers to assess the magnitude of a price based on irrelevant factors such as font size and digit patterns. Given the obvious irrelevance of these factors, it is unlikely that consumers might be relying on these factors intentionally. It seems reasonable to assume that representativeness-based thinking might be influencing price magnitude judgments unintentionally and without consumers' awareness.

Availability heuristic in price cognition
People rely on the ease or the fluency with which information is processed to make judgments, a decision rule referred to as the availability heuristic. To demonstrate the role of the availability heuristic in judgments, Tversky and Kahneman (1974) asked participants whether it is more likely that a word begins with r or that r is the third letter in a word. Because words that begin with r come to mind faster than words with r as the third letter, participants overestimated the number of words that begin with r, and underestimated the words that have r as the third letter. Note that this effect in judgments could have occurred through two distinct mechanisms: (i) participants might have experienced a feeling of ease while retrieving words that begins with r, and might have made inferences based on this experiential information; or (ii) they might have been able to recall more words that start with r. In the former case, the judgment would be based on experiential information, while in the latter case it would be based on declarative information. Subsequent research (see Schwarz et al., 1991) revealed that experiential information by itself can influence judgments: the perceived ease or difficulty of information-processing influences judgments even when the declarative information is inconsistent with the experiential information.

Meanwhile, independent of this stream of research in judgment and decision-making, social and cognitive psychologists have discovered that fluency or ease of processing has remarkable effects on preferences (Zajonc, 1980) and implicit memory (Jacoby et al., 1989). More recent research has identified that different types of fluency – conceptual and perceptual – have distinct effects on judgments (Whittlesea, 1993). These findings have had a substantive impact on research on consumer behavior: researchers have demonstrated that information processing fluency can influence judgments on a range of evaluative dimensions. However, although researchers examining consumer behavior have found that processing fluency can affect evaluations of products (e.g. Janiszewski, 1993; Lee and Labroo, 2004; Menon and Raghubir, 2003), it could be argued that not much work has been done to explore the consequences of processing fluency in the domain of pricing. In this review, we discuss some fluency effects that could be relevant to the understanding of price cognition process. Specifically, we discuss the effects of fluency on willingness to pay (Alter and Oppenheimer, 2006; Mishra et al., 2006) and on judgments of the magnitude of numerical differences (Thomas and Morwitz, forthcoming).

Fluency and willingness to pay Alter and Oppenheimer (2006) suggest that information-processing fluency can affect the price that investors and traders are willing to pay for shares listed on the stock market. They found empirical support for their suggestion in laboratory studies as well in real-world stock market data. In a laboratory experiment, they asked one group of participants to rate a list of fabricated stocks on the ease of pronunciation, as a proxy for fluency. A second group of participants estimated the future performance of the fabricated stocks. As predicted, participants expected more fluently named stocks to outperform the less fluently named stocks. For example, participants predicted that shares of the firm named Yoalumnix (a less fluent name) will depreciate by 11 percent while the shares of Barnings (a fluent name) will appreciate by 12 percent. In a subsequent study, the researchers found similar effects in real-world stock market data: actual performance of shares with easily pronounceable ticker codes were better than those of shares with unpronounceable ticker codes in the short run.

Mishra et al. (2006) suggest that fluency can also influence people's preference for certain denominations of money. Their findings suggest that consumers find processing money in smaller denominations (e.g. five $20 bills) less fluent that processing money in larger denominations (e.g. one $100 bill). The hedonic marking created by such fluency experiences results in a lower inclination to spend money when it is in larger denominations. Together, these studies suggest that fluency experiences can, in a variety of ways, affect buyers' valuations and willingness to pay for goods.

The ease of computation effect Thomas and Morwitz (forthcoming) suggest that the feelings of ease or difficulty induced by the complexity of arithmetic computations systematically affect people's judgments of numerical differences. Usually, the closer the representations of two stimuli on the internal analog scale, the greater the processing difficulty. It is easier to discriminate between two bulbs of 30 and 120 watts of power than to discriminate between bulbs of 70 and 80 watts of power. Likewise, it is more difficult to discriminate between two weights or two sound pitches that are similar to each other than two that are relatively far apart. However, overuse of this ease of processing heuristic can lead to biases in judgments of numerical differences. When presented with two pairs of prices with similar magnitudes of arithmetic difference, participants in Thomas and Morwitz's experiments incorrectly judged the difference to be smaller for pairs with difficult computations (e.g. 4.97–3.96; arithmetic difference 1.01) than for pairs with easy computations (e.g. 5.00–4.00; arithmetic difference 1.00). They show that this ease of computation effect can influence judgments of price differences in several contexts. Ease of computation can influence the perceived price difference between competing products, and can also affect the perceived magnitude of a discount (i.e. the difference between regular and sale prices). Interestingly, they observed that the ease of computation effect is mitigated when participants are made aware that their experiences of ease or difficulty are caused by computational complexity. This finding suggests that the ease of computation effect is unlikely to be due to hedonic marking, and might be due to the nonconscious misattribution of metacognitive experiences.

In conclusion, the evidence we have reviewed suggests that consumers' willingness to pay and judgments of price differences could be influenced by the ease of information-processing. Ease of information-processing can be influenced by several incidental factors such as how easy or difficult it is to pronounce the name of the product, or whether money is held in small or large denominations. The ease of computation effect in judgments of numerical differences reveals that the fluency of information-processing not only influenced affective responses to stimuli, but also influenced cognitive judgments. The empirical regularities we have reviewed are quite counterintuitive. Clearly, no buyer will knowingly invest in a company on the basis of the fluency of its name, or be less willing to spend because of the denominations of wealth. Similarly, people will not knowingly judge that the difference between 4.97 and 3.96 is smaller than that between 5.00 and 4.00. The glaring normative inappropriateness of these judgments suggests that people might be unaware of these fluency effects in their price cognition, and therefore these effects might be occurring unintentionally.

Conclusion
Our objective in this chapter was to examine the psychological mechanisms that underlie the price cognition process. We chose to organize this review around the issues of awareness and intentionality in price cognition. The choice of these issues as the focal theme should not be interpreted as suggesting that all of price cognition occurs without awareness or intention. Demonstrating that the price cognition process is susceptible to unaware and unintended influences is one way to persuade a circumspect reader that price evaluations are not always based on economically valid rule-based reasoning, as portrayed in several models of consumer behavior.

We reviewed two distinct sets of literature to marshal evidence for our proposition that price cognition might entail processes that are not available to introspective analyses. The numerical cognition literature suggests that mental arithmetic relies not only on online computations, but also on activation of patterns of associations stored in the memory. Further, this literature also offers evidence for the existence of a non-verbal numerical cognition system: we can make numerical judgments based on analog representations in much the same way that we judge psychophysical stimuli such as light and sound. Then, drawing on the judgment and decision-making literature, we characterized the heuristics that people use to make price estimates, price magnitude judgments, and judgments of the magnitude of price differences. We showed that people rely on anchoring, availability and representativeness in price cognition, much as they do for other everyday judgments. Relying on the anchoring heuristic makes people incorrectly judge the difference between

6.01 and 5.00 to be smaller than that between 6.00 and 4.99; relying on the representativeness heuristic makes people incorrectly judge $391 534 to be lower than $390 000; relying on the availability heuristic makes people incorrectly judge the difference between 4.97 and 3.96 to be smaller than that between 5.00 and 4.00.

A circumspect reader could argue that the behavioral pricing effects reviewed in this chapter are anomalous deviations that do not represent the usual price cognition processes. Indeed, as we suggested earlier, we do not consider rule-based reasoning and heuristic evaluations of prices as mutually exclusive processes; heuristic processes can co-occur, and sometimes interact, with rule-based thinking. Further, we also acknowledge that rule-based reasoning could account for much of the variance in consumers' responses to prices. However, we believe that delineating the representations and processes that underlie consumers' responses to prices will have substantive and theoretic implications. First, this stream of research can lead to a sound theoretical basis for formulating a price digit policy. The findings in this stream of research highlight that pricing decisions entail more than just deciding the magnitude of the optimal price; managers also have to decide what type of digits to use for the optimal price magnitude. For example, if consumer research and strategic analysis reveals that the optimal price magnitude for a product is $4.50, then the manager is left with the task of deciding whether the final price should have a 9-ending (i.e. $4.49) or whether it should have precise digits (e.g. $4.53) or some other pattern of digits (e.g. $4.44). There is empirical evidence that such decisions can have a significant impact on sales and profits (Anderson and Simester, 2003; Schindler and Kibarian, 1996; Stiving and Winer, 1997). Second, understanding how prices are represented and processed can address the conundrum of how consumers seem to 'know' the prices without being able to recall them (Dickson and Sawyer, 1990; Monroe and Lee, 1999). Finally, this stream of research also promises to augment the pricing literature by providing a unifying framework to discuss the many seemingly unrelated effects reported in the literature.

References

Adaval, Rashmi and Kent B. Monroe (2002), 'Automatic construction and use of contextual information for product and price evaluations', *Journal of Consumer Research*, **28** (March), 572–87.
Anderson, Eric T. and Duncan Simester (2003), 'Effect of $9 price endings on retail sales: evidence from field experiments', *Quantitative Marketing and Economics*, **1** (1), 93–110.
Alter, Adam L. and Daniel M. Oppenheimer (2006), 'Predicting short-term stock fluctuations by using processing fluency', *Proceedings of the National Academy of Science*, **103** (24), 9369–72.
Ashcraft, Mark H. (1995), 'Cognitive psychology and simple arithmetic: a review and summary of new directions', *Mathematical Cognition*, (1), 3–34.
Basu, Kaushik (2006), 'Consumer cognition and pricing in the 9's in oligopolistic markets', *Journal of Economics and Management Strategy*, **15** (1), 125–41.
Bertini, Marco and Luc Wathieu (2008), 'Attention arousal through price partitioning', *Marketing Science*, **27** (2), 236–46.
Bolton, Lisa E., Luk Warlop and Joseph W. Alba (2003), 'Consumer perceptions of price (un)fairness', *Journal of Consumer Research*, **29** (4), 474–91.
Chakravarti, Dipankar, Krish Rajan, Pallab Paul and Joydeep Srivastava (2002), 'Partitioned presentation of multicomponent bundle prices: evaluation, choice and underlying processing effects', *Journal of Consumer Psychology*, **12** (3), 215–29.
Chapman, Gretchen B. and Eric J. Johnson (1999), 'Anchoring, activation and construction of value', *Organizational Behavior and Human Decision Processes*, **79**, 115–53.
Coulter, Keith S. and Robin A. Coulter (2005), 'Size does matter: the effects of magnitude representation congruency on price perceptions and purchase likelihood', *Journal of Consumer Psychology*, **15** (1), 64–76.
Dehaene, Stanislas (1992), 'Varieties of numerical abilities', *Cognition*, **44** (1), 1–42.

Dehaene, Stanislas and Jacques Mehler (1992), 'Cross-linguistic regularities in the frequency of number words', *Cognition*, **43** (1), 1–29.
Dehaene, Stanislas, Emmanual Dupoux and Jacques Mehler (1990), 'Is numerical comparison digital? Analog and symbolic effects in two-digit number comparison', *Journal of Experimental Psychology: Human Perception and Performance*, **16** (3), 626–41.
Dehaene, Stanislas, Serge Bossini and Pascal Giraux (1993), 'The mental representation of parity and number magnitude', *Journal of Experimental Psychology: General*, **122** (3), 371–96.
Dickson, Peter R. and Alan G. Sawyer (1990), 'The price knowledge and search of supermarket shoppers', *Journal of Marketing*, **54** (July), 42–53.
Gabor, Andre (1988), *Pricing: Concepts and Methods of Effective Marketing*, 2nd edn, Aldershot: Gower.
Gallistel, C. Randy and Rochel Gelman (2005), 'Mathematical cognition', in Keith J. Holyoak and Robert G. Morrison (eds), *The Cambridge Handbook of Thinking and Reasoning*, New York: Cambridge University Press, pp. 559–88.
Gilbert, Daniel T. (1999), 'What the mind's not', in Shelly Chaiken and Yaacov Trope (eds), *Dual Process Theories in Social Psychology*, New York: Guilford Press, pp. 3–11.
Gilovich, Thomas and Kenneth Savitsky (2002), 'Like goes with like: the role of representativeness in erroneous and pseudo-scientific beliefs', in Thomas Gilovich, Dale Griffin and Daniel Kahneman (eds), *Heuristics and Biases: The Psychology of Intuitive Judgment*, New York: Cambridge University Press, pp. 617–24.
Henik, Avishai and Joseph Tzelgov (1982), 'Is three greater than five: the relation between physical and semantic size in comparison tasks', *Memory and Cognition*, **10** (4), 389–95.
Jacoby, Larry L., V. Woloshyn and C. Kelley (1989), 'Becoming famous without being recognized: unconscious influences of memory produced by dividing attention', *Journal of Experimental Psychology: General*, **118**, 115–25.
Janiszewski, Chris (1993), 'Preattentive mere exposure effects', *Journal of Consumer Research*, **20** (3), 376–92.
Kahneman, Daniel and Shane Frederick (2002), 'Representativeness revisited: attribute substitution in intuitive judgments', in Thomas Gilovich, Dale Griffin and Daniel Kahneman (eds), *Heuristics and Biases*, New York: Cambridge University Press, pp. 49–81.
Kahneman, Daniel and Amos Tversky (2000), *Choices, Values and Frames*, New York: Cambridge University Press.
Kalyanaram, Gurumurthy and Russell S. Winer (1995), 'Empirical generalizations from reference price research', *Marketing Science*, **14** (Summer), G161–69.
Lee, Angela and Aparna A. Labroo (2004), 'The effect of conceptual and perceptual fluency on brand evaluation', *Journal of Marketing Research*, **41** (May), 151–65.
Lipton, Jennifer S. and Elizabeth S. Spelke (2003), 'Origins of number sense: large number discrimination in human infants', *Psychological Science*, **14** (5), 396–401.
Markman, Arthur (1999), *Knowledge Representation*, Mahwah, NJ: Lawrence Erlbaum.
McCloskey, Michael and Paul Macaruso (1995), 'Representing and using numerical information', *American Psychologist*, **50** (5), 351–63.
Menon, Geeta and Priya Raghubir (2003), 'Ease of retrieval as an automatic input in judgments: a mere accessibility framework?', *Journal of Consumer Research*, **30** (September), 230–43.
Mishra, Himanshu, Arul Mishra and Dhananjay Nayakankuppam (2006), 'Money: a bias for the whole', *Journal of Consumer Research*, **32** (March), 541–9.
Monroe, Kent B. (2003), *Pricing: Making Profitable Decisions*, New York: McGraw-Hill/Irwin.
Monroe, Kent B. and Angela Y. Lee (1999), 'Remembering versus knowing: issues in buyers' processing of price information', *Journal of Academy of Marketing Science*, **27** (2), 207–25.
Morwitz, Vicki, Eric A. Greenleaf and Eric J. Johnson (1998), 'Divide and prosper: consumers' reactions to partitioned prices', *Journal of Marketing Research*, **35** (November), 453–63.
Moyer, Robert S. and Thomas K. Landauer (1967), 'Time required for judgments of numerical inequality', *Nature*, **215**, 1519–20.
Mussweiler, Thomas and Birte Englich (2003), 'Adapting to the euro: evidence from bias reduction', *Journal of Economic Psychology*, **24** (June), 285–92.
Northcraft, G.B. and M.A. Neale (1987), 'Expert, amateurs, and real estate: an anchoring-and-adjustment perspective on property pricing decisions', *Organizational Behavior and Human Decision Processes*, **39**, 228–41.
Nunes, Joseph C. and Peter Boatwright (2004), 'Incidental prices and their effect on willingness to pay', *Journal of Marketing Research*, **41** (1), 457–66.
Raghubir, Priya (2006), 'An information processing review of the subjective value of money and prices', *Journal of Business Research*, **59** (10–11), 1053–62.
Raghubir, Priya and Joydeep Srivastava (2002), 'Effect of face value on monetary valuation in foreign currencies', *Journal of Consumer Research*, **29** (December), 335–47.
Schindler, Robert M. and Patrick N. Kirby (1997), 'Patterns of rightmost digits used in advertised prices: implications for nine ending effects', *The Journal of Consumer Research*, **24** (2), 192–201.

Schindler, Robert M. and Thomas M. Kibarian (1996), 'Increased consumer sales response through use of 99-ending prices', *Journal of Retailing*, **72** (2), 187–99.
Schkade, David A. and Eric J. Johnson (1989), 'Cognitive processes in preference reversals', *Organizational Behavior and Human Decision Processes*, **44**, 203–31.
Schwarz, Norbert, Herbert Bless, Fritz Strack, Gisela Klumpp, Helga Rittenauer-Schatka and Annette Simons (1991), 'Ease of retrieval as information: another look at the availability heuristic', *Journal of Personality and Social Psychology*, **61** (2), 195–202.
Starkey, Prentice and Robert G. Cooper (1980), 'Perception of numbers by human infants', *Science*, **210**, 1033–5.
Stiving, Mark and Russell S. Winer (1997), 'An empirical analysis of price endings with scanner data', *Journal of Consumer Research*, **24** (June), 57–67.
Thomas, Manoj and Geeta Menon (2007), 'When internal reference prices and price expectations diverge: the role of confidence', *Journal of Marketing Research*, **44** (August), 401–9.
Thomas, Manoj and Vicki G. Morwitz (2005), 'Penny wise and pound foolish: the left digit effect in price cognition', *Journal of Consumer Research*, **32** (1), 54–65.
Thomas, Manoj and Vicki G. Morwitz (forthcoming), 'The ease of computation effect: the interplay of metacognitive experience and naive theories in judgments of price difference', *Journal of Marketing Research*.
Thomas, Manoj, Daniel Simon and Vrinda Kadiyali (2007), 'Do consumers perceive precise prices to be lower than round prices? Evidence from laboratory and market data', Working Paper, Cornell University.
Tversky, Amos and Daniel Kahneman (1974), 'Judgment under uncertainty: heuristics and biases', *Science*, **211**, 453–8.
Urbany, Joel E. and Peter R. Dickson (1991), 'Consumer normal price estimation: market versus personal standards', *Journal of Consumer Research*, **18** (June), 45–51.
Viswanathan, Madhubalan and Sunder Narayan (1994), 'Comparative judgments of numerical and verbal attribute labels', *Journal of Consumer Psychology*, **3** (1), 79–101.
Whittlesea, Bruce W.A. (1993), 'Illusions of familiarity', *Journal of Experimental Psychology: Learning, Memory and Cognition*, **19** (6), 1235–53.
Winer, Russell S. (1988), 'Behavioral perspectives on pricing: buyers' subjective perceptions of price revisited', in Timothy Devinney (ed.), *Issues in Pricing: Theory and Research*, Lexington, MA: Lexington Books, pp. 35–57.
Winer, Russell S. (2006), *Pricing*, Cambridge, MA: Marketing Science Institute.
Zajonc, Robert B. (1980), 'Feeling and thinking: preferences need no inferences', *American Psychologist*, **35**, 151–75.
Zbrodoff, N.J. and G.D. Logan (2005), 'What everyone finds: the problem-size effect', in Jamie Campbell (ed.), *Handbook of Mathematical Cognition*, New York: Psychology Press, pp. 331–45.

8 Price cues and customer price knowledge
Eric T. Anderson and Duncan I. Simester

Abstract
A price cue is defined as any marketing tactic used to persuade customers that prices offer good value compared to competitors' prices, past prices or future prices. In this chapter, we review the academic literature that documents the effectiveness of different types of prices cues. The leading economic explanation for why price cues are effective focuses on the role of customer price knowledge and the ability of customers to evaluate whether prices offer good value. We survey the evidence supporting this theory, including a review of the literature on customer price knowledge. Finally, we document the boundaries of when price cues are effective and identify several moderating factors.

Introduction
What is a good price to pay for a 16 ounce package of baking soda? Is $2599 a good price for a 40″ flat-panel television? Classical economic theory assumes that customers have perfect information and can accurately answer such questions. Yet many customers who walk into Best Buy and see a 40″ television priced at $2599 are unsure of both what price Circuit City charges, or whether Best Buy will lower the price in coming weeks. This lack of information provides an opportunity for retailers to influence consumers' price perceptions through the use of 'price cues'.

We broadly define a price cue as any marketing tactic used by a firm to create the perception that its current price offers good value compared to competitors' prices, past prices or future prices (Anderson and Simester, 2003b). A common example is placing a sign at the point of purchase claiming an item is on 'Sale'. However, the definition is broad enough to also include more subtle techniques such as $9 price endings, price-matching guarantees, employee discount promotions and low advertised prices.

Our review of the existing academic research on price cues will focus on seven key results:

1. Many customers have poor price knowledge.
2. Price cues are effective at increasing demand.
3. Price cues are more effective (and actual price changes are less effective) when customers have poor price knowledge.
4. Price cues are most effective on newly introduced items and with newly acquired customers.
5. Price cues are less effective when used more often.
6. It is profitable for firms to place price cues on items for which prices are low.
7. Price cues may lower demand if used incorrectly

The evidence for these results is summarized in Box 8.1. Though not apparent from this summary, this body of research is notable for the range of product categories studied, extending from employee discount promotions for new automobiles to price-matching

BOX 8.1   KEY RESEARCH FINDINGS

1. Many customers have poor price knowledge.
See Monroe and Lee (1999) for a review of 16 studies. Subsequent research includes Vanhuele and Drèze (2002).

2. Price cues are effective at increasing demand.
'Sale' or 'low price' merchandising claims: Guadagni and Little (1983); Inman et al. (1990); Inman and McAlister (1993); Davis et al. (1992); Anderson and Simester (1998 and 2001a); Anderson et al. (2008).
   Employee discount promotions: Busse et al. (2007), who study the impact of the 2005 employee discount promotions in the automobile industry.
   Price-matching guarantees: Jain and Srivastava (2000), who present evidence that price-matching claims lead to favorable price perceptions.
   9-digit price endings: Schindler and Warren (1988); Schindler (1991); Salmon and Ortmeyer (1992); Stiving and Winer (1997); Anderson and Simester (2003a); and Schindler (2006).
   Initial prices: Bagwell (1987) presents an equilibrium model, while Anderson and Simester (2004) compare the long-run impact of offering deep discounts to existing and newly acquired customers.
   Prices of 'signpost items' (for which customers have good price knowledge): Simester (1995) presents both an equilibrium model and data from the Boston dry-cleaning market.
   Prices of related items: Anderson and Simester (2007a and 2007b). See also Xia et al.'s (2004) review of the extensive literature on price fairness and Kalyanaram and Winer's (1995) review of the reference price literature.

3. Price cues are more effective and actual price changes are less effective when customers have poor price knowledge.
Anderson and Simester (1998) present a theoretical model, while Anderson et al. (2008) present empirical evidence from a chain of convenience stores.

4. Price cues are most effective on newly introduced items and with newly acquired customers.
Anderson and Simester (2003a) show that 9-digit price endings are most effective on new items, while Anderson and Simester (2004) present evidence that low initial prices are most effective on new customers.

5. Price cues are less effective when used more often.
This is a central prediction in the Anderson and Simester (1998) model, and is tested empirically in Anderson and Simester (2001a) using data from a variety of sources.

> **6. It is profitable for firms to place price cues on items for which prices are low.**
> This is also a central prediction in the Anderson and Simester (1998) model. For a recent empirical investigation of this issue see Anderson et al. (2008).
>
> **7. Price cues may lower demand if used incorrectly.**
> Including the regular price (when customers expect a larger discount): see the results cited in this chapter.
>   When quality is uncertain: Anderson and Simester (2001b) show that installment billing offers can lower demand.
>   When prices of related items reveal that other customers pay lower prices: see Anderson and Simester (2007a and 2007b) and Xia et al.'s (2004) review.

guarantees for supermarkets. We begin our discussion by reviewing the literature on customer price knowledge. We then discuss both the effectiveness of price cues and theories that explain why consumers are so responsive to them.

Price knowledge
There has been considerable research investigating customer price knowledge. Monroe and Lee (1999) cite over 16 previous studies, most of which focus on measuring customers' short-term price knowledge of consumer packaged goods. In a typical study, customers are interviewed either at the point of purchase or in their home and asked to recall the price of a product, or alternatively, to recall the price they last paid for an item. In one of the earliest studies, Gabor and Granger (1961) conducted in-home interviews with hundreds of housewives in Nottingham, England. They found that consumers were able to provide price estimates for 82 percent of the products in their study. Thus, 18 percent of customers were not able to recall the price of an item. In addition, only 65 percent of customers were able to recall a price within 5 percent of the actual price. These findings have been replicated in later studies, which generally reveal that only half of the customers asked can accurately recall prices (Allen et al., 1976; Conover, 1986; *Progressive Grocer*, 1964, 1975). In perhaps the most frequently cited study, Dickson and Sawyer (1990) asked supermarket shoppers to recall the price of an item shortly after they placed it into their shopping cart. Surprisingly, fewer than 50 percent of consumers accurately recalled the price. Thus, despite the immediate recency of the purchase decision, there is no improvement in the accuracy of the responses.

While price recall taps into consumers' explicit memory, recent research has suggested that consumers may encode and store price knowledge in implicit memory. Monroe and Lee (1999) argue that this implies a clear distinction between what consumers remember about prices versus what they know about prices. They remark that 'the distinction between remembering and knowing contrasts the capacity for conscious recollection about the occurrence of facts and events versus the capacity for non-conscious retrieval of the past event, as in priming, skill learning, habit formation, and classical conditioning' (p. 214). This research suggests that price recall measures do not account for price information stored in consumers' implicit memory.

Building on this research, Vanhuele and Drèze (2002) argue that customers' long-term knowledge of prices is more accurately captured by measuring consumer price recognition and deal recognition. They survey 400 shoppers in a French hypermarket as they arrived at the store. Consistent with past research, they find that consumers have very poor price recall as only 21 percent of customers are within 5 percent of the actual store price. While consumers have poor price recall, the authors also show that they have significantly greater price recognition.[1] This supports the belief that multiple measures may be required to capture all aspects of customer price knowledge.

While Vanhuele and Drèze's (2002) work provides convincing evidence that price recall and price recognition are different constructs, it also leaves several unanswered questions. For example, we do not know the determinants of price recognition or which of these determinants are different from that of price recall. Moreover, the distinction between price recall and price recognition has received only limited attention in the price cue literature. As we shall discuss, the leading economic explanation for the effectiveness of price cues depends critically on lack of customer price knowledge. However, this theory does not distinguish between the inability of customers to recall prices and their inability to recognize them.

We now turn to the price cue literature, starting with the early work measuring whether price cues are effective.

Effectiveness of price cues

Academic research has now documented that price cues can have a large positive impact on demand. For example Inman et al. (1990) simulate a grocery shopping environment and find that price cues significantly increase demand. In one of the first papers to employ scanner data, Guadagni and Little (1983) find that the impact of a price cue (a display or feature) is an order of magnitude greater than price. Subsequent studies of scanner data have replicated this effect and find large, positive effects of in-store features and displays on consumer choice.

One challenge to empirically estimating the effect of a price cue is that price discounts often vary with price cues. Field studies have been used to isolate the impact of a price cue from a change in price. Inman and McAlister (1993) conduct a series of price experiments in a grocery store located on the campus of a major university. In nine categories they find that price cues can increase profits by 10 percent relative to using only price discounts. Anderson and Simester (2001a) report on a number of field tests conducted with direct mail retailers in which they vary price cues. In these experiments, consumers are randomly assigned to a condition and receive different versions of a retail catalog. The catalogs are identical except for the experimental variation in prices or price cues. They repeatedly find large positive effects; for example, demand for a dress increased by 58 percent when a dress includes a 'Sale' sign.

Perhaps surprisingly, the evidence that 'Sale' signs are effective extends beyond consumer packaged goods to include purchases of expensive durable goods. Busse et al. (2007) investigate the 'employee pricing' promotions offered by the three major US

---

[1] The authors measure aided price recognition as the ability of a consumer to tell whether an observed price is the one 'they have in mind' or 'are used to seeing' (see Monroe et al., 1986).

domestic automobile manufacturers during the summer of 2005. These promotions allowed the public to buy new cars at the same prices that employees paid, under a program of discounted prices formerly offered only to employees. While the promotions led to almost unprecedented sales increases, Busse et al. (2007) show that these demand increases cannot be attributed to price changes. All three manufacturers were offering deep discounts in the weeks before the promotion, and for many models the employee prices were *higher* than the prices immediately before the promotion. For these models, prices increased under the promotion, yet even on these models demand increased dramatically under the promotion. After ruling out alternative explanations, such as a change in advertising expenditure, the authors interpret the findings as evidence that the employee discount promotion acted as a price cue, persuading customers to purchase immediately rather than delay in anticipation of future discounts. Although there is evidence that customers engage in extensive price search when purchasing an automobile (see for example Bayus, 1991; Ratchford and Srinivasan, 1993; and Zettelmeyer et al., 2006), customers cannot search on 'future prices', and so they must rely on price cues to evaluate when to purchase. The findings are noteworthy because they demonstrate that customers also respond to price signals in a market in which high dollar values are at stake and customers engage in extensive information search.

Practitioners in the packaged goods industry also recognize that price cues can have a significant, positive impact on demand. For example, in a 1989 interview, a manager at H.E.B. Grocery Company commented:

> Occasionally we attach signs marked 'Everyday Low Price' in front of two randomly selected brands in several product categories throughout our store, leaving their prices unchanged. Even though customers should be accustomed to these signs and realize that the prices are unchanged, sales typically double for those brands that have the signs attached to their displays. I'm just amazed. (Inman et al., 1990, p. 74)

Explanations for why price cues are effective

Researchers have pursued different explanations for the effectiveness of price cues. Inman et al. (1990) extend the elaboration likelihood model (ELM) of Petty and Cacioppo (1986) to explain the consumer response to price cues. They argue that need for cognition plays a role in whether consumers respond to peripheral information, such as a price cue. Their laboratory experiments support this theory; they find that consumers who have low need for cognition are more likely to be influenced by a price cue.[2] The work of Inman et al. (1990) is grounded in psychology and provides a deeper understanding of consumer behavior. However, this research does not incorporate the perspective of the firm. In particular, given that price cues are effective and seemingly inexpensive to use, why not place them on many items?

Anderson and Simester (1998) provide an equilibrium explanation for the role of price cues that includes both the consumer and the firm. In their model, which we depict graphically in Figure 8.1, if customers lack sufficient price knowledge to evaluate whether a price offers good value, then demand does not respond to price changes alone. Instead,

---

[2] Need for cognition (NFC) is measured using the 18-item NFC scale developed by Cacioppo et al. (1984).

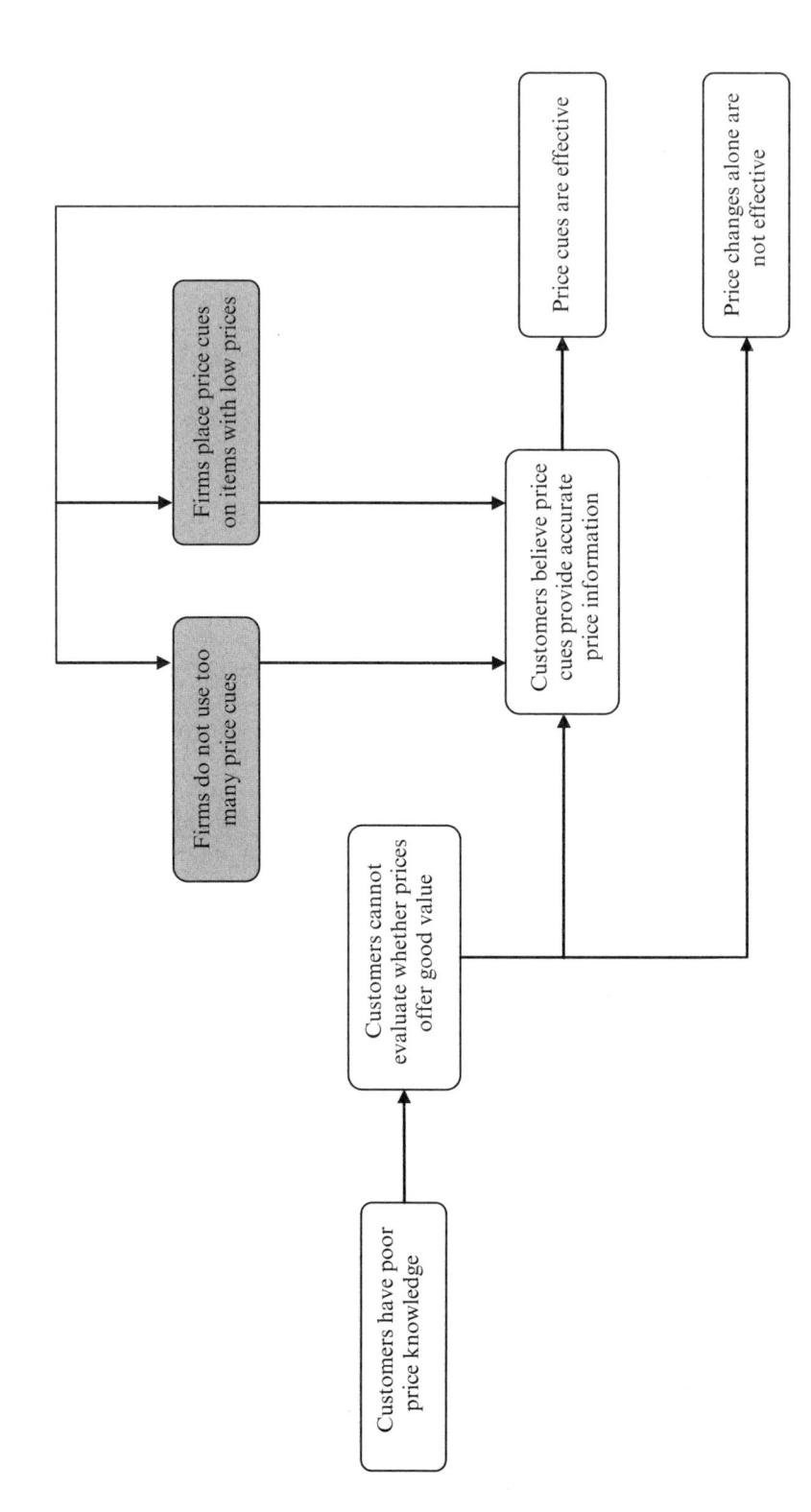

Figure 8.1 The equilibrium theory of price cues

customers turn to price cues to help judge value. Key to their model are the relationships connecting the firm decisions (depicted in the two shaded boxes) with customer decisions. These relationships ensure that retailers' price cue strategies and customers' purchasing behavior are both endogenous and rational. There are two key predictions. First, the model shows that if customers believe that products with price cues are more likely to be relatively low priced, firms prefer to place sale signs on lower-priced products. As a result, customers' beliefs are reinforced and price cues provide a credible source of information. Second, the authors show that if firms use price cues too frequently, customers will attribute less credibility to the cues and they lose their effectiveness. This in turn creates incentives for firms to limit the proliferation of the cues. These two predictions jointly imply that price cues are both self-fulfilling and self-regulating.

In 2001 the same authors (Anderson and Simester, 2001a) tested the second prediction by investigating whether price cues are less effective when used more often. The findings confirm that, holding price constant, overuse of sale signs can diminish their effectiveness. Support for this prediction is found in many industries, including women's apparel, toothpaste, canned tuna fish and frozen orange juice. For example, category demand for frozen orange juice decreases when more than 30 percent of items have sale signs. Similarly, category demand for canned tuna fish and toothpaste decreases when more than 25 percent of the items have sale signs. Notice that this effectively limits firms' use of price cues. Adding one more price cue to an item in a category increases demand for that item, but the other price cues in the category lose their effectiveness. When this second effect is large enough, there is eventually a decrease in category demand, which regulates overuse of the cues.

A recent large-scale field study with a chain of convenience stores has also directly evaluated the first prediction (Anderson et al., 2008). Although we delay a detailed discussion of this study until later in the chapter, the findings both confirm that it is profitable for firms to use price cues on items that are truly low priced, and diagnose why this is optimal.

Notice also that while the equilibrium framework reconciles the consistency of customer beliefs and firm actions, it does not speak to how these beliefs are created. It is sufficient that over time customers have learned to associate price cues with low prices, and that this understanding influences their purchasing behavior. Indeed, it is possible that customers' reactions to price cues occur at a subconscious level, so that they are not always aware that they are responding to the cues. The formation of customer beliefs and the extent to which customer reactions reflect conscious judgments both remain important unanswered research questions.

The role of reputations
Reputations provide another rationale for why firms may not use price cues in a deceptive manner (Tadelis, 1999; Wernerfelt, 1988). A firm's reputation may be irreparably damaged if consumers expect that a price cue signals a promoted price and later discover that the price is not discounted. Data from two competing retailers illustrate the pitfall of using sale signs deceptively. In spring 1997, we collected data from two retailers located approximately one mile apart in Rochester, New York. The retailers sold a broad range of electronics, home appliances and other hard goods. After several visits to both stores, we identified a set of 85 identical items sold by each retailer. We visited

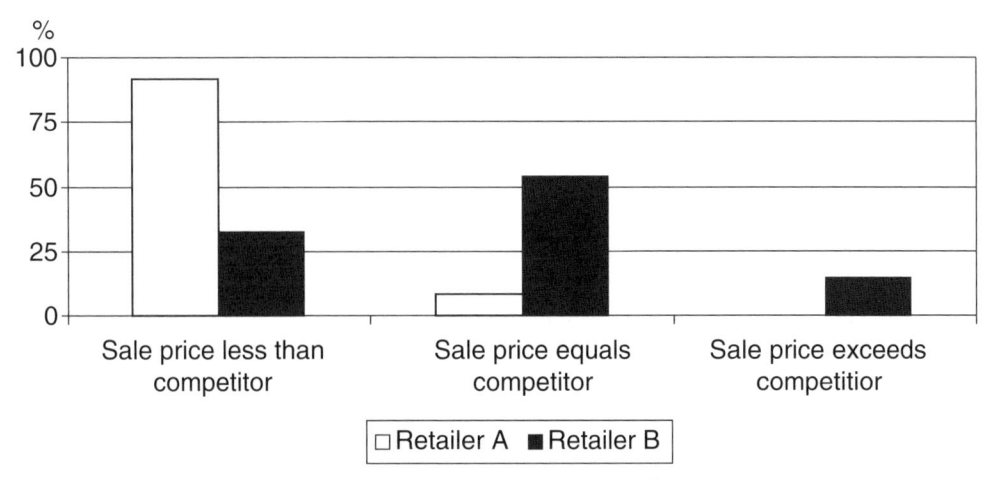

Figure 8.2 Accuracy of sale claims at two competing retailers

each store on the same day and collected the regular price and sale price (if discounted) for all 85 items.

In our analysis of the data we asked: 'Does the presence of a sale sign accurately convey that prices are low compared to a competing retailer?' To answer this question, we identified all cases where a product had a sale sign at one store but none at the competing store. If a sale item is truly low priced, we expect that the sale price should be less than the regular price of a competitor. More importantly, the sale price should never exceed a competing store's regular price. Our results are summarized in Figure 8.2.

The results showed that retailer A used sale signs to accurately signal that the current price was lower than competitors' prices. We found that 92 percent of the items marked as 'Sale' at retailer A were priced lower than at retailer B. For the remaining 8 percent of the observations the prices at the two retailers were identical. In contrast, at retailer B the presence of a sale sign was not nearly as accurate, and in many cases deceptive. We found that only 32 percent of the items marked with a sale sign at retailer B were lower priced that at retailer A. More striking was the fact that 14 percent of the items marked with a sale sign at retailer B had sale prices that exceeded the regular price at retailer A! Thus, while the sale items may have been discounted relative to past prices at retailer B, they were not low priced compared to the alternative of visiting retailer A.

In both cases, the retailers were using the sale signs in a manner that is somewhat 'noisy'. Retailer B was using the signs in a manner that was less informative and potentially misleading. Two years after this study, retailer B declared bankruptcy and went out of business. While we cannot claim a causal link between the retailer's financial distress and price cue policy, the anecdote does suggest that a firm's reputation can be damaged if price cues are used deceptively.

Price cues as information
The Anderson and Simester theory argues that price cues may serve an informational role when consumers have imperfect price knowledge. We consider a series of studies that support this view and illustrate other types of price cues.

Price endings
Academics have been fascinated by the use of 9-digit price endings for over 70 years (Ginzberg, 1936). This is in part due to their widespread use by US retailers – while estimates vary, as many as 65 percent of prices have been estimated to end in the digit 9. Despite this prevalence, there is relatively limited evidence documenting both their effectiveness and their role.

Some of the first evidence that 9-digit price endings can influence demand in retail markets is provided by Anderson and Simester (2003a), who present a series of three field studies in which price endings were experimentally manipulated in women's clothing catalogs. Their results confirm that in all three experiments a $9 price ending increased demand. This prompts the question: why are 9-digit endings effective?

Several competing explanations are reviewed by Stiving and Winer (1997), including the possibility that price endings serve as a price cue. For example, Schindler (1991) suggests that price endings provide information about relative price levels and/or product quality. In this theory, customers pay more attention to the right-most digits because of the information that they convey. This contrasts with the customer's emphasis on the left-most digits in the 'dropping off' theories. In those alternative theories, customers ignore the right-hand digits or place less emphasis on them.

There is both systematic and anecdotal evidence to support the view that price endings convey low prices. For example, Salmon and Ortmeyer (1993) describe a department store that uses a 0-cent ending for regularly priced items and 98-cent endings for clearance items. Similarly, Randall's Department Store uses 95-cent endings on all 'value' priced merchandise, which is 'meant to indicate exceptional value to the customer' (Salmon and Ortmeyer, 1992).

These anecdotes are supported by more systematic academic studies. Schindler and Warren (1988) show that one inference customers may draw from $9 endings is that a price is low, discounted, or on 'Sale'. More recently, Schindler (2006) analyzed prices for hundreds of different products that were advertised in several newspapers. Schindler shows that items priced with a 99-cent price ending are more likely to be in an advertisement that emphasizes price discounts.[3] He argues that this offers a plausible explanation for how consumers form associations between low prices and 9-digit price endings.

Anderson and Simester (2003a) provide further support for the theory that 9-digit prices convey information. They show that the increase in demand from a 9-digit item is greatest for new items that a retailer has not sold in previous years. Because customers have poor price knowledge for these items, this is precisely where price cues should be more effective. The authors also show that $9 price endings are less effective when retailers use 'Sale' cues. This is precisely what we would expect if the 'Sale' sign has already informed customers about whether an item is low priced.

Price promotions for new customers
New customers are typically least informed about prices, and so for these customers deep promotional discounts may act as a price cue and influence their overall price perceptions

---

[3] Schindler refers to these as low-price cues. We do not use this phrase, to avoid confusion with our definition of a price cue.

for a retailer. Bagwell (1987) presents an equilibrium model of initial prices as a cue that signals information about future prices.

There is also field research investigating this possibility (Anderson and Simester, 2004). The research includes three separate field experiments with a direct mail retailer that sells publishing products (books, software etc.). Study A was conducted using 56 000 existing customers. Studies B and C were conducted using 300 000 and 245 000 prospective customers identified from a rented mailing list. Each study used promotion and control versions of a test catalog sent to randomly assigned groups of customers. Prices in the promotion condition were 40 percent lower than in the control condition. The test catalog was otherwise identical and all of the customers received the same catalogs over the subsequent two years.

The results show that deep promotions have different long-run impacts on the behavior of new and established customers. The established customers in Study A reacted in the same manner as documented in other studies (see for example Neslin and Shoemaker, 1989). For these customers the short-run lift in demand was offset by a long-run decrease in demand, which almost certainly reflects the effects of intertemporal demand substitution (forward buying). In contrast, the deep promotions had a positive long-run impact on the demand of new customers (Studies B and C). Receiving deep discounts on their first purchase occasion prompted these customers to return and purchase 10 percent to 21 percent more frequently in the future. Further investigation suggests that the deep promotional discounts influenced the new customers' price perceptions. In this sense, the low initial prices served as a price cue about the overall level of prices.

Signpost items
Consider the purchase of a new tennis racket. The models change frequently and so most customers will be unsure how much a selected model should cost. On the other hand, most tennis players have good price knowledge of tennis balls. If they see a store charging $2 for a can of tennis balls, they may be reassured that they are not overpaying for the tennis racket. However, if the tennis balls are $5 per can, they may be better served purchasing their tennis racket elsewhere. Tennis balls are an example of a 'signpost' item for which many customers have good price knowledge. The price of a signpost item signals information about the prices of items for which price knowledge is poor. Other examples include customers using the prices of bread, milk or Coke to infer whether a supermarket offers good value on baking soda.

Simester (1995) presents an equilibrium model of the signaling role of signpost items. In his model, customers see the prices of a sample of 'advertised' items and use these prices to infer the price of the 'unadvertised' items for which prices are unobserved prior to visiting a store. The underlying signaling mechanism relies on correlation in the underlying costs (to the firm) of the different items. This can be compared with Bagwell's (1987) model of low initial prices, where the information revealed by a price cue depends upon correlation in the firm's costs over time. Simester tests his model using a sample of data from the Boston dry-cleaning market. He shows that the price to launder a man's shirt provides credible information about the cost to dry-clean suits and sweaters.

Price guarantees
A common strategy among retailers is to offer consumers a price guarantee. There are two widely used versions: price-matching policies and best price policies. A price-matching

policy guarantees that prices will be no higher than the prices charged by other retailers. A typical price-matching policy guarantees the consumer a rebate equal to the price (and perhaps more) if the consumer finds the same product offered at lower price by a competing firm within 30 days of purchase. Some firms, such as Tweeter, take the additional step of monitoring competitive prices for the consumer and sending the consumer a rebate automatically. While price-matching policies protect the consumer against price differences among competing retailers, best price policies protect consumers against future discounts within a retail store. For example, when a retailer discounts an item by 25 percent, a best price policy promises to refund this discount to all consumers who purchased the item in the previous 30 days.

Both types of price guarantees are intended to create the perception that an item is low priced compared to competing retailers (price-matching policy) or the firm's future prices (best price policy). Studies measuring the relationship between price guarantees and consumer price perceptions confirm that they can be an effective price cue, leading to more favorable price perceptions (see, e.g., Jain and Srivastava, 2000).

There is also evidence that price guarantees can affect price levels themselves, by influencing the intensity of competition. One stream of theoretical research suggested that these price guarantees may serve as a mechanism that raises market prices (Salop, 1986). Another stream suggested that these policies may increase competition in a market (Chen et al., 2001). These two streams of research show that whether price-matching policies lead to increased competition hinges on the degree of heterogeneity in consumer demand. This research has also highlighted subtle distinctions between price-matching, price-beating and best price policies. The empirical evidence is also mixed. Hess and Gerstner (1991) show that supermarkets that offer price-matching policies have less price dispersion and higher prices. In contrast, there is evidence that retailers who adopt price-matching policies reduce their prices. For example, when Montgomery Ward and Tops Appliance City introduced such policies they significantly lowered their prices (*PR Newswire*, 1989; Beatty, 1995; Halverson, 1995; Veilleux, 1996).

The moderating role of price knowledge
The Anderson and Simester model predicts that price cues will be most effective when consumers lack price knowledge. If consumers know that $4 is a relatively high price for a gallon of milk, then adding a price cue should have little impact on demand. But, if customers are uncertain about the relative price of milk, a price cue may affect purchase behavior. In a recent paper, Anderson et al. (2008) combine survey data and a field experiment to investigate this prediction. In their study, they survey customers and collect price recall measures for approximately 200 products. They then conduct a field experiment in which they randomly assign the same items to one of three conditions. In the control condition, items are offered at the regular retail price. In the price cue condition, a shelf tag with the words 'LOW prices' is used on an item. In the discount condition, the price is offered at a 12 percent discount from the regular price.

The authors show that both price cues and price discounts increase demand. But, consistent with theoretical predictions, they find that price cues are more effective on products for which customers have poor price knowledge. In contrast, price discounts are more effective when customers have better price knowledge. Thus discounting baking soda from 99 cents to 89 cents is unlikely to be effective since customers have poor price knowledge for this product. But an offer of 'Sale 99 cents' may lead to a large increase in demand. Together these results highlight the importance that price knowledge has in determining the effectiveness of price changes and price cues.

Adverse effects of price cues
While price cues are intended to increase demand, retailers must recognize that they can also have an adverse impact on demand. Below we document three situations where a price cue reduced demand.

Regular price
When an item is offered at a discount, many customers are unable to recall the previous price. Including the regular price allows consumers to directly assess whether an item is low priced compared to past prices. One might be tempted to conclude that providing customers with this price cue would be beneficial, but a recent study we conducted with a direct mail company explains why this may not be correct. In this study, we varied the presence or absence of the regular price on a set of five dresses. For example, the regular price of one dress was $120 and it was discounted to $96. Customers who received the control catalog saw this dress offered at 'Sale $96'. Customers who received the test catalog saw 'Regular Price $120, Sale $96'.

The results of this study showed that demand significantly decreased when the regular price was included in the description. The presence of this price cue resolved customer uncertainty about the depth of discount. But the resolution of this uncertainty was unfavorable. In the absence of the regular price, customers expected to receive more than a $24 discount. Thus, while price cues can help resolve customer uncertainty, firms must also ask whether it is profitable to resolve the uncertainty. In some cases, customers may have more favorable price perceptions when they lack perfect information.

Installment billing
If customers lack perfect information about prices, they may also have imperfect knowledge of quality. Price cues are intended to create the perception of a low price and increase demand. But, if the price cue also creates the perception of low quality, then demand may decrease. For example, Fingerhut is a catalog retailer in the USA that offers installment billing on nearly all purchases. While Fingerhut also offers low-priced merchandise, it targets consumers with moderate to low incomes. This raises the possibility that consumers may believe that Fingerhut is positioned to offer both lower-priced and lower-quality items. If the quality inference dominates, then offering installment billing may adversely impact demand.

Anderson and Simester (2001b) document such an effect in a field experiment with a national mail order company. The research was conducted with a catalog that sells expensive gift and jewelry items and competes with retailers such as Tiffany's. In the experiment, customers were randomly mailed either a test or control catalog. The products and prices were identical except that the test catalog offered consumers the option of paying for their purchase with installment billing. For example, if a customer purchased a $500 necklace, the item could be paid for with a series of monthly payments rather than in a single lump sum payment. Installment billing was an optional feature and consumers who received the test catalog were free to select either payment plan (i.e. installment billing or lump sum payment).

The authors show that the installment billing offer led to both a reduction in the number of orders received (13 percent) and a $15 000 reduction in aggregate revenue (5 percent). The sample sizes are very large and so the differences in the number of orders received between the test and control version are statistically significant ($p < 0.01$). The changes were economically significant and persuaded catalog managers not to include installment billing offers in future catalogs.

To further investigate these findings, the catalog agreed to survey their customers to measure how an offer of installment billing affects their customers' price and quality perceptions. Similar to the field test, two versions of a catalog were created and customers were randomly mailed a catalog along with a short survey. Respondents were asked to browse through the catalog and return their responses in a reply paid envelope. The findings confirm that offering installment billing lowers the perceived quality of the items in the catalog. Respondents in the test version were on average significantly more concerned about product quality than respondents in the control version. One respondent in the test version offered the following remarks: 'My reaction to this catalog is that people must be cutting back or not as rich as [the catalog] thought because suddenly everything is installment plan. It makes [the catalog] look tacky to have installment plans – kind of like Franklin Mint dolls.'

These findings contrast with earlier work suggesting that reframing a one-time expense into several smaller expenses can favorably impact demand (see, e.g. Gourville, 1998). The key distinction is the role of quality. In the installment billing study, product quality was not objectively verifiable, and so the installment billing cue not only influenced customers' price perceptions; it also lowered their quality perceptions. The same logic may explain why hospitals rarely use price cues to persuade customers that their prices are low.

Prices paid by other consumers
We have argued that price cues can convey information about competing prices, past prices or future prices. However, research on fairness suggests that whether consumers view a price as a good deal or a bad deal may also depend on what other consumers pay for similar products (Feinberg et al., 2002). Anderson and Simester (2007a) conduct a field experiment with direct mail apparel to investigate this issue. They conducted a split-sample test in which they experimentally varied the price premium on larger-sized women's dresses. In the control condition the prices of dresses did not vary by size. But, in three test conditions a premium of up to $10 was charged for larger-sized 4X and 5X dresses. For example, a size 3X dress may be priced at $39 and a 4X dress priced at $44. The experimental variation in prices enables the authors to examine how the price paid by other consumers affects demand.

The key finding is that customers who demand large sizes react unfavorably to paying a higher price than customers for small sizes. Further investigation suggests that these consumers perceived that the price premium was unfair. This finding is consistent with other evidence from the fairness literature, which contains many documented examples of customers reacting adversely when they perceive that prices are unfair (see, e.g., Xia et al., 2004; Anderson and Simester, 2007b).

Managing price cues

If price cues are effective, how should managers use them? The research reviewed in this chapter suggests that price cues are more effective among customers who lack price knowledge. Because we expect price knowledge to vary among products, a natural response is to use price cues on products for which customers have poor price knowledge. Similarly, price discounts are more effective when customers have better price knowledge. This creates an incentive to discount items for which customers have good price knowledge. Anderson et al. (2008) discuss why this presents a puzzle. For example, consider two items priced at $4 that differ in price knowledge. Suppose a firm lowers the price on an item with high price knowledge and uses a price cue on the other item. If firms pursue this strategy, then rational customers will infer that price cues are associated with products that are relatively high priced!

To address this issue, Anderson et al. (2008) identify three factors that moderate use of price discounts and price cues: total demand, margin and demand sensitivity. Holding all other factors constant, it is less profitable to use a price discount on a high-demand item due to the opportunity cost of a price reduction. Both price discounts and price cues are more profitable on high-margin items and on products with greater demand sensitivity. The question for managers is which of these three factors is most important?

To answer this question, the same authors conduct a large-scale field test with a convenience store chain in which they vary price discounts and price cues on almost 200 items. The authors analyzed which factors best explain the change in profits when a firm uses a price discount or a price cue. The results show that demand sensitivity is the overwhelming factor that drives incremental profits earned from both price cues and price discounts. Moreover, the sensitivity of demand is positively correlated across both treatments, so that items for which there is a greater price response are also items for which there is a greater response to price cues. This finding is important for both managerial practice and the academic theories we have discussed in this chapter. It implies that price cues and price discounts are likely to be used on the same items, and may help to resolve the apparent puzzle, explaining why price cues provide a credible signal of low prices.

A related concern of managers is how to use price cues in a competitive setting. Can price cues be an effective competitive tool? A recent study conducted with a German direct marketer of books examines precisely this question (Anderson et al., 2007). The company owns three different catalog companies that sell primarily books and music CDs. While the companies each have a distinct brand name, they are owned by a single firm. Importantly, from the consumer's perspective the three brands are viewed as competing retailers. This allows the parent company to study how price cues and price changes affect retail book competition.

The retailer conducted a field study in which it varied both prices and price cues on a set of 29 products sold by three different book retailers. The findings reveal that price cues lead to substitution between catalogs, confirming that they can be an effective competitive tool.

The study also showed that customer groups reacted quite differently to price cues and price changes. The company found that price cues were effective at increasing demand among moderate book buyers, but the demand increase did not come at the expense of competing catalogs. Instead, the increased demand from a price cue was incremental. In contrast, among heavy book buyers there was considerable evidence that price cues led to store substitution. This understanding of consumer behavior offers deeper insight into the competitive nature of price cues. Surprisingly, the threat of a competing price cue is greatest among customers who are the heaviest buyers in a category.

Managing price knowledge
Because the effectiveness of price cues is moderated by customers' price knowledge, firms may also try to manage their customers' price knowledge. Indeed, the recent literature on price obfuscation suggests that customers' lack of price information may be partly attributable to the actions of the firms. The role that firms can play in hindering customers' ability to search for price information is investigated by Ellison and Ellison (2004). They argue that price obfuscation can mitigate price competition by reducing the perceived substitutability of the alternatives, and present evidence from the Internet suggesting that obfuscation may sharply increase margins on computer memory modules. They describe a variety of practices that firms use to obfuscate the price, including: introducing shipping costs and other price components; varying warranties, re-stocking fees and other contractual terms; varying prices and products across distribution channels; and/or using 'add-on' pricing in which the base product has inefficiently low quality.

Conclusions
The research on price knowledge reveals that there is an opportunity for firms to influence customers' price perceptions, while the research on price cues documents examples of firms exploiting this opportunity. There are several important conclusions. First, the range of cues available to firms is broad, ranging from explicit claims that prices are discounted to more subtle cues, such as 9-digit price endings, which may work even without customers recognizing their effect. Second, the cues are effective across many product categories. We have reported findings from studies conducted in a wide range of consumer markets, including consumables (toothpaste, canned tuna and frozen juice) and durables (apparel and publishing products). There is even evidence that the cues are effective in the market for new automobiles, where the prices are high and customers engage in extensive price search. Third, there is now a formidable collection of evidence that at least one reason price cues are effective is that they serve a signaling role, allowing customers who are poorly informed about prices to infer whether to search elsewhere for lower prices. This evidence includes investigations of several moderating effects, including: the role of customers' price knowledge, the effects on new versus mature products, and the effect on newly acquired versus established customers. Finally, there is evidence that price cues are not a magic panacea that firms can employ at will. The cues lose effectiveness the more often they are used, and so firms cannot simply place them on every product. Firms also risk lowering demand if they place them on items for which quality is uncertain (few patients are attracted to a cardiologist offering discounts) or if customers can see that other customers have the opportunity to purchase similar items at lower prices. On the other hand, firms that overlook the role of price cues, and focus solely on optimizing prices, forgo an opportunity to optimize profits.

References
Allen, J.W., G.D. Harrell and M.D. Hutt (1976), *Price Awareness Study*, Washington, DC: The Food Marketing Institute.

Anderson, Eric T. and Duncan I. Simester (1998), 'The role of sale signs', *Marketing Science*, **17** (2), 139–55.
Anderson, Eric T. and Duncan I. Simester (2001a), 'Are sale signs less effective when more products have them?', *Marketing Science*, **20** (2), 121–42.
Anderson, Eric T. and Duncan I. Simester (2001b), 'Research note: price discrimination as a signal: why an offer to spread payments may hurt demand', *Marketing Science*, **20** (3), 315–27.
Anderson, Eric T. and Duncan I. Simester (2003a), 'Effects of $9 price endings on retail sales: evidence from field experiments', *Quantitative Marketing and Economics*, **1** (1), 93–110.
Anderson, Eric T. and Duncan I. Simester (2003b), 'Mind your pricing cues', *Harvard Business Review*, **81** (9), 96–103.
Anderson, Eric T. and Duncan I. Simester (2004), 'Long run effects of promotion depth on new versus established customers: three field studies', *Marketing Science*, **23** (1), 4–20.
Anderson, Eric T. and Duncan I. Simester (2007a), 'Does demand fall when customers perceive that prices are unfair? The case of premium pricing for large sizes', *Marketing Science*, **27** (3), 492–500.
Anderson, Eric T. and Duncan I. Simester (2007b), 'Customer antagonism and price stickiness', mimeo, MIT, Cambridge, MA.
Anderson, Eric T., Edward Ku Cho, Bari Harlam and Duncan I. Simester (2008), 'How does consumers' knowledge of prices affect the demand response to price changes and price cues', mimeo, MIT, Cambridge, MA.
Anderson, Eric T., Ralph Elsner, Federico Rossi and Duncan Simester (2007), 'Sale signs and retail competition', Working Paper, Kellogg School of Management.
Bagwell, Kyle (1987), 'Introductory price as a signal of cost in a model of repeat business', *The Review of Economic Studies*, **54** (3), 365–84.
Bayus, Barry L. (1991), 'The consumer durable replacement buyer', *Journal of Marketing*, **55** (January), 42–51.
Beatty, Gerry (1995), 'Tops' ads hail new price policy', *HFN: The Weekly Newspaper for the Home Furnishing Network*, **69** (39), 63–5.
Busse, Meghan R., Duncan Simester and Florian Zettelmeyer (2007), 'The best price you'll ever get: the 2005 employee discount pricing promotions in the U.S. automobile industry', mimeo, MIT, Cambridge, MA.
Cacioppo, John T., Richard E. Petty and Chuan F. Kao (1984), 'The efficient assessment of need for cognition', *Journal of Personality Assessment*, **48** (June), 306–7.
Chen, Yuxin, Chakravarthi Narasimhan and Z. John Zhang (2001), 'Consumer heterogeneity and competitive price-matching guarantees', *Marketing Science*, **20** (3), 300–314.
Conover, Jerry (1986), 'The accuracy of price knowledge: issues in research methodology', in Richard Lutz (ed.), *Advances in Consumer Research*, Vol. 13, Ann Arbor, MI: Association for Consumer Research, pp. 589–93.
Davis, Scott, J. Jeffrey Inman and Leigh McAlister (1992), 'Promotion has a negative effect on brand evaluations: or does it? Additional disconfirming evidence', *Journal of Marketing Research*, **29** (1), 143–8.
Dickson, Peter R. and Alan G. Sawyer (1990), 'The price knowledge and search of supermarket shoppers', *Journal of Marketing*, **54** (July), 42–53.
Ellison, Glenn and Sara Fisher Ellison (2004), 'Search, obfuscation, and price elasticities on the Internet', mimeo, MIT, Cambridge, MA.
Feinberg, Fred M., Aradhna Krishna and Z. John Zhang (2002), 'Do we care what others get? A behaviorist approach to targeted promotions', *Journal of Marketing Research*, **39** (August), 277–91.
Gabor, Andre and C.W.J. Granger (1961), 'On the price consciousness of consumers', *Applied Statistics*, **10** (3), 170–88.
Ginzberg, Eli (1936), 'Customary prices', *The American Economic Review*, **26** (2), 296.
Gourville, John T. (1998) 'Pennies-a-day: the effect of temporal reframing on transaction evaluation', *Journal of Consumer Research*, **24** (4), 395–408.
Guadagni, Peter M. and John D.C. Little (1983), 'A logit model of brand choice calibrated on scanner data', *Marketing Science*, **1** (2), 203–38.
Halverson, Richard (1995), 'Tops touts subdued attitude', *Discount Store News*, **34** (20), 8–9.
Hess, James D. and Eitan Gerstner (1991), 'Price-matching policies: an empirical case', *Managerial and Decision Economics*, **12** (4), 305–15.
Inman, Jeffrey J. and Leigh McAlister (1993), 'A retailer promotion policy model considering promotion signal sensitivity', *Marketing Science*, **12** (4), 339–56.
Inman, Jeffrey J., Leigh McAlister and Wayne D. Hoyer (1990), 'Promotion signal: proxy for a price cut', *Journal of Consumer Research*, **17** (June), 74–81.
Jain, Sanjay and Joydeep Srivastava (2000), 'An empirical and theoretical analysis of price-matching refund policies', *Journal of Marketing Research*, **37** (August), 351–62.
Kalyanaram, Gurumurthy and Russell S. Winer (1995), 'Empirical generalizations from reference price and asymmetric price response research', special issue of *Marketing Science* on empirical generalizations in marketing, **14** (3), G161–G169.

Monroe, Kent B. and Angela Y. Lee (1999), 'Remembering versus knowing: issues in buyers' processing of price information', *Journal of the Academy of Marketing Science*, **27** (2), 207–25.

Monroe, Kent B., Christine P. Powell and Pravat K. Choudhury (1986), 'The influence of price awareness on price perceptions', in R. Lutz (ed.), *Advances in Consumer Research*, Vol. 13, Provo, UT: Association for Consumer Research, pp. 595–9.

Neslin, Scott A. and Robert W. Shoemaker (1989), 'An alternative explanation for lower repeat rates after promotion purchases', *Journal of Marketing Research*, **26** (2), 205–13.

Petty, Richard E. and John T. Cacioppo (1986), *Communication and Persuasion: Central and Peripheral Routes to Attitude Change*, New York: Springer-Verlag.

PR Newswire (1989), 'Montgomery Ward reduces prices on all brand name merchandise', 17 February.

Progressive Grocer (1964), 'How much do consumers know about retail prices?', February, 104–6.

Progressive Grocer (1975), 'Then and now: shopping behavior 10 years apart', October, 37–41.

Ratchford, Brian T. and Narasimhan Srinivasan (1993), 'An empirical investigation of returns to search', *Marketing Science*, **12** (1), 73–87.

Salmon, Walter J. and Gwendolyn K. Ortmeyer (1992), *Randall's Department Stores*, Boston, MA: Harvard Business School Publishing, pp. 1–24.

Salmon, Walter J. and Gwendolyn K. Ortmeyer (1993), *Duncan Department Stores*, Boston, MA: Harvard Business School Publishing, pp. 1–36.

Salop, S. (1986), 'Practices that (credibly) facilitate oligopoly coordination', in J. Stiglitz and F. Mathewson (eds), *New Developments in the Analysis of Market Structure*, Cambridge, MA: MIT Press, pp. 265–90.

Schindler, Robert M. (1991), 'Symbolic meanings of a price ending', *Advances in Consumer Research*, **18**, 794–801.

Schindler, Robert M. (2006), 'The 99-price ending as a signal of a low-price appeal', *Journal of Retailing*, **82** (1), 71–7.

Schindler, Robert M. and Lori S. Warren (1988), 'Effect of odd pricing on choice of items from a menu', *Advances in Consumer Research*, **15**, 348–53.

Simester, Duncan I. (1995), 'Signaling price image using advertised prices', *Marketing Science*, **14** (2), 166–88.

Stiving, Mark and Russell S. Winer (1997), 'An empirical analysis of price endings with scanner data', *Journal of Customer Research*, June, 57–67.

Tadelis, Steven (1999), 'What's in a name? Reputation as a tradeable asset', *The American Economic Review*, **89** (3), 548–63.

Vanhuele, Marc and Xavier Drèze (2002), 'Measuring the price knowledge shoppers bring to the store', *Journal of Marketing*, **66** (October), 72–85.

Veilleux, C.T. (1996), 'Tops loses VP, plans cutbacks', *HFN: The Weekly Newspaper for the Home Furnishing Network*, **70** (24), 67–8.

Wernerfelt, Birger (1988), 'Umbrella branding as a signal of new product quality: an example of signalling by posting a bond', *Rand Journal of Economics*, **19** (3), 458–66.

Xia, Lan, Kent B. Monroe and Jennifer L. Cox (2004), 'The price is unfair! A conceptual framework of price fairness perceptions', *Journal of Marketing*, **68**, 1–15.

Zettelmeyer, Florian, Fiona Scott Morton and Jorge Silva-Risso (2006), 'How the Internet lowers prices: evidence from matched survey and automobile transaction data', *Journal of Marketing Research*, **43** (May), 168–81.

PART II

PRICING DECISIONS AND MARKETING MIX

9 Strategic pricing of new products and services*
Rabikar Chatterjee

Abstract
This chapter organizes and reviews the literature on new product pricing, with a primary focus on normative models that take a dynamic perspective. Such a perspective is essential in the new product context, given the underlying demand- and supply-side dynamics and the need to take a long-term, strategic, view in setting pricing policy. Along with these dynamics, the high levels of uncertainty (for firms and customers alike) make the strategic new product pricing decision particularly complex and challenging. Our review of normative models yields key implications that provide (i) theoretical insights into the drivers of dynamic pricing policy for new products and services, and (ii) directional guidance for new product pricing decisions in practice. However, as abstractions of reality, these normative models are limited as practical tools for new product pricing. On the other hand, the new product pricing tools available are primarily helpful for setting specific (myopic) prices rather than a dynamic long-term pricing policy. Our review and discussion suggest several areas that offer opportunities for future research.

1. Introduction

Pricing of new products is an especially challenging decision, given its critical strategic importance and complexity. Contributing to the complexity are the uncertainty faced by the firm on both demand and supply sides, the dynamic (changing) environment and operating conditions, and the need for a long-term decision-making perspective, given that the firm's pricing decision in the current period is likely to impact future outcomes. Thus this chapter focuses primarily on new product pricing strategies that take a long-term perspective and recognize the dynamics driven by demand- and supply-side conditions over the extended time horizon.

Past reviews of new product pricing models include Kalish (1988), Monroe and Della Bitta (1978), Rao (1984, 1993) and Gijsbrechts (1993) cover new product pricing as part of their broader reviews of pricing. Also relevant are the reviews of new product diffusion models incorporating price and/or other marketing mix elements by Kalish and Sen (1986) and Bass et al. (2000). This chapter provides a selective and updated review and synthesis of strategic new product pricing models, focusing primarily on analytical models, but also describing relevant empirical research.

1.1 Dynamic pricing of new products: skimming versus penetration

Dean's ([1950] 1976) seminal article identifies new product pricing policy as 'the choice between (1) a policy of high initial prices that skim the cream of demand [skimming] and (2) a policy of low prices from the outset serving as an active agent for market penetration [penetration pricing]' (p. 145). The rationale for these two extreme strategies lays the foundation for our subsequent review. As we shall see, some of the policy prescriptions call for

---

* Comments and suggestions from Vithala R. Rao, Jehoshua Eliashberg and an anonymous reviewer are gratefully acknowledged.

a combination of penetration and skimming at different stages of the product life cycle, while others may be nuanced versions of these basic strategies. Dean identifies important elements of the new product pricing problem, including defining the firm's objective in terms of maximizing discounted profits over the planning horizon, taking into account customer and competitive dynamics over that period (see also Dean, 1969).

In a skimming strategy, prices begin high to extract the maximum surplus from customers willing to pay premium prices for the new product. Subsequently, prices decline as more price-sensitive segments are targeted in turn, to implement an intertemporal price discrimination strategy – 'an efficient device for breaking the market up into segments that differ in price elasticity of demand' (Dean [1950] 1976, p. 145). Dean also argues that this is a safer policy given uncertainty about demand elasticity, in that the market is more accepting of prices being lowered over time than the other way round. In addition, costs are likely to drop over time on account of market expansion and improved efficiency through experience (scale economies and experience curve effects). Price skimming helps to recover up-front investments in product development and introductory marketing. On the other hand, the high price level invites competition, unless the firm can extend its monopoly status (e.g. via patent protection).

Under a penetration pricing strategy, the objective is to aggressively penetrate the market by low prices. Some conditions under which penetration pricing makes sense are:

- price-sensitive customers in the mainstream market;
- short- and long-run cost benefits from scale economies and experience curve effects (cost-side learning), respectively;
- product characteristics that are well understood by mainstream customers (suggesting incremental rather than discontinuous innovations); and
- the threat of competitive entry.

Typically, a penetration pricing strategy would require the resources to support the rapid ramp-up in production, distribution and marketing of the product. Strategically, short-run profits are being sacrificed for future benefits – in terms of lower costs and a stronger market position, which can serve as sources of competitive advantage.

1.2 Skimming versus penetration: empirical evidence of managerial practice
When do managers use skimming or penetration pricing strategies in practice? Noble and Gruca (1999) surveyed managers responsible for pricing at firms supplying differentiated, capital goods in business-to-business markets, to learn about management practice and its relationship to theory. For new products, they identify three strategies – price skimming, penetration pricing and experience curve pricing (which is a particular case of penetration pricing).[1] The latter two involve low initial prices and have similar determinants relative to skimming – lower product differentiation, incremental innovation, low costs,

---

[1] Noble and Gruca's study is not limited to new products. They organize the strategies by the pricing situation for both new and mature products and then, for strategies within each pricing situation, by the conditions expected to favor the choice of a particular strategy. The three new product strategies were chosen by 32 percent of all respondents across all situations (skimming 14 percent, penetration 9 percent, and experience curve pricing 11 percent).

price elastic demand and available production capacity. The distinction is the primary source of cost advantage – experience curve pricing exploits learning by doing, while penetration pricing focuses on scale economies.

Managers were more likely to use skimming (with high relative price) in markets with high product differentiation when facing a cost disadvantage due to scale economies. Penetration pricing (with low relative price) was chosen when there was a cost advantage due to scale economies and total market demand was price elastic. Finally, experience curve pricing was used when there was high product differentiation, the product was not a major innovation, and there was low capacity utilization. Thus managerial practice is consistent with theory, except for the finding that experience curve pricing appears to be used in markets with high product differentiation, perhaps because the firms using this strategy are market followers cutting prices now to drive down costs in anticipation of future commoditization of the market.

Turning to a different industry (pharmaceuticals), Lu and Comanor (1998) investigate the temporal price patterns for new drugs and the principal factors affecting prices. Pharmaceutical price behavior appears consistent with Dean's conjecture. Significant innovations follow a modified skimming strategy, with prices at launch displaying substantial premium over existing substitutes, then declining over time. Most 'me too' new products follow a penetration strategy with launch prices below the competition, and then possibly increasing. Competition exerts downward pressure on prices. The nature of the application has pricing implications as well: drugs for acute conditions have larger premiums than those for chronic conditions.[2]

1.3 A framework for reviewing models of new product pricing

In the next two sections, we build on our discussion of skimming and penetration strategies to review analytical models of new product pricing that offer normative guidelines. With this in mind, we identify, in Table 9.1, the product, customer and firm/industry-related dimensions pertinent to the new product pricing decision that we employ to structure our review. Section 2 reviews models in a monopolistic setting, while Section 3 examines competitive models. Section 4 briefly discusses approaches to setting new product prices in practice. We conclude with a summary of the current status and directions for future research, in Section 5.

2. Normative models in a monopolistic setting

We organize our review of monopolistic models on the basis of the specification of the underlying demand model: models using an aggregate-level diffusion model for their demand specification (Section 2.1); models that consider the individual customer adoption decision explicitly in the diffusion process (Section 2.2); models incorporating strategic customers with foresight (Section 2.3); and models focusing on successive generations instead of a single product (Section 2.4). Section 2.5 summarizes the strategic new product pricing implications in a monopoly. Table 9.2 lists the key features and findings of selected monopolistic models.

---

[2] For more on pricing of pharmaceuticals, see the chapter in this volume by Kina and Wosinska (Chapter 23).

Table 9.1 *New product pricing models: key dimensions*

Dimension	Characteristic	Remarks and implications
Product	Nature: frequency of purchase; physical product vs service	The frequency of purchase significantly impacts the dynamics of pricing. With durables, cumulative sales can adversely affect product demand owing to saturation; with nondurables, repeat purchase can build brand loyalty. Differences between physical products and services have pricing implications in general (see chapter).
	Degree of innovativeness	Products can range from radically new or breakthrough at one end of the spectrum to incremental (or 'me too') at the other. This dimension has a critical impact on the demand dynamics, via its influence on customer behavior and competitive advantage.
	Degree of customer involvement	With high-involvement products (e.g. large ticket items), customers are more inclined to make the purchase decision carefully, after collecting information to reduce the high degree of perceived risk, relative to low-involvement products (which are often purchased on impulse). For a new product, adoption behavior and, in the aggregate, the dynamics of demand are affected by the degree of involvement.
	Diffusion (positive network) effects	Positive network effects result in an increase in the value of products as the number of products in use in the market (e.g. fax machines) increases. This is a direct network effect. Similar positive effects can also be indirect – for example, customers' valuations of products (e.g. hardware) may increase from a greater availability of complementary products (e.g. software) as the installed base of customers expands (the 'complementary bandwagon effect', Rohlfs, 2001). The same dynamic of increasing likelihood of adoption with expanding usage base can result on account of 'word of mouth' effect (Rogers, 2003). We use the term *diffusion effect* to refer to the positive impact of market penetration (cumulative sales) on demand, whatever the underlying mechanism driving this dynamic.
Customer	Uncertainty, risk attitude and learning	In the new product context, customer uncertainty about product performance is a pertinent issue. When uncertainty is explicitly considered, customers' attitude toward risk and the possibility of learning to resolve uncertainty become relevant factors as well as influencers of customers' willingness to pay.
	Heterogeneity (in price sensitivity and other characteristics)	While price sensitivity obviously affects price, the heterogeneity in price sensitivity (and, more generally, in preferences) across customers provides opportunities for price-based segmentation, including intertemporal price discrimination. Individual-level price sensitivity may change over time, as in the case of increasing loyalty through product experience. The demand model may be specified at the aggregate level from the outset, or else built up from the

Table 9.1 (continued)

Dimension	Characteristic	Remarks and implications
		disaggregate level. The disaggregate approach allows for explicit consideration of heterogeneity on key behavioral dimensions (such as willingness to pay).
	Type of customer	The degree of customer sophistication (myopic versus far-sighted and strategic) affects the pricing decision. The type of buyer (organizational versus consumer) also affects the nature of buyer behavior, with implications for pricing practices and policy. In particular, organization buyers may be fewer in number but more powerful and sophisticated than individual consumers.
Firm and Industry	Cost structure (static and dynamic)	Apart from the 'static' aspects of the cost structure (fixed versus variable costs and economies of scale), experience curve effects – which result in a lowering of costs with the cumulative volume of units produced and sold – have a dynamic impact on new product pricing policy.
	Uncertainty and learning	There is uncertainty on the firms' part about demand for the new product as well as other aspects of the environment (e.g. the competition). Such uncertainty can impact on firm behavior. There may also be the incentive to learn (e.g. via experimentation).
	Competition	The competitive situation – the presence of competition and its nature – is a critical factor in the pricing decision. We classify new product pricing models on the basis of whether or not they consider competition. Among models considering competition, a distinction can be made between competition among incumbent firms and potential competition from future entrants (Chatterjee et al., 2000).

2.1 Aggregate-level diffusion models

There is a rich stream of literature in marketing on new product pricing models (typically normative in nature) based on aggregate-level diffusion models best exemplified by Bass (1969). A key idea underlying these diffusion models (applied to first-time sales of durables) is that the rate of sales at any point in time depends on the cumulative sales (or market penetration), i.e.

$$dN/dt = f(N(t)) \qquad (9.1)$$

where $N(t)$ is cumulative sales (or penetration), dN/dt is the demand (rate of sales), and $f(\cdot)$ is the function operator. In particular, the Bass model takes the form

$$dN/dt = \left[p + q\frac{N(t)}{\overline{N}}\right][\overline{N} - N(t)] \qquad (9.2)$$

where $\overline{N}$ is the size of the total adopter population, and p and q are the coefficients of innovation and imitation respectively. The underlying demand dynamics are driven by

Table 9.2 Normative models in a monopolistic setting

	(1) Robinson and Lakhani (1975)	(2) Dolan and Jeuland (1981)	(3) Kalish (1983)	(4) Bass and Bultez (1982)	(5) Krishnan et al. (1999)
1. Product characteristics	Durables	Durables and nondurables	Durables	Durables	Durables
2. Customer behavior/demand:					
(a) Demand drivers/sources of demand dynamics	Cumulative sales (diffusion and saturation effects), price	Durable: cumulative sales (diffusion and saturation effects), price. Nondurable (trial plus repeat): cumulative sales and price; saturation effects for trial	Cumulative sales (diffusion and saturation effects) or time (exogenous diffusion pattern), and price	Time (exogenous diffusion pattern), price	Cumulative sales (diffusion and saturation effects), price (current level and rate of change)
(b) Heterogeneity	No (aggregate-level specification)	No (aggregate-level specification)	No (aggregate-level specification)	No (aggregate-level specification)	No (aggregate-level specification)
(c) Uncertainty/ learning?	No	No	No	No	No
(d) Strategic customers?	No	No	No	No	No
3. Firm/industry:					
(a) Experience curve effects?	Yes	Yes	Yes	Yes	Yes
(b) Uncertainty/ learning?	No	No	No	No	No
(c) Decision variable(s)	Price	Price	Price	Price	Price
(d) Type of equilibrium (if customers are strategic)	Not applicable (myopic customers)	Not applicable (myopic customers)	Not applicable (myopic customers)	Not applicable (myopic customers)	Not applicable (myopic customers)

	(6) Chen and Jain (1992)	(7) Raman and Chatterjee (1995)	(8) Huang et al. (2007)	(9) Jeuland (1981)	(10) Kalish (1985)
1. Product characteristics	Durables	Durables	Durables	Durables	Durables and nondurables
2. Customer behavior/demand:					
(a) Demand drivers/sources of demand dynamics	Cumulative sales (diffusion and saturation effects), price, uncertain discrete shock	Cumulative sales (diffusion and saturation effects), price, uncertainty (stochastic disturbance)	Cumulative sales (diffusion and saturation effects), price, reliability	Cumulative sales (information diffusion), distribution of reservation prices	Cumulative aware and cumulative adopters (awareness dynamics with saturation and diffusion effects), distribution of reservation prices
4. Key results/pricing implications	Optimal price may *increase* initially, and then *decline*	Durables: optimal price *increases* initially, and then *declines* if diffusion effect sufficiently strong; otherwise price monotonically *declines* Nondurables: optimal price monotonically *declines* if decline in trial (due to saturation) is greater than growth of repeat, and *increases* otherwise	For durables (with diffusion and saturation effects), optimal price *increases* initially, and then *declines* if diffusion effect sufficiently strong; otherwise price monotonically *declines* In case of exogenously specified life cycle, optimal price monotonically *declines* with experience curve effect on cost	Optimal price monotonically *declines* with decreasing cost (experience curve effect)	Optimal price may *increase* initially (if the diffusion price sensitivity parameter and discount rate are sufficient small), and then *declines*

Table 9.2 (continued)

	(6) Chen and Jain (1992)	(7) Raman and Chatterjee (1995)	(8) Huang et al. (2007)	(9) Jeuland (1981)	(10) Kalish (1985)
(b) Heterogeneity	No (aggregate-level specification)	No (aggregate-level specification)	No (aggregate-level specification)	Heterogeneity in reservation price	No (aggregate-level specification)
(c) Uncertainty/learning?	No	No	No	Yes – information reduces uncertainty	Yes – information reduces uncertainty
(d) Strategic customers?	No	No	No	No	No
3. Firm/industry:					
(a) Experience curve effects?	Yes	Yes	No	Yes	Yes
(b) Uncertainty/learning?	Yes – random, discrete shock (Poisson process); no learning	Yes – demand uncertainty; no learning	No	No	No
(c) Decision variable(s)	Price	Price	Price, length of warranty, product reliability	Price	Price, advertising
(d) Type of equilibrium (if customers are strategic)	Not applicable (myopic customers)	Not applicable (myopic customers)	Not applicable (myopic customers)	Not applicable (myopic customers)	Not applicable (myopic customers)
4. Key results/pricing implications	• Impact of uncertainty on price policy greater if probability and/or magnitude of random shock is larger	• Demand uncertainty – *increases* initial price – *reduces* the price slope (which is declining)	• For particular set of parameter values, price and warranty period *decline* over time	• Same as aggregate-level models, i.e. optimal price *increases* initially, and then *declines* if diffusion effect sufficiently strong; otherwise price	• Industry prices will *increase* when diffusion effect is dominant and *decrease* when saturation effect is dominant

	(11) Horsky (1990)	(12) Besanko and Winston (1990)	(13) Narasimhan (1989)	(14) Moorthy (1988)	(15) Balachander and Srinivasan (1998)
	• Impact of uncertainty can either reinforce or counterbalance price dynamics in deterministic case • Price path experiences jump at time of shock	– reduces sensitivity of initial price and slope to changes in other demand parameters and discount rate		monotonically *declines* • Actual shape of diffusion curve influenced by reservation price distribution	• Lower cost firm will have higher market share (with common industry prices) • Given cost-side learning, high-cost firm will produce more to reduce (or even reverse) cost disadvantage
1. Product characteristics	Household durables	Durables	Durables	Durables	Durables
2. Customer behavior/demand:					
(a) Demand drivers/sources of demand dynamics	Cumulative eligible adopters (saturation and diffusion effects), preference, distribution of wage rates	Distribution of reservation prices, price, future price expectations	Cumulative sales, distribution of reservation prices, price, future price expectations	Distribution of reservation prices, price, future price expectations	Distribution of reservation prices, price, future price expectations
(b) Heterogeneity	Heterogeneity in wage rate	Heterogeneity in reservation price	Heterogeneity in reservation price	Heterogeneity in reservation price	Heterogeneity in reservation price
(c) Uncertainty/learning?	Yes – information (cumulative sales) reduces uncertainty	No	No	Yes – uncertain about cost in Period 1	Yes – uncertain about extent of experience curve effect in Period 1
(d) Strategic customers?	No	Yes – perfect foresight	Yes – perfect foresight	Yes – perfect foresight	Yes – perfect foresight

Table 9.2 (continued)

	(11) Horsky (1990)	(12) Besanko and Winston (1990)	(13) Narasimhan (1989)	(14) Moorthy (1988)	(15) Balachander and Srinivasan (1998)
3. Firm/industry:					
(a) Experience curve effects?	Yes	No	No	No	Yes
(b) Uncertainty/ learning?	No	No	No	No	No
(c) Decision variable(s)	Price	Price	Price	Price	Price
(d) Type of equilibrium (if customers are strategic)	Not applicable	Subgame-perfect Nash	Subgame-perfect Nash	Subgame-perfect Nash	Subgame-perfect Nash
4. Key results/ pricing implications	• Optimal price *declines* monotonically if the diffusion effect is weak. If the diffusion effect is sufficiently strong, then prices start *low* and *increase* before *declining* • If the diffusion effect is especially strong, the initial price may be *lower* than initial cost	• Optimal price for firm facing myopic customers *declines* monotonically over time and is (a) *higher* (in case of myopic customers) and (b) *lower* (in case of strategic customers) in any time period (except last) than single-period optimal price • For any given penetration level, optimal price	• With customer expectations and diffusion, optimal price path follows cyclical pattern. Within each cycle, price declines monotonically • Stronger diffusion effect implies shorter cycles	• It is *not* possible for a low-cost monopolist to signal high cost by charging a high price in Period 1. The optimal decision is to price in Period 1 to reveal true cost	• Low-experience firm credibly signals its cost structure by charging a *higher* first-period price than in full-information case

	(16) Dhebar and Oren (1985)	(17) Judd and Riordan (1994)	(18) Zhao (2000)	(19) Bayus (1992)	(20) Padmanabhan and Bass (1993)
1. Product characteristics	Networked service (e.g. telecom)	Nondurable, experience good	Nondurable, experience good	Successive generations of durables	Successive generations of durables
2. Customer behavior/demand:					
(a) Demand drivers/sources of demand dynamics	Cumulative sales (positive network effect), distribution of reservation prices, subscription price	Distribution of customer's reservation price, product experience, price	Distribution of customer's reservation price, advertising (creates awareness), price	1st gen. (replacement sales only): cumulative 2nd gen. sales, prices, time; 2nd gen: cumulative 2nd gen. sales, prices	1st gen: cumulative firm sales (saturation effect), own price; 2nd gen: cumulative firm sales and own price, plus fraction of 1st gen. demand
(b) Heterogeneity	Heterogeneity in reservation price	Heterogeneity in reservation price	Heterogeneity in reservation price	No (aggregate-level specification)	No (aggregate-level specification)
(c) Uncertainty/ learning?	Yes – uncertain about future network growth (i.e. this can be only partially anticipated)	Yes – uncertain about product quality; learning from product use	Yes – uncertainty about product quality; inference drawn from firm's decisions (price, advertising)	No	No
(d) Strategic customers?	Yes – anticipate future network growth	Yes	Yes	No	No

always *lower* for rational customers relative to myopic customers. Also, price declines at a *lower* rate

Table 9.2 (continued)

	(16) Dhebar and Oren (1985)	(17) Judd and Riordan (1994)	(18) Zhao (2000)	(19) Bayus (1992)	(20) Padmanabhan and Bass (1993)
3. Firm/industry:					
(a) Experience curve effects?	Yes	No	No	No	Yes
(b) Uncertainty/ learning?	No	Uncertainty about quality – resolved by private information	No	No	No
(c) Decision variable(s)	Subscription price	Price	Price, advertising	Price	Price
(d) Type of equilibrium (if customers are strategic)	Subgame-perfect Nash	Bayes–Nash (subgame-perfect)	Separating equilibrium	Not applicable – myopic customers	Not applicable – myopic customers
4. Key results/ pricing implications	• Optimal subscription price monotonically *increases* over time • Anticipation of future network growth by customers and a lower discount rate both *lower* price for a given network size	• When customers are uncertain about product quality and form beliefs based on product experience and price, high-quality monopolist can signal quality by pricing *above* full-information price in Period 1. As consumer learning increases over time, price *declines* toward full-information level	• When customers are uncertain about product quality, a high-quality firm will price *higher* and spend less on advertising than in full-information situation, regardless of the quality–marginal cost relationship	• Optimal price for 2nd gen. *declines* monotonically over time if 2nd gen. sales come from normal and/ or discretionary replacements as long as fraction of normal replacements large enough. Otherwise, 2nd gen. price may be *increasing* initially	• Prior to 2nd gen. entry, diffusion (saturation) effect *decreases (increases)* 1st gen. price • After 2nd gen. entry, higher substitution rate drives 1st gen. and 2nd gen. price closer to, and 2nd gen. price away from, myopic optimum levels. Positive impact of 1st gen. price (sales) on 2nd gen. demand implies *higher (lower)* 1st gen. price

- The firm has incentive for initial investment in temporary quality improvement
- For sufficiently large fraction of replacement sales, 1st gen. price *increases* (*decreases*) if 2nd gen. sales come entirely from discretionary (normal) replacements

	(21) Kornish (2001)
1. Product characteristics	Successive generations of durables
2. Customer behavior/demand:	
(a) Demand drivers/sources of demand dynamics	Prices and qualities of 1st and 2nd gen. distribution of reservation prices
(b) Heterogeneity	Heterogeneity in reservation prices
(c) Uncertainty/learning?	No
(d) Strategic customers?	Yes – perfect foresight

Table 9.2 (continued)

	(21) Kornish (2001)
3. Firm/industry:	
(a) Experience curve effects?	No
(b) Uncertainty/ learning?	No
(c) Decision variable(s)	Price
(d) Type of equilibrium (if customers are strategic)	Subgame-perfect equilibrium
4. Key results/ pricing implications	• With customers with perfect foresight, it is possible for an equilibrium to exist in case there is improvement from 1st to 2nd gen. in real value terms, as long as firm does not offer special upgrade price for 2nd gen. to 1st gen. owners

the diffusion effect captured by the first term on the right-hand side of (9.2), which is increasing in cumulative sales or market penetration, and the saturation effect captured by the second term, which is decreasing in cumulative sales. The diffusion effect drives the dynamics early in the life cycle (when penetration is low), while the saturation effect dominates later – thus demand is increasing in cumulative sales (or market penetration) initially, but decreasing later in the life cycle. The models discussed in this section extend the basic model (9.1) by explicitly incorporating price as a variable influencing demand. Our discussion complements and updates the previous reviews by Kalish (1988); Kalish and Sen (1986); and Bass et al. (2000).

Normative models seek to derive the price trajectory over the planning period to optimize some objective (e.g. the discounted profit stream), given the demand function (based on a diffusion model), and appropriate initial, terminal and/or boundary conditions. Dynamic optimization typically involves the use of calculus of variations or optimal control (Kamien and Schwartz, 1991). Mathematically, the basic version of the problem may be stated as:

$$\max_{p(t)} \int_0^T e^{-rt}[p(t) - c(N(t))](dN/dt)\,dt \qquad (9.3)$$

$$\text{subject to: } dN/dt = f(N(t), p(t)); N(0) = 0; N(T) = \varphi$$

where $c(N(t))$ is the marginal cost, which may decline in cumulative sales under cost-side learning, and φ represents the salvage value. The demand specification usually incorporates price in one of three ways (Kalish and Sen, 1986):

Multiplicative price influence The general form of the demand model is

$$dN/dt = f(N(t)) \cdot h(p(t)) \qquad (9.4)$$

where $h(p(t))$ is a decreasing function of price at time t, $p(t)$. This model was first employed by Robinson and Lakhani (1975; Table 9.2(1)) and later by Dolan and Jeuland (1981; Table 9.2(2)); see also Jeuland and Dolan (1982). Dolan and Jeuland also analyze a non-durable goods model, where the sales rate is the sum of initial purchases given by (9.4) and repeat purchases proportional to the number of users $N(t)$.

Kalish (1983; Table 9.2(3)) considers a variety of demand specifications, including the multiplicative price influence model in (9.4). The Robinson and Lakhani (1975) and Dolan and Jeuland (1981) models are special cases of Kalish's more general formulation. The analysis provides insight into the effects of the different dynamic drivers of long-term profit on the optimal price path for a durable good. We summarize the key implications below:

- If demand is a function of price alone (i.e. there are no demand-side dynamics), the optimal price declines monotonically over time under cost-side learning and a positive discount rate. Cost-side learning reduces the optimal price below the myopic optimum, to trade off short-term profits for lower costs in future. This result applies to both durables and nondurables.

- In the presence of diffusion and saturation effects on demand, and assuming a zero discount rate, the optimal price path increases as long as demand is increasing in market penetration (i.e. the diffusion effect dominates), then decreases when demand begins to decrease with increasing penetration (i.e. the saturation effect dominates). The saturation effect in isolation indicates a higher price at any point in time than the corresponding myopic price, whereas the diffusion effect alone would indicate a lower price (to subsidize the early adopters and thereby stimulate the bandwagon effect for future profits).
- In the more realistic case of nonzero discount rate and cost-side learning, it is still optimal for prices to be increasing initially and then declining, as long as the diffusion effect is sufficiently strong and the discount rate is not too high. It pays to sacrifice early profits by subsidizing the early adopters, as long as the future is not discounted too heavily. Under a high discount rate and/or low diffusion effect, the optimal price path declines monotonically.
- In the case of nondurables (no saturation), the diffusion effect would imply a low initial price, increasing over time. Cost-side learning would also imply a lower price relative to the myopic optimum (at any point in time), but with a decreasing trajectory. Thus, with both diffusion and cost-side learning, the dynamic optimum price would be lower than the myopic optimum because both effects encourage stimulating sales now to drive up future demand and drive down future cost.
- In a trial/repeat model for nondurables, the optimal price declines (increases) monotonically if the decline in trial due to saturation is greater (lower) than the growth in repeat sales.

Multiplicative price influence on exogenous life cycle The general demand specification is

$$dN/dt = g(t) \cdot h(p(t)) \tag{9.5}$$

where $g(t)$ represents an exogenous life cycle, such as that generated by solving the Bass model (2) (Bass, 1980). Bass and Bultez (1982; Table 9.2(4)) and Kalish (1983) analyze this model, and find that the optimal price declines monotonically if there is cost-side learning. In this case, subsidizing early adopters does not help, since the exogenous life cycle specification does not incorporate the dynamic effect of price on demand as fully as the specification in (9.4).

Market potential as a function of price The demand model is of the general form:

$$dN/dt = f(N(t))[\overline{N}(p(t)) - N(t)] \tag{9.6}$$

where the market potential $\overline{N}$ is now modeled as a decreasing function of price and $f(N(t))$ represents the diffusion effect $[p + q[N(t)/\overline{N}]]$. Kalish (1983) examines this demand function as well, and shows that this case implies an initially increasing optimal price if the diffusion effect is sufficiently strong – qualitatively similar to the case of the multiplicative specification (9.4) discussed earlier. However, the condition for an increasing price trajectory is stronger, so that increasing prices will be less prevalent in this case and, where they do occur, brief in their duration. Intuitively, increasing prices will have an adverse impact on the size of the potential adopter population, which is not an issue in the multiplicative price influence demand model.

The generalized Bass model (GBM)   Bass et al. (1994) propose the generalized Bass model (GBM) in which $f(N(t))$ is given by the Bass (1969) model but $h(p(t))$ is replaced by a more general function that the authors term 'current marketing effort'. GBM models the effect of price differently from other multiplicative price influence models.

Krishnan et al. (1999; Table 9.2(5)) employ a slightly modified form of GBM to derive the optimal pricing strategy for new products, with the following current marketing effort function in place of $h(p(t))$ in (9.4):

$$x(t) = 1 + \gamma \ln p(0) + \beta \frac{\frac{dp(t)}{dt}}{p(t)} \quad (9.7)$$

where γ and β are both negative. Note that this specification models the impact of the absolute level as well as the slope of the price path on demand.[3] Under this formulation, the combination (actually, the product) of the diffusion price sensitivity parameter $(-\beta)$ and the discount rate drives the optimal price path. If this combined effect is sufficiently small, the optimal price path is initially increasing and then declining; otherwise the path declines monotonically, as is often observed for many durables. In the multiplicative price influence models discussed earlier (Dolan and Jeuland, 1981; Kalish, 1983; Robinson and Lakhani, 1975), the price dynamics are driven by the demand dynamics (diffusion versus saturation), along with the discount rate and experience curve effects. In contrast, in the GBM formulation, the drivers are the diffusion price sensitivity and the discount rate (acting multiplicatively) and experience curve effects.

Incorporating demand uncertainty   The models discussed above assume that demand is known with certainty over the entire planning horizon; realistically, firms launching new products are uncertain about demand over time. We review two models that explicitly incorporate different types of demand uncertainty. Chen and Jain (1992; Table 9.2(6)) consider uncertainty in the form of discrete shocks or 'jumps'. Raman and Chatterjee (1995; Table 2(7)) focus on demand uncertainty due to imperfect knowledge of the precise impact of explanatory variables included in the model as well as the 'random' impact of excluded variables.

Chen and Jain (1992) extend Kalish's (1983) deterministic model by including random shocks influencing demand. Their occurrence is governed by a Poisson process. Examples of such shocks are sudden changes to the potential market size or in economic conditions. The essential implications of Chen and Jain's analysis are:

---

[3] While Krishnan et al. do not provide a behavioral justification for this specification, consideration of future expectations might suggest the inclusion of the price slope. However, the expectations argument would imply a positive sign for β.

- The impact of uncertainty on pricing policy increases the probability of the occurrence of the event and the magnitude of its after-effect.
- The impact of uncertainty can either reinforce or counterbalance the deterministic dynamic effects (as in Kalish, 1983), depending on whether the 'contingent experience effect' – the expected effect of cumulative sales on profits via its influence on the variation in the contingent state – is in the same or opposite direction as the deterministic experience effect.
- The price path experiences a jump at the time of occurrence of the contingent event.

Raman and Chatterjee (1995) incorporate the effect of demand uncertainty by allowing demand to be subject to stochastic disturbance. They find that, in general, the extent of impact of demand uncertainty on the optimal pricing policy is determined by the interaction among demand uncertainty, demand dynamics (diffusion and/or saturation effects), cost-side learning and the discount rate. For a Bass-type demand model with diffusion and saturation effects, they find (relative to the monotonically declining price path under deterministic demand in their infinite time horizon analysis) that:

- The effect of demand uncertainty is to (a) increase the initial price; (b) decrease the initial slope (that is, the price declines less steeply in cumulative sales); and (c) make the optimal price (both level and slope) less sensitive to changes in the discount rate or the coefficients of innovation and imitation that together determine the magnitude of demand dynamics.

Intuitively, uncertainty moderates the impact of the variables driving optimal price dynamics.

Incorporating the manufacturing–marketing interface In an interesting cross-functional modeling endeavor, Huang et al. (2007; Table 9.2(8)) develop a model that includes product reliability, Bass-type demand-side dynamics and cost-learning effects. The decision variables are product reliability (at the design stage) and dynamic policies over the planning horizon with regard to (i) price and (ii) length of the warranty. Given the complexity of the model, general qualitative implications are difficult to articulate, although the authors identify the direction of the slopes of the price and warranty policy paths for different conditions relating to the current value Hamiltonian and demand dynamics (diffusion versus saturation). Further, they provide numerical examples to demonstrate how dynamic programming may be employed to derive optimal policy. For a particular set of parameter values, it is shown that both optimal price and warranty period decline over time. This model represents a valuable (and rare) effort to capture the cross-functional aspects of decisions involving new products.

2.2 Models considering the individual customer adoption decision

The models discussed in Section 2.1 specify demand at the aggregate level, without really explicitly considering the customer adoption process. We next examine three models proposed by Jeuland (1981), Kalish (1985) and Horsky (1990) (Table 9.2(9), (10) and (11)) that extend the aggregate diffusion model paradigm to include aspects of the adoption process leading to an explicit adoption decision rule at the disaggregate level.

This provides potentially richer implications for new product pricing that augment the findings from the aggregate models. These models postulate that (a) the population is heterogeneous in their reservation price for the new product, (b) potential adopters are uncertain about its performance, lowering their reservation price, (c) information from adopters and other sources reduces this uncertainty, and (d) an individual adopts the product once its price falls below her reservation price.

Jeuland (1981) assumes that uncertain potential adopters believe that there is some probability that product performance will be lower than its true level. Once they are informed of the true performance (through word-of-mouth from adopters), their reservation price jumps up. The dynamics are thus driven by (a) the information diffusion process (which follows a process governed by the model (2) with the coefficient $p = 0$), and (b) the pricing policy. Qualitatively, the optimal pricing policy implications are similar to those for the aggregate-level multiplicative price influence models discussed earlier. However, the distribution of reservation prices across the population affects the specific trajectory of the optimal price path over time.

Kalish (1985) includes an explicit awareness component in his framework. At any point in time, individuals in the population belong to one of three stages: (a) unaware; (b) aware but yet to adopt; and (c) adopter. Awareness of the new product diffuses according to a model similar to (2), with the coefficient of innovation p a function of advertising, and word-of-mouth generated by both groups (b) and (c), with different coefficients of imitation q_1 and q_2, respectively. Aware customers are still uncertain of their valuation; this uncertainty decreases as the number of adopters increases. Aware customers become potential adopters when their risk-adjusted valuations exceed the price. These potential adopters actually adopt the product gradually after this adoption condition is met, with a constant conditional likelihood of adoption (hazard rate). The implications of Kalish's model for durable and nondurable goods are as follows:

- *Durable goods* The optimal price decreases monotonically, unless adopters are highly effective in generating awareness and/or early adopters reduce their uncertainty significantly. In the latter case, prices may increase at product introduction, when customers are the least well informed and the marginal value of information is the highest.
- *Nondurable goods* For constant marginal cost (i.e. no cost-side learning), the optimal price will increase to some steady-state level, if and only if advertising is decreasing, which is the case unless the discount rate is high.

These results for durable and nondurable goods are qualitatively consistent with the implications of the aggregate-level models, with the added insight into the role of uncertainty reduction.

Horsky (1990) uses a household production framework to show that individual (or household) reservation prices depend on product benefits and wage rates. Assuming an extreme value distribution for the wage rate across the population yields a logistic adoption function, dependent on the wage rate distribution parameters and the price. These 'eligible adopters' may delay their purchase because of unawareness, product performance uncertainty, or expectations of a price decline, all of which are assumed to decrease in cumulative sales. The resulting diffusion model reduces to the 'market potential as a

188   *Handbook of pricing research in marketing*

function of price' form in (9.6), with the eligible adopters (obtained from the logistical adopter model) as the potential adopters.

Given the model set-up, the results are consistent with those of the aggregate-level 'market potential as a function of price' model (Kalish, 1983). If the diffusion effect is weak, the optimal price path declines monotonically. If it is sufficiently strong, then prices start lower to subsidize the early adopters and rise before declining. If the effect is especially strong, the initial price may actually be lower than the initial marginal cost, implying negative early contribution.

In summary, the pricing implications of these three models are broadly consistent with the aggregate-level diffusion models discussed in Section 2.1. However, they add nuances to the implications by virtue of their disaggregate-level behavioral assumptions – in particular, the distribution of reservation prices (wage rates in Horsky's model) in the population influences the price trajectory. While these models consider the individual-level adoption decision and thereby incorporate heterogeneity, the dynamics of demand are largely driven by the model components (e.g. awareness) based on an aggregate diffusion model specification, e.g. Bass (1969).

2.3   Models incorporating strategic customers with future expectations
With time-varying price paths, customers may form expectations of future prices (or product performance) and take these future expectations into account while making their current purchase decisions. The models discussed so far effectively ignore the role of customer expectations, assuming that customers act myopically.[4] We now examine models explicitly incorporating customer expectations. These models are commonly based on rational expectations – implying that, in equilibrium, customers correctly predict the pricing policy to be followed by the monopolist. While as a descriptive model of customer behavior the rational expectations assumption is perhaps unrealistic in terms of the implied customer sophistication, its use as a paramorphic ('as if') modeling device in predicting outcomes in dynamic economic systems (including a firm's pricing policy) is widely accepted.

Besanko and Winston (1990; Table 9.2(12)) show how customer foresight influences a durable goods monopolist's price-skimming strategy over multiple time periods. Customers are intertemporal utility maximizers with rational expectations and constant reservation prices that are uniformly distributed over the population. The subgame-perfect Nash equilibrium analysis compares the dynamic pricing implications in the case of rational customers (with perfect foresight) with that of myopic customers.[5] The key findings are as follows:

---

[4]   Kalish (1985) and Horsky (1990) mention future expectations, but do not incorporate them formally in the model.
[5]   A subgame-perfect Nash equilibrium is a Nash equilibrium whose strategies represent a Nash equilibrium for each subgame within the larger game. Limiting the equilibrium to be subgame-perfect rules out unreasonable commitments by the firm (such as committing to not lowering prices in the future, when such lowering will always be profitable).

Strategic pricing of new products and services 189

- The optimal pricing policy for a firm facing myopic customers declines monotonically. The price is higher than the single-period profit-maximizing price in each period except the last.
- The policy for a firm facing rational customers also declines monotonically. However, the price is lower than the single-period profit-maximizing price in each period except the last.
- For a given penetration level, optimal prices are always lower and their decline more gradual, for rational customers. The first-period price for myopic customers is higher, although at some point in time this price may drop below that for rational customers.
- Using a pricing policy that is optimal for myopic customers when the customers are actually rational leads to suboptimally high prices initially and lower profits overall.

Comparing the multi-period versus the single-period case, a higher price in any period but the last makes sense for myopic customers because the firm can sell to those who have not yet bought in a future period, at lower prices. However, with rational customers, this effect is more than offset by the greater price sensitivity of customers who are willing to wait for prices to drop if there are future periods. Thus, with myopic customers, a firm would prefer as many periods (or opportunities to drop its price) as possible within the overall time horizon, for more effective skimming. With rational customers, it is the opposite – a shorter time horizon, or fewer but longer periods within the horizon, is preferred. The challenge for the firm is to be able to credibly commit to holding prices constant over the longer time period.

Besanko and Winston's analysis provides important insights into the impact of customer foresight, in isolation from other dynamics such as positive network effects (which would imply that reservation prices increase with market penetration, rather than being constant).

Narasimhan (1989; Table 9.2(13)) incorporates rational customers along with diffusion effects, assuming two types of customers differing in their reservation prices. New customers enter the market in each period, with the number given by a Bass (1969) type diffusion model. Once they enter the market, customers exit only after making their purchase of the durable. The purchase decision is based on maximizing intertemporal surplus. The key results are as follows:

- The optimal price path follows a cyclical pattern. Over each such cycle, the price declines monotonically from a high level (to sell to the high-valuation customers) and ends at a low level (for one period) to sell to the accumulated stock of low-valuation customers before returning to the high level. Customer expectations limit the price decline within each cycle.
- The length of the price cycles and the depth of discount depend on the relative sizes and valuations of the two segments, and the diffusion model coefficients. A higher coefficient of imitation implies shorter cycles to profit from early market penetration.

While these cyclical pricing implications are interesting, it is not clear if the same effect will persist if the distribution of reservation prices is continuous (e.g. uniform) across the

190 *Handbook of pricing research in marketing*

potential adopters, rather than dichotomous, as assumed. Also, as Narasimhan points out, prices would decline monotonically without cycling if the high-valuation customers entered first, which seems more plausible than both customer types entering in a fixed ratio in each period.

Moorthy (1988; Table 9.2(14)) considers a two-period model with uniformly distributed reservation prices across customers. Customers are uncertain about the cost of the durable, and use the first-period price to form expectations of the second-period price. The question is: can a low-cost monopolist pretend to have a high cost and thereby charge a high price in the first period, before dropping prices in the second period to exploit its low costs? The analysis shows that this is not possible – the firm's optimal decision is to price such that it reveals its true cost in the first period. This result suggests some robustness to the implications of the rational expectations model: the firm cannot 'fool' the customers even if they do not know the product cost.

In a similar vein, Balachander and Srinivasan (1998; Table 9.2(15)) analyze a two-period model in which rational customers with uniformly distributed reservation prices are uncertain about the degree of the firm's cost-side learning (high or low). The first-period price serves as a signal for customers to update their beliefs. The analysis yields a separating equilibrium in which a slow learning firm credibly signals its cost structure by charging a higher first-period price than if customers were fully informed. The signal is credible because a fast learning firm would charge a lower price to benefit from the experience curve effect in the first period.

In contrast to the above models focusing on durables, Dhebar and Oren (1985; Table 2(16)) consider a networked service (such as telecom) where customers can choose to subscribe period by period, with no start-up or termination fee (so that price expectations are not a factor). The value of the service depends on the price (subscription rate) and the number of subscribers. The optimal price path increases monotonically over time, consistent with the results for nondurables in Sections 2.1 and 2.2. Further, by anticipating future network growth, customers lower the equilibrium price (for a given network size) and thereby enlarge the network. A lower discount rate also has the effect of lowering price and enlarging the network.

Dhebar and Oren (1986) extend their 1985 model to consider nonlinear pricing where customers decide on usage volume in addition to subscription. They show that a nonlinear price schedule, consisting of a subscription price and a volume-based usage charge, results in a larger equilibrium network and higher profits than under a policy in which all subscribers pay the same fixed fee irrespective of usage. Dhebar and Oren's research focuses on networked services, which includes an increasing range of applications in today's technology-driven environment.

Price as signal of quality Can price serve as a credible signal of quality when there is uncertainty about quality? Research in economics (e.g. Milgrom and Roberts, 1986; Bagwell and Riordan, 1991) has shown that a high-quality firm may signal its quality via a price higher than the full-information optimum, if the high-quality firm's cost is sufficiently higher than that of the low-cost firm. Judd and Riordan (1994; Table 9.2(17)) use a signal-extraction model of customer behavior to explore this issue in the absence of any cost difference between the low- and high-quality firms. Customers' beliefs about the value of the product depend on their individual experience with the product as well as the inference drawn from the price. The former makes it harder for the firm to deceive the customer. The two-period analysis shows that:

- When customers, uncertain about product quality, form beliefs based on both their product experience and the price, the high-quality monopolist can signal quality by initially pricing above the full-information price even if the high- and low-quality products have the same cost. As consumer learning increases over time, prices decline toward the full-information level.
- Firms have an incentive to invest in temporary enhancement of quality initially, to influence customers' beliefs about quality for future benefit.

Zhao (2000; Table 9.2(18)) includes advertising as a decision variable in addition to price in a quality signaling modeling framework. Advertising serves not just as a signaling device (as in Milgrom and Roberts, 1986), but also as a generator of awareness. The analysis shows that a high-quality firm will price higher and spend less on advertising when customers are uncertain about quality than in the full-information situation. Thus, high price signals high quality in this case, as it does in the price-only models. In contrast to the situation where advertising's only role is to signal quality, it is optimal to spend less on advertising when it also creates awareness.

2.4 Models incorporating successive generations of new products

We next review models focusing on successive generations of a product, where the next generation is an advanced version of the current one, and gradually replaces the latter.

Aggregate-level diffusion models Bayus (1992; Table 9.2(19)) models the sales of a next-generation durable considering the replacement behavior of the previous generation. The time horizon begins with the introduction of the second generation (G2). At the start, there is a fixed population of owners of the first generation (G1). At any point, some proportion of the installed base of G1 will require to be replaced. These 'normal' replacements may be sourced from either G1 or G2. In addition, the rest of the installed base is susceptible to making 'discretionary' (accelerated) replacements on account of the availability of G2 – these sales are influenced by the diffusion effect. Mathematically, sales of G2 are given by:

$$dN(t)/dt = [\overline{N} - N(t)] \{ [1 - \theta(p_1(t), t)] f(N(t)) g(p_2(t))$$
$$+ \theta(p_1(t), t) \varphi(p_1(t), p_2(t)) \} \quad (9.8)$$

where $N(t)$ is cumulative second-generation sales, $\overline{N}$ is the initial market size (G1 installed base at the time of G2 introduction), $p_1(t)$ and $p_2(t)$ are G1 and G2 prices, respectively, $\theta(p_1(t), t)$ is the fraction of G1 installed base making 'normal' replacements at time t, $\varphi(p_1(t), p_2(t))$ is the fraction of 'normal' replacements sourced by G2, and $f(N(t))$ is the diffusion effect. Thus G1 sales equal $[\overline{N} - N(t)] \theta(p_1(t), t) [1 - \varphi(p_1(t), p_2(t))]$. The optimal G1 and G2 price paths can assume various patterns depending on specific conditions, indicating the complexity that consideration of successive generations with overlapping sales adds to the pricing decision. However, for a sufficiently long planning horizon, the following results hold:

- The optimal price for G2 declines monotonically if G2 sales come from only 'normal' or both 'normal' and 'discretionary' replacements; or from only 'discretionary' replacements as long as the fraction of 'normal' replacements θ is sufficiently large. If θ is not large enough, the optimal price may be increasing initially. Thus the G2 price path declines when replacement is important (even without cost-side learning) because the initial G2 sales are sourced by G1 replacements and therefore no subsidization of early adopters is necessary.
- For a sufficiently large fraction of 'normal' replacement sales, the optimal price for G1 monotonically increases [decreases] if G2 sales come entirely from 'discretionary' ('normal') replacements. Thus the G1 price trajectory is heavily influenced by replacement behavior and the source of second-generation sales.

Bayus provides some empirical support for his results, using successive generations of different consumer durables (B&W/color TV; CD/LP record players; corded/cordless/cellular telephones).

Padmanabhan and Bass (1993; Table 9.2(20)) analyze a successive-generations model, with only the first generation (G1) available in the first part of the planning horizon, until the second (advanced) generation (G2) is introduced at some exogenously determined point. The demand specification is fairly general, in order to capture a variety of possible demand dynamics:

$$\text{G1: } dN_1(t)/dt = (1 - \theta)f(N_1)(t), p_1(t) \quad \text{and} \tag{9.9}$$

$$\text{G2: } dN_2(t)/dt = g(N_1(t), N_2(t), p_1(t), p_2(t)) \tag{9.10}$$

where $N_1(t)$, $N_2(t)$ are the cumulative sales of G1 and G2, $p_1(t)$, $p_2(t)$ are the G1 and G2 prices, and θ is the fraction of first-generation sales switching to the second generation ($\theta = 0$ prior to G2 introduction, and some constant value $0 < \theta < 1$ thereafter). Thus, after the introduction of G2, some (fixed) fraction of G1 sales is cannibalized by G2, which also generates sales from its independent market potential. The model may be viewed as a successive-generations extension to Kalish (1983), with the following implications:

- Prior to G2 entry, a positive impact of additional G1 sales on G2 demand (diffusion effect) reduces the G1 price. If the impact on G2 demand is negative (saturation effect), then the G1 price increases. Otherwise, the G1 price slope is in line with Kalish (1983).
- After G2 entry, a higher substitution rate θ drives the G1 price closer to, and the G2 price away from, their myopic optimal levels. Also, if G2 sales are increasing in the G1 price, the latter is higher to sell more of G2. However, a positive impact of G1 sales on G2 demand implies a lower G1 price to stimulate G1 sales. The net effect depends on the relative strengths of these factors. The G2 price trajectory is otherwise in line with Kalish (1983).

One interesting implication of both models is that it may sometimes be optimal to actually increase the price of the first-generation product after the introduction of the next generation: all else equal, a higher G1 price is likely to have a positive impact on G2 demand.

Successive generations and strategic customers with perfect foresight Since customers with perfect foresight can anticipate the introduction of a superior product, what are the implications for strategy? Using a two-period model, Dhebar (1994) shows that if the technology improves too rapidly (so that the product improves in 'present value' terms), there is no equilibrium because the monopolist has the incentive to target customers who did not buy in the first period with low second-period prices. High-end customers are tempted to wait for the improved product. Thus there is a demand-side constraint imposed on the rate of product improvement.

Kornish (2001; Table 9.2(21)) uses a two-period model similar to Dhebar's, but assumes that if both generations were free, customers would be better off having G1 in period 1 and then switching to G2 in period 2 rather than waiting for G2. Under these assumptions, an equilibrium can exist if the successive generations imply improvement in 'real value' terms, as long as the monopolist does not offer a special upgrade price for G2 to current G1 owners. For the monopolist to credibly commit to such a single price in Period 2, he would need to make it impossible for a G1 owner to distinguish herself from a non-owner (e.g. by setting conditions that were either too difficult to prove, or too easy to claim, G1 ownership).

2.5 Normative models in a monopolistic setting: summary of implications

To conclude this section's review of monopolistic models, we summarize the main (and robust) implications for new product pricing strategy from the literature. The dynamic optimum policy is contrasted with the short-term (myopic) optimum that ignores the future profit implications of current decisions. We focus on the effect of individual factors – typically, when several factors operate simultaneously, the net impact depends on their relative strength.

- *Cost-side learning* Experience curve effects lower the optimal price (at any point in time) relative to the myopic optimum, while the dynamic optimal price declines over time.
- *Demand-side learning (diffusion effect)* The diffusion effect lowers the optimal price relative to the myopic optimum; the dynamic optimal price increases over time.
- *Demand saturation (for durables)* Saturation increases the optimal price relative to the myopic optimum; the dynamic optimal price decreases over time.
- *Demand dynamics for durables* For durables, saturation becomes the dominant effect over time relative to diffusion, as the market saturates. If the diffusion effect is sufficiently strong, the optimal price starts low to subsidize early adopters, then increases before declining.
- *Nondurables: net impact of demand- and cost-side learning* The optimal price is lower at any point in time than the myopic optimum, while its slope depends on the strength of demand-side learning (from diffusion and/or learning-by-use) relative to cost-side learning.

- *Random demand shock* The likelihood of a random shock impacts the price path. The degree of impact depends on the probability of occurrence on the event and the magnitude of its after-effect. The price path itself will exhibit a jump at the time of the shock.
- *Demand uncertainty* The impact of demand uncertainty is to make the optimal price less sensitive to the demand dynamics relative to the deterministic case.
- *Customer heterogeneity in willingness to pay in a durable goods market: myopic customers* In the absence of other effects, the optimal price follows the classic skimming strategy, with prices starting high to target the high-valuation segment and then declining over time to target successively lower-valuation segments. In each period, the price is higher than the single-period optimum.
- *Customer heterogeneity in willingness to pay in a durable goods market: strategic customers with perfect foresight* In any period, the optimal price is lower than the single-period optimum if customers have perfect foresight. Relative to the strategy for myopic customers, the starting price is lower and the price decline is more gradual when customers are strategic.
- *Services with positive network effects* The optimal price of a networked service (such as telecom) is monotonically increasing over time. Anticipation of future network growth (by strategic customers) serves to lower the price for a given network size.
- *Signaling cost structure (durable goods)* If customers are uncertain about the firm's cost structure, the firm should set the first period price to reveal its true cost structure, rather than masquerading otherwise. Similarly, if the uncertainty is about the rate of experience-based cost reduction, it may be optimal for a firm with a low learning rate to signal this via an initial price that is higher than the full-information optimum.
- *Signaling by the firm under customer uncertainty about quality (nondurables)* A high-quality firm can signal quality by pricing higher than the full-information optimum. Prices decline over time (toward the full information price) with customer learning.
- *Successive generations (durable goods)*
    - The price of the second generation is more likely to be monotonically declining from the outset than for a single new product, because sales from replacement of the first generation reduce the need to subsidize early adopters.
    - The price of the first generation after introduction of the second generation depends heavily on replacement behavior and the source of second-generation sales.
    - The first-generation price prior to introduction of the second generation decreases (increases) if the impact of additional first-generation sales on the potential market for the second-generation is positive (negative).

3. Normative models in a competitive setting

The models reviewed in Section 2 assume the absence of competition, which may be reasonable for major innovations early in the life cycle, or else if the focus is at the industry level ignoring interfirm competition. The presence of competition, involving incumbent firms or potential entrants, can significantly influence new product pricing strategy.

Section 3.1 briefly introduces the methodology used to analyze competitive models. Section 3.2 reviews models that consider potential competition, with a firm enjoying monopoly status prior to competitive entry, while Section 3.3 reviews models incorporating competition among incumbent firms. Section 3.4 summarizes the strategic new product pricing implications in a competitive setting. Table 9.3 presents the key features and findings of selected competitive models.

3.1 Equilibrium strategies in competitive situations

In a competitive situation, a firm's performance and its best (profit-maximizing) decision is usually affected by the actions of the other competing firms. Analytical models typically employ a game-theoretic framework to obtain a non-cooperative Nash equilibrium solution, such that no firm has an incentive to unilaterally deviate from the equilibrium.[6] As discussed earlier, the new product pricing decision should be in the form of a policy over time, considering the dynamic setting. The competitive counterpart to the optimal control formulation discussed in Section 2.1 is the differential game, which is employed to seek an equilibrium trajectory of the decision variable(s), where the objective of the firms is typically to maximize discounted profits over the planning horizon (Dolan et al., 1986; Dockner et al., 2000).

Two types of Nash equilibria are pertinent in the case of differential games. Open-loop equilibria express the policies as functions of time alone, while closed-loop equilibria are functions of time and the state of the system (e.g. cumulative sales). The strategies under the two equilibria are generally different, as illustrated later. Open-loop strategies are determined and committed to by the competitors at the outset for the entire planning horizon. Closed-loop policies capture the dynamics of competitive interaction by allowing strategies to adapt to the evolving state of the system over time. Closed-loop policies recognize that the best decision for a firm at any point in time is influenced by the positions (states) of its competitors, and are thus more appealing conceptually, though usually more difficult to derive analytically.

3.2 Models considering potential competition

Durable goods models with saturation effects We review two models that address the issue of potential competitive entry in a currently monopolistic market. Eliashberg and Jeuland (1986; Table 9.3(1)) analyze pricing strategies from the perspective of the first entrant, in a durable goods market. This firm enjoys monopoly status, until the second firm enters (at an exogenously specified point). Sales dynamics are driven by saturation effects alone and the price, with the following specification for the monopoly and duopoly periods:

$$\text{Monopoly: } dN_1(t)/dt = [\overline{N} - N_1(t)]\alpha_1[1 - kp_1(t)], \quad 0 < t \leq T_1 \quad (9.11)$$

---

[6] This approach involves the specification of a particular form of firm conduct leading to competitive interaction. Studies in the new empirical industrial organization tradition instead estimate firm conduct rather than making an *a priori* assumption (see, e.g., Kadiyali et al., 1996 for a discussion of this approach).

Table 9.3 Normative models in a competitive setting

	(1) Eliashberg and Jeuland (1986)	(2) Padmanabhan and Bass (1993)	(3) Gabszewicz et al. (1992)	(4) Dockner and Jorgensen (1988)	(5) Rao and Bass (1985)
1. Product characteristics	Durable	Durable, successive generations of innovation introduced by different firms	Nondurable, experience goods for which consumers learn by using product (undifferentiated)	General model, but primary focus on durables	Dynamic industry price and market share paths in an undifferentiated oligopoly, with cost learning
2. Customer behavior/demand:					
(a) Demand drivers/ sources of demand dynamics	Cumulative industry sales (saturation effect), own and cross price	1st gen: cumulative firm sales (saturation effect), own price; 2nd gen.: cumulative firm sales and own price, plus fraction of 1st gen. demand	Distribution of willingness to learn, prices	Cumulative firm/ industry sales' prices (general specification of diffusion model; special cases analyzed)	Cumulative sales (diffusion and saturation effects), industry price
(b) Heterogeneity	No (aggregate-level specification)	No (aggregate-level specification)	Heterogeneity in willingness to learn (to use product)	No (aggregate-level specification)	No (aggregate-level specification)
(c) Uncertainty/ learning?	No	No	Yes: learning through experience	No	Aggregate
(d) Strategic customers?	No	No	No	No	No

3. Firm/industry:						
(a) Experience curve effects?	No	No	No	No	Yes	Yes
(b) Uncertainty/ learning?	'Surprised' monopolist contrasted with correct anticipation of entry	No	No	No	No	No
(c) Competitive setting	Monopoly period followed by duopoly	Monopoly period followed by duopoly	Monopoly period followed by duopoly	Oligopoly	Oligopoly	Oligopoly
(d) Decision variable(s)	Price	Price	Price	Price	Price	Quantity
(e) Type of equilibrium	Nash, open-loop	Nash, open-loop	Nash (Bertrand competition)	Nash, open-loop	Nash, open-loop	Nash, open-loop
4. Key results/pricing implications	• First entrant prices *drop* at point of follower's entry • First entrant who correctly anticipates second entry (a) prices *higher* and decreases prices more gradually than if it were myopic, and (b) prices *lower* than if it did not anticipate the second entry	• 1st gen. price *lower* than for integrated firm producing both generations in monopoly • 1st gen. price *drops* at 2nd gen. entry • After 2nd gen. entry, 1st gen. price *higher* than for integrated firm • 2nd gen. price *equal* to that for integrated firm	• In case of brand-specific learning, pioneer prices *low* in monopoly period; both firms price *above* marginal cost in duopoly period • In case of category-level learning, pioneer chooses monopoly price in first period; both firms forced to price at marginal cost in second period	• Prices may initially *increase* if diffusion effect is sufficiently strong, then *decrease* later • When demand is adversely affected by cumulative sales of competitors, change in slope of price path from positive to negative will tend to be *delayed* • Stronger impact of competition will *lower* prices	• Industry prices will *increase* when diffusion effect is dominant and *decrease* when saturation effect is dominant • Lower-cost firm will have higher market share (with common industry prices) • Given cost-side learning, high-cost firm will produce more to reduce (or even reverse) cost disadvantage	

Table 9.3 (continued)

	(6) Dockner and Gaundersdorfer (1996)	(7) Baldauf et al. (2000)	(8) Dockner and Fruchter (2004)	(9) Chatterjee and Crosbie (1999)	(10) Wernerfelt (1985)
1. Product characteristics	Durable goods (with demand governed by saturation effects)	Durable goods (with demand governed by saturation effects)	Durable goods (with demand governed by saturation effects)	Durable goods (of different quality across firms)	Nondurable, experience goods for which consumers learn by using product
2. Customer behavior/demand:					
(a) Demand drivers/ sources of demand dynamics	Cumulative industry sales (saturation effect) and prices for both firms	Cumulative industry sales (saturation effect) and prices for both firms	Cumulative industry sales (saturation effect) and prices for both firms	Distribution of reservation prices, prices, effect of customer foresight	Market shares of both firms, price difference (also informative and persuasive advertising in extended model)
(b) Heterogeneity	No (aggregate-level specification)	No (aggregate-level specification)	No (aggregate-level specification)	Yes – reservation prices	No (aggregate-level specification)
(c) Uncertainty/ learning?	No	Yes – 2nd period demand uncertain	No	No	Yes – learning through experience
(d) Strategic customers?	No	No	No	Yes – perfect foresight	No
3. Firm/industry:					
(a) Experience curve effects?	No	No	No	No	Yes
(b) Uncertainty/ learning?	No		No	No	No
(c) Competitive setting	Duopoly	Duopoly	Oligopoly	Duopoly	Duopoly
(d) Decision variable(s)	Price	Price	Price	Price	Price, also advertising
(e) Type of equilibrium	Nash, closed-loop	Nash, closed-loop (and open-loop)	Nash, closed-loop	Subgame-perfect (closed-loop)	Nash, open-loop

	(11) Wernerfelt (1986)	(12) Chintagunta et al. (1993)	(13) Chintagunta and Rao (1996)	(14) Bergemann and Välimäki (1997)	(15) Kalra et al. (1998)
4. Key results/pricing implications	• Closed-loop equilibrium price *higher* than myopic price; *drops* toward myopic price as discount rate increases • Prices *decrease* as degree of competition between firms increases	• Prices under closed-loop strategies are *lower* than open-loop strategies. In both cases, prices *decline* over time and are *higher* than myopic prices • When firms use debt financing, the 1st and 2nd period prices are *lower* and *higher*, respectively, relative to the no-debt case	• Closed-loop equilibrium prices are *declining* over time; higher the speed of diffusion, the *lower* the prices (in monopoly case, price independent of speed of diffusion) • Prices *decrease* as number of firms in oligopoly increases	• Prices *decline* over time; customer foresight and competition both act to *lower* prices and *reduce* the rate of decline • Superior performance provides firm with powerful competitive advantage in presence of customer foresight	• Over life cycle, prices generally first decline and then increase
1. Product characteristics	Nondurable, experience goods for which consumers learn by using product	Nondurable, experience goods	Nondurable, experience goods	Nondurable, experience goods – one established brand of known value and one new entrant of uncertain value	Nondurable, experience goods – one established brand of known quality and one new entrant of uncertain quality
2. Customer behavior/demand:					
(a) Demand drivers/ sources of demand dynamics	Market shares, prices (general specification)	Customer preference, consumption experience, advertising, prices	Customer preference, consumption experience, advertising, prices	Distribution of customer valuations, prices	Distribution of customer valuations, prices

Table 9.3 (continued)

	(11) Wernerfelt (1986)	(12) Chintagunta et al. (1993)	(13) Chintagunta and Rao (1996)	(14) Bergemann and Välimäki (1997)	(15) Kalra et al. (1998)
(b) Heterogeneity	No (aggregate-level specification)	Yes – preferences	Yes – price sensitivity (at segment level)	Yes – preference (Hotelling)	Yes – valuation of quality
(c) Uncertainty/ learning?	Brand loyalty through experience	Preferences adjusted through consumption experience	Preferences adjusted through consumption experience	Yes – value of new brand	Yes – quality of new brand
(d) Strategic customers?	No	No	No	Yes	Yes
3. Firm/industry:					
(a) Experience curve effects?	Yes (on variable and fixed costs)	No	No	No	No
(b) Uncertainty/ learning?	No	No	No	Yes – value of new brand (symmetric information between firms and customers)	No
(c) Competitive setting	Oligopoly	Duopoly	Duopoly	Duopoly, with one established and one new brand	Duopoly, with one established and one new brand
(d) Decision variable(s)	Price	Price, advertising	Price	Price	Price
(e) Type of equilibrium	Nash, open-loop	Nash open-loop	Nash open-loop	Markov-perfect equilibrium (closed-loop)	Sequential equilibrium

| 4. Key results/pricing implications | • Prices *decline* in presence of variable cost learning and *increase* over time in presence of demand-side learning (loyalty) and fixed-cost learning | • For identical firms, prices *increase* over time (advertising declines)
• If one firm enjoys higher consumer experience, other firm will price *lower* and advertise more to close gap | • At steady state, the more preferred brand charges the *higher* price | • The expected price path of new product *increases* over time, first at an increasing then at a decreasing rate
• The expected price path of the incumbent *decreases* over time, first at a decreasing and then at an increasing rate | • Under certain conditions, incumbent prices higher (than in full-information case) in first period before dropping prices in second period after entrant's quality is known
• Entrant selects same initial price, whether high or low quality (signal-jamming equilibrium) |

Duopoly: $dN_1(t)/dt = [\overline{N} - (N_1(t) + N_2(t))]\alpha_1[1 - kp_i(t) + \gamma(p_j(t) - p_i(t))]$,

$$i, j = 1, 2; j \neq i, T_1 < t \leq T_2 \qquad (9.12)$$

where $N_i(t)$ and $p_i(t)$ are firm i's cumulative sales and price at time t, and $\overline{N}$ is the potential market size. The firms' objective is to maximize (undiscounted) profits over the entire planning horizon (including both monopoly and duopoly periods for the pioneer), assuming constant marginal cost (no cost-side learning). The open-loop equilibrium analysis shows that the prices for both firms decline monotonically, as expected, given that the dynamics are driven by saturation effects alone. The following results are interesting:

- In the presence of cross-price effects ($\gamma > 0$), there is a discrete drop in the pioneer's price at T_1, when it loses its monopoly status; greater substitutability (larger γ) implies a larger drop.
- The monopolist who correctly anticipates entry at T_1:
  - prices higher, and lowers prices less rapidly, than if he had been myopic because he accounts for the dynamic effects of saturation (greater current sales reduce future sales);
  - prices lower than if he (wrongly) assumes no competitive entry when setting its policy at $t = 0$, to reduce the potential market for the competitor via rapid market penetration.

Padmanabhan and Bass (1993; Table 9.3(2)) contrast the 'integrated monopolist' discussed in Section 2.4 with the case of separate firms introducing the first- and second-generation products (G1 and G2), for example, under technological leapfrogging by the second firm. The authors compare the pricing implications under the two scenarios (integrated and independent), using the following specific demand models in place of the more general forms (9.9) and (9.10):

$$\text{G1: } dN_1(t)/(dt = (1 - \theta)(\overline{N}_1 - N_1)(t))\exp(-k_1p_1(t)), \text{ and} \qquad (9.13)$$

$$\text{G2: } dN_2(t)/dt = [\theta(\overline{N}_1 - N_1(t))\exp(-k_1p_1(t)) + (\overline{N}_2 - N_2(t))]\exp(-k_2p_2(t)) \qquad (9.14)$$

where, as before, $N_1(t), N_2(t)$ are the cumulative G1 and G2 sales, $p_1(t), p_2(t)$ are the G1 and G2 prices, and θ is the fraction of G1 sales switching to G2 ($\theta = 0$ before G2 introduction, and a constant thereafter). $\overline{N}_1$ and $\overline{N}_2$ are the market potentials for G1 and G2.

Note that the demand interrelationship between G1 and G2 in the second period is quite different from that between the competing products in Eliashberg and Jeuland's model, where the interrelationship is more symmetric, reflecting the different scenarios modeled. Padmanabhan and Bass focus on successive generations, with demand for G2 coming from cannibalization of G1 sales and from the independent potential market for G2. The demand for G1 is independent of the G2 price. However, like Eliashberg and Jeuland, Padmanabhan and Bass assume only saturation effects. Under these assumptions, the pricing implications for the independent (competitive) versus integrated cases are as follows:

- G1 and G2 prices decline monotonically over time in both integrated and independent cases, given that the demand dynamics are driven by saturation effects.
- Prior to G2 entry, the G1 price is lower at any point in time in the competitive case, since the first entrant prefers to reduce the potential G1 market remaining when G2 enters.
- At the time of G2's entry, the G1 price drops immediately in both cases.
- After G2's entry, the G1 price is higher in the competitive case, the opposite of the situation before G2 entry; in this model, the fraction of G1 sales cannibalized by G2 is a constant (θ).
- The G2 price is the same in both cases; the G1 price has no impact on the optimal G2 price.

Nondurable goods model In contrast to the above durable goods models with saturation driving demand dynamics, Gabszewicz et al. (1992; Table 9.3(3)) analyze a two-period model for a nondurable, with brand loyalty resulting from consumer learning-by-using. The products from the pioneer and follower are perfectly substitutable, although loyalty serves as a barrier to switching. Consumers are heterogeneous in their willingness to learn how to use the new product. The product must be consumed in the period purchased, and cannot be stored. At the end of the first period, those who bought the product have learned to use it. The authors compare the implications of two cases – brand-specific versus category-level learning:

- If the learning is brand specific, the pioneer uses a low introductory price in the monopoly period. In the second (duopoly) period, both brands price above marginal cost, despite being perfect substitutes; the pioneer brand has the higher price and the higher profits.
- If the learning is at the category level, the pioneer prices at the myopic monopoly price in Period 1 since there is no brand-specific advantage. Without brand loyalty, both firms are forced to price at marginal cost in Period 2, under Bertrand competition.

Thus brand-specific learning provides the pioneer with a first-mover advantage but also softens subsequent price competition via market segmentation, leaving even the follower better off than under category-level learning. The pioneer builds a sustainable competitive advantage via a loyal customer base by pricing low in the monopoly period. (In this model, the pioneer actually raises his price in the duopoly period over the monopoly period.)

3.3 Models incorporating competition against incumbent firms

Durable goods models: dynamics induced by diffusion and/or saturation effects Dockner and Jorgensen (1988; Table 9.3(4)) develop an oligopolistic extension of the Kalish (1983) model discussed in Section 2.1, starting with the following general demand model:

$$dN_i/dt = f_i(N_1(t), N_1(t), N_2(t), \ldots, N_n(t); p_1(t), p_2(t), \ldots, p_n(t)), \quad i = 1, 2, \ldots, n \quad (9.15)$$

where $N_i(t)$ and $p_i(t)$ are the cumulative sales and price for firm i, respectively. They analyze special cases of this general model. In general, the qualitative implications for price trajectories are consistent with the results in Kalish (1983). Case 1 considers price effects only, with dynamics only due to cost-side learning – with positive discount rates, optimal prices decline over time. Case 2 considers own and competitive prices as well as own cumulative sales N_i (but not cumulative industry sales), in a multiplicatively separable formulation:

$$dN_i/dt = f_i(N_i(t)) \cdot h_i(p_1(t), p_2(t), \ldots, p_n(t)), \quad i = 1, 2, \ldots, n \qquad (9.16)$$

In this case, for a zero discount factor, equilibrium prices increase (decrease) over time if df_i/dN_i is positive (negative) for all i. As discussed earlier, df_i/dN_i is likely to be positive early in the life cycle (when the diffusion effect is dominant), and negative later when saturation drives the dynamics. Case 3 is similar to (9.16) except that demand is a function of cumulative industry sales $N = \Sigma_i N_i$ rather than firm-level cumulative sales N_i. Assuming a linear price effect, $h_i = a_i - b_i p_i + \Sigma_i \gamma_{ij}(p_i - p_j)$ and ignoring discounting and cost learning, equilibrium prices increase (decrease) over time if df_i/dN is positive (negative). Finally, Case 4 considers a duopoly, with demand a function of own and competitive cumulative sales but only own price:

$$dN_i/dt = f_i(N_i(t), N_j(t)) \cdot h_i(p_i(t)), \quad i, j = 1, 2; i \neq j \qquad (9.17)$$

Again ignoring discounting and experience effects, equilibrium prices increase (decrease) over time if df_i/dN_i is positive (negative), though the change in slope of the price path (from positive to negative) occurs after the change in sign of df_i/dN_i (from positive to negative) if df_i/dN_j is nonzero. The intuition is that there is a greater incentive to penetrate the market to reduce the potential market for the competitors ($df_i/dN_j < 0$). In summary, the key implications of Dockner and Jorgensen's competitive extension of Kalish's (1983) model are as follows:

- Equilibrium prices tend to increase over time early in the life cycle when the effect of cumulative adopters on demand is positive. Later in the life cycle, equilibrium prices should tend to decline when the effect of cumulative adopters on demand is negative. This robust result holds across a variety of the competitive model variations considered, and is consistent with Kalish's results in the monopoly case.
- When a firm's demand is adversely affected by the cumulative sales of competing brands, the change in the slope of the price path from positive to negative will tend to be delayed.
- In general, the stronger the impact of competition (e.g. a larger cross-price effect on demand), the greater the downward pressure on prices.

In contrast to the models reviewed so far, Rao and Bass (1985; Table 9.3(5)) consider quantity (output) rather than price as the decision variable, in an undifferentiated oligopoly (so that there is a common industry price). The objective is to examine price and market share dynamics in the presence of demand- and cost-side dynamics. The common industry price is a function of cumulative and current industry sales. The authors consider three special cases that isolate the three sources of dynamics in turn: saturation, diffusion and cost-side learning. While the industry price dynamics are in line with other models – price declines (increases) monotonically under a saturation (diffusion) effect alone, and also declines under cost-side learning alone – the analysis reveals interesting results for market share dynamics. Under demand-side dynamics (diffusion and saturation), a lower-cost firm will always have a higher market share than a higher-cost firm. Given cost-side learning, a higher-cost firm is more aggressive than a lower-cost firm in closing the gap in market share over time. Indeed, market share order reversals can occur in cases where the higher-cost firm might find it optimal to produce more than a lower-cost competitor.

Rao and Bass provide an empirical analysis of price dynamics in the semiconductor components industry that generally supports the theoretical results. The assumption of output as the decision variable in an undifferentiated market may be reasonable for industries with essentially commodity-type products (such as certain types of semiconductor components).

Models considering closed-loop equilibria Dockner and Gaundersdorfer (1996; Table 9.3(6)) analyze the properties of closed-loop equilibria for a durable goods duopoly market, considering saturation effects only and an infinite planning horizon. The closed-loop equilibrium price is higher than the myopic price, and drops toward the latter as the discount rate increases. Also, as expected, prices decrease as the products become more substitutable.[7] However, the analysis does not compare open-loop and closed-loop strategies.

Baldauf et al. (2000; Table 9.3(7)) employ a two-period duopoly model with saturation effects to contrast open-loop and closed-loop strategies. They find that:

- When firms choose closed-loop strategies, optimal prices in each period are lower than corresponding open-loop prices. In both cases, prices decline over time and are higher in each period than the corresponding myopic prices.

Closed-loop strategies capture strategic competitive interaction, resulting, in this instance, in lower prices. Next, Baldauf et al. consider the implications of debt financing. Uncertainty is introduced in the second-period demand via a random disturbance term in market potential. The firms' objective is to maximize the expected equity value, concentrating on those states of nature in which there will be no bankruptcy. In this situation, long-term debt has a significant impact:

- When firms use debt financing, second period prices are higher (to avoid possible bankruptcy) while first period prices are lower (to compensate for higher second period prices) relative to their levels in the case of no debt financing.

---

[7] The degree of substitution is captured by the γ parameter, as in Eliashberg and Jeuland (1986) – see (9.14).

Dockner and Fruchter (2004; Table 9.3(8)) investigate the combined effect of the speed of diffusion and competition, using the following demand specification:[8]

$$dN_i(t)/dt = \left[\bar{N} - \sum_{i=1}^{n} N_i(t)\right]\left[a - bp_i(t) + \gamma \sum_{\substack{j=1 \\ j \neq i}}^{n} (p_j(t) - p_i(t))\right], i = 1, \ldots, n \quad (9.18)$$

where the notations are as defined earlier. The speed of diffusion is defined as the percentage increase in the number of adopters corresponding to a 1 percent decrease in the time remaining in the product life cycle (an elasticity-like measure). The key implications are:

- Equilibrium prices decline over time. Given competition, the higher the speed of diffusion (i.e. shorter the life cycle), the lower the prices. In contrast, in a monopoly, the optimal price path is independent of the speed of diffusion.
- The prices decrease as the number of competitors in the oligopoly increases.

Models considering strategic customers with price expectations Chatterjee and Crosbie (1999; Table 9.3(9)) extend Besanko and Winston's (1990) model, discussed in Section 2.3, to a duopoly market, in which firms may sell products differentiated by quality. Customers are rational, with perfect foresight, and heterogeneous in their reservation prices. A subgame-perfect (closed-loop) equilibrium is sought in a discrete time framework. The results, derived partly analytically and partly via numerical simulation, have the following policy implications:

- Equilibrium prices decline over time as customers adopt the durable and leave the market in descending order of their valuations. Customer foresight and competition both lower prices and flatten the declining price path.
- Superior quality can provide a firm with a powerful, even dominant, competitive advantage relative to the case of myopic customers. A strong quality advantage can counteract a competitor's potential advantage from early brand introduction or lower marginal cost.

Nondurable goods models We next review four models that focus on nondurable products for which there is demand-side learning on account of consumption experience. Wernerfelt (1985; Table 9.3(10)) investigates price and market share dynamics over the life cycle in a duopoly, given scale economies and cost-side learning. The demand-side dynamics are modeled as follows. First, the rate of change of market share is proportional to the market shares of the two brands, the price difference, and a term that declines over time to reflect increasing brand loyalty. Next, the rate of change of individual-level consumption decreases in both price and the current consumption level. Finally, a financial constraint is imposed, requiring that some fraction of the funding needed for growth must be generated internally (based on prescriptions from the Boston Consulting Group). Wernerfelt's open-loop equilibrium analysis shows that:

---

[8] This model is a special form of Case 3 in Dockner and Jorgensen (1988), with dynamics from saturation effects.

- Prices first decline and then increase; the larger firm's market share first grows, then declines.

The implications for the slope of the price path over the life cycle are the opposite of those implied by Dockner and Jorgensen's (1988) durable goods model based on diffusion and saturation effects, given the very different demand dynamics in Wernerfelt's model for frequently purchased products. In the case of durables with a finite market, saturation eventually dominates demand-side learning, whereas in Wernerfelt's model, demand-side learning (lowering price sensitivity) continues to grow without the constraint of saturation.

Wernerfelt's (1986) model (Table 9.3(11)) focuses on the implications of experience curves and brand loyalty for pricing policy in an oligopoly. Both fixed and variable costs decline owing to learning and exogenous technical progress. As in Wernerfelt (1985), the market share dynamics depend on current shares, prices and brand loyalty. The implications are that prices should decrease over time if discount rates are high and exogenous declines in variable costs are steep, but increase if fixed costs decline with learning and consumers are brand loyal.

Chintagunta et al. (1993; Table 9.3(12)) analyze dynamic pricing and advertising strategies for a nondurable experience good in a duopoly. Individual-level consumer choice is based on an ideal point preference model. Brand share is obtained by aggregating over consumers, allowing for heterogeneity. Consumers learn about a brand with each successive purchase. The accumulated brand consumption experience obeys Nerlove and Arrow (1962):

$$dG_i(t)/dt = S_i(t) - \delta G_i(t), \quad G_i(0) = G_{i0}, \quad i = 1, 2 \qquad (9.19)$$

where $G_i(t)$ and $S_i(t)$ are firm i's stock of accumulated consumption experience (goodwill) and sales, and δ is the goodwill decay factor. A brand's perceptual location depends on the function of current advertising effort and the accumulated consumption experience, so that higher levels of either imply greater brand preference. The key results, derived via numerical simulation, are:

- If firms are identical, prices increase over time (while advertising decreases).
- If one firm enjoys higher initial consumption experience by being the incumbent, then the other firm will initially market more aggressively by pricing lower (and advertising higher) than the incumbent. Over time, the price and advertising levels for the two brands converge.

In a related paper, Chintagunta and Rao (1996; Table 9.3(13)) develop a duopoly model for nondurable experience goods, with aggregate-level preference evolving according to the Nerlove–Arrow model, similar to the accumulated consumption experience in Chintagunta et al. (1993). At steady state, the more preferred brand charges the higher price. The authors show that managers who are myopic or who ignore customer heterogeneity make suboptimal pricing decisions. An empirical example demonstrates how the model may be estimated (and steady-state price predictions obtained) from longitudinal purchase data.

Competition against an established nondurable Bergemann and Välimäki (1997; Table 9.3(14)) consider the case of a firm introducing a new, differentiated, product to a market for a nondurable experience good currently served by an established firm with a product whose performance is well known.[9] However, the performance of the new product is initially uncertain to customers as well as to the firms. This uncertainty can be resolved only by learning through actual purchases of the second product. Beliefs of product performance are updated gradually in a Bayesian manner. The authors derive the Markov-perfect equilibrium[10] of the infinite horizon differential game, with the following implications, if the new product is of truly high quality:

- The expected price path of the new product is strictly increasing over time, first at an increasing and then at a decreasing rate (i.e. in an S-shaped pattern), while that of of the established product is strictly decreasing, first at a decreasing and then at an increasing rate.

The uncertainty serves to soften competition and increase profits. The incumbent actually values information on new product performance more than the entrant does. Since such information is only available from new product sales, the incentives produce the dynamics noted above.

Kalra et al. (1998; Table 9.3(15)) consider a somewhat similar scenario – an established incumbent and a new entrant whose product is of uncertain quality – to examine whether there is a rationale for the incumbent to react slowly to the entrant as often observed in practice, when the expected response (under full information) would be an immediate price cut. Consumers are initially uncertain about the entrant's quality, and the true quality is revealed over time. Unlike in Bergemann and Välimäki, both firms know the true quality. The analysis, using the sequential equilibrium concept (Krebs and Wilson, 1982) in a two-period model, shows that:

- There are conditions under which the incumbent prices higher than the full-information price to effectively jam the entrant's ability to signal quality via its price. In this signal-jamming equilibrium, the low-quality and high-quality entrants select the same price. The incumbent's price gradually declines to the full-information level as consumers learn about the entrant's true quality.

Thus, whereas a monopolist may use price as a signal of quality (see Section 2.3), a later entrant may not have the ability to do so because of signal-jamming by the incumbent. This is also consistent with the often-observed practice of a delayed or gradual incumbent response. Kalra et al. also provide experimental validity for the premise underlying their result.

---

[9] For other work by the same authors examining implications for strategic pricing in the presence of two-sided learning, see Bergeman and Välimäki (1996, 2000).
[10] See Maskin and Tirole (2001) for a discussion of Markov-perfect equilibrium.

3.4 Normative models in a competitive setting: summary of implications

We conclude this section by summarizing the main implications for new product pricing strategy in a competitive setting, relative to the implications in a monopolistic setting (Section 2.5).

- *General effect of competition*   In general, the stronger the effect of competition (for example, a larger cross-price effect), the lower the prices, all else equal.
- *Anticipating entry in a durable goods market with saturation effect*   Prior to the competitor's entry, the incumbent monopolist's optimal strategy is to price higher and then reduce prices less rapidly over time than the myopic optimum, but price lower than if he does not account for competitive entry. Also, at the point of entry, the incumbent's price drops, with the magnitude depending on the strength of the cross-price effect.
- *Anticipating entry in a nondurable goods market with learning-by-using*   If the learning by customers is mainly brand-specific (rather than at the category level), the pioneer prices below the myopic monopoly price prior to the competitor's entry.
- *Durable goods oligopoly*   When a firm's demand is adversely affected by the cumulative sales of competitors (owing to saturation), there is greater incentive to use penetration pricing early relative to the monopoly situation – thus early prices will be lower and the change of slope of the price path from positive to negative will be delayed.
- *Open-loop versus closed-loop strategies for durable goods market with saturation*   When firms adapt to the evolving state of the system over the planning horizon rather than committing to their strategy at the start of the planning horizon, prices in each period are lower.
- *Strategic customers with perfect foresight in a durable goods market*   Both customer foresight and competition lower prices and make the price decline more gradual.
- *Nondurable goods duopoly with learning-by-using*   Prices may first decline and then increase, or else increase monotonically over time; if one firm enjoys greater consumption experience initially (e.g. as the incumbent), the other firm will be more aggressive in its marketing, including charging lower prices, to close the gap between the firms.
- *Competitive reaction to a new entrant when the entrant's quality is uncertain to customers*   Under certain conditions, the incumbent prices higher than the full-information duopoly price to effectively prevent the entrant from signaling quality to uncertain customers.

4. Setting new product prices in practice

In this section, we briefly discuss some tools and approaches that managers may apply to determine actual pricing policy for new products. A more detailed review of this topic is beyond the scope of this chapter; related issues are covered elsewhere in this volume.

4.1 Conjoint-based methods

Conjoint analysis (Green and Srinivasan, 1978, 1990) provides a popular and widely used methodological tool for assessing customers' willingness to pay for (possibly hypothetical) new products (Jedidi and Zhang, 2002). In particular, conjoint-based methods for optimal pricing (preferably as part of an overall optimization methodology including product design) have been developed and applied (Green et al., 1981; Kohli and Mahajan, 1991; see also Dolan and Simon, 1996).[11] For methodological approaches based on information directly obtained from customers (or from secondary data) to estimate new product demand as a function of price and other demand-drivers, we refer readers to the chapters in this volume on measurement of reservation prices at the disaggregate level (Jedidi and Jagpal, Chapter 2) and demand estimation at a more aggregate level (Liu et al., Chapter 3).

4.2 Field experimentation
In situations in which it is important to track demand dynamics over time, an extended field experiment allows for estimation of a demand model that comes close to capturing reality. An example of such research is the study by Danaher (2002) involving a field experiment to derive a revenue-maximizing pricing strategy for new subscription services (applied to cellular phone market). The study also provides measures of the impact of access and usage prices on volume of usage and customer retention. In the experiment, a panel of homes was recruited to try a new cellular phone service over a year-long period. Both access and usage prices were manipulated systematically across groups within the panel. The model for usage and attrition was developed to fit the data from the experiment while also having the flexibility to describe a subscription service market that is closer to reality than the market in the experiment. It generalizes Hausman and Wise (1979) to deal with bias in the case of attrition. Unobserved heterogeneity is accommodated by employing latent segments. The specification of the revenue (or, more generally, profit) surface as a function of access and usage prices allows for the search of the optimal access and usage price levels.

Danaher's research illustrates a useful practical approach to new product pricing, using experiments that run over a sufficient length of time with manipulation of prices to be able to estimate the key demand dynamics (in this case, usage rates and attrition), in a reasonably realistic setting. In terms of broader findings, the analysis shows that access price primarily affects retention, while usage price affects usage and has an indirect effect on retention via usage (lower usage results in higher attrition).

4.3 Expert opinion/managerial judgment
Clearly, the specific product-market situation will dictate the appropriate choice of methodology for new product pricing. For example, for the pharmaceuticals industry, Woodward et al. (1998) propose a judgment-based approach that solicits experts opinions about the new product's market share under different scenarios based on prices, promotional effort and clinical benefits (as a basis for the product's value proposition and differentiation). The procedure involves a meeting among experts. A spreadsheet-based model returns the profit-maximizing price, promotional effort and value proposition (market differentiation) for each expert and for the group as a whole. The extent of

---

[11] For the interested reader, Sawtooth Software's technical papers library provides a useful set of materials of all aspects of conjoint analysis (http://www.sawtoothsoftware.com/education/techpap.shtml).

disagreement among experts is used to estimate incremental profits from obtaining additional information, via (i) an additional clinical trial (to define a stronger value proposition, possibly by establishing a second clinical indication) and (ii) a demand survey (to better estimate potential sales at different price points).

In summary, customer measurement tools (such as conjoint analysis), experiments (preferably in field settings), and expert opinion/managerial judgment-based approaches (Little, 1970, 2004), have been – and can be – used, possibly in combination, to determine pricing policy for a new product.

5. Conclusion

This chapter has attempted to organize and review the literature on new product pricing, with a primary focus on normative models taking a dynamic perspective. Such a perspective is essential in the new product context, given the underlying demand- and supply-side dynamics and the need to take a long-term, strategic, view in setting pricing policy. Along with these dynamics, the high levels of uncertainty (for firms and customers alike) make the strategic new product pricing decision particularly complex and challenging. We have distilled from our review of normative models the key implications for new product pricing, under various situations. These implications are intended to provide (i) theoretical insights into the drivers of dynamic pricing policy for new products and services, (ii) directional guidance for new product pricing decisions in practice, and (iii) directions for empirical research to test these results.

Given the multiple sources of dynamics and uncertainty, normative models have typically focused on some subset of all the situational factors that might exist in practice, in order to be tractable. Isolating the different effects helps in understanding their individual impact on the price path. However, being abstractions of reality, these models are limited as practical tools for new product pricing. On the other hand, the new product pricing tools available, briefly discussed in Section 4, are primarily helpful for setting short-term prices rather than a dynamic long-term pricing policy, which is what managers really need. Our review and discussion suggests several areas that offer opportunities for future research. Some avenues are discussed below.

5.1 Normative models: possible extensions

Dynamic models incorporating future expectations, successive generations, and current and future competition Today's business environment – characterized by shorter product life cycles, rapidly evolving demand- and supply-side dynamics (including customer tastes, technology and competition), and increasingly sophisticated customers – poses a real challenge for modelers, who must focus on these key drivers simultaneously to obtain managerially relevant pricing implications. Even with better analytical tools, the tradeoff between analytical tractability and richness must be recognized. Numerical methods would typically need to be used in conjunction with analytical approaches in order to derive meaningful results in these circumstances.

Multiple decision variables It is clearly simplistic to focus on price alone as the decision variable. While some dynamic models include additional marketing variables (typically, advertising), real-world new product strategy involves decisions across functional areas. In this regard, the model by Huang et al.(2007) reviewed in Section 2.1 represents an encouraging start, albeit in a monopolistic setting. Again, the tradeoff between tractability and richness (and the use of numerical methods) becomes a germane issue.

5.2 Decision support systems
As observed earlier, the existing tools to support new product pricing decisions are limited in their ability to provide recommendations on dynamic pricing policy. There is an opportunity for developing managerial decision support systems incorporating dynamic models that can be calibrated via managerial judgment, historical data on analogous products, experimentation, or (ideally) some combination thereof to provide dynamic pricing strategy recommendations.

5.3 Nontraditional pricing schemes and other recent advances in pricing
The unique characteristics of services has prompted pricing schemes that include advanced pricing, use-based pricing and pricing for yield management. These topics have received recent attention and are covered in chapters in this volume by Shoemaker and Mattila (Chapter 25) on services, Xie and Shugan (Chapter 21) on advanced pricing, Kimes (Chapter 22) on yield management, and Iyengar and Gupta (Chapter 16) on nonlinear pricing. Further, prompted in part by recent technological advances (including the advent of the Internet), customized pricing of goods and services is now a viable option, prompting increasing use of auctions (and reverse auctions), and pricing to maximize customer lifetime value. Again, these topics are discussed in chapters by Park and Wang (Chapter 19) on mechanisms facilitated by the Internet (including 'name your own price' and auctions) and Zhang (Chapter 14 on price customization).

While these newer pricing topics have generated considerable research interest, there has been little work so far in the context of new products. This is clearly an important and fertile area for research, considering the unique challenges posed by new products, as discussed.

5.4 Takeoff of really new products
An example of an interesting research issue in the new product pricing domain is Golder and Tellis's (1997) study of takeoff in sales of new household consumer durables. The authors argue that the traditional new product diffusion models do not capture the reality of the abrupt sales 'takeoff' for major innovations, at which point sales jump fourfold (or greater). They find that, for 16 post-World War II consumer durable categories, the price at takeoff was 63 percent of the introductory price, on average; furthermore, the takeoff often occurs at specific price points, e.g. $1000, $500, or $100. Also, not surprisingly, the time to takeoff has been decreasing, from 18 years for categories introduced before World War II to six years for those introduced afterwards.

The phenomenon of sales takeoff warrants further attention, given the increasing number of new product introductions, particularly in the technology sector. In particular, the role of strategic pricing (and psychologically important price points, as suggested by Golder and Tellis's findings) in determining new product takeoff is a promising topic for research.

References

Bagwell, K. and M.H. Riordan (1991), 'High and declining prices signal product quality', *American Economic Review*, **81** (1), 224–39.
Balachander, S. and K. Srinivasan (1998), 'Modifying customer expectations of price decreases for a durable product', *Management Science*, **44** (6), 776–86.
Baldauf, A., E.J. Dockner and H. Reisinger (2000), 'The effects of long-term debt on a firm's new product policy in duopolistic markets', *Journal of Business Research*, **50**, 201–7.
Bass, F.M. (1969), 'A new product growth model for consumer durables', *Management Science*, **15** (1), 215–27.
Bass, F.M. (1980), 'The relationship between diffusion, experience curves, and demand elasticities for consumer durable technological innovations', *Journal of Business*, **53**, 557–67.
Bass, F.M. and A.V. Bultez (1982), 'A note on optimal strategic pricing of technological innovations', *Marketing Science*, **1** (4), 371–8.
Bass, F.M., D.C. Jain and T.V. Krishnan (2000), 'Modeling the marketing-mix influence in new-product diffusion', in V. Mahajan, E. Muller and Y. Wind (eds), *New-Product Diffusion Models*, Boston, MA: Kluwer Academic Publishers, pp. 99–122.
Bass, F.M., T.V. Krishnan and D.C. Jain (1994), 'Why the Bass model fits without decision variables', *Marketing Science*, **13** (Summer), 203–23.
Bayus, B.L. (1992), 'The dynamic pricing of next generation consumer durables', *Marketing Science*, **11** (3), 251–65.
Bergemann, D. and J. Välimäki (1996), 'Learning and strategic pricing', *Econometrica*, **5** (September), 1125–49.
Bergemann, D. and J. Välimäki (1997), 'Market diffusion with two-sided learning', *RAND Journal of Economics*, **28** (4), 773–95.
Bergemann, D. and J. Välimäki (2000), 'Experimentation in markets', *Review of Economic Studies*, **67** (2), 213–34.
Besanko, D. and W.L. Winston (1990), 'Optimal price skimming by a monopolist facing rational consumers', *Management Science*, **56** (5), 555–67.
Chatterjee, Rabikar and Peter Crosbie (1999), 'Dynamic pricing strategies and firm performance in a duopoly: the impact of buyer expectations', Working Paper, Katz Graduate School of Business, University of Pittsburgh, Pittsburgh, PA.
Chatterjee, R., J. Eliashberg and V.R. Rao (2000), 'Dymaic models incorporating competition', in V. Mahajan, E. Muller and Y. Wind (eds), *New-Product Diffusion Models*, Boston, MA: Kluwer Academic Publishers, pp. 165–205.
Chen, Y.-M. and D.C. Jain (1992), 'Dynamic monopoly pricing under a Poisson-type uncertain demand', *Journal of Business*, **65** (October), 593–614.
Chintagunta, P.K. and V.R. Rao (1996), 'Pricing strategies in a dynamic duopoly: a differential game model', *Management Science*, **42** (November), 1501–14.
Chintagunta, P.K., V.R. Rao and N.J. Vilcassim (1993), 'Equilibrium pricing and advertising strategies for nondurable experience products in a dynamic duopoly', *Managerial and Decision Economics*, **14**, 221–34.
Danaher, P.J. (2002), 'Optimal pricing of new subscription services: analysis of a marketing experiment', *Marketing Science*, **21** (2), 119–38.
Dean, J. (1950), 'Pricing policies for new products', reprinted in *Harvard Business Review*, **28** (November–December 1976), 141–53.
Dean, J. (1969), 'Pricing pioneering products', *Journal of Industrial Economics*, **17** (3), 165–79.
Dhebar, A. (1994), 'Durable goods monopolists, rational consumers, and improving products', *Marketing Science*, **13** (1), 100–120.
Dhebar, A. and S.S. Oren (1985), 'Optimal dynamic pricing for expanding networks', *Marketing Science*, **4** (4), 336–51.
Dhebar, A. and S.S. Oren (1986), 'Dynamic nonlinear pricing in networks with interdependent demand', *Operations Research*, **34** (3), 384–94.
Dockner, E.J. and G.E. Fruchter (2004), 'Dynamic strategic pricing and the speed of diffusion', *Journal of Optimization Theory and Applications*, **123** (2), 331–48.
Dockner, E.J. and A. Gaundersdorfer (1996), 'Strategic new product pricing when demand obeys saturation effects', *European Journal of Operational Research*, **90**, 589–98.
Dockner, E.J. and S. Jorgensen (1988), 'Optimal pricing strategies for new products in dynamic oligopolies', *Marketing Science*, **7** (Fall), 315–34.
Dockner, E.J., S. Jorgensen, N.V. Long and G. Sorger (2000), *Differential Games in Economics and Management Science*, Cambridge: Cambridge University Press.
Dolan, R.J. and A.P. Jeuland (1981), 'Experience curve and dynamic demand models: implications for optimal pricing strategies', *Journal of Marketing*, **45**, 52–62.

Dolan, R.J. and H. Simon (1996), *Power Pricing*, New York: The Free Press.
Dolan, R.J., A.P. Jeuland and E. Muller (1986), 'Models of new product diffusion: extension to competition against existing and potential firms over time', in V. Mahajan and Y. Wind (eds), *Innovation Diffusion Models of New Product Acceptance*, Cambridge, MA: Ballinger Publishing Company, pp. 117–49.
Eliashberg, J. and A.P. Jeuland (1986), 'The impact of competitive entry in developing markets upon dynamic pricing strategies', *Marketing Science*, **5** (Winter), 20–36.
Gabszewicz, J., L. Pepall and J.-F. Thisse (1992), 'Sequential entry with brand loyalty caused by consumer learning-by-using', *Journal of Industrial Economics*, **40** (4), 397–416.
Gijsbrechts, E (1993), 'Pricing and pricing research in consumer marketing: some recent developments', *International Journal of Research in Marketing*, **10** (2), 115–51.
Golder, P.N. and G.J. Tellis (1997), 'Will it ever fly? Modeling takeoff of really new consumer durables', *Marketing Science*, **16** (3), 256–70.
Green, P.E. and V. Srinivasan (1990), 'Conjoint analysis in marketing: new developments with issues for research and practice', *Journal of Marketing*, **54** (3), 17–37.
Green, P.E. and V. Srinivasan (1978), 'Conjoint analysis in consumer research: issues and outlook', *Journal of Consumer Research*, **5** (2), 103–23.
Green, P.E., J.D. Carroll and S.M. Goldberg (1981), 'A general approach to product design optimization via conjoint analysis', *Journal of Marketing*, **5** (4), 3–19.
Hausman, J.A. and D.A. Wise (1979), 'Attrition bias in experimental and panel data: the Gary income maintenance experiment', *Econometrica*, **47** (March), 455–73.
Horsky, D. (1990), 'A diffusion model incorporating product benefits, price, income, and information', *Marketing Science*, **9** (4), 342–65.
Huang, H.-Z., Z.-J. Liu and D.N.P. Murthy (2007), 'Optimal reliability. Warranty and price for new products', *IIE Transactions*, **39**, 819–27.
Jedidi, K. and Z.J. Zhang (2002), 'Augmenting conjoint analysis to estimate consumer reservation price', *Management Science*, **48** (10), 1350–68.
Jeuland, A.P. (1981), 'Parsimonious models of diffusion of innovation part B: incorporating the variable of price', Working Paper, University of Chicago Graduate School of Business.
Jeuland, A.P. and R.J. Dolan (1982), 'An aspect of new product planning: dynamic pricing', *TIMS Studies in the Management Sciences*, **18**, 1–21.
Judd, K.L. and M.H. Riordan (1994), 'Price and quality in a new product monopoly', *Review of Economic Studies*, **61**, 773–89.
Kadiyali, V., N.J. Vilcassim and P.K. Chintagunta (1996), 'Empirical analysis of competitive product line pricing decisions: lead, follow, or move together?', *Journal of Business*, **69** (4), 459–87.
Kalish, S. (1983), 'Monopolistic pricing with dynamic demand and production cost', *Marketing Science*, **2** (2), 135–59.
Kalish, S. (1985), 'A new product adoption model with price, advertising, and uncertainty', *Management Science*, **31** (December), 1569–85.
Kalish, S. (1988), 'Pricing new products from birth to decline: an expository review', in T. Devinney (ed.), *Issues in Pricing: Theory and Research*, Lexington, MA: Lexington Books, pp. 119–44.
Kalish, S. and S.K. Sen (1986), 'Diffusion models and the marketing mix for single products', in V. Mahajan and Y. Wind (eds), *Innovation Diffusion Models of New Product Acceptance*, Cambridge, MA: Ballinger Publishing Company, pp. 87–116.
Kalra, A., S. Rajiv and K. Srinivasan (1998), 'Response to competitive entry: a rationale for delayed defensive reaction', *Marketing Science*, **17** (4), 380–405.
Kamien, M.I. and N.L. Schwartz (1991), *Dynamic Optimization: The Calculus of Variations and Optimal Control in Economics and Management*, 2nd edn, New York: Elsevier Science.
Kohli, R. and V. Mahajan (1991), 'A reservation-price model for optimal pricing of multiattribute products in conjoint analysis', *Journal of Marketing Research*, **28** (3), 347–54.
Kornish, L.J. (2001), 'Pricing for durable-goods monopolists under rapid sequential innovation', *Management Science*, **47** (11), 1552–61.
Krebs, D.M. and R. Wilson (1982), 'Sequential equilibria', *Econometrica*, **50** (4), 863–94.
Krishnan, T.V., Bass, F.M. and D.C. Jain (1999), 'Optimal pricing strategy for new products', *Management Science*, **45** (12), 1650–63.
Little, J.D.C. (1970), 'Models and managers: the concept of a decision calculus', *Management Science*, **16** (8), B466–B485.
Little, J.D.C. (2004), 'Comments on "Models and managers: the concept of a decision calculus"', *Management Science*, **50** (12), 1854–60.
Lu, Z.J. and W.S. Comanor (1998), 'Strategic pricing of new pharmaceuticals', *Review of Economics and Statistics*, **80** (1), 108–18.

Maskin, E. and J. Tirole (2001), 'Markov perfect equilibrium: 1. Observable actions', *Journal of Economic Theory*, **100**, 191–219.
Milgrom, P. and D.J. Roberts (1986), 'Price and advertising signals of product quality', *Journal of Political Economy*, **94**, 796–821.
Monroe, K.B. and A.J. Della Bitta (1978), 'Models for pricing decisions', *Journal of Marketing Research*, **15** (3), 413–28.
Moorthy, K.S. (1988), 'Consumer expectations and the pricing of durables', in T. Devinney (ed.), *Issues in Pricing: Theory and Research*, Lexington, MA: Lexington Books, pp. 99–114.
Narasimhan, C. (1989), 'Incorporating consumer price expectations in diffusion models', *Marketing Science*, **8** (4), 343–57.
Nerlove, M. and K.J. Arrow (1962), 'Optimal advertising policy under dynamic conditions', *Econometrica*, **29**, 162–75.
Noble, P.M. and T.S. Gruca (1999), 'Industrial pricing: theory and managerial practice', *Marketing Science*, **18** (3), 435–54.
Padmanabhan, V. and F.M. Bass (1993), Optimal pricing of successive generations of product advances', *International Journal of Research in Marketing*, **10**, 185–207.
Raman, K. and R. Chatterjee (1995), 'Optimal monopolist pricing under demand uncertainty in dynamic markets', *Management Science*, **41** (1), 144–62.
Rao, V.R. (1984), 'Pricing research in marketing: the state of the art', *Journal of Business*, **57** (1), S39–S60.
Rao, V.R. (1993), 'Pricing models in marketing', in *Handbooks in Operation Research and Management Science, Volume 5: Marketing*, Amsterdam: North-Holland, pp. 517–52.
Rao, R.C. and F.M. Bass (1985), 'Competition, strategy, and price dynamics: a theoretical and empirical investigation', *Journal of Marketing Research*, **22** (August), 283–96.
Robinson, B. and C. Lakhani (1975), 'Dynamic price models for new-product planning', *Management Science*, **21** (10), June, 1113–22.
Rogers, E.M. (2003), *Diffusion of Innovations*, 5th edn, New York: Free Press.
Rohlfs, J.H. (2001), *Bandwagon Effects in High-Technology Industries*, Cambridge, MA: MIT Press.
Wernerfelt, B. (1985), 'The dynamics of prices and market shares over the product life cycle', *Management Science*, **31** (August), 928–39.
Wernerfelt, B. (1986), 'A special case of dynamic pricing policy', *Management Science*, **32** (December), 1562–6.
Woodward, R.S., L. Amir, M.A. Schnitzler and D.C. Brennan (1998), 'A new product pricing model using intracorporate market perceptions to extract the value of addition information', *Pharmacoeconomics*, **14** (1), 71–7.
Zhao, H. (2000), 'Raising awareness and signaling quality to uninformed consumers: price-advertising model', *Marketing Science*, **19** (4), 390–96.

10 Product line pricing
Yuxin Chen

Abstract

A firm in modern economy is more likely to sell a line of products than a single product. Product line pricing is a challenging marketing mix decision as products in a line demonstrate complicated demand and cost interdependence. In the last three decades researchers from different disciplines have made significant progress in addressing various issues relating to the topic of product line pricing. In this chapter, I discuss the literature on product line pricing with the focus on recent research development.

The discussion starts with a general framework of the product line pricing problem and a brief description of the decision support models for product line pricing. It is then followed with extensive discussions on the pricing of vertically differentiated product lines and the pricing of horizontally differentiated product lines respectively. Finally, I conclude the chapter with a discussion on future research directions.

1. Introduction

A firm in modern economy typically sells a line of products rather than a single product. For example, cars are offered with different powers, yogurts are offered with different flavors, online shopping is offered with different delivery options, and wireless phone service is offered with different plans. This chapter reviews the academic research on product line pricing. Its purpose is to provide a comprehensive discussion on the topic with both the experienced and new researchers as the intended audience. I shall focus on recent research development in this area. Good reviews on the early literature on this topic can be found in Rao (1984, 1993).

To be more precise about the scope of this review, I define a product line as a set of products or services sold by a firm that provide similar functionalities and serve similar needs and wants of customers. This definition sets the topic of product line pricing apart from the more general topic of multi-product pricing. For example, research on bundle pricing, razor-and-blade pricing, and loss-leader pricing in the context of retail assortment management is beyond the scope of this review according to the above definition of a product line.

In addition, to avoid the potential overlap with other chapters in this *Handbook*, I exclude the following topics from this review, even though they can be somewhat related to product line pricing: pricing multiple generations of products, pricing new products with the existence of used goods market, retailer's pricing of a category of products consisting of national and private brands, and quantity discounts. However, some overlap will still occur. This is often inevitable and even desirable because it can be beneficial to look at the same issue from different perspectives. For example, the pricing of different delivery options by an online retailer can be viewed as a problem of product line pricing but also a problem of pricing services if the service aspect is emphasized. Combining the views can provide marketing managers and researchers with more comprehensive understanding on this issue.

Because this chapter contributes to a handbook of pricing research, my discussion will concentrate on the pricing issues conditional on the configurations of product lines. The optimal design of a product line is an important topic but it is beyond the scope of this review. Nevertheless, whenever applicable, I will try to base the discussion on the optimal or equilibrium configurations of product lines as shown in the literature.

The optimal pricing decision of a product line is critically dependent on the relations of the products in the line. In general, products in a line can be vertically differentiated, horizontally differentiated, or both. A product line is vertically differentiated if products in the line are differentiated along a dimension (product attribute) in which consumers have the same preference ranking on each level. That is, all consumers prefer to have more (or less) of the attribute. Such a dimension is typically interpreted as product quality in the literature (Moorthy, 1984; Mussa and Rosen, 1978). Examples of vertically differentiated product lines include iPods with different memory capacities and printers with different speeds. A product line is horizontally differentiated if the products in the line are differentiated along dimensions in which consumers have different preference rankings due to their taste differences. Examples of such product lines include ice creams with different flavors and clothes with different colors. In practice, it is common for a product line to be vertically differentiated along some dimensions but horizontally differentiated along others. For example, a line of automobiles may be vertically differentiated on gas-mileage but horizontally differentiated on colors. In this review, I classify previous studies based on their focus on vertically differentiated or horizontally differentiated product lines and discuss the pricing issues for these two types of product lines respectively in two sections. For papers applicable to both vertically differentiated and horizontally differentiated product lines, I discuss them in either section, depending on their emphasis and main contributions.

The objective of this chapter is to provide a comprehensive review of important research developments in product line pricing. However, due to space and knowledge limitations, this review is far from exhaustive. Readers who are interested in any specific topic of product line pricing research are encouraged to conduct more extensive literature search in that area.

The rest of the chapter is organized as follows. In the next section, I present a general framework for the product line pricing problem and briefly discuss the decision support models for product line pricing. I discuss the pricing of vertically differentiated product lines in Section 3 and horizontally differentiated product lines in Section 4. Finally, I conclude the chapter in Section 5 with a discussion on future research directions.

2. A general framework for product line pricing

Assume a firm sells a product line consisting of m products. The firm's optimal pricing problem can be formulated as

$$\underset{p_1, p_2, \ldots, p_m}{\text{Max }} \pi = \sum_{i=1}^{m} \pi_i = \sum_{i=1}^{m} D_i(p_i, P_{-i}, P_c, X, X_c) p_i - \sum_{i=1}^{m} C_i(D_i, D_{-i}) \quad (10.1)$$

where

π is the total profit of the product line,
π_i is the profit of the ith product in the product line,
D_i is the demand of the ith product,

D_{-i} is a vector of demand of the products other than the ith product in the line,
p_i is the price of the ith product,
P_{-i} is a vector of prices of the products other than the ith product in the line,
P_c is a vector of prices of the products from competing firms,
X is a vector of the firm's marketing mix variables other than prices on all products in the line,
X_c is a vector of the marketing mix variables other than prices from competing firms, and
C_i is the cost of selling D_i units of the ith product

Equation (10.1) reveals two significant differences in pricing a product line as compared to pricing a single product. The first difference comes from the demand interdependence of the products in a line. Unlike the demand in the single-product case, the demand of product i in a line is not only a function of its own price but also a function of the prices of the other products in a line. The second difference comes from the cost interdependence of the products in a line. On the one hand, the economies of scale may reduce the production cost of each product as the number of products in a line decreases. This is because a shorter product line leads to more sales for each product in the line. On the other hand, the economies of scope may lower the cost of each product when more products are added into the product line.

Generally, demand interdependence leads to the cannibalization effect. That is, lowering the price of one product steals the demand from the other products in the line. This is because products in a line are partial substitutes, by our definition of product line. However, under some circumstances, demand among the products in a line can be complementary even though they are substitutes in functionalities. For example, a low price for a product in the line may attract consumers to the line and they may end up buying other products in the line through the 'bait and switch' mechanism (Gerstner and Hess, 1990). As another example, setting a very low price to a product in a line may increase the sales of a high-priced product in the line due to the 'compromise effect', well documented in the consumer behavior literature (Kivetz et al., 2004; Simonson and Tversky, 1992).

The presence of demand and cost interdependence for products in a product line makes the optimal pricing decision a challenging one. There are two main difficulties. First, it is hard to come up with precise specifications of the demand and cost interdependence and estimate their parameters, especially when the number of products in a line is large. Second, it is hard to simultaneously solve for the optimal prices of all products given the complexity of demand and cost interdependence.

Researchers have proposed various mathematical programming and decision support models to obtain optimal prices based on the general framework given in equation (10.1) (Chen and Hausman, 2000; Dobson and Kalish, 1988, 1993; Little and Shapiro, 1980; Reibstein and Gatignon, 1984; Urban, 1969). Generally, the decision support models on product line pricing follow a three-step procedure. The first step is to specify the functional forms of demand and cost. The second step is to estimate parameters in the demand and cost functions. The data source can be sales records, conjoint analysis output and operation/production records. Finally, the third step is to solve the optimization problem mathematically. Given the challenging nature of the product line pricing problem, typically a number of simplifying assumptions have to be imposed in the specifications of demand and cost functions, and heuristic algorithms have to be used in optimization. Some commonly adopted simplifying assumptions include (1) ignoring reactions from the competitors and (2) ignoring interactions between prices and other marketing mix variables. In addition, cost interdependence tends to be ignored or modeled in a less sophisticated fashion than demand interdependence in those models. The primary reason, as stated in Dobson and Kalish (1993, p. 171), is that '(t)he cost structure of a firm can in many cases be very complicated and hard to measure'.

Moreover, the optimization problem as formulated in equation (10.1) is itself a simplified version of the product line pricing problem in general. Two important considerations are ignored in equation (10.1). First, the unit price of each product is assumed to be independent from the number of units purchased. Thus the practice of nonlinear pricing is not taken into account. Second, equation (10.1) is a static model and the potential intertemporal demand and cost interdependence is ignored. If we extend equation (10.1) to consider the issues of nonlinear and dynamic pricing, more complicated decision support models will be required to provide heuristic solutions to the pricing problem.

Besides mathematical programming and decision support models, researchers have also developed various analytical models on product line pricing with stylized assumptions on demand and supply. While the purpose of the decision support models is to obtain optimal prices explicitly based on demand and cost estimations, the objectives of the stylized analytical models are to identify key economic effects that influence the optimal prices and provide directional guidance for optimal product line pricing. We review the analytical models in the literature along with the empirical studies in the next two sections.

3. Pricing vertically differentiated product lines

Recall our definition of vertical differentiation from the Introduction. Examples of the dimension in this case are the power of cars, the processing speed of computers and the purity of chemicals. In the product line pricing literature, researchers typically assume that products are vertically differentiated along a single dimension and interpret such a dimension as product quality.

Firms offer vertically differentiated product lines because consumers are heterogeneous in their willingness to pay for product quality. This gives firms the incentive to conduct second-degree price discrimination, which is achieved by offering a set of products with different quality and prices. In general, there are two possible causes of demand interdependence in a vertically differentiated product line: consumer self-selection and the context effect. Consumer self-selection refers to the fact that each consumer chooses the product to buy that maximizes her net surplus. As a result, the price of one product affects the demand of other products in the line. The context effect refers to the fact that consumers' preferences toward a product can be influenced by the prices of the other products in the line. For example, Petroshius and Monroe (1987) showed that the price range of the products in a line could affect consumers' evaluation on individual products in the line. Simonson and Tversky (1992) showed that the consumers tend to avoid extreme options. Therefore, adding a high price product into a line may increase the demand of a product with a mid-level price.

While the findings from behavioral research on the context effects are interesting and important for product line pricing, most of the studies are descriptive in nature. The analytical and empirical studies on product line pricing have primarily focused on the impact of consumer self-selection. In the rest of this section, I discuss the previous research relating to consumer self-selection and product line pricing in detail.

3.1 Consumer self-selection and product line pricing: the basics

The primary consideration in the literature on pricing a vertically differentiated product line is the demand interdependence resulting from consumer self-selection. The basic modeling framework that captures the self-selection effect is as follows. Suppose a monopoly firm sells a high-quality product (H) and a low-quality product (L). Product H is designed to target consumers with high willingness to pay for quality (the H-type) and product L is designed to target consumers with low willingness to pay for quality (the L-type). If the price of H is too low, then the L-type may want to purchase product H. Similarly, if the price of L is too low, then the H-type may want to purchase product L. Generally speaking, a monopoly firm will not be able to extract consumer surplus fully because the prices of products H and L have to be set to induce consumers to 'self-select' into buying the designated products.

The above idea was formally modeled in the seminal papers by Mussa and Rosen (1978) and Moorthy (1984). While both papers assumed a monopoly seller, the former assumed a continuous distribution of consumer types and the latter assumed a discrete distribution of consumer types. The main insights of both papers are that under general conditions: (1) only the consumers with the highest valuation for quality get the efficient quality (i.e. the quality that would be chosen by a social planner for that segment) and all other segments get lower than the efficient qualities; and (2) the consumers with the lowest valuation for quality are charged with their willingness to pay for the product they buy and other consumers are charged below their willingness to pay for the products they buy. In addition, as pointed out by Verboven (1999), the pricing outcome given in Mussa and Rosen (1978) and Moorthy (1984) implies that the absolute price–cost margins increase with product quality but the percentage price–cost margins typically decrease with product quality.

To illustrate the results from Mussa and Rosen (1978) and Moorthy (1984), let us consider the following numerical example. Suppose that the market consists of one H-type consumer and one L-type consumer, and further assume that the reservation price of the H-type consumer is $3q$ and the reservation price of the L-type consumer is $2.5q$, where q is the product quality. The unit production cost is assumed to be $0.5q^2$. If a monopoly firm sells product H with quality q_H at price p_H to the H-type consumer and sells product L with quality q_L at price p_L to the L-type consumer, the profit of the firm is

$$\pi = (p_H - 0.5q_H^2) + (p_L - 0.5q_L^2) \tag{10.2}$$

If there is no demand interdependence, i.e. the H-type (L-type) consumer can only access product H (L), it will be optimal for the firm to set prices at the reservation prices of the consumers. Therefore the optimal prices are $p_H^* = 3q_H$ and $p_L^* = 2.5q_L$. Then, from (10.2), it is easy to obtain that the optimal quality levels are $q_H^* = 3$ and $q_L^* = 2.5$, and they are socially efficient. Consequently, we have $p_H^* = 9$ and $p_L^* = 6.25$ in this case.

In the situation where consumers have access to both products in the product line, each consumer can choose the one that maximizes her net surplus. In such a case, the demand of the two products becomes interdependent as a result of this consumer self-selection. Notice that the self-selection condition for the H-type consumer to choose product H over product L is

$$3q_H - p_H \geq 3q_L - p_L \tag{10.3}$$

and the condition for the L-type consumer to choose product L over product H is

$$2.5q_L - p_L \geq 2.5q_H - p_H. \tag{10.4}$$

From equations (10.3) and (10.4), we can see that the demand of each product is affected by the prices of both products. Following Moorthy (1984), it is easy to verify that (10.3) has to be binding for profit maximization but (10.4) is not binding. In addition, $p_L^* = 2.5q_L$ still holds. Then, from (10.2), we can obtain that $q_H^* = 3$ and $q_L^* = 2$.[1] Consequently, $p_H^* = 8$ and $p_L^* = 5$. We can see that the consumer with the high valuation for quality still gets the efficient quality but the other consumer gets lower than the efficient quality, and the consumer with the low valuation for quality is charged at her willingness to pay for the product purchased, but the other consumer is charged below her willingness to pay for the product purchased. The above results from the numerical example demonstrate the insights from Mussa and Rosen (1978) and Moorthy (1984). It is also straightforward to verify that the absolute price–cost margins increase with product quality but the percentage price–cost margins decrease with product quality in this case as pointed out by Verboven (1999).[2]

Insights similar to those in Mussa and Rosen (1978) and Moorthy (1984) were also obtained in Maskin and Riley (1984), Katz (1984), and Oren et al. (1984). Following Mussa and Rosen (1978) and Moorthy (1984), the basic idea of pricing a vertically differentiated product line, i.e. maximizing surplus extraction with the quality-based price discrimination under the constraint imposed by consumer self-selection, has been extended into many different contexts. Detailed discussion on the related research is provided below.

3.2 Incorporating competition

A natural extension of the models in Mussa and Rosen (1978) and Moorthy (1984) is to introduce competition into the pricing problem for vertically differentiated product lines. Most papers in this area have focused on the product quality decisions and/or the decisions on the number of products to offer in product lines (Champsaur and Rochet, 1989; De Fraja, 1996; Gilbert and Matutes, 1993; Jing and Zhang, 2007; Johnson and Myatt, 2003). The basic economic force captured by those papers is the tradeoff between product differentiation to mitigate competition and product proliferation along the quality dimension to maximize the benefit from the second-degree price discrimination.

---

[1] Given the parameter values in the example, it is easy to show that it is optimal to offer two products instead of one.
[2] The unit costs are 4.5 and 2 for product H and product L respectively.

As a pioneering paper in this area, Katz (1984) introduced competition by assuming that firms are horizontally differentiated, following the idea of Hotelling (1929). As expected, competition lowers firms' prices and profits. As a result, firms may offer products at different quality levels in order to avoid head-on competition.

The basic intuition behind the result of Katz (1984) can be shown using the numerical example presented in Section 3.1. Assume that there are now two firms with the same cost structure competing in the market described in that example. Further assume that each firm can potentially offer up to two products with $q_H = 3$ and $q_L = 2$. If firms simultaneously decide the number of products to offer before their pricing decisions, neither firm will offer both products in the equilibrium. This is because the Bertrand competition on any common product offered by the firms will lead to zero profit for that product for at least one of the firms. Therefore, in equilibrium one firm will offer product H only and the other firm will offer product L only.[3]

In an interesting paper by Desai (2001), the competition between firms was also modeled following Hotelling (1929) but consumers' horizontal taste differences toward the two competing firms were allowed to be different for the H-type and L-type. Desai (2001) showed that in this setup it was possible for both firms to offer efficient qualities to both consumer segments in equilibrium. The intuition behind this result is that competition lowers the price of product H to the H-type. Consequently, it reduces the incentive of the H-type to buy product L. Therefore firms may not need to lower the quality of product L in order to prevent the H-type from buying product L. Another innovative feature of Desai (2001) was that he allowed the possibility that the market was not fully covered. Under incomplete market coverage, he showed that even a monopoly might offer products with efficient qualities to both consumer segments. This is because the firm in his model faces a downward-sloping demand function instead of a step demand function when the market is not fully covered. As a result, the firm has the incentive to lower its price of product H to attract a large portion of the H-type. This again reduces the incentive of the H-type to buy product L.

Another interesting paper in this area is Verboven (1999). This paper studied a special type of vertically differentiated product line consisting of a base product and a premium product which was the base product plus some add-ons. This type of product line is common in the automobile industry. Under the assumption that consumers were only well informed about the base product prices, Verboven showed that the premium products could have larger percentage markups than the base products in equilibrium. This result was different from the standard result in the literature (e.g. Moorthy, 1984) and it was supported by the empirical findings of the paper.

Closely related empirical work in this area is quite scarce. A noticeable empirical research by Sudhir (2001) examined the competitive product line pricing behavior in the US auto market. He found more-competitive-than-Bertrand pricing behavior in the minicompact and subcompact segment, cooperative pricing behavior in the compact and

---

[3] In this case, there is no pure strategy equilibrium in prices if firms set prices simultaneously. If firms set prices sequentially, the pure strategy equilibrium will be $p_H = 5.5$ and $p_L = 3$ when the first mover produces product H and the second mover produces product L, or $p_H = 5.5$ and $p_L = 2.5$ when the first mover produces product L and the second mover produces product H. We can see that the prices and profits of the firms are lower than those in the monopoly case.

midsize segment and Bertrand pricing behavior in the full-size segment. These findings can be explained by firms' ability to cooperate, which is high in the segment with high concentration, and by firms' motivation to compete, which is high in the segment for entry-level customers (the minicompact and subcompact segment) because firms try to build customer loyalty for long-run probability as those entry-level customers eventually move up to buy large cars. The findings of the paper indicate the importance of the dynamic consideration in firms' product line pricing decisions. Remarkably, such a consideration has been largely ignored in the analytical models.

3.3   Interactions with other marketing mixes

As indicated in equation (10.1), the product line pricing decision is influenced by other marketing mix variables chosen by a firm and its competitors. Recent research on pricing vertically differentiated product lines has examined the interactions of product line pricing with other marketing mixes. Villas-Boas (1998) studied a manufacturer's product line decisions when it sells through a distribution channel with a single retailer. His results show that the main conclusions from Mussa and Rosen (1978) and Moorthy (1984) are reinforced in the channel setting. In fact, the quality of the low-end product is even more distorted than in the case without the retailer. This result is obtained because double marginalization in the channel increases the price to the H-type while the L-type is always charged with the reservation price. Consequently, this increases the incentive of the H-type to buy the low-quality product. To prevent this from happening, the manufacturer has to distort the quality level of the low-end product further down.

As to the interaction between product line decision and advertising, Villas-Boas (2004) studied the situation where the function of advertising is to create product awareness. He showed that in general a monopoly firm would charge a lower price for the high-quality product and a higher price (accompanied by higher quality) for the low-quality product when advertising was costly than when it was costless. The basic intuition is that a low-end consumer is unlikely to buy the high-end product if the high-end product is the only one she is aware of, but a high-end consumer will buy the low-end product if she is only aware of the low-end product. Therefore, when advertising is costly a greater proportion of sales will come from the low-end product. Then the firm has an incentive to increase the price of the low-end product by increasing its quality. To prevent the high-end customer from buying the low-end product when she is aware of both products, the price of the high-end product has to be lowered.

A recent paper by Lin and Narasimhan (2006) studied the interaction between product line decision and persuasive advertising. They suggested that persuasive advertising might increase consumers' willingness to pay for quality. Consequently, they showed that the prices and quality levels of both high- and low-quality products would increase when a firm adopted persuasive advertising strategy.

3.4   Cost-related issues

Researchers have also studied various impacts of cost and cost interdependence on product line pricing. Gerstner and Hess (1987) offered explanations for the empirical phenomenon of quantity discount and quantity premium observed for products in large packs. A product line with the same product sold at different pack sizes can be viewed as a special type of vertically differentiated product line if free disposal is assumed. The authors showed that consumers' storage costs and transaction costs played significant roles in determining quantity discount versus quantity premium for products in large pack sizes. In particular, quantity premium prevails when customers differ only in their storage costs but quantity discount prevails when customers differ only in their transaction costs.

Balachander and Srinivasan (1994) examined the product line pricing by an incumbent firm that used prices to signal its cost advantage in order to deter entry. They found that credible signaling required the firm to offer higher quality and higher price of each product in the line than in the perfect-information case. The intuition is that it is prohibitively costly for a firm without cost advantage to mimic the high quality level of each product in the line. Thus, high quality credibly signals the cost advantage. In contrast to the result from the standard model (e.g. Moorthy, 1984), the quality of the lower-end product can be distorted to a higher than efficient level when quality and price are used to signal cost advantage.

Shugan and Desiraju (2001) studied the optimal adjustments of product prices in a line given the cost change of a product. Somewhat different from the standard assumptions made in the literature (e.g. Moorthy, 1984), their assumptions on demand interdependence were based on the empirical findings by Blattberg and Wisniewski (1989), who suggested that competition between quality tiers was asymmetric. That is, consumers are more likely to switch up to buy the high-quality product when it cuts price than switch down to buy the low-quality product when its price is reduced. Shugan and Desiraju (2001) found that when the cost of high-quality product declined, the prices of all products in the line should decrease. But when the cost of low-quality product declined, the prices of the high-quality product should increase while the price of the low-quality product should decrease. The driving force behind those results is that the high-quality product is mostly immune to the price cut by the low-quality product, so that preventing the H-type from switching down is not a major concern as in the standard case (e.g. Moorthy, 1984).

Desai et al. (2001) examined the pricing implications where products in a line could share common components, which reduced the production costs due to economies of scope. An interesting finding is that the firm has to increase the price of the low-end product and reduce the price of the high-end product if it lets the low-end product share a premium common component used for the high-end product. This is because the quality of the low-end product increases through sharing. This leads to a price increase for the low-quality product. The price of the high-quality product has to decrease in order to prevent the H-type from switching down.

Netessine and Taylor (2007) explored the impacts of production technology and economies of scales on product line decisions. Their model combines the standard product line model as in Moorthy (1984) with the EOQ (economic ordering quantity) production cost model, and allows product line design and production schedule to be optimized simultaneously. They found that the results from their model could be significantly different from the standard results found in Moorthy (1984). The main reason is that, compared to the standard case, a firm is likely to offer fewer products in a line in the presence of inventory costs and economies of scales. This intuition is also obvious from the numerical example discussed in Section 3.1. Given the assumptions made in that example, if the cost of producing the second unit is half the cost of producing the first unit, then only one product will be produced at $q = 2.5$ and $p = 6.25$ with the sales of two units.

4. Pricing horizontally differentiated product lines

Recall our definition of horizontal differentiation from the Introduction. It is interesting that the retail prices for products in a horizontally differentiated product line tend to be uniform. For example, supermarkets typically charge the same price for yogurt with different flavors, department stores typically charge the same price for clothes with different sizes, and video rental stores typically charge the same rental price for new DVDs. Due to the uniform pricing phenomenon, research on pricing horizontally differentiated product lines has focused on the impact of the product line length, i.e. the number of products in the line, or the overall price level of the product line. I discuss this stream of research below, followed by a discussion on the rationales behind the uniform pricing behavior.

4.1 Product line pricing and product line length

According to Lancaster (1990), there are three drivers for firms' product line length decisions: the cost consideration, the demand consideration and the strategic consideration.

The main cost consideration in determining the product line length is economies of scale (Lancaster, 1990). Because of economies of scale, an increase in the product line length leads to an increase in cost, as the demand of each product tends to be lower with more products in the line. This argument suggests that a longer product line is associated with higher price because of the increase in cost. However, if we take the product line length decision as endogenous, a high level of economies of scale would lead to a short product line because of the cost consideration. Then a short product line could imply a high price because the observed product line length resulted from high production costs. The empirical evidence on the actual relation between product line length and production costs is not conclusive. Kekre and Srinivasan (1990) examined this issue using PIMS (profit impact of marketing strategy) data and found no negative effects of broadening product line on production costs. Bayus and Putsis (1999) also investigated this issue using data from the personal computer industry. After controlling for the endogenous nature of the product line length decision, they found support for the positive relation between product proliferation and production costs.

The demand consideration also plays a major role in determining the product line length and price. On the one hand, due to the variety-seeking behavior of individual consumers (Kahn, 1995; McAlister, 1982), heterogeneity in consumer tastes and uncertainty in consumer preference, a product line with a large number of varieties is likely to be preferred by consumers (Hoch et al., 1999; Lancaster, 1990). This preference for varieties suggests a higher price for a longer product line. Evidence from both behavioral and empirical research has provided some support for this claim (Berger et al., 2007; Kahn, 1998; Kekre and Srinivasan, 1990; Kim et al., 2002).

On the other hand, a product line with a large number of varieties may increase consumers' costs of evaluating the alternatives (Shugan, 1980; Hauser and Wernerfelt, 1990) because it requires significant effort to evaluate the options provided by the product line. This consequently reduces the attractiveness of a product line with a large number of varieties. To compensate for this effect, price of the product line has to be lowered. Thus a product line with a very large assortment may actually reduce consumers' purchase probability and has to be charged at a low price. Some recent behavioral and empirical studies have provided evidence on the negative effect of product line length on consumer preference (Boatwright and Nunes, 2001; Chernev, 2003; Dhar, 1997; Iyengar and Lepper, 2000).

Through a set of experiments, Gourville and Soman (2005) showed that product line length could have either positive or negative impacts on consumer preference depending on the assortment type of a product line. They defined two assortment types: alignable and nonalignable. An alignable assortment is one in which the alternatives vary along a single, compensatory product dimension. An example of the alignable assortment is jeans that vary in waist sizes. A nonalignable assortment is one in which the alternatives vary along multiple, noncompensatory product dimensions. For example, a product line consists of a car with sunroof but no alarm system; another one with alarm system but no sunroof can be viewed as a nonlalignable assortment. Gourville and Soman (2005) found that product line length had a positive impact on consumer preference if the assortment was alignable. In contrast, product line length can have a negative impact on consumer preference if the assortment is nonalignable because it increases both the cognitive effort and the potential regret faced by a consumer. The authors also showed that simplifying the information presentation and making the choice reversible could mitigate the negative impact of product line length on consumer preference.

Draganska and Jain (2005) examined the impact of product line length on consumer preference empirically, taking into account product line competition among firms. They developed and estimated a structural model based on utility theory and game theory. In their empirical application for the yogurt category, they found evidence that consumer utility was in an inverse-U relation with the product line length of a firm. This result reconciles the findings in the aforementioned literature that documented either the positive or the negative relation between product line length and consumer preference.

The joint impact of cost and demand factors on optimal product line length and price can be demonstrated with a simple example. Suppose that a firm sells to a unit mass of consumers who are uniformly distributed along a circle of unit length. The product line is also positioned on the circle. The location of a consumer on the circle reflects her preference. If a product is at distance x from a consumer, the consumer's reservation price for the product is $1-x$. The marginal production cost is assumed be to zero but the firm incurs a fixed cost F for adding a product to the line. Given those assumptions, if the length of the product line is n, it is optimal for the firm to position its products evenly around the circle. It can be shown that the optimal price for the product line is $p = 1 - (1/2^n)$. The market is fully covered at this price, i.e. every consumer purchases the closest product, and the total profit of the firm is $\pi = 1 - (1/2^n) - nF$. In this example, the price and profit of the product line increase with its length thanks to the demand effect (as reflected by the term $1/2^n$), but the total profit of the product line can also decrease with its length due to the cost effect (as reflected by the term nF). The optimal length of the product line is determined by the tradeoff between the demand and cost effects. It can be obtained by maximizing the total profit with regard to n.

In addition to the cost and demand considerations, the strategic consideration by firms can have a significant impact on product line length and formation. The strategic consideration can be from three aspects. First, firms' decisions on product line length and formation are influenced by their competitive behavior. On the one hand, firms facing heterogeneous consumers may want to expand their product offerings in order to gain positioning advantage. On the other hand, firms may want to restrict the length of their product lines in order to avoid head-on competition. Theoretical models on competitive product line positioning and pricing generally admit multiple equilibria (Shaked and Sutton, 1990). Brander and Eaton (1984) showed that firms' products could either be positioned in a compartmentalized fashion, with each firm focusing on a segment of the market, or in an interlaced fashion, with competition in every fraction of the market. The price of each firm's product line is expected to be higher in the first case than in the second. The authors further showed that both cases could be Nash equilibrium if firms made product decisions simultaneously, but the first case would be at equilibrium if firms made product decisions sequentially. The model in Brander and Eaton (1984) assumed that each firm was selling a fixed number of products. This assumption was relaxed in Martinez-Giralt and Neven (1988). Their theoretical model showed that firms would shorten their product line to avoid intense price competition. Therefore a shorter product line can be associated with higher price in a competitive setting.

In an empirical study on competition between Procter and Gamble and Lever Brothers in the laundry detergent market, Kadiyali et al. (1996) found that firms seemed to behave in a coordinated way in their product line pricing behavior, with each firm positioning its strong product as the Stackelberg leader in its strategic interaction with the rival's weak product. In their empirical study on the yogurt category, Kadiyali et al. (1999) also found accommodating behavior in product line competition. They showed that a product line extension gave the firm price-setting power in the market but the prices and profits of both the extending firm and its rival increased after the product line extension.

Second, the product line length decision can be made strategically by firms selling through channels. In an interesting paper by Bergen et al. (1996), they showed both theoretically and empirically that offering a large number of branded variants could reduce competition among retailers and lead to high prices and profits for both the manufacturer and the retailers. The intuition of this result is that consumers incur high shopping costs when they compare brands across retailers that carry a large number of branded variants. As a result, fewer consumers engage in comparison-shopping across retailers as the number of branded variants increases. Consequently, the competition among retailers is softened.

Finally, product line length and formation can be used as a strategic tool for entry deterrence, as suggested by Schmalensee (1978). This strategic role of product line length implies a higher price for a longer product line as a long product line deters potential competitive entry. However, Bayus and Putsis (1999) found that the entry deterrence role of product proliferation was not supported by the data used in their empirical study.

4.2 Rationales for the uniform pricing of a product line

As mentioned at the beginning of this section, the products in a horizontally differentiated product line are typically charged with a uniform price, at least at the retail level. This is surprising because one would expect both the demand elasticity and the marginal production costs to be different for different products in a line. Some explanations have been offered in the literature for this puzzling phenomenon. On the supply side, firms may incur large menu costs (Levy et al., 1997) by setting different prices for different product variants. This discourages firms from setting non-uniform prices if the gain from price discrimination is relatively small. Draganska and Jain (2006) and McMillan (2007) found empirical support for this menu-cost-based explanation as they showed that the profit gained from non-uniform pricing was small.

Several demand-side explanations were also proposed in the literature. Kashyap (1995) and Canetti et al. (1998) suggested that many firms believe they face a kinked demand curve where marginal revenue is discontinuous at some 'price points'. If the range of prices is narrow under the potential non-uniform pricing strategy, such a range may contain only one of those price points. Then setting a uniform price at such a price point can be optimal. The fairness concern of consumers (Kahneman et al., 1986; Xia et al., 2004) can also force firms to set uniform prices. Consumers may feel that the prices are unfair if product varieties with similar perceived costs are charged with different prices.

Finally, the uniform pricing policy can result from firms' strategic interactions in competition. In the context of multi-market competition (which can be analogous to product line competition), Corts (1998) showed that firms could soften competition by committing to uniform pricing if they have identical costs but the costs of consumers vary across markets. Chen and Cui (2007) suggested that consumers' fairness concern could serve as a commitment mechanism for firms to set uniform prices. In contrast to Corts (1998), they showed that firms could be better off with uniform pricing even if there were no cost variations across product markets. This is because, besides the competition mitigation effect, uniform pricing can have an additional positive effect on firms' profits as it can expand the market under certain conditions if price elasticity varies across products.

5. Future research directions

As discussed in the previous sections, researchers from many different disciplines, such as marketing, economics, psychology and operations management, have investigated various important topics in product line pricing. While much progress has been made in the last three decades, many issues relating to product line pricing remain to be studied. In this section, I discuss some future research directions that are both important and promising in my own opinion.

First, the existing literature on product line pricing has mainly focused on the cases where prices are set on per unit base. In reality, however, the total price of a product can have both a fixed fee component and a variable price (per unit price) component. A prominent example is the price structure of different wireless phone service plans. Danaher (2002) and Iyengar et al. (2007, 2008) conducted some empirical studies in this area but theoretical study on this topic is still scarce. Future research is expected to help us to better understand the issues relating to pricing product line with a sophisticated price structure.

Second, most analytical models on product line pricing are static in nature, even though the intertemporal nature of consumer behavior such as variety-seeking and brand loyalty can be a key driver for firms' product line decisions. The empirical work by Kadiyali et al. (1999) and Sudhir (2001) discussed early in this chapter indicates that the dynamic interactions among firms can have profound impacts on product line pricing. Future analytical research on product line pricing should incorporate some demand- and/ or supply-side dynamic features.

Third, behavioral research has offered important insights on consumers' reactions toward product line pricing practices (Gourville and Soman, 2005; Petroshius and Monroe, 1987; Simonson and Tversky, 1992). Future analytical and empirical research can benefit from taking into consideration the behavioral aspects of product line pricing, such as the context effect, consumer fairness concern, regret for forgone choices, etc.

Orhun (forthcoming) has taken some initiative in this direction with the attempt to incorporate the context effect into the model of pricing a vertically differentiated product line.

Fourth, as discussed in this chapter, both demand interdependence and cost interdependence among products are critical to the optimal design and pricing of product lines. This suggests that integrating the research approaches from operations and marketing can be a fruitful research direction (Eliashberg and Steinberg, 1993). As shown in Netessine and Taylor (2007), many new insights could be generated by jointly modeling the demand side and the production side of product line decisions.

Fifth, even though this chapter discussed the research on pricing the vertically differentiated product line and the horizontally differentiated product line separately, in many cases the actual product offerings in a line are differentiated both vertically and horizontally. For example, a line of automobiles can be vertically differentiated on their engine powers but also horizontally differentiated on colors and other attributes. With the exception of Shugan (1989), who showed that fewer horizontal variants are offered for high-quality product than for low-quality product, little research has been done to address the issue of pricing a product line with its products interacting both vertically and horizontally. Future research should fill this gap.

Sixth, the number of empirical studies on product line pricing has been far lower than the number of theoretical studies. This imbalance is expected to change in future as high-quality data from many industries become available to academic researchers.

Finally, technology advance and the emerging of the Internet as a marketing platform have made it cost-efficient for retailers to offer a great number of varieties in certain categories, such as music titles available from iTune, books available from Amazon.com and DVDs available from Netflix. This phenomenon of having extremely proliferated product lines was coined as the 'long tail' phenomenon by Anderson (2006). It will be interesting for future research to explore the long tail phenomenon and see whether it may lead to new product line pricing implications.

References

Anderson, Chris (2006), *The Long Tail: Why the Future of Business is Selling Less of More*, New York: Hyperion.
Balachander, S. and K. Srinivasan (1994), 'Selection of product line qualities and prices to signal competitive advantage', *Management Science*, **40** (7), 824–41.
Bayus, B.L. and W.P. Putsis, Jr (1999), 'Product proliferation: an empirical analysis of product line determinants and market outcomes', *Marketing Science*, **18** (2), 137–53.
Bergen, M., S. Dutta and S.M. Shugan (1996), 'Branded variants: a retail perspective', *Journal of Marketing Research*, **33**, 9–19.
Berger, J., M. Draganska and I. Simonson (2007), 'The influence of variety on brand perceptions, choice, and experience', *Marketing Science*, **26** (4), 460–72.
Blattberg, R.C. and K.J. Wisniewski (1989), 'Price-induced patterns of competition', *Marketing Science*, **8**, 291–309.
Boatwright, P. and J.C. Nunes (2001), 'Reducing assortment: an attribute-based approach', *Journal of Marketing*, **65**, 50–63.
Brander, J.A. and J. Eaton (1984), 'Product line rivalry', *The American Economic Review*, **74** (3), 323–34.
Canetti, E., A. Blinder and D. Lebow (1998), *Asking About Prices: A New Approach to Understanding Price Stickiness*, New York: Russell Sage.
Champsaur, P. and J. Rochet (1989), 'Multiproduct duopolists', *Econometrica*, **57** (3), 533–57.

Chen, K.D. and W.H. Hausman (2000), 'Mathematical properties of the optimal product line selection problem using choice-based conjoint analysis', *Management Science*, **46** (2), 327–32.

Chen, Y. and T.H. Cui (2007), 'Fairness and uniform pricing', mimeo, University of Minnesota.

Chernev, A. (2003), 'When more is less and less is more: the role of ideal point availability and assortment in consumer choice', *Journal of Consumer Research*, **30**, 170–83.

Corts, K. (1998), 'Third degree price discrimination in oligopoly: all-out competition and strategic commitment', *RAND Journal of Economics*, **29** (2), 306–23.

Danaher, P. (2002), 'Optimal pricing of new subscription services: analysis of a market experiment', *Marketing Science*, **21** (2), 119–38.

De Fraja, G. (1996), 'Product line competition in vertically differentiated markets', *International Journal of Industrial Organization*, **14** (3), 389–414.

Desai, P.S. (2001), 'Quality segmentation in spatial markets: when does cannibalization affect product line design?', *Marketing Science*, **20**, 265–83.

Desai, P., S. Kekre, S. Radhakrishnan and K. Srinivasan (2001), 'Product differentiation and commonality in design: balancing revenue and cost drivers', *Management Science*, **47**, 37–51.

Dhar, R. (1997), 'Consumer preference for a no-choice option', *Journal of Consumer Research*, **24**, 215–31.

Dobson, G. and S. Kalish (1988), 'Positioning and pricing a product line', *Marketing Science*, **7**, 107–25.

Dobson, G. and S. Kalish (1993), 'Heuristics for pricing and positioning a product-line using conjoint and cost data', *Management Science*, **39** (2), 160–75.

Draganska, M. and D. Jain (2005), 'Product line length as a competitive tool', *Journal of Economics and Management Strategy*, **14** (1), 1–28.

Draganska, M. and D. Jain (2006), 'Consumer preferences and product-line pricing strategies: an empirical analysis', *Marketing Science*, **25** (2), 164–74.

Eliashberg, J. and R. Steinberg (1993), 'Marketing–production joint decision-making', in J. Eliashberg and G.L. Lilien (eds), *Handbooks in Operations Research and Management Science*, Vol. 5, Amsterdam: Elsevier Science, pp. 819–70.

Gerstner, E. and J.D. Hess (1987), 'Why do hot dogs come in packs of 10 and buns in 8s or 12s? A demand-side investigation', *The Journal of Business*, **60** (4), 491–517.

Gerstner, E. and J. Hess (1990), 'Can bait and switch benefit consumers?', *Marketing Science*, **9** (2), 114–24.

Gilbert, R. and C. Matutes (1993), 'Product line rivalry with brand differentiation', *Journal of Industrial Economics*, **41** (3), 223–40.

Gourville, J.T. and D. Soman (2005), 'Overchoice and assortment type: when and why variety backfires', *Marketing Science*, **24**, 382–95.

Hauser, J.R. and B. Wernerfelt (1990), 'An evaluation cost model of consideration sets', *The Journal of Consumer Research*, **16** (4), 393–408.

Hoch, S.J., E.T. Bradlow and B. Wansink (1999), 'The variety of an assortment', *Marketing Science*, **18** (4), 527–46.

Hotelling, H. (1929), 'Stability in competition', *Economic Journal*, **39**, 41–57.

Iyengar, R., A. Ansari and S. Gupta (2007), 'A model of consumer learning for service quality and usage', *Journal of Marketing Research*, **44** (4), 529–44.

Iyengar, R., K. Jedidi and R. Kohli (2008), 'A conjoint approach to multipart pricing', *Journal of Marketing Research*, **45** (2), 195–210.

Iyengar, S.S. and M.R. Lepper (2000), 'When choice is demotivating: can one desire too much of a good thing?', *Journal of Personality and Social Psychology*, **79**, 995–1006.

Jing, B. and J.Z. Zhang (2007), 'Product line equilibrium in a sales model', Working Paper, New York University.

Johnson, J. and D. Myatt (2003), 'Multiproduct quality competition: fighting brands and product line pruning', *American Economic Review*, **93** (3), 748–74.

Kadiyali, V., N. Vilcassim and P. Chintagunta (1996), 'Empirical analysis of competitive product line pricing decisions: lead, follow, or move together?', *Journal of Business*, **69**, 459–88.

Kadiyali, V., N. Vilcassim and P. Chintagunta (1999), 'Product line extensions and competitive market interactions: an empirical analysis', *Journal of Econometrics*, **89**, 339–63.

Kahn, B.E. (1995), 'Consumer variety-seeking among goods and services: an integrative review', *Journal of Retailing and Consumer Services*, **2** (3), 139–48.

Kahn, B.E. (1998), 'Dynamic relationships with customers: high-variety strategies', *Journal of the Academy of Marketing Science*, **26** (1), 45–53.

Kahneman, D., J.L. Knetsch and R. Thaler (1986), 'Fairness as a constraint on profit seeking: entitlements in the market', *American Economic Review*, **76** (4), 728–41.

Kashyap, A.K. (1995), 'Sticky prices: new evidence from retail catalogs', *Quarterly Journal of Economics*, **110** (1), 245–74.

Katz, M.L. (1984), 'Firm-specific differentiation and competition among multiproduct firms', *The Journal of Business*, **57** (1), S149–S166.
Kekre, S. and K. Srinivasan (1990), 'Broader product line: a necessity to achieve success?', *Management Science*, **36**, 1216–31.
Kim, J., G.M. Allenby and P.E. Rossi (2002), 'Modeling consumer demand for variety', *Marketing Science*, **21** (3), 229–50.
Kivetz, R., O. Netzer and V. Srinivasan (2004), 'Alternative models for capturing the compromise effect', *Journal of Marketing Research*, **41**, 237–57.
Lancaster, K. (1990), 'The economics of product variety: a survey', *Marketing Science*, **9** (3), 189–206.
Levy, D., M. Bergen, S. Dutta and R. Venable (1997), 'The magnitude of menu costs: direct evidence from large U.S. supermarket chains', *Quarterly Journal of Economics*, **112** (3), 791–825.
Lin, Y. and C. Narasimhan (2006), 'Persuasive advertising and product line design', Working Paper, Washington University in St Louis.
Little, J.D.C. and J.F. Shapiro (1980), 'A theory for pricing nonfeatured products in supermarkets', *The Journal of Business*, **53** (3), S199–S209.
Martinez-Giralt, X. and D.J. Neven (1988), 'Can price competition dominate market segmentation?', *The Journal of Industrial Economics*, **36** (4), 431–42.
Maskin, E. and J. Riley (1984), 'Monopoly with incomplete information', *The RAND Journal of Economics*, **15** (2), 171–96.
McAlister, L. (1982), 'A dynamic satiation model of variety seeking', *Journal of Consumer Research*, **9**, 141–50.
McMillan, R. (2007), 'Different flavor, same price: the puzzle of uniform pricing for differentiated products', Working Paper, Federal Trade Commission, Bureau of Economics.
Moorthy, K.S. (1984), 'Market segmentation, self-selection, and product line design', *Marketing Science*, **3**, 288–307.
Mussa, M. and S. Rosen (1978), 'Monopoly and product quality', *Journal of Economic Theory*, **18**, 301–17.
Netessine, S. and T.A. Taylor (2007), 'Product line design and production technology', *Marketing Science*, **26**, 101–17.
Oren, S., S. Smith and R. Wilson (1984), 'Pricing a product line', *The Journal of Business*, **57** (1), S73–S99.
Orhun, A.Y. (forthcoming), 'Optimal product line design when consumers exhibit choice set dependent preferences', *Marketing Science*.
Petroshius, S.M. and K.B. Monroe (1987), 'Effect of product-line pricing characteristics on product evaluations', *Journal of Consumer Research*, **13**, 511–19.
Reibstein, D.J. and H. Gatignon (1984), 'Optimal product line pricing: the influence of elasticities and cross-elasticities', *Journal of Marketing Research*, **21** (3), 259–67.
Rao, V.R. (1984), 'Pricing research in marketing: the state of the art', *The Journal of Business*, **57** (1), S39–S60.
Rao, V.R. (1993), 'Pricing models in marketing', in J. Eliashberg and G. L. Lilien (eds), *Handbooks in Operations Research and Management Science, Vol. 5, Marketing*, Amsterdam: North-Holland, pp. 517–52.
Schmalensee, R. (1978), 'Entry deterrence in the ready-to-eat breakfast cereal industry', *Bell Journal of Economics*, **9**, 305–27.
Shaked, A. and J. Sutton (1990), 'Multiproduct firms and market structure', *The RAND Journal of Economics*, **21** (1), 45–62.
Shugan, S.M. (1980), 'The cost of thinking', *The Journal of Consumer Research*, **7** (2), 99–111.
Shugan, S.M. (1989), 'Product assortment in a triopoly', *Management Science*, **35** (3), 304–20.
Shugan, S.M. and R. Desiraju (2001), 'Retail product-line pricing strategy when costs and products change', *Journal of Retailing*, **77** (1), 17–38.
Simonson, I. and A. Tversky (1992), 'Choice in context: tradeoff contrast and extremeness aversion', *Journal of Marketing Research*, **29**, 281–95.
Sudhir, K. (2001), 'Competitive pricing behavior in the auto market: a structural analysis', *Marketing Science*, **20** (1), 42–60.
Urban, G.L. (1969), 'A mathematical modeling approach to product line decisions', *Journal of Marketing Research*, **6** (1), 40–47.
Verboven, F. (1999), 'Product line rivalry and market segmentation', *Journal of Industrial Economics*, **47** (4), 399–425.
Villas-Boas, J.M. (1998), 'Product line design for a distribution channel', *Marketing Science*, **17**, 156–69.
Villas-Boas, J.M. (2004). 'Communication strategies and product line design', *Marketing Science*, **23**, 304–16.
Xia, L., K.B. Monroe and J.L. Cox (2004), 'The price is unfair! A conceptual framework of price fairness perceptions', *Journal of Marketing*, **68**, 1–15.

11 The design and pricing of bundles: a review of normative guidelines and practical approaches
R. Venkatesh and Vijay Mahajan*

Abstract
Bundling, the strategy of marketing products in particular combinations, is growing in significance given the boom in high technology and e-commerce. The seller in these instances typically has to decide which form of bundling to pursue and how to price the bundle and the individual products. We have written this chapter with two main objectives. First, we have sought to draw a set of key guidelines for bundling and pricing from a large body of 'traditional' literature rooted in stylized economic models. Here we have considered factors such as the nature of heterogeneity in consumers' reservation prices, the extent of the underlying correlation in reservation prices, the degree of complementarity or substitutability, and the nature of competition. The key conclusion is that no one form of bundling is always the best. Second, we have attempted to showcase the extant methodologies for bundle design and pricing. The studies that we have considered here have an empirical character and pertain to issues of a 'marketing' nature. In the concluding section, we suggest other avenues for expanding this work.

1. Overview

Bundling – the strategy of marketing two or more products or services as a specially priced package – is a form of nonlinear pricing (Wilson, 1993).[1] The literature identifies three alternative bundling strategies. Under the pure components (or unbundling) strategy, the seller offers the products separately (but not as a bundle);[2] under pure bundling, the seller offers the bundle alone; under mixed bundling, the seller offers the bundle as well as the individual items (see Schmalensee, 1984). The seller's decision involves choosing the particular strategy and the corresponding price(s) that maximize one's objective function. Bundling is significant in both monopolistic and competitive situations, and the guidelines often differ.

Although certain seminal papers on bundling are over four decades old (e.g. Stigler, 1963), the growth in high technology, e-commerce and competition has continually given new meaning to bundling. The rationales for bundling or unbundling (or both!) come from the firm side, demand or consumer side, and the competitor side. The bundles themselves could be of complements (e.g. TV with VCR), substitutes (e.g. a two-ticket combo to successive baseball games) or independently valued products. Indeed, there

---

* The authors thank Vithala Rao and an anonymous reviewer for helpful comments on an earlier version of the chapter.
[1] Multipart tariff, another form of nonlinear pricing, is the focus of Chapter 16 in this volume.
[2] Although pure components and unbundling are essentially the same, Venkatesh and Chatterjee (2006, p. 22) note that unbundling represents 'the strategic uncoupling of a composite product (e.g., a news magazine) into its components'. Pure components is then the slight contrast of offering two naturally separate products in their standalone form.

could be bundles of brands (e.g. Diet Coke with NutraSweet) with more than one vested seller for a product.

We have written this chapter with two main objectives. First, we have sought to draw a set of key guidelines for bundling and pricing from a large body of 'traditional' literature rooted in stylized economic models. Second, we have attempted to showcase the work of marketing scholars. This work emphasizes practical approaches to bundle design and pricing, and includes problems of a 'marketing' nature.

The classical work on bundling by economists has predominantly been of a normative nature. Related studies have examined the role of firm-side drivers such as reduced inventory holding costs by restricting product range (e.g. Eppen et al., 1991), lower sorting and processing costs (e.g. Kenney and Klein, 1983), and greater economies of scope (e.g. Baumol et al., 1982). Price discrimination is the most widely recognized demand-side rationale for (mixed) bundling (e.g. Adams and Yellen, 1976; McAfee et al., 1989; Schmalensee, 1984). Other demand-side drivers include buyers' variety-seeking needs (e.g. McAlister, 1982), desire to reduce risk and/or search costs (e.g. Hayes, 1987), and product interrelatedness in terms of substitutability and complementarity (e.g. Lewbel, 1985). Competitor-driven considerations are most notably linked to tie-in sales (see Carbajo et al., 1990), a predatory bundling strategy in which a monopolist in one category leverages that power by bundling a more vulnerable product with it. Table 11.1 provides real-world examples for the above-mentioned rationales.

At one level, the traditional economics literature has provided the primary impetus to bundling research in marketing, and a subset of marketing articles comprises direct extensions of prior work by economists. On the other hand, and as alluded to earlier, bundling research in marketing has proved novel and complementary in the following ways:

- *New methodologies and empirics* While the bundling research in economics is characterized by stylized analytical models, research in marketing has led to an array of specific approaches to aid decision-makers in optimal bundle design and pricing. Representative approaches are conjoint analysis (Goldberg et al., 1984), balance modeling (Farquhar and Rao, 1976), mixed integer linear programming (Hanson and Martin, 1990), probabilistic modeling (Venkatesh and Mahajan, 1993), and combinatorial methods (e.g. Chung and Rao, 2003). There is a much greater emphasis on empirical work in marketing.
- *'Marketing' problems, concepts and issues* Research in marketing has brought qualitatively different problems and concepts within the purview of bundling, an effort boosted by the emergence of e-commerce. Co-branding (Venkatesh and Mahajan, 1997) or the strategy of offering a bundle of two or more brands, product integration as with copier–printer–scanner–fax machine (see Stremersch and Tellis, 2002), and consolidation or bundling of information goods (see Bakos and Brynjolfsson, 2000) are examples of what we see as 'distinctively' marketing-type contexts.

While considering the entire spectrum of bundling research, we cite only a representative subset of articles. We have oriented the chapter toward certain topics only. First, we emphasize demand- and competitor-side determinants and implications of bundling and pricing. The demand-side factors we consider are the pattern of product demand,

Table 11.1 Select firm-, demand- and competitor-side rationales for (un)bundling

	Practical example	Illustrative articles
Firm-side rationales		
Lower inventory holding costs	Dodge's decision to cut down offerings of the Caravan to a few popular 'bundles'	Eppen et al. (1991)
Lower sorting costs	De Beers selling uncut diamonds as a package and not individually	Kenney and Klein (1983)
Greater economies of scope	Microsoft integrating the development of Windows and Internet Explorer apparently to reduce costs and increase quality	Baumol et al. (1982); Gilbert and Katz (2001)
Demand-side rationales		
Price discrimination (also related to correlation of valuations across consumers)	A sports franchise offering higher-priced tickets for individual events and discounted season tickets	Ansari et al. (1996); Schmalensee (1984); Venkatesh and Mahajan (1993)
Balance within a portfolio; variety-seeking	A TV station or network selecting a subset of TV programs from a broader set of options	Bradlow and Rao (2000); Farquhar and Rao (1976); Rao et al. (1991)
Complementarity	Offering ski rentals and ski lessons as a bundle	Lewbel (1985); Telser (1975); Venkatesh and Kamakura (2003)
Competitor-side rationales		
Tie-in sales and entry deterrence	IBM bundling tabulating machines and cards	Carbajo et al. (1990); Whinston (1990)
Aggregation to reduce buyer heterogeneity	A larger aggregator of information goods outbidding a smaller competitor	Bakos and Brynjolfsson (2000)
Enabling competition through unbundling to facilitate market growth	High-end manufacturer de-linking the sales of stereo receivers and speakers	Wilson et al. (1990); Kopalle et al. (1999)

correlation in reservation prices across consumers, and the degree of complementarity or substitutability. On competition, we contrast the implications of a duopoly in all versus a subset of the product categories. On the firm side, we consider the number of product categories on sale and the level of marginal costs. Second, we draw directly on normative work in bundling to provide a series of guidelines on optimal bundling and pricing. Unless otherwise noted, we treat 'optimal' behavior as one that maximizes the seller's profits in a monopoly or represents equilibrium outcome in competitive settings. Third, we review the extant methods for bundle design and bundle pricing. Our intent here is to highlight the purpose and scope of each approach. Fourth, we refrain from technical and analytical details as much as possible. Finally, we overlook a nascent stream of bundling research in marketing that is motivated by behavioral decision theory.

In Section 2 we discuss the normative bundling guidelines rooted in classical economic theories and axioms. In Section 3 we summarize the key approaches to bundle design and pricing. We conclude with a short chapter summary (Section 4).

2. Normative guidelines on optimal bundling and pricing

By far the largest body of work within the bundling stream is analytical and normative. Articles examining demand-side rationales begin with consumers' valuations for the individual products. The value is often assumed to be deterministic. A consumer's reservation price, an operational measure of value, is simply the maximum price the customer is willing to pay for one unit of a given product (cf. Schmalensee, 1984).[3] The reservation price construct is more nuanced when seen across products for a given consumer, or across consumers. The following two aspects of reservation prices have led to important extensions:

- *Correlation in reservation prices* As price discrimination is a key driver of mixed bundling, the heterogeneity in reservation prices across consumers is of central importance. Reservation prices across consumers for two products could be positively or negatively correlated, or be independent (i.e. uncorrelated). Positive correlation could exist when consumers differ on say their income or importance for quality. Reservation prices for the bundle are the least heterogeneous when component-level reservation prices are perfectly negatively correlated.
- *(Non-)additivity* Additivity means that a consumer's reservation price for a bundle of products is the sum of his or her reservation prices for the individual products. The additivity axiom applies for independently valued products only. For complements (e.g. ski lesson + ski rental), reservation prices are super-additive, i.e. the reservation price for the bundle is greater than the sum of the reservation prices for the individual products. For a bundle of substitutes, the reservation prices are sub-additive, i.e. the bundle reservation price is less than the sum of the product-level reservation prices. Super- or sub-additivity is more generally called non-additivity.

How the component-level reservation prices are stylized has a significant bearing on the bundling and pricing implications. We see four common characterizations and related strengths and weaknesses:

1. *Discrete distributions* (e.g. Adams and Yellen, 1976; Stigler, 1963; Stremersch and Tellis, 2002) Set typically in the two-product case, discrete distributions in bundling represent the reservation prices of two to five potential consumers or segments. The objective of related studies has been to present key conjectures or highlight shortcomings with specific strategies in an anecdotal manner. Comparative statics are irrelevant in these cases and the intent is to be illustrative rather than conclusive.

---

[3] A consumer's reservation price for the second, third, or higher unit of a product is central to the stream on quantity discounts – another form of nonlinear pricing. Normative bundling articles have typically focused on a consumer's unit purchase within a category.

2. *Uniform distribution* (e.g. Matutes and Regibeau, 1992; Venkatesh and Kamakura, 2003) This is the analog of the linear demand function. For a two-product case the distribution of bundle-level reservation prices would be triangular (i.e. unimodal) or trapezoidal. This form is analytically quite tractable, can capture complementarity and substitutability, but is not convenient for modeling correlation (except perfect positive/negative correlation).
3. *Normal (i.e. Gaussian) distribution* (e.g. Bakos and Brynjolfsson, 1999; Schmalensee, 1984) The sum of multiple normal random variables is also normally distributed. Thus any number of components can be considered without making the formulation more complicated. The bivariate normal distribution has the ability to capture the underlying correlation through a single parameter, a property leveraged by Schmalensee (1984). The significant downside is that no closed-form solutions are possible for the optimal price(s), thereby requiring numerical analysis.
4. *Double exponential distribution* (e.g. Anderson and Leruth, 1992; Kopalle et al., 1999) The appeal of random utility theory and logit choice models extends to bundling. Several articles on competition in bundling are rooted in this framework and model heterogeneity through the double-exponential distribution. While complementarity or substitutability can be captured in these models, to our knowledge none of the extant articles captures correlation in reservation prices across consumers through the bivariate double-exponential distribution.

The unit variable costs (or, more generally, the marginal costs) and sub-additivity in these costs are two firm-side variables that matter. Cost sub-additivity means that the unit variable cost of the bundle is less than the sum total of those of the individual items. It most often arises from economies of scope. The number of different products making up the bundle is also a relevant variable in some settings (e.g. digital goods where the number could potentially tend to infinity).

While most normative articles on bundling assume a monopolistic setting – a supposition strengthened by the power of bundling to deter competition – the impact of competition on optimal bundling and pricing is another important research avenue.

We shall consider the above variables and state key extant propositions as guidelines.

2.1 The 'simplest' anecdotal cases
As noted earlier, these are based on discrete distributions of reservation prices. The simplest bundling problem in Stigler (1963) in the context of block booking of movies yields the following guideline (keeping aside legal aspects):

G1: *For a monopolist offering two independent products with perfectly negatively correlated reservation prices across consumers, pure bundling is optimal when marginal costs are 'low'.*[4]

Pure bundling works through reduced buyer heterogeneity in bundle reservation prices. This benefit is maximized with perfect negative correlation in reservation prices,

---

[4] While our guidelines sound definitive, by no means do we rule out exceptions.

Table 11.2 An illustration of the power of pure bundling

Customer	Reservation price ($) for a week's rental of		
	Gone with the Wind (GW)	Getting Gertie's Garter (GGG)	GW+GGG
Theater 1	$8000	$2000	$10 000
Theater 2	$7000	$3000	$10 000

and pure bundling extracts the entire surplus, as illustrated in Table 11.2 with a variation of Stigler's example.

In this example, assuming negligible marginal costs, the seller would have netted $18 000 under pure components by pricing GW at $7000 and GGG at $2000, leaving a surplus of $2000. However, by offering the bundle alone for $10 000, the seller nets $20 000, leaving no surplus behind. Mixed bundling collapses to pure bundling (i.e. component sales are zero). Proposition P2 in Stremersch and Tellis (2002) reinforces this point. Notice that the 'low' marginal cost condition is necessary because if, say, the marginal cost of each extra copy of the movie is $4000, offering GW alone is optimal. A related intuition is discussed below.

Adams and Yellen's (1976) seminal work focuses on both the profit and welfare implications of bundling. Through a number of anecdotal examples the authors show that no one strategy – PC, PB or MB – is always the best from profit and welfare standpoints. The following guideline is significant and could be the reason that pure bundling attracts much legal scrutiny:

G2: *Pure bundling is more prone to over- or undersupply than pure components and mixed bundling.*

In support of the guideline, Adams and Yellen point to the difficulty of adhering to the principle of 'exclusion' with pure bundling in that some individuals whose reservation prices are less than a product's marginal cost may end up buying the product. This oversupply occurs because pure bundling forces the transfer of consumer surplus from one good to another. Undersupply occurs when a consumer who would have bought a subset of the components chooses to forego the bundle as buying it would violate individual rationality.

2.2 Role of marginal costs

Digitized goods and airline seats are examples of products or services with negligible marginal costs. At the other end, electronic equipment and other real hardware have significant marginal costs in relation to consumers' willingness to pay. It would be odd if the bundling and pricing guidelines for such diverse products were the same. Indeed, while it is not uncommon to see marginal costs set to zero for analytical convenience, this section underscores that the level of marginal costs has a profound impact on the attractiveness of alternative bundling strategies.

We assume here that the reservation prices are additive and the correlation coefficient is zero. A commonly used schematic representation of consumers' reservation prices for the two product case and their choices is shown in Figure 11.1 for the alternative bundling strategies.

The upper bounds of the reservation prices for the individual products can theoretically approach infinity. Moreover, the product and bundle prices under mixed bundling need not be the same as those under pure components and pure bundling strategies respectively. There is no implicit assumption in the diagrams on the density of the bivariate distribution.

Consider the case where unit variable costs are additive:

G3: *For a monopolist offering two products with symmetric Gaussian demand and costs:*
   (a) pure bundling is more profitable than pure components when costs are low relative to mean willingness to pay; otherwise, pure components is more profitable;
   (b) as in G2, pure bundling makes the buyers worse off due to over- or undersupply;
   (c) mixed bundling is optimal.

The result comes from Schmalensee (1984). G3(b) is a reinforcement of an earlier guideline. In a sense it drives G3(a): while the seller can effectively force the consumers to buy the bundle without incurring significant marginal costs, the same is not possible when costs are higher. The bundle price would go up significantly to cause severe undersupply; therefore the pure components strategy prevails. On G3(c) – the most significant guideline – Schmalensee (p. S227) points out how mixed bundling is a 'powerful price discrimination device in the Gaussian symmetric case'. This general strategy is able to combine the power of pure bundling to reduce buyer heterogeneity and the ability of pure components to cater to the high-end consumers of one product who care little for the other.

What if the base demand (for a product) is uniform and not Gaussian? Although the uniform and normal distributions can both have low or high standard deviation, given two supports on either side of and equidistant from the mean, the uniform distribution is thicker than the normal near these supports and thinner at the middle. Loosely speaking, the uniform distribution represents greater heterogeneity in reservation prices.

G4: *For a monopolist offering two products with uniform (i.e. linear) demand for each:*
   (a) mixed bundling is optimal when marginal costs are low to moderate; pure components is optimal when marginal costs are high;
   (b) component and bundle prices are both increasing in marginal costs; however, bundle price increases are nonlinear in costs;
   (c) when mixed bundling is optimal, the bundle and component prices are weakly greater than under the corresponding pure strategies.

Supporting evidence comes from Venkatesh and Kamakura (2003, p. 228). When marginal costs are low or negligible, demand-side factors dominate. With mixed bundling, the bundle is targeted at consumers who on average value both products whereas higher-priced components are sold to consumers who value one of the products highly but care little for the other product. As in Schmalensee (1984), mixed bundling can effectively

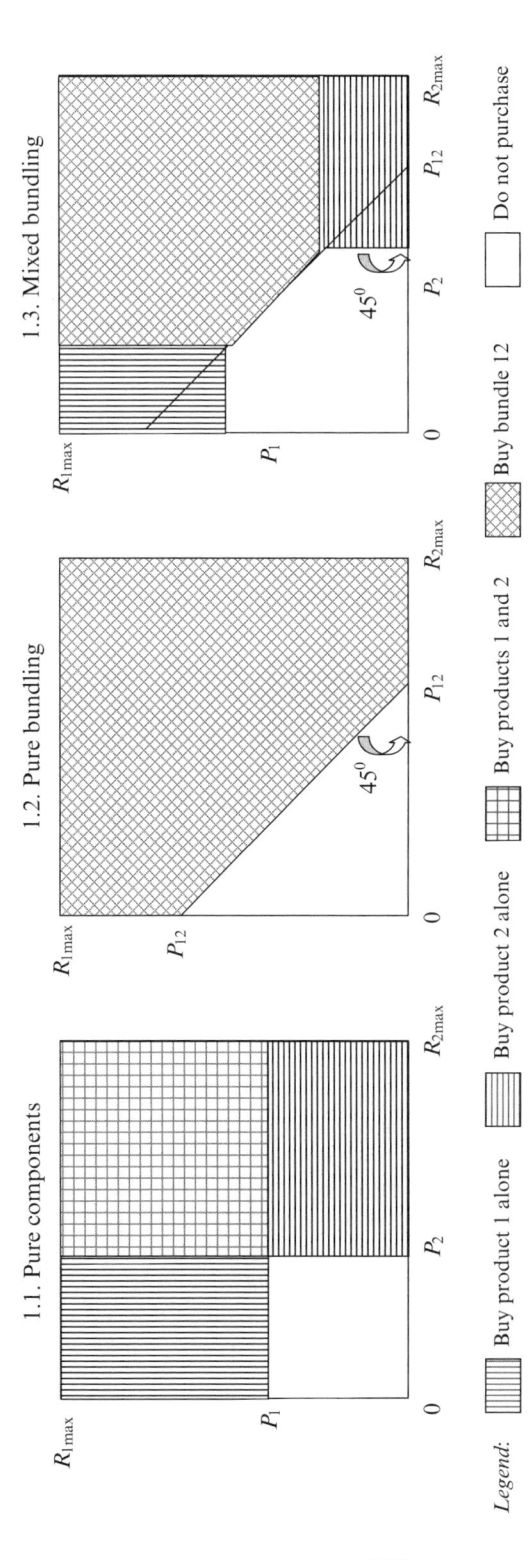

Legend: ▨ Buy product 1 alone   ▨ Buy product 2 alone   ▨ Buy products 1 and 2   ▨ Buy bundle 12   ☐ Do not purchase

Notes:
1. Independently valued products are, by definition, neither complements nor substitutes of each other.
2. The bundle and individual product prices under mixed bundling are likely to be higher than those under the corresponding pure strategies.

Notation: R_{1max}, R_{2max} = Maximum reservation price for products 1 and 2 respectively.
P_1, P_2, P_{12} = Optimal prices of product 1, product 2 and bundle 12 respectively.

Figure 11.1   Bundling with two independently valued products: schematic representation of pricing and penetration

price-discriminate. However, compared to G3, notice that the domain of optimality of mixed bundling is somewhat limited. This relates to the earlier point on the difference between uniform and Gaussian demand. Mixed bundling converges to pure components when marginal costs are high. On G4(b), the reason for the (non)linear increase in product (bundle) price is that the underlying demand function for each product is linear whereas that for the bundle has a kink – reservation prices are more concentrated in the middle. Unlike component prices that increase linearly in marginal costs, there is benefit from increasing bundle prices somewhat slowly when faced with higher costs. G4(c) is an important result on product line pricing. A wider product line – consisting of the bundle and the separate components – means that the offerings are weakly closer to consumers' ideal preferences (than under pure components or pure bundling), and the firm can charge a higher price compared to a case when it offers only a subset of these items.

While G3 and G4 are relevant when the seller has a limited portfolio of 'traditional' products with some level of marginal costs, a seller of information goods – which are numerous and practically costless – can draw on the following guideline.

> **G5:** *For a monopolist offering a large number of products with zero marginal costs, pure bundling is optimal.*

The guideline is based on Bakos and Brynjolfsson (1999). The authors draw on the law of large numbers to point out that for a bundle made up of many goods whose valuations are distributed independently and identically, a considerable fraction of consumers has moderate valuations. This fraction approaches unity as the number of goods gets infinitely large. The assumption of zero (or negligible) marginal costs is crucial because the authors also point out that there is a marginal cost level beyond which bundling becomes less profitable.

It is easy to see that when the marginal cost of the bundle is sub-additive in those of the components, the relative attractiveness of pure bundling is likely to increase.

2.3 Role of correlation in valuations

The nature and extent of correlation in reservation prices across consumers for the product offerings significantly impacts the power of bundling as a price discrimination device.

We rely on Schmalensee (1984) for the following guideline:

> **G6:** *For a monopolist offering two products with symmetric Gaussian demand and costs:*
>   *(a) the attractiveness of pure bundling increases relative to pure components as the correlation coefficient decreases (i.e. tends to -1); however, reservation prices need not be negatively correlated for pure bundling to be more profitable;*
>   *(b) the level of marginal costs in relation to the mean reservation prices of the product and bundle moderate the effectiveness of bundle sales relative to product sales;*
>   *(c) as in G3(c), mixed bundling is optimal.*

The effectiveness of pure bundling comes from the reduced heterogeneity in reservation prices for the bundle. G6(a) from Schmalensee (1984) disproves the myth created by anecdotal examples on bundling that a negative correlation in component-level reservation prices is necessary for reduced bundle-level heterogeneity. With Gaussian demand for the individual products, the benefit of heterogeneity reduction occurs so long as the correlation coefficient is less than +1. Of course, with negative correlation the heterogeneity reduction is greater, and the domain of attractiveness of pure bundling over pure components increases.

A perfectly negative correlation coefficient (of −1) means that the bundle-level reservation prices of all consumers equal the mean value. G6(b) is striking in that even this is not enough to lift pure bundling over pure components. Echoing the point in G1, pure bundling will yield a negative contribution when the marginal cost of the bundle is greater than the mean reservation price. Pure components would prevail.

G6(c) is the succinct generalization from Schmalensee, noted previously in G3. Of course, the share of bundle sales relative to individual product sales depends on the degree of correlation and the level of marginal costs in relation to willingness to pay. When the correlation coefficient approaches +1 (or −1), mixed bundling is expected to converge to pure components (or pure bundling). Of course, the caveat in part (b) will apply.

2.4 Role of complementarity or substitutability

By definition, reservation prices are super- (or sub-) additive for complements (or substitutes). Guiltinan (1987) proposes at least three possible sources of complementarity: (i) search economies, as for oil change performed at the same gas station and at the same time as a filter change; (ii) enhanced customer satisfaction, as for a ski rental accompanied by a lessons package; and (iii) improved total image, as for lawn care services offered with shrub care services (also see Oxenfeldt, 1966). Two products are seen as substitutes when their benefits overlap at least in part (e.g. international business news in the *Financial Times* and *The Wall Street Journal*) or when they compete for similar resources such as a consumer's time. While it may seem at first glance that complements should be bundled and substitutes offered separately, the truth is more nuanced. The normative guidelines that follow are from Venkatesh and Kamakura (2003).

We assume for this subsection that reservation prices across consumers for the two products are uncorrelated. The unit variable costs are additive:

G7: *For a monopolist offering two complements with uniform (i.e. linear) demand for each:*
  (a) pure bundling is more profitable than pure components only when (i) marginal costs are low or (ii) the products are strong complements;
  (b) when all three strategies are available, (i) mixed bundling is optimal for weak complements when the marginal costs are low to moderate; (ii) pure components is optimal for weak complements when marginal costs are high; (iii) pure bundling is optimal for strong complements.

G7(a) underscores that the pure components strategy actually prevails over pure bundling for a wide range of complements, falling short only for strong complements or when the marginal costs are low relative to the market's mean willingness to pay. In the latter case (with low marginal costs), the seller has more flexibility to offer significant discounts on the bundle and induce joint purchase. It is exactly the upward pressure on prices due to higher marginal costs that makes pure bundling less profitable than pure components for low to moderate complements.

The significance of G7(b) is that while the power of mixed bundling extends to moderate complements also when marginal costs are low, it is not a dominating strategy. For strong complements, bundling is so attractive that mixed bundling actually converges to pure bundling. On the other hand, when marginal costs are higher, the lowest possible bundle price is so high that mixed bundling converges to the pure components strategy; offering discounts via the bundle to consumers in the 'middle' (i.e. with moderate reservation prices for both products) is suboptimal.

The following guideline applies for substitutes.

G8: *For a monopolist offering two substitutes with uniform (i.e. linear) demand for each:*
  (a) pure components is optimal for strong substitutes and mixed bundling for weak substitutes;
  (b) when marginal costs are higher, the domain of optimality of pure components relative to mixed bundling is enlarged;
  (c) pure bundling is suboptimal.

Part (c) is intuitive yet significant in that enticing consumers with discounts for the bundle under the pure bundling strategy is suboptimal for substitutes. A better alternative is to focus on consumers who care for one product or the other, and let those who have high prices for both products form their own implicit bundles at higher prices. Indeed, discounted bundles are of such limited appeal that mixed bundling converges to pure components for all but the weak substitutes, a trend amplified under higher marginal costs.

The underlying mechanism for the above guidelines is evident from the pricing patterns discussed below.

G9: *For a monopolist offering two complements or substitutes with uniform (i.e. linear) demand for each:*
  (a) under pure components, optimal prices of complements and most substitutes are weakly higher than those of independently valued products;
  (b) under pure bundling, the optimal bundle price is lower for substitutes and higher for complements than that for independently valued goods;
  (c) under mixed bundling, the bundle and component prices are weakly greater than under the corresponding pure strategies.

The obvious part of the above guideline is that prices under both pure components and pure bundling are increasing in the degree of complementarity; after all, stronger complements are more valuable to consumers and higher prices help extract this higher value. The interesting aspect is that the optimal prices under pure components are higher for substitutes than for independently valued products. Relating back to G8, it actually helps not to encourage joint purchase of a suboptimal combination. Because pure bundling lacks this flexibility (i.e. it can only induce joint purchase), it is dominated. To be sure, mixed bundling is still the best for mild substitutes when the marginal costs are low to moderate.

2.5 Role of competition

Besides price discrimination, the rationale most often attributed to bundling is its ability to deter a new entrant or dislodge an incumbent. Kodak's decision to bundle film with processing, IBM's tie-in of tabulating machines and related cards, and the more recent example of Microsoft's integration of Internet Explorer with its Windows/Vista operating systems are prominent examples. We review a set of proposed guidelines on optimal bundling and pricing.

The simplest example of competition is when firm 1 enjoys a monopoly in product category A but competes with firm 2 in a category B. The available products are A_1, B_1 and B_2. If firm 1 follows pure bundling, a consumer who strongly prefers A_1 and B_2 is forced to buy the bundle $A_1 B_1$ and the product B_2, an obvious case of oversupply. When the two product categories are independent of each other, some consumers may buy B_2 alone. However, if the product categories are strict complements – such as TV and DVD player – the power of the tie-in becomes evident. While the Robinson Patman Act prohibits the use of pure bundling in B2B settings, the same is not true for B2C contexts, especially when firm 1 can justify pure bundling as a prerequisite for ensuring overall quality (as Kodak was once able to argue). We first look at the simplest case with independent demand. All articles cited in this subsection assume uncorrelated valuations across consumers for the products in question.

G10: *Given two product categories with independent uniform (i.e. linear) demand, when a monopolist in the first product category faces a competitor in the second category:*
  (a) given a Bertrand game in the second category, the monopolist in the first category prefers pure bundling when the marginal cost of the monopoly good is 'large enough' compared to that of the other;
  (b) the bundle price of the monopolist in the first category is increasing more rapidly in the marginal cost of the good in the second category;
  (c) the competitor's single product price (for the second product) is higher when the monopolist in the first category prefers pure bundling over pure components.

The guideline comes from Carbajo et al. (1990). The authors point out that in equilibrium, the monopolist pursuing pure bundling is able to clear consumers with the highest reservation prices. Of the remaining consumers, the competitor clears those with the higher reservation prices and excludes those with the lowest reservation prices for the second product. Had the monopolist pursued pure components, the equilibrium prices for the competing products in the second category would have been driven down to marginal costs. Thus the tie-in actually makes both manufacturers better off while aggregate welfare typically suffers.

A more general form of competition is when there is a duopoly in both product categories (e.g. Matutes and Regibeau, 1992; henceforth MR). Consumers could potentially buy two products from the same firm (that MR label 'pure systems') or mix between the two firms (i.e. form 'hybrid systems' as per MR). The following guideline applies:

G11: *In a two-product duopoly with linear demand for each product:*
  (a) pure components dominates pure bundling when the firms offer compatible products; otherwise, pure bundling prevails;

(b) *for compatible products, the choice between pure components and mixed bundling depends on the consumers' valuation of their 'ideal bundle'; when consumers are very particular about their 'ideal bundle', pure components is better.*

The guideline comes from MR. Incompatible offerings from the two firms would mean that the consumer has to make the decision at the system (i.e. bundle) level. Pure bundling prevails. However, with compatible offerings from the two firms, the customer's decision is driven by his or her preference intensity for an ideal combination – the pair that the customer finds the most complementary. If the preference intensity for this combination is very high, the firms are better off with pure components, i.e. giving the customer the most flexibility to put together a hybrid system (i.e. a mix of products from the two manufacturers) or a pure system as desired. There is no need to offer a discounted bundle through mixed bundling because when the complementarity from a pure system is strong enough, the customer is self-motivated to buy both products from the same firm.

Anderson and Leruth (1992) look at a variation of the above problem in which the products from different firms are assumed to be compatible but the heterogeneity in valuations of each product is captured by the double-exponential distribution. Broadly echoing MR, Anderson and Leruth find that if firms can commit to a pricing strategy before setting prices, pure components will be the equilibrium strategy for both firms; otherwise, each firm will pursue mixed bundling.

Building on the above, Kopalle et al. (1999) consider the possibility of market expansion (i.e. an unsaturated market). The key conclusion is that the equilibrium strategies of the firms shift from mixed bundling to pure components when there is limited opportunity for market expansion. The rationale is that when the market is less saturated, each firm can entice more customers by offering a wider product line (i.e. offer both the bundle and the individual products). With saturation, the incentive to entice customers with the discounted bundle is removed.

Given a large number of products in the context of the information economy, we have:

G12: *In a duopoly between bundlers of goods with zero marginal costs and i.i.d. reservation prices:*
  (a) the firm offering the larger bundle will find it more profitable to add an outside good;
  (b) by extension, a firm bundling information goods will be able to deter or dislodge a firm that offers a single information good.

The results are from Bakos and Brynjolfsson (2000), and build on their 1999 study. They invoke the law of large numbers to demonstrate that a firm with a larger bundle of 'costless' information goods is better able to reduce heterogeneity in consumers' valuations. Therefore, in a competition between two firms offering bundles of n_1 versus n_2 goods ($n_1 > n_2$), firm 1 would be better able to extract the consumers' surplus and hence would find it more profitable. The greater power of the larger bundler lets it deter a prospective entrant or dislodge an incumbent firm.

Table 11.3 contains a summary of our above guidelines, the underlying drivers for each guideline, and the articles that provide the supporting evidence.

We see additional linkages such as the following among the above guidelines. Higher

Table 11.3 A summary of normative guidelines on optimal bundling and pricing

Underlying driver(s)	Guidelines	Supporting evidence
Discrete demand (anecdotal cases)	G1: For a monopolist offering two independent products with perfectly negatively correlated reservation prices across consumers, pure bundling is optimal when marginal costs are 'low'.	Stigler (1963) Stremersch and Tellis (2002)
	G2: Pure bundling is more prone to over- or undersupply than pure components and mixed bundling.	Adams and Yellen (1976)
Marginal costs and number of product categories	G3: For a monopolist offering two products with symmetric Gaussian demand and costs: (a) pure bundling is more profitable than pure components when costs are low relative to mean willingness to pay; otherwise, pure components is more profitable; (b) as in G2, pure bundling makes the buyers worse off due to over- or undersupply; (c) mixed bundling is optimal.	Schmalensee (1984)
	G4: For a monopolist offering two products with uniform (i.e. linear) demand for each: (a) mixed bundling is optimal when marginal costs are low to moderate; pure components is optimal when marginal costs are high; (b) component and bundle prices are both increasing in marginal costs; however, bundle price increases are nonlinear in costs; (c) when mixed bundling is optimal, the bundle and component prices are weakly greater than under the corresponding pure strategies.	Venkatesh and Kamakura (2003)
	G5: For a monopolist offering a large number of products with zero marginal costs, pure bundling is optimal.	Bakos and Brynjolfsson (1999)
Correlated valuations	G6: For a monopolist offering two products with symmetric Gaussian demand and costs: (a) the attractiveness of pure bundling increases relative to pure components as the correlation coefficient decreases (i.e. tends to -1); however, reservation prices need not be negatively correlated for pure bundling to be more profitable;	Schmalensee (1984)

Table 11.3 (continued)

Underlying driver(s)	Guidelines	Supporting evidence
	(b) the level of marginal costs in relation to the mean reservation prices of the product and bundle moderate the effectiveness of bundle sales relative to product sales; (c) as in G3(c), mixed bundling is optimal.	
Complements and substitutes	G7: For a monopolist offering two complements with uniform (i.e. linear) demand for each: (a) pure bundling is more profitable than pure components only when (i) marginal costs are low or (ii) the products are strong complements; (b) when all three strategies are available, (i) mixed bundling is optimal for weak complements when the marginal costs are low to moderate; (ii) pure components is optimal for weak complements when marginal costs are high; (iii) pure bundling is optimal for strong complements.	Venkatesh and Kamakura (2003)
	G8: For a monopolist offering two substitutes with uniform (i.e. linear) demand for each: (a) pure components is optimal for strong substitutes and mixed bundling for weak substitutes; (b) when marginal costs are higher, the domain of optimality of pure components relative to mixed bundling is enlarged; (c) pure bundling is suboptimal.	Venkatesh and Kamakura (2003)
	G9: For a monopolist offering two complements or substitutes with uniform (i.e. linear) demand for each: (a) under pure components, optimal prices of complements and most substitutes are weakly higher than those of independently valued products; (b) under pure bundling, the optimal bundle price is the lower for substitutes and higher for complements than that for independently valued goods; (c) under mixed bundling, the bundle and component prices are weakly greater than under the corresponding pure strategies.	Venkatesh and Kamakura (2003)

Competition	G10: Given two product categories with independent uniform (i.e. linear) demand, when a monopolist in the first product category faces a competitor in the second category: (a) given a Bertrand game in the second category, the monopolist in the first category prefers pure bundling when the marginal cost of the monopoly product is 'large enough' compared to that of the other; (b) the bundle price of the monopolist in the first category is increasing more rapidly in the marginal cost of the product in the second category; (c) the competitor's single product price (for the second product) is higher when the monopolist in the first category prefers pure bundling over pure components.	Carbajo et al. (1990)
	G11: In a two-product duopoly with linear demand for each product: (a) pure components dominates pure bundling when the firms offer compatible products; otherwise, pure bundling prevails; (b) for compatible products, the choice between pure components and mixed bundling depends on the consumers' valuation of their 'ideal bundle'; when consumers are very particular about their 'ideal bundle', pure components is better.	Matutes and Regibeau (1992)
	G12: In a duopoly between bundlers of goods with zero marginal costs and i.i.d. reservation prices: (a) the firm offering the larger bundle will find it more profitable to add an outside good; (b) by extension, a firm bundling information goods will be able to deter or dislodge a firm that offers a single information good.	Bakos and Brynjolfsson (2000)

marginal costs appear to increase the significance of the individual components *vis-à-vis* the bundle (and vice versa). This explains why guideline G4(a) on the superiority of pure components over pure bundling for independently valued products with high marginal costs extends even to moderate complements (G7(a)). While the power of pure bundling comes from reduced heterogeneity in the reservation prices for the bundle, guidelines G1 and G6(a) (from Schmalensee, 1984 and Stigler, 1963) together suggest how a negative correlation augments this advantage, a point also made by Salinger (1995, p. 98). The presence of a large number of low-marginal-cost products also aids in reducing buyer heterogeneity for the bundle. Guideline G12 (from Bakos and Brynjolfsson, 2000) points out that an aggregator of a larger number of low-cost products can wield greater power through pure bundling compared to a smaller rival.

3. Approaches for bundle design and pricing

At one level, bundling is a product line decision. Therefore product line design and product line pricing approaches have some relevance to bundling. On the other hand, bundling is different from a product line problem because the latter involves a set of 'similar' or substitute products, such as the line of Toyota cars. The products that make up a bundle could have a broader array of interrelationships such as substitutability, independence or complementarity, and positively or negatively correlated reservation prices. Farquhar and Rao (1976) point to the need for 'balance' among products that make up a bundle. McAlister (1982) links consumers' evaluations of bundles to their variety-seeking needs and proposes the concept of attribute satiation as a driver of portfolio choice. While product line approaches are complicated, approaches to bundling are arguably even more challenging (and cumbersome).

Methodological approaches to bundling come in one of two broad types. Design-oriented approaches (e.g. Bradlow and Rao, 2000; Chung and Rao, 2003; Farquhar and Rao, 1976; Goldberg et al., 1984) help identify which among a feasible set of 'products' should go into the bundle (e.g. the composition of a professional basketball team) or what the levels of specific attributes should be (e.g. designing the make-up of a hotel in terms of the type of room, lounge etc.). Pricing-oriented approaches (e.g. Ansari et al., 1996; Hanson and Martin, 1990; Venkatesh and Mahajan, 1993) typically assume a product portfolio and propose the prices at which the individual items and/or bundles should be offered.

There is of course a design element to pricing-oriented approaches in the sense that if the proposed price of a product is 'too high', it essentially means withdrawing the product from the final set of offerings. However, the design focus is lacking in the sense that if a new component (not in the original portfolio) is added, the model has to be re-estimated (see Chung and Rao, 2003, p. 115). Likewise, while a typical design-oriented approach, say of Chung and Rao, answers certain pricing questions, its pricing focus is typically limited to a subset of strategies – pure bundling in Chung and Rao. By contrast, a component level approach, say Hanson and Martin (1990), provides optimal prices for all three alternative bundling strategies. Thus the distinction between a design versus a pricing emphasis in the extant approaches broadly holds.

Based on Chung and Rao's classification, design-oriented approaches are more likely to be attribute-level approaches (e.g. Bradlow and Rao, 2000) that model the complementarity among product attributes to capture bundle-level valuation. Pricing-oriented approaches are typically component level methodologies (e.g. Hanson and Martin, 1990);

that is, they treat 'components of a bundle as the ultimate unit of analysis in describing the utility of the bundle' (Chung and Rao, 2003, p. 115).

A key input for most pricing-oriented approaches is the consumers' reservation prices for the individual products and the bundle. Indeed, significant bias and/or measurement error in eliciting reservation prices could severely affect the appropriateness of the proposed optimal prices. Several recent studies such as Jedidi et al. (2003), Jedidi and Zhang (2002), Wang et al. (2007), Wertenbroch and Skiera (2002), and Wuebker and Mahajan (1999) propose interesting and effective ways of measuring reservation prices. The reader is referred to Chapter 2 in this book by Jedidi and Jagpal on estimating or eliciting reservation prices.

We now discuss representative design- and pricing-oriented approaches to bundling.

3.1 Design-oriented approaches to bundling

The diversity in the bundles to be designed has led to several types of design-oriented approaches. Our review focuses on the following routes summarized in Table 11.4:

- Hybrid categorical conjoint analysis (Goldberg et al., 1984)
- Balance model (Farquhar and Rao, 1976) and its later adaptations (e.g. Bradlow and Rao, 2000; Chung and Rao, 2003) (Rao and colleagues, hereafter)
- Co-branding approach (Venkatesh and Mahajan, 1997).

Table 11.4 contains the inputs to and outputs from each approach, and its key strengths and weaknesses. We devote this subsection to a discussion of the underpinnings of each approach.

(Hybrid categorical) conjoint approach Conjoint analysis is a well-established methodology in marketing for evaluating consumers' preferences for multi-attribute items and, in turn, as a product development tool. Goldberg et al.'s (1984, GGW) hybrid categorical conjoint approach is an improvement over basic conjoint in that it can deal with correlated attributes (e.g. hotel room price is typically correlated with room size) and provide bundle combinations and price premiums (i.e. express 'the price premiums for each amenity and also for competing bundles of amenities', GGW, p. S112). The GGW approach is preferable especially when a large number of attributes (40+ in their hotel context) and attribute levels (100+) are involved.

The 'hybrid' aspect of GGW's approach comes from simplifying the data collection task while still accounting for certain individual differences. Each respondent evaluates 'the levels of each attribute (one at a time) on some type of desirability scale' (Wind et al., 1989). The respondent is then exposed to a subset of the universal set of profiles so that only the main effects and select interactions are estimated. The 'categorical' element connotes that unlike with 'ordinal' approaches such as LINMAP, the dependent variable capturing preference need not be ordered. GGW's approach is implemented with 'dummy variable canonical correlation'.

The balance modeling approach The original balance model and its variants by Rao and colleagues have two core premises: one, that the selection of products that go into a bundle should consider the interactions among the attributes that define the

Table 11.4 Comparison of alternative approaches to optimal bundle design

Framework and representative articles	Inputs (what the approach needs)	Output (what the approach provides)	Strengths	Limitations
Conjoint analysis • Goldberg et al. (1984) (GGW)	• Respondents' choices at an attribute level, preference importance of attributes, and the likelihood of choosing specific bundles: collected in three phases	• The bundle of amenities and add-ons to be offered, and associated prices (or premiums) • Attribute importance and part-worths	• Extends conjoint analysis to the case of correlated attributes (as in bundling contexts) • A large number of attributes and levels can be handled with categorical hybrid conjoint	• As with traditional conjoint studies, cost of the offerings is not factored in; profit implications of bundle design are unavailable
Balance model • Bradlow and Rao (2000) • Farquhar and Rao (1976)	• Respondents' assessments on which product(s) from a feasible set balances a given (pair of) product(s); pairwise comparisons	• Identification of the best balanced product combinations • Classification of attributes as balancing, non-balancing, or non-essential	• 'Balance', a fundamental driver of consumers' bundle-choice decisions, is captured • Models bundle-level decision as a multi-attribute problem, helps clarify sources of interdependencies	• Pricing is not the focus; determining the makeup of the bundle is • Number of products making up a bundle is exogenous (to keep data collection manageable)
Comparability-based balance model • Chung and Rao (2003)	• Consumers' self-explicated bundle choices in a series of choice tasks, and reservation prices for their 'best' bundle • Consumers' ratings of the products on importance and comparability	• Identification of market segments for candidate bundles • Estimation of consumers' bundle-level reservation prices • Optimal bundle prices	• Integrates the key elements of conjoint analysis and balance model • Considering assortments across product categories improves upon prior balance modeling articles	• Mixed bundling strategy is not considered • Classification of attributes based on their balancing character could overlook perceived differences across consumers

Co-branding approach			
• Venkatesh and Mahajan (1997)	• Consumers' reservation prices for alternative co-branded offerings, and allocation of preference intensities between brands within each offering	• Best alliance partners and product combinations • Optimal prices, profits and (asymmetric) benefits for the respective partners	• By modeling the enrichment or suppression among brands, clarifies the asymmetric returns to alliance partners • General parametric distribution used to capture heterogeneity in valuations and (dis-synergies)	• Model is implemented for a product with two component brands only

products; and two, the bundle so chosen should be one that provides the best balance of features.

Balance represents the 'general harmony [among] the parts of anything, springing from the observance of just proportion and relation' (*Oxford English Dictionary*). Balance, as Rao and colleagues note, could come from homogeneity on some attributes and heterogeneity on others. Setting aside 'non-essential' attributes, the balance approach seeks to classify the remaining essential attributes as balancing and non-balancing. Balancing attributes can be equibalancing or counterbalancing; consumers seek heterogeneity on counterbalancing attributes (e.g. color, as in the assortment of shirts that consumers might like to own) and homogeneity on equibalancing attributes. Non-balancing attributes are those on which consumers wish to maximize (or minimize) aggregate scores as with quality (or costs).

The seminal paper in the stream by Farquhar and Rao (1976) – implemented in the context of scheduling TV programs – takes consumers' self-explicated measures on a series of 'balance'-related questions (see Table 11.3) and uses linear programming to classify attributes and select the most balanced bundle(s) from the possible alternatives.

The extension proposed by Bradlow and Rao (2000) relies on a hierarchical Bayesian model to implement the balance framework at the level of individual consumers as in their magazine or video purchasing behavior. The approach can help managers identify the best prospects for pre-existing product assortments as well as identify the specific bundle that would be appealing to the highest number of customers.

While the above two articles deal with bundle selection in 'homogeneous' categories (e.g. among television programs), the recent article by Chung and Rao (2003) proposes how a bundle of items from across categories could be identified. The approach tackles the possible non-comparability among attributes – a problematic issue for the traditional balance model. The proposed approach gets consumers' input to trifurcate attributes as comparable, partially comparable and non-comparable. Comparable attributes essentially become system-level attributes with possible interaction. Also, while computing sums and dispersion scores, the approach weights the components differently depending on their importance. The authors apply their approach to the context of personal computer systems.

Co-branding approach   Bundles of co-branded products, such as 'Lenovo PCs with Intel Inside', represent an emerging class of product combinations. Such bundles arise out of firms' motivation to emphasize their core competencies and forge alliances with synergistic partners. Unlike the other examples discussed in this subsection, co-branded bundles represent a coming together of two or more firms. The Venkatesh and Mahajan (1997, VM) approach is suitable for partner selection and pricing in co-branded bundles.

VM note that it would not suffice to consider only the aggregate payoffs from the co-branded bundles. Rather, the payoffs attributable to either partner should be distinguished because the benefit or cost from forming the brand alliance could be asymmetric depending on the prior reputation of the two brands and the nature of spillover. The approach defines a positive spillover to a brand as 'enrichment' and a negative spillover as 'suppression'. The heterogeneity in consumers' valuations for the base bundles (those between a branded offering and a generic) and in the perceived spillover effects are used to identify the best partners, the asymmetric benefits to the partners, the optimal prices and premiums for the baseline and co-branded bundles, and the corresponding payoffs. These decisions and outcomes are clarified in the context of the personal computer category and involving Compaq and Intel.

3.2 Approaches to bundle pricing

We devote this subsection to a discussion of the following three significant and diverse approaches to bundle pricing. These are summarized in Table 11.5:

- Mixed integer linear programming (Hanson and Martin, 1990)
- Probabilistic approach (Ansari et al., 1996; Venkatesh and Mahajan, 1993)
- Choice experiment-based hierarchical Bayesian approach (Jedidi et al., 2003)

While each approach's inputs and outputs, and the key strengths and weaknesses, are shown in Table 11.5, our discussion below focuses on the underpinnings and the key empirical findings.

Mixed integer linear programming approach Bundle pricing is a particularly complicated problem when the number of products is three or higher. With n distinct products, the number of possible offerings – consisting of all standalone products and bundles – is 2^{n-1}. Hanson and Martin's (1990) mixed integer linear programming approach is appropriate for a monopolist seeking to set the optimal prices for such a large-scale problem, given the right inputs.

The approach requires consumers' (or their segments') reservation prices and the seller's unit variable costs for all the possible offerings. In the limit, a segment could be made up of a single consumer. Making a reasonable set of assumptions, the article first establishes that a profit-maximizing vector of prices exists provided that each customer will purchase exactly one product or bundle or neither. A disjunctive approach that reduces computational times is used to determine the optimal solution. The approach is implemented with survey data on consumers' preferences for home services such as apartment cleaning.

Probabilistic approach While bundling articles typically assume that the key constraint at the consumer level is the willingness to pay, the probabilistic approach of Venkatesh and Mahajan (1993) and Ansari et al. (1996) is relevant for products such as entertainment or sports events for which other constraints such as available time are also significant in consumers' decision-making. While Venkatesh and Mahajan's approach is aimed at a profit-maximizing monopolist, Ansari et al. extend it to non-profits such as certain symphonies and museums. The components in these instances are the individual events or games, and the bundle is the package of such events. The single and season ticket prices are optimized.

The two studies, based on the same dataset and similar consumer choice processes, are probabilistic in the sense that they recognize potential consumers' uncertainty with finding the time for temporally dispersed events, even when they may have strong tastes for the events in question. The modeling approach translates the dispersion in consumers' reservation prices for the individual events and the heterogeneity in their time-related uncertainty to the bundle level, and provides the optimal single and season ticket prices.

Table 11.5 Comparison of alternative approaches to optimal bundle pricing

Framework and representative articles	Inputs (what the approach needs)	Output (what the approach provides)	Strengths	Limitations
Mixed integer linear programming framework • Hanson and Martin (1990)	• Consumers' reservation prices for components and bundles • Marginal costs of components and bundles	• Optimal prices of the bundle and components • Consumers' choices and surpluses	• Superior to alternatives when a large number of components and bundles is involved • Programming tool developed by authors has interactive, decision support capability	• Focus is on setting actual prices, not on providing strategic insights • Framework is not at the attribute level and hence sensitivity of results to product additions is hard to assess
Probabilistic framework • Ansari et al. (1996) • Venkatesh and Mahajan (1993)	• Distributions of consumers' resources and preferences (e.g. heterogeneity in available time and willingness to pay) • Fixed and variable costs of the bundle/components	• Optimal prices of the bundle and/or components under pure components, pure bundling and mixed bundling • Associated profits and, hence, the optimal bundling strategy	• Integrates consumers' preference intensities (e.g. reservation prices) and constraining resources (e.g. available time) • Suited for time-variant consumption (e.g. concerts) • For-profit and non-profit contexts compared (Ansari et al.)	• Makeup of the bundle is exogenous (i.e. components that go into the bundle are predetermined) • Underlying heterogeneity on any dimension is assumed to be unimodal
Choice experiment/ hierarchical Bayesian framework • Jedidi et al. (2003)	• Consumers' reservation prices inferred through choice experiment • Fixed and variable costs of the bundle/components	• Joint distribution of reservation prices for the individual products and bundle; approach accommodates non-additivity and correlated valuations • Optimal prices, profits and the optimal bundling strategy	• Model is rooted in utility theory and allows for interrelationships among product offerings • No-purchase option captures price expectations and reference effects	• Makeup of the bundle is exogenous, as above • Assuming normal (Gaussian) heterogeneity in component-level valuations is moot for a practical methodology

In the empirical context of a series of entertainment events, Venkatesh and Mahajan find that while mixed bundling is more profitable, the single and season ticket prices have to be optimized simultaneously. That is, starting with the optimal price from pure bundling (say) and sequentially determining the component prices is likely to be suboptimal. Also, ignoring the heterogeneity in available time is likely to bias the prices significantly upward. Ansari et al. find that a non-profit is likely to offer more events and set lower prices. As increasing total attendance is more important for non-profits, pure bundling becomes more attractive than pure components.

Choice experiment-based hierarchical Bayesian approach The above two types of approaches assume that consumers' reservation prices are available, through the use of other approaches. Jedidi et al.'s (2003) choice experiment-based hierarchical Bayesian approach is apt when the seller wishes to arrive at the multivariate distribution of reservation prices for the bundle(s) and the component products, and then apply a built-in algorithmic procedure to arrive at product line prices.

The estimation of the multivariate reservation prices consists of two steps. A (hybrid) choice-based experiment makes up the first step to infer respondents' reservation prices. This part includes a no-purchase option which helps capture competitive and reference price effects, and obtain 'dollarmetric reservation prices' (Jedidi et al., 2003, p. 111). With the choice information and the corresponding price points from the first step, and with the assumption that the true distribution of reservation prices for the offerings is multivariate normal, a hierarchical Bayesian framework is used to estimate the parameters of the joint posterior distribution. Any non-additivity in bundle-level valuations is captured under this approach. The optimization algorithm to obtain the optimal prices of the product line is routine, and requires as input the marginal costs of the various offerings.

The above study by Jedidi et al. yields the following empirical results: charging high prices for the bundle(s) and the individual products is profit maximizing only when there is considerable heterogeneity in the valuations of these offerings. Otherwise, specific products/bundle(s) have to be priced low.

4. Conclusion

Consumers often purchase baskets of products from across product categories. Even when they plan to buy integrated products such as a car, they evaluate its components and how these interact. It is this issue of interrelationships among products that lends meaning and power to the strategy of bundling. Of course, the seller's own desire to reduce costs, increase efficiencies and challenge competition gives added meaning to bundling.

Our objective in this chapter has been to review and synthesize the extant literature on the design and pricing of product bundles. We have looked at the normative guidelines for bundling and pricing as well as the empirical approaches to actually design or price product bundles. Our conclusion from a normative angle is that mixed bundling does not always trump pure bundling and pure components. Indeed, depending on factors such as marginal costs, correlation in reservation prices, complementarity or substitutability, and competition, it may be appealing to the seller to pursue pure components or pure bundling. On the practical approaches, the seller has to be clear about the issues s/he is facing because different approaches apply depending on whether the focus is on design or pricing. Other deciding factors are the number of products in the portfolio, whether these products are predetermined or have to be identified, type of data that are available or can be collected, and so on.

Space constraints have forced us to leave out several other exciting domains of bundling research. Among them are behavioral approaches to bundling that draw on behavioral decision theory and experimental evidence to argue that the assumptions of classical economics may not always hold. For example, Soman and Gourville (2001) show that for bundles of temporally dispersed events (e.g. a four-day ski pass), consumers' likelihood of attending later events (e.g. skiing on the fourth day) is lower than that for earlier events. The authors draw on the sunk cost literature to propose 'transaction decoupling' as the underlying theoretical rationale. Soman and Gourville's findings point to a research opportunity for modelers to propose an approach for overselling and pricing later events in a series. Separately, on the topic of price framing, Yadav and Monroe (1993) find that consumers separate the savings from a bundle into two parts – savings on the individual items if purchased separately, and the additional savings from buying the bundle. An implication is that even when pure bundling is the optimal strategy, a seller should consider offering the individual components as decoys that make the bundle more attractive than what rational behavior might suggest. Analytical research would benefit by recognizing these perspectives.

While we have drawn on some bundling articles motivated by e-commerce, there are several other relevant contributions to bundling (e.g. Rusmevichientong et al., 2006; Venkatesh and Chatterjee, 2006). Indeed, real-world developments in e-commerce and technology offer exciting opportunities for future work on bundling. We urge a closer look at these research avenues.

References

Adams, William J. and Janet L. Yellen (1976), 'Commodity bundling and the burden of monopoly', *Quarterly Journal of Economics*, **90** (August), 475–98.

Anderson, Simon P. and Luc Leruth (1992), 'Why firms may prefer not to price discriminate via mixed bundling', *International Journal of Industrial Organization*, **11**, 49–61.

Ansari, Asim, S. Siddarth and Charles Weinberg (1996), 'Pricing a bundle of products or services: the case of nonprofits', *Journal of Marketing Research*, **33** (February), 86–93.

Bakos, Yannis and Erik Brynjolfsson (1999), 'Bundling information goods: pricing, profits, and efficiency', *Management Science*, **45** (12), 1613–30.

Bakos, Yannis and Erik Brynjolfsson (2000), 'Bundling and competition on the Internet', *Marketing Science*, **19** (1), 63–82.

Bradlow, Eric and Vithala R. Rao (2000), 'A hierarchical Bayes model for assortment choice', *Journal of Marketing Research*, **37** (May), 259–68.

Baumol, W.J., J.C. Panzer and R. Willig (1982), *Contestable Markets and the Theory of Industry Structure*, New York: Harcourt, Brace, Jovanovich.

Carbajo, Jose, David de Meza and Daniel J. Seidmann (1990), 'A strategic motivation for commodity bundling', *The Journal of Industrial Economics*, **38** (March), 283–98.

Chung, Jaihak and Vithala R. Rao (2003), 'A general choice model for bundles with multiple-category products: application to market segmentation and optimal pricing for bundles', *Journal of Marketing Research*, **40** (May), 115–30.

Eppen, Gary D., Ward A. Hanson and R. Kipp Martin (1991), 'Bundling – new products, new markets, low risk', *Sloan Management Review*, (Summer), 7–14.

Farquhar, Peter H. and Vithala R. Rao (1976), 'A balance model for evaluating subsets of multiattributed items', *Management Science*, **22** (5), 528–39.

Gilbert, Richard J. and Michael L. Katz (2001), 'An economist's guide to U.S. vs. Microsoft', Working Paper No. CPC01-19, University of California, Berkeley.

Goldberg, Stephen, Paul E. Green and Yoram Wind (1984), 'Conjoint analysis of price premiums for hotel amenities', *Journal of Business*, **57** (1), S111–32.

Guiltinan, Joseph P. (1987), 'The price bundling of services: a normative framework', *Journal of Marketing*, **51** (2), 74–85.

Hanson, Ward and R. Kipp Martin (1990), 'Optimal bundle pricing', *Management Science*, **36** (2), 155–74.
Hayes, Beth (1987), 'Competition and two-part tariffs', *Journal of Business*, **60** (1), 41–54.
Jedidi, Kamel and John Z. Zhang (2002), 'Augmenting conjoint analysis to estimate consumer reservation price', *Management Science*, **48** (10), 1350–68.
Jedidi, Kamel, Sharan Jagpal and Puneet Manchanda (2003), 'Measuring heterogeneous reservation prices for product bundles', *Marketing Science*, **22** (1), 107–30.
Kenney, Roy W. and Benjamin Klein (1983), 'The economics of block booking', *Journal of Law and Economics*, **26** (October), 497–540.
Kopalle, Praveen, Aradhna Krishna and João Assunção (1999), 'The role of market expansion on equilibrium bundling strategies', *Managerial and Decision Economics*, **20** (7), 365–77.
Lewbel, Arthur (1985), 'Bundling of substitutes or complements', *International Journal of Industrial Organization*, **3** (1), 101–7.
Matutes, Carmen and Pierre Regibeau (1992), 'Compatibility and bundling of complementary goods in a duopoly', *The Journal of Industrial Economics*, **40** (March), 37–54.
McAfee, R. Preston, John McMillan and Michael D. Whinston (1989), 'Multiproduct monopoly, commodity bundling, and correlation of values', *Quarterly Journal of Economics*, **104**, 371–83.
McAlister, Leigh (1982), 'A dynamic attribute satiation model of variety-seeking behavior', *Journal of Consumer Research*, **9** (2), 141–50.
Oxenfeldt, Alfred (1966), 'Product line pricing', *Harvard Business Review*, 44 (July–August), 135–43.
Rao, Vithala R., Vijay Mahajan and Nikhil Varaiya (1991), 'A balance model for evaluating firms for acquisition', *Management Science*, **37** (3), 331–49.
Rusmevichientong, Paat, Benjamin Van Roy and Peter W. Glynn (2006), 'A nonparametric approach to multiproduct pricing', *Operations Research*, **54** (1), 82–98.
Salinger, Michael (1995), 'A graphical analysis of bundling', *Journal of Business*, **68**, 85–98.
Schmalensee, Richard (1984), 'Gaussian demand and commodity bundling', *Journal of Business*, **57** (1), S211–S230.
Soman, Dilip and John T. Gourville (2001), 'Transaction decoupling: how price bundling affects the decision to consume', *Journal of Marketing Research*, **38** (February), 30–44.
Stigler, George (1963), 'United States vs. Loews' Inc.: a note on block-booking', *Supreme Court Review*, 152–7.
Stremersch, Stefan and Gerard Tellis (2002), 'Strategic bundling of products and prices: a new synthesis for marketing', *Journal of Marketing*, **66** (1), 55–72.
Telser, L.G. (1979), 'A theory of monopoly of complementary goods', *Journal of Business*, **55** (2), 211–30.
Venkatesh, R. and Rabikar Chatterjee (2006), 'Bundling, unbundling, and pricing of multiform products: the case of magazine content', *Journal of Interactive Marketing*, **20** (2), 21–40.
Venkatesh, R. and Wagner Kamakura (2003), 'Optimal bundling and pricing under a monopoly: contrasting complements and substitutes from independently valued products', *Journal of Business*, **76** (2), 211–31.
Venkatesh, R. and Vijay Mahajan (1993), 'A probabilistic approach to pricing a bundle of products and services', *Journal of Marketing Research*, **30** (November), 494–508.
Venkatesh, R. and Vijay Mahajan (1997), 'Products with branded components: an approach for premium pricing and partner selection', *Marketing Science*, **16** (2), 146–65.
Wang, Tuo, R. Venkatesh and Rabikar Chatterjee (2007), 'Reservation price as a range: an incentive compatible measurement approach', *Journal of Marketing Research*, **44** (May), 200–213.
Wertenbroch, Klaus and Bernd Skiera (2002), 'Measuring consumer willingness to pay at the point of purchase', *Journal of Marketing Research*, **39** (2), 228–41.
Whinston, Michael D. (1990), 'Tying, foreclosure, and exclusion', *American Economic Review*, **80** (4), 837–59.
Wilson, Lynn O., Allen M. Weiss and George John (1990), 'Unbundling of industrial systems', *Journal of Marketing Research*, **27** (May), 123–38.
Wilson, Robert B. (1993), *Nonlinear Pricing*, New York: Oxford University Press.
Wind, Yoram, Paul E. Green, Douglas Shifflet and Marsha Scarbrough (1989), 'Courtyard by Marriott: designing a hotel facility with consumer-based marketing models', *Interface of Marketing and Strategy*, **19**, 317–37.
Wuebker, Georg and Vijay Mahajan (1999), 'A conjoint analysis based procedure to measure reservation price and to optimally price product bundles', in Ralph Fuerderer, Andreas Herrmann and Georg Wuebker (eds), *Optimal Bundling: Marketing Strategies for Improving Economic Performance*, Berlin: Springer-Verlag, pp. 157–76.
Yadav, Manjit S. and Kent Monroe (1993), 'How buyers perceive savings in a bundle price: an examination of a bundle's transaction value', *Journal of Marketing Research*, **30** (3), 350–58.

12 Pricing of national brands versus store brands: market power components, findings and research opportunities
*Koen Pauwels and Shuba Srinivasan**

Abstract

Among the most important activities for supermarket retailers is the creation and marketing of store brands, also known as private label brands. Given the increasing quality-equivalence between national brands and store brands, they have become direct competitors, and pricing decisions should take this into account. In most cases, national brands still possess some degree of pricing and market power over store brands. In this chapter, we define three components of market power for national brands versus store brands: (1) price premium; (2) volume premium; and (3) margin premium. Our chapter proceeds along the following lines. First, we delineate the factors that are the most important drivers of the three components of premium. Second, we discuss managerial implications about key success factors in the pricing of national brands and store brands. A key contribution of this chapter is that we incorporate emerging insights from the marketing literature on the pricing and market power of national brands versus store brands. Finally, we conclude by offering important future research directions.

1. Introduction

1.1 Importance of store brands

One of the most important activities for supermarket retailers is the creation and marketing of store brands, also known as own labels, distributor-owned brands or private labels. Although store brands have been around for about a century, despite some exceptions (such as Marks & Spencer's St Michael brand), store brands were seen as poor cousins to the manufacturer brands, with a small market share that was considered unlikely to become significant. Recently, store brands have enjoyed tremendous success at the expense of national brands. For example, in an analysis of over 225 categories during the period 1987 to 1994, Hoch and Lodish (2001) found that the average annual share of sales for store brands increased by 1.12 percent, while the average shares of the top three national brands in each category fell by 0.20 percent. According to the Private Label Manufacturers' Association (PLMA), store brands now account for one in every five items sold in US supermarkets and represent nearly a $50 billion segment of the retailing business (Hansen et al., 2006). This trend has also occurred in international markets. A striking example is Germany, Europe's largest and the world's third-largest economy. Over the last three decades, store brand share tripled from 12 percent to 34 percent. Worldwide, the six largest retailers obtain between 24 percent and 50 percent of their revenue from store brands, while the tenth-largest retailer, Aldi, stocks its stores almost exclusively with store brands (Kumar and Steenkamp, 2007, p. 3).

---

* The authors are listed in alphabetical order. The authors thank Marnik Dekimpe, Vincent Nijs, Raj Sethuraman, the editor and an anonymous reviewer for their excellent input and suggestions.

No longer are store brands only for recessionary times, to be discarded once the economy has picked up again (Lamey et al., 2007). Although traditionally store brands were perceived to be low-quality brands and inexpensive versions of generics, they have made great strides in quality in recent years (Quelch and Harding, 1996; Dunne and Narasimhan, 1999). Increasingly, retailers are differentiating themselves and building customer loyalty by offering quality products that are unavailable elsewhere, for example through multi-tiered offerings such as premium versus value store brands (Zimmerman et al., 2007). For instance, *Consumer Reports* magazine ranked Winn-Dixie's chocolate ice cream ahead of Breyers, Wal-Mart's Sam's Choice better than Tide detergent, and Kroger's potato chips tastier than Ruffles and Pringles. At the 2005 annual Christmas wine Oscars in the UK, Tesco Premier Cru, at less than £15 a bottle, was named the best non-vintage champagne. It beat in blind taste tests famous names such as Taittinger and Lanson that can cost twice as much. A German study across 50 consumer product categories (reported in Kapferer, 2003) found that in over half of these categories, the hard discounter store brands (e.g. Aldi, Lidl) rivaled or exceeded the quality of manufacturer brands. A US study (Apelbaum et al., 2003) reports that the average quality of store brands exceeds the average quality of national brands in 22 out of 78 categories. In sum, store brands are becoming largely quality-equivalent to national brands (Soberman and Parker, 2006), although national brand manufacturers have been slow to face up to this new market reality in their planning and marketing decisions (Kumar and Steenkamp, 2007).

From a strategic pricing perspective, three sets of players are affected by store brands and interact to create their net impact: (i) the retailers, (ii) the manufacturers, and (iii) the consumers. For the retailers, store brands typically provide greater (percentage) margins (Hoch and Banerji, 1993; Sayman et al., 2002; Narasimhan and Wilcox, 1998; Pauwels and Srinivasan, 2004). Since store brands by definition can be exclusively sold by the retailer that carries them, many retailers attempt to use this exclusivity to differentiate themselves from the competition (Ailawadi et al., 2008; Walters and Rinne, 1986). Moreover, store brands change the retailer–national brand manufacturer interaction from one of cooperation to one of competition for consumer dollars (Chintagunta et al., 2002). Retailer performance is linked to all the brands in the category (Raju, 1992; Sayman et al., 2002), and, as such, this changing competitive environment may induce reconsideration of how store brands and national brands should be priced. Indeed, categories with larger store brand share tend to get more retailer pricing attention with more extensive use of demand-based pricing rather than past-price dependence and higher-category profits (Nijs et al., 2007; Srinivasan et al., 2008).

For the national brand manufacturers, the growing competitive element in the manufacturer–retailer relationship may change the strategic interaction between the two parties (Mills, 1995; Steiner, 2004). For example, national brand manufacturers may increasingly respond to store brands with changes in regular prices (Hauser and Shugan, 1983) and with changes in price promotions (Lal, 1990; Quelch and Harding, 1996). The advent of 'premium' store brands adds quality competition to the picture and brings the fight from lower-tier national brand to premium-tier national brands (Kumar and Steenkamp, 2007; Pauwels and Srinivasan, 2004). Therefore national brands increasingly find themselves in a battle for market share with their own customers: retailers.

The responses of consumers define the demand side. Store brands often make it more affordable to buy into the category, and thus may increase primary demand, creating room for win–win scenarios among entrant and incumbent brands (Hauser and Shugan, 1983). Alternatively, the introduction of store brands may result in brand switching, drawing buyers away from the existing brands (Dekimpe et al., 1997; Srinivasan et al., 2000). Moreover, long-term price sensitivity may change due to the different competitive market structure over time.

Given the increasing quality-equivalence between national brands and store brands, they have become direct competitors, and their pricing decisions should take this into account. In most cases, national brands still possess some degree of market power over store brands. In this chapter, we identify the components of such power: (1) price premium, (2) volume premium, and (3) margin premium. We discuss the main drivers of these components and their implications for retailers and national brand manufacturers. To this end, we draw upon the extant literature in marketing and economics on national brands versus store brands.

2. Framework for pricing national brands versus store brands

In industrial economics, a brand is said to have market power when it is able to charge prices exceeding marginal costs (Besanko and Braeutigam, 2005). In a perfectly competitive market, price equals marginal costs, and brands have no market power. However, producers of differentiated products (and monopolists) will, in general, be able to charge prices that exceed marginal costs, and, hence, have market power. In the context of the packaged goods industry, the relative market power of retailers versus manufacturers determines how total channel profit is split between the two (e.g. Kadiyali et al., 2000).

Market power of national brands can arise from a variety of sources. Two natural dimensions are the ability to outprice and outsell the store brand, and can be measured as the price and volume premium, respectively (Ailawadi and Harlam, 2004).

2.1 Price premium
We define the price premium[1] as the difference in price between a specific national brand and a corresponding specific store brand offered by the retailer:

$$Price\ premium_{NB} = Price_{NB} - Price_{SB} \qquad (12.1)$$

2.2 Volume premium
We define the volume premium as the difference in the volume between a specific national brand[2] and a corresponding specific store brand offered by the retailer:

---

[1] This metric is based on the price premium charged in the market and is not the same as the price premium metric commonly used in the literature. The latter is defined as the maximum price consumers will pay for a national brand relative to a store brand expressed as the proportionate price differential that consumers report that they are willing to pay for a national brand over a private label, and is usually obtained from survey data (Sethuraman and Cole, 1999).

[2] Moreover, it is important to note that typically, only leading national brands in a category command a volume premium over the private label good. For the other national brands in the category, the situation could vary on a case-by-case basis, and the volume premium could well be negative for specific national brands.

$$\text{Volume premium}_{NB} = \text{Volume}_{NB} - \text{Volume}_{SB} \qquad (12.2)$$

Both retailers and manufacturers consider the likely impact of their pricing decisions on volume premiums, although the many complexities are not yet well understood (Sayman and Raju, 2007).

2.3 Margin premium

Ultimately, retailers and manufacturers should make pricing decisions that optimize their overall profits (Kumar and Steenkamp, 2007; Raju et al., 1995a).

$$\text{Retailer margin premium}_{NB} = \text{Retailer profit contribution}_{NB}$$
$$- \text{Retailer profit contribution}_{SB} \qquad (12.3)$$

$$\text{Manufacturer margin premium}_{NB} = \text{Mfr profit contribution}_{NB}$$
$$- \text{Mfr profit contribution}_{SB} \qquad (12.4)$$

Evidently, the key to price premiums, volume premiums and margin premiums is the price/quality positioning of store brands, in relation to the quality and price of national brands (Sayman and Raju, 2007). Table 12.1 provides a scheme to understand the extent to which three main types of prevalent private label brands, generic private labels, copycat private labels and premium private labels differ in terms of their characteristics from national brands.

Examples of premium-tier (lower-tier) store brands are Sam's Choice (Great Value) and Archer Farms (Market Pantry) at Wal-Mart and Target, respectively. The most common strategy is an imitation or copycat strategy, accounting for more than 50 percent of the store brand introductions (Scott Morton and Zettelmeyer, 2004).

2.4 Illustrative numerical example

To illustrate the problem of pricing store brands versus national brands, we consider the fictional numerical example of a store brand entering a category in a retail store with two incumbent national brands with retail prices of $2.00 and $3.00 and wholesale prices of $1.50 and $2.00, respectively. In this market, the retailer sells 300 units of each brand, yielding category revenues of $1500 and a margin of $450. The retailer considers introducing a store brand that falls into one of the following three categories:

(a) a generic store brand, SB_1 at a price of $1.50; i.e. lower than any other brand;
(b) a copycat store brand SB_2 at a price of $2.50; i.e. right in between the national brand prices;
(c) a premium store brand, SB_3, at a price of $3.00; i.e. at the highest end of the market.

Because of the different quality of the ingredients, these store brand options also differ in wholesale price: $0.90 for the generic brand, $1.25 for the copycat brand and $1.80 for the premium store brand. How will these options impact short-term retailer revenues, manufacturer revenues and category margin? We start from a very simple formal model

Table 12.1 *Price premium, volume premium and margin premium of national brand versus store brand*

Examples	Characteristics	Illustrative papers	Price premium	Volume premium	Margin premium
Generic store brands	No brand name products Example – generic sugar	Steenkamp and Kumar (2007)	Large; sell 20%–50% below national brand	Moderate to high, depending on price sensitivity of potential customers	High; they have a very low price and suffer from low margins relative to national brands
Copycat brands	Me-too brand copying a strong brand leader Example – Walgreens Shampoo	Pauwels and Srinivasan (2004) Soberman and Parker (2006) Sayman et al. (2002)	Moderate; 5%–25% below national brand	Moderate to low, depending on the copycat execution and the loyalty for the emulated brand	Moderate; their cost structure is similar to imitated national brands
Premium store brands	Premium store brand offered as best products on market Example – Archer Farms (Target)	Corstjens and Lal (2000) Steenkamp and Kumar (2007)	Zero or even negative; sometimes priced higher than national brands	Moderate to high, depending on the retailer's ability to convince consumers of premium-tier status	Moderate to low; critically depends on sales success given similar retail and wholesale price

to derive the initial effect on sales and margin. Consider the Hotelling competitive positioning model in which consumers are uniformly distributed in their ideal points for quality/price positions (e.g. Lilien et al., 1992, p. 233). Figure 12.1 visualizes our pre-entry situation, in whom the incumbent national brands split the current number of shoppers for whom the buying utility exceeds the price of second-tier national brand NB_1. All shoppers to the left of this point X_1 do not buy in the category (i.e. the 'outside good'), while all customers to the right of point X_2 prefer the premium national brand NB_2. As usual in this model, we assume complete information (i.e. full consumer awareness/knowledge of all brands and perceived quality equals objective quality).

What happens when a store brand gets introduced into this market? When the retailer enters with the generic store brand SB_1, it expands the category by moving X_1 to the left (from X_1 to X_1'). Moreover, it steals share from NB_1, not from NB_2. In contrast, entering with the copycat SB_2 does not expand the category. Instead, the introduction steals share from both NB_1 and NB_2. Finally, premium-tier brand SB_3 competes directly with the premium national brand NB_2 and steals share from it. Table 12.2 calculates how the three options differently impact key performance indicators for retailers, consumers and manufacturers.

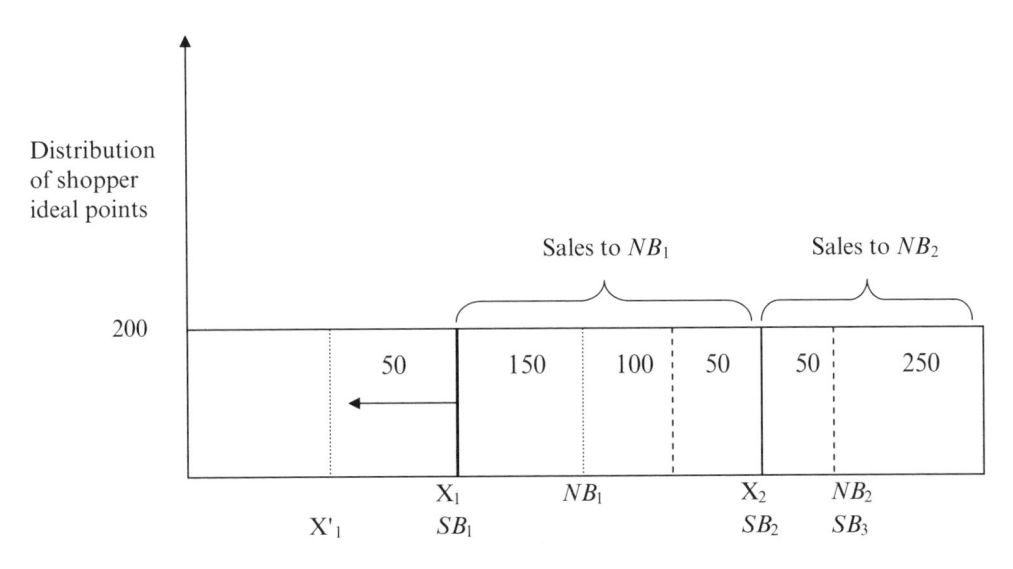

Figure 12.1 Simple model of sales of national brands versus store brands

2.4.1 Retailer's perspective When the generic store brand SB_1 is introduced, it obtains 200 customers and a healthy margin of $120. For the total category, demand grows from 600 to 650, and retailer gross margin increases from $450 to $495. In contrast, the copycat store brand does not expand category demand and obtains a smaller customer base (100), but with a higher store brand margin of $125. Category margin grows to $500. Finally, the premium store brand does not expand demand but obtains a customer base of 150 and obtains the highest store brand margin ($180). However, retailer category margin increases only to $480. Thus it appears that in this case, the copycat store brand strategy yields the highest contribution to retailer profits. The important point is that this revelation of the optimal store brand strategy for the retailer requires a category management perspective; it would not derive from a simple assessment of the sales and margin contribution of the store brand itself. Indeed, the generic store brand is the clear winner in terms of store brand sales and category traffic, while the premium option yields the highest margin from the store brand itself.

2.4.2 Consumer's perspective From the consumer's perspective, the average price before the introduction is $2.50. This average price stays the same for the copycat and premium store brand options but lowers to $2.30 with the introduction of the generic store brand. Thus price-sensitive shoppers, in particular those that now become new-category customers, benefit from the generic store brand introduction, leading to category expansion. No such benefit occurs for the copycat brand and, in our example, for the premium store brand. We return later to possible store loyalty effects of high-quality store brands.

2.4.3 Manufacturer's perspective Store brand entry hurts the sales of at least one national brand in our example, with the extent of the damage depending on store brand price/quality positioning. Would supplying the store brand overcome the margin loss for

Table 12.2 Illustrative example on pricing of national versus store brands

Variable	Retailers			Manufacturers	
	Store brands			National brands	
	SB_1	SB_2	SB_3	NB_1	NB_2
Retail price	$1.50	$2.50	$3.00	$2.00	$3.00
Wholesale price	$0.90	$1.25	$1.80	$1.50	$2.00
Manufacturer cost	$0.70	$1.00	$1.50	$1.00	$1.50
Before introduction					
Sales				300	300
Manufacturer revenue				$450	$600
Retailer revenue				$600	$900
Retailer margin				$150	$300
Category sales = 600, retailer category revenues = $1500, retailer category margin = **$450**					
After introduction of SB1 (generic store brand)					
Sales	200			150	300
Manufacturer revenue	$180			$225	$600
Retailer revenue	$300			$300	$900
Retailer margin	$120			$75	$300
Category sales = 650, retailer category revenues = $1500, retailer category margin = **$495**					
After introduction of SB_2 (copycat store brand)					
Sales		100		250	250
Manufacturer revenue		$125		$375	$500
Retailer revenue		$250		$500	$750
Retailer margin		$125		$125	$250
Category sales = 600, retailer category revenues = $1500, retailer category margin = **$500**					
After introduction of SB_3 (Premium store brand)					
Sales			150	300	150
Manufacturer revenue			$270	$450	$300
Retailer revenue			$450	$600	$450
Retailer margin			$180	$150	$150
Category sales = 600 retailer category revenues = $1500, retailer category margin = **$480**					

the national brand manufacturer? This appears unlikely given the competitive nature of the store brand procurement market (Kumar and Steenkamp, 2007). In all of our scenarios, the manufacturer margin on the national brand remains higher than that for the store brand (which is $40, $25 and $45). Table 12.3 shows the components of price premium, volume premium and retailer margin premium of each national brand over the three store brand options.

Even in this stylized example, the observed scenarios are relatively complex: national brands may have positive or negative price premium, volume premium and margin premium over a store brand. And, of course, actual markets involve several issues that further influence the impact of store brands, including (1) varying retailer success in bridging the gap between perceived versus objective store brand quality, (2) consumer

Table 12.3   Illustrative example on pricing of national versus store brands

Examples	Price Premium	Volume Premium	Margin Premium
After introduction of SB_1 (generic store brand)			
Second-tier national brand (NB_1)	$0.50	−50	−$45
Premium-tier national brand (NB_2)	$1.50	100	$180
After introduction of SB_2 (copycat store brand)			
Second-tier national brand (NB_1)	−$0.50	150	$0
Premium-tier national brand (NB_2)	$0.50	150	$125
After introduction of SB_3 (premium store brand)			
Second-tier national brand (NB_1)	−$1.00	150	−$30
Premium-tier national brand (NB_2)	$0.00	0	−$30

involvement with and perceived risk in the category and (3) national brand manufacturers' reaction in terms of product, price and advertising. We next turn to these drivers of the premium components.

3. Findings on pricing of national brands versus store brands

Despite the high and increasing importance of store brands for both retailers and manufacturers, we have seen relatively little academic research on pricing of national brands versus store brands. This is probably because of the mindset of both marketing academicians and executives in manufacturer companies, who tend to consider store brands as inferior goods and hence focus on competition between national brands (Kumar and Steenkamp, 2007). As a result, we believe it is too early to give exact recommendations on how to price national brands versus store brands. However, as argued, this decision will depend on the three components of market power. The last two decades have yielded influential articles on the importance, presence and drivers of the three premiums mentioned, as shown in Table 12.4.

Table 12.5 shows how the various drivers influence price, volume and margin premiums, and also offers some generalizations on these effects in the last column. Clearly, this is an area where more research is needed to make specific predictions on pricing, so we conclude in Section 4 with suggestions for future research.

3.1   Price premium

3.1.1   Importance   The price premium of a national brand over a store brand is of major importance to both manufacturers and retailers (Hoch and Banerji, 1993). In the absence of pricing mistakes, it reflects consumer willingness to pay for the different brands. For manufacturers, keeping consumer prices high is a main objective. Consider the typical economics of a S&P500 company (Kumar and Steenkamp, 2007): 19.2 percent of all revenues are needed to cover fixed costs, 68.3 percent to cover variables costs, leaving a profit margin of 12.5 percent. All other things equal, a price increase of 2 percent would

Table 12.4 Illustrative papers on price, volume and margin premiums

Paper – authors/ year of study	Substantive issue	Data	Key contribution
1. Price premium			
Raju et al. (1995a)	Decision to introduce a store brand into a category	IRI data on 438 product categories	Store brands are more likely to be introduced in categories where the price competition is low, and when the number of national brands is high.
Raju et al. (1995b)	Price differential of national brands	Numerical simulations of data	Results show that a store brand can obtain a high market share even with a low price differential when the cross-price sensitivity is high.
Hoch and Lodish (2001)	Optimal price gap	Two consumer studies and two in-market pricing tests	Most retailers would improve profits by maintaining national brand pricing and closing the gap by raising store brand prices.
Sethuraman and Cole (1999)	Factors influencing the price premium	Random survey of 350 households	Perceived quality differential is the most important driver of price premiums.
Apelbaum et al. (2003)	Extent to which quality premiums drive price premiums	*Consumer Reports* data for 78 product categories	For 75% of the categories considered, the average quality of national brands was higher than that of store brands, and price premiums for national brands prevail regardless of their command of quality premium or not.
Sayman et al. (2002)	Retailer's store brand positioning problem	Data from 19 product categories	In categories with high-quality store brands, the store brand and the leading national brand compete more intensely with each other than with the secondary national brand.
2. Volume premium			
Hoch and Banerji (1993)	Cross-category differences in private label share	185 grocery categories	Six variables (quality relative to national brands, quality variability, category revenue, percentage gross margins, number of national brand manufacturers, and national advertising expenses) explain 70% of the variance in market shares.
Dhar and Hoch (1997)	Store brand penetration variations across retailers	34 food categories for 106 major chains	Store brand penetration increases with retailer size, commitment to quality, category expertise, the use of own name on the store brands, breadth of store brand offerings, premium store brand offerings, and promotional support for the store brand.

Table 12.4 (continued)

Paper – authors/ year of study	Substantive issue	Data	Key contribution
Hansen et al. (2006)	Drivers of store brand purchase across categories	10 food and non-food product categories	Household-level traits which are no-category-specific explain variation in store brand shares across categories.
Cotterill et al. (2000)	Factors that drive market shares of private label brands	143 food categories in 59 geographic markets	Feature and display promotions are more effective than price cuts for private labels to gain share from national brands.
Deleersnyder et al. (2005)	Factors that drive national brand success	400 brands in 6 stores in 3 countries	Large price gaps benefit both manufacturers and retailers since they signal that the brands are targeted at different consumers/purchase occasions.
Erdem et al. (2004)	Factors that drive store brand shares	Scanner data for 3 countries (UK, USA, and Spain)	Quality uncertainty is the key determinant of store brand market share across countries, more important than price sensitivity.
3. Margin premium			
Ailawadi and Harlam (2004)	The effect of store brand share on margins of the retailer	Retail data from a grocery and a drug retail chain for multiple categories	Retailers' percentage margin on store brands is higher than on national brands, even though dollar margin per unit may be lower for store brands.
Pauwels and Srinivasan (2004)	Impact of store brand entry on retailer margins	Data from 4 food and non-food categories with store brand entry	Store brand entry raises retailers' margins due to high unit margins on the store brand as well as on the national brands.
Ailawadi et al. (2008)	Impact of store brand use on store loyalty	Consumer hand-scan panel: all categories	Store brand use and store loyalty (share of wallet) have an inverted U-shaped relationship.

thus raise profits by 16 percent, and vice versa. Evidently, the net effect will depend on the resulting volume changes, and manufacturers need to understand both own and cross-price elasticities in the market, including that of their brand with the store brand. For retailers, the price premium, also known as the price gap between a national brand and the store brand, is a key driver of the gross dollar margin from the store brand, but also of the total category's profit to the retailer. Papers in economics have argued that the magnitude of the ratio of national brand to store brand prices can be used to measure the markup of the retailer (Scherer and Ross, 1990; Carlton and Perloff, 1994; Barsky et al., 2001).

3.1.2 Presence In all studied countries, even those leading in store brand quality and penetration, a price premium still exists between national brands and store brands

Table 12.5 *Generalizations on drivers of price premiums, volume premiums and margin premiums*

Premium components	Drivers	Illustrative papers	Generalization
A. Price premium	Perceived quality	Sethuraman and Cole (1999); Hoch and Banerji (1993); Apelbaum et al. (2003)	Brands with higher perceived quality command higher price premiums.
	Innovation	Pauwels and Srinivasan (2004); Steiner (2004)	Innovative national brands command higher price premiums.
	Imagery/feelings	Wills and Mueller (1989); Connor and Peterson (1992)	Brands high on imagery command higher price premiums.
	Promotional activity	Cotterill et al. (2000)	Higher price promotional activity in a category leads to lower price premiums.
	Category characteristics	Ailawadi et al. (2008); Steenkamp and Dekimpe (1997)	Category characteristics are related to price premiums.
	Retailer store brand strategy	Meza and Sudhir (2002); Soberman and Parker (2006)	Price premiums of national are largest vs generic store brands, followed by copy-cat brands and least vs premium store brands.
B. Volume premium	Prices of national vs private labels	Dhar and Hoch (1997); Hoch and Lodish (2001); Geyskens et al. (2007)	Negative impact for within-category changes; positive impact across categories as high-selling store brands allow the retailer to charge more.
	Availability of brands	Srinivasan et al. (2004); Ailawadi et al. (2008); Kumar and Steenkamp (2007)	Availability of popular national brands drives volume premiums.
	Usage occasions	Pauwels and Joshi (2007)	Volume premium depends on usage occasions.
C. Margin premium	Wholesale prices	Ailawadi (2001); Sethuraman (2006); Ailawadi and Harlam (2004)	Higher wholesale prices of national brands result in lower margin premiums.

Table 12.5 (continued)

Premium components	Drivers	Illustrative papers	Generalization
	Price premiums	Pauwels and Srinivasan (2004); Kumar and Steenkamp (2007)	Factors that drive the price drive premium of the national brand will margin premiums.
	Brand switching patterns	Pauwels et al. (2007); Rangan and Bell (2002)	Retailer gross margin depends on the switching patterns among brands.
	Category expansion and store traffic	Bronnenberg and Mahajan (2001)	Category expansion and store traffic effects of enhanced retailer profitability for store brands.
	Store image	Corstjens and Lal (2000)	Store brands enhance store image and retailer margins.

in general (Pauwels and Srinivasan, 2004; Dhar and Hoch, 1997). Based on IRI (Information Resources Inc.) pricing data, the current price premiums across all US retailers between national and store brands is about 25–30 percent (Hoch and Lodish, 2001). Kumar and Steenkamp (2007) report an average price premium of 37 percent in situations where the store brand is quality-equivalent with the national brand. Moreover, Apelbaum et al. (2003) report a 29 percent price premium in categories where average store brand quality exceeds average national brand quality and a 50 percent price premium in other categories. However, this price premium appears under siege. For instance, a recent survey by AC Nielsen (2005) revealed that only 29 percent of US consumers agree that manufacturer brands are worth the price premium. Several driving forces may explain why the price premium has been going down over time (Kumar and Steenkamp, 2007).

3.1.3 Drivers of price premium In general, consumers compare the price of a product to the utility they derive from buying and consuming it. This utility may have both rational and emotional components, also known as performance perceptions and judgments versus imagery and feeling in the customer-based brand equity framework (Keller, 1993). Research has shown that the range of acceptable prices depends on the product characteristics such as brand familiarity (Monroe, 1976) and on customer perceptions of price and value (Raju et al., 1995b).

DRIVER 1: PERCEIVED QUALITY Branded and private label versions of a product cannot be identical, as that would violate the law of one price (Barsky et al., 2001). Despite the increasing quality-equivalence of national brands and store brands in general, certain national brands do succeed in maintaining superior perceived quality. Perceived quality of the national brand versus the store brand is a key driver of the price premium because most consumers care more about quality than about price (Steenkamp, 1989; Sethuraman and Cole, 1999; Hoch and Banerji, 1993). French data revealed that in categories where manufacturer quality exceeds store brand quality, the price premium for national brands is 56 percent; in quality-equivalent categories, it is 37 percent; and in categories where store brand quality is higher, the price premium is 21 percent (Kumar and Steenkamp, 2007). In the USA, the numbers are similar: quality-equivalence yields a 37 percent price premium for national brands, and a 1 percent quality gap results in a 5 percent price gap (Apelbaum et al., 2003). Therefore both national brand manufacturers and retailers should carefully monitor the perceived quality of their brands. In fact, empirical evidence suggests that as store brands improve their quality, national brands lose some of the pricing power, and the price premium they command relative to the store brand decreases (Rao and Monroe, 1996). If the manufacturer fails to convince consumers of its higher quality, it is tough to justify a high price premium. Likewise, if the retailer fails to convince quality-sensitive consumers of its high store brand quality, it is left with only the price-sensitive buyers and consequently has to charge a lower price for its store brand. This is especially true when consumers believe it is only fair that the store brand charges them less because it costs less to the retailer, for instance because of the lower quality of the ingredients. Interestingly, though, quality is not the full story: US consumers perceive store brands to be quality-equivalent in 33 percent of cases, but are only willing to pay the same price in 5 percent of all cases (AC Nielsen, 2005).

DRIVER 2: INNOVATION Besides enhanced quality, national brands may also contain desirable new features that are not (yet) present in store brands. For instance, Pauwels and Srinivasan (2004) find that, faced with store brand entry and resulting price competition at the low end of the market, some manufacturers take the high road and introduce innovative, higher-priced SKUs (stock-keeping units). In contrast, due to their reliance on low prices, store brands are not typically engaged in expensive product innovations, and thus score low on innovativeness (Steiner, 2004). As such, a highly innovative national brand will clearly stand out and be able to command a higher price premium (Deleersnyder et al., 2007). In contrast, categories with few national brand innovations allow the store brand to easily close the quality and price gap (Hoch and Banerji, 1993).

DRIVER 3: IMAGERY/FEELINGS The emotional components of product utility are known under many labels: brand feelings, image, emotional bond, love, engagement, etc. National brand manufacturers use their large advertising budgets and brand-building experience to create and sustain these elements of brand equity. Specifically, research has found that advertising has a positive effect on the price of national brands relative to store brands (Wills and Mueller, 1989; Connor and Peterson, 1992). Kumar and Steenkamp (2007) report that the typical price premium for brand image is 23 percent. In France, categories high on imagery obtain an average price premium of 61 percent compared to only 38 percent in categories low on imagery. However, creative marketing can and has achieved high image in such categories as baked beans and paper towels (ibid.). While such imagery used to be generated by television advertising, future success may be more readily obtained through such new communication channels as videogame marketing, 'underground marketing' (e.g. Red Bull giving free samples to trendsetting people and bars, but refusing them to others), word-of-mouth marketing, Internet community marketing (e.g. Trusov et al., 2007), and the like. Manufacturers appear to have a substantial advantage over retailers in this regard. Once retailers move beyond simple copycat strategies for their store brands, they may find creative ways to build their own imagery components, instead of merely attempting to demote the imagery of national brands.

DRIVER 4: PROMOTIONAL ACTIVITY   While non-price-oriented promotions by national brands may benefit their price premium, price-oriented promotions appear 'fast but faulty'. In the short run, price promotions may enable national brands to keep price-sensitive consumers from trying store brands (e.g. Lal, 1990) and thus help sustain their price premium at regular levels. In the long run, however, price promotions may teach consumers to 'lie in wait' for deals (Mela et al., 1997) and focus on price instead of quality as a buying criterion (Kalwani and Yim, 1992; Wathieu et al., 2004). Moreover, price promotional activity in a category not only lowers prices but is also a more effective way for store brands to gain share from national brands (Cotterill et al., 2000).

DRIVER 5: CATEGORY CHARACTERISTICS   Despite increasing quality and consumer acceptance of store brands, willingness to pay for them still varies substantially by category (Steenkamp and Dekimpe, 1997; Ailawadi et al., 2008). The first author of this chapter analyzed a European dataset where the price premium of the store band versus the leading national brand varied from virtually zero (e.g. aluminum foil and canned vegetables) to over 80 percent (e.g. shampoo and bodymilk). These variations in price premium were associated with consumer involvement with the category: the price premium is higher for categories that connect to consumers' ego and self-image (Assael, 1998), with higher hedonic value (Holbrook and Hirschman, 1982), and with a higher social expressive or sign value (McCracken, 1986). Other important characteristics may include the risk and credence nature of the product category.

DRIVER 6: RETAILER SIZE AND STRATEGY   First, retail consolidation reduces the price premium of national brands (Cotterill et al., 2000). Second, we know that the price premium of national brands depends on the store brand strategy of the retailer. Kumar and Steenkamp (2007) show that 'generic store brands' and 'value innovators' have a large discount (20–50 percent), 'copycat' brands have a moderate discount (5–25 percent) compared to brand leaders, while 'premium store brands' are priced close to or higher than the brand leaders. Recent research suggests that when it comes to copycat store brands, retailers may behave non-optimally by increasing the price of the national brand imitated by the store brand and by maintaining a high price differential between the copycat store brand and the national brand (Meza and Sudhir, 2002; Soberman and Parker, 2006). Importantly, 'despite all the buzz surrounding premium store brands, we should not forget that traditional store brands – generics and copycats– are still the dominant types of store brands around the world' (Kumar and Steenkamp, 2007, p. 29). Even so-called 'premium' store brands are typically not 'premium-price' (priced above leading manufacturer brands) but 'premium-lite', i.e. of similar/higher quality than manufacturer brands but at a lower price. Moreover, even truly premium-price retailer brands are still necessarily mass-market, and consequently may be priced below a niche manufacturer brand. Increasingly, retailers maintain a portfolio of store brands similar to Tesco's three-tier strategy (Buckley, 2005): low-priced Tesco Value (lowest price: 34 percent of its store brand volume), Tesco (standard quality: 61 percent of its store brand volume), and Tesco's Finest (highest quality: 5 percent of its store brand volume).

3.2 Volume premium

3.2.1 Importance Because manufacturers face substantial fixed costs (on average, 19 percent of revenues at full capacity), it is very important to keep volumes up and, thus, keep factories running. Higher volumes also mean better bargaining power with suppliers and with retailers, who prefer to stock and promote leading manufacturer brands (e.g. Pauwels, 2007). Retailers care about volume for similar scale and scope reasons, and several studies have investigated factors that lead to successful store brands (Hoch and Banerji, 1993; Dhar and Hoch, 1997; Hoch et al., 2002).

3.2.2 Presence In the USA, the leading national brand typically still has a volume premium over the store brand, but this is no longer true in several categories and in several European countries. Kumar and Steenkamp (2007) project a store brand share of 40–50 percent: increasing retailer consolidation and globalization will increase current store brand shares, but after a certain point, higher store brand share will turn off consumers looking for choice and will not be beneficial to the retailer (Ailawadi et al., 2008). Still, an expected store brand share of 40–50 percent implies a substantial loss of volume premium, as has been demonstrated across 225 consumer-packaged goods categories in Hoch et al. (2002), who find that store brands capture most of the category growth and steal away share, especially from the smaller national brands.

3.2.3 Drivers of volume premium Evidently, the volume premium may be affected by the same drivers as those identified for price premium. Additional drivers include prices, availability and usage occasions as detailed below.

DRIVER 1: PRICES OF NATIONAL BRAND AND STORE BRAND   The relation between the price gap and store brand sales depends on whether one considers within-category effects (over time) versus cross-category relations (Raju et al., 1995b; Sayman and Raju, 1997). Focusing on within-category effects, research finds that a 10 percent change in the price gap fraction results in a 0.8 percent change in the store brand share (Dhar and Hoch, 1997). In contrast, cross-category comparisons find a higher store brand share with a smaller price gap (Mills, 1995; Sethuraman, 1992), apparently because store brand popularity in a category allows the retailer to price it close to the national brands (Raju et al., 1995b). Moreover, Dhar and Hoch (1997) argue that a high price differential leads (some) consumers to infer that the store brand has substantially lower quality, outweighing the positive direct price effect. The situation gets more complex in the presence of compromise, similarity and attraction effects (e.g. Geyskens et al., 2007).

DRIVER 2: AVAILABILITY   Distribution is a key driver of store brand share and growth (Dhar and Hoch, 1997; Kumar and Steenkamp, 2007; Sayman and Raju, 2007). Indeed, European store brands may derive their strength from championing by large, consolidated retailers (Hoch and Banerji, 1993) versus smaller manufacturers. However, even the largest retailer is not the only game in town and thus typically fails to obtain the quasi-universal availability of popular national brands. This provides an important edge to national brands, which they should strive to maintain. In principle, retailers could overcome this advantage by either licensing their store brands to other retailers (e.g. President's Choice) or creating such a strong preference for their store brands that most consumers will seek them out at the expense of other retailers. With a few notable exceptions, either scenario appears unlikely. Licensing to competitors reduces the differentiation a retailer achieves with its store brand, and price-sensitive shoppers tend to look intelligently for deals wherever they are and thus are 'loyal' to store brands in general rather than to the store brand of a specific retailer (Ailawadi et al., 2008). Related to the retailer distribution strength, research has shown that the higher the retailer's private label share in a category, the lower the revenue benefits a national brand obtains from its own promotions (Srinivasan et al., 2002; 2004).

DRIVER 3: RETAILER POSITIONING   Dhar and Hoch (1997) find that store brand penetration increases with retailer commitment to quality, category expertise, the use of own name on the store brands, premium store brand offerings and promotional support for the store brand.

DRIVER 4: USAGE OCCASIONS   As long as consumers associate certain usage occasions with certain brands, the volume premium also depends on the frequency of such usage occasions. For one snack category, Pauwels and Joshi (2007) find that 'entertaining friends' and 'afternoon lift' occasions were associated with the national brand. However, the typical 'store brands for myself, national brands for conspicuous consumption' attitude is not set in stone, as consumers in some countries (such as Germany, the UK and the Netherlands) proudly display their smart, best-value shopping (Kumar and Steenkamp, 2007). Even in the USA, only 6 percent of consumers feel uncomfortable serving store brands in their homes (AC Nielsen, 2005). Therefore, to safeguard their volume premium, manufacturers may strive to 'set the agenda' in terms of usage occasions and their link to the national brand.

3.3   Margin premium

3.3.1   Importance   The manufacturer margin premium is especially important if a given manufacturer is (or is considering) supplying both national brands and store brands (Kumar and Steenkamp, 2007). The retailer margin premium is obviously relevant to retailers, as they want to carry the optimal assortment of brands to maximize their overall profitability. Moreover, national brand manufacturers need the retailer's cooperation for a host of activities that affect the national brand's performance: sufficient and appropriately located shelf space, promotional pass-through, launch and promotion of new products, etc. Negotiations on such activities are easier when the manufacturer can demonstrate and quantify the contribution of these activities to the retailer's profitability.

3.3.2   Presence   Little is known about the margin premium for national brand manufacturers, mostly because they do not spread the word that they are also producing store brands (Kumar and Steenkamp, 2007). Therefore the presence and drivers of this manufacturer margin premium are a key topic for future research. In contrast, it is now well documented that store brands give retailers a better percentage margin than national brand manufacturers do (Ailawadi and Harlam, 2004; Handy, 1985; Hoch and Banerji, 1993). Sethuraman (2006) reports that the average retailer's margin from store brands is about 34 percent compared to the margin of 24 percent that retailers obtain from national brands. However, virtually unanswered is the more relevant question about how much each brand contributes to the category's gross margin and to retailer overall profitability (Ailawadi and Harlam, 2004; Ailawadi et al., 2008). Several factors need to be considered to determine each brand's margin contribution to the retailer, and our numerical example in Section 2 and recent research demonstrates that the margin premium may substantially vary depending on several drivers.

3.3.3 Drivers of margin premium

DRIVER 1: WHOLESALE PRICES   Wholesale prices are almost always lower for store brands, even compared to small national brands (e.g. Sethuraman, 2006; Ailawadi and Harlam, 2004). The key reasons are the competitive nature of the store brand procurement market and the much lower marketing and advertising costs faced by store brands as compared to national brand manufacturers. As to the competitive nature of the market, most store brand suppliers are fairly small companies, especially compared to their retail customers. They specialize in a few product categories, product differentiation is virtually absent, optimal scale of production is low, and they sell their products to powerful, well-informed, professional retail buyers. Furthermore, the marketing and advertising costs are much higher for national brands, as they are building consumer-based brand equity (Keller, 1993) by creating and maintaining awareness, relevance and differentiation in consumers' minds.

DRIVER 2: RETAIL PRICES   As long as national brands sell at higher retail prices than store brands, their unit dollar margins may be higher even if their percentage margins are lower than the store brands'. Indeed, real-life cases (e.g. Rangan and Bell, 2002) and our numerical example illustrate the situations in which the dollar margins of the store brand are lower than those of at least one national brand: the generic store brand has only a $0.60 margin as compared to $1.00 for the premium national brand. Evidently, retail prices depend both on the pricing decisions of the retailer and on consumer willingness to pay for a brand. Often, the dollar margin on the store brand is higher than on that of second-tier national brands – especially if the retailer decides to drop its retail prices in the face of store brand growth (Pauwels and Srinivasan, 2004). Likewise, factors that drive the price premium of the national brand, such as innovation and advertising, will help maintain retail prices and thus dollar margins. On the other hand, the dollar margin benefit erodes with successful retailer efforts to increase willingness to pay for the store brand. Moreover, retailers may further reduce their store brand costs in terms of logistics, rental, overhead, marketing, personnel, etc. 'Value innovator' store brands like Aldi's are especially successful in lowering process costs by passing on shopping functions to the consumer and focusing on a limited assortment to compensate for lower dollar margin with high turnover and supply chain negotiating power (Kumar and Steenkamp, 2007).

DRIVER 3: BRAND SWITCHING PATTERNS   Given the tradeoffs in dollar margins, retailer gross margin in the category will critically depend on the switching patterns among brands. Every purchase going from a higher dollar-margin national brand to the store brand will actually reduce retailer gross margin (and related measures such as profit per square foot). Such a situation creates an interesting dilemma for the retailer: if the store brand does not expand category consumption, its sales growth at the expense of national brands may lower total category retail margin. This realization induced HEB Foods managers to consider cheaper sourcing and to reposition the store brand against a low-margin instead of a high-margin national brand (Rangan and Bell, 2002). More generally, both retailers and manufacturers influence these brand-switching patterns. Retailers often emulate a specific national brand (e.g. the brand leader as recommended in Sayman et al., 2002) and promote direct comparison by shelf placement, displays, features, etc. Manufacturers choose to get closer to or further away from the store brand by introducing new products with similar or very different features from those of the store brand (Pauwels et al., 2007) and by pricing their brand closer to or further away from the store brand (Pauwels and Srinivasan, 2004).

DRIVER 4: CATEGORY EXPANSION AND STORE TRAFFIC   Besides inducing brand switching within the category, store brands may also induce shoppers to buy in the category or even to come into the store – thus enhancing retailer store profitability. Traditionally, popular and expensive national brands are believed to be more successful in doing so (Bronnenberg and Mahajan, 2001; Pauwels, 2007); witness the loss-leaders in key retail categories. Likewise, Kumar and Steenkamp (2007) note that the velocity (or shelf-space turnover) of national brands is typically 10 percent higher than that for store brands. As a result of the above factors, recent papers argue that store brands are not as profitable as national brands (Corstjens and Corstjens, 1995). A private Price Waterhouse study commissioned by Pepsi in Canada showed that the national brand is typically more profitable than store brands once all factors, including deal allowances, warehousing, transportation and in-store labor were accounted for (Corstjens and Lal, 2000).

However, store brands clearly have the potential to increase category demand and store traffic. As to the former, low-end store brands make the category affordable to budget-restrained shoppers, while premium store brands may attract shoppers who value their quality and/or unique features (e.g. Tesco's Finest). As to the latter, Corstjens and Lal (2000) argue that retailers can attract shoppers with quality store brands, and they report that store brand penetration is positively related to store loyalty and customer share of wallet at the chain. Moreover, Sudhir and Talukdar (2004) find that a household buying store brands in more categories spends more at the store. In contrast, Uncles and Ellis (1989) question the role of store brands in store loyalty, and Richardson (1997) finds no evidence of store brand differentiation in five product categories. A recent study accounts for reciprocity and nonlinearities in the relationship between store brand buying and store loyalty for all categories of a leading supermarket chain (Ailawadi et al., 2008). Their analysis finds that the relationship is inverted U-shaped, with the highest benefits to store loyalty at around 40 percent of store brand share. Stores with lower store brand shares may thus increase store loyalty by pushing their own brands, but only up to a point. Anecdotal evidence suggests that pushing store brands (especially in terms of shelf space) at the expense of national brands may generate a backlash from consumers who value freedom of choice (ibid.). In sum, the ability of either national brand or store brand to bring in truly new purchases depends not just on their individual consumer appeal but also on the current ratio of consumer purchases and shelf space devoted to store brands.

DRIVER 5: STORE IMAGE   At the category level, US consumers still believe that manufacturer brands are better than store brands in 89 percent of categories (Aimark, 2006). In general, the introduction of store brands with high objective quality may be beneficial to the retailer even if there is no margin advantage for the store brand because quality store brands increase store differentiation (Corstjens and Lal, 2000). Just like manufacturers, some retailers spot a 'hole in the market' for a product with a unique feature currently not offered by competitors. For instance, Tesco is able to offer freshly squeezed orange juice in its stores, which is not logistically feasible for the likes of Tropicana and Minute Maid (Kumar and Steenkamp, 2007). Retailers do not compromise on quality of store brands because they cannot really afford to put their store name or their own brand name on a product that is inferior (Fitzell, 1998). For example, if Dominick's were to use its name on a product that is inferior, there would likely be a negative spillover effect on all products and stores carrying that label.

3.4 Pricing implications

3.4.1 What is the preferred price gap for the manufacturer?
It differs for premium versus second-tier brands, which face different own and cross-price elasticities with the store brand. This is graphically illustrated by Kumar and Steenkamp (2007, p. 202) and empirically demonstrated in Pauwels and Srinivasan (2004). First, premium brands get a substantially smaller sales increase from a price drop because their customers are more niche and less price-sensitive. At the same time, a price cut from the store brand won't affect them much, either. The recommendation is to keep prices high while justifying the price premium by continuous improvement in the identified drivers of market power (quality, imagery, innovation, association with specific usage occasions, category and store traffic drawing power). Moreover, the manufacturer can add a low-end brand to fight the store brand (e.g. P&G added Mister Clean detergent to its leading Ariel brand in Germany). Second-tier brands face a tough dilemma: they typically cannot win a price war with the store brand, so such brands need to choose between upgrading the brand (a large and uncertain investment) versus head-on value competition with the store brand. The latter strategy is impeded by the absence of the true leverage that national brand manufacturers possess to determine the price gap with store brands: while they can set recommended prices and send consumer coupons, the retailer decides on promotional pass-through and may engage in 'price shielding' by promoting the store brand at the same time (Hoch and Lodish, 2001). In some cases, the manufacturer may be better off divesting in such second-tier brands to focus its resources on a portfolio of leading brands. Unilever, for instance, decided to cut 75 percent of its brands because it had insufficient brand power, defined as the potential to be number one or two in its market and to be a must-carry brand to drive retailer's store traffic (Kumar, 2004).

3.4.2 What is the preferred price gap for the retailer?
Answering this question requires knowledge of the performance criterion for the retailer. If only store brand volume is of

interest, larger price gaps may yield more immediate success even though smaller price gaps, accompanied by the necessary investments in store brand quality and the communication thereof, should yield higher sales in the long run (Dhar and Hoch, 1997). Moreover, as argued earlier, store brand volume is only part of the retailer profitability equation. Therefore retailers need to consider the effect of the price gap on category revenues and gross margin. If the price gap is too big, the retailer may lose both manufacturer brand revenue and store brand revenue! In a rigorous field experiment, Hoch and Lodish (2001) found that increasing the price gap from 33 percent to 50 percent for analgesics increases category sales units but reduces revenue as the price elasticity for store brand is low: −0.56. In summary, we obtain consistent advice for retailers aiming to increase (long-run) store brand sales and category performance: strive for smaller price gaps. To this end, the above-identified drivers suggest that retailers should strive to reduce the gap in (perceived) quality, innovation and imagery; increase the store brand's availability and associated usage occasions; and position store brands to expand the category, improve store image, and thus, traffic and basket size in the chain (van Heerde et al., 2008).

In principle, the retailer can manipulate the price gap by changing the retail price of either the store brand or the manufacturer brands. However, the latter is often not a realistic option: increasing national brand prices may induce shoppers to buy them at other retailers, and reducing national brand prices eats away the retailer's margin on them unless the retailer can negotiate for lower wholesale prices. If store brand purchases are being driven by the price component only to a small degree, then the retailer can lower the price gap between the store and national brand and improve profitability (Hoch and Lodish, 2001). In order to do so, the retailer would have to know the answer to the question of which store brand purchases are being driven by brand preferences versus price considerations (Hansen et al., 2006).

4. Future research directions

Our review has emphasized the role of price premium, volume premium and margin premium in national brands versus private label brands. As Table 12.4 indicates, empirical work in this area has been expanding rapidly. These previous studies have dealt primarily with understanding the drivers of price premium or volume premium for national brands versus store brands. Recently, however, we have witnessed research in this area addressing a new set of strategic questions on national brands versus store brands, five of which we briefly examine below:

4.1 What are the most important drivers of the premiums?

While several of the above-mentioned drivers have been well documented in isolation (or within a small subset of candidate drivers), we know little about the relative importance of the major classes of drivers. Are the premiums mostly driven by national brand characteristics and actions, and thus largely under the control of national brand manufacturers? Or do retailer characteristics and actions yield most influence on the price, volume and margin premium of national brands over store brands? Alternatively, do (external changes to) consumer characteristics determine the fate of national and store brands in a category? Answering these questions requires a comprehensive study, including the following variables:

(a) Brand manufacturers: prices, quality, innovation, imagery, distribution, promotions, packaging, marketing communication spending, volume versus margin goals.
(b) Category characteristics: category concentration, size, growth, etc.
(c) Retailer characteristics: size, marketing spending, quality and price image, EDLP versus Hi-Lo, country and format type (e.g. grocery store, drug store versus mass merchandisers), store brand portfolio, store brand experience, etc.
(d) Consumer characteristics: quality and price sensitivity, brand loyalty, innovation proneness, product usage occasions and their importance for consumers' self-image (Assael, 1998), hedonic value (Holbrook and Hirschman, 1982), and social expressive or sign value (McCracken, 1986), etc.

4.2 To what extent do store brand investments benefit the investing retailer?
While many retailers appear to believe they reap the full benefits of investments in store brands, recent research has called this into question. First, it appears that most store brand shoppers are 'loyal' to store brands in general, not to the store brands of any specific retailers (Ailawadi et al., 2008). Because store-brand-prone shoppers may not be most profitable for a retailer (Ailawadi and Harlam, 2004), pushing the store brand at the expense of national brands may not be best strategy to increase retailer profitability. Moreover, Szymanowski and Gijsbrechts (2007) find that investments in store brand quality and reputation by one retailer appear to benefit other retailers. Reputation spillovers constitute a pitfall, as they limit the potential of store brands to differentiate retailers. As such, retailers wishing to use store brands as a differentiating strategy need to pursue a quality leadership strategy with their store brands. Such an approach diminishes subsidizing of rival brands or suffering from negative quality perception spillovers from these brands.

4.3 Can manufacturers manage premiums with product line extensions and contractions?
With the growth of their store brand programs, retailers are willing to carry those manufacturer brand assortments that result from successful product innovation and are able to command price and volume premiums. In this context, it has been increasingly important for manufacturers to add SKUs that enhance brand equity while at the same time deleting SKUs that do not enhance brand equity. A recent paper by Pauwels et al. (2007) examines the impact on brand price premium and volume premiums with a focus on manufacturer product assortment decisions. Specifically, they analyze the weekly short-term and long-term effects of SKU additions and deletions on the components of brand equity – brand price premium and brand sales volume premium – over the store brand. From a manufacturer perspective, SKU additions with similar attribute levels as the store brand are found to lower market-based brand equity while SKU additions are especially beneficial in categories with a high store brand share.

4.4 Do store brands provide a reference price for how much a basic product should cost?
The store brand's price could be an important external reference price against which the national brand price is evaluated (Deleersnyder et al., 2007). Many researchers (Ailawadi et al., 2003) have suggested the use of store brands as the comparison brands for national brands. This is important for novices and could shape their price image of the retailer. Despite its managerial relevance, store price image research in the marketing literature

has remained quite scarce, and research is needed to generate guidelines for retailers on how to manage store price image (Lourenço et al., 2007).

4.5 Are multi-tier store brands the holy grail for retailers?

Consultants and retailers alike believe that adding premium store brands is the number one growth priority, but preliminary evidence suggests complex and surprising substitution patterns in the presence of such store brands (Geyskens et al., 2007). Given the growth of multi-tier store brand portfolio strategies, it is increasingly important for retailers to understand whether a three-tier store brand strategy enhances their store brands to make them stronger competitors to manufacturer brands. Will the introduction of a premium store brand versus an economy store brand reinforce the standard store brand's position in the eyes of the consumer, or will it cannibalize the retailer's existing store brand offering? Or will the economy store brand simply steal share from the incumbent standard store brand and possibly even backlash on the image of the retailer's standard store brand line (Kumar and Steenkamp, 2007)? Addressing these questions, Geyskens et al. (2007) show that whereas incumbent store brands have borne the brunt of the negative impact in terms of consumer preferences, the introduction of economy and premium store brands may actually be beneficial for premium and secondary national brands.

Overall, store brands affect the pricing of national brands in complex ways. In this new environment, where retailers have succeeded in building up trusted store brands, manufacturers and retailers need to find 'win–win' situations in order to be successful in the market. In order to make further inroads, retailers will, for example, increasingly need to adopt a portfolio approach to managing their product lines. Manufacturers will be able to recapture their significance to consumers by continuing to innovate and use SKU assortment strategies that enhance brand equity. The findings in this chapter are important because they show the empirical realization of mutual benefits and because they identify marketing strategies that lead to such win–win situations. Ultimately, the nature of the competitive/cooperative interactions between manufacturers and retailers helps determine success versus failure in tomorrow's marketplace.

References

AC Nielsen (2005), 'Consumer attitudes toward private label: a 38 country online consumer opinion survey', presentation, available at: http://www2.acnielsen.com/press/documents/ACNielsen_PrivateLabel_GlobalSummary.pdf.

Ailawadi, Kusum (2001), 'The retail power–performance conundrum: what have we learned?', *Journal of Retailing*, **77** (3), 299–318.

Ailawadi, Kusum and Bari Harlam (2004), 'An empirical analysis of the determinants of retail margins: the role of store-brand share', *Journal of Marketing*, **68** (January), 147–65.

Ailawadi, Kusum, Donald R. Lehmann and Scott A. Neslin (2003), 'Revenue premium as an outcome measure of brand equity', *Journal of Marketing*, **67** (4), 1–17.

Ailawadi, Kusum, Koen Pauwels and Jan-Benedict Steenkamp (2008), 'Store brands and store loyalty', *Journal of Marketing*, **72** (November), 19–30.

Aimark (2006), 'Perceived quality gap between manufacturer and store brands', available at http//www.aimark.org.

Apelbaum, Eidan, Eitan Gertsner and Prasad Naik (2003), 'The effects of expert quality evaluations versus brand name on price premiums', *Journal of Product & Brand Management*, **12** (3), 154–65.

Assael, Henry (1998), *Consumer Behavior and Marketing Action*, 6th edn, Cincinnati, OH: SouthWestern College Publishing.

Barsky, Robert, Mark Bergen, Shantanu Dutta and Daniel Levy (2001), 'What can the price gap between branded and generic tell us about markups?', in R. Feenstra and M. Shapiro (eds), *Scanner Data and Price Indexes*, Chicago, IL: Chicago University Press, pp. 165–228.

Besanko, David and Ronald R. Braeutigam (2005), *Microeconomics: An Integrated Approach*, 2nd edn, New York: John Wiley & Sons.

Bronnenberg, Bart J. and Vijay Mahajan (2001), 'Unobserved retailer behavior in multimarket data: joint spatial dependence in market shares and promotion variables', *Marketing Science*, 20 (3), 284–99.

Buckley, Sophie (2005), 'The brand is dead; long live the brand', *Financial Times*, 4 April.

Carlton, Dennis W. and Jeffrey M. Perloff (1994), *Modern Industrial Organization*, New York: HarperCollins.

Chintagunta, Pradeep K., Andrew Bonfrer and Inseong Song (2002), 'Investigating the effects of store brand introduction on retailer demand and pricing behavior', *Management Science*, 48 (10), 1242–67.

Connor, John M. and Everett B. Peterson (1992), 'Market-structure determinants of national brand–private label price differences of manufactured food products', *Journal of Industrial Economics*, 40 (2), 157–71.

Corstjens, Judy and Marcel Corstjens (1995), *Store Wars*, New York: John Wiley.

Corstjens, Marcel and Rajiv Lal (2000), 'Building store loyalty through store brands', *Journal of Marketing Research*, 37, 281–91.

Cotterill, Ronald W., William P. Putsis and Ravi Dhar (2000), 'Assessing the competitive interaction between private labels and national brands', *Journal of Business*, 73 (1), 109–38.

Deleersnyder, Barbara, Marnik G. Dekimpe, Jan-Benedict E.M. Steenkamp and Oliver Koll (2007), 'Win–win strategies at discount stores', *Journal of Retailing and Consumer Services*, 14 (5), 309–18.

Dekimpe, Marnik, Jan-Benedict E-M. Steenkamp, Martin Mellens and Piet Vanden Abeele (1997), 'Decline and variability in brand loyalty', *The International Journal of Research in Marketing*, 14 (5), 405–20.

Dhar, Sanjay and Stephen Hoch (1997), 'Why store brand penetration varies by retailer', *Marketing Science*, 16 (3), 208–27.

Dunne, David and Chakravarthi Narasimhan (1999), 'The new appeal of private labels', *Harvard Business Review*, May–June, 41–52.

Erdem, Tulin, Ying Zhao and Ana Valenzuela (2004), 'Performance of store brands: a cross-country analysis of consumer store brand preferences, perceptions, and risk', *Journal of Marketing Research*, February, 86–100.

Fitzell, Philip (1998), *The Explosive Growth of Private Labels in North America*, New York: Global Books.

Geyskens Inge, Katrijn Gielens and Els Gijsbrechts (2007), 'Proliferating private label portfolios: how introducing economy and premium private labels influences brand choice', Working Paper, Tilburg University.

Handy, C.R. (1985), 'Surveying private and national brand prices', *National Food Review*, Winter–Spring, 14–17.

Hansen, Karsten, Vishal Singh and Pradeep Chintagunta (2006), 'Understanding store brand purchase behavior across categories', *Marketing Science*, 25 (1), 75–90.

Hauser, John R. and Steven M. Shugan (1983), 'Defensive marketing strategies', *Marketing Science*, 2 (4), 319–60.

Hoch, Stephen J. and Shumeet Banerji (1993), 'When do private labels succeed?', *Sloan Management Review*, 34 (4), 57–67.

Hoch, Stephen J. and Leonard M. Lodish (2001), 'Store brands and category management', Working Paper, Wharton School, University of Pennsylvania.

Hoch, Stephen, Alan Montgomery and Young-Hoon Park (2002), 'Long-term growth trends in private label market share', Working Paper, Wharton School, University of Pennsylvania.

Holbrook, Morris B. and Elizabeth C. Hirschman (1982), 'The experiential aspects of consumption: consumer fantasies, feelings, and fun', *Journal of Consumer Research*, 9 (September), 132–40.

Kadiyali, Vrinda, Pradeep Chintagunta and Naufel Vilcassim (2000), 'Manufacturer–retailer channel interactions and implications for channel power: an empirical investigation of pricing in a local market', *Marketing Science*, 19 (2), 127–48.

Kalwani, Manohar U. and Chi Kin Yim (1992), 'Consumer price and promotion expectations: an experimental study', *Journal of Marketing Research*, 29, 90–100.

Kapferer, Jean-Noel (2003), *The New Strategic Brand Management*, 3rd edn, Dover, NH: Kogan Page.

Keller, Kevin Lane (1993), 'Conceptualizing, measuring, and managing customer-based brand equity', *Journal of Marketing*, 57 (January), 1–22.

Kumar, Nirmalya (2004), *Marketing as Strategy: Understanding the CEO's Strategy for Driving Growth and Innovation*, Cambridge, MA: Harvard Business School Press.

Kumar, Nirmalya and Jan-Benedict E.M. Steenkamp (2007), *Private Label Strategy*, Cambridge, MA: Harvard Business School Press.

Lal, Rajiv (1990), 'Price promotions: limiting competitive encroachment', *Marketing Science*, 9 (3), 247–62.

Lamey, Lien, Barbara Deleersnyder, Marnik G. Dekimpe and Jan-Benedict E.M. Steenkamp (2007), 'Cyclical sensitivity of private label share', *Journal of Marketing*, 71 (January), 1–15.

Lilien, Gary L., Philip Kotler and K. Sridhar Moorthy (1992), *Marketing Models*, Englewood Cliffs, NJ: Prentice Hall.
Lourenço, Carlos, Els Gijsbrechts and Richard Paap (2007), 'Dynamic store price image formation and category pricing', Working Paper, Tilburg University.
McCracken, Grant (1986), 'Culture and consumption: a theoretical account of the structure and movement of the cultural meaning of consumer goods', *Journal of Consumer Research*, **13**, 71–84.
Mela, Carl F., Sunil Gupta and Donald R. Lehmann (1997), 'The long-term impact of promotion and advertising on consumer brand choice', *Journal of Marketing Research*, **34** (May), 248–61.
Meza, Sergio and K. Sudhir (2002), 'The role of strategic pricing by retailers in the success of store brands', Working Paper, Yale University.
Mills, David E. (1995), 'Why retailers sell private labels', *Journal of Economics and Management Strategy*, **4** (3), 509–28.
Monroe, Kent B. (1976), 'The influence of price differences and brand familiarity on brand preferences', *Journal of Consumer Research*, **3** (1), 42–9.
Narasimhan, Chakravarthi and Ronald T. Wilcox (1998), 'Private labels and the channel relationship: a cross-category analysis', *Journal of Business*, **71** (4), 573–600.
Nijs, Vincent, Shuba Srinivasan and Koen Pauwels (2007), 'Retail-price drivers and retailer profits', *Marketing Science*, **26** (4), 473–87.
Pauwels, Koen (2004), 'How dynamic consumer response, competitor response, company support and company inertia shape long-term marketing effectiveness', *Marketing Science*, **23** (4), 596–610.
Pauwels, Koen (2007), 'How retailer and competitor decisions drive the long-term effectiveness of manufacturer promotions for fast moving consumer goods', *Journal of Retailing*, **83** (3), 297–308.
Pauwels, Koen and Amit Joshi (2007), 'Counting what will count: does your dashboard predict?', Working Paper, Tuck School of Business at Dartmouth, Hanover, NH.
Pauwels, Koen and Shuba Srinivasan (2004), 'Who benefits from store brand entry?', *Marketing Science*, **23** (3), 364–90.
Pauwels, Koen, Vincent Nijs and Shuba Srinivasan (2007), 'Managing brand equity with product line extensions and contractions', paper presented at the Marketing Dynamics Conference, University of Groningen, 22–24 August.
Quelch, John A. and D. Harding (1996), 'Brands versus private labels, fighting to win', *Harvard Business Review*, January/February, 99–109.
Raju, Jagmohan (1992), 'The effect of price promotions on variability in product category sales', *Marketing Science*, **11** (Summer), 207–20.
Raju, Jagmohan, Raj Sethuraman and Sanjay Dhar (1995a), 'The introduction and performance of store brands', *Management Science*, **41** (6), 957–78.
Raju, Jagmohan, Raj Sethuraman and Sanjay Dhar (1995b), 'National brand-store brand price differential and store brand market', *Pricing Strategy and Practice*, **3** (2), 17–24.
Rangan, Kasturi V. and Marie Bell (2002), 'H-E-B own brands', Harvard Business School Case 9-502-053.
Rao, Akshay R. and Kent B. Monroe (1996), 'Causes and consequences of price premiums', *Journal of Business*, **69**, 511–35.
Richardson, Paul S. (1997), 'Are store brands perceived to be just another brand?', *Journal of Product & Brand Management*, **6** (6), 388–404.
Sayman, Serdar and Jagmohan S. Raju (2007), 'Store brands: from back to the future', in N.K. Malhotra (ed.), *Review of Marketing Research*, Vol. 3, New York: M.E. Sharpe.
Sayman, Serdar, Steve Hoch and Jagmohan S. Raju (2002), 'Positioning of store brands', *Marketing Science*, **2** (4), 378–97.
Scherer, Frederick M. and David Ross (1990), *Industrial Market Structure and Economic Performance*, Boston, MA: Houghton Mifflin.
Scott Morton, Fiona and Florian Zettelmeyer (2004), 'The strategic positioning of store brands in retailer–manufacturer negotiations', *Review of Industrial Organization*, **24**, 161–94.
Sethuraman, Raj (1992), 'The effect of marketplace factors on private-label penetration in grocery products', Working Paper, Marketing Science Institute, Cambridge, MA.
Sethuraman, Raj (2006), 'Private label marketing strategies in packaged goods: management beliefs and research insights', Working Paper, Marketing Science Institute, Cambridge, MA.
Sethuraman, Raj and Catherine Cole (1999), 'Factors influencing the price premiums that consumers pay for national brands over store brands', Pricing Strategy and Practice, *Journal of Brand and Product Management*, **8** (4), 340–51.
Soberman, David A. and Philip M. Parker (2006), 'The economics of quality-equivalent store brands', *International Journal of Research in Marketing*, **23** (2), 125–39.
Srinivasan, Shuba, Peter T.L. Popkowski and Frank M. Bass (2000), 'Market share response and competitive

interaction: the impact of temporary, evolving and structural changes in prices', *International Journal of Research in Marketing*, **17**, 281–305.

Srinivasan, Shuba, Koen Pauwels and Vincent Nijs (2008), 'Demand-based pricing versus past-price dependence: A cost–benefit analysis', *Journal of Marketing*, **72** (2), March, 15–27.

Srinivasan, Shuba, Koen Pauwels, Dominique M. Hanssens and Marnik G. Dekimpe (2002), 'Who benefits from price promotions?', *Harvard Business Review*, September, 22–3.

Srinivasan, Shuba, Koen Pauwels, Dominique M. Hanssens and Marnik G. Dekimpe (2004), 'Do promotions benefit manufacturers, retailers or both?', *Management Science*, **50** (5), 617–29.

Steenkamp, Jan-Benedict E.M. (1989), *Product Quality: An Investigation into the Concept and How it is Perceived by Consumers*, Assen: Van Gorcum.

Steenkamp, Jan-Benedict E.M. and Marnik G. Dekimpe (1997), 'The increasing power of store brands: building loyalty and market share', *Long Range Planning*, **30** (6), 917–30.

Steiner, Robert L. (2004), 'The nature and benefits of national brand/private label competition', *Review of Industrial Organization*, **24**, 105–27.

Sudhir, K. and Debabrata Talukdar (2004), 'Does store brand patronage improve store patronage?', *Review of Industrial Organization*, **24** (2), 143–60.

Szymanowski, Maciej and Els Gijsbrechts (2007), 'Conditional cross-brand learning: when are private labels really private?', Working Paper, Tilburg University.

Trusov, Michael, Randolph E. Bucklin and Koen Pauwels (2007), 'Estimating the dynamic effects of online word-of-mouth on member growth of a social network site', Working Paper, UCLA Anderson School.

Uncles, Mark and Kartina Ellis (1989), 'The buying of own labels', *European Journal of Marketing*, **23** (3), 57–70.

van Heerde, Harald, Els Gijsbrechts and Koen Pauwels (2008), 'Winners and losers in a major price war', *Journal of Marketing Research*, **45** (5), October, 499–518.

Walters, Rockney G. and Heikki Rinne (1986), 'An empirical investigation into the impact of price promotions on retail store performance', *Journal of Retailing*, **62** (3), 237–66.

Wathieu, Luc, A.V. Muthukrishnan and Bart J. Bronnenberg (2004), 'The asymmetric effect of brand positioning on post-promotion preference', *Journal of Consumer Research*, **31** (3), 652–7.

Wills, R.L. and W.F. Mueller (1989), 'Brand price and advertising', *Southern Economic Journal*, **56**, 383–95.

Zimmerman, Ann, David Kesmodel and Julie Jargon (2007), 'From cheap stand in to shelf star', *The Wall Street Journal*, 29 August.

13 Trade promotions*
Chakravarthi Narasimhan

Abstract

Trade promotions are price incentives given by manufacturers of products and services to their intermediaries such as a dealer, distributor and retailer as part of their overall marketing strategy. In this chapter past research on trade promotion is examined and issues relating to the rationale behind these, the potential impact on the channel partners and managerial aspects of implementation are discussed. Key research issues for researchers working in this area are highlighted.

1. Introduction

In many B2C markets manufacturers distribute their products and services through a set of intermediaries. These are retailers, distributors and brokers. See Figure 13.1. Whether there is only a retailer between the manufacturer and consumer or multiple layers of channel members might depend on the size of the retailer and other factors. Manufacturers use multiple instruments to promote their products to their customers (retailers) and consumers (end users) to stimulate demand and grow. Promotional instruments directed at consumers include advertising, consumer promotions such as coupons, contests, special packages and other incentives. Incentives directed at the trade are trade promotions, category management initiatives such as assistance with planograms, merchandising support, demand forecasts, inventory support etc. Trade promotions are incentives given by a manufacturer of products and services to its supply chain partners, distributors/dealers/retailers, to promote its products to the ultimate end users. Trade promotion spending has been averaging around 14 percent of sales over the last 15 years or so (AC Nielsen Co., 2004). A similar report by AC Nielsen in 2004 states that 53 percent of manufacturers and retailers report 'a measurable increase' in trade promotion spending, while 35 percent and 36 percent of manufacturers and retailers respectively are satisfied with the value they get out of trade promotions. An Accenture report on 'Capturing and sustaining value opportunities in trade promotion' (2001) reports that while advertising, consumer promotion and trade promotion account for 23 percent of sales in 2005, trade promotion alone accounts for 13 percent of sales, quite consistent with the AC Nielsen report. Whether trade promotions are effective in delivering the stated goals for the manufacturers is debatable. The above-cited Accenture report, for example, claims that while CPG (consumer packaged goods) manufacturers spent in excess of $25 billion on trade promotion in 2005, the incremental revenue was only $2–4 billion, suggesting that, at the aggregate, trade promotions lost money for the manufacturers. Citing a Forrester Research report, Inforte Corp. claims in its report that in 2002 manufacturers spent $80 billion on trade promotion with an annual growth rate of 5–8 percent (Inforte

---

* I would like to thank Tingting He and Sudipt Roy for their assistance in assembling the Reference section. I thank Vithala Rao and an anonymous reviewer for their valuable comments and suggestions.

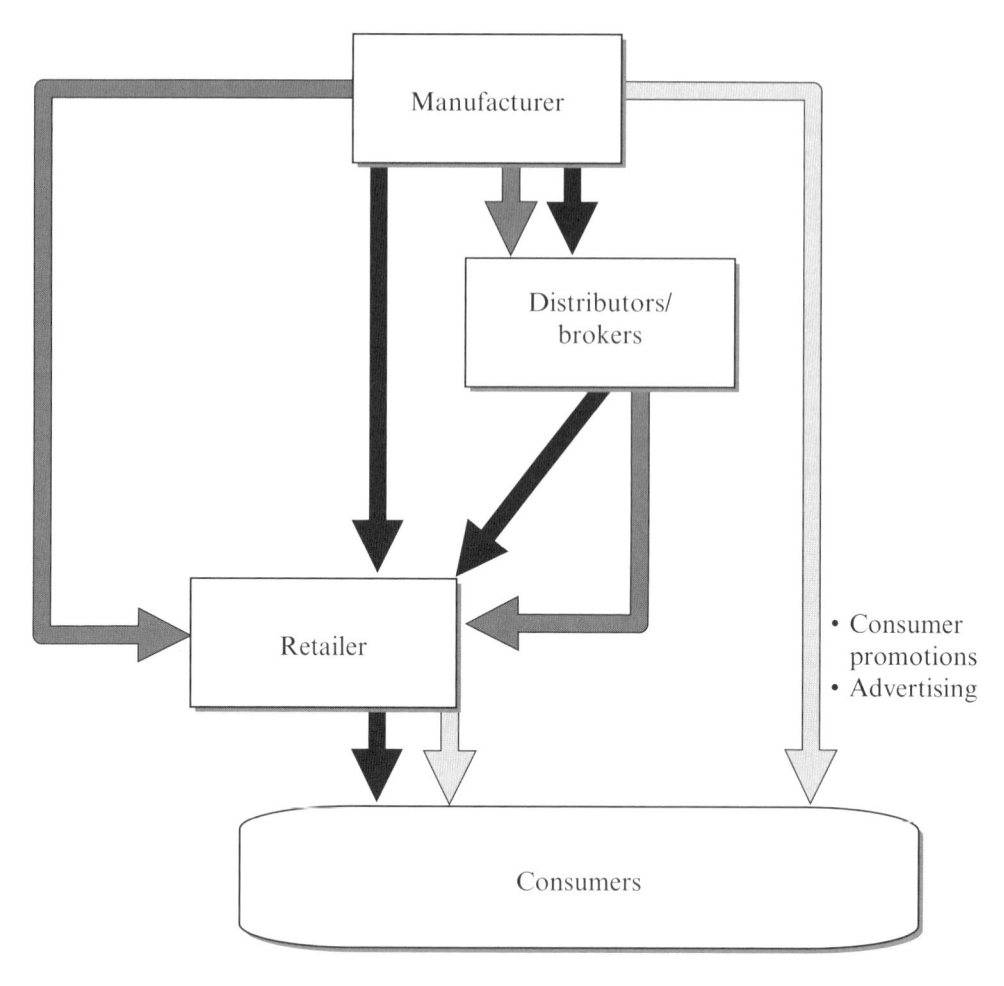

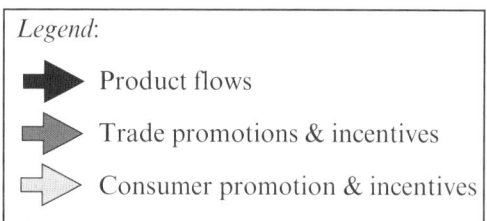

Figure 13.1   Manufacturer–consumer link in a supply chain

Corp., 2005). A recent Booz Allen Hamilton report states that 'manufacturers are so focused in generating additional volume that the overall efficiency of their trade investment is low', and goes on to claim that manufacturers lose a third of the money spent on trade promotions (Booz Allen Hamilton, 2003). This report also states that trade promotion is the second-largest item in the profit and loss account next only to COGS (cost of goods sold). While in nominal terms the money spent has been increasing, as a percentage

Trade promotions 285

of sales, at least in CPG, it has been in a narrow range between 13 and 15 percent. From these industry studies reported in the popular press and research reports by various agencies it seems clear that trade promotion is an important marketing mix variable, CPG manufacturers predominantly use it, these promotions take different forms, and their efficiency in delivering the stated goals of the manufacturers is debatable.

In this chapter I summarize the extant academic literature on trade promotions and identify key research issues relevant to academics and practitioners. The reminder of the chapter is organized as follows. In Section 2, I provide some background on the types and forms of incentives that manufacturers provide to the trade. In Section 3, I examine analytical and empirical literature on retailer behavior relating to such practices and manufacturers' incentives to offer trade promotions. In Section 4, I discuss issues that pertain to the evaluation of the efficacy and profitability of trade promotions. In Section 5, I discuss literature on the role of trade promotion as part of the marketing mix. I conclude the chapter with a discussion of key issues.

2. Types of trade incentives and objectives of trade promotions

If we define trade incentives as broadly any money or allowance provided to the trade, then these incentives take many forms. Blattberg and Neslin (1990) list several different types of trade incentives for durable and non-durable products. Among the main ones are:

1. *Slotting and renewable allowances*   These are payments made to the trade for stocking a manufacturer's product, often on a per SKU (stock-keeping unit) per store basis. While stocking fee or allowance is normally associated with new products, renewable allowances are sometimes paid on existing products as well.
2. *Display or feature allowance*   Money paid for setting up special displays of a manufacturer's product or advertising the product.
3. *Co-op advertising allowances*, where the manufacturer lets the retailer participate in a manufacturer's advertising or pays part of the cost.
4. *Off-invoice allowance*   Here the manufacturer sells a product, as many units as the retailer desires, at a lower price than given on a regular list price. Such a promotion may last anywhere from one to several weeks.
5. *Scanback allowance*   Here the manufacturer reimburses the retailer an amount on every unit sold over a specified period. Thus, while off-invoice is a price reduction on every unit bought, scan-back allowance is on every unit sold by the retailer over a specified period.
6. *Free goods*   Usually a case free for every n cases bought by the retailer. For all practical purposes this is almost like an off-invoice promotion but forces the retailer to buy n cases before he can get the price reduction.
7. *Volume discounts*, based on the past year's purchases.

These incentives are usually accompanied by certain 'requirements' that retailers have to meet. For example, cigarette manufacturers pay promotion money depending on facings, types of display, in-store advertising etc. (Bloom, 2001). The extent of these promotions varies depending on the type of retail outlet, such as supermarkets, drug stores, mass merchandisers/discounters, convenience stores and warehouse clubs, and type of categories, such as CPG, cigarettes and drugs. Similarly, slotting allowances would require a minimum level of facings, inventory support and so on. Unfortunately there is very little systematic documentation of these and their trends over time. As stated in the Introduction, the level of these promotions has increased over time. Thus, while there are many types of trade incentives, the term 'trade promotions' as used in marketing refers to per unit reduction in wholesale price, and for most of the remainder of this chapter I review and consider research that focuses on this type of incentive.

2.1 Strategic objectives of trade promotions
There are several objectives of trade promotion. I list the major ones below.

1. *Liquidating excess inventory* When demand and supply are out of sync, a firm may be saddled with excess inventory in the supply chain and needs to get rid of it. Common examples are seasonal items such as snow throwers and lawn mowers, and end-of season model clearances in apparel, certain electronic items and automobiles.
2. *Introducing new product* Trade promotions provide a discount from a reference price to convey to consumers and the trade that the product is sold at an introductory discount. If the retailers in turn choose to pass through some or the entire discount, this could stimulate initial trial.
3. *Stimulate demand* If there are segments of consumers that would react differently to retail promotions, then trade promotions can be an effective tool to reach them.
4. *Competitive response* In response to trade promotions offered by competing manufacturers, a firm may choose to offer trade promotions. Of course this begs the question as to why the other manufacturers offered trade promotions to start with.

2.2 Trade promotion as part of the overall pricing strategy
In marketing their products to the ultimate end users through a set of intermediaries (see Figure 13.1), manufacturers use the entire marketing mix to gain acceptance of their products by the trade and to penetrate the end user market. Conditional on product quality, assortment, flavors or product line, and branding, the marketing mix used to achieve these objectives is price, advertising, and consumer and trade promotions. Thus the role of trade promotions needs to be understood in the larger context of brand competition, supply chain power and brand equity or brand strength. There is clearly a tradeoff between using more of one type of promotion versus another or advertising or a lower price.

In the early 1990s, for example, P&G made a strategic choice to streamline their product offerings by reducing the massive amount of trade and consumer incentives and adopting an EDLP strategy for many of their products. Similarly, recent empirical evidence suggests that slotting allowance, a form of trade incentive offered by firms to gain distribution for new products, has been on the rise. If the result of a trade promotion is to stimulate demand by encouraging retailers to promote the product in turn, a natural question that must be asked and answered is 'Why are these promotions temporary and why not set a low "regular" price rather than periodically providing discounts to the trade?' Thus firms should strategically choose the level of importance and amount of money spent on trade promotion as a part of their overall mix, and not in isolation or as an afterthought. This means that the strategic objectives of trade promotion should be understood and the allocation to trade promotion should be made in conjunction with the regular price. We revisit this issue in the final section.

3. Retail response to manufacturers' promotions

Before I offer plausible reasons why manufacturers may want to give promotions to the trade, it is instructive to examine how a retailer might respond and the documented evidence in support of this. Almost the entire academic literature considers only price-off promotions, i.e. either off-invoice or scanback promotions, and I shall therefore confine myself to these types of promotion.

When a manufacturer offers a price-off incentive, what would be the response of the retailer in terms of the retail price he charges? By this we mean what is the impact of a trade promotion on the retail price of the promoted product and perhaps even other products in the category? Most retailers are multiproduct retailers. A retailer also competes with other retailers in his trading area. If we assume that retailers want to maximize the total store profit, then a retailer's response to a manufacturer's promotion would depend on a host of factors that include the brand strength of the promoted product, its ability to attract consumers, the available substitutes and complements and the margins on these, the potential action of other retailers etc. From an analytical point of view it is worthwhile to characterize the role of these drivers and reconcile these with the empirical facts. We start with the empirical papers.

3.1 Empirical facts and documented evidence

The empirical literature on retail response has addressed two issues. What is the rate of retail pass-through and what are some factors that affect this? By pass-through we mean the percentage of money that is received from a manufacturer that is passed through to the ultimate consumers, or, more specifically, the change in the retail price due to a change in the wholesale price. Thus 100 percent pass-through means that every penny that is received via a wholesale price reduction is reflected as a penny reduction in the retail price.

Chevalier and Curhan (1976) examined over 990 trade promotions received by a single grocery chain and found that the chain supported only about one-third of the products with any kind of promotional support in the form of a price cut, display or feature advertising. Over 45 percent of the products for which the chain got trade promotions did not receive any retail support. But, conditional on promoting through a price reduction, the average retail pass-through rate was 126 percent. Moreover, the authors found that the sales movement of the brand had a significant impact on the retail support while package size, rank of a product in its category or the amount of money received had no predictable impact. Somewhat contrary to this, Walters (1989), using data from two grocery chains, found that the size of the incentive has a positive effect on the level of retail support. In addition he found that sales volume (consistent with Chevalier and Curhan), compliance requirements (such as manufacturer-paid feature or display support) and price elasticity of the brand affect positively the level of retail support. Armstrong (1991) also documents that across many categories pass-through rates vary, and can be greater than 100 percent.

More recently Besanko et al. (2005) examined own-brand and cross-brand retail pass-through using data from a supermarket chain in 11 categories and 78 products. They estimate a reduced-form model of the following form:

$$P\{i\} = f(c\{i\}, c\{-i\}, \delta) \qquad (13.1)$$

where $P\{i\}$ is the retail price of brand i, $c\{i\}$ is the wholesale price of brand i, $c\{-i\}$ is a vector of wholesale prices of all other brands in the category and δ is a vector of exogenous shift variables. They estimate the above model using liner, log linear and a flexible polynomial specification. The estimates of interest are the marginal change in $P\{i\}$ with respect to a small change in $c\{i\}$ and $c\{-i\}$, that is own- and cross-brand pass-through. They estimate (13.1) for each product, using the three specifications mentioned, by pooling data across different price zones of the chain and including shift variables to control for interzone heterogeneity. They report that nearly 70 percent of the estimates of pass-through are significant and positive. This pass-through rate varies significantly across categories with beer and detergent getting larger pass-through than categories such as toothpaste and paper towel. The range is quite large, with average pass-through rate of 22 percent in toothpaste to over 550 percent in beer. The pass-through rate on own brand is on average more than 60 percent in most of the categories they examined. They find the cross-brand pass-through to be positive and negative. They find that market share, and a brand's importance or contribution to the category profit positively influence pass-through. Moreover, a large brand's promotion is less likely to generate cross-brand pass-through on smaller brands than the other way around.

The data used by Besanko et al. come from a chain where the recorded wholesale price is not the actual wholesale price but rather is an 'average acquisition cost' (see Peltzman, 2000) that is based on a weighted average of past prices and past inventory. Thus it is not the strategic choice variable of the manufacturer. This leads to a potential bias towards overstating the pass-through effect and the size of the bias is unknown. Meza and Sudhir (2006) claim that in the presence of forward buying by a retailer, using this acquisition cost measure as a proxy for true wholesale price leads to less of a bias than not using the inventory data at all. McAlister (2005) takes issue with Besanko et al.'s methodology and conclusions. She argues that a typical retailer carrying around 30000 SKUS will be unable to optimize as the model claims; manufacturers would rationally withhold trade promotion support if they know that their brands' retail prices can fluctuate depending on their competitors' promotions; variability of promotional deals masks the true wholesale prices; measurement errors exist in accounting for promotions etc. Conducting a more detailed analysis of the detergent data Besanko et al. used, McAlister offers further support for the view that the significance of cross-brand promotions is overstated.

Meza and Sudhir (2006) criticize earlier empirical studies for the methodology used to uncover the pass-through rate. Since a typical grocery product category is subjected to seasonal demand shocks, retail prices could be adjusting to these shocks independent of any wholesale price fluctuations and therefore this needs to be accounted for in determining pass-through rates. Starting with a random utility model at the individual level and aggregating to the store-level demand for a brand, they estimate store-level market share equations using the same database as Besanko et al. However, they estimate using only two categories: tuna, which was used by Besanko et al., and beer, which was not used by Besanko et al. By estimating a demand model with data from 94 stores over 400 weeks they infer the pass-through rates and show that loss leaders receive a higher pass-through than other products, and that this rate is lower during periods of high demand.

To summarize, the empirical literature documents the following:

- Not all trade promotions are reflected in retail promotions or pass-through.
- There is considerable variation in this pass-through across brands and across categories.
- The pass-through rates can be more than 100 percent and often, in some categories, substantially more.
- A brand's market share and sales volume affect positively the rate of pass-through.
- There is some evidence that the cross-brand pass-through and a smaller brands trade promotion might lead to pass-through on a larger brand. But more analysis is needed to establish this more convincingly. Similarly, certain categories, due to their importance in attracting store traffic, could potentially receive a higher pass-through.

Thus, while we have evidence on the variability of pass-through, a more systematic analysis of the behavior of wholesale prices and retail prices needs to be conducted to make accurate inferences about the impact of wholesale prices on retail prices. This means that we need econometric models grounded in theory that simultaneously account for the behavior of wholesale and retail prices so that we can make inferences about the impact of the former on the latter. Notwithstanding my admonition, how can these tentative 'facts' be reconciled with optimal behavior of market players? To assess this, we turn to the analytical literature.

3.2 Analytical models of retail response to trade promotions

Tyagi (1999) characterized the optimal response of a single-product monopoly retailer faced with a trade promotion, i.e. reduction in the wholesale price. The retailer is a Stackelberg follower in pricing, and takes the wholesale price as given and sets the retail price. He showed that if the retail demand function is concave or quasi concave, the pass-through rate is <100 percent and if convex, such as a constant elasticity demand function, then the pass-through rate is greater than 100 percent. His paper thus offers support for >100 percent pass-through based purely on the shape of the demand function. Kumar et al. (2001), in their attempt to explain the empirical facts, consider a single manufacturer–retailer dyad selling a single product. The elements of their model are as follows:

- There are two segments of consumers, low valuation and high valuation, that derive net utility of $v - p$ and $\delta^* v - p$ respectively, where v is the intrinsic utility for the single product in the market, p is the price and $\delta > 1$.
- Consumers know the frequency (α) with which manufacturers offer trade promotions, and on observing the retail price at the focal retailer make inference about whether the retailer is being opportunistic (not passing on the trade promotion) or whether the wholesale price is really high and consequently the retail price is at its regular level.
- Based on this, consumers decide to buy from this retailer or choose an outside option, which is to buy from another retailer.

- The manufacturer can use advertising to mitigate the retailer's opportunism by choosing to inform a fraction (φ) of the market about the trade promotion offer.
- The game sequence is as follows. The manufacturer selects φ, the retailer selects the likelihood he would offer a consumer promotion. Consumers observe φ and the retail price and decide whether or not to buy from this retailer.

Kumar et al. show that, in this world, the retailer does not always pass through and is less likely to pass through the greater the level of discount (inconsistent with Walters, 1989), lower the frequency of trade promotions, and lower the manufacturer support through advertising of the promotions (consistent with Walters, 1989).

Lal and Villas-Boas (1998) consider more complex consumer heterogeneity in the presence of retail and manufacturer competition, with each manufacturer selling a single product. There are two manufacturers selling one product each through two retailers and consumers can be in one of nine segments (size): a most price-sensitive segment (S) that buys the cheapest product in the market, two retailer-loyal segments (R) that buy from a single retailer the lowest-priced product, two manufacturer-loyal segments (M) that buy from the cheapest retailer, and four retailer–manufacturer-loyal (that is they are loyal to one retailer and one brand) segments (I). All consumers buy one unit of the product as long as the price is less than the common reservation value r. The game is set as follows:

- Manufacturers set wholesale prices simultaneously to maximize profits.
- Retailers take the wholesale prices as given and set retail prices simultaneously to maximize their profits.
- Consumers decide on the store and brand to buy.

When there is no retailer loyalty ($R = I = 0$), there is no retailer power and retail prices equal wholesale prices, which follows the equilibrium described in Narasimhan (1988). Similarly, when there is no manufacturer loyalty ($M = I = 0$), the manufacturers have no market power, wholesale prices equal marginal cost and now the retail prices track Narasimhan's model. When the market consists of no manufacturer switchers, i.e. $R = S = 0$, all prices are equal to r. If there are no retail switchers, i.e. $M = S = 0$, retail prices equal r and manufacturers randomize as in Narasimhan's model.

In the more general cases Lal and Villas-Boas show that the retail equilibrium can be quite complex depending on the relative magnitudes of the segments, and in some cases, it is possible for the retailer not to promote a brand when that brand's wholesale price is lowered, i.e. under trade promotion. Moreover, in some cases the brand that has the highest wholesale price can have the lowest retail price. An important contribution of this paper is to show when results from prior work such as Narasimhan (1988) will continue to hold and when the equilibrium will be qualitatively different.

Moorthy (2005) extends this literature by considering multiproduct retailers and retail competition. Consider for example two retailers carrying two brands, each with one brand common between the two and the other an exclusive brand that can be interpreted as a private label. Unlike in much of the literature, the demand functions are assumed continuous functions of all prices. In addition to wholesale price changes, the author considers variety of cost shocks that could lead to a change in retail price. The profit function for retailer i can be written as

$$\Pi^i(\mathbf{P}) = (p_{i1} - w_1 - c_{i1} - c_i - c) D^{i1}(\mathbf{P}) + (p_{i2} - c_{i2} - c_i - c) D^{i2}(\mathbf{P}) \quad (13.2)$$

where $\mathbf{P}$ is the vector of all prices

w_1 is the wholesale price of the brand that is common among retailers
c_{i1} and c_{i2} are retailer i's brand-specific marginal costs
c_i is retailer i's non-brand-specific marginal cost such as labor cost
c is a non-brand, non-retailer-specific cost such as excise cost
D^{i1} and D^{i2} are the demand functions for product 1 and 2 respectively at retailer i.

Moorthy examines how, if the retailer maximizes category profits, retail prices will change with respect to wholesale price and the different marginal costs. He shows that the response due to a trade promotion is always positive, leading to a retail promotion. This pass-through would be greater with retail competition and the adoption of category management by the retailers. He also shows that cross-brand effects are ambiguous, i.e. can be both positive and negative, a conclusion supported by Besanko et al.

To summarize, analytical models explain how optimizing retailers' behavior can lead to (i) pass-through of trade promotion, (ii) the pass-through can be greater than 100 percent depending on the shape of the demand function, (iii) in some instances the retailer may not pass through at all, and (iv) cross-brand pass-through can arise but its direction can be positive or negative.

3.3 Manufacturers' incentives to offer trade promotions

At the heart of trade promotions is the question: why do manufacturers offer temporary reduction in wholesale prices? Notice that there are two questions here: (i) why is the incentive tied to the wholesale price as opposed to lump sum payment such as a display support or feature support, and (ii) why are these promotions temporary? The null hypothesis on the second question is: why not offer a permanent reduction in wholesale price? Clearly, if there are demand (seasonality, mismatch between forecast and realization of demand etc.) shocks or supply shocks (crop prices, labor costs) we should observe a temporary fluctuation on wholesale prices. But most trade promotions cannot be dismissed as arising out of these random shocks. There must be consumer, supply chain and competitive factors that lead to such promotions. This second question takes on added importance when we factor in the direct and indirect costs of trade promotion (see Buzzell et al., 1990). One of these costs is the opportunity cost or foregone profit if retailers forward buy on trade promotions. If retailers buy more than what they require to meet the compliance requirements and use the additional quantity to sell the product at its normal regular price, this represents a loss or cost of that trade promotion. We examine the answers provided by analytical models of consumers, intermediaries and manufacturers.

Jeuland and Narasimhan (1985) offered a model of two parties – a monopoly firm and consumers – to explain the occurrence of promotions. There are two segments of consumers who differ in their preferences and inventory costs. The demand for a product at the segment level is given by

$$Q_i = \alpha_i - \beta * P \tag{13.3}$$

where Q_i is the demand for segment i and P is the retail price, α_i is the segment specific parameter and β is the price sensitivity parameter.

The authors assume that the segment with higher α has a higher holding cost for inventorying this product, only buys for current consumption and does not forward-buy. The consumers with lower α, when faced with a retail promotion, respond by increasing their consumption and forward buying the product when it is on sale. They show that the optimal strategy for the monopolist is to conduct periodic sales and solve for the frequency and depth of promotion. The contribution of this paper is to show that consumer heterogeneity in inventory costs and demand elasticity, and correlation between these, can drive periodic promotion by a manufacturer. While they didn't identify the consumers as retailers, they could apply their model to trade promotions as well. As long as there are enough customers able to expand their demand and forward-buy, it is optimal for the firm to offer trade promotions. Lal (1990) offers a model with two competing manufacturers marketing one brand each through a retailer who offers a store brand. He shows that in an infinitely repeated game the manufacturers take turns to offer a trade deal to the retailer. Thus in a non-cooperative game the manufacturers collude to limit the encroachment by the store brand into their franchises. Lal et al. (1996) consider a model of two competing manufacturers selling one product each through a common retailer. The manufacturer incurs a selling cost of promotion and the retailer, if he accepts the promotion, incurs a fixed cost. The retailer can buy the product either at the regular price or at the promoted price and can forward-buy products for future use. The demand model has features similar to models without a retailer (see Narasimhan, 1988). As in earlier models, manufacturers use a randomized strategy in offering discounts to induce the retailer to inventory their products. An important contribution of this paper is to show that even when the retailer forward-buys, manufacturers find it profitable to offer a trade deal. The reason is that holding inventory leads to less intense price competition since smaller deals are less attractive to the retailer when he has inventory and larger deals become unprofitable to the manufacturers. So the manufacturers compete over a narrower range of trade deals, which means that the probability of beating your opponent (i.e. the retailer will accept the deal) is lower and therefore the manufacturers are less aggressive.

A paper that models manufacturer promotion not as a wholesale price reduction but as a lump sum transfer is by Kim and Staelin (1999), who consider a model of two manufacturers selling one product each and two retailers who sell two products each. Trade promotion is captured through a lump sum allowance that a manufacturer provides a retailer. Each retailer selects the retail prices and a common pass-through rate for the two brands. The 'pass-through rate' is the proportion of this allowance spent on merchandising activity that affects demand positively. Retail demand for brand i at the retailer is given by the following:

> Demand for brand 1 at store 1 = f (prices of all brands at store 1, pass-through rate at store 1*difference in the promotional allowance of brand 1 in store 1, difference in promotional allowances across stores, pass-through rate at store1*promotional allowance at store1)

Thus the demand function captures the effect of prices, own- and cross-brand pass-through, store switching and category expansion. The game proceeds as follows. Each manufacturer simultaneously chooses wholesale price and promotional allowance for his brand, anticipating the actions of the retailers. In the second stage, retailers simultaneously choose retail prices and pass-through rates. Two broad conclusions emerge from this paper. First, it offers analytical support to the evidence and argument made earlier by Messinger and Narasimhan (1995) that even when manufacturers provide greater concessions to the retailers, because of retail competition these concessions are passed along aggressively by the retailers. Second, the authors show that even though retailers pass through less than they receive, manufacturers provide the side payments to the retailers.

A different rationale for the existence of trade promotions and allowances is provided by the research stream that examines the channel relationship when the retailer not only distributes manufacturers' products but also markets a store brand. Narasimhan and Wilcox (1998) consider a manufacturer–retailer channel where the retailer is able to procure a private label in a competitive market. There are two segments of consumers, one loyal to the national brand and another that is composed of national brand–private label switchers. All consumers buy one unit of either the national brand or the private label as long as the price of that product is less than r, the reservation price. A randomly chosen consumer in the switching has a preference for the national brand but will buy the private label if the retail price of the private label is l less than the national brand. They assume that l is distributed $U(0, L)$. The manufacturer sets his wholesale price anticipating retailer's pricing behavior in relation not only to the national brand but also to the private label. They compute the equilibrium prices with and without private labels. They show that the retail margin on the national brand is positively related to the size of the switching segment and is negatively related to the heterogeneity of the switching segment. The first result is obvious. The second result arises due to the fact that as the heterogeneity in the switching segment increases, it is more costly for the retailer to attract the same proportion of switchers away from the national brand, which leads to lower concession from the manufacturer. The authors thus show that not only does a private label have a direct effect in terms of attracting more customers in the market; it also has a strategic effect of eliciting better wholesale price concessions from the manufacturer. They offer empirical support to their predictions.

To summarize, we have the following predictions from the analytical models:

- Retailers in general will pass through manufacturers' incentives. Greater than 100 percent pass-through is predicated upon the shape of the demand curve.
- Ignoring menu costs and adjustment costs of changing prices, cross-brand pass-through is likely to occur.
- Even if retailers forward-buy, in a competitive world we should see trade promotions.
- Retail competition forces retailers to pass through more than they would normally have passed through based on demand and cost curves.
- Trade promotions or concessions from manufacturers can arise when retailers market store brands or private labels.

4. Profitability and efficacy of trade promotions

In this section we discuss two key managerial issues: (i) how should one evaluate the profitability of trade promotions and (ii) how can one make trade promotions more effective in achieving stated objectives?

4.1 Evaluating the profitability of trade promotions

At first glance this seems a very simple task. Compare the profits with and without promotion and if the latter are greater than the former, declare victory because the promotion is profitable. But closer examination reveals that it is not simple: evaluation of promotion is fraught with many measurement and data problems. To understand the difficulties, let us think about what happens when a promotion occurs by focusing on off-invoice promotion. If retailers anticipate that such promotions are temporary, they are likely to be strategic and engage in forward-buying. Likewise there is a large body evidence that consumers, when faced with retail promotions, forward-buy; more recent evidence (see, e.g., Van Heerde et al., 2003; Chan et al., 2008) seems to suggest that such stockpiling behavior accounts for a major portion of the sales spike. The amount that is forward bought is potentially an opportunity loss since these units could have been sold at the regular price at some point later in time. Of course not all of it is a loss since there is no guarantee that the retailer would have bought the same amount in future. Moreover, wholesale demand and retail demand of a product are subject to random shocks and competitive actions. Given all this, determining incremental sales due to a promotion is a complicated task. If consumers and retailers act strategically, examining shipments data in a 'before versus after' promotion analysis will be misleading. Next is the question of identifying direct and indirect costs of promotion. What are the direct costs of running a trade promotion? What about the indirect or opportunity costs of accumulating higher inventory in preparation for a promotion etc? Thus, even if one can estimate the incremental sales, identifying the direct and indirect costs to evaluate profitability of promotions is daunting. Two papers tried to tackle the profitability of promotion using sales and shipment data.

Blattberg and Levin (1987) use a three-equation model and an accounting identity to predict shipments and consumer sales as below:

$$\text{Shipments } \{t\} = f1 \text{ (inventory } \{t-1\}, \text{ trade promotions, other factors)}$$

$$\text{Retail promotions } \{t\} = f2(\text{trade promotions } \{t\}, \text{ trade promotions } \{t-1\}, \text{ inventories } \{t-1\})$$

$$\text{Consumer sales } \{t\} = g \text{ (trade promotions } \{t\}, \text{ retail promotions } \{t-1\}, \text{ other factors } \{t\}, \text{ other factors } \{t-1\})$$

$$\text{Inventories } \{t\} = h \text{ (inventories } \{t-1\}, \text{ shipments } \{t\}, \text{ consumer sales } \{t\})$$

They estimate the model using data from ten products and three markets. Using the estimates, one can simulate what will happen when a trade promotion is offered to shipments and retail sales. This model, by being theoretically sound in that it relies on a process model of the flow of goods and money in the system, gives confidence as to face validity. While this is a good beginning, note that they were not able to estimate separately, due to data problems, the second equation above to uncover the factors that drive retail promotions. Moreover, there was no attempt to explicitly control for or model within-category competitive effects or interstore competition. Finally, the consumer sales model can be enriched to include drivers under the control of the retailers such as feature and display support etc.

Abrahim and Lodish (1987) develop an expert system to evaluate the impact of promotion. Their focus is on identifying baseline sales, those that would result in the absence of promotional effects. They define sales at time t as

$$S(t) = T(t) * SI(t) * X(t) \, (b(t) + p(t) + e(t))$$

where T, SI, X are trend, seasonal and 'exception' indices, b, p are the base-level sales and promotional bump after removing trend, seasonality and 'exceptions', and finally e is an error term. Through data analysis and judgment the baseline sales is estimated and, using that, the incremental sales and profitability of any promotion can be estimated. Unlike the Blattberg and Levin model, this model is purely data driven and the statistical property of the baseline sales is not known. Further, the procedure for identifying exceptions seems not to follow from any structure but rather depend on the analyst's judgment. For example, the authors report that category-level and competitive effects are captured by the exception index but it is not made clear how; nor is the robustness of this index measured.

To summarize, there have been some attempts to model the profitability of trade promotions. Largely due to the type of data available and the cost of conducting this exercise, we have not seen more of this type of research but it remains an important area.

4.2 Drivers of effective trade promotions

What are the drivers that improve the effectiveness of trade promotions? How can we use these drivers to optimize the timing and characteristics of promotional offers? To answer the first question, we should develop metrics for effectiveness. Is it just profitability, or are there other measures that we should examine? Hardy (1986) explored this issue through a survey of managers from a sample of 27 Canadian packaged good companies on 103 trade promotions. Each manager was asked to complete the survey instrument for one successful and one unsuccessful promotion. Using these data, Hardy examines through a multiple regression model the drivers for the following four dependent variables: short-term volume, long-term market share, build-up of trade inventories and increased consumer trial. He found that trade support had a predictable impact on all the four metrics. The level of incentives affected positively the short- and long-term share goals while competitive promotion affected negatively the build-up of inventories, with the trade, of the focal brand. These results are intuitive. Blattberg and Neslin (1990), based on a study by Curhan and Kopp (1986), identify the following four factors as influencers on the level of support the retailers would provide:

1. Economic structure of promotions such as amount of discount, terms, requirements and restrictions.
2. Item importance, including volume, category size and competitive retail activity.
3. Manufacturer's reputation.
4. Promotional elasticity.

Murry and Heide (1998) consider the issue of retailer participation and compliance with manufacturer-initiated promotions such as POP programs. They theorize that both interpersonal relationship and incentives matter in retailers' decisions. They designed a conjoint study that included four factors (two levels each) to capture both organizational and incentive drivers. The study was administered using a full factorial design to liquor and grocery store managers. They found that incentive factors are more important in the decisions of the retailers, and that strength of interpersonal relationship does not diminish this importance.

Which type of trade promotions would be best and what are the drivers? This is somewhat of an underresearched area. Given the structure of these promotional incentives, it is not surprising that manufacturers tend to favor performance-based promotions such as scan-backs while the retailers favor straight off-invoice promotions. Drèze and Bell (2003) show analytically that if the terms of the deals are identical, the above result is valid, but a manufacturer can redesign the scan-back promotion to leave the retailer no worse off while improving his profitability. This is because under scan-back there is no excess ordering and retail price is lowered, resulting in higher retail sales. In their model there is no manufacturer or retail competition, so it is not clear how these added institutional details would change the result.

5. Trade promotion as part of the marketing mix

As any marketing student knows, firms have multiple instruments to stimulate demand and to respond to competitive and channel initiatives. So where does trade promotion fit as part of the overall marketing strategy? How should managers address the problem of budget allocation? I explore these issues in this section.

Narasimhan (1989) explores the factors that are perceived to be important in deciding on consumer and trade promotions. He conducted a survey of brand managers to assess this. He identified three factors that drive the importance attached to trade promotions. These are goal oriented (achieving sales targets, introducing new products, motivating sales force), defensive (maintaining shelf space, meeting competition), and penetration (increasing usage rate and getting more retailer push). The factors for consumer promotion were similar except that there were two goal factors, one short and one long term. He found that the managers' beliefs about the importance of these factors were correlated with category and brand variables such as category, volume, growth rate, shelf life, purchase frequency, market share, rank etc. Finally, he finds that the decision to allocate money between trade and consumer promotions is based not only on category and brand variables but also on the perceived importance of the factors.

Neslin et al. (1995) consider a market consisting of a single manufacturer–retailer dyad and consumers. The manufacturer can advertise the product to consumers and trade-promote to its retailers. Advertising affects retail sales through the pull effect and retail promotion also affects retail sales. The manufacturer is assumed to maximize its net profit over a year by deciding on the optimal allocation between advertising and trade promotions. Unlike the standard analytical models, they do not use a game-theoretic set-up. The amount to be ordered by the retailers, the intensity of promotion at retail level etc., do not come from maximizing behavior by the retailer but rather are written down as exogenous decisions. A demand equation describes the total sales at the retail outlet. They use numerical optimization methods to arrive at an optimal policy for the manufacturer. In the base case, for example, they show that periodic trade promotions and constant advertising expenditures except in the period before a trade promotion is an optimal strategy. While this kind of exercise incorporates a level of richness that is not found in standard analytical models, the non-strategic behavior of retailers and consumers is a limitation of such an exercise.

Gomez et al. (2007) evaluate the drivers behind the allocation of the trade promotion budget and its components. They hypothesize that the amount of money allocated to trade promotion increases is positively (negatively) correlated with the size of retailer and the brand power of retailer (size of manufacturer, brand strength) while the effect of private label penetration is ambiguous. Similarly, allocation of money between off-invoice and performance-based scan-backs is also driven by these factors. Using survey data from 36 supermarkets in the USA, they test their hypotheses and find support. It is interesting and somewhat intuitive that they find that, with greater retailer size, positioning and power through private label, retailers are able to elicit better concessions from the manufacturer through off-invoice promotions, a point made earlier by Narasimhan and Wilcox (1998).

Gerstner and Hess (1991, 1995) consider the dual role of trade promotions and consumer promotions through coupons or rebates. They consider a manufacturer–retailer dyad with no competition at either level. Consumers are of two types, H and L. The H type has a higher reservation price than the L type. All consumers desire at most one unit of the product as long as the price is less than their reservation price. The manufacturer distributes the product through a retailer and decides on the wholesale price first and, conditional on this, the retailer decides his retail price. As long as the L-type segment size is below a critical level, the manufacturer's optimal strategy is to cater only to the H type. But as the L type grows it is optimal for the manufacturer and for the channel as a whole to sell to both types. But in the standard Stackleberg leader–follower game, if the manufacturer lowers the wholesale price, the retailer has every incentive not to pass along the lowered price to attract the L type due to the standard double marginalization problem. Gerstner and Hess show how the use of pull promotions through rebate or coupon can coordinate the channel. They go on to discuss the effect of coupons and what happens if perfect targeting of low-value consumers is not possible. This paper doesn't capture the essence of trade promotions, which are temporary reductions in wholesale price. These papers offer insights into when a wholesale price reduction is necessary and how other marketing mix variables play a role in enhancing the effectiveness of such a policy. These papers make two interesting points. Consumer promotions in conjunction with trade promotion can coordinate the channel. Pull promotions, in addition to any discriminatory or segmentation effect among end users, can serve an added role in the presence of an intermediary.

Agrawal (1996) considers the effect of brand loyalty on advertising and trade promotion. He constructs a theoretical model that captures two competing manufacturers distributing one brand each and a common retailer that distributes both brands. Consumers desire at most one unit of either product as long as the retail price is less than $\$r$. There are two segments of consumers each loyal to one of the two brands, but each will switch to the other brand if the price of the other brand is lower than a threshold relative to its favorite brand. The retail demand for brand i ($i = 1, 2; j = 3 - i$) can be written as

$$D_i(p_i, p_j) = \begin{cases} 1 & \text{if} \quad p_i < p_j - l_j \\ M_i & \text{if} \quad p_i - l_i \leq p_j \leq p_i + l_j \\ 0 & \text{if} \quad p_j < p_i - l_i \end{cases} \quad (13.4)$$

where p_i and p_j are retail prices, and l_i and l_j represent the threshold the competing brand has to overcome. A firm's own advertising expenditure raises, at a diminishing rate, the threshold the other firm has to overcome but competitive advertising lowers this threshold. So firm i's advertising raises l_i while firm j's advertising lowers l_i and vice versa. The author assumes that the thresholds for two brands are sufficiently different so that the brand with a larger l is called the stronger brand and the other the weaker brand. The game proceeds in four stages. In stage one, the two manufacturers simultaneously decide on their respective advertising levels. In stage two they simultaneously set wholesale prices, in stage three the retailer sets the retail prices for the two brands and in stage four consumers observe all the prices and make their choices. He finds that the retailer, similar to Narasimhan's results, promotes the stronger brand more frequently than the weaker brand. Turning to the manufacturer, he finds that there are several equilibria, depending on the marginal cost of advertising, where the stronger brand does not advertise but the weaker brand advertises and the promotional strategy is one of the following:

(a) Neither manufacturer promotes.
(b) Both promote and the weaker brand spends less.
(c) Both promote and the weaker brand spends more.

On pass-through of trade promotions the author finds that the stronger brand enjoys greater pass-through in terms of frequency but not on the size of the discount. Some of these results, especially on the pass-through, seem to be inconsistent with the empirical evidence cited earlier. Using scanner panel data, he examines some of the predictions from his model. To test these predictions he first estimates the size and strength of loyalty for each of 54 brands in seven different categories. Using linear regression he estimates the following three modes at the brand level:

$$\text{Advertising expenditure} = \alpha_0 + \alpha_1 \times \text{loyalty} + \alpha_2 \times \text{size} + \text{category dummies} + \varepsilon_1$$

$$\text{Average retail discount} = \beta_0 + \beta_1 \times \text{loyalty} + \beta_2 \times \text{advertising expenditure} + \text{category dummies} + \varepsilon_2$$

$$\text{Frequency of retail promotions} = \gamma_0 + \gamma_1 \times \text{loyalty} + \gamma_2 \times \text{advertising expenditure} + \text{category dummies} + \varepsilon_3$$

Consistent with his theoretical predictions, he finds that high loyalty leads to lower advertising expenditures, lower retail discount and greater frequency of retail promotions, and loyal segment size is positively related to the manufacturer's advertising expenditure. The contribution of this paper is in considering trade promotions as part of the overall mix in conjunction with advertising and promotions at both the wholesale and retail level.

6. Discussion

In this chapter I discuss several research streams examining the role of trade promotions, the incentives of trading partners in offering and accepting these, the drivers of the efficacy of trade promotions, evaluating the profitability of trade promotions and how trade promotions may interact with other marketing variables.

Manufacturers, especially CPG manufacturers, have been allocating a greater share of the promotional budget to trade promotions over time. We are also seeing a shift in the allocation among the types of promotions, partly driven by improvements in IT that have lead to better data capture, analysis and monitoring.

Existing research has evolved along the following streams:

- Documenting retailer acceptance and pass-through rates.
- Empirically identifying the drivers of retailer acceptance.
- Analytical models exploring the rationale behind trade promotions in monopoly and competitive contexts.
- Analytical models characterizing the impact of promotions on retailers and their propensity to accept these.
- Models evaluating profitability.
- Understanding the drivers to improve the efficacy and impact of trade promotion.
- Role of trade promotion as part of the marketing mix.

Several conclusions emerge from the extant literature:

- Retailers are selective in passing the money they receive from the manufacturers to the consumers. Surprisingly, several instances have been documented where the retailers pass through more than they receive.
- A brand's strength and its ability to pull sales or increase store traffic (Lal and Narasimhan, 1996), item importance, size and structure of incentives are key predictors of retailer compliance.
- Retail competition increases the pass-through rate.
- Trade promotions can arise even if retailers forward-buy.
- The presence of store brands or private labels acts as an important driver for the manufacturers to offer concessions to trade, often in the form of trade promotions.
- Cross-brand pass-through can occur, although the empirical evidence seems to be somewhat scant or mixed.

Based on this, I expect future research to continue to build on this important topic along the following lines:

- A broader assessment of the empirical regularities across many categories and markets such as in international markets.
- Exploring in greater depth the efficacy and profitability of trade promotions by explicitly modeling retailer characteristics such as size, market share, reputation etc. in the empirical models.
- Extending and checking for robustness of the findings in non-grocery markets such as apparel, electronic goods, toys etc. Some studies have looked at trade promotions in durable goods (Bruce et al., 2005) and dealer promotions in automobiles (Busse et al., 2006). More work along these dimensions would help us to understand

and establish robust drivers for the incidence, acceptance and pass-through of these trade promotions.
- Examining analytically and empirically the promotion incentives, acceptance and performance when there are multiple channels such as brick-and-mortar and online channels.
- Examining the strategic role of trade promotions as part of the overall pricing strategy. How exactly do or should firms design trade incentives and an overall pricing strategy including a regular list price?

References

Abrahim, M. and L. Lodish (1987), 'PROMOTOR: an automated promotion evaluation system', *Marketing Science*, **6**, 101–23.
AC Nielson Co. (2004), 'Summary: 2003 trade promotion practices', *Consumer Insight*, Summer, available at: http://www2.acnielsen.com/pubs/documents/2004_q3_ci_tpp.pdf.
Agrawal, D. (1996), 'Effect of brand loyalty on advertising and trade promotions: a game theoretic analysis and empirical evidence', Marketing Science, **15** (1), 86–106.
Armstrong, M.K.S. (1991), 'Retail response to trade promotion: an incremental analysis of forward buying and retail promotion', Doctoral Dissertation, UT Dallas.
Besanko, D., J.-P. Dubé and S. Gupta (2005), 'Own-brand and cross-brand retail pass-through', *Marketing Science*, **24** (1), 123–37.
Blattberg, R.C. and A. Levin (1987), 'Modeling the effectiveness and profitability of trade promotions', *Marketing Science*, **6**, 124–46.
Blattberg, R.C. and S.A. Neslin (1990), *Sales Promotion: Concepts, Methods, and Strategies*, Englewood Cliffs, NJ: Prentice Hall.
Bloom, P.N. (2001), 'Role of slotting fees and trade promotions in shaping how tobacco is marketed in retail stores', *TC online*, **10**, 340–44.
Booz Allen Hamilton (2003), 'Boosting the bottom line through improved trade promotion effectiveness', Report, McLean, VA: Booz Allen Hamilton.
Bruce, N., P. Desai and R. Staelin (2005), 'The better they are, the more they give', *Journal of Marketing Research*, February, 54–66.
Busse, M., J. Silva-Risso and F. Zettelmeyer (2006), '$1,000 cash back: the pass through of auto manufacturer promotions', *American Economic Review*, September, 1253–70.
Buzzell, R.D., J.A. Quelch and W.J. Salmon (1990), 'The costly bargain of trade promotions', *Harvard Business Review*, March–April, 2–9.
Chan, T., C. Narasimhan and Q. Zhang (2008), 'Decomposing purchase elasticity with a dynamic structural model of flexible consumption', *Journal of Marketing Research*, **45** (4), August, 487–98.
Chevalier, M. and R.C. Curhan (1976), 'Retail promotions as a function of trade promotions: a descriptive analysis', *Sloan Management Review*, Fall, 19–32.
Curhan, R.C. and R.J. Kopp (1986), 'Factors influencing grocery retailers' support of trade promotions', Report No. 86-104, Marketing Science Institute.
Drèze, X. and D.R. Bell (2003), 'Creating win–win trade promotions: theory and empirical analysis of scan-back trade deals', *Marketing Science*, **22** (1), 16–39.
Gerstner, E. and J.D. Hess (1991), 'A theory of channel price promotions', *The American Economic Review*, **81** (4), 872–86.
Gerstner, E. and J.D. Hess (1995), 'Pull promotions and channel coordination', *Marketing Science*, **14** (1), 43–60.
Gomez, M.I., V.R. Rao and E.W. McLaughlin (2007), 'Empirical analysis of budget allocation of trade promotions in the US supermarket industry', *Journal of Marketing Research*, **44** (3), 410–24.
Hardy, K.G. (1986), 'Key success factors for manufacturers' sales promotions in package goods', *Journal of Marketing*, **50** (3), 13–23.
Inforte Corp. (2005), 'Point of view: trade promotion effectiveness', Report, Chicago: Inforte Corp.
Jeuland, A.P. and C. Narasimhan (1985), 'Dealing – temporary price cuts – by sellers as a buying discrimination mechanism', *Journal of Business*, **58** (3) 295–308.
Kim, S.Y. and R. Staelin (1999), 'Manufacturer allowances and retailer pass-through rates in a competitive environment', *Marketing Science*, **18** (1), 59–76.
Kumar, N., S. Rajiv and A. Jeuland (2001), 'Effectiveness of trade promotions: analyzing the determinants of retail pass through', *Marketing Science*, **20** (4), 382–404.

Lal, R. (1990), 'Manufacturer trade deals and retail price promotions', *Journal of Marketing Research*, **27** (4), 428–44.
Lal, R., J.D.C. Little and J.M. Villas-Boas (1996), 'A theory of forward buying, merchandising, and trade deals', *Marketing Science*, **15** (1), 21–37.
Lal, R. and C. Narasimhan (1996), 'The inverse relationship between manufacturer and retailer margins: a theory', *Marketing Science*, **15** (2), 132–51.
Lal, R. and J.M. Villas-Boas (1998), 'Price promotions and trade deals with multiproduct retailers', *Management Science*, **44** (7), 935–49.
McAlister, L. (2005), 'Cross-brand pass-through? Not in grocery retailing', Working Paper, MSI Reports, 05-003.
Messinger, P.R. and C. Narasimhan (1995), 'Has power shifted in the grocery channel?', *Marketing Science*, **14** (2), 189–221.
Meza, S. and K. Sudhir (2006), 'Pass-through timing', *Quantitative Marketing and Economics*, **4** (4), December, 351–82.
Moorthy, S. (2005), 'A general theory of pass-through in channels with category management and retail competition', *Marketing Science*, **24** (1), 110–22.
Murry, J.P. and J.B. Heide (1998), 'Managing promotion program participation within manufacturer–retailer relationships', *Journal of Marketing*, **62** (1), 58–68.
Narasimhan, C. (1989), 'Managerial perspectives on trade and consumer promotions', *Marketing Letters*, **1** (3), 239–51.
Narasimhan, C. (1988), 'Competitive promotional strategies', *Journal of Business*, **61** (4), 427–49.
Narasimhan, C. and R.T. Wilcox (1998), 'Private labels and the channel relationship: a cross-category analysis', *Journal of Business*, **71** (4), 573–601.
Neslin, S.A., S.G. Powell and L.S. Stone (1995), 'The effects of retailer and consumer response on optimal manufacturer advertising and trade promotions strategies', *Management Science*, **41** (5), 749–66.
Peltzman, S. (2000), 'Prices rise faster than they fall', *Journal of Political Economy*, **108** (3), 466–502.
Tyagi, R.K. (1999), 'A characterization of retailer response to manufacturer trade deals', *Journal of Marketing Research*, **36** (4), 510–16.
Van Heerde, H.J., S. Gupta and D.R. Wittink (2003), 'Is 75% of the sales promotion bump due to brand switching? No, only 33% is', *Journal of Marketing Research*, **40**, 481–91.
Walters, R.J. (1989), 'An empirical investigation into retailer response to manufacturer trade promotions', *Journal of Retailing*, **65** (2), 253–72.

14 Competitive targeted pricing: perspectives from theoretical research*
Z. John Zhang

Abstract
With an unprecedented capability to store and process consumer information, firms today can tailor their pricing to individual consumers based on consumer preferences and past buying behaviors. In this chapter, we discuss this nascent practice of targeted pricing from a theoretical perspective. We focus on three main questions that are relevant to assessing the future of this practice. First, is targeted pricing beneficial to practicing firms? Second, if a firm decides to embrace targeted pricing, what should be its targeting strategy in terms of whom to target and with what incentives? Third, is targeted pricing beneficial to the society as a whole? We draw on the existing literature on targeted pricing to offer some preliminary answers to these questions.

1. Introduction

Targeted pricing, as the term is commonly used by practitioners, refers to the practice where a firm tailors its prices of a product to individual customers based on some discernible differences in their preferences, willingness to pay, buying behaviors, etc. For instance, when selling magazines, a publisher may decide to offer a discount to a new subscriber, but withhold the same discount from someone who has been a loyal subscriber for years. In the famous battle for market share between AT&T and MCI in the early 1990s, AT&T successfully persuaded many MCI customers to switch carriers by offering them personalized checks in the amounts of $25 to $100 depending on each consumer's long-distance calling history and experience with AT&T (Turco, 1993). Today, many industries adopt some form of targeted pricing when they have actionable customer information, and such practices are also variably called 'one-to-one pricing', 'personalized pricing', 'tailored pricing', and sometimes 'dynamic pricing'.

On the surface, targeted pricing is nothing new and merely a form of price discrimination. The textbook definitions for different forms of price discrimination we use today came from the English economist Arthur C. Pigou (1877–1959). In his book *Economics of Welfare*, originally published in 1920, Pigou articulated three forms of price discrimination that a monopolist could implement. To use Pigou's words,

> A first degree would involve the charge of a different price against all the different units of commodity, in such wise that the price exacted for each was equal to the demand price for it, and no consumers' surplus was left to the buyers. A second degree would obtain if a monopolist were able to make n separate prices, in such wise that all units with a demand price greater than x were sold at a price x, all with a demand price less than x and greater than y at a price y, and so on. A third degree would obtain if the monopolist were able to distinguish among his customers n different groups, separated from one another more or less by some practicable mark, and could charge a separate monopoly price to the members of each group. (Pigou, 1929, p. 278)

---

* The author thanks Christophe van Den Bulte, Vithala Rao, Preyas Desai, David Bell, Eric Bradlow and Raghu Iyengar for their constructive comments on this chapter.

However, targeted pricing as practiced in industries today frequently does not fit any of these different forms of price discrimination. For instance, when amazon.com targets its loyal customers with a high price for a book, while charging a new, occasional purchaser a low price for the same, it implements a pricing scheme that cuts across all three forms of price discrimination and, arguably, goes beyond what has been understood to be the standard practices of price discrimination. First, amazon.com's pricing scheme is based primarily on past buying behaviors, rather than on any invariable 'practicable mark' such as gender, age and other demographics. Therefore this practice of targeted pricing is not exactly the third degree of price discrimination where customers with the same characteristics, say being students or senior citizens, are charged the same price. Second, it is not exactly the second degree of price discrimination, either, as both loyal and occasional purchasers are buying the same amount. In addition, it is amazon.com that is assigning a price to individual customers, and customers do not have a chance to self-select in terms of what they end up paying. Finally, this pricing practice is almost certainly not first-degree price discrimination, as the pricing scheme does not tap into variations in willingness to pay that must exist among loyal as well as among occasional customers.

It is perhaps not surprising that a classification scheme developed nearly a century ago can no longer encompass an ever-increasing number of different schemes of price discrimination concocted today by increasingly sophisticated practitioners. In the area of price discrimination, two market forces drive today's practitioners to become ever more inventive. First, the availability of new information technologies and sophisticated database analytics, and the widespread use of Internet transactions allow firms to gather and process detailed customer information on a large scale and in a timely and cost-effective manner. Consequently, firms are having ever-sharper pictures of individual customers so that they can move away from a labor-intensive targeting approach (Desai and Purohit, 2004) and go beyond static, obvious variables such as demographics and purchasing quantities in designing their price discrimination schemes. They can look into consumer preferences, loyalties and other psychographics, as well as geographic and other discernible and quantifiable differences among customers. Second, as the marketplace is becoming increasingly competitive, firms need to tune their pricing schemes constantly to stay ahead of competition when searching and capturing the last pockets of profitability in the marketplace.[1]

The proliferation of targeted pricing practices challenges not only the standard taxonomy of price discrimination, but also much of the conventional wisdom about price discrimination. One such piece of conventional wisdom is that price discrimination should always benefit the practicing firm whether it implements first-, second- or third-degree price discrimination. After all, a firm, by being a monopoly, has the choice not to implement any price discrimination. However, in today's market environment, this logic is no longer valid, and certainly not in the industries where we frequently observe targeted pricing. For example, in the case of AT&T mentioned above, competition is a driving force behind its practice of targeted pricing. Indeed, AT&T's primary targets for its switching checks were MCI's customers. Armed with customer usage information in

---

[1] Of course, even with conventional price discrimination schemes, competition intensity in a market plays an important role, as shown in Desai (2001).

addition to customer addresses and demographics, AT&T could identify the switchable customers who were served by MCI and gauge the strength of their preferences for MCI to determine the right incentives required to induce them to switch. In this case, price discrimination was implemented based on consumer relative preferences. In addition, targeted pricing did not and could not take place in an insulated market where AT&T could ignore any competitive reactions. As a matter of fact, MCI implemented its own targeted pricing campaign to switch AT&T's customers, too. As a result of competitive targeted pricing, millions of customers switched (perhaps multiple times) between the two firms as they cashed the switching checks received from both firms.

In this new reality of price discrimination, three fundamental questions arise that are of interest to practitioners and marketing scholars alike. First, can firms benefit from targeted pricing in oligopolistic markets? Many practitioners and experts may be tempted to offer a quick 'yes'. However, the answer is not that obvious, considering the complexity involved in implementing targeted pricing in terms of costs, competitive reactions and consumer responses. Yet the answer to this question gives us a perspective to guide the practice of targeted pricing and to assess its future. For instance, if firms become worse off because of targeted pricing, they may not have much incentive to invest in their targeting capability or they may want to seek ways to restrain targeted pricing in their industry. The answer to this question also offers some strategic prescriptions as to whether a firm should adopt targeted pricing and how it should prepare itself for such a future.

Second, if a firm decides to implement targeted pricing, what should be its targeting strategy? In other words, if a firm can identify consumers and charge different prices to different consumers, how should it deploy its capabilities? More concretely, should the firm target its competitor's customers with a discount, its own customers, or both? Our answer to this question can help us to understand the current practice of targeted pricing and offer some strategic guidance to practitioners.

Third, does targeted pricing improve social welfare? Marketers need to pay attention to this question because welfare implications do have regulatory implications, and our answer to this question may affect the legal environment in which targeted pricing is conducted.

In this chapter, we take a brief tour of the recent literature on targeted pricing to see how it answers those three questions. Before we start on that tour, three points are worth noting. First, targeted pricing is a nascent practice. Few data are available that can help us to address those three questions. For that reason, empirical research on targeted pricing mostly focuses on how a firm can or should implement targeted pricing given that it has a certain kind of customer information (Rossi and Allenby, 1993; Rossi et al., 1996; Dong et al., 2006; and Zhang and Wedel, 2007). Theoretical research, in contrast, is uniquely suited for addressing all three questions in a competitive context. Therefore, in this chapter, we focus exclusively on the theoretical literature on targeted pricing.

Second, targeted pricing is an evolving practice, and new ways to implement targeted pricing emerge all the time. Therefore it is infeasible and perhaps even unwise to try to catalog all of the existent practices. The theoretical literature on targeted pricing so far mostly focuses on preference-based and behavior-based targeted pricing and we shall do the same in this chapter. Third, most of the theoretical studies on targeted pricing are fairly complex technically. Such technical complexity has sometimes rendered the literature inaccessible to a broad audience. Therefore, in our opinion it is desirable to discuss the messages of the literature without being unduly encumbered by technicalities.

Towards that objective, we shall use simplified models instead of the original models, whenever possible, to illustrate the basic economics behind the main conclusions of this literature. In what follows, we take up each of the three questions in turn.

2. Would firms benefit from targeted pricing?

The simple answer to this question is 'it depends'! That is, of course, the easy part of the answer. The difficult part is to figure out what it depends on. Many researchers, such as Thisse and Vives (1988), Shaffer and Zhang (1995), Bester and Petrakis (1996), Chen (1997), Fudenberg and Tirole (2000), and Taylor (2003), have investigated this question with different models. We can use a simple model to capture the gist of their arguments.

In any market where targeted pricing is implemented, consumers must be heterogeneous in their preferences and firms must be selling a differentiated product. We can use the standard Hotelling (1929) model to capture both market conditions. Concretely, consider two firms located respectively at 0 and 1 of a unit Hotelling line and set their prices independently. For simplicity, we assume away all production costs. Consumers in the market are uniformly distributed along the unit line and we normalize the number of consumers to one, so we do not need to carry a constant around in our computations. To follow convention, we further assume that each consumer in the market makes at most only a single unit purchase if such a purchase generates positive surplus.

Before a consumer makes a purchase, she will compare the surplus she would get from Firm 1 with that from Firm 2, and choose the firm that provides the most surplus. To make the choice decision more concrete, let V stand for the reservation price that consumers are willing to pay for their 'ideal' product and let t denote the unit transportation cost that a consumer must incur to purchase a non-ideal product. Then, for a consumer located at $x \in [0, 1]$, if she purchases from Firm 1 at the price p_1, the surplus she obtains is $V - p_1 - tx$. If she purchases from Firm 2 at the price p_2, her surplus is $V - p_2 - t(1 - x)$. Thus, depending on the location x, even if both firms charge the same price to a consumer, the consumer will have a definite preference in terms of where she prefers to make the purchase – she will purchase the product that is closer to her ideal product. This preference heterogeneity gives rise to the possibility of using targeted pricing to compete for customers.

To isolate the effect of targeted pricing, let us first establish the benchmark of uniform pricing where each firm can only charge one price to all consumers. In this case, we can easily identify the location of marginal consumers $\tilde{x}$ such that to the left of $\tilde{x}$, all consumers purchase from Firm 1 and, to the right, all consumers purchase from Firm 2. From $V - p_1 - t\tilde{x} = V - p_2 - t(1 - \tilde{x})$, we have

$$\tilde{x} = \frac{p_2 - p_1 + t}{2t} \qquad (14.1)$$

Then it is easy to write down each firm's payoff function and they are, respectively, $\pi_1 = p_1\tilde{x}$ and $\pi_2 = p_2(1 - \tilde{x})$. As each firm sets its price to maximize its payoffs, we can derive the equilibrium prices and profits from the first-order conditions and they are, respectively, $p_1 = p_2 = t$ and $\pi_1 = \pi_2 = t/2$. The equilibrium is illustrated in Figure 14.1.

In this equilibrium of uniform pricing, the two competing firms share the market equally, i.e. $\tilde{x} = \frac{1}{2}$. A firm has no incentive to price more aggressively to gain a larger market share in this case because by cutting its price to lure marginal consumers away from the competition, the firm also cuts its price to all consumers who would have purchased from the

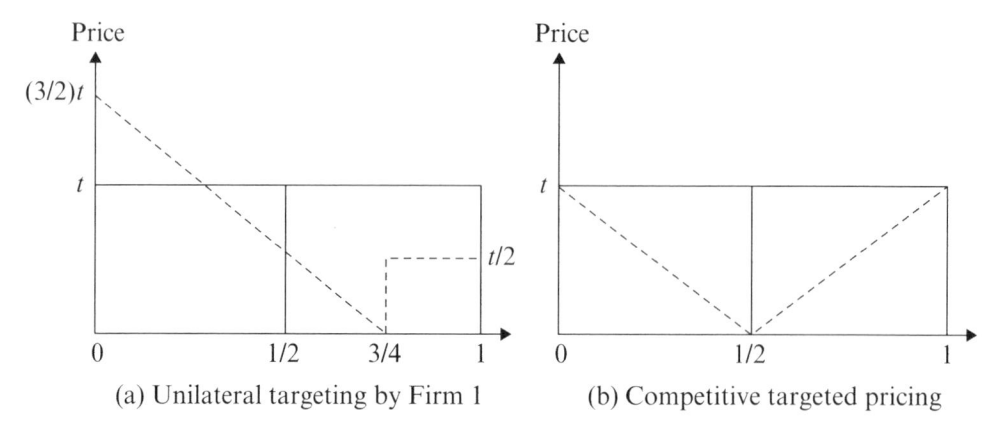

Figure 14.1 Equilibrium prices and market share

Note: The benchmark case of uniform pricing is illustrated with solid lines in both cases.

(a) Unilateral targeting by Firm 1

(b) Competitive targeted pricing

firm without the price cut. In other words, without the flexibility of charging different customers at different locations a different price, a firm must leave more money on the table for those non-marginal customers in order to generate more incremental sales. However, targeted pricing gets a firm out of that bind and gives it the needed flexibility.

To see this, suppose that Firm 1 suddenly gains the capability of implementing targeted pricing in the sense that it can set location-specific prices $p_1(x)$ for all $x \in [0, 1]$, but Firm 2 cannot. In this case, in any equilibrium, there still exists an $\tilde{x}$ such that all consumers located to the right of $\tilde{x}$ will purchase from Firm 2 and to the left from Firm 1. Then, at $\tilde{x}$, given that Firm 1 can charge a location-specific price $p_1(\tilde{x})$, it must be the case that Firm 1 sets $p_1(\tilde{x}) = 0$, which is Firm 1's marginal cost. Otherwise, Firm 1 can always lower its $p_1(\tilde{x})$ slightly to secure the patronage of the consumers located at $\tilde{x}$ and increase its profit. This means that for any given p_2, we can obtain the location of the marginal consumers for this case of unilateral targeting by replacing p_1 in equation (14.1) with 0, i.e. $\tilde{x} = (p_2 + t)/2t$.

To determine Firm 1's prices for consumers located at $x < \tilde{x}$, we note that Firm 1 has no incentives to offer to anyone a price that is lower than what is needed to make a consumer indifferent between buying from Firm 1 and from Firm 2. In other words, the equilibrium $p_1(x)$ is determined by setting $V - p_1(x) - tx = V - p_2 - t(1-x)$ for $x < \tilde{x}$. Therefore, we should have in equilibrium

$$p_1(x) = \begin{cases} p_2 + t(1-2x) & \text{if } x \leq \tilde{x}, \\ 0 & \text{if otherwise} \end{cases} \quad (14.2)$$

Firm 1's payoff is then given by $\pi_1 = \int_0^{\tilde{x}} p_1(x)dx$ and Firm 2's payoff by $\pi_2 = p_2(1 - \tilde{x})$. By taking the first-order condition with respect to Firm 2's payoff,[2] we can easily

---

[2] Here, we follow the example in Thisse and Vives (1988) to treat Firm 1 as a price follower when it implements targeted pricing because of its pricing flexibility.

determine the optimal price for Firm 2 and hence the optimal pricing schedule for Firm 1. We illustrate this equilibrium of unilateral targeting in Figure 14.1(a).

In this equilibrium of unilateral targeted pricing, Firm 1 is better off, with its profit increasing from $t/2$ in the case of uniform pricing to $\frac{9}{16}t$. From Figure 14.1(a), we can see that Firm 1 is better off for two reasons. First, Firm 1 can tailor its prices to customers based on their strength of preference, offering varying discounts to those who have progressively stronger preferences for Firm 2. This flexibility in pricing helps Firm 1 to increase its market share from $\frac{1}{2}$ to $\frac{3}{4}$ (see Figure 14.1a). This is 'the market share effect'. Second, Firm 1 can also charge progressively higher prices to those who have progressively stronger preferences for its own product. This is 'the price discrimination effect'. Because of these two effects, most practitioners and experts have intuitively come to the conclusion that targeted pricing will always benefit the practicing firm.

However, this need not be the case. In Figure 14.1(a), we get a hint as to why a practicing firm may not benefit in a competitive context. When both firms adopts uniform pricing, they each set their price at t. However, when Firm 1 has the capability of deploying targeted pricing, Firm 2 responds by lowering its price from t to $t/2$ in an effort to counter the threat of targeted pricing from Firm 1. In other words, targeted pricing can potentially trigger more intense price competition. We can see this 'price competition effect' more clearly if we also allow Firm 2 to implement targeted pricing so that we have competitive targeted pricing in the market.

When both firms can set a location-specific pricing schedule, respectively $p_1(x)$ and $p_2(x)$, we can follow the similar steps as in the case of unilateral targeted pricing to derive the equilibrium pricing schedules, which are given below and illustrated in Figure 14.1(b).

$$p_1(x) = \begin{cases} t(1-2x) & \text{if } x \leq \frac{1}{2} \\ 0 & \text{if otherwise} \end{cases} \quad (14.3)$$

$$p_2(x) = \begin{cases} t(2x-1) & \text{if } x \geq \frac{1}{2} \\ 0 & \text{if otherwise} \end{cases} \quad (14.4)$$

In this equilibrium, the market share effect disappears, as the competing firms share the market equally (see Figure 14.1(b)). The price discrimination effect is still present, as we can see from the above pricing schedules. However, it is not strong enough to outweigh the price competition effect. This is reflected in the fact that both firms' pricing schedules are uniformly below t, the price that both firms set in the benchmark case of no targeted pricing. As a result, both firms are worse off with a lower profit of $t/4$.

The fact that competitive targeted pricing could make practicing firms worse off is perhaps not very surprising in hindsight. As pointed out by Corts (1998, p. 321), 'Competitive price discrimination may intensify competition by giving firms more weapons with which to wage their war.' When competing firms all have the flexibility of targeted pricing, they can target each other's customers with great accuracy and efficiency, and they will all have to compete for each individual customer in the market. For that reason, the intensity of price competition increases to the detriment of both firms. Also for that reason, the early studies on competitive targeted pricing, such as Thisse and Vives (1988), Shaffer and Zhang (1995), Bester and Petrakis (1996), Chen (1997), Fudenberg and Tirole (2000), and Taylor (2003), have all come to the same conclusion, in varying institutional contexts and with different models, that competitive targeted pricing will make practicing firms worse off.

This conclusion, of course, does not bode well for the future of targeted pricing. However, some reflection based on the analysis we have conducted so far tells us that this conclusion is not inevitable. This is because even if the flexibility compels firms to wrestle each other for each customer in the market, it does not give all firms an equal chance to win each wrestling match. In fact, if a firm is a 'Sumo wrestler' to start with, the flexibility may give it a chance to wrestle for each customer and win each customer, too. In that asymmetrical case, the market share effect can be enhanced and the price discrimination effect can be amplified so that the Sumo wrestler can be better off with targeted pricing than without. Then the question is what kind of firms might be Sumo wrestlers? Shaffer and Zhang (2002) address that question.

To illustrate the argument in that article, consider the following simple model where Firm 1 sells a high-quality product and Firm 2 sells a low-quality product. Suppose that all consumers are willing to pay V for a low-quality product, but $V + \theta$ for the high-quality product, where $\theta \in [0, 1]$ follows a uniform distribution. In other words, the willingness to pay for the low-quality product is constant, but that for the high-quality product varies among consumers. For simplicity, we still maintain the assumption that all costs are zero. Thus, if both high- and low-quality firms charge a single price, respectively p_l and p_h, we must have the payoff functions for both firms given respectively by $\pi_l = p_l(p_h - p_l)$ and $\pi_h = p_h(1 - p_h + p_l)$. From first-order conditions, we can easily determine equilibrium prices and profits. They are $p_l = \frac{1}{3}, p_h = \frac{2}{3}, \pi_l = \frac{1}{9}$, and $\pi_h = \frac{4}{9}$. In this equilibrium, the high-quality firm gets two-thirds of the market and the low quality firm one-third.

Now imagine that both firms can costlessly implement targeted pricing. In this case, it is easy to see that in equilibrium the high-quality firm can corner all consumers by charging θ, the premium that a consumer is willing to pay for a high-quality product. The low-quality firm will charge zero (the marginal cost) to all consumers, but sell to none. Here, the low-quality firm makes zero profit under competitive targeted pricing and the high-quality firm's profit is $\pi_h = \frac{1}{2} > \frac{4}{9}$. The high-quality firm is the Sumo wrestler!

The model used in Shaffer and Zhang (2002) is more general than this simple model suggests, and it incorporates the four main features of targeted pricing: individual addressability, personalized incentives, competition and costs of targeting (Blattberg and Deighton, 1991; Schultz, 1994). The model also allows customers to be loyal to different firms in a competitive context and introduces differences in the size of customer groups loyal to the respective firms.

Their analysis shows that a firm can benefit from competitive targeting after all, even if all consumers are perfectly addressable. The firm that commands a larger loyal following, i.e. that has more customers who are willing to pay a premium for its product, will be the one that benefits. This is because under competitive targeted pricing, a firm's expected payoff from consumers who are contested by competing firms comes only from the loyalty that these consumers have for the firm's brand. Although a firm is always able to outbid its competitor for the consumers who prefer its brand, targeted pricing dissipates all potential rents except for the premiums that contested consumers are willing to pay for a brand. Therefore, in an information-intensive marketing environment where a firm's customers are not anonymous to competition, the last line of defense in a firm's battle to acquire or retain a customer is the customers' relative preference for the firm.

In this context, one can readily appreciate the vital importance of individual (rather than average) consumer loyalty in the information age and hence the need for a firm to invest in enhancing consumer brand loyalty through quality, relationship, satisfaction, one-to-one marketing etc.

More recently, Liu and Zhang (2006) have shown that in a channel context, manufacturers are typically such Sumo wrestlers if they are in a position to dictate the wholesale prices for retailers. This is because, without targeted pricing at the retail level, a retailer can always commit to a single price markup and leverage the market coverage to get the manufacturer to charge a low wholesale price. In other words, the retailer can credibly threaten to raise its retail price to all end users automatically and sell to far fewer customers if the manufacturer charges a high wholesale price. To alleviate 'the double marginalization problem', the manufacturer will not charge too high a wholesale price. However, with the ability to implement targeted pricing at the retail level, the retailer loses such a leverage somewhat, as it will use variable markups to sell to end users. This means that the manufacturer can raise its wholesale price without worrying too much about worsening the double marginalization problem.

Of course, the existence of a Sumo wrestler, or asymmetry in competition, is a more obvious situation where a firm can benefit from competitive targeted pricing. A tougher question to answer is, whether in a situation where competing firms are equally matched and they all implement targeted pricing, can any of them become better off? This is a situation where the early literature has shown that the market share effect of targeted pricing disappears and the price competition effect dominates. More recently, however, Chen et al. (2001) have concluded that a firm, indeed all competing firms, can become better off in that situation.

Chen et al. (2001) note that targeted pricing in practice is imperfect in that competing firms can never distinguish different types of customers in a market with certitude.[3] For instance, a firm's own loyal customer may be mistaken for a switcher because of a firm's imperfect targetability. When firms compete with imperfect targetability, what they term the 'mistargeting effect' will be at work, which can help to moderate price competition to the benefit of all competing firms. More concretely, firms always want to charge a high price to price-insensitive loyal customers and a low price to price-sensitive switchers. Due to imperfect targetability, each firm will mistakenly classify some price-sensitive switchers as price-insensitive loyal customers and charge them all a high price. These misclassifications thus allow its competitors to acquire those mistargeted customers without lowering their prices and, hence, reduce the rival firm's incentive to cut prices. This effect softens price competition in the market, which benefits all competing firms. Of course, the magnitude of this effect will depend on targetability, and at a sufficiently high targetability, say perfect targetability, this effect can be weakened to the extent that neither firm can benefit from competitive targeted pricing.

Thus this study narrows down the conditions under which competing firms cannot benefit from competitive targeted pricing. There are two: firm symmetry and (sufficiently) high targetability. In addition, the article points out that imperfect targetability also

---

[3] Interestingly, Chen and Iyer (2002) show that competing firms may even purposefully underinvest in their targetability so that they do not identify consumers perfectly.

qualitatively changes the incentive environment for competing firms engaging in targeted pricing. For instance, superior knowledge of individual customers can be a competitive advantage, but competing firms may all benefit from exchanging individual customer information with each other at the nascent stage of targeted pricing when firms' targetability is low. Indeed, under certain circumstances, a firm may even find it profitable to give away this information unilaterally. In terms of competitive dynamics, Chen et al. (2001) suggest that competitive targeted pricing does not doom small firms. In fact, targeted pricing may provide a good opportunity for a small firm to leapfrog a large firm. The key to leapfrogging is a high level of targetability or customer knowledge. In other words, small firms can also become the Sumo wrestler if they manage to gain a high level of targetability first.

The literature has also looked into behavior-based targeted pricing. When consumers with varying brand preferences are all passive recipients of a targeted price and they do not react when a firm takes away their surplus, firms can understandably become better off. However, when more and more consumers become aware of the practice of targeted pricing, many of them will start to react to the practice and behave strategically (Feinberg et al., 2002). For instance, a price-insensitive customer may fake being a price-sensitive customer by refusing to pay a high price. In that case, could targeted pricing still benefit a practicing firm? Villas-Boas (2004) offers an intriguing answer to that question.

Villas-Boas (2004) shows that if a firm targets a consumer based on the consumer's past buying behavior and the consumer knows about it, the consumer may start to behave strategically: choosing to forego a purchase today to avoid being recognized as a price-insensitive customer and hence to avail herself of a low price targeted at new buyers. Such strategic waiting on the part of consumers can hurt a firm both through reducing the benefit of price discrimination and through foregone sales. As a result, even a monopoly cannot benefit from targeted pricing.[4] A more recent study by Acquisti and Varian (2005) has come to a similar conclusion from the perspective of the revelation mechanism design, showing that it is never profitable for a monopolist to condition its pricing on purchase history, unless a sufficient number of consumers are not sophisticated enough to see through the seller's targeting strategy or the firm can provide enhanced services to boost consumer valuation subsequent to a purchase. In a competitive context, however, a firm cannot benefit from targeted pricing based on consumer purchase history at all.

Both studies have pointed to the difficulty in implementing price discrimination when consumers can anticipate future prices and make intertemporal adjustments. Without the benefit of price discrimination, targeted pricing will most likely make a firm worse off. However, just as there are reasons to believe that the existence of rational, forward-looking consumers can reduce the benefit of targeted pricing, there are also reasons to believe that their existence may enhance that benefit, too. For instance, in a two-period game, Fudenberg and Tirole (2000) show that a firm always has the incentive to offer discounts to the rival firm's customers who have revealed, through their prior purchase, their preference for the rival firm's product. In other words, once a firm figures out who is buying from whom, the firm always has an incentive to poach the rival's customers with a low price. Anticipating such a poaching discount, consumers should become less price

---

[4] In an earlier paper, Villas-Boas (1999) also shows that competing firms can all be worse off.

sensitive when they make their initial purchases, and this demand-driven effect should help to sustain high initial prices in the market. These high initial prices in turn should benefit competing firms.

On the supply side, the pursuit of targeted pricing can also generate some strategic benefits. In practice, firms frequently need to 'experiment' with their prices in order to gauge customer price sensitivities. A long stream of research on price experimentation shows that a firm may optimally experiment with its pricing decision at the cost of its current profit in order to enhance the informativeness of the observed market demand, and such information can help the firm to increase its future profit (Kihlstrom et al., 1984; Mirman et al., 1993). Interestingly, Mirman et al. (1994) subsequently show that such information always helps a monopolist, but may be detrimental to competing firms. Chen and Zhang (forthcoming) have recently extended the analysis to the case where firms may experiment with their prices not to gauge an uncertain market demand more accurately but to recognize the individual segments of a certain market demand for the purpose of implementing targeted pricing.

Chen and Zhang (forthcoming) show that the pursuit of customer recognition by competing firms based on consumer purchase history can moderate price competition in a market. This is because, as a firm strives to glean more accurate, actionable customer information for subsequent targeted pricing, it must seek to sell to a small number of customers, or to achieve 'exclusivity'. Exclusivity can come only with a high price, relative to the rival's price, such that not all consumers will purchase from the firm. Consequently, the firm has a strategic incentive to raise its price in its pursuit of customer recognition and price discrimination, to the benefit of all competing firms. In fact, Chen and Zhang (forthcoming) show that, paradoxically, a monopolist can become worse off because of the firm's quest for customer recognition, similar to Villas-Boas (1999), but competing firms can all become better off when they all actively pursue customer recognition. This is because competition amplifies what they term as 'the price-for-information' effect, as with competition the rise in one firm's price will, in turn, induce the increase in the rival's price and vice versa.

From all these discussions, we can draw one clear conclusion about targeted pricing: firms do not automatically benefit from this practice. There are mitigating factors, such as competition, strategic customers and mature markets that would prevent a firm from benefiting from this flexible, competitive form of price discrimination. Only those firms that command customer loyalty through product quality, branding, service, relationship marketing etc., and those that have an information advantage, are positioned to reap the benefits of targeted pricing.

3. What is the optimal targeting strategy?

To benefit from targeted pricing, a firm must target the right customers with the right incentives. Who are the right customers to target with discounts: a firm's own customers or the competition's? The literature has shed a good deal of light on this question.

Intuitively, to any firm, the customers who are currently buying from the competition are those who will deliver incremental sales if they are switched over. Therefore a firm should generate most incremental sales and get the most bang out of its discount dollars if it targets the competition's customers. It turns out that poaching with targeted pricing or the strategy of 'paying customers to switch' can be the optimal strategy in a competitive equilibrium (Shaffer and Zhang, 1995; Chen, 1997; Fudenberg and Tirole, 2000). This is perhaps why magazines offer new subscribers' discounts, and why AT&T and MCI target each other's customers with switching checks.

However, some reflection here should reveal that this strategy cannot be optimal all the time or for all firms. For instance, MCI may very well benefit from poaching AT&T's customers, as AT&T had a bigger market share and hence more (marginal) customers to lose, but why should AT&T follow the same strategy by poaching MCI's customers? Doesn't it make more sense for AT&T to adopt the strategy of 'paying customers to stay'?

Shaffer and Zhang (2000) develop a model where consumers differ in their preferences and competing firms have different installed customer bases. In this model, firms cannot target individual customers, but only their own or the competition's customer base. From the analysis of this model, they come to the conclusion that the benefits of 'paying customers to switch' do not carry over to markets where competing firms are not equally matched. When firms are asymmetric, it can be optimal for a firm to use the strategy of 'paying customers to stay', but surprisingly the identity of this firm cannot be determined by firm size alone. Either the smaller firm or the bigger firm, but not both, may find it optimal to charge a lower price to its own customers. What determines a firm's targeting strategy is whether the firm's own customers are more price elastic than the rival's customers from the firm's own perspective.

To use the example in Shaffer and Zhang (2000, p. 413) to illustrate the point, suppose Pizza Hut and Domino's can both price-discriminate between own customers and the rival's customers. In this case, we might expect that for both firms, the customers located further away from a firm tend to be more price elastic and the customers located near a firm are more price inelastic. Then, regardless of its market share, each firm should pay customers to switch, poaching the customers on the competition's turf. On the other hand, suppose Domino's delivers, but Pizza Hut does not. Then, because Domino's delivers, customers close to Pizza Hut incur little cost to switch to Domino's, while the cost for Domino's customers (who live far from Pizza Hut) to switch to dining in at Pizza Hut is significant, so that few of them will switch even when offered a substantial discount. In this case, Pizza Hut should pay customers to stay, while Domino's Pizza should pay customers to switch.

The analysis in Shaffer and Zhang (2000) also generates three additional insights into how a firm should implement its targeted pricing. First, the firm with the higher regular price should offer the larger discount (e.g. AT&T will offer a larger discount than MCI). Second, the firm with the higher regular price always pays customers to switch. In other words, if a firm's optimal pricing strategy is pay to stay, it must have the lower regular price, too. However, the converse is not true: depending on parameters, the firm with the lower regular price may either want to pay customers to switch (MCI's strategy) or pay customers to stay (Sprint's strategy). Third, if each firm offers a discount to the same consumer group, the firm that is paying customers to switch will have the higher discount. This partially reflects the fact that it is more difficult to acquire the customers who prefer the rival's product in the first place.

Of course, this clear division of own versus competition's customers loses much of its significance when firms can identify and address each individual customer in the market and all consumers are potentially contested for by all competing firms. In that case, as shown in Shaffer and Zhang (1995 and 2000), firms need to pursue both offensive and defensive targeting simultaneously: they must offer well-tailored incentives to pay customers to stay as well as to switch.

Concretely, in situations where the targeting cost is quite significant, firms should never target all consumers and they should only target consumers in a well-selected 'targeting zone' – the customers who can be profitably contested. Furthermore, they should target both their own and their competitors' customers in the targeting zone with a certain amount of randomness. As targeting costs decrease, firms should move away from offensive targeting to defensive targeting. The reason is that, as costs decrease, a firm has an incentive to target more of the rival's customers. However, the more it does so, the more consumers with stronger loyalty to the rival's product are targeted, so that offensive targeting becomes less effective in switching these consumers. This explains why the intensity of a firm's offensive targeting should level off as the cost of targeting decreases. In contrast, as a firm's more loyal customers are exposed to the rival's targeting due to a lower targeting cost, the firm faces increasingly more incentives to retain these profitable customers through defensive targeting. For that reason, the intensity of defensive targeting should pick up as the cost of targeting decreases.

One side effect of broad targeting is this phenomenon of massive customer churn, where a large number of customers switch to a less-preferred product because of targeted discounts. Shaffer and Zhang (2000) provide a fresh perspective on this phenomenon and suggest that customer churn need not always cause undue alarm. This is because customer churn results from firms taking chances with their loyal customers in order to capture as much consumer surplus from them as possible. From this perspective, it should not be eliminated. In addition, enhancing consumer loyalty should not always lead to churn reduction. This is because a higher consumer loyalty should also give competing firms more incentives to take chances with their loyal customers. The optimal way to manage customer churn is to engage in more defensive targeting (e.g. loyalty programs) as the cost of targeting decreases.

The cost of targeting and the strength of consumer preferences are but two out of many parameters to which firms should pay attention in adjusting their offensive and defensive targeting strategies. In a recent article, Fruchter and Zhang (2004) develop a differential game of competitive targeted pricing and show that a firm's optimal targeting strategies, both offensive and defensive, depend on its actual market share, the relevant redemption rate of its targeted promotions, customer profitability and the effectiveness of its targeted promotions. In the short run, a firm should operationalize its targeting strategies by adjusting its planned promotional incentives on the basis of the observed differences between actual and planned market shares, and between actual and planned redemption rates. In the long run, a focus on customer retention is not an optimal strategy for all firms in a competitive context. A firm with a sufficiently large market share should focus on customer retention (defensive targeting), whereas a firm with a sufficiently small market share should stress customer acquisition (offensive targeting). This is the case regardless of whether or not the firm is more effective in targeting its current customers. When market shares are more evenly divided, the optimal strategy for a firm is to focus more on customer acquisition than retention.

However, no matter how thoughtful and diligent a firm is in implementing its targeting strategy, it may still be doomed to fail if it ignores the customers' emotional reactions to

Table 14.1   Parameter estimates and effects tests

	Behaviorist	No switching	No loyalty	No betrayal	No Jealousy	Strong	None
		$s = 0$	$l = 0$	$b = 0$	$j = 0$	$bj = 0$	All = 0
s	0.2341	–	0.1434	0.2612	0.1875	0.2300	–
l	0.2040	0.1535	–	0.2416	0.1832	0.2030	–
b	0.1241	0.1950	0.1607	–	0.1679	–	–
j	0.1187	0.0796	0.0539	0.1626	–	–	–
p versus behaviorist	–	*	*	*	*	*	*
p versus strong	*	a	a	*	*	–	*
p versus none	*	*	*	*	*	*	–

Notes:
a As these do not nest the strong-rationality model, they are not directly comparable.
* $p < 0.001$.

Source: Feinberg et al. (2002), table 6.

targeted pricing. When more and more customers become aware of the practice of targeted pricing, a practicing firm cannot simply assume that consumers will calmly accept whatever price a firm imposes on them. Indeed, amazon.com learned the hard way, when it experimented in 2000 with using targeted pricing to sell DVDs and books, that 'Few things stir up a consumer revolt quicker than the notion that someone else is getting a better deal' (*The Washington Post*, 27 September 2000, p. A1). Amazon.com had a PR disaster on its hands when some consumers found out through Internet chat rooms and media reports that they were willfully subjected to higher prices than others who did not necessarily deserve a discount. Should a firm still use targeted pricing when consumers become aware? Feinberg et al. (2002) look into that question.

Through experiments, Feinberg et al. show that consumers care about not only the prices they themselves have to pay, but also the prices other groups of potential purchasers pay at the same firm. As shown in Table 14.1, by comparing statistical results for nested models, Feinberg et al. establish that targeted pricing in a competitive context can generate two behavioral effects among customers. First, 'consumers' preference for their favored firm will decrease if it offers a special price to switchers (the other firms present customers) and not to loyals (their own firm's present customers)'. Because of this, loyals are less likely to purchase from their favored firm. This is what they term as 'the betrayal effect', which has a sizable magnitude of 0.1241, as indicated in Table 14.1. Second, 'Consumers' preference for their favored firm will decrease if another firm offers a special price to its own loyals.' This is 'the jealousy effect', which also tends to reduce the likelihood of consumers' purchases at their favored firm. The magnitude of this effect is comparable to that of the betrayal effect (0.1187). However, the presence of the two effects in the marketplace does not mean that a firm should never use targeted pricing. All it means is that a firm should think through its strategies carefully and take advantage of those effects when they are favorable and mitigate them when they are not. In general, this involves a firm recognizing these psychological effects and adjusting its targeting strategy from a more offensive-oriented to a more defensive-oriented strategy. This analysis was recently extended by the same authors to an environment of competitive price increase (Krishna et al., 2007).

4. Does social welfare improve?

Many researchers have argued that targeted pricing can potentially harm social welfare (Shaffer and Zhang, 1995; Chen, 1997; Fudenberg and Tirole, 2000). This is because targeted pricing can distort consumer choices and motivate consumers to buy products that are less preferred. By implication, regulatory interventions might be warranted. However, this line of reasoning works only when the market size is fixed, firms do not make any other non-price adjustments because of targeted pricing, and strategic consumers do not exist in the market. In the real world, it would be difficult to find a market where all three conditions are present.

When the size of a market is expandable, it is easy to see why social welfare may improve due to competitive targeted pricing. Targeted pricing will allow all competing firms to lower their prices to 'marginal consumers' who would otherwise not purchase from any firm. The increased sales will increase social welfare, as firms will never sell at a price below its marginal cost and consumers will never purchase a product that does not provide a positive surplus.

Even if the size of a market cannot expand, social welfare can still improve if competing firms make long-term adjustments, say changing their product locations to compete for customers. Lederer and Hurter (1986) investigate that possibility in an elegant, but rather involved, model. Here, we can use a much simpler model to illustrate that possibility.

Consider again the simple Hotelling model that we used in Section 2. Instead of assuming that two competing firms are located at the respective ends of the Hotelling line, we now assume that two firms can choose their respective locations a and b on the line, where $0 \leq a \leq b \leq 1$, before they make their pricing decisions. In other words, firms know each other's locations before they make their respective pricing decisions. To make sure that for any pair of locations (a, b), the equilibrium exists for the pricing game, we further assume that consumer transportation cost is quadratic in the distance traveled. Thus, for a consumer located at $x \in (a, b)$, her utility from buying from Firm 1 and Firm 2 is given by $V - p_1 - t(x - a)^2$ and $V - p_2 - t(b - x)^2$ respectively. We shall maintain all other assumptions about the Hotelling model that we made in Section 2.

As D'Aspremont et al. (1979) have shown, if the two firms are restricted to uniform pricing, each charging a single price, the firms will choose their product locations respectively at 0 and 1 in equilibrium. In other words, the competing firms want to follow 'the principle of maximum differentiation', maximally differentiating themselves to moderate price competition in the market. In equilibrium, the two firms share the market equally, with the indifferent customers being located at $\frac{1}{2}$, and they each charge a price of t. In this market, given that the total demand is fixed, any change in social welfare will depend only on the total disutility (or the total transportation cost) that consumers in the market must suffer, which is $\frac{1}{12}t$.

Now imagine that in this market both firms adopt targeted pricing. Then, for any pair of locations (a, b), if the consumers located at x purchase from Firm 1, the price they are paying must be the premium they are willing to pay for Firm 1's product because of their location, which is the difference in transportation costs between traveling to Firm 1 and to Firm 2. Thus competitive targeted pricing introduces the incentives for a firm to minimize the costs for consumers to travel to the firm in its location decision, as doing so will allow the firm to charge higher prices subsequently. Then competing firms will choose their locations at $\frac{1}{4}$ and $\frac{3}{4}$ respectively, the locations that will minimize the total disutility in the market. At these socially optimal locations, the total disutility in the market is only $\frac{1}{48}t$ and thus competitive targeted pricing improves social welfare by $\frac{3}{48}t$.

Intuitively, competitive targeted pricing will expose all consumers to competition, and what each firm can charge will depend on how happy individual consumers are about a firm relative to its rival. Therefore firms will have to make customers happy to keep themselves profitable and hence comes social welfare improvement. Clearly, this source of social welfare improvement is generalizable to other situations and even to many other decisions that competing firms have to make. For instance, social welfare also improves by the same amount if firms were to pursue 'the principle of minimum differentiation' prior to the introduction of targeted pricing (Zhang, 1995). It is also likely that because of competitive targeted pricing, a firm's service provisions (Armstrong and Vickers, 2001), marketing expenditures, quality improvements, market entry etc. may also be at the socially optimal levels or close to them (Choudhary et al., 2005; Ghose and Huang, 2006; Liu and Serfes, 2004, 2005).

Finally, as shown in Chen and Zhang (forthcoming), the existence of strategic consumers in the market can also provide an opportunity for competitive targeted pricing to improve social welfare. This is because targeted pricing allows a firm to price-discriminate and hence to discourage strategic consumers from waiting for or foregoing purchases. As a result, sales increase even if no new customer enters the market.

Of course, there could be other reasons on the cost side or demand side as to why targeted pricing may or may not improve social welfare. However, the literature seems to suggest, on balance, that competitive targeted pricing is social welfare improving. At the minimum, there does not seem to be any solid economic ground at this point to call for any regulatory intervention in targeted pricing.

5. Conclusion

Competitive targeted pricing is a practice that is still evolving rapidly. The theoretical research in the past decade or so has generated some insightful perspectives, which allow us to peer into its future, notwithstanding the fact that the literature itself is also fast evolving. From these theoretical studies, we can perhaps draw three general conclusions about competitive targeted pricing.

First, the practice of targeted pricing has gone significantly beyond the traditional concept of price discrimination. With new information technologies becoming available, practitioners are redefining what is feasible in price discrimination and they have broken out of the confines of traditional practices. Looking into the future, we should not be surprised to see more and more sophisticated, unconventional schemes in targeted pricing. Indeed, as we are marching further into the Information Age, only practitioners' creativity, information technologies and consumer privacy concerns can limit the popularity and varieties of targeted pricing.

Second, unlike the conventional practices of price discrimination where the firm is thought always to benefit, competitive targeted pricing does not always benefit practicing firms. The reason is that better customer targeting by competing firms exposes more consumers to competition. As a result, consumers may all benefit from competitive targeted pricing and social welfare may also improve.

Third, perhaps most interestingly, competitive targeted pricing rewards the 'right' firms with 'right' strategies. The conventional wisdom is that price discrimination benefits monopolistic firms who are deft enough to exploit their market power. In contrast, competitive targeted pricing forces competing firms to contest for, potentially, all consumers. Only the firms that have earned customer liking and command customer loyalty will have the upper hand in winning individual contests and hence benefit from targeted pricing. This cannot help but encourage firms to become more customer and market oriented in the long run.

These three conclusions bode well for the future of competitive targeted pricing. This means that the literature also needs to move forward to facilitate the coming of that future. On the empirical side, a pressing need is to document the benefits of targeted pricing to a firm with some actual performance data, even though from a theoretical perspective there is a compelling logic for such benefits to exist. On the theory side, much research is still needed to understand how targeted pricing may change and interact with other decisions in the marketing mix.

References

Acquisti, Alessandro and Hal R. Varian (2005), 'Conditioning prices on purchase history', *Marketing Science*, **24** (3), 367–81.
Armstrong, Mark and John Vickers (2001), 'Competitive price discrimination', *RAND Journal of Economics*, **32** (4), 579–605.
Bester, H. and E. Petrakis (1996), 'Coupons and oligopolistic price discrimination', *International Journal of Industrial Organization*, **14**, 227–42.
Blattberg, R. and J. Deighton (1991), 'Interactive marketing: exploiting the age of addressability', *Sloan Management Review*, 22 September, 5.
Chen, Yongmin (1997), 'Paying customers to switch', *Journal of Economics and Management Strategy*, **6**, 877–97.
Chen, Yuxin and Ganesh Iyer (2002), 'Research note: consumer addressability and customized pricing', *Marketing Science*, **21** (2), 197–208.
Chen, Yuxin and Z. John Zhang (forthcoming), 'Dynamic targeted pricing with strategic consumers', *International Journal of Industrial Organization*.
Chen, Yuxin, Chakravarthi Narasimhan and Z. John Zhang (2001), 'Individual marketing with imperfect targetability', *Marketing Science*, **20** (1), 23–41.
Choudhary, V., A. Ghose, T. Mukhopadhyay and U. Rajan (2005), 'Personalized pricing and quality differentiation', *Management Science*, **51** (7), 1120–30.
Corts, K. (1998), 'Third-degree price discrimination in oligopoly: all-out competition and strategic commitment', *RAND Journal of Economics*, **29**, 306–23.
D'Aspremont, C., J.J. Gabszewicz and J.F. Thisse (1979), 'On Hotelling's "Stability in competition"', *Econometrica*, **47**, 1145–50.
Desai, Preyas (2001), 'Quality segmentation in spatial markets: when does cannibalization affect product line design?', *Marketing Science*, **20** (3), 265–83.
Desai, Preyas S. and Devavrat Purohit (2004), '"Let me talk to my manager": haggling in a competitive environment', *Marketing Science*, **23** (2), 219–33.
Dong, Xiaojing, Puneet Manchanda and Pradeep K. Chintagunta (2006), 'Quantifying the benefits of individual level targeting in the presence of firm strategic behavior', Working Paper, University of Chicago.
Feinberg, Fred, Aradhna Krishna and Z. John Zhang (2002), 'Do we care what others get? A behaviorist approach to targeted promotions', *Journal of Marketing Research*, **39** (August), 277–91.
Fruchter, Gila and Z. John Zhang (2004), 'Dynamic targeted promotions: a customer retention and acquisition perspective', *Journal of Service Research*, **7** (1), 3–19.
Fudenberg, D. and J. Tirole (2000), 'Customer poaching and brand switching', *RAND Journal of Economics*, **31**, 634–57.

Ghose, A. and K. Huang (2006), 'Personalized pricing and quality customization', Working Paper, New York University.
Hotelling, H. (1929), 'Stability in competition', *Economic Journal*, **39**, 41–57.
Kihlstrom, Richard, Leonard J. Mirman and A. Postlewaite (1984), 'Experimental consumption and the "Rothschild effect"', in M. Boyer and R.E. Kihlstrom (eds), *Bayesian Models of Economic Theory*, Amsterdam: Elsevier, pp. 279–302.
Krishna, Aradhna, Fred Feinberg and Z. John Zhang (2007), 'Should price increases be targeted? Pricing power and selective versus across-the-board price increases', *Management Science*, **53** (9), September, 1407–22.
Lederer, P. and A. Hurter, Jr (1986), 'Competition of firms: discriminatory pricing and location', *Econometrica*, **54**, 623–40.
Liu, Qihong and Konstantinos Serfes (2004), 'Quality of information and oligopolistic price discrimination', *Journal of Economics and Management Strategy*, **13** (4), 671–702.
Liu, Qihong and Konstantinos Serfes (2005), 'Imperfect price discrimination, market structure, and efficiency', *Canadian Journal of Economics*, **38** (4), 1191–203.
Liu, Yunchuang and Z. John Zhang (2006), 'Research note: the benefits of personalized pricing in a channel', *Marketing Science*, **25** (1), 97–105.
Mirman, Leonard J., Larry Samuelson and Amparo Urbano (1993), 'Monopoly experimentation', *International Economic Review*, **34**, 549–63.
Mirman, Leonard J., Larry Samuelson and Edward E. Schlee (1994), 'Strategic information manipulation in duopolies', *Journal of Economic Theory*, **62**, 363–84.
Pigou, Arthur C. (1929), *The Economics of Welfare*, 3rd edn, London: Macmillan and Co..
Rossi, P.E. and G.M. Allenby (1993), 'A Bayesian approach to estimating household parameters', *Journal of Marketing Research*, **30**, 171–82.
Rossi, P.E., R.E. McCulloch and G.M. Allenby (1996), 'The value of purchase history data in target marketing', *Marketing Science*, **15**, 321–40.
Schultz, D. (1994), 'Driving integration is what IT is all about', *Marketing News*, 10 October, 12.
Shaffer, Greg and Z. John Zhang (1995), 'Competitive coupon targeting', *Marketing Science*, **14** (4), 395–416.
Shaffer, Greg and Z. John Zhang (2000), 'Pay to switch or pay to stay: preference-based price discrimination in markets with switching costs', *Journal of Economics and Management Strategy*, **9** (Fall), 397–424.
Shaffer, Greg and Z. John Zhang (2002), 'Competitive one-to-one promotions', *Management Science*, **48** (9), 1143–60.
Taylor, C. (2003), 'Supplier surfing: competition and consumer behavior in subscription markets', *The RAND Journal of Economics*, **34** (2), 223–46.
Thisse, J.F. and X. Vives (1988), 'On the strategic choice of spatial price policy', *American Economic Review*, **78**, 122–37.
Turco, F. (1993), 'Call is on to switch long-distance firms: pennies, $100 checks among lures', *Arizona Republic*, 7 April, A1.
Villas-Boas, J. Miguel (1999), 'Dynamics competition with customer recognition', *RAND Journal of Economics*, **30**, 604–31.
Villas-Boas, J. Miguel (2004), 'Price cycles in markets with customer recognition', *RAND Journal of Economics*, **35** (3), 486–501.
Zhang, Jie and Michel Wedel (2007), 'The effectiveness of customized promotions in online and offline stores', Working Paper, University of Maryland.
Zhang, Z. John (1995), 'Price-matching policy and the principle of minimum differentiation', *Journal of Industrial Economics*, **43** (3), 287–99.

15 Pricing in marketing channels*
K. Sudhir and Sumon Datta

Abstract
This chapter provides a critical review of research on pricing within a channel environment. We first describe the literature in terms of increasing time horizons of decision-making in a channel setting: (1) retail pass-through (2) pricing contracts and (3) channel design, all of which occur within a given market environment. We then describe the emerging empirical literature on structural econometric models of channels and its use in (1) inferring channel participant behavior and (2) policy simulations in a channel setting. We also discuss potential areas for future research in each area.

'Price' and 'channel' are two of the four elements of the marketing mix that managers control, yet they differ fundamentally in how managers can use them to impact market demand. While price is the most flexible, in that managers can change it most easily to impact short-run demand, the distribution channel through which firms reach their end consumer is the least flexible and perhaps the costliest to change in the short run. Therefore channel design is viewed as part of a firm's long-run strategy. Most importantly, in the presence of a typically decentralized distribution channel, an upstream price change by a manufacturer does not affect consumer demand directly, but only through how this upstream price change affects the retail price set downstream in the channel.

In his review of the pricing literature, Rao (1984) stated that 'the issues of pricing along the distribution channel . . . have not received much attention in the literature'. However, over the last 25 years, this gap has been remedied substantially. The tools of game theory have revolutionized the theoretical analysis of pricing within the channel and clarified the many issues about how prices are set within a channel; more importantly, these analyses have offered insights into the optimal long-term channel strategy, given how prices will be set within the channel. A smaller but emerging empirical literature on structural models of channels has provided insights on the behavior of channel participants and tools to perform policy analysis in a channel setting. The purpose of this chapter is to provide a critical review of this literature, identify the key themes of understanding that have emerged from research to date and identify important gaps in our knowledge that would benefit from future research.

Given the short-run nature of price and the long-run nature of the channel, we organize the literature in terms of three key issues of managerial interest that progressively increase in their time horizons for the decision. The three questions are:

1. Conditional on the distribution channel (which is fixed in the short run) and other market characteristics, how can a change in upstream price affect the downstream price seen by the end consumer? This question of 'pass-through' is the most short

---

* We thank the editor Vithala Rao and Jiwoong Shin for comments and suggestions on the chapter.

Market environment

- Channel design
  - Pricing contracts
    - Pass-through

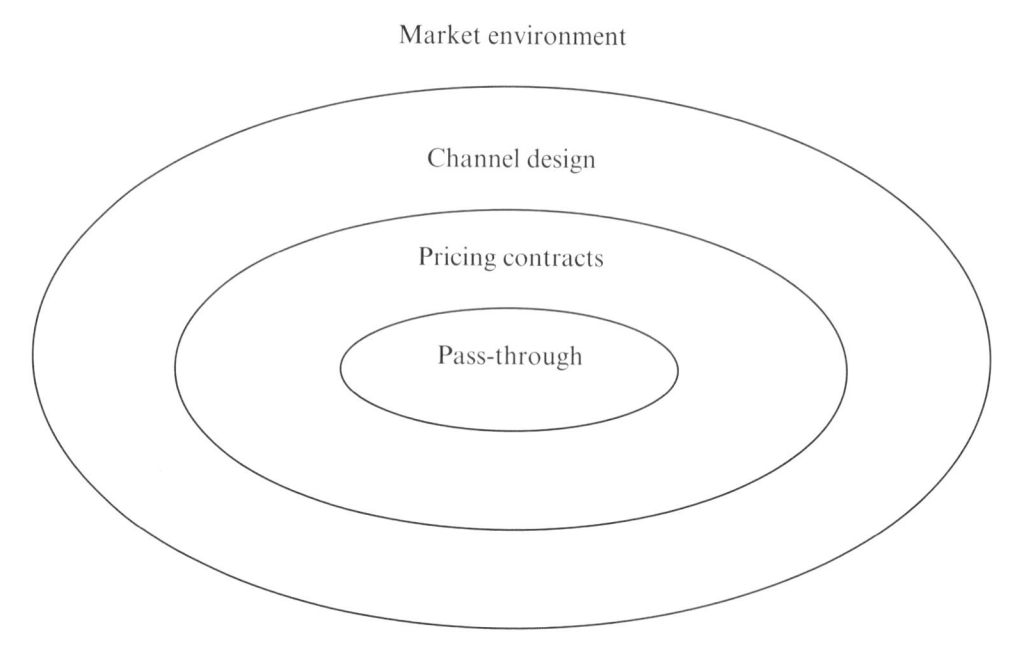

Figure 15.1 Pricing within a channel: key issues

term of the three sets of decisions we consider. Pass-through is of interest to an upstream manager because it determines the extent to which the upstream manufacturer will change prices.

2. Conditional on the distribution channel (which is fixed in the short run) and other market characteristics, what is the best pricing contract to offer to the downstream channel member? This is a medium-term decision, where managers set the 'rules of their interactions' within the existing channel structure. These contracts affect the objective function of the market participants; and managers seek contracts that maximize their profits given a chosen channel structure. Pricing contracts can include linear tariffs, two part-tariffs, quantity discounts, slotting allowances, resale price maintenance (RPM) etc. Note that the types of pricing contracts that can be used may be constrained by law.

3. Finally, given the market characteristics, what is the optimal channel structure and the pricing contract? This is a long-term consideration where managers decide on the nature of channel ownership given the market characteristics. Should a firm vertically integrate or decentralize? Or would a mixed strategy of partial integration, with the manufacturer directly selling along with independent retailers, be optimal? The emergence of the Internet as a sales channel has brought the issue of partial forward integration again into focus in recent years. Since the optimality of the channel structure depends on the nature of pricing contracts that are available to the manufacturer, channel structure design is intimately linked to the pricing strategy.

Finally, all of these decisions are embedded in the market environment in which the firms operate. A schematic way of thinking about these three sets of managerial decisions embedded within a market environment is given in Figure 15.1, where we have laid out each of these questions within concentric circles. The answers to the pass-through questions are linked to the pricing contracts, which are in turn linked to the questions about channel design, which in turn are linked to the market environment in which the firms operate. Since no one contribution can exhaust all possible combinations within the above framework to give us a complete understanding of the tradeoffs involved, one objective of this chapter is to identify generalizable themes across multiple papers that model different combinations of market environments, channel structures and pricing contracts (see Table 15.1). This exercise should also help us identify key gaps in the literature.

We also describe the complementary empirical literature on structural models of channels that have emerged over the last decade. Such models serve (1) to describe manufacturer–retailer interactions that best describe the market and (2) to perform policy analysis of various channel decisions.

Section 2 describes a basic game-theoretic model of channels to illustrate the key modeling issues. Section 3 discusses the pass-through literature, Section 4 discusses the pricing contracts and Section 5 discusses the literature on optimal channel structures. Section 6 reviews the literature on structural econometric models. Section 7 concludes.

2. An illustrative game-theoretic model of channels: the bilateral monopoly

McGuire and Staelin (1983) laid the foundation for game-theoretic analysis of channels in marketing. At the heart of the channel pricing game-theoretic literature is the concept of double marginalization (Spengler, 1950). The concept is applicable whenever there are multiple decision-makers setting prices in stages; but to make the idea concrete we illustrate double marginalization in the simplest setting of a bilateral monopoly.

Consider the following bilateral monopoly setting as shown in Figure 15.2: a manufacturer who produces at a unit cost c sets a wholesale price w to his retailer who in turn sets a retail price p to the consumer. Consumer demand follows a linear demand model: $q = 1 - p$.

Given the sequential nature of the game, we solve for the optimal retail and wholesale prices by backward induction. We begin by choosing retail price p to maximize the

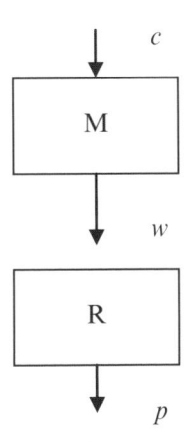

Figure 15.2   A model of bilateral monopoly

Table 15.1 Features modeled in selected papers on channels

Papers	Market characteristics: deterministic/uncertain demand (DD/UD); (durable/nondurable (D/ND)/non-specifiable (NS)	Manufacturers: monopoly/competition (M/C); observed/hidden action (O/H); non-price action (NP)	Retailers: monopoly/competition (M/C); single/multiple (SP/MP); observed/hidden action (O/H); non-price action (NP)	Pricing contract: linear pricing (LP); 2-part tariff (TT)/qty discount (QD)/RPM/slotting allow (SA)	Model characteristics: demand model: linear(L)/nonlinear (NL): logit exponential/general; manufacturer/retailer stackelberg/vertical Nash (MS/RS/VN)
Jeuland and Shugan (1983)	DD, ND	M, O	M, SP, O	LP, QD	L, MS
McGuire and Staelin (1983)	DD, ND	C, O	C, SP, O	LP	L, MS
Coughlan (1985)	DD, ND	C, O	C, SP, O	LP	L, concave, convex, MS
Choi (1991)	DD, ND	C, O	(C, SP); (M, MP), O	LP	L, NL, MS, RS, N
Trivedi (1998)	DD, ND	C, O	C, MP, O	LP	L, MS, RS, N
Desai et al. (2004)	DD, D	M, O	M, SP, O	TT	L, MS
Iyer (1998)	DD, ND	M, O	C, NP		
Moorthy (1987)	DD, ND	M, O	M, SP, O	TT	L, MS
Ingene and Parry (1998)	DD, ND	M, O	C, non-identical, SP, O	TT	L, MS
Iyer and Villas-Boas (2003)	UD, NS	M, O	M, SP, H	TT, bargaining	NL
Romano (1994)	DD, ND	M, H, NP	M, SP, H, NP	RPM	NL, N
Lal (1990)	DD, ND	C, O	M, MP, O	LP, TD	L, N
Gerstner and Hess (1995)	DD, ND	M, O	M, SP, O	LP, manufacturer rebates/coupons	2 segments of high and low valuation, MS
Lal and Villas-Boas (1998)	DD, ND	C, O	C, MP, O	LP, TD	4 segments, MS
Bruce et al. (2005)	DD, D	C, O	C, SP, O	LP, TD	2 segments of high and low valuation, MS
Moorthy (2005)	DD, ND	C, O	C, MP, O	LP, TD	General, MS

Tyagi (1999a)	DD, ND	M, O	M, SP, O	LP, TD	L, concave, convex, MS
Sudhir and Rao (2006)	DD, ND	C, O	M, MP, O	SA	L
Shaffer (1991)	DD, ND	C, O	C, MP, O	LP, SA, RPM	General, MS
Kim and Staelin (1999)	DD, ND	C, O	C, MP, O, NP	LP, SA	L, MS
Chen (2003)	DD, ND	M, O	C, SP, one dominant retailer, O	TT	General, MS
Dukes et al. (2006)	DD, ND	C, O	C, MP, O	Bargaining	L
Chiang et al. (2003)	DD, ND	M, O, direct channel	M, SP, O	LP	L, MS
Kumar and Ruan (2006)	DD, ND	C, O, direct channel	M, MP, O, NP	LP	2 segments of store/brand loyal, L, MS
Purohit (1997)	DD, D	M, O	C, SP, O	LP	Rent vs buy, MS

retailer's objective function: $\Pi^R = (p - w)q(p) = (p - w)(1 - p)$. Taking the first-order conditions with respect to p gives

$$\frac{\partial \Pi^R}{\partial p} = 1 + w - 2p = 0 \Rightarrow p = \frac{1 + w}{2}$$

Therefore retail pass-through measured in this model is given by

$$\frac{\partial p}{\partial w} = \frac{1}{2}$$

The manufacturer then chooses wholesale price w to maximize the manufacturer's objective function:

$$\Pi^M = (w - c)q(p(w)) = (w - c)\left(1 - \frac{1 + w}{2}\right) = (w - c)\left(\frac{1 - w}{2}\right)$$

Taking the first-order conditions with respect to w gives

$$\frac{\partial \Pi^M}{\partial w} = \frac{1 + c - 2w}{2} = 0 \Rightarrow w = \frac{1 + c}{2}$$

Hence retail price is

$$p = \frac{1}{2} + \frac{1 + c}{4} = \frac{3 + c}{4}$$

At the chosen retail and wholesale prices, the manufacturer and retailer profits are

$$\Pi^M = \left(\frac{1 - c}{2}\right)\left(\frac{1 - c}{4}\right) = \frac{(1 - c)^2}{8}; \quad \Pi^R = \left(\frac{1 - c}{4}\right)\left(\frac{1 - c}{4}\right) = \frac{(1 - c)^2}{16}$$

The total channel profit is

$$\Pi^M + \Pi^R = \frac{3}{16}(1 - c)^2$$

As a point of comparison, it is useful to compare the retail prices and total channel profits if the manufacturer owned the retailer and set the final retail price. In that case, the manufacturer's (or the channel's) optimal price is obtained by maximizing $\Pi^c = (p - c)q(p) = (p - c)(1 - p)$. Taking the first-order conditions with respect to p gives

$$\frac{\partial \Pi^c}{\partial p} = 1 + c - 2p = 0 \Rightarrow p = \frac{1 + c}{2}$$

The total channel profit is given by

$$\Pi^c = \frac{(1 - c)^2}{4}$$

The total profit from the vertically integrated channel is therefore greater than profit from the decentralized channel.

The key takeaways from the above model are: first, the price in the vertically integrated channel is lower than the price in the decentralized channel; i.e. in the decentralized channel the retail price is distorted upward from the price that would be observed in the integrated channel. At each stage the monopolist marks up the price; therefore in the integrated channel there is only one monopoly markup, while there are two markups in the channel (one by the manufacturer and one by the retailer). This 'double markup' is referred to as the 'double marginalization' and lends itself to the joke: 'From the consumer's point of view, what is worse than a monopoly? A chain of monopolies.' Second, the total channel profit with vertical integration is greater than the profits in the decentralized channel; therefore in this case, it would be optimal for the manufacturer to set up an integrated channel if it were feasible. Finally, given that $\partial p/\partial w = \frac{1}{2}$ in equilibrium, only 50 percent of the change in wholesale prices is passed through to the consumer.

In this model, we allowed for only a linear price contract between the manufacturer and the retailer. Suppose the manufacturer could use another contract such as a two-part tariff, where the retailer pays not only a unit cost, but also a fixed fee. In such a scenario, it is easy to see from the earlier analysis that the optimal strategy for the manufacturer would be to set the wholesale price at the manufacturer's marginal cost c, and the retailer would set the price at the vertically integrated retail price of $(1 + c)/2$. The manufacturer can then extract the entire profits that would result $[(1 + c)^2]/4$ in the form of fixed fees. Thus, using a two-part tariff, the manufacturer can obtain the vertically integrated channel outcome without having to integrate the channel.

The above illustrative model outlines the issues involved in the three managerial questions raised in the introduction. First, the pass-through with either a linear contact or two-part tariff is 50 percent. Second, the optimal pricing contract for the manufacturer between a unit price and two-part tariff is the two-part tariff. Finally, the profit from the vertically integrated channel and the bilateral monopoly structure is identical for the manufacturer when allowing for both a linear price contract and two-part tariff. But if the manufacturer is restricted to a linear price contract, the total channel profit is greater with a vertically integrated structure.

In the bilateral monopoly model above, a single manufacturer sold a single product at a linear unit price to a single retailer, who in turn sold only that product to the end customer. The demand was modeled using a linear demand model. It was also deterministic, and so there was no uncertainty about the market demand. Finally, manufacturers and retailers had no ability to affect demand, except through the change in price.

Markets of course can differ on every one of the dimensions described above. For instance, there could be competition among manufacturers, and competition among retailers. Each manufacturer or retailer could sell more than one product. Market participants may use objectives such as category profit maximization or only choose to maximize profits of any given product without considering the externalities on other products.

Rather than a linear price, the manufacturers could use other pricing contracts. Examples include nonlinear quantity discounts and two-part tariffs, which are common among franchisers. They could also impose a maximum retail price that retailers can charge, i.e. employ resale price maintenance (RPM). In the short term, they could also offer trade promotions or slotting allowances that involve transfers from manufacturers to the retailer.

Finally, uncertainty in demand can be important. If manufacturers and retailers can affect demand through their actions such as better service, then in the presence of demand uncertainty, the issue of whether participants put in the optimal level of effort to create

Table 15.2 Key characteristics modeled in current research

Channel structure	Manufacturers	• Monopoly/competition • Single/multiple products • Observability of actions
	Retailer	• Monopoly/competition/provision of exclusive territories • Single/multiple products/provision of exclusive dealing • Observability of actions/types
Pricing contracts		• Linear pricing • Two-part tariffs • Quantity discount • Resale price maintenance • Trade promotions • Slotting allowances
Market environment		• Deterministic versus uncertain demand • Relative power between manufacturers and retailers • Presence of store brands • Appropriate model of demand: linear, logit, exponential etc.

demand becomes a challenge. The issues of moral hazard and free-riding in terms of services at both the manufacturer and retailer level becomes critical. Researchers have also observed that the functional form used to model demand affects retail pass-through and optimal equilibrium strategies. Indeed, the range of possible institutional and market characteristics is very large. We summarize the key characteristics that have been modeled in current research in the Table 15.2 above.

3. Retail pass-through

The theoretical literature on pass-through follows two broad streams. The first stream assumes that manufacturers change wholesale prices in response to changing demand and cost conditions (e.g. Moorthy, 2005). The second is based on the price discrimination motive; here trade promotions serve to price-discriminate between price-sensitive and brand-loyal customers (e.g. Lal and Villas-Boas, 1998). In practice, both reasons coexist in the market. Empirical research typically has not drawn a distinction between the different reasons.

3.1 Models where wholesale price changes due to changes in demand and costs
As in our illustrative example in Section 2, own pass-through for a product, j, is typically measured using the comparative static $\partial p_j/\partial w_j$ (e.g. Tyagi, 1999a; Sudhir, 2001; Moorthy, 2005). With multiple products, the extent to which a retailer changes the price of another product i in response to a wholesale price change for product j is termed cross pass-through and is operationalized as $\partial p_i/\partial w_j$.

The literature has highlighted five factors that affect pass-through: (1) retailer objective/pricing rule; (2) demand characteristics; (3) manufacturer–retailer interaction; (4) manufacturer competition; and (5) retail competition. We organize the discussion of the results along these factors. Table 15.3 provides a summary of the key results in the literature.

Depending on the retailer's sophistication, a retailer may use a simple markup rule (a constant markup would imply 100 percent own pass-through and 0 percent cross pass-through) or maximize profits. The theoretical literature on pass-through is based on the assumption that the retailer maximizes a profit objective. Retailers may maximize brand profits, category profits, or, when cross-category effects are important, profits across categories.

A profit-maximizing retailer sets the retail price where marginal cost equals marginal revenue. A reduction in the wholesale price reduces the retailer's marginal cost, and therefore it must reduce its price to reduce its marginal revenue by the same amount. As the responsiveness of the marginal revenue to a change in retail price depends on the concavity of the demand function, the change in retail price corresponding to a change in wholesale price, or the pass-through, depends on the functional form of demand (Lee and Staelin, 1997; Tyagi, 1999a).[1]

Lee and Staelin create a typology of vertical strategic interactions between channel members with pass-through between 0 and 100 percent ($0 < \partial p_i/\partial w_i < 1$, which they refer to as vertical strategic substitutability), pass-through over 100 percent ($\partial p_i/\partial w_i > 1$, vertical strategic complementarity) and pass-through of 100 percent ($\partial p_i/\partial w_i = 0$, vertical strategic independence). Tyagi characterizes demand functions with pass-through greater than or below 100 percent in terms of the convexity of the demand curve. While standard demand functions, such as the linear and the logit (or any concave function), lead to vertical strategic substitutes, the multiplicative demand function (and other, but not all, convex demand functions) leads to vertical strategic complements (also see Sudhir, 2001). When a retailer carrying multiple products maximizes category profits, the magnitude of own pass-through is independent of the product's market share in a linear demand specification (Shugan and Desiraju, 2001) but is inversely proportional to own share in a logit demand specification (Sudhir, 2001).

The level of competition between manufacturers (or products from the same manufacturer) affects cross pass-through. Shugan and Desiraju (2001) show that with a linear demand function the cross pass-through depends on the substitutability of the products. If the cross-price slopes are asymmetric, then cross pass-through will be positive for one product and negative for the other, depending on the direction of asymmetry.

In terms of the effect of manufacturer–retailer relationship on pass-through, the three common relationships studied are: (1) manufacturer Stackelberg, where the manufacturers set the wholesale prices and the retailer takes these wholesale prices as given when setting the retail price; (2) vertical Nash, where manufacturers and retailers set prices simultaneously; and (3) retailer Stackelberg, where the retailer sets the retail price and the manufacturer responds with a wholesale price.

Finally, Moorthy (2005) extends the pass-through results to the case of competing retailers (see also Basuroy et al., 2001). Moorthy studies both the linear and nested logit model,[2]

---

[1] See Tyagi (1999a) for a more detailed explanation as to how the demand function influences pass-through.
[2] In the nested model, consumers make a retailer choice in the first stage and a brand choice in the second stage.

Table 15.3 Summary of pass-through results in the literature

Paper	Market structure	Demand model	Vertical strategic interaction	Retailer objective	Implications for own-brand pass-through ($\partial P_j/\partial w_j$)	Implications for cross-brand pass-through ($\partial P_i/\partial w_j$)
Besanko et al. (1998)	Multiple manufacturers, single retailer	Homogeneous logit	Vertical Nash	Maximize category profits	• Equal to 1	• Equal to 0
Tyagi (1999a)	Single manufacturer, single retailer	Linear; concave; convex	Manufacturer Stackelberg	Maximize profits (only one product)	• Greater or less than 100% depending on demand model	• Not applicable (only one product)
Sudhir (2001)	Multiple manufacturers, single retailer	Homogeneous logit	Manufacturer Stackelberg	Maximize category profits	• Between 0 and 1 • Inversely proportional to own share s_j	• Between 0 and -1 • Magnitude is directly proportional to promoting brand share s_j • Unrelated to s_i
		Homogeneous logit (two brands + outside good)	Manufacturer Stackelberg	Maximize brand profits	• Positive • Inversely related to own share s_j	• Positive • Magnitude is directly proportional to promoting brand share s_j • Directly related to s_i
Shugan and Desiraju (2001)	Multiple manufacturers, single retailer	General linear	Not specified	Maximize category profits	• Between 0 and 1 • Does not vary with share	• 0 if cross-price effects in demand are equal • Positive or negative, depending on direction of asymmetry in cross-price effects in demand • In a product pair cross-brand pass-through rates have opposite signs

Moorthy (2005)	Two manufacturers and two retailers	Linear demand Hotelling-like model	Manufacturer Stackelberg	Maximize category profits	• Between 0 and 1 w/o retail competition	• Positive with retail competition • Without retail competition, brand asymmetry needed for cross-pass-through, positive for stronger brand and negative for weaker brand
	Two manufacturers and two retailers	Nested logit	Manufacturer Stackelberg	Maximize category profits	• Positive	• Negative cross pass-through w/o retail competition • Can be greater or less than 100% depending on demand model

and arrives at a large number of results on pass-through and cross pass-through. For the nested logit model, which brand gets a greater pass-through from a retailer depends not so much on its strength *vis-à-vis* the other brand (as in Sudhir, 2001), but rather on the relative strengths of the brands at the two retailers. In particular, he finds that pass-through at a retailer for the nested logit model can be greater than or less than 100 percent, depending on whether the brand has lower or greater market share at that retailer.

Moorthy's results show that pass-through for a brand is linked to the extent of retail competition in the market. If retail competition is limited, as is probably true in categories that are not major drivers of store traffic, one can use the predictions of the single retailer models. For categories that drive store traffic, retail competition can be critically important, and therefore the extent of pass-through needs to consider relative brand strengths at the retailers.

Cross pass-through also depends on the extent of retail competition (see Table 15.3 for key results). Moorthy also discusses the cases when wholesale price changes are retailer specific or common across retailers. When wholesale price changes are retailer specific, own pass-through is less than 100 percent and cross pass-through is always negative. But when wholesale price changes are common, cross pass-through can be positive or negative. These differences in results suggest intriguing possibilities about how manufacturers should time trade deals (synchronously or asynchronously) to different retail chains within the market.

3.2 Models where wholesale price changes induce price discrimination

Varian (1980) and Narasimhan (1988) introduce models that seek to discriminate between brand-loyal and price-sensitive customers through promotions. In these models, promotions are characterized as mixed-strategy equilibria. Hence wholesale prices may change with the motive of price discrimination and not necessarily as a result of changes in demand or costs. In contrast to the models that are concerned with demand functional forms (or models like the Hotelling model that generate linear demands), the analytical literature on price discrimination explicitly models consumer segments in terms of their price sensitivity and loyalty.

Lal and Villas-Boas (1998) study price promotions in the context of two competing retailers. Consumers may be loyal to manufacturers, retailers, both or none. A retailer is guaranteed retailer-loyal customers (denoted by R) and the brand-retailer-loyal customers who are committed to the brand (manufacturer) and the retailer (MR). But the retailer has to compete for brand- or manufacturer-loyal customers (M) who are not loyal to a particular retailer, and the completely price-sensitive customer group who are neither loyal to a brand nor to a retailer (S). Whether to promote a high-priced brand is based on the relative ratio of the customers the retailer has to fight for (M), relative to the guaranteed customers (MR). In contrast, the decision to promote a low-priced brand is based on the relative ratio of the customers the retailer has to fight for ($M + S$), relative to the guaranteed customers ($MR + R$). The main insight of the paper is that the retailer has the incentive to promote the higher-priced brand when $(M/MR) > (M + S/MR + R)$.

Thus the decision to pass through a trade deal for the retailer is based on the extent of both retailer and brand loyalty. Interestingly, retailer loyalty has the opposite effect of brand loyalty. Greater brand loyalty allows greater pass-through, while greater retailer loyalty reduces pass-through. Note that these results about how brand loyalty affects pass-through are critically dependent on retail competition. If there were no retail competition, brand loyalty would not lead to greater pass-through, because the retailer would find the brand-loyal customer to be captive and only the price-sensitive customer needs to be wooed by price promotions.

Kumar et al. (2001) suggest that information asymmetry between customers and firms might be a reason for low pass-through. In a model where customers differ in their valuations and have search costs to find the lowest price, they argue that retailers will pass through a trade promotion only probabilistically in a mixed-strategy equilibrium. This is because in any given week, the consumer may not know if a better price may be available at another retailer who may pass through the trade promotion. The authors show that manufacturers can increase pass-through by advertising their trade promotions to consumers. This relationship between asymmetry and pass-through is consistent with the findings in Busse et al. (2006), who show that pass-through increases when asymmetric information is reduced in the context of trade promotions versus consumer promotions in the car market.

Another suggestion about how to improve pass-through is made in Gerstner and Hess (1991, 1995). They show that manufacturers can use consumer rebates (pull promotion), targeted towards the low-valuation segment, in combination with trade promotions (push promotions) to improve pass-through. Consumer promotions increase the low-valuation segment's willingness to pay. This encourages retailers to participate in trade promotions and serve this segment. Also, consumers are better off with retail price reductions motivated by trade promotions than with large consumer rebates alone. With only consumer rebates, the retailer increases the retail price by the value of the rebate so that the consumer has to pay a higher price in addition to the transaction cost of using the rebate.

3.3 Empirical results on pass-through

Empirical research on pass-through has mostly been on grocery markets, because of the availability of data. Theoretical models show that pass-through is affected by retail competition. But for groceries, even though there is retail competition at the basket level (Bell et al., 1998; Gauri et al., 2007), retail competition is not as strong at the individual-product level (Walters and MacKenzie, 1988). Hence a significant body of empirical research on pass-through has assumed a monopoly retailer.

Based on research in Chevalier and Curhan (1976), Curhan and Kopp (1987/88), Walters (1989) and Blattberg and Neslin (1990), Blattberg et al. (1995) conclude that the finding, 'pass-through rates are less than 100 percent', is an empirical generalization. However, Armstrong (1991), Walters (1989) and Besanko et al. (2005) find that pass-through rates can be greater than 100 percent for certain products. While Armstrong and Walters use a multiplicative functional form for demand (which, as we discussed earlier, leads to greater than 100 percent pass-through), Besanko et al. estimate a reduced-form regression for pass-through across products in several categories without making any assumptions about the functional form of demand or retailers' objectives (category or brand profit maximization). For a single store chain, they find that pass-through rates are greater than 100 percent for 14 percent of the products. In most categories, brands with larger market shares get greater pass-through, suggesting the effect of differences in manufacturers' bargaining power on pass-through. Pass-through rates are also found to be greater in markets with older and more ethnic populations and in markets with larger households and greater home values. This may be an evidence for the findings of Lal and Villas-Boas (1998) if consumers in these markets have low retailer loyalty.

Does retail competition affect pass-through? Besanko et al. find that distance from the competitor does not affect pass-through. While one possible interpretation of this result is that retail competition has no impact on pass-through, the more likely explanation is that retailers of the same store chain do not adjust their prices across stores because of practical difficulties of having different specials at different stores. In fact, Besanko et al. find that only 2 percent of their pass-through variations can be explained by price zones. But the result that brands with greater market shares have greater pass-through offers indirect support for the role of retail competition. If market shares are correlated with strong brand loyalty, then the result that brands with stronger market share get greater pass-through suggests that retailers do consider retail competition when deciding on pass-through (see the discussion in Lal and Villas-Boas, 1998). Alternatively, this could be because the retail chain is weaker for the brands with the larger market share (Moorthy, 2005). Additional research needs to resolve these alternative reasons for the empirical results.

How do retailer objectives affect pass-through? The retailer objective affects the magnitudes of own and cross pass-through, and, in case of a logit demand specification, even the sign of the cross pass-through. Sudhir (2001) shows that, without retail competition, the cross pass-through is negative for category profit maximization and positive for brand profit maximization. He finds that category profit maximization by the retailer fits the price data better than brand profit maximization for the analyzed categories. Basuroy et al. (2001) evaluate how pricing behavior changed when a retailer shifted from a brand management to a category management behavior. They find that retail pricing in terms of own and cross pass-through changed in a manner predicted by the theory, suggesting that a manufacturer should take into account the retailer's price-setting rules when setting optimal wholesale prices.

A retailer could strategically vary its pricing strategy over high and regular demand periods. Chevalier et al. (2003) show that retail margins for specific goods fall during peak demand periods for that good. Meza and Sudhir (2006) account for the differences in levels of demand and price sensitivity between regular and high demand periods, and show that pass-through varies over the year and the average measures of pass-through for the entire year may be misleading. They use two categories: tuna, which has peak demand during Lent, and beer, which has peak demand during holiday and major sports weekends, to study differences in pass-through between high- and low-demand periods. They find an interesting difference between the two categories. Tuna's peak demand is not correlated with peak purchases in other complementary categories. Hence, while a tuna promotion can draw customers into the store, it does not provide many spillover benefits. In contrast, peak beer demand is correlated with peak purchases in complementary high-margin categories such as snacks. Hence the benefit of passing through promotions is greater for beer than for tuna during peak periods, and accordingly pass-through is greater for beer than for tuna during peak demand. Further, they find that retailers follow a narrow but deep pass-through strategy (only pass-through for the most popular size/brand 'pull items') in regular periods, but a broad but shallow pass-through strategy (lower but similar pass-through for all items) in peak periods.

With respect to cross pass-through, Besanko et al. (2005) find that about two-thirds of the cross pass-through effects are statistically different from zero. Slightly more than one-third of these effects are negative, while slightly less than one-third are positive. However, McAlister (2007) shows that these significant effects do not exist once we account for the high correlation in prices (0.9) across the stores in the data. Essentially, she argues that these significant effects are an artifact of the additional degrees of freedom due to using repeated price observations at the zone level (that do not vary independently over time). Hence further research is required on cross pass-through effects. One possibility as to why the cross pass-through effects are insignificant could be because extant pass-through research has not included prices from competing retailers in the model (as argued by Moorthy, 2005). Future research needs to study cross pass-through effects in greater detail.

Busse et al. (2006) show support for the information asymmetry effect on pass-through in the car market and may be considered indirect support for the findings of Kumar et al. (2001). They show that consumers obtain about 70–90 percent of the value of a consumer rebate, while they get only about 30–40 percent of a dealer promotion. As the authors acknowledge, the result is also consistent with a prospect theory argument. When consumers see a consumer promotion, the reference price shifts downwards, but with a trade promotion, the consumer is unaware of the price discount and the reference price is not affected. This differential effect on consumers' reference prices may explain the differences in pass-through. Future research needs to separate the role of consumer reference point effects and information asymmetry on pass-through.

3.4 Future research

In practice, price discrimination and demand and cost changes both affect wholesale prices. The extant analytical literature on pass-through has studied these cases separately, but it would be worthwhile to see how the predictions might change when both of these effects coexist, as in real markets. This can help create better hypotheses of pass-through in future research. In terms of empirical research, structural models that simultaneously develop both the demand side and the supply side (e.g. Villas-Boas and Zhao, 2005) could potentially incorporate heterogeneity in consumers' price sensitivity or brand and retailer loyalty, and thus tie in the price discrimination motive along with cost changes on the supply side. As we discuss in a subsequent section, a structural model to this effect would not only enable us to test some of the theoretical predictions but would also allow us to perform counterfactual simulations to understand channel member reactions and their impacts under different scenarios.

Several issues are important to address in empirical research on pass-through, for example: (1) how does retail competition affect pass-through?; (2) how does demand specification (brand/retailer loyalty; functional forms etc.) affect pass-through?; (3) how does pass-through behavior vary across categories?; (4) how does pass-through change over time?; (5) how is pass-through measured?; (6) how does pass-through behavior differ across types of trade promotions?

Moorthy (2005) and Lal and Villas-Boas (1998) have shown how pass-through is critically dependent on the extent of retail competition. Empirical research on pass-through has mostly assumed that retail competition is not strong at the individual product level (Walters and MacKenzie, 1988). Further, data from multiple competing retailers are hard to obtain. Hence empirical evidence for the effects of competition is scarce. However, there could be variations in shopping behavior, across categories within consumers' shopping baskets. For example, a consumer might always buy her produce from the same retailer but search across retailers for best prices on paper goods. Such category-based consumer shopping behavior would be critical for a retailer whose objective is to maximize profits across categories. The issue of share-of-wallet across retailers and its influence on pass-through, for different categories and different retail formats, has not been sufficiently explored. Such analysis would of course require a rich dataset that has information on consumer behavior at a disaggregate level, and across retail chains and retail formats. Future research needs to investigate the implications of retail competition either directly, by acquiring data across competing retailers, or indirectly, by appropriately approximating retail competition in terms of geographical locations of consumers and retail stores of the same or different formats in the market.

For retail competition it is important to consider the differences in retail formats. On the cost or the supply side, this is important because manufacturers could use nonlinear pricing contracts (as we discuss in the next section) which could result in different marginal costs for different retailers and, hence, different pass-through behaviors. In addition, manufacturers could time trade deals synchronously or asynchronously to different retailers, which has different implications for pass-through (Moorthy, 2005). Also, as we have seen, pass-through varies over regular and peak demand periods. The extant literature on pass-through has assumed that the manufacturer and the retailer marginal costs are independent of order quantities and frequencies. If the operating costs of the manufacturer and the retailer are misaligned, or if they are different for different retailers (as may be the case for supermarkets versus club stores), this could have implications for pass-through when demand varies over time.

On the demand side, brand and retailer loyalty and competition could vary across store formats. For example, consumers who tend to visit supermarkets may be less price sensitive, and more retailer or brand loyal, whereas consumers who frequent discount or club stores could be more price sensitive, and less retailer and brand loyal. There could be such idiosyncratic differences in consumers across retail formats because of the different assortment of products in different store formats or because of their different pricing policies (e.g. small pack sizes versus bulk quantities and Hi-Lo versus EDLP). This could have some interesting implications for the nature of competition between different formats and the resulting pass-through behavior across retail formats and brands. Further, retailer and brand loyalty may differ over time as infrequent customers enter markets in peak periods. Systematic research needs to be done across store formats and time to test some of the existing theories and to present managers with descriptive insights into pass-through. For instance, most store chains have a loyalty program. Analysis of store loyalty card data, in conjunction with the overall sales data, could be used to test some of the conclusions in Lal and Villas-Boas (1998).

As the analytical literature has shown, results on pass-through are conditional on the demand-functional forms. Hence adopting specific structural models in empirical research could impose specific constraints on possible pass-through rates. A systematic investigation of which functional forms are supported in the pricing and pass-through data in a given setting can be useful to understand which models should be used for decision support systems for setting wholesale and retail prices.

Pass-through has been measured in many ways. Much of the theoretical literature has focused on the comparative static $\partial p_i/\partial w_i$ to study pass-through (e.g. Tyagi, 1999a), while some has looked at the proportion of trade deals passed through (Kumar et al., 2001). In the context of forward buying and consumer stockpiling, one may need a different definition of pass-through such as the fraction of the total discount that gets passed through to the consumer. Meza and Sudhir (2006) show that using the weighted average wholesale price (rather than the true current promotional price) gets us closer to a true estimate of pass-through in the presence of forward buying and stockpiling than the actual prices. Testing this using data on true marginal wholesale price and actual shipping data as in Abraham and Lodish (1987) and Blattberg and Levin (1987) would be useful validation of extant research using readily available weighted average wholesale price.

Lal et al. (1996) study forward buying, merchandising and trade deals in a single retailer context. They find that while such forward buying reduces pass-through for manufacturers, it is beneficial for manufacturers because it reduces competition among them. Future research should look at how these effects manifest in terms of pass-through when there is retail competition.

Pass-through research has mostly been on grocery markets. It is obvious that there are interesting issues in the context of durable goods, services, industrial buying situations etc. As discussed earlier, Busse et al. (2006) is an exception. Bruce et al. (2005) note that secondary markets matter with durable goods. They find that trade promotions can mitigate the double marginalization problem better for manufacturers of more durable goods. In their model, retailers do not compete with each other. Hence, how these results translate in markets with retail competition needs to be investigated.

Much research on pass-through is based on off-invoices, with unconditional wholesale price reductions. Gomez et al. (2007) study different types of trade deals. They find that only 25.9 percent of discounts are off-invoices. Scanbacks and accruals (31 percent) are negotiated with retailers; these require retailers to attain a quantity level to get the allowance. Scanbacks and accruals may therefore be considered similar to a quantity discount in terms of our discussion of pricing contracts below. Billbacks (3.1 percent) are similar to scanbacks, but based on items that are purchased, not sold, and therefore leave open the option for forward buying. A systematic investigation of how pass-through changes when different pricing contracts are used would be a very useful area of research.

4. Optimal pricing contracts

Manufacturers (or upstream firms) can decide the pricing contract they offer to the retailer (or downstream firm). Researchers have evaluated a number of pricing contracts such as linear wholesale price, quantity discounts, two part-tariffs and resale price maintenance. Typically, the upstream manufacturer structures the pricing contract in a way that is most profitable for it. When the upstream firm does not have the power (for example with large retailers), either the downstream player will set the terms of the pricing contract or it may be an outcome of bargaining negotiations.

4.1 Linear wholesale prices

The simplest and most common pricing contract is the linear wholesale price. This leads to the familiar double marginalization problem discussed in the illustrative example of Section 2. The double marginalization problem results in lower total channel profits (the

336 *Handbook of pricing research in marketing*

size of the pie) than what it could have been under channel coordination. A long stream of literature on channels of distribution has emphasized pricing contracts where the double marginalization problem can be minimized and the channel can be coordinated.[3] We discuss these contracts below.

4.2 Quantity discounts and two-part tariffs

Quantity discounts and two-part tariffs can coordinate the channel. With quantity discounts, the per-unit costs to the retailer fall with quantity purchases. Jeuland and Shugan (1983) show that quantity discounts can be used as a means by which a manufacturer can coordinate the channel in a bilateral monopoly setting.

Moorthy (1987) argues that the Jeuland–Shugan quantity–discount coordination requires only that the retailer's marginal cost equal the marginal revenue at the channel's optimal quantity; its value at quantities other than the channel's optimal quantity can be almost anything. This leeway in choosing the retailer's effective marginal cost away from the channels' optimal quantity leads to a variety of potential pricing schemes (e.g. two-part tariff) that can also be optimal. In a two-part tariff, the retailer makes a fixed payment and pays a per-unit charge for the product. The fixed fee and the per-unit charge are set such that the sales volume and total profit of the channel members is the same as when maximizing total channel profit. For instance, in the bilateral monopoly model discussed in Section 2, the manufacturer can set the wholesale price (w) equal to his marginal cost (c) and then extract the retailer's profit completely with a fixed fee. This will maximize total channel profit and also help the manufacturer maximize his profit.

Researchers have shown that two-part tariffs can be optimal in a wide range of market scenarios such as (1) when retailers have to provide non-contractible services as with franchising services with potential for moral hazard as in Lal (1990); (2) when retailers have to complement the product with another input and then sell a composite output (Vernon and Graham, 1971); (3) when retailers carry a product line (Villas-Boas, 1998); (4) when there is demand uncertainty (e.g. Rey and Tirole, 1986); (5) when manufacturers and retailers have private information (e.g. Desai and Srinivasan, 1995; Tirole, 1988, p. 176).

Iyer and Villas-Boas (2003) however argue that two-part tariffs are not optimal if the product is not completely specifiable. They show that in a model of bargaining between manufacturers and retailers when products are not completely specifiable and demand is uncertain (as is typical in almost all channel models, they also assume retail actions are unobservable), two-part tariffs will not be a part of the market contract even in a simple one manufacturer–one retailer channel. This is because the fixed fee in the two-part tariff does not affect the opportunistic behavior on the part of the manufacturer and, therefore, will not be accepted by the retailer. In their bargaining model, a linear wholesale price contract emerges as the equilibrium outcome. They also note that empirically the use of

---

[3] Channel coordination can also be brought about by non-pricing mechanisms. For a simple bilateral monopoly case, Shugan (1985) shows that implicit understandings between channel members can be a partial substitute for formal agreements. Also see Fugate et al. (2006) for a discussion on the different types of coordination mechanisms.

two-part tariffs is considerably small, despite prior findings in the theoretical literature about the optimality of two-part tariffs in a broad range of settings.[4]

When else might a two-part tariff or a quantity discount not work? Ingene and Parry (1995a, 1995b, 1998, 2000) have studied the case of a manufacturer setting a wholesale price schedule for its retailers who differ in their demand and cost structures. They show that when these non-identical retailers compete on price, channel coordination can still be achieved with an appropriately specified quantity discount schedule but not with a simple two-part tariff. A quantity discount schedule can be designed such that the effective marginal cost is different for different retailers and is equal to their marginal revenue, given their differences. In contrast, a two-part tariff offers each retailer the same per-unit charge. Since the Robinson–Patman Act does not allow manufacturers to discriminate between different retailers by charging retailer-specific wholesale prices, a menu of two-part tariffs, where retailers can select whichever tariff they want, can overcome this legal problem, and also coordinate the channel. Interestingly, the authors show that, from the perspective of a profit-maximizing manufacturer, a non-coordinating 'Sophisticated Stackelberg' two-part tariff that simultaneously optimizes the per-unit fee and the fixed fee in light of the difference in retailers' fixed costs may be preferred over channel coordination. The optimal pricing policy is dependent on (1) the retailers' fixed costs, (2) the relative size of the retailers, and (3) the degree of retail competition.

Models in marketing typically assume the manufacturer and retailer marginal costs as constant and fixed. There is a literature at the interface of marketing and operations that addresses optimal pricing contracts when it affects retailer operating costs. When the operating costs of the retailer and the manufacturer are a function of the order quantities, the manufacturer needs to motivate the retailer to choose both retail prices and order quantities that will simultaneously maximize the retailer's profit and the joint profit of the retailer and the manufacturer (Weng, 1995). A simple quantity discount cannot achieve this, and the manufacturer will have to use a fixed franchise fee in combination with the quantity discount. When a supplier caters to multiple non-identical retailers, Chen et al. (2001) show that the same optimum level of channel-wide profits as in a centralized system can be achieved in a decentralized system, but only if coordination is achieved via a unique wholesale pricing policy – periodically charged fixed fees, and a discount pricing scheme under which the discount given to a retailer is the sum of three discount components based on the retailer's (i) annual sales volume, (ii) order quantity, and (iii) order frequency.

4.3 Resale price maintenance (RPM)
RPM is a method of vertical control where the upstream firm dictates pricing policies at subsequent stages of the distribution channel. By setting a price ceiling (maximum RPM), the upstream firm can control the retailer's margin, so that it can eliminate the double marginalization problem and reduce the retail price. Setting a price floor (minimum RPM) can also achieve channel coordination by reducing price competition

---

[4] Through a laboratory experiment, Ho and Zhang (2008) show that, with a reference-dependent utility function, retailers perceive the up-front fixed fee in a two-part tariff as a loss, and the subsequent sales proceeds as a gain. Hence, if retailers are loss averse, a two-part tariff may not be able to coordinate the channel.

among retailers and diverting competition into non-price dimensions such as service (Telser, 1960; Mathewson and Winter, 1984; Iyer, 1998) or product quality (Marvel and McCafferty, 1984).[5]

The issue of RPM is pertinent in cases of demand uncertainty, information asymmetry and moral hazard: (1) when retailers have private information about an uncertain state of the demand (Gal-Or, 1991); (2) both the upstream and downstream firms make a non-price choice (e.g. advertising, sales effort, etc.) subject to moral hazard – double or two-sided (Romano, 1994); and (3) when the manufacturer faces uncertain demand (Butz, 1997).

Iyer (1998) examines a channel with two symmetric retailers engaging in price and non-price competition (e.g. provision of product information, after-sales service etc.). Consumers are heterogeneous in their locations (as in the spatial models of horizontal differentiation) and in their willingness to pay for retail services (as in the models of vertical differentiation). When the diversity in willingness to pay is relatively greater than locational differentiation, neither quantity discounts nor a menu of two-part tariffs are sufficient to coordinate the channel. A complicated menu of contractual mechanisms is necessary that can induce retail differentiation so that all retailers don't compete only for consumers with low willingness to pay (by engaging in price competition) or only for consumers with high willingness to pay (by engaging in non-price competition). An example of such a menu is one consisting of retail price restraints linked to particular wholesale prices and fixed fees.

In general, RPM restricts the resellers' freedom to set prices. Minimum RPM can be anticompetitive by acting as a monitoring or an enforcing mechanism that facilitates collusion of an upstream or downstream cartel or by facilitating third-degree price discrimination by a monopolistic manufacturer (Gilligan, 1986). Although maximum RPM is traditionally viewed as reducing retail price,[6] it could reduce consumer welfare by reducing the number of retailers (Perry and Groff, 1985) or facilitate manufacturer opportunism, whereby it may drive prices down enough so that the retailers almost fail and then the manufacturer may exploit such retailers (Blair and Lafontaine, 1999). Hence both forms of RPM are viewed unfavorably by the US Supreme Court.

Since 1911, and until recently, either form of RPM was *per se* illegal under Section 1 of the Sherman Antitrust Act. This meant that a violation of Section 1 had been established once the government or private plaintiff proved that the defendant manufacturer had implemented an explicit or implicit plan to maintain a resale price. However, the last few years have seen legal cases where a price maintenance agreement between an upstream supplier and a downstream distributor is judged on its unique circumstances. In its *State Oil Company, Petitioner v. Barkat U. Khan and Khan & Associates, Inc.* decision of 1997, the Court returned the antitrust treatment of maximum RPM to the 'rule of reason', so that now a defendant manufacturer can defend itself by demonstrating that, in its case, maximum RPM has pro-competitive effects that benefit the consumers (Roszkowski,

---

[5] On a different note, Perry and Porter (1990) show that minimum RPM can result in excessive retail service or induce new entry because of the reduced price competition.

[6] When the manufacturer can set both a franchise fee and a wholesale price, Perry and Besanko (1991) show that the traditional view that maximum RPM will lower retail prices and that minimum RPM will raise retail prices may be reversed.

1999). More recently, in June 2007, the Supreme Court's decision in *Leegin Creative Leather Products Inc. v. PSKS Inc.* established that courts should also evaluate minimum RPM according to the 'rule of reason'.[7]

4.4 Slotting allowances

Unlike fixed fees that retailers pay to manufacturers in two-part tariffs, slotting allowances are payments made by manufacturers to retailers. They include a wide assortment of fixed transfers from manufacturers to retailers that are not linked to quantities sold. These have been variously called pay-to-stay fees, failure fees, premium shelf-placement fees, share of shelf-space fees etc.

Sullivan (1997) argues that as the cost of developing new products falls, more new products are supplied; slotting allowances emerge as a means by which to ration shelf space efficiently to the most profitable products. Another argument often used is that when shelf space is a scarce resource, slotting allowances serve to shift the risk of failure from the retailers to the manufacturer. This risk-shifting becomes particularly important in the presence of private information about the success of the product in the hands of the manufacturer. Lariviere and Padmanabhan (1997) and Desai (2000) argue that slotting allowances are means by which manufacturers signal to retailers their private information about the quality of their products. Desai (2000) shows that slotting allowances can be pro-competitive as it serves to enhance retailer participation because it reduces the demand uncertainty of retailers and increases their profitability. But Shaffer (1991) argues that slotting allowances are anticompetitive because they reduce retail competition and increase prices.

While Shaffer assumes that manufacturers are in a perfectly competitive market and therefore have no power and the retailer sets the terms of trade, in Desai's model, the manufacturer sets the terms of trade. In both models, wholesale prices are higher in the presence of slotting allowances. But with manufacturers setting the terms of trade and using slotting allowances as a signaling device, the likelihood of slotting allowances falls when there is greater market potential (as understood by both manufacturers and retailers). This is because retailers find it worthwhile to participate in the market even without slotting allowances when the market is profitable. However, when the retailer seeks to exercise power, the retailer can extract the manufacturers' entire surplus through slotting allowances. Then slotting allowances should increase with market potential.[8]

In terms of empirical research, Bloom et al. (2000) and Wilkie et al. (2002) use surveys of manufacturers and retailers to identify key reasons why slotting allowances are used. However, the results are inconclusive because retailers and manufacturers have somewhat opposing views. Rao and Mahi (2003) survey manufacturers and retailers about each transaction they were involved in. They find that slotting allowances increase with greater retailer power, but acknowledge that the results may be due to their inability to control for manufacturer–retailer power at the level of each transaction due to pooling transactions across a wide range of manufacturers and retailers.

---

[7] *Source*: Knowledge@Wharton, 08 August 2007.
[8] Chu (1992) develops a screening model where retailers use slotting allowances to screen new products for their potential. Again, with this model where the retailer has power, slotting allowances increase with the potential of the product.

Sudhir and Rao (2006) use a database of all new products offered to a particular retailer, some of which received slotting allowances and others that did not. By using such a universe of accepted and non-accepted products, they are able to control for any potential issues of selection involved in using only accepted products. They also had internal ratings data of retailer buyers on the potential for success. These data enabled them to study which of the rationales are supported in their data by sidestepping the common problems of selection and levels of information asymmetry for any new product. Broadly, Sudhir and Rao find support for the efficiency rationales: opportunity costs, information asymmetry, signaling and retail participation. They do not find support for the retail power and retail competition mitigation (with an anticompetitive rationale) hypotheses.

Israelevich (2004) shows evidence based on a policy analysis using a structural model that slotting allowances (pay to fees) serve to put products on retailer shelves that may not be profitable purely through the revenues they generate for the retailer; thus slotting allowances may serve to increase consumer variety. The question of whether other better products that could be more in demand by consumers are being pushed out from the shelves due to slotting fees is yet to be resolved.

Slotting allowances for existing products may also be given to enhance retailer participation in activities such as in-store service or merchandising. These allowances may be called display allowances or advertising allowances, and may fall under the broad rubric of slotting allowances. Kim and Staelin (1999) show that with greater store substitutability, manufacturers will 'freely' give retailers side payments to increase merchandising. If a retailer passes through a greater portion of these side payments to the consumer, then the manufacturer increases the side payment to this retailer. In addition, the competing retailers will react by lowering their retail margin and, thus, regular retail price. The authors present comparative static results for how changes in consumer sensitivity to pricing and promotional activities affect prices, side payments, and both retailer and manufacturer profits.

4.5 Future research
As we have seen, manufacturers might use any of the several possible pricing schemes or they could even use a combination of pricing schemes. Future research needs to address: (1) what are the implications of different pricing contracts for pass-through?; (2) how does retail competition, manufacturer competition and the overall channel structure influence the choice of pricing contract?; and (3) what combination of pricing schemes might be used under what market situations?

Different pricing schemes would have different implications for how pass-through is defined and measured. Specifically, when wholesale prices are not observed, the researcher should be wary that, with a nonlinear pricing scheme, the marginal cost could be different for different retailers. This could, in turn, result in different pass-through behaviors across competing retailers. Also, researchers should be cautious about using directly observed wholesale prices if, say, side payments or slotting allowances, which are not observed by the researcher, change the effective wholesale price for the retailer. Inferring pass-through behavior through a structural model that tests different hypotheses on the contracting and pricing relationships between manufacturers and retailers could be one potential solution.

It would be interesting to see if retailers' pass-through behavior might influence the pricing contract set by manufacturers. While the causality between the pricing contract and the pass-through behavior may be difficult to tease out, it is nonetheless interesting to explore this issue. For instance, it is known that pass-through behavior changes between regular and peak demand periods. What terms might a manufacturer want to incorporate in the pricing contract (e.g. RPM) to guard itself against these variations? How might a manufacturer want to set the contract differently when retailers' objective is brand profit maximization versus when retailers' objective is category profit maximization?

Heterogeneity among retailers (Ingene and Parry, 2000), and the relative bargaining power of manufacturers and retailers (Iyer and Villas-Boas, 2003; Shaffer, 1991; Desai, 2000) have implications for the terms of the pricing contract. Different retail formats (supermarkets versus discount stores or club stores) carry an assortment of products and attract different kinds of consumers, and hence face very different demand structures. Hence the bargaining power of a retailer may not only depend on the extent of retail competition in the market but also on the store format. Future research should analyze pricing contracts in the context of differences in demand structures and bargaining power of competing retailer formats.[9]

Chen (2003) studies the situation where an upstream supplier uses two-part tariffs for its downstream retailers, which include a dominant retailer and competitive fringe retailers. The dominant retailer is more efficient at a large scale of operation (i.e. it has a cost advantage). In order to offset the reduction in profits caused by the rise in the dominant retailer's power, the manufacturer seeks to boost the fringe retailers' sales by lowering wholesale prices to them. This in turn leads to greater retail competition and lower prices. Dukes et al. (2006) consider a bilateral bargaining situation of competing manufacturers and competing multiproduct retailers. In this setting, manufacturers raise prices to the weaker retailer in order to boost sales through the more efficient retailer, which is also more profitable. This in turn reduces retailer competition and raises retail prices. Manufacturers' increased bargaining power over the weaker retailer allows them to accrue, in part, the additional extracted consumer surplus. These findings need to be empirically tested in view of their implications for pass-through behavior of dominant versus weak retailers, with and without manufacturer competition.

Both Chen (2003) and Dukes et al. (2006) assume that the manufacturers can charge different prices to the powerful and weak retailers, but, as pointed out earlier, manufacturers could instead use menu pricing schemes to overcome the limitations imposed by the Robinson–Patman Act. While the Robinson–Patman Act does not allow a manufacturer to discriminate between retailers, different manufacturers might offer different contracts to the same retailer. Hence, with regard to upstream competition, it would be interesting to understand when competing manufacturers might offer different pricing contracts or pricing schemes to their retailers. For example, would a national brand and a local brand always offer the same pricing scheme to a retailer? If not, then when might they differ?

Future research should investigate how different channel structures influence pricing contracts. For instance, as will be discussed in the next section, the presence of a direct channel that is owned by the manufacturer (a partially integrated channel) could strain

---

[9] One source of retail power has been the emergence of store brands. We refer the reader to the companion chapter on store brands in this handbook for a survey of issues relating to store brands.

the manufacturer–retailer relationship. What is the optimal pricing contract under such a scenario? Also a distribution channel could evolve over time because of mergers or because manufacturers and retailers enter or exit the market. This would change the extent of competition upstream or downstream, and also the demand for individual retailers. How should the pricing contract be designed to adjust for such potential changes in the channel structure?

Iyer and Villas-Boas (2003) note that empirically the use of two-part tariffs is considerably small despite findings in the theoretical literature about the optimality of such tariffs. While bargaining between the channel members could be a possible reason, an alternate reason could be that the real-world settings are far more complex, and as the findings of Chen et al. (2001) and Iyer (1998) suggest, manufacturers might be using more complicated pricing schemes. Future research thus needs to incorporate more efficiently the characteristics of channel members, characteristics of the product and consumer behavior in analyzing the issue of setting a wholesale pricing contract, while allowing for the use of a combination of different pricing schemes.

5. Channel structure

The channel structure is a long-term decision where managers decide on the structure of the distribution channel given the market characteristics. Managers can decide whether to have an integrated channel (sell directly to the consumer) or a decentralized channel (use intermediaries such as retailers, dealers etc.) or a combination of both – a partially integrated channel (e.g. use a direct online channel and traditional retailers). For a channel with intermediaries, managers can not only decide the number of players at each level; they can also choose among different options such as exclusive dealers (EDs), exclusive territories (ETs) and independent profit-maximizing retailers. While making such a decision, managers need to take into account the optimal pricing strategy that can be implemented in the resulting channel structure, given the market characteristics (e.g. competition, demand uncertainty, power structure).

5.1 Vertical integration and decentralization

In the illustrative model of Section 2, we found that vertical integration (VI) can solve the double marginalization problem and the associated pricing inefficiency from an independent retailer (Jeuland and Shugan, 1983). VI can lower retail prices for other channel structures as well – upstream monopolists selling through multiple downstream monopolists (Romano, 1987), a duopoly channel structure with exclusive dealers (McGuire and Staelin, 1983; Coughlan, 1985), and a 'full channel' structure with two competing manufacturers both selling through both competing retailers (Trivedi, 1998).[10]

Although VI can internalize the double marginalization problem, when the retail market is highly competitive (as a result of, say, high product substitutability[11]), manufacturers may be better off if they can shield themselves from the competitive environment by inserting privately owned profit-maximizers (retailers) between themselves and the

---

[10] The integrated structure has two manufacturers selling directly to consumers.
[11] Product substitutability is defined as the ratio of the rate of change of quantity with respect to the competitor's price to the rate of change of quantity with respect to own price.

ultimate retail markets (McGuire and Staelin, 1983; Coughlan, 1985; Lin, 1988).[12] This is because marketing middlemen soften manufacturer competition as the effect of a price change by a manufacturer on final retail demand is weakened by the intermediary. Other channel restraints such as exclusive dealing (Trivedi, 1998) and exclusive territories (Rey and Stiglitz, 1995) can also reduce manufacturer competition.

Moorthy (1988) showed that retail competition is not necessary for decentralization to be a Nash equilibrium. What is critical is the nature of coupling between demand dependence and strategic dependence. The author shows that decentralization is a Nash equilibrium only if one of the following (mutually exclusive) conditions are satisfied: (1) the manufacturers' products are demand substitutes at the retail level and strategic complements at the manufacturer or retailer levels; (2) the manufacturers' products are demand complements at the retail level and strategic substitutes at the manufacturer or retailer levels.

In general, with pure price competition, a mixed channel structure where one firm vertically integrates while another decentralizes is not an equilibrium. However, when retailers engage in price and non-price competition (e.g. provision of product information, after-sales service etc.), Iyer (1998) shows that a mixed channel structure can be an equilibrium in markets with weak brand loyalty. Although the decentralized retailer will charge higher prices than those chosen by the vertically integrated firm, adopting a high-end service position helps the retailer to differentiate and support the higher price. Hence the corresponding manufacturer's incentive to decentralize is reinforced in equilibrium.

We have already mentioned that demand functional form and manufacturer–retailer interactions affect pass-through. Choi (1991) and Trivedi (1998) analyze the effect of demand functional forms and manufacturer relationship on channel structure. The two papers find a rich set of results on how channel structure decisions are affected by functional form and manufacturer–retailer interactions.

The channel structure may also evolve over time with the entry of new players into the market. Tyagi (1999b) shows demand conditions where, contrary to conventional wisdom, entry of a new downstream firm lowers the downstream market output and increases the consumer price. This is because the upstream firms gain bargaining power with downstream entry, raising their wholesale price, and this effect can overcome the competitive effect of entry. But he also shows that for a class of widely used demand functions – linear, constant elasticity and a variety of convex and concave demand functions – the supplier's optimal price is invariant to the entry/exit of downstream firms. Similarly, Corbett and Karmarkar (2001) model competition and entry into different levels of a multiple-tier serial channel structure with a price-sensitive linear deterministic demand and find that price per unit, in a tier, falls with the number of entrants in any upstream tier, but is unchanged with the number of entrants in a downstream tier.

Desai et al. (2004) discuss the role of the intermediary in the context of durable goods. There are two issues with durable goods: (1) the presence of secondary market competition; and (2) the Coase problem, where the manufacturer's inability to commit to a future price causes consumers to wait and the market to fail. Desai et al. show that by pre-committing the retailer to a two-part contract that covers both periods, the manufacturer can solve

---

[12] They all find conditions under which decentralization is a Nash equilibrium strategy of manufacturers.

both problems. With pre-committed wholesale prices, the channel can replicate the sales schedule under a consumer-pricing commitment. Interestingly, in this contract, the manufacturer charges a wholesale price above marginal cost in both periods and earns higher profits by selling through a retailer than by selling the product directly to the consumers.

5.2 Partial integration

Manufacturers may also consider partial integration (PI) – taking over part of the downstream industry – as a channel design strategy. The popular argument for this strategy is the manufacturer's incentive to raise rivals' (independent retailers') costs. Romano (1987) considers the case when an upstream monopolist services two downstream monopolists. Through PI, the upstream monopolist can not only (partially) eradicate the pricing inefficiency associated with successive monopolies, but also practice implicit price discrimination towards the non-integrated downstream firm. Hastings and Gilbert (2005) focus on the 1997 acquisition by Tosco of Unocol's West Coast refining and retail assets. They empirically examine the reaction of Tosco's wholesale prices in 13 metropolitan areas to differential increases in competition with independent retailers resulting from the merger. The upstream firms (refineries) have market power and the downstream products (gasoline from different refineries) are strategic complements. The authors find that an increase in the degree of integration is associated with higher wholesale prices to competing retailers.

The emergence of the Internet as a sales channel has brought the issue of partial forward integration into focus again in recent years. The growth of the Internet has made it very easy for manufacturers to directly connect with the final consumer through an online store (direct channel). While the direct channel reduces the manufacturer's dependence on retailers and eliminates pricing inefficiencies due to double marginalization, it is also likely to steal customers from retailers. This might strain the manufacturer–retailer relationship and may cause retailers to react in a way that adversely affects the manufacturer. It has been shown that firms can control the competition between the online channel and the traditional retailers by controlling the amount of information made available on the online channel (Balasubramanian, 1998; Zettelmeyer, 2000; Brynjolfsson and Smith, 2000).

The online channel, however, may not always be detrimental to the non-integrated retailers. Chiang et al. (2003) analyze the price-setting game between a direct channel of a manufacturer and its independent retailer. They find that, depending on consumers' acceptance of direct channel purchases (for low acceptance), the introduction of the direct channel may be accompanied by a wholesale price reduction (as a result of low direct channel prices).

Kumar and Ruan (2006) consider the case when a retailer carries products of competing manufacturers and maximizes category profits. Consumers in the market are one of two types – they are either brand loyal or store loyal. In addition to the retail price, the retailer is also allowed to set the level of merchandising support, which impacts the demand for the manufacturer's product. They find conditions under which a manufacturer may get higher margins from brand-loyal customers online, and then offer higher margins to the retailer to get better merchandising support and a greater share of the store-loyal consumers. Thus, under certain conditions, the online channel not only serves to increase the level of retail support and manufacturers' profits, but it may also increase retailers' profits.

5.3 Future research

The literature on channel structure in marketing has typically assumed that consumer demand is deterministic. However, the operations literature typically highlights the variability in consumer demand. Small levels of consumer demand variability are amplified across a channel and lead to the well-known 'bullwhip effect', and harm channel efficiency (Lee et al., 1997). Thus a decentralization decision may depend on demand variability, which is typically abstracted away from in the traditional channel structure literature in marketing. It is critical to understand the tradeoffs when designing channels in the presence of demand uncertainty, retailer/manufacturer moral hazard etc.

While there has been a large volume of theoretical research on issues of channel structure, the volume of empirical research on this issue has been very limited. This is partly because channel structure decisions tend to be long term and therefore researchers cannot get variation in the data. The emergence of the Internet has provided opportunities to study the effect of a change in channel structure, and empirical researchers should take advantage of this natural variation in the data.

6. Structural econometric models of pricing in a channel

In this section, we discuss the emerging literature on structural econometric models of channels. We begin by discussing an illustrative model. In recent years, a number of papers have used the structural econometric framework to model the marketing channel. Such models serve to (1) depict manufacturer–retailer interactions that best describe the market and (2) perform policy analysis in markets where a channel intermediary needs to be modeled. We discuss these two types of models in turn.

6.1 An illustrative structural econometric model of channels

We illustrate a basic structural econometric model of the channel using a logit demand model to highlight the key aspects of developing a structural econometric model of the marketing channel.

Demand Consider a market where households can choose between two brands (sold by two different manufacturers) denoted by $i = 1, 2$ and a no-purchase option denoted by $i = 0$. The utility for a brand i to household h in period t is given by

$$U_{hit} = \beta_{0i} + X_{it}\beta - \alpha p_{it} + \xi_{it} + \varepsilon_{hit}, \quad i = 1, 2 \qquad (15.1)$$
$$= \delta_{it} + \varepsilon_{hit}, \quad i = 1, 2$$

where X_{it} is a vector of observable (to the firm and the econometrician) attributes and marketing variables (for, e.g., display and feature activity for the brand) and p_{it} is the retail price. β_{0i} is the intrinsic preference of consumers for brand i, and ξ_{it} is the unobservable (to the econometrician, but observable to the firm and the consumer) component of utility. This term captures the variation in consumer preferences for brands across time that is induced by manufacturer advertising and consumer promotions. ε_{hit} is household h's idiosyncratic component of utility which is unobserved by the firm and is assumed to be independent and identically distributed as a Type I extreme value distribution across consumers. This assumption leads us to the familiar multinomial logit model of demand. Denote the deterministic part of the utility that is observed by the firm by the term δ_{it} and, normalizing the deterministic component of utility for no purchase (δ_{0t}) to zero, we have the familiar equation for market share for the brand

$$s_{it} = \frac{\exp(\delta_{it})}{1 + \sum_{k=1}^{2}\exp(\delta_{kt})}, \quad i = 0, 1, 2 \qquad (15.2)$$

It is therefore easy to see that

$$\ln(s_{it}/s_{0t}) = \delta_{it} = \beta_{0i} + X_{it}\beta - \alpha p_{it} + \xi_{it}, \quad i = 1, 2$$

This equation serves as the demand-side estimation equation. The term ξ_{it} serves as the error term in the estimation equation. It can capture the effects of manufacturer advertising and consumer promotions, and other unobserved demand shocks that are not explicitly modeled.

The supply (or channel) model
Assume that the two manufacturers set wholesale prices and the retailer then sets retail prices to maximize its category profits in period t. Then the retailer's objective function is given by

$$\Pi^R_t = (p_{1t} - w_{1t})s_{1t}M_t + (p_{2t} - w_{2t})s_{2t}M_t$$

where p_{1t} and p_{2t} are the retail prices of products 1 and 2, w_{1t} and w_{2t} are the wholesale prices of products 1 and 2 set by the manufacturers, and s_{1t} and s_{2t} are the shares of products 1 and 2 defined in the demand model (note that $s_{0t} = 1 - s_{1t} - s_{2t}$ is the share of the outside good) and M_t is the size of the market. The t subscript refers to the period t.

The first-order conditions for the retailer are given by

$$\frac{\partial \Pi^R_t}{\partial p_{it}} = s_{it} + (p_{1t} - w_{1t})\left[\frac{\partial s_{1t}}{\partial p_{it}}\right] + (p_{2t} - w_{2t})\left[\frac{\partial s_{2t}}{\partial p_{it}}\right] = 0, \quad i = 1, 2$$

Taking the derivatives of market share with respect to prices, we have

$$\frac{\partial s_t}{\partial p_t} = \begin{pmatrix} \dfrac{\partial s_{1t}}{\partial p_{1t}} & \dfrac{\partial s_{2t}}{\partial p_{1t}} \\ \dfrac{\partial s_{1t}}{\partial p_{2t}} & \dfrac{\partial s_{2t}}{\partial p_{2t}} \end{pmatrix} = \alpha \begin{pmatrix} -s_{1t}(1 - s_{1t}) & s_{1t}s_{2t} \\ s_{1t}s_{2t} & -s_{2t}(1 - s_{2t}) \end{pmatrix} \qquad (15.3)$$

Solving the first-order conditions, we get the formula for retail prices that is written in matrix form.

$$p_t = w_t + \frac{1}{\alpha(1 - s_{1t} - s_{2t})} \quad \text{where } p_t = \begin{pmatrix} p_{1t} \\ p_{2t} \end{pmatrix} \text{ and } w_t = \begin{pmatrix} w_{1t} \\ w_{2t} \end{pmatrix} \qquad (15.4)$$

If the wholesale prices can be observed, the equation above can serve as the supply side equation for the retailer. One could potentially capture unobservable retailer costs as an error on the supply equation.

Alternatively one may wish to actually write out an equation to describe the wholesale prices in order to structurally model the wholesale price choices. In that case, one will write out the manufacturers' pricing model. To illustrate different types of manufacturer pricing behavior, consider the two alternatives of (1) tacit collusion and (2) Bertrand competition. The objective function of manufacturer i selling brand i in period t is given by

$$\Pi^M_{it} = (w_{it} - c_{it})s_{it}M_t + \theta(w_{jt} - c_{jt})s_{jt}M_t - F_{it}, \quad i = 1, 2; j \neq i$$

where w_{it} is the wholesale price for brand i that the manufacturer charges the retailer and c_{it} is the marginal cost of brand i. F_{it} is the fixed cost to the manufacturer (it can include costs that are not related to the marginal sales of the brand, for, e.g., slotting allowances). Note that $\theta = 1$ for the case of tacit collusion and $\theta = 0$ for the case of Bertrand competition. Let the marginal cost of brand i be $c_{it} = \gamma_i + \omega_{it}$, where γ_i is the brand-specific marginal cost, and ω_{it} is the brand-specific unobservable marginal cost at time t. Note that ω_{it} is unobservable to the researcher, but observable to the manufacturers.

The first-order conditions for the manufacturer are given by

$$\frac{\partial \Pi^M_{it}}{\partial w_{it}} = s_{it} + (w_{it} - c_{it})\left[\frac{\partial s_{it}}{\partial p_{1t}}\frac{\partial p_{1t}}{\partial w_{it}} + \frac{\partial s_{it}}{\partial p_{2t}}\frac{\partial p_{2t}}{\partial w_{it}}\right] +$$

$$\theta(w_{jt} - c_{jt})\left[\frac{\partial s_{jt}}{\partial p_{1t}}\frac{\partial p_{1t}}{\partial w_{it}} + \frac{\partial s_{jt}}{\partial p_{2t}}\frac{\partial p_{2t}}{\partial w_{it}}\right] = 0, \quad i = 1, 2; j \neq i$$

$$s_t + \left[\left(\frac{\partial p_t}{\partial w_t}\frac{\partial s_t}{\partial p_t}\right).*\Theta\right](w_t - c_t) = 0$$

where

$$\Theta = \begin{pmatrix} 1 & 1 \\ 1 & 1 \end{pmatrix} \text{ for tacit collusion and } \Theta = \begin{pmatrix} 1 & 0 \\ 0 & 1 \end{pmatrix} \text{ for Bertrand competition. The .*}$$

operator denotes element by element multiplication of a matrix.

We can thus solve for the wholesale prices as

$$w_t = c_t + \left[\left(-\frac{\partial p_t}{\partial w_t}\frac{\partial s_t}{\partial p_t}\right).*\Theta\right]^{-1} s_t \quad (15.5)$$

where the term in brackets after c_t is the vector of margins that manufacturers choose for their brands. The retailer's reactions to manufacturers' wholesale prices are obtained by taking the derivatives of the retail prices in (15.4). It can be shown that (see Sudhir, 2001 for the proof)

$$\frac{\partial p_t}{\partial w_t} = \begin{pmatrix} \frac{\partial p_{1t}}{\partial w_{1t}} & \frac{\partial p_{2t}}{\partial w_{1t}} \\ \frac{\partial p_{1t}}{\partial w_{2t}} & \frac{\partial p_{2t}}{\partial w_{2t}} \end{pmatrix} = \begin{pmatrix} 1 - s_{1t} & -s_{1t} \\ -s_{2t} & 1 - s_{2t} \end{pmatrix}$$

If we observe wholesale prices and retailer prices, we can model the supply side by fitting both equations. However, typically, wholesale prices are not observed and most researchers in marketing substitute the wholesale price equation into the retail pricing equation and fit the following retailer pricing equation to the data:

$$p_t = \underbrace{c_t}_{\text{Manufacturer cost}} + \underbrace{\left[\left(-\frac{\partial p_t}{\partial w_t}\frac{\partial s_t}{\partial p_t}\right).*\Theta\right]^{-1} s_t}_{\text{Wholesale margin}} + \underbrace{\frac{1}{\alpha(1 - s_{1t} - s_{2t})}}_{\text{Retail margin}} \quad (15.6)$$

$$\underbrace{\phantom{c_t + \left[\left(-\frac{\partial p_t}{\partial w_t}\frac{\partial s_t}{\partial p_t}\right).*\Theta\right]^{-1} s_t}}_{\text{Wholesale price } (w_t)}$$

There are some key aspects that should be highlighted in the derivation of the structural econometrics models. First the demand-side error is incorporated into the supply-side equations through the observed market shares. Note that, in contrast to the game-theoretic models of Section 2.1, where the retailer and wholesale pricing equations are characterized completely in terms of the primitive demand and cost parameters, the pricing equations here (15.4 and 15.5) are characterized in terms of the observable market shares. The advantage of incorporating observed market shares is that demand-side errors (which are observable to the consumers and firms) are allowed to affect prices. In this sense, the structural econometric specification acknowledges that econometric errors have structural meaning and are accounted for in the specification.

In summary, a standard structural econometric model of channels is a simultaneous equation model with demand and supply pricing equations (could be one equation for manufacturer and retailer each or combined into one), both specified in terms of behavioral primitives. The demand equation relates quantity purchased to retail price, product characteristics and unobserved demand determinants. While many types of demand models can be used, the random coefficients logit model remains the most popular because of its flexibility in capturing substitution patterns, while still providing closed-form solutions that do not require integration for individual-level choice probabilities (see Dubé et al., 2002 for discussion). The supply equation relates prices to a markup and to observed and unobserved cost determinants. The structural econometric model can be used to either infer the consumers' and firms' decision rules from observable retail price–quantity pairs, or to perform policy simulations on how the equilibrium will evolve in response to actions by firms.

6.2 Descriptive models of channels

Sudhir (2001) demonstrated how to construct a structural econometric model of the channel under alternative assumptions of manufacturer–retailer interaction. In his analysis of competition among manufacturers selling through a single retailer, he finds that the manufacturer Stackelberg model of vertical interactions fits the data better than the vertical Nash model. He also finds that the category profit maximization objectives fit the data better than brand profit maximization objectives. He finds that the logit model fits the data better than a constant elasticity multiplicative model of demand, suggesting that even though multiplicative models fit the data well, they are less useful in retail decision support systems, because the implied markups are less consistent with the data.

Berto Villas-Boas (2007) expands the analysis to vertical interactions between multiple manufacturers and multiple retailers using a general random coefficients logit model. She finds that wholesale prices are close to marginal cost, but retailers have pricing power in the market. This could be consistent with either retail power or nonlinear pricing contracts. Bonnet and Dubois (2008) explicitly model nonlinear contracts involving two-part tariffs and resale price maintenance, and find that manufacturers use two-part tariffs with RPM.[13] Unlike Berto Villas Boas, they find that retailers price at marginal cost.

Berto Villas-Boas, and Bonnet and Dubois do not observe wholesale prices. Using a conjectural variations framework, Kadiyali et al. (2000) take advantage of the fact that wholesale prices can be observed in their data and estimate the extent of channel power. Their findings suggest that channel participants deviate from the prices predicted by 'standard' games such as manufacturer–retailer Stackelberg and vertical Nash, and retailers have power in that they obtain the larger share of channel profits. While this is consistent with a two-part tariff, they find that neither manufacturers nor retailers charge zero markups. Similar to Kadiyali et al., Meza and Sudhir (2007) estimate both a retail and wholesale price equation, but explicitly look for departures from the short-term profit-maximizing prices predicted by the standard models. They find that retailers strategically deviate from short-term profit-maximizing retail prices to support their store brands, but manufacturer margins are consistent with a manufacturer-Stackelberg model. Again both manufacturers and retailers have non-zero markups.

There appears to be a discrepancy in extant research: when wholesale prices are observed, Kadiyali et al. and Meza and Sudhir observe positive markups by manufacturers and retailers; when wholesale prices are not observed, Berto Villas-Boas and Bonnet and Dubois find evidence of zero markup for either manufacturer or retailer. While the differences may be artifacts of the specific markets studied, the differences in inference of markups when wholesale prices are not observed should be explored systematically in future work.

In contrast to the above analysis using aggregate data, Villas-Boas and Zhao (2005) use household-level data in a particular local market to evaluate the degree of manufacturer competition, retailer–manufacturer interactions, and retailer product category pricing in the ketchup market in a certain city using household level data. Che et al. (2007) also use individual data to model manufacturer and retailer behavior in the presence of consumer state dependence. Given the dynamics involved, they study the extent to which firms are forward looking in their pricing behavior. They find that firms are boundedly rational in that they look only one period ahead when setting prices.

6.3 Policy analysis within a channel setting

Several papers have also applied the structural econometric framework of channels in performing policy simulations on a wide range of marketing mix questions. These analyses have addressed product, pricing, promotions and channel issues.

Goldfarb et al. (forthcoming) use the structural econometric channel framework to measured brand equity. They estimate a demand model and then assess how prices and profits will change within a competitive setting in the presence of a channel when a brand

---

[13] They study the market for bottled water in France.

loses its intangible equity (as represented by the relative value of the intercept with respect to a base brand such as the store brand).

Israelevich (2004) addresses the issue of product variety and the role of slotting fees within a distribution channel. As discussed earlier, he finds that slotting fees have served to enhance the available product variety at a retailer, because the policy analysis indicates that retailers do not find all products to be intrinsically profitable. This result, suggesting two-part tariffs, where manufacturers are offering retailers allowances, is different from the pricing strategies suggested in the analysis of Berto Villas-Boas and Bonnet and Dubois. Clearly more research on the types of pricing contracts used for different types of products is required.

Besanko et al. (2003) study optimal targeted pricing on the part of manufacturers in the presence of retailers, using aggregate data within a competitive setting. Pancras and Sudhir (2007) study the optimal marketing strategies of a customer data intermediary, which needs to consider the value of its target pricing services to manufacturers in the presence of a retailer who sets retail prices. Hartmann and Nair (2007) estimate a demand system for tied good (razors and razor blades) when consumers shop across stores with different retail formats. Consumers buy razors disproportionately at grocery and drug stores, but the razor blades at club stores. As cross-elasticities between the two products are moderated by the retail channel, a policy analysis requires modeling the retail channel behavior. Chu et al. (2007) study the pricing behavior in the PC market and are able to assess the value of different distribution channels. They perform a variety of policy analyses on how dropping a distribution channel will affect firms. They also investigate the effect of the HP–Compaq merger using their estimates.

6.4 Future research

In summary, the structural models of channels literature has been able to map game-theoretic models to the data to both provide descriptions of the equilibrium interactions in the market, and perform policy analysis. As we pointed out earlier, there are some discrepancies in the inferences of power within the channel, depending on whether wholesale prices are observed or not. Further, there has been limited research on describing channel behavior in the presence of nonlinear contracts, because fixed transfers are typically not observed. More empirical research is needed in describing channel behavior in such markets.

While much extant research has focused on pricing as the key variable, future research should address other strategic variables such as manufacturer advertising and push versus pull promotions. Also current methodologies can deal with continuous strategic variables such as price, but new methodologies need to endogenize discrete decisions such as the retailer's decision to carry a product, introduce a new store brand etc. This would be in contrast to Israelevich's model, where he takes product acceptance decisions as exogenous. Such models can shed additional light on aspects such as how pricing contracts such as slotting allowances and trade deals affect product attractiveness and the decision to carry the product. Such advances not only require modeling advances, but also additional data on retailer product acceptance and rejection decisions (e.g. Sudhir and Rao, 2006) that would help us to learn about market behavior.

Far more challenging would be to model asymmetric information among channel members and how this may affect pricing contracts within a channel. This would require us to have access to a variety of contracts entered into by a firm at alternative levels of information asymmetry. Such data, however, are hard to obtain. But detailed data from a particular retailer (manufacturer) about the pricing contracts it enters with different manufacturers (retailers) can be very useful in developing appropriate methodologies and obtaining insights into how channel members arrive at pricing contracts.

Overall, the ratio of empirical to theoretical research on pricing across channels is low. This situation is being remedied as more data on both consumer choices across channels and retailer pricing become available and new empirical tools for analyzing retailer behavior are being developed. We hope these tools will provide greater insights into consumer behavior across channels, channel structure and relationships, and the behavior of channel participants in the near future.

7. Conclusion

This chapter surveyed the analytical and structural econometric literature on pricing in a channel. We described the analytical literature on channels in terms of the time horizons of decision-making: pass-through, pricing contracts and channel structure. We described the econometric literature in terms of its two major applications: description and policy analysis. The chapter also discussed gaps in the literature in each of the areas, and offered suggestions for future research.

References

Abraham, M.M. and L.M. Lodish (1987), 'PROMOTER: an automated promotion evaluation system', *Marketing Science*, **6**, 101–23.
Armstrong, M.K. (1991), 'Retailer response to trade promotions: an incremental analysis of forward buying and retail promotion', unpublished doctoral dissertation, University of Texas at Dallas, TX.
Balasubramanian, S. (1998), 'Mail versus mall: a strategic analysis of competition between direct marketers and conventional retailers', *Marketing Science*, **17**, 181–95.
Basuroy, S., M.K. Mantrala and R.G. Walters (2001), 'The impact of category management on retailer prices and performance: theory and evidence', *Journal of Marketing*, **65**, 16–32.
Bell, D.R., T.H. Ho and C.S. Tang (1998), 'Determining where to shop: fixed and variable costs of shopping', *Journal of Marketing Research*, **35**, 352–69.
Berto Villas-Boas, S. (2007), 'Vertical relationships between manufacturers and retailers: inference with limited data', *The Review of Economic Studies*, **74**, 625–52.
Besanko, D., S. Gupta and D. Jain, (1998), 'Logit demand estimation under competitive pricing behavior: an equilibrium framework', *Management Science*, **44**, 1533–47.
Besanko, D., J.-P. Dubé and S. Gupta (2003), 'Competitive price discrimination strategies in a vertical channel using aggregate retail data', *Management Science*, **49**, 1121–38.
Besanko, D., J.-P. Dubé and S. Gupta (2005), 'Own-brand and cross-brand retail pass-through', *Marketing Science*, **24**, 123–37.
Blair, R.D. and F. Lafontaine (1999), 'Will *Khan* foster or hinder franchising? An economic analysis of maximum resale price maintenance', *Journal of Public Policy and Marketing*, **18**, 25–36.
Blattberg, R.C. and A. Levin (1987), 'Modelling the effectiveness and profitability of trade promotions', *Marketing Science*, **6**, 124–47.
Blattberg, R.C. and S.A. Neslin (1990), *Sales Promotion Concepts, Methods, and Strategies*, Englewood Cliffs, NJ: Prentice-Hall.
Blattberg, R.C., R. Briesch and E. Fox (1995), 'How promotions work', *Marketing Science*, **14**, G122–G132.
Bloom, P.N., G.T. Gundlach and J.P. Cannon (2000), 'Slotting allowances and fees: schools of thought and the views of practicing managers', *Journal of Marketing*, **64**, 92–108.
Bonnet, C. and P. Dubois (2008), 'Inference on vertical contracts between manufacturers and retailers allowing for nonlinear pricing and resale price maintenance', Working Paper, Toulouse School of Economics.
Bruce, N., P.S. Desai and R. Staelin (2005), 'The better they are the more they give: trade promotions of consumer durables', *Journal of Marketing Research*, **42**, 54–66.
Brynjolfsson, E. and M.D. Smith (2000), 'Frictionless commerce? A comparison of internet and conventional retailers', *Management Science*, **46**, 563–85.

Busse, M., J. Silva-Risso and F. Zettelmeyer (2006), '$1,000 cash back: the pass-through of auto manufacturer promotions', *The American Economic Review*, **96**, 1253–70.
Butz, D.A. (1997), 'Vertical price controls with uncertain demand', *Journal of Law and Economics*, **40**, 433–59.
Che, H., K. Sudhir and P.B. Seetharaman (2007), 'Bounded rationality in pricing under state dependent demand: do firms look ahead, and if so, how far?', *Journal of Marketing Research*, **44**, 434–49.
Chen, F., A. Federgruen and Y. Zheng (2001), 'Coordination mechanisms for a distribution system with one supplier and multiple retailers', *Management Science*, **47**, 693–708.
Chen, Z. (2003), 'Dominant retailers and the countervailing-power hypothesis', *RAND Journal of Economics*, **34**, 612–25.
Chevalier, M. and R.C. Curhan (1976), 'Retail promotions as a function of trade promotions: a descriptive analysis', *Sloan Management Review*, **18**, 19–32.
Chevalier, A.J., A.K. Kashyap and P.E. Rossi (2003), 'Why don't prices rise during periods of peak demand? Evidence from scanner data', *The American Economic Review*, **93**, 15–37.
Chiang, W.K., D. Chhajed and J.D. Hess (2003), 'Direct marketing, indirect profits: a strategic analysis of dual-channel supply-chain design', *Management Science*, **49**, 1–20.
Choi, S.C. (1991), 'Price competition in a channel structure with a common retailer', *Marketing Science*, **10**, 271–96.
Chu, J., P. Chintagunta and N. Vilcassim (2007), 'Assessing the economic value of distribution channels: an application to the personal computer industry', *Journal of Marketing Research*, **44**, 29–41.
Chu, W. (1992), 'Demand signaling and screening in channels of distribution', *Marketing Science*, **11**, 324–47.
Corbett, C.J. and U.S. Karmarkar (2001), 'Competition and structure in serial supply chains with deterministic demand', *Management Science*, **47**, 966–78.
Coughlan, A.T. (1985), 'Competition and cooperation in marketing channel choice: theory and application', *Marketing Science*, **4**, 110–29.
Curhan, R.C. and R.J. Kopp (1987/88), 'Obtaining retailer support for trade deals: key success factors', *Journal of Advertising Research*, **27**, 51–60.
Desai, P.S. (2000), 'Multiple messages to retain retailers: signaling new product demand', *Marketing Science*, **19**, 381–9.
Desai, P.S. and K. Srinivasan (1995), 'Demand signaling under unobservable effort in franchising: linear and nonlinear price contracts', *Management Science*, **41**, 1608–23.
Desai, P.S., O. Koenigsberg and D. Purohit (2004), 'Strategic decentralization and channel coordination', *Quantitative Marketing and Economics*, **2**, 5–22.
Dubé, J.-P., P. Chintagunta, A. Petrin, B. Bronnenberg, G. Ron, P.B. Seetharaman, K. Sudhir, T. Raphael and Y. Zhao (2002), 'Structural application of the discrete choice model', *Marketing Letters*, **13**, 207–20.
Dukes, A.J., E. Gal-Or and K. Srinivasan (2006), 'Channel bargaining with retailer asymmetry', *Journal of Marketing Research*, **43**, 84–97.
Fugate, B., F. Sahin and J.T. Mentzer (2006), 'Supply chain management coordination mechanisms', *Journal of Business Logistics*, **27**, 129–61.
Gal-Or, E. (1991), 'Optimal franchising in oligopolistic markets with uncertain demand', *International Journal of Industrial Organization*, **9**, 343–64.
Gerstner, E. and J.D. Hess (1991), 'A theory of channel price promotions', *The American Economic Review*, **81**, 872–86.
Gerstner, E. and J.D. Hess (1995), 'Pull promotions and channel coordination', *Marketing Science*, **14**, 43–60.
Gilligan, T.W. (1986), 'The competitive effects of resale price maintenance', *RAND Journal of Economics*, **17**, 544–56.
Goldfarb, A., Q. Lu and S. Moorthy (forthcoming), 'Measuring brand value in an equilibrium framework', *Marketing Science*.
Gomez, M.I., V.R. Rao and E.W. McLaughlin (2007), 'Empirical analysis of budget and allocation of trade promotions in the U.S. supermarket industry', *Journal of Marketing Research*, **44**, 410–24.
Hartmann, W. and H. Nair. (2007), 'Retail competition and the dynamics of consumer demand for tied goods', Working Paper, Stanford Graduate School of Business.
Hastings, J.S. and R.J. Gilbert (2005), 'Market power, vertical integration and the wholesale price of gasoline', *The Journal of Industrial Economics*, **53**, 469–92.
Ho, T.H. and J. Zhang (2008), 'Designing pricing contracts for boundedly rational customers: does the framing of the fixed fee matter?', *Management Science*, **54**, 686–700.
Ingene, C.A. and M.E. Parry (1995a), 'Channel coordination when retailers compete', *Marketing Science*, **14**, 360–77.
Ingene, C.A. and M.E. Parry (1995b), 'Coordination and manufacturer profit maximization: the multiple retailer channel', *Journal of Retailing*, **71**, 129–51.

Ingene, C.A. and M.E. Parry (1998), 'Manufacturer-optimal wholesale pricing when retailers compete', *Marketing Letters*, **9**(1), 65–77.
Ingene, C.A. and M.E. Parry (2000), 'Is channel coordination all it is cracked up to be?', *Journal of Retailing*, **76**, 511–47.
Israelevich, G. (2004), 'Assessing supermarket product-line decisions: the impact of slotting fees', *Quantitative Marketing and Economics*, **2**, 141–67.
Iyer, G. (1998), 'Coordinating channels under price and nonprice competition', *Marketing Science*, **17**, 338–55.
Iyer, G. and J.M. Villas-Boas (2003), 'A bargaining theory of distribution channels', *Journal of Marketing Research*, **40**, 80–100.
Jeuland, A.P. and S.M. Shugan (1983), 'Managing channel profits', *Marketing Science*, **2**, 239–72.
Kadiyali, V., P. Chintagunta and N. Vilcassim (2000), 'Manufacturer–retailer interactions and implications for channel power: an empirical analysis of pricing in a local market', *Management Science*, **19**, 127–48.
Kim, S.Y. and R. Staelin (1999), 'Manufacturer allowances and retailer pass-through rates in a competitive environment', *Marketing Science*, **18**, 59–76.
Kumar, N. and R. Ruan (2006), 'On manufacturers complementing the traditional retail channel with a direct online channel', *Quantitative Marketing and Economics*, **4**, 289–323.
Kumar, N., S. Rajiv and A. Jeuland (2001), 'Effectiveness of trade promotions: analyzing the determinants of retail pass through', *Marketing Science*, **20**, 382–404.
Lal, R. (1990), 'Manufacturer trade deals and retail price promotions', *Journal of Marketing Research*, **27**, 428–44.
Lal, R. and J.M. Villas-Boas (1998), 'Price promotions and trade deals with multiproduct retailers', *Management Science*, **44**, 935–49.
Lal, R., J.D.C. Little and J. Villas-Boas (1996), 'A theory of forward buying, merchandising, and trade deals', *Marketing Science*, **15**, 21–37.
Lariviere, M.A. and V. Padmanabhan (1997), 'Slotting allowances and new product introductions', *Marketing Science*, **16**, 112–28.
Lee, E. and R. Staelin (1997), 'Vertical strategic interaction: implications for channel pricing strategy', *Marketing Science*, **16**, 185–207.
Lee, H.L., V. Padmanabhan and S. Whang (1997), 'Information distortion in a supply chain: the bullwhip effect', *Management Science*, **43**, 546–58.
Lin, J. (1988), 'Oligopoly and vertical integration: note', *The American Economic Review*, **78**, 251–4.
Marvel, H.P. and S. McCafferty (1984), 'Resale price maintenance and quality certification', *RAND Journal of Economics*, **15**, 346–59.
Mathewson, G.F. and R.A. Winter (1984), 'An economic theory of vertical restraints', *RAND Journal of Economics*, **15**, 27–38.
McAlister, L.M. (2007), 'Cross-brand pass-through: fact or artifact?', *Marketing Science*, **26**, 876–98.
McGuire, T.W. and R. Staelin (1983), 'An industry equilibrium analysis of downstream vertical integration', *Marketing Science*, **2**, 161–91.
Meza, S. and K. Sudhir (2006), 'Pass-through timing', *Quantitative Marketing Economics*, **4**, 351–82.
Meza, S. and K. Sudhir (2007), 'The role of strategic pricing by retailers in the success of store brand', Working Paper, University of Toronto.
Moorthy, S. (1987), 'Managing channel profits: comment', *Marketing Science*, **6**, 375–9.
Moorthy, S. (1988),' Strategic decentralization in channels', *Marketing Science*, **7**, 335–55.
Moorthy, S. (2005), 'A general theory of pass-through in channels with category management and retail competition', *Marketing Science*, **24**, 110–22.
Narasimhan, C. (1988), 'Competitive promotional strategies', *Journal of Business*, **61**, 427–50.
Pancras, J. and K. Sudhir (2007), 'Optimal marketing strategies for a customer data intermediary', *Journal of Marketing Research*, **44**, November, 560–78.
Perry, M.K. and D. Besanko (1991), 'Resale price maintenance and manufacturer competition for exclusive dealership', *The Journal of Industrial Economics*, **39**, 517–44.
Perry, M.K. and R.H. Groff (1985), 'Resale price maintenance and forward integration into a monopolistically competitive industry', *Quarterly Journal of Economics*, **100**, 1293–311.
Perry, M.K. and R.H. Porter (1990), 'Can resale price maintenance and franchise fees correct suboptimal levels of retail service?', *International Journal of Industrial Organization*, **8**, 115–41.
Purohit, D. (1997), 'Dual distribution channels: the competition between rental agencies and dealers', *Marketing Science*, **16**, 228–45.
Rao, V.R. (1984), 'Pricing research in marketing: the state of the art', *The Journal of Business*, **57**, S39–S60.
Rao, A.R. and H. Mahi (2003), 'The price of launching a new product: empirical evidence on factors affecting the relative magnitude of slotting allowances', *Marketing Science*, **22**, 246–68.
Rey, P. and J. Stiglitz (1995), 'The role of exclusive territories in producers' competition', *RAND Journal of Economics*, **26**, 431–51.

Rey, P. and J. Tirole (1986), 'The logic of vertical restraints', *American Economic Review*, **76**, 921–39.

Romano, R.E. (1987), 'A note on vertical integration: price discrimination and successive monopoly', *Economica*, **55**, 261–8.

Romano, R.E. (1994), 'Double moral hazard and resale price maintenance', *RAND Journal of Economics*, **25**, 455–66.

Roszkowski, M.E. (1999), 'State oil company v. Khan and the rule of reason: the end of intrabrand competition?', *Antitrust Law Journal*, **66**, 613–41.

Shaffer, G. (1991), 'Slotting allowances and retail price maintenance: a comparison of facilitating practices', *RAND Journal of Economics*, **22**, 120–35.

Shugan, M.S. (1985), 'Implicit understandings in channels of distribution', *Management Science*, **31**, 435–60.

Shugan, S. and R. Desiraju (2001), 'Retail product line pricing strategy when costs and products change', *Journal of Retailing*, **77**, 17–38.

Spengler, J.J. (1950), 'Vertical integration and antitrust policy', *The Journal of Political Economy*, **58**, 347–52.

Sudhir, K. (2001), 'Structural analysis of manufacturer pricing in the presence of a strategic retailer', *Marketing Science*, **20**, 244–64.

Sudhir, K. and V.R. Rao (2006), 'Do slotting allowances enhance efficiency or hinder competition?', *Journal of Marketing Research*, **43**, 137–55.

Sullivan, M.W. (1997), 'Slotting allowances and the market for new products', *Journal of Law and Economics*, **40**, 461–93.

Telser, L.G. (1960), 'Why should manufacturers want fair trade?', *Journal of Law and Economics*, **3**, 86–105.

Tirole, J. (1988), *The Theory of Industrial Organization*, Cambridge, MA: MIT Press.

Trivedi, M. (1998), 'Distribution channels: an extension of exclusive retailership', *Management Science*, **44**, 896–909.

Tyagi, R.K. (1999a), 'A characterization of retailer response to manufacturer trade deals', *Journal of Marketing Research*, **36**, 510–16.

Tyagi, R.K. (1999b), 'On the effects of downstream entry', *Management Science*, **45**, 59–73.

Varian, H.R. (1980), 'A model of sales', *American Economic Review*, **70**, 651–9.

Vernon, J.M. and D.A. Graham (1971), 'Profitability of monopolization by vertical integration', *Journal of Political Economy*, **79**, 924–5.

Villas-Boas, J.M. (1998), 'Product line design for a distribution channel', *Marketing Science*, **17**, 156–69.

Villas-Boas, J.M. and Y. Zhao (2005), 'Retailer, manufacturers, and individual consumers: modelling the supply side in the ketchup marketplace', *Journal of Marketing Research*, **42**, 83–95.

Walters, R.G. (1989), 'An empirical investigation into retailer response to manufacturer trade promotions', *Journal of Retailing*, **65**, 253–72.

Walters, R.G. and S.B. MacKenzie (1988), 'A structural equations analysis of the impact of price promotions on store performance', *Journal of Marketing Research*, **25**, 51–63.

Weng, K. (1995), 'Channel coordination and quantity discounts', *Management Science*, **41**, 1509–22.

Wilkie, W.L., D.M. Descrochers and G.T. Gundlach (2002) 'Marketing research and public policy: the case of slotting fees', *Journal of Public Policy and Marketing*, **21**, 275–88.

Zettelmeyer, F. (2000), 'Expanding to the Internet: pricing and communications strategies when firms compete on multiple channels', *Journal of Marketing Research*, **37**, 292–308.

16 Nonlinear pricing
Raghuram Iyengar and Sunil Gupta

Abstract
A nonlinear pricing schedule refers to any pricing structure where the total charges payable by customers are not proportional to the quantity of their consumed services. We begin the chapter with a discussion of the broad applicability of nonlinear pricing schemes. We note that the primary factor for the use of such schemes is the heterogeneity of the customer base. Such heterogeneity of preferences leads customers to choose different pricing plans based on their expected demand. We describe past analytical and empirical research. Past analytical work is categorized based on whether it is in a monopoly setting or a more general oligopoly context. Most past research has found two-part tariffs to be optimal in many settings. More recent research has begun to investigate the limits of such optimality and when a more general pricing scheme can be optimal. In the summary of empirical research on multi-part tariffs, we note that while nonlinear pricing schemes are popular, any analysis of demand under such schemes is nontrivial. One important reason is the two-way relationship between price and consumption in multi-part tariffs – the pricing scheme influences consumption and the level of consumption determines the applicable per-unit price. We describe how researchers have addressed this and other such issues and then show a modeling framework that integrates all the issues. We end by discussing empirical generalizations, which also suggest some promising areas for future research.

1. Introduction

A nonlinear pricing schedule refers to any pricing structure where the total charges payable by customers are not proportional to the quantity of their consumed services. The most common form is quantity discount for the purchase of large volumes. Several other forms of such pricing schemes exist across different industries. The following examples show the ubiquitous nature of this pricing strategy.

1. *Telecommunications* Most long-distance providers charge customers based on a combination of fixed fees (for access to the service) and per-minute price for each minute of a long-distance call. Wireless companies also charge customers in a similar manner for consumption of minutes but typically include some free minutes of consumption, along with a service plan.
2. *Consumer packaged goods* Quantity discounts are common in the consumer packaged goods industry. Typically, the per-unit price declines with package size. For instance, a recent search on Netgrocer.com showed that an 8 oz can of original B & M baked beans cost $1.39, which translates to $0.17/oz. A 16 oz can of the same baked beans cost $2.19, which is $0.14/oz. Some past research such as Nason and Della Bitta (1983) shows that consumers expect such quantity discounts.
3. *Electricity and water supply* Utility companies also offer quantity discounts. For instance, higher levels of consumption cost less for each kilowatt of consumption. In addition, energy rates for business users are different from those for residential users. Business users also incur varying rates based on peak versus off-peak electricity consumption.

4. *Business-to-business transactions* Many businesses offer quantity discounts to their customers. For instance in the electricity industry, customers purchasing large quantities of power have a high utilization as well. A quantity discount acknowledges the lower cost of idle capacity for such customers. Similar instances occur in the newspaper advertising industry, where businesses that advertise with a high frequency get charged at a lower rate per advertisement. See Dolan (1987) for a detailed discussion of various aspects of quantity discounts.
5. *Magazine subscriptions* Most magazines offer a lower rate for a two- or three-year subscription compared to the one-year subscription rate.

These examples show that nonlinear pricing takes many different forms. The purpose of this chapter is to summarize the research on nonlinear pricing. In Section 2, we explain the different kinds of nonlinear pricing schemes and discuss why such pricing schemes are used. Section 3 discusses the relevant managerial decisions for implementing such schemes. This is followed by a discussion in Section 4 on the theoretical findings on nonlinear pricing. In Section 5, we focus on empirical studies. Section 6 concludes the chapter.

2. Nonlinear pricing schemes – applications and motivation

Nonlinear pricing can be broadly classified in two categories – increasing block and decreasing block. In an increasing block pricing scheme, the marginal (per-unit) prices increase with quantity, whereas in a decreasing block scheme the marginal prices decrease with quantity. Figure 16.1 shows a few examples of increasing and decreasing block tariffs.

An increasing block tariff promotes conservation by penalizing excess consumption of units. A recent application of a multi-tier increasing block tariff for conservation is the electricity tariff in California. After the financial crisis in 2001, the California Public Utilities Commission imposed a new five-tier increasing block structure (see Reiss and White, 2005, p. 875 for more details). The new pricing scheme was implemented to encourage energy conservation. It was also expected to raise supplementary revenue for the state. Some evidence suggests that there was indeed a significant reduction in electricity consumption in 2001 as compared to the year before (Goldman et al., 2002).

A typical example of a decreasing block tariff is a quantity discount. For instance, Table 16.1 shows the rates that the *New York Times* charges in various categories (NYTimes Advertising Rates, 2008). Note that the rates decrease as the frequency of advertisement increases. This is essentially a mechanism for price discrimination – the advertisers who will commit to placing ads several times a year will get a cheaper rate than those customers who place only a one-time ad.

2.1 Reasons for nonlinear pricing

There are several reasons for firms to adopt a nonlinear pricing scheme. Here we discuss a few of the salient ones. See Wilson (1993) for a more detailed discussion.

1. *Price discrimination* Heterogeneity among customers is the primary reason to implement a nonlinear pricing scheme. This pricing structure can be thought of as a menu of quantities and corresponding charges. Each customer is expected to self-select the quantity–charge combination that is most appealing to him. As there is demand heterogeneity among customers, customers buy their ideal total quantity

Figure 16.1   Examples of nonlinear pricing schemes

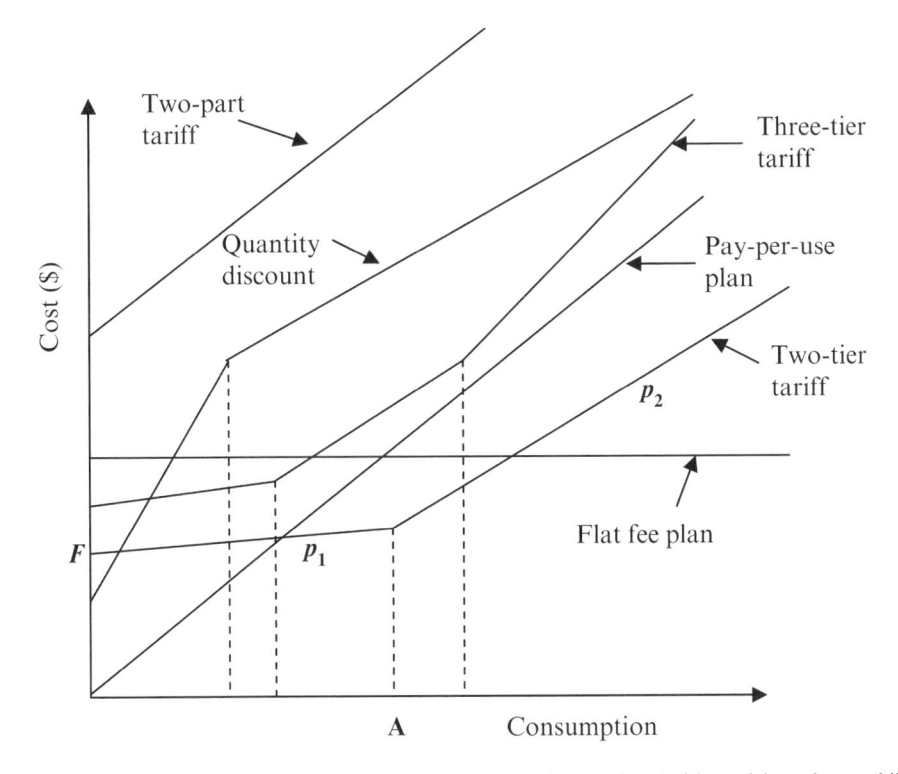

Note: In the figure, the intercept on the vertical axis is the fixed fee associated with a pricing scheme while the slopes are the per-unit (marginal) prices. For the two-tier tariff, F refers to the access fee, p_1 and p_2 are per-unit (marginal) prices and A is the kink point when the per-unit price changes from p_1 to p_2.

Table 16.1   Advertising rates in the New York Times *for different categories*

Frequency (times/year)	Line rates ($)		
	Computer Services	Healthy Living	Home/Garden Guide
13	37.00	38.00	37.25
26	36.50	35.25	36.75
52	34.75	34.75	36.25

Source: New York Times website. See http://www.nytadvertising.com/was/ATWWeb/ProcessorAction.do.

based on how the per-unit rates vary with each incremental unit. Table 16.2 shows the wireless service plans offered by Verizon in the Philadelphia region. Note that these plans are an example of a two-tier (or three-part) tariff scheme.

Table 16.2 shows that there is significant variation in the number of free minutes among plans and thus can appeal to a wide customer base. In addition, plans are designed to offer a quantity discount to heavy users.

Table 16.2 Verizon wireless plans within Philadelphia, PA

Plans	Monthly access fee ($)	Overage rate ($/min)	Free minutes per month
1	39.99	0.45	450
2	59.99	0.40	900
3	79.99	0.35	1350
4	99.99	0.25	2000
5	149.99	0.25	4000
6	199.99	0.20	6000

Source: Verizon wireless website. See www.verizonwireless.com.

2. *Cost considerations* Decreasing block pricing schemes such as quantity discounts offer incentives for customers to stockpile and transfer the inventory of units from the firm to the customer. If the inventory cost for a firm is high, then such discounts offer a way of reducing its costs. Wilson (1993, pp. 15–16) gives an example from the electric utilities industry. In that industry, customers purchasing large quantities of power have a high utilization as well. A quantity discount acknowledges the lower cost of idle capacity for such customers.

The pricing scheme within the package delivery industry provides another illustration of where the pricing scheme reflects cost considerations. Federal Express charges different rates depending on the weight of package and speed of delivery. Figure 16.2 shows the shipping charges for delivering a package from San Francisco to New York. These shipping charges increase with the weight of the package and the speed of delivery.

3. *Competitive pressures* Competitive pressures lead firms to use innovative nonlinear pricing schemes to entice customers. For instance, frequent flier miles began with each airline trying to acquire and retain business customers. Similarly, in the package delivery industry, many competitors of Federal Express such as UPS offer competitive nonlinear pricing schemes to draw customers. Figure 16.3 shows the package delivery charges from UPS for the same route (i.e. from San Francisco to New York).

A comparison of the UPS and Federal Express rates shows that they are similar, although the latter's prices are marginally lower. It is interesting to note that Federal Express also offers more alternatives – this can help customers to discriminate between companies even more. This suggests that the optimal design of a portfolio of nonlinear pricing plans involves the choice of number of plans as well as the pricing scheme for each plan.

3. Managerial decisions

The following example from long-distance telecommunications will provide a concrete context for the relevant decisions that a manager needs to make to set up a nonlinear pricing scheme.

Long-distance service providers typically price calling plans using a combination of

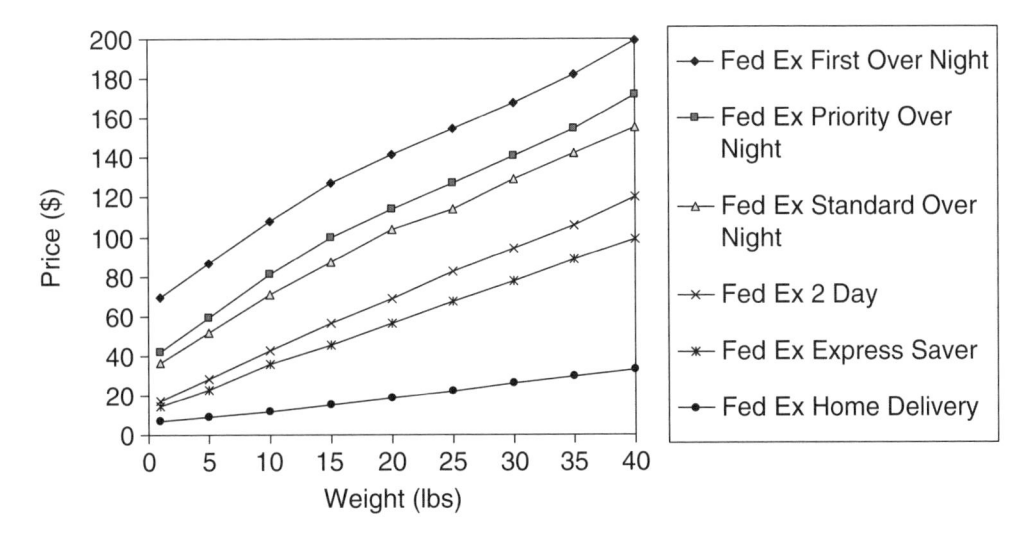

Figure 16.2 Federal Express delivery charges for shipping a package from San Francisco to New York

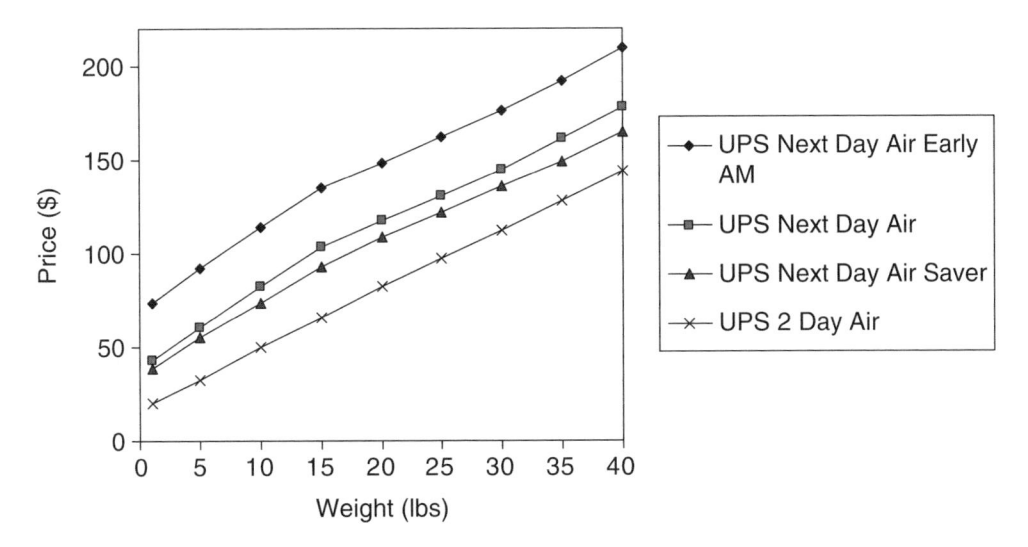

Figure 16.3 UPS delivery charges for shipping a package from San Francisco to New York

fixed fees (for access to the service) and per-minute price for each minute of a long-distance call. For instance, within New York State, Verizon offers several different callings plans. Table 6.3 illustrates these long-distance calling plans.

The table shows that there is some variation among the offered plans. For instance, the Timeless Plan has a fixed fee of $2.00 per month and a 10 c/minute rate for any consumption of long-distance minutes. This type of plan is termed a 'two-part tariff', with

Table 16.3 Verizon long-distance plans for New York State

Plan	Type of pricing plan	Monthly fee ($)	Detail of per-minute pricing
Timeless Plan	Two-part tariff	2.00	State-to-state and in-state calls: 10c/minute
E-Values	Two-part tariff	2.50	State-to-state and in-state calls: 10c/minute weekdays 7c/minute weekends
TalkTime 30	Three-part tariff	5.00	First 30 minutes free. Unused minutes do not carry over. State-to-state and in-state calls: 10c/minute after 30 minutes.
Verizon Five Cents Package Plan	Two-part tariff	6.00	State-to-state calls: 5c/minute In-state calls: 7c /minute
Verizon Freedom Value	Flat fee plan	34.99–39.99	Free

Source: Verizon website. See http://www22.verizon.com/Residential/Phone/Long+Distance/Long+Distance.htm.

the access fee and the per-minute price forming the two parts. Both Verizon Five Cents and E-Values have a similar structure but charge different prices for in-state and state-to-state calls. The remaining two plans (TalkTime 30 and Verizon Freedom Value) have a slightly different structure.

The Verizon Freedom Value Plan has an access fee ($34.99–$39.99) and any usage of long-distance minutes is free. Such type of plan is termed a 'flat fee' plan. Finally, the TalkTime 30 has three distinct components – an access fee ($5.00), per-minute rate (10 c/minute) and free minutes (30 minutes). Such a tariff is termed a 'three-part tariff'. Another popular term for this pricing scheme is a 'two-tier increasing block' tariff. Here, the term two-tier refers to the fact that there are two consumption regions based on different per-minute prices – region 1, when the consumption is less than 30 minutes, has a zero per-minute price and region 2, when the consumption is greater than 30 minutes, has a per-minute price of 10 c/minute. The term 'increasing block' signifies that the per-minute price in region 2 (10 c/minute) is greater than the per-minute price in region 1 (0 c/minute). Readers can immediately see that a two-tier increasing block tariff can be extended to a pricing scheme that has multiple tiers, which can be either increasing or decreasing block.

This example shows that nonlinear pricing schemes appear in many different forms – at one extreme, there is the special case of a flat fee plan and, on the other, there are multi-tier tariffs. Such a wide spectrum of plans can enable Verizon to appeal to different types of customers. When the pricing scheme involves a flat fee or in case of a two-part tariff, a relatively higher monthly access fee combined with a lower per-minute charge, heavy users are more likely to sign up for that plan. In contrast, light users will prefer the pricing scheme that has a relatively lower monthly access fee but a higher per-minute charge. This example also highlights the key managerial questions that have to be answered prior to designing a nonlinear pricing scheme. We show these decisions in Figure 16.4. There are three broad sets of decisions:

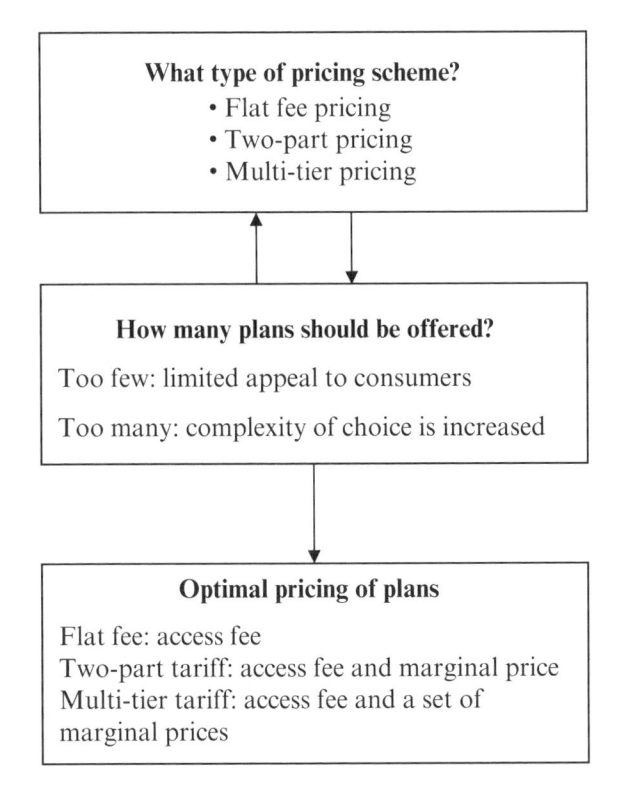

```
┌─────────────────────────────────────────┐
│      What type of pricing scheme?       │
│         • Flat fee pricing              │
│         • Two-part pricing              │
│         • Multi-tier pricing            │
└─────────────────────────────────────────┘
              ▲    │
              │    ▼
┌─────────────────────────────────────────┐
│      How many plans should be offered?  │
│  Too few: limited appeal to consumers   │
│  Too many: complexity of choice is      │
│            increased                    │
└─────────────────────────────────────────┘
                   │
                   ▼
┌─────────────────────────────────────────┐
│          Optimal pricing of plans       │
│  Flat fee: access fee                   │
│  Two-part tariff: access fee and        │
│    marginal price                       │
│  Multi-tier tariff: access fee and a    │
│    set of marginal prices               │
└─────────────────────────────────────────┘
```

Figure 16.4 Managerial questions for implementing a nonlinear pricing scheme

1. *Type of pricing schemes* A typical portfolio of plans can have a flat fee, two-part tariff and even a few multi-tier tariffs. Much analytical work has investigated the optimality of two-part tariffs (Schmalensee, 1981; Stole, 1995; Armstrong and Vickers, 2001; Rochet and Stole, 2002). Are such two-part tariffs optimal in every circumstance or does the presence of competition and customer heterogeneity affect the optimality of a pricing scheme? Similar questions can be asked about multi-part tariffs.

2. *Number of plans* One of the primary motivations of nonlinear pricing is consumer heterogeneity, and thus offering too few plans limits its appeal to a wide range of customers. At the same time, past research suggests that increasing the number of plans might not be the answer either (Iyengar and Lepper, 2000; Iyengar et al., 2004). This line of work suggests that consumers are less motivated to make a decision if there are too many alternatives. The optimal number of plans, which would differ from one context to another, will then emerge from modeling the tradeoff between a firm's desire to offer many alternatives to appeal to the heterogeneous customer base and consumers' motivation to process all the information. In addition, as Figure 16.4 shows, the two decisions, i.e. the number of plans and type of pricing scheme for each plan, are interlinked.

3. *Optimal pricing of plans* Given a set of plans, a firm has to choose the access fees and marginal prices for each of these plans. These decisions have to consider the impact

362 *Handbook of pricing research in marketing*

of pricing structure on consumers' choice, consumption and retention. The presence of competition (see the earlier example of Fed Ex© and UPS©) can further complicate the situation.

Next, we discuss an example that shows how a firm designed a nonlinear pricing scheme.

3.1 Illustrative Example Deutsche Bahn AG

We discuss how Deutsche Bahn AG, the German railroad corporation, implemented a two-part tariff pricing scheme and also highlight the type of data collection and analysis required for designing such a scheme. This example is adapted from Dolan and Simon (1996, p. 164), where it is discussed in much greater detail.

Duetsche Bahn AG faced stiff competition from the automobile industry. It charged DM 0.36 per kilometer for first-class rail travel and DM 0.24 per kilometer for second-class travel. Compared to these prices, the typical gasoline price in Germany was about DM 0.15 per kilometer. Thus it was cheaper for everyone to drive and indeed most people did perceive the prices for rail travel to be too high. In addition, the company also did not price-discriminate in any other way among its customers. For instance, an obvious price segmentation strategy is based on frequency of travel, with heavy and light users being charged at a different rate. It is the possibility of implementing such usage-based price discrimination that led to the concept of BahnCard – a card that would have an annual fee and, once purchased, would lead to discounted trips. Such a pricing scheme is a two-part tariff as there is a fixed fee for access to the card and then a per-kilometer charge for any travel. Further, the two-part tariff scheme of the card would be designed such that it can be a viable alternative to attract people away from just driving to their destination. Intuitively, it would be the heavy users who will be drawn towards such a card.

On route to designing the pricing plan, the management of the railroad corporation struggled with several key questions:

(a) What percentage discount over the regular per-kilometer rate should be granted to BahnCard buyers?
(b) What should be the price of the BahnCard?
(c) How should the price be varied by class and special groups such as elderly and students?

The answers to these questions were critical to optimally designing the pricing plan and required extensive data collection from customers and potential customers of the railroad system. This data collection, in the form of responses to a conjoint design, measured the willingness to pay for varying levels of discounts. In addition, a model was developed to simulate the effects of the different pricing structures on customer segments and thereafter to estimate optimal pricing. This model took into account various tradeoffs, such as that a low price for the card may sell a high volume but the overall revenue may be negative as otherwise the full-paying heavy usage segment will pay a lower price. On the other hand, a high price for access to the card will deter many potential customers and even current customers might not increase their usage.

The analysis resulted in the set of optimal prices for both the fixed fee (access to the card) and the marginal price (percentage discount per kilometer) of the two-part tariff. The discount was set at 50 percent, i.e. the per-kilometer rate for first-class travel was DM 0.18 and for second-class travel, at DM 0.12. The fixed fee for the BahnCard for first- (second-) class travel was determined to be DM 440 (220). Finally, for elderly and the students, the card was offered at half the regular price.

We can analyze the attractiveness of this pricing scheme from the viewpoint of a second-class traveler. If the customer purchases a BahnCard, then he pays an initial fee of DM 220 and receives a rate of DM 0.12 per kilometer. Thus, for the first 100 kilometers, the customer pays a total of DM 232 (= DM 220 + 0.12*100). This translates to a rate of DM 2.32 per kilometer. If the customer did not purchase a BahnCard, he would be charged at the uniform rate of DM 0.24 per kilometer. At this rate, for the first 100 kilometers, he would pay only DM 24. The break-even point between paying the uniform rate and buying the BahnCard, and getting the discount rate occurs at around 1833 kilometers. If the customer is going to travel more than 1833 km annually, then it would be cheaper for him to purchase the BahnCard. Next, we compare the cost for a BahnCard customer with his cost for driving to his destination. As mentioned before, the typical gasoline charge was about DM 0.15 per kilometer. In this case, if the customer does not buy the BahnCard, then it would never be economical to travel by train. However, after purchasing the BahnCard, he receives a discounted per-kilometer rate that is lower than the per-kilometer rate for driving. The break-even point between driving and train travel occurs around 7333 km. If the customer is going to travel more than 7333 km annually, then it will cheaper for him to purchase the BahnCard.

Since its introduction in 1993, BahnCard has been a spectacular success. In 2004, there were about 3.2 million BahnCards sold, giving Deutsche Bahn AG an overall revenue of $450 million.

4. Theoretical research

Analytical work has focused on the issue of optimality of certain nonlinear pricing schemes under different market conditions such as monopoly and oligopoly. We begin with some broad findings applicable in monopoly settings.

4.1 Monopoly

In a classic paper, Oi (1971) addressed the following question: as an owner of Disneyland, should you charge a high entry (fixed) fee and give the individual rides for free or should you let people come in for free but charge a high price per ride (marginal price)? These two alternatives represent two extremes: either charge a flat fee for entry or a per-ride rate. Oi considered the different roles played by the entry fee and price per ride. He noted that if the monopolist desired to have all consumers in the marketplace be interested in its product, then the entry fee has to be equal to the smallest of consumer surpluses. Next, as the marginal price and entry fee together determine the demand and the overall profit, there is an implicit relationship between the two prices. He showed that a two-part tariff (as opposed to a flat fee or a per-ride rate) will allow a monopolist to be both efficient in allocation and profit maximizing. The allocation efficiency comes from setting the usage price close to the marginal cost and the profit maximization occurs by using the access (or fixed) fee to extract all or most consumer surplus. In addition, the resulting pricing scheme can be such that a few consumers might be left out of the market (i.e. the entry fee is higher than the minimum of consumer surplus). This reduction in market coverage is compensated by a lower per-ride fee and the subsequent increase in demand for rides from the rest of the market.

In later work, Schmalensee (1981) and Varian (1985) have extended this analysis for situations where the monopolist can price-discriminate and investigated how it changes the welfare implications. Welfare change is the sum of monopoly profits and consumer surplus changes. They found that there is an increase in welfare from a simple monopoly to a price-discriminating monopoly only if the total quantity produced increases. In another extension, Rochet and Stole (2002) showed that even with random participation constraints, the optimal nonlinear pricing scheme takes the form of a two-part tariff.

Recent work has investigated the conditions that can alter the optimal combination of the fixed fee and marginal price in a two-part tariff. Essegaier et al. (2002) consider the dual roles of capacity constraints and usage heterogeneity in the customer base for optimal pricing of access services (e.g. services such as AOL, sports clubs, resorts and cable TV services). They make the following modeling assumptions: there are two consumer segments in the market – heavy users, who account for a fraction α of the market and use d_h units of capacity, and the rest $(1-\alpha)$ are light users who use d_l $(d_l < d_h)$ units of capacity. These usage rates are assumed to be independent of price. Thus the maximum usage rate (assuming the number of customers in the market is normalized to 1) is given by $\bar{d} = \alpha d_h + (1-\alpha)d_l$. This is the maximum capacity that is required to service the entire market. For any given fee (f) and usage price (p), light users pay $P_l = f + pd_l$ and heavy users pay $P_h = f + pd_h$. In addition, they model customer heterogeneity in preference by using the Hotelling line – a consumer who is located at x ($0 \leq x \leq 1$) has a linear transportation cost of tx to access the monopolist's service, where t is the unit transportation cost. In addition, V is the reservation price for the service (which is assumed to be the same for the two segments).

With these assumptions, they show that in the case of no capacity constraints, a monopolist will charge a flat fee such that it can cover the entire market. This flat fee price is $f = V - t$. The more interesting case arises when there are capacity constraints. The following constrained maximization problem captures the managerial decision:

$$\underset{(f,p)}{\text{Max}} \ (1-\alpha)x_l(f + pd_l) + \alpha x_h(f + pd_h),$$

$$\text{subject to } 0 \leq x_l \leq 1, 0 \leq x_h \leq 1, \quad (16.1)$$

$$\text{and } (1-\alpha)x_l d_l + \alpha x_h d_h \leq K.$$

Here, K is the capacity of the provider which satisfies, $0 \leq K \leq \bar{d}$ and x_l is $(V - f - pd_l)/t$, which is the location of marginal light users who are just indifferent between buying and not buying. Similarly, x_h is $(V - f - pd_h)/t$, which is the location of heavy users who are just indifferent between buying and not buying. The above maximization problem can be used to calculate what the optimal f and p should be as the capacity K changes. Essegaier et al. perform such an analysis and find that the two pricing components (f, p) should be negatively correlated. The flat fee is an effective way of extracting surplus from light users whereas the heavy users are more sensitive to the usage rate.

Thus, when customers have different usage rates, the pricing policy determines the customer mix that will be present and how much of the constrained capacity will be used. See Oren et al. (1985) and Scotchmer (1985) for other research that relates nonlinear pricing with capacity constraints.

An important question is whether firms should have a fixed fee and other nonlinear pricing plans together in their portfolio of offered plans. Sundararajan (2004) offers some guidelines in this regard. He analyzed a scenario where a firm associated with information goods offered both a fixed fee and a usage-based pricing plan under incomplete information. He found that if there are transaction costs associated with administering the usage-based pricing scheme, then offering a fixed fee pricing scheme (in addition to the usage-based scheme) is always profit improving. In fact, there may be situations (such as an information market in its early stages with a high concentration of low-usage customers) wherein a pure fixed fee pricing is optimal. What about the optimality of other types of nonlinear pricing schedules within a monopolistic setting? In a recent work, Masuda and Whang (2006) show that a portfolio comprising special forms of three-part tariff plans wherein, upon payment of a fixed fee, consumers receive certain units of the service for free and then are charged on a per-unit rate delivers as good a performance as any other nonlinear pricing schedule. Such special forms of three-part tariff are commonly used in the wireless telecommunications industry.

The examples described so far have considered a firm selling only a single product. What happens if the firm sells multiple products? Is a two-part tariff still optimal under some conditions? Armstrong (1999) attacked such a problem with a model that assumed consumers had multiple latent preference parameters, which might or might not be correlated across the products. He finds that if the preference parameters are independently distributed across products, the almost optimal tariff is a two-part tariff. If, however, there is a correlation in the preferences across products, the almost optimal tariff can be implemented as a menu of two-part tariffs. Thus a correlation of consumers' preferences induces a change in the overall optimal pricing scheme. See other work such as Mirman and Sibley (1980) and Wilson (1991) for other examples of optimal multiproduct pricing.

In this section, we have described only a small fraction of the enormous amount of research that has been done in monopoly settings. See Wilson (1993) for a more detailed discussion of such work.

4.2 Oligopoly

For oligopoly settings, researchers have tried to ascertain whether an increase in competition changes the structure of offered nonlinear pricing schemes. The typical modeling framework in such settings has both vertical and horizontal differentiation – the horizontal component captures the preferences of consumers across competitors while the vertical component captures differences in quality (Stole, 1995; Villas-Boas and Schmidt-Bohr, 1999; Armstrong and Vickers, 2001; Ellison, 2005). Stole (1995) showed that as competition increases, the quality distortion (i.e. the classic result that a monopolist will distort the quality level of its offered products to extract higher profits) decreases. Other work (Rochet and Stole, 2002; Armstrong and Vickers, 2001) have also found a similar result. In addition, both Rochet and Stole and Armstrong and Vickers show that, with some simplifying conditions such as full market coverage, the nearly optimal pricing scheme is again a two-part tariff scheme. One salient aspect of research in oligopoly settings is the rapid increase in mathematical complexity, which constrains researchers from obtaining simple closed-form solutions.

While the two-part tariff scheme can be nearly optimal under many conditions, several firms use more complex pricing schemes. Are such schemes optimal under any circumstance? The recent work of Jensen (2006) provides some direction, albeit in a much simpler duopoly setting. Jensen shows that implementation of simple two-part tariffs may not be a feasible strategy as the optimal nonlinear tariff exhibits a convexity for lower quantities. She shows that an optimal outcome can be implemented if firms use a tariff with inclusive consumption, i.e. a two-tier tariff where consumption on the first tier is free. This is exactly the type of pricing scheme used in wireless services. Such a finding clearly points to some future research that can investigate the implementation of other, more complex, pricing schemes.

5. Empirical research

While theoretical work has addressed the optimality of nonlinear pricing schemes under different conditions, the other two issues – the number of plans and the determination of optimal access fee and marginal prices – are empirically driven (see Section 3). Some researchers have begun to address these latter two questions and we describe such work in this section. To a large extent, however, empirical researchers have been concerned with several critical intermediate steps in modeling demand under nonlinear pricing schemes. Table 16.4 shows a summary of various studies in chronological order. In the table, we also indicate the key issue that a study considered and its main findings. Here we discuss a few of these studies in more detail within the broader framework of key issues.

5.1 Simultaneity of price and consumption

Services typically charge based on some form of a multi-part tariff. Such multi-part pricing induces a two-way dependence of price and consumption – the price influences consumption while the level of consumption depends on the prices charged by a provider. This two-way dependence occurs in many contexts. Examples are utilities such as electricity and water supply (Taylor, 1975; Nordin, 1976; Hausman et al., 1979; Billings and Agthe, 1980; Hewitt and Hanemann, 1995; Reiss and White, 2005), landline telephone services (Park et al., 1983; Train et al., 1987; Kling and Van der Ploeg, 1990; Kridel et al., 1993; Miravete, 2002; Danaher, 2002; Narayanan et al., 2007) and cellular phone (Miravete and Roller, 2004; Miravete, 2007; Iyengar et al., 2007a).

Research on addressing this simultaneity has its roots in labor economics (Hall, 1973; Rosen, 1976; Burtless and Hausman, 1978; Wales and Woodland, 1979; Hausman, 1985; Blomquist, 1996; Moffitt, 1990; Van Soest, 1995; Van Soest et al., 2002). Labor economists are concerned with the prediction of changes in the labor supply when a new tax structure is imposed on people. The early work on labor supply (Hall, 1973) used an ordinary least squares (OLS) approach with hours of work as a dependent variable and the applicable federal income tax rate as an explanatory variable. While OLS is attractive because of its simplicity, it is clearly not a viable option for this application because of the endogeneity of tax rate. When such endogeneity is present, researchers have typically used an instrumental variables (IV) approach (Hausman and Wise, 1976; Hausman et al., 1979). The biggest issue with the IV approach is that in practice it is often difficult to find

Table 16.4 Summary of empirical research on nonlinear pricing

Authors	Objective	Data	Model	Key Findings
Hall (1973)	Establish a relationship between the nonlinearity in tax schedules and number of hours that people work	Survey of Economic Opportunity (SEO) – hourly wage rates, personal characteristics of respondents	Ordinary least squares (OLS)	Effects of demographics, such as age, gender, race on number of work hours
Taylor (1975)	Survey of econometric literature on demand for electricity	Description of several studies	–	Appropriate modeling of demand under nonlinear pricing schemes involves an inclusion of marginal and average prices
Burtless and Hausman (1978)	Demand model with a nonlinear budget set arising from changes in tax rates	Consumer-level work hours, tax rates, wages, non-wage compensation and personal characteristics	Utility-based economic model that allows for maximization under a nonlinear budget	Much lower wage elasticities from tax rate changes than previous reduced-form approaches
Hausman et al. (1979)	Forecast consumer-level electricity usage	Household electricity consumption data	Economic demand model using budget constraints	Electricity usage under both time-of-day and declining block rate are predicted well
Park et al. (1983)	Calculate price elasticity for local telephone calls	Number of calls and minutes of local calls	Heteroskedastic and autocorrelated regression	Very small (about 0.1 or less) price elasticities for both calls and minutes
Dubin and McFadden (1984)	Analysis of residential electricity appliance holdings and consumption	Household-level appliance and electricity consumption data	Discrete/continuous demand model	Estimating demand using OLS without modeling appliance choice leads to an overestimation of the elasticity of demand
Train et al. (1987)	Forecast plan choice and demand for local telephone service	Number and average duration of local calls for a sample of customers	Nested logit	Households respond to a price change by changing their calling patterns more than their calling plans

Table 16.4 (continued)

Authors	Objective	Data	Model	Key Findings
Nunes (2000)	How consumers anticipate product usage during purchase deliberation and how it affects the choice of flat fee versus measured plan	Experimental data/ health club visitation records	NBD model	Consumers employ a break-even model – if expected usage is greater than the break-even, they choose a flat fee plan, otherwise they choose a measured plan
Danaher (2002)	Empirically derive a revenue-maximizing strategy for a two-part tariff with customer defection	Monthly usage and retention data	Regression model which also accounts for attrition	Access and usage prices have different relative effects on demand and attrition
Miravete (2002)	Analyze choice of plan and demand for local telephone service with consumer uncertainty	Monthly usage data on number and duration of calls	Demand model with a distinction between *ex ante* and *ex post* consumer types	There is evidence for *ex ante* and *ex post* asymmetry of information. This has implications for optimal design of plans
Lambrecht and Skiera (2007)	Understand the antecedents of flat fee and pay-per-use bias	Customer transaction data and survey data from an Internet service provider	Binomial logit model	Underestimation of usage is a major reason for pay-per-use bias. In addition, flat fee bias does not significantly increase customer defection
Allenby et al. (2004)	Model consumer choice for packaged goods and account for discrete quantities and quantity discounts	Scanner panel data	Discrete/continuous demand model	Model provides a valid measure of utility to assess changes in consumer welfare with assortment changes

Lambrecht et al. (2007)	Analyze the effect of consumer uncertainty on choice among three-part tariff plans	Customer transaction data from an Internet service provider	Discrete/continuous model	Demand uncertainty decreases consumer surplus and increases provider revenue. Access fee is the main driver of tariff choice
Iyengar et al. (2007a)	Incorporate consumer uncertainty on both quality and usage and model choice among three-part tariffs	Consumer-level monthly usage from a wireless service provider	Discrete/continuous model	Consumer learning can be a win–win for both consumers and provider. There is a 35% increase in customer lifetime value with learning than without
Narayanan et al. (2007)	Incorporate consumers' usage uncertainty and model choice between flat fee and measured plan	Consumer-level monthly usage for local telephone service	Discrete/continuous model	Consumers learn about their usage rapidly when they are on a measured plan and learn very slowly when on a fixed plan
Iyengar et al. (2007b)	Incorporate consumer uncertainty in expected usage and model choice among three-part tariffs	Choice-based conjoint	Utility-based economic model, with an underlying latent usage, in the presence of a nonlinear budget	Utility-based discrete choice model with inferred usage predicts significantly better than a traditional conjoint model

proper instruments and justify their use. Given the deficiency of the IV approach, other methods based on the selectivity bias literature (Heckman, 1979) have been developed (Heckman and MaCurdy, 1981; Reiss and White, 2005).

In a seminal paper, Burtless and Hausman (1978) suggested a technique, which combined theory with econometrics, to address this problem. In a pricing context, an application of this technique involves maximizing a specified utility function subject to the constraints imposed by the pricing scheme. With suitable assumptions on the utility function (quasi-concavity) and under increasing block pricing schemes, such maximization can yield a unique optimal solution. The actual consumption is then modeled as a deviation from this optimal solution. Thus it is not the observed consumption that results from an optimization but rather depends on the optimal consumption, which in turn is influenced by the pricing scheme. Burtless and Hausman termed the deviation between the optimal consumption and actual consumption as the 'optimization error'. A detailed explanation of all past research can be found elsewhere (Hausman, 1985; Moffitt, 1990).

Note that uniqueness of the optimal solution requires the presence of an increasing block pricing scheme. This is because these schemes translate to convex constraints and the maximization of a quasi-concave utility function subject to such constraints has a unique optimum (Hausman, 1985). This uniqueness is not ensured if the pricing scheme is decreasing block (e.g. a quantity discount). In such a case, multiple optima might exist. Thus the utility function will have to be directly evaluated to calculate the overall optimum. See Allenby et al. (2004) for such analysis where they evaluate the effect of quantity discounts on overall demand.

5.2 Endogenous choice and consumption decisions
In many service settings, consumers typically choose from a portfolio of nonlinear pricing tariffs. Thus they not only consume under a nonlinear pricing tariff but also choose that tariff (Dubin and McFadden, 1984; Train et al., 1987; Narayanan et al., 2007). For example, in a wireless service context, consumers choose a calling plan and then decide how many minutes to consume under that chosen plan. Such a process suggests two salient points. One, there is a temporal difference between the two decisions. Two, the choice and consumption decisions are endogenous (Hanemann, 1984; Chiang, 1991; Chintagunta, 1993).

Early research had modeled these two decisions as simultaneous. For instance, Train et al. (1987) used a nested logit model to captures households' choices among local telephone options and the relationship between the choice and the number and average duration of local calls. Here, they assume that choice and usage are simultaneous decisions. Similarly, Dubin and McFadden (1984) model the demand of consumer durables and the use of electricity. Here too, they assume that the two decisions are contemporaneous.

More recent research has focused on how to capture the intertemporal nature of the choice and consumption decisions. For instance, Miravete (2002) investigates how consumers choose between a flat fee and a measured tariff for local telephone service and then consume under the chosen tariff. He models the time lag and any uncertainty in consumers that arises by distinguishing between *ex ante* and *ex post* consumer types. A consumer knows only her *ex ante* type when she makes a choice among the different plans. After making the choice, she receives a shock, which alters her *ex ante* type to the *ex post* type. It is the *ex post* type that in turn influences the subsequent usage decision. This difference between the *ex ante* type and the *ex post* type captures any change in the information set of consumers due to the sequential nature of the decisions. Specifically, Miravete assumes the following relationship between the *ex ante* and the *ex post* type:

$$\theta = \theta_1 \theta_2, \qquad (16.2)$$

where θ is the consumer's *ex post* type, θ_1 is the *ex ante* type (known to the consumer at the tariff choice stage) and θ_2 is the shock. Thus the distribution of the *ex post* type is composed of the distribution of the *ex ante* type and the shock.

For model tractability, he makes the following distributional assumptions:

$$\theta_1 \sim Beta\left(1, \frac{1}{\lambda_1}\right). \qquad (16.3)$$

and

$$\theta_2 \sim Beta\left(1 + \frac{1}{\lambda_1}, \frac{1}{\lambda} - \frac{1}{\lambda_1}\right). \qquad (16.3)$$

With these assumptions, the consumer's *ex post* type has a Beta distribution as well:

$$\theta \sim Beta\left(1, \frac{1}{\lambda}\right). \qquad (16.4)$$

With these distributional assumptions, these consumer types are similar to probabilities. The demand function for the telephone service is dependent on the *ex post* type and is specified as follows:

$$x(p, \theta) = \theta_0 + \theta - p, \qquad (16.6)$$

where the parameter θ_0 is a parameter large enough to ensure that the demand is always positive and p is the per-minute price. This demand function, together with the distributional assumptions on the *ex post* type, then help Miravete test several hypotheses about how uncertainty plays a role in the sequential decision-making nature of the problem.

A different means for capturing this sequential nature of consumer decisions comes from extending the Burtless and Hausman model to incorporate the choice decision. The intuition is that consumers ascertain the optimal consumption under each available option, evaluate the utility of the different options with that option-specific optimal consumption and then choose the alternative that provides the highest utility. Subsequent to plan choice, consumers' actual consumption deviates from their optimal consumption due to optimization error. Thus the earlier decision of plan choice is influenced by optimal consumption and not the actual consumption. See Section 5.4 for an illustration of this modeling framework.

5.3 Usage uncertainty and learning

The sequential nature of decisions indicates that the information set of consumers could differ from when they are making a choice among different alternatives to when they

372 *Handbook of pricing research in marketing*

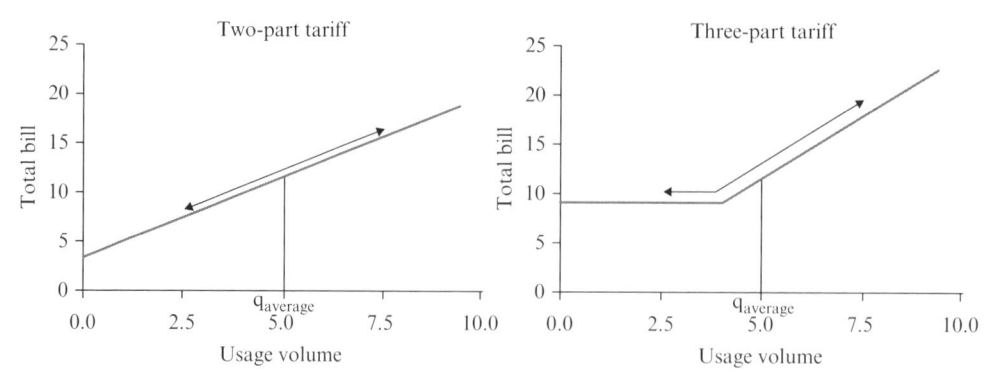

Source: Lambrecht et al. (2007), p. 11.

Figure 16.5 *Symmetric deviations of usage under a two-part tariff and three-part tariff scheme*

are consuming under a chosen plan. Further, if they have the opportunity to engage in repeated choice and usage decisions, their information set might alter over time as they 'learn' and resolve the uncertainty about their own usage patterns.

Lambrecht et al. (2007) use a simple example to show how such usage uncertainty can affect consumer choice. They consider symmetric distributions of usage under a two-part tariff and a three-part tariff. Figure 16.5 shows these deviations. The figure shows that usage deviations under a two-part tariff leave the expected bill unaffected, i.e. the expected bill is the same with low or high levels of uncertainty in usage. This is not so under a three-part tariff – under such pricing schemes, the higher the uncertainty in usage given the same level of mean usage, the higher is the overall bill. This clearly suggests that, under a three-part tariff and more complex multi-part tariffs, consumers' usage expectation can influence their choice of service plan.

Several researchers have found evidence to support this hypothesis (Nunes, 2000; Lemon et al., 2002; Lambrecht and Skiera, 2006). For instance, Nunes (2000) explores the cognitive process of how people anticipate service usage and how they integrate their expectations of usage to choose between a flat fee plan and a measured (pay-per-use) plan. He proposes that consumers calculate a break-even number and then see whether the break-even implies a choice of flat fee plan or a measured plan. Similarly, Lemon et al. (2002) show that consumer expectations of future usage influence their decision to stay with or leave a service provider.

Other researchers have quantitatively investigated consumers' usage uncertainty and learning using sophisticated models that incorporate Bayesian updating. For instance, Goettler and Clay (2007) capture consumer uncertainty and learning about the quality of an online retailer. Similarly, Narayanan et al. (2007) analyze data from an experiment conducted by South Central Bell. In this experiment, people had a choice between a flat rate pricing scheme and a two-part tariff. They find that consumer learning is very rapid when consumers are on the two-part tariff scheme but is very low while on the flat fee plan. Specifically, they make the following modeling assumption for the conditional indirect utility function for consumer i, plan j and time t:

$$V^j_{it} = (y_i - f^j) + \frac{\theta_{it}}{\beta}\exp(-\beta p^j_t). \tag{16.7}$$

Here, y_i is the income, θ_{it} is the consumer-specific and time-specific type (similar in spirit to the consumer type proposed by Miravete (2002)), f^j and p^j_t are the access fees and per-unit usage price and the parameter $-\beta$ is the price coefficient.

In addition, Narayanan et al. decompose the type parameter (θ_{it}) in the following manner:

$$\ln(\theta_{it}) = \alpha_i + \gamma Z_{it} + \eta_{it} + \nu_{it} \tag{16.8}$$

Here, the first component α_i is consumer specific but time invariant, the term $(\gamma Z_{it} + \eta_{it})$ captures the component observed by the consumer at the time of plan choice and finally, the shock ν_{it} is unobservable to the consumer during plan choice but is known at the time of usage decision. This framework captures the sequential nature of choice and consumption decisions. To capture learning, Narayanan et al. assume that consumers have beliefs over the parameter α_i, and these beliefs get updated as they observe their choices and the consumption signal.

Note that the above model is developed for a choice between a flat fee and a two-part tariff scheme. It is not straightforward to extend it to a setting where the pricing scheme has multiple tiers. Recently, Iyengar et al. (2007) developed a model that captured consumer learning and uncertainty within the context of more general pricing schemes. They found that consumer learning can lead to a win–win situation for both consumers and the firm – consumers leave fewer minutes on the table while the firm sees an increase in overall customer lifetime value (CLV). In particular, they estimated that there is about a 35 percent increase in CLV (about $75) in the presence of consumer learning. The key driver of this difference is the change in the retention rate with and without consumer learning.

Such quantitative models shed light on how different aspects of the pricing scheme and past choice and consumption decisions can affect consumers' information set and thereby influence their future decisions. While such work provides a direction, there are still many unresolved issues. For instance, within service settings, all models of consumer learning assume that each month's usage gives a signal to the consumer to better understand their own consumption pattern. However, there is research in a scanner data context that suggests that consumers have thresholds of insensitivity (Han et al., 2001). It is certainly plausible to assume that this might be the case within service contexts as well, i.e. perhaps only usage signals that are either above or below some threshold (which could be a function of how many free minutes are associated with the plan) have the potential to affect consumer learning. Such questions have much managerial significance given that consumer uncertainty and learning can affect their decision to defect from a service provider and thereby impact their overall lifetime value.

Thus far, we have given examples of how different researchers have addressed each of the issues associated with modeling consumer decisions under nonlinear pricing schemes. Next, we illustrate an integrated modeling framework that captures all three issues. See Iyengar et al. (2007) for more details. For this example, we use the context of wireless services.

374 *Handbook of pricing research in marketing*

5.4 Integrated modeling framework – example from wireless services

Consider a wireless service that has a two-tier increasing block pricing structure characterized by a fixed fee and two marginal prices. This scheme was graphically shown in Figure 16.1. Suppose F represents the access price for the service and the applicable marginal price is p_1 for consuming an additional unit before the kink is less than the marginal price, p_2, for consuming after the kink.

When consumers choose a wireless service, they do not make this decision in isolation from their other consumption decisions. At any point in time, they have several consumption opportunities and they allocate their income among these opportunities. This tradeoff across goods can be appropriately represented using a budget set representation. Such a budget set corresponding to an increasing two-tier pricing scheme is shown in Figure 16.6. The vertical axis in the figure corresponds to the consumption of the outside good (z) and the horizontal axis corresponds to the consumption of units of the service (x).

Figure 16.6 shows that the two-tier increasing block pricing structure of the service results in a piecewise linear budget set with a kink point (A). A consumer who subscribes to the service faces a convex budget set, and her income (I) is lowered by the sum of the access fee (F) and the variable charges for any consumed service. If, however, she does not subscribe to the service, then the entire income is used for consuming the outside good. If the marginal price of the outside good is normalized to 1 (numeraire), then the following equations represent the piecewise budget set.

$$p_1 x + z \leq I - F \quad \text{if } x > 0 \text{ and } x \leq A \tag{16.9}$$

$$p_2(x - A) + z \leq I - F - p_1 A \quad \text{if } x > A \tag{16.10}$$

In the wireless communications industry, a restricted form of such a two-tier increasing block pricing scheme, where p_1 is 0, is widely used. Therefore the consumption of an addi-

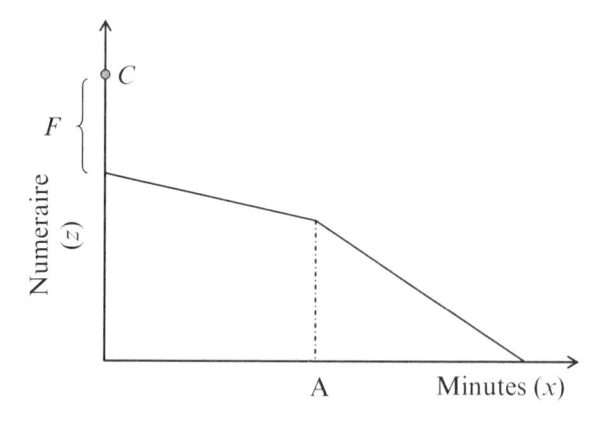

Note: F refers to the access fee, A is the kink point (free minutes) and C is the total income used for consuming the outside good if the consumer does not subscribe to the plan.

Figure 16.6 A budget set representation of a two-tier increasing block pricing scheme

tional minute before the kink point is costless. Next, we specify the utility that a consumer receives when he/she uses the wireless service.

Utility function Let U_{ijt} be the direct utility function for a consumer *I* for consuming x_{ijt} minutes under a plan *j* and a quantity z_{ijt} of the numeraire commodity during period *t*. We specify U_{ijt} as

$$U_{ijt}(x_{ijt}, z_{ijt}) = \hat{a}_{ij} + \acute{a}_{i1}x_{ijt} + \acute{a}_{i2}z_{ijt} + \acute{a}_{i3}x_{ijt}^2 + \mathring{a}_{ijt}. \tag{16.11}$$

The terms $\hat{a}_{ij}$, $\acute{a}_{i1}$, $\acute{a}_{i2}$ and $\acute{a}_{i3}$ are individual-level parameters[1] and the random choice errors are contained in $\mathring{a}_{ijt}$. We assume that this choice error is double exponential.

The optimal consumption, x^*, which maximizes the direct utility in Equation (16.11) subject to the non-linear pricing constraints imposed by plan *j*, can be written as follows:

$$\max_x U_{ijt}(x, z(x))$$

subject to Constraint I: $p_{1j}x + z = I_i - F_j$, if $0 < x \le A_j$,

Constraint II: $p_{2j}(x - A_j) + z = I_i - F_j - p_{1j}A_j$, if $A_j < x < B$. (16.12)

To ensure a unique solution to the above maximization problem, the utility function should be quasi-concave. This requires the Slutsky constraints – $\acute{a}_{i2} > 0$ and $\acute{a}_{i3} < 0$ on the parameters of the utility function. For a quasi-concave utility function and a convex budget set, the unique optimal solution x^* can be at an interior point (between 0 and A_j or between A_j and B) or one of the end points – 0, A_j and B. The two candidates for an interior optimal solution can be found by maximizing the utility function subject to the two linear constraints. The first-order conditions yield the following two interior candidate optima:

$$x^{candopt,I} = \frac{\acute{a}_{i2}p_{1j} - \acute{a}_{i1}}{2\acute{a}_{i3}},$$

$$x^{candopt,II} = \frac{\acute{a}_{i2}p_{2j} - \acute{a}_{i1}}{2\acute{a}_{i3}}, \tag{16.13}$$

In the above equations, $x^{candopt,I}$ ($x^{candopt,II}$) refers to the candidate optimal consumption when the utility function is maximized with Constraint I (Constraint II).

Given the uniqueness of the solution, at most one of the two candidates will be attainable, i.e. will lie in the consumption interval where its applied constraint holds. As Constraint I holds for any positive consumption less than A_j minutes, even though $x^{candopt,I}$ can lie anywhere on the real line, it is attainable only if it lies between 0 and A_j minutes. Similarly, $x^{candopt,II}$ is attainable only if it lies between A_j minutes and B. It is, however, possible that none of two candidates for an interior solution is attainable. Then, one of end points (0, A_j or B) might be chosen. These cases are mutually exclusive and, together with any possible

---

[1] The term $\hat{a}_{ij}$ represents an individual and plan-specific intercept. The parameter $\acute{a}_{i1}$ represents the main effect of consumption of minutes and $\acute{a}_{i2}$ represents the effect of consuming a unit of the numeraire. The term $\acute{a}_{i3}$ captures the effect of differential marginal impact of consuming an additional minute.

interior solution, form an exhaustive solution set, i.e. $x^* \in \{0, A_j, B, x^{candopt,I}, x^{candopt,II}\}$. We denote this optimal quantity for consumer i, plan j and time t by x^*_{ijt}.

Let the actual demand under plan j for consumer i at time t be x^{act}_{ijt}, then the optimal demand is related to the actual demand in the following manner:

$$x^{act}_{ijt} = x^*_{ijt} + \eta_{ijt}. \tag{16.14}$$

Here, the demand error, η_{ijt}, is assumed to be normally distributed with a mean 0 and variance δ^2. Thus the actual demand is a function of the optimal demand, which in turn is dependent on the budget constraints imposed by the pricing scheme. Equation (16.14) can then be used to determine the likelihood of consuming a certain number of minutes under a given plan.

Note that we developed this model for a scenario where consumers were facing an increasing block pricing scheme. As discussed earlier, such a scheme results in a convex budget set, and together with a quasi-concave utility function, we obtain a unique optimal quantity. This uniqueness is not ensured if the pricing scheme is decreasing block (e.g. a quantity discount). In such a case, multiple optima might exist and the algorithm for finding the optima (see equation 16.12 and the following discussion) will not be applicable. Thus the utility function will have to be directly evaluated to calculate the overall optimum. See Allenby et al. (2004) for such analysis where they evaluate the effect of quantity discounts on overall demand.

In addition, the above example shows that the Burtless and Hausman model primarily investigated demand under a nonlinear budget set. In several service contexts, however, such a model captures only one part of consumers' decisions. For example, in the wireless service context, consumers choose a calling plan among several alternatives and then consume under the chosen plan. Next, we describe how the above model can be extended to include the choice decision.

5.4.1 Inclusion of choice decision To incorporate the choice decision within the above framework, we calculate the optimal consumption associated with every plan. Thus, for every service plan k ($k = 1 \ldots J$), let the optimal consumption be x^*_{ikt}. Next, we determine the utility corresponding to this optimal consumption. This is the maximum utility that consumer i will receive if he or she chooses alternative k. Let the systematic component be denoted by V_{ikt}. Thus

$$U^{max}_{ikt}(x^*_{ikt}) = V_{ikt} + å_{ikt}. \tag{16.15}$$

Recall that we assumed that the choice error is double exponential distributed. This assumption gives the familiar logit expression for the probability of choice:

$$P_{ijt} = \frac{e^{V_{ijt}}}{\sum_k e^{V_{ikt}}} \tag{16.16}$$

Equations (16.14) and (16.16) together give the likelihood of choosing plan j and consuming x^{act}_{ijt} minutes. In this model, the choice and consumption decisions are related via the optimal quantity, which in turn is determined by maximizing the utility function subject to the budget constraints. Thus both consumer decisions stem from a single utility function. In addition, the choice decision occurs before the consumption decision and is influenced by optimal consumption.

Note that so far in this framework, we have assumed that consumers are completely certain of their optimal consumption under the different plans. Next, we show a way in which such uncertainty can be incorporated within the model.

5.4.2 Consumption uncertainty
If consumers have uncertainty in their consumption, then it renders the utility function stochastic. In such situations, consumers will use expected utility for making any decisions. This can be represented as follows:

$$EU_{ijt} = E^t_{usage}[g(x_{ijt}, z_{ijt})] + \mathring{a}_{ij} + \mathring{a}_{ijt},$$

$$g(x_{ijt}, z_{ijt}) = \mathring{a}_{i1}x_{ijt} + \mathring{a}_{i2}z_{ijt} + \mathring{a}_{i3}x^2_{ijt}.$$

(16.17)

Here, EU_{ijt} refers to the expected utility for consumer i and plan j and the term $E^t_{usage}[g(x_{ijt}, z_{ijt})]$ is the expectation with respect to a consumer's beliefs about his/her own usage. For each plan j we can assume an individual-specific belief distribution denoted by $f^{usage}_{ijt}(x)$. We subscript this belief distribution by time 't' to denote that it might be changing over time due to consumer learning. Different assumptions made for this belief distribution can investigate its sensitivity on the findings.

Thus, using the quantity belief distribution and the plan-specific budget constraints, the component, $E^t_{usage}[.]$, can be computed. The budget constraints for the plan impose a relationship between the consumed minutes (x_{ijt}) and the numeraire (z_{ijt}) as shown in equations (16.9 and 16.10). For example, if Constraint I holds, then $z_{ijt} = I_i - F_j - p_{1j}x_{ijt}$. Similarly, if Constraint II holds, then $z_{ijt} = I_i - F_j - p_{1j}A_j - p_{2j}(x_{ijt} - A_j)$. In other words, we can rewrite $g(x_{ijt}, z_{ijt})$ as a function of x_{ijt} only. Let $g(x_{ijt}, z_{ijt})$ be denoted by $h_1(x_{ijt})$ if $x_{ijt} \leq A_j$ and by $h_2(x_{ijt})$ if $x_{ijt} > A_j$. The quantity expectation is as follows:

$$E^t_{usage}[g(x_{ijt}, z_{ijt})] = \int_0^{A_j} h_1(x) f^{usage}_{ijt}(x) dx + \int_{A_j}^{\infty} h_2(x) f^{usage}_{ijt}(x) dx. \quad (16.18)$$

This expected quantity can be re-inserted in equation (16.17) to give the overall utility function. As before, if we continue to assume that the choice errors are double exponential distributed, then we can write the probability of choice for a plan with the familiar logit expression. This probability expression now would incorporate the effect of consumption uncertainty on plan choice. This completes our integrated modeling framework.

5.5 Key empirical results
Several empirical studies have focused on how consumers behave under nonlinear pricing schemes and then capture how the different components of a multi-part pricing scheme affect their behavior. Here, we summarize some key empirical results.

5.5.1 Flat fee bias
A robust finding across many empirical studies is that many consumers prefer a tariff with a flat fee even though their overall expense will be lower on

378   *Handbook of pricing research in marketing*

a pay-per-use plan (Kling and Van der Ploeg, 1990; Kridel et al., 1993; Nunes, 2000; Lambrecht and Skiera, 2006). This is referred to as the 'flat fee' bias. For instance, within the context of long-distance telephone service, Kridel et al. (1993) had found that 65 percent of consumers showed a flat fee bias. Similarly, in an application involving the use of an Internet service, Lambrecht and Skiera (2006) find that about 48 percent of consumers show a flat rate bias.

Lambrecht and Skiera (2006) also systematically consider the various causes for this bias and suggest that there are four reasons for its existence: insurance effect, taxi meter effect, convenience effect and overestimation effect. Insurance effect refers to the notion that consumers might want to choose a flat fee option as they want to 'insure' against future variation in their usage. The taxi meter effect captures the fact that many consumers can find their use of the service less enjoyable if they are paying by the minute. The term 'convenience effect' points to consumers choosing a status quo tariff to minimize any mental hassle associated with calculating the expected cost under the different available alternatives. Finally, the overestimation effect refers to the empirical finding that consumers can overestimate their demand, thereby biasing their choice towards a plan with a flat fee. In their study, Lambrecht and Skiera find that the insurance, taxi meter and overestimation effects account for the flat fee bias. Clearly, the level of consumers' usage uncertainty can moderate which of the four factors will have an influence on his/her choice decision.

5.5.2   Differential effect of access fee/marginal price   A second empirical generalization is that the different components of a pricing scheme indeed have a differential impact on customer behavior. We discuss two aspects: price elasticity and the use of the multi-part tariff for discrimination.

1. *Price elasticity*   Several studies across different contexts have investigated the price elasticity of different components of a multi-part pricing scheme. They have typically found price elasticity ranging from 0.1 to 1.0. Danaher (2002) describes a market experiment for a new telecommunication product (like a wireless service) in which the pricing scheme (a two-part tariff) was systematically manipulated. Consumers had to make a decision whether to continue using the product and if so, how much to use it. In that context, he found that both access fee and marginal price elasticity to be lower than 1.0. Within wireless services, Reiss and White (2007) also find that the mean price elasticity is less than one (1.00) and estimate it to be −0.44. Two studies in the context of local telephone service find very similar numbers – Park et al. (1983) and Train et al. (1987) found the price elasticity to be between 0.1 and 1.0. See Manfrim and Da Silva (2007) for a summary of estimated price elasticity across several different studies.
2. *Price discrimination*   Iyengar (2007) reports that changes in access fee have a much larger impact on customer lifetime value (CLV) as compared to that from changes in marginal price. He analyzed consumers' choice among four wireless service plans and their decision to leave the service provider. Each of these plans had a three-part tariff structure – access fee, associated free minutes and a per-minute rate for any consumed minutes beyond the free minutes. Table 16.5 shows the details of the pricing scheme for the four plans. After estimating the model parameters, he then

Table 16.5 Elasticity of customer lifetime value with increase or decrease in prices

Plan	Access fee ($)	Free minutes	Per-minute rate ($/min)	Access fee		Per-minute rate	
				up	down	up	down
1	30	200	0.40	−1.18	1.08	−0.02	0.09
2	35	300	0.40	−0.09	0.09	−0.06	0.08
3	40	350	0.40	−0.48	0.25	−0.12	0.10
4	50	500	0.40	0.06	−0.09	−0.22	0.16

Source: Iyengar (2007).

performed simulation studies to capture consumers' choice and consumption decisions (which provide revenue to the service provider) and their decision to stay with or leave the provider (consumers' defection decision). He then combined the generated revenue and consumers' defection decision to determine their CLV. In addition, he calculated the elasticity of CLV with respect to both access fee and marginal price. In these simulations, he changed (either increased or decreased) the access fee and marginal prices of the four plans, one plan at a time. Table 16.5 shows the results of the simulations.

The table shows that, in general, a price decrease for a plan leads to a higher CLV than that from an equivalent price increase. A price increase for a plan results in higher average revenue per user (ARPU) but negatively affects retention. In contrast, a price decrease for a plan enhances retention but lowers the revenue. The CLV results suggest that an increase in retention is more effective for increasing the CLV than an increase in the revenue. He also finds that for all plans but Plan 4, the elasticity of CLV with respect to the access price for a plan is higher than with respect to its marginal price. Thus service providers can affect the CLV more by changing the access fee than by altering the marginal prices.

An analysis of the effects of changing the access price on the CLV shows that a decrease in the access price for Plan 1 has the highest effect. This effect on CLV can be decomposed into the effect on revenue and retention. Table 16.6 shows this decomposition.

The table shows that the primary contributor for this result is an increase in retention of the 'light users' on Plan 1. Interestingly, he finds that an increase in the access price for Plan 4 leads to a higher CLV than that arising from a price decrease. This result can be explained based on the tradeoff between the ARPU and retention. The table shows that for a change in the access price of Plan 4, the ARPU is more elastic than retention is. Hence the increase in the ARPU due to an increase in the access fee dominates the decrease in retention and thereby yields a higher CLV than that of the base case scenario. An analysis of the effects of changing the marginal price on the CLV reveals that an increase in the marginal price for Plan 4 has the highest effect. This result is due to the increase in the defection rate of 'heavy users' on Plan 4. These consumers have a high consumption of minutes and can only respond to a price increase by defecting since downgrading to lower plans is not attractive. In contrast, a decrease in the marginal price for Plan 4 generates an incentive for

Table 16.6 *Elasticity of ARPU and retention with increase or decrease in prices*

Plan	Elasticity of ARPU				Elasticity of retention			
	Access fee		Per-minute rate		Access fee		Per-minute rate	
	up	down	up	down	up	down	up	down
1	0.23	−0.24	0.16	−0.07	−0.68	0.58	−0.08	0.07
2	0.11	−0.12	0.02	−0.01	−0.10	0.10	−0.03	0.04
3	0.24	−0.27	0.01	−0.01	−0.34	0.24	−0.05	0.04
4	0.10	−0.09	0.01	−0.02	−0.03	0.01	−0.11	0.08

Source: Iyengar (2007).

these heavy users to stay longer with the company. These findings suggest that the different components of a multi-part pricing scheme can be effectively used for price discrimination.

Iyengar et al. (2007b) provide additional evidence in support of the differing effect of access fee and marginal prices on consumers' choice decisions. With data from a choice-based conjoint task using multi-part tariffs, they build an economics-based model to investigate how changes in the pricing scheme of plans affect its probability of choice. They find that changes in access fee affect the plan choice probability in a way that differs both qualitatively and quantitatively from those by changes in the marginal prices. Specifically, they find that above a certain threshold, an increase in marginal price of plan does not have any effect on the consumer choice decision. In contrast, any increase in access fee of a plan always reduces the probability of choice of that plan.

Iyengar et al. also address questions regarding optimal (profit-maximizing) values of access fee and marginal price for the available plans. They use individual-level parameter estimates, e.g. price sensitivity, to account for customer heterogeneity and calculate the value of access fee and marginal prices for a portfolio of plans, which would lead to maximum overall profit. Such an analysis combines economic theory with customer behavior under such a pricing structure to yield profit-maximizing values for the various components of the pricing scheme.

In summary, these findings suggest that components of a pricing scheme can have a systematically differential impact on customer behavior. It is only recently that researchers have started investigating such effects, which suggests that this area holds much promise for future investigations.

6. Conclusions

In this chapter, we discussed several aspects of nonlinear (or multi-part) pricing. Such pricing schemes are very common in the service industry. We began the chapter by discussing several reasons for the use of such schemes and noted that the primary factor is the heterogeneity of the customer base. Such heterogeneity of preferences leads customers to choose different pricing plans based on their expected demand.

Next, we discussed findings from analytical work on nonlinear pricing. Here, we categorized past research based on whether it was in a monopoly setting or a more general oligopoly context. Most past research has found that two-part tariffs are optimal in many settings. Researchers have now begun to investigate the limits of optimality of two-part tariffs and when a more general pricing scheme can be optimal.

Thereafter, we summarized the past work on empirical research on multi-part tariffs. We noted that while nonlinear pricing schemes are popular, any analysis of demand under such schemes is nontrivial. A primary reason is that within multi-tier pricing schemes, there is a two-way relationship between price and consumption – the pricing scheme influences consumption and the level of consumption determines the applicable per-unit price. Two other issues are especially relevant within service contexts. First, the linkage between the choice of a service plan and usage under the chosen plan has to be appropriately specified. Two, there is a need to incorporate consumption uncertainty within any demand model. We discussed how researchers have addressed these issues and then showed a modeling framework that integrates all three issues. We ended by discussing some empirical generalizations, which also suggested some promising areas for future research.

References

Allenby, Greg M., Thomas S. Shively, Sha Yang and Mark J. Garratt (2004), 'A choice model for packaged goods: dealing with discrete quantities and quantity discounts', *Marketing Science*, **23** (1), 95–108.
Armstrong, Mark (1999), 'Price discrimination by a many-product firm', *Review of Economic Studies*, **66** (1), 151–68.
Armstrong, Mark and John Vickers (2001), 'Competitive price discrimination', *RAND Journal of Economics*, **32** (4), 579–605.
Billings, Bruce R. and Donald E. Agthe (1980), 'Price elasticities for water: a case of increasing block rates', *Land Economics*, **56**, 73–84.
Blomquist, N. Soren (1996), 'Estimation methods for male labor supply functions: how to take care of non-linear taxes', *Journal of Econometrics*, **70**, 383–405.
Burtless, Gary and Jerry Hausman (1978), 'The effects of taxation on labor supply: evaluating the Gary income tax maintenance experiment', *Journal of Political Economy*, **86**, 1103–30.
Chiang, Jeongwen (1991), 'A simultaneous approach to the whether, what and how much to buy questions', *Marketing Science*, **10** (4), 297–315.
Chintagunta, Pradeep (1993), 'Investigating purchase incidence, brand choice and purchase quantity decisions of households', *Marketing Science*, **12** (2), 184–208.
Danaher, Peter J. (2002), 'Optimal pricing of new subscription services: analysis of a market experiment', *Marketing Science*, **21** (2), 119–38.
Dolan, Robert J. (1987), 'Quantity discounts: managerial issues and research opportunities', *Marketing Science*, **6** (1), 1–22.
Dolan, Robert J. and Hermann Simon (1996), *Power Pricing*, New York: The Free Press.
Dubin, Jeffrey A. and Daniel L. McFadden (1984), 'An econometric analysis of residential electric appliance holdings and consumption', *Econometrica*, **52** (2), 345–62.
Ellison, Glenn (2005), 'A model of add-on pricing', *Quarterly Journal of Economics*, **120**, 1349–72.
Essegaier, Skander, Sunil Gupta and Z. John Zhang (2002), 'Pricing access services', *Marketing Science*, **21** (2), 139–59.
Goettler, Ron L. and Karen Clay (2007), 'Price discrimination with experience goods: sorting-induced biases and illusive surplus', Working Paper, Carnegie Mellon University.
Goldman, Charles A., Joseph H. Eto and Galen L. Barbose (2002), 'California customer load reductions during the electricity crisis: did they help to keep the lights on?', Ernest Orlando Lawrence Berkeley National Laboratory, Paper No: LBNL-49733.
Hall, Robert (1973), 'Wages, income and hours of work in the U.S. labor force', in Glen Cain and Harold Watts (eds), *Income Maintenance and Labor Supply*, Chicago, IL: Markham Press, pp. 102–62.
Han, Sangman, Sunil Gupta and Donald R. Lehmann (2001), 'Consumer price sensitivity and price thresholds', *Journal of Retailing*, **77** (4), 435–56.
Hanemann, Michael W. (1984), 'Discrete/continuous models of consumer demand', *Econometrica*, **52**, 541–61.
Hausman, Jerry (1985), 'The econometrics of non-linear budget sets', *Econometrica*, **53**, 1255–82.

Hausman, Jerry and David Wise (1976), 'The evaluation of results of truncated samples: the New Jersey income maintenance experiment', *Annals of Economic and Social Measurement*, **5**, 421–45.
Hausman, Jerry, M. Kinnucan and Daniel L. McFadden (1979), 'A two level electricity demand model: evaluation of the Connecticut time-of-day pricing test', *Journal of Econometrics*, **8**, 263–89.
Heckman, James J. (1979), 'Sample selection bias as a specification error', *Econometrica*, **47**, 153–67.
Heckman, James and Thomas MaCurdy (1981), 'New methods for estimating labor supply functions: a survey', in Ronald Ehrenberg (ed.), *Research in Labor Economics*, Vol. 4, Greenwich, CT: JAI Press, pp. 65–102.
Hewitt, Julie A. and W. Michael Hanemann (1995), 'A discrete/continuous choice approach to residential water demand under block rate pricing', *Land Economics*, **7**, 173–92.
Iyengar, Raghuram (2007), 'A structural demand model for wireless services', Working Paper, University of Pennsylvania.
Iyengar, Raghuram, Asim M. Ansari and Sunil Gupta (2007a), 'A model of consumer learning for service quality and usage', *Journal of Marketing Research*, **44** (4), 529–44.
Iyengar, Raghuram, Kamel Jedidi and Rajeev Kohli (2007b), 'A conjoint approach to multi-part pricing', *Journal of Marketing Research*, **45** (2), 195–210.
Iyengar, Sheena S. and Mark R. Lepper (2000), 'When choice is demotivating: can one desire too much of a good thing?', *Journal of Personality and Social Psychology*, **79**, 995–1006.
Iyengar, Sheena S., Wei Jeing and Gur Huberman (2004), 'How much choice is too much?: Determinants of individual contributions in 401K retirement plans', in O.S. Mitchell and S. Utkus (eds), *Pension Design and Structure: New Lessons from Behavioral Finance*, Oxford: Oxford University Press, pp. 83–95.
Jensen, Sissel (2006), 'Implementation of competitive nonlinear pricing: tariffs with inclusive consumption', *Review of Economic Design*, **10** (1), 9–29.
Kling, John P. and Stephen S. Van der Ploeg (1990), 'Estimating local telephone call elasticities with a model of stochastic class of services and usage choice', in A. de Fontenay, M. Shugard and D. Sibley (eds), *Telecommunications Demand Modeling*, Amsterdam: North Holland, pp. 119–36.
Kridel, Donald J., Dale E. Lehman and Dennis L. Weisman (1993), 'Option value, telecommunications demand and policy', in *Information Economics and Policy*, New York: Elsevier, pp. 125–44.
Lambrecht, Anja and Bernd Skiera (2006), 'Paying too much and being happy about it: existence, causes and consequences of tariff-choice biases', *Journal of Marketing Research*, **43** (2), 212–23.
Lambrecht, Anja, Katja Seim and Bernd Skiera (2007), 'Does uncertainty matter? Consumer behavior under three-part tariffs', *Marketing Science*, **6** (5), 698–710.
Lemon, Katherine N., Tiffany B. White and Russell S. Winer (2002), 'Dynamic customer relationship management: incorporating future considerations into the service retention decision', *Journal of Marketing*, **66**, 1–14.
Manfrim, Gustavo and Sergio Da Silva (2007), 'Estimating demand elasticities of fixed telephony in Brazil', *Economics Bulletin*, **12** (5), 1–9.
Masuda, Yasushi and Seungjin Whang (2006), 'On the optimality of fixed-up-to tariff for telecommunication service', *Information Systems Research*, **17** (3), 247–53.
Miravete, Eugenio J. (2002), 'Estimating demand for local telephone service with asymmetric information and optional calling plans', *The Review of Economic Studies*, **64**, 943–71.
Miravete, Eugenio J. (2007), 'Competing with menus of tariff options', Working Paper, University of Texas at Austin.
Miravete, Eugenio J. and Lars Frederick Roller (2004), 'Estimating markups under nonlinear pricing competition', *Journal of the European Economic Association*, **2**, 526–35.
Mirman, Leonard J. and David S. Sibley (1980), 'Optimal nonlinear prices for multiproduct monopolies', *The Bell Journal of Economics*, **11**, 659–70.
Moffitt, Robert (1990), 'The econometrics of kinked budget sets', *The Journal of Economic Perspectives*, **4** (2), 119–39.
Narayanan, Sridhar, Pradeep Chintagunta and Eugenio J. Miravete (2007), 'The role of self selection, usage uncertainty and learning in the demand for local telephone service', *Quantitative Marketing and Economics*, **5**, 1–34.
Nason, Robert W. and Albert J. Della Bitta (1983), 'The incidence and consumer perceptions of quantity surcharges', *Journal of Retailing*, **59** (2), 40–53.
Nordin, John A. (1976), 'A proposed modification of Taylor's demand analysis: comment', *Bell Journal of Economics*, **7**, 719–21.
Nunes, Joseph C. (2000), 'A cognitive model of people's usage estimation', *Journal of Marketing Research*, **37**, 397–409.
NYTimes Advertising Rates (2008), http://www.nytadvertising.com/was/files/others/05-3419-8_General Classified.pdf.
Oi, Walter Y. (1971), 'A Disneyland dilemma: two-part tariffs for a Mickey Mouse monopoly', *Quarterly Journal of Economics*, **85**, 77–96.

Oren, Shmuel S., Stephen S. Smith and Robert B. Wilson (1985), 'Capacity pricing', *Econometrica*, **53**, 545–66.
Park, Rolla E., Bruce M. Wetzel and Bridger M. Mitchell (1983), 'Price elasticities for local telephone calls', *Econometrica*, **51** (6), 1699–730.
Reiss, Peter C. and Matthew W. White (2005), 'Household electricity demand, revisited', *Review of Economic Studies*, **72** (3), 853–83.
Reiss, Peter C. and Matthew W. White (2007), 'Evaluating welfare with nonlinear prices', Working Paper, University of Pennsylvania.
Rochet, Jean-Charles and Lars A. Stole (2002), 'Nonlinear pricing with random participation', *Review of Economic Studies*, **69** (1), 277–311.
Rosen, Harvey (1976), 'Taxes in a labor supply model with joint wage-hours determination', *Econometrica*, **44**, 485–507.
Schmalensee, Richard (1981), 'Monopolistic two-part pricing arrangements', *Bell Journal of Economics*, **12**, 445–66.
Scotchmer, Suzanne (1985), 'Two-tier pricing of shared facilities in a free entry equilibrium', *RAND Journal of Economics*, **16**, 456–72.
Stole, Lars A. (1995), 'Nonlinear pricing and oligopoly', *Journal of Economic Management Strategy*, **4** (4), 529–62.
Sundararajan, Arun (2004), 'Nonlinear pricing of information goods', *Management Science*, **50** (12), 1660–73.
Taylor, Lester D. (1975), 'The demand for electricity: a survey', *Bell Journal of Economics*, **6** (1), 74–110.
Train, Kenneth E., Daniel L. McFadden and Moshe Ben-Akiva (1987), 'The demand for local telephone service: a fully discrete model of residential calling patterns and service choices', *RAND Journal of Economics*, **18** (1), 109–23.
Van Soest, Arthur (1995), 'Discrete choice models of family labor supply', *Journal of Human Resources*, **30**, 63–88.
Van Soest, Arthur, Marcel Das and Xiadong Gong (2002), 'A structural labor supply model with nonparametric preferences', *Journal of Econometrics*, **107** (1–2), 345–74.
Varian, Hal R. (1985), 'Price discrimination and social welfare', *American Economic Review*, **74** (4), 870–75.
Villas-Boas, Miguel and Udo Schmidt-Mohr (1999), 'Oligopoly with asymmetric information: differentiation in credit markets', *RAND Journal of Economics*, **30** (3), 375–96.
Wales, Terence and Anthony Woodland (1979), 'Labor supply and progressive taxes', *Review of Economic Studies*, **46**, 83–95.
Wilson, Robert B. (1991), 'Multiproduct tariffs', *Journal of Regulatory Economics*, **3**, 5–26.
Wilson, Robert B. (1993), *Nonlinear Pricing*, Oxford: Oxford University Press.

17 Dynamic pricing
P.B. (Seethu) Seetharaman

Abstract
This chapter reviews pricing issues that are relevant to oligopolistic firms competing in markets characterized by demand dynamics, i.e. state dependence and reference price effects. Normative models of dynamic pricing predict that (1) in inertial markets, competing firms have an incentive to compete fiercely using low prices in the early (growth) stages, but tacitly collude on high prices in the later (mature) stages, (2) variety-seeking markets always sustain higher prices for competing firms, and (3) markets with reference prices show cyclical pricing, which is more profitable for competing firms as long as enough consumers weigh price gains more heavily than price losses. Descriptive models of dynamic pricing show that (1) competing firms in inertial and variety-seeking markets indeed account for the future effects, in addition to current effects, of their current pricing decisions, and (2) such firms behave in a boundedly rational manner in the sense of looking into a few future periods only. Descriptive models of dynamic pricing in the presence of reference price effects need to be estimated in future research.

1. Introduction

When pricing strategies of firms recognize the future (i.e. long-term) implications – for consumers and/or competitors – of their current prices, dynamic pricing is said to exist. Such dynamic pricing incentives arise, for example, for the following reasons: (1) consumers learn about a brand's attributes by repeatedly buying it over time, and eventually form stable preferences for the brand, which suggests that using low prices to encourage brand trial may speed up, for example, the brand's market penetration; (2) consumers provide word of mouth – positive or negative – for previously tried brands, which suggests that targeting low initial prices at 'opinion leaders' may pay off for brands in the long run; (3) declining prices erode brand equity, which suggests that high prices may be necessary for firms to positively cultivate their brand strength in the long term; (4) seasonality or excess production capacity leads firms to adopt clearance pricing strategies for their brands etc. All of these reasons typically apply to markets involving new brands. Interestingly, however, dynamic pricing incentives also arise for mature brands when conditions of 'demand dynamics' exist. This is the focus of this chapter, on which we now elaborate.

1.1 Demand dynamics

In order to effectively price their brands in mature product categories, brand managers must understand how prices of competing brands influence consumers' brand choices within the product market. Some product markets are characterized by demand dynamics that arise due to the effects of state dependence or/and reference prices in consumers' brand choices. We explain these effects below.

State dependence The probability that a given consumer is likely to buy Coke or Pepsi on a visit to the store is partly a function of which cola brand the consumer bought on their previous visit. One consumer may buy Coke on consecutive purchase occasions 'out of habit' (even if Pepsi were on sale at the second purchase occasion), while another consumer may switch from Coke to Pepsi (even if Coke were on sale at the second purchase occasion) just to try 'something different'. The first consumer's brand choices are said to exhibit positive state dependence or 'inertia', while the second consumer's brand choices are said to exhibit negative state dependence or 'variety-seeking'.

Reference prices The probability that a given consumer is likely to buy Coke or Pepsi on a visit to the store is a function of not only the current values of the two cola brands' prices, but also their relative values when compared to the brands' historical prices, as perceived by the consumer, referred to as 'reference prices'. For example, a consumer may buy Coke even when it is higher priced than Pepsi because Coke's price is lower than its reference price, while Pepsi's price is higher than its reference price. Such reference prices for brands are generally formed on the basis of what the consumer has observed during previous shopping trips.

When state dependence or reference price effects, as explained above, are present, market shares of brands in the corresponding market will tend to be serially correlated over time. We refer to such serial correlations as demand dynamics. This chapter deals with pricing decisions of competing firms in markets characterized by such demand dynamics.

1.2 Pricing implications of demand dynamics

Under demand dynamics, a brand's demand in a given period is not just a function of the brand's price in that period, but also a function of the brand's price or/and demand in previous periods. A pricing implication of demand dynamics that arises due to inertia is that reducing the price for one's brand in the current period may increase the brand's market share not only in the current period but also in the subsequent period when the price reduction on the brand has been retracted (assuming no competitive responses in prices). A pricing implication of demand dynamics that arises due to either variety-seeking or reference prices is that reducing the price for one's brand in the current period may increase the brand's market share in the current period, but may hurt in the subsequent period when the price reduction is retracted. For example, in the reference price case, the subsequent high price may be evaluated negatively when compared to the previous lower price. In the variety-seeking case, an increased market share in the current period may lead to decreased market share in the subsequent period when consumers switch away from the previously tried brand. In other words, for a given brand, price reductions may be more attractive in the presence of inertia, while price increases may be more attractive in the presence of reference prices or variety-seeking, when compared to markets where such demand dynamics are absent. A game-theoretic equilibrium analysis of oligopolistic prices under demand dynamics will shed light on this issue.

1.3 Econometric models of dynamic pricing

When setting prices for their brands in markets characterized by demand dynamics, brand managers must know both (1) the actual extent of demand dynamics in the market, and (2) the pricing techniques that are actually adopted by competing brand managers. Analyzing historical market-level data on market shares and prices of competing brands over time will enable brand managers to obtain an accurate understanding of (1) and (2). Brand managers can then set prices based on their understanding of these two elements.

386 *Handbook of pricing research in marketing*

The rest of this chapter is organized as follows. We briefly review empirical findings on demand dynamics in Section 2. In Section 3, we discuss theoretical results pertaining to the pricing implications of demand dynamics that have been derived using game-theoretic equilibrium analyses. Section 4 discusses empirical findings on firms' pricing strategies in the presence of demand dynamics, which have been obtained using econometric models of dynamic pricing. Section 5 concludes.

2. Demand dynamics

Since the seminal empirical study of Guadagni and Little (1983), dynamic considerations have generally been shown to govern consumers' brand choices in packaged goods categories. These dynamics operate in the sense that a consumer's probability of buying a brand in the current period is a function of, among other things, whether or not the consumer has bought the same brand in previous periods, as well as the brand's previously observed prices. The first influence is that of state dependence effects, while the second is that of reference prices. We next discuss the existing empirical findings pertaining to these two effects.

2.1 State dependence

A positive effect of past consumption of a brand on the consumer's current probability of buying the brand is referred to as 'inertia', while a negative effect is referred to as 'variety-seeking'. For example, to the extent that it is cognitively expensive for consumers to 'think' extensively about their brand choice decisions, they may routinize their brand purchases by buying the same brand repeatedly over time. This means that a previously chosen brand has a higher probability of being chosen in the current period than other brands, all else being equal. This is called inertia. In contrast, consumers may satiate themselves on attributes contained in previously chosen brands and, therefore, switch to new brands that contain new, untried attributes. In such a scenario, a previously chosen brand has a lower probability of being chosen in the current period than other brands, all else being equal. This is called variety-seeking.

The effects of inertia and variety-seeking on consumers' brand choices have been documented in numerous empirical studies over the years (Jeuland, 1979; McAlister, 1982; Givon, 1984; Kahn et al., 1986; Bawa, 1990; Fader and Lattin, 1993; Trivedi et al., 1994; Allenby and Lenk, 1995; Erdem, 1996). These effects have been shown to persist even after accounting for the effects of marketing variables and unobserved heterogeneity on brand choices in a flexible manner (Keane, 1997; Gupta et al., 1997; Seetharaman and Chintagunta, 1998; Seetharaman et al., 1999; Ailawadi et al., 1999; Abramson et al., 2000; Erdem and Sun, 2001; Moshkin and Shachar, 2002).

2.2 Reference prices

Consumers often evaluate the price of a brand at the store with respect to some summary statistic representing the brand's historically observed prices from the past, which is referred to as the brand's reference price. When the brand's observed price is higher than its reference price, the brand is perceived by the consumer as less attractive than when the brand's observed price is lower than the reference price, all else being equal. This means that frequent price cuts may have a hurtful consequence to the brand in the long run since they are likely to reduce the brand's reference price and, therefore, consumers' evaluations of future prices of the brand. In this sense, demand dynamics arise on account of the long-run effects of brands' pricing decisions.

The effects of reference prices on consumers' brand choices have been extensively documented since the late 1980s (Winer, 1986; Lattin and Bucklin, 1989; Rajendran and Tellis, 1994; Briesch et al., 1997; Chang et al., 1999). Reference price effects have been shown to be consistently larger for price losses than for price gains, i.e. the negative impact of a price increase (loss) is greater in magnitude than the positive impact of an equal-sized price decrease (gain), on a consumer's probability of buying the brand (Kalwani et al., 1990; Kalwani and Yim, 1992; Mayhew and Winer, 1992; Krishnamurthi et al., 1992; Hardie et al., 1993; Kalyanaram and Little, 1994; Mazumdar and Papatla, 1995, 2000; Bell and Lattin, 2000; Erdem et al., 2001; Han et al., 2001).

In the presence of demand dynamics – intertemporal linkages in demand for brands that arise due to the effects of inertia, variety-seeking and reference prices – a managerial question that arises pertains to the long-term effectiveness of pricing. Past empirical studies have quantified the magnitudes of long-term 'spillover' effects of price cuts in markets with inertia, variety-seeking or reference prices (Lattin and Bucklin, 1989; Roy et al., 1996; Seetharaman, 2003, 2004). For example, Seetharaman (2004) shows that ignoring inertia underestimates the total incremental impact of a price cut by as much as 35 percent. This suggests that the reduced profit margin for a brand during a period of a price cut may be offset by increases in brand volume not just during the period of promotion but also in future periods. But these findings are predicated on the assumption that competitive responses are absent. In reality, however, price changes on a brand would have not only direct effects on its sales, but also indirect effects through the changes triggered in competitive brands' prices. A game-theoretic analysis of price competition between brands in markets with demand dynamics will throw light on this issue. We discuss this in the next section.

3. Pricing implications of demand dynamics

Game-theoretic models are typically used to provide insights into the nature of price competition in oligopolistic markets. In the presence of demand dynamics, such as those discussed in Section 2, these game-theoretic models are rendered dynamic. Such dynamic pricing models are also called state-space pricing models, in which firms' pricing actions in one period shift their payoffs (profits) in subsequent periods. One of two common informational assumptions are typically invoked to solve for firms' optimal pricing strategies in such state-space pricing models: (1) open-loop, i.e. firms commit to their pricing actions in the initial period, (2) closed-loop, i.e. firms' pricing actions are functions of all payoff relevant information ('state'), which are typically the most recent period and market shares. An open-loop pricing equilibrium is a Nash equilibrium in open-loop strategies and is, therefore, static. A closed-loop equilibrium is a sub-game-perfect equilibrium and is, therefore, dynamic. Since closed-loop strategies are much more difficult to solve analytically than open-loop strategies (since each firm's pricing actions enters the opponent's pricing decision rules and affects their future choices), one analytical simplification that is typically made is to restrict attention to 'stationary strategies', i.e. pricing strategies that do not depend on time and only on brands' most recent market shares (see Slade, 1992 for insightful discussions of these issues). Many theoretical studies have employed one or more of these concepts to solve state-space pricing models in the presence of demand dynamics. We discuss them below.

3.1 Pricing implications of state dependence

Klemperer (1987a) derives the normative pricing implications of demand inertia in an undifferentiated duopoly using a two-period game-theoretic framework, and shows that the non-cooperative pricing equilibrium in the second period is the same as the collusive outcome in an otherwise identical market without inertia. In other words, two competing firms in a mature market characterized by inertia – each firm with an installed base of customers from the previous period – face demand functions that are relatively price inelastic compared to their counterparts in an identical mature market without inertia. This decreased price elasticity reduces the price rivalry among the firms, leading to higher prices for the brands of both firms. Klemperer (1987a) also shows that the pricing power that the two firms gain in the second period leads to vigorous price competition in the first period, which may more than dissipate the firms' extra monopolistic returns from the second period. In other words, in the early growth stages of a market characterized by inertia, competing firms would engage in fierce price competition to build market shares for their brands.

Klemperer (1987b) shows that the central implications of Klemperer (1987a), discussed above, also apply for a differentiated duopoly. Klemperer (1987b) also extends the modeling framework to allow for rational (i.e. 'forward-looking') consumers, and shows that first-period prices of the two firms become less competitive because consumers who realize that firms with higher market shares will charge higher prices in the future are less price elastic than naive consumers.

The two-period game-theoretic models of Klemperer (1987a, 1987b) do not tell us what to expect from price competition over many periods when old (locked-in) customers and new (uncommitted) customers are intermingled and firms cannot discriminate between these groups of customers. Will firms' temptation to exploit their current customer bases lead to higher prices, or will firms' desire to attract new customers lead to lower prices than in the case of no inertia? In order to answer this question, Beggs and Klemperer (1992) extend the duopoly pricing model of Klemperer (1987b) to the infinite-period case, where new consumers arrive and a fraction of old consumers leaves in each period. Beggs and Klemperer (1992) show, over a wide range of parametric assumptions, that firms obtain higher prices and profits compared to those in the absence of inertia. The authors find that prices rise as (1) firms discount the future more, (2) consumers discount the future less, (3) turnover of consumers decreases, and (4) the rate of growth of the market decreases.

In contrast to the discrete-time, game-theoretic framework adopted by Beggs and Klemperer (1992), Wernerfelt (1991) adopts a continuous-time, game-theoretic framework to study price competition between firms in inertial markets. Consistent with the findings in Beggs and Klemperer (1992), Wernerfelt (1991) also derives higher equilibrium prices for firms, as well as a positive effect of the extent of firms' future discounting behavior on equilibrium prices, in inertial markets. This shows that the equilibrium pricing results are robust to whether the game-theoretic pricing models are solved in discrete or continuous time.

As in Wernerfelt (1991), Chintagunta and Rao (1996) also study the normative pricing implications of demand dynamics using a continuous-time, game-theoretic framework. The authors show that in the presence of demand inertia, the firm with the higher baseline preference level will charge the higher price in steady state. They also show that myopic pricing strategies of firms that fail to recognize the long-run impact of their current prices lead to prices that are 100–200 percent higher than those implied by dynamic pricing strategies.

Seetharaman and Che (forthcoming) extend the two-period game-theoretic frameworks of Klemperer (1987a, 1987b) to derive the normative pricing implications of variety-seeking in a duopoly. Unlike the inertia case of Klemperer (1987a, 1987b), where the positive effects of a tacitly collusive pricing equilibrium in the second period could effectively unravel on account of vigorous price competition in the first period, the variety-seeking case implies tacitly collusive prices among firms in both periods. This is because in the early growth stages of a market characterized by variety-seeking, competing firms have no incentive to build market shares for their brands since each firm recognizes that its customers have an incentive to defect to the competing firm in the future on account of variety-seeking. In later stages, firms exploit the fact that previous customers of competitors will buy their brands in a search for variety and, therefore, again end up charging high prices. Once the model allows for rational (i.e. 'forward-looking') consumers, first-period prices of the two firms become even less competitive.

3.2 Pricing implications of reference prices
Greenleaf (1995) derives the normative pricing implications of reference price effects for a retailer. He finds that a price promotion on a brand can increase retail profit if the retailer's gain in the promotion period – from increased demand for the promoted brand at the lower price – outweighs the retailer's loss in future periods – from a lowered reference price for the brand in the future. He derives conditions under which the optimal pricing policy for the retailer is cyclical, i.e. involves periodic price promotions.

Kopalle et al. (1996) derive the normative pricing implications of reference price effects in a duopoly involving two manufacturers. Assuming a linear demand function and allowing for two consumer segments – one that weighs price gains more heavily than losses, and another that does the opposite – in the analysis, the authors derive a Markov-perfect Nash equilibrium in prices. They derive the sufficient condition, i.e. the relative sizes of the two consumer segments, for cyclical pricing to be optimal for both manufacturers. They find that the existence of the first consumer segment (i.e. those who weigh gains more heavily than losses) is necessary for cyclical pricing to be an optimal policy.

While the models discussed in this section throw light on how prices in an oligopoly ought to be in the presence of demand dynamics, a pertinent question that arises next is how prices actually operate in real-world markets with demand dynamics. In other words, do real-world manufacturers and retailers indeed account for demand dynamics while setting prices for their brands? We cover this issue in the next section.

4. Econometric models of dynamic pricing
Econometric models of dynamic pricing – pricing models that are necessary in the presence of demand dynamics – require both (1) the solution of discrete-time, stochastic dynamic optimization problems for each firm, where a firm chooses from a continuum of possible prices, and the (2) fixed point to the game-theoretic problem of multiple

firms employing their best pricing responses to each other's pricing choices. Recently proposed techniques in the econometric literature – Pakes and McGuire (1994); Berry and Pakes (2000); Pakes and McGuire (2001) – enable the estimation of such dynamic pricing models while successfully circumventing the challenges posed by the large dimensionality of each firm's pricing choices, as well as the possibility of the existence of multiple pricing equilibria.

Chan and Seetharaman (2004) investigate price competition between cola brands – Coke and Pepsi – using two years of IRI's scanner panel data (from June 1991 to June 1993) on household purchases in the cola category in a metropolitan market in a large US city. The authors first estimate the extent of demand dynamics in the product category using a stochastic brand choice model of state dependence. This model incorporates the effects of households' intrinsic brand preferences, as well as responsiveness to marketing variable – in addition to the effects of inertia and variety-seeking – and allows all parameters to be heterogeneous across households in a flexible manner. Using the estimated brand choice model, along with estimates of interpurchase times in the product category, the authors then construct a predictive model of brand sales. This brand sales model is assumed to serve as an input for the pricing decisions of firms. The authors develop a game-theoretic dynamic pricing model, which is based on the idea that firms compete on prices in an infinite-period, repeated game with discounting. This dynamic pricing game – which uses the predictive brand sales model as an input – is estimated using historical data on brands' prices in the market, adopting a recently proposed estimation technique (Berry and Pakes, 2000). The estimates of the dynamic pricing model are compared to those obtained using (1) a myopic pricing model that assumes that firms are not forward looking (even though firms recognize the existence of demand dynamics in the market), and (2) a static pricing model that assumes that firms ignore demand dynamics altogether when pricing their products. The authors show that the dynamic pricing model better fits and predicts the observed prices, and also yields more intuitively reasonable estimates of brand-specific marginal costs and, therefore, profit margins (about 20 percent for each brand), when compared to the myopic and static pricing models (which yield brand-specific average margins of about 100 percent and 70 percent, respectively).

Che et al. (2007) investigate price competition between breakfast cereals brands, as well as the nature of strategic pricing interactions between breakfast cereals manufacturers and the retailer, using two years of IRI's scanner panel data (from June 1991 to June 1993) on household purchases in the breakfast cereals category in a metropolitan market in a large US city. For this purpose, the authors extend the econometric methodology of Berry et al. (1995) to handle the dynamic aspects of the manufacturers' and the retailer's pricing problems. The authors study whether firms look ahead, as well as to what extent, while setting prices. The authors find that (1) omission of demand dynamics biases the econometrician's inference of manufacturer behavior, i.e. one erroneously infers tacit collusion among cereals manufacturers when firms are competitive, and (2) the observed retail prices are consistent with a pricing model in which both cereals manufacturers and the retailer are forward looking, but the firms' time horizon when setting prices is short term, i.e. firms look ahead by only one period, suggesting that firms are boundedly rational in their dynamic pricing behavior. The authors also find that 94 percent of the additional explanatory power of the dynamic pricing model over the static pricing model (that ignores state dependence effects) arises from the firm's accounting for the effects of lagged demand on current demand, while only 6 percent arises from the firm's looking into the future when setting current prices.

While the above-mentioned studies estimate pricing decisions of oligopolistic firms in the presence of state dependence, no econometric study has looked at firms' pricing decisions in the presence of reference prices. This is a notable omission in the literature on dynamic pricing and merits further study.

5. Conclusions

This chapter discusses pricing models in the presence of demand dynamics that arise due to the effects of state dependence and reference prices in consumers' brand choices over time. One notable omission in the existing literature on these dynamic pricing models pertains to the estimation of pricing decisions of competitive firms in the presence of reference price effects. While normative models of what firms must do have been proposed by Kopalle et al. (1996), no descriptive model of what firms actually do in practice has been estimated so far. Addressing this is an important avenue for future research. Future econometric research on pricing should also systematically investigate how alternative sources of demand dynamics – such as consumer stockpiling, retailer forward buying, consumer learning, word of mouth, price expectations etc. – affect strategic pricing decisions of firms in practice. Future research should also focus on the implications of dynamic pricing for firms' distribution channel or contracting strategies.

References

Abramson, C., I.S. Currim and J.M. Jones (2000), 'Parameter bias from unobserved effects in the multinomial logit model of consumer choice', *Journal of Marketing Research*, **37** (4), 410–26.

Ailawadi, K.L., K. Gedenk and S.A. Neslin (1999), 'Heterogeneity and purchase event feedback in choice models: an empirical analysis with implications for model building', *International Journal of Research in Marketing*, **16** (3), 177–98.

Allenby, G.M. and P.J. Lenk (1995), 'Reassessing brand loyalty, price sensitivity and merchandising effects on consumer brand choice', *Journal of Business and Economic Statistics*, **13** (3), 281–9.

Bawa, K. (1990), 'Modeling inertia and variety-seeking tendencies in brand choice behavior', *Marketing Science*, **9** (3), 87–96.

Beggs, A. and P. Klemperer (1992), 'Multi-period competition with switching costs', *Econometrica*, **57** (3), 651–66.

Bell, D.R. and J.M. Lattin (2000), 'Looking for loss aversion in scanner panel data: the confounding effect of price response heterogeneity', *Marketing Science*, **19** (2), 185–200.

Berry, S., J. Levinsohn and A. Pakes (1995), 'Automobile prices in market equilibrium', *Econometrica*, **63** (4), 841–90.

Berry, S. and A. Pakes (2000), 'Estimation from the optimality conditions for dynamic controls', Working Paper, Yale University, New Haven, CT.

Briesch, R.A., L. Krishnamurthi, T. Mazumdar and S.P. Raj (1997), 'A comparative analysis of reference price models', *Journal of Consumer Research*, **24** (2), 202–14.

Chan, T. and P.B. Seetharaman (2004), 'Estimating dynamic pricing decisions in oligopolistic markets: an empirical approach using micro- and macro-level data', Working Paper, Washington University in St Louis.

Chang, K., S. Siddarth and C.B. Weinberg (1999), 'The impact of heterogeneity in purchase timing and price responsiveness on estimates of sticker shock effects', *Marketing Science*, **18** (2), 178–92.

Che, H., K. Sudhir and P.B. Seetharaman (2007), 'Bounded rationality in pricing under state dependent demand: do firms look ahead? How far ahead?', *Journal of Marketing Research*, **44** (3), 434–49.

Chintagunta, P.K. and V.R. Rao (1996), 'Pricing strategies in a dynamic duopoly: a differential game model', *Management Science*, **42** (11), 1501–14.

Erdem, T. (1996), 'A dynamic analysis of market structure based on panel data', *Marketing Science*, **15** (4), 359–78.

Erdem, T. and B. Sun (2001), 'Testing for choice dynamics in panel data', *Journal of Business and Economic Statistics*, **19** (2), 142–52.
Erdem, T., G. Mayhew and B. Sun (2001), 'Understanding reference-price shoppers: a within- and cross-category analysis', *Journal of Marketing Research*, **38** (4), 445–57.
Fader, P. and J.M. Lattin (1993), 'Accounting for heterogeneity and non-stationarity in a cross-sectional model of consumer purchase behavior', *Marketing Science*, **12** (3), 304–17.
Givon, M. (1984), 'Variety-seeking through brand switching', *Marketing Science*, **3** (1), 1–22.
Greenleaf, E.A. (1995), 'The impact of reference price effects on the profitability of price promotions', *Marketing Science*, **14** (1), 82–104.
Guadagni, P. and J.D.C. Little (1983), 'A logit model of brand choice calibrated on scanner data', *Marketing Science*, **2** (3), 203–38.
Gupta, S., P.K. Chintagunta and D.R. Wittink (1997), 'Household heterogeneity and state dependence in a model of purchase strings: empirical results and managerial implications', *International Journal of Research in Marketing*, **14** (4), 189–213.
Han, S., S. Gupta and D.R. Lehmann (2001), 'Consumer price sensitivity and price thresholds', *Journal of Retailing*, **77** (4), 435–56.
Hardie, B.G.S., E.J. Johnson and P.S. Fader (1993), 'Modeling loss aversion and reference dependence effects on brand choice', *Marketing Science*, **12** (4), 378–94.
Jeuland, A. (1979), 'Brand choice inertia as one aspect of the notion of brand loyalty', *Management Science*, **25** (3), 671–82.
Kahn, B.E., M.U. Kalwani and D.G. Morrison (1986), 'Measuring variety seeking and reinforcement behaviors using panel data', *Journal of Marketing Research*, **23** (2), 89–100.
Kalwani, M.U. and C.K. Yim (1992), 'Consumer price and promotion expectations: an experimental study', *Journal of Marketing Research*, **29** (1), 90–100.
Kalwani, M.U., C.K. Yim, H.J. Rinne and Y. Sugita (1990), 'A price expectations model of customer brand choice', *Journal of Marketing Research*, **27** (3), 251–62.
Kalyanaram, G. and J.D.C. Little (1994), 'An empirical analysis of latitude of price acceptance in consumer package goods', *Journal of Consumer Research*, **21** (3), 408–18.
Keane, M.P. (1997), 'Modeling heterogeneity and state dependence in consumer choice behavior', *Journal of Business and Economic Statistics*, **15** (3), 310–27.
Klemperer, P. (1987a), 'Markets with consumer switching costs', *The Quarterly Journal of Economics*, **102** (4), 375–94.
Klemperer, P. (1987b), 'The competitiveness of markets with switching costs', *RAND Journal of Economics*, **18** (1), 138–50.
Kopalle, P.K., J.L. Assunção and A. Rao (1996), 'Asymmetric reference price effects and dynamic pricing policies', *Marketing Science*, **15** (1), 60–85.
Krishnamurthi, L., T. Mazumdar and S.P. Raj (1992), 'Asymmetric response to price in consumer brand choice and purchase quantity decisions', *Journal of Consumer Research*, **19** (3), 387–400.
Lattin, J.M. and R.E. Bucklin (1989), 'Reference effects of price and promotion on brand choice behavior', *Journal of Marketing Research*, **26** (3), 299–310.
Mayhew, G.E. and R.S. Winer (1992), 'An empirical analysis of internal and external reference prices using scanner data', *Journal of Consumer Research*, **19** (1), 62–70.
Mazumdar, T. and P. Papatla (1995), 'Loyalty differences in the use of internal and external reference prices', *Marketing Letters*, **6** (2), 111–22.
Mazumdar, T. and P. Papatla (2000), 'An investigation of reference price segments', *Journal of Marketing Research*, **37** (2), 246–58.
McAlister, L. (1982), 'A dynamic attribute satiation model for choices made across time', *Journal of Consumer Research*, **9** (3), 141–50.
Moshkin, N. and R. Shachar (2002), 'The asymmetric information model of state dependence', *Marketing Science*, **22** (4), 1–20.
Pakes, A. and P. McGuire (1994), 'Computing Markov-perfect Nash equilibria: numerical implications of a dynamic differentiated product model', *The RAND Journal of Economics*, **25** (4), 555–89.
Pakes, A. and P. McGuire (2001), 'Symmetric Markov-perfect equilibrium, stochastic algorithms and the curse of dimensionality', *Econometrica*, **69** (5), 1261–81.
Rajendran, K.N. and G.J. Tellis (1994), 'Contextual and temporal components of reference price', *Journal of Marketing*, **58** (1), 22–34.
Roy, R., P.K. Chintagunta and S. Haldar (1996), 'A framework for investigating habits, the hand of the past, and heterogeneity in dynamic brand choice', *Marketing Science*, **15** (3), 280–99.
Seetharaman, P.B. (2003), 'Probabilistic versus random utility models of state dependence: an empirical comparison', *International Journal of Research in Marketing*, **20** (1), 87–96.

Seetharaman, P.B. (2004), 'Modeling multiple sources of state dependence in random utility models: a distributed lag approach', *Marketing Science*, **23** (2), 263–71.
Seetharaman, P.B., A. Ainslie and P.K. Chintagunta (1999), 'Investigating household state dependence effects across categories', *Journal of Marketing Research*, **36** (4), 488–500.
Seetharaman, P.B. and H. Che (forthcoming), 'Pricing behavior in markets with consumer variety seeking', *Marketing Science*.
Seetharaman, P.B. and P.K. Chintagunta (1998), 'A model of inertia and variety seeking with marketing variables', *International Journal of Research in Marketing*, **15** (1), 1–17.
Slade, M.E. (1992), 'Vancouver's gasoline price wars: an empirical exercise in uncovering supergame strategies', *Review of Economic Studies*, **59** (2), 257–76.
Trivedi, M., F.M. Bass and R.C. Rao (1994), 'A model of stochastic variety seeking', *Marketing Science*, **13** (3), 274–97.
Wernerfelt, B. (1991), 'Brand loyalty and market equilibrium', *Marketing Science*, **10** (3), 229–45.
Winer, R. (1986), 'A reference price model of brand choice for frequently purchased products', *Journal of Consumer Research*, **13** (2), 250–56.

PART III

SPECIAL TOPICS

18 Strategic pricing: an analysis of social influences*
Wilfred Amaldoss and Sanjay Jain

Abstract

Social factors influence our everyday life in many ways. For example, consumers purchase conspicuous goods to satisfy not only material needs but also social needs such as prestige. In an attempt to meet these social needs, producers of conspicuous goods such as cars, perfumes and watches highlight the exclusivity of their products. In this chapter, we discuss a model of conspicuous consumption and examine how purchase decisions are affected by the desire for exclusivity and conformity. We show that snobs can have an upward-sloping demand curve but only in the presence of consumers who are (weakly) conformists. The influence of these social needs on firms' profits is moderated by the structure of market. In a monopoly, conformism is conducive to profits while snobbishness hurts profits. We find that the results are reversed in a duopoly. We also investigate how social needs may influence the prices and qualities of the products that consumers choose to buy. A series of laboratory tests lends support for our some of model predictions.

1. Introduction

At the very core of social psychological theory and research is the notion that we function in a social context that influences our thoughts, feelings and actions (Ross and Nisbett, 1991; see Taylor, 1998 for a review). While several theories have been advanced on the essence of social being, we focus on two basic social needs: a need for uniqueness and the countervailing need to conform (Fromkin and Snyder, 1980; Brewer, 1991). Consider, for example, the purchase of a conspicuous good. We buy these goods not just to meet our material needs but also to satisfy social needs (see for example Belk, 1988). In an attempt to satisfy such social needs, firms advertise the exclusivity of their products. For example, Ferrari promises that it will not produce more than 4300 vehicles per year despite more than a two-year waiting list for its cars (Betts, 2002). Some firms restrict the availability of their products by using exclusive distribution channels and even legal action. For example, Christian Dior sued supermarkets for carrying its products, fearing that wide availability could hurt its exclusive image (*Marketing Week*, 3 July 1997).

In an effort to understand how social needs may influence firm behavior, we discuss a theoretical model of conspicuous consumption. We capture consumers' desire for exclusivity and conformity by allowing the utility derived from a product to depend not only on its intrinsic value but also on consumption externality. Following Leibenstien (1950), we model snobs as consumers whose utility from a product decreases as more people consume the same product. For example, a BMW in every driveway could dilute the value of the car to potential buyers (cf. Bagwell and Bernheim, 1996). We model conformists as consumers whose utility from a product increases as more people consume the product (Ross et al., 1976; Jones, 1984; also see Becker, 1991 for a similar formulation).

---

* This chapter is based on Amaldoss and Jain (2005a and 2005b), which were published in *Management Science* and *Journal of Marketing Research*, respectively. Both authors have contributed equally to the chapter.

Teenagers, for example, often view MTV because their friends watch it (Sun and Lull, 1986). For similar reasons, consumers purchase popular books, toys and garments.

Our theoretical analysis suggests that if a market comprises only snobs or conformists, then consumers will not demand more as price increases. However, if a market comprises both snobs and conformists, then more snobs may buy as price increases. Consistent with this result, we find that the demand curve is upward sloping for visible cosmetics such as lipsticks and mascara (Chao and Schor, 1998). Next we show that the profits of a monopolist increase as conformism increases but decline as snobbishness increases. The results, however, are reversed in a duopoly. Finally, we investigate how social factors may influence the quality of the products consumers choose to purchase. We find that sometimes snobs purchase high-quality products not because of snobbishness but despite it.

Our model relies on strong behavioral assumptions such as rational expectations. However, human beings are only boundedly rational. In an attempt to validate the predictions of our model, we subject our monopoly model to a laboratory test. The experimental investigation shows that more snobs buy as price rises, even though the products have neither quality differences nor any signal value. Furthermore, we find some support for the rational expectations framework at the aggregate level. An analysis of the first trial data shows that subjects' behavior is qualitatively consistent with model predictions, and on average subjects were probably capable of three to four steps of iterative reasoning. Their behavior in subsequent trials, however, can be explained using adaptive learning mechanisms.

This chapter draws heavily from the work of Amaldoss and Jain (2005a, 2005b). In Section 2, we review related literature. In Section 3, we describe a model of conspicuous consumption and examine its implications. Section 4 discusses a laboratory test of the model. Finally, Section 5 concludes the chapter by outlining some directions for future research.

2. Literature on social influences

Several researchers have investigated the role of products in expressing an individual's self (Belk, 1988). This body of research has identified the existence of two competing social needs among consumers: a need for uniqueness and a countervailing need for similarity (Brewer, 1991; Fromkin and Snyder, 1980). These needs form the basis of what we refer to as the desire for exclusivity and conformity. Prior research has examined from a psychological perspective how these needs influence consumer choice processes (Lynn, 1991; Snyder, 1992; Simonson and Nowlis, 2000). Another related construct is the notion of reference groups. For example, the elite seek goods that will distinguish them from the masses. But the masses, who look up to the elite, want to emulate their choices (Simmel, 1957; Bourdieu, 1984; Bryson, 1996). Reference group effects have been examined by several marketing researchers. Bearden and Etzel (1982), for example, examined product and brand decisions of a panel of 645 consumers and found that reference group effects are stronger for publicly consumed brands. Childers and Rao (1992) obtained similar results in a sample of 345 American and Thai consumers. This behavioral literature, however, does not examine how social factors influence firm behavior.

A stream of research in economics incorporates social factors in formal economic analysis. Veblen (1899) and Leibenstein (1950) emphasized the importance of studying the role of social factors in consumption. Becker (1991) used conformism to explain why similar restaurants might eventually experience vastly different sales patterns. Specifically, using a model in which consumers demand increases as the sales of the product increases, he shows that the demand curve for conformists could be upward sloping; but the equilibrium is not stable. Karni and Levin (1994) extend Becker's model by explicitly modeling individual consumer decisions. Basu (1987) proposes a model where consumers' desire for a product increases if there is excess demand for the product. Using this stylized model, he explains why firms may find it unprofitable to raise prices even when there is excess demand for their products.

There are several signaling models on conspicuous consumption. In these models consumers purchase certain goods to signal their status or wealth. For example, consumers who have higher income could purchase more expensive items and thereby signal their wealth. This need to signal could lead to behavior which looks as if consumers are conformists. Bernheim (1994), for example, showed that when status is sufficiently important relative to intrinsic utility, many individuals conform to a single standard of behavior, despite heterogeneous underlying preferences. Bagwell and Bernheim (1996) examine whether a desire to signal status could lead to the Veblen effect. In other words, can the desire to achieve status lead to consumers' demand curve to be upward sloping? They find that these effects cannot arise under the usual 'single-crossing' condition. However, if this condition fails, then Veblen effects could arise. Corneo and Jeanne (1997) consider a model in which consumers could engage in conspicuous consumption to signal their wealth. They show that under a signaling framework, snobbish behavior cannot lead to an upward-sloping demand curve. The intuition for this result is that if more consumers buy the good, then the signal value of the good must decrease for snobs. Consequently, the firm needs to reduce prices in order to increase demand, implying a downward-sloping demand curve. Pesendorfer (1995) shows that the desire to signal status could lead to fashion cycles. These cycles are induced as new designs dilute the signal value of old designs and make them obsolete. Stock and Balachander (2005) show that excess demand for a product could be a signal of quality. Consequently, we may observe firm-induced scarcity.

Another stream of research in economics investigates herding behavior (e.g. Banerjee, 1992; Bikhchandani et al., 1992). In these models, consumers observe the actions of other consumers and then infer the (unknown) quality of the product. In such a sequential decision-making context, Banerjee (1992) shows that rational consumers may follow the actions of other consumers even when their private information would suggest that they should not do so. Consequently, we may observe informational cascades; but these cascades may be fragile (Bikhchandani et al., 1992).

Word of mouth can be a useful vehicle for transmitting product knowledge within a social network. Godes and Mayzlin (2004) show that online chats can be an effective indicator of word-of-mouth effects. Mayzlin (2006) shows online chats can be persuasive and may encourage firms to spend more on promoting inferior goods. This stream of research, however, is yet to examine the impact of word-of-mouth behavior on pricing.[1] Next we discuss a model of conspicuous consumption and its implications

---

[1] A related stream of research is the work on diffusion, which implicitly considers positive word-of-mouth effects. This research has examined the issue of optimal pricing (see for example Kalish, 1985).

3. A model of conspicuous consumption

Using a monopoly model, we delineate the effect of prices on demand. Then we examine how the degree of consumer desire for uniqueness or conformism influences equilibrium prices and profits. We explore this issue in the context of a duopoly and contrast our findings with the results obtained in a monopoly model. This analysis sheds light on the role of market structure in equilibrium behavior. Third, we examine how social factors may moderate the effect of product quality on prices and profits.

Effect of prices on demand

Consider a market comprising one seller and two types of consumers. We label the two types of consumers snobs and conformists. Snobs value exclusivity, and consequently the utility they derive from a product depends not only on its base value but also on the number of people expected to purchase the product. Hence the expected (indirect) utility of purchasing a product is given by

$$U(z^e, p) = v - p - g(z^e) \tag{18.1}$$

where v is the base valuation, p is the price for the product, and z^e is the expected number of buyers. Note that snobs value the product less as more people buy it. We capture this characteristic of snobs by assuming that $g(0) = 0$, $g(z^e) \geq 0 \ \forall z^e > 0$, $g(1) < \infty$, and $g'(\cdot) \geq 0$. We assume that each consumer purchases at most one unit of the product. This is a reasonable assumption for many durable conspicuous goods such as cars. Further, assume that v is distributed in the population according to a continuous distribution $F_s(\cdot)$ with pdf $f_s(\cdot)$.

We model conformists as consumers who like to follow others. The expected (indirect) utility of such a consumer is given by

$$U(z^e, p) = v - p + h(z^e) \tag{18.2}$$

where $h(0) = 0$, $h(1) < \infty$, $h(\cdot) \geq 0$ and $h' \geq 0$. Thus conformists value a product more as more people purchase it. We assume that the valuations of conformists are drawn from a continuous distribution $F_c(\cdot)$ with pdf $f_c(\cdot)$. Further, these value distributions are common knowledge. Note that in our formulation we allow for the possibility that the two groups of consumers could have different value distributions.

The snobs account for $\beta \in [0, 1]$ fraction of the consumers and the remaining $(1 - \beta)$ consumers are assumed to be conformists. Thus the number of snobs who will buy the product is given by

$$x = \beta (1 - F_s(p + g(z^e))) \tag{18.3}$$

where z^e is the expected sales of the product. Similarly, the number of conformists who buy the product is given by

$$y = (1 - \beta)(1 - F_c(p - h(z^e))) \tag{18.4}$$

Using (18.3) and (18.4), we obtain the total demand z for the product:

$$z = \beta(1 - F_s(p + g(z^e))) + (1 - \beta)(1 - F_c(p - h(z^e))) \qquad (18.5)$$

We assume that consumers form expectations about the number of people who will buy the product. Further, these expectations are rational, implying that they are correct in equilibrium (see for example Becker, 1991; Katz and Shapiro, 1985). Thus

$$z - z^e = 0. \qquad (18.6)$$

Now using (18.5) and (18.6) we obtain

$$\Lambda_1(z) = z - \beta(1 - F_s(p + g(z))) + (1 - \beta)(1 - F_c(p - h(z))) = 0 \qquad (18.7)$$

Equation (18.7) implicitly describes the total demand $z(p)$ under the rational expectations equilibrium. If equation (18.7) defines a unique z for a given p, then it follows from (18.4) and (18.5) that for any given price p there will be unique numbers x and y which will define the sales to the snobs and the conformists, respectively. The proofs for the different results in this chapter can be seen in Amaldoss and Jain (2005a, 2005b). The following lemma establishes the condition for existence and uniqueness.

Lemma 18.1 *There exists a rational expectations equilibrium that satisfies (18.7). The equilibrium is unique if and only if (iff)*

$$h'(z)f_2[p - h(z)] < \frac{1 + \beta f_1[p + g(z)]g'(z)}{(1 - \beta)} \qquad (18.8)$$

where z is the equilibrium total demand at price p.

Note that the condition included in the above lemma imposes an upper bound on the size of conformism, namely $h'(\cdot)$ When conformism grows very large, we may observe bandwagons wherein all consumers buy or none buys the product. Further, we may face multiple equilibria in such situations. However, if conformism is absent we will still obtain a unique rational expectations equilibrium. Note that the lemma places no upper bound on the level of snobbishness. In fact, a higher desire for exclusivity will make it easier to satisfy condition (18.8).

Assuming that the condition specified in Lemma 18.1 is satisfied, we analyzed how changes in price affect the aggregate demand as well as the demand from snobs and conformists. A key finding is summarized in the following proposition:

Proposition 18.1 *If the market consists of only snobs or conformists, then the market demand always decreases with price. However, if the market consists of both snobs and conformists, then the demand from snobs will increase with price iff*

$$(1 - \beta)f_2[p - h(z)](h'(z) + g'(z)) > 1. \qquad (18.9)$$

However, the demand curve for conformists and the total demand curve are downward sloping.

This finding is very different from the results reported in the network externality or congestion externality literature, which has traditionally examined only one type of externality. In the presence of only one type of externality, we will only observe a downward-sloping demand curve according to Proposition 18.1. However, in a model that includes both negative and positive externalities, consumers experiencing negative externalities can have an upward-sloping demand curve. To clarify the intuition for this proposition, we first study a market consisting only of snobs ($\beta = 1$). Then we consider a market consisting of both snobs and conformists, that is $\beta \in (0, 1)$.

According to Proposition 18.1, if the market comprises only snobs ($\beta = 1$), then demand will decline as price rises. Note that if $\beta = 1$, then $z^e = x^e$. In this case, the utility that a snob receives from consuming a product is

$$U_s = v - p - g(x^e) \tag{18.10}$$

The impact of price on the consumer's utility is given by

$$\frac{\partial U_s}{\partial p} = -1 - g'(x^e)\frac{\partial x^e}{\partial p} \tag{18.11}$$

Consumers' expectations are likely to be shaped by what they observe in their everyday lives. For example, the sales of typical grocery items decline when price increases. If so, consumers are likely to expect demand to decline as price rises, implying that $\partial x^e/\partial p$ will be negative. Further, if $g'(\cdot)$ is sufficiently large, then consumer utility may increase with price. Consequently, as the price increases, the total number of consumers who will buy the product would increase – thus giving rise to an upward-sloping demand curve, that is $\partial x/\partial p > 0$. Note that there is an internal inconsistency in this line of reasoning. Specifically, if consumers expect $\partial x^e/\partial p < 0$, the outcome will lead to $\partial x^e/\partial p > 0$, contradicting the requirement for a rational expectations equilibrium. Therefore the only equilibrium that is consistent with the rational expectations equilibrium in this case is the one in which demand is downward sloping ($\partial x/\partial p < 0$). A similar argument can establish that if the market consists of only conformists, then the demand curve will again be downward sloping.

Now consider a market that consists of both snobs and conformists, that is $\beta \in (0, 1)$. On examining the effect of price on utility derived by snobs, we find that

$$\frac{\partial U_s}{\partial p} = -1 - g'(z^e)\frac{\partial z^e}{\partial p} \tag{18.12}$$

If the consumer expects the total demand to drop as price increases, then for a sufficiently large $g'(\cdot)$ consumer utility may increase with price, implying an upward-sloping demand curve for snobs. Thus it is possible that the total demand curve is downward sloping ($\partial z^e/\partial p < 0$), while the demand from snobs is growing as price increases. To illustrate the possibility that there exist situations in which (18.8) and (18.9) are satisfied, consider the case where $f_1(\cdot)$ and $f_2(\cdot)$ are uniform with range $(0, 1)$, $\beta = 1/2$ and $g(\cdot)$ and $h(\cdot)$ are linear with $g' \equiv \lambda_1 = 0.8$ and $h' \equiv \lambda_2$. In this case it can be shown that (18.8) is always satisfied and furthermore (18.9) will be satisfied as long as $\lambda_2 > 1.2$.

Conventional wisdom suggests that snobs (not conformists) will demand more as price increases. Proposition 18.1 offers a potential basis for this common belief: the demand curve can be upward sloping at the equilibrium price for snobs, but not for conformists. Further, an upward-sloping demand curve for snobs is likely to be observed only when the market includes a group of consumers who are (weakly) conformists. Specifically, the demand curve for snobs could be upward sloping even if $h' \equiv 0$; that is, there exists a segment of consumers whose utility is unaffected by the choices of other consumers. Our finding goes against the grain of Leibenstein's claim (1950) that the demand curve for snobs will always be downward sloping.

Interestingly, the demand curve for conspicuous cosmetics such as lipsticks, mascara and eyeshadow is upward sloping for college-educated women (Chao and Schor, 1998). Specifically, for women with a college degree the price coefficient is +0.117. However, the price coefficient for the overall market is −0.157. It is useful to note that the correlation between quality and price in this category is zero, implying that price is probably not a signal of quality. Similar results were observed in the case of mascara and eyeshadow. To the extent that college-educated women are more likely to be status conscious and desire exclusivity, these empirical findings are consistent with our theoretical results.

Effect of snobbishness and conformism
Next we investigate how the degree of snobbishness or conformism influences equilibrium profits. To help us better appreciate how the nature of competition can potentially moderate these effects, we first study a duopoly model. Later we contrast the duopoly results with those obtained in a monopoly model.

Consider a duopoly where firms are located at the opposite ends of a Hotelling line, with firm 1 positioned at 0 and firm 2 at 1. As discussed earlier, the market comprises snobs and conformists, with snobs accounting for β fraction of the consumers.

Consider a snob located at θ on the Hotelling line. The (expected) indirect utility derived by this snob on purchasing product 1 is given by

$$U_s(z_1^e, p_1) = \omega_s v_1 - p_1 - \theta t_s - \lambda_s z_1^e, \qquad (18.13)$$

where v_1 is the base quality level for firm 1's product, p_1 is the price for product 1, and z_1^e is the expected total number of buyers for product 1. In this utility formulation ω_s reflects the extent to which snobs are sensitive to quality, while t_s captures the sensitivity of snobs to product characteristics (Grossman and Shapiro, 1984). The degree to which the consumers desire uniqueness is reflected in $\lambda_s \geq 0$. As λ_s increases, the consumer values uniqueness more. The corresponding indirect utility derived by the consumer from buying product 2 is given by

$$U_s(z_2^e, p_2) = \omega_s v_2 - p_2 - (1-\theta) t_s - \lambda_s z_2^e \qquad (18.14)$$

As in the monopoly model, we denote the value distribution for snobs by a continuous distribution $F_s(\cdot)$ with a corresponding pdf $f_s(\cdot)$. Further, each consumer buys at most one unit of the product. Therefore, the number of snobs who will buy product 1 is

$$x_1 = \beta F_s(\theta_s(z_1^e)) \qquad (18.15)$$

where $\theta_s(z_1^e)$ is the location of the snob who is indifferent between the two products for a given sales expectation z_1^e. $\theta_s(z_1^e)$ is given by

$$\theta_s(z_1^e) = \frac{t_s + \omega_s(v_1 - v_2) + (p_2 - p_1) + \lambda_s(1 - 2z_1^e)}{2t_s} \quad (18.16)$$

The other group of consumers in the market is labelled conformists. The indirect utility derived from product 1 by a conformist located at θ is

$$U_c(z_1^e, p_1) = \omega_c v_1 - p_1 - \theta t_c + \lambda_c z_1^e \quad (18.17)$$

where v_1 is the base quality level, p_1 is the price for product 1, and z_1^e is the expected number of buyers for product 1. The parameters ω_c and t_c reflect the sensitivity of conformists to the quality and horizontal differentiation of a product, respectively, whereas $\lambda_c (\lambda_c \geq 0)$ captures the degree of consumer desire for conformity. Similarly, the utility of buying product 2 is given by

$$U_c(z_2^e, p_2) = \omega_c v_2 - p_2 - (1 - \theta)t_c + \lambda_c z_2^e \quad (18.18)$$

Assume that the value distribution for conformists is given by a continuous distribution $F_c(\cdot)$ with a corresponding pdf $f_c(\cdot)$, and that the full market is covered. Then the number of conformists who will buy product 1 is given by

$$y_1 = (1 - \beta)F_c(\theta_c(z_1^e)) \quad (18.19)$$

where $\theta_c(z_1^e)$ is the location of the conformist who is indifferent between the two products for a given expectation z_1^e, and $\theta_c(z_1^e)$ is given by

$$\theta_c(z_1^e) = \frac{t_c + \omega_c(v_1 - v_2) + (p_2 - p_1) - \lambda_c(1 - 2z_1^e)}{2t_c} \quad (18.20)$$

On assuming that consumers are forming rational expectations, we have

$$z_1 = x_1 + y_1 = z_1^e \quad (18.21)$$

Using (18.15), (18.19) and (18.21), we derive the rational expectations equilibrium. The relevant equation is

$$\Omega(z_1) = \beta F_s\left(\frac{t_s + \omega_s(v_1 - v_2) + (p_2 - p_1) + \lambda_s(1 - 2z_1)}{2t_s}\right)$$

$$+ (1 - \beta)F_c\left(\frac{t_c + \omega_c(v_1 - v_2) + (p_2 - p_1) - \lambda_c(1 - 2z_1)}{2t_c}\right) - z_1 = 0 \quad (18.22)$$

Note that equation (18.22) implicitly describes the demand $z_1(p_1, p_2)$ if consumers form rational expectations. The following lemma establishes the condition under which there exists a unique rational expectations equilibrium for any price pair (p_1, p_2).

Lemma 18.2 *There exists a unique rational expectations equilibrium for any given pair of prices (p_1, p_2) if and only if*

$$-\frac{\beta \lambda_s f_s(\theta_s)}{t_s} + \frac{(1 - \beta)\lambda_c f_c(\theta_c)}{t_c} - 1 < 0 \quad (18.23)$$

at the equilibrium point where

$$\theta_s = \frac{t_s + \omega_s(v_1 - v_2) + (p_2 - p_1) + \lambda_s(1 - 2z_1)}{2t_s} \quad (18.24)$$

$$\theta_c = \frac{t_c + \omega_c(v_1 - v_2) + (p_2 - p_1) - \lambda_c(1 - 2z_1)}{2t_c} \quad (18.25)$$

Condition (18.23) suggests that there is a unique rational expectations equilibrium if the net conformism effect, which is $(1 - \beta)\lambda_c f_c / t_c$, is small. It is easy to see that the net conformism effect will become small if the proportion of snobs in the population (β) and the horizontal differentiation (t_c) increase. The net conformism effect would also decrease if λ_c and $f_c(\cdot)$ diminish.[2] Lemma 18.1 raises a natural question: what would happen if the net conformism effect were large? In such a case, even a small change in price could induce a bandwagon effect, and we would have multiple Nash equilibria. More precisely, when condition (18.23) is not satisfied, then we may obtain corner solutions that are asymmetric solutions, even when the firms are completely symmetric *a priori*. For example, consider the case when the market consists of only conformists ($\beta = 0$). Also assume that $t_c = 1$ and f_c is uniform $(0,1)$ and prices are the same. In this case, if $\lambda_c > 1$, then the condition in Lemma 18.1 is violated. In such a situation, one firm sells to the entire market and the other firm has zero sales. We confine our attention to cases where (18.23) holds, so that we have a unique rational expectations equilibrium.

For analytical tractability, we assume that f_s and f_c are uniform. Although this assumption guarantees the existence of a unique Nash equilibrium in prices, it is not a necessary condition. In fact, a weaker condition that ensures that the solutions are unique and stable is that $|\partial^2 \Pi_i / \partial p_i^2| > |\partial^2 \Pi_i / \partial p_i \partial p_j|$ and $\partial^2 \Pi_i / \partial p_i^2 < 0$. These conditions imply that the profit functions are concave and that own-price effects are stronger than cross-price effects. Such conditions on the reduced-form profit functions hold for a wide variety of models.

We also assume that the marginal costs for both products are the same and equate them to zero. Note that, in our model, f_s and f_c could be different, implying that snobs could have a higher mean valuation for the products than conformists and vice versa. Also, as before, snobs and conformists could differ in their sensitivity to quality and horizontal product differentiation.

Now on studying how equilibrium profits and prices are affected by snobbishness and conformity in a monopoly as well as a duopoly, we have the following result:

Proposition 18.2 *In a monopoly, the equilibrium profits are increasing in conformity and decreasing in snobbishness. In a duopoly, however, the results are reversed.*

The intuition for the first part of the proposition is easy to appreciate. Note that in a monopoly, as snobbishness increases, each additional sale exerts a greater negative externality on the sale of other units. Further, we know that

---

[2] For example, if $f_c(\cdot)$ is uniform, then the conformism effect decreases when the range of the uniform distribution increases

$$\frac{\partial \Pi^*}{\partial \lambda_s} = p\frac{\partial z}{\partial \lambda_s} < 0. \qquad (18.26)$$

Thus the monopolist's profits are hurt by the negative impact of snobbish behavior on the demand. Similarly,

$$\frac{\partial \Pi^*}{\partial \lambda_c} = p\frac{\partial z}{\partial \lambda_c} > 0. \qquad (18.27)$$

Thus, as conformism has a positive effect on demand, it helps to improve monopolists' profits.[3]

The duopoly results are different from the monopoly results. The intuition for this can be understood by noting how conformity and snobbishness change the complexion of competition. First, consider the impact of conformity. As the number of consumers who buy product 1 grows, the value of the product increases for the conformists and therefore the relative value of product 2 decreases. This implies that a unit reduction in price by firm 1 affects its total demand in two ways. First, the price reduction makes firm 1's product relatively more attractive than firm 2's product, and so the demand for product 1 increases. Second, as the consumers can rationally expect the demand for product 1 to increase, the value of the product for the conformists increases, and therefore they find it even more attractive to buy product 1. Thus, as the degree of conformity increases, duopolists are lured to cut prices. The ensuing price competition causes the equilibrium prices to drop.

Next let us understand how increased snobbishness affects a duopolist's profits. Now if firm 1 decreases its prices, it expects to get more consumers. However, this increase in demand reduces the value of the product for the snobs, and they are less likely to buy the product. Therefore, as the degree of snobbishness increases, reducing prices becomes less attractive to both the firms. The consequent reduction in price competition helps firms to charge higher prices and make more profits. Next we proceed to understand how quality difference between the firms in a duopoly affects equilibrium behavior.[4]

Effect of quality differences
Assume that the base quality of product 2 is better than that of product 1 ($v_1 < v_2$). To facilitate exposition, we first consider the case where both snobs and conformists value quality equally ($\omega_s = \omega_c$) and the marginal costs of the two products are the same ($c_1 = c_2$). Later, we study the case where snobs value quality more than conformists. We have

---

[3] In order to see this consider the following numerical example. Assume $\beta = 1/2$ and that the value distribution is uniform with range (0,1). In this case, absent social effects, a monopolist (who does not serve the full market) will charge a price 1/2 and make profits of 1/4. However, if $\lambda_s = 0.2$, $\lambda_c = 0$, the profits are reduced to 0.22 while the profits are 0.27 if $\lambda_c = 0.2$, $\lambda_s = 0$.

[4] To see this, assume that $\beta = 1/2$ and v is sufficiently large so that the market is fully covered. In this case, absent social effects, a duopolist will charge a price 1 and make profits of 1/2. However, if $\lambda_c = 0.2$, $\lambda_s = 0$, the prices and profits reduce to 0.90 and 0.45 respectively. On the other hand, if $\lambda_s = 0.2$, $\lambda_c = 0$, then prices and profits increase to 0.55 and 1.1 respectively.

Proposition 18.3 *If $v_1 < v_2$ and $\omega_s = \omega_c$, then:*
(a) *The higher-quality firm charges a higher price and has a larger total market share. Furthermore, as λ_c increases (or λ_s decreases), the higher-quality firm's market share increases.*
(b) *The higher-quality firm has a larger market share among conformists.*
(c) *There exists a λ_s^* such that if $\lambda_s > \lambda_s^*$, then the higher-quality firm has a lower market share among snobs.*

The above result shows that the higher-quality firm charges a higher price and has a larger total market share. Thus increased conformism makes it profitable for the high-quality firm to pursue market share. On the other hand, increased snobbishness reduces market share differences between the firms. This is because snobbishness motivates the higher-quality firm to raise prices rather than go after market share.

Further, if snobbishness is sufficiently large, then a majority of the snobs may purchase the low-quality product. It is important to note that, in our model, snobs prefer higher-quality products to lower-quality products keeping all other things constant. Thus, as a product becomes more attractive due to its improved quality, the snobs correctly expect more consumers to buy the product. Hence the high-quality product becomes less attractive to snobs. Consequently, snobs may well buy a lower-quality product to differentiate themselves from others.

As this finding is very counterintuitive, we explore the conditions under which this result may hold. Note that Proposition 18.3 assumes that the snobs and conformists value quality equally and that the costs for each firm are the same even though they have different qualities. Next we examine whether demand-side effects, such as differences in consumer valuation for quality, can reverse the result. Later we study how supply-side effects, such as differences in manufacturing costs, could potentially change our results.

Proposition 18.4 *If $v_1 < v_2$ and $\omega_s > \omega_c$, then for sufficiently low values of λ_c and λ_s and high values of ω_s, we find that the high-quality firm has a lower market share among the conformists and a higher market share among the snobs.*

The intuition for this finding is that, if snobs value quality highly, they will be willing to pay such a high price for the product that the product will become unattractive to the conformists, who value quality less. Consequently, in contexts where snobs have a strong preference for quality, most of the snobs will buy the higher-quality product at a higher price whereas the conformists may purchase the lower-quality product at a lower price.

To explore whether supply-side factors can reverse the results in Proposition 3, consider the case where the costs for the two products are different and it costs more to produce a higher quality product. Specifically, assume that the marginal cost for producing a product of quality v is $c(v)$ where $c'(\cdot) \geq 0$. Further assume that the fixed costs for producing a product of quality v is $C(v)$ with $C'(\cdot) \geq 0$. We have

Proposition 18.5 *If $v_1 < v_2$ and $\omega_s = \omega_c = \omega$, then the high-quality firm has a smaller market share among snobs and a larger market share among the conformists if $\lambda_s > \lambda_s^*$, as long as $\omega \geq c'(v_1)$. If $\omega < c'(v_1)$ and $\lambda_s > \lambda_s^*$, then the higher-quality firm has a higher market share among snobs and a lower market share among the conformists.*

It is useful to note that in Proposition 18.3, $c'(\cdot) = 0$. The preceding result clarifies that the results of Proposition 18.3 would be reversed by cost effects only under the rather strong condition that the marginal costs of quality are higher than the marginal value of quality to the consumer. To the extent that this condition is unlikely to be satisfied, this result adds strength to the claim made in Proposition 18.3.[5]

It is commonly believed that snobs tend to buy high-quality products at high prices. Propositions 18.3, 18.4 and 18.5 provide a useful clarification of the theoretical basis for such a behavior. We are likely to observe such behavior when snobs value quality much more than others. In reality, it is quite likely that ω_s is higher than ω_c in many contexts. So we might often see snobs buying high-quality products at high prices. It is useful to note that our results suggest that snobs purchase high-quality products despite snobbishness and not because of it.

Now we examine how sensitivity to product quality, either among snobs or conformists, affects firms' profits.

Proposition 18.6 *If $v_1 < v_2$, then as ω_1 or ω_2 increases the profits of firm 1 decrease and the profits of firm 2 increase.*

The result is intuitive. As expected, a firm with a quality advantage benefits as consumers become more sensitive to quality.

Discussion We have analyzed how some social factors such as desire for uniqueness and conformism may influence the behavior of firms and consumers. First we established that more snobs may purchase a conspicuous good when its price increases. However, the overall demand and the demand from conformists decline as price increases. This finding also holds in the case of a duopoly (see Amaldoss and Jain, 2005b), implying that market structure does not drive this result. On the other hand, the effect of snobbishness and conformism on equilibrium profits is moderated by market structure. In a monopoly, profits increase with conformism but decline with snobbishness. The converse holds in the case of a duopoly. Finally, we found that the firm offering a higher-quality product is likely to charge a higher price and gain a larger market share, especially among conformists. But when snobbishness is sufficiently high the snobs may well buy the lower-quality product. Our analysis also clarifies that snobs may purchase a high-quality product not because of their snobbishness but despite it.

A central assumption of our theoretical model is that consumers form rational expectations. Simple introspection tells us that it not easy for individuals to do so. Further, several studies reject the possibility that individual people can form rational expectations (Schmalensee, 1976; Garner, 1982; Williams, 1987; Smith et al., 1988). Market-level experimental studies, however, suggest that people can form adaptive expectations and still move toward the rational expectations equilibrium (see Sunder, 1995 for a review). A related question is whether individuals merely forming adaptive expectations can converge to the rational expectations equilibrium predictions of our model. To explore

---

[5] To see why this condition is too strong, consider the case when $c'(v_1) > \omega$. It can then be shown that firm 1 can benefit by choosing a lower quality.

this issue theoretically, we studied the case where consumers form adaptive beliefs using the Cournot learning process. Our analysis shows that if consumers play according to Cournot dynamics, then the equilibrium demand converges to that under the rational expectations equilibrium (see Amaldoss and Jain, 2005a for more details).

Note that experimental economics literature suggests that consumer learning is often not purely guided by a belief-based mechanism (e.g. Cournot mechanism). Learning could well be influenced by reinforcement of past choices. The experience-weighted attraction (EWA) learning model proposed by Camerer and Ho (1999) is a hybrid model that includes features of both reinforcement and belief learning. On using EWA parameter estimates of 4×4 constant sum games reported in Camerer and Ho (1999, p. 852, column 3), we find that adaptive learning can converge toward the rational expectations equilibrium. This raises hope that our equilibrium predictions may survive in a market despite the bounded rationality of consumers.

4. Model validation

It is a challenge to test our model in a field setting because consumers may not be forthcoming with their social preferences. Alternatively, we can estimate the social effects from the actions of consumers. This avenue faces several econometric issues. For example, the simultaneity in the actions of strategic players makes it difficult to separate the endogenous and exogenous interactions in the model. Furthermore, unobserved group characteristics may be correlated with the exogenous variables. In an attempt to circumvent such econometric issues and directly test the model, we pursue a different path. In the tradition of experimental economics literature, we test our model under controlled laboratory conditions. The experimental investigation addresses two key questions:

1. *Do more snobs buy as price increases?* In our laboratory test, more snobs purchased the product when price increased. In addition to finding strong support for the qualitative predictions of the model, we have moderate support for the point predictions. Our theory also predicts that the demand curves for conformists and the total market should be downward sloping, and we also find support for this claim.
2. *Are the expectations of subjects consistent with the rational expectations model?* We tracked the beliefs that guided the purchase decisions of subjects in every trial of the experiment. On average, the expected demand was consistent with the actual demand and the rational expectations equilibrium predictions. We observe variation in the behavior of individual subjects, implying that the model prediction survives at the aggregate level rather than at the individual level.

Our analytical model assumes a continuous distribution in values, but it is difficult to validate such a model in a laboratory setting with a small sample of subjects. As our theory does not crucially depend on the continuity assumption, we next outline a discrete version of our model and test its predictions.

Empirical model
We use a discrete distribution of valuations that is conducive to test the model with a population of 20 subjects. The approach of testing a continuous model using a discrete version is common in experimental economics (e.g. Smith, 1982). Table 18.1 presents the

Table 18.1 Value distribution for the empirical model

	S_1^A	S_2^A	S_3^A	S_4^A	S_5^A	S_6^A	S_7^A	S_8^A	S_9^A	S_{10}^A
Type A	2	3	4	5	6	9.5	10.1	10.6	11.2	11.4
	S_1^B	S_2^B	S_3^B	S_4^B	S_5^B	S_6^B	S_7^B	S_8^B	S_9^B	S_{10}^B
Type B	0.1	0.2	0.5	0.55	0.7	1.5	2	2.5	3.5	5

Note: S_j^i refers to Subject j of Type i.

distribution of valuations for ten snobs (labeled Type A buyers in our experiment) and ten conformists (Type B buyers in our experiment).[6] We used $g(z) = 0.5z$ and $h(z) = 0.6z$. The resulting equilibrium demand curve for snobs is (weakly) upward sloping, while it is (weakly) downward sloping for conformists and the total market. In our initial study, we use two price points to trace the slope of the demand curve. Later, in Studies 2 and 3, we will use three price points to trace the demand curve.

Procedure
To test the model, we used a within-subject design with two levels of prices. Using price points 5.9 and 6.9 francs, we traced the changes in demand among snobs and conformists. We ran two groups comprising 20 subjects each. In Group 1 the price was low in the first 30 trials and high in the next 30 trials. In Group 2 the order of price presentation was reversed.

We recruited business school students for the study promising them a show-up fee of $5 and additional monetary reward contingent on their performance. All transactions were in an experimental currency called 'francs' which were converted into US dollars at the end of the experiment.

In our experiment, we simulated the retail market environment where the seller posts price and promises to supply its product to all buyers who are willing to pay the posted price (see Smith, 1982 for a discussion on the posted prices market, and its implications for market efficiency). The computer played the role of seller, and buyers could not negotiate the price with the seller.

Each subject was randomly assigned to play the role of either a Type A or Type B buyer. Type A buyers value the product less when more people own the product. Consequently, the actual value of the product systematically drops below the base value when more people choose to buy it. For example, consider the Type A buyer whose base valuation for the product is 9.5 francs. If a total of five Type A and Type B buyers purchase the product, the actual value of the product will fall to 7 francs (that is, $9.5 - (0.5 \times 5) = 7$).

On the other hand, Type B buyers value the product more when more people own it. Hence the actual value of the product rises above the base value when more people choose to buy it. For example, consider the Type B buyer whose base valuation is 2 francs. If

---

[6] We named the two types of buyers as Type A and Type B buyers, rather than as snobs and conformists, so that the behavior of subjects is guided purely by the negative and positive externality captured in our model.

a total of five Type A and Type B buyers purchase the product, the actual value of the product will increase to 5 francs (that is, 2 + (0.6 × 5) = 5).

At the start of every trial, subjects were endowed with 7 francs so that they had sufficient funds to afford the product. As our model is a complete information game, subjects were informed of $g(z)$, $h(z)$, the value distributions, and price of the product. Detailed instructions can be seen in Amaldoss and Jain (2005a). The type of subjects, the total number of subjects and the base valuations remained fixed in all trials.

In every trial, each subject had to decide whether or not to purchase the product. Subjects were asked to provide demand projections. Then, using these demand projections, the computer showed the expected value of the product. Subjects could revise their demand projections, and obtain new estimates of the likely value of the product. We used the demand projections to track the expectations that guided the decisions of the subjects.

After all the buyers had made their decisions, the computer counted the total number of subjects who purchased the product. Then, based on this, the actual value of the product for each subject was assessed. The payoff to a subject who bought the product was obtained by adding the endowment to the actual value of the product and then deducting the price paid. The subjects who did not buy the product kept the endowment. At the end of every trial, each subject was informed of the number of Type A and Type B buyers who purchased the product, and the payoff for the trial.

In order to make subjects familiar with the structure of the game, they were allowed to play three practice trials for which they received no monetary reward. Then they played 60 trials, and the price condition changed after 30 trials. At the end of 60 trials, subjects were paid according to their cumulative earnings. Finally, they were debriefed and dismissed.

Results

First, we study the quantity demanded by snobs and conformists. Then we investigate the expectations that could have shaped the decisions of our subjects. The experimental results are consistent with the predictions of the model. We observe an upward-sloping demand curve for Type A buyers (snobs), and a downward-sloping demand curve for Type B buyers (conformists). On average, the expected demand is also consistent with the rational expectations equilibrium solution. However, we observe variations in the beliefs and actions of individual subjects.

Analysis of aggregate demand The empirical results are consistent with the qualitative predictions of the equilibrium solution. However, we see some departures from the point predictions of the model. Also, there is a significant trend in the demand pattern over the several iterations of the game. Table 18.2 presents the mean quantity demanded by the two types of buyers, and the corresponding equilibrium predictions.

QUALITATIVE PREDICTIONS The model makes four qualitative predictions. First, the demand for the product among Type A buyers (snobs) should grow as the price increases. The average demand was 1.53 units, when the product was priced 5.9 francs. But when the price increased to 6.9 francs, the demand rose to 3.57 units. We can reject the null hypothesis that these demand levels are the same ($F_{(1,118)} = 92.83$, $p < 0.0001$). We obtain

412 *Handbook of pricing research in marketing*

Table 18.2 Mean demand

Price	Type A buyers (snobs)				Type B buyers (conformists)			
	Actual demand			Prediction	Actual demand			Prediction
	Group 1	Group 2	Both		Group 1	Group 2	Both	
5.9	1.33 (0.78)	1.93 (1.08)	1.53 (1.02)	1	9.03 (0.67)	9.2 (0.87)	9.12 (0.78)	10
6.9	3.43 (1.04)	3.70 (1.49)	3.57 (1.28)	4	2.90 (1.02)	3.26 (2.31)	3.08 (1.79)	2

Note: The standard deviations are presented in parentheses.

similar results in each of the two groups. In Group 1, the average demand grew from 1.33 to 3.43 units, as the price rose from 5.9 to 6.9 francs, and this difference in demand is significant ($F_{(1,58)} = 94.25$, $p < 0.0001$). In Group 2, the mean demand correspondingly increased from 1.93 to 3.7 units ($F_{(1,58)} = 27.66$, $p < 0.0001$).

Second, in equilibrium the Type B buyers (conformists) should demand less as the price increases. In actuality, the average demand of Type B buyers across the two groups declined from 9.12 to 3.08 units, when the price rose from 5.9 to 6.9 francs. This shift in demand is significant ($F_{(1,118)} = 573.31$, $p < 0.0001$). We see similar results at the level of individual groups. In Group 1, on average the demand dropped from 9.03 to 2.9 units ($F_{(1,58)} = 749.48$, $p < 0.0001$). In Group 2, the demand declined from 9.2 to 3.26 units, as the price increased ($F_{(1,58)} = 171$, $p < 0.0001$).

Third, the model predicts that the overall demand should fall as price increases. The mean actual demand dropped from 10.65 to 6.65 units, when price rose from 5.9 to 6.9. This change in average demand is significant ($F_{(1,118)} = 199.93$, $p < 0.0001$). We obtain similar results in each of the two groups (Group 1: $F_{(1,58)} = 134.81$, $p < 0.0001$; Group 2: $F_{(1,58)} = 89.67$, $p < 0.0001$).

Fourth, when the price is 5.9 francs, conformists should demand the product more than snobs. Consistent with this prediction, the conformists demanded on average 9.12 units across both groups. On average, snobs demanded only 1.53 units. A paired comparison of the units demanded by snobs and conformists reveals that the observed difference in demands is significant ($t = 42.15$, $p < 0.0001$). We observe similar results in both Group 1 and Group 2. In Group 1, the average demand of conformists was 9.03, which is more than the 1.13 units demanded by snobs ($t = 45.10$, $p < 0.0001$). In Group 2, the conformists and snobs bought on the average 9.2 and 1.93 units, respectively ($t = 23.69$, $p < 0.0001$).

Finally, when the price is 6.9 francs, snobs should demand more than conformists. On average across the two groups, snobs and conformists bought 3.56 and 3.08 units, respectively. We cannot reject the null hypothesis that these quantities are the same ($t = 1.5$, $p > 0.13$). On closer examination, we note that the difference in demand is marginally significant in Group 1, but not in Group 2. In Group 1, the mean quantity purchased by snobs and conformists is 3.43 and 2.9 units, respectively ($t = 1.97$, $p < 0.058$). In Group 2, snobs and conformists purchased 3.7 and 3.26 units, respectively ($t = 0.73$, $p > 0.2$).

DISTRIBUTION OF AGGREGATE DEMAND   The equilibrium solution provides point predictions about demand, but the actual demand varies over the several trials of the experiment.

The model predicts that if the price is 5.9 francs, then one snob should buy the product. Over the 60 trials across the two groups, the actual quantity demanded ranges from 0 to 4, with mean = 1.53, median = 2 and mode = 2. But if the price rises to 6.9 francs, then in theory four snobs should buy the product. We observe that the actual demand ranges from 1 to 6, with mean = 3.56, median = 4 and mode = 4.

In equilibrium, the conformists should demand ten units when the price is 5.9 francs. The actual demand ranged from 7 to 10 units, with mean = 9.11, median = 9 and mode = 9. If the price is increased to 6.9 francs, then in theory the demand should drop to 2 units. The observed demand ranged from 0 to 8 units, with mean = 3.08, median = 3 and mode = 2. This suggests that, although the observed behavior is consistent with the qualitative predictions of the model, there are departures from the point predictions of the equilibrium solution.

TRENDS IN AGGREGATE DEMAND   In the analyses discussed above, we have aggregated the demand across groups and trials, which could mask trends in demand. Now we compute the mean for each block of five trials across the two groups. These block means were computed across the two groups. Statistical analysis of the block means suggests that conformists evince a significant trend in demand, when the price is 6.9 francs ($F_{(5,20)}$ = 9.76, $p < 0.0001$), but only a marginal trend when the price is 5.9 francs ($F_{(5,20)}$ = 2.34, $p < 0.08$). The trends in the demand pattern of snobs are much weaker. It is marginally significant at 6.9 francs ($F_{(5,20)}$ = 2.87, $p < 0.05$), and not significant at 5.9 francs ($p < 0.2$). This suggests that we observe some learning in the experiment.

These trends raise an interesting question: how did our subjects behave in the very first trial? We find that three Type A buyers and two Type B buyers bought the product at 6.9 francs in Group 1. In the other group, three buyers of each type purchased the product at 6.9 francs. Thus the actual aggregate demand was quite close to the predicted total demand of six units. When the price was 5.9, we find that one Type A buyer and nine Type B buyers bought the product in the first trial in Group 1, whereas three Type A and eight Type B buyers purchased the product in Group 2. Again, the actual total demand is not very different from the predicted demand of eleven units. On examining the segment-level demand, we see some departures from the predicted behavior. However, the demand patterns are directionally consistent with the predictions of the theory. In particular, the average demand from Type A buyers (snobs) increased from two to three units as price increased, while the demand from conformists decreased from 8.5 to 2.5 as price increased. This informal analysis of the first trial data suggests that through introspection subjects were able to behave in a manner consistent with the aggregate equilibrium predictions. The purchases in the subsequent trials could be tracked by adaptive decision-making. Amaldoss and Jain (2005a) provide more details on how well adaptive learning models can be fitted to our data.

VARIATION BY VALUATION   Whether or not a subject buys the product depends on her base valuation and the number of people she expects to buy the product. In equilibrium, each player should play a pure strategy, and that strategy changes with the base value of the product. For instance, when the price is 5.9 francs, only the Type A buyer with a base value of 11.4 francs should buy the product. All others should not buy the product. On the other hand, when the price is 6.9 francs, only the Type A buyers with the four top base valuations should buy the product. Subjects did not always play the predicted strategies,

Table 18.3 Mean expected demand

Price	Type A buyers (snobs)				Type B buyers (conformists)			
	Expected demand			Prediction	Expected demand			Prediction
	Group 1	Group 2	Both		Group 1	Group 2	Both	
5.9	1.40 (1.19)	1.86 (1.59)	1.63 (1.42)	1	8.82 (1.34)	7.35 (3.52)	8.08 (2.76)	10
6.9	3.56 (1.24)	3.20 (1.72)	3.38 (1.51)	4	3.17 (1.40)	3.86 (2.47)	3.52 (2.04)	2

Note: The standard deviations are presented in parentheses.

as predicted. Yet the aggregate behavior is directionally consistent with the model prediction. We observe similar behavior among Type B buyers.

Analysis of expectations Thus far we have examined how purchase behavior conforms to the rational expectations equilibrium solution. In every trial of the experiment, subjects were asked to guess the number of Type A and Type B buyers who might purchase the product. Using these demand projections, we can explore whether the expectations of our subjects are consistent with the outcomes and the equilibrium solution. Note that each subject forecast the number of Type A and Type B buyers who would purchase the product. The mean expected demand is computed by averaging the expectations of all the subjects. Table 18.3 presents the mean expected demand, along with the rational expectations equilibrium solution. It is reassuring to observe that the expected demand is congruent with the observed outcomes and the qualitative predictions of the model, but there is a wide variation in expectations. Further, we discern a trend in expectations over multiple iterations of the game.

QUALITATIVE PREDICTIONS In keeping with the theory, our subjects expected snobs to buy more when the price was high. Across the two groups, the mean expected demand of snobs increased from 1.63 to 3.38 units as the price rose from 5.9 to 6.9 francs ($F_{(1,2398)} = 853.65, p < 0.0001$). On the other hand, conformists were expected to buy less as the price rose. The average expected demand dropped from 8.08 to 3.52 units as the price increased ($F_{(1,2398)} = 2126.39, p < 0.0001$). The changes in expected demand follow a similar pattern within each group. Finally, consistent with theory, the mean aggregate demand was expected to drop as price increased ($F_{(1,2398)} = 554.01, p < 0.0001$). The results are similar within each group.

The model assumes that expectations are correct; that is, the actual demand and the expected demand are the same. Indeed, the mean observed demand and the expected demands are similar. When the price was 6.9 francs, the average actual and expected total demands were 6.65 and 6.89 units, respectively. We cannot reject the null hypothesis that these demands are the same ($t = 0.11, p > 0.2$). When the price dropped to 5.9 francs, the actual and expected demand were on average 8.45 and 9.11 units, respectively. Again, we cannot reject the null hypothesis that these demands are the same ($t = 0.39, p > 0.2$).

DISTRIBUTION OF EXPECTATIONS In equilibrium, one snob should buy if the price is 5.9 francs. The expectations range from 0 to 10, with mean = 1.63, median = 1 and mode

= 1. In theory, the demand should be four units, if the price is increased to 6.9 francs. We note that the expectations range from 0 to 10, with mean = 3.38, median = 3 and mode = 4. Thus, although the expectations vary widely, they conform to the qualitative predictions of the model.

Our subjects expected anywhere from none to all of the conformists to buy the product at both prices. Yet, as before, the distributions of expectations are qualitatively consistent with the equilibrium solution. If the price is 5.9, all conformists should buy. The corresponding expectations followed a distribution with mean = 8.86, median = 9 and mode = 9. But if the price is 6.9, then two conformists should buy. The expectations were distributed with mean = 3.51, median = 3 and mode = 3.

TRENDS IN EXPECTATIONS   We also examined the trends in expected demand over blocks of five trials. An analysis of variance suggests that the block means are significantly different for snobs (Price = 5.9: $F_{(5,780)} = 66.79, p < 0.001$; Price = 6.9: $F_{(5,780)} = 4.35, p < 0.001$). The results are similar for conformists.

Discussion   The experimental results show that in a market comprising both snobs and conformists we could observe an upward-sloping demand curve as predicted by the rational expectations equilibrium. In this study, we used two price points to trace the demand curve. Assessing the demand at three price points using a within-subject experimental design could add to the robustness of the experimental finding. In Study 2, presented in Amaldoss and Jain (2005a), we used three price points to trace the demand curve. Furthermore, in contrast to Study 1, we provided subjects additional monetary incentive for making accurate demand forecasts. The payoff based on purchase decision was similar to the experiment described earlier. The additional payoff based on accuracy of the total demand projection $= 5 - (|e|/2)$ where e is the difference between actual and forecasted demand. The findings of this additional study are consistent with the theoretical predictions.

Another interesting implication of our theory is that, if the market comprises only snobs, then it exhibits a downward-sloping demand curve. We find experimental support for this prediction (see Study 3 in Amaldoss and Jain, 2005a for more details). A related question is whether or not more snobs will purchase a product as price increases in a duopoly market. The answer is yes. Interested readers can find theoretical and experimental support for this claim in Amaldoss and Jain (2005b).

5. Summary and directions for future research

In this chapter, we attempted to explore how social needs may influence strategic pricing. The theoretical and empirical analysis offers some useful insights about pricing of conspicuous goods.

1. *What is the effect of consumer desire for uniqueness or conformity on the demand pattern for conspicuous goods?* We show that in a market comprising snobs and conformists, demand among snobs may increase as the price of a product increases. However, the demand among conformists, as well as the total market demand, may decrease as price rises. The intuition for this result is that snobs prefer a higher-priced product if they expect the overall demand to be lower at the higher price, and such

an expectation will be rational only if the conformists have a downward-sloping demand curve. Hence, in a market comprising either only snobs or conformists, the demand curve is downward sloping. It is useful to note that our result does not rely on signaling either product quality or wealth of consumers.[7] We find support for our model predictions in our experiments and also in the empirical research of Chao and Shor (1998).

2. *How does consumer desire for uniqueness or conformity affect firms prices and profits?* In a monopoly, conformism is conducive to firms' profits, whereas snobbishness hurts firms' profits. In a duopoly, on the other hand, the desire for uniqueness leads to higher prices and profits. The intuition for this result is as follows. As the price of a product falls, this attracts more buyers, and thereby makes the product less appealing to the snobs. Thus firms are less inclined to cut prices as snobbishness increases. The resulting softening in price competition increases firm profits. In contrast, conformism encourages price competition and thus reduces firm profits.

3. *Do consumers buy high-quality products because of their desire for uniqueness?* It is commonly believed that snobs buy high-quality products at high prices. In contrast to this perception, we find that when snobbishness is sufficiently large, snobs might actually buy a lower-quality product. However, if snobbishness is low and snobs have a strong preference for quality, then we might observe them buying high-quality products. Hence snobs purchase high-quality products despite snobbishness and not because of it.

There are several avenues to further investigate how social factors may influence firm behavior. Next we discuss some of these research opportunities.

The theoretical model discussed in this chapter is a single-period game. As producers of conspicuous goods typically make multiple pricing decisions over a long time horizon, it would be useful to investigate how social effects affect firms' pricing policies over time. For example, it is plausible that desire for conformity could lead to penetration pricing. We also did not examine how heterogeneity among consumers in the need for uniqueness or conformity could impact the results, and it is useful to explore such issues. We note that, while there is a large body of research on reference groups, extant research has yet to investigate the implications of these social groups for firm behavior. Our theoretical model can be adapted to formally study reference group effects (for one such attempt see Amaldoss and Jain, 2007).

The issue of brand equity has attracted the attention of marketing scholars for a long time. Researchers have examined the factors that determine the success of brand extensions (see Aaker and Keller, 1990; Reddy et al., 1994), and the impact of failed brand extensions on the parent brand (e.g. Keller and Aaker, 1992). It is possible to modify the framework proposed in this chapter to examine how social effects can moderate the success of brand extensions. It would also be interesting to investigate how firms should price multiple product lines in the presence of social effects.

Word of mouth is well recognized as an important source of information. While

---

[7] In fact, an explanation based on signaling status cannot account for an upward-sloping demand curve for snobs (see Corneo and Jeanne, 1997).

previous research has examined the issue of product adoption and advertising in the presence of word of mouth (see for example Mayzlin, 2006), researchers have not examined the issue of pricing in markets where word of mouth is the primary means of communication. Finally, it would be useful to test our model predictions using field data on consumption of conspicuous goods.

References

Aaker, D. and K. Keller (1990), 'Consumer evaluations of brand extensions', *Journal of Marketing*, **54** (1), 27–41.
Amaldoss, W. and S. Jain (2005a), 'Conspicuous consumption and sophisticated thinking', *Management Science*, **51** (10), 1449–66.
Amaldoss, W. and S. Jain (2005b), 'Pricing of conspicuous goods: a competitive analysis of social effects', *Journal of Marketing Research*, **42** (1), 30–42.
Amaldoss, W. and S. Jain (2007), 'Trading up: an analysis of reference group effects', mimeo.
Bagwell, L. and D. Bernheim (1996), 'Veblen effects in a theory of conspicuous consumption', *American Economic Review*, **86**, 349–73.
Banerjee, A. (1992), 'A simple model of herd behavior', *The Quarterly Journal of Economics*, **C108** (3), 797–817.
Basu, K. (1987), 'Monopoly, quality uncertainty and "Status" Goods', *International Journal of Industrial Organization*, **5** (4), 435–46.
Bearden, W. and M. Etzel (1982), 'Reference group influence on product and brand purchase decision', *Journal of Consumer Research*, **9** (2), 183–94.
Becker, G. (1991), 'A note on restaurant pricing and other examples of social influences on price', *Journal of Political Economy*, **99** (5), 1109–16.
Belk, R. (1988), 'Possessions and the extended self', *Journal of Consumer Research*, **15** (2), 139–68.
Bernheim, B. (1994), 'A theory of conformity', *The Journal of Political Economy*, **102** (5), 841–77.
Betts, P. (2002), 'National hero bearing the burden of success', *Financial Times*, 11 April.
Bikhchandani, S., D. Hirshleifer and I. Welch (1992), 'A theory of fads, fashion, custom, and cultural change as informational cascades', *Journal of Political Economy*, **100** (5), 992–1026.
Bourdieu, Pierre (1984), *Distinction: A Social Critique of the Judgment of Taste*, Cambridge, MA: Harvard University Press.
Brewer, M. (1991), 'The social self: on being the same and different at the same time', *Personality and Social Psychology Bulletin*, **17**, 475–82.
Bryson, Bethany (1996), 'Anything but heavy metal: symbolic exclusion and musical dislikes', *American Sociological Review*, **61**, 884–99.
Camerer, C.F. and T.-H. Ho (1999), 'Experience-weighted attraction learning in games', *Econometrica*, **87** (July), 827–74.
Chao, A. and J. Schor (1998), 'Empirical tests of status consumption: evidence from women's cosmetics', *Journal of Economic Psychology*, **19**, 107–31.
Childers, Terry and Akshay Rao (1992), 'The influuence of familial and peer-based reference groups on consumer decisions', *Journal of Consumer Research*, **19** (2), 198–211.
Corneo, G. and O. Jeanne (1997), 'Conspicuous consumption, snobbism and conformism', *Journal of Public Economics*, **66**, 55–71.
Fromkin, H. and C. Snyder (1980), 'The search for uniqueness and the valuation of scarcity', in K. Gergen et al. (eds), *Social Exchange: Advances in Theory and Research*, New York: Plenum, pp. 57–75.
Garner, C. (1982), 'Experimental evidence on the rationality of intuitive forecasters', *Research in Experimental Economics*, **2**, 113–28.
Godes, D. and D. Mayzlin (2004), 'Using online conversations to study word-of-mouth communication', *Marketing Science*, **23** (4), 545–60.
Grossman, G. and C. Shapiro (1984), 'Informative advertising with differentiated products', *The Review of Economic Studies*, **51** (1), 63–81.
Jones, S. (1984) *Economics of Conformism*, Oxford: Blackwell.
Kalish, S. (1985), 'A new product adoption model with price, advertising, and uncertainty', *Management Science*, **31** (12), 1569–85.
Karni, E. and D. Levin (1994), 'Social attributes and strategic equilibrium: a restaurant pricing game', *The Journal of Political Economy*, **102** (4), 822–40.
Katz, M. and C. Shapiro (1985), 'Network externalities, competition, and compatibility', *The American Economic Review*, **75** (3), 424–40.

Keller, K. and D. Aaker (1992), 'The effects of sequential introduction of brand extensions', *Journal of Marketing Research*, **29** (1), 35–50.
Leibenstein, H. (1950), 'Bandwagon, snob, and Veblen effects in the theory of consumer demand', *Quarterly Journal of Economics*, **64**, 183–207.
Lynn, M. (1991), 'Scarcity effect on value: a quantitative review of the commodity theory literature', *Psychology and Marketing*, **8**, 43–57.
Mayzlin, D. (2006), 'Promotional chat on the Internet', *Marketing Science*, **25** (2), 155–64.
Pesendorfer, W. (1995), 'Design innovation and fashion cycles', *American Economic Review*, **85** (4), 771–92.
Reddy, S., S. Holak and S. Bhat (1994), 'To extend or not to extend: success determinants of line extensions', *Journal of Marketing Research*, **31** (2), 243–52.
Ross, L. and R. Nisbett (1991), *The Person and Situation: Perspectives of Social Psychology*, New York: McGraw-Hill.
Ross, L., G. Bierbrauer and S. Hoffman (1976), 'The role of attribution processes in conformity and dissent: revisiting the Asch situation', *American Psychologist*, **31**, 148–57.
Schmalensee, R. (1976), 'An experimental study of expectation formation', *Econometrica*, **44**, 17–41.
Simmel, George (1957) 'Fashion', *American Journal of Sociology*, **62** (6), 541–58.
Simonson, I. and S. Nowlis (2000), 'The role of explanations and need for uniqueness in consumer decision making', *Journal of Consumer Research*, **27**, 49–68.
Smith, V. (1982), 'Markets as economizers of information: experimental investigation of Hayek's hypothesis', *Economic Inquiry*, **20**, 165–79.
Smith, V., G. Suchanek and A. Williams (1988), 'Bubbles, crashes and endogenous expectations in experimental spot asset markets', *Econometrica*, **56**, 1119–51.
Snyder, C. (1992), 'Product scarcity by need for uniqueness interaction: a consumer catch-22 carousel?', *Basic and Applied Social Psychology*, **13**, 9–24.
Stock, A. and S. Balachander (2005), 'The making of a "hot product": a signaling explanation of marketer's scarcity strategy', *Management Science*, **51** (8), 1181–92.
Sun, W. and J. Lull (1986), 'The adolescent audience for music videos and why they watch', *Journal of Communication*, **36** (1), 115–25.
Sunder, S. (1995), 'Experimental assets markets: a survey', in J. Kagel and A. Roth (eds), *The Handbook of Experimental Economics*, Princeton, NJ: Princeton University Press, pp. 445–500.
Taylor, S. (1998), 'The social being in social psychology', in D. Gilbert, S. Fiske and G. Lindzey (eds), *The Handbook of Social Psychology*, Vol. 1, New York: McGraw-Hill, ch. 2.
Veblen, T. (1899), *The Theory of Leisure Class: An Economic Study of Institutions*, London: Unwin.
Williams, A. (1987), 'The formation of price forecasts in experimental markets', *Journal of Money, Credit, and Banking*, **19**, 1–18.

19 Online and name-your-own-price auctions: a literature review
Young-Hoon Park and Xin Wang*

Abstract
With the explosive growth of activity in online auctions, considerable recent research studies this market mechanism. We survey recent theoretical, empirical and experimental research on the effects of auction design parameters (including minimum price, buy price and duration) and bidding strategies (including reference price, auction fever and dynamic bidding behavior) in online auctions, as well as literature dealing with competition in online auctions. We also discuss the name-your-own-price mechanism, in which the buyer determines the price, which the seller can either accept or reject. The review concludes with a proposed agenda for future research.

1. Introduction

The growth of the Internet has transformed markets for antiques, collectibles, consumer electronics and jewelry, to name just a few. In particular, online auctions have become popular and important venues for conducting business transactions. eBay Inc., the most widely recognized and largest online auction venue, has witnessed tremendous growth during the past decade, as shown in Figure 19.1.[1] From its humble origins as a trading post for Beanie Babies' collectors, eBay achieved 222 million confirmed registered users in the fourth quarter of 2006, representing a growth rate of 23 percent. These users generated a total of 610 million listings, and the listings helped drive eBay gross merchandise volume, or the total value of all successfully closed items on its trading platforms, to $14.4 billion, for a growth rate of 20 percent.[2]

In addition, the emergence of the Internet and its extensive electronic commerce provides companies with the opportunity to experiment with various innovative pricing models. A well-known example is the name-your-own-price (NYOP) model and, more generally, the concept of online haggling. In an NYOP setting, instead of posting a price, the seller waits for an offer by a potential buyer that he or she can then accept or reject. The relative ease of transacting in electronic markets makes this pricing mechanism viable, especially in the emergence of several new price intermediaries, such as Priceline. com, which implemented an NYOP model for selling airline tickets, rental cars and vacation packages.

Concurrent with this explosive growth of activity in online and NYOP auctions comes considerable research in recent years to study these market mechanisms. The enormous

---

* We would like to thank Vithala Rao and an anonymous reviewer for their comments and suggestions.
[1] eBay Inc. financial releases from second quarter 1998 to first quarter 2007 are available at http://investor.ebay.com/results.cfm.
[2] eBay Inc. financial releases from fourth quarter 2006 are available at http://investor.ebay.com/results.cfm.

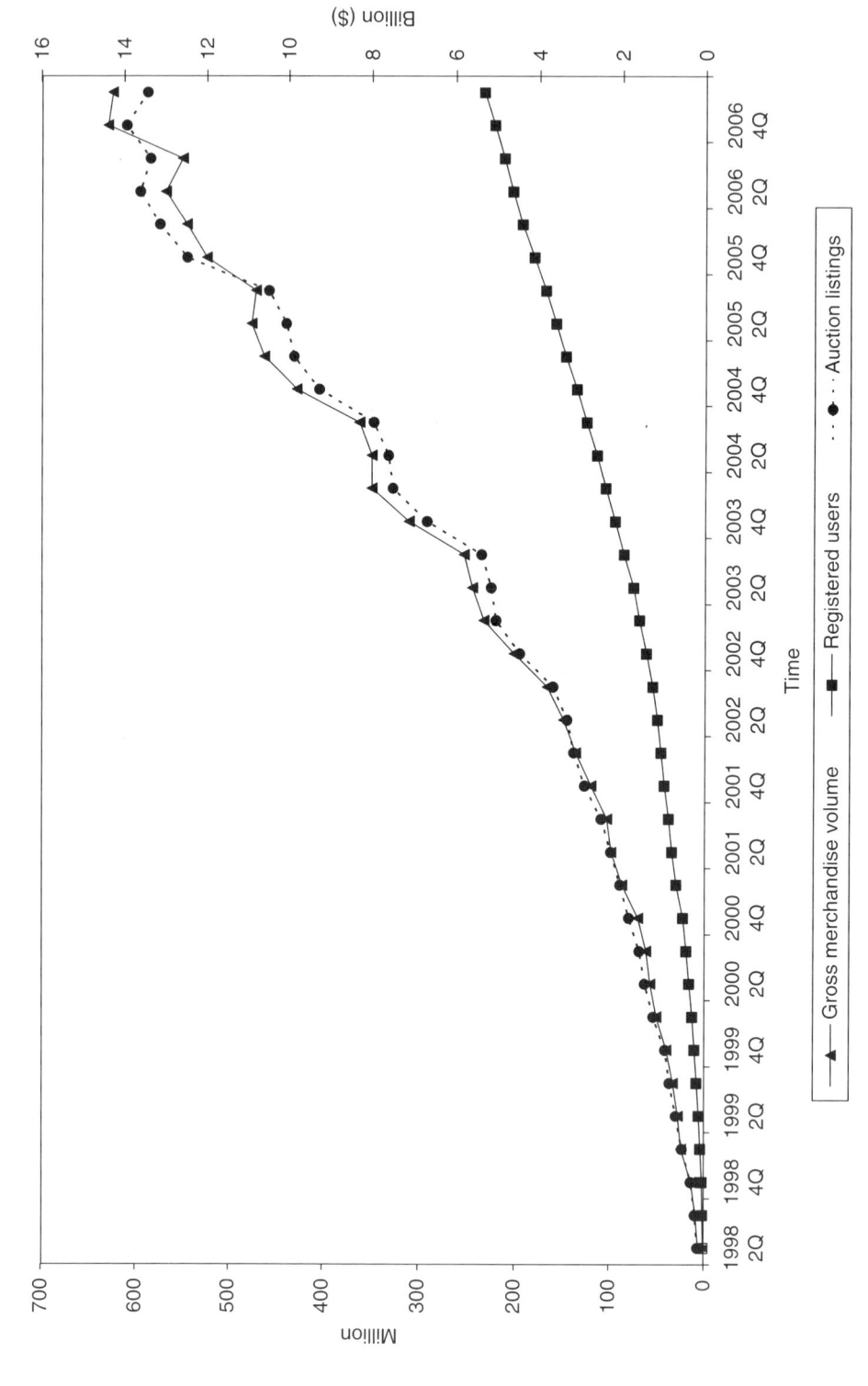

Figure 19.1 Registered users, auction listings and gross merchandise volume on eBay

amount of readily available field data, emergence of innovative auction design features, and precise and simple rules for bidders and sellers on auction platforms such as eBay have created excellent research opportunities. This chapter reviews that recent research on online and NYOP auctions and thus provides an overview of theoretical, empirical and experimental research. We limit the scope of this chapter to recent research in the marketing field. In particular, we organize this review according to two major areas: online auctions (including auction designs, bidder behavior and competition) and NYOP auctions. Although we attempt to cover all major aspects of research in the field, we exclude the reputation construct, because most research into the relationship between feedback ratings and auction outcomes is conducted by economists and is well documented in economics literature (e.g. Bajari and Hortaçsu, 2004). We refer interested readers to Bajari and Hortaçsu (2004) for a review of Internet auctions in economics literature.[3] Interested readers also may choose to peruse a few recent review articles (e.g. Ockenfels et al., 2006; Pinker et al., 2003) and discussion papers (e.g. Chakravarti et al., 2002; Cheema et al., 2005) pertaining to online auctions.

The rest of this chapter is organized as follows. In Section 2, we discuss research findings pertaining to the effects of auction design parameters (e.g. minimum bid, buy price, duration) on auction outcomes. Then, in Section 3, we detail research findings that show that bidders are susceptible to both static and dynamic context effects and allow situational factors or irrelevant cues to influence their decisions. This section includes insights from recent research regarding the influence of reference prices, auction fever and bidding dynamics on bidding outcomes. In Section 4, we discuss the impact of competition on bidding behavior in online auctions. In addition, we present research findings on the NYOP auction mechanism in Section 5. We conclude with directions for future research in Section 6.

2. Auction design in online auctions

Online auctions have precise and simple rules, which greatly facilitates theoretical analyses because it limits the complexity of strategic decisions by market participants. The huge amount of data readily available in electronic form further facilitates empirical studies. As a result, literature on online auctions has quickly produced insights into the effects of online auction design parameters on a variety of auction outcomes. In this section, we discuss research findings regarding the effects of the seller's design parameters (e.g. minimum price, buy price, duration) on auction outcomes on the basis of a mixture of empirical, experimental and theoretical research in online auctions.

Minimum price
Minimum price (or starting or minimum bid) represents a form of reserve price, usually publicly observable and contractual. When a seller sets the minimum bid below her valuation, she often combines this strategy with either a secret reserve price or shill bidding.

---

[3] We also exclude research on traditional auctions. Several important articles in economics discuss auction theory in general (e.g. Milgrom, 1989; Milgrom and Weber, 1982; Riley and Samuelson, 1981; Vickrey, 1963). Although these articles are crucial for understanding auction theory as it relates to online auctions, they are not specifically concerned with online auctions *per se* and thus are not included in this research.

422 *Handbook of pricing research in marketing*

The latter two are not made public; shill bidding is a type of fraud. However, both have similar effects on the minimum price: a trade occurs only if the final highest bid is above the secret reserve price or the shill bid. Although the details may differ, theoretical models share a few predictions that represent some of the earliest ideas studied in the field. The first basic hypothesis states that reserve prices (whether public or secret) should reduce the number of bids and bidders in an auction. The second hypothesis posits that the number of auctions that end without a trade should increase with the use of reserve prices.

Reiley (2006) tests hypotheses regarding reserve prices in first-price, sealed-bid auctions on Internet newsgroups, using field experiments of collectible trading cards from the game 'Magic: The Gathering'. By systematically varying the reserve-price levels as a fraction of each card's book value while keeping everything else constant, he finds that imposing a public reserve price can reduce the number of bidders and increase the chance of goods being unsold. However, conditional on a transaction taking place, having a reserve price increases the revenues received on the goods. Moreover, bidders clearly exhibit strategic behavior in their reactions to public reserve prices. High-value bidders, for example, raise their bids above the reserve in anticipation that rival bidders will do the same. The increased reserve-price level also seems to reduce the number of bidders and the probability of sale, although auctions with a reserve price tend to receive higher revenue than those without, conditional on sale.

Similarly, through field experiments, Ariely and Simonson (2003) document a positive correlation between the minimum price and the auction price. In particular, their experiment suggests that a high minimum price generates a higher auction price when bidders cannot compare the prices of two items. Furthermore, although low minimum prices tend to draw more bidders, the bids generally are low and insufficient to create a price war. Therefore low minimum prices often lead to lower auction prices.

Another role of minimum price is signaling. On eBay, as on most online auction sites, bidders know that an auction has a secret reserve and whether that reserve has been met. In an interesting contrast, traditional, live auction houses such as Christie's and Sotheby's do not inform bidders whether any secret reserve price has been exceeded. Bajari and Hortaçsu (2003) examine the effects of minimum prices and secret reserve prices using field data associated with collectible coin auctions and find that a secret reserve deters entry less than does a public reserve and has a positive effect on revenue. Therefore these authors suggest that a combination of a low minimum bid and a secret reserve probably represents the optimal configuration from a seller's point of view, especially in auctions of high-value items.

In the comprehensive descriptive model proposed by Park and Bradlow (2005), which models several key components of the bidding process (e.g. whether an auction prompts any bids; if so, who bids, when they bid, and how much they bid), the authors find a minimum price in general relates positively to bidder valuations in the context of a first-price ascending notebook auction. Using the same data set, Bradlow and Park (2007) find that the minimum price relates negatively to bid time increments. That is, a lower minimum price leads to the faster arrival, and thus greater concentration, of bids.

Behaviorally, Greenleaf (2004) identifies two emotional effects (anticipated regret and rejoicing) that a seller might experience while setting a reserve at auctions. Regret occurs when the highest bid exceeds the seller's value for the product but remains below the reserve, whereas rejoicing occurs when the reserve forces the winning bidder to pay a higher price. When asked to make reserve price decisions repeatedly over a series of open English auctions, sellers deliberate over their reserve decisions and adjust them considerably. This finding suggests that seller learning takes place. The result also indicates that sellers use a frequency heuristic, and both anticipated regret and rejoicing are significant for the seller's learning process.

Suter and Hardesty (2005) also investigate the relationship between price fairness perceptions and minimum prices. A high minimum price has a positive impact on the fairness perceptions of winning bidders but an adverse effect on losing bidders. This finding implies that sellers receive greater earnings, as well as no adverse price fairness perceptions from winning bidders, when they set minimum prices higher.

In most online auctions, the seller can make strategic choices not only about the amount of the reserve price but also whether to make it secret or public, and, if public, at what point in the auction it should be revealed. Although this scenario violates the formal rules of the auction game on eBay and most other online auction sites, the seller also may effectively camouflage and dynamically adjust the reserve price during the auction by using shill bids, or bids covertly placed by the seller or the seller's confederates to inflate the final sale price artificially. The seller could use any of these strategic options (or combinations thereof) to increase expected revenues from the auction. For example, Sinha and Greenleaf (2000) examine sellers' optimal reserve and shilling, as well as the effect of bidder's aggressiveness on these strategies, in the specific contexts of discrete bidding in private value English auctions, in which the bidders can bid only in increments rather than continuously. These auctions thus closely resemble online auctions. When they assess the utility implications of shilling for both sellers and bidders and compare them with those of using a reserve, they find that the optimal reserve strategy is affected by the relative bidding aggressiveness of the highest-valuation bidder compared with the remaining bidders, as well as the number of bidders.

Buy price
An interesting auction feature, unique to online auctions, involves the seller's ability to post a buy price at the auction, at which the product may be sold without bidding. Buy price auctions are ubiquitous in online auction markets. Starting with Yahoo!Auctions' Buy-Now in 1999, all major auction sites currently have similar features (e.g. 'Buy-It-Now' on eBay, 'Take-It-Price' on Amazon), though variations in buy-now auction formats appear in the online auction market. For example, on Yahoo and Amazon, the buy price stays throughout the auction, as long as the buy-now option is not exercised; in eBay's buy-now auction, in contrast, the buy price disappears after the first qualifying bid (i.e. higher than the reserve price).

The growing importance of selling auction items through the buy-now feature has attracted the attention of academic researchers and motivated studies on rationales for its existence. Various theories attempt to explain this seemingly irrational phenomenon, which explicitly limits the final price by imposing a fixed price at auction. One argument involves risk aversion, in that bidders might be risk averse to losing an item for various reasons, such as if the item is rare or they have lost items in the past and therefore are wary about losing a desired auction item again. In this case, a seller can exploit and appeal the bidder's risk aversion by offering the buy-now option so that the bidder can circumvent bidding (e.g. Budish and Takayama, 2001). Therefore, the higher the risk aversion among bidders, the higher the buy price a seller can demand for an item, which implies that risk-averse bidders are not better off in buy-now auctions (e.g. Hidvégi et al., 2006). Reynolds and Wooders (2009) study buy prices in both eBay and Yahoo auctions and find that introducing a buy price generally increases the seller's revenue when she faces risk-averse bidders. Moreover, Yahoo's buy-now auction can generate more revenue than eBay's with the same reserve and buy prices.

Other explanations regarding why sellers use a buy price in online auctions include waiting costs and the impatience of bidders. Wang et al. (2008) use a game-theoretical model to study the effect of endogenous participation on a seller's use of buy-now prices and argue that potential bidders endogenously make auction participation decisions. Because bidding entails costs (e.g. waiting, monitoring, cognitive efforts) and valuations vary across bidders, not everyone can afford or should participate in the auction. Instead, the decision should reflect a utility-maximizing outcome determined from a comparison of the utility of bidding versus not bidding. Similarly, when a price is posted at the auction, bidders base their choice on the expected utilities of bidding and exercising the buy option. In analyzing eBay's buy-now auctions, these authors find that because of endogenous participation, the seller can extract more surplus from the bidders, which would be lost in a pure auction. However, because of the dynamic nature of the buy-now feature, the seller should take extra care in setting the price level; when the costs of bidding are high, the seller should adjust the buy-now price downward to avoid the situation in which the buy-now auction reverts to a pure auction.

Sellers also might prefer to set low buy prices for their own reasons. Parallel to bidder risk aversion, sellers might be risk averse, such as if they are inexperienced, their items have unobservable quality, or they do not want to spoil their reputation as a reliable seller. Similarly, sellers might suffer high waiting costs. A similar argument indicates that sellers' impatience can motivate the use of a buy price. However, in all these cases, sellers might set the buy prices too low, which leads to the exercise of the buy-now option and lower revenues. In addition, Qiu et al. (2005) empirically analyze the use of buy prices by both sellers and bidders on the basis of eBay and experimental data. Their study shows that when bidders experience uncertainty about the value of the product, the buy price serves as an external reference price. Therefore the seller can use the buy price to signal the quality of the product and improve the auction outcome. Sellers with good reputations might be able to implement this method better than those without credibility. In addition, the signaling effect diminishes as the buy price increases and loses its own credibility.

Using notebook PC data in first-price ascending auctions, Chan et al. (2006) propose an integrated framework that examines sellers' decisions about whether and where to set buy prices, which are displayed throughout the auction. Bidders' regular bidding and buy-now decisions get modeled jointly, and the model contains several other distinctive features. First, bidders' willingness to pay is a function of their demographics and experience. Second, the effect of buy price (relative to expected price) on willingness to pay is modeled explicitly. This impact also has been explored in behavioral literature pertaining to how price may have an anchoring effect on willingness to pay, as well as in economic literature regarding how price can provide a signal if bidders are uncertain about quality. Third, the model does not assume that all sellers already optimize their buy-now decisions. Instead, the authors compute the optimal prices on the basis of estimation results and compare them with the data. If the sellers are risk averse, the observed buy price should be lower than the optimal level, but if bidders are willing to pay more for the buy-now option, the observed buy prices should be higher than the optimal level estimated by the model. Similar to Qiu et al. (2005), this research finds that a buy price higher than the 'expected price' increases bidders' willingness to pay. Furthermore, a large proportion of notebook PC sellers (62 percent) set their buy prices suboptimally from a revenue maximization perspective: approximately 15 percent of sellers set their buy prices too high, more than half (about 54 percent) set their buy prices too low, perhaps as a result of misestimations of competition across auctions. In addition, the authors show how sellers can use the model to set optimal buy prices.

On eBay, identical goods often sell simultaneously by two different mechanisms, that is, auctions and posted prices. Zeithammer and Liu (2006) propose and empirically test four possible reasons why sellers choose auctions versus posted prices, including sellers' indifference to selling mechanisms, price discrimination, an exogenous partitioning of the eBay market into posted price and auction markets, and sellers' heterogeneity. Using a data set that captures individual seller behavior across categories and allowing for various sources of seller heterogeneity, these authors find no empirical support for the first three hypotheses. In contrast, they indicate that both observed and unobserved seller heterogeneity represent important correlates of mechanism choice. Thus the coexistence of pure auctions and posted price selling is largely due to sellers' heterogeneity in, for example, their inventories.

Duration
Different rules mark auction ending times on various online auction sites. For example, the duration of an Amazon auction is automatically extended if bidding remains active; that is, if a new bid occurs within ten minutes of the previous bid. Hence the auction does not have a hard ending time. In contrast, eBay adopts a hard ending time and accepts no bids after the closing time specified by the seller. Roth and Ockenfels (2002) compare last-minute bidding behavior in eBay and Amazon auctions and find that late bidding occurs more frequently in the presence of hard-ending rules such as on eBay, in categories that require more expertise, and from more experienced bidders. Ockenfels and Roth (2006) also examine bidding strategies under the hard-ending rule in second-price online auctions and find that snipe bidding (i.e. bidding during the last ten minutes of an auction) arises as both equilibrium and an off-equilibrium outcome. Using data from completed auctions, they conclude that the extent of sniping is much more pronounced on eBay than Amazon, and that it largely occurs as a best response to incremental bidding.

Research findings regarding the impact of duration on auction outcomes are mixed. Ariely and Simonson (2003) argue that even though shorter durations may attract fewer bidders, they also can lead to increased competition. They document in a field experiment that auction duration relates negatively to auction price. By viewing bids as a sequence of record-breaking observations, Bradlow and Park (2007) empirically study auction duration as one of three key design variables, along with image placement and minimum price. Their results indicate that auction duration negatively affects the number of latent bidders; furthermore, auctions of shorter duration tend to have larger bid increments and marginally larger bid variations.

Borle et al. (2006) analyze the degree of multiple bidding and late bidding in online auctions using more than 10 000 eBay auctions across 15 different consumer product categories. Large variation occurs in late bidding and multiple bids across product categories, and in general, experienced bidders refrain from submitting multiple bids. In contrast to findings in existing literature on late bidding, the authors report that experienced bidders tend to bid either at the beginning or near the end of the auction.

In addition to these research findings regarding auction design parameters under the seller's control, a few researchers study the role of the seller in shaping demand for auctions. In particular, Yao and Mela (2008) estimate a structural model of buyer and seller behavior that incorporates heterogeneities in both bidder and seller costs. Thus they infer how changes in the listing behavior of the seller affect each bidder's likelihood of bidding in any given auction. Using data on Celtic coins, they find that buyer valuations are influenced by item, seller and auction characteristics; buyer costs are affected by bidding behavior and seller costs are influenced by item characteristics and the number of listings. On the basis of their model estimates, the authors assess the effects of an auction house's pricing strategy on the market equilibrium number of listings, bids and closing prices in the product category studied. This investigation is particularly useful because it provides explicit guidance to auction houses regarding their fees. Specifically, they find commission elasticities are higher than per-item fee elasticities because they target high-value sellers and enhance the likelihood that they will list.

3. Bidder behavior in online auctions

While an auction is in progress, participants are influenced by various types of value signals, which in turn can affect their decision dynamics for the auction item. In addition, economic, social and psychological factors might alter bidding behavior (e.g. Cheema et al., 2005). In this section, we discuss research findings that reveal that consumers violate principles of value maximization and consistency and are susceptible to both static and dynamic context effects, in that they allow situational factors and irrelevant cues to influence their decisions.

Reference price
Various price cues may systematically affect bidding behavior in an auction marketplace. Some researchers consider price cues within the focal product category, whereas others address them across product categories. Kamins et al. (2004) investigate the impact of two external reference points (reserve price and minimum price) under the seller's control on the final price of an auction and the number of bidders. In a field experiment, they find that when a seller specifies a high external reference price (reserve price), the final bid is higher than when it specifies a low external reference price (minimum price). When the seller provides both high and low reference prices, the former influences the final bid more, although a low reference price leads to a lower outcome than when the seller does not communicate any reference price. In addition, the number of bidders influences outcomes in the absence of seller-supplied reference prices. Finally, auctions with only reserve prices specified tend to attract more bidders than those with both reserve and minimum prices, which illustrates further the asymmetric role of the two reference prices.

In addition to reserve prices, other price cues can influence a consumer's willingness to pay. For example, Nunes and Boatwright (2004) examine how the prices of products that buyers unintentionally encounter can serve as anchors that affect their willingness to pay for the product they intend to buy. According to real-world auction data, the price tag on a relatively expensive car alters bidders' willingness to pay for a lower-priced car that subsequently appears on the auction block. This effect increases as the price of the anchor increases.

Building on the notion that loss aversion is more pronounced for explicit compared with implicit comparisons, Dholakia and Simonson (2005) propose that the existence of explicit instructions to make particular comparisons induces more risk-averse and cautious choice and bidding behavior among consumers. Their field experiment involves real online auctions, in which buyers either viewed comparisons among listings provided spontaneously by bidders or were encouraged by an explicit instruction to compare the focal auction with an adjacent listing. They find that an explicit reference point reduces the influence of adjacent auctions' minimum prices on the focal auction's price; induces bidders to submit fewer, lower and later bids; increases the tendency for sniping and bidding on multiple items at the same time; and reduces bidding frenzies.

Chan et al. (2007) also incorporate closed auction prices in their willingness-to-pay model. They find that the impact of a previous closing price on willingness to pay is negative, possibly because the bidder with the highest willingness to pay has been eliminated after purchasing the product, which means willingness to pay decreases among the pool of remaining bidders.

Auction fever
Auction fever refers to an excited and competitive state of mind in which the thrill of competing against other bidders increases a bidder's willingness to pay, beyond what the bidder would pay in a posted-price setting. Because auction fever depends on the thrill of competition, the effect should increase with the number of active bidders. This theory also may explain why some sellers prefer low minimum prices; a lower opening bid may attract more competitive bidders who are looking for a bargain, even though it increases the risk of underselling.

Ku et al. (2005) explore field and survey data of live and online auctions to find evidence of competitive arousal, such as rivalry, time pressure, social facilitation and first-mover advantages. They find considerable support for competitive arousal and escalation models but no support for rational choice predictions. In addition to evidence of auction fever, the authors find overbidding due to an attachment effect, such that long bidding durations and other sunk costs intensify the desire to win the auction and thus increase revenues for the seller. Both effects also emerge in a controlled laboratory experiment that varies the sunk cost parameter and the number of bidding rivals.

Heyman et al. (2004) also examine these two phenomena of competition and attachment, using the opponent effect to describe the arousal prompted by competing with others and quasi-endowment to represent the increased valuation due to having been attached to the item as the high bidder. In two experiments, one involving hypothetical bids and the other real-money bids, they vary the number of rival bids and duration of the quasi-endowment (i.e. time spent as the high bidder). Increases in both the number of rival bids and the duration of the quasi-endowment have positive effects on the final price; therefore the authors conclude that sellers may be able to increase their revenues by increasing the total auction duration and lowering the minimum price to induce more feverish bidding.

The evidence to date thus suggests that auction fever is a real phenomenon, which implies that sellers might increase revenues by setting a very low minimum price that increases the number of active bidders. Although this specific prediction has not been tested directly, several researchers report that lower minimum bids increase the number of latent bidders for auction items, which in turn increases the final auction price (e.g. Bradlow and Park, 2007).

Dynamic bidding
Although bidding behavior is inherently dynamic during an auction, research commonly assumes bidder rationality, such that bidders do not change their valuations while an auction is in progress. Most researchers focus on summary outcomes (e.g. final auction price) in an auction (e.g. Ariely and Simonson, 2003; Chakravarti et al., 2002) rather than explaining bidding behavior across the duration of the auction.

Park and Bradlow (2005) study bidding behavior over the entire sequence of bids by building a latent, time-varying construct of consumer willingness to bid, in which bidders may update a particular auction item over the course of the auction. They therefore incorporate and model simultaneously four key components of the bidding process within an integrated framework: whether an auction receives a bid at all; if so, who bids, when they bid, and how much they bid over the entire sequence of bids in an auction. The authors impose no structural assumption on bidder rationality or equilibrium behavior; instead, they derive the model using a probabilistic modeling paradigm. With a database of notebook PC auctions, they demonstrate that this general (yet parsimonious) model captures the key behavioral patterns of bidding behavior established in existing literature. Furthermore, they provide a tool for auction site managers to conduct customer relationship management efforts, which requires an evaluation of the goodness of the listed auction items (whether bids occur), as well as the potential bidders in their online auctions (who, when, and how much to bid).

A recent modeling advance in the field of dynamic bidding comes from Bradlow and Park (2007), who consider a sequence of bids in online auctions with an analogy of record-breaking events, in which only data points that break an existing record come into play. They investigate stochastic versions of the classical record-breaking problem, for which they apply Bayesian estimation to predict observed bids and bid times in online auctions. They address these data through data augmentation, with the assumption that participants (bidders) have dynamically changing valuations for the auctioned item but that the latent number of bidders competing in the events is unknown. Significant variations are identified in the number of latent bidders across auctions. In addition, the analysis indicates that there are many latent bidders relative to observed bidders. Given a previous bid, the number of remaining latent bidders is much smaller compared to that of new entrants. Moreover, both larger bid and time increments significantly influence the bidding participation behavior.

4. Competition in online auctions

In online auctions, both buyers and sellers have more opportunity to obtain the best value in the marketplace, compared with traditional auctions. Sellers have access to a much larger pool of potential bidders, unconstrained by information access or time restrictions. Similarly, buyers can consider more auction items in a given product category, which enables them to find the object of their search. The level of competition among auction items and bidders probably matters in terms of consumers' willingness to pay, which in turn affects the final auction price. Therefore we discuss the impact of competition on bidding behavior next.

Dholakia and Soltysinski (2001) provide evidence of herd behavior bias – the tendency to gravitate toward and bid for auction listings with one or more existing bids while ignoring comparable or even more attractive unbid auction listings within the same product category and available at the same time. To elaborate on this bias, they posit two distinct psychological mechanisms – the use of others' bidding behaviors as cues for pre-screening and the escalation of commitment after the first bid – as responsible for herd behavior. On the basis of auction listings in four product categories (portable CD players, Italian silk ties, Mexican pottery and Playstation consoles), they report that herd behavior bias gets attenuated by increasing bid prices but increases with the difficulty of evaluating quality. Dholakia et al. (2002) further investigate two specific types of herding bias moderators: auction attributes (volume of listing activity and posting of reservation prices) and agent characteristics (seller and bidder experience). They find that greater experience mitigates bias susceptibility among both sellers and bidders. As in traditional exchange arenas, for which behavioral decision research shows consumers are influenced by contextual informational cues when they make choices, consumers still violate the principles of value maximization and consistency and make suboptimal bidding decisions in online auction marketplaces.

In studying the extent to which people search for prices and the influence of the minimum price on the magnitude of bids, Ariely and Simonson (2003) find that higher minimum prices cause participants to bid more for the goods, but only when there are no immediate comparisons. Thus the measure of the amount of supply offered by other sellers interacts with the effect of the minimum price on auction prices. When many sellers offer identical or similar items at the same time, auctions with both high and low minimum prices end at roughly the same price. That is, a high degree of supply reduces the effect of the public reserve price; however, when few other sellers offer the same item, a high minimum price yields empirically higher auction prices.

To model a bidder's willingness to pay in ascending first-price auctions, Chan et al. (2007) consider two-dimensional market competition. These authors use breadth and depth measures to characterize marketing competition in online auctions; they define the former as the number of items with product attributes (except for brand name) similar to the focal item and the latter as the number of items with the same brand as the focal item that come from the pool of auction items with similar product attributes. The elasticities for breadth and depth are informative. An increase in breadth reduces willingness to pay about four times as much as an increase in depth, even after they control for brand effects (and other brand interaction effects) in the willingness-to-pay estimates. Therefore consumers appear to value breadth, because it helps them determine their willingness to pay by reducing their search and comparison shopping costs (especially if the same seller provides multiple listings of the same brand). This explanation is consistent with literature in psychology and marketing regarding consumer consideration and choice set formation and decision-making.

In online auctions, nearly identical goods often sell in a sequence of auctions, which allows bidders to focus on the auction that will end first while accounting for the presence of subsequent auctions. Zeithammer (2006) analytically and empirically studies this forward-looking behavior in online auctions with a model that extends existing literature on sequential auctions by allowing consumers to take into account the exact product information for future auctions. He assumes that bidders know not only the type of the current product on which they bid but also the type that will be sold next and when. The expected future surplus, and hence the opportunity cost of winning now, is a function of the available information about what will be sold at what point in the future. Actual data from eBay's MP3 and DVD categories test the theoretical model, and the empirical results suggest that bidders pay close attention to future products and auction timing, and adjust their bidding strategies accordingly.

5. NYOP auctions

'Name your own price' refers to a pricing mechanism in which the buyer, instead of the seller, determines the price. The buyer makes a bid, and the seller decides to accept or reject it. In an NYOP auction, any consumer who bids above a seller's unrevealed threshold price receives the product at the price of his or her bid. In the case of limited availability, consumers who are the first to bid above the threshold are served first. In contrast, a standard auction determines the winning bidder as the one who places the highest bid (if bidding to buy) or the lowest (if bidding to sell) among rival bids.

Chernev (2003) examines consumers' willingness to pay in an online environment by comparing two price elicitation strategies: price generation (i.e. 'name your price') and price selection (i.e. 'select your price'). The former approach, advanced by Priceline.com for example, asks consumers to state their willingness to pay for the product under consideration. In the latter approach, consumers consider a set of possible prices and select the price they find most acceptable. Contrary to popular belief that more choice is better, this research demonstrates that consumers often prefer a price elicitation task that offers less flexibility and is more restrictive in allowing consumers to express their willingness to pay. Moreover, Chernev shows that the presence of a readily available reference price moderates consumer price generation processes. This reference price, either externally or internally generated, can strengthen consumer preferences for the price generation process by mitigating the negative affect associated with it such as due to complexity of the task.

In an NYOP channel, no consensus exists about how to structure the market interactions optimally. For example, Priceline and eBay Travel allow consumers to place only a single bid for a given item, whereas sites such as All Cruise Auction openly allow consumers to continue bidding if their previous offer was rejected. To understand the effects of restrictions on the possible number of bids consumers can submit on an NYOP, Fay (2004) develops an analytical model and compares the single-bid model with one in which experienced consumers can submit multiple bids at Priceline. The analysis indicates that both market structures yield the same expected profit if all consumers have the same bidding options (single bid versus multiple bids). However, some consumers may know how to circumvent the single-bid rule and submit multiple bids (sophisticated bidders). The author argues that if it is impossible to completely prevent consumers from 'surreptitious rebidding', then the NYOP firm may be better off by encouraging rebidding. The benefit is determined by the proportion of the sophisticated bidders.

From the consumer point of view, repeatedly revising bids is not costless. Hann and Terwiesch (2003) study this cost, which they call frictional costs in NYOP, defined as the disutility that the consumer experiences when conducting an online transaction, such as submitting an offer. Thus consumers trade off direct financial value for frictional costs. The authors show that frictional costs in electronic markets are substantial, with mean (median) values ranging from EUR 4.84 (3.54) for a portable digital music player to EUR 7.95 (6.08) for a personal digital assistant. They also report that socio-demographic variables do not explain variations in frictional costs. Spann et al. (2004) develop and empirically test a model that simultaneously estimates individual willingness to pay and frictional costs on the basis of consumers' bidding behavior at an NYOP seller. Their results show significant consumer heterogeneity that enables sellers to segment the market and indicates an opportunity for sellers to increase profits further through price discrimination. Moreover, they find that restricting consumers to a single bid may reduce the seller's revenue. Thus providers of NYOP mechanisms should be very concerned about the particular design of this mechanism.

Terwiesch et al. (2005) present a model of consumer haggling between an NYOP retailer and a set of individual buyers. In an NYOP setting, instead of posting a price, the retailer waits for potential buyers to submit offers and then chooses to accept or reject them. Consumers whose offers have been rejected can invest in additional haggling effort and incrementally increase their next offers. Using transaction data from an NYOP retailer, these authors show that the retailer must choose a threshold price above which all offers will be accepted. If consumers are very heterogeneous with respect to their valuations and haggling abilities, haggling can lead to higher profits than posted prices.

According to the notion that real-life bidders do not behave as game theory prescribes they should, Ding et al. (2005) formally incorporate the emotions evoked by an auction process similar to Priceline's, including the excitement of winning if a bid is accepted and the frustration of losing if it is not. They identify the important role that emotions play in bids revisions, which has been ignored by classic economic models. It is found that emotions dynamically influence the direction of such revisions, particularly according to the bidding outcome of the previous round. In addition, the authors characterize the optimal bidding strategies depending on the bidder's propensity to bid.

The behavior of consumers in NYOP auctions has also been empirically investigated and compared with the predictions of economic theories. Spann and Tellis (2006) find that a majority of bidding sequences are inconsistent with the theoretical prediction in that the bids in a sequence do not increase monotonically at a decreasing rate. Empirical evidence is found of overbidding, which suggests that consumers are paying a higher than efficient price. Interestingly, the authors find that bidders' experience (measured by the number of products bid on) does not increase the chance of rational bidding. A large number of bids and long inter-bid times increase the chance of irrational bidding.

The literature on NYOP auctions remains quite sparse. Some studies focus on the specific design of an NYOP channel but do not provide empirical data (Chernev, 2003; Ding et al., 2005; Fay, 2004). Other studies analyze consumer characteristics on the basis of data from such auctions but do not examine whether consumer behavior is rational (Hann and Terwiesch, 2003; Spann et al., 2004). Spann and Tellis (2006) analyze the empirical behavior of consumers and assess the extent of irrationality reflected in the bids submitted. Although NYOP channels have rapidly become a familiar business model in the e-commerce landscape, uncertainty about the survival of these new electronic markets on the Internet remains. Thus it is critical to study how best to structure this sales mechanism and design user interface. To this end, behavioral aspects should be considered in additional research of NYOP mechanisms.

6. Conclusions and future research

In this chapter, we focus on effects of auction design parameters on auction outcomes, irrational bidder behavior, and competition among online auctions, as well as research findings pertaining to NYOP auctions. Although we acknowledge that a more complete literature review is possible, this chapter captures the key results from existing literature about online and NYOP auctions and thus provides a strong overview.

Extant literature covers much ground and attempts to answer various questions. After assessing that literature, we note several avenues for the further exploration of online auctions. First, current empirical research mainly focuses on understanding the effects of various auction design parameters. Most research examines design variables in lieu of competition, whether from other auctions or from alternative options such as the retail channel. Incorporating these aspects would not only clarify the actual decision-making process of bidders more accurately but also provide more relevant insights for managers as they develop pricing strategies, in terms of both price format and price levels.

Second, a new theme has been formed in online auction research, namely, the behavior of bidders, especially how bidders form their willingness to pay. Economic models typically assume that in private value auctions, bidders *a priori* possess a valuation (signal) that remains invariant to other signals. Increasingly, however, researchers identify various influences on this valuation and the process by which it forms. Continued research into how consumers form their willingness to pay in online auctions has great value for business managers, because it can help them identify potential buyers and increase the efficiency of their business operations. This topic might be explored in more detail through controlled lab or field experiments.

Third, bidder learning represents yet another promising research area. Prior research examines sellers' feedback ratings and links them to auction outcomes; more recent work also considers bidders' experience, also measured through feedback ratings, as a means to explain bidding behavior and the formation of willingness to pay. Additional research is needed in this area, because understanding how bidding strategies within a product category, as well as across product categories, evolve as a result of experience will be crucial for online auctions to evaluate the lifetime value of bidders (both winners and losers). Because buyers and sellers interact in an auction marketplace, further research should develop integrated frameworks to study both buyer and seller behavior, instead of presuming that seller behavior is exogenous (e.g. Yao and Mela, 2008).

The Internet provides a fertile ground for studying consumer behavior, particularly in the cases of online and NYOP auctions. Not only do these new trading platforms make the market more efficient, but they also provide generous amounts of data and information that can inform our understanding of human behavior, especially with regard to decision-making processes associated with transactions. Research developments pertaining to online and NYOP auctions have been fruitful; we hope this review further accelerates the development of theoretical, empirical and experimental research on online and NYOP auctions.

References

Ariely, Dan and Itamar Simonson (2003), 'Buying, bidding, playing or competing? Value assessment and decision dynamics in online auctions', *Journal of Consumer Psychology*, **13** (4), 113–23.
Bajari, Patrick and Ali Hortaçsu (2003), 'Winner's curse, reserve prices, and endogenous entry: empirical insights from eBay auctions', *RAND Journal of Economics*, **34** (2), 329–55.
Bajari, Patrick and Ali Hortaçsu (2004), 'Economic insight from Internet auctions', *Journal of Economic Literature*, **42** (2), 457–86.
Borle, Sharad, Peter Boatwright and Joseph Kadane (2006), 'The timing of bid placement and extent of multiple bidding', *Statistical Science*, **21** (2), 194–205.
Bradlow, Eric T. and Young-Hoon Park (2007), 'Bayesian estimation of bid sequences in Internet auctions using a generalized record breaking model', *Marketing Science*, **26** (2), 218–29.
Budish, Eric and Lisa Takayama (2001), 'Buy prices in online auctions: irrationality on the Internet?', *Economics Letters*, **72** (3), 325–33.
Chakravarti, Dipankar, Eric Greenleaf, Atanu Sinha, James C. Co, Daniel Friedman, Teck H. Ho, R. Mark Isaac, Andrew Mitchell, Amnon Rapoport, Michael H. Rothkorf, Joydeep Srivastava and Rami Zwick (2002), 'Auctions: research opportunities in marketing', *Marketing Letters*, **13** (3), 281–96.
Chan, Tat Y., Vrinda Kadiyali and Young-Hoon Park (2006), 'The exercise of buy-it-now pricing in auctions: seller revenue implications', Working Paper, Johnson Graduate School of Management, Cornell University.
Chan, Tat Y., Vrinda Kadiyali and Young-Hoon Park (2007), 'Willingness to pay and competition in online auctions', *Journal of Marketing Research*, **44** (2), 324–33.
Cheema, Amar, Peter T.L. Popkowski Leszczyc, Rajesh Bagchi, Richard P. Bagozzi, James C. Cox, Utpal M. Dholakia, Eric A. Greenleaf, Amit Pazgal, Michael H. Rothkopf, Michael Shen, Shyam Sunder and Robert Zeithammer (2005), 'Economics, psychology, and social dynamics of consumer behavior in auctions', *Marketing Letters*, **16** (3), 401–13.
Chernev, Alexander (2003), 'Reverse pricing and online price elicitation strategies in consumer choice', *Journal of Consumer Psychology*, **13** (1–2), 51–62.
Dholakia, Utpal M. and Itamar Simonson (2005), 'The effect of explicit reference points on consumer choice and online bidding behavior', *Marketing Science*, **24** (2), 206–17.
Dholakia, Utpal M. and Kerry Soltysinski (2001), 'Coveted or overlooked? The psychology of bidding for comparable listings in digital auctions', *Marketing Letters*, **12** (3), 225–37.
Dholakia, Utpal M., Suman Basuroy and Kerry Soltysinski (2002), 'Auction or agent (or both)? A study of moderators of the herding bias in digital auctions', *International Journal of Research in Marketing*, **19** (2), 115–30.
Ding, Min, Jehoshua Eliashberg, Joel Huber and Ritesh Saini (2005), 'Emotional bidders – an analytical and experimental examination of consumers' behavior in a Priceline-like reverse auction', *Management Science*, **51** (3), 352–64.
Fay, Scott (2004), 'Partial-repeat-bidding in the name-your-own-price channel', *Marketing Science*, **23** (3), 407–18.
Greenleaf, Eric A. (2004), 'Reserves, regret and rejoicing in open English auctions', *Journal of Consumer Research*, **31** (2), 264–73.
Hann, Il-Horn and Christian Terwiesch (2003), 'Measuring the frictional costs of online transactions: the case of a name-your-own-price channel', *Management Science*, **49** (11), 1563–79.
Heyman, James E., Yesim Orhun and Dan Ariely (2004), 'Auction fever: the effect of opponents and quasi-endowment on product valuations', *Journal of Interactive Marketing*, **18** (4), 7–21.
Hidvégi, Zoltán, Wenli Wang and Andrew Whinston (2006), 'Buy-price English auction', *Journal of Economic Theory*, **129**, 31–56.
Kamins, Michael A., Xavier Drèze and Valerie S. Folkes (2004), 'Effects of seller-supplied prices on buyers' product evaluations: reference prices in an Internet auction context', *Journal of Consumer Research*, **30** (4), 622–8.
Ku, Gillian, Deepak Malhotra and J. Keith Murnighan (2005), 'Towards a competitive arousal model of decision-making: a study of auction fever in live and internet auctions', *Organizational Behavior and Human Decision Processes*, **96**, 89–103.
Milgrom, Paul R. (1989), 'Auctions and bidding: a primer', *Journal of Economic Perspectives*, **3** (3), 3–22.
Milgrom, Paul R. and Robert J. Weber (1982), 'A theory of auctions and competitive bidding', *Econometrica*, **50** (5), 1089–122.
Nunes, Joseph C. and Peter Boatwright (2004), 'Incidental prices and their effect on willingness to pay', *Journal of Marketing Research*, **41** (4), 457–66.
Ockenfels, Axel and Alvin Roth (2006), 'Late and multiple bidding in second price Internet auctions: theory and evidence concerning different rules for ending an auction', *Games and Economic Behavior*, **55** (2), 297–320.

Ockenfels, Axel, David Reiley and Abdolkarim Sadrieh (2006), 'Online auctions', in Terrence Hendershott (ed.), *Economics and Information Systems*, Amsterdam: Elsevier Science, pp. 571–628.

Park, Young-Hoon and Eric T. Bradlow (2005), 'An integrated model for bidding behavior in Internet auctions: whether, who, when, and how much', *Journal of Marketing Research*, **42** (4), 470–82.

Pinker, Edieal J., Abraham Seidmann and Yaniv Vakrat (2003), 'Managing online auctions: current business and research issues', *Management Science*, **49** (11), 1457–84.

Qiu, Chun, Peter T.L. Popkowski Leszczyc and Yongfu He (2005), 'The signal effect of buy-now price in Internet auctions', Working Paper, School of Business, University of Alberta.

Reiley, David (2006), 'Field experiments on the effects of reserve prices in auctions: more magic on the Internet', *RAND Journal of Economics*, **37** (1), 195–211.

Reynolds, Stanley and John Wooders (2009), 'Auctions with a buy price', *Economic Theory*, **38** (1), 9–39.

Riley, John G. and William F. Samuelson (1981), 'Optimal auctions', *American Economic Review*, **71** (3), 381–92.

Roth, Alvin E. and Axel Ockenfels (2002), 'Last-minute bidding and the rules for ending second-price auctions: evidence from eBay and Amazon auctions on the Internet', *American Economic Review*, **92** (4), 1093–103.

Sinha, Atanu and Eric A. Greenleaf (2000), 'The impact of discrete bidding and bidder aggressiveness on seller's strategies in open English auctions: reserves and covert shilling', *Marketing Science*, **19** (3), 244–65.

Spann, Martin, Bernd Skiera and Björn Schäfers (2004), 'Measuring individual frictional costs and willingness-to-pay via name-your-own-price mechanisms', *Journal of Interactive Marketing*, **18** (4), 22–36.

Spann, Martin and Gerard J. Tellis (2006), 'Does the Internet promote better consumer decisions? The case of name-your-own-price auctions', *Journal of Marketing*, **70** (January), 65–78.

Suter, Tracy A. and David M. Hardesty (2005), 'Maximizing earnings and price fairness perceptions in online consumer-to-consumer auctions', *Journal of Retailing*, **81** (4), 307–17.

Terwiesch, Christian, Sergei Savin and Il-Horn Hann (2005), 'Online haggling at a name-your-own-price retailer: theory and application', *Management Science*, **51** (3), 339–51.

Vickrey, William S. (1963), 'Counter-speculation auctions and competitive sealed tenders', *Journal of Finance*, **41** (1), 8–37.

Wang, Xin, Alan Montgomery and Kannan Srinivasan (2008), 'When auction meets fixed price: a theoretical and empirical examination of buy-it-now auctions', *Qualitative Marketing and Economics*, **6** (4), 339–70.

Yao, Song and Carl F. Mela (2008), 'Online auction demand', *Marketing Science*, **27** (5), 861–85.

Zeithammer, Robert (2006), 'Forward-looking bidding in online auctions', *Journal of Marketing Research*, **43** (3), 462–76.

Zeithammer, Robert and Pengxuan Liu (2006), 'When is auctioning preferred to posting a fixed selling price?', Working Paper, Graduate School of Business, University of Chicago, IL.

20 Pricing under network effects
Hongju Liu and Pradeep K. Chintagunta

Abstract
Pricing in markets characterized by network effects is a topic that has recently been attracting considerable interest from researchers in both marketing and economics. Early literature on static pricing under network effects focused on the importance of consumer expectations and the multiple equilibria problem. In a dynamic setting, penetration pricing has been found to be optimal under various scenarios. After reviewing the analytical literature on pricing under network effects, we discuss its connections to other literatures. Empirical studies have been relatively scarce. One obstacle is the computational burden in solving for the optimal pricing policies. We illustrate the issues involved in empirical studies and suggest directions for future research.

Network effects arise when the utility of an agent from consumption of a good increases with the number of other agents consuming the same good. A classic example is communication networks – telephones, fax machines, or e-mail accounts become more valuable as more people join the network, i.e. adopt the product.

Network effects can be direct or indirect. Under direct network effects, the utility that a consumer derives from a good depends directly on its installed base, or equivalently the cumulative unit sales of the good. The communication networks mentioned above are examples of direct network effects. They are in contrast with indirect network effects, under which consumers care about the installed base only because a large installed base of the good will increase the availability of a complementary good. For example, a person purchasing a video game console will be concerned with the number of other people purchasing the same hardware because a more popular game console will induce more games to be developed for it. Such a hardware–software paradigm applies to many other industries such as compact disks (CDs), digital video disks (DVDs), personal computers (PCs), personal digital assistants (PDAs), video cassette recorders (VCRs) and so on.

A wide range of industries are characterized by network effects. Some of these network effects may appear in more subtle ways. For example, more people going to a shopping mall can make it more crowded. On the other hand, a more popular shopping mall may attract more and better-quality stores. If the second effect dominates, the utility of going to the shopping mall increases with the number of people going there, which gives rise to the indirect network effect. In the case of QWERTY keyboards, there is a direct effect because people like to be able to type on others' keyboards. There may also be an indirect effect because the dominant keyboard design will draw more compatible products and services.

Network effects add interesting dimensions to firms' strategies: should the new product generation be compatible with the old one? Should the new system standard be proprietary or open to other firms? But pricing continues to be a critical element for firms that compete in these markets. In the following sections, we discuss the issues that require special attention for pricing under network effects.

The rest of this chapter is organized as follows. We first introduce the issues involved in static pricing, dynamic pricing and nonlinear pricing under network effects. Then we

1. Static pricing

We start from simple static pricing in a monopoly market, which introduces the important issues of consumer expectations and multiple equilibria. Rohlfs (1974) provides an early treatment of such issues in the context of a communication network, although the fulfilled-expectations demand curve has been discussed in Leibenstein (1950). We discuss them below.

Consumer expectations play an important role in the adoption of network products. At the time of making purchase decisions, consumers do not know exactly how many people will adopt the product. Such information is needed while making purchase decisions since a consumer's utility from the product depends on the network size. Therefore consumers' purchase decisions are based on the expected size of the network.

One commonly proposed restriction to be placed on expectations is that they will be fulfilled in the sense that consumer expectations are consistent with the actual outcome in the market (see, e.g., Leibenstein, 1950; Rohlfs, 1974; Katz and Shapiro, 1985; Economides, 1996). That is, on the induced fulfilled-expectations demand curve, each price p corresponds to those quantities q such that, when consumers expect quantity q, there will be just q consumers purchasing at price p. Leibenstein (1950) derives such a demand curve from fixed-expectations demand curves. Assume a fixed-expectations demand curve $q=D^x(p)$ if all consumers believe the total demand is x. Varying x will result in a set of fixed-expectations demand curves. On each $D^x(p)$, there is a point where the actual demand is consistent with consumers' expectations, i.e. $x=D^x(p)$. As illustrated in Figure 20.1, the locus of all these points forms the fulfilled-expectations demand curve $D(p)$. Leibenstein argues that such a demand curve is more elastic than any of the fixed-expectations demand curves from which it is derived.

Multiple equilibria may occur even if we restrict attention to fulfilled expectations. Intuitively, if each consumer believes that no other consumer buys the network product, then it may result in the case that no one will buy it, which leads to a fulfilled-expectations equilibrium with zero sales. However, if each consumer expects many others to purchase the product, then many people will purchase, and this outcome is another fulfilled-expectations equilibrium.

Multiple equilibria show up graphically as multiple intersections between the fulfilled-expectations demand curve and the horizontal line corresponding to a given price level. Implicitly this means that the demand curve has both upward-sloping segments and downward-sloping ones. For reasons explained by Rohlfs (1974), the equilibria located on the upward-sloping segments may be ruled out because they are unstable. However, there could still be multiple equilibria which are stable, and hence the exact demand at any given price level has to be determined carefully.

If multiple equilibria are possible, firms will try to affect consumer expectations so that the largest equilibrium quantity can be achieved at a given price level. Shapiro and Varian (1998) discuss various tactics in managing consumer expectations. In particular, a low introductory price, or penetration pricing, can help convince consumers that the

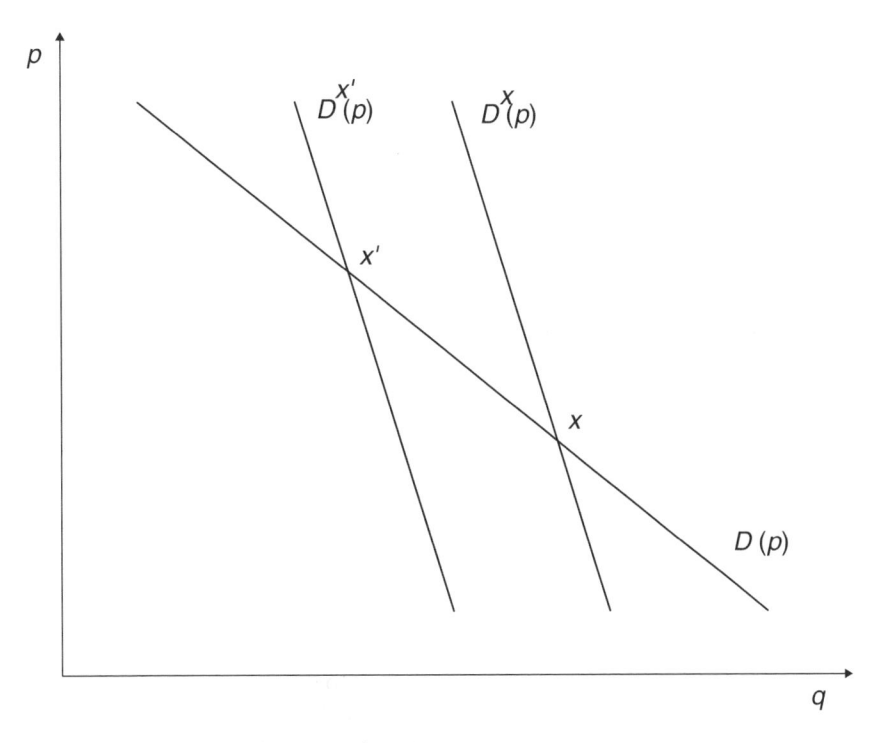

Source: Adapted from Leibenstein (1950), Figure 1.

Figure 20.1 Fulfilled-expectations demand curve

product will be successful in the future. Further discussion on penetration pricing follows in the next section.

2. Dynamic pricing

The diffusion of a network product takes place over time. During the life cycle of the product, firms may want to charge different prices according to evolving market conditions. Thus firms' pricing strategies can be better captured through a dynamic model.

When a network product is just launched, it may not be very attractive to consumers because of its limited network size. This provides an incentive for the firm to set a low initial price in order to encourage consumer adoptions. Once many consumers have joined the network and hence the product has become more attractive, the price can be raised. This low-high pricing scheme is often referred to as penetration pricing.

According to Cabral et al. (1999), the early telephone network provides a good example of penetration pricing. Bell's 1876 patents created a monopoly over the telephone service until the expiration of these patents in 1893. In this period, average monthly fees charged by the unregulated telephone companies rose steadily.

Monopoly pricing
In a monopoly market for durable goods, firms' incentives for penetration pricing are in contrast with the Coase conjecture (Coase, 1972). Coase (1972) argues that durable-goods

monopolists have incentives to keep cutting prices in order to further penetrate the market. Anticipating this, forward-looking consumers will delay purchases until prices equal marginal costs. Therefore, unless there is a way for these monopolists to credibly commit to future prices, they will not be able to exercise any market power. But under network effects, if indeed a monopolist finds it optimal to engage in penetration pricing and as a result prices keep rising, the Coasian dynamics (Hart and Tirole, 1988) may no longer be applicable.

Bensaid and Lesne (1996) study the optimal pricing policy of a monopolist selling a durable good. They start with a two-period model and then extend it to an infinite number of periods. In each period the network benefit is assumed to be proportional to the previous installed base. They find equilibrium prices to be increasing over time when the network effect is of sufficient magnitude.

Using a two-period model, Cabral et al. (1999) study when and why a monopolist would set a low introductory price. They find that, when consumers are price-takers, Coasian dynamics tend to predominate over penetration pricing if there is complete information. Penetration pricing occurs when each consumer's valuation of the product is her private information, or when consumers are not perfectly informed about the firm's unit cost.

Mason (2000) develops a continuous-time, infinite-horizon model in which a monopolist chooses output to maximize the present value of profits from production of a durable good. Consumers decide whether to adopt according to the current price and the expected network benefit. Under this configuration they show that the monopolist prices at marginal cost, as predicted by Coase (1972).

Gabszewicz and Garcia (2005) solve explicitly for the optimal price path in a monopoly market with a finite number of time periods. A somewhat unusual feature in their framework is that consumers are 'short-lived' in the sense that there is a different cohort of consumers making purchase decisions in each new time period. They find an increasing price path, i.e. penetration-like pricing, to be optimal.

Competition
Many papers on dynamic pricing under network effects have focused on monopoly markets. Dealing with competition in the market adds to the complexities in solving for firms' optimal policies. In general, the incentives for penetration pricing still exist in oligopoly markets. However, one difference is that competition would limit the market power of each firm.

If penetration pricing does occur, competition might push initial prices to be even lower than those under monopoly. But on the other hand, there is splintering of the market under oligopoly but not under monopoly. Thus a monopolist may expect more profits in the second period than oligopolists, and hence may be willing to cut initial prices even lower. Therefore it is unclear whether monopoly or oligopoly leads to lower initial prices.

Katz and Shapiro (1986) study the adoption pattern of competing technologies depending on whether these technologies are sponsored or not. If a technology is sponsored, an entity owns property rights to the technology and hence is willing to make investments to promote it. In the absence of a sponsor, free entry into the supply of a technology will lead to marginal cost pricing. Katz and Shapiro consider two periods or generations of homogeneous consumers, and two incompatible technologies. In each period consumers choose to adopt one of the two standards. If both standards are sponsored, they find that the firm with the superior standard in the second period may decide to price below cost in the first period in order to attract consumers to join its network.

Xie and Sirbu (1995) model the dynamic pricing behaviors of an incumbent and a later entrant. They incorporate network effects into a diffusion model with finite horizon and continuous time. The dynamic potential demand depends on the current network sizes. They establish optimal pricing policies with open-loop controls, i.e. firms set a one-shot price trajectory without feedback effects. This is as opposed to closed-loop controls, in which case firms set a state-contingent pricing policy and adjust for any changes in market conditions. Xie and Sirbu show that, under strong network effects, an increasing price path can be optimal. Also, with strong network effects and a small installed base, the incumbent profits from a compatible entry.

Nondurable goods

The aforementioned studies concentrate on durable-goods markets, in which a consumer will drop out of the market after making a purchase. In these markets a consumer's utility is affected by the cumulative sales of the durable product. This may not be true for nondurable-goods markets.

For example, consider Xbox Live, a subscription service offered by Microsoft for online gaming. In each month, some consumers may join or drop out of the network. So the subscription level fluctuates over time. When a potential customer decides whether to subscribe to the service, she cares about how many people she can play with, i.e. the current subscription level.

If consumers' utilities are affected by the current subscription level, not historical levels, then it seems that there is no intertemporal price effect, and the producer can set prices to maximize single-period profits only. However, past prices or quantities may affect current demand through consumer expectations or usage experiences. Therefore the producer's pricing problem may still be dynamic, and it turns out that an increasing price path can be optimal for nondurable goods as well.

Dhebar and Oren (1985) analyze a monopolist's intertemporal pricing decision for a new subscription service. In each time period all consumers decide whether to subscribe based on the previous level of subscription and their anticipation about the network growth. The potential demand is defined as $d^\alpha(x, p)$, where x is the previous subscription level and p is the price. $\alpha \in [0, 1]$ governs consumer expectations on network growth. $\alpha = 1$ indicates that consumers have rational expectations and $\alpha = 0$ indicates that consumers are myopic and base their subscription decisions on the previous subscription level only.

The monopolist sets a price trajectory $p(t)$ by solving the following optimization problem:

$$\underset{p(t)}{\text{Max}} \int_0^\infty e^{-\delta t}[px - c(x)]dt$$

subject to

$$x(0) = x_0,$$
$$x'(t) = G(d^\alpha, x)$$

Here $G(d^e, x)$ describes the product diffusion process. Standard control theory is then applied to solve for the optimal price trajectory. They demonstrate that typically the price path is increasing and the firm may set initial prices below marginal costs. It is also shown that higher growth anticipations and a lower discount rate result in a lower equilibrium price and a larger network.

Consumer expectations
Under network effects, consumers' adoption decisions critically depend on their expectations on future network sizes. The assumption of fulfilled expectations or rational expectations indicates that consumers can perfectly predict the future network sizes if there is perfect information and no uncertainty, and when there is imperfect information or uncertainty, consumers can use all available information to make the best possible predictions. This might require too much faith in consumers' cognitive processing power.

In dynamic settings, firms are forward looking in the sense that they maximize the present discounted value of total profits over a planning horizon. Regarding consumer adoption decisions, however, past studies have made various assumptions ranging from completely myopic to perfectly rational.

For example, Xie and Sirbu (1995) assume myopic consumers in the sense that consumers' adoption decisions are based on the current prices and network sizes, not the expected future ones.

Bensaid and Lesne (1996) assume that the value of the product is a function of the existing network size, but consumers still form rational expectations about the future network size in order to decide when to purchase the product.

In the Dhebar and Oren (1985) model, a consumer's adoption decision depends on the expected network size. However, fulfilled expectations are not enforced. Instead, the expected network size is allowed to vary between the existing network size and fulfilled future network size.

Radner and Sundararajan (2005) examine how the predictions would change if the assumption of unbounded rationality were relaxed in a monopoly market for a subscription service. They assume that consumers are boundedly rational in two aspects. First, not all consumers observe a price change immediately. Only a fraction of consumers respond to new prices, while others make no adjustment. Second, consumers are not able to make accurate forecasts on future demand. In particular, they examine a model with myopic consumers and then extend it to other cases.

They use a continuous-time, infinite-horizon model to study the dynamic pricing problem of a network monopolist. They find that the price is zero when the product user base is below a specific threshold. Once this threshold is crossed, the price is chosen to keep user base stationary. They show that this pricing policy is robust to several alternative models of bounded rationality.

3. Nonlinear pricing

So far we have restricted our attention to those markets in which each consumer buys at most one unit of the network good. In such markets only uniform pricing is relevant. However, in some other markets it may happen that different consumers buy variable quantities of the product. As pointed out by Sundararajan (2003), software purchases from the business segment often fall into this category.

Table 20.1 Analytical studies on pricing under network effects

Pricing Scheme	Market	Paper
Static	Monopoly	Leibenstein (1950)
		Rohlfs (1974)
		Sundararajan (2003)
	Oligopoly	Katz and Shapiro (1985)
		Economides (1996)
Dynamic	Monopoly	Dhebar and Oren (1985)
		Dhebar and Oren (1986)
		Bensaid and Lesne (1996)
		Cabral et al. (1999)
		Mason (2000)
		Gabszewicz and Garcia (2005)
		Radner and Sundararajan (2005)
	Oligopoly	Katz and Shapiro (1986)
		Xie and Sirbu (1995)

For example, the market for PC operating systems exhibits indirect network effects through the availability of compatible software applications. In this market, a company usually buys many copies of an operating system for the computers owned by the company. So the magnitude of the network effect increases with the installed base of an operating system, rather than the total number of buyers. Also, the network benefit to a buyer depends on the quantity she will buy, in addition to the product installed base.

In such scenarios firms have incentives to charge a different price to different quantities. That is, a nonlinear pricing scheme can be designed to extract more consumer surplus and raise profits.

Sundararajan (2003) presents a static model of nonlinear pricing in a monopoly market with fulfilled expectations. It is shown that optimal pricing includes discounts that increase with quantity, and can also involve a two-part tariff. While network effects generally raise prices, consumption may or may not rise.

In the context of a subscription service, Dhebar and Oren (1986) analyze a monopolist's pricing schedule over quantity and time. In each period, a usage-sensitive nonlinear pricing policy is used to induce heterogeneous consumers to self-select different quantities at different marginal prices. Using a numerical example, they show that nonlinear pricing results in a larger equilibrium network because on average it offers consumption access at a lower subscription fee than uniform pricing. Also, nonlinear pricing leads to higher producer surplus, higher total surplus, but smaller consumer surplus than uniform pricing.

Studies on pricing with network effects are summarized in Table 20.1.

4. Indirect network effects and two-sided markets

In our previous discussion we do not distinguish between two types of network effects, direct network effects and indirect network effects, because the models and the results apply to both. In most studies that we have discussed, consumers' utility functions take the general form of $u(p,x)$, where p is price and x is the installed base of the network product. This may seem to include direct network effects only, because under indirect network effects, a consumer's utility, $u(p,y)$, depends on y, the availability of the complementary product, and not directly on x, the installed base of the network product itself. However, we can argue that the availability of the complementary product will be a function of the installed base of the network product, i.e.

$$y = f(x)$$

This function f is determined by the market structure for the complementary good. Now the utility function under indirect network effects becomes

$$u'(p, x) = u(p, f(x))$$

which is no different from the general form.

Applying this approach to study the pricing dynamics under indirect network effects, we focus on how a firm would price its network good to consumers, and take the market structure for the complementary good as given. Therefore the two-sidedness of the market is hidden behind the function f that governs the provision of the complementary good.

However, this function f may not be exogenous to the model because it is often the case that a firm has some control over both sides of the market. For example, in the video game industry, console makers (Microsoft, Sony, Nintendo) set the prices of their game consoles (Xbox 360, PS3, Wii), but they also decide the royalties that they charge to the games developed for their consoles. The royalty structure will in turn affect how many games will be provided to each console. Therefore firms may strategically affect the function f through royalty fees, or, more generally, firms may set prices to both sides of the market.

How firms should price to both sides of the market in order to get both sides on board is the central question of a growing literature on two-sided markets. The literature on indirect network effects and the literature on two-sided markets are closely related because conceptually indirect network effects must operate in two-sided markets. The two literatures seem to have different focuses, though. In some sense dynamic pricing under indirect network effects is about a firm's incentive to price-discriminate between early adopters and late adopters, while studies on two-sided markets emphasize a firm's incentive to price-discriminate between two sides of the market.

Indeed, firms often treat two sides of the market asymmetrically. For example, most credit card holders do not have to pay for usage, while merchants are usually charged for each transaction. In contrast, firms that develop PC operating systems adopt the opposite business model. They decide to make money on consumers, not on software application developers. Actually in two-sided markets it is common to see one side pays zero or below cost. Rochet and Tirole (2006) argue that the defining feature of two-sided markets is that the economic outcome is affected by the price structure. In other words, a market is two-sided if the platform can affect the volume of transactions by charging more to one side of the market but reducing the price paid by the other side by the same amount.

A number of studies have examined the market structure in different two-sided markets, e.g. Rochet and Tirole (2002), Schmalensee (2002) on payment cards, Caillaud and

Jullien (2003) on matchmakers, Economides and Katsamakas (2006), Economides and Viard (2006) on operating systems, McCabe and Snyder (2007) on academic journals.

In a general framework, Rochet and Tirole (2003) study how the price allocation between the two sides of the market is affected by a number of factors, including industry structure (monopoly versus duopoly) and governance structure (for-profit versus non-profit). They find that, under both monopoly and duopoly, one side that creates large externalities on the other side will be targeted aggressively by lowering prices. As the number of captive buyers increases, the price to buyers increases while the price to sellers decreases. In the case of competing nonprofit associations, an increase in multi-homing (users access more than one platform) of buyers raises the price to buyers and lowers the price to sellers.

Armstrong (2006) extends the analysis by Rochet and Tirole (2006) and focuses on how the price structure is determined by three main factors: relative size of cross-group externalities, fixed fees or per-transaction charges, single-homing or multi-homing.

Pricing in two-sided markets may look similar to pricing with complementarities. For example, Gillette often sets a low price on its razors but makes money on blades later (Hartmann and Nair, 2007). Nevertheless, there is a subtle difference – in two-sided markets there are complementarities between different customers' consumption decisions.

5. Relationship to other literatures

Switching costs

Switching costs and network effects are two distinct terms. Switching costs affect a consumer's choice between competing products when she makes repeated purchase decisions. In contrast, the network effect describes the connection between different consumers' purchase decisions on the same product. Farrell and Klemperer (2007) provide a comprehensive survey on the literatures of both switching costs and network effects.

However, there is an analogy between switching costs and network effects. In both cases, early adopters of a product increase the *ex post* market power of its producer. Under switching costs, firms can exercise market power over the same consumers who have been locked in to their products. Under network effects, the market power is over other consumers who have not purchased before.

Therefore, in both cases firms compete *ex ante* for the *ex post* market power, which provides an incentive for penetration pricing. But one difference is that, under switching costs, firms sell to both old and new customers after the first period. If a single price has to be set for both groups of customers, the bargain-then-ripoff incentive might be weakened.

Switching costs and network effects can exist for the same product. We mentioned that the market for the QWERTY keyboard exhibits network effects because a user benefits from a large installed base of the same keyboard design. Additionally there also exist switching costs in this market because it is costly for a user to get used to a different keyboard design.

Doganoglu and Grzybowski (2005) study the dynamic duopoly competition in the presence of both network effects and switching costs, by introducing network effects into the Klemperer (1987) framework of switching costs. Following a Hotelling model, heterogeneous consumers make repeated purchase decisions in two periods. It is assumed that consumers form rational expectations on future prices and network sizes. They show that stronger network effects imply lower prices in both periods while the impact of switching costs is ambiguous. Also, when network effects are strong and switching costs are moderate, prices in both periods may be lower than those in a market without network effects and switching costs.

Economies of scale
Economies of scale characterize a production process in which the average cost is a decreasing function of the quantity produced. As more consumers adopt a product, the producer may benefit from both economies of scale and network effects, but in different ways. On the production side, economies of scale reduce average costs, while on the demand side, network effects lead to even larger demand. Therefore the network effect is also referred to as demand-side economies of scale.

Due to their similarities, one may expect economies of scale and network effects to have similar implications for firms' pricing policies. Actually this may or may not be true depending on the sources of the scale economies.

Economies of scale tend to occur in industries with high upfront fixed costs, and such fixed costs will be distributed across all the units produced. Thus the larger the quantity, the smaller the average cost. In this case, the resulting economies of scale may not have the same implications on pricing as network effects, because when setting prices, a profit-maximizing firm will ignore the fixed costs and base its pricing decision on the marginal costs only. Without other factors at play, this type of scale economies does not have any direct impact on firms' pricing decisions.

Another important source of scale economies is learning by doing, which means that a firm becomes more efficient in its production process as more units are produced. Therefore a larger quantity results in a lower marginal cost. This creates an incentive for penetration pricing similar to the one under network effects.

Since Robinson and Lakhani (1975) there have been many studies on dynamic pricing under learning by doing, or experience effects. Robinson and Lakhani (1975) discuss a monopolist's dynamic pricing policy under experience effects and product diffusion. Using an illustrative example, they show that initial prices could be well below the initial costs, which suggests that penetration pricing can be completely justified for the sake of long-run profits.

Since learning by doing and network effects have similar implications for pricing, some researchers include learning by doing as one type of network effects (e.g. Bensaid and Lesne, 1996). However, it is still important to recognize the distinction that learning by doing reduces production costs while network effects increase product values.

6. Empirical research
As evidenced by the large number of studies, the topic of pricing under network effects has been examined extensively in the theoretical literature. It is shown that network effects provide an incentive for firms to engage in penetration pricing. Under certain conditions an increasing price path can be optimal in both monopoly and oligopoly settings. Compared with this rich theoretical literature, empirical studies on this topic have been scarce. Thus we are still not well equipped to provide normative guidance on firms' pricing strategies in real industry settings.

On the demand side, however, there have been many empirical papers that show the existence of network effects in various markets (e.g. Nair et al., 2004 on PDAs (personal digital assistants); Clements and Ohashi, 2005 on video game consoles). These demand-side models can be extended in order to establish firms' optimal pricing strategies on the supply side.

In such an attempt, Liu (2006) studies the dynamics of pricing in the video game console market. Clearly the existence of indirect network effects provides an incentive for penetration pricing for game consoles. But due to the rapid decline in costs, this incentive does not lead to increasing console prices. Instead, we observe decreasing prices but increasing markups over time. On the other hand, consumers put different valuations on game consoles, which create an incentive for price-skimming. Based on the increasing markups, this incentive for price-skimming seems to be dominated by the competing incentive for penetration pricing due to indirect network effects.

To explain the observed price and markup patterns, Liu estimates a demand model similar to those in Nair et al. (2004) and Clements and Ohashi (2005). He then solves for the optimal pricing policies of competing console makers (i.e. Sony and Nintendo in the time period under study). It is shown that the optimal pricing policies are consistent with the observed price and markup patterns.

For empirical studies, the demand systems are relatively complicated. This often makes it infeasible to obtain analytical solutions to firms' dynamic pricing problems. As demonstrated by Liu (2006), numerical dynamic programming techniques prove useful in solving these dynamic pricing problems.

Special attention is needed on the function form of the network effects. Linear network effects are often assumed in analytical models (e.g. Bensaid and Lesne, 1996; Cabral et al., 1999; Mason, 2000; Gabszewicz and Garcia, 2005). That is, the value that a network provides increases linearly with its installed base. Although this could be a good approximation at initial stages of a product life cycle, decreasing marginal network benefits may eventually take place. For example, when the use of the telephone was less common, it was important that one million people joined the telephone network, but today it is probably not a big deal whether one million people join or quit the telephone network. Swann (2002) argues that linear network effects can only be generated under very restrictive conditions, and most communication networks exhibit decreasing marginal network benefits. Therefore it is important for future empirical work to allow for flexible specifications of network effects.

7. An illustrative example

We illustrate the issues involved in empirical studies using the following example. Assume there are M potential consumers and J competing products in a durable-goods market characterized by network effects. Each product j is sold by a single-product firm j for T time periods.

The demand for product j in period t can be written as

$$Q_{jt}(p_t, n_t, M_t)$$

where p_t is the vector of prices, n_t is the vector of network sizes, and the network size of product j is simply its cumulative unit sales:

$$n_{jt} = \sum_{\tau=1}^{t-1} Q_{j\tau}$$

M_t is the market size, or equivalently the number of consumers who have not bought any of the J products. M_t and n_t are related since

$$M_t = M - \sum_{j=1}^{J} n_{jt}$$

Naturally the demand for product j decreases with its own prices but increases with its own network sizes and the market size, i.e.

$$\frac{\partial Q_{jt}}{\partial p_{jt}} < 0, \quad \frac{\partial Q_{jt}}{\partial n_{jt}} > 0, \quad \frac{\partial Q_{jt}}{\partial M_t} > 0$$

Firms' current prices affect not only their current demand, but also their future demand through future network sizes and future market sizes. Therefore, when setting prices each firm will look beyond the current period and maximize the expected present value of all current and future profits:

$$E\left[\sum_{\tau=t}^{T} \delta^{\tau-t} \pi_{j\tau}\right]$$

where δ is a discount factor, and the profit function is

$$\pi_{jt} = (p_{jt} - c_{jt}) Q_{jt}$$

Although firms' pricing decisions could potentially depend on the entire history of past states and actions, for simplicity it is often assumed that firms set prices based on the current state only. Let S_t be the state vector, which consists of all the current payoff relevant variables including M_t, n_{jt} and c_{jt}. The evolution of S_t is governed by a Markov transition density $F(S_{t+1} | S_t, p_t)$ conditional on current prices.

First we consider a monopoly market with $J = 1$. Subscript j can be omitted in this case. Define the value function

$$V_t(S_t) = \max_{p_t} E\left[\sum_{\tau=t}^{T} \delta^{\tau-t} \pi_\tau(S_\tau, p_\tau) | S_t, p_t\right]$$

The optimal pricing policy can be obtained by solving the following Bellman equation

$$V_t(S_t) = \max_{p_t}\{\pi_t(S_t, p_t) + E[V_{t+1}(S_{t+1}) | S_t, p_t]\}$$

Each value function $V_t(S_t)$ is associated with an optimal pricing policy $p_t(S_t)$. Usually it is infeasible to solve the dynamic pricing problem analytically, and hence numerical dynamic programming techniques need to be applied.

If the time horizon T is finite, we can start from the last time period and solve backwards in time. With an infinite horizon $T = \infty$, the form of the value function V_t does not change across time periods. Therefore the Bellman equation becomes

$$V(S) = \max_{p}\{\pi(S, p) + E[V(S') | S, p]\}$$

Starting from an initial guess of the value function, we can iterate on the Bellman equation until it converges to the final solution. Rust (1994) shows that, under fairly weak regularity conditions, the above Bellman equation has a unique solution.

Consumers are assumed to be heterogeneous so that some of them are willing to pay more than others. Suppose marginal costs remain constant over time. In the absence of network effects, in which case Q_{jt} is independent of n_t, the monopolist has incentives to set a high price initially and cut it later. Thus price-skimming may be the optimal strategy.

However, in the presence of network effects, there is a competing incentive to price low initially in order to build up the network. This incentive for penetration pricing may or may not dominate the incentives for price-skimming depending on the strength of network effects. As a result, prices can be increasing or decreasing.

To make the above discussion concrete, we consider a simple demand system. The indirect utility that a consumer i derives from a product is specified as

$$U_{it} = \alpha_i + \beta p_t + \gamma n_t^\lambda + \varepsilon_{it}$$

Here consumers differ in their intrinsic preferences toward the product according to a distribution function $F(\alpha_i)$. A consumer's individual taste, ε_{it}, follows a Type I extreme-value distribution. The outside option is normalized to have a mean utility of zero net of an individual taste. Therefore the demand function is given by

$$Q_t(p_t, n_t, M_t) = M_t \int \frac{\exp(\alpha_i + \beta p_t + \gamma n_t^\lambda)}{1 + \exp(\alpha_i + \beta p_t + \gamma n_t^\lambda)} dF(\alpha_i)$$

To solve for the optimal pricing policy, we assume a potential market size of 200 and a discrete distribution on α_i: 10 percent of consumers have $\alpha = -2$ and the rest have $\alpha = -5$. For other parameters we assume $\beta = -0.02$, $\gamma = 1$, $\lambda = 0.3$ and a discount factor of 0.995. These parameter values are consistent with the estimates for the Palm Vx PDA in Nair et al. (2004).

After solving for the optimal pricing policy with a finite horizon of 24 time periods, we simulate the market evolution and plot the price path in Figure 20.2. It indicates an increasing price path under network effects. But without network effects, we would see decreasing prices over time.

Now consider an oligopoly market in which each firm's pricing decision has to take into account the pricing policies of other firms. We need to solve the dynamic pricing game for the equilibrium pricing policies. The equilibrium concept often in use is the Markov-perfect equilibrium (MPE) in pure strategies. Maskin and Tirole (2001) provide a concise treatment of the MPE concept.

Given other firms' pricing policies, a particular firm's pricing policy can be obtained by following a similar algorithm to the one used for a monopoly market. We can then iterate through all firms' pricing policies until convergence. Unlike the single-agent dynamic optimization problem, there is no general result that guarantees the existence and uniqueness of an equilibrium. In practice, the convergence of the solution algorithm confirms the existence, and starting the algorithm from different initial values may help find evidence of multiple equilibria.

In an oligopoly market, incentives for both price-skimming and penetration pricing

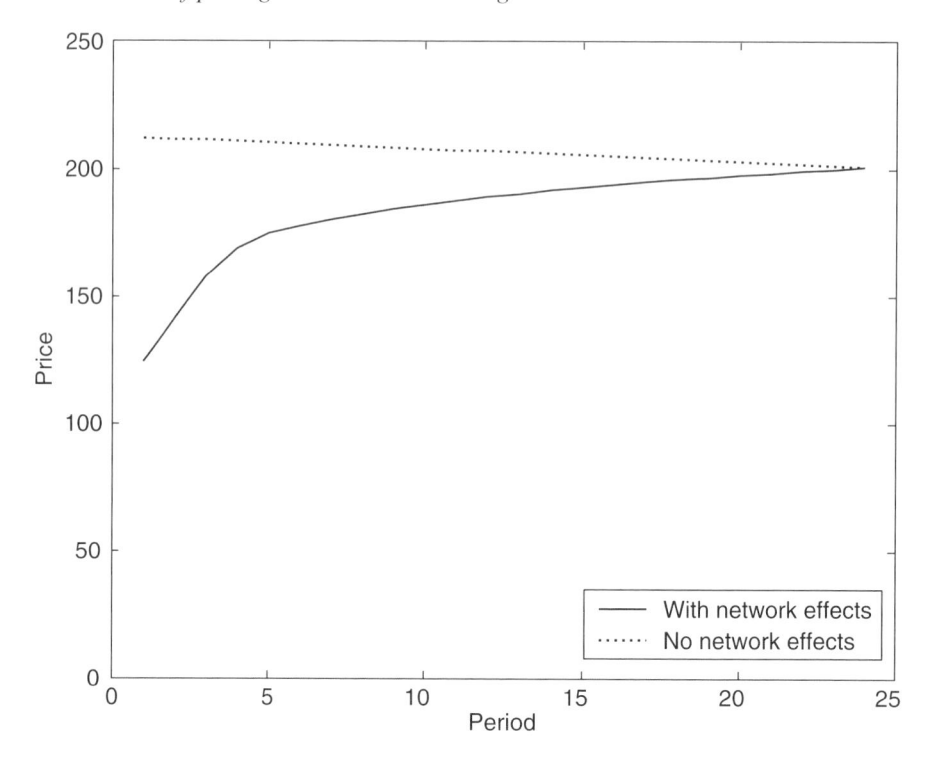

Figure 20.2 Simulated prices with and without network effects

still exist, just as in a monopoly market. Competition may push initial prices lower than those under monopoly. But as we explained previously, a monopolist may expect more profits in future periods than oligopolists, and hence may be willing to cut initial prices even deeper. Therefore an oligopoly does not necessarily lead to lower initial prices.

If the market exhibits learning by doing, or experience effects, marginal costs will decline as more units are produced. This adds to the incentives for penetration pricing since a low initial price brings the additional benefit of reducing unit production costs. It should be noted that, despite stronger incentives for penetration pricing, an increasing price path does not become more likely because costs are declining. Therefore it might be useful to examine the unit markups. Even if prices decrease, the incentives for penetration pricing could still be revealed by increasing markups.

In order to fit this model to empirical data, generally there are two sets of parameters to be estimated. On the demand side, there may be parameters in the demand function Q_{jt}. On the supply side, there may be parameters in the cost function c_{jt}. A joint estimation of demand and supply is attractive in terms of efficiency. But, recognizing the computational burden in solving the dynamic pricing game, we may resort to a two-step approach. In the first step, we can use data on quantities, prices and other covariates to estimate the demand parameters. In the second step, we can use the optimal pricing model to estimate the parameters on the supply side.

It should be mentioned that, if the costs are estimated in this way, implicitly firms are assumed to set prices optimally. This may or may not be an issue depending on the purpose of the study. If we want to analyze firms' current pricing strategies and provide guidance on how firms should set prices, then optimality assumption is not appropriate and cost estimates should come from other sources. In such cases a two-step approach is required.

8. Conclusions and future research

Firms' pricing strategies are intrinsically dynamic under network effects. Various issues on dynamic pricing of network goods have been examined carefully by a number of theoretical studies. In particular, the incentive for penetration pricing is emphasized. This literature is closely related to the literatures on two-sided markets, switching costs and economies of scale.

Due to the asymmetry between a rich theoretical literature and a limited empirical one, further empirical research might be fruitful in this area. In addition, there have been abundant examples of new products characterized by network effects, such as online gaming (e.g. Xbox Live), instant messaging software (e.g. AOL Instant Messenger, MSN Messenger, Yahoo! Messenger), etc. which provide exciting markets and issues for empirical studies.

As we have mentioned in the previous section, network effects are often assumed to be linear in network sizes. With empirical data, we can allow for a flexible specification of the network effect and uncover any decreasing marginal network benefits. A nonlinear network effect could affect firms' pricing policies differently from a linear effect.

In most network industries, firms' pricing decisions are affected by certain other factors besides network effects. The incentive for penetration pricing induced by network effects can be either strengthened or weakened by other factors. For example, learning by doing could provide a similar incentive for penetration pricing to network effects, while consumers' heterogeneous valuations could provide a competing incentive for price-skimming. Empirically we can estimate the magnitude of such factors and identify the effect of each on firms' pricing policies.

Consumer expectations play an important role in the diffusion of network products. Consumers' adoption decisions may depend on their expectations on future prices and network sizes. Different assumptions can be made on these expectations, ranging from completely myopic to perfectly forward looking. In an empirical model, we often rely on numerical techniques to solve firms' dynamic pricing problems. If consumers are perfectly forward looking, their expectations will be consistent with future states of the market in equilibrium. Such a model could be challenging to solve. However, Dubé et al. (2008) have made significant progress on this front recently.

References

Armstrong, M. (2006), 'Competition in two-sided markets', *RAND Journal of Economics*, **37**, 668–91.
Bensaid, B. and J.P. Lesne (1996), 'Dynamic monopoly pricing with network externalities', *International Journal of Industrial Organization*, **14**, 837–55.
Cabral, L.M.B., D.J. Salant and G.A. Woroch (1999), 'Monopoly pricing with network externalities', *International Journal of Industrial Organization*, **17**, 199–214.
Caillaud, B. and B. Jullien (2003), 'Chicken & egg: competition among intermediation service providers', *RAND Journal of Economics*, **34**, 309–28.
Clements, M.T. and H. Ohashi (2005), 'Indirect network effects and the product cycle: video games in the U.S., 1994–2002', *Journal of Industrial Economics*, **53**, 515–42.
Coase, R.H. (1972), 'Durability and monopoly', *Journal of Law and Economics*, **15**, 143–9.
Dhebar, A. and S.S. Oren (1985), 'Optimal dynamic pricing for expanding networks', *Marketing Science*, **4**, 336–51.

Dhebar, A. and S.S. Oren (1986), 'Dynamic nonlinear pricing in networks with interdependent demand', *Operations Research*, **34**, 384–94.
Doganoglu, T. and L. Grzybowski (2005), 'Dynamic duopoly competition with switching costs and network externalities', Working Paper, University of Munich.
Dubé, J.-P., G.J. Hitsch and P. Chintagunta (2008), 'Tipping and concentration in markets with indirect network effects', Working Paper, University of Chicago.
Economides, N. (1996), 'The economics of networks', *International Journal of Industrial Organization*, **14**, 673–99.
Economides, N. and E. Katsamakas (2006), 'Two-sided competition of proprietary vs. open source technology platforms and the implications for the software industry', *Management Science*, **52**, 1057–71.
Economides, N. and V.B. Viard (2006), 'Pricing of complements and network effects', Working Paper, New York University.
Farrell, J. and P. Klemperer (2007), 'Coordination and lock-in: competition with switching costs and network effects', in M. Armstrong and R. Porter (eds), *Handbook of Industrial Organization*, vol. 3, Amsterdam: Elsevier, pp. 1967–2072.
Gabszewicz, J.J. and F. Garcia (2005), 'A note on expanding networks and monopoly pricing', Working Paper, Université catholique de Louvain.
Hart, O. and J. Tirole (1988), 'Contract renegotiation and Coasian dynamics', *Review of Economics Studies*, **55**, 509–40.
Hartmann, W. and H. Nair (2007), 'Retail competition and the dynamics of consumer demand for tied goods', Working Paper, Stanford University.
Katz, M.L. and C. Shapiro (1985), 'Network externalities, competition and compatibility', *American Economic Review*, **75**, 424–40.
Katz, M.L. and C. Shapiro (1986), 'Technology adoption in the presence of network externalities', *Journal of Political Economy*, **94**, 822–41.
Klemperer, P. (1987), 'The competitiveness of markets with switching costs', *RAND Journal of Economics*, **18**, 138–50.
Leibenstein, H. (1950), 'Bandwagon, snob, and Veblen effects in the theory of consumers' demand', *Quarterly Journal of Economics*, **64**, 183–207.
Liu, H. (2006), 'Dynamics of pricing in the video game console market: skimming or penetration?', dissertation, University of Chicago.
Maskin, E. and J. Tirole (2001), 'Markov perfect equilibrium', *Journal of Economic Theory*, **100**, 191–219.
Mason, R. (2000), 'Network externalities and the Coase conjecture', *European Economic Review*, **44**, 1981–92.
McCabe, M.J. and C.M. Snyder (2007), 'Academic journal prices in a digital age: a two-sided market model', *B.E. Journal of Economic Analysis & Policy*, **7**, Article 2.
Nair, H., P. Chintagunta and J.-P. Dubé (2004), 'Empirical analysis of indirect network effects in the market for personal digital assistants', *Quantitative Marketing and Economics*, **2**, 23–58.
Radner, R. and A. Sundararajan (2005), 'Dynamic pricing of network goods with boundedly rational consumers', Working Paper, New York University.
Robinson, B. and C. Lakhani (1975), 'Dynamic price models for new-product planning', *Management Science*, **21**, 1113–22.
Rochet, J.C. and J. Tirole (2002), 'Cooperation among competitors: some economics of payment card associations', *RAND Journal of Economics*, **33**, 1–22.
Rochet, J.C. and J. Tirole (2003), 'Platform competition in two-sided markets', *Journal of the European Economic Association*, **1**, 990–1029.
Rochet, J.C. and J. Tirole (2006), 'Two-sided markets: a progress report', *RAND Journal of Economics*, **37**, 645–67.
Rohlfs, J. (1974), 'A theory of interdependent demand for a communications service', *Bell Journal of Economics*, **5**, 16–37.
Rust, J. (1994), 'Structural estimation of Markov decision processes', in R.F. Engle and D.L. McFadden (eds), *Handbook of Econometrics, Volume IV*, Amsterdam: Elsevier Science, pp. 3081–143.
Schmalensee, R. (2002), 'Payment systems and interchange fees', *Journal of Industrial Economics*, **50**, 103–22.
Shapiro, C. and H.R. Varian (1998), *Information Rules: A Strategic Guide to the Network Economy*, Cambridge, MA: Harvard Business School Press.
Sundararajan, A. (2003), 'Network effects, nonlinear pricing and entry deterrence', Working Paper, New York University.
Swann, P. (2002), 'The functional form of network effects', *Information Economics and Policy*, **14**, 417–29.
Xie, J. and M. Sirbu (1995), 'Price competition and compatibility in the presence of positive demand externalities', *Management Science*, **41**, 909–26.

21 Advance selling theory
Jinhong Xie and Steven M. Shugan

Abstract

The term 'advance selling' refers to a marketing practice in which the seller offers opportunities for buyers to make purchase commitments before the time of consumption. New developments in technology are overcoming many difficulties that have hindered the usefulness of advance selling in the past and are making it economically efficient for sellers in many industries. Traditional explanations for advance selling generally require some unique industry characteristics. Recent developments in advance selling theory illustrate that the profit advantage of advance selling is far more general than previously realized; it does not require specific industry structures, such as capacity constraints and the existence of early arrivals with low valuation and late arrivals with high valuation. This suggests that offering advance sales can improve profit simply because advance selling separates purchase from consumption, which creates buyer uncertainty about their future product/service valuation and removes the seller's information disadvantage. Since such buyer uncertainty occurs in almost all markets, the profit advantage of advance selling is generally applicable to sellers in many, if not all, industries. Moreover, this recent theory explains how various factors, such as seller credibility, marginal cost, capacity constraints, competition and refunds, affect the profit advantage of advance selling, and suggests specific selling strategies under different market/product conditions. Finally, this theory also demonstrates how advance selling can improve sellers' profit without necessarily reducing buyer surplus.

Overview

The term 'advance selling' refers to a marketing practice in which the seller offers opportunities for buyers to make purchase commitments before the time of consumption. For example, providers in different service industries can advance-sell services (e.g. concerts, sports, vacation packages, training courses, park passes) that are to be delivered at a specified future date or time period. Two recent changes have greatly increased the significance of advance selling as a general marketing strategy. First, new developments in technology are changing marketing activities (Shugan, 2004) and, specifically, are overcoming many difficulties that have hindered the usefulness of advance selling in the past. These developments are making advance selling economically efficient, less costly for sellers in many industries and inhibiting barriers to advance selling such as arbitrage. Second, recent developments in advance selling theory (e.g. Shugan and Xie, 2000, 2005; Xie and Shugan, 2001) have illustrated that the conditions necessary for a profit advantage from advance selling are far more general than previously thought. For example, consider traditional price discrimination explanations for advance selling that are often implemented with yield management systems. These systems hold capacity for late purchasers who are sometimes willing to pay more than those who buy in advance. However, these traditional explanations require specific relationships between price sensitivity and time of purchase (i.e. charging less to the price-sensitive leisure customers who often purchase early). This requirement is only met in a few industries, such as the travel industry (Desiraju and Shugan, 1999). New developments in advance selling theory, however, illustrate that the profit advantage

452 *Handbook of pricing research in marketing*

of advance selling does not require specific industry structures, such as capacity constraints and the existence of early arrivals with low valuation and late arrivals with high valuation that we often observe in travel-related industries. It suggests that offering advance sales can improve profit simply because advance selling separates purchase from consumption, which creates buyer uncertainty about their future product/service valuation and removes the seller's information disadvantage (caused by the buyer knowing more about their own valuation than the seller does). Since such buyer uncertainty occurs in almost all markets, the profit advantage of advance selling is generally applicable to sellers in many, if not all, industries. Moreover, this recent theory explains how various factors, such as seller credibility, marginal cost, capacity constraints, competition and refunds, affect the profit advantage of advance selling, and suggests specific selling strategies under different market/product conditions. Finally, this theory also demonstrates how advance selling can improve sellers' profit without necessarily reducing buyer surplus.

In Section 1 of this chapter, we discuss how and why advances in technology are creating new opportunities for implementing advance selling strategies. In Section 2, we review various reasons for offering advance sales. We devote the next three sections to the theory of advance selling driven by buyer uncertainty concerning future valuations or consumption states. We introduce the basic idea of the theory in Section 3 and discuss factors affecting the profit advantage of advance selling in Section 4. We focus on 'when' and 'how' to advance sell and discuss six specific selling strategies applicable to sellers facing different market/product conditions in Section 5. Finally, we provide a summary and state our conclusions in Section 6.

1. New technologies facilitate advance selling

1.1 Past impediments
Although some sellers have been practicing advance selling for some time, particularly those with access to institutional channels for the purpose, older technologies continue to limit the usefulness of advance selling for at least three important reasons. First, the seller has had difficulties in controlling/limiting arbitrage, which has often dramatically reduced the profitability of advance selling. For example, consider the case where an amusement park advance sells a park pass for future admission at a discounted price. An arbitrageur could buy the discounted park passes in advance and then make a profit by reselling them at a higher price to customers who otherwise would have been willing to buy directly from the seller at high prices at the gate. Consequently, the seller lowers profits by offering advance sales. Second, until recently, many sellers lacked efficient ways of implementing advance selling, which increased transaction costs of advance sales for both sellers and buyers. For example, in order to complete a transaction in the advance period, either the buyer had to make an extra visit to the seller or the seller had to use a complicated and costly central database system and/or specialized physical distribution channel (e.g. a travel agency). It was impractical for many services to establish such a centralized database and distribution networks. Finally, the high cost of content presentation and constrained buyer–seller interaction (e.g. without travel agents) have limited traditional advance selling to the simplest and most standardized transactions.

Advance selling theory 453

1.2 New technology
Many recent technological advances, such as Internet websites, electronic tickets and smart cards, are overcoming these limitations and making advance selling possible and indeed desirable for many service providers. These new technological developments facilitate advance selling by providing the following benefits:

1. *Limiting arbitrage* Electronic tickets and smart cards (i.e. credit card sized tickets with computer chips) can store and dynamically update relevant information such as the value, the quantity, the number and kind of pre-paid services, the valid duration of the pre-paid services, any restrictions on the pre-paid services and the quantity of services already consumed. Such encrypted information is making it difficult or impossible for arbitrageurs to resell the pre-purchased services (e.g. arbitrageurs are unable to certify to potential buyers that resold tickets provide the claimed services and have not expired). Smart cards provide more ample capacity for storing personal information (e.g. a digital picture of the user, biometric information) and are able to offer high-level encryption and sophisticated security protocols to identify users. These new technologies link a buyer's identity with specific purchases, which significantly increases a seller's ability to limit/control the degree of arbitrage. National Ticket Company, for example, prints personalized bar-coded redemption tickets (www.nationalticket.com). Amusement parks are beginning to place usage information on magnetic ticket strips that are updated electronically at the gate. Disney is using biometric palm readers and fingerprint scanners to identify season-pass holders (Rogers, 2002).

2. *Lowering transaction costs of advance sales* New technologies benefit advance selling by lower transaction costs for several reasons. First, widespread access to Internet websites allows sellers to make transactions and communicate with buyers remotely, without the need for physical presence. Second, new technologies are making it possible for sellers to avoid the use of a central database and the infrastructure necessary to allow real-time communication with that database. As ticketing technology becomes 'smarter', it is possible to record transaction records securely within a ticket. An electronic reader at any remote or decentralized location can obtain a customer's transaction records from the ticket itself. For example, a dry cleaning service could sell a $20 ticket good for $25 worth of future services and the ticket keeps track of the remaining balance. For a more complex example, consider a ticket for an under-hood automotive service that could contain credits for three oil changes, one tune-up and two brake inspections. As a customer consumes the services, a local device debits the ticket so that that ticket is kept current. When the customer advance-buys additional services, a credit is added to the ticket. The ticketing technology does the accounting and no communication with a central database is required.

3. *Allowing far more complex advance offerings* In addition to discouraging arbitrage and lowering transaction costs, new technologies allow far more complex transactions involving service packages with nonlinear pricing, bundling and variable consumption periods. For example, a hotel package can provide many different and complicated options, e.g. a bundle of a three-night stay with a dinner, a breakfast and, perhaps, tickets to local events; a two-night stay to be used during a specified time period that may include blackout dates; or a five-night stay that may not be

contiguous. Moreover, in addition to changes in package components, prices can continuously change over time as the service provider learns of demand and available capacity changes (e.g. due to cancellations). The service provider can now instantaneously adjust to changing conditions. In fact, it may be possible to make contingent sales, which allow buyers to make advance purchases for the right to use the service contingent on availability. Such sophisticated communications provide many benefits as well as satisfying the conditions that make advance selling profitable by creating more complex advance offerings. Complex advance offerings allow the seller to sufficiently differentiate advance offerings to avoid direct competition with other advance sellers. Moreover, complex advance offerings can focus on less constrained and more predictable dimensions of capacity. In sum, more sophisticated communication allows construction of very complex advance offerings that would be too costly to implement without the help of new technologies.

2. Why advance-sell?

Various factors can cause sellers to offer advance sales, some of which are simple and intuitive. For example, for many services, offering advance sales can prevent long lines at the gate or ticket counters on the day of service delivery, which is desirable for both buyers and service providers (e.g. amusement parks, theaters, studios, museums, auto shows, airlines and railroads). Offering advance sales may also be necessary for service providers who need time to make logistic arrangements. For instance, requiring advance registrations allows conference organizers sufficient time to arrange meeting rooms, transportation, beverages and meals, and to prepare printed materials for participants.

For example, Moe and Fader (2002) show that advance selling can provide sellers with important information that allows better forecasting of future demand. Gale and Holmes (1993) argue that advance selling allows sellers to divert demand from high-demand peak periods to off-peak periods with lesser demand. For a review of this literature, see Anderson and Dana (2005). Other causal factors, however, may be less straightforward. In this section, we focus on several important economic factors that motivate advance selling.

2.1 Advance selling driven by price discrimination

Until recently, advance selling theory has largely focused on the benefits of price discrimination and has been applied mostly in travel-related industries (Borenstein and Rose, 1994; Stavins, 2001). Although price discrimination usually requires monopoly power, Dana (1998) argues that, despite a lack of market power, firms might still use advance purchase sales to sell to low-valuation customers at lower prices as predicted by traditional models of second-degree price discrimination. Hence, when potential buyers differ in their willingness to pay and the certainty with which they will need the service, advance selling allows sellers to charge a lower price to buyers with lower valuations and a larger probability of needing the service.

Second-degree price discrimination can be an important factor motivating advance selling in these industries because these industries possess some specific characteristics, such as capacity constraints and the existence of two unique segments, 'leisure travelers' and 'business travelers', of which the former are typically more price sensitive and buy earlier and the latter are typically less price sensitive but buy later. Hence, by offering customers the options of purchasing in advance at a low price or waiting to buy when close to the time of service delivery at a high price, the seller creates opportunities to segment the market based on buyer heterogeneity.

As noted earlier, Dana (1998) shows that advance selling can allow the seller to segment the market based on heterogeneity in buyer demand certainty when the transaction costs of using spot prices to clear markets are excessively high (i.e. firms may employ some alternative rationing rules to clear the market). Specifically, Dana (1998) considers the situation where customers differ in certainty about their future need for the service and, consequently, their valuation. Dana (1998) considers potential buyers who differ in their willingness to pay and the certainty with which they will need the service. Advance selling allows sellers to charge a lower price to buyers with lower valuations and a larger probability of needing the service. Hence, when there is a negative correlation between demand certainty and valuation (i.e. buyers with more certain demands have a low valuation, but buyers with a less certain demand value the service more highly), customers with more certain demands and low valuation prefer to buy in advance to avoid the chance of being rationed in the spot market, especially when rationing of the item (e.g. airline seats) favors customers with low demand certainty and high valuation.

Gale and Homes (1992) provide another potential application of price discrimination when proposing that advance selling can both segment the market based on buyer heterogeneity in the strength of their preference and allow diversion of some buyers to off-peak services. Specifically, they consider the case where an airline operates two flights with departures at different times. In the advance period, all customers are uncertain about which flights they prefer, although some customers have a strong preference and others a weak one. Customers with a weak preference (e.g. with more time flexibility) prefer to buy in advance at a lower price, even though this leads to a higher risk of being ticketed on their less preferred flight (because they have bought their tickets before knowing which flight they prefer). Customers with a strong preference, on the other hand, choose to delay their purchase decision until the date of departure (i.e. after they have learned which flight fits their schedule best), even though they have to pay a higher price. Advance selling induces customers with weak preferences to buy in advance, which offers those with strong preferences a higher chance to get their preferred flight and increase their willingness to pay. Gale and Holmes (1993) further show that such discrimination provides an efficient allocation of capacity because it shifts buyers from peak to off-peak flights.

2.2 Advance selling driven by efficient capacity utilization
While advance selling at discount prices allows the seller to price-discriminate against high-valuation customers who arrive late, efficiently allocating capacity between different fare classes is extremely challenging for industries where the sellers face both capacity constraints and demand uncertainty (i.e. travel-related industries). In these industries, advance selling is often associated with yield management (also called revenue management), which utilizes heuristics and tools for capacity allocation (Weatherford and Bodily, 1992; Chatwin, 2000; Subramanian et al., 1999). As pointed out by Desiraju and Shugan (1999), yield management systems can assist advance selling only in industries with binding capacity and those that exhibit some special buyers characteristics (e.g. the inverse relationship between consumers' price sensitivity and their arrival time). Desiraju

and Shugan (1999) explain that, despite popular belief that yield management lowers prices, the actual intent of yield management is to save capacity for the late buyer who will pay lower prices. Otherwise, without capacity constraints, the seller could simply sell to meet demand.

One important yield management tool is overbooking – advance selling tickets for more seats than are actually available (Biyalogorsky et al., 1999; Chatwin, 2000; Subramanian et al., 1999). Overbooking maximizes capacity utilization and avoids revenue loss from 'no shows', but can suffer from the cost of compensating customers with confirmed seats who are bumped from an overbooked service.

Biyalogorsky and Gerstner (2004) show that in markets where low-valuation buyers arrive early and high-valuation buyers arrive late, advance selling under contingent pricing can enhance capacity utilization in the presence of both capacity constraints and demand uncertainty. In such markets, spot selling leads to low capacity utilization and decreased profits. Specifically, if capacity is reserved for spot sales at high prices, the reserved capacity will remain unsold if the high-valuation buyer fails to appear. If capacity is reserved for spot sales at low prices, the high-valuation buyer may not obtain the capacity even if she shows up, and the seller loses the opportunity to receive a high price for the purchase. However, if the seller advance sells under a contingent pricing contract, i.e. offering a low price in advance, but canceling the sales to low-paying advance buyers if high-valuation customers show up later, the seller can maximize capacity utilization and increase profit. Biyalogorsky et al. (2005) illustrate that providers with multi-class services (e.g. airlines offering first-class and coach-class seats) can increase capacity utilization by advance selling 'upgradeable tickets' to low-valuation buyers. The advance buyers of such tickets will be upgraded to a higher class of service (e.g. a hotel room with an ocean view) at the time of service delivery only if the reserved higher-class capacity remains unsold.

2.3 Advance selling driven by multiple selling limited capacities
Xie and Gerstner (2007) show that in the presence of capacity constraints, advance selling can not only be used to minimize unused capacity, as discussed earlier, but can also be used to sell a limited capacity multiple times. Advance buyers may find other alternatives after they have made advance purchases. If the alternative is sufficiently attractive, they are willing to pay a cancellation fee to terminate their pre-paid contracts. This implies that the seller has the opportunity to sell the same capacity twice, i.e. collecting fees from advance buyers who cancel and then reselling the freed slots. Multiple selling can be profitable even if the canceled unit was originally sold to high-valuation customers at a premium price and has to be resold to low-valuation customers at a low price as long as the refund offered for cancellation is lower than the resell price. Note that some consumer-added surplus is created when customers find new alternatives, which is why the advance buyers would be willing to pay a cancellation fee to get out of their paid-in-advance contract. Advance selling allows the seller to capture such consumer-added surplus – a profit potential that is not possible under a spot-selling strategy.

2.4 Advance selling driven by buyer uncertainty
All of the economic motivation factors previously discussed require either buyer heterogeneity or capacity constraints (or both), because the profit advantages from advance

selling in these cases are fundamentally driven by enhanced price discrimination or increased capacity utilization. Shugan and Xie (2000) proposed a theory of advance selling driven by buyer uncertainty, which suggests that conditions for a profit advantage are more general than previously thought and do not require the benefit of price discrimination and improved capacity utilization. Unlike research exploiting differences between consumers on their uncertainty for merely implementing price discrimination (e.g. Courty and Hau, 2000), Shugan and Xie (2000) proved that advance selling can increase profits simply because consumers have uncertainty about their future consumption states (whether consumers differ on uncertainty or not). Their proof requires conditions satisfied in almost all markets. Xie and Shugan (2001) further develop this theory by analyzing the impact of various factors affecting the profit potential of advance selling, such as seller credibility, buyer risk aversion, capacity constraints and refunds, and they offer specific guidelines for advance selling in different market/product conditions. Shugan and Xie (2005) extend the theory to competitive markets and examine how competition affects the profit advantage of advance selling. We now use a simple example to illustrate the core idea of this theory of advance selling. We then devote the next three sections to examine this theory in more detail and discuss its implications.

Consider a local river cruise line offering a 'Friday Moonlight Dance Cruise' that departs at 9:00 p.m. and returns at 1:00 a.m. The value of the dance cruise to a given customer on a given Friday may depend on many personal factors, including whether she is in a good mood for such a late-night entertainment or has an unexpected schedule conflict. When the Friday arrives, the customer knows these factors and forms a valuation (willingness to pay). Several weeks before the Friday, however, this future valuation is uncertain.

We first consider the case where the cruise line sells the ticket on the day of the cruise departure (i.e. when consumers have resolved their valuation uncertainty). We call this case 'spot selling'. Suppose, on a given Friday evening, 100 potential customers are equally likely to be in a favorable consumption state for the cruise (e.g. in good health and/or mood for enjoying a late-night dance party on the river) or an unfavorable consumption state (e.g. feeling tired, facing a deadline at work, or interested in some other activities, such as a late comedy show performed on the same Friday night). Suppose customers are willing to pay $60 when in a favorable state, but only $30 in the unfavorable state (of course, any number of states is possible). Also suppose that the cruise line has enough capacity to service 100 people on any given night and the average variable cost of serving a customer is $10. With spot selling, the cruise line has two possible optimal strategies: (1) charge the higher price of $60 and sell to only 50 customers who are in the favorable state, which leads to a profit of $(60–10) × 50 = $2500; or (2) charge the low price of $30 and sell to all 100 customers, which leads to a profit of $(30–10) × 1000 = $2000. Clearly, under spot selling, the optimal price is $60 and the maximum profit is $2500. Notice that, under the optimal spot price of $60, total consumer surplus is zero because all buyers pay a price equal to their valuation (i.e. $60).

Next, we shall see what happens if the cruise line offers the cruise tickets three weeks before the Friday evening (i.e. when customers have some uncertainty about their valuation). We call this case 'advance selling'. Given an equal chance to be in the favorable and unfavorable states, all customers expect to have a valuation of $60 × 0.5 + $30 × 0.5 =

$45 for the dance cruise. Hence, by charging a discounted price of $45, the seller will be able to advance-sell to all 100 potential customers and earn a profit of $(45 − 10) × 100 = $3500. Hence, with advance selling, the seller achieves a profit improvement over spot selling of ($3500 − $2500)/($2000) = 40%. Furthermore, as in the case of spot selling, the total consumer surplus under advance selling is zero (i.e. 50 buyers in favorable state receive a total positive surplus of $(60 − 45) × 50 = $750, and 50 buyers in unfavorable state receive a total negative surplus of $(30 − 45) × 50 = −$750).

Finally, we consider the ideal case where the seller is able to implement first-degree price discrimination, such that each customer pays their respective true willingness to pay (i.e. the customers who are in a favorable state pay $60, and the customers who are in an unfavorable state pay $30). With such perfect price discrimination, the seller is able to earn a profit of $(60 − 10) × 50 + $(30 − 10) × 50 = $3500, which is exactly the same profit that she achieves under advance selling!

The above example reveals the following intriguing facts:

1. Under both advance- and spot-selling strategies, a single price is charged to all customers (i.e. $60 under spot selling and $45 under advance selling), suggesting that the 40 percent profit advantage of advance selling is *not* achieved by enhanced price discrimination or price discrimination of any kind (all consumers pay the same price).
2. Under both advance- and spot-selling strategies, the seller has enough capacity to serve all potential customers, suggesting that the 40 percent profit advantage of advance selling is *not* due to the benefit of yield management.
3. Advance selling increases the cruise line's profit by 40 percent but has no impact on total consumer surplus, suggesting that advance selling can help the seller without hurting buyers.
4. Advance selling allows the cruise line to achieve the amount of profit only possible under first-degree price discrimination (i.e. $3500), suggesting that the profit advantage of advance selling can be enormous.
5. This example is not dependent on these particular numbers. In fact, Xie and Shugan (2001) show that increased profits of 100 percent are possible. Moreover, advance selling can increase profits with or without positive variable costs.

These facts are intriguing because they cannot be explained by the previous theory of advance selling and raise many important questions. For example, without the benefit of price discrimination and yield management, what is the fundamental source for the 40 percent profit improvement? How can advance selling benefit the seller without harming the buyer? How can the seller achieve the profit of first-degree price discrimination without either knowing the individual consumers' consumption states or charging them different prices? Furthermore, do these intriguing facts only hold for this specific example, or are they generally applicable to many more realistic settings (e.g. when consumers have more than two discrete consumption states, differ in their arrival times, or are risk averse, when the seller has capacity constraints or faces competition, or when refunds have to be offered to consumers who want to cancel advance purchases)? Finally, it is important to understand how sellers facing different market/product conditions should advance-sell. For example, when should we offer advance sales? How do we decide the price of advance and spot sales? When should we limit the capacity for advance sales? We answer these questions in the next three sections.

3. A theory of advance selling driven by buyer uncertainty

3.1 Buyer state-dependent utility

The consumption utility of a given product or service for a given consumer may not be fixed, but may vary from time to time even if the quality of the product or service is constant (Hauser and Wernerfelt, 1990). The reason is that individual consumers can have multiple consumption states, and the level of realized utility from consuming a product or enjoying a service depends on the state of the consumer at the time of consumption or service delivery. Buyer consumption states are often affected by many personal factors, including health, mood, finances, work schedule and family situation. For example, the value of a dinner buffet at a Chinese restaurant to a given customer on a given Saturday evening could be affected by how much the customer craves Chinese food and the magnitude of the customer's hunger. The value of a summer holiday vacation package to a given family will be higher if the family is in a more favorable consumption state (e.g. healthy, in the mood for a vacation, and with no significant conflict) and lower in a less favorable state (e.g. a child has a cold, the roof of the house is leaking after major rainfall, a close friend is coming to town, or the family is facing some financial difficulty). The factors determining the true state of the customer for the specific consumption (e.g. a Chinese buffet dinner on a specific night or the vacation package for specified days and location) are often known to the customer only when close to the time of consumption. This is known as state-dependent consumption utility.

For example, consider the valuation of a soft drink. States might be not thirsty, somewhat thirsty, thirsty and very thirsty. As we move from the first state to the last, the buyer is willing to pay more for the soft drink. Close to the time of consumption, the buyer knows their own state (i.e. how thirsty they are). However, when buying in advance for future consumption, say a day in advance, the buyer has beliefs only about their future states, which we capture with state probabilities.

3.2 Spot selling: seller information disadvantage

State-dependent consumption utility can have significant implications for the seller, especially when the buyer has limited control over the time of consumption. These situations occur in many service markets (e.g. concerts, sports, cruises, group tours, educational programs, flights and trains, conferences, trade shows) where the service delivery time is scheduled by service providers rather than by each individual buyer.[1] In these situations, the buyer's willingness to pay depends on unobserved factors known only to the buyer with certainty at the time of consumption. From a seller's perspective, this implies that the seller faces an information disadvantage when close to the time of consumption (i.e. the spot period) because, at that point, the buyers know their

---

[1] The value of a bottle of water to a customer may vary depending on whether or not she is thirsty; however, the realized utility of the bottle of water may not vary much if she can always decide when to drink it.

consumption states while sellers do not. Such an information disadvantage can potentially reduce seller profit.

3.3 Advance selling: creating buyer uncertainty

By offering sales in advance, sellers can separate purchase and consumption, usually creating buyer uncertainty at the point of purchase around future consumption states and future valuations. Consequently, sellers can sell in advance to buyers with only uncertain future valuations or spot-sell to buyers with known valuations or do both. For example, when consumers advance purchase services (e.g. a Broadway show ticket, a summer camp sign-up, a SAT (standardized aptitude test) preparation course registration, a skating rink pass, or a tour bus voucher), they may be uncertain about their future valuation associated with the consumption of the service. Such buyer uncertainty creates an opportunity for profit improvement because it removes the seller information disadvantage. We shall see that advance selling also usually allows increased market participation because some buyers will have higher future valuations while others will have lower future valuations.

3.4 Profit advantage of advance selling

We now use a simple model to illustrate how buyer uncertainty creates a profit advantage for advance selling. To rule out the possibility of price discrimination, we consider a homogeneous market where all consumers arrive at the same time and have exactly the same distribution for their future valuation of the service. Specifically, assume that all consumers arrive in advance and have a q probability to be in a favorable state associated with a high valuation of H and a $1 - q$ probability to be in an unfavorable state associated with a low valuation of L, where $H > L$. There are absolutely no restrictions on the number of possible states and we only assume two states to illustrate the general intuition. Suppose both buyers and sellers know the distribution of buyer valuations. Let c denote the marginal cost, where $c \leq L$, and M denote the number of total potential customers. To eliminate any confusion with yield management, suppose the seller has sufficient capacity to serve all M customers.

In the case of spot selling, the seller offers sales in the spot period, in which q fraction of customers are in a favorable state and are willing to pay H and $1 - q$ fraction of customers are in an unfavorable state and are willing to pay only L. Customers decide whether to buy based on the spot price and their realized valuation. Note that customers have different realized valuations in the spot period (i.e. H or L), which is their private information unknown to the seller. The seller considers two spot-selling strategies: charging a high spot price of H or a low spot price of L.[2] We call these two spot-selling strategies 'high-price spot selling' and 'low-price spot selling', respectively. The profits under the two spot-selling strategies are given in the first two columns of Table 21.1. In the case of advance selling, the seller offers sales in the advance period, in which customers, like the seller, do not know their future consumption state. Given such buyer uncertainty, customers make purchase decisions based on their expected valuation

---

[2] Spot selling at any price between L and H is dominated by spot selling at a price of H; spot selling at any price below L is dominated by spot selling at a price of L.

Table 21.1 Profit advantage of advance selling

	High-price spot selling	Low-price spot selling	Advance selling	First-degree price discrimination (FPD) in the spot period
Price	H	L	$EV = qH + (1-q)L$	H (to those in favorable state) L (to those in unfavorable state)
Sales	qM	M	M	M
Profit	$qM(H-c)$	$M(L-c)$	$M(qH + (1-q)L - c)$	$M(qH + (1-q)L - c)$
Lost profit compared to FPD	$M(1-q)(L-c)$	$Mq(H-L)$	0	N/A
Consumer surplus	0	$Mq(H-L)$	0	0

EV, where $EV = qH + (1-q)L$. The seller offers advance sales at a price of EV.[3] The profit under 'advance selling' is presented in the third column of Table 21.1.[4]

To understand the sources of the profit advantage of advance selling, we compare each of the selling strategies with the ideal situation where the seller is able to implement first-degree price discrimination (FPD), i.e. charging buyers in a favorable state a high price of H and buyers in an unfavorable state a low price of L. We present the case of first-degree price discrimination in the last column of Table 21.1. We show the price, sales and profit under each case in the first three rows and the lost profit of each selling strategy compared with the case of FPD in the fourth row of Table 21.1. We also presents consumer surplus under each case in the last row of Table 21.1.

Table 21.1 reveals that, compared with the case of first-degree price discrimination, the two spot-selling strategies lead to lower profits. Specifically, the profit lost under high-price spot selling strategy is $M(1-q)(L-c)$. This profit decrease occurs because under high-price spot selling, the seller fails to capture demand from customers in an unfavorable state although their valuation is higher than the cost, $L > c$. This profit decline is greater when the profit margin from selling to these consumers increases (i.e. $L - c$ is higher) or when more customers will be in an unfavorable state (i.e. q is smaller). The profit decrease under low-price spot selling is $Mq(H-L)$. This profit decrease occurs because, under low-price spot selling, the seller charges the same price to all consumers

---

[3] Advance selling at any price above EV generates zero sales; and advance selling at any price below EV leads to the same sales but a lower profit margin compared with advance selling at a price of EV.

[4] Note that the seller can also consider offering sales both in advance and spot periods such as advance selling at a price of EV and spot selling at a price of H, or advance selling at a price of EV and spot selling at a price of L. However, the former is equivalent to advance selling only at EV because all consumers will buy in advance, and the latter is equivalent to spot selling only at L because all consumers will wait.

although those in a favorable state have a higher valuation than those in an unfavorable state, $H > L$. This profit decline is greater when the difference between valuations associated with favorable and unfavorable states increases (i.e. $H - L$ is larger) or when more consumers will be in a favorable state (i.e. q is higher).

The profit decreases under spot selling shown in Table 21.1 are not surprising given that the seller has neither the knowledge of individual consumers' consumption states nor the market power to charge different prices to consumers in different consumption states. However, it is surprising to see in Table 21.1 that, with the same seller knowledge and market power, the advance selling strategy allows the seller to achieve the profit that would be possible only under first-degree price discrimination (i.e. the lost profit under advance selling is zero), regardless of the specific values of H, L, q and c. (Notice that our early example of the local river cruise line is a special case of Table 21.1, where $H = 60, L = 30, q = 0.5, c = 10$.)

The advantages of advance selling over spot selling illustrated in Table 21.1 are fundamentally driven by buyer uncertainty that only occurs in the advance period but not in the spot period. The seller has an information disadvantage in the spot period given that the buyer's consumption state is known to the buyer but not to the seller. As a result of such an information disadvantage, the seller has to either give up the potential demand from consumers in an unfavorable state (as in the case of high-price spot selling) or give up the high profit margin from consumers in a favorable state (as in the case of low-price spot selling). However, as shown in Table 21.1, moving the transaction time from the spot period (i.e. when buyers have no uncertainty) to the advance period (i.e. when buyers have uncertainty) allows the seller to achieve both the benefits of a larger demand and a higher margin. This is because buyer uncertainty motivates consumers to change their decision criterion, i.e. rather than making purchase decisions based on realized utility in the spot period, they make those decisions based on expected utility in the advance period. Note that customers' realized utility is an individual consumer's private information unavailable to the seller; however, their expected utility can be constructed based on the seller's knowledge about the distribution of consumer valuation using the aggregate sales data. Without an informational disadvantage in the advance period, the seller is capable of reaching full market coverage (i.e. selling to all M customers) at a price higher than the valuation associated with an unfavorable state, $EV > L$. Note that if the same price of $EV = qH + (1 - q)L$ is offered in the spot period, the seller can only generate a demand of qM and is unable to reach full market coverage.

Finally, Table 21.1 shows that consumer surplus under advance selling is the same as that under high-price spot selling but lower than that under low-price spot selling. This implies that advance selling improves profit without reducing buyer surplus as long as the seller prefers high-price spot selling over low-price spot selling, which is the case when the favorable-state probability (q) is sufficiently high, the valuation difference between favorable and unfavorable states ($H - L$) is sufficiently high, or the profit margin from selling to customers in an unfavorable state ($L - c$) is sufficiently low. In sum, advance selling increases market participation, which increases profits without affecting consumer surplus.

It is important to note that although the simple model presented here has only two possible consumption states (i.e. a favorable state and an unfavorable state), the profit advantage of advance selling driven by buyer uncertainty applies for any distribution of consumer valuations provided that expected valuations are above cost (see Shugan and Xie, 2004 for a formal analysis of a general distribution of consumer valuation). Furthermore, although the profit advantage of advance selling does not require buyer heterogeneity in the advance period (e.g. our simple model assumes the same distribution of valuation for all potential buyers), buyer heterogeneity can make advance selling even more profitable. For example, Shugan and Xie (2004) show that when buyers differ in their distribution of valuation, advance selling can future-improve profits by price discrimination between different segments with a combination strategy: advance selling at a discounted price and spot selling at a high price (see also Xie and Shugan, 2001 for a formal analysis of the case where consumers arrive at different times).[5]

4. Important factors affecting advance selling

We have shown in the previous section that the profit advantage of advance selling does not require price discrimination nor yield management and can be driven simply by buyer uncertainty. In this section, we discuss some important factors affecting the profit potential of advance selling.

4.1 Seller credibility

The first important factor is the seller's ability to credibly offer a discounted advance price. To motivate an advance purchase, the seller must often offer a discounted advance price. Unless consumers believe that a higher price will be charged in the future, they may decide to wait rather than make an advance purchase. This situation can create problems for sellers, especially when buyers expect that sellers will offer both advance and spot sales – a likely outcome when some customers fail to plan ahead for various reasons and enter the market only in the spot period (see Xie and Shugan, 2001 for a formal analysis of this case). In general, the seller's ability to credibly commit to a high spot price is a crucial condition for inducing advance sales. At least three types of sellers can establish such credibility:

1. *Sellers with high marginal costs* When it is very costly to serve each customer, it is in the seller's best interest to charge a higher rather than a lower spot price because the benefit of serving customers in low valuation may not be sufficient to compensate for its cost. If customers were aware of a high service cost, they would expect a higher spot price. As a result, a high cost can help the seller to establish endogenous

---

[5] Table 21.1 assumes that all customers arrive in the advance period. In the case where customers arrive in both the advance and spot period, the advance purchase decision by the early arrivals will be affected by their expected future spot price, $\tilde{p}_S$. When buyer valuations are H and L with probabilities q and $1-q$, respectively, the maximum price inducing an advance purchase is $p_A^{max} = q\tilde{p}_S + (1-q)L$ for $\tilde{p}_S \leq H$ and $p_A^{max} = EV$, otherwise. Furthermore, consider a general density function $f(r)$ for buyer valuations where $L < r < H$. Let p_A denote the price in the advance period. The maximum advance price (buyers will pay) can be derived by equating the early arrivals' expected surplus from advance purchase, $ESA = \int_L^H rf(r)dr - p_A$, with their expected surplus from waiting, $ESW = \int_{\tilde{p}_S}^H (r - \tilde{p}_S)f(r)dr$. Solving for p_A, we obtain $p_A^{max} = \tilde{p}_S - \int_L^{\tilde{p}_S} (\tilde{p}_S - r)f(r)dr$ for a general distribution. Readers interested in models of advance selling strategy should consult Xie and Shugan (2001) and Shugan and Xie (2005).

credibility. This reasoning is a consequence of imposing the rationality condition on consumers.

2. *Sellers with limited capacity* The optimal spot price is determined based on both the demand and the available capacity in the spot period. Sellers with limited capacity benefit little from offering low spot prices because the capacity is insufficient to satisfy the large demand. Consequently, when consumers know capacity is limited, they will expect high spot prices. Limited capacity also implies that, if the early arrivals wait, they may not be able to purchase in the spot period. A 'no capacity' situation is equivalent to one in which the spot price is infinite. Hence use of capacity constraints is another way for the seller to gaining endogenous credibility. By selling sufficient capacity in advance, the seller credibly commits to a high spot price.

3. *Sellers with established exogenous credibility* Even when sellers have very low costs and sufficient capacity, it is still possible to establish exogenous credibility. For example, many sellers, such as Disneyland, The Lake Erie Speedway and The Delaware Valley Bluegrass Festival, offer both a discounted 'Advance Price' and a regular 'Gate Price' simultaneously and routinely. A potential buyer has the option to pay a low 'Advance Price' for a future ticket or pay a high 'Gate Price' for a ticket good for the day of purchase. The fact that the future spot price is observable at the time when customers are making advance purchases allows the seller to establish exogenous credibility. Finally, persistently maintaining a reputation for a high spot price might also be sufficient for exogenous credibility when buyers expect sellers to guard zealously their reputations or face future loses.

4.2 Marginal cost

The second important factor is the marginal cost. On the one hand, a sufficiently low marginal cost is necessary to make advance selling at a discounted price profitable. As discussed earlier, advance selling allows sales to buyers who would be in unfavorable states later and would not purchase under a high spot price. Selling to those buyers, however, is unprofitable when the value of the product/service is less to them than its cost. When costs are too high (e.g. when $c > L$ in Table 21.1), advance selling fails to improve profits (see 'Strategy III: same low advance and spot prices' in the next section). We call the requirement of a sufficiently low cost the 'profitability condition' of advance selling. On the other hand, for sellers without capacity constraints, too low a cost may destroy the 'credibility' condition of advance selling, under which the customers believe the advance price is discounted from the spot price. A marginal cost that is too low may also motivate customers to wait rather than to purchase in the advance period because, under such conditions, they will expect a low spot price.

4.3 Capacity constraints

Capacity constraints affect advance selling strategies in several ways. First, they can facilitate advance selling. As mentioned earlier, without capacity constraints, a sufficiently high marginal cost is necessary to make a high spot price credible. Without that high spot price, buyers would not purchase in advance. However, in the presence of capacity constraints, the seller can credibly commit to a high spot price despite a zero marginal cost, because lack of availability implies an infinite spot price.

Second, capacity constraints allow sellers to charge a premium for advance purchase (see 'Strategy V: PREMIUM advance selling' in the next section). Without capacity constraints, buyers will pay no more in advance than the expected spot price. In the presence of capacity constraints, however, advance buyers must consider both the spot price and the likelihood of lack of availability in the spot period if they wait. They may be willing to pay a higher price in advance rather than compete with later arrivals in the spot period if the chance of obtaining capacity is sufficiently low. In general, premium advance selling is possible when the capacity is sufficiently large to make a low spot price optimal, but also sufficiently small to make the likelihood of availability in the spot period sufficiently low.

Third, although limited capacity can create the ability to advance-sell or even offer the opportunity for charging premium advance prices, it can also reduce the incentive for the seller to offer advance sales. For example, when capacity constraints are severe, the seller can easily sell out at a high spot price, implying that it is in the seller's best interest to offer only spot sales (see 'Strategy II: high spot prices without advance sales' in the next section). When capacity constraints are not too severe, the seller may benefit by offering limited advance sales at discount prices and reserve sufficient capacity for spot sales at high prices (see 'Strategy IV: discount advance selling, limit on advance sales' in the next section).[6]

4.4 Refunds for cancellations

Can the seller still benefit from advance selling if refunds are offered to advance buyers who wish to cancel their advance purchase at a later time because their state (ability to enjoy the service) becomes unfavorable? Surprisingly, as we show below, despite lower sales with refunds, advance selling with partial refunds can provide more profit than advance selling without refunds.

The benefit of offering refunds can be cost driven. To illustrate this we extend our basic model by allowing three possible consumption states that are associated with three different valuations, $\{H, L, V_0\}$, where $H > L > c > V_0$. We assume that the buyer is equally likely to be in any of the three states. Under a no-refund policy, in advance period, consumer expected valuation is $EV_{NR} = (H + L + V_0)/3$. By offering the advance sales at the price of EV_{NR}, all M potential consumers buy. The seller's maximum profit under advance selling without refunds is

$$\pi_{NR} = \left(\frac{H + L + V_0}{3} - c\right)M$$

Now consider advance selling with a partial refund, R, where $L > R > V_0$. Under such a partial refunds policy, advance buyers request refunds when in their worst state (i.e. a valuation of V_0), but otherwise enjoy the service. In the advance period, the consumer's expected valuation is $EV_R = (H + L + R)/3$. By offering advance sales at the price of EV_R, all M potential consumers will buy. Among them, two-thirds will enjoy the service,

---

[6] A formal analysis of capacity constraints on advance selling can be found in Xie and Shugan (2001).

but one-third will cancel the purchase later and will receive a refund of R. The seller's profit of advance selling with refunds is

$$\pi_R = \left\{ \left(\frac{H+L+R}{3} - c \right) \frac{2}{3} + \left(\frac{H+L+R}{3} - R \right) \frac{1}{3} \right\} M = \left\{ \frac{H+L}{3} - \frac{2c}{3} \right\} M$$

Now consider the difference in the profit from advance selling with (π_R) and without refunds (π_{NR}), i.e.

$$\pi_R - \pi_{NR} = \left(\frac{H+L}{3} - \frac{2c}{3} \right) M - \left(\frac{H+L+V_0}{3} - c \right) M = \left(\frac{V_0 - c}{3} \right) M$$

Profits with refunds are greater when $\pi_R > \pi_{NR}$ or $c > V_0$. This suggests that offering partial refunds increases the profitability of advance selling as long as the seller's marginal cost of offering the service is higher than the value of the service to the consumer who wants to cancel. Note that in this situation, offering partial refunds increases profits not by increasing revenues, but by cost savings from not serving customers in extremely low value states. Also note that offering refunds increases the buyer's expected utility, and thus their willingness to pay for advance sales. The seller can charge a higher advance price under the refund policy (i.e. $EV_R = (H+L+R)/3$ than that under the no-refund policy (i.e. $EV_{NR} = (H+L+V_0)/3$). This higher advance price under refunds compensates for the actual cost of the refunds. Recall our early example of the river cruise line. It is possible that some customers may be in states associated with very low or even zero value for the late-night dance cruise on a given Friday night (e.g. having severe back pain). The above discussion suggests that the cruise line can earn a higher profit by offering refunds to encourage advance buyers who value the cruise less than the cost of serving them ($c = \$10$). Such a refund policy also allows the cruise line to charge a higher advance price.

In addition to the benefit of refunds due to cost saving, refunds may also be used as a way of generating more revenue for sellers with capacity constraints. Xie and Gerstner (2007) show that allowing customers who find better alternatives to escape service contracts for a fee creates opportunities to sell the capacity-constrained service multiple times. The better the alternative that motivates a cancellation, the more profitable is a refund-for-cancellations policy compared with a no-refund policy that 'locks in' customers. The seller can benefit from offering refunds despite the willingness of advance buyers to abandon the service for no refund (i.e. they fail to arrive and claim the service). The role of the refund is to motivate these customers to notify the seller about their cancellations (instead of merely failing to arrive), which allows the seller to resell the service. For example, a buyer might purchase one of the best seats for a very popular concert at $120 one month in advance. One week before the performance, however, a commitment might arise that prevents the buyer from attending the performance. In this situation, the capacity would go unused unless the buyer notified the seller of the situation. Without refunds, the highly desirable seat would be wasted. A partial refund (e.g. 50 percent of ticket value or $60) could motivate the buyer to inform the seller of the cancellation, which allows the seller to resell the seat. It is important to note that the benefit of offering refunds for multiple selling requires capacity constraints. Sellers with sufficient capacity do not benefit from reselling returned capacity given that the seller has sufficient capacity to satisfy all potential demand.

4.5 Competition
Competition weakens or eliminates the effectiveness of many marketing strategies (e.g. bundling, quantity discounts, coupons and loyalty programs intended to exploit price discrimination). We might wonder whether the same negative effect of competition applies to advance selling. Recent work by Shugan and Xie (2005) shows that the profit advantage of advance selling driven by consumer uncertainty can not only survive competition, but also be greater in a competitive market than in a monopoly market, because, unlike many other marketing strategies, advance selling is not driven by price discrimination. Competition weakens other marketing strategies that exploit price discrimination because competitors target those being discriminated against. As a result, the profit advantages of marketing strategies based on price discrimination are often weaker for a seller facing competitors than for a monopoly seller. The profit advantage of an advance selling strategy, however, as shown in this chapter, does not require price discrimination. It can be driven simply by consumers' uncertainty about their future consumption states. Competition may not diminish the advantage of advance selling because consumer uncertainty applies to all consumers in the advance period; thus a competitor is unable to focus attention on only one group of consumers. It is possible, though, that the existence of a competitor can make it harder to satisfy the credibility condition of advance selling (i.e. consumers believe a high price will be charged in the spot period) because such competition may force the seller to lower spot prices. Shugan and Xie (2005) find that under some market conditions, advance selling can increase both the competitors' profits and the consumers' surplus because advance selling leads to greater market coverage. For example, suppose that buyer preferences for one competitor over another become apparent only in the spot period. Then, competition could raise spot prices as buyers only purchase from their preferred competitor (e.g. see Hauser and Shugan, 1983 for examples of how competition can raise prices). As noted earlier, higher spot prices can facilitate advance sales because advance prices are unable to exceed spot prices. Hence competition can create conditions profitable for advance selling.

4.6 Buyer risk aversion
Finally, will the profit advantage diminish or disappear when buyers are risk averse? Intuitively, buyer risk aversion could make advance purchasing less attractive because future valuations are uncertain. Sellers might need to take deeper discounts in the advance period, thereby making advance selling less profitable. Xie and Shugan (2001) examine the impact of buyer risk aversion on advance selling and find that the profit advantage of advance selling does not depend on risk neutrality. Buyer risk aversion can either increase or reduce the profitability of advance selling. Risk aversion increases the profitability from advance selling when buyers associate a greater loss with not enjoying discounted prices in favorable states than paying more than their valuations in unfavorable states.

5.   When and how to advance-sell: six specific selling strategies
In the previous sections, we have explained why buyer uncertainty can turn advance selling into a profit advantage, and we have discussed some important factors affecting the profit potential of an advance-selling strategy. In this section, we focus on when and how to advance-sell. We discuss six specific selling strategies and provide guidelines for sellers who face different product/market conditions. Xie and Shugan (2001) develop a formal

468   Handbook of pricing research in marketing

model to derive these selling strategies, which states the explicit conditions under which each strategy is optimal. We illustrate these strategies here by providing several numerical examples in Table 21.2. As defined earlier, H and L denote consumer valuation in favorable and unfavorable states, respectively; q denotes the probability that a consumer will be in a favorable state, and c denotes the marginal cost. Furthermore, the model allows consumers to enter the market at different times. For example, some vacationers are 'early arrivals' who plan their vacation and thus have the opportunity to make advance purchases. There are also 'later arrivals', those who wait until the last minute to make a decision concerning their vacation and thus often miss opportunities for advance sales. Specifically, for the examples in Table 21.2 (except Example 1), consider the case where there are a total of M potential buyers, and $N = M/2$ buyers arrive in each of the two periods (i.e. the advance and spot periods). Finally, T denotes the level of capacity. To highlight the impact of the two important factors, capacity constraints and marginal cost, we set the same values for H and L in all of these examples ($H = 50$, $L = 30$, i.e. the consumer is willing to pay \$50 in a favorable state and \$30 in an unfavorable state) but vary N, T and c.

5.1   Strategy I: advance sales only

Under this strategy, the seller offers only advance sales. This strategy is best when there are no late arrivals, capacity is not a binding constraint, and the seller can credibly claim that spot sales are not available. That credibility occurs, for example, because the seller would probably suffer future losses in reputation from deceiving customers by making an advance announcement of no spot sales and later reneging on that statement. Our subsequent examples will explore the case without this form of exogenous credibility. Without exogenous credibility, consumers believe only seller announcements that are consistent with the seller's best strategy within the stated problem. For instance, consumers believe an announcement of no spot sales only when it is, in fact, more profitable for the seller to have no sales in the spot period than to spot-sell.

Let us consider a three-hour cruise at Clearwater Beach with a boat passenger capacity of $T = 200$ people. Assume that a potential customer is equally likely to be in a favorable state (e.g. a valued companion can also participate) or an unfavorable state (e.g. the companion is unable to participate), that is, $q = 0.5$. The customer will pay $H = \$50$ in a favorable state and $L = \$30$ in an unfavorable state. During the high season, many tourists may be interested in such a boat trip. Suppose that a total of $M = 200$ potential customers are interested in a given trip and all arrive in the advance period. In this case, the highest advance price the seller can charge is the customers' expected valuation, $\$50 \times 0.5 + \$30 \times 0.5 = \$40$. Hence, if costs are zero, $c = \$0$, then the seller would always prefer to sell all 200 tickets at the advance price of \$40, yielding a profit of $\$40 \times 200 = \$8000$. Spot selling at \$50 would yield a profit of only $\$50 \times 100 = \$5000$ and spot selling at \$30 would yield a profit of only $\$30 \times 200 = \$6000$. This case is Example 1 in Table 21.2.

5.2   Strategy II: high spot prices without advance sales

Under this strategy, the seller offers spot sales at a high price and does not offer advance sales. This strategy is best if either the capacity is sufficiently small or the cost is sufficiently high. A sufficiently small capacity occurs when all capacity can be sold at high spot prices. Sufficiently high costs occur when producing advance sales requires advance prices below marginal costs.

Table 21.2 Examples of six specific selling strategies

Example 1: $H = 50$, $L = 30$, $q = 0.5$, $M = 200$ (all arrive in the advance period), $T = 200$, $c = 0$
→**Strategy I (advance sales only) is optimal**

Strategy	Profit
High spot price ($50) only	$50 × 0.5 × 200 = $5000
Low spot price ($30) only	$30 × 200 = $6000
Advance price ($40) only	$40 × 200 = $8000←**Optimal**
High advance price & low spot price	Same profit as low spot price because all buyers wait to buy spot

Example 2: $H = 50$, $L = 30$, $q = 0.5$, $N = 100$, $T = 85$, $c = 25$
→**Strategy II (high spot prices without advance sales) is optimal**

Strategy	Profit
High spot price ($50) only	$(50–25) × 85 = $2125←**Optimal**
Low spot price ($30) only	$(30–25) × 85 = $425
Advance price ($40) only	$(40–25) × 85 = $1275
Advance price ($40) & spot price ($50)	Same profit as advance selling only ($40)
Same low spot & advance price ($30)	Same profit as spot selling at $30
Same high spot & advance price ($50)	Same profit as spot selling at $50

Example 3: $H = 50$, $L = 30$, $q = 0.5$, $N = 100$, $T = 200$, $c = 0$
→**Strategy III (same low advance and spot prices) is optimal**

Strategy	Profit
High spot price ($50) only	$50 × 0.5 × (100 + 100) = $5000
Low spot price ($30) only	$30 × (100 + 100) = $6000←**Optimal**
Advance price ($40) only	Not credible – all consumers wait to buy spot at $30
Advance price ($40) & spot price ($50)	Not credible – $30 is the optimal spot price
Low advance price ($30) & spot price ($30)	($30 × 100) + ($30 × 100)=$6000←**Optimal**

Example 4: $H = 50$, $L = 30$, $q = 0.5$, $N = 80$, $T = 85$, $c = 0$
→**Strategy III (discount advance selling, limit on advance sales) is optimal**

Strategy	Profit
High spot price ($50) only	$50 × 0.5 × (80 + 80)= $4000
Low spot price ($30) only	$30 × 85 = $2550
Advance price ($40) only	$40 × 80 = $3200
Advance price ($40) & spot price ($50)	($40 × 80) + $50 × (85–80)= $3450
Discounted advance price ($40) with limited advance sales of 10 units & high spot price ($50)	• Set advance limit to be S • Remaining spot capacity is 85–S • Spot sales are (0.5)(80 + 80–S) • Solve for the optimal limit: 85–S = (0.5)(80 + 80–S), S = 10 • Profit=($40 × 10) + ($50 × 0.5 × (80 + 80–10)) = $4150←**Optimal**

Table 21.2 (continued)

Example 5: $H = 50$, $L = 30$, $q = 0.5$, $N = 55$, $T = 85$, $c = 0$
→**Strategy IV (discount advance selling, no limit on advance sales) is optimal**

Strategy	Profit
High spot price ($50) only	$50 × 0.5 × (55 + 55) = $2750
Low spot price ($30) only	$30 × 85 = $2550
Advance price ($40) only	$40 × 55 = $2200
Discounted advance price ($40) without limiting advance sales & high spot price ($50)	$40 × 55 + $50 × 0.5 × 55 = $3575←**Optimal**

Example 6: $H = 50$, $L = 30$, $q = 0.44$, $N = 55$, $T = 85$, $c = 0$
→**Strategy V (PREMIUM advance selling) is optimal**

Strategy	Profit
High spot price ($50) only	$50 × 0.44 × (55 + 55) = $2420.00
Low spot price ($30) only	$30 × 85 = $2550
Advance price (0.44 × 50 + 0.56 × 30 = $38.80) & spot ($30)	Not credible – all consumers wait & try to buy at $30
Premium advance price ($32) advance sales & low spot price ($30)	• Probability of available spot capacity given everyone tries to spot-buy: 85/(55+55) = 17/22 • Spot probability of both a favorable state & no available spot capacity: 0.44 × (1− (17/22)) = 0.10 • Advance price inducing sales: 0.10 × 50 + (1 − 0.10) × 30 = $32 • $32 × 55 + $30 × (85 − 55) = $2660←**Optimal**

Note: H, L = valuation in favorable and unfavorable states; q = the probability to be in favorable states; N = the number of arrivals in each period; T = capacity, c = the marginal cost.

Again, let us consider the same cruise, this time with a capacity of $T = 85$ people. For this and subsequent examples, assume half of the $M = 200$ customers arrive in the advance period ($N = M/2$) and the remainder arrive in the spot period. In this case, with $q = 0.5$, the highest advance price the seller can charge is the customers' expected valuation, $50 × 0.5 + 30 × 0.5 = 40. Note that a total of 100 customers will be in a favorable state in the spot period and are willing to pay $50, but the seller has only a total of 85 units for sale. Hence the seller would always prefer to sell all 85 tickets at the higher spot price of $50 and sell no tickets at the lower advance price of $40 given a constant marginal cost. Advance selling should also be avoided when the marginal cost is too high (i.e. failing to satisfy the profitability condition discussed earlier). For example, if it costs more than $40 to serve each customer on board (e.g. variable costs including refreshments), it is more profitable for the seller to charge a high spot price without offering advance sales at a discounted price, even if the capacity is sufficient to satisfy all demand. Example 2 in Table 21.2 provides numerical details for this example ($H = 50$, $L = 30$, $q = 0.5$, $N = 100$, $T = 85$, $c = 25$), in which selling only at a high spot price is best.

5.3 Strategy III: same low advance and spot prices

This strategy, which involves advance and spot selling at the same low price that induces purchases from all buyers and is equivalent to selling only at a low spot price, works best when the seller has both unlimited capacity and very low costs. With neither capacity constraints nor high marginal costs, a low spot price is often optimal because the large capacity and low cost make it more profitable to sell to all customers at a low price than to sell to customers in the favorable state only at a higher price. Early arrivals expect such a low price in the spot period and will only advance-buy at prices equal to the low spot price. Thus advance selling at that price generates no more profit than spot selling alone when we require endogenous credibility. Consider Example 3 in Table 21.2 ($H = 50$, $L = 30$, $q = 0.5$, $N = 100$, $T = 200$, $c = 0$), which differs from Example 2 in the value of two parameters: (1) the seller now has sufficient capacity to serve all 200 potential customers (i.e. $T = 200$) and (2) the boat offers neither beverages nor entertainment and thus bears a near zero marginal cost (e.g. $c = 0$). In this case, if the seller adopts Strategy II, i.e. spot selling at a high price without offering advance sales, the profit is $(50 \times 100) = \$5000$. However, by offering the same price of \$30 in both the advance and spot periods, the profit is $\$30 \times 100 + \$30 \times 100 = \$6000$. Note that an advance price higher than \$30 fails to induce advance sales because consumers wait to spot buy at the low spot price of \$30. Of course, if the seller had some other means to guarantee a spot price of \$50, similar to Example 1, then advance selling would again become more profitable than solely spot selling.

5.4 Strategy IV: discount advance selling, limit on advance sales

Under this strategy, the seller advance-sells at a discount from the spot price, but limits the number of advance sales in order to reserve sufficient capacity for sales in the spot period. This strategy is best when (a) the cost is sufficiently low to satisfy the profitability condition of advance selling, and (b) the capacity is sufficient to serve all late arrivals who are in a favorable state but insufficient to satisfy all additional advance demand. Consider Example 4 in Table 21.2 ($H = 50$, $L = 30$, $q = 0.5$, $N = 80$, $T = 85$, $c = 0$), which differs from Example 2 only in the value of two parameters: (1) there is a total of 160 (i.e. $N = 80$) rather than 200 (i.e. $N = 100$) potential customers for a given boat trip; hence the seller faces a less severe capacity constraint compared with Example 2, and (2) the marginal cost is zero. In this case, if the seller should adopt Strategy II by spot selling at a price of \$50 without offering advance sales, 80 customers in the favorable state will buy and the seller earns a profit of $\$50 \times 80 = \$4000$. It is easy to see that this strategy is not optimal because there is still some unsold capacity and unfulfilled demand. Alternatively, all 85 tickets can be sold in the spot period under a low spot price of \$30; however, this strategy leads to a still lower profit of $\$30 \times 85 = \$2550$. Now suppose that the seller offers advance sales at a price of \$40 and spot sales at \$50. Under this strategy, 80 tickets will be sold in the advance period and five tickets will be sold in the spot period, earning a profit of $\$(40 \times 80 + 50 \times 5) = \$3450$. Although this profit represents a significant improvement over the two spot-selling strategies, the seller can further increase profit by limiting the number of tickets offered for sale in advance. Specifically, it is optimal to offer only ten tickets for sale in advance at a price of \$40.

We set this limit on advance sales, denoted S, by equating spot demand with available capacity. Selling S units in the advance period leaves $85 - S$ capacity in the spot period.

Spot demand will consist of 50 percent, i.e. the percentage in a favorable state, of the total number of consumers remaining in the spot period, which is $80 + 80 - S$, because we have already sold S in the advance period. Hence we solve $85 - S = 0.5 \times (80 + 80 - S)$ to find that $S = 10$ units.

With this limit, ten customers will purchase tickets in advance at a discounted price and the remaining 150 customers (i.e. 70 advance arrivals plus 80 later arrivals) will make purchase decisions in the spot period. Of these 150 consumers, 75 will be willing to pay the high spot price of $50 given their favorable consumption state. Hence the seller earns a higher total profit of $(\$40 \times 10) + (\$50 \times 0.5 \times (80 + 80 - 10)) = \$4150$ by advance selling and limiting advance sales, in this case to ten units.

5.5 Strategy V: discount advance selling, no limit on advance sales

Under this strategy, the seller does not limit advance sales. This strategy is optimal if the cost is sufficiently low to satisfy the profitability condition and the capacity is sufficiently large to serve all early arrivals as well as all later arrivals who are in a favorable state. Consider Example 5 in Table 21.2 ($H = 50, L = 30, q = 0.5, N = 55, T = 85, c = 0$), which differs from Example 4 only in the number of potential customers, i.e. there is a total of $M = 110$ ($N = 55$) rather than $M = 160$ ($N = 80$) potential customers for a given trip. Hence the seller faces less severe capacity constraints in Example 5 than in Example 4. In this case, the capacity of 85 is sufficient to serve all 55 early arrivals plus 30 later arrivals in a favorable state and the cost is lower than the valuation of customers in an unfavorable state. Hence the optimal strategy is to sell tickets to all early arrivals at the discounted price of $40 and to later arrivals at a higher spot price of $50. The seller's profit under this strategy is $\$(40 \times 55 + 50 \times 0.5 \times 55) = \$3575$, which is higher than any strategy that excludes advance sales (i.e. without offering advance sales, the profit is $\$50 \times 0.5 \times (55 + 55) = \$2750$ under a high spot price and $\$30 \times 85 = \$2550$ under a low spot price). The higher spot profit for higher-price tickets makes the high spot price credible without the need for any form of exogenous credibility

5.6 Strategy VI: PREMIUM advance selling

This is a unique strategy under which advance sales are priced at a premium rather than discounted from the spot price. This strategy is best when the capacity is sufficiently large to make a low spot price optimal but also sufficiently small to make the likelihood of availability in the spot period sufficiently low. We might wonder why buyers would be willing to pay a premium in the advance period over the spot price when waiting is an option. As we show in the following analysis, charging a higher advance price is possible when early arrivals receive a greater benefit (surplus) by securing their capacity at a higher price, compared with competing for capacity with later arrivals in the spot period. Although this reasoning resembles risk aversion, it does not require risk aversion. We demonstrate that fact by providing an example with risk-neutral buyers. Consider Example 6, ($H = 50, L = 30, q = 0.44, N = 55, T = 85, c = 0$), which differs from Example 5 in only one way – the probability that a customer will be in a favorable state is 44 percent ($q = 0.44$) rather than 50 percent. In this case, in the advance period, a customer's expected valuation is $\$50 \times 0.44 + \$30 \times (1 - 0.44) = \$38.80$ for the boat trip.

In this case, however, the seller is unable to induce advance sales at an advance price of $38.80 because early arrivals do not believe a high price of $50 will be charged in the spot period (i.e. the high spot price of $50 is not credible). Specifically, the profits from only spot selling at a high price of $50 are $50 × 0.44 × (55 + 55) = $2420 because only 44 percent of the 110 total arrivals will buy. Meanwhile, the profit from simply offering the low spot price of $30 is $30 × 85 = $2550, because there is insufficient capacity to sell to more than 85 customers. Since the low spot price provides greater profit ($2550) for the seller than does a high spot price ($2420), early arrivals expect that a low spot price of $30 will be offered if they wait. In that case, they get a positive expected surplus because they receive $(50 − 30) = $20 if in a favorable state (and obtaining capacity), and zero surplus otherwise. Hence an advance price of $38.80 fails to induce advance sales simply because early arrivals receive a positive expected surplus from waiting but an expected surplus of zero from purchasing in advance at a price of $38.80.

However, early arrivals may be willing to purchase in advance at a price lower than $38.80 but still higher than the low spot price of $30 (i.e. advance purchase at a premium price) because, with limited availability, not all potential buyers will obtain spot capacity. Specifically, if all 55 + 55 = 110 buyers attempt to spot buy, the probability of getting capacity is only 85/110 given capacity of 85. For this reason, early arrivals may be willing to pay a higher price in the advance period in order to guarantee capacity. Limited capacity is not a problem for the buyer when she is in an unfavorable state, because in that instance the buyer receives no surplus regardless of whether or not she buys at $30 or fails to get capacity. In contrast, limited capacity is a problem for the buyer in a favorable state, because she would pay considerably more than $30 (in fact up to $50) to buy but may be unable to do so. In the advance period, the probability of this event (wanting to buy in a favorable state but not getting capacity) is $(1 − (85/110)) \times 0.44 = 0.1$. Given this probability, we can compute the amount the buyer would be willing to pay to avoid this event, which is the maximum advance price that the seller can charge to induce advance sales. Specifically, the buyer would be willing to advance buy at $0.1 \times \$50 + (1 − 0.1) \times \$30 = \$32$, which is lower than $38.80 but still higher than $30.[7]

We can also obtain the maximum advance price, denoted $P_A^{\max}$, by finding the advance price that makes the buyer's surplus from advance purchase, $0.44 \times (\$50 − P_A^{\max}) + (1 − 0.44) \times (\$30 − P_A^{\max})$, equal to the buyer's surplus from waiting, $0.44 \times (85/110) \times (\$50 − \$30) + (1 − 0.44) \times (\$30 − \$30)$. This leads to $P_A^{\max} = \$32$.

---

[7] There are three technical points here. The reader may skip these points, but completeness requires them. First, we used the probability 85/110 as that for obtaining capacity when we calculated the maximum advance price (i.e. $32). At that price, early arrivals would advance buy to guarantee capacity. Now, if the probability of obtaining capacity is smaller than 85/110, then our conclusions survive and early arrivals will still advance-buy because the smaller probability increases the likelihood of the event of being in a favorable state with no available capacity. Second, when one or more consumers advance-buy, the probability of obtaining spot capacity is no longer $85/110 = 0.773$. For example, if one buyer advance-buys, the probability for obtaining spot capacity decreases to $(85 − 1)/(110 − 1) = 0.771$. If 55 buyers advance-buy, the probability of not obtaining spot capacity decreases further to $(85 − 55)/(110 − 55) = 0.55$. Hence, regardless of the way we compute the probability of obtaining capacity, an advance price of $32 will induce advance sales. Third, if all 55 early arrivals advance-buy, the probability of wanting to buy in a favorable state but not getting capacity is $(1 − (85 − 55)/(110 − 55)) \times 0.44 = 0.2$ rather than $(1 − 85/110) \times 0.44 = 0.1$. The maximum advance price then becomes $0.2 \times \$50 + (1 − 0.2) \times \$30 = \$34$. Hence consumer expectations about other consumers' behavior influence optimal prices.

474 Handbook of pricing research in marketing

```
                                                          Get ticket
                                                                        ◁ 50 – 30 = 20
                            In favorable state            0.773
                                                          No ticket
                            0.44                                        ◁ 0
            Wait                                          0.227
                                                          Get ticket
                                                                        ◁ 30 – 30 = 0
                            In unfavorable state          0.773
                                                          No ticket
Boat trip                   0.56                                        ◁ 0
                                                          0.227
                                                          In favorable state
                                                                        ◁ 50 – 32 = 18
            Advance-buy     Get ticket                    0.44
                                                          In unfavorable state
                            1.00                                        ◁ 30 – 32 = –2
                                                          0.56
```

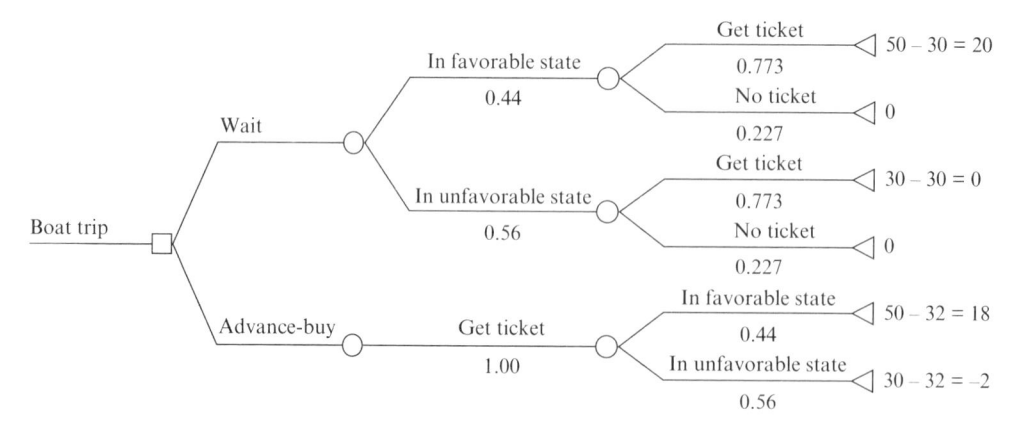

Figure 21.1   *Early arrivals receive the same surplus from advance purchase at a price of $32 or from waiting to buy in the spot period at a price of $30*

Figure 21.1 illustrates the buyer's decision. Specifically, it illustrates the consumer's surplus in different states under different conditions given different actions. We shall show that an advance price of $32 and a spot price of $30 make the consumer indifferent to either advance buying or spot buying, given a probability of 85/110 = 0.773 of obtaining capacity.

If early arrivals advance-buy, they pay $32. There is a 44 percent chance that their valuation will be $50 and they will enjoy a surplus of $50 − $32 = $18. There is a 1−44 percent = 56 percent chance that their valuation will be $30 and they will suffer a loss of $30 − $32 = −$2. The expected surplus from advance buying, therefore, is (0.44 × $18) − (0.56 × $2) = $6.80.

If early arrivals wait, there is a 1−44% = 56% chance of being in the unfavorable state which always results in zero surplus whether the consumer buys at $30 or does not buy at all (because the consumer valuation is $30). If early arrivals wait, there is a 44 percent chance of being in the favorable state and a probability of 85/110 = 0.773 of getting a ticket. Obtaining a ticket provides a surplus of $50 − $30 = $20 because the consumer would be willing to pay $50. The expected surplus of waiting, therefore, is 0.44 × (0.773) × ($50 − $30) = $6.80.

We see that the surplus from waiting exactly equals the surplus from advance buying. Hence, $32, or just slightly less, is the optimal advance price (to break the indifference), to induce advance buying. As shown in Example 6 in Table 21.2, premium advance selling at $32 and spot selling at $30 is superior to other strategies and produces a profit of $32 × 55 + $30 × (85 − 55) = $2660.

It is important to notice that, although 'discounted advance selling' fails to improve profit in this case, 'premium advance selling' is more profitable than any spot-selling strategy. In general, the optimality of premium advance selling depends upon the amount of available capacity, the distribution of consumer valuation, the marginal cost of the service and consumer expectation.

6. Conclusion

Advance selling is a powerful marketing tool worthy of considerable future research. We have shown that advance selling can be profitable with or without price discrimination, with or without capacity constraints, with or without competition, with or without refunds, with or without buyer uncertainty, and under other robust conditions. However, when buyer uncertainty concerning future consumption states is present, that condition alone can allow advance selling to increase profits by up to 100 percent over the profits from spot selling only at the optimal spot price. Buyer uncertainty in the advance period that would be resolved in the spot period would create private information in the spot period for the buyer. Hence the seller benefits from selling in the advance period when buyers often lack that specific private information. For the common case when buyer uncertainty about future consumption states motivates advance selling, we show that the profits from advance selling come from increased market participation rather than price discrimination. Hence advance selling for this reason, unlike price discrimination, does not necessarily reduce buyer surplus and might actually increase it. Given our enthusiasm for advance selling, we might wonder why firms are not already exploiting advance-selling tools. We argue that, for many industries, only recent technological advances have made advance selling profitable.

As noted earlier, research has just begun to explore many topics related to advance selling and many topics await future research. Geng et al. (2007) study situations of advance selling when sellers allow resales. The consequences and profitability of advance selling in many unexplored situations deserve further research. For example, we have discussed only future uncertain consumption states that influence buyer valuations for a service. It is possible that, in competitive markets, this future uncertainty is related to which competitor best matches buyer preferences. Hence buyers know which competitor best meets their needs only in the spot period. Another situation worth exploration is when sellers have a better estimate of buyer valuations in the advance period than the buyers do themselves. This situation is common when sellers have extensive experience while buyers are usually buying for the first time. Still another situation is when buyers realize that other buyers are also acting strategically and that their ability to obtain future capacity depends on the behavior of these other buyers. In this case, buyers must anticipate how other buyers will behave given particular advance-selling strategies and buyers might attempt to influence other buyers. Finally, but certainly not the only other avenue for research, we might consider the situation when sellers are offering different advance prices at different points in time before the spot period. In other words, we could consider situations with multiple advance periods.

References

Biyalogorsky, Eyal and Eitan Gerstner (2004), 'Contingent pricing to reduce price risks', *Marketing Science*, **23** (1), 146–55.

Biyalogorsky, Eyal, Eitan Gerstner, Dan Weiss and Jinhong Xie (2005), 'Economics of service upgrades', *Journal of Service Research*, **7** (3), 234–44.

Biyalogorsky, Eyal, Ziv Carmon, Gila Fruchter and Eitan Gerstner (1999), 'Overselling with opportunistic cancellations', *Marketing Science*, **18** (4), 605–10.

Borenstein, Severin and Nancy L. Rose (1994), 'Competition and price dispersion in the U.S. airline industry', *The Journal of Political Economy*, **102** (4), 653–83.

Chatwin, Richard E. (2000), 'Optimal dynamic pricing of perishable products with stochastic demand and a finite set of prices', *European Journal of Operational Research*, **125** (1), 149–74.

Courty, Pascal and Hau Li (2000), 'Sequential screening', *Review of Economic Studies*, **67**, 697–717.
Dana, J.D., Jr (1998), 'Advanced-purchase discounts and price discrimination in competitive markets', *Journal of Political Economy*, **106**, 395–422.
Dana, James, Jr and Eric Anderson (2005), 'When is price discrimination profitable?', Working Paper, Northwestern University.
Desiraju, Ramarao and Steven M. Shugan (1999), 'Strategic service pricing and yield management', *Journal of Marketing*, **63** (January), 44–56.
Gale, Ian L. and T. Holmes (1992), 'The efficiency of advance-purchase discounts in the presence of aggregate demand uncertainty', *International Journal of Industrial Organization*, **10** (September), 413–37.
Gale, Ian L. and Thomas J. Holmes (1993), 'Advance-purchase discounts and monopoly allocation of capacity', *American Economic Review*, **83** (1), 135–46.
Geng, Xianjun, Ruhai Wu and Andrew B. Whinston (2007), 'Profiting from partial allowance of ticket resale', *Journal of Marketing*, **71** (April), 184–95.
Hauser, John and Steven M. Shugan (1983), 'Defensive marketing strategy' *Marketing Science*, **2** (4), 319–60.
Hauser, John. R. and Birger Wernerfelt (1990), 'An evaluation cost model of consideration sets', *Journal of Consumer Research*, **16** (March), 393–408.
Moe, Wendy W. and Peter S. Fader (2002), 'Using advanced purchase orders to forecast new product sales', *Marketing Science*, **21** (3), 347–64.
Rogers, M. (2002), 'The practical futurist: halt! Who goes there?', *Newsweek*, 7 February.
Shugan, Steven M. (2004), 'The impact of advancing technology on marketing and academic research', *Marketing Science*, **23** (4), 469–75.
Shugan, Steven M. and Jinhong Xie (2000), 'Advance pricing of services and other implications of separating purchase and consumption', *Journal of Service Research*, **2** (February), 227–39.
Shugan, Steven M. and Jinhong Xie (2004), 'Advance selling for services', *California Management Review*, **46** (3), 37–55.
Shugan, Steven M. and Jinhong Xie (2005), 'Advance-selling as a competitive marketing tool', *International Journal of Research in Marketing*, **22**, 351–73.
Stavins, Joanna (2001), 'Price discrimination in the airline market: the effect of market concentration', *The Review of Economics and Statistics*, **83** (1), 200–202.
Subramanian, Janakiram, Shaler Shaler and Conrad J. Lautenbacher (1999), 'Airline yield management with overbooking, cancellations, and no-shows', *Transportation Science*, **33** (2), 147–67.
Weatherford, L.R. and S.E. Bodily (1992), 'A taxonomy and research overview of perishable-asset revenue management: yield management, overbooking, and pricing', *Operations Research*, **40**, 831–44.
Xie, Jinhong and Eitan Gerstner (2007), 'Service escape: profiting from customer cancellations', *Marketing Science*, **26** (Spring), 18–30.
Xie, Jinhong and Steven M. Shugan (2001), 'Electronic tickets, smart cards, and online prepayments: when and how to advance sell', *Marketing Science*, **20** (3), 219–43.

22 Pricing and revenue management
Sheryl E. Kimes

Abstract

The focus of this chapter is on the strategic role of price in revenue management (RM). In order to successfully use price as a strategic weapon, firms must address two questions: what prices to charge and how to determine which customers or market segments should be offered those prices. In addition, companies must study and understand both customer and competitive reaction to their use of RM pricing. In this chapter, I address these questions through a review of the relevant literature and of current practice.

Introduction

The focus of this chapter is on the strategic role of price in revenue management (RM). I will first review the revenue management literature and present some of the most commonly used models. Following that, I will discuss how prices are set in practice and provide a review of the relevant literature on how customers react to variable pricing.

Revenue management

Revenue management (RM) has been practiced in the airline (Smith et al., 1992), hotel (Hanks et al., 1992) and car rental industries (Carroll and Grimes, 1995; Geraghty and Johnson, 1997) for over 20 years, and has more recently attracted attention in other industries, including broadcasting (Secomandi et al., 2002), golf (Kimes, 2000), health care (Born et al., 2004), and restaurants (Kimes et al., 1998). RM is applicable to any business that has a relatively fixed capacity of perishable inventory (i.e. seats, rooms, tee times), that inventories demand (either through reservations or wait lists), has a high fixed cost and low variable costs, and that has varying customer price sensitivity. Industries using RM typically report revenue increases of 2–5 percent (Hanks et al., 1992; Kimes, 2004; Smith et al., 1992).

The ability to effectively implement RM strategies in different industries is subject to the various combinations of duration control and variable pricing that exist within each industry (Kimes and Chase, 1998). Figure 22.1 illustrates the various combinations of price and duration and specifies the type of industries that correspond to each combination. The most effective applications of RM are generally found in industries in which both duration and price can be managed (see Quadrant 2). Consequently, it is not surprising that industries traditionally associated with RM (i.e. hotels, airlines, car-rental firms and cruise lines) are those that are able to apply variable pricing for a product or service that has a specified or predictable duration. On the other hand, some businesses (e.g. movie theaters, performing-arts centers, arenas and convention centers) charge a fixed price for a product of predictable duration (Quadrant 1), while still others (e.g. restaurants and golf courses) charge the same price for all customers purchasing a particular product or service, but face a relatively unpredictable duration of customer use (Quadrant 3). Finally, a few industries, such as health care, charge variable prices (e.g. Medicare versus private pay), but do not know the duration of customer use, even though

		PRICING	
		Few	Many
DURATION	Controlled	Quadrant 1 Movies Stadiums/arenas Convention centers Spas	Quadrant 2 Hotels Airlines Rental cars Cruise lines
	Uncontrolled	Quadrant 3 Restaurants Golf courses	Quadrant 4 Continuing care hospitals

Figure 22.1   Typical pricing and duration positioning of selected service industries

some may try to control that duration (Quadrant 4). The lines dividing the quadrants are broken because in reality no fixed demarcation point exists between quadrants; thus an industry may have attributes from more than one quadrant.

As discussed above, companies using RM can deploy two strategic levers, price and duration control (Kimes and Chase, 1998). Pricing can be used in two ways: to determine the optimal prices and to determine who should pay which price (typically through the development of appropriate rate fences). What makes RM pricing different is the presence of excess (or unconstrained) demand. When unconstrained demand exists, firms can select the customers willing to pay the most. Because of this, companies that are successful with RM generally show a strong positive correlation between their capacity utilization percentage and their average rate per person (Canina and Enz, 2006).

Duration can be controlled by better managing customer arrivals (i.e. overbooking and wait list management) or by better managing duration (i.e. length of usage controls). Most of the early (pre-1995) RM research focused on the duration aspect of RM and more specifically focused on various facets of the arrival management question including (1) the forecasted demand for different price categories, (2) the inventory allocation decision (the amount of inventory – whether seats, rooms or cars – to allocate to different price categories) and (3) the overbooking decision. The question of duration control, whether in the context of the multiple flight legs for the airline industry or the multiple-day usage patterns of the car-rental and hotel industries, was not addressed until the early 1990s (Baker and Collier, 1999; Smith et al., 1992; Williamson, 1992). The implementation of this research was slowed because of the need to develop the necessary level of forecast detail (Smith, 2001). For an excellent review of RM research see McGill and van Ryzin (1999) and Boyd and Bilegan (2003).

RM research has been conducted since the late 1950s (Beckmann, 1958), but did not become widespread until the 1990s. Early research (e.g. Littlewood, 1972) focused on the seat inventory allocation problem in the airline industry. Belobaba (1987, 1989), in his work on the expected marginal seat revenue (EMSR) model, further developed Littlewood's earlier research.

The EMSR model considers both fare categories (f_i) and the expected demand for each fare category (d_i). Demand is assumed to be normally distributed and customers booking lower fare classes are assumed to book earlier than those booking higher fare classes. The EMSR model is as follows:

$$\text{EMSR}_i(d_i) = f_i * P_i(d_i)$$

where f_i is the average fare level of the fare class i; and $P_i(d_i)$ is the probability of selling d or more inventory units at a given price.

The model is solved iteratively to set booking limits for each fare class, and the booking limit for the full fare is assumed to be equal to the remaining capacity. Note that the fare classes are considered as a given. Belobaba (1992) later modified the EMSR to better account for the relationship between fare classes. This revision, termed the EMSRb, is one of the most commonly used seat allocation heuristics used in the airline industry.

Linear programming methods have also been used as a basis for RM models. The objective is generally to maximize revenue given capacity and demand constraints over time. Again, rate classes are taken as a given. The basic linear programming formulation is as follows:

$$\text{Max} \sum_{j=1}^{m} \sum_{i=1}^{n} \sum_{t=1}^{p} R_{ij} * A_{ijt}$$

$$\text{Subject to } \sum_{j=1}^{m} \sum_{i=1}^{n} A_{ijt} \leq C_t \text{ for all } t$$

$$A_{ijt} \leq D_{ijt}$$

$$A_{ijt} \geq 0$$

where

i = rate class
j = length of stay
t = time period
A_{ijt} = the number of inventory units to sell for each rate class i, length of stay j, time period t combination,
R_{ij} = the revenue from rate class i and length of stay j combination,
C_t = the capacity at time period t,
D_{ijt} = the forecasted demand for each rate class i length of stay j, time period t combination.

The linear programming formulation is generally approached in one of two ways: (1) as an allocation method in which the decision variables are the number of inventory units to allocate to each rate class; or (2) as a shadow price approach in which the shadow prices associated with the capacity constraints are used to determine which (if any) of the rate classes should be available (Baker and Collier, 1999; Simpson, 1989; Talluri and van Ryzin, 1998; Williamson, 1992). The shadow price approach (also referred to as the network bid price approach) can be used to develop duration controls and allow a firm to move from Quadrant 4 (multiple prices and little duration control) to Quadrant 3 (multiple prices and increased duration control).

Dynamic programming models have also been proposed and allow for better inclusion of the multiple decisions needed over a set time horizon than linear programming-based models (Badinelli, 2000; Bitran and Mondschein, 1995; Lee and Hersh, 1993). Although theoretically appealing, the dynamic programming approach has been stymied because of the size of the problem and the intensive computation required.

Interestingly, very little of the research published before 1995 included price as a variable. Price was considered to be an exogenous variable that was provided by a third party and there appears to have been little consideration for the fact that price might drive demand or that the prices provided may not be optimal. Given that any RM decision is a function of both price and duration, it is essential that RM models include information on the relationship between price and demand, and consider the potential impact of that relationship on revenue maximization.

Most research on integrating the pricing and allocation decision began in the mid-1990s and both deterministic and stochastic models for both the single- and multiple-product problems have been proposed. For an excellent review of pricing research in an RM context, see Bitran and Caldentey (2003) or Elmaghraby and Keskinocak (2003).

Ladany and Arbel (1991), in their article on RM in the cruise line industry, were some of the first to consider the role of price in RM. Weatherford (1997) developed a simultaneous pricing/inventory allocation decision model, but the complexity of his formulation led to the need for simulation to develop reasonable solutions.

Gallego and van Ryzin (1994) studied the optimal pricing decision in situations with stochastic and price-sensitive demand where a firm is trying to maximize revenue. Gallego (1996) developed a simple deterministic model to analyze pricing and market segmentation decisions and presented optimality conditions.

Gallego and van Ryzin (1997) and Zhao and Zheng (2001) studied the problem of dynamically pricing products over a given time so that a firm can maximize revenue. Other studies have looked at similar problems in the retail context (e.g. Bitran et al., 1998; Heching et al., 2002).

Beyond developing an optimal set of prices, a firm must decide on the number of prices (or price buckets) that should be offered (Bitran and Caldentey, 2003; Quain et al., 1999); the maximum number of price changes to make over the selling horizon (Bitran and Caldentey, 2003); the strategy for integrating markdowns, markups and promotions (Bitran and Caldentey, 2003; Bitran et al., 1998; Heching et al., 2002) and the potential impact of price on bundled products (Morwitz et al., 1998; Xia and Monroe, 2004).

The change in research orientation parallels the changes in RM practice. During the 1980s and 1990s, the primary way that RM professionals used price was to ask the marketing department to provide prices and then used their RM system to determine how to best allocate demand to those prices. During the past ten years, RM practice has moved from an operations focus to much more of a marketing orientation in which revenue managers try to develop products/services for particular market segments and price them accordingly. Not surprisingly, this change has also resulted in the movement of the RM function from operations-related departments to sales and marketing departments.

How prices are set in practice
Although some of the pricing research previously described has been adopted by firms in the airline, hotel, car-rental and retail industries, the majority of pricing practices are still non-mathematically based. In practice, most RM prices are set either with competitive pricing or through negotiation. This results in a large number of prices that generally have to be placed into rate categories (or buckets) so that they can be controlled by the RM system.

Competitive pricing
Competitive pricing has become even more important with the growth in the online travel market (Green, 2006). Customers can easily compare prices among competitors by going to any of the large Internet travel sites such as Expedia.com, Travelocity.com or Orbitz.com and specify the date(s) of travel, the location (or origin–destination of the flight) and a particular quality level (hotel type, car type, class of service). They can also compare the price for a particular company across distribution channels (including the company's own website).

Travel firms have mixed feelings about these third-party intermediaries: they like them because of the increased visibility and sales of their products, but do not like the associated cost (often 20–30 percent). In addition, when a company uses multiple distribution channels, they must maintain the same price in each channel because of the potential impact on customer satisfaction. A number of travel firms have instituted lowest rate guarantees in an attempt to reassure customers that the company always offers the best rate available (Rohlfs and Kimes, 2007).

Firms generally obtain competitive information from four sources: (1) phone calls to competitors ('shopping'); (2) global distribution systems (GDS); (3) third-party data providers; and (4) various electronic distribution channels (e.g. Expedia and Travelocity). This information is useful for adjusting overall price levels, but does not really provide detailed competitive pricing information by market segment.

- *Shopping* Many hotels and car-rental companies call their competitors on a daily basis to inquire about rates and availability. Generally, these calls are made as if they were made by a potential customer, but in many cases, the source of the call is known. This information is then used to evaluate the current pricing policies.
- *Global distribution systems (GDS)* Many airline pricing analysts rely on the fares listed in the various GDSs (Sabre, Amadeus, Worldspan and Galileo) to determine what the competition is charging for different origin–destination pairs and use this information to make adjustments in their prices.
- *Third-party data providers* A variety of third-party systems such as Electrobug (www.Electrobug.com), RateGain (www.rategain.com) and TravelClick (www.travelclick.com) search competitive websites on at least a daily basis and provide clients with information on what their competition is charging in various markets. This information is then used to evaluate current pricing policies.
- *Electronic distribution systems* Many of the online travel distribution systems (e.g. Expedia (www.expedia.com) and Travelocity (www.travelocity.com)) provide their suppliers with competitive pricing information. Again, as with the other sources of data, this can be used to evaluate current pricing policies.

Negotiation
Prices for a considerable portion of airline, hotel, car-rental and cruise line industry inventory are set through negotiation. Group and tour operator prices are generally negotiated as are the rates offered to large corporate accounts. The prices are based on demand, the forecasted number of inventory units that will be used, when usage is likely to occur, the ancillary revenue associated with the business, and the long-term value of the business to the firm.

Determining who gets which price
If a company decides to charge multiple prices for essentially the same product, it must differentiate those prices so that customers feel as if they are purchasing different products. For example, consider a hotel that charges three rates ($75, $100 and $125). Customers paying the $125 rate may receive additional services such as 'free breakfast', more desirable rooms and late check-out while those paying the discounted $75 rate may be required to make their reservations well in advance and receive less desirable rooms. The conditions associated with different rate categories (or prices) are referred to as rate fences. Essentially, a rate fence is the reason why people pay different prices.

Rate fences take five basic forms: physical, controlled availability, customer characteristics, transaction characteristics and product line (Dolan and Simon, 1996; Kimes and Wirtz, 2003). Traditionally, rate fences were not always apparent to customers seeking to make a reservation. For example, a car-rental firm could offer lower rates to government employees or to senior citizens, but most customers might not be aware of these lower rates. Internet prices make rate fences much more transparent to customers and, if not well managed, may lead to questions as to why particular groups are given lower rates that may not be available to other customers.

Understanding customer reaction to revenue management pricing
Although better pricing decisions can lead to increased revenue, firms must also consider the impact of pricing on customer satisfaction. Customer satisfaction with pricing is affected by the perceived fairness of those prices (Bolton et al., 2003; Kahneman et al., 1986a, 1986b; Xia et al., 2004), notions of procedural and distributive justice (Smith et al., 1999; Sparks and McColl-Kennedy, 2001; Tax et al., 1998), familiarity with the pricing practice (Kahneman et al., 1986a, 1986b; Wirtz and Kimes, 2007), the relative advantage received from the pricing practice (Xia et al., 2004; Wirtz and Kimes, 2007) and the framing of the prices (Kimes and Wirtz, 2003; Wirtz and Kimes, 2007).

Perceived fairness
If customers believe that a company is behaving in an unfair fashion, they are unlikely to patronize that firm in the future (Kahneman et al., 1986a, 1986b). For example, consider customer reaction to high prices after a natural disaster or high hotel room rates during an important sporting event such as the Olympics or World Cup (Campbell, 1999).

Perceived fairness is strongly affected by the reference price and the reference transaction (Kahneman et al., 1986a, 1986b; Thaler, 1985). When companies use RM, they may alter the reference price and reference transaction and, if they do not carefully plan how to present their pricing practices to customers, may run the risk of customer dissatisfaction.

The principle of dual entitlement (Kahneman et al., 1986a) states that customers believe that they are entitled to a reasonable price and that companies are entitled to a reasonable profit. When this relationship becomes unbalanced in favor of the company, perceptions of unfairness may occur. Based on their research on the principle of dual entitlement, Kahncman et al. (1986a, 1986b) found that: (1) price increases arc seen as acceptable when costs increase; (2) price increases are seen as unacceptable if costs have not increased; and (3) maintaining a price increase is acceptable even if costs go back to their original, lower levels.

There are three ways to offer multiple prices without upsetting customers: raise the reference price, obscure the reference price, and attach restrictions or benefits with different prices (Kahneman et al., 1986a, 1986b):

- *Raise the reference price*   If the reference price (for airlines, this would be the full fare; for hotels, this would be rack rate) is raised, other prices will be seen as relatively low compared to the reference price. For example, airlines frequently use this practice when they offer 'super-saver' fares representing a substantial discount off of the full fare. Since less than 5 percent of airline passengers actually pay full fare, the discount seems a lot better than it actually is.
- *Obscure the reference price*   Firms with excess inventory that they would like to sell at a lower price are often concerned that an extremely low price might send the wrong signal to current and potential guests. If an airline can package a lower-priced airfare with other products (such as a hotel room or rental car), it can obscure the reference price since customers will not know how much the flight actually costs. Tour operators and, more recently, Expedia.com and Travelocity.com, have been very successful at offering packages and allowing travel firms to distribute their inventory while obscuring the actual price of the product.

    In addition, some online travel distribution channels such as Priceline (www.priceline.com) and Hotwire (www.hotwire.com) allow travel firms to easily dispose of their distressed inventory while obscuring the identity of the firm. Companies using these 'opaque' sites (so called because the identity of the company selling the inventory is obscured) can specify the number of inventory units available and the minimum acceptable price. Customers then place bids for an inventory unit in a particular city or for a particular flight, but do not know the identity of the companies providing inventory. If a bid is higher than the minimum acceptable price, it is accepted and the customer is then given the company name. In addition, all of these reservations are non-refundable: if a bid is accepted, the customer's credit card is immediately charged.
- *Benefits and restrictions*   If companies include certain benefits (such as a larger car or free Internet access) with higher rates and attach restrictions (such as time of booking or change penalties) to lower rates, they can effectively differentiate not only the price, but also the inventory unit.
- *Procedural and distributive justice*   Customers also evaluate the fairness of a policy (procedural justice) and the fairness of the outcome of that pricing policy (distributive justice) (Smith el al., 1999; Sparks and McColl-Kennedy, 2001; Tax et al., 1998). It is possible that a customer could consider a policy to be fair (procedural justice), but the outcome resulting from its implementation to be unfair

(distributive justice), and vice versa. For example, customers may feel that a car-rental company's Internet pricing policies are fair but that it is unfair that some people pay more than others.

Familiarity
Perceived fairness is affected by community norms (Monroe, 1976), and perceived fairness of a pricing practice is judged relative to these community norms (i.e. a reference price provides a basis for fairness judgments because it is normal, not necessarily because it is just (Kahneman et al., 1986a, 1986b). This means that reference prices are not static but continually adapt to market conditions (Wirtz and Kimes, 2007).

In an RM context, there is evidence to suggest that customers are shifting their fairness perceptions to community norms. For example, Kimes (1994) showed that RM pricing practices were considered more acceptable for airlines than for hotels in 1994. Interestingly, in a follow-up study eight years later, Kimes and Noone (2002) found that there were no longer significant differences between the acceptability of these same practices in both industries. US golfers and diners are also more accepting of RM practices and find them relatively fair (Kimes and Wirtz, 2002, 2003). As a market becomes more familiar with RM practices, the unfairness perceptions of those practices may decline over time (Wirtz and Kimes, 2007).

Relative advantage
Xia et al. (2004) suggest that perceived price differences can lead to perceptions of advantaged inequality (i.e. the consumer pays less than the reference price or another consumer) or disadvantaged inequality (i.e. the consumer pays more). Every RM pricing practice can be seen from two perspectives: that of the person paying the higher price (e.g. a non-student who pays a full price and cannot take advantage of a special student rate); and that of the person who can take advantage of a lower price through the same fencing mechanism (e.g. a student who pays the discounted student rate).

When there is a wide variation in the prices charged (as is the case with airlines, car-rental companies and hotels), customers are likely to compare the prices they pay with the prices paid by other customers (Bolton et al., 2003; Chen et al., 1998; Martins and Monroe, 1994), and customers who receive a lower price may be seen as receiving an unfair advantage (Adams, 1963). Wirtz and Kimes (2007) found that customers who are familiar with RM pricing practice do not consider relative advantage when assessing the perceived fairness of that practice.

Framing
Price differences can either be presented as a premium or as a discount to regular prices. For example, a restaurant may decide to charge higher prices for weekend dinners. They can either present the higher price as a premium over regular menu prices, or they can position the regular menu price as a discount from the higher weekend prices.

Prospect theory holds that price differences framed as a customer gain (i.e. discounts) as fairer than those framed as a customer loss (i.e. premiums or surcharges), even if the situations are economically equivalent (Chen et al., 1998; Kahneman and Tversky, 1979; Thaler, 1985). RM research has shown that customers view prices presented as a discount as fairer than those presented as a surcharge (Kimes and Wirtz, 2002, 2003; Wirtz and Kimes, 2007).

Summary and conclusion

In this chapter, I have reviewed the literature on RM allocation and pricing models, discussed how RM prices are set in practice and reviewed the literature on customer reaction to prices. As RM practice becomes more sophisticated and as the Internet becomes the customer booking engine of choice, we can expect price to become an even more important component of an RM strategy. The technical pricing models discussed are likely to become much more widely adopted, and models that incorporate competitive reactions to price changes are likely to be developed. Still, as pricing becomes an even more important part of an RM strategy, companies must carefully monitor customer reaction to these policies since a reduction in customer satisfaction may result in lower long-term profitability.

References

Adams, J.S. (1963), 'Towards an understanding of inequity', *Journal of Abnormal and Social Psychology*, **67**, 422–36.
Badinelli, R.D. (2000), 'An optimal, dynamic policy for hotel yield management', *European Journal of Operational Research*, **121**, 476–503.
Baker, T.K. and D.A. Collier (1999), 'A comparative revenue analysis of hotel yield management heuristics', *Decision Sciences*, **30** (1), 239–56.
Beckmann, M.J. (1958), 'Decision and team problems in airline reservations', *Econometrica*, **26** (1), 134–45.
Belobaba, P.P. (1987), 'Airline yield management: an overview of seat inventory control', *Transportation Science*, **21** (2), 63–73.
Belobaba, P.P. (1989), 'Application of a probabilistic decision model to airline seat inventory control', *Operations Research*, **37** (2), 183–97.
Belobaba, P.P. (1992), 'Optimal vs. heuristic methods for nested seat allocation', AGIFORS, Cambridge, MA, USA.
Bitran, G. and R. Caldentey (2003), 'An overview of pricing models for revenue management', *Manufacturing and Service Operations Management*, **5** (3), 203–339.
Bitran, G. and S.V. Mondschein (1995), 'An application of yield management to the hotel industry considering multiple day stays', *Operations Research*, **43** (3), 427–43.
Bitran, G., R. Caldentey and S. Mondschein (1998), 'Coordinating clearance markdown sales of seasonal products in retail chains', *Operations Research*, **46** (5), 609–24.
Bolton, L.E, L. Warlop and J.W. Alba (2003), 'Consumer perceptions of price (un)fairness', *Journal of Consumer Research*, **29** (4), 474–92.
Born, C., M. Carbajal, P. Smith, M. Wallace, K. Abbott, S. Adyanthaya, E. Andrew Boyd, C. Keller, J. Liu, W. New, T. Rieger, B. Winemiller and R. Woestemeyer (2004), 'Contract optimization at Texas Children's Hospital', *Interfaces*, **34** (1), 51–8.
Boyd E.A. and I.C. Bilegan (2003), 'Revenue management and e-commerce', *Management Science*, **49** (10), 1363–86.
Campbell, M.C. (1999), 'Perceptions of price unfairness: antecedents and consequences', *Journal of Marketing Research*, **36** (2), 187–99.
Canina, L. and C.A. Enz (2006), 'Revenue management in US hotels', Cornell University Center for Hospitality Research Report.
Carroll, W.J. and R.C. Grimes (1995), 'Evolutionary change in product management: experiences in the car rental industry', *Interfaces*, **25** (5), 84–104.
Chen, Shih-Fen S., K.B. Monroe and Y. Lou (1998), 'The effects of framing price promotion messages on consumers' perceptions and purchase intentions', *Journal of Retailing*, **74** (3), 353–72.
Dolan, R.J. and H. Simon (1996), *Power Pricing*, New York: The Free Press.
Elmaghraby, W. and P. Keskinocak (2003), 'Dynamic pricing, research overview, current practices and future directions', *Management Science*, **49** (10), 1287–96.
Gallego, G. (1996), 'A demand model for yield management', Technical Report, Columbia University: Department of Industrial Engineering and Operations Research, New York.

Gallego, G. and G. van Ryzin (1994), 'Optimal dynamic pricing of inventories with stochastic demand over finite horizons', *Management Science*, **40** (10), 999–1020.
Gallego, G. and G. van Ryzin (1997),'A multiproduct dynamic pricing problem and its applications to network yield management', *Operations Research*, **45** (1), 24–41.
Geraghty, M.K. and E. Johnson (1997), 'RM saves National Car Rental', *Interfaces*, **27** (1), 107–27.
Green, C.E. (2006), 'Demystifying distribution: building a distribution strategy one channel at a time', TIG Global Special Report, Hospitality Sales and Marketing Institute.
Hanks, R.D., R.G. Cross and R.P. Noland (1992), 'Discounting in the hotel industry: a new approach', *Cornell Hotel and Restaurant Administration Quarterly*, **33** (February), 15–23.
Heching, A., G. Gallego and G. van Ryzin (2002), 'Mark-down pricing: an empirical analysis of policies and revenue potential at one apparel retailer', *Journal of Revenue and Pricing Management*, **1** (2), 139–60.
Kahneman, D. and A. Tversky (1979), 'Prospect theory: an analysis of decision under risk', *Econometrica*, **47** (2), 263–91.
Kahneman, D., J.L. Knetsch and R.H. Thaler (1986a), 'Fairness as a constraint on profit seeking: entitlements in the market', *American Economic Review*, **76**, 728–41.
Kahneman, D., J.L. Knetch and R.H. Thaler (1986b), 'Fairness and the assumptions of economics', *Journal of Business*, **59** (4), 285–300.
Kimes, S.E. (1994), 'Perceived fairness of yield management', *Cornell Hotel and Administration Quarterly*, **35** (1), 22–9.
Kimes, S.E. (2000), 'Revenue management on the links: applying yield management to the golf-course industry', *Cornell Hotel and Restaurant Administration Quarterly*, **41** (1), 120–27.
Kimes, S.E. (2004), 'Revenue management: implementation at Chevys Arrowhead', *Cornell Hotel and Restaurant Administration Quarterly*, **44** (4), 52–67.
Kimes, S.E. and R.B. Chase (1998), 'The strategic levers of yield management', *Journal of Service Research*, **1** (2), 156–66.
Kimes, S.E. and B.M. Noone (2002), 'Perceived fairness of yield management: an update', *Cornell Hotel and Restaurant Administration Quarterly*, **43** (1), 28–9.
Kimes, S.E. and J. Wirtz (2002), 'Perceived fairness of RM in the U.S. golf industry', *Journal of Revenue and Pricing Management*, **1** (4), 332–44.
Kimes, S.E. and J. Wirtz (2003), 'Has RM become acceptable? Findings from an international study on the perceived fairness of rate fences', *Journal of Service Research*, **6** (2), 125–35.
Kimes, S.E., R.B. Chase, S. Choi, E.N. Ngonzi and P.Y. Lee (1998), 'Restaurant revenue management', *Cornell Hotel and Restaurant Administration Quarterly*, **39** (3), 40–45.
Ladany, S.P. and A. Arbel (1991), 'Optimal cruise-liner passenger cabin pricing policy', *European Journal of Operational Research*, **55**, 136–47.
Lee, T.C. and M. Hersh (1993), 'A model for dynamic airline seat inventory control with multiple seat bookings', *Transportation Science*, **27** (3), 252–65.
Littlewood, K. (1972), 'Forecasting and control of passenger bookings', AGIFORS Symposia.
Martins, M. and K.B. Monroe (1994), 'Perceived price fairness: a new look at an old construct', *Advances in Consumer Research*, **21**, 75–8.
McGill, J.I. and G.J. van Ryzin (1999), 'Revenue management: research overview and prospects', *Transportation Science*, **33** (2), 233–56.
Monroe, K.B. (1976), 'The influence of price differences and brand familiarity on brand preferences', *Journal of Consumer Research*, **3** (June), 42–9.
Morwitz, Vicki G., Eric A. Greenleaf and Eric J. Johnson (1998), 'Divide and prosper: consumers' reactions to partitioned prices', *Journal of Marketing Research*, **35**: 453–68.
Quain, W.J., M. Sansbury and D. Quinn (1999), 'Revenue enhancement, Part 2', *Cornell Hotel and Restaurant Administration Quarterly*, **40** (2), 76–81.
Rohlfs, K.V. and S.E. Kimes (2007), 'Customer perceptions of best available rates', *Cornell Hotel and Restaurant Administration Quarterly*, **48** (2), 151–62.
Secomandi, N., K. Abbott, T. Atam and E.A. Boyd (2002), 'From revenue management concepts to software systems', *Interfaces*, **32** (2), 1–11.
Simpson, R.W. (1989), 'Using network flow techniques to find shadow prices for market and seat inventory control', Cambridge, MA, MIT Flight Transportation Laboratory.
Smith, A., R. Bolton and J. Wagner (1999), 'A model of customer satisfaction with service encounters involving failure and recovery', *Journal of Marketing Research*, **34**, 356–72.
Smith, B.C. (2001), Personal communication.
Smith, B.C., J.F. Leimkuhler and R.D. Darrow (1992), 'Yield management at American Airlines', *Interfaces*. **22** (1): 8–31.
Sparks, B.A. and J. McColl-Kennedy (2001), 'Justice strategy and options for increased customer satisfaction in a services recovery setting', *Journal of Business Research*, **54** (3), 209–18.

Talluri, K. and G. van Ryzin (1998), 'An Analysis of bid-price controls for network revenue management', *Management Science*, **44** (11), 1577–93.
Tax, S., S. Brown and M. Chandrashekaran (1998), 'Customer evaluation of service complaint experiences: implications for relationship marketing', *Journal of Marketing*, **62** (2), 60–76.
Thaler, R.F. (1985), 'Mental accounting and consumer choice', *Marketing Science*, **4** (3), 199–214.
Weatherford, L.R. (1997), 'Optimization of joint pricing and allocation perishable revenue management problems with cross-elasticity', *Journal of Combinatorial Optimization*, **1**, 277–304.
Williamson, E.L. (1992), 'Airline network seat inventory control: methodologies and revenue impacts', MIT Flight Transportation Laboratory Report.
Wirtz, J. and S.E. Kimes (2007), 'The moderating role of familiarity in fairness perceptions of revenue management pricing', *Journal of Service Research*, **9** (3), 229–40.
Xia, Lan and Kent B. Monroe (2004), 'Price partitioning on the Internet', *Journal of Interactive Marketing*, **18**(4), 63–73.
Xia, L., K.B. Monroe and J.L. Cox (2004), 'The price is unfair! A conceptual framework of price fairness perceptions', *Journal of Marketing*, **68** (October), 1–15.
Zhao, W. and Y. Zheng (2001), 'A dynamic model for airline seat allocation with passenger diversion and no-shows', *Transportation Science*, **35**(1), 80–98.

23 Pharmaceutical pricing
*Samuel H. Kina and Marta Wosinska**

Abstract
In this chapter, we discuss the multiple institutional characteristics that affect prescription drug pricing. We organize our discussion around the 5Cs that define the prescription drug industry: companies (the innovative process), competitors (the limits of patent protections), customers (how insurance markets affect pricing), collaborators (roles played by physicians and various channel players), and context (government regulation of pricing). We conclude the chapter with implications for drug pricing research. We categorize areas for future research in three distinct areas. First, future research should continue to clarify the nature of the current market. Second, we believe that more research is needed on how to optimize the current system. Finally, given the dynamic nature of the regulatory and institutional environment that defines the pharmaceutical industry, continued research on how these changes influence pricing will be needed as the industry continues to evolve.

1. Introduction

The reader might ask at this point why devote a special chapter to pharmaceuticals and make it the only chapter in the whole book devoted to a specific category. The answer to this question is twofold. First, the pharmaceutical industry is of particular interest not only because of its sheer size (five times the entire cosmetics industry and ten times the personal computers industry) and its leading place in marketing expenditures (it spends more on sales force than any other industry and it ranks among the most advertised to consumers), but also due to availability of detailed data that allow researchers to study many general marketing phenomena such as sales force effectiveness, product adoption, social networks, or optimal marketing mix allocation. The caveat is that it is an industry with many institutional characteristics that affect pricing. This leads us to the second and perhaps the primary reason for this chapter – a diligent researcher must understand how industry dynamics affect the critical aspect of pricing, whether or not it is the primary focus of his or her research.

In our exploration, we focus on four critical facets that contribute to how pharmaceutical prices are determined. First, in contrast to the case for most other products, consumers of prescription drugs rarely make consumption decisions on their own. Rather, many different actors influence which drugs patients consume. Patients use physicians as learned intermediaries whose education, experience and access to specialized tools allow them to diagnose the patient's health problem and determine the appropriate treatment. The physician acts as an agent for the patient, but this agency may be imperfect because the objectives of the physician and patient may not coincide.[1] Insurers and pharmacy

---

* Disclaimer: this chapter was prepared by the authors in their private capacities. No official support or endorsement by the US Food and Drugs Administration is intended or should be inferred.
[1] For example, suppose two drugs, A and B, treat a given condition. All else equal, an insured patient may prefer the cheaper drug A (as determined by the benefit manager), but his physician may prefer to prescribe drug B because she believes it to be of higher quality, she is more familiar

benefit managers (PBMs), who often administer drug benefits for insurers, also influence consumption patterns by determining what patients need to pay out-of-pocket for various drug alternatives.

Second, widespread insurance coverage shields patients from the true cost of prescription drugs. In the USA, over 80 percent of people have some form of prescription drug coverage, and high levels of private or public insurance coverage are common in many other nations. The discrepancy between patient prices and retail prices distorts consumer demand for prescription drugs. Aside from the increase in consumption levels, insurance also distorts choices between different drugs when patients do not face the true price differences among different drugs. Perhaps because out-of-pocket payments for insured patients have so little to do with actual retail prices, it is standard terminology to refer to 'patient costs' rather than 'patient prices'.

Third, pharmaceutical prices are influenced by the presence of the patent system, which ensures products a degree of market power while the patent is active but also imposes a well-defined life cycle to the product. A product will face dramatically different pricing environments over its life cycle, with greater ability to maintain higher markups while the patent is active, and then by operating in a highly competitive environment, which is created when generic competitors enter the market.

Fourth, many countries regulate prices of prescription drugs because of their payer role and the political importance of healthcare to voters. However, the standard notion of efficient pricing at marginal cost of production – the goal of regulators in other contexts – is not sustainable in a research-intensive industry like pharmaceuticals where the marginal cost is negligible while R&D is incredibly costly. This extreme divergence between marginal cost of production and fixed costs creates a tension between static and dynamic efficiency. Pricing at marginal cost would maximize static efficiency but would halt future development in the industry. Higher price, on the other hand, promotes dynamic efficiency, giving pharmaceutical firms an incentive to invest in R&D and introduce new products (Berndt, 2002) while lowering current consumer welfare.

In our presentation, we follow the 5Cs framework so commonly used in marketing analyses, organizing our discussion around the companies, competitors, customers, channels and context that define the prescription drug industry. We begin in Section 2 by discussing some high-level industry statistics before turning to the innovative process and the typical product life cycle imposed by patents. In Section 3, we expand on this discussion with a description of the competitive framework that the drug patent system presents. We then explore how the insurance market affects pricing in Section 4. The subsequent discussion of collaborators is divided into two parts: in Section 5 we discuss the role of physicians and then follow that with a detailed discussion of channel players and their role in drug pricing in Section 6. To complete our 5Cs analysis, in Section 7 we analyze the regulatory constraints placed on pharmaceutical prices. We conclude the chapter with implications for pricing research.

As a final note, we would like to point out that, for several reasons, we primarily focus on the US market. First, the USA is the largest national market for prescription drugs,

---

with that product, she is influenced by detailing for drug B, etc. See McGuire (2000) for an exhaustive review of the physician–patient relationship.

with more than 40 percent of global sales (IMS Health, 2006). Second, facing less regulation, the US market presents greater opportunities for marketing research than is more generally applicable to other product categories. For example, there is significantly less government regulation of pricing in the USA and it is also one of only two countries that allow direct-to-consumer advertising. Finally, we expect that most marketing researchers will have access to US data reinforcing our focus on this market. Therefore, unless we make specific references to international markets, the reader can assume that our discussion pertains to the US market. For similar reasons we focus on drugs available through the retail channel rather than physician-administered drugs such as oncology drugs.

2. Companies

The pharmaceutical industry comprises companies that develop, manufacture, distribute and market branded and generic drugs. In general, companies focus on developing either branded drugs or generics because the respective business models are sufficiently different. For example, the branded drug business model requires very heavy investments in R&D and marketing, while the generic drug model requires particularly strong competence in manufacturing, channel management and patent litigation.

Global pharmaceutical sales have grown on the order of 10 percent per year, rising to $602 billion in 2005 with the top ten firms accounting for 45 percent of this total (Forbes. com, 2006; IMS Health, 2006). Because of the discrepancy in general price levels between branded and generic drugs, dollar sales are weighted more towards branded drugs and thus are a better representation of drug spending, while unit sales better represent actual utilization. Although prescription drugs, both branded and generic, account for only about 10 percent of total health spending in the USA, it is the fastest-growing segment of health care spending, and in 2005, 20 percent of all out-of-pocket spending was for prescription drugs compared to 17 percent for physicians and clinical services, and 8 percent for hospital care.[2]

A new prescription drug is the outcome of a process that can take many years from discovery to regulatory approval, cost hundreds of millions of dollars, and tie up valuable capital that could be used in other ventures. Firms that bring these products to market spend heavily on R&D, and, although patents impose a finite lifespan on brand name pharmaceuticals, the profit opportunities that they furnish encourage such investments.

2.1 R&D

Product innovation in the pharmaceutical industry is characterized by high research and development costs. DiMasi and colleagues (2003) surveyed ten large manufacturers and estimate that the average economic cost of bringing a new drug to market is $802 million.[3] This probably overestimates the average development cost for all patented drugs because it focuses only on new chemical entities (NCEs) and does not consider the cost of reformulations of existing products, such as extended release versions of a pill (Frank, 2003). Nonetheless it does capture the fact that bringing a new product to

---

[2] Authors' calculations from the National Health Accounts (http://www.cms.hhs.gov/NationalHealthExpendData)

[3] Economic costs include the opportunity cost of capital that is tied up in the R&D process.

market can be exceedingly expensive even though pharmaceutical research is now potentially more efficient than ever, thanks to more effective methods and technologies such as high-throughput screening and rational drug design. What counteracts improvements in research methods is the reality that many of the foremost targets of pharmaceutical research are more complex than the pharmacological challenges of years past. The most common explanation for this is that all of the low-hanging fruit has been picked, and the recent drop in Food and Drug Administration (FDA) approvals for NCEs would seem to support this contention.[4] These high research costs are coupled with the regulatory pressures to have even more extensive and expensive clinical trials, thereby further driving up development costs.

The high cost of bringing a new product to market influences the pricing dynamics we observe in the pharmaceutical industry. First, R&D costs represent an imposing barrier to entry that limits the competition that firms face, which in turn allows incumbents to sustain higher prices. Second, because R&D costs are so high, firms must be able to expect significant profits if they are to continue investing in innovation. The relationship between profitability and innovation is well documented (Abbott and Vernon, 2005; Giaccotto et al., 2005; Scherer, 2001). Patents are an important tool through which governments attempt to mitigate the innovation problems that arise when lower expected returns make continued investments in R&D less attractive.

2.2 The product life cycle

Governments use patents to compensate for the potential dynamic inefficiency that stems from high development costs. Patents encourage innovation by granting a limited period of market exclusivity to firms that develop new pharmaceutical products. This shapes the characteristic life cycle for pharmaceutical products that can end within months of patent expiration depending on how quickly generic competitors enter the market. Patents remain active for 20 years from the date of filing, but because firms file patents before beginning clinical trials, the average effective patent life is 11.5 years (PhRMA, 2006). While a patent can forestall direct competition, it does not secure monopoly power because a patented molecule has to compete with other distinct molecules approved to treat the same general condition.

Patent holders may attempt to extend the patent life of their drugs in a variety of ways. For example, generic entry could be delayed if patents were staggered so that, for example, the molecule patent expires at a different time than the patent on the production process or delivery method.[5] Occasionally firms obtain patent extensions for reasons unrelated to changes in the underlying product – consider the relatively common six-month extension for filing a pediatric indication or the two-year extension Claritin received in an addendum to the 1994 GATT treaty.[6] Brand name manufacturers can also introduce new presentations (e.g. change dosage strength, delivery mechanism, or form)

---

[4] See Cockburn (2006) for a discussion of productivity in the pharmaceutical industry.
[5] Many drugs hold multiple patents, which are filed and approved on different dates. Information on patents is available from the FDA Orange Book, which lists information about all approved patents for prescription drugs. http://www.fda.gov/cder/ob/.
[6] Stephen Hall, 'The Claritin effect', *New York Times Magazine*, 11 March 2001.

of an existing product in the year prior to patent expiration.[7] This subsequently requires that competing firms either incur higher entry costs as they develop generic versions of each formulation or risk reducing the potential market share that they can capture. In addition, patent holders sometimes launch their own authorized generic products, license authorized generics to another generic manufacturer, or reduce the price of their branded product prior to patent expiration.

3. Competitors

Patents protect pharmaceutical products from direct competition of same-molecule copycats for a period of time – 20 years in the USA. However, patents cannot completely foreclose competition, because they do not prevent competing manufacturers from bringing to market distinct molecules to treat the same condition. Once patents expire, generic manufacturers are free to introduce products that are virtually undifferentiated from the branded product, which heightens competition, reduces the average price for a molecule, and ultimately often results in a shrinking market because of diminished marketing support by manufacturers.

3.1 Brand name drugs

While a prescription drug is under patent protection, the market conditions it faces can best be described as an oligopoly with a number of differentiated, patent-protected products competing within a therapeutic class. As distinct molecules, they may work through a different chemical pathway and thus vary in efficacy, they may target patients with different risk factors or slightly different symptoms, and they may have different side-effect profiles. Because of high entry costs associated with developing a distinct drug molecule, entry into a given therapeutic class is limited, although larger markets tend to attract more entrants (Scott Morton, 1999).

Brand name products are often categorized as either innovative or 'me-too' drugs based on how much therapeutic advantage they represent over existing drugs in a therapeutic class. This distinction is a significant factor explaining launch prices of drugs (Lu and Comanor, 1998). Drugs that represent significant therapeutic advantages over existing drugs in a therapeutic class launch, on average, at prices three times higher than other brand name drugs in that class. 'Me-too' drugs, on the other hand, generally introduce modest improvements over existing products, and therefore add a measure of price competition into the market. Lu and Comanor (1998) find that launch prices of me-too drugs are comparable to the average price of existing drugs in the market. They also find that the number of drugs in a therapeutic class reduces entry prices and that long-run pricing strategies differ by drug type. Innovative drugs in their sample drugs followed a skimming strategy with high initial prices that fall over time, while 'me-too' drugs employed a penetration strategy with entry prices low, in order to gain market share, but rising over time.

---

[7] Ellison and Ellison (2000) find that firms are most likely to deter entry in medium-sized markets. They explain that entry deterrence is less common in small and large markets because it is not worthwhile to deter entry in small markets that attract fewer generic entrants, and deterrence strategies will not be effective in large markets where the payoff to entry is sufficiently high.

Non-price competition is equally, if not more, important. Researchers looking at strategies related to the order of entry have found that 'me-too' entrants into a therapeutic class would launch at prices similar to the breakthrough incumbent but they would pursue non-price competition in the form of heavy physician marketing (Berndt et al., 1997). In fact new drug introduction is always accompanied by large investments in product promotion regardless of the type of therapeutic advantage that a new product brings to market. Bhattacharya and Vogt (2003) empirically support a model showing that pharmaceutical manufacturers do this to build product recognition and consumer goodwill, which helps facilitate rising prices later in the product life cycle.

3.2 Generic competition

The competitive environment facing a prescription drug changes considerably with patent expiration. The rules governing the launch of generic pharmaceutical products in the USA were set forth in the Drug Price Competition and Patent Term Restoration Act of 1984 (the so-called Hatch–Waxman Act). Hatch–Waxman altered the FDA's approval process so that generic entrants need only to demonstrate that their product is bioequivalent to the brand name product without having to conduct costly safety and efficacy trials. Moreover, under the Hatch–Waxman rules, generic manufacturers are allowed to produce the patented molecule, and submit their marketing applications to the FDA while the original patent is still in effect. This significantly lowers barriers to entry, thereby opening the market up to potentially intense competition. In markets with at least one generic molecule, own- and cross-price elasticities for branded products appear to be higher than in markets with no generic competition (Ellison et al., 1997). In other words, demand is much more sensitive to the prices of a drug and its competitors in the presence of generic products.

Even when a patent expires, generic entry may not have an immediate effect on the prices that consumers pay for a given molecule. Under the Hatch–Waxman rules, the first generic entrant to obtain FDA approval can earn a market exclusivity period of 180 days and thereby delay the further entry of competing generic products.[8] During this period, the generic manufacturer shares the market only with the original innovator company, which may or may not choose to compete directly with the generic. The generally higher level of pricing sustained during the exclusivity period creates an incentive to be the first to gain FDA approval. During this exclusivity period, the first generic entrant tends to set a price equal to about 80 percent of the brand name price (Berndt et al., 2007; Reiffen and Ward, 2005).

Generic drug prices fall as additional entrants come into the market (Caves et al., 1991; Grabowski and Vernon, 1992; Frank and Salkever, 1997) and approach marginal cost only after several generic firms enter the market (Reiffen and Ward, 2005). But this need not happen in all markets because intense competition depends on the attractiveness of market entry, which varies across therapeutic categories. Not surprisingly, large markets are the most attractive (Ellison and Ellison, 2000). Drugs that treat chronic conditions and drugs that are administered in inpatient settings are also attractive targets for generic entry because consumers have more elastic demand, so they are more likely to switch to

---

[8] http://www.fda.gov/cder/about/smallbiz/generic_exclusivity.htm.

the generic product (Scott-Morton, 1999). Mandatory substitution laws and the emergence of pharmacy benefit managers (PBMs) that encourage switching to generic products encourage a fairly rapid rate of generic penetration, which further boosts generic entry.[9]

Most of the evidence pertaining to how incumbent prices respond to generic entry is based on data that pre-date the rise of managed care. In addition, the findings conflict on how manufacturers respond to entry, perhaps because the data used in these studies do not properly capture off-invoice price concessions. Caves et al. (1991) model markups for prescription drugs as a function of a drug's age, patent status, and drug-specific effects such as the type of condition that it treats and where the drug is primarily dispensed. They test their model using the prices of a sample of drugs that lost patent protection between 1978 and 1987 and find that, while the prices of some brand name drugs continued to rise after patent expiration, they increased more slowly than they would have in the absence of generic entry. They find that brand name list prices are declining in the number of generic entrants, and list prices faced by hospitals are much more sensitive to generic entry than are retail list prices. In contrast, Grabowski and Vernon (1992) and Frank and Salkever (1992, 1997) use pricing data from a similar period of time (1983–87 and 1984–87 respectively) and find that over time brand name list prices rise relative to those of generic drugs. Frank and Salkever propose that market segmentation explains this pricing behavior. Once generic firms enter, brand name manufacturers focus on less elastic segments of the market rather than trying to compete with generic products. Thus volume falls, but pharmaceutical firms are able to raise prices for the less elastic customers that remain.

These segmentation-based pricing patterns are probably less attractive now that most states have generic substitution laws that allow pharmacists to fill prescriptions with generic drugs when available. (Note that these generic substitution laws apply only to same-molecule switches and not cross-molecule substitutions.) Even without such laws, the majority of insured patients carry plans that utilize formularies to encourage switching to generic products by increasing the co-payment for the branded version and lowering the co-payment for the generic versions of a drug. As managed care has become more prevalent, the inelastic share of the market has shrunk considerably, and it may no longer be profitable to target this share of the market upon patent expiry.

An alternative strategy to increasing brand name price upon patent expiration is for brand name manufacturers to introduce their own generic products and directly compete with generic copycats. Because there would be no entry costs, this is a winning proposition if the firm can earn more profits during the generic exclusivity period than if they were to focus on the inelastic side of the market. In 2006 Merck followed a similar strategy when it negotiated a deal with United Healthcare and Blue Shield of California to dramatically lower the price in exchange for more favorable consumer-level pricing, which is opposite to what is typically done. When the branded version of a drug loses patent, insurers usually require that patients pay more out of pocket for the brand version of that drug (Won Tesoriero and Martinez, 2006). How such a strategy plays out remains

---

[9] Berndt and colleagues give the example of Paxil, which lost 70 percent of its market share to generic entrants within two months (Berndt et al., 2007).

to be seen, but this kind of competitive threat from a branded manufacturer could lower incentives for generic manufacturers to challenge patents.

4. Customers

In the market for pharmaceutical products, the end-user, payer and decision-maker roles are shared by distinct parties: patients, insurance companies and physicians. In this section we focus on distinctions between the end-user and payer roles and on their implications for pricing.

4.1 Insurance

In most industrialized countries, national governments are the predominant source of health insurance coverage. This contrasts with the USA, where employers provide health insurance coverage and, in almost all cases, prescription drug benefits for approximately 60 percent of the population. Twenty-seven percent of the US population receives some form of government health insurance such as Medicare for those 65 years and older (13.7 percent), Medicaid for the disabled and qualified low-income citizens (13.0 percent) or military health insurance (3.8 percent).[10] There is some overlap between the employer and government-sponsored groups, as some Medicare beneficiaries also obtain supplementary retirement coverage through their former employers or are eligible for Medicaid. Both Medicaid and Medicare cover prescription drugs, but prior to the 2006 implementation of the prescription drug benefit for the elderly (the so-called Medicare Part D), more than a quarter of the population eligible for Medicare lacked any sort of prescription drug coverage.[11]

Insurance distorts consumption patterns by creating a divergence between what a patient pays and what a retail pharmacy charges for the drug. As a result, insurance may effectively lower the elasticity of demand for pharmaceuticals. Because insurance reduces the out-of-pocket cost, it may also increase the quantity of pharmaceutical products consumed as insured patients may choose to take drugs that they might not have been willing to pay for were they facing their full cost.

Many private insurers and government-sponsored plans use a variety of cost management strategies to influence patient behavior to mitigate the adverse effect of health insurance coverage. Once such measure is the drug formulary – a preferred list of drugs that a PBM selects based on efficacy, side-effect profile, and cost-effectiveness. Being a list, it will affect utilization patterns only if it is aligned with proper incentives. Common tiered formularies require varying levels of cost-sharing from patients. A common structure for a tiered formulary is to require no or minimal cost-sharing for generic drugs (e.g. a flat fee of $5 for a 30-day supply of pills), higher for brand name drugs that have 'preferred' designation (e.g. $15 for a 30-day supply), and often significantly higher for drugs that are not on the preferred list (e.g. $45 for a monthly supply). When cost-sharing relies on a fixed dollar fee for each prescription, it is referred to as co-payment. This is in contrast

---

[10] US Census Bureau, 'Income, poverty, and health insurance coverage in the United States: 2005', http://www.census.gov/prod/2006pubs/p60-231.pdf. Percentages do not add up because some people are eligible for more than one type of coverage.

[11] Kaiser Family Foundation, Prescription Drug Trends Fact Sheet, November 2005, http://www.kff.org/insurance/upload/3057-04.pdf.

to co-insurance, which requires patients to pay a defined percentage of the total cost, usually also increasing with tier preference.

4.2 Effects of insurance on price sensitivity

Much of the early empirical evidence on the effect of health insurance on prescription drug consumption comes from the RAND Health Insurance Experiment (Newhouse and the Insurance Experiment Group, 1993), which assigned people to plans with different levels of prescription drug coverage and found that those who were enrolled in plans with higher cost-sharing requirement consumed fewer prescription drugs.

Gibson et al. (2005) provide a review of recent research on the effects of cost-sharing on drug consumption. As a whole, the evidence that they review supports the notion that insurers can use tiered formularies to alter patient consumption patterns. It has been found, for example, that increasing the number of tiers in a formulary and thus the out-of-pocket prices for some drugs, changes the mix of drugs consumed but not the total volume of drugs consumed (Huskamp et al., 2005). Other research reports that elasticity of demand varies across different therapeutic classes and types of treatment. In particular, demand elasticity ranges from -0.1 to -0.16 for chronic conditions and from -0.6 to -0.24 for acute conditions (Landsman et al., 2005; Goldman et al., 2004).

The studies above show that insurers can influence both the total amount of drugs consumed and choices among drugs by changing the out-of-pocket costs that patients pay. While these studies do not consider prices charged by manufacturers, their results imply that, by influencing consumer behavior, changes in out-of-pocket costs could lead to downward pressure on drugs prices. Pavcnik (2002) explicitly addresses this question, taking advantage of a change in reimbursement practices in Germany in 1989 to analyze how drug prices respond to changes in out-of-pocket spending. These new reimbursement rules made patients responsible for the full cost difference of a specific drug in a therapeutic class and other, more expensive drugs that they might wish to consume. Using a sample of anti-diabetics and anti-ulcer drugs, Pavcnik demonstrates that the policy change led to lower prices for all drugs in those classes by 10 percent to 26 percent, with particularly dramatic decreases occurring among branded drugs.

4.3 Search and switching behavior

The existence of search costs and switching costs in a market leads to higher prices and greater price dispersion. Search costs are a feature of prescription drug markets that is particularly relevant for cash-paying customers who potentially face price dispersion among like drugs across different pharmacies. Sorensen (2000) models search behavior for patients consuming prescription drugs, where a patient will continue going from one pharmacy to the next if the expected benefits from searching exceed the cost of searching. The patient will stop searching once they believe that they cannot make themselves any better off through shopping around. Sorensen documents considerable price dispersion and high search costs for cash-paying customers. The findings are telling – even when patients are responsible for the full cost of the drugs that they consume, they are either not willing to or not able to gather enough information about prescription drugs on their own to limit price dispersion.

Patients who have insurance coverage do not face this kind of price dispersion because their co-payments are pegged to the formulary status of the drug rather than its retail price. However, insured patients also face costs in their search for the best drug match for them. Gaining the requisite knowledge to effectively evaluate products can be costly for patients, and, indeed, this is one of the reasons why patients rely on physicians to make the choice for them. As we discuss in more detail below, physicians also face search costs that may influence their prescribing choices. Crawford and Shum (2005) observe a sample of patients taking anti-ulcer drugs in Italy and find that very few patients diverge from the initial prescription. This suggests that either the initial prescription is a good match, that there is considerable risk aversion towards switching among patients or doctors, or that search costs of finding a better match are too high. It is important to note that patients are weighing the search cost against the expected benefit, which may not be accurate if patients are not well informed about the quality or existence of different products. Because search costs dampen price shopping, high search costs could contribute to higher prices even when several products exist within a therapeutic class.

5. Collaborators

For the most part, physicians neither consume nor pay for the drugs they prescribe for their patients, but they nonetheless have an institutionalized role as the primary decision-maker. After diagnosing a problem, physicians determine not only whether drug therapy is appropriate, but also what drug and dose should be prescribed. Presumably, physicians' primary objective is to offer their patients a level of care consistent with broadly accepted best practices, but it is not so clear that they have the incentive to account for economic considerations when prescribing a drug. The most medically effective care may not necessarily be the most cost-effective care, and when applied to prescribing behavior, this could be manifested in prescriptions whose marginal value is less than the marginal cost over another drug that treats the same condition. Furthermore, physicians face severe time constraints, making it costly for them to take the time to learn about new pharmaceutical products. While brand name drugs are heavily marketed, generic manufacturers do not promote their products, so it takes relatively more effort for physicians to learn about new generic products.

Despite their lack of direct financial involvement in the decision, research shows that physicians do sometimes alter their behavior in response to cost considerations. There are several reasons for this. First, insurers and PBMs can directly entice physicians to prescribe certain drugs over others. This approach is particularly effective in settings where physician salary is tied to performance on the cost-effectiveness front, as in the case of staff health maintenance organizations. Patients' economic considerations also play a role, despite the general belief to the contrary. According to the Kaiser Family Foundation (2006), 53 percent of physicians frequently discuss out-of-pocket costs with patients when they prescribe drugs. This finding is supported by research showing that tiered patient co-payments matter (Huskamp et al., 2005). This is especially apparent when patients have no insurance coverage or have limited resources (Reichert et al., 2000; Hux and Naylor, 1994).

Nonetheless, physicians neither fully internalize the patient's price incentives nor the insurer's cost burden. This further exacerbates the incentive distortion posed by insurance. This effect is also magnified by the fact that physicians tend to prescribe habitually, with many doctors persistently prescribing brand name drugs after generics have become available (Hellerstein, 1998). The stickiness of prescribing patterns allows brand name firms to maintain higher prices upon generic entry; although, in the case of generics, the impact of this behavior is mitigated somewhat by the fact that pharmacists are generally allowed to substitute generics when available.[12] Habitual prescribing also helps differentiate products within a therapeutic class, which, according to economic theory, should lead to higher prices.

6. Channels

Because the resale of prescription drugs is closely regulated, pharmaceutical manufacturers can charge very different prices to different buyers without facing the threat of arbitrage (Frank, 2001). These negotiated prices are commonly not available to parties outside the agreement. Therefore, when describing channel structures in the pharmaceutical industry, it is worthwhile to distinguish between the channel structure for the physical product distribution and the financial flow. The former has the typical channel structure that involves wholesalers and retailers. The latter is complicated by the existence of the insurance system, which introduces new players and payments that sidestep the channel partners involved in the physical distribution of the product. We follow this logic after a brief introduction of the various players involved in the distribution and reimbursement of prescription drugs. The discussion in this chapter draws heavily on conversations with industry insiders, on recent reports by the CBO and the Kaiser Family Foundation (CBO, 2007; Kaiser Family Foundation, 2005), and on Kolassa (1997). We summarize some of the key pricing terms in Box 23.1.

6.1 Channel players

Wholesalers Approximately two-thirds of all US prescription drug sales flow through wholesalers (CBO, 2007). The wholesale function is highly concentrated in the top three firms, McKesson, Cardinal Health and AmerisourceBergen, holding an 80 percent market share in 2005 (Kaiser Family Foundation, 2005). Wholesalers distribute products to different types of pharmacies and to some non-retail buyers such as hospitals and nursing homes.

Pharmacies There is a wide spectrum of pharmacy ownership forms: chain pharmacies (e.g. CVS, Duane Reade, Walgreens), mass merchandisers (e.g. Costco, Wal-Mart, Target), food supermarkets (e.g. Safeway, Albertsons), independent pharmacies and mail order pharmacies. Chain pharmacies account for the largest share of the market with over 40 percent of the dollar and unit share (see Table 23.1). The fastest-growing pharmacy segment includes mail pharmacies, of which the largest ones are owned by PBMs. Because mail pharmacy prescriptions are generally for 90 days rather than the standard 30 days in retail, they represent a disproportionate share of dollars (relative to units measured by prescriptions). In addition, these pharmacies dispense a disproportionate share of typically newer and more expensive drugs that treat chronic conditions (Wosinska and Huckman, 2004).

---

[12] Line extensions, such as 'extended release' or 'extra strength' may limit the effect of such mandatory substitution laws because such formulations are not affected by them.

BOX 23.1 KEY PRICING TERMS

Average manufacturer price (AMP) AMP is the average price that wholesalers pay to manufacturers for a drug that is distributed through the retail pharmacy channel. AMP incorporates all discounts that the wholesaler negotiates with the manufacturer, but does not include any rebates that insurers or PBMs negotiate. Congress established the AMP in 1990 as a way to calculate rebates for Medicaid prescription drug expenditures.

Wholesale acquisition cost (WAC) WAC is generally the price that manufacturers charge wholesalers. This price does not include any of the discounts that the wholesaler receives.

Average wholesale price (AWP) AWP does not actually represent any average price and it does not reflect what wholesalers pay. Instead, it is best thought of as a benchmark price that may be used as a reference for negotiating discounts and rebates. For example, prior to the 2003 Medicare Modernization Act, CMS set the prices for Medicare Part B drugs as a percentage of AWP. Now CMS uses ASP as its reference point since that price better reflects actual prices that manufacturers receive. (ASP is analogous to AMP for physician-administered drugs.)

Chargeback Sometimes wholesalers provide drugs to organizations that have negotiated discounts directly with the manufacturer. In these cases, the wholesaler offers the drug to these organizations at the lower, negotiated price. The chargeback, which wholesalers receive from manufacturers, is the difference between the WAC and the discounted price that the wholesaler receives.

Rebate Manufacturers pay rebates to customers after the customers have purchased the drug. PBMs, insurers and pharmacies may all negotiate rebates with the manufacturer, and the rebate allows the manufacturer to retroactively lower the net prices that different customers pay. The AWP is commonly used as a starting point in these negotiations. These rebates are confidential.

Non-retail buyers The class of non-retail buyers includes parties such as hospitals, select HMOs (such as Kaiser Permanente) and nursing homes. These health care providers both purchase and administer prescription drugs, and CBO (2005) estimates that they dispense around 28 percent of the prescription market measured in dollars. Non-retail buyers distinguish themselves from other members of the distribution chain in that they can influence consumption patterns. Concordantly, non-retail buyers are able to negotiate significant discounts from manufacturers.

Pharmacy benefit managers Most health insurance plans use separate entities called pharmacy benefit managers (PBMs) to administer prescription drug coverage. While

Table 23.1 Sales, market share and pharmacy type in the USA (2005–06)

Pharmacy type	Sales ($ billions)		Dollar share (%)		Unit share (%)	
	2006	2005	2006	2005	2006	2005
Chain	102.83	94.49	41.2	40.7	47.2	46.6
Mass merchandiser	24.34	22.48	9.7	9.7	11.0	10.9
Supermarket	28.82	27.64	11.5	11.9	13.9	14.2
Independent	43.48	41.90	17.4	18.1	21.1	21.5
Mail order	50.37	45.50	20.2	19.6	6.8	6.8

Source: National Association of Chain Drug Stores, 'Industry facts at a glance'.

many PBMs began as claims processors, they have evolved into full service entities that develop formularies, negotiate prices with manufacturers, establish pharmacy networks (lists of pharmacies where covered patients can fill prescriptions), and offer mail order pharmacy services. Although the PBM industry is not as concentrated as the drug wholesale industry, most of its activity is consolidated in a small number of large multi-billion-dollar firms. In 2005, four PBMs accounted for half of all covered lives: Caremark Rx (19 percent), Medco Health Solutions (13 percent), Express Scripts (11 percent) and WellPoint Pharmacy Management (7 percent) (AIS, 2006). Outside of their mail order operations, PBMs rarely take possession of drugs, but they play a critical role in determining the net price of pharmaceuticals.

Insurers and employers Some private insurers and employers do not outsource the management of pharmacy benefits to PBMs, but rather run them internally. In some cases, self-insured employers form coalitions, such as Rx Collaborative, to improve their bargaining power against manufacturers. In this chapter, our references to PBMs also encompass these entities that perform the PBM functions internally.

6.2 Channel partners involved in physical product distribution

The physical distribution of drugs presented in Figure 23.1 is straightforward – wholesalers purchase drugs from manufacturers and then sell these drugs to pharmacies, which in turn dispense to patients. Any potential discounts and the ability to extract higher markups earned by these channel partners depend on their value added, in particular their ability to affect downstream demand.

The first party downstream from manufacturers – wholesalers – are not able to negotiate substantial discounts for branded pharmaceuticals because of their inability to move market share. They are, however, able to negotiate discounts for volume, prompt payment, and for taking on products close to expiration, but these discounts are minimal. A system of 'chargebacks' allows a manufacturer to offer negotiated discounts to end customers without the risk of arbitrage by the wholesaler. Under this system, the amount that wholesalers generally pay to manufacturers for inventory is an undiscounted invoice or list price, often referred to as wholesale acquisition cost (WAC)

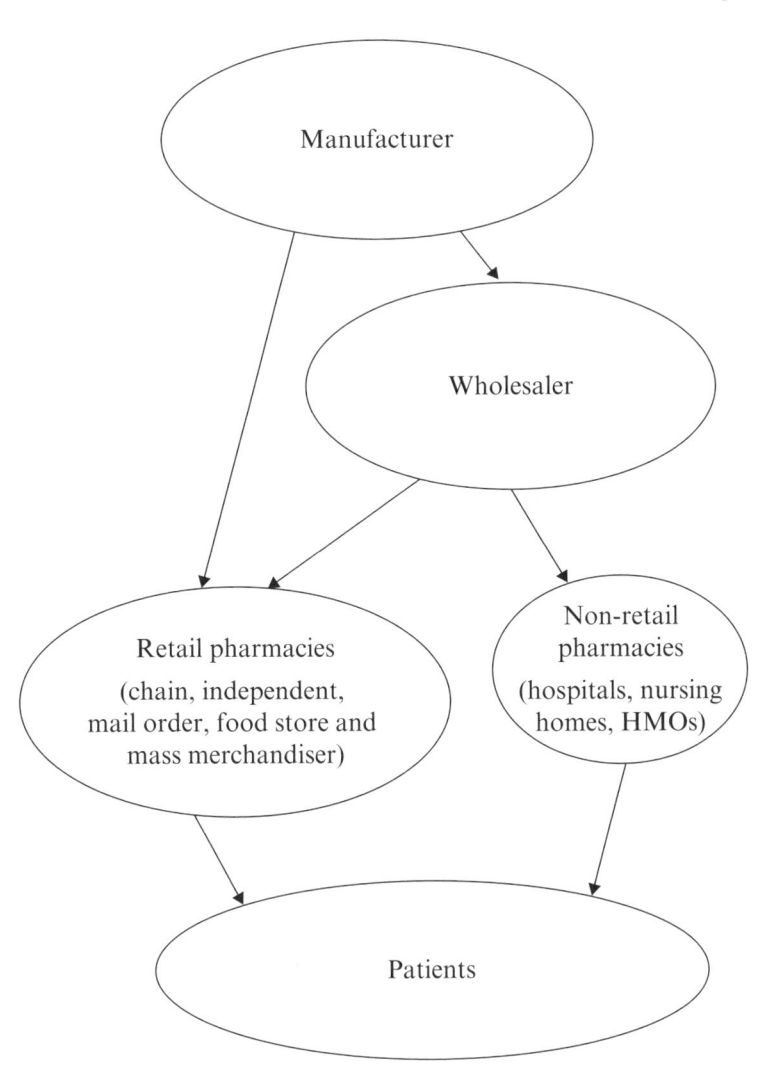

Figure 23.1   Product flows

(Schweitzer, 1997, p. 11). The end purchaser obtains its contractual discount immediately from the wholesaler at the time of purchase, while the wholesaler subsequently is reimbursed for the amount of the discount after submitting a claim to the manufacturer. This payment, known as the chargeback, is mainly used in sales of branded drugs to non-retail entities and sales of generic drugs to retail pharmacies. The net price that the wholesaler pays to the manufacturer is typically the WAC price net of discounts and chargebacks. Customers that do not have discount agreements with the manufacturer typically pay prices near WAC because that is the cost of inventory on hand for the wholesaler.

At the retail level, pharmacy acquisition costs and margins differ drastically between branded and generic drugs and across pharmacy ownership types. In all cases, they are driven by the ability to influence consumer demand. In the case of branded drugs, pharmacies simply fulfill demand by stocking a wide variety of drugs. In the case of generic drugs, pharmacies make decisions about which manufacturer's generic version to stock. In addition, third-party payers have exhausted their bargaining power with pharmacies for generic markups because any threat to steer patients away from generics would not be credible. Differences in bargaining power across pharmacy types also drive variation in pharmacy acquisition price levels. While independent pharmacies buy almost all of their drugs from wholesalers, chain pharmacies purchase a large share of drugs from their own warehouses, which results in a price differential to the benefit of large retailers. Mail order pharmacies are able to achieve consistently lower prices than other dispensers not only because they are able to take advantages of efficiencies in distribution, but they can ensure a higher degree of formulary compliance.

The amounts that pharmacies receive for drugs vary from payer to payer and also depend on whether the drug is branded or generic. Payments to pharmacies for branded drugs are generally fixed in a formulaic fashion based on the acquisition cost plus a pharmacy margin, which consists of a fixed percentage markup on the drug and a flat dispensing fee. For generic drugs, payers frequently impose a fixed maximum allowable cost (MAC) for reimbursement plus a flat dispensing fee that may vary by payer or drug type. Nevertheless, pharmacies are often able to earn higher margins on generic drugs because they can perform switches from brand to generic. A recent study by the Congressional Budget Office (CBO, 2004) makes that point explicit. The study measured the difference between the average manufacturer price (AMP) and the average price paid by independent pharmacies, which represents both wholesale and pharmacy markups, and found that markups per prescription were $3.80 for brand name drugs, $5 for new generics and $1.40 for old generics. The report also stated that wholesalers retain most of the markup for branded, on-patent drugs while pharmacies keep most of the markup for post-patent branded drugs and generics. The pharmacy markup also depends on a patient's insurance status.

6.3 Payments by entities not involved in physical product distribution

Because of insurance and formularies, the flow of money from the patient back to the manufacturer is more complex than the physical product distribution would suggest (see Figure 23.2). For one, the revenues that pharmacies receive are based on patient co-payments and payments from insurance companies, which are most commonly handled by PBMs. In addition, formularies give PBMs an ability to negotiate manufacturer discounts to bring down the net price they pay to the retail channel.

There are two reasons why PBMs and the insurers they represent are able to bargain with manufacturers. First, an individual PBM represents a large number of health plans and thus pools a large share of the prescription market. Second, PBMs not only influence the formulary line-up, but are also actively involved in enforcing it by mapping it to patient out-of-pocket costs, educational programs, prior authorization requirements, and drug utilization reviews. Ellison and Snyder (2003) argue that it is the ability to manipulate patient behavior, and not size, that confers bargaining power to PBMs. Formularies improve buyers' positions when they negotiate drug prices because they provide a credible means to punish a drug manufacturer for not offering an attractive price. The ability to affect purchase patterns through the formulary is also the reason why

Pharmaceutical pricing 503

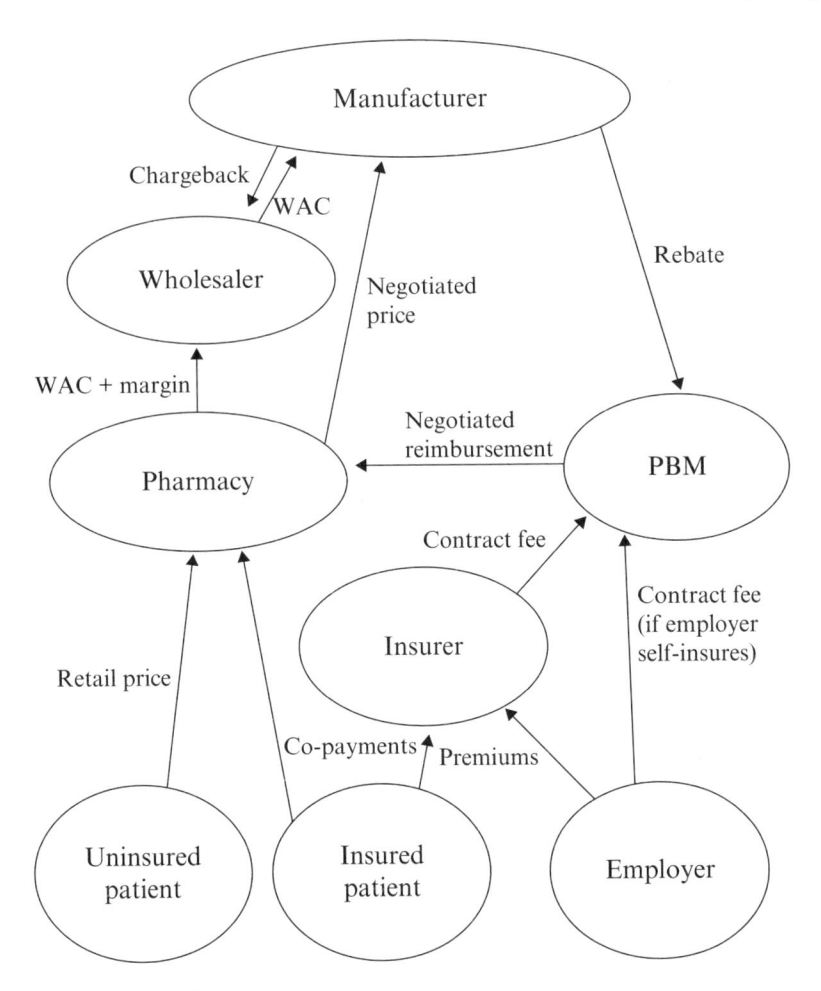

Figure 23.2 Payment flows

hospitals and other non-retail buyers can obtain discounts from the retail price found in pharmacies.

Rebates are a form of *ex post* discounting that PBMs may be able to obtain. Unlike chargebacks, rebates often bypass market intermediaries and change hands after retail transactions are completed. For example, one type of rebate that can flow from manufacturers to payers or PBMs is called a formulary rebate. Such rebates may be tied directly to performance metrics such as achievement of market share goals. Since these metrics cannot be computed until well after transactions are completed (often on a quarterly basis), they are not generally reflected in transactional data. Moreover, in this example, the rebate goes to the payer or PBM and bypasses the pharmacy and wholesaler, which means that transactional data from those entities would not reflect the full discounted prices that PBMs and insurers obtain for their formulary performance – a fact that could bias elasticity estimates based on such data. In addition, mapping rebates to specific transactions is very difficult if not impossible because a rebate may pertain to purchases aggregated over a long period of time or to a bundle of products.

In addition to bargaining with manufacturers, PBMs use their ability to define which retail pharmacies participate in a network as a way to negotiate lower payments to pharmacies.

7. Context

Pharmaceuticals, together with other health care segments, tend to generate much political interest and therefore regulation. An important reason is the influence that drug quality has on someone's physical well-being in a way that other products do not, and the fact that adverse effects of going without treatment are very different from the adverse effects of going without, say, a new operating system on your computer. Furthermore, because health care accounts for a large share of public spending in the USA and other countries, policy-makers face pressure to limit prices, especially on pharmaceuticals, which represent a fast-growing segment of health care spending.

7.1 Forms of price regulation

In the USA, the main regulatory agency for the industry, the Food and Drug Administration (FDA), regulates the development, approval and marketing of prescription and over-the-counter medicines. It does not, however, regulate pricing. This is in contrast to most other industrialized countries where a single government purchaser is responsible for administering drug benefits. Differences stem from the fact that while many industrialized nations have universal or single-payer health care systems, the USA relies on a system that is predominantly financed by employers.

Methods of price regulation fall into the following general categories: price ceilings, reference pricing and profit regulation (GAO, 2007). Price ceilings, where the government sets a maximum price, are used in France and Australia. If non-governmental purchasers are free to negotiate lower prices than those set by the regulator, then the established price becomes a price ceiling. A related practice, reference pricing, occurs when the regulator links reimbursement to price levels of other drugs in the therapeutic class (as in Germany) or of the same drug in other countries (as in Canada or Australia). Profit or rate of return regulation, which is practiced in the UK, allows pharmaceutical manufacturers to earn a specified rate of return across a portfolio of products sold in the country, and manufacturers are free to set prices for each drug so long as they stay within the acceptable profit corridor. If profits exceed a specified level, the drug company would have to lower prices to bring profits within an acceptable range, and the drug companies can request price increases if profits are too low.

In general, the US government does not regulate the market prices of prescription drugs, although it plays an important role as the largest payer for prescription drugs, primarily through the Medicaid program for the disabled and low-income and the relatively new Medicare program for the elderly (Medicare Part D). State and federal agencies are responsible for financing a considerable amount of prescription drug spending in the USA. A large share of federally financed drug spending flows through private insurance plans and PBMs that are responsible for administering Medicare Part D.

In addition to Medicare Part D and Medicaid, the government finances prescription drugs under the auspices of Medicare Part B (which primarily covers drugs administered in physician clinics), the relatively small programs in the Veterans' Administration (VA), and the Department of Defense (DOD). These programs directly negotiate with manufacturers or follow legislated reimbursement rules and are able to obtain highly discounted prices. The Congressional Budget Office (2005) estimated that the average prices that the DOD and VA pay for prescription drugs are 41 and 42 percent of the average wholesale price (AWP) respectively. The average price that Medicaid pays is 51 percent of AWP relative to a best price in the private sector of about 63 percent of AWP.

7.2 Firm response to price regulation

The intent of any price regulation is to secure lower prices for prescription drugs. However, consequences unintended by regulators can result from poorly conceived regulation. Exactly how a pharmaceutical manufacturer responds to pricing regulation depends on the regulatory approach taken, but a growing body of evidence suggests that price regulation does not necessarily lead to lower drug costs and it can have adverse effects on both the short- and long-term supply of prescription drugs.

Medicaid's adoption of a 'most-favored-customer' pricing rule in 1991 is a good example of how price regulation can influence industry dynamics. Because Medicaid was a passive payer, it was not securing the same discounts that private purchasers were able to negotiate. In response, the US Congress established that Medicaid price net of rebates would be the lesser of the AMP minus 15.1 percent or the lowest price made available to any private purchaser. In turn, manufacturers responded by offering smaller discounts to private purchasers (Congressional Budget Office, 2004; Scott-Morton, 1997). Furthermore, the pricing regulation created an incentive to introduce new versions of drugs as a way to skirt price regulation because launch prices are not regulated (Duggan and Scott-Morton, 2004). This led to an inefficiently high rate of incremental innovation for certain drugs and effectively raised spending as Medicaid programs began to pay for new and more expensive presentations of the same drugs (Duggan and Scott-Morton, 2004).

Ekelund and Persson (2003) provide an example from Sweden of how regulation changes pricing in the pharmaceutical industry. Using the model of Lu and Comanor (1998), they investigate launch price strategies for innovative and me-too drugs. The model predicts that the profit-maximizing strategy for me-too drugs is setting a low entry price that would rise over time, while the best strategy for unique drugs entails setting a high entry price that would fall over time. However, the Swedish government negotiates prices with manufacturers, who are then prohibited from raising them without government approval. In such a regulated regime, a penetration strategy is not possible because firms cannot raise prices freely. Ekelund and Persson find that launch prices are higher for drugs that represent more significant therapeutic advances, and they find that the relative launch prices are higher in the regulated market. Because regulation does not affect launch prices, they do find evidence for skimming strategies for all drug types.

In similar vein, Danzon and Chao (2000b) argue that regulating prescription drug prices reduces competition. They find that price competition among generic drugs is more robust in less regulated markets, while highly regulated markets have less generic entry and, in turn, higher prices for off-patent drugs. Kyle (2007) finds that firms tend to delay entry into markets where prices are highly regulated, which is consistent with the studies above, which show that price regulation reduces price competition. That price regulation reduces price competition is a somewhat obvious conclusion. Price regulation, after all, fixes prices or at least binds prices within some range.

So, does price regulation lower prices or does it raise prices? The answer to this depends on how the regulator sets prices. Price regulation will surely lead to lower prices for existing drugs, but it is not clear that regulation leads to lower prices for newer products. Ekelund and Persson's (2003) findings suggest that in a regulated market, the me-too drug sets its price higher than it would do in an unregulated market, so now the average price for treating the condition when two products exist is higher in the regulated market than it would be in the unregulated market. However, price regulation will only have a chilling effect on competition if prices are set upon market entry and renegotiated infrequently or not at all. If regulators can renegotiate prices when substitutes become available, they can induce price competition among firms.

One further concern with price regulation is that, if it depresses prices and current revenues, it will lead to less innovation. Pharmaceutical innovation is funded through both internal revenues and external venture capital, and profit-reducing price regulation can reduce access to both sources of R&D funding. Furthermore, firms may find it more profitable to divert funds towards product promotion if the returns to R&D fall as a result of price regulation. Again, this is not necessarily a bad thing from a regulator's perspective. Both innovation and low prices are valuable to public welfare, but there is a tradeoff between innovation and profits (Abbott and Vernon, 2005; Scherer, 2001). The goal of the regulator is to strike a balance between these two objectives.

7.3 International price variation and arbitrage

Just as there is price variation among different purchasers within the USA, there is substantial international price variation. Price variation among consumers in the USA is sustained by purchasers' inability to resell the drugs that they purchase. Similar restrictions exist in international markets, which partly explains why average prices can differ so much across countries.

Measuring exactly how much prices vary is a difficult task. Danzon and Chao (2000a) and Danzon and Furukawa (2003) discuss some of the difficulties involved with comparing prices for prescription drugs across countries and explain that many comparisons of prices overstate differences. But a consistent finding from the literature on cross-country pricing differences is that the USA and Japan have higher prices than other countries. This is generally attributed to the fact that these countries do not regulate prices and do not take advantage of parallel imports that arbitrage such price differences.

In general, international price variation is sustained by global patent laws that restrict the movement of prescription drugs across borders. The European Union (EU) represents an exception to this rule because of free movement of goods among EU states. Interestingly, this is in spite of patent laws that would restrict such movement. The resulting parallel imports of drugs allow EU governments to arbitrage the existing price variation. When Ganslandt and Maskus (2004) measured the effect that parallel imports had on prices in Sweden after its 1995 EU entry, they found that prices fell between 12 and 19 percent for drugs that faced competition from parallel imports.

Whether the experience from Sweden generalizes to other countries is an open question. In fact, economic theory suggests that while parallel importation could reduce prices in high-priced, importing countries, this effect would be mitigated if pharmaceutical manufacturers raised prices in exporting countries, or credibly threatened to foreclose a market altogether if their reservation price was not met.[13] At the same time, the exporting country can sometimes credibly threaten to either nullify a drug's patent or require that it be licensed in country. With few exceptions, such compulsory licensing is prohibited by the Agreement on Trade Related Aspects of Intellectual Property Rights (TRIPs), but Thailand recently responded to high prescription drug prices by licensing the production of generic versions of Plavix, a drug that treats heart disease, and HIV/AIDS drugs Efevirens, Kaletra and Stocrin (Fuller, 2007).[14]

Even when parallel trade is restricted, prices across different countries seem correlated. Chintagunta and Desiraju (2005) look at pricing and detailing levels for three antidepressants and find significant across-market interactions in the pricing of these drugs in the USA, the UK and Italy. They present anecdotal evidence that local and global units of pharmaceutical firms work together when setting prices, and explain that when firms compete in multiple markets, a global, rather than a regional, approach to pricing would generate the observed across-market effects.

Political pressure in key markets, such as the USA, could also explain correlation of prices across countries. When markets are perfectly segmented, profit-maximizing firms with market power will set prices according to the willingness to pay in each market. Large disparities in prices among countries could invite legislative action in high-priced countries that would be unfavorable to pharmaceutical firms. For example, firms may feel that if prices are too low in one country, legislators in the USA could respond by imposing price controls or permitting importation. When setting prices across countries, pharmaceutical firms consider the possibility of inviting such political backlash. Kremer (2002) explains that this is one factor that helps explain the shortage of prescription drugs in the developing world.

8. Areas for future research

From our discussion in this chapter, it should be clear that the pharmaceutical industry is unique, and pricing in this environment merits special attention. A substantial literature addresses pricing in the pharmaceutical industry, but several avenues for future research exist. We would categorize areas for future research in three distinct areas. First, future research should continue to clarify the nature of the current market. Second, we believe that more research is needed on how to optimize the current system. Finally, given the dynamic nature of the regulatory and institutional environment that defines the pharmaceutical industry, continued research on how these changes influence pricing will be needed as the industry continues to evolve.

Research that focuses on the actual measures of price would facilitate a better

---

[13] Grossman and Lai (2006) and Pecorino (2002) outline game-theoretic models of pharmaceutical pricing when drug importation is allowed. The key insight of these models is that drug imporation changes the possible payoffs for both the drug manufacturers and price-regulating governments. The different payoffs change behavior relative to a regime where drug importation is not allowed.

[14] Under TRIPs, countries are permitted to manufacture a patented drug under a compulsory license if the drug is necessary to address a national emergency and the government cannot otherwise obtain the drug. TRIPs does not clearly define what constitutes a national emergency.

understanding of the industry today. As Figure 23.2 illustrates, payment flows are anything but straightforward. The payment system is made up of several different agents, each of which pays a unique price. Some of these prices are negotiated, but most of the observable prices are list prices. The multiplicity of different price measures can be confusing to the uninitiated. Should one consider the out-of-pocket cost that the patient pays, the pharmacy acquisition price, pharmacy retail price, wholesaler's net price, AWP or WAC? The answer depends on the issue at heart and the segment of the market in question. But it is worth noting that one important price, the price that the manufacturer receives net of rebates, is unobserved because of the private nature of negotiations among drug manufacturers and various purchasers. While this situation is not necessarily unique to the pharmaceutical industry, in the absence of a direct measure, researchers must make do with the price measures available and hope that these prices are at least correlated with the price of interest.

In addition, much of the extant literature on pharmaceutical pricing utilizes data from the 1980s and early 1990s, but, as the market has changed considerably since that time, there is a need for research that demonstrates how and whether these changes have influenced competitive pricing dynamics in the industry. As managed care companies began to actively participate in the pharmaceutical market during the 1990s, pricing in the pharmaceutical industry evolved to the three-tiered co-payment systems we see today. More recently it has been affected by the widespread adoption of PBMs. Through their use of formularies and other negotiating tactics, PBMs injected market power into the buyer side of the market. While it is well known that PBMs secure significant rebates, research that quantifies this effect would be a welcome addition to the literature. This could however be a difficult task, given the confidential nature of the rebates that PBMs negotiate.

Besides improving our understanding of current industry dynamics, research is needed on the optimal way to structure or restructure the systems and contracts that determine prescription drug prices. On the one hand, the growing role that PBMs perform, coupled with their expanded capabilities, could create conflicting incentives for the clients they represent. On the patient-insurer front, misalignment of incentives also is present because the structure of pharmacy benefits has clear implications for patients' drug utilization. These structures are often overly simplistic; for example patients usually face the same co-payment structure regardless of therapeutic category or can fill 90-day scripts through mail pharmacy for both chronic and episodic conditions (e.g. hay fever). We expect that much of this line of research may necessarily be theoretical, although we believe that researchers should also seek out the rare natural or controlled experiments because of their power to aid decision-making.

Finally, the political and therefore regulatory context in which the industry functions is constantly evolving. The introduction of Medicare prescription drug benefits for the elderly will have a substantive impact on industry dynamics and this will undoubtedly be a ripe area for research. The anticipated public release of average manufacturer prices (AMP) is likely to increase transparency in the marketplace, which will probably impact competitive dynamics although the direction of that impact appears ambiguous (CBO, 2008). Even the change in political party controlling the US government's policy is likely to impact the type and likelihood of price regulation. All these changes will provide plentiful opportunities for relevant policy research.

Outside of the USA, several interesting questions are left unanswered. Compulsory licensing and the free trade of prescription drugs across borders significantly changes how pharmaceutical firms think about patents and will change the way they set prices across countries. Pharmaceutical firms charge different prices for the same drug in different countries, but it is not clear that these prices are completely uncorrelated. A small amount of research investigates the correlation of prices across markets, but this is an area that is open for continued research and will become more important if changes in international agreements influence how patents operate internationally.

Aside from the ever-shifting regulatory pressures, advances in the science that drives the industry will affect pricing dynamics in the industry and indirectly fuel regulatory interest. Many newer pharmaceutical and biological products target very specific populations, and the introduction of these highly specialized drugs could place upward pressure on prices. The increased use of biologics may also alter the generic industry dynamics because these complex compounds are difficult to replicate cheaply and consistently.

As noted in the introduction, spending on prescription drugs constitutes an increasingly important share of spending on both the personal and national level. Together with the fact that prescription drugs influence a consumer's well-being like few other products, it is self-evident that a clear understanding of pricing in this industry is important, but research in this area may have a broader appeal. Perhaps because the pharmaceutical industry is regulated on many fronts, many of the transactions are closely recorded, providing a wealth of data that researchers can use to investigate consumer behaviors such as responses to marketing or decision-making when product attributes are not well known. We leave it to the authors of other chapters in this book to identify some of the important areas for such research.

References

Abbott, T.A. and J.A. Vernon (2005), 'The cost of US pharmaceutical price reductions: a financial simulation model of R&D decisions', NBER Working Paper, No. 11114.
AIS Market Data (2006), 'PBM market share by enrollment (covered lives)', http://www.aishealth.com/MarketData/PharmBenMgmt/PBM_market01.html, accessed 30 January 2007.
Berndt, E.R. (2002), 'Pharmaceuticals in U.S. health care: determinants of quantity and price', *Journal of Economic Perspectives*, **16** (4), 45–66.
Berndt, E.R., L. Bui, D.R. Reiley and G.L. Urban (1997), 'Information, marketing, and pricing in the U.S. antiulcer drug market', *American Economic Review*, **85** (2), 100–105.
Berndt, E.R., R. Mortimer, A. Bhattacharjya, A. Parece and E. Tuttle (2007), 'Authorized generic drugs, price competition, and consumers' welfare', *Health Affairs*, **26** (3), 790–99.
Bhattacharya, J. and W.B. Vogt (2003), 'A simple model of pharmaceutical price dynamics', *Journal of Law and Economics*, **46** (2), 599–626.
Caves, R., M. Whinston and M. Hurwitz (1991), 'Patent expiration, entry, and competition in the U.S. pharmaceutical industry', *Brookings Papers on Economic Activity: Microeconomics*, pp. 1–66.
Chintagunta, P.K. and R. Desiraju (2005), 'Strategic pricing and detailing behavior in international markets', *Marketing Science*, **24** (1), 67–80.
Cockburn, I.M. (2006), 'Is the pharmaceutical industry in a productivity crisis?', in Adam B. Jaffe, Josh Lerner and Scott Stern (eds), *Innovation Policy and the Economy*, vol. 7, Cambridge, MA: MIT Press, pp. 1–32.
Congressional Budget Office (2004), *Medicaid Reimbursements to Pharmacies for Prescription Drugs*, Washington, DC: Government Printing Office.
Congressional Budget Office (2005), *Prices for Brand-name Drugs under Selected Federal Programs*, Washington, DC: Government Printing Office.
Congressional Budget Office (2007), *Prescription Drug Pricing in the Private Sector*, Washington, DC: Government Printing Office.
Congressional Budget Office (2008), *Increasing Transparency in the Pricing of Health Care Services and Pharmaceuticals*, Washington, DC: Government Printing Office.

Crawford G.S. and M. Shum (2005), 'Uncertainty and learning in pharmaceutical demand', *Econometrica*, **73** (4), 1137–73.
Danzon, P. and L.W. Chao (2000a), 'Cross-national price differences for pharmaceuticals: how large, and why?', *Journal of Health Economics*, **19** (2), 158–95.
Danzon, P. and L.W. Chao (2000b), 'Does price regulation drive out competition in pharmaceutical markets?', *Journal of Law and Economics*, **43** (2), 311–57.
Danzon, P. and M. Furukawa (2003), 'Prices and availability of pharmaceuticals: evidence from nine countries', *Health Affairs*, Web Exclusive W3-521.
DiMasi, J.A., R.W. Hansen and H.G. Grabowski (2003), 'The price of innovation: new estimates of drug development costs', *Journal of Health Economics*, **22** (2), 151–85.
Duggan, M. and F. Scott Morton (2004), 'The distortionary effects of government procurement: evidence from Medicaid prescription drug purchasing', NBER Working Paper No. 10930.
Ekelund, M. and B. Persson (2003), 'Pharmaceutical pricing in a regulated market', *The Review of Economics and Statistics*, **85** (2), 298–306.
Ellison, G. and S.F. Ellison (2000), 'Strategic entry deterrence and the behaviour of pharmaceutical incumbents prior to patent expiration', mimeo, MIT.
Ellison, S.F. and C.M. Snyder (2003), 'Countervailing power in wholesale pharmaceuticals', Working Paper, available at http://gsbwww.uchicago.edu/research/workshops/wae/chris1.pdf.
Ellison, S.F., I.M. Cockburn, Z. Griliches and J. Hausman (1997), 'Characteristics of demand for pharmaceutical products: an examination of four cephalosporins', *RAND Journal of Economics*, **28** (3), 426–46.
Forbes (2006), 'Forbes 2000, the world's leading companies, drugs & biotechnology', http://www.forbes.com/2004/03/24/04f2000land.html, accessed 7 January 2007.
Frank, R.G. (2001), 'Prescription drug prices: why do some pay more than others do?', *Health Affairs*, **20** (2),115–28.
Frank, R.G. (2003), 'New estimates of drug development costs', *Journal of Health Economics*, **22** (2), 325–30.
Frank, R.G. and D.S. Salkever (1992), 'Pricing, patent loss and the market for pharmaceuticals', *Southern Economic Journal*, **59** (2), 165–79.
Frank, R.G. and D.S. Salkever (1997), 'Generic entry and the pricing of pharmaceuticals', *Journal of Economics and Management Strategy*, **6** (1), 75–90.
Fuller, T. (2007), 'Thailand takes on drug industry, and may be winning', *International Herald Tribune*, 11 April, available at http://www.iht.com/articles/2007/04/11/news/pharma.php.
Ganslandt, M. and K. Maskus (2004), 'Parallel imports and the pricing of pharmaceutical products: evidence from the European Union', *Journal of Health Economics*, **23** (5), 1035–57.
Giaccotto, C., R.E. Santerre and J.A. Vernon (2005), 'Drug prices and research and development investment behavior in the pharmaceutical industry', *Journal of Law and Economics*, **48** (1), 195–214.
Gibson, T.B., R.J. Ozminski and R.Z. Goetzel (2005), 'The effects of prescription drug cost sharing: a review of the evidence', *The American Journal of Managed Care*, **11** (11), 730–40.
Goldman, D.P., G.F. Joyce, J.J. Escarce et al. (2004), 'Pharmacy benefits and the use of drugs by the chronically ill', *Journal of the American Medical Association*, **291** (19), 2344–50.
Government Accountability Office (2007), *Prescription Drugs: An Overview of Approaches to Negotiate Drug Prices Used by Other Countries and U.S. Private Payers and Federal Programs*, Testimony before the Committee on Finance, US Senate, GAO-07-358T.
Grabowski, H.G. and J.M. Vernon (1992), 'Brand loyalty, entry, and price competition in pharmaceuticals after the 1984 Drug Act', *Journal of Law and Economics*, **35** (2), 331–50.
Grossman, G. and E. Lai (2006), 'Parallel imports and price controls', NBER Working Paper No. 12423.
Hellerstein, J. (1998), 'The importance of the physician in the generic versus trade-name prescriptions decision', *RAND Journal of Economics*, **29** (1), 108–36.
Huskamp, H., R.G. Frank, K. McGuigan and Y. Zhang (2005), 'The impact of three-tier formulary on demand response for prescription drugs', *Journal of Economics & Management Strategy*, **14** (3), 729–53.
Hux, J.E. and C.D. Naylor (1994), 'Drug prices and third party payment: do they influence medication selection?', *Pharmacoeconomics*, **5** (4), 343–50.
IMS Health (2006), 'IMS Health reports 5.4 percent dollar growth in 2005 U.S. prescription sales', Press release, 22 February, available at http://www.imshealth.com/ims/portal/front/articleC/0,2777,6599_3665_77180090,00.html.
Kaiser Family Foundation (2005), *Follow the Pill: Understanding the U.S. Commercial Pharmaceutical Supply Chain*, Washington, DC: Kaiser Family Foundation, publication 7296.
Kaiser Family Foundation (2006), *Prescription Drugs: Advertising, Out-of-Pocket Costs, and Patient Safety from the Perspective of Doctors and Pharmacists*, Washington, DC: Kaiser Family Foundation, publication 7583.
Kolassa, E.M. (1997), *Elements of Pharmaceutical Pricing*, New York: The Pharmaceutical Products Press.

Kremer, M. (2002), 'Pharmaceuticals and the developing world', *Journal of Economic Perspectives*, **16** (4), 67–90.

Kyle, M.K. (2007), 'Pharmaceutical price controls and entry strategies', *Review of Economics and Statistics*, **89** (1), 88–99.

Landsman, P.B., W. Yu, X. Liu, S.M. Teutsch and M.L. Berger (2005), 'Impact of 3-tier pharmacy benefit design and increased consumer cost-sharing on drug utilization', *American Journal of Managed Care*, **11** (10), 621–8.

Lu, Z.J. and W.S. Comanor (1998), 'Strategic pricing of new pharmaceuticals', *The Review of Economics and Statistics*, **80** (1), 108–18.

McGuire, T.G. (2000), 'Physcian agency', in Joseph Newhouse and Anthony Culyer (eds), *Handbook of Health Economics*, vol. 1A, Amsterdam: Elsevier, pp. 461–536.

Newhouse, J.P. and the Insurance Experiment Group (1993), *Free for All? Lessons from the RAND Health Insurance Experiment*, Cambridge, MA: Harvard University Press.

Pavcnik, N. (2002), 'Do pharmaceutical prices respond to potential patient out-of-pocket expenses?', *RAND Journal of Economics*, **33** (3), 469–87.

Pecorino, P. (2002), 'Should the US allow prescription drug reimports from Canada?', *Journal of Health Economics*, **21** (4), 699–708.

PhRMA (2006), Pharmaceutical Industry Profile 2006, www.phrma.org, Washington, DC.

Reichert, S., T. Simon and E.A. Halm (2000), 'Physicians' attitudes about prescribing and knowledge of the costs of common medications', *Archives of Internal Medicine*, **160** (18), 2799–803.

Reiffen, D. and M.R. Ward (2005), 'Generic drug industry dynamics', *The Review of Economics and Statistics*, **87** (1), 37–49.

Scherer, F.M. (2001), 'The link between gross profitability and pharmaceutical R&D spending', *Health Affairs*, **20** (5), 216–20.

Schweitzer, Stuart D. (1997), *Pharmaceutical Economics and Policy*, New York: Oxford University Press.

Scott Morton, F. (1999), 'Entry decisions in the generic pharmaceutical industry', *RAND Journal of Economics*, **30** (3), 421–40.

Scott Morton, F. (1997), 'The strategic response by pharmaceutical firms to the Medicaid most-favored-customer rules', *RAND Journal of Economics*, **28** (2), 269–90.

Sorensen, A. (2000), 'Equilibrium price dispersion in retail markets for prescription drugs', *Journal of Political Economy*, **108** (4), 833–50.

Won Tesoriero, H. and B. Martinez (2006), 'Cut-rate deals for branded Zocor worry generics makers', *The Wall Street Journal*, 14 July, p. A9.

Wosinska, M and R.S. Huckman (2004), 'Generic dispensing and substitution in mail and retail pharmacies', *Health Affairs*, Web Exclusives, W4, 409-416.

24 Pricing for nonprofit organizations
Yong Liu and Charles B. Weinberg*

Abstract
Pricing decisions are particularly challenging for nonprofit organizations. They have a social rather than a for-profit objective function, they must obey a legal restriction not to distribute possible financial surpluses to those who control the organization's assets, and they have the opportunity to receive donations. While historically nonprofits have not developed their pricing capabilities as fully as they might have, pricing is becoming increasingly important, especially as many nonprofit organizations face declining support from government and are unable to increase private giving significantly. The goal of this chapter is to discuss pricing practice and pricing research in the nonprofit sector. We demonstrate how theoretical models of pricing strategies for nonprofits are different from those of for-profit businesses. Moreover, although only limited empirical data on nonprofit pricing are available, the data we do have suggest that nonprofits charge different (and usually lower) prices than similarly situated businesses. We survey the literature of nonprofit pricing to discuss important theoretical and empirical findings, and highlight the unique characteristics of nonprofits and the various modeling issues they generate for pricing research. We also discuss unresolved problems and potential research opportunities in nonprofit pricing.

Overview of nonprofit organizations and pricing behavior
Nonprofit organizations are precluded from distributing possible financial surplus to those who control the use of organizational assets (Hansmann, 1980). Such restrictions are imposed by external regulation or their own governance structure (Steinberg, 2006). As a whole, nonprofits are referred to as the third sector of the economy, next to private for-profit firms and the governments. While the existence of nonprofits varies widely across industries, the markets where nonprofits are the most active include arts and culture, education, health, human services, public and societal benefit (Boris and Steuerle, 2006). In some industries, nonprofits are a major provider of services. For example, Salamon and Anheier (1998) report that nonprofits account for 51 percent of all US hospitals.

In the USA, there were more than 1.6 million registered nonprofits in 1998 (Boris and Steuerle, 2006). Their numbers have been growing at a steady rate of about 25 000 new nonprofits annually. Figure 24.1, which is based on data from Hall and Burke (2006), illustrates this trend.

Not only are nonprofits involved in some of the most important sectors of modern life; they also account for an increasingly large share of economic activities. Nonprofits produce one-fifth of research and development (Lakdawalla and Philipson, 2006) and, in 2001, employed 11.7 million individuals, which represents 8.5 percent of total US civilian employment (Leete, 2006).

---

* The financial support of the Social Sciences and Humanities Research Council of Canada is gratefully acknowledged.

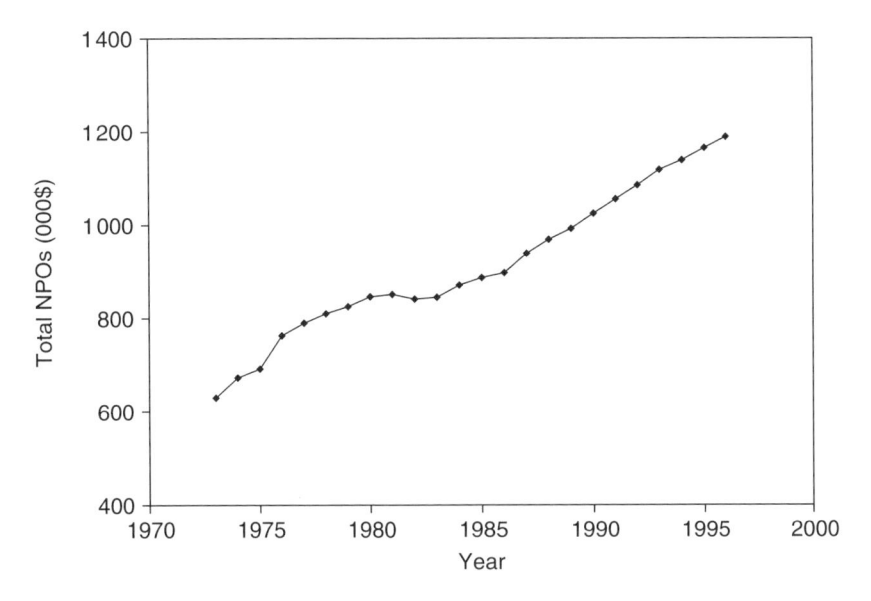

Source: Hall and Burke (2006).

Figure 24.1 Growth of nonprofit organizations (1973–96)

Characteristics of nonprofits

Nonprofits differ from for-profit firms in several important ways. It is these distinctive features that have made the existence and behavior of nonprofits an important phenomenon for researchers, public policy makers and managers. In anticipation of the pricing focus in this chapter, we discuss four fundamental features of nonprofits that have important implications for their pricing strategies: the objective functions; the nondistribution constraint; being able to seek grants and donations; and increased reliance on marketing tools to survive and grow.

Different from for-profit firms, nonprofits tend to pursue socially beneficial causes that are not profit-oriented. This is a crucial justification for why certain nonprofits are tax-exempted and their donors can receive tax breaks for their contributions. While profit maximization is typically assumed for for-profit firms and plays a significant role in their pricing behavior, the nonprofit objective functions are more complex. The literature provides some theoretical guidance on this issue. As summarized by Steinberg (1986), possible nonprofit objective functions include the maximization of output (or service), budget, prestige, quality and employee income, or a combination of these.

Which of these objectives are observed most frequently is an empirical question. Focusing on service versus budget maximization, Steinberg (1986) tests this family of nonprofit objective functions for about 2200 nonprofit organizations:

$$\text{Max } U = \lambda S + (1 - \lambda) B \tag{24.1}$$

Among other things, a large budget brings greater power and higher prestige for the organization (and its managers). In the equation, S is service spending in the amount of

$x + D(r) - r$, where x is the exogenous resources endowed to the nonprofit organization, r is the fundraising expenditure, and $D(r)$ is the donation or fundraising response function. B is the total budget composed of endowment and funds raised: $B = x + D(r)$. As a result, $\lambda = 0$ indicates budget maximization and $\lambda = 1$ indicates service maximization.

The first-order condition of equation (24.1) is $dD/dr = \lambda$; thus the marginal rate of donation with regard to fundraising expense can be used as the instrument to test whether the nonprofits are service maximizers or budget maximizers. Steinberg shows that public welfare, education and arts nonprofits are service maximizers, and health firms are budget maximizers. In a later study, Brooks (2005) replicated the main finding that most nonprofits are service maximizers with more recent data from 190 000 nonprofits.

Note that in these studies, financial revenue comes from two sources: donation (which is costly for the nonprofits to solicit) and exogenous income. The decision variable for the nonprofits is the level of fundraising expenses. Price is not an issue since sales of goods are not considered. For many nonprofits, one may argue that fundraising decisions may not be the driving force of organizational behavior. Instead, the decision about pricing, as well as what kinds of products or service to provide (e.g. variety and quality) and distribution decisions, can be more fundamental than fundraising. To differentiate the types of models discussed in Steinberg and Brooks from the pricing models we discuss later in the chapter, we shall term them 'fundraising models'.

In other studies, Jacobs and Wilder (1984) find that the pricing patterns of the Red Cross's blood service units are consistent with output maximization (subject to a break-even constraint). Gapinski (1984) finds that the Royal Shakespeare Company, a non-profit performing arts organization in the UK, produced more output and set lower prices than would a profit maximizer. Evidence for service or output maximization can also be found in studies such as Rose-Ackerman (1987), Liu and Weinberg (2004) and Weinberg (1980).

In typical models of profit maximization, optimality is obtained at an output level where marginal revenue equals marginal cost. It is useful to illustrate how the consideration of output in an organization's utility function might change this principle. Similar to the model of Lakdawalla and Philipson (2006) for an arbitrary organization, we can assume that profit maximization and output maximization are the two relevant factors in its objective function:

$$\text{Max } U = f(q, \pi(q)) \qquad (24.2)$$

where q is nonprofit output, π is profit in the amount of $\pi(q) = p(q)q - c(q)$, $p(q)$ is the inverse demand function, and $c(q)$ is cost. The first-order condition is $f_q + f_\pi \pi_q = 0$; f_q and f_π reflect the priorities of the organization ($f_q \geq 0$, $f_\pi \geq 0$); $f_q = 0$ indicates a typical for-profit and $f_\pi = 0$ indicates a nonprofit that is concerned with output.

Substituting the derivatives in the first-order condition, we have $p_q q + p = c_q - f_q/f_\pi$. That is, the organization's preference for quantity (q) reduces the value on the right-hand side of the equality, making it possible to sell greater quantity at reduced marginal revenue. Lakdawalla and Philipson (2006) call this the 'effective' marginal cost. In the case of a profit maximizer ($f_q = 0$), the equality restores to the traditional outcome that marginal revenue equals marginal cost.

The nondistribution constraint is another fundamental characteristic of nonprofits

(Hansmann, 1980). Because of this constraint, nonprofits cannot use their revenue to compensate board members, trustees, or other owners beyond an economic salary. This implies that a nonprofit has to use all its resources for purposes compatible with its non-financial objectives. Financial surplus, if any, is 'either retained (as endowment, reserves, or temporarily restricted funds), reinvested (in organizational expansion or the provision of charitable services), or given to other nonprofit organizations (as grants)' (Steinberg, 2006, p. 118). In the literature, nondistribution of surplus is typically modeled as a zero-profit constraint on nonprofit behavior (e.g. James, 1983; Schiff and Weisbrod, 1993; Rose-Ackerman, 1987). The following specification is representative of the nondistribution constraint:

$$pq + D(q,r) - r - c(q) = 0 \qquad (24.3)$$

where p is the price of goods or service per unit, q is the quantity of goods or services provided, and $c(q)$ is the cost function for quantity q. Note that the donation amount received is assumed to be dependent upon both the fundraising expense (r) and the quantity q (Schiff and Weisbrod, 1993; Rose-Ackerman, 1987), implying that potential donors care about the effectiveness of the nonprofit in providing mission-related products or service.

As suggested in the discussion of nonprofit objective functions and the nondistribution constraint, nonprofits differ from for-profits in that their socially beneficial nature enables them to seek support from donors and government agencies. A useful way of looking at how most nonprofits function is to view the customers of nonprofits as belonging to two different groups – donors and product or service users. (In addition, nonprofits also market to volunteers who provide time and talent to the organization.) Nonprofits try to appeal to both customer groups at the same time. The two groups are related to each other through the donors' concern about how well the nonprofits serve the users. A general literature in economics has started to address such 'two-sided' markets (Rochet and Tirole, 2004; Evans and Schmalensee, 2005). Even for firms maximizing profits, the two-sided market structure may lead to unusual pricing behavior. For instance, Evans and Schmalensee (2005) suggest that firms with two customer groups may find it profit maximizing to charge prices for one customer group that are below marginal cost or even negative, an argument that has direct implications for the nonprofit sector.

The implication of donations for pricing behavior of nonprofits is mainly through the nondistribution constraint. Everything else being equal, a nonprofit should be able to lower the price of its products or services if it receives donations to offset overall expenses. Nevertheless, this is contingent upon the fundraising response function – nonprofits are only willing to solicit donations up to the point where fundraising expense no longer helps improve their objective function.[1]

---

[1] Nonprofit organizations, in practice, often spend less than the optimal amount as indicated by a marginal analysis: some rating agencies only give approval ratings to nonprofit organizations for which fundraising (or total administration costs) is below a certain percentage of funds raised (or total spending). For example, the Better Business Bureau's Wise Giving Alliance gives its approval only to organizations for which the ratio of fundraising expenses to funds raised is less than 35 percent. See www.give.org for further details.

Finally, an important characteristic in the nonprofit sector is that many nonprofits face declining support from government and are unable to increase private giving significantly (Schiff and Weisbrod, 1993, Simon et al., 2006). As a result, nonprofits are increasingly turning to commercial activities by selling products or service for revenue in order to maintain their non-deficit status (Dees, 1998; Dart and Zimmerman, 2000). In fact, revenue from sales is the dominant source of income for nonprofits in many large subsectors (Brown and Slivinski, 2006). The Urban Institute and the NCCS/GuideStar National Nonprofit Database report that in 2000, arts and culture organizations derived 29 percent of their revenue from fees for goods and services. This percentage is 49 percent for human services, 47 percent for education, 22 percent for environment groups, 21 percent for public and societal benefit organizations, 85 percent for health care, and 27 percent for religious groups (Boris and Steuerle, 2006). These revenues include both primary products and other activities that support the primary mission of the organization.

Both James (1983) and Schiff and Weisbrod (1993) examine how nonprofits make tradeoffs between products or services that are of different values to the organization. In their models, the nonprofits derive positive utility from one product or service but negative utility from another. These are termed 'exempt output' versus 'commercial good' by Schiff and Weisbrod (1993), and 'core mission activities' versus 'ancillary services' by Oster et al. (2003). The basic economic principle is that the nonprofit sells commercial goods in order to subsidize activities that produce exempt output. For example, zoos and museums use the revenue from gift shops to subsidize exhibitions and collections, which are also supported by admission revenue. As another example, many universities and colleges use the revenue from bookstores and cafeteria to support academic activities. This type of product line decisions can be difficult for nonprofits since it involves pursuing commercial activities that may be counter to their preference (see Krug and Weinberg, 2004 for a portfolio model approach to help nonprofits manage such product line issues). Furthermore, the existence of donors and their concern about non-mission-related activities make such decisions more crucial.

To provide a clear context for the pricing issues in this chapter, we follow Schiff and Weisbrod (1993) and Oster et al. (2003) to distinguish mission-related products or service from non-mission-related ones. To accommodate discussion and in anticipation of the later analyses of nonprofits competing with for-profits, we shall terms these 'nonprofit outputs' versus 'commercial outputs'. Although pricing can be relevant for both outputs, our focus will be on the pricing strategy for the nonprofit output. As a result, our discussion will be closer to the model of James (1983) than to that of Schiff and Weisbrod (1993). In practice, prices for these nonprofit outputs can be the (subscription or single-ticket) admission price charged by nonprofit arts organizations, the annual membership fee for museums, the tuition fees for colleges and universities, the hourly rate for non-profit daycare centers, or the charges for many hospital services.

Nonprofit pricing practice
As an extremely diversified economic sector, nonprofits differ considerably in the ways they distribute products or services to target customers. As we discussed earlier, many nonprofits have found it necessary to charge at least some fee for their nonprofit output. It is important to note that to many people, pricing conveys a commercial interest or intent. Pricing behavior is often perceived to be counter to a nonprofit's objective. It is

thus not surprising that the nonprofit sector overall is not experienced with pricing practice. For example, McCready (1988) points out that there is only a sparse literature on the issue of pricing for nonprofits. Rentschler et al. (2007), in the context of museums, notes that the use of pricing as an element of the marketing mix seems to be particularly problematic.

Nevertheless, Oster et al. (2003) suggest several situations that are conducive to pricing by nonprofits. Charging prices is suitable when demand is relatively inelastic, when collecting fees is practical, and when such fees do not violate organizational norms. They also provide several rationales as to why pricing may have several positive effects on the nonprofit organization in addition to providing financial revenue. For instance, charging a fee helps reduce service bottlenecks and congestion, can motivate staff and client behavior, and can yield positive behavioral effects on the clients. When charging a price, nonprofits need to consider how to serve those who cannot afford to pay at all. One approach is to make the service available for free or at minimal cost to some (as universities do with financial aid) or to have free events, programs, or services. Consider, for example, the offering of free events by arts organizations; many museums offer one night a week in which admission is free. This is possible due to two effects. First, the price charged on regular days enhances the nonprofit's ability to offer free service on other days. Second, the value of a free day may be perceived to be higher by some customers when the service is not free on other days.

When a price is not charged, other methods must sometimes be used to achieve some of the positive effects of pricing. For example, Steinberg and Weisbrod (1998) suggest that nonprofits are more likely than businesses to use waiting lists (rather than pricing) to allocate demand when capacity is inadequate to meet demand.

Pricing strategies adopted by nonprofit organizations can be broadly classified into two categories. The first involves simple rules of thumb, which are mostly passive reactions to either cost or demand factors. Some nonprofits charge users a price that is based on costs. The price may equal the marginal cost of providing the product or service, leaving aside all fixed costs to be covered by foundation funding, government subsidies and development funds (Oster et al., 2003). Alternatively it may include part or all of the fixed costs. A good example of cost-based pricing is the Red Cross Blood Bank that charges all users a processing fee based on the 'irreducible cost of recruiting, processing, collecting, and distributing the blood to the hospital' (Weinberg, 1984, p. 264). Others nonprofits may use fair pricing; that is, they simply charge whatever price other organizations providing similar products or services are charging. For example, McCready (1988), through a survey of social service providers, finds that some children's centers serving particular consumers (e.g. special needs children) charge fees comparable to those offered by other nearby centers dealing with a non-special need clientele. Other nonprofit agencies act 'as a substitute for publicly-provided services (e.g., transportation) but service a particular clientele (the disabled)' at the same price as the public transit system. Finally, some nonprofits such as museums have adopted the practice of 'pay what you can, but pay something'. In such cases, museums have found that suggesting the typical voluntary entrance fee has a significant effect on the average amount that visitors voluntarily pay.

The second category of nonprofit pricing practice involves more complex pricing decisions and, in many cases, explicit price discrimination. For example, many nonprofit daycare centers use a sliding scale that ties the rate a family has to pay to its annual income level. Another example is the use of a two-part tariff (Bilodeau and Steinberg, 1999), which requires a joint pricing decision on both the fixed fee and the per-usage charge. Public universities typically charge different amounts for in-state and out-of-state residents; both public and private universities use a complex system of scholarships, loans and work-study programs to attract a mix of students with differing abilities and willingness to pay for a university education.

While dealing with complex pricing issues is new to many nonprofits, others first started grappling with such issues many years ago. Consider San Francisco's American Conservatory Theater (ACT); founded in 1965, it is one of the most prominent repertory theater companies in the USA. Its 'current performance, education, and outreach programs annually reach more than 250,000 people in the San Francisco Bay Area', and 'the company continues to produce challenging theater in the rich context of symposia, audience discussions, and community interaction'.[2] During a critical stage of its development in the early 1970s, the management decided to conduct a major research study to help in its strategic planning. One of the pricing issues involved was that the management was unsure whether or not to drop the subscription discount of seven tickets for the price of six. On the one hand, it is critical to maintain a sizable subscriber base to keep a steady flow of revenue and a satisfying audience size. On the other hand, the audience seemed to be upscale and had been renewing subscriptions at a fairly high rate. As a result, careful considerations of both users and organizational objectives were critical in making a decision about the price discount. The research study surveyed approximately 9000 season subscribers, and found that the discount itself was not a major factor in subscription decisions. As a result, ACT dropped the discount from its pricing scheme, starting with the 1976–77 season. Neither the percentages of subscriptions renewed nor the total subscription revenue in subsequent years were negatively affected by this change. While many theater companies need to offer a discount in order to acquire and retain subscribers, a combination of market research and market testing can lead to better understanding of the demand function and more informed pricing decisions.

Literature and basic nonprofit pricing models
Although pricing is now used more often by nonprofits, and brings in valuable revenue to keep them operating, there has been very limited research on pricing issues in this sector. Much of the published research is either conceptual or industry specific (mostly focusing on the health care market). Other studies, despite including price as a factor in the model, abstract from the pricing issue by assuming exogenous price levels (e.g. Schiff and Weisbrod, 1993). The following studies, mostly situated in a monopoly setting, illustrate several basic properties of nonprofit pricing models.

In an early work modeling nonprofit behavior, James (1983) considers the service mix decision together with pricing, formally showing that the nonprofits' involvement in non-mission-related (revenue-generating) activities is not necessarily an indication of the pursuit of commercial interests.

---

[2] Information and quotes were obtained from the ACT website http://act-sf.org/index.cfm?s_id=&pid=abt_act, 5 June 2007. Other information about this study was obtained from Ryans and Weinberg (1978).

To bridge the gap between nonprofit optimization and neoclassical profit maximization, Lakdawalla and Philipson (2006) proposed a monopoly model for an arbitrary organization that includes profit maximization and quantity maximization in the objective function. As we discussed earlier, their basic theory is that the nonprofit's altruism would enable it to have a lower 'effective' marginal cost and thus provide greater output than a comparable for-profit.[3] To derive this result, the nondistribution constraint is not necessary.

McCready (1988) investigates the applicability of Ramsey pricing to social service organizations. In contrast to profit-maximizing pricing practice, Ramsey pricing generates zero-profit prices that are Pareto optimal and leads to greater demand for the nonprofit output. However, McCready did not find evidence of such pricing practice in the Ontario, Canada sample of social service agencies that he studies.

Ansari et al. (1996) focus on the issue of service bundling, which includes both how many items to bundle and what prices to charge for different bundles. Besides finding that usage-maximizing nonprofits charge a lower price and hold more events to attract customers, they point to the critical role of fixed cost in nonprofits' pricing decisions. This is distinctive from for-profit optimizations, in which fixed cost matters only for entry/exit decisions but not pricing.

Steinberg and Weisbrod (2005) model nonprofit pricing based on the assumption that nonprofits care about the amount and distribution of consumer surplus. They show that price discrimination often arises in equilibrium. Weinberg (1984) provides a more comprehensive model of nonprofit pricing decisions. He includes three decision variables for a nonprofit monopolist: price, marketing expenditure to users, and marketing expenditure to donors. Marketing expenditure to users can be interpreted as, for instance, the promotional expenditure or the cost of product quality.

Below we use Weinberg (1984)'s main model and results to illustrate the basic properties of nonprofit pricing. Similar to that of for-profits, both price (p) and marketing expenditure (v) influence the demand for nonprofit output. A general nonprofit pricing model can be specified as follows:

$$\text{Max } q = f(p, v) \qquad (24.4)$$

$$\text{subject to } pf(p, v) + D(q, r) - r - c(q) - v - F = 0$$

where $f(p, v)$ is the demand function at price p and marketing expenditure v. As in equations (24.2) and (24.3), q is the corresponding quantity, $c(q)$ is the cost function, $D(q, r)$ is the donation response to quantity q and fundraising expense r. F is the fixed cost of running the nonprofit organization. As compared to the typical for-profit pricing situation in which marginal cost is the most important factor and fixed cost F does not influence the optimal price levels, F is relevant to nonprofit pricing. This occurs due to the inclusion of F in the non-deficit constraint as shown in equation (24.4). Moreover, in contrast to the fundraising models discussed earlier, equation (24.4) highlights the need

---

[3] Rose-Ackerman (1996) provides a more general discussion about how altruism influences nonprofit behavior.

by nonprofits to obtain sales revenue to support their mission. The donation function is dependent upon both the level of fundraising effort and the number of users of the service.

A for-profit, in contrast, has the typical objective function of profit maximization, Max $\pi = pq - c(q) - v$, where $q = f(p, v)$. Solving the constrained optimization problem for the nonprofits involves finding the values of p^*, v^* and r^* that jointly maximize $f(p,v)$. The for-profit's optimization involves solving the typical first-order conditions $\partial\pi/\partial v = 0$ and $\partial\pi/\partial p = 0$. Particular formats can be specified for the functions in equation (24.4) so that closed-form optimal solutions can be derived.

For the demand and fundraising response functions, Weinberg (1984) adopts the power function that is used frequently in empirical research. It becomes the popular double-log function through log transformations. The cost function is assumed linear with marginal cost c:

$$\begin{cases} q = f(p, v) = \alpha_0 p^{-\alpha_1} v^{\alpha_2} \\ D(q, r) = \beta_0 q^{\beta_1} r^{\beta_2} \\ c(q) = cq \end{cases} \quad (24.5)$$

where $\alpha_1, \alpha_2, \beta_1, \beta_2 > 0$. To illustrate the nature of these results and to make concrete the comparison between the nonprofit and the for-profit sectors, Weinberg further assumes that $\alpha_1 + \alpha_2 = 2$ and $2\beta_1 + \beta_2 = 1$. An important benefit of these assumptions is that analytical solutions can be obtained to illustrate how optimal pricing decisions (together with other decisions such as marketing expense) are determined by the relevant factors.[4]

The optimal price for the for-profit is straightforward: $p_f^* = c\alpha_1/(\alpha_1 - 1)$. Closed-form solutions for the nonprofit are in more extensive format. For example, the optimal nonprofit price is $p_n^* = (k - \sqrt{k^2 - 4cFk_2})/2F$, where $k = k_2 - k_1 + k_3$, $k_1 = (\alpha_0\alpha_2/\alpha_1)^{1/(1-\alpha_2)}$, $k_2 = (\alpha_1 k_1)/\alpha_2$, and $k_3 = [2\beta_1(\beta_0\beta_2)^{1/2\beta_1}\sqrt{k_2}]/\beta_2$. If there is no fixed cost ($F = 0$), then $p_n^* = ck_2/(k_2 - k_1)$. Weinberg (1984) uses various numerical examples to illustrate the patterns of these analytical solutions. Table 24.1 provides some of these examples to highlight the key features of the nonprofit price model.

First, nonprofit optimal price is lower than that of the for-profit, and the difference increases as the donation is more responsive to fundraising effort and the levels of nonprofit output. Consistent with the pricing models discussed earlier, the optimal nonprofit output is greater than that of the for-profit.

Second, fixed cost matters for the nonprofit pricing decision. Many discussions and debates concerning nonprofit management focus on the issues of efficiency and innovativeness. Fixed cost is one of the major factors that have direct implication for these issues. As shown here, and as we discuss further below, nonprofits are more directly influenced by fixed cost than are for-profits, and thus it is likely that they are more constrained in the ability to utilize newer technology than comparable for-profits.

---

[4] In practice, the estimation of demand functions may lead to parameter values that do not lead to closed-form solutions. In such cases, numerical methods can be used.

Table 24.1 Optimal decisions by nonprofit versus for-profit monopolist

Organization type	Fixed cost (F)	Donation response (β_0)	Price (p^*)	Output (q^*)	Marketing expense to users (v^*)	Market expense to donors (r^*)	Profit from users
Nonprofit	0	10	1.25	25 327	7 915	378	−1 512
	0	50	0.90	48 838	10 984	3 922	−15 687
	5 000	10	1.72	13 402	5 763	275	−1 101
	5 000	50	1.02	38 062	9 705	3 466	−13 862
For-profit	0	–	2.67	5 574	3 720	–	5 581
	5 000	–	2.67	5 574	3 720	–	581

Source: Weinberg (1984), p. 268. Other parameter values: $\alpha_0 = 1000$, $\alpha_1 = 1.6$, $\alpha_2 = 0.4$, $\beta_1 = 0.4$, $\beta_2 = 0.2$, $c = 1.0$. Minor discrepancies are due to rounding errors.

Third, the nonprofit may spend more on marketing expenditures than a similarly situated for-profit would. This has direct implications for nonprofits' marketing management practice. It has been the tradition that nonprofits do not rely as much on commercial techniques such as advertising as for-profits do (or perhaps they just use donated advertising space by policy, as is the case with the Red Cross). However, this result indicates they may actually benefit from adopting these techniques, using them even more than comparable for-profits do. If marketing expense is interpreted as the cost of product quality, the model here provides analytical guidance for the empirical research that tests how the quality levels differ between for-profits and nonprofits in specific markets (Chou, 2002; Luksetich et al., 2000; Schlesinger, 1998; Krashinsky, 1998).

Weinberg's result lends support to the finding that, at least in some markets, the quality of the nonprofit's output can be higher than that of a comparable for-profit. More importantly, this result is derived from a perspective that is very different from the typical 'contract failure' rationale behind the quality differential between nonprofits and for-profits. Contract failure refers to the information asymmetry between the seller and buyer. As Hansmann (1987, p. 29) states, in situations where it is difficult for consumers to evaluate the true quality of a product or service,

> a for-profit firm has both the incentive and the opportunity to take advantage of customers by providing less service to them than was promised or paid for. A nonprofit firm, in contrast, offers consumers the advantage that, owing to the nondistribution constraint, those who control the organization are constrained in their ability to benefit personally from providing low-quality services and thus have less incentive to take advantage of customers than do managers of a for-profit firm.

Lastly, while charging a price to help increase operating revenue, the nonprofit may have negative profit from users for some products due to donations and cross subsidization (e.g. James, 1983). Interestingly, a more responsive donation function can potentially benefit the nonprofit in all operational aspects – a lower price, more people served and greater marketing (e.g. quality) expenditures. Further empirical testing of these results would be highly instructive.

We now present an example of how pricing can be set in a nonprofit organization (Weinberg, 1990). The major elements in this case involve the estimation of the demand function and the choice of a nonprofit objective. The organization (name, location and other details are disguised) is the Korona Community Center (KCC), located in the Midwestern USA. The pricing issue for the KCC is to decide the admission price for its Levy Auditorium, where various performing arts events are held, jointly with the appropriate advertising budget levels. The KCC needs to pay $4 per seat sold to the performing art group and an additional $6 per seat to cover other operational expenses. It is also responsible for local advertising to promote the performing art groups and the events. To focus on the pricing issues, we do not consider the opportunity of fundraising for this specific event or the fixed cost of producing it. An extensive operational record kept by the KCC included tickets sold, price and advertising budget information for various events. Using these data, the demand function for the KCC is estimated to be

$$TICKETS = 5014 PRICE^{-1.54} ADV^{0.35}$$

The optimal marketing mix of price and advertising depends on the objective function. Here we consider two objectives – the maximization of attendance (i.e. tickets sold, subject to the non-deficit constraint) and the maximization of profit (i.e. the for-profit case). The number of tickets sold is maximized approximately at a price of $13 and an advertising budget of $6130. These will generate a demand of 2040 tickets sold and KCC will be able to break even (approximately). On the other hand, if the organization behaves like a for-profit, the optimal price should be set at about $28.50 and advertising spending should be $3600. This strategy should sell about 500 tickets for a profit of approximately $5800. While setting a lower price (than the for-profit) to increase attendance, KCC should also spend more on advertising to attract an audience for this event.

Besides illustrating the price-setting process for nonprofits, the KCC example suggests the importance of data in enhancing the efficiency of organizational decision-making. Similar to the situation of for-profit firms where data collection, storage and computing technologies have enabled the accumulation of large amounts of consumer data, the value of such data to the nonprofits should not be overlooked. While many nonprofits have retained extensive data on their fundraising activities, relatively few have substantial databases with which to analyze market demand.

Competition and nonprofit pricing
The monopoly models discussed in the previous section illustrate the distinctive features of nonprofit pricing, such as objective functions, nondistribution constraint, donations, and the joint decisions of pricing, fundraising and marketing expenses. In this section, we turn to competitive situations that involve at least one nonprofit. An important reason to account for competition in nonprofit pricing is the reality that most nonprofits operate in a competitive environment. In many markets, nonprofits not only compete with other nonprofits for revenue and donation; they also compete with for-profits that sell similar products or services. The trend of decreasing public funding and relatively stable private contributions makes such competition only more critical for the nonprofits (e.g. Rose-Ackerman, 1990).

The markets where nonprofits and for-profits coexist are many. They include, for

Pricing for nonprofit organizations   523

example, health care, education, child daycare, family counseling and performing arts. In these 'mixed' markets, what drives the pricing behavior of nonprofits has important managerial and public policy implications, since most nonprofits receive tax and other regulatory advantages that are not available to for-profits. These advantages can be the exemption from corporate income tax, reductions or elimination of state and local property taxes, and a lower postal rate.

Analytical work addressing competitive issues faced by nonprofits is growing, but the literature is still in its infancy. As mentioned before, most nonprofit models focus on the fundraising issues and, if price is involved, an exogenous price is typically assumed (e.g. Schiff and Weisbrod, 1993). Given the trend of nonprofits seeking more revenue from sales of products and services, pricing and price competition appear to be particularly promising issues for modeling.

We focus on a duopoly market to address two different types of price competition – a nonprofit competing with another nonprofit, and a nonprofit competing with a for-profit. We follow the modeling framework of Liu and Weinberg (2004), who examine the degree to which a for-profit's competitive disadvantage, if any, can be attributed to the favorable policy and regulatory treatments received by the competing nonprofit. In contrast, in this chapter we will highlight the pricing principles of the nonprofit in competitive situations and market structure issues such as entry and exit.

We discuss the following issues of nonprofit pricing in a competitive environment: (1) nonprofit price reaction functions; (2) Stackelberg price leadership; (3) the roles of fixed cost and entry/exit in a mixed market where nonprofits and for-profits compete on price; and (4) price levels in various markets that have implications for empirical research. The first three issues are addressed in a mixed duopoly market served by a nonprofit and a competing for-profit. The fourth issue involves such mixed markets and also the markets where the duopoly competitors are both nonprofits. Since our focus is on pricing issues, the price competition models discussed here differ significantly from the literature on the public or government organizations (e.g. Beato and Mas-Colell, 1984; Cremer et al., 1989). Many models there are Cournot games based on quantity competition, and pricing plays a much more passive role.

We keep the previous assumption that the nonprofits' objective function is the maximization of output, and to focus on pricing decisions, we abstract from the donation and the marketing expenditure problems.[5] However, we model product differentiation following the well-known approach used, for example, by Shubik and Levitan (1980) and Raju et al. (1995). (See equation 24.6 below.) Modeling heterogeneous products is particularly useful for a mixed market where nonprofits and for-profits coexist. Rose-Ackerman (1996) suggests that due to their different priorities and managerial preferences, for-profits and nonprofits may choose to serve different market segments with differentiated products or services.

Product differentiation can be captured with an (exogenous) parameter in the demand model

---

[5] Liu and Weinberg (2004) discuss the robustness of the duopoly model to these assumptions. They show that the structure of the competitive model and its main results do not change for a wide range of nonprofit objective functions and donation response functions.

524 *Handbook of pricing research in marketing*

$$q_i = \frac{1}{2}[1 - p_i + \theta(p_j - p_i)] \tag{24.6}$$

where q_i is the demand for firm i's product at price p_i, and θ is the degree of product differentiation ($\theta > 0$). A higher θ implies more similar products and thus greater competition. Using the subscript f to indicate a for-profit firm, the subscript n to indicate a nonprofit, and retaining the cost factors from the nonprofit monopoly model, the optimization problems for the nonprofit and the for-profit can be specified as follows.

The nonprofit optimization problem is

$$\text{Max } q_n = \frac{1}{2}[1 - p_n + \theta(p_f - p_n)] \tag{24.7}$$

$$\text{subject to } pq_n - cq_n - F = 0$$

The for-profit optimization problem is

$$\text{Max } \pi_f = p_f q_f - cq_f - F \tag{24.8}$$

Price is the decision variable for both competitors.

Nonprofit price reaction in the duopoly model
Liu and Weinberg (2004) show that this demand system leads to well-behaved isoprofit curves. Solving equations (24.7) and (24.8) separately yields the price reaction functions of the nonprofit and the for-profit. Figure 24.2 illustrates the unique pattern of the nonprofit's price reaction and how it differs from that of the for-profit.

If Firm 1 is a for-profit, its price reaction curve will be line BC, an upward-sloping curve following the well-known 'strategic complement' pattern documented for price competition (Bulow et al., 1985; Tirole, 1988, pp. 207–8). However, if Firm 1 is a nonprofit, its

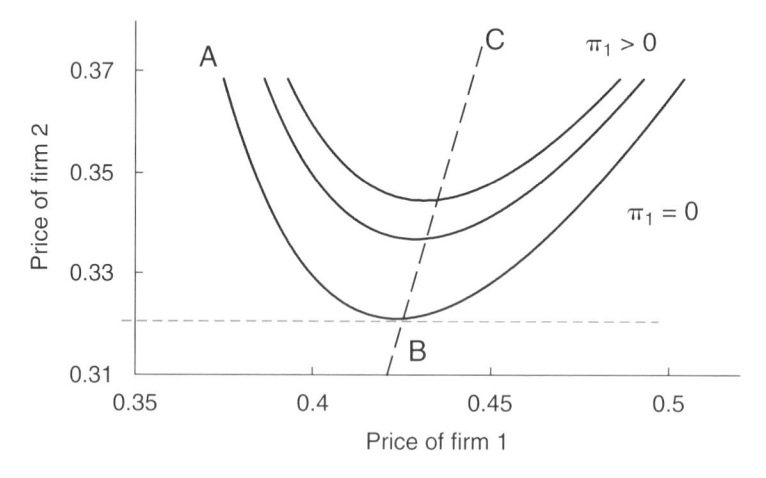

Source: Based on Liu and Weinberg (2004), Figure 1.

Figure 24.2 *Isoprofit curves of the duopoly model and the price reaction functions of Firm 1*

reaction curve will be AB, where B is the lowest point on the zero isoprofit curve $\pi_1 = 0$. This is the case since only the isoprofit curve representing zero profit is relevant to the nonprofit due to the nondistribution constraint. The downward-sloping pattern of AB makes the nonprofit price reaction curve distinct from that of the for-profit. It is similar to the 'strategic substitute' pattern that has been mainly found for quantity response functions in theoretical models of profit maximization.

The distinct price reaction pattern is the result of the nonprofit maximizing output subject to the nondistribution constraint. Thus, in a duopoly market, if a competitor increases its price, the nonprofit will lower its price to gain more customers. If the competitor reduces its price in an attempt to increase demand, the nonprofit will have to raise its own price. This happens since the nonprofit is operating at the break-even level.

One implication of this finding is that nonprofits can be particularly vulnerable in competitive markets if their demand models are not accurate. Consistent with the arguments advanced by Gallagher and Weinberg (1991), nonprofits typically do not have as much protection from the 'risk cushion' that for-profits can accumulate from earned profits. As a result, nonprofit management may need to adopt more long-term orientations to build up their capability of dealing with uncertainties. From the point of view of regulation and public policy, nonprofits may survive and grow more easily in a competitive environment if they are encouraged to keep sufficient retained assets as a cushion against unforeseen events.

Stackelberg price leadership
Stackelberg price leadership assumes that one firm has knowledge or foresight of its competitor's reaction to its price policies. As a result, the firm may credibly announce a price in anticipation of the competitor's reaction. In contrast to a simultaneous game in which both firms act at the same time, the Stackelberg price leader benefits from this foresight and is normally better off than in the simultaneous game. In for-profit pricing models, this happens since the price leader can search the competitor's reaction function to find a price level that maximizes its profit (Tirole, 1988). Not surprisingly, this price is usually higher than its equilibrium price in the simultaneous game. Recall that in for-profit competitions, the pricing pattern is usually strategic complement; thus a higher price by the Stackelberg leader will lead to a higher price by its competitor (Stackelberg follower). The consumers will then be worse off due to these higher prices. As we shall see, different results hold when one of the competitors is a nonprofit.

Two questions are relevant here. First, if the for-profit is the Stackelberg price leader, how will its behavior be different now that its competitor is a nonprofit organization? Second, if the nonprofit is the price leader, how may it change its behavior from the equilibrium in the simultaneous game? Figure 24.3 summarizes Liu and Weinberg (2004)'s findings for both questions. It includes the isoprofit curves of the Stackelberg price leader (which can be either a for-profit or a nonprofit), and the price reaction curves of both competitors. Note that, as the intersection of the price reaction curves, p_f^* and p_n^* are the equilibrium prices in the simultaneous game, $p_f^*(p_n)$ is the price reaction function of the for-profit, and $p_n^*(p_f)$ is that of the nonprofit.

Figure 24.3(a) shows the case of for-profit being the Stackelberg leader. As the level of product differentiation (captured by parameter θ in the demand functions) varies, different isoprofit curves are in effect that, in turn, lead to different equilibrium results. Higher

526 *Handbook of pricing research in marketing*

(a) For-Profit Stackelberg

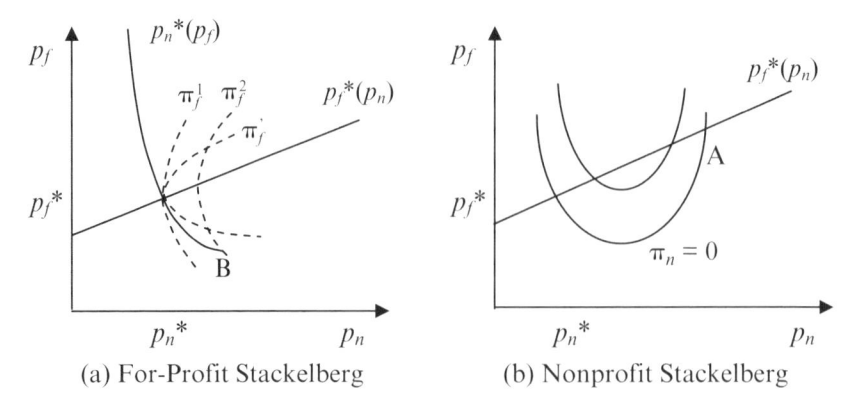

(b) Nonprofit Stackelberg

Source: Based on Liu and Weinberg (2004), Figure A1.

Figure 24.3 *The effects of Stackelberg price leadership*

levels of θ are associated with curves such as π_f^1 and π_f^2 ($\pi_f^2 > \pi_f^1$) and lower levels of θ lead to curves similar to π_f'. The fundamental difference between these two situations is whether the for-profit's isoprofit curves, when moved along its price reaction curve, would be able to intersect with the nonprofit's price reaction curve and lead to greater profits for the for-profit. When the market is more competitive (i.e. high θ), this is possible. The for-profit earns a maximum level of profit π_f^2 obtained at B, the lowest end-point of $p_n^*(p_f)$. Interestingly, at point B, the for-profit's equilibrium price is lower than p_f^*, its equilibrium price in the simultaneous game (which obtains at the intersection between reaction curves $p_f^*(p_n)$ and $p_n^*(p_f)$). As discussed earlier, the nonprofit's equilibrium price will be increased accordingly. When the market is not sufficiently competitive (i.e. isoprofit curves similar to π_f' are in effect), the for-profit will not be able to take advantage of the Stackelberg price leadership to improve its profit level.

Figure 24.3(b) illustrates the situation of the nonprofit being the Stackelberg price leader. Since the zero-profit curve is the one that matters, and the left branch of it makes up the nonprofit's price reaction function, the nonprofit will not change its pricing behavior from the simultaneous case. As a result, when the nonprofit is the Stackelberg price leader, or when the for-profit is the leader but the degree of product differentiation is not great, consumers will face the same price levels at equilibrium as they do when the nonprofit and for-profit compete simultaneously.

These Stackelberg results are different from (and in many cases opposite to) those obtained in purely for-profit competition games. They add new situations of price reaction curves and price leadership results to the literature on competitive strategies and industrial organization. They also suggest that organizations' objective functions matter a great deal for the competitive outcome. In this sense, the nonprofit sector, due to its diversified organizational goals, provides a good opportunity for examining the robustness of traditional monopoly and competitive results obtained in the for-profit context.[6]

---

[6] Even in the for-profit world where profit maximization is the default objective, one may want to be cautions when modeling firm behavior at different stages of the product life cycle. For

The effect of fixed cost
By solving through the price reaction functions, closed-form price equilibrium solutions can be obtained for the mixed market. They are in very complex algebraic format, but we can write them as functions of the parameters: $p_f^* = p_f(\theta, c, F)$ and $p_n^* = p_n(\theta, c, F)$. As we discussed earlier in the chapter, fixed cost matters for nonprofit pricing behavior due to the nondistribution constraint. Because of the strategic interactions in the duopoly competition, the for-profit's equilibrium price is affected by F as well.

The impact of F on the structure of the mixed market depends upon its magnitude. Ranking from low to high levels, there are three critical values, denoted as F_1, F_2 and F_3. For comparatively low levels of F ($F < F_1$), the price equilibrium exists so that the for-profit earns positive profit and the nonprofit is able to break even with a positive level of output. As F becomes greater, it becomes more difficult for both organizations to compete.

When $F_1 < F < F_2$, the price equilibrium technically exists but the for-profit's profit is negative. Therefore, if market entry is modeled as the first step in a dynamic game, the for-profit will not want to compete in this market and the duopoly equilibrium does not hold. On the other hand, the nonprofit is able to break even with positive demand, even when the for-profit decides to enter. Liu and Weinberg (2004) term this range as the 'reserved market' for the nonprofit.

When $F_2 < F < F_3$, neither the for-profit nor the nonprofit can survive in the duopoly market. Each of them can, however, survive if there is no competitor – the for-profit can earn positive profits and the nonprofit can break even as a monopolist. For this situation, the market structure will probably be determined by who is the first mover to enter the market. When one organization establishes itself in the market, its commitment to the market will be a credible signal to deter the other one from entering. As a result, this level of fixed cost leads to a 'first-mover monopoly' situation.

Taking this result to empirical testing, one would expect that certain market situations could be related to a comparatively high level of entry cost that is conducive to early-mover monopoly. For example, nonprofits are historically 'early movers' in markets such as health care, family counseling, arts and education. If the fixed cost of operating on some of these markets can be shown to be within this range, nonprofits should be expected to continue to dominate these markets.

When $F > F_3$, fixed cost is so high that neither the for-profit nor the nonprofit can survive even as a monopolist. Over the ranges of the fixed cost, it can be seen that as long as the market (or consumers) is appropriate for nonprofits, they are more likely to be in the market than a comparable for-profit. The existence of the 'reserved market' for nonprofits is an interesting question for empirical research. As Rose-Ackerman (1996) summarizes, in industries where nonprofits and for-profits coexist, the nonprofits are on average larger than the for-profits both in terms of the number of employees and in terms of revenue.

---

example, Mahajan and Venkatesh (2000) propose several intriguing research questions about marketing modeling for e-business. One of the 'model setup-related challenges' they discuss focuses on the objective of e-business firms – 'firms in e-business typically seem more concerned with maximizing customer share [at least] in the short term' (p. 220).

Liu and Weinberg (2004) further point out that when fixed cost is prohibitively high for socially desirable products or services, governments and private donors may respond by helping nonprofits overcome the entry barrier. One well-known example of this situation is the provision of accommodation for families of sick children who are receiving treatment for very serious illnesses at tertiary-level children's hospitals. For example, in Vancouver, Canada, two specially built facilities were opened to provide just such accommodation for families of children at the British Columbia Children's Hospital. The Easter Seals House provides 53 rooms at a rate of $18 per night and the Ronald MacDonald House offers 14 rooms at a rate of $12 per night; while the Ronald MacDonald house has a different mission ('for families of seriously ill children; priority given to children with cancer and bone marrow transplants') from that of the Easter Seal House, both are within walking distance of the hospital. These rooms provide kitchen facilities and other amenities. Clearly, no for-profit company can offer these facilities at such a low price; the nearest hotel charges $99 for a room in the off-season.[7]

The issue of why nonprofit organizations are more frequently observed in some markets than in others has stimulated a great deal of research. Perhaps the most popular explanation is based on the nonprofit's value to the society when market failure occurs. Steinberg (2006) provides a comprehensive review of this issue, considering the roles of nonprofits together with those of for-profits and governments. He suggests that as market failure happens due to the inefficiency resulting from for-profit provision of goods and services, governments and nonprofits will respond to regulate or restore the market. As a result, nonprofits can be observed more often in markets where the problem of market (and government) failure is more severe. The issues of contract failure and information asymmetry discussed earlier could be good examples of market situations that are conducive to nonprofit operations. Related empirical evidence suggests that in some industries, such as day care and medical services, nonprofits are more trusted than the for-profits by customers (e.g. Krashinsky, 1998; Brown and Slivinski, 2006). The findings we discuss in this chapter regarding the effects of fixed cost provide a different perspective on market entry and exit that is distinct from these theories.

Nonprofits competing with nonprofits
In many markets, nonprofits compete with other nonprofits for revenue and donations. If we focus on the revenue side of the competition, it is useful to compare the price equilibrium with that obtained in the mixed market. One benefit of doing so is to provide guidance for empirical research. For example, in a market where there is a for-profit daycare and a nonprofit daycare, will the prices of the two organizations be higher or lower than those in a market where there are two nonprofit daycare centers? As another example, empirical research based on such analytical results can cast light on the important issue of whether some nonprofits are just 'for-profit in disguise' (Weisbrod, 1988).

Liu and Weinberg (2004) compare the magnitude of four equilibrium prices: p_f^* and p_n^* from the mixed duopoly market, p^n from the market with two nonprofits, and p^f from the market served by two for-profits. They find the following ranking for all parameter values of the demand function: $p^f > p_f^* > p^n > p_n^*$. The most interesting and in many ways

---

[7] All rates are from website www.bcchildrens.ca, accessed on 5 June 2007.

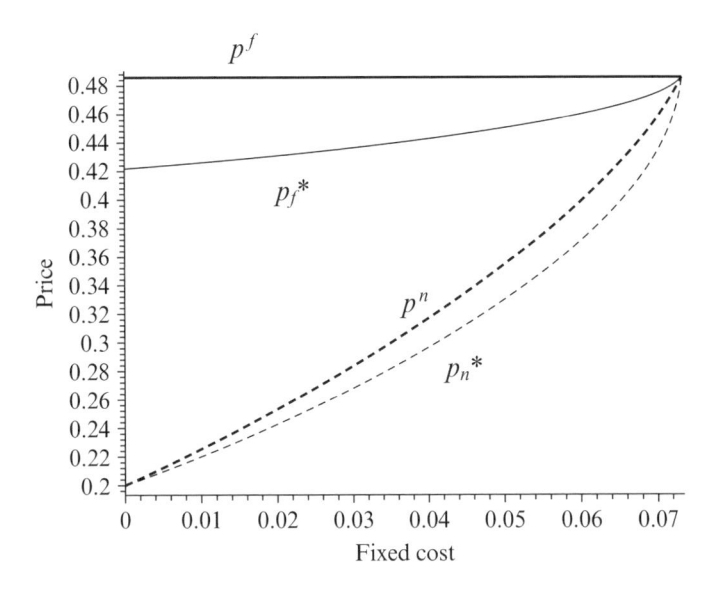

Figure 24.4 Comparison of equilibrium prices in three different duopoly markets ($\theta = 0.8, c = 0.2$)

Notes: p^f: for-profit equilibrium price when both duopolists are for-profits.
p_f^*: for-profit equilibrium price when the competitor is a nonprofit.
p^n: nonprofit equilibrium price when both duopolists are nonprofits.
p_n^*: nonprofit equilibrium price when the competitor is a for-profit.

surprising result is probably the comparison of p^n and p_n^* – a nonprofit charges a higher price when it competes with another nonprofit than when it competes with a for-profit. This happens since the nonprofit has more flexibility in setting its price when the competitor is a profit-oriented firm rather than an equally low-price-oriented nonprofit organization. The need to survive (i.e. break even) in a highly competitive market drives up p^n to be higher than p_n^*. Figure 24.4 shows how these four equilibrium prices compare with each other as fixed cost changes.

Concluding discussion and future research issues

Nonprofit pricing decisions differ significantly from those of for-profit businesses due to the unique features of nonprofit organizations. The objective function and nondistribution constraint play particularly important roles in formulating models of pricing and in exploring their intuition and implications. As noted by Weinberg (1983), nonprofits' deviation from profit maximizing complicates any optimum-seeking algorithm. Researchers working on studying business decisions have developed demand systems and price models that depend on several critical features of the demand function (e.g. a well-behaved profit curve and specific functional forms) to allow for tractable analyses. Even for the (presumably) simplest objective of maximizing nonprofit output, closed-form solutions can be complicated to achieve. Nevertheless, as demonstrated in this chapter, an appropriately specified demand system can be very useful in examining the pricing behavior of nonprofits under a variety of circumstances in both the monopoly and duopoly cases.

In the for-profit sector, issues of dynamic pricing have become increasingly important. The areas covered include pricing at various stages of the product life cycle, prices in response to changing cost structures, and pricing to reflect and influence temporal patterns of demand. Such issues are important for nonprofit organizations as well, but we could identify no papers specifically addressing such issues in the nonprofit sector. An additional factor for nonprofits is how to modify the no-deficit constraint so that it has meaning in a dynamic setting. It would seem that considerations other than simply applying a cumulative non-deficit constraint (with a present value discount factor) are pertinent. For example, if a nonprofit accumulates a surplus in the early years, how does it value the result that some potential clients may not be served due to the imposition of this constraint?

Donations are not explicitly included in the competition model discussed earlier. Conceptually, donations have an impact on nonprofits' pricing decisions through two distinct mechanisms. One is the effect of increasing funds available, thus reducing pricing pressure and, if quality decisions are involved, helping to improve quality. The other is the usage of funds for fundraising campaigns, which works in the opposite direction to increase the pricing pressure and reduce potential quality levels. Of course, the amount spent raising donations should not exceed the amount raised. Therefore an appropriately specified donation response function is critical to derive useful results for the pricing problem. Empirical research with regard to donations is facilitated by the availability of public data sources. For example, a large data set of revenues and expenditures of nonprofits, which was collected from the IRS 990 forms filed annually by 501(c)(3) organizations, can be accessed through the National Center for Charitable Statistics (NCCS) at the Urban Institute (nccsdataweb.urban.org). Boris and Steuerle (2006) provide a list of major IRS nonprofit data sources.

A very common role of pricing in the for-profit world is to implement price discrimination. Many models assume consumers can be differentiated along two fundamental dimensions of preference, namely horizontal differentiation and vertical differentiation. The former refers to the preference space where buyers have heterogeneous ideal points (e.g. Hotelling, 1929), while the latter refers to that where 'the more, the better' holds true for everyone (e.g. Shaked and Sutton, 1982). Models have also been constructed for firms competing on both dimensions (e.g. Neven and Thisse, 1990). Related to these two dimensions are the typical issues of consumer taste and willingness to pay. While both are straightforward in for-profit pricing models, they are no longer so for nonprofits.

First, the taste for nonprofit products or service may not be as clearly defined as for commercial products. For instance, it is easy to assume that consumers may prefer different styles of cars (e.g. color, size, or a 'sporty' image), but it is not easy to conceptualize the taste for performing arts or family counseling services. This issue becomes particularly complex when the researcher wants to consider the different (and sometimes conflicting) preference of nonprofit managers and donors. For example, Rose-Ackerman (1987) explicitly models the donor's preference for a qualitative index of nonprofit output, which may differ from the preference of the nonprofit manager. Voss et al. (2000) distinguish five organizational value dimensions for arts organizations: pro-social, artistic, financial, market and achievement. They suggest that there exist underlying tensions between competing values in cultural organizations, such as the pressure to be both artistic and market oriented.

Second, consumer willingness to pay is no longer a simple factor for segmentation and positioning models. It is commonly observed in the commercial world that firms pursue different segments of consumers by offering differentiated products, such as high-quality firms selling to the consumers with higher willingness to pay (for quality) and low-quality firms selling to the remaining consumers (Moorthy, 1988). Due to the socially beneficial nature of nonprofit outputs, it is unclear whether consumer willingness to pay is an appealing factor to all nonprofits. There are certainly situations where the nonprofits want to ensure that the poor or needy population will be able to receive their products or services regardless of their financial capability. This is in many ways reflected in the output-maximizing goal of nonprofits – social service agencies measure success in part by clients-served levels, and museums by attendance (Oster et al., 2003). As a matter of policy, many nonprofits prefer to serve the low-willingness-to-pay population. This is, again, different from business models in which the ultimate profit earned drives firm behavior.

Increasingly business managers are recognizing that consumers' reactions to prices involve such factors as mental accounting, price–perceived quality relationships, and perceived fairness. These findings are likely to be important for pricing decisions in the nonprofit sector as well. For example, in the research stream on price–perceived quality relationships, Scitovsky (1945) was the first to formally suggest that price is both an index of sacrifice and an index of quality to consumers. Subsequent studies show that the use of price as an indicator of quality is widespread across consumers and product categories (Lichtenstein and Burton, 1989; Peterson and Wilson, 1985). The behavioral literature establishes that when it is often difficult for consumers to judge quality before purchase, they tend to infer quality based on relevant cues (Lichtenstein and Burton, 1989; Monroe, 1973). It is then an interesting issue how consumers in the nonprofit market evaluate both price and the nonprofit status as signals of quality (Ryans and Weinberg, 1978). Furthermore, while some businesses may employ such behavioral findings to enhance their profitability, nonprofits, with their focus on social ends, may seek to pursue pricing policies that seek to remove such biases from the consideration of prices.

Another critical issue for nonprofit pricing research is consumer surplus. In the for-profit world, consumer surplus is based on the difference between the amount consumers are willing to pay (the demand curve) and what they actually pay. Graphically this is the area below the demand curve but above the prevailing market price. For the same price, richer consumers will, on average, derive a greater amount of consumer surplus than poor consumers. A simple maximization of consumer surplus has the problem of ignoring the distribution issue – it may counter some nonprofits' goal of serving the needy population.

Pricing is still a new phenomenon in nonprofit management. While some nonprofits adopt pricing practice voluntarily (see Oster et al., 2003 for the potential benefit of pricing), others do so due to financial pressure. Given that nonprofits have several other more traditional choices when it comes to the distribution or allocation of nonprofit output (such as waiting lists and rationing), it is useful to examine the efficiency of pricing relative to these other mechanisms in achieving nonprofit objectives. Steinberg and Weisbrod (1998) pioneered this area of research by looking at the waiting lists versus prices as the rationing mechanism. It is possible that pricing is more efficient for certain nonprofit types or objectives than for others.

Finally, we want to highlight the issue of product and service quality as a joint decision factor together with pricing for nonprofits. Similar to the product line decision by for-profits, the product mix decision can be critical to the managers of many nonprofits (e.g. Newhouse, 1970; James, 1983; Rose-Ackerman, 1987; Ansari et al., 1996). Among these decisions, product or service quality has received a great deal of attention. A number of empirical studies test how the quality levels differ between for-profits and nonprofits in markets such as nursing homes (Chou, 2002; Luksetich et al., 2000), healthcare facilities and hospitals (Schlesinger, 1998), and daycare centers (Krashinsky, 1998). Analytical work in this area appears to be particularly promising. For example, if the nonprofit can offer differentiated products or services, how should it position and price them? As another example, given their different objectives and financial goals, how do for-profits and nonprofits differentiate themselves in price and quality in mixed markets?

References

Ansari, A., S. Siddarth and C. Weinberg (1996), 'Pricing a bundle of products or services: the case of nonprofits', *Journal of Marketing Research*, (February), 86–93.

Beato, P. and A. Mas-Colell (1984), 'The marginal cost pricing as a regulation mechanism in mixed markets', in M. Marchand, P. Pestieau and H. Tulkens (eds), *The Performance of Public Enterprises*, Amsterdam: North-Holland, pp. 81–100.

Bilodeau, M. and R. Steinberg (1999), 'Ransom of the opera', Typescript, Indiana University and Purdue University at Indianapolis.

Boris, E.T. and C.E. Steuerle (2006), 'Scope and dimensions of the nonprofit sector', in W. Powell and R. Steinberg (eds), *The Nonprofit Sector: A Research Handbook*, 2nd edn, New Haven, CT and London, Yale University Press, pp. 66–88.

Brooks, A.C. (2005), 'What do nonprofit organizations seek? (and why should policymakers care?)', *Journal of Policy Analysis and Management*, **24** (3), 543–58.

Brown, E. and A. Slivinski (2006), 'Nonprofit organizations and the market', in W. Powell and R. Steinberg (eds), *The Nonprofit Sector: A Research Handbook*, 2nd edn, New Haven, CT and London, Yale University Press, pp. 140–58.

Bulow, J., J. Geanakoplos, and P. Klemperer (1985), 'Multimarket oligopoly: strategic substitutes and complements', *Journal of Political Economy*, **93** (3), 488–511.

Chou, S. (2002), 'Asymmetric information, ownership and quality of care: an empirical analysis of nursing homes', *Journal of Health Economics*, **21** (2), 293–311.

Cremer, H., M. Marchand, and J.F. Thisse (1989), 'The public firm as an instrument for regulating an oligopolistic market', *Oxford Economic Papers*, **41**, 283–301.

Dart, R. and B. Zimmerman (2000), 'After government cuts: insights from two Ontario enterprising nonprofits', in K. Banting (ed.), *The Nonprofit Sector in Canada*, Kingston, Ont.: Queen's University School of Policy Studies, pp. 107–48.

Dees, J. (1998), 'Enterprising nonprofits', *Harvard Business Review*, **76** (1), 55–67.

Evans, D. and R. Schmalensee (2005), 'The industrial organization of markets with two-sided platforms', Working Paper, National Bureau of Economic Research.

Gallagher, K. and C. Winberg (1991), 'Coping with success: new challenges for nonprofit marketing', *Sloan Management Review*, **33** (Fall), 27–42.

Gapinski, J. (1984), 'The economics of performing Shakespeare', *American Economic Review*, **74** (3), 458–66.

Hall, P.D. and C.B. Burke (2006), *Historical Statistics of the United States*, millennial edition, New York: Cambridge University Press.

Hansmann, H. (1980), 'The role of nonprofit enterprises', *Yale Law Journal*, **89**, 835–901.

Hansmann, H. (1987), 'Economic theories of nonprofit organization', in W. Powell (ed.), *The Nonprofit Sector: A Research Handbook*, New Haven, CT: Yale University Press, pp. 27–42.

Hotelling, H. (1929), 'Stability in competition', *The Economic Journal*, **39**, 41–57.

Jacobs, P. and R. Wilder (1984), 'Pricing behavior of nonprofit agencies', *Journal of Health Economics*, **3** (1), 49–61.

James, E. (1983), 'How nonprofits grow: a model', *Journal of Policy Analysis and Management*, **2** (3), 350–66.

Krashinsky, M. (1998), 'Does auspice matter? The case of day care for children in Canada', in W. Powell and E. Clemens (eds), *Private Action and the Public Good*, New Haven, CT: Yale University Press, pp. 114–23.

Krug, K. and C. Weinberg (2004), 'Mission, money, and merit: strategic decision making by nonprofit managers', *Nonprofit Management and Leadership*, **14** (3), 325–42.

Lakdawalla, D. and T. Philipson (2006), 'The nonprofit sector and industry performance', *Journal of Public Economics*, **90** (8–9), 1681–98.

Leete, L. (2006), 'Work in the nonprofit sector', in W. Powell and R. Steinberg (eds), *The Nonprofit Sector, A Research Handbook*, 2nd edn, New Haven, CT and London: Yale University Press, pp.159–79.

Lichtenstein, D. and S. Burton (1989), 'The relationship between perceived and objective price-quality', *Journal of Marketing Research*, **26** (November), 429–43.

Liu, Y. and C. Weinberg (2004), 'Are nonprofits unfair competitors for businesses? An analytical approach', *Journal of Public Policy and Marketing*, **23** (1), 65–79.

Luksetich, W., M. Edwards and T. Carroll (2000), 'Organizational form and nursing home behavior', *Nonprofit and Voluntary Sector Quarterly*, **29**, 255–79.

Mahajan, V. and R. Venkatesh (2000), 'Marketing modeling for e-business', *International Journal of Research in Marketing*, **17**, 215–25.

McCready, D. (1988), 'Ramsey pricing: a method of setting fees in social service organizations', *American Journal of Economics and Sociology*, **47** (1), 97–110.

Monroe, K. (1973), 'Buyers' subjective perceptions of price', in Harold H. Kassarjian and Thomas S. Robertson (eds), *Perspectives in Consumer Behavior*, Glenview, IL: Scott, Foresman, pp. 23–42.

Moorthy, K. (1988), 'Product and price competition in a duopoly', *Marketing Science*, **7** (2), 141–68.

Neven, D. and J.F. Thisse (1990), 'On quality and variety competition', in J. Gabszewicz, J.-F. Richard and L. Wolsey (eds), *Economic Decision Making: Games, Econometrics and Optimization*, Amsterdam: North-Holland, pp. 175–99.

Newhouse, J. (1970), 'Toward a theory of nonprofit institutions: an economic model of a hospital', *American Economic Review*, **60** (1), 64–74.

Oster, S., C. Gray and C. Weinberg (2003), 'Pricing in the nonprofit sector', in D. Young (ed.), *Effective Economic Decision-Making for Nonprofit Organizations*, New York: Foundation Center, pp. 27–46.

Peterson, R. and W. Wilson (1985), 'Perceived risk and price reliance schema as price-perceived quality mediators', in J. Jacoby and J. C. Olson (eds), *Perceived Quality: How Consumers View Stores and Merchandise*, Lexington, MA: D.C. Heath, pp. 247–68.

Raju, J., R. Sethuraman, and S. Dhar (1995), 'The introduction and performance of store brands', *Management Science*, **41** (6), 957–78.

Rentschler, R., A. Hede and T. White (2007), 'Museum pricing: challenges to theory development and practice', *International Journal of Nonprofit and Voluntary Sector Marketing*, **12**, 163–73.

Rochet, J. and J. Tirole (2004), 'Two sided-markets: an overview', Working Paper, IDEI and GREMAQ, Toulouse.

Rose-Ackerman, S. (1987), 'Ideals versus dollars, donors, charity managers, and government grants', *Journal of Political Economy*, **95** (4), 810–23.

Rose-Ackerman, S. (1990), 'Competition between non-profits and for-profits: entry and growth', *Voluntas*, **1** (1), 13–25.

Rose-Ackerman, S. (1996), 'Altruism, nonprofits, and economic theory', *Journal of Economic Literature*, **34** (June), 701–28.

Ryans, A. and C. Weinberg (1978), 'Consumer dynamics in nonprofit organizations', *Journal of Consumer Research*, **5** (September), 89–95.

Salamon, L. and H.K. Anheier (1998), 'The third route: government–nonprofit collaboration in Germany and the United States', in W. Powell and E. Clemens (eds), *Private Action and the Public Good*, New Haven, CT: Yale University Press, 151–62.

Schiff, J. and B. Weisbrod (1993), 'Competition between for-profit and nonprofit organizations in commercial markets', in Avner Ben-Ner and Benedetto Gui (eds), *The Nonprofit Sector in the Mixed Economy*, Ann Arbor, MI: The University of Michigan Press, pp. 127–47.

Schlesinger, M. (1998), 'Mismeasuring the consequences of ownership: external influences and the comparative performance of public, for-profit and private nonprofit organizations', in W. Powell and E. Clemens (eds), *Private Action and the Public Good*, New Haven, CT: Yale University Press, pp. 85–113.

Scitovsky, T. (1945), 'Some consequences of the habit of judging quality by price', *Review of Economic Studies*, **12**, 100–105.

Shaked, A. and J. Sutton (1982), 'Relaxing price competition through product differentiation', *Review of Economic Studies*, **49**, 3–13.

Shubik, M. and R. Levitan (1980), *Market Structure and Behavior*, Cambridge, MA: Harvard University Press.

Simon, J., H. Dale and L. Chisolm (2006), 'The federal tax treatment of charitable organizations', in W. Powell and R. Steinberg (eds), *The Nonprofit Sector: A Research Handbook*, 2nd edn, New Haven, CT and London: Yale University Press, pp. 267–306.

Steinberg, R. (1986), 'The revealed objective functions of nonprofit firms', *RAND Journal of Economics*, **17** (Winter), 508–26.

Steinberg, R. (2006), 'Economic theories of nonprofit organizations', in W. Powell and R. Steinberg (eds), *The Nonprofit Sector: A Research Handbook*, 2nd edn, New Haven, CT and London: Yale University Press, pp. 117–39.

Steinberg, R. and B. Weisbrod (1998), 'Pricing and rationing by nonprofit organizations with distributional objectives', in B. Weisbrod (ed.), *To Profit or Not to Profit: The Commercial Transformation of the Nonprofit Sector*, Cambridge, New York and Melbourne: Cambridge University Press, pp. 65–82.

Steinberg, R. and B. Weisbrod (2005), 'Nonprofits with distributional objectives, price discrimination and corner solutions', *Journal of Public Economics*, **89**, 2205–30.

Tirole, J. (1988), *The Theory of Industrial Organization*, Cambridge, MA: The MIT Press.

Voss, G., D. Cable and Z. Voss (2000), 'Linking organizational values to relationships with external constituents: a study of nonprofit professional theatres', *Organization Science*, **11** (3), 330–47.

Weinberg, C. (1980), 'Marketing mix decision rules for nonprofit organizations', in J. Sheth (ed.), *Research in Marketing*, Vol. 3, Greenwich, CT: JAI Press, pp. 191–234.

Weinberg, C. (1984), 'Marketing mix decisions for nonprofit organizations: an analytical approach', in C. Lovelock and C. Weinberg (eds), *Public and Nonprofit Marketing: Cases and Readings*, Palo Alto, CA: Scientific Press, pp. 261–9.

Weinberg, C. (1990), 'Korona Community Center: auditorium rental', in C. Lovelock and C. Weinberg (eds), *Public & Nonprofit Marketing: Cases & Readings*, 2nd edn, Palo Alto, CA: Scientific Press, pp. 187–8.

Weisbrod, B. (1988), *The Nonprofit Economy*, Cambridge, MA: Harvard University Press.

Weisbrod, B. (1998), 'Institutional form and organizational behavior', in W. Power and E. Clements (eds), *Private Action and the Public Good*, New Haven, CT: Yale University Press, pp. 69–84.

25 Pricing in services
Stowe Shoemaker and Anna S. Mattila

Abstract
Most existing frameworks of pricing were developed in the context of consumer goods and, as such, they fail to explain how to price complex service offerings. In this chapter, the authors explain the characteristics of services that make services pricing different from goods. Relying on theory from both the general pricing literature and from services research, they develop a conceptual model of pricing of services. This framework incorporates critical pricing elements from both the consumer's and the service provider's perspective. The authors also explain how consumers form value perceptions in the context of service offerings and how such knowledge can be used for developing pricing strategies for various types of services. The chapter concludes with a discussion on measuring price sensitivity in service, competitive pricing and areas for future research.

Introduction
Today, the service sector comprises 80 percent of US employment and 64 percent of US gross domestic product (WTO, 2007). It is well known that the professional disciplines required to manage the marketing function of service firms are different from those used in the marketing of goods. Consider for example an automobile manufacturing plant and the marketing of the cars produced by that plant. Now consider a law firm, the marketing of the services provided by the law firm and the individual lawyers in the firm. Finally consider both how the customer determines which car to buy and which lawyer to hire, and how this customer evaluates the purchase afterward. The many differences that exist between the marketing functions of these two types of industries, and the impact of these differences on pricing, are the subject of this chapter.

Customers will only give money for an item – whether it is a product or a service – if they believe that the value they are receiving is greater or equal to the price they pay for the desired product or service. This presents a challenge for those selling services (e.g. hospitality business, doctors, lawyers, consultants etc.) because the purchaser cannot evaluate services prior to purchasing them. Many services (e.g. vacations, hospital visits and restaurant meals) are high in experience qualities while other services (e.g. those high in credence qualities) are difficult to evaluate even after purchase and consumption (Darby and Karni, 1973; Nelson, 1970, 1974) and consumers often lack sufficient knowledge to assess the services received. This inability to evaluate services creates uncertainty about the utility of consumption, a factor that has direct bearing on the pricing of services. Intangibility (inability to touch and feel) is another characteristic of a service that makes pricing extremely difficult to determine if the item a customer is receiving is greater than or equal to what they are paying. These two characteristics of services, as well as other characteristics of services that will be discussed, introduce much risk into the purchase decision.

The main objective of this chapter is to show how firms both manage the heightened risk associated with service purchase and how they incorporate customers' beliefs (both real and imagined) and knowledge into the pricing decision. The chapter is organized as follows: first, we discuss the many different types of pricing in services. We then discuss a framework for setting prices in services. Third, we review how services are different from goods. In this third section we also include a discussion of the implications of these differences between the perspectives of marketers and customers. We then explore different pricing strategies employed by service firms. This is followed by a discussion on how to assess customers' value perceptions. We end with a discussion on measuring price sensitivity in services, competitive pricing and areas for future research.

The many different types of service pricing

Definition of price and role of non-monetary costs
From the customers' viewpoint, price can be defined as 'what he or she must give up to purchase the product or service'. The 'what' may include actual money, time (e.g. the time it takes to search for a doctor or lawyer), a product or service (e.g. an exchange of rooms for free advertising), mental or cognitive effort, and transaction cost (steps necessary to take actual possession of the product or service). Customers will often pay more for a reduction in both cognitive effort and search time by adopting such strategies as always buying the same brand (e.g. higher prices for in-room mini bars in hotels relative to a grocery store, and using an insurance agent that is around the corner rather than one further away).

Pricing in services
Pricing in services goes by many names (Ng, 2007). Table 25.1 provides examples of the terms used for the pricing of services. For instance, consumers pay 'entrance fees', 'cover charges' and 'green fees' when they purchase visits to museums, entrance to dance clubs and rounds of golf. To receive the knowledge of an attorney, one pays 'a retainer' and to attend college one pays 'tuition'. These activities are intangible and have experiential quality to them; therefore they require a different approach to pricing than is typically found with the pricing of goods.

Framework for setting prices for services

Figure 25.1 provides a framework for price formation organized into two sections. The left section relates to the consumers' role in determining price, while the right section refers to the firms' role in price formation. The critical element in Figure 25.1 is the direct relationship between the 'reservation price' (the maximum price the customer will pay for a product) on the consumer side and the 'final price' on the service provider side. The difference between these two prices is the consumer surplus. Firms attempt to price exactly at the reservation price in order to extract the entire 'consumer surplus'. If they do not, they will be 'leaving money on the table'. The challenge for firms is to determine this reservation price and then get customers to happily pay this price. An additional challenge is to move this reservation price higher. While these challenges are also true for goods, the characteristics of services make it more complicated.

The model proposes that consumers' 'reservation price' is influenced by both the perceived fairness of the offer and the value consumers place on the offer. These features are influenced by the perceived risk of the purchase, which is a result of the consumers'

Table 25.1 *The many different terms for price in services*

Organization	What consumer is buying	Term used for price
Museum, theater, sports team, dance club, golf course	Performance, entertainment	Entrance fee, cover charge, green fee
Office buildings, apartments	Space	Rent
Hotel, resort	Comfortable place to sleep, entertainment, experience	Room rate
Bank	Access to capital	Interest rate
Telecommunications	Ability to communicate	Tariff
Consultant, doctor, educator	Advice, knowledge	Retainer, tuition

Source: Based on a table in Ng (2007).

characteristics, their reasons for purchase, the type of purchase, the non-monetary costs associated with the purchase, and finally the characteristics of the service. The 'final price' charged is influenced not only by consumers' reservation price, but also by how and if the product is bundled, the demand and supply characteristics, how the purchase is framed, competitors' prices, and costs to produce. We discuss each of these components next.

Consumer side: characteristics of services
The characteristics of services differ from the characteristics of manufactured goods in four important ways: intangibility, perishability, heterogeneity, and simultaneous production and consumption. In addition, unlike most consumer products, services provide only temporary possessions (Lovelock and Gummesson, 2004). These differences impact how service firms approach the pricing function, as shown in Table 25.2.

Intangibility Intangibility is believed to comprise three dimensions: physical intangibility, generality, and mental intangibility. The more intangible the service, the more risk there is for buyers. This makes pricing decisions difficult. The price has to be high enough to ensure confidence, but not too expensive that consumers will refuse to purchase (Zeithaml et al., 1996; Rust and Zahorik, 1993).

The inability to touch and feel the service before the purchase suggests that consumers make choice decisions based on their expectations of service delivery and by cues put forth by the seller. One cue is price. The higher the price, the higher the expectations that service quality will be delivered (Zeithaml et al., 1996). For instance, whom would you want to defend you against a crime you did not commit – a $150 per hour lawyer or a $1000 per hour lawyer? A second cue is the uniform worn by the service provider. Doctors wear white gowns not because they make them better doctors, but because of the impression the coats give to the patients; namely, authority, cleanliness and professionalism.

Perishability Services such as airline seats or hotel rooms, information sold by news services, and the time availability of a consultant are perishable. If the service is not sold, the revenue for that service is lost forever. Perishability is compounded by the fact that most services have fixed capacity and most are unable to increase their capacity in the short run. The challenge is to 'manage' both demand and capacity by getting customers

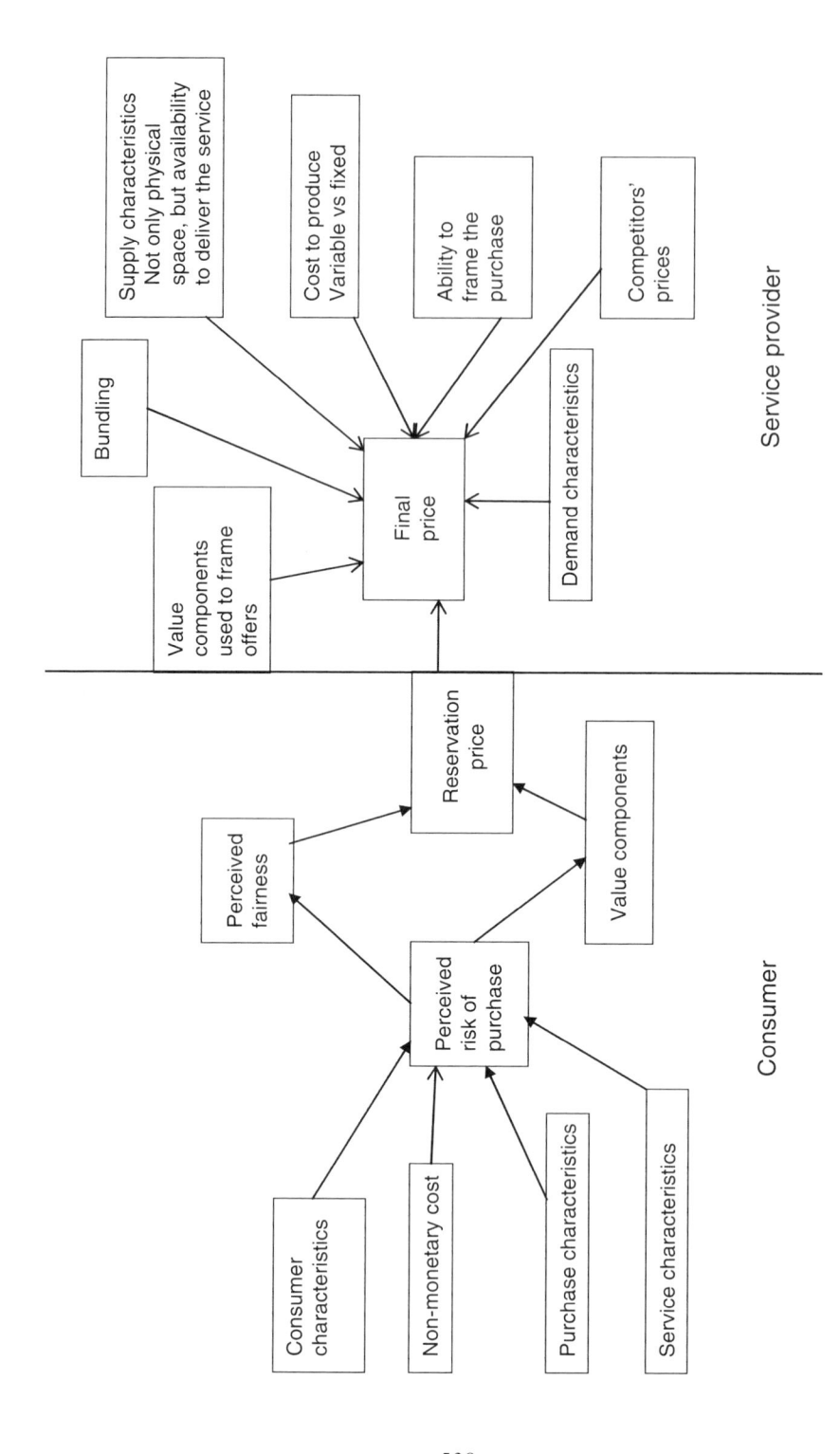

Figure 25.1 Model for pricing of services

Table 25.2   Distinctive features of services and price challenges for firm and customer

Distinctive features of services	Definition	Example	Resulting price challenges: firm
Intangibility	Incapable of being touched or perceived by touch. Also defined as being unable or difficult to be perceived by the five senses	Consulting services, teaching, law advice, medical diagnosis	Not easy to display and communicate intangible service offerings. Prices help set consumers' expectations.
Perishability	If service unit is not sold one day, the same service unit cannot be stored and sold next day	Hotel rooms, airline seats, personal athletic trainer, billing hour of an attorney	Firms needs to set price that guarantees sale but does not 'leave money on the table'; leads to revenue management.
Heterogeneity	The variation and lack of uniformity in the service being performed	Moments of truth in the service encounter. Person one day can give great service, but next day provide totally different service	Customers' heterogeneity impacts how they judge the quality of the purchase; employees' heterogeneity indicates there is an element of risk in the purchase.
Simultaneous production and consumption	The purchase and the delivery occur at the same time	Ordering dinner in a restaurant, hiring consulting service, visiting a lawyer or doctor	Customers may be less willing to pay higher prices unless they believe they will receive what they pay for.

to change their behavior so the firm can manage supply and demand. This is being accomplished more often by dynamic pricing, which is defined as setting prices based on the customer's willingness to pay and buying habits (Kannan and Kopalle, 2001; Huang et al., 2004). Dynamic pricing can be thought of as 'tell me what you want to pay, and I will tell you when you can use the service'. 'Tell me when you want to use the service, and I will tell you what you need to pay.'

Heterogeneity   Heterogeneity of services refers to the variation in the service as a result of individual differences among employees of a service firm. Customers also contribute to heterogeneity as they often act as partial employees (Bateson, 1985; Bowen and Schneider, 1985). Although such co-production of services can greatly reduce employees' workload, it also creates another layer of uncertainty in service quality. The customer's knowledge, experience and proficiency or lack of it can affect how they judge the quality of the purchase. Uncertainty about performance quality tends to increase consumers' reliance on price as a cue for forming expectations (Dodds et al., 1991; Rao and Monroe, 1988). Since most services suffer from performance heterogeneity, service firms need to truly understand price–performance inconsistencies from the consumer's perspective (Voss et al., 1998). Moreover, the price–perceived quality literature suggests that consumers who have limited prior knowledge tend to use price to assess product quality more than consumers who have a moderate degree of prior knowledge (e.g. Zeithaml, 1981). Novice consumers easily interpret higher prices as indicators of higher value (Gerstner, 1985; Rao and Monroe, 1988).

Conversely, knowledgeable consumers tend to be less likely to use high prices as surrogate cues of high quality (Leavitt, 1954; McConnell, 1968). Due to their well-developed cognitive structures, experts are able to use intrinsic cues to evaluate quality (Marks and Olson, 1981). Consequently, for these consumers, there may be a decreased reliance on extrinsic information such as price in the evaluation of service quality.

For the service firm, the emphasis should be placed on understanding the customer, not the service. Many service firms offer their services in varying degrees of customization (e.g. consulting, software development) and consumers tend to be willing to pay a higher price for such customized services (Broekhuizen and Alsem, 2002; Jiang, 2002). Negotiating the price with the customer, as opposed to a fixed price scheme, is often used when the service involves a set of customized procedures (Roth et al., 2006).

Simultaneity of production and consumption and purchase The characteristic of simultaneous production and consumption is unique to services. As the attorney produces the information, the customer 'consumes' the information. Unlike goods, where the customer can examine the item she wants to purchase prior to purchase, in the services the purchase and the delivery occur at the same time. To ensure customer satisfaction, some organizations empower their employees to take appropriate action on the spot and advertise this, some offer service guarantees.

The purpose of the service guarantee is to remove pre-purchase risk and to convey a message that management takes complaints seriously and wants to fix the issues not just in the short term, but making sure the failure does not happen again. The service guarantee typically allows firms to charge more money, as the guarantee assures the consumer that quality will be delivered. One example of the service guarantee is the one offered by Starwood Hotels and Resorts, which promises to fix any defect on the spot, if possible, or offer a menu of 'rewards' (e.g. free lodging, airline miles etc.) to compensate for the troubles caused. Satisfaction guarantees are also offered by other service firms such as 1&1 (www.1and1.com/web-hosting), which bills itself as the world's largest web hosting service, and offers a 90-day complete money-back guarantee, and buy-dissertations.net (http://www.buy-dissertations.net/BuyDissertation/guarantee.asp), which claims that not only will you get your masters, doctorate-level dissertation or research paper on time, but they will revise it if you are not happy with the content.

Consumer influence: consumer characteristics

Lack of pricing knowledge One consumer characteristic is the lack of pricing knowledge of a service that arises due to four reasons: (i) the firm offers multiple services at different levels (e.g. prices for an airline flight by class, time of day/week); (ii) difficulty for service providers to quote exact rates in advance until they begin to understand the customers' exact needs (as in the case of attorney fees); (iii) availability of multiple options available to fulfill a need (e.g. a multitude of doctors are available in a given area) (Miao and Mattila, 2007); and (iv) the fact that service prices are often not visible (Zeithaml et al., 2006). An example of this last point is American Express Financial Services, which found in a study of its customers that many did not know the prices of the services they were buying.

The lack of price knowledge suggests that consumers will use other cues besides price to determine the best option. Examples of such cues are lawyers locating their offices in expensive office buildings, real-estate agents driving expensive cars and doctors displaying their diplomas with the brand names of their medical schools. In all these examples, the firm attempts to make tangible that which is intangible; and at the same time, convey the belief that consumers should be willing to pay more for their services.

Consumer influence: purchase characteristics
The characteristics of the purchase situation also impact the perceived risk of purchase. For instance, the time of purchase influences the price. One way to think about revenue management is in terms of the following two statements: 'Tell me when you want to use the service and I will tell you what you need to pay'; 'Tell me what you want to pay and I will tell you when you can use the service.' Consumers needing to be somewhere at a specific time are less price sensitive than those who have much flexibility. At the time of the use of the service, prices tend to rise, as supply usually decreases.

At times, it may be advantageous to separate the purchases from consumption (Shugan and Xie, 2000). One such way is to offer advance selling. When consumers feel uncertain about the future availability of the service, they might place higher value on it and thus be willing to pay a higher price at an earlier date. For instance, music fans might be willing to pay more for a concert ticket purchased two months in advance as the anticipation of the experience enhances its value. This often happens with vacation travel, especially cruises. With limited inventory, consumers are willing to pay in advance to guarantee that availability.

Consumer influence: perceived fairness
Charging different prices for essentially the same product or service raises concerns about fairness when dynamic pricing strategies are evaluated by consumers (Garbarion and Lee, 2003; Grewal et al., 2004). Unfair prices are a considerable cause for customer defections (Keaveney, 1995). Consumers evaluate price fairness based on three anchor points: past prices, competitors' prices and production costs (Bolton and Myers, 2003). According to Xia et al.'s (2004) framework of fairness perceptions, transaction similarity is the key in prompting fairness judgments. When the degree of similarity between two transactions is high, consumers have little additional information to explain a price discrepancy. In such situations, they tend to believe that they are entitled to equal prices and hence consider price variations as unfair. Revenue management practices try to buffer the negative impact of differential pricing by using rate fences or framing to present price fluctuations in a more favorable light (Wirtz and Kimes, 2007). Wirtz and Kimes (2007) show that consumers' familiarity with revenue management practices might moderate the effect of fencing and framing on consumers' fairness perceptions.

To counter this issue of fairness, in the lodging sector major lodgings now offer 'rate integrity', which means that prices are the same regardless of the channel (Internet, central reservations etc.) through which the reservation came.

Table 25.3 *The components of value*

Value component	Definition	Implication
Financial	Actual currency (dollars, euros, etc.) exchanged for purchase of a service	Degree of service differentiation between competing firms, price relative to household income, and ease of switching all impact price sensitivity.
Temporal	Amount of time required to purchase and use a service	Adage 'time is money' is relevant here as customers continue to have less and less time. Consumers will pay more to save time.
Functional	Ability of the service to meet or exceed customers' expectations. Components are reliability, assurance, tangibility, empathy and responsiveness	Customers need to see or feel the components of functional value to know expectations are being met or exceeded. If they are, will both pay more and be more accepting of price paid.
Experiential	Also known as the hedonic aspects. Occurs when guests are active participants in the service experience	Need to create opportunities for guests to become active participants; for example, 'chef's table' in restaurant, ability to exchange frequency points for 'trophy' rewards.
Emotional	Ability of the service to make customers' feel special or provide a certain level of comfort	Emotional bonding is a major driver of brand loyalty. Strong brands are less vulnerable to competitive attacks such as price discounts or other promotional tactics.
Social	Ability to enjoy the service with others – either your referent group or people you meet while consuming the service	Social interaction and the desire to please one's referent group helps create experiential and emotional value. The more perceived social value, the less price sensitive.
Trust	The belief that organization has customers' best interest in mind	The more the customers feel they can trust the organization, the less price sensitive they are.
Identification with the organization	Customers and organization share similar beliefs	The more the customers feel identification with the organization, the less price sensitive they are.

Consumer influence: value components
The final influence from the consumer side of the model is the components of value. There are eight components of value, presented in Table 25.3. Each of the value components listed has implications for pricing. For instance, consider 'temporal value'. This is based on the notion that 'time is money' and in order to save time, consumers will be willing to spend more money. The total price of a shopping basket at a traditional grocery (i.e. not a Wal-Mart Super Center) store is much higher than if the consumer shopped in multiple stores. Consumers typically shop in just one store because of its convenience. Firms can increase prices by understanding how much their customers' time is worth and then

determining how much of that figure customers would be willing to give back in order to save time.

Next, consider 'social value'. The theory of reasoned action (Ajzen and Fishbein, 1980) states that behavior is a function of two constructs: (1) the attitude towards performing the action and (2) the influence of the group norms. It is this second component that influences pricing. The desire to please one's referent group leads consumers to spend more money. Social value is also related to 'experiential' and 'emotional' value. D'Aveni (2007) revealed in research on restaurants the desire for customers to have a wonderful 'customer experience' and their willingness to pay additional funds for such experiences.

Functional value pertains to the belief that the service does what it is designed to do. A doctor who cures an illness is an example of functional value, as is the lawyer who keeps his client away from legal troubles. As discussed earlier, service guarantees play an important part in assuring the customer that the service will work as it was designed.

Other examples of pricing and consumer value can be seen in Table 25.3.

Service provider and setting prices
Setting prices is a complex exercise, with any number of strategic and tactical implications. Service firms generally have fixed costs that need to be covered. Sometimes firms have to work with these costs and set prices accordingly. This is called product-driven pricing or cost-based pricing.[1] The problem with these methods of pricing is that the final price offered to the consumer may be less than the customer is willing to pay. The reason is that the only component of the price is from the firm's perspective and does not consider what the customer values. Firms need to consider what the customer values when setting pricing. It is for this reason that the value components 'box' is connected to both the consumer and the service provider.

Value-based pricing can be considered the antithesis of cost-based pricing. It involves choosing a price after developing estimates of how potential customers perceive the value of the product or service. It has nothing to do with the cost to produce the item. Value-based pricing has the advantage that it forces managers to keep in touch with the needs and preferences of customers.

Service provider: value and framing
Prospect theory (Kahneman and Tversky, 1979) argues that when people make decisions about buying products or services, they do so by examining the changes in their well-being that occur. This well-being is considered by examining changes from a neutral reference point. A positive change (or value) is considered a gain, while a negative change is considered a loss. Consumers are more likely to make decisions that avoid losses rather than make gains. How the consumer 'looks at the decision' – or the decision frame – can determine whether the outcome is in the domain of gain or loss. Decision frames are

---

[1] Types of cost-based pricing: 'cost-plus pricing' involves establishing the total cost of a product, including a share of the overhead, plus a predetermined profit margin. 'Cost percentage or markup pricing' features either a dollar markup on the variable ingredient cost of the item, a percentage markup based on the desired ingredient cost percentage, or a combination of both. 'Contribution margin' pricing occurs when pricing is used to help cover costs.

controlled by the formulation of the problem and by the norms, habits and characteristics of the decision-maker. While the firm can do little to control the idiosyncrasies of the decision-maker, it can change how the consumer frames the decision problem so that the outcome becomes favorable to the firm.

Decision frames are currently being used in the airline industry as the legacy carriers battle the low-cost carriers (LCC). LCCs are believed to be cheaper (a gain), while the legacy carriers are thought to be more expensive (a loss). Yet the truth is more complex. On certain flights the legacy carriers may actually be cheaper. The challenge for the legacy carriers is to stay price competitive and at the same time move the frame of reference away from price to something on which they can compete; for example, pre-assigned seating, no luggage restrictions, landing at airports close to cities, etc. British Airways is currently running advertisements in Europe highlighting how they offer these options while the LCCs do not. These advertisements highlight the problems of flying with a low-cost carrier, not the benefits of flying BA (they are implied.).

As service firms move more of their information to the web, they need to consider how to use decision frames to gain customer compliance. Because consumers come to the website with different frames of reference, information needs to be presented in such a way ('framed') that price no longer becomes the dominant reference point. In the travel industry, firms are beginning to use reservation calendars that clearly show customers dates of availability and the corresponding lowest prices for those dates. Because price is clearly transparent, customers can consider other features, such as when they want to travel and what amenities they want included. As they 'click through' the calendar they are able to customize their purchase, which leads to higher prices.

Contextual pricing is another implication of prospect theory. Contextual pricing implies that the context in which the purchase is made will have an impact on the overall price paid. Essentially, the context changes the reference point. Consider going to dinner with a significant other for a special occasion versus going to dinner for a 'quick bite', or choosing an attorney for estate planning versus choosing an attorney to defend you in a civil suit. In both cases the reservation price will go up. Service firms should attempt to determine the context of the purchase prior to quoting a price.

Service provider: price bundling
Bundling or marketing two or more services in a single package for a special price is a common practice in many segments of the service industry (Guiltnan, 1987; Johnson et al., 1999). Bundling can be a great way to maximize revenues (Dolan and Simon, 1996; Guiltnan, 1987) and to increase customers' value perceptions (Yadav and Monroe, 1993; Soman and Gourville, 2001). From the consumer's perspective, bundling minimizes cognitive effort and also reduces the direct association between costs and benefits (Soman and Gourville, 2001).

Bundling works because consumers have different reservation prices for different components of a package. Bundling also works for the firm because it can protect its published prices; in many cases it is impossible for the consumer to tell what each part of the bundle costs.

Prospect theory suggests that losses should be bundled. The rationale is that once a consumer has agreed to spend $159, getting them to spend an additional $30 for another feature (e.g., free Internet access) is not difficult, as the psychological difference between

$159 and $189 is not that great. However, should the consumer wish to purchase the $30 item at a later date, now the frame of reference is $0 and the jump to $30 (because the item is purchased at a later date) seems more expensive.

This idea of bundling, combined with how the issue is framed, has been profitable for firms. For example, in an unpublished study, a major hotel in Las Vegas bundled both the hotel room and a guaranteed Las Vegas Strip view for a total price of $189. If the guest did not want a strip view, the rate was $159. To test the impact of this bundling and the impact of the framing of the bundle, telephone reservation agents were divided into two groups. One group quote a rate of $159 to stay anywhere in the hotel (view not bundled). If, however, the guest wanted a guaranteed Las Vegas Strip view, there would be a $30 additional fee. This could be paid at time of booking (e.g. bundled) or purchased at time of check-in if available. A second group was quoted the $189 with a guaranteed view (view bundled). If such a view was not included, the rate was $159. Results revealed that when the $159 unbundled rate was quoted, 13.6 percent elected to pay an additional $30 at the time of booking. When the $189 was quoted first, 20.1 percent elected to take the bundled option. By including the view as part of the bundle, revenues increased $31 878 per month – revenue that went directly to the bottom line. While this may not seem like a big figure, on an annual basis it is $382 536.

Service provider: role of competition
Although the notion of customer centricity is highly recognized in the service literature (e.g. Shah et al., 2006), most models focusing on value fail to incorporate competitive factors (Leone et al., 2006). Those that do incorporate competitive factors often use positioning maps to understand pricing from the customer's viewpoint. For instance, D'Aveni (2007) used positioning maps in part to understand that restaurants with dance floors charged $4.50 – $7.25 more for a meal than restaurants without. He also saw the pricing power of these restaurants rise over the three years, as they understood this price relationship.

Shoemaker (2007) shows how hospitality firms have used competitive positioning maps to determine their pricing strategies. This methodology is shown in Table 25.4 and data to illustrate the technique are shown in Table 25.5. The resulting positioning map is shown in Figure 25.2. Notice in Figure 25.2 that the prices charged are plotted on the vertical axis and the customer competitive index (CCI), which shows how the firm is perceived relative to the competition in terms of what features are important to the customer and how well the firm performs on those features, is plotted on the horizontal axis. The firm undertaking this analysis plots its price in the center of the *Y*-axis and its CCI score in the center of the *X*-axis. This makes it easy to tell which competitors are below or above the firm both in terms of CCI scores and price.

Figure 25.2 shows the Rio (the base hotel) positioned in the center with a rate of $179 and a CCI of approximately 60.0. The positioning map reveals that Bally's and Caesars have higher rates than the Rio ($185 and $189, respectively). More important, both of these brands have a CCI lower than that of the Rio. This indicates that the Rio could probably raise its prices because its customers are generally more satisfied than are those of Bally's and Caesars, which are both earning a higher rate than the Rio. Boulder Station could also probably charge a higher rate because its CCI score is the highest. This analysis should be done for each market segment.

Table 25.4 *Developing competitive positioning maps for pricing hotel rooms (calculation of customer competitive index)*

Column feature	Importance	Brand A		Brand B	
		Performance rating	Score	Performance rating	Score
	A Scale: 1–10	B Scale: 1–10	C A × B	D Scale: 1–10	E A × D
It is a place friends like to go	7.30	7.60	55.48	6.40	46.72
Atmosphere is very pleasant	8.80	7.70	67.76	7.63	66.88
One place seems to have better odds	7.40	6.80	50.32	6.00	44.40
Slot machines filled in a timely manner	7.50	6.80	51.00	6.80	51.00
Types of promotions offered	7.40	7.70	56.98	6.80	50.32
Total	38.4		281.54		259.32
Index			73.32*		67.53

Note: * Sum all numbers in the column; divide sum by total in column A. Multiply by 10; index based on 100.

Questions used to determine importance and performance

Importance question
Next, please think for a moment about the reason for visiting a specific legalized gambling establishment in Las Vegas. Please tell me how important each reason is for you in your decision to choose one specific property over another. Please use a 1 to 10 scale where a 1 means the reason is not at all important and a 10 means the reason is very important. You may use any number on this 1 to 10 scale. Do you understand how this 1 to 10 scale works? How important is _____ in your decision to choose one place to visit over another?

Performance question
Now I am going to read you a list of features that may or may not describe some of the casinos in the Las Vegas area. We'll use a 1 to 10 scale where 1 means it 'does not describe the casino at all' and 10 means it 'describes the casino perfectly'. If you have not been to the casino personally, please base your answers on what you have heard or what you believe to be true. The first feature is _____. How well does this feature describe casino _____?

Although the method is simple, it has proven quite useful in the hotel industry and the airline industry to better understand competitors.

Selected current pricing examples

Pay-for-performance pricing
Pay-for-performance, or performance-based pricing, is 'an arrangement in which the seller is paid based on the actual performance of its product or service' (Shapiro, 1998, p. 2). This form of pricing is gaining popularity in particular in services based on agency–client

Table 25.5 Example of data collected on multiple firms in a market and average rate charged per room

	Feel safe there	Friendly employees	Place my friends like to go	Always have good entertainment	Drink orders taken in timely manner	Cashier lines are short	Restaurants offer great value	Can get change quickly	Slot machines filled in timely manner	Like the promotions offered	You can get complimentaries	Overall average
Importance	8.20	8.20	6.27	4.80	6.12	6.37	7.49	6.33	5.67	4.80	6.15	6.40
Rio	7.26	6.60	6.49	6.47	5.93	5.91	5.70	5.54	5.35	5.05	4.96	5.93
Bally	6.55	5.28	3.96	4.59	5.11	5.05	4.05	4.70	4.60	3.75	4.20	4.71
Boulder	7.40	6.88	6.40	5.74	6.50	5.90	6.54	6.11	5.89	6.16	6.05	6.32
Caesar	7.19	5.85	6.15	5.81	5.37	5.43	4.32	4.82	5.07	3.62	3.97	5.24
Circus	4.70	4.60	4.07	4.24	4.59	4.63	4.55	4.15	4.21	3.80	3.81	4.30
Excalibur	6.61	5.64	5.01	4.89	5.03	5.42	5.01	5.19	5.04	4.06	4.47	5.12
Fiesta	6.19	6.00	4.75	4.64	5.48	5.43	5.61	5.60	5.34	4.66	5.25	5.36

	Rate	CSI
Rio	$179.00	59.97
Bally	$185.00	47.91
Boulder	$160.00	63.92
Caesar	$189.00	53.16
Circus	$159.00	43.41
Excalibur	$140.00	52.07
Fiesta	$155.00	54.3

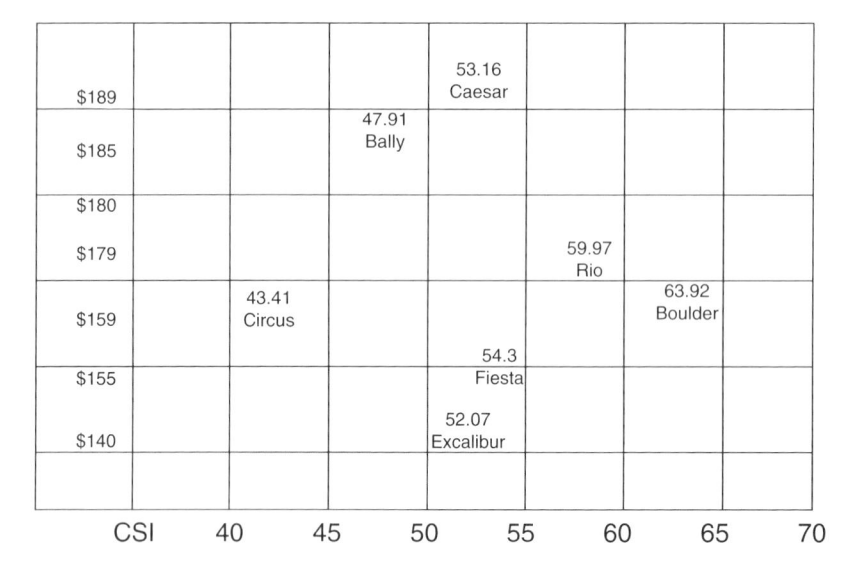

	CSI	40	45	50	55	60	65	70
$189				53.16 Caesar				
$185				47.91 Bally				
$180								
$179						59.97 Rio		
$159			43.41 Circus				63.92 Boulder	
$155					54.3 Fiesta			
$140					52.07 Excalibur			

Figure 25.2 Fictional data to illustrate competitive positioning

relationships such as advertising, consulting and industrial services. Pay-for-performance pricing enables the goals of the buyer and the seller to be aligned through the negotiation process. Careful negations are in fact a prerequisite for a successful implementation of pay-for-performance-based pricing. In sum, pay-for-performance pricing maximizes value for both the customer and the service provider since customers pay only for what they value and suppliers can reduce costs by eliminating non-value-added components of their services.

Yet its applicability to a wide range of services is limited. There is also a great deal of uncertainty involved in this pricing method since the actual dollar amount cannot be determined in advance. Finally, pay-for-performance pricing is not appropriate in cases where short-term cash flows are an integral part of the company's success (e.g. most startup companies).

Modularity pricing
To overcome the challenges caused by intangibility, many service firms have turned to modularity pricing (Docters et al., 2004). For this pricing strategy to work, it is crucial to determine the full range of services that the firm's customers might want. Modular service bundles can then be developed to meet individual customer needs and wants. The mixing and matching allows the service firm to charge for components of its service delivery system that might otherwise be offered free of charge. Airlines, for example, have mastered modularity pricing – they not only charge for passengers, but also for excess baggage, pets, special ticketing, alcoholic beverages, and snacks, and even sometimes for pillows.

Modularity pricing enables companies to reflect both customer needs and their own cost structures, thus creating a potential win–win situation. A wide spectrum of prices for different components of the service also makes it harder for customers to compare prices across competitors. However, for modular packages to succeed, it is important that there is minimal overlap among the service components – no customer is willing to pay twice for the same part of service!

Examples of complex service pricing
We next provide three examples of complex service pricing. One example is from the business process outsourcing industry, the second is from the healthcare field and the third is from the legal profession.

In the business process outsourcing industry, prices are normally based on a fixed rate, where the rate is based upon an agreed metric (e.g. a 'per-call basis', a 'per-minute basis', or a 'monthly per-head basis' (Shoemaker, 2007). Price estimates are based upon client-supplied historical data of call volumes, arrival patterns and average handle time. Call centers also earn additional fees for meeting or exceeding specific service targets (e.g. 80 percent of calls answered within 120 seconds and exceeding customer satisfaction goals). Call centers are penalized (bonuses) up to 10 percent of the base contract price for not meeting (exceeding) the targets.

A leading computer manufacturer has recently taken a more radical approach and has asked that bids be based on a 'per-resolution basis', regardless of how long it takes to resolve the customer's issue. To accurately create a bid price, call centers have a target of a certain number of minutes, on average, to resolve customer issues. This method of pricing not only limits the client's cost, but also results in higher customer satisfaction, as there is an incentive to solve the problem as quickly as possible. This is an example of performance pricing at its best.

The second example comes from healthcare (Shoemaker, 2007). Since the 1980s the federal government has become the key player in determining healthcare pricing. Most pricing in today's environment is driven by the Medicare diagnostic related groups (DRGs), which are set by Medicare, Medicaid and other government programs (e.g. Champus, Tricare). The healthcare provider and the insurance company use these prices to assign fee schedules for each procedure. Insurance premiums are set in part by the total number of units of service provided by each of the providers in that healthcare 'experience'. Most insurance contracts have a 'stop loss' clause where after a threshold dollar amount is met, additional payments will be at a discounted charge.

Doctors' offices have standardized billing codebooks for each type of service provided, such as a patient visit, a procedure etc., and the bill becomes a claim, or the 'gross charge'. In the case of hospitals, the patient (patient co-pay plus company contribution) pays $1 of premium to the insurance company and typically 15–18 percent of that premium goes to the hospital (acute care, sub-acute care, rehab etc.), 15–19 percent to the doctor, 10 percent to outpatient pharmacy and 15–20 percent to insurance administration and sales.

Differentiating services is the key to successful pricing. Typically, around 14 percent of healthcare services involve highly specialized services while the rest of the services reflect standard services that fall under 'commodity' pricing. The main challenge for healthcare organizations is to be able to increase prices in tandem for both the highly profitable commodity business and proprietary services. To that end, firms differentiate highly specialized services via special certification (i.e. stroke center, 'center of excellence'), specific complex procedures, and state-of-the-art technology.

Law firms typically bill their clients by the hour, partly because that is how business has always been done. In addition to the professional code of ethics, competitive prices become a key consideration in determining the hourly rate. The billable hour method often causes dissatisfaction among clients as it doesn't tie costs to value and it fails to make lawyers accountable for the results. To address these concerns, some law firms are moving towards alternative fee arrangements including fixed fees, result-based fees, retainers, blended hourly rates and capped fees. Yet there is a great deal of resistance to change in the profession. One of the key issues to be addressed is risk and reward allocation. Who should bear the risk of a cost overrun, the risk of bad outcome or the risk of compromised quality due to alternative fee structures? Creating hybrid models with risk corridors might provide an alternative that satisfies both the law firm and the client. These more relationship type fee arrangements have started to gain popularity in recent years.

Ways to access consumers' reservation prices in services

Reference prices and reservation prices
'Reference price' is the standard against which the price of a service is judged (Monroe, 1973) or the price at which consumers believe the product should sell. Consumers use both prior expectations and contextual information when forming reference prices (Mazumdar et al., 2005), resulting in multiple conceptualizations, including those based on predictive expectations (Kalyanaram and Weiner, 1995), normative expectations or fairness (Bolton and Lemon, 1999; Campbell, 1999; Xia et al., 2004). In other words, the reference price is formed when consumers consider such things as the following: price last paid, price of similar items, price considering the brand name, real or imagined cost to produce the item, and perceived cost of product failure. The last item is of considerable importance because it reflects consumers' imaginations of what could go wrong. For example, the reference price for a meal at which one is celebrating a special occasion is higher than the reference price for a meal with some old college friends, even though the restaurant may be the same. The risk of failure is critical in the first case and less critical in the second. Moreover, the internal reference price is crucial for continuously provided services such as healthcare, utilities, insurance and membership-based services (Mazumdar et al., 2005). For these types of services, consumers are likely to focus on payment equity (i.e. are they using the service enough, given the price charged; Bolton and Lemon, 1999). Hence, a high fixed fee might induce consumers to use the service more while a variable fee might have an opposite effect on service consumption (Mazumdar et al., 2005).

The second definition firms need to understand is 'reservation price', which was introduced at the beginning of this chapter. It is the maximum price the customer will pay for a product.

Price sensitivity measurement
One way to assess customers' willingness to pay is through price sensitivity measures (Gabor and Granger, 1966; Travers, 1983). This method is based on psychological and sociological principles, and aims to examine price perception by determining levels of customer resistance as they relate to quality perceptions and the market range of acceptable

prices for a specific product or service. For each specific product or service, four questions are asked:

1. At what price on the scale do you consider the product or service to be cheap?
2. At what price on the scale do you consider the product or service to be expensive?
3. At what price on the scale do you consider the product or service to be too expensive, so expensive that you would not consider buying it?
4. At what price on the scale do you consider the product or service too cheap, so cheap that you would question the quality?

A fifth question is sometimes asked: what price do you expect to pay?

Answers to the above questions are then plotted to reveal the information necessary to determine the appropriate price to charge. The responses to question 3, 'too cheap' and question 4, 'too expensive' are typically graphed with the reversed cumulative distributions of 'cheap' and 'expensive', which are then labeled 'not cheap' and 'not expensive'. The intersection of these two curves is the point of marginal cheapness (PMC). This is the point where the number of respondents who feel the service is too cheap is equal to the number of respondents who feel it is not cheap. The intersection of the 'not expensive' and 'too expensive' curves is the point of marginal expensiveness (PME). This is the point where the number of respondents who feel the product or service is too expensive is equal to the number of respondents who feel it is not expensive. The range of acceptable prices (RAP) has the PMC as its lower price limit and the PME as its upper price limit. It would be unwise to price outside this range unless there is real change in the perceived value or positioning of the product or service.

Lewis and Shoemaker (1997) show how hotel firms can use this technique to determine the range of acceptable prices for the association meeting market. This technique has been used quite successfully in proprietary studies conducted by the lead author of this chapter for a large international hotel company for hotel room pricing, a multi-unit restaurant and pie shop to determine the pricing of individual pies, an international restaurant chain to price its tacos, a major university for the pricing of its executive education programs, as well as other service firms.

Conjoint analysis is another common way to estimate consumers' willingness to pay. For example, Marriott Hotels used conjoint analysis to build and price its Courtyard brand (Goldberg et al., 1984). Conjoint analysis has also been used extensively in the cable and the travel industry to determine specific combinations of packages to offer and at what price.

Unresolved issues and future research directions
We have identified several research topics that require conceptual and empirical attention to better understand pricing of services. First, our conceptual framework needs to be empirically tested. Should our model 'work' as we expect, it would provide practitioners with a clear set of tools that could be used to price more efficiently.

Second, what is the relationship between price–value and satisfaction in the context of services? Recent research suggests that satisfaction generates free word of mouth, thus greatly reducing the need for costly marketing campaigns (e.g. Luo and Homburg, 2007). Exploring some other key moderators such as emotional reactions to service offering

(Ladhari, 2007) or consumers' loyalty status would be highly beneficial for deepening our understanding of word of mouth in the context of intangible services. This knowledge will in turn help us understand how word of mouth influences consumers' willingness to pay. While formulas exist to calculate the value of word of mouth (Hallowell, 2001), these formulas are often based on the current price charged. The question of interest is: does word of mouth influence the price that can be charged, and if so, by what amount?

Third, the notion of fairness is an area that warrants future research. Although some attention has been paid to fair prices in the context of revenue management, the territory is largely uncovered (Wirtz and Kimes, 2007). For example, what is the role of the Internet (e.g. blogs and consumer review cites) in informing consumers of differential pricing policies? Do social comparisons made available via technology make fairness an even bigger issue for services? In a similar vein, how do self-service technologies (SSTs) (e.g. self-service kiosks) modify consumers' value perceptions of services? For example, do customer preferences for SSTs vary across market segments (Ding et al., 2007)? And if SSTs are used, does the consumer consider this to be a 'time saver' and hence is willing to pay more for the service, or does s/he feel that since the organization is providing less service, the customer should pay less? This is not a trivial question as more and more services are relying on self-service technologies.

Four, what is the role of framing in influencing customer perceptions of service offerings? Although discounts have been shown to have a positive impact on consumers' perceptions of deal value (e.g. Darke and Chung, 2005), service providers might need to be cautious about potential negative effects on quality inferences. Price bundling has been effectively used in many service settings (e.g. Soman and Gourville, 2001) to increase the perceptions of value, but separating the discounts in multiple savings might also be useful in enhancing customers' value perceptions (Ha, 2006; Johnson et al., 1999). Making sure that consumers use the regular price rather than discounted prices as price reference might be the key to boosting consumers' price perceptions (Krishna et al., 2002). For example, would reference prices change if on all invoices the following information were presented: normal price, discount, price you pay? Currently most invoices only present the price paid. Similarly, how does the rationale for the discount impact reference price and perceived fairness? This notion of reference price formation in the context of services warrants further research (Mazudmar et al., 2005).

Five, technology has made many service firms less labor intensive. Consider for instance how computer-aided design programs have automated many of the design functions of engineering firms. If such firms charge by the hour, the price charged should also go down, especially after all necessary computer software and equipment has been paid for. How should firms account for this decrease? How much reduction in price do consumers expect, if any?

Six, as more price information becomes more readily available, researchers need to understand what is the impact of this information on reference price and price acceptability. And, is this impact the same for all services or does it vary by type of service?

Seven, our model has proposed that the eight components of value detailed in Table 25.3 influence both the reservation price and the final price. Future research needs to investigate each of these components in more detail as well as the relative influence of each of the specific components on the reservation price and the final price for services. For instance, Mathwick et al. (2001) developed an experiential value scale that they used to understand differences in perceived value for catalog versus Internet shopping. It would be useful to test this scale for the different services presented in Table 25.1. More important would be to test if a relationship existed between the scale score and the price paid; and, if such a relationship existed, how could the information be used in pricing?

Temporal value also needs to be investigated further. Leclerc et al. (1995) investigated the impact of time versus money and found in two studies that the value of time seemed to be highly context dependent. The two contexts investigated were (1) short wait time versus long wait time; and (2) a good or service with a high monetary value versus a good or service with a low value. The marginal value of time was higher in the short wait time context and the high monetary value context. They also found that time is nonfungible, which means that time savings and time losses cannot easily be transferred and exchanged. The natural question is: how do consumers trade off time for money and does this vary by service situation?

Much research has investigated what is known as the 'pennies-a-day' strategy (Gourville, 1998, 2003; Nagle and Holden, 2002). This strategy states that 'reframing a large aggregate expense as a small daily expense helps to reduce the perceived cost of a transaction' (Gourville, 2003, p. 125). This strategy has been found successful in terms of charitable notations, cellular telephone service, and health club memberships. A question that has not been investigated is how this strategy can be applied to the framing of one's time. For instance, a television commercial for a large tour operator in Europe shows a man lying on a chair that he moves to follow the sun. The voice-over talks about the number of hours this man had to work for each day in the sun. The implication is that it takes a lot of time to earn a vacation and therefore it is worth paying more to make sure the vacation is a good one. In this example the 'pennies-per-day' strategy is used not to minimize the cost, but to maximize it. This approach has yet be investigated in the published literature and a natural question is: 'Does this approach get customers to pay more money than they normally would?'

Another value worth investigating is 'identification with the organization'. The question here is: will consumers pay more to purchase from a firm that has similar values? This is an important question given that many firms now promote that they are 'carbon neutral' and that their organization is 'green'. Ginsberg and Bloom (2004) state that consumers are willing to pay more for organic foods because they believe them to be safer and healthier. They also state that consumers have been willing to pay price premiums for energy-efficient appliances.

An eighth issue for future research is the presentation of the reservation calendar. Currently these calendars present exact prices, which imply that consumers must make the calculations necessary to examine the price differences between traveling one day versus another. No research has investigated the impact on pricing if a base price is presented and then each day shows the differential from this base. Research could investigate the use of a low base price and an increase for other days or the use of a high base price and a decrease for other days.

A final issue pertains to service guarantees. Service guarantees might influence consumers' value or price perceptions. Companies that consider fixing service failures as a serious business practice might induce higher satisfaction and repurchase intent levels than their counterparts that offer no risk buffers. The interesting question is: will this increase in satisfaction and repurchase intent lead to a willingness to pay higher prices?

Another question of interest pertains to the relationship between what the firm gives back to the customer in terms of a service failure and how much, if anything, the customer will be willing to pay extra for these guarantees. For instance, Starwood Hotels and Resorts provide a sliding scale depending upon what is wrong. For instance, inconveniences such as missing bath amenities or slow check-in are worth $15, a large problem that can be fixed is worth anywhere from $25 to $75, and a large problem that cannot be fixed is worth a free night's stay. Essentially this is an insurance policy for the guest and, like all insurance policies, the amount of 'coverage' translates into higher premiums. Again, modeling the relationship between service guarantees (the coverage) and the price a firm can charge (the premium) is worth investigating.

References

Ajzen, Icek and Martin Fishbein (1980), *Understanding Attitudes and Predicting Social Behavior*, Englewood Cliffs, NJ: Prentice-Hall.

Bateson, John (1985), 'Self-service consumer: an exploratory study', *Journal of Retailing*, **61** (3), 49–76.

Bolton, Ruth N. and Katherine N. Lemon (1999), 'A dynamic model of customers' usage of services: usage as an antecedent and consequence of satisfaction', *Journal of Marketing Research*, **36** (May), 171–86.

Bolton, Ruth N. and Matthew B. Myers (2003), 'Price-based global market segmentation for services', *Journal of Marketing*, **67** (3), 108–18.

Bowen, David E. and Benjamin Schneider (1985), 'Boundary spanning role employees and the service encounter: some guidelines for management and research', in John Czepiel, Michael Solomon and Carol Surprenant (eds), *Service Business*, Lexington, MA: Lexington Books, pp. 127–48.

Broekhuizen, L.J. Thijs and Karel J. Alsem (2002), 'Success factors for mass customization: a conceptual model', *Journal of Market Focused Management*, **5** (4), 309–30.

Campbell, Margaret C. (1999), 'Perceptions of price unfairness: antecedents and consequences', *Journal of Marketing Research*, **36** (May), 187–99.

D'Aveni, Richard A. (2007), 'Mapping your competitive position', *Harvard Business Review*, **85** (11), 110–20.

Darby, Michael R. and Edi Karni (1973), 'Free competition and the optimal amount of fraud', *Journal of Law and Economics*, **16**, 67–88.

Darke, Peter R. and Cindy M.Y. Chung (2005), 'Effects of pricing and promotion on consumer perceptions: it depends on how you frame it', *Journal of Retailing*, **81** (1), 35–47.

Ding, Xin, Rohit Verma and Zafar Iqbal (2007), 'Self-service technology and online financial service choice', *International Journal of Service Industry Management*, **18** (3), 246–68.

Docters, Rob, Mile Reopel, Jeanne-May Sun and Steve Tanny (2004), 'Capturing the unique value of services: why pricing services is different', *Journal of Business Strategy*, **25** (2), 23–8.

Dodds, William B., Kent B. Monroe and Dhruv Grewal (1991), 'The effects of price, brand and store information on buyers' product evaluations', *Journal of Marketing Research*, **28** (August), 307–19.

Dolan, Robert J. and Hermann Simon (1996), *Power Pricing: How Managing Price Transforms the Bottom Line*, New York: Free Press.

Gabor, Andre and Clive W.J. Granger (1966), 'Prices as an indicator of quality: report on an enquiry', *Economica*, **33**, 43–70.

Garbarion, Ellen and Olivia F. Lee (2003), 'Dynamic pricing in Internet retail: effects of consumer trust', *Psychology & Marketing*, **20** (6), 495–513.

Gerstner, Eitan (1985), 'Do high prices signal higher quality?', *Journal of Marketing Research*, **22** (May), 207–15.

Ginsberg, Jill Meredith and Paul Bloom (2004), 'Choosing the right green marketing strategy', *MIT Sloan Management Review*, **46** (1), 79–84.

Goldberg, Stephen M., Paul E. Green and Yoram Wind (1984), 'Conjoint analysis of price premiums for hotel amenities', *Journal of Business*, **57** (1), 111–32.

Gourville, John T. (1998), 'Pennies-a-day: the effect of temporal reframing on transaction evaluation', *Journal of Consumer Research*, **24** (4), 395–408.

Gourville, John T. (2003), 'The effects of monetary magnitude and level of aggregation on the temporal framing of price', *Marketing Letters*, **14** (2), July, 125–35.

Grewal, Dhruv, Gopalkrishnan R. Iyer and Michael Levy (2004), 'Internet retailing: enablers, limiters and consequences', *Journal of Business Research*, **57** (7), 703–13.

Guiltnan, Joseph P. (1987), 'The price bundling of services: a normative framework', *Journal of Marketing*, **51** (2), 74–85.

Ha, Hong-Youl (2006), 'An exploratory study and consumers' perceptions of e-reverse bundling price in online retailing', *Journal of Strategic Marketing*, **14** (3), 211–28.

Hallowell, Roger (2001), 'Word-of-mouth referral: module note', Product No. 801332, Harvard Business School Publishing.

Huang, Jen-Hung, Ching-Te Chang and Cathy Chen (2004), 'Perceived fairness of pricing on the Internet', *Journal of Economic Psychology*, **26** (3), 343–61.

Jiang, Pingjun (2002), 'Exploring consumers' willingness to pay for online customization and its marketing outcomes', *Journal of Targeting, Measurement and Analysis for Marketing*, **11** (2), 168–83.

Johnson, Michael D., Andreas Herrmann and Hans H. Bauer (1999), 'The effects of price bundling on consumer evaluations of product offerings', *International Journal of Research in Marketing*, **16**, 129–42.

Kahneman, Daniel and Amos Tversky (1979), 'Prospect theory: an analysis of decision under risk', *Econometrica*, **47** (2), 263–91.

Kalyanaram, Gurumurthy and Russell Weiner (1995), 'Empirical generalizations from reference price research', *Marketing Science*, **14** (3), 161–9.

Kannan, P.K. and Praveen K. Kopalle (2001), 'Dynamic pricing on the Internet: importance and implications for consumer behavior', *International Journal of Electronic Commerce*, **5** (3), 63–83.

Keaveney, Susan M. (1995), 'Customer switching behavior in service industries: an exploratory study', *Journal of Marketing*, **59** (2), 71–82.

Krishna, Aradhna, Richard Briesch and Donald R. Lehmann (2002), 'A meta-analysis of the impact of price presentation on perceived savings', *Journal of Retailing*, **78** (2), 101–18.

Ladhari, Riadh (2007), 'The effect of consumption emotions on satisfaction and word-of-mouth communications', *Psychology & Marketing*, **24** (12), 1085–93.

Leavitt, Harold J. (1954), 'A note on some experimental findings about the meaning of price', *Journal of Business*, **27**, 205–10.

Leclerc, France, Bernd Schmitt and Laurette Dubé (1995), 'Waiting time and decision making: is time like money?', *Journal of Consumer Research*, **22** (1), 110–19.

Leone, Robert P., Vithala R. Rao, Kevin Lane Keller, Anita Man Luo, Leigh McAlister and Rajendra Srivastava (2006), 'Linking brand equity to customer equity', *Journal of Service Research*, **9** (2), 125–38.

Lewis, Robert C. and Stowe Shoemaker (1997), 'Value pricing: another view and a research example', *Cornell Hotel and Restaurant Administration Quarterly*, **38** (2), 44–54.

Lovelock, Christopher and Evert Gummesson (2004), 'Whither services marketing?', *Journal of Service Research*, **7** (1), 20–41.

Luo, Xueming and Christian Homburg (2007), 'Neglected outcomes of customer satisfaction', *Journal of Marketing*, **71** (2), 133–42.

Marks, Larry J. and Jerry C. Olson (1981), 'Towards a cognitive structure conceptualization of product familiarity', *Advances in Consumer Research*, **8**, 145–50.

Mathwick, Charla, Naresh Malhotra and Edward Rigdon (2001), 'Experiential value: conceptualization, measurement and application in the catalog and Internet shopping environment', *Journal of Retailing*, **77**, 39–59.

Mazumdar, Tridib, S.P. Raj and Indrajit Sinha (2005), 'Reference price research: review and propositions', *Journal of Marketing*, **69** (4), 84–102.

McConnell, J. Douglas (1968), 'An experimental examination of the price–quality relationship', *Journal of Business*, **41**, 439–44.

McConnell, J. Douglas (1973), 'Buyers' subjective perceptions of price', *Journal of Marketing Research*, **10** (February), 70–80.

Miao, Li and Anna Mattila (2007), 'How and how much to reveal? The effects of price transparency on consumers' price perceptions', *Journal of Hospitality & Tourism Research*, **31** (4), 530–45.

Monroe, Kent (1973), 'Buyers' subjective perceptions of price', *Journal of Marketing Research*, **10** (February), 70–80.

Nagle, Thomas T. and Reed K. Holden (2002), *The Strategy and Tactics of Pricing: A Guide to Profitable Decision Making*, 3rd edn, Upper Saddle River, NJ: Pearson Education.

Nelson, Phillip (1970), 'Information and consumer behavior', *Journal of Political Economy*, **78**, 311–29.

Nelson, Phillip (1974), 'Advertising as information', *Journal of Political Economy*, **81**, 729–54.

Ng, Irene C.L. (2007), *The Pricing and Revenue Management of Services: A Strategic Approach*, New York: Routledge Advances in Management & Business Studies.

Rao, Akshay R. and Kent B. Monroe (1988), 'The moderating effect of prior knowledge on cue utilization in product evaluations', *Journal of Consumer Research*, **15**, 253–64.

Roth, Stefan, Herbert Woratschek and Sven Pastowski (2006), 'Negotiating prices for customized services', *Journal of Service Research*, **8** (4), 316–29.

Rust, Roland T. and Anthony J. Zahorik (1993), 'Customer satisfaction, customer retention and market share', *Journal of Retailing*, **69** (2), 193–215.

Shah, Denish, Roland T. Rust, A. Parasuraman, Richard Staelin and George S. Day (2006), 'The path to customer centricity', *Journal of Service Research*, **9** (2), 113–24.
Shapiro, Benson P. (1998), 'Precision pricing for profit in the new world order', Product No. 999003, Harvard Business School Publishing.
Shoemaker, Stowe (2007), Personal correspondence with Wasim Shiehk, May and August.
Shoemaker, Stowe (2007), Personal correspondence with John Evler, May.
Shugan, Steven and Jinhong Xie (2000), 'Advance pricing of services and other implications of separating purchase and consumption', *Journal of Service Research*, **2** (3), 227–39.
Soman, Dilip and John T. Gourville (2001), 'Transaction decoupling: how price bundling affects the decision to consume', *Journal of Marketing Research*, **38** (1), 30–44.
Travers, Kenneth (1983), *PSM: A New Technique for Determining Consumer Sensitivity to Pricing*, Los Angeles, CA: Plog research.
Voss, Glenn, A. Parasuraman and Dhruv Grewal (1998), 'The roles of price, performance, and expectations in determining satisfaction in service exchanges', *Journal of Marketing*, **62** (4), 46–61.
Wirtz, Jochen and Sheryl E. Kimes (2007), 'The moderating role of familiarity in fairness perceptions of revenue management pricing', *Journal of Service Research*, **9** (3), 229–40.
WTO (2007), 'Revised U.S. services offer to the WTO' (accessed 9 November), available http://www.ustr.gov/Trade_Sectors/Services/2005_Revised_US_Services_Offer/Section_Index.html.
Xia, Lan, Kent B. Monroe and Jennifer L. Cox (2004), 'The price is unfair! A conceptual framework of price fairness perceptions', *Journal of Marketing*, **68** (October), 1–15.
Yadav, Manjit and Kent B. Monroe (1993), 'How buyers perceive savings in a bundle price: an examination of a bundle's transaction value', *Journal of Marketing Research*, **30** (3), 350–64.
Zeithaml, Valarie A. (1981), 'How consumer evaluation processes differ between goods and services', in Christopher Lovelock (ed.), *Services Marketing*, Englewood Cliffs, NJ: Prentice Hall, pp. 191–9.
Zeithaml, Valarie A., Mary Jo Bitner and Dwayne D. Gremler (2006), *Services Marketing*, 4th edn, New York: McGraw-Hill.
Zeithaml, Valarie A., Leonard L. Berry and A. Parasuraman (1996), 'The behavioral consequences of service quality', *Journal of Marketing*, **60** (2), 31–46.

26 Strategic pricing response and optimization in operations management
Teck H. Ho and Xuanming Su

Abstract
This chapter reviews how rational customers or buyers should respond to firms' pricing decisions and how firms should optimize prices as a consequence of these strategic responses. The key departure from standard economic and marketing pricing research is that either customers or firms are simultaneously faced with other operational choices, such as capacity sizing and inventory control, which are of central interest to operations management researchers. The chapter covers four broad areas and it is intended to serve as a selective rather than comprehensive review of the extensive literature.

1. Introduction

The main purpose of this chapter is to provide a selective review of pricing models, with an emphasis on issues that are of interest to operations management researchers. Apart from pricing decisions, these models tend to explicitly incorporate supply-side considerations that reflect physical characteristics of production processes, such as inventory control, capacity constraints and demand uncertainty. In such settings, there are two broad questions: how should rational customers respond to firms' pricing decisions, and how should firms optimize prices to maximize profits?

In this review, we focus on the following four broad areas. The first two areas cover pricing and inventory decisions, and the last two areas cover pricing in the presence of capacity constraints.

1. *EOQ inventory models* The classic economic ordering quantity (EOQ) model is an inventory model that is typically applied to products with a relatively stable consumption pattern over time. One main advantage is that this model applies to the buyer as both a consumer and producer. The model shows how the buyer should react operationally in response to the seller's pricing decisions. On the consumer side, the model addresses questions such as optimal shopping frequency and stockpiling decisions. On the producer side, the model addresses issues such as fixed costs (e.g. due to batch production or transportation costs) and inventory carrying costs. This class of models studies producers' pricing and inventory decisions as well as consumers' purchase and inventory decisions in response to sellers' pricing decisions.
2. *Newsvendor inventory models* The newsvendor model is another classic inventory model in operations management. It is ideally suited for analyzing a business-to-business setting where a retailer must cope with demand uncertainty by ordering from a manufacturer that has long production lead times before the short selling season begins. The central dilemma captured by newsvendor models is the tradeoff between excess inventory that remains unsold and profit losses due to insufficient orders. Here, we explore how pricing (demand-side control) can complement inventory ordering decisions (supply-side control) to improve the retailer's profits.

3. *Dynamic pricing models* For many products, the firm has a finite capacity that cannot be replenished. Examples include airplane tickets, hotel rooms, and even fashion apparel. In these settings, revenue management tactics are commonly used to optimize prices over time in response to sales performance. Apart from dynamic pricing by firms, we also review models that consider consumers' dynamic responses to these prices, i.e. whether they should buy or wait for discounts. Here, we focus on the effect of finite capacity, which creates additional considerations for firms (since unsold units have little to no value) as well as for consumers (since the item may be sold out if the consumer waits too long).
4. *Queueing models* In operations management, queueing models are typically used to capture capacity constraints in service settings. Unlike the dynamic pricing models above (where a customer may either get the item or not), queueing models admit intermediate outcomes. Here, the waiting time dimension is used to reflect various forms of service degradation associated with excess demand, relative to available capacity. Pricing can then be used to influence demand to improve profits for the firm. These models study firms' pricing decisions in queueing contexts, and also address consumers' decisions (e.g. whether to enter the queue given the price, how much 'work' to send to the queue, which priority level to choose, and so on).

In each of the areas listed above, we shall highlight the significance of operational considerations. One common theme across all areas is that consumers are active decision-makers and respond strategically to these operational issues (so we refer to them as rational or strategic consumers). For example, in EOQ models, consumers choose purchase quantities and make stockpiling decisions, and in the dynamic pricing models, consumers choose the timing of their purchases. As a result, firms' pricing decisions serve as an important strategic lever to shape consumer behavior and optimize profits. To draw a stark comparison, we occasionally compare the above models with their counterparts that do not have the corresponding operational issues. The next four sections review the four areas listed above. We provide some closing remarks and suggest broad directions for future research in the concluding section.

2. EOQ-based pricing models

The standard economic ordering quantity (EOQ) model is perhaps one of the most fundamental models in operations management. In the standard EOQ setup, a seller charges a time-invariant price p. A rational customer who has a constant consumption r per unit time must decide how much (Q) to order to minimize her total costs over time.[1] The ordering policy must consider three cost components: the purchase cost (p per unit); the fixed cost in placing an order, such as traveling cost (denoted by K); and the cost associated with inventory holding (h per unit per time period). This implicitly assumes that holding cost h does not depend on price or quantity purchased. As a result, this model does not account for the cost of capital associated with holding inventory (e.g. financial holding cost).

---

[1] There is an equivalent utility maximization problem. Since the consumption rate is exogenous and fixed over time, the ordering policy that minimizes the total cost also maximizes the utility.

The rational customer's decision is to choose an optimal ordering quantity Q to minimize the total cost (TC) per unit time. Note that the rational customer places orders at an interval of Q/r and at the time when the inventory is zero. The objective function of the optimization problem is

$$TC(Q) = p \cdot r + \frac{Kr}{Q} + h \cdot \frac{Q}{2} \quad (26.1)$$

where the first term on the left-hand side gives the purchase cost per unit time, the second term is the fixed cost per unit time and the last term is the average holding cost per unit time. Solving the problem yields the optimal economic ordering quantity as follows:

$$Q^* = \sqrt{\frac{2Kr}{h}} \quad (26.2)$$

Note that the optimal economic ordering quantity does not depend on the firm's pricing decision p even though the optimal total cost increases linearly with p. Let us illustrate the above formula with a numerical example. Let the consumption rate (r) be 5 units per month, the setup cost per order (K) be \$10, and the holding cost be \$1 per unit per month. Using equation (26.2), we compute the optimal ordering quantity Q^* as 10 units per order. That is, the consumer must place an order of 10 units every two months.

Ho et al. (1998) extend the EOQ model to investigate how a rational customer should strategically respond when the firm's pricing policy fluctuates over time (i.e. p is a random variable). The fluctuation of the price is described by a time-invariant probability distribution that consists of S scenarios (i.e. a general discrete distribution with pricing scenario p_s occurs with a probability π_s). The rational customer has knowledge of the price distribution but is unaware of the price realization before incurring the fixed cost (or in their context a shopper traveling to visit a grocery store). Once the fixed cost is sunk, the customer observes the price p_s and then chooses purchase quantity Q_s. Let $\mu_P = \sum_{s=1}^{S} \pi_s \cdot p_s$ and $\sigma_P^2 = \sum_{s=1}^{S} \pi_s \cdot (p_s - \mu_p)^2$ be the mean and variance of the distribution respectively. The customer's ordering policy is to decide how much to order under each pricing scenario s, Q_s. As before, the total cost per unit time under pricing scenario s is given by

$$TC(Q_s) = \frac{Kr}{Q_s} + p_s \cdot r + \frac{h \cdot Q_s}{2} \quad (26.3)$$

It can be shown that the long-run average cost per unit time is given by

$$\mu_{TC}(Q_1,\ldots,Q_s) = \frac{K + \sum_{s=1}^{S}[\pi_s \cdot p_s \cdot Q_s + \pi_s \cdot h \cdot Q_s^2/(2 \cdot r)]}{\sum_{s=1}^{S} \pi_s \cdot Q_s/r} \quad (26.4)$$

The customer must select a purchase quantity under each scenario s in order to minimize the above long-run average cost per unit time.

The optimal ordering quantity under pricing scenario s shown to be

$$Q_s^* = \sqrt{\frac{2K^*r}{h}} - \frac{r}{h} \cdot (p_s - \mu_P) \quad (26.5)$$

where $K^* = K - (r/2h) \cdot \sigma_P^2$. Consequently, the expected economic ordering quantity is given as follows:

$$\mu_Q^* = \sqrt{\frac{2K^*r}{h}} \qquad (26.6)$$

Note that the optimal ordering quantity is no longer independent of price once the latter is random. It is now linear in price p_s. This linear ordering rule states that the ordering quantity in scenario s is proportional to the difference between the reference price (the average price μ_p) and the price of scenario p_s. Interestingly, the expected ordering quantity is decreasing in the variance of the price (σ_P^2). So a higher price fluctuation induces the customer to place more but smaller orders by providing an option value (or ordering flexibility) that effectively reduces the fixed cost of placing an order. Consequently, the rational customer shops more often and places a smaller order when variance of the price increases. The authors test these predictions on an extensive dataset from a grocery chain and find strong support for them. The authors also extend the model by allowing the customer to adjust her consumption rate r in response to price fluctuation. They show that it is optimal for the customer to increase her consumption rate if variance of the price increases.[2]

Let us use the same example above to examine the influence of price variability. Assume there are two pricing scenarios (i.e. regular ($10) and discounted ($8)), each occurring with equal probability of 0.5. Consequently, the price variance is $\sigma_P^2 = 1$ and the revised setup cost is $K^* = 10 - (5/2.1) \cdot 1 = 7.5$. Using equation (26.6), the average ordering quantity becomes 8.67 units, which is smaller than the average ordering quantity of ten units under no price variability. Given the same consumption rate, the consumer must shop more frequently.

Assunção and Meyer (1993) consider a similar problem but in a shopping context where there is no fixed cost associated with placing an order (e.g. $K = 0$). In their setting, the customer pays periodic visits to the store (and hence the travel costs are sunk) and must decide in each period how many units to order and consume given a current inventory holding level (Z) and observed price (p). The price fluctuation is assumed to follow a Markov process (i.e. the immediate future price is only a function of the most recent observed price). Formally, the customer must solve the following dynamic programming problem:

$$V(Z,p) = \max_{Q,r} \{U(r) - p \cdot Q - h(Z + Q - r) + \beta \cdot E[V(Z + Q - r, p_{t+1}) | p]\} \qquad (26.7)$$

where $U(.)$ is the utility from consumption and is concave in r and $h(.)$ is the holding cost of inventory. The authors provide structural results on the optimal purchase and consumption policies. They show that the customer should order in a period only if the current inventory level Z is below a threshold level $I(p)$ (which is a function of price only).

---

[2] It is assumed that utility is concave in consumption and the customer maximizes the net utility, which is the difference between utility from consumption per unit time and the long-run average cost per unit time.

The optimal ordering quantity is given by $I(p) - Z$ (i.e. order up to $I(p)$). The optimal consumption is shown to be always increasing in the current inventory (Z) level independent of the observed price p.[3] The customer buys less and consumes more if the holding cost increases. Also, both purchase and consumption are decreasing in the observed price p as long as some sensible assumptions about future price expectations hold.

Kunreuther and Richard (1971) extend the EOQ model to consider the situation where the customer is a retailer who must simultaneously decide how many units to order (Q) from the distributor and how much to charge the product to a group of end customers. The end-customer demand per unit time and the retail price have a one-to-one mapping so that the retailer's pricing decision is mathematically equivalent to its consumption or sales rate decision (r). Formally, the retailer's profit function is given by

$$\Pi(Q, r) = R(r) - \frac{K \cdot r}{Q} - \frac{h \cdot Q}{2} - p \cdot r \tag{26.8}$$

where $R(r)$ is the retailer's revenue when it sells r units per period. Differentiating the profit function with respect to Q and r yields the following two simultaneous equations:

$$Q^* = \sqrt{\frac{2 \cdot K \cdot r^*}{h}} \tag{26.9}$$

$$\frac{dR(r)}{dr} = p + \sqrt{\frac{K \cdot h}{2 \cdot r^*}} \tag{26.10}$$

where $(R(r)/dr)$ is the marginal revenue per unit time from the last unit sold when the sales rate is r^*. The authors use the above results to investigate the costs of sequential decision-making (or lack of coordination). They consider an environment where the marketing department first chooses r^* ignoring the fixed and inventory holding costs. The purchase department then chooses an ordering quantity taking the sales rate r^* as given (i.e. solving the standard EOQ problem). They find that the costs of sequential decision-making can be high if the product of fixed cost and holding cost $K \cdot h$ is high and the optimal sales rate r^* is small.

Blattberg et al. (1981) show that an economic reason that a retailer might offer special sales or deals on its products is the transfer of inventory holding costs from the firm to its customers. Their model framework consists of two sub-models, one for retailer and one for the customer. The idea here is to solve for an equilibrium with each party seeking to minimize its total costs. In their customer model (and with usual notations), customer i chooses a order quantity Q_i in order to minimize the total cost over a purchasing cycle of Q_i/r_i given below:

$$TC(Q_i) = \frac{h_i \cdot Q_i}{2} \cdot \frac{Q_i}{r_i} - d \cdot Q_i \tag{26.11}$$

where the second term of the left-hand side is the total cost saving due to price deals d over the purchase cycle. Note that there is no fixed cost associated with placing an order (i.e.

---

[3] This positive relationship between consumption and inventory is used by Bell et al. (2002) in their model of customer behavior.

562   *Handbook of pricing research in marketing*

$K = 0$). Solving, we obtain the optimal ordering quantity (Q^*) and the optimal purchase period (t^*) as follows:

$$Q_i^* = \frac{d \cdot r_i}{h_i} \tag{26.12}$$

$$t^* = \frac{d}{h_i} \tag{26.13}$$

Customers are segmented into two groups: the first with high holding costs (h_H) and the second with lower holding costs (h_L). All customers have the same consumption rate r. There is a total of N customers of which an α ($0 < \alpha < 1$) fraction has low holding costs. It is assumed that only customers with low holding costs buy on deals. Consequently, the aggregate quantity bought on deal is

$$Q_D = \alpha \cdot N \cdot Q_2^* = \alpha \cdot N \cdot \frac{d \cdot r}{h_L} \tag{26.14}$$

In their retailer model setup, the retailer must choose a deal amount d and the length of reordering period T (i.e. retailer's ordering quantity divided by its sales rate) in order to minimize its total cost per unit time. The total cost consists of a fixed cost per order K_R, a holding cost (h_R per unit per unit time), and costs associated with sales. They show that the optimal deal amount and the reorder period are given as follows:

$$d^* = \left[\frac{K_R \cdot h_L}{N \cdot r(\alpha + (1 - \alpha) \cdot \frac{h_R}{2 \cdot h_L})} \right]^2 \tag{26.15}$$

$$T^* = \frac{d^*}{h_L} \tag{26.16}$$

Besides the optimal deal amount d^*, the optimal dealing frequency (f^*) is the number of deals offered in any given time interval τ and is simply $(\tau/t^*) = \tau \cdot (h_L/d^*)$. The predictions of the overall model are: (1) the deal amount increases when the holding cost to the customer (h_L) and the fixed cost (K_R) cost increase. It decreases as the the total consumption rate ($N \cdot r$) increases; and (2) the deal frequency increases when the holding cost (h_L) and the total consumption rate increase and when the fixed cost decreases. The authors find support for these predictions using a panel dataset and hence establish the transfer of inventory explanation as a plausible rationale for price promotion.

Jeuland and Narasimhan (1985) consider a similar problem and study how a monopolist firm should set its price when it serves two groups of customers with different consumption rates. Each group of customers i has a consumption rate r_i conditioned on the firm's price p given as follows:

$$r_i = \alpha_i - p \tag{26.17}$$

where $\alpha_1 > \alpha_2 > 0$. That is, given a price p, group 1 customers consume more than group 2 customers. A key assumption is that the high-demand (i.e. group 1) customers have a higher inventory holding cost so that the two groups shop differently when faced with price promotion. Customers are assumed to make periodic visits to the firm so that travel costs are sunk (i.e. customers have zero fixed costs, $K = 0$). The firm gives a discount d once every T periods.

Because of high inventory holding cost, group 1 customers never stockpile or forward-buy, so they purchase and consume in a deal period a quantity given by $r_{1d} = \alpha_1 - p + d$. During nondeal periods, these customers purchase and consume $r_{1n} = \alpha_1 - p$. Group 2 customers always forward-buy during the deal period for consumption in all periods. These customers consume at a rate of $r_2 = \alpha_2 - p + d - (hT/2)$ in every period, where h is the inventory cost per unit per period.[4] The authors establish that it is indeed possible and profitable for the firm to price-discriminate between the two groups of customers by offering promotion deals occasionally. This work provides a theoretical reason why a firm might want to give discount deals in practice. It highlights a necessary condition (i.e. high consumption rate must be accompanied by high inventory cost) for such a promotion strategy to be successful.

Bell et al. (2002) extend Jeuland and Narasimhan's model and study how homogeneous firms should engage in price promotion in a competitive setting where customers might increase their consumption as a result of inventory holding. They consider a two-period model in which rational customers must decide how much to buy in each period. A customer has two choices, buy either one unit or two units in the first period depending on the observed price. If the customer buys one unit, she consumes one unit and must incur a fixed cost K to visit the store again in the second period. In she buys two units, there are two possible consumption scenarios. In the first consumption scenario (which occurs with probability $(1 - \theta)$), the customer consumes one unit and must incur a cost h to hold the second unit for consumption in the second period. The customer does not visit the store in the second period. In the second consumption scenario (which occurs with probability θ), the customer consumes two units and must incur a cost K to visit the store in the second period. The authors show that the symmetric equilibrium profits for each firm are

$$\Pi^* = \frac{v \cdot [v + h(1 - \theta)] \cdot N}{[v - h(1 - \theta)] \cdot n} \tag{26.18}$$

where v is the per unit utility of the product to a customer, N is the total number of customers and n is the total number of firms in the industry.

It can be readily shown that equilibrium profits decrease as θ increases. That is, increased consumption effect due to price fluctuation intensifies price competition. This phenomenon occurs because the increased consumption leads to deeper price discounts and an increase in the frequency of promotions. They examine both predictions using purchase data of eight categories from a grocery chain. Some categories (e.g. bacon, soft drinks etc.) are likely to have a higher consumption effect (i.e. higher θ) while others (e.g. bathroom tissue, detergent etc.) are likely to have a smaller consumption effect (a lower θ). Overall, they find support for their predictions.

3. Newsvendor-based pricing models

Like the EOQ model, the newsvendor model is a celebrated and classic model in operations management. Here, we consider a retailer who must order a product with a short

---

[4] Note that the average inventory holding cost reduces the consumption rate.

life cycle from a distributor in order to serve a group of end customers. The end-customer demand is random, following a well-behaved cumulative distribution given by $F(.)$ and a density function and distribution given by $f(.)$ and $F(.)$ respectively. The retailer buys the product at price w and sells it at price p. It has a short and well-defined selling cycle so that any unsold product must be salvaged. The retailer must place an order of size Q before it knows the actual demand. The retailer faces two possible scenarios after the demand realization.[5] In the first scenario, the actual demand is higher than the order. Here the retailer experiences a foregone profit of $(p - w)$ per unit of unfulfilled demand. In the second scenario, the retailer has an overstock of supply because the actual demand is smaller than the order. Consequently the firm incurs a cost of $(w - s)$ per unit of leftover supply where s is the unit salvage value of the product. Let the unit underage cost $C_u = (p - w)$ and the unit overage cost $C_o = (w - s)$. Formally, the retailer chooses an ordering quantity in order to minimize the total expected costs as follows:

$$EC(Q) = C_o \int_0^Q (Q - q) \cdot f(q) \cdot dq + C_u \int_Q^\infty (q - Q) \cdot f(q) \cdot dq \quad (26.19)$$

It can be shown that the optimal ordering quantity (Q^*) is given by

$$F(Q^*) = P(D \leq Q^*) = \frac{C_u}{C_u + C_o} \quad (26.20)$$

That is, the retailer should order at a level Q^* that sets the probability of serving all customers to the ratio given by $(C_u/C_u + C_o)$ (i.e. the relative underage cost). Readers are referred to Porteus (2002) for more details. Let us use a numerical example to illustrate the formula given in equation (26.20). Let $w = \$2$, $p = \$4$ and $s = \$1$. Then $C_u = 4 - 2 = \$2$ and $C_o = 2 - 1 = \$1$. Consequently, we have $F(Q^*) = (2/2 + 1) = (2/3)$. If demand follows a normal distribution with mean 100 and standard deviation of 20, then the optimal ordering quantity becomes $Q^* = 100 + 0.435 \cdot 20 = 108.7$ units.

Petruzzi and Dada (1999) extend the standard newsvendor problem by allowing the retailer to choose the stocking quantity and price simultaneously. Randomness in demand is captured in either an additive or a multiplicative form as follows:

$$D(p, \varepsilon) = y(p) + \varepsilon = a - b \cdot p + \varepsilon \quad (26.21)$$

$$D(p, \varepsilon) = y(p) \cdot \varepsilon = a \cdot p^{-b} \cdot \varepsilon \quad (26.22)$$

where ε has a support $[L, H]$, a density function $f(.)$, and a distribution function $F(.)$. It is assumed that leftovers are disposed at the unit cost α and shortages experience a per-unit penalty cost of β. If α is negative (i.e. leftovers have a salvage value), then $|\alpha| = s$ (as defined above). Also, if $\beta > 0$, there is a loss in goodwill (i.e. the basic newsvendor problem assumes $\beta = 0$). That is, the underage and overage costs are given as $C_u = (p - w + \beta)$ and $C_o = w + \alpha$ respectively.

The profit $\Pi(Q, P)$ can be written as

---

[5] We assume both order and demand are continuous so that the probability that the order is identical to demand is zero.

$$\Pi(Q, p) = \begin{cases} p \cdot D(p, \varepsilon) - w \cdot Q - \alpha \cdot [Q - D(p, \varepsilon)] & \text{if } D(p, \varepsilon) \leq Q \\ p \cdot Q - w \cdot Q - \beta \cdot [D(p, \varepsilon) - Q] & \text{if } D(p, \varepsilon) > Q \end{cases} \quad (26.23)$$

Consider the additive case and define the stocking factor $z = Q - y(p)$. Then the profit function can be rewritten as a function of (z, p) as

$$\Pi(z, p) = \begin{cases} P \cdot [y(p) + \varepsilon] - w \cdot [y(p) + z] - \alpha \cdot [z - \varepsilon] & \text{if } \varepsilon \leq z \\ p \cdot [y(p) + z] - w \cdot Q[y(p) + z] - \beta \cdot [\varepsilon - z] & \text{if } \varepsilon > z \end{cases} \quad (26.24)$$

Expected profit is:

$$E[\Pi(z, p)] = \int_L^z (p \cdot [y(p) + x] - \alpha \cdot [z - x]) \cdot f(x) \cdot dx$$
$$+ \int_z^H (p \cdot [y(p) + z] - \beta \cdot [x - z]) \cdot f(x) \cdot dx - w \cdot [y(p) + z] \quad (26.25)$$

$$= \Phi(p) - L(z, p) \quad (26.26)$$

where $\Phi(p) = (p - c) \cdot [y(p) + E(\varepsilon)]$ and $L(z, p) = C_o \cdot \Theta(z) + C_u \cdot \Omega(z)$ where $\Theta(z) = \int_L^z (z - x) \cdot f(x) \cdot dx$ and $\Omega(z) = \int_z^H (x - z) \cdot f(x) \cdot dx$.

Let $p^o = (a + b \cdot w + E(\varepsilon)/2b)$. If $y(p) = a - b \cdot p$, then the optimization problem can be solved sequentially as follows:

1. For a fixed z, the optimal price is determined uniquely as $p^* = p(z) = p^o - (\Omega(z)/2b)$.
2. The optimal stocking quantity Q^* is given by $Q^* = y(p^*) + z^*$, where p^* is determined as above and z^* is determined as follows:
   (a) If $F(.)$ is an arbitrary distribution, an exhaustive search over all possible values of z in the region $[L, H]$ will determine z^*.
   (b) If $F(.)$ satisfies the condition that $2r(z)^2 + (dr(z)/dz) > 0$, where $r(z) = (f(z)/[1 - F(.)])$ is the hazard rate, then z^* is the largest z in the region $[L, H]$ that satisfies $(dE(\Pi(z, p(z)))/dz) = 0$.
   (c) If the condition for (b) is met and $a - b(w - 2\alpha) + L > 0$, then z^* is the unique z that satisfies $(dE(\Pi(z, p(z)))/dz) = 0$.

In the multiplicative case, we have $D(p, \varepsilon) = y(p) \cdot \varepsilon = a \cdot p^{-b} \cdot \varepsilon$. Let $z = (Q/y(p))$, then the expected profit function can be rewritten like before as a sum of a deterministic profit term and an expected loss function term:

$$E[\Pi(z, p)] = \Phi(p) - L(z, p) \quad (26.27)$$

where $\Phi(p) = (p - c) \cdot y(p) \cdot E(\varepsilon)$ and $L(z, p) = y(p) \cdot [C_o \cdot \Theta(z) + C_u \cdot \Omega(z)]$.

Let $p^1 = (b \cdot w/b - 1)$. As before, the optimization problem can be solved sequentially as follows:

1. For a fixed z, the optimal price is determined uniquely as $p^* = p(z) = p^1 + (b/b - 1) \cdot [(C_o \cdot \Theta(z) + \beta \cdot \Omega(z)/E(\varepsilon) - \Omega(z))]$.

2. The optimal stocking quantity Q^* is given by $Q^* = y(p^*) \cdot z^*$, where p^* is determined as above and z^* is determined as follows:
   (a) If $F(.)$ is an arbitrary distribution, an exhaustive search over all possible values of z in the region $[L, H]$ will determine z^*.
   (b) If $F(.)$ satisfies the condition that $2r(z)^2 + (dr(z)/dz) > 0$, where $r(z) = (f(z)/[1 - F(.)])$ is the hazard rate and $b \geq 2$, then z^* is the unique z that satisfies $(dE(\Pi(z, p(z)))/dz) = 0$.

The authors provide a unifying interpretation of the above results by introducing the notion of a base price and showing that the optimal price in both the additive and multiplicative cases can be interpreted as the base price plus a premium.

Su and Zhang (2008) extend the standard newsvendor problem by allowing the retailer to choose the price and customers to choose their timing of purchase (either during the selling season or at the end of the season). In their model setup, the firm sells the product during the selling season at price p_r (or regular price) and at the end of the selling season at a salvage price p_s (the latter is exogenously fixed). Customers have valuation V for the product. They form an expectation of product availability and believe that they will obtain the product with a probability E_ϕ at the end of the selling season. Therefore, customers will only buy the product during the selling season if $V - p_r \geq (V - p_s) \cdot E_\phi$ or, equivalently, $p_r \leq V - (V - p_s) \cdot E_\phi$.

The retailer holds a rational expectation that all customers will not buy the product during selling season unless $p_r \leq V - (V - p_s) \cdot E_\phi$. Given this expectation, the retailer sets $p_r^* = V - (V - p_s) \cdot E_\phi$. Also, it chooses Q^* to maximize its profit given below:

$$\pi(Q|p_r^*) = p_r^* \cdot \min\{d, Q\} - w \cdot Q + p_s \cdot [Q - d]^+ \quad (26.28)$$

or $\quad \pi(Q|p_r^*) = (p_r^* - p_s) \cdot \min\{d, Q\} - (w - p_s) \cdot Q \quad (26.29)$

where, as before, d is the demand and has a probability and distribution function given by $f(.)$ and $F(.)$ respectively.

If customers' expectation is rational (i.e. $E\theta = F(Q^*)$ or the expectation of product availability equals to the actual fill rate during the selling season), then it can be shown that the optimal regular price and stocking quantity are

$$p_r^* = p_s + \sqrt{(V - p_r) \cdot (w - p_r)} \quad (26.30)$$

$$F(Q^*) = 1 - \sqrt{\frac{w - p_s}{V - p_s}} \quad (26.31)$$

Note that the optimal regular price is between w and V. Interestingly, the equilibrium stocking quantity Q^* is lower than that of the standard newsvendor problem. The following inequality shows this result:

$$F(Q^0) = 1 - \frac{w - p_s}{V - p_s} > 1 - \sqrt{\frac{w - p_s}{V - p_s}} = F(Q^*) \quad (26.32)$$

where Q^0 is the optimal stocking quantity in the standard newsvendor problem.

Using the same numerical example for the optimal ordering quantity (26.20) in the basic newsvendor model above, we have $p_s = s = \$1$ and $V = p = \$4$. Hence $F(Q^*) = 1 - \sqrt{(2 - 1/4 - 1)} = 0.5774$, implying an optimal ordering quantity of 94:12 units (i.e. $100 - 0{:}294 \cdot 20$). Notice that this optimal quantity is smaller than 108.7 units obtained before.

Dana and Petruzzi (2001) extend Petruzzi and Dada's (1999) model by allowing customers to actively choose whether or not to visit the retailer depending on its price p and stocking quantity Q, which are assumed to be known to the customers before they make their visit decision. Customers are heterogenous in two ways. First, they have a value of either $V > 0$ or $V = 0$ for the product. Second, each customer has an outside option u. The number of customers with a positive value V (assumed to be continuous), d, has a support of $[L, H]$ and a probability and distribution function of $f(.)$ and $F(.)$ respectively. The expected number of customers with positive value is $\mu = E(d)$. Similarly, the outside option value has a probability and distribution function of $g(.)$ and $G(.)$. The retailer must choose its price and stocking quantity *ex ante* (i.e. before observing the realizations of d and u).

Let $\hat{u}$ be the outside option of the marginal customer, the person who is indifferent between the outside option and visiting the store. Then the retailer's total demand is $d \cdot G(\hat{u})$. Its total sales is $\min(Q, d \cdot G(\hat{u}))$, so the expected demand and sales are

$$E[Demand(\hat{u})] = \int_L^H x \cdot G(\hat{u}) \cdot f(x) \cdot dx = \mu \cdot G(\hat{u}) \qquad (26.33)$$

$$E[Sales(Q, \hat{u})] = \int_L^H \min(Q, x \cdot G(\hat{u})) \cdot f(x) \cdot dx = \mu \cdot G(\hat{u}) - E[d \cdot G(\hat{u}) - Q]^+ \qquad (26.34)$$

Note that $\hat{u}$ is a function of the retailer's price and stocking quantity. In fact $\hat{u}$ solves the following implicit function:

$$\hat{u} = \phi(Q, \hat{u}) \cdot (V - p) \qquad (26.35)$$

where $\phi(Q, \hat{u})$ is the probability that a random customer is served (i.e. fill rate). It is the ratio of the expected sales and demand and is given by $(E[Sales(Q, \hat{u})]/E[Demand(\hat{u})]) = 1 - (E[d - (Q/G(\hat{u}))]^+/\mu)$. The retailer's expected profit is

$$p \cdot E[Sales(Q, \hat{u})] - w \cdot Q \qquad (26.36)$$

Let $z = (Q/G(\hat{u}))$. Then the fill rate can be rewritten as $\Phi(z) = 1 - (E[d - z]^+/\mu)$ and $\hat{u}$ can be solved using the revised implicit function $\hat{u} = \Phi(z) \cdot (V - p)$. Since $p = V - (\hat{u}/\Phi(z))$, the retailer's optimization problem is to choose $\hat{u}$ and z to maximize the expected profit given below:

$$\pi(z, \hat{u}) = \left[V - \frac{\hat{u}}{\Phi(z)}\right] \cdot G(\hat{u}) \cdot \left[\mu - \int_z^H [1 - F(x)]dx\right] - w \cdot z \cdot G(\hat{u}) \qquad (26.37)$$

The authors first consider the case where the price is set exogenously. Here they show that a retailer that takes into account the effect of its stocking quantity on customers' visit decision carries more inventories, attracts more customers, and earns a higher expected profit than a retailer that ignores this effect. When price is set endogenously, they show that the two-dimensional optimization problem can be reduced to two, sequential, one-dimensional optimization problems by first solving for z^* locally and then given z^* solving for u^* globally.

Deneckere and Peck (1995) extend the standard newsvendor problem by incorporating competition. In their model setup, there are n firms and each firm i simultaneously chooses a stock quantity Q_i and the price p_i. Customers know both the stocking quantities and prices of all firms before making their store visit decision. It is assumed that leftovers are disposed at zero cost and there is no loss in goodwill associated with shortages (i.e. $\alpha = \beta = 0$ or $C_o = w$ and $C_u = p - w$). Note that the outside option of a customer for each firm is defined by other firms' strategies. As before, the number of customers has a probability and distribution function of $f(.)$ and $F(.)$ respectively. The mean number of customers is denoted by μ. At equilibrium, customers choose a mixed strategy $(ms_1, \ldots, ms_n)$ and ms_i represents the probability that a customer visits firm i. The fill rate of firm i given a stocking quantity Q_i and ms_i is

$$\phi(Q_i|ms_i) = E\left[\frac{\min(Q_i, ms_i \cdot d)}{ms_i \cdot d}\right] \quad (26.38)$$

Hence, firm i's expected profit is given by

$$\Pi_i(p_i, Q_i) = p_i \cdot \mu \cdot ms_i \cdot \phi(Q_i|ms_i) - w \cdot Q_i \quad (26.39)$$

The authors show that an equilibrium in which all firms choose pure strategies, if it exists, is unique and is characterized as follows:

$$Q_i^* = \frac{F^{-1}\left(1 - \frac{w}{V}\right)}{n} \quad (26.40)$$

$$p_i^* = \frac{w \cdot F^{-1}\left(1 - \frac{w}{V}\right) \cdot \frac{n}{n-1}}{\mu \cdot \phi\left(F^{-1}\left(1 - \frac{w}{V}\right)\right) + w \cdot \frac{\phi\left(F^{-1}\left(1 - \frac{w}{V}\right)\right)}{v \cdot (n-1)}} \quad (26.41)$$

$$ms_i = \frac{1}{n} \quad (26.42)$$

The authors show that if n is sufficiently large, the above equilibrium always exists. In addition, they show that the optimal stocking quantity decreases with the purchase cost w, increases with the customer value V and is independent of the number of firms n. The optimal price, on the other hand, increases with V and decreases with n and is ambiguous with respect to w.

Dana (2001) extends Deneckere and Peck's (1995) model by making stocking quantities unobservable before customers visit a firm. As before, let ms_i denote the probability with which a random customer visits firm i. Customers visit only one firm. There is no loss in goodwill for shortages and leftovers can be disposed at zero cost. The author consider two closely related models. In the first model (Bertrand model), firms commit to observable prices before they choose their stocking levels. In the second model (Cournot model), firms commit to their stocking levels before they choose their prices. Here, a firm's price acts as a 'signal' of the stocking level it chooses.

In the Bertrand model, taking prices and consumers' subgame-perfect equilibrium strategies $(ms_1, \ldots, ms_n)$ as given, firm i solves

$$\max_{Q_i, p_i} \cdot \int_L^H \min(Q_i, ms_i \cdot d) \cdot f(x) \cdot dx - w \cdot Q_i \qquad (26.43)$$

to determine the stocking quantity. The optimal stocking quantity $Q^*(p_i, ms_i)$ is solved by the standard newsvendor condition given by $F(Q^*((p_i ms_i)/ms_i)) = (p_i - w/p_i)$. Consequently, it can be shown that each firm sets a price to maximize consumer surplus. That is, $p^* = \arg\max_{p \geq w} (V - p) \cdot \phi(F^{-1}((p - w/p)))$, where $\phi(.)$ is the fill rate as defined above.

In the Cournot model, it is assumed that customers conjecture that each firm has chosen the optimal stocking level given the firm's observed price and its competitors' equilibrium prices. Given this assumption, the author proves that there exists a unique symmetric pure-strategy equilibrium in which every firm offers a common price and consumers' equilibrium strategies satisfy $ms_i = (1/n)$ (similar to the results of Deneckere and Peck's 1995 model.) The authors then show that the Cournot equilibrium price is always higher than the Bertrand price and that the difference depends on the number of firms. As the number of firms increases, the equilibrium price of the Cournot model converges to that of the Bertrand model. In both cases, it is shown that industry profits are strictly positive even when there are arbitrarily many firms.

4. Dynamic pricing

In many situations, pricing decisions can be revised periodically in response to current information or market conditions. Static models that yield a single fixed price would not be adequate in providing guidance on how prices should be adjusted over time. In this section, we review several dynamic pricing models and highlight the managerial insights that they provide.

We first discuss the dynamic pricing model developed by Gallego and van Ryzin (1994). They consider a monopolist seller operating in a finite time horizon of length T. The seller has a finite inventory of N units to sell over the time horizon. The seller may adjust prices $p(t)$ dynamically over time $t \in [0, T]$. Demand arrives according to a Poisson process with rate λ. Each arriving customer has i.i.d. (independent and identically distributed) valuations for the product that follow distribution F. Therefore sales occur (at prevailing prices) according to a variable-rate Poisson process with intensity $\lambda(p) = \lambda(1 - F(p))$ dependent on the current price. In other words, during the small time interval $[t, t + \varepsilon)$, a customer arrives with probability $\lambda \varepsilon$, and given that the current price is $p(t)$, this arrival purchases with probability $1 - F(p(t))$. Units remaining at the end of the time horizon have no value. This model captures constraints in both inventory and time, and can be applied to travel industries (airlines and hotels), fashion retailing, as well as other seasonal or perishable items.

For this model, the seller's pricing problem can be formulated as follows. Let $J(n, t)$ denote the value function, representing the seller's optimal continuation payoff at time t and with n units of inventory remaining. Consider a small time interval $[t; t + \varepsilon)$. The Hamilton–Jacob–Bellman (HJB) equation for this stochastic control problem can be written as

$$J^*(n,t) = \sup_p \{\lambda(p)\varepsilon[p + J^*(n-1, t+\varepsilon)] + (1 - \lambda(p)\varepsilon)J^*(n, t+\varepsilon) + o(\varepsilon) \quad (26.44)$$

Rearranging and taking limits, we obtain

$$-\frac{\partial J^*(n, t)}{\partial t} = \lim_{\varepsilon \to 0} \frac{J^*(n, t) - J^*(n, t+\varepsilon)}{\varepsilon} \quad (26.45)$$

$$= \sup_p \lambda(p)[p + J^*(n-1, t) - J^*(n, t)] = 0 \quad (26.46)$$

where we have assumed regularity conditions (to interchange limits and supremums) and the last equality follows from the zero-derivative first-order condition. The boundary conditions are $J^*(n, T) = 0$ (since remaining units have zero value) and $J^*(0, t) = 0$ (there is nothing to sell). With these boundary conditions and the HJB equation, we can numerically compute the optimal price $p^*(n, t)$ corresponding to having n units on hand at time t. However, for a general demand intensity $\lambda(p)$, the optimal price does not admit an explicit characterization. Nevertheless, there is an intuitive interpretation of equation (26.46). The rate of change of the value function $J^*(n, t)$ is determined by two terms: the revenue accrued from consummating a sale at price p; and a loss of $J^*(n, t) - J^*(n-1, t)$, which can be interpreted as the option value of retaining the nth unit for sale in the future.

In their analysis, Gallego and van Ryzin provide additional results. They show that the optimal prices $p^*(n, t)$ are decreasing in both n and t. Put differently, as the inventory level n increases, the optimal price drops; similarly, as we have less time to sell, the risk of having unsold units increases and thus the optimal price also falls. In addition, the authors consider a deterministic version of the problem. In this version, the instantaneous demand rate is now deterministic at $\lambda(p)$; that is, given price p, units are sold at this constant rate. They demonstrate that for this deterministic problem, the optimal solution is to set a fixed price for the entire time interval. This optimal price is the maximum of p^* and p^0, where the p^* is the price that maximizes the revenue rate $p\lambda(p)$ and p^0 is the 'run-out' price under which all N units will be sold out at exactly time T, i.e. $\lambda(p^0) = N/T$. This result is intuitive because when there is sufficient inventory, charging p^* maximizes revenue, but when inventory is too low, it is preferable to sell all units at a higher price p^0. (Here, an assumption that the revenue function $p\lambda(p)$ is quasi-concave is used.)

Let us now summarize the insights from the Gallego and van Ryzin model. First, optimal prices can be determined by assessing the tradeoff between sales at the current price and the option value of unsold units. Since this option value decreases with more inventory and also as time passes, optimal prices should also follow these trends. Second, the price dynamics in this model are driven primarily by demand uncertainty. In an analogous setup with deterministic demand, we see that a single fixed price is optimal. Therefore, this model is useful in isolating the price dynamics that are important in environments with high demand uncertainty as well as other operational considerations such as inventory and time horizon constraints.

Next, we turn to another class of dynamic pricing models. These models study intertemporal price discrimination by durable goods monopolists. The basic setup involves a monopolist firm selling a durable product to a fixed market of consumers with heterogeneous valuations. The monopolist's problem is to set prices optimally over time so that consumers are willing to buy. In particular, consumers form rational expectations over future prices and thus are not willing to buy if they anticipate more attractive purchase opportunities in the future. Therefore, while the previous class of models focuses on managing uncertainties in the demand process, intertemporal price discrimination models focus on the strategic interactions with rational consumers.

We first review the two-period model of Bulow (1982), which makes the analysis rather transparent. In this model, the monopolist faces demand curve of the form $p = \alpha - \beta q$ and sells over two periods. In other words, if a quantity q_1 is sold in the first period, the effective demand curve in the second period is $p = (\alpha - \beta q_1) - \beta q$, so the firm maximizes revenue from second-period sales by producing $q_2 = (\alpha - \beta q_1)/(2\beta)$ units and selling them at price $p_2 = (\alpha - \beta q_1)/2$. Therefore rational consumers, upon observing that q_1 units are sold in the first period, will expect the second-period price to fall to p_2. Now, the crucial step is to recognize that in order for q_1 units to be sold in period 1, the price p_1 must be chosen such that the marginal consumer (who has valuation $\alpha - \beta q_1$) is indifferent between buying and waiting. In other words, assuming the discount factor δ, we need

$$\alpha - \beta q_1 - p_1 = \delta(\alpha - \beta q_1 - p_2) = \delta(\alpha - \beta q_1)/2 \qquad (26.47)$$

$$p_1 = (1 - \delta/2)(\alpha - \beta q_1). \qquad (26.48)$$

Finally, we maximize the total revenue over both periods by solving

$$\operatorname*{Max}_{q_1, q_2}(1 - \delta/2)(\alpha - \beta q_1)q_1 + \delta(\alpha - \beta q_1 - \beta q_2)q_2 \qquad (26.49)$$

The key to this type of analysis is to characterize the reservation prices of consumers who form rational expectations over future prices by predicting the monopolist's optimal actions. Given these reservation price constraints, the monopolist's dynamic pricing problem can then be formulated and solved. As an illustration, consider the following example with $\alpha = \beta = \$1$ and $\delta = 0.5$. At the profit-maximizing solution, the monopolist sells $q_1 = 0.4$ units at price $p_1 = \$0.45$ in period 1 and sells $q_2 = 0.3$ units at price $p_2 = \$0.3$ in period 2. The total profit earned is \$0.225.

The two-period model above can be extended to infinite horizon settings. This was the setting considered by Coase (1972), who first proposed the durable goods monopoly problem. He conjectures that durability eliminates monopoly power because as long as prices remain above marginal cost, the monopolist will have the incentive to lower the price (to sell additional units) after some consumers have bought, so these consumers will not be willing to buy in the first place. Stokey (1981) solves the infinite-horizon pricing problem and characterizes the monopolist's optimal falling price path. In a related analysis, Stokey (1979) assumes that the monopolist commits to the temporal price schedule and finds that a single fixed price is optimal; this suggests that if the monopolist could commit, he would prefer not to price-discriminate over time. This point is evident from the numerical example above: if the monopolist could commit not to lower prices in period 2, he essentially faces a single-period monopoly pricing problem, for which the optimal solution is to sell 0.5 units at price $0.50, yielding profit $0.25 (which is higher than $0.225 above). Besanko and Winston (1990) isolate the effect of consumer rational expectations by comparing a model with strategic consumers (similar to Stokey, 1981) to a model with myopic consumers (in which consumers are not forward looking and purchase as soon as the price is below their valuations). They show that relative to the static monopoly price, prices are uniformly lower with strategic consumers and prices are uniformly higher with myopic consumers. In addition, prices start higher and fall faster when there are myopic consumers, as compared to strategic consumers.

A related model by Conlisk et al. (1984) studies intertemporal price discrimination when there is a continual influx of new consumers. (The models reviewed in the previous two paragraphs assume that all consumers are present at the start of the time horizon.) In some sense, this demand structure is similar to the customer arrival processes in the Gallego and van Ryzin setup, although customer inflows are deterministic here (i.e. N consumers enter the market each period). There are two customer types: a fraction α are high-types with valuation V_H and the rest are low-types with valuation V_L. The discount factor is β per period. Consumer rational expectations and heterogeneous valuations continue to play a major role. In this environment, the authors show that the optimal solution involves cyclic pricing. Each price cycle, of duration n periods, is characterized by

$$p_j = (1 - \beta^{n-j}) V_H + \beta^{n-j} V_L \tag{26.50}$$

for $j = 1, \ldots, n$. There are periodic 'sales' (when $j = n$) through which the monopolist 'harvests' the low-valuation consumers that have accumulated in the market; prices subsequently return to the 'regular price' level at the start of each cycle ($j = 1$) and gradually decline until the next sale at the end of the cycle ($j = n$). In each price cycle, the price path is chosen so that high-valuation customers are willing to buy rather than wait for the sale; thus prices are higher the further away the anticipated sale is. Time discounting is quite important in driving the price cycles in this model. Another important element is the assumption that the monopolist is unable to commit to future prices. Sobel (1991) analyzes the case in which commitment is feasible, and he shows that the seller's optimal solution is to commit to a fixed price, similar to the above case where there is a fixed market of consumers. This suggests that commitment power diminishes the usefulness of dynamic pricing when selling to strategic consumers.

Observe that the durable goods monopoly models described above do not involve inventory or time constraints. The firm is able to sell as many units as demanded at each price. Moreover, most models have infinite time horizons. This is in contrast to the Gallego and van Ryzin setup, in which there is a finite inventory to sell over a limited time period, so each unsold unit has a dynamically evolving option value that shapes the optimal prices. The stark difference between these two strands of work motivates a third class of models, which incorporates both perspectives into a single framework. These relatively more recent models contain two main ingredients: operational constraints (i.e. in time and inventory) as well as strategic constraints (i.e. consumer rational expectations and sequential rationality). Aviv and Pazgal (2008) develop a model with Poisson customer arrivals and analyze the optimal timing of a single price discount. Su (2007) uses a simpler deterministic demand structure to study the firm's dynamic pricing problem.

We review the basic model by Su (2007). The setup is based on the deterministic setting in Gallego and van Ryzin, where there is a finite inventory N to sell over a finite time horizon T. This puts the operational constraints in place. Next, the main ingredient of durable goods monopoly models is added: strategic customers, who arrive according to a deterministic flow process, form rational expectations of future prices and optimally choose between buying versus waiting. This behavior generates incentive constraints that prices must satisfy in order to induce purchases. The derivation of these incentive constraints is similar in spirit to the analysis in (26.47)–(26.48). With both operational and incentive constraints in place, the firm's pricing problem can then be formulated and the optimal prices characterized. In this model, there is a mixture of strategic customers (with rational expectations) and myopic customers (who purchase as soon as prices are below their reservation values). Moreover, consumers may have high valuations (V_H) or low valuations (V_L). This creates four consumer segments: strategic-highs, strategic-lows, myopic-highs and myopic-lows. Depending on the relative sizes of these four segments, the optimal price path may take one of two forms: (1) prices start at V_L and jump to V_H at some point during the selling season; or (2) prices start high at V_H and drop to an intermediate price $p \varepsilon (V_L, V_H)$ before the end of the season, when prices fall to V_L. These results can also be extended to incorporate time discounting in the form of waiting costs (i.e. customers may face waiting costs when delaying purchases).

Two surprising results emerge from this model. First, note that a remarkably robust finding from the stream of revenue management literature following Gallego and van Ryzin is that optimal prices (on average) tend to fall as time passes. This is intuitive, given that the option value of unsold units declines over time. However, once strategic customer behavior is added to the picture, the optimal price path may either increase or decrease over time. This endogenous structure of optimal price paths depends on the composition of the customer population, and in particular, on the correlation between strategic behavior and reservation prices. The main result is that, when strategic customers have higher reservation prices than myopic customers, optimal prices increase over time. However, in the reverse case, decreasing prices (e.g. markdowns) serve as an intertemporal price discrimination device because the seller is able to extract higher revenues from myopic customers who do not wait. This suggests that option value considerations (which generate declining price paths) are no longer dominant when there are strategic interactions in the marketplace. Second, a common finding in the durable goods monopoly literature is that strategic customers with rational expectations hurt seller profits. In the extreme case of the Coase conjecture, monopoly profits are completely eroded. However, by incorporating operational constraints, the model demonstrates that strategic behavior may benefit the seller. This is because low-valuation customers, by competing with high-valuation customers for product availability, may increase their willingness to pay. This effect is driven by the operational constraints, because otherwise there would be no notion of 'product availability'. In essence, with limited inventory and limited time, rational consumers need not only consider future prices, but also future availability.

5. Queueing models

For many situations, queueing models provide a useful way to capture capacity limitations. We begin this section with a description of a standard textbook queueing model, and then review the classic work that incorporates pricing effects into queueing models.

Consider a single-server queue facing a stream of customers who arrive over time according to a Poisson process of rate λ. Service is rendered in a first-come-first-served basis, and service times for each customer are independently, identically and exponentially distributed with rate μ. We denote $\rho = \lambda/\mu$ and assume $\rho < 1$. It is well known that the average time spent in the queue, including service time, is $1/(\mu - \lambda)$. Therefore we may interpret the customer arrival rate λ as demand and the service rate μ as the capacity of the queue. Then, increasing demand generates congestion effects that lead to longer waits for all customers. Observe that queueing models exhibit 'soft' capacity constraints in the sense that all customers will eventually be served. This is in contrast to operations models with finite inventory, in which some customers may not obtain the product in the event of a stock-out, so there are 'hard' capacity constraints. For this reason, queueing models are often applied to service contexts where the consequences of capacity limitations are more subtle. The waiting time that customers face as a result of queueing capacity μ may also be interpreted as a degradation in other dimensions of service quality.

The classic model that considers pricing in queueing models is proposed by Naor (1969). The fundamental premise is that customers, upon arrival and observing the current state of the queue, may choose whether to join. Customers earn a reward of R upon completion of service at the queueing station but incur waiting costs at a rate of C per unit time. Thus, if a customer arrives at a queue with n other customers in line, the expected payoff from joining is $R - nC/\mu$ (compared to zero from departing). This implies that the customer leaves the queue whenever the queue length exceeds a particular threshold, $k = \lfloor R\mu/C \rfloor$. Now, suppose that the server charges some price p. By the same logic, customers will now adopt the threshold strategy

$$k(p) = \lfloor (R - p)\mu/C \rfloor \tag{26.51}$$

i.e. join if $n \leq k(p)$ and leave if $n > k(p)$. This sets up the framework to study pricing effects in queues. Given a particular price p, we can characterize the resulting demand pattern. Consider the following numerical example. Suppose that customers arrive to a coffee stand at a rate of $\lambda = 1$ customer per minute, and that they can be served at a rate of $\mu = 2$ customers per minute. Further, customers value their coffee at $R = \$10$ but assess waiting costs to be $C = \$1$ per minute. Then, we see from equation (26.51) that customers are willing to wait in line for free coffee (i.e. when the price is $p = 0$) as long as there are no more than $k = 20$ customers in line. However, when the price $p = \$5$ is charged, customers are no longer willing to wait in line when there are more than $k = 10$ people waiting.

From a revenue maximization perspective, the queue manager should optimally balance the tradeoff between a high price and the consequent reduction in demand. Corresponding to price p, customers join the queue only when the queue length is less than or equal to threshold $k(p)$. From queueing theory (see, e.g., Gross and Harris, 1998; Wolff, 1989), the probability that a customer joins the queue is $(1 - \rho^{k(p)}/1 - \rho^{k(p)+1})$. In other words, the demand function is

$$D(p) = \lambda \frac{1 - \rho^{k(p)}}{1 - \rho^{k(p)+1}}. \tag{26.52}$$

The manager should charge the optimal price p^* that maximizes the expected revenue rate $pD(p)$. This induces the customer threshold strategy $k^* = k(p^*)$ that maximizes the firm's revenue.

Alternatively, from a social planner perspective, we may write down the social welfare function as

$$SW(p) = RD(p) - CN(p) \tag{26.53}$$

$$= \lambda R \frac{1 - \rho^{k(p)}}{1 - \rho^{k(p)+1}} - C\left[\frac{\rho}{1-\rho} - \frac{(k(p)+1)\rho^{k(p)+1}}{1 - \rho^{k(p)+1}}\right] \tag{26.54}$$

The first term is the rate at which reward is earned, and the second term is the rate at which waiting cost is incurred; here, $N(p)$ denotes the average number of customers in the queue at any point in time and can be expressed in terms of $k(p)$ as shown above. Therefore the first-best can be attained if the firm charges the price that maximizes social welfare $SW(p)$. Let us denote the first-best price as p^{FB} and the resulting customer threshold as $k^{FB} = k(p^{FB})$.

Apart from laying out the framework above, Naor (1969) also provides the following comparative results. He shows that

$$k^* < k^{FB} < k_0 \tag{26.55}$$

where k_0 denotes customers' queue-joining threshold strategy in the absence of prices (i.e. $p = 0$). Analogously, the following also holds:

$$p^* > p^{FB} > 0. \tag{26.56}$$

Using our numerical example above, we find that the revenue-maximizing price is $p^* = \$8.50$ while the socially efficient price is $p^{FB} = \$5$. Equivalently, the revenue-maximizing and first-best queue-joining thresholds are $k^* = 3$ and $k^{FB} = 10$.

There are two key insights. First, revenue maximization leads to prices above the socially efficient level, and second, achieving first-best requires positive prices (above marginal cost). The first is consistent with standard monopoly pricing models, but the second is not. This is due to the negative congestion externality that is present in queueing models. Customers make their joining decisions in self-interest even though their current decisions will influence the well-being of future arrivals. In this situation, pricing can be used to address such externalities and attain first-best.

Thus far, we have assumed that customers are served in a first-come-first-served order. In an interesting analysis, Hassin (1985) considers the opposite extreme of last-come-first-served priority rules. In this case, since all future arrivals will be placed in front of current customers, these current customers will take them into consideration. The consequence is that equilibrium-joining behavior will be socially optimal even in the absence of pricing. However, Hassin points out a strategic difficulty involved with last-come-first-served queues. Now, customers have the incentive to leave and re-enter the join, presumably disguised as a new arrival. In the analysis, such behavior is assumed away, but in practice, substantial monitoring may be required. Certainly, there are also equity and fairness issues that have not been accounted for.

This modeling framework has been shown to be robust along several dimensions. The restriction to customer threshold joining strategies is an important simplification but currently holds only under the assumption of Poisson customer arrivals. Yechiali (1971) extends this setup to general arrival processes and shows that threshold-type policies is without loss of generality. In another paper, Yechiali (1972) extends the analysis to multi-server systems. While we have considered only linear waiting costs and linear rewards, Knudsen (1972) analyzes general nonlinear cost and reward structures and shows that the basic insights still hold. Lippman and Stidham (1977) introduce discounting and also consider finite time horizons; they also find that the structure of the results remains unchanged. This line of research demonstrates that for economic and managerial analysis, it is usually sufficient to focus on simple models, such as single-server exponential systems. Nevertheless, even for such 'simple' models, there is usually a high degree of technical complexity involved. This is because for most dynamic queueing processes, characterizing performance measures (such as waiting time and number of customers in queue) is not an easy task.

Another modeling approach is to consider a static steady-state analysis of queueing systems. Here, we review the framework proposed by Mendelson (1985). The starting point is a value function $V(\lambda)$, which represents the total value of performing the service when the aggregate arrival rate is λ. We assume that V is concave, as this captures the decreasing marginal value of each additional unit of customers served. In other words, the value of service to the marginal customer is $V'(\lambda)$. Apart from the service rewards, there are also waiting costs due to capacity constraints. Letting $W(\lambda)$ denote the average wait time and C denote the waiting cost (per unit time), we see that corresponding to arrival rate λ, the waiting cost incurred by each customer is $CW(\lambda)$. Therefore, in the absence of pricing, equilibrium arrival rates chosen by the customer population satisfies

$$V'(\lambda) = CW(\lambda) \qquad (26.57)$$

Similarly, when each customer faces an admission fee p, the equilibrium arrival rate is $\lambda(p)$ given implicitly by

$$V'(\lambda(p)) = p + CW(\lambda(p)) \qquad (26.58)$$

We stress that for any price p, the equilibrium is unique since V is concave in λ (so V' is decreasing in λ) and W is increasing in λ. Therefore, there is a one-to-one relationship between prices and equilibrium arrival rates, and we may use $p(\lambda)$ to denote the price that can be used to induce arrival rate λ. In this setup, the implicit assumption is that customers do not observe queue lengths when making joining decisions, but instead base their decisions on the expected steady-state queue lengths. This simplifies the analysis since customer decisions no longer dynamically depend on the evolution of the stochastic queueing system.

Using this modeling approach, we may proceed to study profit-maximizing pricing schemes and compare them to the first-best. For a given price p, the firm's revenue rate is

$$\Pi(p) = \lambda(p) \cdot p = \lambda(p) \cdot [V'(\lambda(p)) - CW(\lambda(p))] \qquad (26.59)$$

In terms of λ, we have

$$\Pi(\lambda) = [V'(\lambda) - CW(\lambda)]. \quad (26.60)$$

Therefore, we may maximize this expression to find the profit-maximizing arrival rate λ^*. The firm's optimal price is then given by $p^* = p(\lambda^*)$. Similarly, we now characterize the first-best outcome. In terms of arrival rate λ, the social welfare function is

$$SW(\lambda) = V(\lambda) - \lambda CW(\lambda) \quad (26.61)$$

Maximizing this expression over λ, we obtain the first-best arrival rate λ^{FB}. This can be sustained in equilibrium by imposing the first-best price $p^{FB} = p(\lambda^{FB})$. Consistent with Naor's model, this setup also yields $p^* > p^{FB} > 0$.

This modeling framework has been extended to incorporate multiple customer classes. In Mendelson and Whang (1990), there are multiple customer classes, each with different value functions V_i and waiting costs C_i. Customer classes are unobservable, so this is a hidden information problem. The authors analyze a priority pricing mechanism; that is, paying different prices corresponds to receiving different priorities in the queue and thus incurring different waiting times. The pricing mechanism can be designed to be incentive compatible and socially optimal. This analysis highlights an interesting feature of queueing models: with just a single server (producing a single good), the addition of priorities essentially introduces multiple different goods, which can be used to price discriminate amongst different customer classes. Subsequently, Lederer and Li (1997) extend this analysis to a competitive setting. In another paper, Van Mieghem (2000) introduces methodology to treat the case of convex delay costs (rather than linear delay costs assumed above). This modeling framework is quite flexible and can be extended to include another dimension of choice by customers: apart from choosing whether to join the queue, customers may also choose how much service to request. In some sense, this resembles a quantity decision. Ha (2001) studies this scenario and derives optimal incentive-compatible pricing mechanisms.

6. Conclusions

In this chapter, we introduce four broad areas of research in operations management that relate to pricing. A central theme that cuts across all areas is that customers are active and strategic, and they maximize their utility by choosing an appropriate buying and/or operational action. In reviewing each area, we first describe a classic model in operations management and show how subsequent research extends these standard models. Our review is deliberately selective because we want to show how research and model development accumulates in the literature. Our primary goal is to expose marketing and economic researchers to the rapidly growing areas of research in operations management that relate to pricing.

Table 26.1 summarizes the main findings and insights in this chapter when consumers are strategic and actively engage in operational decision-making. In the EOQ inventory models, we show that pricing variability leads to higher shopping frequency and smaller average purchase quantities. Promotions can serve as an effective vehicle to transfer inventory-holding costs from the seller to consumers, and to price-discriminate between

Table 26.1 *Summary of results and insights when buyers are customers*

Area	Key operational consideration(s)	Consumer decisions	Role of pricing	Applications
EOQ inventory models	• holding cost • fixed cost	• how much to buy	• Price variance induces consumers to shop more frequently at smaller quantities. • Deals transfer holding costs to consumers who stockpile. • Periodic promotions allow firms to price-discriminate between consumers with high and low holding costs.	• Food products • Household items
Newsvendor inventory models	• availability	• whether to visit the store	• Low prices attract consumers to visit the store (and face the risk of stock-outs). • High prices signal high availability.	• Fashion • Electronics
Dynamic pricing models	• limited capacity • limited time	• when to buy	• Stable prices discourages strategic timing of purchases and increases firm profits. • Prices should be adjusted dynamically to reflect the option value of unsold units. • Dynamic pricing serves as a price discrimination device when consumers have different propensities to wait.	• Airlines • Hotels • Fashion
Queueing models	• congestion	• whether to join the queue	• The price that attains first-best is higher than the marginal cost; at this price, existing customers will consider the externality they impose on future arrivals. • The firm may price-discriminate by establishing priorities and charging different prices.	• Services

different consumers. In the newsvendor inventory models, we show that low prices attract more store visits by consumers while high prices signal high product availability. In the dynamic pricing models, it is shown that stable prices increase profits because they discourage strategic timing of purchases. Dynamic pricing can also be effective if consumers have different propensities to wait. Another consideration is that prices should be adjusted dynamically to reflect the option value of unsold units over the selling horizon. In the queuing models, we show that pricing above marginal cost induces customers to consider the externality they impose on future customer arrivals, and that firms can price-discriminate by establishing service priorities.

Besides making the problem contexts more realistic and richer, operational considerations often influence the optimal price of the firm significantly. Also, these considerations frequently generate more realistic equilibrium outcomes in competitive settings. While they are typically accompanied by more challenging analyses, the payoffs seem worthwhile because we begin to see an accumulation of knowledge and insights. The current approaches make a major step forward by focusing on making customers active (i.e. or in game-theoretic terms, they are players in the model). This is accomplished by making them more strategic and rational. Clearly, we do not need to restrict to these standard assumptions. In fact, research in psychology and experimental economics suggests that these assumptions are routinely violated even when customers are motivated by substantial monetary incentives.

A promising and perhaps more radical approach is to assume that active customers are boundedly rational. One can extend the equilibrium analysis to include situations where mistakes are allowed but in the way that more costly mistakes are made less frequently than less costly mistakes (see McKelvey and Palfrey, 1995), and where a lack of rational expectation in belief formation among players is possible (see Camerer et al., 2004). Also, consumers care both about the final outcomes as well as the changes in outcomes with respect to a target outcome, they are impatient in that they prefer instant gratification, and they care about being treated fairly (see Ho et al., 2006 for a comprehensive review).

References

Assunção, J.L. and R.J. Meyer (1993), 'The rational effect of price promotions on sales and consumption', *Management Science*, **39** (5), 517–35.
Aviv, Y. and A. Pazgal (2008), 'Optimal pricing of seasonal products in the presence of forward-looking consumers', *Manufacturing and Service Operations Management*, **10** (3), 339–59.
Bell, D.R., G. Iyer and V. Padmanabhan (2002), 'Price competition under stockpiling and flexible consumption', *Journal of Marketing Research*, **39** (3), 292–303.
Besanko, D. and W.L. Winston (1990), 'Optimal price skimming by a monopolist facing rational consumers', *Management Science*, **36** (5), 555–67.
Blattberg, R.C., G.D. Eppen and J. Lieberman (1981), 'A theoretical and empirical evaluation of price deals for consumer nondurables', *Journal of Marketing*, **45** (1), 116–29.
Bulow, J.I. (1982), 'Durable-goods monopolists', *Journal of Political Economy*, **90** (2), 314–32.
Camerer, C.F., T.H. Ho and J.K. Chong (2004), 'A cognitive hierarchy model of games', *Quarterly Journal of Economics*, **119** (3), 861–98.
Coase, R.H. (1972), 'Durability and monopoly', *Journal of Law & Economics*, **15** (1), 143–49.
Conlisk J., E. Gerstner and J. Sobel (1984), 'Cyclic pricing by a durable goods monopolist', *Quarterly Journal of Economics*, **99** (3), 489–505.
Dana, J.D. (2001), 'Competition in price and availability when availability is unobservable', *RAND Journal of Economics*, **32** (3), 497–513.
Dana, J.D. and N.C. Petruzzi (2001), 'The newsvendor model with endogenous demand', *Management Science*, **47** (11), 1488–97.

Deneckere, R. and J. Peck (1995), 'Competition over price and service rate when demand is stochastic: a strategic analysis', *RAND Journal of Economics*, **26** (1), 148–62.
Gallego, G. and G. van Ryzin (1994), 'Optimal dynamic pricing of inventories with stochastic demand over finite horizons', *Management Science*, **40** (8), 999–1020.
Gross, D. and C.M. Harris (1989), *Fundamentals of Queueing Theory*, 3rd edn, New York: John Wiley & Sons.
Ha, A.Y. (2001), 'Optimal pricing that coordinates queues with customer-chosen service requirements', *Management Science*, **47** (7), 915–30.
Hassin, R. (1985), 'On the optimality of first come last served queues', *Econometrica*, **53** (3), 201–2.
Ho, T.H., C.S. Tang and D.R. Bell (1998), 'Rational shopping behavior and the option value of variable pricing', *Management Science*, **44** (12), S145–S160.
Ho, T.H., N. Lim and C.F. Camerer (2006), 'Modeling the psychology of firm and consumer behavior with behavioral economics', *Journal of Marketing Research*, **43**, 307–31.
Jeuland, A.P. and C. Narasimhan (1985), 'Dealing – temporary price cuts – by seller as a buyer discrimination mechanism', *Journal of Business*, **58** (3), 295–308.
Knudsen, N.C. (1972), 'Individual and social optimization in a multiserver queue with a general cost–benefit structure', *Econometrica*, **40** (3), 515–28.
Kunreuther, H. and J.F. Richard (1971), 'Optimal pricing and inventory decisions for non-seasonal items', *Econometrica*, **39** (1), 173–5.
Lederer, P.J. and L. Li (1997), 'Pricing, production, scheduling, and delivery-time competition', *Operations Research*, **45** (3), 407–20.
Lippman, S.A. and S. Stidham (1977), 'Individual versus social optimization in exponential congestion systems', *Operations Research*, **25** (2), 233–47.
McKelvey, R.D. and T.R. Palfrey (1995), 'Quantal response equilibria for normal form games', *Games and Economic Behavior*, **10**, 6–38.
Mendelson, H. (1985), 'Pricing computer services: queueing effects', *Communications of the ACM*, **28** (3), 312–21.
Mendelson, H. and S. Whang (1990), 'Optimal incentive-compatible priority pricing for the M/M/1 queue', *Operations Research*, **38** (5), 870–83.
Naor, P. (1969), 'The regulation of queue size by levying tolls', *Econometrica*, **37** (1), 15–24.
Petruzzi, N. and M. Dada (1999), 'Pricing and the newsvendor problem: a review with extensions', *Operations Research*, **47**, 183–94.
Porteus, E.L. (2002), *Foundations of Stochastic Inventory Theory*, Stanford, CA: Stanford University Press.
Sobel, J. (1991), 'Durable goods monopoly with entry of new consumers', *Econometrica*, **59** (5), 1455–85.
Stokey, N.L. (1979), 'Intertemporal price discrimination', *Quarterly Journal of Economics*, **93** (3), 355–71.
Stokey, N.L. (1981), 'Rational expectations and durable goods pricing', *Bell Journal of Economics*, **12** (1), 112–28.
Su, X. (2007), 'Intertemporal pricing with strategic customer behavior', *Management Science*, **53** (5), 726–41.
Su, X. and F. Zhang (2008), 'Strategic customer behavior, commitment, and supply chain performance', *Management Science*, **54** (10), 1759–73.
Van Mieghem, J.A. (2000), 'Price and service discrimination in queuing systems: incentive compatibility of Gc scheduling', *Management Science*, **46** (9), 1249–67.
Wolff, R.W. (1989), *Stochastic Modeling and the Theory of Queues*, Englewood Cliffs, NJ: Prentice Hall.
Yechiali, U. (1971), 'On optimal balking rules and toll charges in the GI/M/1 queuing process', *Operations Research*, **19** (2), 349–70.
Yechiali, U. (1972), 'Customers' optimal joining rules for the GI/M/s queue', *Management Science*, **18** (7), 434–43.

Index

Titles of publications are in *italics*.

Abraham, M.M. 295, 335
access fee effect, nonlinear pricing 378–80
accruals 335
Acquisti, A. 310
Adams, W.J. 237
Adaval, R. 141
additivity, consumer reservation price 235
advance selling 451–75
   and buyer uncertainty 459–63
   factors affecting 463–7
   reasons for 454–9
   of services 541
   strategies 467–74
   use of new technology 452–4
advertising 101
   and brand loyalty 297–8
   and product line pricing 223
agent's uncertainty, structural models 122–3
aggregate-level diffusion models 173–86, 191–3
Agrawal, D. 297–8
Ailawadi, K. 128, 267
Ainslie, A. 70
Allenby, G.M. 61–73, 368, 370, 376
Alter, A.L. 145
Amaldoss, W. 397–417
amazon.com 303, 314
AMP (average manufacturer price) 499
analog representations of numbers 136–9
anchoring in price cognition 140–42
Anderson, C. 229
Anderson, E.T. 150–64
Anderson, J.C. 37
Anderson, S.P. 244
Anheier, H.K. 512
Ansari, A. 253, 255, 519
Apelbaum, E. 266, 269
Arbel, A. 480
arbitrage
   effect of new technology 453
   pharmaceutical industry 506–7
Arentze, T. 102
Ariely, D. 39, 104, 422, 425, 429
Armstrong, M. 365, 443
Armstrong, M.K. 287, 331
Arora, N. 70, 89
Arrow, K.J. 207
Ashcraft, M.H. 135

associative processes in cognitive arithmetic 135–6
Assunção, J.L. 560
AT&T 302, 303–4
auction-based WTP measurement 47–51
auction fever 427–8
auctions 419–32
   name-your-own-price 419, 430–32
   online auctions 419, 421–30
availability heuristic in price cognition 144–6
average manufacturer price (AMP) 499
average wholesale price (AWP) 499
Aviv, Y. 572
Avlonitis, G.J. 12, 13
AWP (average wholesale price) 499

Bagwell, K. 101, 159
Bagwell, L. 399
Bajari, P. 128, 421, 422
Bakos, Y. 103, 104, 240, 244
Balachander, S. 177–8, 190, 224, 399
balance model approach to bundling 249, 252
Baldauf, A. 198–9, 205
Balistreri, E.C. 51
Banerjee, A. 399
Banerji, S. 266
Bass, F.M. 173, 174–5, 179–80, 184, 185, 192, 196–7, 202, 204–5
Basu, K. 141, 399
Basuroy, S. 332
Baye, M. 96, 103
Bayesian analysis 64
   and data pooling 69–71
Bayus, B.L. 179–81, 191–2, 225, 227
BDM method, WTP measurement 49
Bearden, W. 398
Becker, G. 398–9
Beggs, A. 388
behavior-based targeted pricing 310
behavioral pricing 76–89
Bell, D.R. 68, 563
Beloba, P.P. 478–9
Bensaid, B. 438, 440
Bergemann, D. 199–201, 208
Bergen, M. 227

Berkowitz, E.N. 81
Bernheim, B. 399
Bernheim, D. 399
Berry, S. 390
Berto Villas-Boas, S. 349
Bertrand model 569
Besanko, D. 109, 114–27, 177–9, 188–9, 287–8, 328, 332, 333, 350, 572
best price policies 160
Bewley, T. 12
Bhattacharya, J. 493
bidder behaviour, online auctions 426–8
bilateral monopoly model 321–6
billbacks 335
Bishop, R. 43
Biswas, A. 87
Biyalogorsky, E. 456
Blattberg, R.C. 224, 285, 294, 295, 331, 335, 561
Blinder, A.S. 12
Bloom, P. 339, 553
Boatwright, P. 134, 141, 426–7
Bonnet, C. 349
Borle, S. 425
Bradlow, E.T. 44, 70, 252, 422, 425, 428
brand equity 349–50
brand loyalty, effect on advertising and promotions 297–8
brand name drugs 492–3
brand perceptions and consumer search 93
brand switching patterns as drivers of margin premium 275
Brander, J.A. 227
Bresnahan, T.F. 124–5
Briesch, R. 87
Brooks, A.C. 514
Brown, J. 103
Bruce, N. 335
Brynjolfsson, E. 103, 240, 244
Bucklin, R.E. 87
Bulow, J.I. 571
Bultez, A.V. 174–5, 184
bundle design and pricing 232–56
  design-oriented approaches 249–53
  normative guidelines 235–48
  pricing approaches 253–5
  services 544–5
  and willingness to pay 52–3
Burtless, G. 367, 370
business process outsourcing, service pricing 549
business-to-business transaction, nonlinear pricing 356
Busse, M. 153–4, 331, 333
buy price, online auctions 423–5

buyers
  buyer consumption state, and advance selling 459
  buyer risk aversion and advance selling 467
  buyer uncertainty and advance selling 456–63
  see also consumers; customers

Cabral, L.M.B. 437, 438
Cameron, T.A. 42
Campbell, M.C. 79
cancellation refunds 465–6
Canetti, E. 228
cannibalization effect 39, 218
capacity constraints and advance selling 464–5
capacity utilization as driver for advance selling 455–6
Carbajo, J. 243
Carlson, J. 95, 99, 105
category characteristics as driver of price premium 271
category expansion as driver of margin premium 275
Caves, R. 494
ceiling reservation price 40
Chan, T. 108–29, 390
Chan, T.Y. 424, 427, 429
channel structure 342–5
channels, pharmaceutical industry 498–504
Chao, L.W. 505, 506
chargeback 499
Chatterjee, R. 169–212
Che, H. 109, 129, 349, 389, 390
Chen, F. 337
Chen, Y. 216–29, 309, 310, 311, 316
Chen, Y.-M. 175–7, 185–6
Chen, Z. 341
Chernev, A. 430
Chevalier, A.J. 332
Chevalier, M. 287
Chiang, J. 68
Chiang, W.K. 344
Childers, T. 398
Chintagunta, P.K. 68, 72, 109, 122, 199–201, 207, 388–9, 435–49, 507
Cho, E.K. 160, 163
Choi, S.C. 343
choice and consumption decision 370–71
choice-based conjoint analysis, WTP measurement 44–6
choice experiment-based approach to bundle pricing 255
Chu, C.H. 110
Chu, J. 350
Chung, J. 252

Clay, K. 372
closed-loop equilibria 195, 205, 387
clustering, and price searching 102
Coase, R.H. 437–8, 571
co-branding approach to bundling 252–3
Cobb–Douglas utility function 67
cognitive miserliness 141–2
Cole, C. 266
collaborators, pharmaceutical industry 497–8
Comanor, W.S. 171, 492
companies, pharmaceutical industry 490–92
Compeau, L.D. 87
competition
  and advance selling 467
  and bundling 243–4
  and network effects 438–9
  and new product pricing 194–209
  and nonlinear pricing 358
  between nonprofit organizations 528–9
  and nonprofit pricing 522–4
  in online auctions 428–30
  pharmaceutical industry 492–5
  and price cues 163–4
  and product line pricing 221–3
  and service pricing 545–6
competitive pricing 481
competitive targeted pricing, see targeted pricing
complementarity, reservation prices 241–2
complex service pricing 549–50
computational ease, effect on price cognition 145–6
conformism and strategic pricing 397–416
conjoint analysis, WTP measurement 44–7
conjoint-based methods for new product pricing 210–11
Conlin, M. 128
Conlisk, J. 572
conspicuous consumption model 397–8, 400–415
consumer search and pricing 91–105
  information sources 100–104
  Internet searching 102–4
  models 92–4
  pharmaceutical products 496–7
consumer self-selection and product line pricing 219–21
consumer surplus, nonprofit organizations 531
consumers
  expectations and network effects 436, 440
  influences, service pricing 540–43
  objective function 117
  preferences 115–16
  rational expectations 572
  reference prices, see reference prices
  reservation prices, see reservation prices
  searching, see consumer search and pricing
  social influences 397–9
  and store brands 259–60, 263
  taste and nonprofit organizations 530–31
  uncertainty 119
  see also buyers; customers
consumption uncertainty 377
context, pharmaceutical industry 504–7
context effect, product line pricing 219
contextual pricing, services 544
contingent valuation methods
  compared with choice-based conjoint analysis 46
  WTP measurement 42–4
Cooper, R.G. 137
Corbett, C.J. 343
Corneo, G. 399
Cornille, D. 12
correlation in reservation prices 235, 240–41
Corstjens, M. 275
Corts, R. 307
cost interdependence and product line pricing 218, 223–4
cost-based pricing
  nonprofit organizations 517
  services 543
cost-plus pricing 26–9
costs and nonlinear pricing 358
Cotterill, R.W. 267
Coulter, K.S. 143
Coulter, R.A. 143
Cournot model 569
Crawford, G.S. 497
Crosbie, P. 198–9, 206
cross pass-through 330, 333
cross-price effects measurements 61–73
Cui, T.H. 228
Curhan, R.C. 287, 295
customers
  expectations of future prices 188–91
  pharmaceutical industry 495–7
  price knowledge 152–3, 160–61
  reaction to revenue management pricing 482–4
  see also buyers; consumers

D'Aspremont, C. 315
Da Silva, S. 378
Dada, M. 564–6
Dahlby, B. 97, 98
Dana, J.D. 454, 455, 567–8, 568
Danaher, P.J. 228, 368, 378
Danzon, P. 505, 506
data pooling 69–73

Datta, S. 319–51
deal characteristics 81, 85
Dean, J. 169–70
decentralization and vertical integration 342–4
decision frames 543–4
decreasing block tariffs 356
Dehaene, S. 137, 138, 139, 143
Deleersnyder, B. 267
demand, effect of prices 400–403
demand dynamics 384–91
  econometric models 385–6, 389–91
  pricing implications 385, 387–9
demand interdependence of products 218, 219–21
DemandTec 70
Deneckere, R. 568
Desai, P.S. 222, 224, 339, 343–4
descriptive models of channels 348–9
design-oriented approaches to bundling 248–53
Desiraju, R. 72, 224, 327, 328, 455–6, 507
Deutsche Bahn, nonlinear pricing 362–3
Dhar, S. 266, 272, 273
Dhebar, A. 179–80, 190, 439, 440, 441
Dholakia, U.M. 427, 429
Diamantopoulos, A. 13
Dickson, P. 99, 152
diffusion models, aggregate 173–86
digit pattern representativeness 143–4
DiMasi, J.A. 490
Ding, M. 51, 431
direct network effects 435
discount advance selling 471–2
discrete choice models 68
distributor-owned brands, *see* store brands
Dockner, E.J. 196–7, 198–9, 203–4, 205, 206
Doganoglu, T. 443
Dolan, R.J. 174–5, 183
donations, nonprofit organizations 530
Dossche, M. 12
double-bounded dichotomous choice questions 43
Draganska, M. 110, 226, 227
Drèze, X. 153
drivers
  for advance selling 454–9
  of effective trade promotions 295–6
  of margin premium 274–6
  of price premium 269–72, 277–8
  of volume premium 272–3
dual entitlement principle 483
Dubé, J.-P. 69
Dubin, J.A. 367, 370
Dubois, P. 349
Dukes, A.J. 341

duopoly model, nonprofit price reaction 524–5
durable goods models 187, 195, 202–3, 203–5
duration, online auctions 425–6
Dutch auctions 47
dynamic bidding, online auctions 428
dynamic price effects 73
dynamic pricing 384–91, 437–40
  models 117, 129, 389–91, 558, 569–73
  new products 169–70
dynamic programming models, revenue management 480

Eaton, J. 227
eBay 419
Eckstein, Z. 94
econometric estimation of structural models 123–6
econometric models of dynamic pricing 385–6, 389–91
economic models for pricing 62–9
economic ordering quantity (EOQ) model 557, 558–63
Economics of Welfare (A.C. Pigou) 302
economies of scale and network effects 444
Ehrlich, I. 97, 101
Ekelund, M. 505, 506
elaboration likelihood model (ELM) 154
Eliashberg, J. 195–7, 202
Ellis, K. 275
Ellison, G. 164
Ellison, S.F. 164, 502
Elsner, R. 163
emotion as driver of price premium 270–71
emotional effect, online auctions reserve prices 422
employee pricing promotions 153–4
EMSR (expert marginal seat model) 478–9
endogenous choice and consumption decisions 370–71
Englich, B. 140
English auction 48
EOQ inventory models 557, 558–63
equilibrium price dispersion 95
equilibrium strategies in competitive situations 195
Erdem, T. 94, 99, 267
Essegaier, S. 364
Etzel, M. 398
Evans, D. 515
expectations, analysis of 414–15
experience curve pricing 171
experimental auctions and WTP measurement 47–51
expert judgment, new product pricing 210–11

expert marginal seat model (EMSR) 478–9
external reference prices 87

Fader, P.S. 454
fair pricing, nonprofit organizations 517
fairness, service pricing 552
familiarity and revenue management pricing 484
Farquhar, P.H. 248, 252
Farrell, J. 443
Feinberg, F. 79, 314
Fennell, G. 61
field experimentation for new product pricing 210
firms
    objective function 117, 119
    see also manufacturers; retailers
first-price, sealed-bid auction 47–8
Fisher, L. 97, 101
fixed cost effect, nonprofit organizations 527–8
flat fee bias 377–8
floor reservation price 40
fluency and willingness to pay 145
font size, effect on price cognition 143
Ford, G. 100
formulary rebate 503
Fox, E. 99, 104
framing
    price differences 484
    and service pricing 552
Frank, R.G. 494
Frederick, S. 134, 143
frictional costs, NYOP auctions 430–31
Fruchter, G. 198–9, 206, 313
Frykblom, P. 51
Fudenberg, D. 310
functional value, services 543
Furukawa, M. 506

Gabor, A. 152
Gabszewicz, J. 196–7, 203, 438
Gale, I.L. 454, 455
Gallego, G. 480, 569–70
Gallet, C.A. 43
Gallistel, C.R. 138
game-theoretic model of channels 321–6
Ganslandt, M. 506
Gapinski, J. 514
Garbarino, E. 103
Garcia, F. 438
Gasmi, F. 121
Gaunsdorfer, A. 198–9, 205
Gauri, D. 99, 104
GBM (generalized Bass model) 185
Gelman, R. 138

generalized Bass model (GBM) 185
generalized method of moments (GMM) 124
generic pharmaceutical products 493–5
Geng, X. 475
Gerstner, E. 102, 160, 223–4, 297, 331, 456, 466
Geyskens, I. 279
GGW approach, conjoint analysis 249
Gieseke, R. 99
Gilbert, R.J. 344
Gilovich, T. 142
Ginsberg, J.M. 553
Ginter, J.L. 70
GMM (generalized method of moments) 124
Godes, D. 399
Goettler, R.L. 372
Goldberg, S. 249
Goldfarb, A. 349
Gomez, M.I. 297, 335
Goolsbee, A. 103
Gourville, J.T. 77, 226, 256
Grabowski, H.G. 494
Granger, C.W.J. 152
Greenleaf, E.A. 389, 422, 423
Grewal, D. 87
Gruca, T.S. 11, 12, 13, 170
Grzybowski, L. 443
Guadagni, P.M. 153
Guiltinan, J.P. 241
Gupta, S. 355–81

Ha, A.Y. 577
Hall, R. 10, 367
Hann, I.-H. 430–31
Hansen, K. 267
Hansmann, H. 521
Hanson, W. 253
Hardesty, D.M. 423
Hardie, B.G.S. 88
Hardy, K.G. 295
Harlam, B. 267
Hartmann, W. 350
Hassin, R. 575
Hastings, J.S. 344
Hatch–Waxman Act 493
Hauser, J.R. 39
Hausman, J. 367, 370
hazard models of consumer search 93–4
healthcare pricing 549
Heberlein, T.A. 43
Heide, J.B. 295–6
Henderson, T. 89
herd behavior 399
    online auctions 429
Hess, J.D. 102, 160, 223–4, 297, 331

heterogeneity, services 539–40
heuristics
  in numerical cognition 132–47
  in price cognition 139–46
Heyman, J.E. 427
Hitch, C. 10
Ho, T.H. 557–79
Hoch, S. 99, 104, 258, 266, 272, 273, 277
Holmes, T.J. 454, 455
Hong, H. 98
Hooley, G. 11
horizontal product differentiation 217, 225–8
Horsky, D. 99, 177–8, 187–8
Hortaçsu, 128, 421, 422
household panel data and WTP measurement 40
Huang, H.-Z. 175–6, 186
Hurter, A. 315
hybrid categorical conjoint analysis for bundling 249

identification, structural pricing models 125
IIA (independence of irrelevant alternative) constraints 65–6
imagery as driver of price premium 270–71
incentive-compatible methods, WTP measurement 49, 51–2
increasing block tariffs 356
independence of irrelevant alternative (IIA) constraints 65–6
indifference reservation price 40
indirect network effects 435, 441–3
Indounas, K.A. 12, 13
information asymmetry 119–20
  effect on pass-through 333
information processing fluency, and willingness to pay 145
information role of price cues 157–60
information sources 100–104
Ingene, C.A. 337
Inman, J.J. 153, 154
innovation as driver of price premium 270
installment billing and price cues 161–2
instruments, structural pricing models 124–5
insurance and pharmaceutical pricing 489, 495–6, 500
intangibility, services 537
integrated modeling framework, nonlinear pricing 374–7
internal reference prices 87
international price variation, pharmaceuticals 506–7
Internet auctions 419–32
Internet price searching 102–4
Internet pricing 14

Internet selling and partial integration 344
Internet shopping agents (ISAs) 103
Israelevich, G. 340, 350
Iyengar, R. 110, 228, 355–81
Iyer, G. 96, 103, 336, 338, 342, 343

Jacobs, P. 514
Jagpal, S. 37–59
Jain, D.110, 175–7, 185–6, 226, 227
Jain, S. 397–417
James, E. 516, 518
James, M.D. 42
Jeanne, O. 399
Jedidi, K. 37–59, 255
Jensen, S. 366
Jeuland, A.P. 174–5, 175–7, 183, 187, 195–7, 202, 291, 336, 562
Jobber, D. 11
Jorgensen, S. 196–7, 203–4
Joshi, A. 273
Judd, K.L. 179–81, 190
judgement and decision-making (JDM) 134
judgment-based approach, new product pricing 210–11

Kadiyali, V. 108–29, 227, 228, 349
Kahneman, D. 132, 134, 140, 142, 143, 144, 483
Kalish, S. 174–5, 175–7, 183, 184, 187
Kalra, A. 199–201, 208
Kalwani, M.U. 88
Kalyanaram, G. 87
Kamakura, W. 238, 241
Kamins, M.A. 426
Karmarkar, U.S. 343
Karni, E. 399
Kartono, B. 9–35
Kashyap, A.K. 228
Katz, M.L. 222, 438–9
Keane, M. 99
Kekre, S. 225
Kim, J. 67
Kim, S.Y. 292, 340
Kimes, S.E. 477–85, 541
Kina, S.H. 488–509
Kirby, P.N. 77
Klein, L. 100
Klemperer, P. 388, 443
Knudsen, N.C. 576
Kohli, R. 39
Kopalle, P. 73, 244, 389
Kopp, R.J. 295
Kornish, L.J. 181–2, 193
Kremer, M. 507
Kridel, D.J. 378

Krishna, A. 76–89
Krishnamurthi, L. 88
Krishnan, T.V. 174–5, 185
Ku, G. 427
Kumar, N. 269, 270, 271, 272, 275, 276, 289–90, 331, 344
Kunreuther, H. 561
Kyle, M.K. 505

lack of pricing knowledge, consumers 540–41
Ladany, S.P. 480
Lakdawalla, D. 514, 519
Lakhani, C. 174, 183, 444
Lal, R. 103, 275, 290, 292, 330, 333, 335
Lambrecht, A. 110, 368, 369, 372, 378
Lancaster, K. 225
Lanzillotti 10, 12
Lariviere, M.A. 339
Lattin, J.M. 87
leader pricing 33–4
learning and non-linear pricing 371–3
learning by doing 444
Leclerc, F. 553
Lederer, P. 315, 577
Lee, A.Y. 152
Lee, E. 327
Lee, T. 44
legal profession, service pricing 550
Leibenstein, H. 398, 436
Lenk, P.J. 70
Leruth, L. 244
Leslie, P. 111
Lesne, J.P. 438, 440
Levin, A. 294, 335
Levin, D. 399
Lewis, R.C. 551
Li, L. 577
Lien, S.M. 12
limited capacity and advance selling 464
Lin, Y. 223
linear programming methods, revenue management 479
linear wholesale prices 335–6
Lippman, S.A. 576
List, J.A. 43
Little, J.D.C. 87, 153
Littlewood, K. 478
Liu, H. 435–49
Liu, P. 425
Liu, Q. 61–73
Liu, Y. 309, 512–32
location-specific pricing 306–7
Lodish, L.M. 258, 266, 277, 295, 335
Lu, Z.J. 171, 492

Lusk, J.L. 51
Lynch, J. 104

Mahajan, V. 39, 232–56
Mahi, H. 339
management decisions
 new product pricing 210–11
 nonlinear pricing 358–63
 price cues 163–4
 price knowledge 164
Manfrim, G. 378
manufacturer initiated price discrimination 127
manufacturer Stackelberg (MS) game 121
manufacturers
 incentives for trade promotions 291–3
 objective function 117
 and price regulation, pharmaceutical industry 505–6
 and store brands 259, 263–4, 276
margin premium 261, 273–6
marginal costs
 and advance selling 463–4
 and bundling pricing 237–40
marginal price effect, nonlinear pricing 378–80
market expansion effect 39
market mavens 100–101
marketing channels and pricing 319–51
Markov chain Monte Carlo (MCMC) estimation 65
Martin, R.K. 253
Martinez-Giralt, X. 227
Maskin, E. 447
Maskus, K. 506
Mason, R. 438
Masuda, Y. 365
Mathews, B. 13
Mathwick, C. 552–3
Mattila, A.S. 535–54
Mayzlin, D. 399
McAfee, R. 95, 105
McAlister, L. 153, 248, 288, 333
McCready, D. 517, 519
McFadden, D.L. 367, 370
McGuire, P. 390
McGuire, T.W. 321
MCI, competition from AT&T 302, 303–4
McManus, B. 111
McMillan, R. 227
me-too drugs 492
Medicaid 495, 505
Mehler, J. 143
Mehta, R. 99–100
Mela, C.F. 426
Mendelson, H. 576, 577

Menon, G. 138
Messinger, P. 101–2, 293
meta-analysis of price presentation effects 79–87
Meyer, R.J. 560
Meza, S. 288, 332, 335, 349
minimum price, online auctions 421–3
Miravete, E.J. 120, 368, 370–71
Mishra, H. 145
mixed bundling 232
mixed integer linear programming approach to bundle pricing 253
mixed strategy model, consumer search 96
moderating role of price knowledge 160–61
modularity pricing 548–9
Moe, W.W. 454
monopoly settings
  and network effects 437–8
  new product pricing 171–94
  nonlinear pricing 363–5
Monroe, K. 141, 152, 219, 256
Montgomery, A. 67, 70
Moorthy, K.S. 177–8, 190, 220
Moorthy, S. 93, 290–91, 327, 329, 330, 333, 336, 343
Morgan, J. 96, 103
Morwitz, V.G. 77, 132–47
multi-tier store brands 271–2, 279
multinomial logit (MNL) model 46
multiple equilibria 436
multiple pricing 482–4
multiple selling of limited capacities 456
Murry, J.P. 295–6
Murthi, B. 99
Mussa, M. 220
Mussweiler, T. 140

Nair, H. 129, 350
name-your-own-price auctions 419–21, 430–32
Naor, P. 574–5
Narasimhan, C. 96, 101–2, 128, 177–8, 189, 223, 283–300, 330, 562
Narayanan, S. 111, 369, 372–3
national brands and store brands 258–79
Natter, M. 64
Neale, M.A. 140
negotiation, revenue management 482
Nerlove, M. 207
Neslin, S.A. 285, 295, 296
Netessine, S. 224, 229
network effects in pricing strategies 435–49
Neven, D.J. 227
new customers, price promotions 158–9
new product pricing 169–212
newsvendor models 557, 563–9

9-digit price endings 77, 158
Noble, P.M. 11, 12, 13, 170
nondurable goods
  models 187, 203, 206–8
  network effects 439–40
nonlinear pricing 355–81, 440–41
  and willingness to pay 53
nonlinear utility functions 69
nonprofit organizations 512–32
  characteristics 513–18
  and competition 522–4, 528–9
  pricing models 518–22
  pricing practice 516–18
nontraditional pricing schemes 212
non-verbal processing of numbers 136–9
Noone, B.M. 484
Northcraft, G.B. 140
nth-price, sealed-bid auction 48–9
numeric priming 141–2
numerical cognition
  heuristics in 132–47
  and pricing 134–9
Nunes, J.C. 134, 141, 368, 372, 426–7
NYOP (name-your-own-price) auctions 419–21, 430–32

objective functions, structural models 117–19
Ockenfels, A. 425
Oi, W.Y. 363
oligopoly settings, nonlinear pricing 365–6
one-stop shopping 101–2
online auctions 419–32
online chats and product knowledge transmission 399
open-loop equilibria 195
open-loop pricing equilibrium 387
operations management, strategic pricing response 557–79
Oppenheimer, D.M. 145
ordinal restrictions 64
Oren, S.S. 179–80, 190, 439, 440, 441
Orhun, A.Y. 229
Ortmeyer, G.K. 158
Oster, S. 516
Otter, T. 61–73
overbooking 456
own labels, *see* store brands
own-price effects measurements 61–73

Padmanabhan, V. 179–80, 192, 196–7, 202, 339
Pakes, A. 390
Pan, X. 98
Pancras, J. 111, 350
parity pricing 30–31

Park, R.E. 367, 378
Park, Y.-H. 52, 419–32
Parry, M.E. 337
partial integration, channel design 344
partitioned prices 77
pass-through 287–9, 319–20, 326–35
patents, pharmaceutical industry 489, 491–2
Pauwels, K. 258–79
pay-for-performance pricing 546, 548
Pazgal, A. 96, 103, 572
Peck, J. 568
penetration pricing 170–71, 437–8
pennies-a-day strategy 553
perceived fairness
　revenue management pricing 482–4
　service pricing 541
perceived quality as driver of price premium 269–70
perceived value pricing 29–30
performance-based pricing, services 546, 548
perishability of services 537, 539
Persson, B. 505, 506
Pesendofer, W. 399
Petroshius, S.M. 219
Petruzzi, N.C. 564–6, 567–8
pharmaceutical pricing 488–509
　channels 498–504
　collaborators 497–8
　companies 490–92
　competitors 492–5
　context 504–7
　customers 495–7
pharmacies, role in pharmaceutical industry 498
pharmacy benefit managers (PBM) 499–500, 502–4
Philipson, T. 514, 519
physicians, role in pharmaceutical pricing 497–8
Pigou, A.C. 302
point of marginal cheapness (PMC) 551
point of marginal expensiveness (PME) 551
policy analysis
　structural pricing models 127–8
　within a channel setting 349–50
pooling, data 69–73
Porter, R. 125
Pratt, J. 97
prediction models using consumer reference prices 87–8
preferred price gap 276–7
premium advance selling 472–4
premium pricing 32–3
presentation effects 79–87
price as signal of quality 190–91

price bundling, *see* bundle design and pricing
price ceilings, pharmaceutical industry 504
price cognition 132–3
　heuristics in 139–46
　model 139
price-consumption simultaneity 366–70
price cues
　adverse effects 161–2
　as competitive tool 163–4
　effectiveness 153–6
　as information 157–60
price discrimination
　as driver for advance selling 454–5
　and nonlinear pricing 356–7, 378–80
　nonprofit organizations 517–18, 530
price dispersion 91, 94–8
price effects measurement 61–73
price elasticity and nonlinear pricing 378
price endings 77, 158
price expectations of customers 188–91
price fairness 79
price gap preferences 276–7
price guarantees 159–60
price incentives, trade promotions 283–300
price knowledge 152–3, 160–61
price-matching policies 159–60
price premium of national brands 260, 265–72
　drivers of price premium 269–72
price presentation effects 79–87
price promotions
　as driver of price premium 271
　for employees 153–4
　for new customers 158–9
price regulation, pharmaceutical industry 504–6
price sensitivity measurement, services 550–51
price-setting interactions, modeling 121
price signaling 31–2
price stickiness 12
prices, effect on demand 400–403
prices paid by others 162
pricing contracts 320, 335–42
pricing decisions, conceptual framework 13–15
pricing objectives and strategies 9–35
　cost-plus pricing 26–9
　determinants 20–23
　leader pricing 33–4
　parity pricing 30–31
　perceived value pricing 29–30
　premium pricing 32–3
　price signalling 31–2
　survey 17–19
pricing-oriented approaches to bundling 248, 253–5
private labels, *see* store brands

probabilistic approach to bundle pricing 253–5
product differentiation, nonprofit organizations 523–4
product-driven pricing, *see* cost-based pricing
product generations, pricing 191–3
product life cycle, pharmaceuticals 491–2
product line length and pricing 225–7
product line pricing 216–29
　and willingness to pay 55
profit advantage of advance selling 460–63
profit regulation, pharmaceutical industry 504
profitability of trade promotions 293–5
promotions, *see* price promotions
purchase characteristics, services 541
purchase data and WTP measurement 40–41
pure bundling 232, 236–7
Putler, D.S. 88
Putrevu, S. 99
Putsis, W.P. 225, 227

Qiu, C. 424
quality
　effect of quality differences 406–9
　indicated by price 190–91
quantity discounts 336–7, 355
　and willingness to pay 53–5
queuing models 558, 573–7

Radner, R. 440
Raju, J. 266
Raman, K. 175–7, 185, 186
Ramey, G. 101
Rao, A. 398
Rao, A.R. 339
Rao, R.C. 196–7, 204–5
Rao, V.R. 9–35, 70, 199–201, 207, 248, 249, 252, 319, 340, 388–9
Ratchford, B.T. 91–105
rate of return regulation, pharmaceutical industry 504
rating-based conjoint WTP measurement 44
rebates, pharmaceutical industry 499, 503–4
reduced-form pricing models 108, 113, 128–9
reference groups 398
reference prices 385, 386–7
　and bidder behaviour 426–7
　in choice models 87–8
　manipulation of 483
　pharmaceutical industry 504
　pricing implications 389
　services 550
refunds, advance selling 465–6
regular price and price cues 161
regulation, pharmaceutical prices 504–6
Reiley, D. 422

Reiss, P.C. 123, 378
relative advantage, revenue management pricing 484
Rentschler, R. 517
representativeness heuristic in price cognition 142–4
reputation of firm, and price cues 156–7
resale price maintenance (RPM) 337–9
research and development, pharmaceutical industry 490–91
researcher's uncertainty 122–3
reservation prices 38–40, 235
　services 550–51
reserve price, online auctions 421–3
retail agglomeration effects 102
retail competition, effect on pass-through 332, 333–4
retail pass-through 287–9, 319–20, 326–35
retail prices as drivers of margin premium 274
retailers
　objective functions 117
　objectives, effect on pass-through 332
　and price discrimination 127
　and price searching 101–2
　reputation and use of price cues 156–7
　response to manufacturers' promotions 287–93
　size and strategy as driver of price premium 271–2
　and store brands 259, 263, 276–7
revenue management and pricing 477–85
reverse auctions 50
Reynolds, S. 424
Richard, J.F. 561
Richards, T.J. 111
Richardson, P.S. 275
Riordan, M.H. 179–81, 190
Robinson, B. 174, 183, 444
Robinson–Patman Act 341
Rochet, J.-C. 364, 365, 442, 443
Rohlfs, J. 436
Romano, R.E. 344
Rose-Ackerman, S. 523, 527, 530
Rosen, S. 220
Rossi, P.E. 67, 68, 70
Roth, A.E. 425
Roy, A. 112
RPM (resale price maintenance) 337–9
Ruan, R. 344
Rust, J. 447

Salamon, L. 512
Salkever, D.S. 494
Salmon, W.J. 158
Salop, S. 96

Samiee, S. 10–11
Sarvary, M. 103
Savitsky, K. 142
Sawtooth Software 70–71
Sawyer, A. 99
Sawyer, A.G. 152
Sayman, S. 266
scanbacks and accruals 335
Schiff, J. 516
Schindler, R.M. 77, 158
Schmalensee, R. 227, 238, 240, 364, 515
Schroeder, T.C. 51
Scitovsky, T. 531
search, *see* consumer search
Seetharaman, P.B. 384–91
self-stated WTP 41–2
seller credibility and advance selling 463–4
service guarantees 540, 553–4
services 535–54
   complex service pricing 549–50
   consumer reservation prices 550–51
   modularity pricing 548–9
   pay-for-performance pricing 546–8
   pricing framework 536–43
   setting prices 543–6
Sethuraman, R. 266
shadow price approach 479–80
Shaffer, G. 308, 312–13, 339
Shapiro, C. 436, 438–9
Sherman Antitrust Act 338
Shipley, D.D. 10
Shoemaker, S. 535–54
Shogren. J.F. 51
Shrinivasan, N. 99
Shugan, S.M. 224, 229, 327, 328, 336, 451–75
Shum, M. 98, 497
signaling role of minimum price, online auctions 422
signpost items 159
Simester, D.I. 150–64
Simonson, I. 219, 422, 425, 427, 429
simultaneity of price and consumption 366–70
simultaneity of production and consumption 540
Sinha, A. 423
Sirbu, M. 439, 440
situational factors, price presentation 79, 85
size of physical price representation 143
Skiera, B. 41, 49, 51, 368, 378
skimming strategy 170–71
slotting allowances 339–40
Smith, M. 103
SNARC (spatial–numerical association) 138
snobbishness 397–416
Snyder, C.M. 502

Sobel, J. 572
social influences on pricing 397–417
social value, services 543
social welfare effects of targeted pricing 315–16
Soltysinski, K. 429
Soman, D. 226, 256
Sorenson, A. 97, 98, 496
sources of information 100–104
Spann, M. 431
spatial orientation and numerical information 138
specification analysis, structural pricing models 126–7
spot selling 457
   seller information disadvantage 459–60
Srinivasan, K. 99, 177–8, 190, 224, 225
Srinivasan, N. 93–4, 99, 104
Srinivasan, S. 258–79
Sriram, S.119
Stackelberg price leadership 525–6
Staelin, R. 292, 321, 327, 340
Starkey, P. 137
starting bid, online auctions 421–3
state dependence and demand 384–5, 386
   pricing implications 388–9
state-space pricing models 387
static models 117
static pricing 436–7
Steenkamp, J.-B.E.M. 269, 270, 271, 272, 275, 276
Steinberg, R. 513–14, 517, 519, 528, 531–2
Stidham, S. 576
Stigler, G. 91, 92, 236
Stiglitz, J. 96
Stiving, M. 77, 142, 158
Stock, A. 399
Stokey, N.L. 571
Stole, L.A. 364, 365
store brands and national brands 258–79
store image as driver of margin premium 276
store traffic as driver of margin premium 275–6
strategic pricing
   new products and services 169–212
   operations management 557–79
   social influences 397–417
Stremersch, S. 237
structural models
   of channels 345–51
   consumer search 94
   of pricing 108–29
Su, X. 557–79
sub-additivity, consumer reservation price 235

subjective price 77
substitutability, reservation prices 241–2
Sudhir, K. 111, 112, 222–3, 228, 275, 288, 319–51
Sullivan, M.W. 339
Sundararajan, A. 365, 440
super-additivity, consumer reservation price 235
Suter, T.A. 423
Swann, P. 445
switching costs
   and network effects 443–4
   pharmaceutical products 496–7

takeoff of new products 212
Talukdar, D. 275
targeted pricing 302–17
   effects 305–11
   optimal strategy 311–15
   social welfare effects 315–16
Taylor, L.D. 367
Taylor, T.A. 224, 229
technology and advance selling 452–4
telecommunications, nonlinear pricing 355, 358–62, 374–7
Tellis, G. 13, 237, 431
temporal price discrimination model 96
temporal pricing 77
temporal value, services 542–3
Terwiesch, C. 430, 431
Thaler, R.H. 77
Thomadsen, R. 113
Thomas, M. 132–47
Tirole, J. 310, 442, 443, 447
trade promotions 283–300
   incentives for 291–3
   and marketing strategy 296–8
   objectives 286
   and pricing strategy 286–7
   profitability and efficacy 293–6
   retail response 287–93
Train, K.E. 367, 370, 378
translog approach 68
travel tickets, nonlinear pricing 362–3
Trivedi, M. 343
Tversky, A. 132, 140, 142, 144, 219
two-part tariffs 336–7
two-sided markets 441–3
Tyagi, R.K. 289, 327, 328

unaware anchoring in price cognition 140–41
uncertainty, structural models 119
Uncles, M. 275
uniform pricing of a product line 227–8

unintentional anchoring, price cognition 141
Urban, G.L. 39
usage uncertainty, nonlinear pricing 371–3

Välimäki, J. 199–201, 208
value and framing, service pricing 543–4
value components, services 542–3
Van Mieghem, J.A. 577
van Ryzin, G. 480, 569–70
Vanhuele, M. 153
Varian, H. 96, 103
Varian, H.R. 39, 310, 330, 364, 436
Veblen, T. 398
Venkatesh, R. 232–56
Verboven, F. 112, 222
Verizon 359–60
Vernon, J.M. 494
vertical integration and decentralization 342–4
vertical product differentiation 217, 219–24
Vickers, J. 365
Vickery auctions 48–9
Villas-Boas, J.M. 223, 290, 310, 330, 333, 336, 342, 349
Vogt, W.B. 493
volume premium 260–61, 272–3
Voss, G. 530–31

Walters, R.G. 331
Walters, R.J. 287
Walton, J.R. 81
Wang, S.S. 119
Wang, T. 39–40
Wang, X. 419–32
Wang, Y. 79
Warren, L.S. 158
Weatherford, L.R. 480
Weinberg, C.B. 512–32
Weisbrod, B. 516, 517, 519, 531–2
Weitzman model of search 92–3
Wernefelt, B. 102, 198–201, 206–7, 388
Wertenbroch, K. 41, 49, 51
West, D. 97, 98
Whang, S. 365, 577
White, M.W. 378
wholesale acquisition cost (WAC) 499
wholesale prices
   as drivers of margin premium 274
   and price discrimination 330–31
wholesalers, pharmaceutical industry 498
Wilcox, R.T. 293
Wilder, R. 514
Wilkie, W.L. 339
willingness to pay (WTP) 37–59

definitions 38–40
effect of information processing fluency 145
measurement 40–52
nonprofit products 531
online auctions 429, 430
and pricing decisions 37–8, 52–8
Winer, R.S. 77, 87, 142, 158
Winston, W.L. 177–9, 188–9, 572
Wirtz, J. 484, 541
Wisniewski, K.J. 224
Wolak, F.A. 123
Wolpin, K. 94
Wooders, J. 424
Woodward, R.S. 210
word of mouth as information source 100–101, 399
Wosinska, M. 488–509
WTP, *see* willingness to pay

Xia, L. 484, 541
Xiao, P. 108–29
Xie, J. 439, 440, 451–75

Yadav, M.S. 256
Yao, S. 426
Yechiali, U. 576
Yellen, J.L. 237

Zeithaml, V.A. 81
Zeithammer, R. 425, 429–30
Zettelmeyer, F. 103
Zhang, F. 566
Zhang, Z.J. 38–9, 41, 45, 302–17
Zhao, H. 179–80, 191
Zhao, W. 480
Zhao, Y. 349
Zheng, Y. 480